VideoNote

LOCATION OF VIDEONOTES IN THE TEXT

Second Edition

Starting Out with

Games & Graphics
in C++

Tony Gaddis

Haywood Community College

PEARSON

Boston   Columbus   Indianapolis   New York   San Francisco   Upper Saddle River
Amsterdam   Cape Town   Dubai   London   Madrid   Milan   Munich   Paris   Montreal   Toronto
Delhi   Mexico City   Sao Paulo   Sydney   Hong Kong   Seoul   Singapore   Taipei   Tokyo

Editorial Director: Marcia Horton
Acquisitions Editor: Matt Goldstein
Editorial Assistant: Jenah Blitz-Stoehr
Director of Marketing: Christy Lesko
Marketing Manager: Yez Alayan
Marketing Coordinator: Kathryn Ferranti
Director of Production: Erin Gregg
Managing Editor: Jeff Holcomb
Production Project Manager:
    Kayla Smith-Tarbox
Operations Supervisor: Nick Sklitsis
Manufacturing Buyer: Lisa McDowell
Art Director: Anthony Gemmellaro
Cover Designer: Studio Montage
Manager, Visual Research: Karen Sanatar

Photo Researcher: Christa Tilly
Manager, Rights and Permissions:
    Michael Joyce
Text Permission Coordinator: Sara Smith,
    Creative Compliance
Cover Illustration/Art: Studio Montage
Lead Media Project Manager: Renata Butera
Full-Service Project Management:
    Aptara®, Inc.
Composition: Aptara®, Inc.
Printer/Binder: RR Donnelley
Cover Printer: RR Donnelley
Text Font: Sabon LT Std

Credits and acknowledgments borrowed from other sources and reproduced, with permission, in this textbook appear on the appropriate page within text.

Many of the designations by manufacturers and sellers to distinguish their products are claimed as trademarks. Where those designations appear in this book, and the publisher was aware of a trademark claim, the designations have been printed in initial caps or all caps.

Library of Congress Cataloging-in-Publication Data

Gaddis, Tony.
    [Starting out with games and graphics in C++]
    Gaddis starting out with games and graphics in C++ / Tony Gaddis, Haywood Community College. —2e.
        pages cm
    Includes bibliographical references and index.
    ISBN 978-0-13-312807-9 (alk. paper)—ISBN 0-13-312807-5 (alk. paper)
    1. Computer programming.   2. Computer games—Programming.   3. Computer graphics.   4. C++ (Computer program language)   I. Title.
        QA76.6.G3148 2014
        005.13'3—dc23

                                                                2012034982

3 16

ISBN 10: 0-13-312807-5
ISBN 13: 978-0-13-312807-9

Contents

Preface

Welcome to the second edition of *Starting Out with Games and Graphics in C++*. This book teaches the traditional topics of an introductory programming course using C++, along with simple game development using a library known as the App Game Kit. Students using this book will start writing traditional, console-based programs with Microsoft Visual C++. Once the fundamentals of procedural programming have been covered, the student learns to use the App Game Kit library to develop simple games in C++, as well as programs that use graphics and animation. The examples and assignments are designed to excite and motivate students and to keep them engaged throughout the semester.

New to This Edition

- The second edition of this book is a complete revision of the first edition. Reviewers of the first edition overwhelmingly expressed that their students needed more knowledge of standard C++ to be adequately prepared for subsequent courses. To address this concern, the second edition is divided into two parts:
  - Part 1 (Chapters 1 through 6) covers the fundamentals of procedural programming using standard C++.
  - Part 2 (Chapters 7 through 11) covers graphics and game programming using C++ and the App Game Kit. Part 2 also covers file I/O and introduces object-oriented programming.
- Another change in the second edition is the use of the App Game Kit Tier 2, instead of the Dark GDK. The App Game Kit is the latest development environment from The Game Creators. It is designed to create games for Windows, as well as a variety of smartphones and tablets. The App Game Kit is available in two "tiers."
  - Tier 1 provides an integrated development environment that supports a BASIC-like programming language.
  - Tier 2 provides a C++ library that is compatible with Microsoft Visual C++ 2010. In Part 2 of this book we use the App Game Kit Tier 2, along with Microsoft Visual C++ 2010. (Although the App Game Kit is a commercial product, The Game Creators provide a free trial version that includes Tier 2. The trial version is not time restricted, but it does display a small watermark on the screen. You can use either the trial version or the full commercial version with this book.)
- A set of online VideoNotes have also been developed for use with this book. The VideoNotes provide short explanations of various topics in the book, coding demonstrations, and walkthroughs of selected programming problems at the end of each chapter.

Required Software

To use this book, you will need the following software and files:

- **Microsoft Visual C++ 2010**

  See Appendix A for instructions for downloadig Microsoft Visual C++ 2010 Express Edition.

- **The App Game Kit (AGK) Tier 2**

  The App Game Kit Tier 2 must be downloaded and installed from The Game Creators' Web site. A free trial version is available, as well as a commercial version. See Appendix A for specific instructions.

- **Sample Source Code and Media Files**

  The source code for the book's example programs, as well as graphics, audio files, and game case studies, are available for download from the publisher's Web site. See Appendix A for instructions.

Brief Overview of Each Chapter

PART 1: INTRODUCTION TO STANDARD C++

Chapter 1: Introduction to Computers and Programming

This chapter begins by giving a very concrete and easy-to-understand explanation of how computers work, how data is stored and manipulated, and why we write programs in high-level languages. Step-by-step tutorials are given that get the student started using Visual C++.

Chapter 2: C++ Fundamentals

This chapter introduces the student to the fundamental concepts needed to write simple C++ programs that display output, gather input, and perform calculations. Variables, data types, literals, and named constants are introduced. The student learns to use stream input and output and write math expressions.

Chapter 3: Decision Structures and Boolean Logic

In this chapter the student learns about relational operators and Boolean expressions and is shown how to control the flow of a program with decision structures. The `if`, `if-else`, and `if-else-if` statements are covered. Nested decision structures, logical operators, and the `switch` statement are also discussed.

Chapter 4: Repetition Structures

This chapter shows the student how to create repetition structures using the `while` loop, the `do-while` loop, and `for` loop. Examples are shown using counters, accumulators, and running totals.

Chapter 5: Functions

In this chapter the student first learns how to write and call void functions, showing the benefits of using functions to modularize programs. Then, the student learns to pass arguments to functions. Passing by value and by reference are discussed. Local and global variables and constants are also discussed. Finally, the student learns to write value-returning methods.

Chapter 6: Arrays

In this chapter the student learns to create and work with one- and two-dimensional arrays. Many examples of array processing are provided, including examples illustrating how to find the sum, average, and highest and lowest values in an array. Programming techniques using parallel arrays are also demonstrated.

PART 2: INTRODUCTION TO GAME PROGRAMMING WITH C++ AND APP GAME KIT

Chapter 7: Using the App Game Kit with C++

This chapter introduces the student to program development using Visual C++ and the App Game Kit (AGK) Tier 2. It starts by introducing the structure of a C++ program that is written with the AGK, including the game loop. The game loop is a special loop that constantly runs, controlling all the action in a game. The screen coordinate system that is used by the AGK to map the locations of pixels is introduced. The student learns to load graphic images from files and create sprites that can be displayed and manipulated on the screen. The student also learns how colors are produced using the RGB color system and how an alpha channel determines transparency. The student learns about simple AGK functions for displaying text, and generating random numbers.

Chapter 8: Input, Animation, and Sound

This chapter introduces various ways to get user input in a game or other program developed with the AGK. Functions and programming techniques for using the mouse, virtual buttons, virtual joysticks, and reading keystrokes on the keyboard are covered. Then, the chapter discusses techniques for displaying animations using animated sprites and texture atlases. A discussion of playing music and sound in a program is presented. The chapter concludes with the BugZapper game, in which the user attempts to click randomly appearing bugs as fast as possible.

Chapter 9: Text, Collisions, and the Vulture Trouble Game

This chapter begins with a discussion of text objects, which give the programmer greater control over text that is displayed in an AGK window. Next, the chapter discusses collision detection between sprites and demonstrates a simple game named PizzaBot. Next the student learns how perform the calculations necessary to simulate the motion of an object falling toward Earth. This is all finally brought together in the Vulture Trouble game. Vulture Trouble is a high-quality video game that incorporates all the programming skills that the student has learned to this point.

Chapter 10: Using Files and Arrays with the AGK

This chapter begins by discussing sequential file input and output, using the AGK file functions. Examples include storing a set of random colors in a file, saving a game's high score, and writing a log file. Next, the chapter discusses how arrays can be used to hold sprite or image indices, using examples that simulate dealing, shuffling, and sorting a deck of cards. The chapter also demonstrates how to use two-dimensional arrays to map tiles (small rectangular images) to the screen to make the background for a game.

Chapter 11: Object-Oriented Programming

This chapter compares procedural and object-oriented programming practices. It covers the fundamental concepts of classes and objects. Member variables, member functions, access specification, constructors, accessors, and mutators are discussed. The chapter also introduces inheritance. An object-oriented game named Balloon Target is presented.

Appendix A: Downloading and Installing the Required Software

This appendix is a guide for downloading and installing all the software and files that are necessary to use this book.

Answers to Checkpoints (available online)

This file gives the answers to the checkpoint questions that appear throughout the text.

Features of the Text

Concept Statements. Each major section of the text starts with a concept statement. This statement concisely summarizes the main point of the section.

Example Programs. Each chapter has an abundant number of complete and partial example programs, each designed to highlight the current topic.

VideoNote

VideoNotes. Online videos developed specifically for this book are available for viewing at www.pearsonhighered.com/gaddis. Icons appear throughout the text alerting the student to videos about specific topics.

In the Spotlight. Numerous *In the Spotlight* sections appear throughout the book. These provide detailed discussions and examples of how certain programming techniques can be applied to specific applications.

NOTE: Notes appear at several places throughout the text. They are short explanations of interesting or often misunderstood points relevant to the topic at hand.

WARNING: Warnings caution students about programming techniques or practices that can lead to malfunctioning programs or lost data.

Checkpoint. Checkpoints are questions placed at intervals throughout each chapter. They are designed to query the student's knowledge quickly after learning a new topic.

Review Questions. Each chapter presents a thorough and diverse set of review questions and exercises. They include Multiple Choice, True/False, Algorithm Workbench, and Short Answer.

Programming Exercises. Each chapter offers a pool of programming exercises designed to solidify the student's knowledge of the topics currently being studied.

Supplements

Microsoft Visual Studio 2010 Express Edition

See Appendix A for instructions for downloadig Microsoft Visual C++ 2010 Express Edition.

Online Resources

This book's online resource page contains numerous student supplements. To access these supplements, go to www.pearsonhighered.com/gaddis, and click on the image of this book's cover. You will find the following items:

- A link to download the trial version of the App Game Kit
- Source code for all the book's example programs
- Graphics and audio files that can be used in student projects
- Access to the book's companion VideoNotes
- Answers to the Checkpoint questions

Instructor Resources

The following supplements are available to qualified instructors only:

- Answers to the Review Questions
- Solutions for the exercises
- PowerPoint presentation slides for each chapter

Visit the Pearson Instructor Resource Center (www.pearsonhighered.com/irc) or send an e-mail to computing@pearson.com for information on how to access them.

Acknowledgments

I would like to thank The Game Creators for developing the App Game Kit, a powerful game development environment that is simple enough for beginning students. I would also like to thank Christopher Rich for his invaluable contributions to this book. His work on the second half of the book, knowledge of the App Game Kit, and original artwork and media helped make this book what it is. Thanks Chris!

I also want to thank everyone at Pearson Education for making the *Starting Out with* series so successful. I have worked so closely with the team at Pearson Education that I consider them among my closest friends. I am extremely grateful that Matt Goldstein is my editor. He and Emma Snider, editorial assistant, guided me through the

I consider them among my closest friends. I am extremely grateful that Matt Goldstein is my editor. He and Emma Snider, editorial assistant, guided me through the process of revising this book. I am also fortunate to have Yez Alyan as marketing manager and Kathryn Ferranti as marketing coordinator. They do a great job getting my books out to the academic community. The production team, led by Kayla Smith-Tarbox, worked tirelessly to make this book a reality. Thanks to you all!

About the Author

Tony Gaddis is the principal author of the *Starting Out with* series of textbooks. Tony has nearly twenty years of experience teaching computer science courses, primarily at Haywood Community College. He is a highly acclaimed instructor who was previously selected as the North Carolina Community College "Teacher of the Year" and has received the Teaching Excellence award from the National Institute for Staff and Organizational Development. The *Starting Out with* series includes introductory books covering C++, Java™, Microsoft® Visual Basic®, Microsoft® C#®, Python, Programming Logic and Design, and Alice, all published by Pearson Education.

1

Introduction to Computers and Programming

TOPICS

1.1 Introduction

The goal of this book is to teach computer programming in a fun and interesting way. It is assumed that you are a beginner, with little or no programming experience. You might have noticed that this book is divided into two parts. In Part 1, you will learn to write simple C++ programs that display text on the screen, read input from the keyboard, and perform basic calculations. In Part 2, you will advance your knowledge by writing programs that are graphical, interactive, and game-like.

A *program* is a set of instructions that a computer follows to perform a task. Programs are commonly referred to as *software*. Software is essential to a computer because without software, a computer can do nothing. All the software that we use to make our computers useful (and entertaining) is created by individuals known as programmers or software developers. A *programmer*, or *software developer*, is a person with the training and skills necessary to design, create, and test computer programs. Computer programming is an exciting and rewarding career. In addition to creating computer games, you will find programmers working in business, medicine, government, law enforcement, agriculture, academics, telecommunications, and almost every other field.

Before we begin to explore the concepts of programming, you need to understand a few basics about computers and how they work. This chapter will build a solid foundation of knowledge that you will continually rely on as you study computer science. First, we will discuss the physical components of computers. Next, we will look at how computers store data and how programs work. Finally, we will discuss the specific tools that you will use in this book to create games and graphical programs: the C++ language and the App Game Kit library.

1.2 Hardware

CONCEPT: The physical devices that a computer is made of are referred to as the computer's hardware. Most computer systems are made of similar hardware devices.

The term *hardware* refers to all the physical devices, or *components*, of a computer. A computer is not one single device, but rather a system of devices that work together. Like the different instruments in a symphony orchestra, each device in a computer plays its own part.

If you have ever shopped for a computer, you've probably seen sales literature listing components such as microprocessors, memory, disk drives, video displays, graphics cards, and so forth. Unless you already know a lot about computers, or at least have a friend who does, understanding what these different components do might be challenging. As shown in Figure 1-1, a typical computer system consists of the following major components:

- The central processing unit (CPU)
- Main memory
- Secondary storage devices
- Input devices
- Output devices

Let's take a closer look at each of these components.

Figure 1-1 Typical components of a computer system

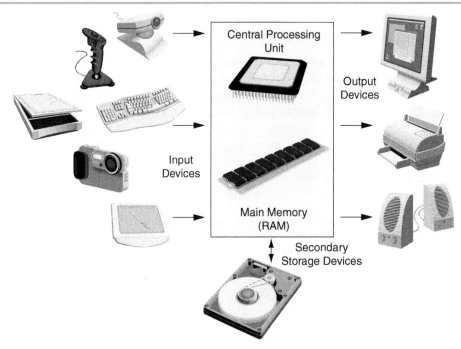

The CPU

When a computer is performing the tasks that a program tells it to do, we say that the computer is *running* or *executing* the program. The *central processing unit*, or *CPU*, is the part of a computer that actually runs programs. The CPU is the most important component in a computer because without it, the computer could not run software.

In the earliest computers, CPUs were huge devices made of electrical and mechanical components such as vacuum tubes and switches. Figure 1-2 shows such a device. The two women in the photo are working with the historic ENIAC computer. The *ENIAC* is considered by many as the world's first programmable electronic computer and was built in 1945 to calculate artillery ballistic tables for the U.S. Army. This machine, which was primarily one big CPU, was 8 feet tall and 100 feet long and weighed 30 tons.

Figure 1-2 The ENIAC computer (U.S. Army photo)

Today, CPUs are small chips known as *microprocessors*. Figure 1-3 shows a lab technician holding a modern-day microprocessor. In addition to being much smaller than the old electromechanical CPUs in early computers, microprocessors are also much more powerful.

Main Memory

You can think of *main memory* as the computer's work area. This is where the computer stores a program while the program is running, as well as the data that the program is working with. For example, suppose you are using a word processing program to write an essay for one of your classes. While you do this, both the word processing program and the essay are stored in main memory.

Figure 1-3 A lab technician holds a modern microprocessor (photo courtesy of Intel Corporation)

Main memory is commonly known as *random-access memory*, or *RAM*. It is called this because the CPU is able to access data stored at any random location in RAM quickly. RAM is usually a *volatile* type of memory that is used only for temporary storage while a program is running. When the computer is turned off, the contents of RAM are erased. Inside your computer, RAM is stored in chips, similar to the ones shown in Figure 1-4.

Figure 1-4 Memory chips

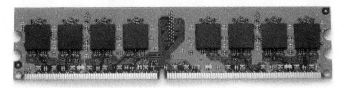

Secondary Storage Devices

Secondary storage is a type of memory that can hold data for long periods of time, even when there is no power to the computer. Programs are normally stored in secondary memory and loaded into main memory as needed. Important data, such as word processing documents, payroll data, and inventory records, is saved to secondary storage as well.

The most common type of secondary storage device is the disk drive. A *disk drive* stores data by magnetically encoding it onto a circular disk. Most computers have a disk drive mounted inside their case. External disk drives, which connect to one of the computer's communication ports, are also available. External disk drives can be used to create backup copies of important data or to move data to another computer.

In addition to external disk drives, many types of devices have been created for copying data and for moving it to other computers. For many years floppy disk drives were popular. A *floppy disk drive* records data onto a small floppy disk, which can be removed from the drive. Floppy disks have many disadvantages, however. They hold only a small amount of data, and are very slow. The use of floppy disk drives has declined dramatically in recent years, in favor of superior devices such as universal serial bus (USB) drives. *USB drives* are small devices that plug into a computer's USB port and appear to the system as a disk drive. These drives do not actually contain a disk, however. They store data in a special type of memory known as *flash memory*. USB drives, which are also known as *memory sticks* and *flash drives*, are inexpensive, reliable, and small enough to be carried in your pocket.

Optical devices such as the *CD* (compact disc) and the *DVD* (digital versatile disc) are also popular for data storage. Data is not recorded magnetically on an optical disc, but is encoded as a series of pits on the disc surface. CD and DVD drives use a laser to detect the pits and thus read the encoded data. Optical discs hold large amounts of data, and because recordable CD and DVD drives are now common, they are good mediums for creating backup copies of data.

Input Devices

Input is any data the computer collects from people and from other devices. The component that collects the data and sends it to the computer is called an *input device*. Common input devices are the keyboard, mouse, joystick, scanner, microphone, and digital camera. Disk drives and optical drives can also be considered input devices because programs and data are retrieved from them and loaded into the computer's memory.

Output Devices

Output is any data the computer produces for people or for other devices. It might be a sales report, a list of names, or a graphic image. The data is sent to an *output device*, which formats and presents it. Common output devices are video displays and printers. Disk drives and CD/DVD recorders can also be considered output devices because the system sends data to them in order to be saved.

 Checkpoint

> 1.1. What is a program?
>
> 1.2. What is hardware?
>
> 1.3. List the five major components of a computer system.
>
> 1.4. What part of the computer actually runs programs?

1.5. What part of the computer serves as a work area to store a program and its data while the program is running?

1.6. What part of the computer holds data for long periods of time, even when there is no power to the computer?

1.7. What part of the computer collects data from people or other devices?

1.8. What part of the computer formats and presents data for people or other devices?

1.3   How Computers Store Data

CONCEPT: All data that is stored in a computer is converted to sequences of 0s and 1s.

A computer's memory is made of tiny storage locations known as *bytes*. One byte is only enough memory to store a letter of the alphabet or a small number. To do anything meaningful, a computer has to have lots of bytes. Most computers today have billions of bytes of memory.

Each byte is made of eight smaller storage locations known as bits. The term *bit* stands for *binary digit*. Computer scientists usually think of bits as tiny switches that can be either on or off. Bits aren't actual "switches," however, at least not in the conventional sense. In most computer systems, bits are tiny electrical components that can hold either a positive or a negative charge. Computer scientists think of a positive charge as a switch in the *on* position and a negative charge as a switch in the *off* position. Figure 1-5 shows the way a computer scientist might think of a byte of memory: as a collection of switches that are each flipped to either the on or off position.

Figure 1-5 Think of a byte as eight switches

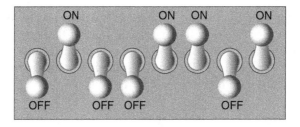

When a piece of data is stored in a byte, the computer sets the eight bits to an on/off pattern that represents the data. For example, the pattern shown on the left in Figure 1-6 shows how the number 77 would be stored in a byte, and the pattern on the right shows how the letter A would be stored in a byte. In a moment you will see how these patterns are determined.

Figure 1-6 Bit patterns for the number 77 and the letter A

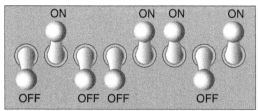
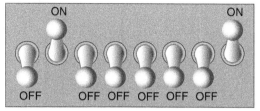

The number 77 stored in a byte.   The letter A stored in a byte.

Storing Numbers

A bit can be used in a very limited way to represent numbers. Depending on whether the bit is turned on or off, it can represent one of two different values. In computer systems, a bit that is turned off represents the number 0, and a bit that is turned on represents the number 1. This corresponds perfectly to the *binary numbering system*. In the binary numbering system (or *binary*, as it is usually called), all numeric values are written as sequences of 0s and 1s. Here is an example of a number that is written in binary:

    10011101

The position of each digit in a binary number has a value assigned to it. Starting with the rightmost digit and moving left, the position values are 2^0, 2^1, 2^2, 2^3, and so forth, as shown in Figure 1-7. Figure 1-8 shows the same diagram with the position values calculated. Starting with the rightmost digit and moving left, the position values are 1, 2, 4, 8, and so forth.

Figure 1-7 The values of binary digits as powers of 2

Figure 1-8 The values of binary digits

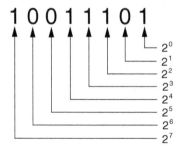
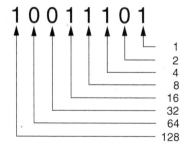

To determine the value of a binary number you simply add up the position values of all the 1s. For example, in the binary number 10011101, the position values of the 1s are 1, 4, 8, 16, and 128. This is shown in Figure 1-9. The sum of all of these position values is 157. So, the value of the binary number 10011101 is 157.

Figure 1-9 Determining the value of 10011101

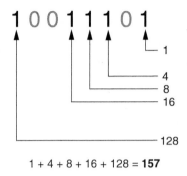

$1 + 4 + 8 + 16 + 128 = \mathbf{157}$

Figure 1-10 shows how you can picture the number 157 stored in a byte of memory. Each 1 is represented by a bit in the on position, and each 0 is represented by a bit in the off position.

Figure 1-10 The bit pattern for 157

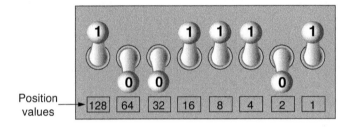

$128 + 16 + 8 + 4 + 1 = \mathbf{157}$

When all the bits in a byte are set to 0 (turned off), then the value of the byte is 0. When all the bits in a byte are set to 1 (turned on), then the byte holds the largest value that can be stored in it. The largest value that can be stored in a byte is $1 + 2 + 4 + 8 + 16 + 32 + 64 + 128 = 255$. This limit exists because there are only eight bits in a byte.

What if you need to store a number larger than 255? The answer is simple: Use more than one byte. For example, suppose we put two bytes together. That gives us 16 bits. The position values of those 16 bits would be 2^0, 2^1, 2^2, 2^3, and so forth, up through 2^{15}. As shown in Figure 1-11, the maximum value that can be stored in two bytes is 65,535. If you need to store a number larger than this, then more bytes are necessary.

> **TIP:** If you are feeling overwhelmed by all this, relax! You will not actually have to convert numbers to binary while programming. Knowing that this process is taking place inside the computer will help you as you learn, and in the long term this knowledge will make you a better programmer.

Figure 1-11 Two bytes used for a large number

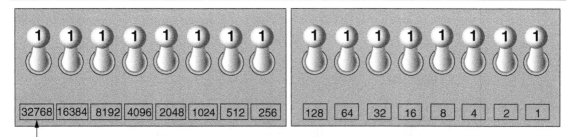

32768 + 16384 + 8192 + 4096 + 2048 + 1024 + 512 + 256 + 128 + 64 + 32 + 16 + 8 + 4 + 2 + 1 = **65535**

Position values

Storing Characters

Any piece of data that is stored in a computer's memory must be stored as a binary number. This includes characters, such as letters and punctuation marks. When a character is stored in memory, it is first converted to a numeric code. The numeric code is then stored in memory as a binary number.

Over the years, different coding schemes have been developed to represent characters in computer memory. Historically, the most important of these coding schemes is *ASCII*, which stands for the *American Standard Code for Information Interchange*. ASCII is a set of 128 numeric codes that represent the English letters, various punctuation marks, and other characters. For example, the ASCII code for the uppercase letter *A* is 65. When you type an uppercase *A* on your computer keyboard, the number 65 is stored in memory (as a binary number, of course). This is shown in Figure 1-12.

Figure 1-12 The letter A is stored in memory as the number 65

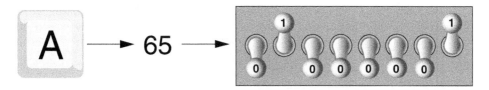

TIP: The acronym ASCII is pronounced "askee."

In case you are curious, the ASCII code for uppercase B is 66, for uppercase C is 67, and so forth. Appendix B shows all the ASCII codes and the characters they represent.

The ASCII character set was developed in the early 1960s and eventually was adopted by all computer manufacturers. ASCII is limited, however, because it defines codes for only 128 characters. To remedy this, the Unicode character set was developed in the early 1990s. *Unicode* is an extensive encoding scheme that not only is compatible with ASCII, but also can represent all the characters of most of the languages in the world. Today, Unicode is quickly becoming the standard character set used in the computer industry.

Negative Integers

Perhaps it has occurred to you by now that the binary numbering technique we have been discussing can represent only integer values, beginning with 0. Negative numbers cannot be represented using this simple technique. To store negative integers in memory, computers use *two's complement arithmetic*. In two's complement arithmetic, a negative integer is encoded so it can be represented as a binary number.

Real Numbers

You might also have realized that the binary numbering technique we have been discussing cannot be used to store real numbers with a fractional part (such as 3.14159). To store a number with a fractional part in memory, computers typically use floating-point notation. In *floating-point* notation, a real number is encoded so it can be represented as a binary number. They are called floating-point numbers because no fixed number of digits comes before or after the decimal point. Floating-point notation can be used to represent real numbers such as 2176.6 or 1.3783652.

Real numbers sometimes have many digits, or even an infinite number of digits, appearing after the decimal point. For example, when we convert the fraction ⅓ to a decimal, we get 1.333333..., with an infinite number of 3s after the decimal point. Storing a value such as ⅓ in memory is problematic because there is no exact way to represent such values using binary numbers. So, floating-point numbers are stored in memory with a specified precision. The *precision* is the total number of digits (both before and after the decimal point) that are stored in memory.

For example, if we use seven digits of precision when storing a floating-point number, it means that only seven digits are stored in memory. If we try to store a real number that has more than seven digits, it will be rounded to seven digits. For example, the number 1.23456789 (which has nine digits) would be rounded to 1.234568.

Other Types of Data

Computers are often referred to as digital devices. The term *digital* can be used to describe anything that uses binary numbers. *Digital data* is data that is stored in binary, and a *digital device* is any device that works with binary data. In this section, we have discussed how numbers and characters are stored in binary, but computers also work with many other types of digital data.

For example, consider the pictures that you take with your digital camera. These images are composed of tiny dots of color known as *pixels*. (The term pixel stands for *picture element*.) As shown in Figure 1-13, each pixel in an image is converted to a numeric code that represents the pixel's color. The numeric code is stored in memory as a binary number.

Figure 1-13 A digital image is stored in binary format

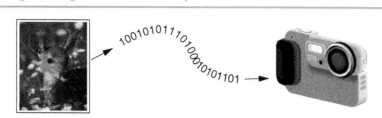

The music that you play on your CD player, iPod, or MP3 player is also digital. A digital song is broken into small pieces known as *samples*. Each sample is converted to a binary number, which can be stored in memory. The more samples a song is divided into, the more it sounds like the original music when it is played back. A CD-quality song is divided into more than 44,000 samples per second!

 Checkpoint

1.9. What amount of memory is enough to store a letter of the alphabet or a small number?

1.10. What do you call a tiny "switch" that can be set to either on or off?

1.11. In what numbering system are all numeric values written as sequences of 0s and 1s?

1.12. What is the purpose of ASCII?

1.13. What encoding scheme is extensive enough to represent the characters of most of the languages in the world?

1.14. What do the terms "digital data" and "digital device" mean?

1.4 How a Program Works

CONCEPT: A computer's CPU only understands instructions that are written in machine language. Because people find it very difficult to write entire programs in machine language, other programming languages have been invented.

Earlier, we stated that the CPU is the most important component in a computer because it is the part of the computer that runs programs. Sometimes the CPU is called the "computer's brain" and is described as being "smart." Although these are common metaphors, you should understand that the CPU is not a brain, and it is not smart. The CPU is an electronic device that is designed to do specific things. In particular, the CPU is designed to perform operations such as the following:

- Reading a piece of data from main memory
- Adding two numbers
- Subtracting one number from another number
- Multiplying two numbers

- Dividing one number by another number
- Moving a piece of data from one memory location to another location
- Determining whether one value is equal to another value
- And so forth...

As you can see from this list, the CPU performs simple operations on pieces of data. The CPU does nothing on its own, however. It has to be told what to do, and that's the purpose of a program. A program is nothing more than a list of instructions that cause the CPU to perform operations.

Each instruction in a program is a command that tells the CPU to perform a specific operation. Here's an example of an instruction that might appear in a program:

```
10110000
```

To you and me, this is only a series of 0s and 1s. To a CPU, however, this is an instruction to perform an operation.[1] It is written in 0s and 1s because CPUs only understand instructions that are written in *machine language*, and machine language instructions are always written in binary.

A machine language instruction exists for each operation that a CPU is capable of performing. For example, there is an instruction for adding numbers; there is an instruction for subtracting one number from another; and so forth. The entire set of instructions that a CPU can execute is known as the CPU's *instruction set*.

NOTE: Several microprocessor companies today manufacture CPUs. Some of the more well-known microprocessor companies are Intel, AMD, and Motorola. If you look carefully at your computer, you might find a tag showing the logo of its microprocessor company.

Each brand of microprocessor has its own unique instruction set, which is typically understood only by microprocessors of the same brand. For example, Intel microprocessors understand the same instructions, but they do not understand instructions for Motorola microprocessors.

The machine language instruction that was previously shown is an example of only one instruction. It takes a lot more than one instruction, however, for the computer to do anything meaningful. The operations that a CPU knows how to perform are very basic in nature; therefore, a meaningful task can be accomplished only if the CPU performs many operations. For example, if you want your computer to calculate the amount of interest that you will earn from your savings account this year, the CPU will have to perform a large number of instructions, carried out in the proper sequence. It is not unusual for a program to contain thousands, or even a million or more machine language instructions.

Programs are usually stored on a secondary storage device such as a disk drive. When you install a program on your computer, you might download it to your computer's disk drive from a Web site or an app store, or possibly copy it to your computer's disk drive from a CD-ROM, or a DVD.

---

[1]The example shown is an actual instruction for an Intel microprocessor. It tells the microprocessor to move a value into the CPU.

Although a program can be stored on a secondary storage device such as a disk drive, it has to be copied into main memory, or RAM, each time the CPU executes it. For example, suppose you have a word processing program on your computer's disk. To execute the program you use the mouse to double-click the program's icon. This causes the program to be copied from the disk into main memory. Then, the computer's CPU executes the copy of the program that is in main memory. This process is illustrated in Figure 1-14.

Figure 1-14 A program is copied into main memory and then executed

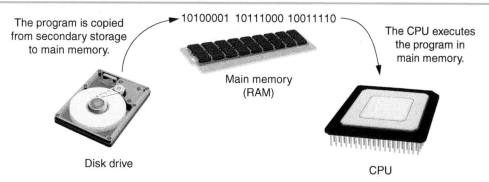

The program is copied from secondary storage to main memory.

10100001 10111000 10011110

The CPU executes the program in main memory.

Main memory (RAM)

Disk drive

CPU

When a CPU executes the instructions in a program, it is engaged in a process that is known as the *fetch–decode–execute cycle*. This cycle, which consists of three steps, is repeated for each instruction in the program, as follows:

1. **Fetch**   A program is a long sequence of machine language instructions. The first step of the cycle is to fetch, or read, the next instruction from memory into the CPU.

2. **Decode**   A machine language instruction is a binary number that represents a command that tells the CPU to perform an operation. In this step, the CPU decodes the instruction that was just fetched from memory, to determine which operation it should perform.

3. **Execute**   The last step in the cycle is to execute, or perform, the operation.

Figure 1-15 illustrates these steps.

Figure 1-15 The fetch–decode–execute cycle

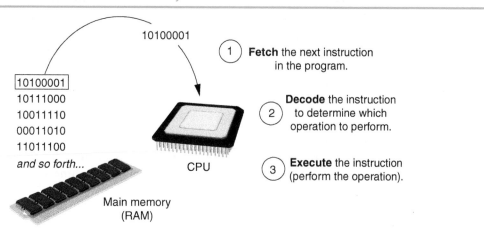

10100001

1. **Fetch** the next instruction in the program.

10100001
10111000
10011110
00011010
11011100
and so forth...

CPU

2. **Decode** the instruction to determine which operation to perform.

3. **Execute** the instruction (perform the operation).

Main memory (RAM)

From Machine Language to Assembly Language

Computers can only execute programs that are written in machine language. As previously mentioned, a program can have thousands, or even a million or more, binary instructions, and writing such a program would be very tedious and time consuming. Programming in machine language would also be very difficult because putting a 0 or a 1 in the wrong place will cause an error.

Although a computer's CPU only understands machine language, it is impractical for people to write programs in machine language. For this reason, in the early days of computing[2] *assembly language* was created as an alternative to machine language. Instead of using binary numbers for instructions, assembly language uses short words that are known as *mnemonics*. For example, in assembly language, the mnemonic add typically means to add numbers, mul typically means to multiply numbers, and mov typically means to move a value to a location in memory. When a programmer uses assembly language to write a program, he or she can write short mnemonics instead of binary numbers.

> **NOTE:** There are many different versions of assembly language. It was mentioned earlier that each brand of CPU has its own machine language instruction set. Each brand of CPU typically has its own assembly language as well.

Assembly language programs cannot be executed by the CPU, however. The CPU only understands machine language, so a special program known as an *assembler* is used to translate an assembly language program into a machine language program. This process is shown in Figure 1-16. The machine language program that is created by the assembler can then be executed by the CPU.

Figure 1-16 An assembler translates an assembly language program into a machine language program

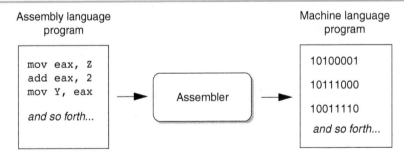

High-Level Languages

Although assembly language makes it unnecessary to write binary machine language instructions, it is not without difficulties. Assembly language is primarily a direct substitute for machine language, and like machine language, it requires

[2]The first assembly language was most likely the one developed in the 1940s at Cambridge University for use with an historic computer known as the EDSAC.

that you know a lot about the CPU. Assembly language also requires that you write a large number of instructions for even the simplest program. Because assembly language is so close in nature to machine language, it is referred to as a *low-level language.*

In the 1950s, a new generation of programming languages known as *high-level languages* appeared. A high-level language allows you to create powerful and complex programs without knowing how the CPU works and without writing large numbers of low-level instructions. In addition, most high-level languages use words that are easy to understand. For example, a programmer using COBOL (which was one of the early high-level languages created in the 1950s) would write the following instruction to display the message *Hello world* on the computer screen:

```
DISPLAY "Hello world"
```

Doing the same thing in assembly language would require several instructions and an intimate knowledge of how the CPU interacts with the computer's video circuitry. As you can see from this example, high-level languages allow programmers to concentrate on the tasks they want to perform with their programs rather than on the details of how the CPU will execute those programs.

Since the 1950s, thousands of high-level languages have been created. Table 1-1 lists several of the more well-known languages.

Table 1-1 Programming languages

Language	Description
Ada	Ada was created in the 1970s, primarily for applications used by the U.S. Department of Defense. The language is named in honor of Countess Ada Lovelace, an influential and historic figure in the field of computing.
BASIC	Beginners All-purpose Symbolic Instruction Code is a general-purpose language that was originally designed in the early 1960s to be simple enough for beginners to learn. Today, there are many different versions of BASIC.
FORTRAN	FORmula TRANslator was the first high-level programming language. It was designed in the 1950s for performing complex mathematical calculations.
COBOL	Common Business-Oriented Language was created in the 1950s and was designed for business applications.
Pascal	Pascal was created in 1970 and was originally designed for teaching programming. The language was named in honor of the mathematician, physicist, and philosopher Blaise Pascal.
C and C++	C and C++ (pronounced "c plus plus") are powerful, general-purpose languages developed at Bell Laboratories. The C language was created in 1972. The C++ language, which was based on the C language, was created in 1983.
C#	Pronounced "c sharp." This language was created by Microsoft around the year 2000 for developing applications based on the Microsoft .NET platform.

(continues next page)

Table 1-1 Programming languages *(continued)*

Language	Description
Java	Java was created by Sun Microsystems in the early 1990s. It can be used to develop programs that run on a single computer or over the Internet from a Web server.
JavaScript	JavaScript, created in the 1990s, can be used in Web pages. Despite its name, JavaScript is not related to Java.
Python	Python is a general-purpose language created in the early 1990s. It has become popular in business and academic applications.
Ruby	Ruby is a general-purpose language that was created in the 1990s. It is increasingly becoming a popular language for programs that run on Web servers.
Visual Basic	Visual Basic (commonly known as VB) is a Microsoft programming language and software development environment that allows programmers to create Windows-based applications quickly. VB was originally created in the early 1990s.

Key Words, Operators, and Syntax: An Overview

Each high-level language has its own set of predefined words that the programmer must use to write a program. The words that make up a high-level programming language are known as *key words* or *reserved words*. Each key word has a specific meaning and cannot be used for any other purpose. In this book we use the C++ programming language. Table 1-2 shows the C++ key words.

Table 1-2 The C++ key words

and	continue	goto	public	try
and_eq	default	if	register	typedef
asm	delete	inline	reinterpret_cast	typeid
auto	do	int	return	typename
bitand	double	long	short	union
bitor	dynamic_cast	mutable	signed	unsigned
bool	else	namespace	sizeof	using
break	enum	new	static	virtual
case	explicit	not	static_cast	void
catch	export	not_eq	struct	volatile
char	extern	operator	switch	wchar_t
class	false	or	template	while
compl	float	or_eq	this	xor
const	for	private	throw	xor_eq
const_cast	friend	protected	true	

NOTE: As you look at Table 1-2, you might be wondering if you will have to memorize these key words or learn what all of them are used for. The answer is no! As you learn to program in C++, you will find that you frequently use a handful of these key words, and you will quickly learn what they do. Even experienced programmers occasionally have to look up the proper usage of a key word that they do not use often.

In addition to key words, programming languages have *operators* that perform various operations on data. For example, all programming languages have math operators that perform arithmetic. In C++, as well as in most other languages, the + sign is an operator that adds two numbers. The following adds 12 and 75:

```
12 + 75
```

Numerous other operators are in the C++ language, many of which you will learn about as you progress through this book.

In addition to key words and operators, each language also has its own *syntax*, which is a set of rules that must be strictly followed when writing a program. The syntax rules dictate how key words, operators, and various punctuation characters must be used in a program. When you are learning a programming language, you must learn the syntax rules for that particular language.

The individual instructions that you use to write a program in a high-level programming language are called *statements*. A programming statement can consist of key words, operators, punctuation, and other allowable programming elements, arranged in the proper sequence to perform an operation.

Compilers and Interpreters

Because the CPU understands only machine language instructions, programs that are written in a high-level language must be translated into machine language. Depending on the language that a program has been written in, the programmer will use either a compiler or an interpreter to make the translation.

A *compiler* is a program that translates a high-level language program into a separate machine language program. The machine language program can then be executed any time it is needed. This is shown in Figure 1-17. As shown in the figure, compiling and executing are two different processes.

Some languages use an *interpreter*, which is a program that both translates and executes the instructions in a high-level language program. As the interpreter reads each individual instruction in the program, it converts it to a machine language instruction and then immediately executes it. This process repeats for every instruction in the program. This process is illustrated in Figure 1-18. Because interpreters combine translation and execution, they typically do not create separate machine language programs.

NOTE: The C++ language uses a compiler to make the translation from C++ to machine language.

Figure 1-17 Compiling a high-level program and executing it

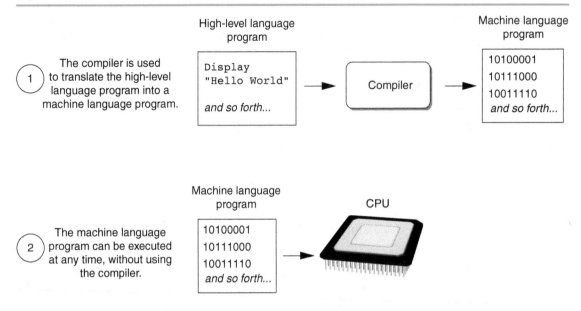

Figure 1-18 Executing a high-level program with an interpreter

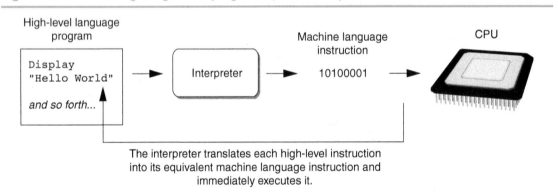

The statements that a programmer writes in a high-level language are called *source code*, or simply *code*. Typically, the programmer types a program's code into a text editor and then saves the code in a file on the computer's disk. Next, the programmer uses a compiler to translate the code into a machine language program or an interpreter to translate and execute the code. If the code contains a syntax error, however, it cannot be translated. A *syntax error* is a mistake, such as a misspelled key word, a missing punctuation character, or the incorrect use of an operator. If this happens, the compiler or interpreter displays an error message, indicating that the program contains a syntax error. The programmer corrects the error and then attempts again to translate the program.

> **NOTE:** Human languages also have syntax rules. Do you remember when you took your first English class, and you learned all those rules about commas, apostrophes, capitalization, and so forth? You were learning the syntax of the English language.
>
> Although people commonly violate the syntax rules of their native language when speaking and writing, other people usually understand what they mean. Unfortunately, compilers and interpreters do not have this ability. If even a single syntax error appears in a program, the program cannot be compiled or executed.

Checkpoint

1.15. A CPU understands instructions that are written only in what language?

1.16. A program has to be copied into what type of memory each time the CPU executes it?

1.17. When a CPU executes the instructions in a program, it is engaged in what process?

1.18. What is assembly language?

1.19. What type of programming language allows you to create powerful and complex programs without knowing how the CPU works?

1.20. Each language has a set of rules that must be strictly followed when writing a program. What is this set of rules called?

1.21. What do you call a program that translates a high-level language program into a separate machine language program?

1.22. What do you call a program that both translates and executes the instructions in a high-level language program?

1.23. What type of mistake is usually caused by a misspelled key word, a missing punctuation character, or the incorrect use of an operator?

1.5 C++ and the App Game Kit Library

CONCEPT: C++ is a high-level programming language, and the App Game Kit provides a library of prewritten code that can be used in C++ to write games and graphical programs.

As previously mentioned, we will be using the C++ programming language in this book. C++ is one of the most popular programming languages used by professional programmers and is widely used by game developers.

The C++ programming language was based on the C programming language. C was created in 1972 by Dennis Ritchie at Bell Laboratories for writing system software. *System software* controls the operation of a computer. For example, an operating system like Windows, Linux, or Mac OS X is system software. Because system software must be efficient and fast, the C programming language was designed as a high-performance language.

The C++ language was created by Bjarne Stroustrup at Bell Laboratories in the early 1980s as an extension of the C language. C++ retains the speed and efficiency of C and adds numerous modern features that make it a good choice for developing large applications. Today, many commercial software applications are written in C++. Game programmers especially like C++ because speed and performance are critical in game programming.

The Core Language and Libraries

The C++ language consists of two parts: The core language and the standard library. The *core language* is the set of key words that you saw in Table 1-2. Each of the key words in the table has a specific meaning and cannot be used for any other purpose. These key words allow a program to perform essential operations, but they do not perform input, output, or other complex procedures. For example, the core language does not have key words for displaying output on the screen or reading input from the keyboard. To perform these types of operations you use a library. A *library* is a collection of prewritten code that exists for some specific purpose. The C++ language has a *standard library* that contains code for performing common operations such as input and output. In Part 1 of this book you will be using the standard library extensively.

In Part 2 of this book, you will begin to use another library known as the App Game Kit. The App Game Kit library is a collection of code that can be used with C++ for handling graphics and writing game programs. App Game Kit was developed by The Game Creators, a software company based in the United Kingdom.

The Software You Will Need

To use this book you will need to install the following software and files:

- **Microsoft Visual Studio 2010, or Microsoft Visual C++ 2010 Express.** The express edition of this software is available for free from Microsoft. See Appendix A for instructions on downloading and installing it.
- **App Game Kit.** Starting in Part 2 of this book you will use App Game Kit (AGK), along with Visual Studio, or Visual C++ 2010 Express. The trial version of App Game Kit works very well with this book, and it does not have a time limit. You can download the App Game Kit trial version from the Game Creators Web site. See Appendix A for instructions.
- **Sample Source Code and Media Files.** These files comprise all of the example programs in the book, as well as graphics and audio files that you can use in your projects. Appendix A provides instructions for downloading the files from the publisher's Web site.

Before going any further, you should make sure that you have downloaded and installed the necessary software and files on your computer. Once you have done that, go through the following tutorials. In the following *In the Spotlight*, you will write a C++ program and execute it. The steps that you will follow in the tutorial will be the same for most of the programs that you will write as you work through Part 1 of this book. In the second *In the Spotlight*, you will open and execute one of the book's example programs.

In the Spotlight:

Writing Your First Program with
Visual C++ 2010 Express

VideoNote

**Writing your first
program with
Visual C++ 2010
Express**

Step 1:   Start Visual Studio, or Visual C++ 2010 Express. (You can find it by clicking the *Start* button, then selecting *All Programs*, then selecting *Visual Studio 2010 Express*, then selecting *Visual C++ 2010 Express*.)

Visual C++ 2010 Express appears similar to Figure 1-19 when it first
starts up. The screen shown in the figure is the *Start Page*.

Figure 1-19 The Visual C++ Start Page

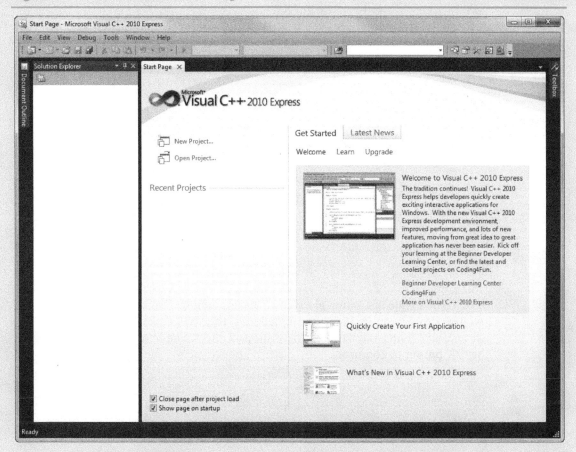

Step 2:   To write a program in Visual C++, you need to create a project. A *project* is
a group of one or more files that make up a software application. (Even if
your program consists of no more than a single source code file, it still must
belong to a project.)

To start a new project, click *File* on the menu bar, then *New*, then
Project. The *New Project* window appears, as shown in Figure 1-20. In the
center section of the window, select *Win32 Console Application*.

Figure 1-20 The New Project dialog box

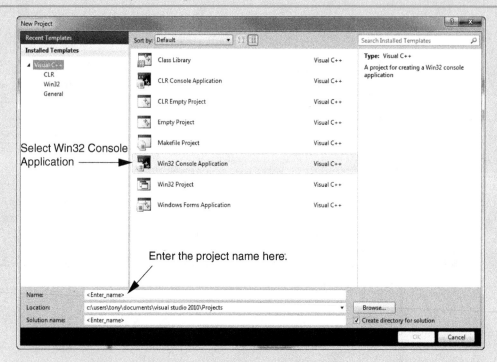

Each project must have a name. Notice that an entry field for the project's name appears at the bottom of the dialog box. As shown in Figure 1-20, this field is initially set to *<Enter_name>*. Change this to `MyFirstProgram`, and then click the *OK* button to continue.

TIP: When your instructor gives you a programming assignment, you will want to give the project a name that identifies the assignment, such as `Lab6`, or `Assignment7`. Enter the name of the project in the *Name* text box, and then click the *OK* button to continue.

NOTE: When you create a project, Visual C++ creates a folder where all the project files are stored. This folder is referred to as the *project folder*, and it has the same name as the project. The *Location:* entry field lets you specify a location on your system where the project folder will be created. You will probably want to keep the default location, but if not, click the *Browse...* button to select a different one.

Step 3: The *Win32 Application Wizard* window appears next, as shown in Figure 1-21. Click *Application Settings*.

Figure 1-21 The Win32 Application Wizard window

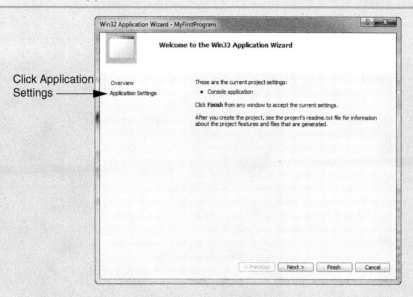

Click Application Settings

Step 4:   The *Application Settings* window appears next, as shown in Figure 1-22. As shown in the figure, make sure *Console Application* is selected, and check *Empty project*. Click *Finish*.

Figure 1-22 The Application Settings window

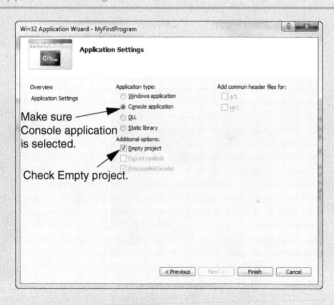

Make sure Console application is selected.

Check Empty project.

Step 5:   Visual C++ has a *Solution Explorer* window that shows a list of all the files in your project. Figure 1-23 shows the *Solution Explorer*, which should be visible. If you do not see the *Solution Explorer*, click *View* on the menu bar, then select *Other Windows*, and then click *Solution Explorer*.

Figure 1-23 The Solution Explorer

The Solution Explorer →

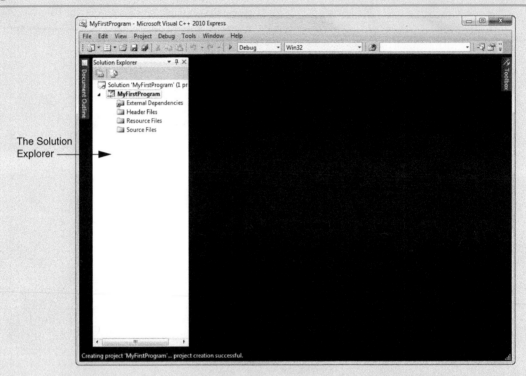

Step 6: Notice that one of the folders shown in the *Solution Explorer* is named *Source Files*. Right-click the *Source Files* folder, then select *Add*, then click *New Item*. Figure 1-24 shows the pop-up menus.

Figure 1-24 Adding a source file

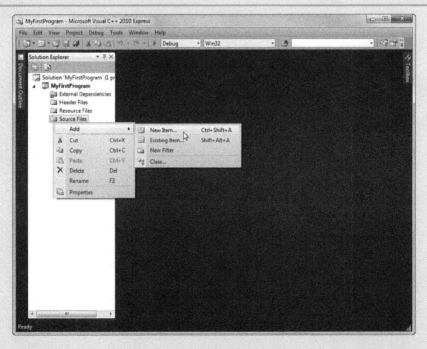

Step 7: The *Add New Item* window appears next, as shown in Figure 1-25. Select *C++ File (.cpp)* in the center section of the window. Notice that an entry field for the source file's name appears at the bottom of the window. This field is initially set to *<Enter_name>*. Change this to `MyFirstProgram`, and then click the *Add* button to add the new source file to the project.

Figure 1-25 The Solution Explorer

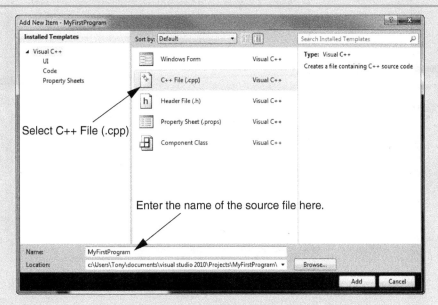

Select C++ File (.cpp)

Enter the name of the source file here.

NOTE: Notice that in this example, we named both the project and the source file `MyFirstProgram`. You do not have to use the same name for both the project and the source file, but it's a common practice to do so.

Step 8: In the *Solution Explorer*, you should now see the file `MyFirstProgram.cpp` listed, as shown in Figure 1-26. A text editing window should also be opened, as shown in the figure. This text editing window is where you will type the C++ code for the file.

TIP: If the text editing window is not opened, you can double-click `MyFirstProgram.cpp` in the *Solution Explorer*. This will open the text editing window.

Type the following C++ code, exactly as it appears, in the text editing window. (For now, do not worry about what the code does. This exercise is merely meant to give you practice working with Visual C++.)

```cpp
#include <iostream>
using namespace std;

int main()
{
    cout << "This is my first program!" << endl;
    return 0;
}
```

Figure 1-26 The `MyFirstProgram.cpp` file added to the project

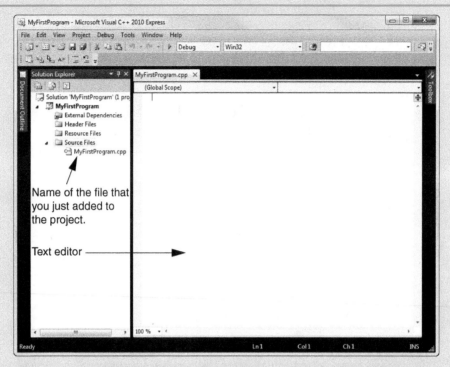

When you have finished typing the code, the text editing window should appear as shown in Figure 1-27.

Figure 1-27 Code typed into the text editing window

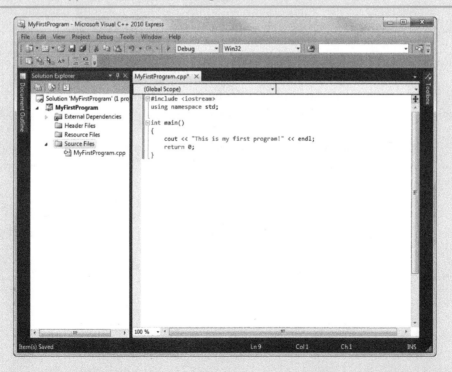

Step 9: Click *File* on the menu bar, then click *Save All* to save the project. (Anytime you are writing a program, it is a good idea to save the project often.)

Step 10: Now you will compile and execute the program. Earlier in this chapter, you read that compiling and executing are two separate processes. Visual C++, however, can compile a program and immediately execute it, as long as there are no errors in the program. That is what you will do in this step.

Press Ctrl+F5 on the keyboard. Next, you will see the dialog box, as shown in Figure 1-28. Click the *Yes* button.

Figure 1-28 Confirmation dialog box

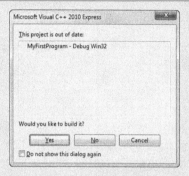

Step 11: If you typed the program with no mistakes, you should see the program execute, as shown in Figure 1-29. The program simply prints the following message: *This is my first program!* Press any key on the keyboard to end the program.

Figure 1-29 `MyFirstprogram.cpp` running

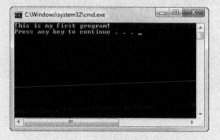

If you did not type the program exactly as it was shown, you will probably see the following error message: *There were build errors. Would you like to continue and run the last successful build?* If you see this, click the *No* button, then compare the code that you typed with the code shown in Step 8. Make sure your code is exactly like the code we have given you. After correcting any mistakes, repeat Steps 10 and 11.

Step 12: To exit Visual C++, click *File* on the menu bar, then click *Exit*.

In the Spotlight:
Opening and Executing an Example Program

VideoNote

**Opening and
Executing an
Example Program**

As you work through this book you will see many example programs. Program 1-1 shows how an example program will appear. (For now, do not worry about what the program does. We are merely using it for demonstration purposes.)

Program 1-1   (Welcome.cpp)

```cpp
#include <iostream>
using namespace std;

int main()
{
    cout << "Welcome to the world of C++ programming." << endl;
    return 0;
}
```

Notice that the program's name, Welcome.cpp, is shown at the top of the program listing. Assuming you have downloaded the student source code files from the publisher's Web site (www.pearsonhighered.com/gaddis), you can follow these steps to open, compile, and execute the program.

Step 1:   Start Visual C++ 2010 Express.

Step 2:   Click *File* on the menu bar, then select *Open*, then select *Project/Solution*. The *Open Project* dialog box will appear. Navigate to the location on your system where you saved the student source code files, and locate the source code folder for Chapter 1. Inside that folder you will see another folder named *Welcome*. Open that folder, and you will see a file named *Welcome. sln*, as shown in Figure 1-30. Select the *Welcome.sln* file and click *Open*.

Figure 1-30 The Open Project dialog box

Step 3: You have just opened the project that contains the Welcome.cpp program. Locate the entry for the *Welcome.cpp* file in the *Solution Explorer* window, as shown in Figure 1-31. (If the *Solution Explorer* window is not visible, click *View* on the menu bar, then select *Other Windows*, then click *Solution Explorer*.) Double-click the entry for the *Welcome.cpp* file to open it in the text editing window, as shown in Figure 1-32.

Figure 1-31 The Welcome.cpp file's entry in the Solution Explorer

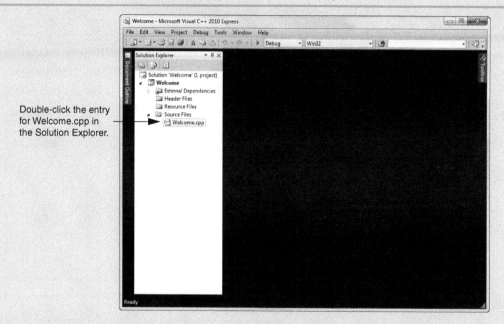

Double-click the entry for Welcome.cpp in the Solution Explorer.

Figure 1-32 The Welcome.cpp file opened in the text editing window

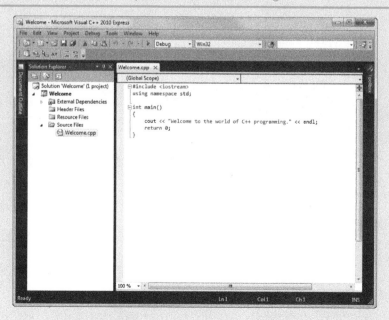

Step 4:   Press Ctrl+F5 on the keyboard to compile and execute the program. If the dialog box that was previously shown in Figure 1-28 appears, click the *Yes* button. You should see the program execute, as shown in Figure 1-33. Pressing any key on the keyboard will end the program.

Figure 1-33 The Welcome.cpp program executing

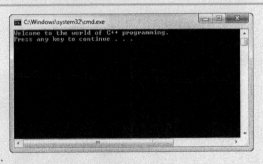

Review Questions

Multiple Choice

1. A(n) _____ is a set of instructions that a computer follows to perform a task.
   a. compiler
   b. program
   c. interpreter
   d. programming language

2. The physical devices that a computer is made of are referred to as _____.
   a. hardware
   b. software
   c. the operating system
   d. tools

3. The part of a computer that runs programs is called _____.
   a. RAM
   b. secondary storage
   c. main memory
   d. the CPU

4. Today, CPUs are small chips known as _____.
   a. ENIACs
   b. microprocessors
   c. memory chips
   d. operating systems

5. The computer stores a program while the program is running, as well as storing the data that the program is working with, in _____.
   a. secondary storage
   b. the CPU
   c. main memory
   d. the microprocessor

6. This is a volatile type of memory that is used only for temporary storage while a program is running: _____.
   a. RAM
   b. secondary storage
   c. the disk drive
   d. the USB drive

7. A type of memory that can hold data for long periods of time—even when there is no power to the computer is called _____.
   a. RAM
   b. main memory
   c. secondary storage
   d. CPU storage

8. A component that collects data from people or other devices and sends it to the computer is called _____.
   a. an output device
   b. an input device
   c. a secondary storage device
   d. main memory

9. A video display is a(n) _____ device.
   a. output device
   b. input device
   c. secondary storage device
   d. main memory

10. A _____ is enough memory to store a letter of the alphabet or a small number.
    a. byte
    b. bit
    c. switch
    d. transistor

11. A byte is made up of eight _____.
    a. CPUs
    b. instructions
    c. variables
    d. bits

12. In a(n) _____ numbering system, all numeric values are written as sequences of 0s and 1s.
    a. hexadecimal
    b. binary
    c. octal
    d. decimal

13. A bit that is turned off represents the following value: _____.
    a. 1
    b. −1
    c. 0
    d. "no"

14. A set of 128 numeric codes that represent the English letters, various punctuation marks, and other characters is _____.
    a. binary numbering
    b. ASCII
    c. Unicode
    d. ENIAC

15. An extensive encoding scheme that can also represent the characters of most of the languages in the world is _____.
    a. binary numbering
    b. ASCII
    c. Unicode
    d. ENIAC

16. Negative numbers are encoded using the _____ technique.
    a. two's complement
    b. floating-point
    c. ASCII
    d. Unicode

17. Real numbers are encoded using the _____ technique.
    a. two's complement
    b. floating-point
    c. ASCII
    d. Unicode

18. The tiny dots of color that digital images are composed of are called _____.
    a. bits
    b. bytes
    c. color packets
    d. pixels

19. If you look at a machine language program, you will see _____.
    a. C++ code
    b. a stream of binary numbers
    c. English words
    d. circuits

20. In the _____ part of the fetch–decode–execute cycle, the CPU determines which operation it should perform.
    a. fetch
    b. decode
    c. execute
    d. immediately after the instruction is executed

21. Computers can only execute programs that are written in _____.
    a. Java
    b. assembly language
    c. machine language
    d. C++

22. The _____ translates an assembly language program to a machine language program.
    a. assembler
    b. compiler
    c. translator
    d. interpreter

23. The words that make up a high-level programming language are called _____.
    a. binary instructions
    b. mnemonics
    c. commands
    d. key words

24. The rules that must be followed when writing a program are called _____.
    a. syntax
    b. punctuation
    c. key words
    d. operators

25. A(n) _____ program translates a high-level language program into a separate machine language program.
    a. assembler
    b. compiler
    c. translator
    d. utility

True or False

1. Today, CPUs are huge devices made of electrical and mechanical components such as vacuum tubes and switches.

2. Main memory is also known as RAM.

3. Any piece of data that is stored in a computer's memory must be stored as a binary number.

4. Images, like the ones you make with your digital camera, cannot be stored as binary numbers.

5. Machine language is the only language that a CPU understands.

6. Assembly language is considered a high-level language.

7. An interpreter is a program that both translates and executes the instructions in a high-level language program.

8. A syntax error does not prevent a program from being compiled and executed.

9. The C++ language has built-in features for writing games and graphical programs.

10. C++ is a good language for game programming because it is fast and efficient.

Short Answer

1. Why is the CPU the most important component in a computer?

2. What number does a bit that is turned on represent? What number does a bit that is turned off represent?

3. What would you call a device that works with binary data?

4. What are the words that make up a high-level programming language called?

5. What are the short words that are used in assembly language called?

6. What is the difference between a compiler and an interpreter?

7. What language was the C++ language based on?

8. What is the difference between the C++ core language and the standard library?

Programming Exercises

VideoNote

Programming
Exercise 1:
Creating a
new program

1. This exercise will give you additional practice using Visual C++ to create a project. Before attempting this exercise you should complete the steps in the first *In the Spotlight* in this chapter.

Use the steps that you followed in the first *In the Spotlight* in this chapter to create a new project named MyProgram. When you add a C++ source code file to the project (as you did in Step 4 of the first *In the Spotlight*), name it `MyProgram.cpp`. Then, type the following code into the file. (Be sure to type the code exactly as it appears here.)

```cpp
#include <iostream>
using namespace std;

int main()
{
    cout << "Programming is fun!" << endl;
    return 0;
}
```

Save the project, then compile and execute it. If you typed the code exactly as shown, the window shown in Figure 1-34 should appear. Press any key on the keyboard to exit the program.

If you did not type the program exactly as shown, you will probably see the following error message: *There were build errors. Would you like to continue and run the last successful build?* If you see this, click the *No* button, then compare the code that you typed with the code shown in the book. Make sure your code is exactly like the code we have given you. After correcting any mistakes, save the project, then try to compile and execute it again.

Figure 1-34 Output of the `MyProgram.cpp` program

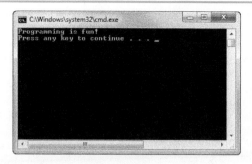

2. Use what you've learned about the binary numbering system in this chapter to convert the following decimal numbers to binary:

   11
   65
   100
   255

3. Use what you've learned about the binary numbering system in this chapter to convert the following binary numbers to decimal:

   1101
   1000
   101011

4. Use the Web to research the history of computer games, and answer the following questions:

   • From your research, what was the first computer game?
   • Have computer games that do not use graphics ever been created?
   • What is a serious game?

2 C++ Fundamentals

2.1 The Parts of a C++ Program

CONCEPT: Your first step in learning C++ is to learn the basic parts of a C++ program.

As you work through Part 1 of this book, all the C++ programs that you will write will contain the following code:

```cpp
#include <iostream>
using namespace std;

int main()
{
    return 0;
}
```

You can think of this as a skeleton program. As it is, it does absolutely nothing. But you can add additional code to this program to make it perform an operation. Let's take a closer look at the parts of the skeleton program.

> **NOTE:** At this point, it is not critical that you understand everything about the skeleton program. The description that follows is meant to demystify the code, at least a little. Because you are a beginning programmer, you should expect that some of the following concepts will be unclear. As you dig deeper into the C++ language, you will understand these concepts. So, don't despair! Your journey is just beginning.

The first line reads:

```
#include <iostream>
```

This is called an *include directive*. It causes the contents of a file named `iostream` to be included in the program. The `iostream` file is known as a *header file*, and it contains a prewritten code that allows a C++ program to display output on the screen and read input from the keyboard. The next line reads:

```
using namespace std;
```

A program usually contains several items that have names. C++ uses *namespaces* to organize the names of program entities. The statement `using namespace std;` declares that the program will be accessing entities whose names are part of a namespace called `std`. The reason the program needs access to the `std` namespace is because every name created by the `iostream` file is part of that namespace. For a program to use the entities in `iostream`, it must have access to the `std` namespace. (Notice that the statement ends with a semicolon. More about that in a moment.)

The following code appears next:

```
int main()
{
    return 0;
}
```

This is called a *function*. You will learn a great deal about functions later, but for now, you simply need to know that a function is a group of programming statements that collectively has a name. The name of this function is `main`. Every C++ program must have a function named `main`, which serves as the program's starting point.

Notice that a set of curly braces appears below the line that reads `int main()`. The purpose of these braces is to enclose the statements that are in the `main` function. In this particular program, the `main` function contains only one statement, which is

```
return 0;
```

This statement returns the number 0 to the operating system when the program finishes executing. When you write your first C++ programs, you will write other statements inside the main function's curly braces, as indicated in Figure 2-1.

> **NOTE:** C++ is a case-sensitive language. That means it regards uppercase letters as being entirely different characters than their lowercase counterparts. In C++, the name of the `main` function must be written in all lowercase letters. C++ doesn't see `Main` the same as `main`, or `INT` the same as `int`. This is true for all the C++ key words.

Figure 2-1 The skeleton program

```
#include <iostream>
using namespace std;

int main()
{                        ←——————————  You will write other C++
                                       statements in this area.
    return 0;
}
```

Semicolons

In C++, a complete programming *statement* ends with a semicolon. You'll notice that some lines of code in the skeleton program do not end with a semicolon, however. For example, the include directive does not end with a semicolon because, technically speaking, directives are not statements. The main function header does not end with a semicolon because it marks the beginning of a function. Also, the curly braces are not followed by a semicolon because they are not statements, as they form a container that holds statements. If this is confusing, don't despair! As you practice writing C++ programs more and more, you will develop an intuitive understanding of the difference between statements and lines of code that are not considered statements.

 Checkpoint

2.1. Rearrange the following statements to make a skeleton C++ program:

```
int main()
return 0;
}
#include <iostream>
{
using namespace std;
```

 2.2 **Displaying Screen Output**

CONCEPT: You write cout statements to display output in a console window.

VideoNote
Using cout

In this section you will learn to write programs that produce output on the screen. The simplest type of screen output that a program can display is *console output*, which is merely plain text. The word *console* is an old computer term. It comes from the days when a computer operator interacted with the system by typing on a terminal. The terminal, which consisted of a simple screen and keyboard, was known as the *console*.

On modern computers, running graphical operating systems such as Windows or Mac OS, console output is usually displayed in a window such as the one shown in Figure 2-2.

Figure 2-2 A console window

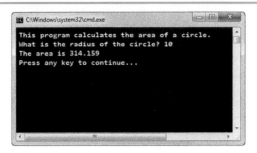

To display console output in C++, you write a cout statement (pronounced *see out*). A cout statement begins with the word cout, followed by the << operator, followed by an item of data that is to be displayed. The statement ends with a semicolon. Program 2-1 demonstrates.

NOTE: The line numbers that are shown at the beginning of each line are *not* part of the program. This book shows line numbers in each program because it makes it easier to refer to specific parts of the program. When you are typing code, however, do not type line numbers into your programs!

Program 2-1   (**HelloWorld.cpp**)

```
1 #include <iostream>
2 using namespace std;
3
4 int main()
5 {
6    cout << "Hello world";
7    return 0;
8 }
```

Program Output

```
Hello world
```

The << operator is known as the *stream insertion operator*. It always appears on the left side of the item of data that you want to display. Notice that in line 6, the << operator appears to the left of the message *Hello world*, which is enclosed in a set of quotation marks. The quotation marks are not to be displayed. They simply mark the beginning and the end of the text that we wish to display. When the program runs, *Hello world* is displayed.

Programs almost always work with data of some type. For example, Program 2-1 uses the following piece of data, in line 6:

```
"Hello world"
```

This piece of data is a sequence of characters. In programming terms, a sequence of characters that is used as data is called a *string*. When a string appears in the actual code of a program, it is called a *string literal*. In program code, a string literal is enclosed in quotation marks. As mentioned earlier, the quotation marks simply mark where the string begins and ends.

You can display multiple items with a single cout statement, as long as a << operator appears to the left of each item. Program 2-2 shows an example. In line 6, three items of data are being displayed: the string literal "Programming ", the string literal "is ", and the string literal "fun.". Notice that the << operator appears to the left of each item.

Program 2-2   (MultipleItems.cpp)

```
1 #include <iostream>
2 using namespace std;
3
4 int main()
5 {
6    cout << "Programming " << "is " << "fun.";
7    return 0;
8 }
```

Program Output

```
Programming is fun.
```

Take a closer look at line 6 of Program 2-2:

```
                    Notice the space.
                          ↓
  cout << "Programming " << "is " << "fun.";
                                ↑
                    Notice the space.
```

Notice that the string literal "Programming " ends with a space, and the string literal "is " ends with a space. That is because in the program output, we want a space to separate the words, as shown here:

```
      Notice the space.
            ↓
  Programming is fun.
                ↑
      Notice the space.
```

Without the spaces in the string literals, the words would appear jammed together in the output. For example, if the statement in line 6 had been written like this:

```
  cout << "Programming" << "is" << "fun.";
```

Then, the output would appear as:

```
  Programmingisfun.
```

Using the endl Manipulator

When you display output with cout, the output is displayed as one continuous line on the screen. For example, look at Program 2-3. Even though the program has three cout statements, its output appears on one line.

Program 2-3 (OneLine.cpp)

```
1 #include <iostream>
2 using namespace std;
3
4 int main()
5 {
6    cout << "Programming ";
7    cout << "is ";
8    cout << "fun.";
9    return 0;
10 }
```

Program Output

```
Programming is fun.
```

The output comes out as one long line is because the cout statement does not start a new line unless told to do so. One way to instruct cout to start a new line is to use the endl manipulator. (You pronounce endl as "end L," or "end line.") Program 2-4 shows an example.

Program 2-4 (ThreeLines.cpp)

```
1 #include <iostream>
2 using namespace std;
3
4 int main()
5 {
6    cout << "Programming" << endl;
7    cout << "is" << endl;
8    cout << "fun." << endl;
9    return 0;
10 }
```

Program Output

```
Programming
is
fun.
```

 NOTE: The last character in endl is the lowercase letter *L*, *not* the number one.

Every time cout encounters an endl stream manipulator, it advances the output to the beginning of the next line for subsequent printing. The manipulator can be inserted anywhere in the stream of characters sent to cout, outside the double quotes. The following statements show an example.

```
cout << "My pets are" << endl << "dog";
cout << endl << "cat" << endl << "bird" << endl;
```

Using the \n Escape Sequence

Another way to cause cout to go to a new line is to insert an *escape sequence* in the string literal itself. An escape sequence starts with the backslash character (\) and is followed by one or more control characters. It allows you to control the way output is displayed by embedding commands within a string literal. Program 2-5 is an example.

Program 2-5   (EscapeSequence.cpp)

```
 1 #include <iostream>
 2 using namespace std;
 3
 4 int main()
 5 {
 6    cout << "The following items were top sellers\n";
 7    cout << "during the month of June:\n";
 8    cout << "Computer games\nCoffee";
 9    cout << "\nAspirin\n";
10    return 0;
11 }
```

Program Output

```
The following items were top sellers
during the month of June:
Computer games
Coffee
Aspirin
```

The *newline escape sequence* is \n. When cout encounters \n in a string, it doesn't print it on the screen, but interprets it as a special command to advance the output cursor to the next line. In many situations, using the \n escape sequence within a string literal requires less typing than using endl.

A common mistake made by beginning C++ students is to use a forward slash (/) instead of a backslash (\) when trying to write an escape sequence. This will not work. For example, look at the following code.

```
// Error!
cout << "Four Score/nAnd seven/nYears ago./n";
```

In this code, the programmer accidentally wrote /n when he or she meant to write \n. The statement will simply display the /n characters on the screen. This code will display the following output:

```
Four Score/nAnd seven/nYears ago./n
```

Another common mistake is to forget to put the \n inside quotation marks. For example, the following code will not compile.

```
// Error! This code will not compile.
cout << "Good" << \n;
cout << "Morning" << \n;
```

This code will result in an error because the \n sequences are not inside quotation marks. We can correct the code by placing the \n sequences inside the string literals, as shown here:

```
// This will work.
cout << "Good\n";
cout << "Morning\n";
```

C++ has many escape sequences. They give you the ability to exercise greater control over the way information is output by your program. Table 2-1 lists a few of them.

Table 2-1 Common Escape Sequences

Sequence	Name	Description
\n	Newline	Causes the cursor to go to the next line for subsequent printing.
\t	Horizontal tab	Causes the cursor to skip over to the next tab stop.
\a	Alarm	Causes the computer to beep.
\b	Backspace	Causes the cursor to back up, or move left one position.
\r	Return	Causes the cursor to go to the beginning of the current line, not the next line.
\\	Backslash	Causes a backslash to be printed.
\'	Single quote	Causes a single quotation mark to be printed.
\"	Double quote	Causes a double quotation mark to be printed.

 WARNING! When using escape sequences, do not put a space between the backslash and the control character.

When you type an escape sequence in a string literal, you type two characters (a backslash followed by another character). However, an escape sequence is stored in memory as a single character. For example, consider the following string literal:

```
"One\nTwo\nThree\n"
```

The diagram in Figure 2-3 breaks this string literal into its individual characters. Notice how each of the \n escape sequences are considered one character.

Figure 2-3 Characters stored in memory

O n e \n T w o \n T h r e e \n

Checkpoint

2.2. What will the following statement display?

```
cout << "one" << "two" << "three" << endl;
```

2.3. What will the following statement display?

```
cout << "one"
     << "two"
     << "three"
     << endl;
```

2.4. What will the following statement display?

```
cout << "one"
     << endl
     << "two"
     << endl
     << "three"
     << endl;
```

2.5. What will the following statement display?

```
cout << "one\n" << "two\n" << "three\n";
```

2.6. What will the following statement display?

```
cout << "one\ntwo\nthree\n";
```

2.3 More about the `#include` Directive

CONCEPT: The `#include` directive causes the contents of another file to be inserted into the program.

Now is a good time to expand our discussion of the `#include` directive. The following line has appeared near the top of every example program:

```
#include <iostream>
```

As mentioned earlier, this directive causes the contents of a file named `iostream` to be included in the program. When you compile a C++ source code file, a program known as the *preprocessor* first reads the C++ source code, looking for lines that begin with the `#` symbol. These lines are special directives that the preprocessor executes. The `#include` directive causes the preprocessor to copy the contents of the file that is named inside the angled brackets (<>) into the C++ program. Files such as `iostream`, which are included by the preprocessor, are known as *header files*.

The `iostream` header file must be included in any program that uses `cout` to display output. This is because `cout` is not part of the core C++ language. Specifically, it is part of the *input–output stream library*. The header file, iostream, contains code that must be included in any program that uses cout.

Preprocessor directives are not C++ statements. They are commands to the preprocessor, which runs prior to the compiler (hence the name "preprocessor"). The preprocessor's job is to set programs up in a way that makes life easier for the programmer.

WARNING! Do not put semicolons at the end of processor directives. Because preprocessor directives are not C++ statements, they do not require semicolons. In many cases an error will result from a preprocessor directive terminated with a semicolon.

NOTE: When a header file is included in a C++ program by the preprocessor, you don't actually see the contents of the header file appear in the program. The contents of the header file are only temporarily inserted into the C++ program for the purpose of compiling the program.

2.4 A First Look at Variables

CONCEPT: A variable is a storage location in memory that is represented by a name.

Quite often a program needs to store data in the computer's memory so it can perform operations on that data. For example, consider the typical online shopping experience: You browse a Web site and add the items that you want to purchase to the shopping cart. As you add items to the shopping cart, data about those items is stored in memory. Then, when you click the checkout button, a program running on the Web site's computer calculates the total of all the items you have in your shopping cart, applicable sales taxes, shipping costs, and the total of all these charges. When the program performs these calculations, it stores the results in the computer's memory.

Programs use variables to store data in memory. A *variable* is a storage location in memory that is represented by a name. For example, a program that calculates the sales tax on a purchase might use a variable named tax to hold that value in memory. And a program that calculates the distance from Earth to a distant star might use a variable named distance to hold that value in memory.

In C++, you must declare a variable in a program before you can use it to store data. You do this with a *variable declaration*, which specifies two things about the variable:

1. The variable's data type, which is the type of data the variable will hold
2. The variable's name

A variable declaration statement is written in this general format:

    DataType VariableName;

Let's take a closer look at each of these.

Data Type

A variable's *data type* indicates the type of data that the variable will hold. Before you declare a variable, you need to think about the type of values that will be stored in the variable. For example, will the variable hold a number or a string? If it will hold a number, what kind of number will it be, an integer or a real number? When you have determined the kind of data that the variable will hold, you select one of the data types that C++ provides for variables. The C++ language provides many data types for storing fundamental types of data, such as integers, real numbers, and characters. We will look at several of them in this chapter.

Variable Name

A *variable name* identifies a variable in the program code. When naming a variable, you should always choose a meaningful name that indicates what the variable is used for. For example, a variable that holds the temperature might be named `temperature`, and a variable that holds a car's speed might be named `speed`. You may be tempted to give variables short, nondescript names such as `x` or `b2`, but names such as these give no clue to the purpose of the variables.

In addition, you must follow these rules when naming a variable:

- The first character must be one of the letters *a* through *z* or *A* through *Z* or an underscore character (_).
- After the first character, you may use the letters *a* through *z* or *A* through *Z*, the digits 0 through 9, or underscores.
- The name cannot contain spaces.

Table 2-2 lists some potential variable names and indicates whether each is legal or illegal in C++.

Table 2-2 Legal and Illegal Variable Names

Name	Legal or Illegal?
dayOfWeek	Legal
3rdQuarterSales	Illegal because identifiers cannot begin with a digit.
customer*first*name	Illegal because the * character is not allowed.
totalPoints	Legal
sales tax total	Illegal because identifiers cannot contain spaces.

Because a variable's name should reflect the variable's purpose, programmers often find themselves creating names that are made of multiple words. For example, consider the following variable names:

```
grosspay
payrate
hotdogssoldtoday
```

Unfortunately, these names are not easily read by the human eye because the words aren't separated. Because we can't have spaces in variable names, we need to find another way to separate the words in a multiword variable name and make it more readable to the human eye.

One way to do this is to use the underscore character to represent a space. For example, the following variable names are easier to read than those previously shown:

```
gross_pay
pay_rate
hot_dogs_sold_today
```

Another way to address this problem is to use the *camelCase* naming convention. camelCase names are written in the following manner:

- You begin writing the name with lowercase letters.
- The first character of the second and subsequent words is written in uppercase.

For example, the following variable names are written in camelCase:

```
grossPay
payRate
hotDogsSoldToday
```

> **NOTE:** This style of naming is called camelCase because the uppercase characters that appear in a name are sometimes reminiscent of a camel's humps.

Commonly Used Data Types

Table 2-3 lists some of the C++ data types, gives their memory size in bytes, and describes the type of data that each can hold. Note that in Part 1 of this book we will primarily use the int, double, and string data types.[1]

Table 2-3. Some of the C++ Data Types

Data Type	Size	What It Can Hold
short	2 bytes	Integers in the range of −32,768 to +32,767
int	4 bytes	Integers in the range of −2,147,483,648 to +2,147,483,647
long	4 bytes	Integers in the range of −2,147,483,648 to +2,147,483,647
float	4 bytes	Floating-point numbers in the range of $\pm3.4\times10^{-38}$ to $\pm3.4\times10^{38}$, with 7 digits of accuracy
double	8 bytes	Floating-point numbers in the range of $\pm1.7\times10^{-308}$ to $\pm1.7\times10^{308}$, with 15 digits of accuracy
char	1 byte	Can store integers in the range of −128 to +127. Typically used to store characters.
string	Varies	Strings of text.
bool	1 byte	Stores the values true or false

[1]To use the string data type, you must write the directive #include <string> at the top of your program. To be correct, string is not a data type in C++, it is a class. We use it as a data type, though.

The int, float, and double Data Types

C++ provides several data types for storing numbers, but most of the time, you will use the int data type to store integers and the float and double data type to store real numbers. In Part 1 of this text, we will primarily use the int and double data types. Here are examples of how you would declare an int and a double variable:

```
int speed;
double distance;
```

The first statement declares an int variable named speed. The second example declares a double variable named distance.

In code, you use an *assignment statement* to store a value in a variable. For example, suppose you have declared an int variable named speed, as previously shown. The following assignment statement assigns the value 60 to the speed variable:

```
speed = 60;
```

The equal sign (=) is known as the *assignment operator*. It assigns the value that appears on its right side to the variable that appears on its left side. In this example, the item on the left side of the assignment operator is the speed variable.

Let's look at another assignment statement example. Suppose you have declared a double variable named distance, as previously shown. The following assignment statement assigns the value 27.5 to the distance variable:

```
distance = 27.5;
```

> **WARNING!** When writing assignment statements, remember that the variable receiving the value must be on the left side of the = operator. For example, assuming that speed is a variable that has been declared, the following statement will cause an error when you compile the program:
>
> ```
> 60 = speed;    ← ERROR!
> ```

Once you have assigned a value to a variable, you can use cout to display the variable's value. For example, assuming the speed variable has been declared and a value has been assigned to it, the following statement displays its value:

```
cout << speed << endl;
```

Notice that the variable name is not enclosed in quotation marks. Only string literals are enclosed in quotation marks. For example, the following statement does not display the value of the speed variable. Instead, it displays the string "speed" on the screen:

```
cout << "speed" << endl;  ← Does not display the value of the speed variable!
```

The code in Program 2-6 demonstrates how variables are declared, assigned values, and their values displayed on the screen.

Program 2-6   (**VariableDemo.cpp**)

```
1 #include <iostream>
2 using namespace std;
3
4 int main()
5 {
6    int speed;
7    double distance;
8
9    speed = 60;
10   distance = 27.5;
11   cout << "The car's speed was " << speed
12        << " miles-per-hour and it traveled "
13        << distance << " miles.\n";
14   return 0;
15 }
```

Program Output

```
The car's speed was 60 miles-per-hour and it traveled 27.5 miles.
```

Let's take a closer look at this program.

- Line 6 declares an int variable named speed.
- Line 7 declares a double variable named distance.
- Line 9 assigns the value 60 to the speed variable.
- Line 10 assigns the value 27.5 to the distance variable.
- The cout statement in lines 11 through 13 displays a message that includes the values of the speed and distance variables.

Declaring Variables Inside a Function

Notice that the speed and distance variables in Program 2-6 are declared inside the main function. Variables that are declared inside a function are known as local variables. A *local variable* belongs to the function in which it is declared, and only statements inside that function can access the variable. (The term *local* is meant to indicate that the variable can be used only locally, within the function in which it is declared.)

For now, all the programs that you will write will have only one function, main. In Chapter 5, you will learn to write programs with multiple functions, and you will be able to declare variables in each function.

Declare Variables Before Using Them

Notice in Program 2-6 that the variable declarations (in lines 6 and 7) appear before any other statements in the function. The purpose of a variable declaration is to tell the compiler that you plan to use a variable of a specified name to store a particular type of data in the program. A variable declaration statement causes the variable to be created in memory. For this reason, a variable's declaration statement must appear *before* any other statements in the function that use the variable. This makes perfect sense because you cannot store a value in a variable if the variable has not been created in memory.

Variable Initialization

You can optionally initialize a variable with a value when you declare the variable. A variable declaration and initialization statement is written in this general format:

```
DataType VariableName = value;
```

In the general format, *value* is the starting value that the variable should be initialized with. For example, the following statement declares an `int` variable named `speed`, initialized with the value 60:

```
int speed = 60;
```

Program 2-7 shows an example. In this program, the `speed` and `distance` variables are declared and initialized in lines 6 and 7.

Program 2-7   **(VariableInit.cpp)**

```cpp
 1 #include <iostream>
 2 using namespace std;
 3
 4 int main()
 5 {
 6    int speed = 60;
 7    double distance = 27.5;
 8
 9    cout << "The car's speed was " << speed
10         << " miles-per-hour and it traveled "
11         << distance << " miles.\n";
12    return 0;
13 }
```

Program Output

```
The car's speed was 60 miles-per-hour and it traveled 27.5 miles.
```

You are not required to initialize a variable when you declare it, but it is usually a good idea to do so. If a local variable is declared, but not initialized, it will contain an unpredictable value. For this reason, it is almost certain that an error will result if a program uses an uninitialized local variable.

Declaring Multiple Variables with One Statement

You can declare multiple variables of the same data type with one declaration statement. Here is an example:

```
int month, day, year;
```

This statement declares three `int` variables named `month`, `day`, and `year`. Notice that commas separate the variable names. Here is an example of how we can declare and initialize the variables with one statement:

```
int month = 5, day = 4, year = 1865;
```

Remember, you can break up a long statement so it spreads across two or more lines. Sometimes you will see long variable declarations written across multiple lines, like this:

```
int month = 5,
    day = 4,
    year = 1865;
```

Numeric Literals

A *numeric literal* is a number that is written into a program's code. When you know, at the time that you are writing a program's code, that you want to store a specific number in a variable, you can assign that number as a numeric literal to the variable. For example, assuming `speed` is an `int` variable, the following statement assigns the numeric literal 60 to the `speed` variable:

```
speed = 60;
```

When you write a numeric literal in a program's code, the numeric literal is automatically assigned a data type by the compiler. In C++, if a numeric literal is an integer (not written with a decimal point), and it fits within the range of an `int` (see Table 2-3 for the minimum and maximum values), then the numeric literal is treated as an `int`. A numeric literal that is treated as an `int` is called an *int literal*. For example, each of the following statements initializes a variable with an `int` literal:

```
int hoursWorked = 40;
int unitsSold = 650;
int score = -23;
```

If a numeric literal is written with a decimal point, and it fits within the range of a `double` (see Table 2-3 for the minimum and maximum values), then the numeric literal is treated as a `double`. A numeric literal that is treated as a `double` is called a *double literal*. For example, each of the following statements initializes a variable with a `double` literal:

```
double distance = 28.75;
double testScore = 87.3;
double temperature = -10.0;
```

`int` Variables and Assignment Compatibility

You can assign `int` values to `int` variables, but you cannot assign `double` values to `int` variables. For example, look at the following declarations.

```
int hoursWorked = 40;   ← This works
int score = -25.5;      ← ERROR!
```

The first declaration works because we are initializing an `int` variable with an `int` value. The second declaration will cause an error, however, because you cannot assign a double value to an `int` variable.

You cannot assign a `double` value to an `int` variable because such an assignment could result in a loss of data. Here are the reasons:

- `double` values may be fractional, but `int` variables can hold only integers. If you were allowed to store a fractional value in an `int` variable, the fractional part of the value would have to be discarded.
- `double` values may be much larger or much smaller than allowed by the range of an `int` variable. A `double` number can potentially be so large or so small that it will not fit in an `int` variable.

`double` Variables and Assignment Compatibility

You can assign either `double` or `int` values to `double` variables. For example, look at the following declarations.

```
double distance = 28.75;  ← This works
double speed = 75;        ← This works
```

In the first declaration we are initializing a `double` variable with a `double` value. In the second declaration we are initializing a `double` variable with an `int` value. Both of these statements work. It makes sense that you are allowed to assign an `int` value to a `double` variable because any number that can be stored as an `int` can be converted to a `double` with no loss of data. When you assign an `int` value to a `double` variable, the `int` value is implicitly converted to a `double`.

A Variable Holds One Value at a Time

Variables can hold different values while a program is running, but they can hold only one value at a time. When you assign a value to a variable, that value will remain in the variable until you assign a different value to the variable. For example, look at Program 2-8.

Program 2-8   (OneValue.cpp)

```cpp
 1 #include <iostream>
 2 using namespace std;
 3
 4 int main()
 5 {
 6     double price = 29.95;
 7
 8     cout << price << endl;
 9     price = 12.95;
10     cout << price << endl;
11     return 0;
12 }
```

Program Output

```
29.95
12.95
```

In the program, line 6 declares a `double` variable named `price`, initialized with the value 29.95. Line 8 displays the value of the `price` variable, which is 29.95. Then, line 9 assigns the value 12.95 to the `price` variable. This value replaces the value that was previously assigned to the variable. Line 10 displays the variable's value, which is now 12.95.

Program 2-8 illustrates two important characteristics of variables:

- A variable holds only one value at a time.
- When you store a value in a variable, that value replaces the previous value that was in the variable.

Scope

Programmers use the term *scope* to describe the part of a program in which a variable may be accessed. A variable is visible only to statements inside the variable's scope.

A local variable's scope begins at the variable's declaration and ends at the end of the function in which the variable is declared. A local variable cannot be accessed by statements that are outside the function in which the variable is declared. In addition, a local variable cannot be accessed by code that is inside the function, but before the variable's declaration.

Duplicate Variable Names

You cannot declare two variables with the same name in the same scope. For example, if you declare a variable named `productNumber` in a function, you cannot declare another variable with that name in the same function.

The `float` Data Type

You can use the `float` data type, as well as the `double` data type, to store real numbers. If you refer to Table 2-3, you will see that the `float` data type uses less memory than the `double` data type, but the `double` data type can store a much wider range of numbers and has more accuracy. In Part 1 of this book we use the `double` data type to store real numbers because the C++ standard library primarily uses it when working with floating-point numbers. In Part 2, however, we will use the `float` data type extensively because the App Game Kit library uses it as the primary data type for storing floating-point numbers.

 Checkpoint

2.7. What is the purpose of a variable?

2.8. What two items do you specify with a variable declaration?

2.9. Summarize the rules for naming variables in C++.

2.10. Indicate whether each of the following is a legal variable name. If it is not, explain why.
   a. `pay_Rate`
   b. `speed Of Sound`
   c. `totalCost`
   d. `1stPlaceScore`

2.11. For each of the following items, determine whether the data type should be `int` or `double`.
  a. The number of apples picked from an apple tree
  b. The amount of sales tax for a purchase
  c. An average of several test scores
  d. The number of items sold

2.12. Describe the camelCase naming convention.

2.13. Does it matter where you write the variable declarations inside a function?

2.14. What is variable initialization?

2.15. What is an uninitialized variable?

2.16. Do uninitialized variables pose any danger in a program?

2.17. What happens when you assign a `double` value to an `int` variable?

2.18. Write a declaration statement for a variable named `testScore`. The data type should be `double`, and the variable should be initialized with the value 87.5.

2.19. Write a declaration statement for a variable named `points`. The data type should be `int`, and the variable should be initialized with the value 0.

2.5 Reading Keyboard Input

CONCEPT: You write `cin` statements to read input from the keyboard.

VideoNote
Reading Input with `cin`

The programs you have seen so far use built-in data, such as numeric literals. Without giving the user an opportunity to enter his or her own data, you have initialized the variables with the necessary starting values. In reality, most programs require the user to enter values that will be assigned to variables. For example, a program that calculates payroll for a small business might ask the user to enter the employee's hours worked and the employee's hourly pay rate. When that employee's pay has been calculated, the program could start over again and ask for the next employee's hours worked and hourly pay rate.

To read keyboard input in C++ you write a `cin` statement (pronounced *see in*). A `cin` statement begins with the word `cin`, followed by the `>>` operator, followed by the name of a variable. The statement ends with a semicolon. When the statement executes, the program will wait for the user to enter input at the keyboard and press the Enter key. When the user presses Enter, the input will be assigned to the variable that is listed after the `>>` operator. (The `>>` operator is known as the *stream extraction operator*.) Assuming that `value` is the name of a variable that has already been declared, here is an example of such a statement:

```
cin >> value;
```

This statement causes the program to wait for the user to enter an item of data at the keyboard and then press the Enter key. The item that was entered will be stored in the `value` variable. Program 2-9 demonstrates.

Program 2-9   **(InputExample.cpp)**

```
1 #include <iostream>
2 using namespace std;
3
4 int main()
5 {
6    int age;
7
8    cout << "What is your age? ";
9    cin >> age;
10   cout << "I would never have guessed that you are "
11        << age << " years old!" << endl;
12   return 0;
13 }
```

Program Output with Example Input Shown in Bold

What is your age? **25 [Enter]**
I would never have guessed that you are 25 years old!

Let's take a closer look at the program:

- Line 6 declares an int variable named age.
- Line 8 displays a message asking the user what his or her age is.
- Line 9 uses cin to read a value from the keyboard. When this statement executes, the program waits until the user presses the Enter key. When that happens, the value entered at the keyboard is assigned to the age variable.
- Lines 10 and 11 display a message that includes the value of the age variable.

The program shown in Program 2-10 uses cin statements to read a double and an int.

Program 2-10   **(SimplePayroll.cpp)**

```
1 #include <iostream>
2 using namespace std;
3
4 int main()
5 {
6    double payRate;
7    int hours;
8
9    cout << "Enter your hourly pay rate: ";
10   cin >> payRate;
11   cout << "Enter the number of hours worked: ";
12   cin >> hours;
13
14   cout << "Here are the values that you entered:" << endl;
15   cout << "Hourly pay rate: " << payRate << endl;
16   cout << "Hours worked: " << hours << endl;
17   return 0;
18 }
```

Program Output with Example Input Shown in Bold

```
Enter your hourly pay rate: 25 [Enter]
Enter the number of hours worked: 40 [Enter]
Here are the values that you entered:
Hourly pay rate: 25
Hours worked: 40
```

Prompting the User

Getting keyboard input from the user is normally a two-step process:

1. Display a prompt on the screen.
2. Read a value from the keyboard.

A *prompt* is a message that tells (or asks) the user to enter a specific value. For example, Program 2-10 gets the user to enter his or her hourly pay rate with the following statements:

```
cout << "Enter your hourly pay rate: ";
cin >> payRate;
```

A cin statement reads keyboard input, but does not display instructions on the screen. It simply causes the program to pause and wait for the user to type something on the keyboard and then press the Enter key. For this reason, whenever you write a cin statement to read keyboard input, you should also write a cout statement just before it that tells the user what to enter. Otherwise, the user will not know what he or she is expected to do. For example, suppose we remove the cout statements in lines 9 and 11 from Program 2-10, as follows:

```
cin >> payRate;
cin >> hours;
```

Can you see what would happen when the program runs? The screen would appear blank because the first cin statement would cause the program to wait for something to be typed on the keyboard. The user would probably think the computer was malfunctioning.

The term *user-friendly* is commonly used in the software industry to describe programs that are easy to use. Programs that do not display adequate or correct instructions are frustrating to use and are not considered user-friendly. One of the simplest things that you can do to increase a program's user-friendliness is to make sure that it displays clear, understandable prompts prior to each statement that reads keyboard input.

 Checkpoint

2.20. Write a cin statement that reads an item of input and stores that item in a variable named myvar.

2.21. What is a prompt?

2.22. Write code that prompts the user to enter his or her checking account balance and then stores the user's input in a variable named balance.

2.6 Comments, Blank Lines, and Indentation

CONCEPT: Comments are brief notes that are placed in a program's source code, explaining how parts of the program work. Programmers commonly use blank lines and indentation in program code to give the code visual organization and make it easier to read.

Comments are short notes that are placed in different parts of a program, explaining how those parts of the program work. Comments are not intended for the compiler. They are intended for programmers to read, to help them understand the code. The compiler skips all the comments that appear in a program.

As a beginning programmer, you might resist the idea of writing a lot of comments in your programs. After all, it's a lot more fun to write code that actually does something! However, it's crucial that you take the extra time to write comments. They will almost certainly save you time in the future when you have to modify or debug the program. Even large and complex programs can be made easy to read and understand if they are properly commented.

C++ uses two types of comments: single-line and multiline. Let's briefly discuss each type.

Single-Line Comments

To create a single-line comment, simply place two forward slashes (//) where you want the comment to begin. The compiler ignores everything from that point to the end of the line. Program 2-11 shows that single-line comments may be placed liberally throughout a program.

Program 2-11 (SingleLineComment.cpp)

```
 1 // This program calculates gross pay.
 2 #include <iostream>
 3 using namespace std;
 4
 5 int main()
 6 {
 7    double payRate; // To hold the hourly pay rate
 8    int hours;      // To hold the hours worked
 9
10    // Get the hourly pay rate.
11    cout << "Enter your hourly pay rate: ";
12    cin >> payRate;
13
14    // Get the number of hours worked.
15    cout << "Enter the number of hours worked: ";
16    cin >> hours;
17
18    // Display the values entered.
```

```
19    cout << "Here are the values that you entered:" << endl;
20    cout << "Hourly pay rate: " << payRate << endl;
21    cout << "Hours worked: " << hours << endl;
22    return 0;
23 }
```

Program Output with Example Input Shown in Bold

```
Enter your hourly pay rate: 25 [Enter]
Enter the number of hours worked: 40 [Enter]
Here are the values that you entered:
Hourly pay rate: 25
Hours worked: 40
```

Multiline Comments

The second type of comment in C++ is the multi-line comment. *Multiline comments* start with /* (a forward slash followed by an asterisk) and end with */ (an asterisk followed by a forward slash). Everything between these markers is ignored. Program 2-12 shows an example of a multiline comment in lines 1 through 4.

Program 2-12   **(MultilineComment.cpp)**

```
 1 /*
 2    This program gets the user's age
 3    and displays it in a message.
 4 */
 5 #include <iostream>
 6 using namespace std;
 7
 8 int main()
 9 {
10    int age;
11
12    cout << "What is your age? ";
13    cin >> age;
14    cout << "I would never have guessed that you are "
15        << age << " years old!" << endl;
16    return 0;
17 }
```

Program Output with Example Input Shown in Bold

```
What is your age? 25 [Enter]
I would never have guessed that you are 25 years old!
```

Remember the following advice when using block comments:

- Be careful not to reverse the beginning symbol (/*) with the ending symbol (*/).
- Do not forget the ending symbol.

Using Blank Lines and Indentation to Make Your Code Easier to Read

Programmers commonly use blank lines and indentations in their code to create a sense of visual organization. This is similar to the way that authors visually arrange the text on the pages of a book. Instead of writing each chapter as one long series of sentences, they break it into paragraphs that are visually separated on the page. This does not change the information in the book, but it makes it easier to read.

For example, look at the following code sample. Notice that we have inserted a blank line to visually separate the code into two sets of statements. The blank line is not required, but it makes the code easier for humans to read. Programmers commonly insert blank lines at various places to make the code easier to read.

```
// Display the number of hours worked.
cout << hoursWorked;

// Display the gross pay.
cout << grossPay;
```

Programmers also use indentation to visually organize code. You may have noticed that in the code editor, all the statements that appear inside a set of braces ({ }) are indented. For example, all the statements inside a function are indented. In fact, Visual Studio is normally set up to automatically indent the code that you write in this fashion.

Although the indentation is not required, it makes your code much easier to read. By indenting the statements inside a function, you visually set them apart. As a result, you can tell at a glance which statements belong to the function. This practice of indentation is a convention that virtually all programmers follow.

 Checkpoint

2.23. What purpose do comments serve?

2.24. How are line comments and multiline comments different?

2.25. What should you be careful to remember about the beginning and ending symbols of multiline comments?

2.26. Why do programmers insert blank lines and indentations in their code?

 2.7 Performing Calculations and Working with Numbers

CONCEPT: To perform calculations in a C++ program, you use math operators to create math expressions.

Most programs require calculations to be performed. A programmer's tools for performing calculations are *math operators*. The C++ math operators are shown in Table 2-4.

Table 2-4 C++'s Math Operators

Symbol	Operation	Description
+	Addition	Adds two numbers
–	Subtraction	Subtracts one number from another
*	Multiplication	Multiplies two numbers
/	Division	Divides one number by another and gives the quotient
%	Remainder, or Modulus	Divides one integer by another and gives the remainder

Programmers use the operators shown in Table 2-4 to create math expressions. A *math expression* performs a calculation and gives a value. The following is an example of a simple math expression:

```
12 + 2
```

The values on the right and left of the + operator are called *operands*. These are values that the + operator adds together. The value that is given by this expression is 14.

Variables may also be used in a math expression. For example, suppose we have two variables named hours and payRate. The following math expression uses the * operator to multiply the value in the hours variable by the value in the payRate variable:

```
hours * payRate
```

VideoNote

Assignment Statements and Simple Math Expressions

When we use a math expression to calculate a value, normally we want to save that value in memory so we can use it again in the program. We do this with an assignment statement. Here are some examples of statements that use an arithmetic operator to calculate a value and assign that value to a variable:

```
total = price + tax;
sale = price - discount;
population = population * 2;
half = number / 2;
leftOver = 17 % 3;
```

Program 2-11 shows an example program that performs mathematical calculations.

Program 2-11   **(SalePrice.cpp)**

```
 1 #include <iostream>
 2 using namespace std;
 3
 4 int main()
 5 {
 6    // Declare variables
 7    double retailPrice,
 8           discount,
 9           salePrice;
10
11    // Get the retail price and discount.
```

```
12    cout << "Enter the item's retail price: ";
13    cin >> retailPrice;
14    cout << "Enter the amount of the discount: ";
15    cin >> discount;
16
17    // Calculate and display the sale price.
18    salePrice = retailPrice - discount;
19    cout << "The sale price is: " << salePrice << endl;
20    return 0;
21 }
```

Program Output with Example Input Shown in Bold

```
Enter the item's retail price: 100 [Enter]
Enter the amount of the discount: 25 [Enter]
The sale price is: 75
```

The Order of Operations

It is possible to build mathematical expressions with several operators. The following statement assigns the sum of 17, the variable x, 21, and the variable y to the variable answer.

```
answer = 17 + x + 21 + y;
```

Some expressions are not that straightforward, however. Consider the following statement:

```
outcome = 12 + 6 / 3;
```

What value will be stored in outcome? The number 6 is used as an operand for both the addition and division operators. The outcome variable could be assigned either 6 or 14, depending on when the division takes place. The answer is 14 because the *order of operations* dictates that the division operator works before the addition operator does.

The order of operations in C++ can be summarized as follows:

1. Perform any operations that are enclosed in parentheses.
2. Perform any multiplications, divisions, or modulus operations as they appear from left to right.
3. Perform any additions or subtractions as they appear from left to right.

Mathematical expressions are evaluated from left to right. When two operators share an operand, the order of operations determines which operator works first. Multiplication and division are always performed before addition and subtraction, so the statement

```
outcome = 12 + 6 / 3;
```

works like this:

1. 6 is divided by 3, yielding a result of 2.
2. 12 is added to 2, yielding a result of 14.

It could be diagrammed as shown in Figure 2-4.

Figure 2-4 The order of operations at work

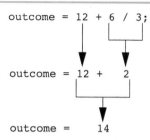

Table 2-5 shows some other sample expressions with their values.

Table 2-5 Some expressions and their values

Expression	Value
5 + 2 * 4	13
10 / 2 - 3	2
8 + 12 * 2 - 4	28
6 - 3 * 2 + 7 - 1	6

Grouping with Parentheses

Parts of a mathematical expression may be grouped with parentheses to force some operations to be performed before others. In the following statement, the variables a and b are added together, and their sum is divided by 4:

```
result = (a + b) / 4;
```

Without the parentheses, however, b would be divided by 4 and the result added to a. Table 2-6 shows more expressions and their values.

Table 2-6 More expressions and their values

Expression	Value
(5 + 2) * 4	28
10 / (5 - 3)	5
8 + 12 * (6 - 2)	56
(6 - 3) * (2 + 7) / 3	9

Integer Division

Be careful when dividing an integer by another integer. In C++, when an integer is divided by another integer, the result will also be an integer. This behavior is known as *integer division*. For example, look at the following code:

```
double number;
number = 3 / 2;
```

The assignment statement divides 3 by 2 and assigns the result to the number variable. What will be assigned to number? You would probably assume that 1.5 would be assigned to number because that's the result your calculator shows when you divide 3 by 2. However, that's not what will happen in C++. Because the numeric literals 3 and 2 are both treated as ints, the fractional part of the result will be thrown away. (Throwing away the fractional part of a number is called *truncation*.) As a result, the statement will assign the value 1 to the number variable, not 1.5.

In the previously shown code, it doesn't matter that number is declared as a double because the fractional part of the result is discarded before the assignment takes place. For a division operation to return a fractional value, at least one of the operands must be of a floating-point data type, such as double. For example, the previously shown statement could be written as:

```
double number;
number = 3.0 / 2;
```

In this code the numeric literal 3.0 is interpreted as a double, so the division operation will return a double. The value 1.5 will be assigned to number.

The Remainder (Modulus) Operator

In C++, the % symbol is the remainder operator. (This is also known as the *modulus operator*.) The remainder operator performs division, but instead of returning the quotient, it returns the remainder. The following statement assigns 2 to leftover:

```
leftover = 17 % 3;
```

This statement assigns 2 to leftover because 17 divided by 3 is 5 with a remainder of 2. The remainder operator is useful in certain situations. It is commonly used in calculations that convert times or distances, detect odd or even numbers, and perform other specialized operations. For example, Program 2-12 gets a number of seconds from the user, and it converts that number of seconds to hours, minutes, and seconds. For example, it would convert 11,730 seconds to 3 hours, 15 minutes, and 30 seconds.

Program 2-12   (SecondsConverter.cpp)

```
 1 // This program converts a number of seconds to
 2 // hours, minutes, and seconds.
 3 #include <iostream>
 4 using namespace std;
 5
 6 int main()
 7 {
 8    int totalSeconds,   // Total number of seconds
 9        hours,          // Number of hours
10        minutes,        // Number of minutes
11        seconds;        // Number of seconds
12
13    // Get the total number of seconds.
14    cout << "Enter a number of seconds: ";
```

```
15    cin >> totalSeconds;
16
17    // Calculate the number of hours.
18    // Note: This calculation uses integer division.
19    hours = totalSeconds / 3600;
20
21    // Calculate the number of minutes.
22    // Note: This calculation also uses integer division.
23    minutes = (totalSeconds / 60) % 60;
24
25    // Calculate the number of remaining seconds.
26    seconds = totalSeconds % 60;
27
28    // Display the results.
29    cout << "Here is the time in hours, minutes, and seconds:\n";
30    cout << "Hours: " << hours << endl;
31    cout << "Minutes: " << minutes << endl;
32    cout << "Seconds: " << seconds << endl;
33    return 0;
34 }
```

Program Output with Example Input Shown in Bold

```
Enter a number of seconds: 11730 [Enter]
Here is the time in hours, minutes, and seconds:
Hours: 3
Minutes: 15
Seconds: 30
```

Let's take a closer look at the program:

- Line 14 prompts the user for a number of seconds, and line 15 stores the user's input in the totalSeconds variable.
- Line 19 calculates the number of hours in the specified number of seconds. There are 3600 seconds in an hour, so this statement divides totalSeconds by 3600. Notice that this statement performs integer division (because both totalSeconds and the numeric literal 3600 are int values). This is intentional because we want the number of hours with no fractional part. The result is assigned to the hours variable.
- Line 23 calculates the number of remaining minutes. This statement first uses the / operator to divide totalSeconds by 60. (Once again, we are intentionally performing integer division.) This gives us the total number of minutes. Then, it uses the % operator to divide the total number of minutes by 60 and get the remainder of the division. The result is the number of remaining minutes, and that value is assigned to the minutes variable.
- Line 26 calculates the number of remaining seconds. There are 60 seconds in a minute, so this statement uses the % operator to divide the totalSeconds by 60 and get the remainder of the division. The result is the number of remaining seconds, and that value is assigned to the seconds variable.
- Lines 29 through 32 display the number of hours, minutes, and seconds.

Combined Assignment Operators

Sometimes you want to increase a variable's value by a certain amount. For example, suppose you have a variable named number and you want to increase its value by 1. You can accomplish that with the following statement:

```
number = number + 1;
```

The expression on the right side of the assignment operator calculates the value of number plus 1. The result is then assigned to number, replacing the value that was previously stored there. Effectively, this statement adds 1 to number. For example, if number is equal to 6 before this statement executes, it will be equal to 7 after the statement executes.

Similarly, the following statement subtracts 5 from number:

```
number = number - 5;
```

If number is equal to 15 before this statement executes, it will be equal to 10 after the statement executes. Here's another example. The following statement doubles the value of the number variable:

```
number = number * 2;
```

If number is equal to 4 before this statement executes, it will be equal to 8 after the statement executes.

These types of operations are very common in programming. For convenience, C++ offers a special set of operators known as *combined assignment operators* that are designed specifically for these jobs. Table 2-7 shows the combined assignment operators.

Table 2-7 Combined assignment operators

Operator	Example Usage	Equivalence
+=	x += 5;	x = x + 5;
-=	y -= 2;	y = y - 2;
*=	z *= 10;	z = z * 10;
/=	a /= b;	a = a / b;
%=	c %= 3;	c = c % 3;

As you can see, the combined assignment operators do not require the programmer to type the variable name twice. Also, they give a clear indication of what is happening in the statement.

Mixed-Type Expressions and Data Type Conversion

When you perform a math operation on two operands, the data type of the result will depend on the data type of the operands. C++ follows these rules when evaluating mathematical expressions involving int and double values:

- When an operation is performed on two int values, the result will be an int.
- When an operation is performed on two double values, the result will be a double.

- When an operation is performed on an int and a double, the int value will be temporarily converted to a double, and the result of the operation will be a double. (An expression that uses operands of different data types is called a *mixed-type expression*.)

The first two situations are straightforward: operations on ints produce ints, and operations on doubles produce doubles. Let's look at an example of the third situation, which involves mixed-type expressions:

```
double number;
number = 5 * 2.0;
```

When the assignment statement executes, the value 5 will be converted to a double (5.0) and then multiplied by 2.0. The result, 10.0, will be assigned to number.

The int to double conversion that takes place in the previous statement happens implicitly. If you need to explicitly perform a conversion, you can use a *type cast expression*. The general format of a type cast expression is

```
static_cast<DataType>(Value)
```

In the general format, *Value* is a variable or literal value that you wish to convert, and *DataType* is the data type you wish to convert *Value* to. Here is an example of code that uses a type cast expression:

```
double dvalue = 3.7;
int ivalue;
ivalue = static_cast<int>(dvalue);
```

This code declares two variables: dvalue, a double, and ivalue, an int. The type cast expression in the third statement returns a copy of the value in dvalue, converted to an int. When a double is converted to an int, the fractional part is thrown away, or truncated, so this statement stores 3 in ivalue. The original value in dvalue is not changed, however.

Type cast expressions are useful in situations where C++ will not perform the desired conversion automatically. Program 2-13 shows an example where a type cast expression is used to prevent integer division from taking place. The statement that uses the type cast expression is in line 21.

Program 2-13   **(TypeCast.cpp)**

```
1 // This program uses a type cast to avoid integer division.
2 #include <iostream>
3 using namespace std;
4
5 int main()
6 {
7    int books;      // Number of books to read
8    int months;     // Number of months spent reading
9    double perMonth; // Average number of books per month
10
11   // Get the number of books the user plans to read.
12   cout << "How many books do you plan to read? ";
13   cin >> books;
```

```
14
15    // Get the number of months it will take.
16    cout << "How many months will it take you to read them? ";
17    cin >> months;
18
19    // Calculate and display the average number of
20    // books per month.
21    perMonth = static_cast<double>(books) / months;
22    cout << "That is " << perMonth << " books per month.\n";
23    return 0;
24 }
```

Program Output with Example Input Shown in Bold

```
How many books do you plan to read? 9 [Enter]
How many months will it take you to read them? 2 [Enter]
That is 4.5 books per month.
```

The variable books is an int, but in line 21 its value is converted to a double before the division takes place. Without the type cast expression, integer division would have been performed resulting in an incorrect result.

> **NOTE:** Suppose the statement in line 21 of Program 2-13 had been written like this:
>
> ```
> perMonth = static_cast<double>(books / months);
> ```
>
> This statement will produce an incorrect result because integer division will take place. The result of the expression books / months is 4. When 4 is converted to a double, it is 4.0. To prevent the integer division from taking place, only one of the operands of the division operation should be converted to a double prior to the division operation. This forces C++ to automatically convert the value of the other operand to a double.

In the Spotlight:
Calculating Percentages and Discounts

Determining percentages is a common calculation in computer programming. Although the % symbol is used in general mathematics to indicate a percentage, most programming languages (including C++) do not use the % symbol for this purpose. In a program, you have to convert a percentage to a floating-point number, just as you would if you were using a calculator. For example, 50 percent would be written as 0.5 and 2 percent would be written as 0.02.

Let's look at an example. Suppose you earn $6,000 per month, and you are allowed to contribute a portion of your gross monthly pay to a retirement plan. You want to determine the amount of your pay that will go into the plan if you contribute 5 percent, 7 percent, or 10 percent of your gross wages. To make this determination, you write the program shown in Program 2-14.

Program 2-14   **(Percentages.cpp)**

```cpp
 1 #include <iostream>
 2 using namespace std;
 3
 4 int main()
 5 {
 6    // Variables to hold the monthly pay and the
 7    // amount of contribution.
 8    double monthlyPay = 6000.0, contribution;
 9
10    // Calculate and display a 5% contribution.
11    contribution = monthlyPay * 0.05;
12    cout << "5 percent is $" << contribution
13         << " per month.\n";
14
15    // Calculate and display a 7% contribution.
16    contribution = monthlyPay * 0.07;
17
18    cout << "7 percent is $" << contribution
19         << " per month.\n";
20
21    // Calculate and display a 10% contribution.
22    contribution = monthlyPay * 0.1;
23    cout << "10 percent is $" << contribution
24         << " per month.\n";
25    return 0;
26 }
```

Program Output

```
5 percent is $300 per month.
7 percent is $420 per month.
10 percent is $600 per month.
```

In the Spotlight:
Calculating an Average

Determining the average of a group of values is a simple calculation: You add all the values and then divide the sum by the number of values. Although this is a straightforward calculation, it is easy to make a mistake when writing a program that calculates an average. For example, let's assume that a, b, and c are double variables. Each of the variables holds a value, and we want to calculate the average of those values. If we are careless, we might write a statement such as the following to perform the calculation:

```cpp
average = a + b + c / 3.0;
```

Can you see the error in this statement? When it executes, the division will take place first. The value in c will be divided by 3.0, and then the result will be added to the sum of a + b. That is not the correct way to calculate an average. To correct this error, we need to put parentheses around a + b + c, as shown here:

```
average = (a + b + c) / 3.0;
```

Let's step through the process of writing a program that calculates an average. Suppose you have taken three tests in your computer science class, and you want to write a program that will display the average of the test scores. Here are the general steps the program must take:

Get the first test score.
Get the second test score.
Get the third test score.
Calculate the average by adding the three test scores and dividing the sum by 3.
Display the average.

In the first three steps we prompt the user to enter three test scores. Let's say we store those test scores in the double variables test1, test2, and test3. Then in the fourth step we calculate the average of the three test scores. We will use the following statement to perform the calculation and store the result in the average variable, which is a double:

```
average = (test1 + test2 + test3) / 3.0;
```

The last step is to display the average. Program 2-15 shows the program.

Program 2-15   **(AverageScore.cpp)**

```cpp
 1 #include <iostream>
 2 #include <cmath>
 3 using namespace std;
 4
 5 int main()
 6 {
 7    double test1, test2, test3; // To hold the scores
 8    double average;             // To hold the average
 9
10    // Get the three test scores.
11    cout << "Enter the first test score: ";
12    cin >> test1;
13    cout << "Enter the second test score: ";
14    cin >> test2;
15    cout << "Enter the third test score: ";
16    cin >> test3;
17
18    // Calculate the average of the scores.
19    average = (test1 + test2 + test3) / 3.0;
20
21    // Display the average.
22    cout << "The average score is: " << average << endl;
23    return 0;
24 }
```

Program Output with Input Shown in Bold

```
Enter the first test score: 90 [Enter]
Enter the second test score: 80 [Enter]
Enter the third test score: 100 [Enter]
The average score is 90
```

 Checkpoint

2.27. Summarize the mathematical order of operations.

2.28. Assume `result` is a double variable. When the following statement executes, what value will be stored in `result`?

```
result = 4 + 10 / 2;
```

2.29. Assume `result` is a double variable. When the following statement executes, what value will be stored in `result`?

```
result = (2 + 5) * 10;
```

2.30. Assume `result` is a double variable. When the following statement executes, what value will be stored in `result`?

```
result = 5 / 2;
```

2.31. Rewrite the following statements using combined assignment operators:
   a. `x = x + 1;`
   b. `lowerY = lowerY − 5;`
   c. `radius = radius * 10;`
   d. `length = length / 2;`

2.8 Named Constants

CONCEPT: A named constant is a name that represents a value that cannot be changed during the program's execution.

Assume that the following statement appears in a banking program that calculates data pertaining to loans:

```
amount = balance * 0.069;
```

In such a program, two potential problems arise. First, it is not clear to anyone other than the original programmer what 0.069 is. It appears to be an interest rate, but in some situations fees are associated with loan payments. How can the purpose of this statement be determined without painstakingly checking the rest of the program?

The second problem occurs if this number is used in other calculations throughout the program and must be changed periodically. Assuming the number is an interest rate, what if the rate changes from 6.9 percent to 7.2 percent? The programmer would have to search through the source code for every occurrence of the number.

Both of these problems can be addressed by using a named constant. A *named constant* is a name that represents a value that cannot be changed during the program's execution. The following is an example of how you can declare a named constant in C++:

```
const double INTEREST_RATE = 0.129;
```

This statement declares a named constant named INTEREST_RATE initialized with the value 0.129. It looks like a regular variable declaration, except that the word const appears before the data type name, and the name of the variable is written in upper-case characters. The keyword const is a qualifier that tells the compiler to make the variable read only. If a statement attempts to change the constant's value, an error will occur when the program is being compiled. When you declare a named constant, an initialization value is required.

It is not required that the constant name be written in uppercase letters, but many programmers prefer to write them this way so they are easily distinguishable from regular variable names. When you are reading a program's code and see an uppercase identifier, you know instantly that it is a constant.

An advantage of using named constants is that they make programs more self-explanatory. The statement

```
amount = balance * 0.069;
```

can be changed to read

```
amount = balance * INTEREST_RATE;
```

A new programmer can read the second statement and know what is happening. It is evident that balance is being multiplied by the interest rate. Another advantage to this approach is that widespread changes can easily be made to the program. Let's say the interest rate appears in a dozen different statements throughout the program. When the rate changes, the initialization value in the declaration of the named constant is the only value that needs to be modified. If the rate increases to 7.2 percent, the declaration can be changed to the following:

```
const double INTEREST_RATE = 0.072;
```

The new value of 0.072 will then be used in each statement that uses the INTEREST_RATE constant.

Named constants can also help prevent typographical errors in a program's code. For example, suppose you use the number 3.14159 as the value of *pi* in a program that performs various geometric calculations. Each time you type the number 3.14159 in the program's code, there is a chance that you will make a mistake with one or more of the digits. As a result, the program will not produce the correct results. To help prevent a mistake such as this, you can define a named constant for *pi*, initialized with the correct value, and then use that constant in all the formulas that require its value. Program 2-16 shows an example. It calculates the circumference of a circle that has a diameter of 10.

Program 2-16   (`NamedConstant.cpp`)

```cpp
 1  // This program calculates the circumference of a circle.
 2  #include <iostream>
 3  using namespace std;
 4
 5  int main()
 6  {
 7     // Constants
 8     const double PI = 3.14159;
 9     const double DIAMETER = 10.0;
10
11     // Variable to hold the circumference
12     double circumference;
13
14     // Calculate the circumference.
15     circumference = PI * DIAMETER;
16
17     // Display the circumference.
18     cout << "The circumference is: " << circumference << endl;
19     return 0;
20  }
```

Program Output

```
The circumference is: 31.4159
```

Let's take a closer look at the program. Line 8 defines a constant `double` named `PI`, initialized with the value 3.14159. This constant will be used for the value of *pi* in the program's calculation. Line 9 defines a constant `double` named `DIAMETER`, initialized with the value 10. This will be used for the circle's diameter. Line 12 defines a `double` variable named `circumference`, which will be used to hold the circle's circumference. Line 15 calculates the circle's circumference by multiplying `PI` by `DIAMETER`. The result of the calculation is assigned to the `circumference` variable. Line 18 displays the circle's circumference.

 Checkpoint

2.32. Write statements using the `const` qualifier to create named constants for the following literal values:

Literal Value	Description
2.71828	Euler's number (known in mathematics as *e*)
5.256E5	Number of minutes in a year
32.2	The gravitational acceleration constant (in feet per second^2)
9.8	The gravitational acceleration constant (in meters per second^2)
1609	Number of meters in a mile

2.9 Math Functions in the Standard Library

CONCEPT: The C++ standard library provides several functions for performing advanced mathematical operations.

The C++ standard library provides numerous functions that perform common mathematical operations. To use these functions you need to write the following include directive at the top of your program:

```
#include <cmath>
```

One of the math functions is named pow, and it raises a number to a power. Here is an example of how you use it:

```
area = pow(4.0, 2.0);
```

This statement *calls* the pow function. Notice that inside the parentheses, two numbers appear that are separated with a comma. The numbers inside the parentheses are *arguments*, which are pieces of data being sent to the function. In this case, the first argument is 4.0, and the second argument is 2.0. The pow function always raises the first argument to the power of the second argument. In this example, 4.0 is raised to the power of 2.0. The result is *returned* from the function. In this case, the value 16 is returned from the pow function and assigned to the area variable. This is illustrated in Figure 2-5.

Figure 2-5 Using the pow function

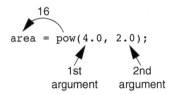

Program 2-17 solves a simple math problem. It asks the user to enter the radius of a circle and then calculates the area of the circle. The formula for finding the area of a circle is

$$area = \pi r^2$$

which is expressed in the program as

```
area = PI * pow(radius, 2.0);
```

Program 2-17   (PowFunction.cpp)

```
1 // This program demonstrates the pow function.
2 #include <iostream>
3 #include <cmath>
4 using namespace std;
5
6 int main()
7 {
8     double radius, area;
```

```
 9     const double PI = 3.14159;
10
11     // Get the circle's radius.
12     cout << "Enter the circle's radius: ";
13     cin >> radius;
14
15     // Calculate and display the circle's area.
16     area = PI * pow(radius, 2.0);
17     cout << "The circle's area is: " << area << endl;
18     return 0;
19 }
```

Program Output with Example Input Shown in Bold

```
Enter the circle's radius: 10 [Enter]
The circle's area is: 314.159
```

NOTE: Program 2-15 is presented as a demonstration of the pow function. In reality, there is no reason to use the pow function in such a simple operation. The math statement could just as easily be written as

```
    area = PI * radius * radius;
```

The pow function is useful, however, in operations that involve larger exponents.

Table 2-8 lists several of the C++ math functions.

Table 2-8 Some of the C++ math functions

Function	Description
acos(x)	Returns the arc cosine of x, in radians. The argument and the return value are doubles.
asin(x)	Returns the arc sine of x, in radians. The argument and the return value are doubles.
atan(x)	Returns the arc tangent of x, in radians. The argument and the return value are doubles.
ceil(x)	Returns the smallest whole number that is greater than or equal to x. The argument and the return value are doubles.
cos(x)	Returns the cosine of x in radians. The argument and the return value are doubles.
exp(x)	Returns e^x. The argument and the return value are doubles.
floor(x)	Returns the largest whole number that is less than or equal to x. The argument and the return value are doubles.
log(x)	Returns the natural logarithm of x. The argument and the return value are doubles.
log10(x)	Returns the base-10 logarithm of x. The argument and the return value are doubles.
pow(x, y)	Returns the value of x raised to the power of y. The arguments and the return value are doubles.
sin(x)	Returns the sine of x in radians. The argument and the return value are doubles.
sqrt(x)	Returns the square root of x. The argument and the return value are doubles.
tan(x)	Returns the tangent of x in radians. The argument and the return value are doubles.

2.10 Working with Strings

> **CONCEPT:** You use the standard library's string class to create objects that can hold strings.

C++ does not have a built-in data type for storing strings, but the C++ standard library does provide something called the *string class*. You can use the string class to create objects in memory that work like string variables.

The first step in using the string class is to include the string header file. This is accomplished with the following preprocessor directive:

```
#include <string>
```

The next step is to declare a string object. For example, the following statement declares a string object named movieTitle.

```
string movieTitle;
```

You can initialize the object with a string literal when you declare it, as shown here:

```
string movieTitle = "Wheels of Fury";
```

You can also assign a string literal to the object with the assignment operator, as shown here:

```
movieTitle = "Midnight in the Library";
```

You can use cout to display the value of a string object, as shown here:

```
cout << "My favorite movie is " << movieTitle << endl;
```

Program 2-18 is a complete program that demonstrates some of the preceding statements.

Program 2-18   (StringExample.cpp)

```
 1 // This program demonstrates the string class.
 2 #include <iostream>
 3 #include <string>
 4 using namespace std;
 5
 6 int main()
 7 {
 8    string movieTitle = "Wheels of Fury";
 9
10    cout << "My favorite movie is " << movieTitle << endl;
11    return 0;
12 }
```

Program Output

```
My favorite movie is Wheels of Fury
```

You can use cin to read string input from the keyboard, as shown in Program 2-19.

Program 2-19   (`StringInput1.cpp`)

```
 1  // This program demonstrates string input.
 2  #include <iostream>
 3  #include <string>
 4  using namespace std;
 5
 6  int main()
 7  {
 8      string name;
 9
10      // Get the user's name.
11      cout << "Enter your name: ";
12      cin >> name;
13
14      // Display the user's name.
15      cout << "Your name is: "
16           << name << endl;
17      return 0;
18  }
```

Program Output with Example Input Shown in Bold

```
Enter your name: Liza [Enter]
Your name is: Liza
```

There is a limitation to using cin to read string input: A cin statement can read only one word. For example, when Program 2-17 runs, if the user enters *Liza Smith*, only the word *Liza* will be read by cin and stored in the name object. The program would display *Your name is: Liza*. Program 2-20 demonstrates how two cin statements are needed if we want the program to read both the user's first and last names.

Program 2-20   (`StringInput2.cpp`)

```
 1  // This program demonstrates string input.
 2  #include <iostream>
 3  #include <string>
 4  using namespace std;
 5
 6  int main()
 7  {
 8      string firstName, lastName;
 9
10      // Get the user's first and last names.
11      cout << "Enter your first name: ";
```

```
12    cin >> firstName;
13    cout << "Enter your last name: ";
14    cin >> lastName;
15
16    // Display the user's first and last names.
17    cout << "Your name is: "
18        << firstName << " "
19        << lastName << endl;
20    return 0;
21 }
```

Program Output with Example Input Shown in Bold

Enter your first name: **Liza** [*Enter*]
Enter your last name: **Smith** [*Enter*]
Your name is: Liza Smith

The + operator also works with string objects. You have already seen how the + operator adds two numbers. Because strings cannot be added, when the + operator is used with strings, it *concatenates* them, or joins them together. The following demonstrates:

```
string greeting = "Hello " + "world";
```

This statement declares a string object named greeting. The object will be initialized with the string "Hello world". The following shows another example:

```
string str1 = "Hello ";
string str2;
string str3 = "World";
string str4 = "People";
str2 = str1 + str3;    // str2 now holds "Hello World"
str1 = str1 + str4;    // str1 now holds "Hello People"
```

Checkpoint

2.33. What header file must you include to use string objects?

2.34. Write a statement that declares a string object named myName, initialized with your name.

2.35. Look at the following code sample, and assume that the user enters *Cheryl Green* as input. What will the last cout statement display?

```
string name;
cout << "Enter your name? "
cin >> name;
cout << name << endl;
```

2.36. What will be stored in the message object after the following statement is executed?

```
string message = "He" + "ll" + "o!";
```

2.11 The char **Data Type**

CONCEPT: You use the char data type to store individual characters in memory.

The char data type is used to store individual characters. A variable of the char data type can hold only one character at a time. Here is an example of how you might declare a char variable:

```
char letter;
```

This statement declares a char variable named letter, which can store one character. In C++, *character literals* are enclosed in single quotation marks. Here is an example, showing how we would assign a character to the letter variable:

```
letter = 'g';
```

This statement assigns the character 'g' to the letter variable. Because char variables can hold only one character, they are not compatible with strings. For example, you cannot assign a string to a char variable, even if the string contains only one character. The following statement, for example, will not compile because it attempts to assign a string literal to a char variable.

```
letter = "g";  // ERROR! Cannot assign a string to a char
```

It is important that you do not confuse character literals, which are enclosed in single quotation marks, with string literals, which are enclosed in double quotation marks. Program 2-21 demonstrates how character literals are assigned to a char variable.

Program 2-21   (CharLiterals.cpp)

```
 1 #include <iostream>
 2 using namespace std;
 3
 4 int main()
 5 {
 6    char letter;
 7
 8    letter = 'A';
 9    cout << letter << endl;
10
11    letter = 'B';
12    cout << letter << endl;
13
14    letter = 'C';
15    cout << letter << endl;
16    return 0;
17 }
```

Program Output

```
A
B
C
```

Review Questions

Matching

1. Which of the following include directives is correct?
   a. `#include (iostream)`
   b. `#include {iostream}`
   c. `#include <iostream>`
   d. `#include [iostream]`

2. A _____ is a storage location in memory that is represented by a name.
   a. mnemonic
   b. data type
   c. namespace
   d. variable

3. In C++, you must _____ a variable before you can use it to store data.
   a. cite
   b. associate
   c. declare
   d. instance

4. A variable's _____ indicates the type of data that the variable will hold.
   a. name
   b. data type
   c. scope
   d. value

5. A _____ identifies a variable in the program code.
   a. binary number
   b. variable name
   c. unique global identifier
   d. hexadecimal value

6. An operation that is performed on strings using the + operator is _____, or appending one string to the end of another string.
   a. addition
   b. merging
   c. concatenation
   d. tying

7. Programmers use the term _____ to describe the part of a program in which a variable may be accessed.
   a. range
   b. scope
   c. focus
   d. field

8. Short notes placed in different parts of a program explaining how those parts of the program work are called _____.
   a. comments
   b. reference manuals

   c. tutorials
   d. external documentation

9. You can use a _____ to explicitly convert a value from one numeric data type to another, even if the conversion might result in a loss of data.
   a. transpose statement
   b. type cast expression
   c. conversion operator
   d. literal conversion

10. The process of dropping a number's fractional part is called _____.
   a. data downgrading
   b. two's complement
   c. numeric rounding
   d. truncation

11. A programmer's tools for performing calculations are _____.
   a. math operators
   b. numeric literals
   c. local variables
   d. parsed literals

12. A _____ performs a calculation and gives a value.
   a. numeric literal
   b. math expression
   c. machine instruction
   d. programming statement

13. In the expression 12 + 7, the values on the right and left of the + symbol are called _____.
   a. operands
   b. operators
   c. arguments
   d. math expressions

14. C++ offers a special set of operators known as _____ that are designed specifically for changing the value of a variable without having to type the variable name twice.
   a. combined assignment operators
   b. advanced math operators
   c. variable modifiers
   d. assignment sequencers

15. A _____ is a name that represents a literal value and cannot be changed during the program's execution.
   a. named literal
   b. named constant
   c. variable signature
   d. key term

16. The _____ data type is used to store individual characters in memory.
    a. character
    b. alpha
    c. char
    d. letter

True or False

1. In C++, uppercase and lowercase letters are considered the same.
2. A semicolon must appear at the end of an include directive.
3. Comments are ignored by the compiler.
4. When you declare a named constant, an initialization value is required.
5. In a math expression, multiplication and division takes place before addition and subtraction.
6. Variable names can have spaces in them.
7. In C++ the first character of a variable name can be a number.
8. String literals are enclosed in double quotation marks.
9. char literals are enclosed in double quotation marks.

Short Answer

1. What two things does a variable declaration specify about a variable?
2. Give an example of a programming statement that uses string concatenation.
3. What is the term used for a number that is written into a program's code?
4. Write a programming statement that assigns an integer literal to a variable.
5. Is the following comment written using single-line or multiline comment symbols?

    ```
    /* This program was written by M. A. Codewriter*/
    ```

6. Is the following comment written using single-line or multiline comment symbols?

    ```
    // This program was written by M. A. Codewriter
    ```

7. What standard library function do you use to raise a number to a power? What include directive must you write to use the function?

Algorithm Workbench

1. Assume the following code is part of a complete program. What will it display?

    ```
    cout << "Be careful\n";
    cout << "This might/n be a trick ";
    cout << "question\n";
    ```

2. What would the following code display if it were part of a complete program?

    ```
    int a = 5;
    int b = 2;
    int c = 3;
    int result = a + b * c;
    cout << result << endl;
    ```

3. What would the following code display if it were part of a complete program?

```
int num = 99;
num = 5;
cout << num << endl;
```

4. Assume that a, b, and c are variables that have been declared. Write assignment statements that perform the following operations:

    a. Adds 2 to a and assigns the result to b
    b. Multiplies b times 4 and assigns the result to a
    c. Divides a by 3.14 and assigns the result to b
    d. Subtracts 8 from b and assigns the result to a

5. Write a C++ code that prompts the user to enter his or her height and assigns the user's input to a variable named height.

6. Write a C++ code that prompts the user to enter the name of his or her favorite color and assigns the user's input to a string object named color.

7. Rewrite the following statements using combined assignment operators.

```
x = x + 5;
total = total + subtotal;
dist = dist / rep;
ppl = ppl * period;
inv = inv - shortage;
num = num % 2;
```

Programming Exercises

1. **Personal Information**
   Write a program that displays the following information:
   - Your name
   - Your address, with city, state, and ZIP
   - Your telephone number
   - Your college major

2. **Sales Prediction**
   A company has determined that its annual profit is typically 23 percent of total sales. Write a program that asks the user to enter the projected amount of total sales, and then displays the profit that will be made from that amount. *Hint: Use the value 0.23 to represent 23 percent.*

3. **Land Calculation**
   One acre of land is equivalent to 43,560 square feet. Write a program that asks the user to enter the total square feet in a tract of land and calculates the number of acres in the tract. *Hint: Divide the amount entered by 43,560 to get the number of acres.*

VideoNote

Solving the Total Purchase Programming Problem

4. **Total Purchase**
   A customer in a store is purchasing five items. Write a program that asks for the price of each item, and then displays the subtotal of the sale, the amount of sales tax, and the total. Assume the sales tax is 6 percent.

5. **Distance Traveled**

   Assuming there are no accidents or delays, the distance that a car travels down the interstate can be calculated with the following formula:

   Distance = Speed × Time

   A car is traveling at 60 miles per hour. Write a program that displays the following:

   - The distance the car will travel in 5 hours
   - The distance the car will travel in 8 hours
   - The distance the car will travel in 12 hours

6. **Sales Tax**

   Write a program that will ask the user to enter the amount of a purchase. The program should then compute the state and county sales tax. Assume the state sales tax is 4 percent and the county sales tax is 2 percent. The program should display the amount of the purchase, the state sales tax, the county sales tax, the total sales tax, and the total of the sale (which is the sum of the amount of purchase plus the total sales tax). *Hint: Use the value 0.02 to represent 2 percent, and 0.04 to represent 4 percent.*

7. **Miles-per-Gallon**

   A car's miles-per-gallon (MPG) can be calculated with the following formula:

   MPG = miles ÷ gallons

   Write a program that asks the user for the number of miles driven and the gallons of gas used. It should calculate the car's MPG and display the result.

8. **Tip, Tax, and Total**

   Write a program that calculates the total amount of a meal purchased at a restaurant. The program should ask the user to enter the charge for the food and then calculate the amount of a 18 percent tip and 7 percent sales tax. Display each of these amounts and the total.

9. **Celsius to Fahrenheit Temperature Converter**

   Write a program that converts Celsius temperatures to Fahrenheit temperatures. The formula is as follows:

   $F = 1.8 \times C + 32$

   In the formula, F stands for the Fahrenheit temperature, and C stands for the Celsius temperature. The program should ask the user to enter a temperature in Celsius and then display the temperature converted to Fahrenheit.

10. **Stock Transaction Program**

    Last month Joe purchased some stock in Acme Software, Inc. Here are the details of the purchase:

    - The number of shares that Joe purchased is 1,000.
    - When Joe purchased the stock, he paid $32.87 per share.
    - Joe paid his stockbroker a commission that amounted to 2 percent of the amount he paid for the stock.

Two weeks later Joe sold the stock. Here are the details of the sale:

- The number of shares that Joe sold is 1,000.
- He sold the stock for $33.92 per share.
- He paid his stockbroker another commission that amounted to 2 percent of the amount he received for the stock.

Write a program that displays the following information:

- The amount of money Joe paid for the stock.
- The amount of commission Joe paid his broker when he bought the stock.
- The amount that Joe sold the stock for.
- The amount of commission Joe paid his broker when he sold the stock.
- Display the amount of money that Joe had left when he sold the stock and paid his broker (both times). If this amount is positive, then Joe made a profit. If the amount is negative, then Joe lost money.

3 Decision Structures and Boolean Logic

3.1 Control Structures

CONCEPT: Control structures affect the order in which statements execute. The three main types of control structures are sequence, decision, and repetition.

A *control structure* determines the order in which a set of statements executes. Back in the 1960s a group of mathematicians proved that only three control structures are needed to write any type of program: the sequence structure, the decision structure, and the repetition structure. The simplest of these structures is the *sequence structure*, which is a set of statements that executes in the order that they appear. Without realizing it, you have already used the sequence structure many times. For example, look at the following `main` function:

```
int main()
{
    cout << "Hello, world." << endl;
    cout << "This is a simple program." << endl;
    return 0;
}
```

The statements inside the function are a sequence structure because they execute in the order that they are written, from the top of the function to the bottom of the function.

When programmers design programs, they sometimes draw diagrams known as flowcharts, which show a program's logical flow of execution. Figure 3-1 shows a flowchart for the main function previously shown. The elliptical symbols at the top and bottom of the flowchart are known as *terminals* because they mark starting and ending points. The symbols that appear between the terminals are the steps taken in the program. Notice that the symbols are connected by arrows that represent the flow of execution. To step through the program's actions, you begin at the *Start* terminal and follow the arrows until you reach the *Return 0* terminal. As you can see, this flowchart depicts a sequence structure because the steps are taken one after another, from the beginning to the end.

> **NOTE:** Flowcharts are planning tools that programmers sometimes use to design a program's logic. Notice that no actual code is written in Figure 3-1. The steps are written as informal statements that simply describe the actions that must take place. Once the programmer has determined all the actions that must take place and the order in which they must be performed, the programmer can refer to the flowchart while writing the code.

Figure 3-1 Flowchart for a sequence structure

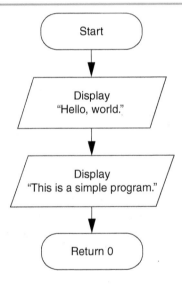

Although the sequence structure is heavily used in programming, it cannot handle every type of task. This is because some problems simply cannot be solved by performing a set of ordered steps, one after the other. In some programs, a set of statements must be executed only under certain circumstances. If those circumstances do not exist, the statements should be skipped. For example, consider a company payroll program that determines whether an employee has worked overtime. If the employee has worked more than 40 hours, he or she is paid extra for all the hours over 40. Otherwise, the overtime calculation should be skipped. This can be accomplished with a *decision structure*.

Suppose the same payroll program calculates pay for all employees. This means it has to perform the same steps for each employee. This requires a repetition structure. A *repetition structure*, which is also known as a *loop*, is a structure that repeats a set of statements as many times as necessary.

In this chapter you will learn how to write decision structure code in C++. In Chapter 4, you will learn to write repetition structure code.

Pseudocode

In addition to flowcharts, programmers often use *pseudocode* (pronounced "sue doe code") to design their programs. The word *pseudo* means fake, so pseudocode is fake code. It is an informal language that has no syntax rules and is not meant to be compiled or executed. Because programmers don't have to worry about syntax errors while writing pseudocode, they can focus all their attention on the program's logic. Once a satisfactory design has been created with pseudocode, the pseudocode can be translated directly to actual code.

The following example shows pseudocode for a program that calculates an employee's gross pay:

Display "Enter the number of hours the employee worked."
Input hours
Display "Enter the employee's hourly pay rate."
Input payRate
*grossPay = hours * payRate*
Display grossPay

Each statement in the pseudocode represents an operation that can be translated to C++. (This pseudocode is a sequence structure because the steps takes place one after the other.) Throughout this book you will see other examples of pseudocode and how it can be translated into actual C++ code.

 Checkpoint

3.1. What does a control structure determine?

3.2. Name three types of control structures.

3.3. What type of control structure have you used so far working through this book?

3.2 Writing a Decision Structure with the if Statement

VideoNote
The if Statement

CONCEPT: The if statement is used to create a decision structure, which allows a program to have more than one path of execution. The if statement causes one or more statements to execute only when a Boolean expression is true.

In a decision structure's simplest form, a specific action is performed only if a certain condition exists. If the condition does not exist, the action is not performed. Figure 3-2

Figure 3-2 A simple decision structure

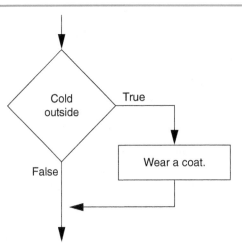

shows part of a flowchart. The figure shows how the logic of an everyday decision can be diagrammed as a decision structure. The diamond symbol represents a true/false condition. If the condition is true, we follow one path, which leads to an action being performed. If the condition is false, we follow another path, which skips the action.

In the flowchart, the diamond symbol indicates some condition that must be tested. In this case, we are determining whether the condition *Cold outside* is true or false. If this condition is true, the action *Wear a coat* is performed. If the condition is false, the action is skipped. The action is *conditionally executed* because it is performed only when a certain condition is true.

Programmers call the type of decision structure shown in Figure 3-2 a *single alternative decision structure*. This is because it provides only one alternative path of execution. If the condition in the diamond symbol is true, we take the alternative path. Otherwise, we exit the structure. Figure 3-3 shows a more elaborate example, where three actions are taken only when it is cold outside. It is still a single alternative decision structure because only one alternative path of execution is given.

In C++ you use the `if` statement to write a single alternative decision structure. Here is the general format of the `if` statement:

```
if (expression)
{
    statement;
    statement;
    etc;
}
```

The statement begins with the word `if`, followed by an *expression* that is enclosed in a set of parentheses. Beginning on the next line is a set of statements that are enclosed in curly braces.

The *expression* that appears inside the parentheses is a Boolean expression. A *Boolean expression* is an expression that can be evaluated as either true or false. When the `if`

Figure 3-3 A decision structure that performs three actions if it is cold outside

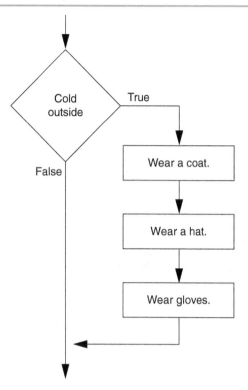

statement executes, the Boolean expression is tested. If it is true, the statements that appear inside the curly braces are executed. If the Boolean expression is false, however, the statements inside the curly braces are skipped. We say that the statements inside the curly braces are conditionally executed because they are executed only if the Boolean expression is true.

If you are writing an if statement that has only one conditionally executed statement, you do not have to enclose the conditionally executed statement inside curly braces. Such an if statement can be written in the following general format:

```
if (expression)
    statement;
```

When an if statement written in this format executes, the Boolean expression is tested. If it is true, the one statement that appears on the next line will be executed. If the Boolean expression is false, however, that one statement is skipped.

Although the curly braces are not required when there is only one conditionally executed statement, it is still a good idea to use them, as shown in the following general format:

```
if (expression)
{
    statement;
}
```

This is a good style for writing `if` statements because it cuts down on errors. Remember, if you have more than one conditionally executed statement, those statements *must* be enclosed in curly braces. If you get into the habit of always enclosing the conditionally executed statements in a set of curly braces, it's less likely that you will forget them.

Boolean Expressions and Relational Operators

The value of a Boolean expression can be either true or false. Boolean expressions are named in honor of the English mathematician George Boole. In the 1800s Boole invented a system of mathematics in which the abstract concepts of true and false can be used in computations.

Typically, the Boolean expression that is tested by an `if` statement is formed with a relational operator. A *relational operator* determines whether a specific relationship exists between two values. For example, the greater than operator (>) determines whether one value is greater than another. The equal to operator (==) determines whether two values are equal. Table 3-1 lists the relational operators that are available in C++.

Table 3-1 Relational operators

Operator	Meaning
>	Greater than
<	Less than
>=	Greater than or equal to
<=	Less than or equal to
==	Equal to
!=	Not equal to

The following is an example of an expression that uses the greater than (>) operator to compare two variables, `length` and `width`:

```
length > width
```

This expression determines whether the value of the `length` variable is greater than the value of the `width` variable. If `length` is greater than `width`, the value of the expression is true. Otherwise, the value of the expression is false. The following expression uses the less than operator to determine whether `length` is less than `width`:

```
length < width
```

Table 3-2 shows examples of several Boolean expressions that compare the variables `x` and `y`.

The >= and <= Operators

Two of the operators, >= and <=, test for more than one relationship. The >= operator determines whether the operand on its left is greater than *or* equal to the operand on

Table 3-2 Boolean expressions using relational operators

Expression	Meaning
x > y	Is x greater than y?
x < y	Is x less than y?
x >= y	Is x greater than or equal to y?
x <= y	Is x less than or equal to y?
x == y	Is x equal to y?
x != y	Is x not equal to y?

its right. The <= operator determines whether the operand on its left is less than *or* equal to the operand on its right.

For example, assume the variable a is assigned 4. All the following expressions are true:

```
a >= 4
a >= 2
8 >= a
a <= 4
a <= 9
4 <= a
```

The == Operator

The **==** operator determines whether the operand on its left is equal to the operand on its right. If the values of both operands are the same, the expression is true. Assuming that a is 4, the expression a == 4 is true, and the expression a == 2 is false.

NOTE: The equality operator is two = symbols together. Don't confuse this operator with the assignment operator, which is one = symbol.

The != Operator

The != operator is the not-equal-to operator. It determines whether the operand on its left is not equal to the operand on its right, which is the opposite of the == operator. As before, assuming a is 4, b is 6, and c is 4, both a != b and b != c are true because a is not equal to b, and b is not equal to c. However, a != c is false because a is equal to c.

Putting It All Together

Let's look at the following example of the `if` statement:

```
if (sales > 50000)
{
    bonus = 500;
}
```

This statement uses the > operator to determine whether sales is greater than 50,000. If the expression sales > 50000 is true, the bonus variable is assigned 500. If the expression is false, however, the assignment statement is skipped. Figure 3-4 shows a flowchart for this section of code.

Figure 3-4 Example decision structure

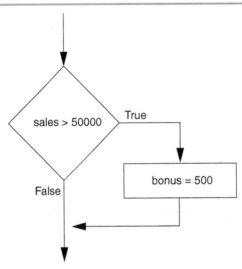

The following example conditionally executes three statements. Figure 3-5 shows a flowchart for this section of code.

```
if (sales > 50000)
{
    bonus = 500.0;
    commissionRate = 0.12;
    cout << "You met your sales quota!" << endl;
}
```

Notice that in both of the previous if statement examples, the conditionally executed statements were indented. This indentation is not required, but it makes the code easier to read and debug. By indenting the conditionally executed statements, you visually set them apart from the surrounding code. This allows you to tell at a glance what part of the program is controlled by the if statement. Most programmers use this style of indentation when writing if statements.

The following code uses the == operator to determine whether two values are equal. The expression balance == 0 will be true if the balance variable is assigned 0. Otherwise, the expression will be false.

```
if (balance == 0)
{
    // Statements appearing here will
    // be executed only if balance is
    // equal to 0.
}
```

Figure 3-5 Example decision structure

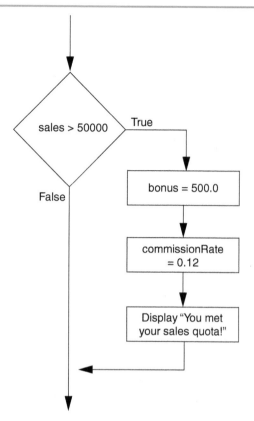

The following code uses the `!=` operator to determine whether two values are *not* equal. The expression `choice != 5` will be true if the `choice` variable is not equal to 5. Otherwise the expression will be false.

```
if (choice != 5)
{
    // Statements appearing here will
    // be executed only if choice is
    // not equal to 5.
}
```

In the Spotlight:

Using the `if` Statement

Kathryn teaches a science class, and her students are required to take three tests. She wants to write a program that her students can use to calculate their average test score. She also wants the program to congratulate the student enthusiastically if the average is greater than 95. Here is the algorithm in pseudocode:

Get the first test score
Get the second test score

> *Get the third test score*
> *Calculate the average*
> *Display the average*
> *If the average is greater than 95*
> > *Congratulate the user*

Program 3-1 shows the code for the program.

Program 3-1   (TestAverage.cpp)

```
 1 // This program prompts the user to enter three test
 2 // scores. It displays the average of those scores and
 3 // and congratulates the user if the average is 95
 4 // or greater.
 5 #include <iostream>
 6 using namespace std;
 7
 8 int main()
 9 {
10    // Variables
11    double test1,            // To hold test score #1
12           test2,            // To hold test score #2
13           test3,            // To hold test score #3
14           average;          // To hold the average
15
16    // Constant for a high average.
17    const double HIGH_AVERAGE = 95.0;
18
19    // Get the three test scores.
20    cout << "Enter the score for test 1: ";
21    cin >> test1;
22    cout << "Enter the score for test 2: ";
23    cin >> test2;
24    cout << "Enter the score for test 3: ";
25    cin >> test3;
26
27    // Calculate the average test score.
28    average = (test1 + test2 + test3) / 3.0;
29
30    // Display the average.
31    cout << "The average score is: "
32         << average << endl;
33
34    // If the average is high, congratulate
35    // the user.
36    if (average >= HIGH_AVERAGE)
37    {
38       cout << "Congratulations!" << endl;
39       cout << "That's a great average!" << endl;
40    }
41
42    return 0;
43 }
```

Program Output (with Input Shown in Bold)

```
Enter the score for test 1: 82 [Enter]
Enter the score for test 2: 76 [Enter]
Enter the score for test 3: 91 [Enter]
The average score is 83
```

Program Output (with Input Shown in Bold)

```
Enter the score for test 1: 93 [Enter]
Enter the score for test 2: 99 [Enter]
Enter the score for test 3: 96 [Enter]
The average score is 96
Congratulations!
That's a great average.
```

 Checkpoint

3.4. What is a control structure?

3.5. What is a decision structure?

3.6. What is a single alternative decision structure?

3.7. What is a Boolean expression?

3.8. What types of relationships between values can you test with relational operators?

3.9. Write an if statement that assigns 0 to the x variable if the y variable is equal to 20.

3.10. Write an if statement that assigns 0.2 to the commission variable if the sales variable is greater than or equal to 10000.

3.3 The if-else Statement

VideoNote
The if-else
Statement

CONCEPT: An if-else statement will execute one block of statements if its Boolean expression is true or another block if its Boolean expression is false.

The previous section introduced the single alternative decision structure (the if statement), which has one alternative path of execution. Now we will look at the *dual alternative decision structure*, which has two possible paths of execution—one path is taken if a Boolean expression is true, and the other path is taken if the Boolean expression is false. Figure 3-6 shows an example flowchart for a dual alternative decision structure.

Figure 3-6 A dual alternative decision structure

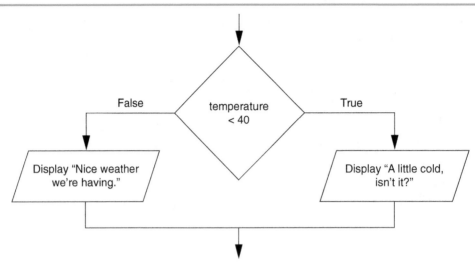

The decision structure in the flowchart tests the expression `temperature < 40`. If this expression is true, the message "A little cold, isn't it?" is displayed. If the expression is false, the message "Nice weather we're having." is displayed.

In code we write a dual alternative decision structure as an `if-else` statement. Here is the general format of the `if-else` statement:

```
if (expression)
{
    statement;
    statement;
    etc;
}
else
{
    statement;
    statement;
    etc;
}
```

An `if-else` statement has two parts: an `if` clause and an `else` clause. Just like a regular `if` statement, the `if-else` statement tests a Boolean expression. If the expression is true, the block of statements following the `if` clause is executed, and then control of the program jumps to the statement that follows the `if-else` statement. If the Boolean expression is false, the block of statements following the `else` clause is executed, and then control of the program jumps to the statement that follows the `if-else` statement. This action is described in Figure 3-7.

The `if-else` statement has two sets of conditionally executed statements. One set is executed only under the condition that the Boolean expression is true, and the other set is executed only under the condition that the Boolean expression is false.

Figure 3-7 Conditional execution in an `if-else` statement

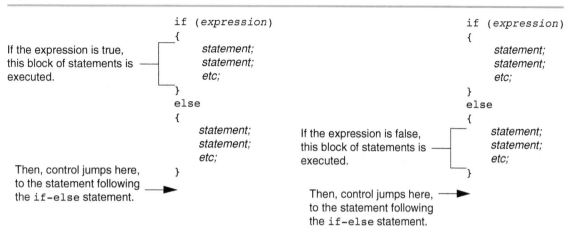

Under no circumstances will both sets of conditionally executed statement be executed.

If either set of conditionally executed statements contains only one statement, the curly braces are not required. For example, the following general format shows only one statement following the `if` clause and only one statement following the `else` clause:

```
if (expression)
    statement;
else
    statement;
```

Although the curly braces are not required when there is only one conditionally executed statement, it is still a good idea to use them, as shown in the following general format:

```
if (expression)
{
    statement;
}
else
{
    statement;
}
```

When we were discussing the regular `if` statement we mentioned that this is a good style of programming because it cuts down on errors. If more than one conditionally executed statement follows either the `if` clause or the `else` clause, those statements *must* be enclosed in curly braces. If you get into the habit of always enclosing the conditionally executed statements in a set of curly braces, it's less likely that you will forget them.

In the Spotlight:
Using the `if-else` Statement

Chris owns an auto repair business and has several employees. If any employee works over 40 hours in a week, he pays them 1.5 times their regular hourly pay rate for all hours over 40. He has asked you to design a simple payroll program that calculates an employee's gross pay, including any overtime wages. You design the following algorithm:

> *Get the number of hours worked.*
> *Get the hourly pay rate.*
> *If the employee worked more than 40 hours,*
>   *Calculate and display the gross pay with overtime.*
> *Else*
>   *Calculate and display the gross pay as usual.*

The code for the program is shown in Program 3-2. Notice that two named constants are created in lines 16 and 17. BASE_HOURS is assigned 40.0, which is the number of hours an employee can work in a week without getting paid overtime. OT_MULTIPLIER is assigned 1.5, which is the pay rate multiplier for overtime hours. This means that the employee's hourly pay rate is multiplied by 1.5 for all overtime hours.

Program 3-2   **(AutoRepairPayroll.cpp)**

```cpp
 1 // This program calculates payroll, including overtime
 2 // if the hours worked are more than 40.
 3 #include <iostream>
 4 using namespace std;
 5
 6 int main()
 7 {
 8    // Variables
 9    double hoursWorked,      // Number of hours worked
10           payRate,          // Hourly pay rate
11           overtimeHours,    // Number of overtime hours
12           overtimePay,      // Amount of overtime pay
13           grossPay;         // Amount of gross pay
14
15    // Constants
16    const double BASE_HOURS = 40.0;    // Base hours per week
17    const double OT_MULTIPLIER = 1.5;  // Overtime multiplier
18
19    // Get the number of hours worked.
20    cout << "Enter the number of hours worked: ";
21    cin >> hoursWorked;
22
23    // Get the hourly pay rate.
24    cout << "Enter the hourly pay rate: ";
25    cin >> payRate;
26
27
28    // Calculate the gross pay.
29    if (hoursWorked > BASE_HOURS)
30    {
```

```
31        // Calculate the number of overtime hours worked.
32        overtimeHours = hoursWorked - BASE_HOURS;
33
34        // Calculate the amount of overtime pay.
35        overtimePay = overtimeHours * payRate * OT_MULTIPLIER;
36
37        // Calculate the gross pay.
38        grossPay = BASE_HOURS * payRate + overtimePay;
39     }
40     else
41     {
42        // Calculate the gross pay (no overtime).
43        grossPay = hoursWorked * payRate;
44     }
45
46     // Display the gross pay.
47     cout << "The gross pay is $" << grossPay << endl;
48     return 0;
49 }
```

Program Output with Example Input Shown in Bold

```
Enter the number of hours worked: 40 [Enter]
Enter the hourly pay rate: 20 [Enter]
The gross pay is $800
```

Program Output with Example Input Shown in Bold

```
Enter the number of hours worked: 50 [Enter]
Enter the hourly pay rate: 20 [Enter]
The gross pay is $1100
```

 Checkpoint

3.11. Describe how a dual alternative decision structure works.

3.12. In an `if-else` statement, under what circumstances are the statements that appear after the `else` clause executed?

3.13. Write an `if-else` statement that determines whether y is less than 0. If this is true, set x to 0. Otherwise, set x to 320.

 3.4 Nested Decision Structures
and the `if-else-if` Statement

CONCEPT: To test more than one condition, a decision structure can be nested inside another decision structure.

In Section 3.1, we mentioned that a control structure determines the order in which a set of statements executes. Programs are usually designed as combinations of different control structures. For example, Figure 3-8 shows a flowchart that combines a decision structure with two sequence structures.

Figure 3-8 Combining sequence structures with a decision structure

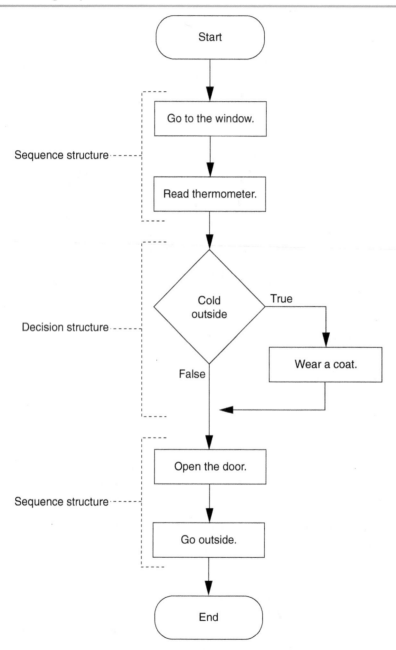

The flowchart in the figure starts with a sequence structure. Assuming you have an outdoor thermometer in your window, the first step is *Go to the window*, and the next step is *Read thermometer*. A decision structure appears next, testing the condition *Cold outside*. If this is true, the action *Wear a coat* is performed. Another sequence structure appears next. The step *Open the door* is performed, followed by *Go outside*.

Quite often, structures must be nested inside other structures. For example, look at the partial flowchart in Figure 3-9. It shows a decision structure with a sequence structure nested inside it. The decision structure tests the condition *Cold outside*. If that condition is true, the steps in the sequence structure are executed.

Figure 3-9 A sequence structure nested inside a decision structure

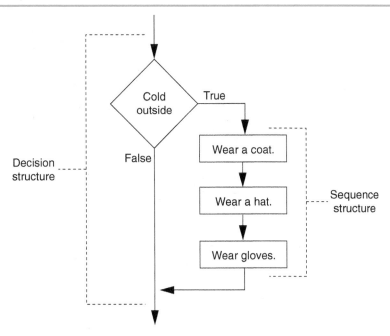

You can also nest decision structures inside other decision structures. This is commonly done in programs that need to test more than one condition. For example, consider a program that determines whether a bank customer qualifies for a loan. To qualify, two conditions must exist: (1) the customer must earn at least $30,000 per year, and (2) the customer must have been employed at his or her current job for at least two years. Figure 3-10 shows a flowchart for a program that could be used in such a program. Assume that the `salary` variable is assigned the customer's annual salary, and the `yearsOnJob` variable is assigned the number of years that the customer has worked on his or her current job.

If we follow the flow of execution, we see that the condition `salary >= 30000` is tested. If this condition is false, there is no need to perform further tests; we know that the customer does not qualify for the loan. If the condition is true, however, we need to test the second condition. This is done with a nested decision structure that tests the condition `yearsOnJob >= 2`. If this condition is true, then the customer qualifies for the loan. If this condition is false, then the customer does not qualify. Program 3-3 shows the code for the complete program.

Figure 3-10 A nested decision structure

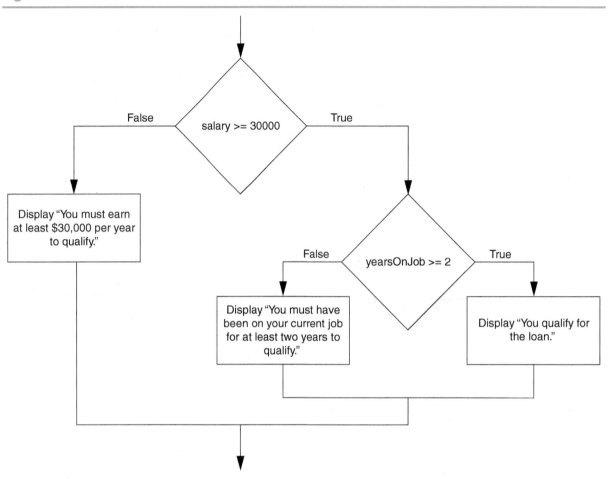

Program 3-3   (LoanQualifier.cpp)

```
 1 // This program determines whether a bank customer
 2 // qualifies for a loan.
 3 #include <iostream>
 4 using namespace std;
 5
 6 int main()
 7 {
 8     // Variables
 9     double salary;    // Applicant's salary
10     int yearsOnJob;   // Years on the job
11
12     // Constants
13     const double MIN_SALARY = 30000.0;  // Minimum salary
14     const int MIN_YEARS = 2;            // Minimum years
15
16     // Get the applicant's salary.
```

```
17      cout << "Enter your annual salary: ";
18      cin >> salary;
19
20      // Get the applicant's years on the current job.
21      cout << "Enter the number of years on your current job: ";
22      cin >> yearsOnJob;
23
24
25      // Determine whether the customer qualifies.
26      if (salary >= MIN_SALARY)
27      {
28         if (yearsOnJob >= MIN_YEARS)
29         {
30            cout << "You qualify for the loan." << endl;
31         }
32         else
33         {
34            cout << "You must have been on your current" << endl;
35            cout << "job for at least " << MIN_YEARS
36                 << " years to qualify." << endl;
37         }
38      }
39      else
40      {
41         cout << "You must earn at least $" << MIN_SALARY
42              << " to qualify." << endl;
43      }
44      return 0;
45 }
```

Program Output with Example Input Shown in Bold

```
Enter your annual salary: 35000 [Enter]
Enter the number of years on your current job: 1 [Enter]
You must have been on your current
job for at least 2 years to qualify.
```

Program Output (with Input Shown in Bold)

```
Enter your annual salary: 25000 [Enter]
Enter the number of years on your current job: 5 [Enter]
You must earn at least $30000 to qualify.
```

Program Output (with Input Shown in Bold)

```
Enter your annual salary: 35000 [Enter]
Enter the number of years on your current job: 5 [Enter]
You qualify for the loan.
```

Look at the `if-else` statement that begins in line 26. It tests the condition `salary >= MIN_SALARY`. If this condition is true, the `if-else` statement that begins in line 28 is executed. Otherwise the program jumps to the `else` clause in line 39 and executes the cout statement in lines 41 and 42. The program then leaves the decision structure.

For debugging purposes, it is important to use proper alignment and indentation in a nested decision structure. This makes it easier to see which actions are performed by each part of the structure. For example, the following code is functionally equivalent to lines 26 through 43 in Program 3-3. Although this code is logically correct, it would be very difficult to debug because it is not properly indented.

```cpp
if (salary >= MIN_SALARY)
{
if (yearsOnJob >= MIN_YEARS)
{
cout << "You qualify for the loan." << endl;
}
else
{
cout << "You must have been on your current" << endl;
cout << "job for at least " << MIN_YEARS
    << " years to qualify." << endl;
}
}
else
{
cout << "You must earn at least $" << MIN_SALARY
    << " to qualify." << endl;
}
```

Proper indentation and alignment also makes it easier to see which `if` and `else` clauses belong together, as shown in Figure 3-11.

Figure 3-11 Alignment of `if` and `else` clauses

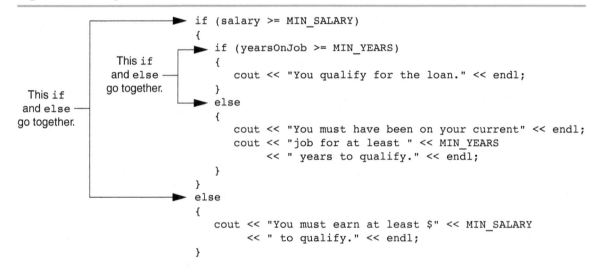

Testing a Series of Conditions

In the previous example you saw how a program can use nested decision structures to test more than one condition. It is not uncommon for a program to have a series of conditions to test and then perform an action depending on which condition is true. One way to accomplish this it to have a decision structure with numerous other decision structures nested inside it. For example, consider the program presented in the following *In the Spotlight* section.

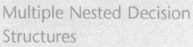

In the Spotlight:
Multiple Nested Decision Structures

Dr. Suarez teaches a literature class and uses the following 10-point grading scale for all of his exams:

Test Score	Grade
90 and above	A
80–89	B
70–79	C
60–69	D
Below 60	F

He has asked you to write a program that will allow a student to enter a test score and then display the grade for that score. Here is the algorithm that you will use:

Ask the user to enter a test score
If the score is greater than or equal to 90, then the grade is A
  Else, if the score is greater than or equal to 80, then the grade is B
    Else, if the score is greater than or equal to 70, then the grade is C
      Else, if the score is greater than or equal to 60, then the grade is D
        Else, the grade is F

You decide that the process of determining the grade will require several nested decisions structures, as shown in Figure 3-12. Program 3-4 shows the code for the program. The code for the nested decision structures is in lines 15 through 43.

Figure 3-12 Nested decision structure to determine a grade

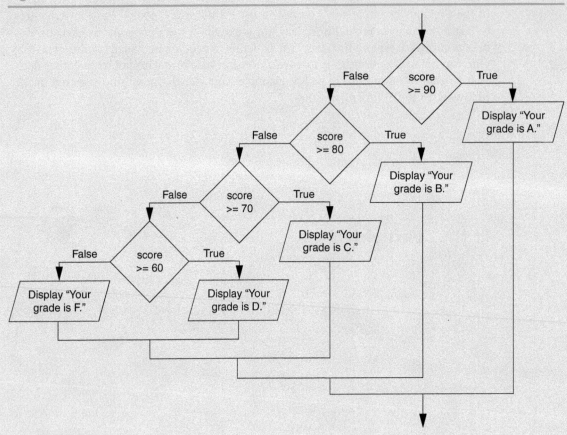

Program 3-4   (Grader.cpp)

```
 1  // This program gets a numeric test score from the
 2  // user and displays the corresponding letter grade.
 3  #include <iostream>
 4  using namespace std;
 5
 6  int main()
 7  {
 8      int testScore;
 9
10      // Get the test score.
11      cout << "Enter your test score: ";
12      cin >> testScore;
13
14      // Determine the letter grade.
15      if (testScore >= 90)
16      {
17          cout << "Your grade is A." << endl;
18      }
19      else
```

```
20    {
21        if (testScore >= 80)
22        {
23            cout << "Your grade is B." << endl;
24        }
25        else
26        {
27            if (testScore >= 70)
28            {
29                cout << "Your grade is C." << endl;
30            }
31            else
32            {
33                if (testScore >= 60)
34                {
35                    cout << "Your grade is D." << endl;
36                }
37                else
38                {
39                    cout << "Your grade is F." << endl;
40                }
41            }
42        }
43    }
44    return 0;
45 }
```

Program Output (with Input Shown in Bold)

```
Enter your test score: 78 [Enter]
Your grade is C.
```

Program Output (with Input Shown in Bold)

```
Enter your test score: 84 [Enter]
Your grade is B.
```

The `if-else-if` Statement

VideoNote

The if-else-if Statement

Even though Program 6-3 is a simple example, the logic of nested decision structures can become complex. C++ provides a special version of the decision structure known as the `if-else-if` statement, which makes this type of logic simpler to write. Here is the general format of the `if-else-if` statement:

```
if (BooleanExpression_1)
{
    statement;
    statement;
    etc.
}
```

```
        else if (BooleanExpression_2)
        {
            statement;
            statement;
            etc.
        }
```

Insert as many else if clauses as necessary.

```
        else
        {
            statement;
            statement;
            etc.
        }
```

When the statement executes, `BooleanExpression_1` is tested. If `BooleanExpression_1` is true, the block of statements that immediately follow is executed, and the rest of the structure is ignored. If `BooleanExpression_1` is false, however, the program jumps to the very next else-if clause and tests `BooleanExpression_2`. If it is true, the block of statements that immediately follows is executed, and the rest the structure is then ignored. This process continues until a condition is found to be true, or no more else-if clauses are left. If none of the conditions are true, the block of statements following the else clause is executed.

The code shown in Program 3-5 is a revision of the test score grading program shown in Program 3-4. This version of the program uses an if-else-if statement instead of nested if-else statements. The output is the same as that of Program 3-4.

Program 3-5   (`Grader2.cpp`)

```cpp
 1 // This program gets a numeric test score from the
 2 // user and displays the corresponding letter grade.
 3 #include <iostream>
 4 using namespace std;
 5
 6 int main()
 7 {
 8     int testScore;
 9
10     // Get the test score.
11     cout << "Enter your test score: ";
12     cin >> testScore;
13
14     // Determine the letter grade.
15     if (testScore >= 90)
16         cout << "Your grade is A." << endl;
17     else if (testScore >= 80)
18         cout << "Your grade is B." << endl;
19     else if (testScore >= 70)
20         cout << "Your grade is C." << endl;
21     else if (testScore >= 60)
22         cout << "Your grade is D." << endl;
```

```
23    else
24       cout << "Your grade is F." << endl;
25    return 0;
26 }
```

Program Output (with Input Shown in Bold)

Enter your test score: 78 [*Enter*]
Your grade is C.

Program Output (with Input Shown in Bold)

Enter your test score: 84 [*Enter*]
Your grade is B.

Notice the alignment and indentation that used with the `if-else-if` statement: The if, `else-if`, and `else` clauses are all aligned, and the conditionally executed statements are indented.

You never have to use the `if-else-if` statement because its logic can be coded with nested `if-else` statements. However, a long series of nested `if-else` statements has two particular disadvantages when you are debugging code:

- The code can grow complex and become difficult to understand.
- Because indenting is important in nested statements, a long series of nested `if-else` statements can become too long to be displayed on the computer screen without horizontal scrolling. Also, long statements tend to "wrap around" when printed on paper, making the code even more difficult to read.

The logic of an `if-else-if` statement is usually easier to follow than a long series of nested `if-else` statements. And, because all the clauses are aligned in an `if-else-if` statement, the lengths of the lines in the statement tend to be shorter.

 Checkpoint

3.14. How does a dual alternative decision structure work?

3.15. What statement do you use in C++ to write a dual alternative decision structure?

3.16. When you write an `if-else` statement, under what circumstances does the block that appears after the `else` clause execute?

3.17. Convert the following code to an `if-else-if` statement:

```
if (number == 1)
{
    cout << "One" << endl;
}
else
{
    if (number == 2)
    {
        cout << "Two" << endl;
    }
```

```
            else
            {
               if (number == 3)
               {
                  cout << "Three" << endl;
               }
               else
               {
                  cout << "Unknown" << endl;
               }
            }
         }
```

3.5 Logical Operators

CONCEPT: The logical AND operator and the logical OR operator allow you to connect multiple Boolean expressions to create a compound expression. The logical NOT operator reverses the truth of a Boolean expression.

The C++ language provides a set of operators known as *logical operators*, which you can use to create complex Boolean expressions. Table 3-3 describes these operators.

Table 3-3 Logical operators

Operator	Meaning
&&	This is the logical AND operator. It connects two Boolean expressions into one compound expression. Both subexpressions must be true for the compound expression to be true.
||	This is the logical OR operator. It connects two Boolean expressions into one compound expression. One or both subexpressions must be true for the compound expression to be true. It is only necessary for one of the subexpressions to be true, and it does not matter which.
!	This is the logical NOT operator, which is a unary operator, meaning it works with only one operand. The operand must be a Boolean expression. The NOT operator reverses the truth of its operand. If it is applied to an expression that is true, the operator returns false. If it is applied to an expression that is false, the operator returns true.

Table 3-4 shows examples of several compound Boolean expressions that use logical operators.

Table 3-4 Compound Boolean expressions using logical operators

Expression	Meaning
x > y && a < b	Is x greater than y AND is a less than b?
x == y || x == z	Is x equal to y OR is x equal to z?
! (x > y)	Is the expression x > y NOT true?

The && Operator

The && operator takes two Boolean expressions as operands and creates a compound Boolean expression that is true only when both subexpressions are true. The following is an example of an if statement that uses the && operator:

```
if (temperature < 20 && minutes > 12)
    cout << "The temperature is in the danger zone." << endl;
```

In this statement, the two Boolean expressions temperature < 20 and minutes > 12 are combined into a compound expression. The cout statement will be executed only if temperature is less than 20 and minutes is greater than 12. If either of the Boolean subexpressions is false, the compound expression is false, and the message is not displayed.

Table 3-5 shows a truth table for the && operator. The truth table lists expressions showing all the possible combinations of true and false connected with the && operator. The resulting values of the expressions are also shown.

Table 3-5 Truth table for the and operator

Expression	Value of the Expression
true && false	false
false && true	false
false && false	false
true && true	true

As the table shows, both sides of the && operator must be true for the operator to return a true value.

The || Operator

The || operator takes two Boolean expressions as operands and creates a compound Boolean expression that is true when either of the subexpressions is true. The following is an example of an if statement that uses the || operator:

```
if (temperature < 20 || temperature > 100)
    cout << "The temperature is in the danger zone." << endl;
```

The cout statement will execute only if temperature is less than 20 or temperature is greater than 100. If either subexpression is true, the compound expression is true. Table 3-6 shows a truth table for the || operator.

Table 3-6 Truth table for the || operator

Expression	Value of the Expression
true || false	true
false || true	true
false || false	false
true || true	true

All it takes for an || expression to be true is for one side of the || operator to be true. It doesn't matter if the other side is false or true.

Short-Circuit Evaluation

Both the && and || operators perform *short-circuit evaluation*. Here's how it works with the && operator: If the expression on the left side of the && operator is false, the expression on the right side will not be checked. Because the compound expression will be false if only one of the subexpressions is false, it would waste CPU time to check the remaining expression. So, when the && operator finds that the expression on its left is false, it short-circuits and does not evaluate the expression on its right.

Here's how short-circuit evaluation works with the || operator: If the expression on the left side of the || operator is true, the expression on the right side will not be checked. Because it is only necessary for one of the expressions to be true, it would waste CPU time to check the remaining expression.

The ! Operator

The ! operator is a unary operator that takes a Boolean expression as its operand and reverses its logical value. In other words, if the expression is true, the ! operator returns false, and if the expression is false, the ! operator returns true. The following is an if statement using the ! operator:

```
if (!(temperature > 100))
    cout << "This is below the maximum temperature." << endl;
```

First, the expression (temperature > 100) is tested, and a value of either true or false is the result. Then the ! operator is applied to that value. If the expression (temperature > 100) is true, the ! operator returns false. If the expression (temperature > 100) is false, the ! operator returns true. The previous code is equivalent to asking: "Is the temperature not greater than 100?"

NOTE: In this example, we have placed parentheses around the expression temperature > 100. This is to make it clear that we are applying the ! operator to the value of the expression temperature > 100, not just to the temperature variable.

Table 3-7 shows a truth table for the ! operator.

Table 3-7 Truth table for the ! operator

Expression	Value of the Expression
! true	false
! false	true

Precedence of the Logical Operators

We mentioned earlier that the ! operator has higher precedence than the relational operators. The && and || logical operators have lower precedence than the relational operators. For example, look at the following expression:

```
creditScore > 700 || accountBalance > 9000
```

When this expression is evaluated, the > operators work first, and then the || operator works. The expression is the same as the following:

```
(creditScore > 700) || (accountBalance > 9000)
```

Many programmers choose to enclose the expressions that are to the left and the right of a logical operator in parentheses, as shown here. Even though the parentheses are not required in many situations, using them makes the compound expression easier to understand.

Checking Numeric Ranges with Logical Operators

Sometimes you will need to write code that determines whether a numeric value is within a specific range of values or outside a specific range of values. When determining whether a number is inside a range, it is best to use the && operator. For example, the following if statement checks the value in x to determine whether it is in the range of 20 to 40:

```
if (x > 20 && x < 40)
{
    cout << "The value is in the acceptable range." << endl;
}
```

The compound Boolean expression being tested by this statement will be true only when x is greater than 20 *AND* less than 40. The value in x must be between the values of 20 and 40 for this compound expression to be true.

When determining whether a number is outside a range, it is best to use the || operator. The following statement determines whether x is outside the range of 20 through 40:

```
if (x < 20 || x > 40)
{
    cout << "The value is outside the acceptable range." << endl;
}
```

It is important not to get the logic of the logical operators confused when testing for a range of numbers. For example, the compound Boolean expression in the following code would never test true:

```
// This is an error!
if (x < 20 && x > 40)
{
    cout << "The value is outside the acceptable range." << endl;
}
```

Obviously, x cannot be less than 20 and at the same time be greater than 40.

Checkpoint

3.18. What is a compound Boolean expression?

3.19. The following truth table shows various combinations of the values true and false connected by a logical operator. Complete the table by circling *T* or *F* to indicate whether the result of such a combination is true or false.

Logical Expression	Result (circle true or false)	
true && false	T	F
true && true	T	F
false && true	T	F
false && false	T	F
true || false	T	F
true || true	T	F
false || true	T	F
false || false	T	F
! true	T	F
! false	T	F

3.20. Assume the variables a = 2, b = 4, and c = 6. Circle *T* or *F* for each of the following conditions to indicate if it is true or false.

```
a == 4 || b > 2        T    F
6 <= c && a > 3        T    F
1 != b && c != 3       T    F
a >= -1 || a <= b      T    F
!(a > 2)               T    F
```

3.21. Explain how short-circuit evaluation works with the && and || operators.

3.22. Write an `if` statement that displays the message "The number is valid" if the variable speed is within the range 0 through 200.

3.23. Write an `if` statement that displays the message "The number is not valid" if the variable speed is outside the range 0 through 200.

3.6 The `switch` Statement

CONCEPT: The `switch` statement lets the value of a variable or an expression determine which path of execution the program will take.

The `switch` *statement* is a *multiple alternative decision structure*. It allows you to test the value of an integer variable or an expression and then use that value to determine which statement or set of statements to execute. Figure 3-13 shows an example of how a `switch` statement looks in a flowchart.

In the flowchart, the diamond symbol contains the name of an integer variable named month. If the variable contains the value 1, then "January" is displayed. If the variable contains the value 2, then "February" is displayed. If the variable contains the value 3, then "March" is displayed. If the variable contains none of these values, the box labeled *Default* is executed. In this case, the message "Error: Invalid month" is displayed.

Figure 3-13 A switch statement

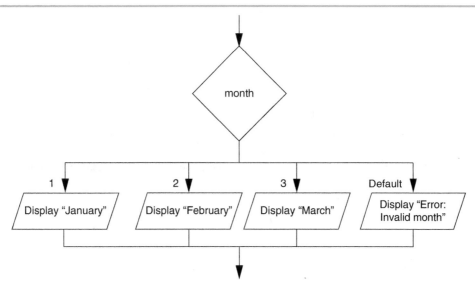

Here is the general format of the switch statement in C++ code:

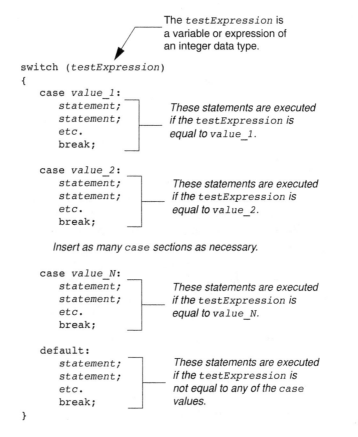

The first line of the structure starts with the word *switch*, followed by a *testExpression*, which is enclosed in parentheses. The testExpression is usually an integer variable, but it can also be any expression that gives an integer value. Beginning at the next line is a block of code enclosed in curly braces. Inside this block of code is one or more *case sections*. A case section begins with the word `case`, followed by a value, followed by a colon. Each case section contains one or more statements, followed by a `break` statement. At the end is an optional *default section*.

When the `switch` statement executes, it compares the value of the `testExpression` with the values that follow each of the `case` statements (from top to bottom). When it finds a case value that matches the `testExpression`'s value, the program branches to the `case` statement. The statements that follow the `case` statement are executed until a break statement is encountered. At that point the program jumps out of the `switch` statement. If the `testExpression` does not match any of the case values, the program branches to the `default` statement and executes the statements that immediately follow it.

For example, the following code performs the same operation as the flowchart in Figure 3-13:

```
switch (month)
{
    case 1:
        cout << "January" << endl;
        break;

    case 2:
        cout << "February" << endl;
        break;

    case 3:
        cout << "March" << endl;
        break;

    default:
        cout << "Error: Invalid month" << endl;
}
```

In this example the `testExpression` is the `month` variable. If the value in the `month` variable is 1, the program will branch to the `case 1:` section and execute the `cout` statement that immediately follows it (displaying "January"). If the value in the `month` variable is 2, the program will branch to the `case 2:` section and execute the `cout` statement that immediately follows it (displaying "February"). If the value in the `month` variable is 3, the program will branch to the `case 3:` section and execute the `cout` statement that immediately follows it (displaying "March"). If the value in the `month` variable is not 1, 2, or 3, the program will branch to the `default:` section and execute the `cout` statement that immediately follows it (displaying the error message).

Here are some important points to remember about the `switch` statement:

- The `testExpression` must be a variable that is of an integer data type, or an expression that gives an integer value.
- The value that follows a `case` statement must be an integer literal or an integer constant. It cannot be a variable.
- The `break` statement that appears at the end of a case section is optional, but in most situations you will need it. If the program executes a case section that does not end with a `break` statement, it will continue executing the code in the very next case section.

- The default section is optional, but in most situations you should have one. The default section is executed when the testExpression does not match any of the case values.
- Because the default section appears at the end of the switch statement, it does not need a break statement.

In the Spotlight:
Using a switch Statement

Lenny, who owns Lenny's Stereo and Television, has asked you to write a program that lets the customer pick one of three TV models and then displays the price and size of the selected model.

Here is the algorithm:

> *Get the TV model number*
> *If the model is 100, then display the information for that model.*
>   *Otherwise, if the model is 200, then display the information for that model.*
>   *Otherwise, if the model is 300, then display the information for that model.*

At first you consider designing a nested decision structure to determine the model number and display the correct information. But you realize that a switch statement will work just as well because a single value, the model number, will be used to determine the action the program will perform. The model number can be stored in a variable, and that variable can be tested by a switch statement. Assuming that the model number is stored in a variable named modelNumber, Figure 3-14 shows

Figure 3-14 Flowchart for the switch statement

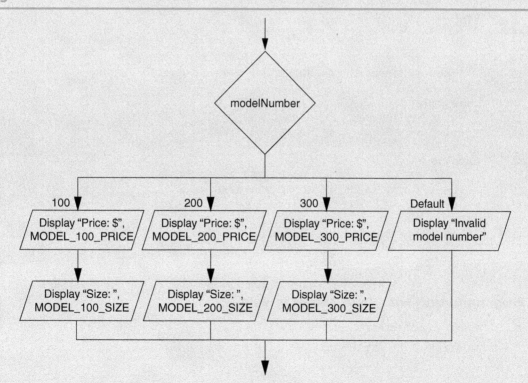

a flowchart for the switch statement. Program 3-6 shows the C++ code for the program.

Program 3-6 **(SwitchExample.cpp)**

```cpp
 1 // This program demonstrates the switch statement.
 2 #include <iostream>
 3 using namespace std;
 4
 5 int main()
 6 {
 7    // Constants for the TV prices
 8    const double MODEL_100_PRICE = 199.99;
 9    const double MODEL_200_PRICE = 269.99;
10    const double MODEL_300_PRICE = 349.99;
11
12    // Constants for the TV sizes
13    const int MODEL_100_SIZE = 24;
14    const int MODEL_200_SIZE = 27;
15    const int MODEL_300_SIZE = 32;
16
17    // Variable for the model number
18    int modelNumber;
19
20    // Get the test score.
21    cout << "Which TV are you interested in?" << endl;
22    cout << "The model 100, 200 or 300? ";
23    cin >> modelNumber;
24
25    // Display the price and size.
26    switch (modelNumber)
27    {
28    case 100:
29       cout << "Price: " << MODEL_100_PRICE << endl;
30       cout << "Size: " << MODEL_100_SIZE << endl;
31       break;
32    case 200:
33       cout << "Price: " << MODEL_200_PRICE << endl;
34       cout << "Size: " << MODEL_200_SIZE << endl;
35       break;
36    case 300:
37       cout << "Price: " << MODEL_300_PRICE << endl;
38       cout << "Size: " << MODEL_300_SIZE << endl;
39       break;
40    default:
41       cout << "Invalid model number." << endl;
42    }
43    return 0;
44 }
```

Program Output with Input Shown in Bold

```
Which TV are you interested in?
The 100, 200, or 300? 100 [Enter]
```

```
Price: $199.99
Size: 24
```

Program Output with Input Shown in Bold

```
Which TV are you interested in?
The 100, 200, or 300? 200 [Enter]
Price: $269.99
Size: 27
```

Program Output with Input Shown in Bold

```
Which TV are you interested in?
The 100, 200, or 300? 300 [Enter]
Price: $349.99
Size: 32
```

Program Output with Input Shown in Bold

```
Which TV are you interested in?
The 100, 200, or 300? 500 [Enter]
Invalid model number
```

 Checkpoint

3.24. Convert the following if-else-if code to a switch statement.

```cpp
if (choice == 1)
{
    cout << "You chose 1." << endl;
}
else if (choice == 2)
{
    cout << "You chose 2." << endl;
}
else if (choice == 3)
{
    cout << "You chose 3." << endl;
}
else
{
    cout << "Make another choice." << endl;
}
```

3.7 bool Variables

CONCEPT: A bool variable can hold one of two values: true or false. Variables of the bool data type are commonly used as flags, which indicate whether specific conditions exist.

The C++ language provides a special data type named `bool` that you can use to create variables that hold true or false values. Here is an example of the declaration of a `bool` variable:

```
bool grandMaster;
```

This declares a `bool` variable named `grandMaster`. In the program we can assign the special values `true` or `false` to the variable, as shown here:

```
if (points > 5000)
{
    grandMaster = true;
}
else
{
    grandMaster = false;
}
```

Variables of the `bool` data type are commonly used as flags. A *flag* is a variable that signals when some condition exists in the program. When the flag variable is set to `false`, it indicates that the condition does not yet exist. When the flag variable is set to `true`, it means the condition does exist. For example, the previous code might be used in a game to determine whether the user is a "grand master." If he or she has earned more than 5,000 points, we set the `grandMaster` variable to true. Otherwise, we set the variable to `false`. Later in the program we can test the `grandMaster` variable, like this:

```
if (grandMaster)
{
    powerLevel += 500;
}
```

This code performs the following: If `grandMaster` is true, add 500 to `powerLevel`. Here is another example:

```
if (!grandMaster)
{
    powerLevel = 100;
}
```

This code performs the following: If `grandMaster` is not true, set `powerLevel` to 100.

 Checkpoint

3.25. What values can you store in a `bool` variable?

3.26. What is a flag variable?

3.8 Comparing Strings

CONCEPT: C++ allows you to compare strings. This allows you to create decision structures that test the value of a string.

You saw in the preceding examples how numbers can be compared in a decision structure. You can also compare strings. For example, look at the following code:

```
string name1 = "Mary";
string name2 = "Mark";
if (name1 == name2)
{
    cout << "The names are the same." << endl;
}
else
{
    cout << "The names are NOT the same." << endl;
}
```

The == operator compares name1 and name2 to determine whether they are equal. Because the strings "Mary" and "Mark" are not equal, the else clause will display the message "The names are NOT the same."

Let's look at another example. Assume month is a string object. The following code uses the != operator to determine whether the value of month is not equal to "October".

```
if (month != "October")
{
    cout << "This is the wrong time for Octoberfest!" << endl;
}
```

Program 3-7 is a complete program demonstrating how two strings can be compared. The program prompts the user to enter a password and then determines whether the string entered is equal to "prospero".

Program 3-7   **(CompareStrings.cpp)**

```
 1 // This program compares strings.
 2 #include <iostream>
 3 #include <string>
 4 using namespace std;
 5
 6 int main()
 7 {
 8     string password;
 9
10     // Get a password from the user.
11     cout << "Enter the password: ";
12     cin >> password;
13
14     // Determine whether the password is correct.
15     if (password == "prospero")
16     {
17         cout << "Password accepted." << endl;
18     }
19     else
```

```
20   {
21       cout << "Sorry, that's the wrong password." << endl;
22   }
23   return 0;
24 }
```

Program Output with Input Shown in Bold

Enter the password: **ferdinand** [*Enter*]
Sorry, that's the wrong password.

Program Output with Input Shown in Bold

Enter the password: **prospero** [*Enter*]
Password accepted.

String comparisons are case sensitive. For example, the strings "saturday" and "Saturday" are not equal because the s is lowercase in the first string, but uppercase in the second string. The following sample session with Program 3-7 shows what happens when the user enters Prospero as the password (with an uppercase P).

Program Output with Input Shown in Bold

Enter the password: **Prospero** [*Enter*]
Sorry, that is the wrong password.

Review Questions

Multiple Choice

1. A _____ structure can execute a set of statements only under certain circumstances.
   a. sequence
   b. circumstantial
   c. decision
   d. Boolean

2. A _____ structure provides one alternative path of execution.
   a. sequence
   b. single alternative decision
   c. one path alternative
   d. single execution decision

3. A(n) _____ expression has a value of either true or false.
   a. binary
   b. decision
   c. unconditional
   d. Boolean

4. The symbols >, <, and == are all _____ operators.
   a. relational
   b. logical
   c. conditional
   d. ternary

5. A(n) _____ structure tests a condition and then takes one path if the condition is true or another path if the condition is false.
   a. `if statement`
   b. single alternative decision
   c. dual alternative decision
   d. sequence

6. You use a(n) _____ statement to write a single alternative decision structure.
   a. `test-jump`
   b. `if`
   c. `if-else`
   d. `if-call`

7. You use a(n) _____ statement to write a dual alternative decision structure.
   a. `test-jump`
   b. `if`
   c. `if-else`
   d. `if-call`

8. `&&`, `||`, and `!` are _____ operators.
   a. relational
   b. logical
   c. conditional
   d. ternary

9. A compound Boolean expression created with the _____ operator is true only if both of its subexpressions are true.
   a. `&&`
   b. `||`
   c. `!`
   d. `both`

10. A compound Boolean expression created with the _____ operator is true if either of its subexpressions is true.
    a. `&&`
    b. `||`
    c. `!`
    d. `either`

11. The _____ operator takes a Boolean expression as its operand and reverses its logical value.
    a. `&&`
    b. `||`
    c. `!`
    d. `either`

12. This statement allows you to test the value of an integer variable or expression and then use that value to determine which statement or set of statements to execute:
    a. menu.
    b. branch.
    c. select.
    d. switch.

13. This section of a switch statement is branched to if none of the case values match the test expression:
    a. else.
    b. default.
    c. case.
    d. otherwise.

14. A _____ is a Boolean variable that signals when some condition exists in the program.
    a. flag
    b. signal
    c. sentinel
    d. siren

15. You use the _____ operator to determine whether two strings are equal.
    a. !=
    b. @=
    c. ==
    d. $=

True or False

1. You can write any program using only sequence structures.

2. A program can be made of only one type of control structure. You cannot combine structures.

3. A single alternative decision structure tests a condition and then takes one path if the condition is true or another path if the condition is false.

4. A decision structure can be nested inside another decision structure.

5. A compound Boolean expression that has two subexpressions connected with the && operator is true only when both subexpressions are true.

6. A compound Boolean expression that has two subexpressions connected with the || operator is true only when both subexpressions are true.

7. The test expression in a switch statement must have an integer value.

Short Answer

1. Explain what is meant by the term *conditionally executed*.

2. You need to test a condition and then execute one set of statements if the condition is true. If the condition is false, you need to execute a different set of statements. What structure will you use?

3. Briefly describe how the `&&` operator works.

4. Briefly describe how the `||` operator works.

5. Briefly describe how the `!` operator works.

6. What is a flag, and how does it work?

7. If you need to test the value of an integer variable and use that value to determine which statement or set of statements to execute, which statement would be a good choice?

Algorithm Workbench

1. Write an `if` statement that assigns 20 to the variable y and assigns 40 to the variable z if the variable x is greater than 100.

2. Write an `if` statement that assigns 0 to the variable b and assigns 1 to the variable c if the variable a is less than 10.

3. Write an `if-else` statement that assigns 0 to the variable b if the variable a is less than 10. Otherwise, it should assign 99 to the variable b.

4. The following code contains several nested `if-else` statements. Unfortunately, it was written without proper alignment and indentation. Rewrite the code and use the proper conventions of alignment and indentation.

```
if (score < 60)
{
cout << "Your grade is F.";
}
else
{
if (score < 70)
{
cout << "Your grade is D.";
}
else
{
if (score < 80)
{
cout << "Your grade is C.";
}
else
{
if (score < 90)
{
cout << "Your grade is B.";
}
else
{
cout << "Your grade is A.";
}}}}
```

5. Write nested decision structures that perform the following: If amount1 is greater than 10 and amount2 is less than 100, display the greater of amount1 and amount2.

6. Write an if-else statement that displays "Speed is normal" if the speed variable is within the range of 24 to 56. If the speed variable's value is outside this range, display "Speed is abnormal".

7. Write an if-else statement that determines whether the points variable is outside the range of 9 to 51. If the variable's value is outside this range, it should display "Invalid points." Otherwise, it should display "Valid points."

8. Rewrite the following if-else if statement as a switch statement.

```
if (selection == 1)
    cout << "You selected A." << endl;
else if (selection == 2)
    cout << "You selected 2." << endl;
else if (selection == 3)
    cout << "You selected 3." << endl;
else if (selection == 4)
    cout << "You selected 4." << endl;
else
    cout << "Not good with numbers, eh?" << endl;
```

9. Write a switch statement that tests the month variable and does the following:
   - If the month variable is set to 1, it displays "January has 31 days."
   - If the month variable is set to 2, it displays "February has 28 days."
   - If the month variable is set to 3, it displays "March has 31 days."
   - If the month variable is set to anything else, it displays "Invalid selection."

10. Write an if statement that sets the variable hours to 10 if the flag variable minimum is set to true.

Programming Exercises

1. **Roman Numerals**

   Write a program that prompts the user to enter a number within the range of 1 through 10. The program should display the Roman numeral version of that number. If the number is outside the range of 1 through 10, the program should display an error message. The following table shows the Roman numerals for the numbers 1 through 10:

Number	Roman Numeral
1	I
2	II
3	III
4	IV
5	V
6	VI
7	VII
8	VIII
9	IX
10	X

2. **Areas of Rectangles**

   The area of a rectangle is the rectangle's length times its width. Write a program that asks for the length and width of two rectangles. The program should tell the user which rectangle has the greater area, or if the areas are the same.

3. **Mass and Weight**

   Scientists measure an object's mass in kilograms and its weight in Newtons. If you know the amount of mass of an object, you can calculate its weight, in Newtons, with the following formula:

   Weight = mass × 9.8

   Write a program that asks the user to enter an object's mass and then calculates its weight. If the object weighs more than 1000 Newtons, display a message indicating that it is too heavy. If the object weighs less than 10 Newtons, display a message indicating that it is too light.

4. **Book Club Points**

   Serendipity Booksellers has a book club that awards points to its customers based on the number of books purchased each month. The points are awarded as follows:

   - If a customer purchases 0 books, he or she earns 0 points.
   - If a customer purchases 1 book, he or she earns 5 points.
   - If a customer purchases 2 books, he or she earns 15 points.
   - If a customer purchases 3 books, he or she earns 30 points.
   - If a customer purchases 4 or more books, he or she earns 60 points.

   Write a program that asks the user to enter the number of books that he or she has purchased this month and displays the number of points awarded,

5. **Software Sales**

   A software company sells a package that retails for $99. Quantity discounts are given according to the following table:

Quantity	Discount
10–19	20%
20–49	30%
50–99	40%
100 or more	50%

   Write a program that asks the user to enter the number of packages purchased. The program should then display the amount of the discount (if any) and the total amount of the purchase after the discount.

6. **Shipping Charges**

   The Fast Freight Shipping Company charges the following rates:

Weight of Package	Rate per Pound
2 pounds or less	$1.10
Over 2 pounds but not more than 6 pounds	$2.20
Over 6 pounds but not more than 10 pounds	$3.70
Over 10 pounds	$3.80

Write a program that asks the user to enter the weight of a package and then displays the shipping charges.

7. **Body Mass Index**

Write a program that displays a person's body mass index (BMI). The BMI is often used to determine whether a person is overweight or underweight for their height. A person's BMI is calculated with the following formula:

$$BMI = weight \times 703/height^2$$

In the formula, weight is measured in pounds, and height is measured in inches. After the program displays the user's BMI, it should display a message indicating whether the person has optimal weight, is underweight, or is overweight. A person's weight is considered to be optimal if his or her BMI is between 18.5 and 25. If the BMI is less than 18.5, the person is considered to be underweight. If the BMI value is greater than 25, the person is considered to be overweight.

8. **Time Calculator**

VideoNote

Solving the Time Calculator Problem

Write a program that asks the user to enter a number of seconds and works as follows:

- There are 60 seconds in a minute. If the number of seconds entered by the user is greater than or equal to 60, the program should display the number of minutes in that many seconds.
- There are 3,600 seconds in an hour. If the number of seconds entered by the user is greater than or equal to 3,600, the program should display the number of hours in that many seconds.
- There are 86,400 seconds in a day. If the number of seconds entered by the user is greater than or equal to 86,400, the program should display the number of days in that many seconds.

Repetition Structures

4.1 Introduction to Repetition Structures

CONCEPT: A repetition structure causes a statement or set of statements to execute repeatedly.

Programmers commonly have to write code that performs the same task over and over. For example, suppose you have been asked to write a program that calculates a 10 percent sales commission for several salespeople. Although it would not be a good design, one approach would be to write the code to calculate one salesperson's commission, and then repeat that code for each salesperson. For example, look at the following pseudocode:

```
// Variables for sales and commission.
double sales, commission;

// Constant for the commission rate.
const double COMMISSION_RATE = 0.15;

// Get the amount of sales.
cout << "Enter the amount of sales." << endl;
cin >> sales;

// Calculate the commission.
commission = sales * COMMISSION_RATE;

// Display the commission.
cout << "The commission is $"
     << commission << endl;
```

This calculates the first salesperson's commission.

131

```
// Get the amount of sales.
cout << "Enter the amount of sales."
cin >> sales;

// Calculate the commission.
commission = sales * COMMISSION_RATE;

// Display the commission.
cout << "The commission is $"
     << commission << endl;
```

This calculates the second salesperson's commission.

And this code goes on and on...

As you can see, this code is one long sequence structure containing a lot of duplicated code. The several disadvantages to this approach include the following:

- The duplicated code makes the program large.
- Writing a long sequence of statements can be time consuming.
- If part of the duplicated code has to be corrected or changed, then the correction or change has to be done many times.

Instead of writing the same sequence of statements over and over, a better way to repeatedly perform an operation is to write the code for the operation once, and then place that code in a structure that makes the computer repeat it as many times as necessary. This can be done with a *repetition structure*, which is more commonly known as a *loop*.

Condition-Controlled and Count-Controlled Loops

In this chapter we will look at two broad categories of loops: condition-controlled and count-controlled. A *condition-controlled loop* uses a true/false condition to control the number of times that it repeats. A *count-controlled loop* repeats a specific number of times. We will also discuss the C++ statements that allow you to construct these types of loops.

 Checkpoint

4.1. What is a repetition structure?

4.2. What is a condition-controlled loop?

4.3. What is a count-controlled loop?

 4.2 **Condition-Controlled Loops: The while and do-while Loops**

CONCEPT: Both the while and do-while loops cause a statement or set of statements to repeat as long as a condition is true.

The while Loop

The while loop gets its name from the way it works: *While a Boolean expression is true, do some task.* The loop has two parts: (1) a Boolean expression that is tested for a true or false value, and (2) a statement or set of statements that is repeated as long as the Boolean expression is true. Figure 4-1 shows the logic of a while loop.

Figure 4-1 The logic of a while loop

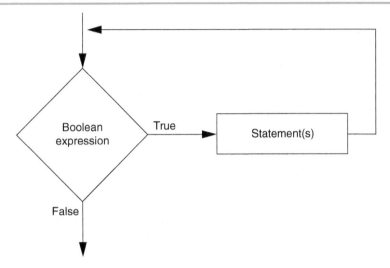

The diamond symbol represents the Boolean expression that is tested. Notice what happens if the Boolean expression is true: One or more statements are executed, and the program's execution flows back to the point just above the diamond symbol. The Boolean expression is tested again, and if it is true, the process repeats. If the Boolean expression is false, the program exits the loop. Each time the loop executes its statement or statements, we say the loop is *iterating*, or performing an *iteration*.

Here is the general format of the while loop:

```
while (BooleanExpression)
{
    statement;
    statement;
    etc;
}
```

We will refer to the first line as the while *clause*. The while clause begins with the word while, followed by a Boolean expression that is enclosed in parentheses. Beginning on the next line is a block of statements that are enclosed in curly braces. This block of statements is known as the *body* of the loop.

When the while loop executes, the Boolean expression is tested. If the Boolean expression is true, the statements that appear in the body of the loop are executed, and then the loop starts over. If the Boolean expression is false, the loop ends, and the program resumes execution at the statement immediately following the loop.

We say that the statements in the body of the loop are conditionally executed because they are executed only under the condition that the Boolean expression is true. If you are writing a `while` loop that has only one statement in its body, you do not have to enclose the statement inside curly braces. Such a loop can be written in the following general format:

```
while (BooleanExpression)
    statement;
```

When a `while` loop written in this format executes, the Boolean expression is tested. If it is true, the one statement that appears on the next line will be executed, and then the loop starts over. If the Boolean expression is false, however, the loop ends.

Although the curly braces are not required when the loop's body contains only one statement, it is still a good idea to use them, as shown in the following general format:

```
while (BooleanExpression)
{
    statement;
}
```

When we discussed the various `if` statements, we mentioned that this is a good style of programming because it cuts down on errors. If you have more than one statement in the body of a loop, those statements *must* be enclosed in curly braces. If you get into the habit of always enclosing the conditionally executed statements in a set of curly braces, it's less likely that you will forget them.

You should also notice that the statements in the body of the loop are indented. As with `if` statements, this indentation makes the code easier to read and debug. By indenting the statements in the body of the loop, you visually set them apart from the surrounding code. Most programmers use this style of indentation when writing loops.

Program 4-1 shows how we might use a `while` loop to write the commission calculating program that was described at the beginning of this chapter.

Program 4-1   **(Commissions.cpp)**

```
1 // This program calculates sales commissions.
2 #include <iostream>
3 #include <string>
4 using namespace std;
5
6 int main()
7 {
8     // Variables
9     double sales, commission;
10    string keepGoing = "y";
11
12    // Constant for the commission rate
13    const double COMMISSION_RATE = 0.10;
14
15    // Determine the commissions.
```

```
16      while (keepGoing == "y")
17      {
18         // Get the amount of sales.
19         cout << "Enter the amount of sales: ";
20         cin >> sales;
21
22         // Calculate the commission.
23         commission = sales * COMMISSION_RATE;
24
25         // Display the commission
26         cout << "The commission is $"
27              << commission << endl;
28
29         cout << "Do you want to calculate another" << endl;
30         cout << "commission? (Enter y for yes): ";
31         cin >> keepGoing;
32      }
33      return 0;
34 }
```

Program Output with Input Shown in Bold

```
Enter the amount of sales: 10000 [Enter]
The commission is $1000
Do you want to calculate another
commission? (Enter y for yes): y [Enter]
Enter the amount of sales: 5000 [Enter]
The commission is $500
Do you want to calculate another
commission? (Enter y for yes): y [Enter]
Enter the amount of sales: 12000 [Enter]
The commission is $1200
Do you want to calculate another
commission? (Enter y for yes): n [Enter]
```

In line 9 we declare the sales variable, which will hold the amount of sales, and the commission variable, which will hold the amount of commission. Then, in line 10 we declare a string variable named keepGoing. Notice that the variable is initialized with the value "y". This initialization value is important, and in a moment you will see why. In line 13 we declare a constant, COMMISSION_RATE, which is initialized with the value 0.10. This is the commission rate that we will use in our calculation.

Line 16 is the beginning of a while loop, which starts like this:

```
while (keepGoing == "y")
```

Notice the expression that is being tested: keepGoing == "y". The loop tests this expression, and if it is true, the statements in the body of the loop (lines 18 through 31) are executed. Then, the loop starts over at line 16. It tests the expression keepGoing == "y" and if it is true, the statements in the body of the loop are executed again. This cycle repeats until the expression keepGoing == "y" is tested in line 16 and found to be false. When that happens, the program exits the loop. This is illustrated in Figure 4-2.

Figure 4-2 The while loop

This expression is tested.

```
while (keepGoing == "y")
{
    // Get the amount of sales.
    cout << "Enter the amount of sales: ";
    cin >> sales;

    // Calculate the commission.
    commission = sales * COMMISSION_RATE;

    // Display the commission
    cout << "The commission is $"
         << commission << endl;

    cout << "Do you want to calculate another" << endl;
    cout << "commission? (Enter y for yes): ";
    cin >> keepGoing;
}
```

If the expression is true, these statements are executed, and then the loop starts over.

If the expression is false, these statements are skipped and the program exits the loop.

For this loop to stop executing, something has to happen inside the loop to make the expression keepGoing == "y" false. The statements in lines 29 through 31 take care of this. Lines 29 and 30 display a message asking, "Do you want to calculate another commission (Enter y for yes)." Then, the cin statement in line 31 reads the user's input and assigns it to the keepGoing variable. If the user enters y (and it must be a lower-case y), then the expression keepGoing == "y" will be true when the loop starts over. This will cause the statements in the body of the loop to execute again. But, if the user enters anything other than lowercase y, the expression will be false when the loop starts over, and the program will exit the loop.

Now that you have examined the code, look at the program output in the sample run. First, the program prompted the user to enter the amount of sales. The user entered 10000, and then the program displayed the commission for that amount, which is $1000. Then, the user is prompted, "Do you want to calculate another commission? (Enter y for yes)." The user entered y, and the loop starts these steps over. In the sample run, the user goes through this process three times. Each execution of the body of a loop is known as an iteration. In the sample run, the loop iterated three times.

The while Loop Is a Pretest Loop

The while loop is known as a *pretest* loop, which means it tests its condition *before* performing an iteration. Because the test is done at the beginning of the loop, you usually have to perform some steps prior to the loop to make sure that the loop executes at least once. For example, the loop in Program 4-1 starts like this:

```
while (keepGoing == "y")
```

The loop will perform an iteration only if the expression keepGoing == "y" is true. To make sure the expression is true the first time that the loop executes, we declared and initialized the keepGoing variable in line 10 as follows:

```
string keepGoing = "y";
```

If keepGoing had been initialized with any other value (or not initialized at all), the loop would never execute. This is an important characteristic of the while loop: It will never execute if its condition is false to start with. In some programs, this is exactly what you want. The following *In the Spotlight* section gives an example.

In the Spotlight:

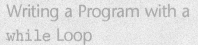

Writing a Program with a while Loop

A project currently underway at Chemical Labs, Inc. requires that a substance be continually heated in a vat. A technician must check the substance's temperature every 15 minutes. If the substance's temperature does not exceed 102.5, then the technician does nothing. However, if the temperature is greater than 102.5, the technician must turn the vat's thermostat down, wait five minutes, and check the temperature again. The technician repeats these steps until the temperature does not exceed 102.5. The director of engineering has asked you to write a program that guides the technician through this process.

Here is the algorithm that you designed:

1. Get the substance's temperature.
2. Repeat these steps as long as the temperature is greater than 102.5:
   a. Tell the technician to turn the thermostat down, wait five minutes and check the temperature again.
   b. Get the substance's temperature.
3. After the loop finishes, tell the technician that the temperature is acceptable and to check it again in 15 minutes.

After reviewing this algorithm, you realize that steps 2a and 2b should not be performed if the test condition (temperature is greater than 102.5) is false to begin with. The while loop will work well in this situation because it will not execute even once if its condition is false. Program 4-2 shows the code for the program.

Program 4-2   **(PretestWhileLoop.cpp)**

```
1 // This program demonstrates the pretest while loop.
2 #include <iostream>
3 using namespace std;
4
5 int main()
```

```
 6 {
 7     // Variable to hold the temperature
 8     double temperature;
 9
10     // Constant for the maximum temperature
11     const double MAX_TEMP = 102.5;
12
13     // Get the substance's temperature.
14     cout << "Enter the substance's temperature: ";
15     cin >> temperature;
16
17     // If necessary, adjust the thermostat.
18     while (temperature > MAX_TEMP)
19     {
20        cout << "The temperature is too high." << endl;
21        cout << "Turn the thermostat down and wait" << endl;
22        cout << "five minutes. Take the temperature" << endl;
23        cout << "again and enter it here: ";
24        cin >> temperature;
25     }
26
27     // Remind the user to check the temperature
28     // again in 15 minutes.
29     cout << "The temperature is acceptable." << endl;
30     cout << "Check it again in 15 minutes." << endl;
31     return 0;
32 }
```

Program Output with Input Shown in Bold

```
Enter the substance's temperature: 104.7 [Enter]
The temperature is too high.
Turn the thermostat down and wait
five minutes. Take the temperature
again and enter it here: 103.2 [Enter]
The temperature is too high.
Turn the thermostat down and wait
five minutes. Take the temperature
again and enter it here: 102.1 [Enter]
The temperature is acceptable.
Check it again in 15 minutes.
```

Program Output with Input Shown in Bold

```
Enter the substance's temperature: 102.1 [Enter]
The temperature is acceptable.
Check it again in 15 minutes.
```

Infinite Loops

In all but rare cases, loops must contain a way to terminate within themselves. This means that something inside the loop must eventually make the test condition false. The loop in Program 4-1 stops when the expression keepGoing == "y" is false. If a loop does not have a way of stopping, it is called an *infinite loop*. An infinite loop continues to repeat until the program is interrupted. Infinite loops usually occur when the programmer forgets to write code inside the loop that makes the test condition false. In most circumstances, you should avoid writing infinite loops.

Program 4-3 demonstrates an infinite loop. This is a modified version of the commission calculating program. In this version, we have removed the code that modifies the keepGoing variable in the body of the loop. Each time the expression keepGoing == "y" is tested in line 9, keepGoing will contain the string "y". As a consequence, the loop has no way of stopping.

Program 4-3   (InfiniteLoop.cpp)

```cpp
 1 // This program has an infinite loop!
 2 #include <iostream>
 3 #include <string>
 4 using namespace std;
 5
 6 int main()
 7 {
 8    // Variables
 9    double sales, commission;
10    string keepGoing = "y";
11
12    // Constant for the commission rate
13    const double COMMISSION_RATE = 0.10;
14
15    // Warning! Infinite loop!
16    while (keepGoing == "y")
17    {
18       // Get the amount of sales.
19       cout << "Enter the amount of sales: ";
20       cin >> sales;
21
22       // Calculate the commission.
23       commission = sales * COMMISSION_RATE;
24
25       // Display the commission
26       cout << "The commission is $"
27            << commission << endl;
28    }
29    return 0;
30 }
```

The do-while Loop: A Posttest Loop

You have learned that the while loop is a pretest loop, which means it tests its Boolean expression before performing an iteration. The do-while loop is a *posttest* loop. This means it performs an iteration before testing its Boolean expression. As a result, the do-while loop always performs at least one iteration, even if its Boolean expression is false to begin with. The logic of a do-while loop is shown in the flowchart in Figure 4-3.

Figure 4-3 The logic of a do-while loop

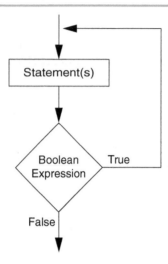

In the flowchart, one or more statements are executed, and then a Boolean expression is tested. If the Boolean expression is true, the program's execution flows back to the point just above the first statement in the body of the loop, and this process repeats. If the Boolean expression is false, the program exits the loop.

In code, the do-while loop looks something like an inverted while loop. Here is the general format of the do-while loop:

```
do
{
    statement;
    statement;
    etc;
} while (BooleanExpression);
```

As with the while loop, the braces are optional if only one statement is in the body of the loop. This is the general format of the do-while loop with only one conditionally executed statement:

```
do
    statement;
while (BooleanExpression);
```

Notice that a semicolon appears at the very end of the do-while statement. This semicolon is required, and leaving it out is a common error.

The do-while loop is a posttest loop. This means it does not test its Boolean expression until it has completed an iteration. As a result, the do-while loop always performs at least one iteration, even if the expression is false to begin with. This differs from the behavior of a while loop. For example, in the following while loop, the cout statement will not execute at all:

```cpp
int number = 1;
while (number < 0)
{
    cout << number << endl;
}
```

But, the cout statement in the following do-while loop will execute one time because the do-while loop does not test the expression number < 0 until the end of the iteration.

```cpp
int number = 1;
do
{
    cout << number << endl;
} while (number < 0);
```

Checkpoint

4.4. What is a repetition structure?

4.5. What is a condition-controlled loop? What is a count-controlled loop?

4.6. What is a loop iteration?

4.7. What is the difference between a pretest loop and a posttest loop?

4.8. Does the while loop test its condition before or after it performs an iteration?

4.9. Does the do-while loop test its condition before or after it performs an iteration?

4.10. What is an infinite loop?

4.3 The Increment and Decrement Operators

CONCEPT: To increment a variable means to increase its value, and to decrement a variable means to decrease its value. C++ provides special operators to increment and decrement variables.

To *increment* a variable means to increase its value, and to *decrement* a variable means to decrease its value. Both of the following statements increment the variable num by one:

```cpp
num = num + 1;
num += 1;
```

And num is decremented by one in both of the following statements:

```cpp
num = num - 1;
num -= 1;
```

Incrementing and decrementing is so commonly done in programs that C++ provides a set of simple unary operators designed just for incrementing and decrementing variables. The increment operator is ++, and the decrement operator is --. The following statement uses the ++ operator to add 1 to num:

```
num++;
```

After this statement executes, the value of num will be increased by one. The following statement uses the -- operator to subtract 1 from num:

```
num--;
```

NOTE: The ++ operator is pronounced "plus plus," and the -- operator is pronounced "minus minus." The expression num++ would be pronounced "num plus plus," and the expression num-- would be pronounced "num minus minus."

In these examples, we have written the ++ and -- operators after their operands (or, on the right side of their operands). This is called *postfix mode*. The operators can also be written before (or, on the left side) of their operands, which is called *prefix mode*. Here are examples:

```
++num;
--num;
```

When you write a simple statement to increment or decrement a variable, such as the ones shown here, it doesn't matter if you use prefix mode or postfix mode. The operators do the same thing in either mode. However, if you write statements that mix these operators with other operators or with other operations, there is a difference in the way the two modes work. Such complex code can be difficult to understand and debug. When we use the increment and decrement operators, we will do so only in ways that are straightforward and easy to understand, such as the statements previously shown.

We introduce these operators at this point because they are commonly used in certain types of loops. In the next section, which discusses the for loop, you will see these operators used often.

Checkpoint

4.11. When you increment or decrement a variable, what are you doing?

4.12. After the following code executes, what value will be stored in the number variable?

```
int number = 5;
number++;
```

4.13. After the following code executes, what value will be stored in the number variable?

```
int number = 5;
number--;
```

4.4 **Count-Controlled Loops: The for Loop**

CONCEPT: A count-controlled loop iterates a specific number of times. In C++ the
for loop is commonly used as a count-controlled loop.

As mentioned earlier, a count-controlled loop iterates a specific number of times.
Count-controlled loops are commonly used in programs. For example, suppose a
business is open six days per week, and you are going to write a program that calculates the total sales for a week. You will need a loop that iterates exactly six times.
Each time the loop iterates, it will prompt the user to enter the sales for one day.

The way a count-controlled loop works is simple: The loop keeps a count of the number
of times it iterates, and when the count reaches a specified amount, the loop stops. A count-
controlled loop uses a variable known as a *counter variable*, or simply *counter*, to store the
number of iterations that it has performed. Using the counter variable, the loop performs
the following three actions, which are known as the *initialization*, *test*, and *increment*:

1. **Initialization:** Before the loop begins, the counter variable is initialized to a starting value. In many situations the starting value will be 0, or possibly 1, but it
   can be other values depending on the nature of the problem.
2. **Test:** The loop tests the counter variable by comparing it to a maximum value.
   If the counter variable has not reached the maximum value yet, the loop iterates.
   If the counter has reached the maximum value, the program exits the loop.
3. **Increment:** To increment a variable means to increase its value. During each
   iteration, the loop increments the counter variable by adding one to it.

Figure 4-4 shows the general logic of a count-controlled loop. The initialization, test,
and increment operations are indicated with the ①, ②, and ③ callouts.

In the flowchart, assume that counter is an int variable. The first step is to set counter
to the value 1. Then, we determine whether counter is less than or equal to a maximum value. If this is true, we execute the body of the loop. Otherwise, we exit the
loop. Notice that in the body of the loop we execute one or more statements, and then
we add one to counter. Adding one to the counter variable is critical because without
this step, the loop would iterate an infinite number of times.

Using the logic shown in the flowchart, the maxValue that we use in the comparison
will be the number of times we want the loop to iterate. For example, if we want the
loop to iterate six times, we will test the expression counter <= 6. Likewise, if we
want the loop to iterate 100 times, we will test the expression counter <= 100.

Count-controlled loops are so common that C++ provides a type of loop just for
them. It is known as the *for loop*. The for loop is specifically designed to initialize,
test, and increment a counter variable. Here is the general format of the for loop:

```
for (InitializationExpression; TestExpression; IncrementExpression)
{
    statement;
    statement;
    etc.
}
```

Figure 4-4 Logic of a count-controlled loop

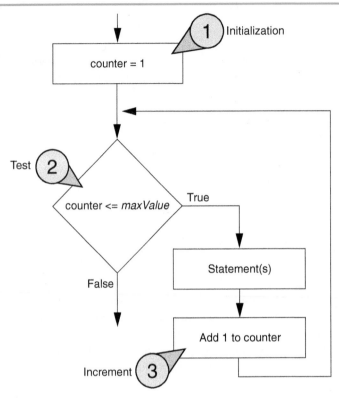

The statements that appear inside the curly braces are the body of the loop. These are the statements that are executed each time the loop iterates. As with other control structures, the curly braces are optional if the body of the loop contains only one statement, as shown in the following general format:

```
for (InitializationExpression; TestExpression; IncrementExpression)
    statement;
```

As with other control structures, we always recommend using the curly braces, even if there is only one statement in the body of the loop. Let's look at each part of the loop.

The first line of the for loop is the *loop header*. After the key word for, three expressions are inside the parentheses, separated by semicolons. (Notice there is not a semicolon after the third expression.)

The first expression is the *initialization expression*. It is normally used to initialize a counter variable to its starting value. This is the first action performed by the loop, and it is only done once. The second expression is the *test expression*. This is a Boolean expression that controls the execution of the loop. As long as this expression is true, the body of the for loop will repeat. The for loop is a pretest loop, so it evaluates the test expression before each iteration. The third expression is the *increment expression*. It executes at the end of each iteration. Typically, this is a statement that increments the loop's counter variable.

Here is an example of a simple for loop that prints "Hello" five times:

```
for (counter = 1; counter <= 5; counter++)
{
    cout << "Hello" << endl;
}
```

In this loop, the initialization expression is counter = 1, the test expression is counter <= 5, and the increment expression is counter++. The body of the loop has one statement, which is a cout statement. This is a summary of what happens when this loop executes:

1. The initialization expression counter = 1 is executed. This assigns 1 to the counter variable.
2. The expression counter <= 5 is tested. If the expression is true, continue with step 3. Otherwise, the loop is finished.
3. The statement cout << "Hello" << endl; is executed.
4. The increment expression counter++ is executed. This adds 1 to the counter variable.
5. Go back to step 2.

Figure 4-5 illustrates this sequence of events. Notice that steps 2 through 4 are repeated as long as the test expression is true.

Figure 4-5 Sequence of events in the for loop

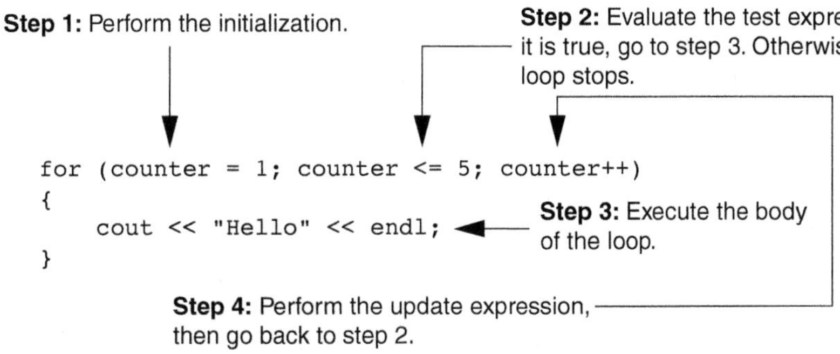

Okay, we've explained enough! Let's look at an actual program. Program 4-4 uses a for loop to display the string "Hello world" five times.

Program 4-4   (ForLoop.cpp)

```
1 // This program demonstrates the for loop.
2 #include <iostream>
3 using namespace std;
4
5 int main()
6 {
7     int counter;
8     const int MAX_VALUE = 5;
```

```
 9
10    for (counter = 0; counter < MAX_VALUE; counter++)
11    {
12       cout << "Hello world" << endl;
13    }
14    return 0;
15 }
```

Program Output

```
Hello world
Hello world
Hello world
Hello world
Hello world
```

Line 7 declares an int variable that will be used as the counter variable. You do not have to name the variable counter (you are free to name it anything you wish), but in many cases that is an appropriate name. Line 8 declares a constant named MAX_VALUE that will be used as the counter's maximum value. The for loop begins in line 10. This is what's happening in the loop header:

- The initialization expression is count = 0. This assigns 0 to the count variable.
- The test expression is count < MAX_VALUE.
- The increment expression is count++.

As a result of these expressions, the loop will iterate five times. As the loop iterates, the count variable will be assigned the values 0 through 4. Each time it iterates, it displays "Hello world".

Notice that the loop does not contain a statement to increment the counter variable. This happens automatically in a for loop, at the end of each iteration. For that reason, you should be careful not to place a statement that modifies the counter variable inside the body of a for loop. Doing so will usually disrupt the way the for loop works.

> **NOTE:** There are different ways to set up the counter variable in a for loop to achieve the same results. For example, the loop in Program 4-4 could have started like this:
>
> ```
>     for (counter = 1; counter <= MAX_VALUE; counter++)
> ```
>
> In this example counter is initialized with the value 1, and the loop iterates as long as counter is less than or equal to MAX_VALUE. This loop will also iterate five times, but the counter variable will be assigned the values 1 through 5.

Declaring the Counter Variable in the Initialization Expression

Not only may the counter variable be initialized in the initialization expression, but it may also be declared there as well. The following code shows an example.

```cpp
const int MAX_VALUE = 5;
for (int counter = 0; count < MAX_VALUE; counter++)
{
    cout << "Hello" << endl;
}
```

In this loop, the counter variable is both declared and initialized in the initialization expression. If the variable is used only in the loop, it makes sense to define it in the loop header. This makes the variable's purpose more clear.

When a variable is declared in the initialization expression of a for loop, the scope of the variable is limited to the loop. This means you cannot access the variable in statements outside the loop. For example, the following code would cause a compiler error because the last statement (the last cout statement) cannot access the count variable.

```cpp
const int MAX_VALUE = 5;
for (int count = 0; count < MAX_VALUE; count++)
{
    cout << "Hello" << endl;
}
cout << "The value of the counter is " << count << endl;
```

Using the Counter Variable in the Body of the Loop

In a count-controlled loop, the primary purpose of the counter variable is to store the number of times that the loop has iterated. In some situations, it is also helpful to use the counter variable in a calculation or other task within the body of the loop. For example, suppose you need to write a program that displays the numbers 1 through 10 and their squares in a table similar to this:

Number	Square
1	1
2	4
3	9
4	16
5	25
6	36
7	49
8	64
9	81
10	100

This can be accomplished by writing a count-controlled loop that iterates 10 times. During the first iteration, the counter variable will be set to 1, during the second iteration it will be set to 2, and so forth. Because the counter variable will take on the values 1 through 10 during the loop's execution, you can use it in the calculation inside the loop. Program 4-5 demonstrates this logic.

Program 4-5   **(Squares.cpp)**

```
1 // This program prints a table showing the squares
2 // of the numbers 1 through 10.
3 #include <iostream>
4 using namespace std;
5
6 int main()
7 {
8    const int MAX_VALUE = 10;
9
10   // Display the table headings.
11   cout << "Number\t\tSquare" << endl;
12
13   for (int number = 1; number <= MAX_VALUE; number++)
14   {
15      cout << number << "\t\t"
16           << (number * number) << endl;
17   }
18   return 0;
19 }
```

Program Output

Number	Square
1	1
2	4
3	9
4	16
5	25
6	36
7	49
8	64
9	81
10	100

First, take a closer look at line 11, which displays the table headings:

```
cout << "Number\t\tSquare" << endl;
```

Notice that two \t escape sequences appear inside the string literal, between the words *Number* and *Square*. The \t escape sequence is like pressing the Tab key: it causes the output cursor to move over to the next tab position. This causes the spaces that you see between the words *Number* and *Square* in the sample output.

The for loop begins in line 13. During the first iteration, number will be assigned 1, during the second iteration number will be assigned 2, and so forth, up to 10. Inside the loop, the statement in lines 15 and 16 displays the value of number, tabs over twice, and then displays the value of number * number. (Tabbing over twice, with the two \t escape sequence causes the numbers to be aligned in two columns in the output.)

Other Forms of the Update Expression

You are not limited to using increment statements in the update expression. Here is a loop that displays all the even numbers from 2 through 100 by adding 2 to its counter variable:

```
for (int counter = 2; counter <= 100; counter += 2)
    cout << counter << endl;
```

And here is a loop that counts backward from 10 down to 0:

```
for (int counter = 10; counter >= 0; counter--)
    cout << counter << endl;
```

In the Spotlight:

Writing a Count-Controlled for Loop

Your friend Amanda just inherited a European sports car from her uncle. Amanda lives in the United States, and she is afraid she will get a speeding ticket because the car's speedometer indicates kilometers per hour. She has asked you to write a program that displays a table of speeds in kilometers per hour with their values converted to miles per hour. The formula for converting kilometers per hour to miles per hour is

$$MPH = KPH * 0.6214$$

In the formula, MPH is the speed in miles per hour, and KPH is the speed in kilometers per hour.

The table that your program displays should show speeds from 60 kilometers per hour through 130 kilometers per hour, in increments of 10, along with their values converted to miles per hour. The table should look something like this:

KPH	MPH
60	37.3
70	43.5
80	49.7
etc....	
130	80.8

After thinking about this table of values, you decide that you will write a for loop that uses a counter variable to hold the kilometer-per-hour speeds. The counter's starting value will be 60, its ending value will be 130, and you will add 10 to the counter variable after each iteration. Inside the loop you will use the counter variable to calculate a speed in miles-per-hour. Program 4-6 shows the code.

Program 4-6   (`SpeedConverter.cpp`)

```cpp
 1  // This program converts the speeds 60 kph through
 2  // 130 kph (in 10 kph increments) to mph.
 3  #include <iostream>
 4  using namespace std;
 5
 6  int main()
 7  {
 8     // Constants for the speeds
 9     const int START_KPH = 60,    // Starting speed
10               END_KPH = 130,     // Ending speed
11               INCREMENT = 10;    // Speed increment
12
13     // Constant for the conversion factor
14     const double CONVERSION_FACTOR = 0.6214;
15
16     // Variables
17     int kph;        // To hold speeds in kph
18     double mph;     // To hold speeds in mph
19
20     // Display the table headings.
21     cout << "KPH\tMPH" << endl;
22     cout << "----------------" << endl;
23
24     // Display the speeds.
25     for (kph = START_KPH; kph <= END_KPH; kph += INCREMENT)
26     {
27        // Calculate mph
28        mph = kph * CONVERSION_FACTOR;
29
30        // Display the speeds in kph and mph.
31        cout << kph << "\t" << mph << endl;
32     }
33     return 0;
34  }
```

Program Output

```
KPH       MPH
---------------
60        37.284
70        43.498
80        49.712
90        55.926
100       62.14
110       68.354
120       74.568
130       80.782
```

Letting the User Control the Number of Iterations

In many cases, the programmer knows the exact number of iterations that a loop must perform. For example, recall Program 4-5, which displays a table showing the numbers 1 through 10 and their squares. When the code was written, the programmer knew that the loop had to iterate 10 times. A constant named MAX_VALUE was initialized with the value 10, and the loop was written as follows:

```
for (int number = 1; number <= MAX_VALUE; number++)
```

As a result, the loop iterates exactly 10 times. Sometimes, however, the programmer needs to let the user decide the number of times that a loop should iterate. For example, what if you want Program 4-4 to be a bit more versatile by allowing the user to specify the maximum value displayed by the loop? The code in Program 4-7 shows how you can accomplish this.

Program 4-7   **(UserSquares.cpp)**

```
 1 // This program prints a table of numbers
 2 // and their squares.
 3 #include <iostream>
 4 using namespace std;
 5
 6 int main()
 7 {
 8     int upperLimit;
 9
10     // Get the upper limit.
11     cout << "This program displays numbers, starting at 1," << endl;
12     cout << "and their squares. How high should I go? ";
13     cin >> upperLimit;
14
15     // Display the table headings.
16     cout << "Number\t\tSquare" << endl;
17
18     // Display the values.
19     for (int number = 1; number <= upperLimit; number++)
20     {
21        cout << number << "\t\t"
22             << (number * number) << endl;
23     }
24     return 0;
25 }
```

Program Output with Input Shown in Bold
This program displays numbers, starting at 1,
and their squares. How high should I go? **5 [Enter]**

Number	Square
1	1
2	4
3	9
4	16
5	25

Lines 11 and 12 ask the user how high the numbers in the table should go, and the statement in line 13 assigns the user's input to the upperLimit variable. Then, the for loop uses the upperLimit variable as the counter's ending value:

```
for (int number = 1; number <= upperLimit; number++)
```

As a result, the counter variable starts with 1 and ends with the value in upperLimit.

Checkpoint

4.14. What is a counter variable?

4.15. What three actions do count-controlled loops typically perform using the counter variable?

4.16. What would the following code display?

```
for (int counter = 1; count <= 5; count++)
{
   cout << counter << endl;
}
```

4.17. What would the following code display?

```
for (int counter = 0; count <= 500; count += 100)
{
   cout << counter << endl;
}
```

4.5   Calculating a Running Total

CONCEPT: A running total is a sum of numbers that accumulates with each iteration of a loop. The variable used to keep the running total is called an accumulator.

Many programming tasks require you to calculate the total of a series of numbers. For example, suppose you are writing a program that calculates a business's total sales for a week. The program would read the sales for each day as input and calculate the total of those numbers.

Programs that calculate the total of a series of numbers typically use two elements:

- A loop that reads each number in the series.
- A variable that accumulates the total of the numbers as they are read.

The variable that is used to accumulate the total of the numbers is called an *accumulator*. It is often said that the loop keeps a *running total* because it accumulates the total as it reads each number in the series. Figure 4-6 shows the general logic of a loop that calculates a running total.

Figure 4-6 Logic for calculating a running total

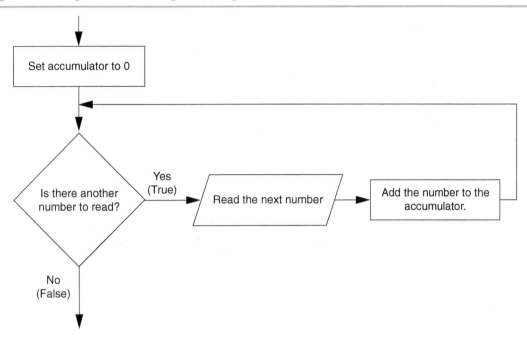

When the loop finishes, the accumulator will contain the total of the numbers that were read by the loop. Notice that the first step in the flowchart is to set the accumulator variable to 0. This is a critical step. Each time the loop reads a number, it adds it to the accumulator. If the accumulator starts with any value other than 0, it will not contain the correct total when the loop finishes.

Let's look at a program that calculates a running total. The code shown in Program 4-8 allows the user to enter five numbers, and it displays the total of the numbers entered.

Program 4-8　　(SumOfNumbers.cpp)

```
1 // This program calculates the sum of a series of numbers.
2 #include <iostream>
3 using namespace std;
4
5 int main()
6 {
7    // Variables
8    int number,      // To hold each number
9        total = 0;   // Accumulator, initialized with 0
10
11   // Constant for the number of numbers
12   const int MAX_NUMS = 5;
13
14   // Explain the program's purpose.
15   cout << "This program calculates the total" << endl;
16   cout << "of " << MAX_NUMS << " numbers." << endl;
```

```
17
18    // Get the numbers and accumulate them.
19    for (int counter = 0; counter < MAX_NUMS; counter++)
20    {
21        cout << "Enter a number: ";
22        cin >> number;
23        total += number;
24    }
25
26    // Display the total.
27    cout << "The total is: " << total << endl;
28    return 0;
29 }
```

Program Output with Input Shown in Bold

```
This program calculates the total of 5 numbers.
Enter a number: 2 [Enter]
Enter a number: 4 [Enter]
Enter a number: 6 [Enter]
Enter a number: 8 [Enter]
Enter a number: 10 [Enter]
The total is: 30
```

First, let's look at the variable declarations. The number variable, declared in line 8, will be used to hold a number entered by the user. The total variable, declared in line 9, is the accumulator. Notice that it is initialized with the value 0. The for loop, in lines 19 through 24, does the work of getting the numbers from the user and calculating their total. Line 21 prompts the user to enter a number, and line 22 gets the user's input and stores it in the number variable. Then, the following statement in line 23 adds number to total:

```
total += number;
```

After this statement executes, the value in the number variable will be added to the value in the total variable. When the loop finishes, the total variable will hold the sum of all the numbers that were added to it. This value is displayed in line 27.

 Checkpoint

4.18. A program that calculates the total of a series of numbers typically has what two elements?

4.19. What is an accumulator?

4.20. Should an accumulator be initialized to any specific value? Why, or why not?

4.21. Look at the following code. If it were a real program, what would it display?

```
int counter, total = 0;
const int MAX = 6;
for (int counter = 1; counter < MAX; counter++)
{
    total += counter;
}
cout << total << endl;
```

4.6 Nested Loops

CONCEPT: A loop that is inside another loop is called a nested loop.

A nested loop is a loop that is inside another loop. A clock is a good example of something that works like a nested loop. The second hand, minute hand, and hour hand all spin around the face of the clock. The hour hand, however, only makes one revolution for every 12 of the minute hand's revolutions. And it takes 60 revolutions of the second hand for the minute hand to make one revolution. This means that for every complete revolution of the hour hand, the second hand has revolved 720 times. Here is code with a loop that partially simulates a digital clock. It displays the seconds from 0 to 59:

```cpp
const int MAX_SECONDS = 60;
for (int seconds = 0; seconds < MAX_SECONDS; seconds++)
{
    cout << seconds << endl;
}
```

To count the minutes as well as the seconds, we can nest the preceding loop inside another loop that cycles through 60 minutes:

```cpp
const int MAX_SECONDS = 60;
const int MAX_MINUTES = 60;
for (int minutes = 0; minutes < MAX_MINUTES; minutes++)
{
    for (int seconds = 0; seconds < MAX_SECONDS; seconds++)
    {
        cout << minutes << ":"
             << seconds << endl;
    }
}
```

To make the simulated clock complete, another loop can be added to count the hours:

```cpp
const int MAX_SECONDS = 60;
const int MAX_MINUTES = 60;
const int MAX_HOURS = 24;
for (int hours = 0; hours < MAX_HOURS; hours++)
{
    for (int minutes = 0; minutes < MAX_MINUTES; minutes++)
    {
        for (int seconds = 0; seconds < MAX_SECONDS; seconds++)
        {
            cout << hours << ":"
                 << minutes << ":"
                 << seconds << endl;
        }
    }
}
```

If this code were part of a complete program, its output would be:

```
0:0:0
0:0:1
0:0:2
```

. (The program will count through each second of 24 hours.)

.

.

```
23:59:59
```

The innermost loop will iterate 60 times for each iteration of the middle loop. The middle loop will iterate 60 times for each iteration of the outermost loop. When the outermost loop has iterated 24 times, the middle loop will have iterated 1,440 times, and the innermost loop will have iterated 86,400 times!

The simulated clock example brings up a few points about nested loops:

- An inner loop goes through all its iterations for every single iteration of an outer loop.
- Inner loops complete their iterations faster than outer loops.
- To get the total number of iterations of a nested loop, multiply the number of iterations of all the loops.

In the Spotlight:
Using Nested Loops to Print Patterns

One interesting way to learn about nested loops is to use them to display patterns on the screen. Let's look at a simple example. Suppose we want to print asterisks on the screen in the following rectangular pattern:

```
******
******
******
******
******
******
******
******
```

If you think of this pattern as having rows and columns, you can see that it has eight rows, and each row has six columns. The following code can be used to display one row of asterisks:

```
const int COLS = 6;
for (int col = 0; col < COLS; col++)
{
    cout << "*";
}
cout << endl;
```

If we run this code in a program, it will produce the following output:

```
******
```

To complete the entire pattern, we need to execute this loop eight times. We can place the loop inside another loop that iterates eight times, as shown here:

```
1        const int COLS = 6;
2        const int ROWS = 8;
3        for (int row = 0; row < ROWS; row++)
4        {
5           for (int col = 0; col < COLS; col++)
6           {
7              cout << "*";
8           }
9           cout << endl;
10       }
```

The outer loop iterates eight times. Each time it iterates, the inner loop iterates six times. (Notice that in line 9, after each row has been printed, the statement cout << endl; appears. We have that statement to advance the screen cursor to the next line at the end of each row. Without that statement, all the asterisks will be printed in one long row on the screen.)

We could easily write a program that prompts the user for the number of rows and columns, as shown in Program 4-9.

Program 4-9   **(RectangularPattern.cpp)**

```
1  // This program displays a rectangular pattern
2  // of asterisks.
3  #include <iostream>
4  using namespace std;
5
6  int main()
7  {
8     int rows, cols;
9
10    // Get the number of rows and columns.
11    cout << "How many rows? ";
12    cin >> rows;
13    cout << "How many columns? ";
14    cin >> cols;
15
16    // Display the pattern.
17    for (int r = 0; r < rows; r++)
18    {
19       for (int c = 0; c < cols; c++)
20       {
21          cout << "*";
22       }
23       cout << endl;
```

```
24    }
25    return 0;
26 }
```

Program Output with Input Shown in Bold

```
How many rows? 5 [Enter]
How many columns? 10 [Enter]
**********
**********
**********
**********
**********
```

Let's look at another example. Suppose you want to print asterisks in a pattern that looks like the following triangle:

```
*
**
***
****
*****
******
*******
********
```

Once again, think of the pattern as being arranged in rows and columns. The pattern has a total of eight rows. In the first row is one column. In the second row are two columns. In the third row are three columns. This continues to the eighth row, which has eight columns. Program 4-10 shows the program that produces this pattern.

Program 4-10   (TrianglePattern.cpp)

```cpp
1 // This program displays a triangle pattern.
2 #include <iostream>
3 using namespace std;
4
5 int main()
6 {
7     const int BASE_SIZE = 8;
8
9     for (int r = 0; r < BASE_SIZE; r++)
10    {
11        for (int c = 0; c < (r+1); c++)
12        {
13            cout << "*";
14        }
```

```
15        cout << endl;
16    }
17    return 0;
18 }
```

Program Output

```
*
**
***
****
*****
******
*******
********
```

The outer loop (which begins in line 9) will iterate 8 times. As the loop iterates, the variable r will be assigned the values 0 through 7.

For each iteration of the outer loop, the inner loop will iterate r+1 times. So,

- During the outer loop's 1st iteration, the variable r is assigned 0. The inner loop iterates one time, printing one asterisk.
- During the outer loop's 2nd iteration, the variable r is assigned 1. The inner loop iterates two times, printing two asterisks.
- During the outer loop's 3rd iteration, the variable r is assigned 2. The inner loop iterates three times, printing three asterisks.
- And so forth.

Let's look at another example. Suppose you want to display the following stair-step pattern:

The pattern has six rows. In general, we can describe each row as having some number of spaces followed by a # character. Here's a row-by-row description:

First row:	0 spaces followed by a # character.
Second row:	1 space followed by a # character.
Third row:	2 spaces followed by a # character.
Fourth row:	3 spaces followed by a # character.
Fifth row:	4 spaces followed by a # character.
Sixth row:	5 spaces followed by a # character.

To display this pattern, we can write code containing a pair of nested loops that work in the following manner:

- The outer loop will iterate six times. Each iteration will perform the following:
  - The inner loop will display the correct number of spaces, side-by-side.
  - Then, a # character will be displayed.

Program 4-11 shows the C++ code.

Program 4-11   (StairStepPattern.cpp)

```cpp
 1 // This program displays a stair-step pattern.
 2 #include <iostream>
 3 using namespace std;
 4
 5 int main()
 6 {
 7    const int NUM_STEPS = 6;
 8
 9    for (int r = 0; r < NUM_STEPS; r++)
10    {
11       for (int c = 0; c < r; c++)
12       {
13          cout << " ";
14       }
15       cout << "#" << endl;
16    }
17    return 0;
18 }
```

Program Output

```
#
 #
  #
   #
    #
     #
```

The outer loop (which begins in line 9) will iterate six times. As the loop iterates, the variable r will be assigned the values 0 through 5.

For each iteration of the outer loop, the inner loop will iterate r times. So,

- During the outer loop's 1st iteration, the variable r is assigned 0. The inner loop will not execute at this time.
- During the outer loop's 2nd iteration, the variable r is assigned 1. The inner loop iterates one time, printing one space.
- During the outer loop's 3rd iteration, the variable r is assigned 2. The inner loop iterates two times, printing two spaces.
- And so forth.

Review Questions

Multiple Choice

1. A _____-controlled loop uses a true/false condition to control the number of times that it repeats.
   a. Boolean
   b. condition
   c. decision
   d. count

2. A _____-controlled loop repeats a specific number of times.
   a. Boolean
   b. condition
   c. decision
   d. count

3. Each repetition of a loop is known as a(n) _____.
   a. cycle
   b. revolution
   c. orbit
   d. iteration

4. The while loop is a _____ type of loop.
   a. pretest
   b. no-test
   c. prequalified
   d. posttest

5. The do-while loop is a _____ type of loop.
   a. pretest
   b. no-test
   c. prequalified
   d. posttest

6. A(n) _____ loop has no way of ending and repeats until the program is interrupted.
   a. indeterminate
   b. interminable
   c. infinite
   d. timeless

7. This type of loop always executes at least once:
   a. pretest.
   b. posttest.
   c. condition-controlled.
   d. count-controlled.

8. This is a variable that keeps a running total:
   a. sentinel.
   b. sum.
   c. total.
   d. accumulator.

9. The expression x++ uses the increment operator in _____ mode.
   a. automatic
   b. prefix
   c. postfix
   d. infix

True or False

1. A condition-controlled loop always repeats a specific number of times.

2. The while loop is a pretest loop.

3. An infinite loop will automatically stop after 256 seconds.

3. The do-while loop is a pretest loop.

4. You should not write code that modifies the contents of the counter variable in the body of a for loop.

5. You cannot display the contents of the counter variable in the body of a loop.

6. It is not possible to increment a counter variable by any value other than 1.

7. The ++ operator adds 2 to its operand.

8. It is not necessary to initialize accumulator variables.

9. In a nested loop, the inner loop goes through all its iterations for every single iteration of the outer loop.

10. To calculate the total number of iterations of a nested loop, add the number of iterations of all the loops.

Short Answer

1. What is a condition-controlled loop?

2. What is a count-controlled loop?

3. What is an infinite loop? Write the code for an infinite loop.

4. Describe the difference between pretest loops and posttest loops.

5. What three actions do count-controlled loops typically perform using the counter variable?

6. Why is it critical that accumulator variables are properly initialized?

7. What would the following code sample display?
   ```
   int number = 9;
   number++;
   cout << number << endl;
   number--;
   cout << number << endl;
   ```

Algorithm Workbench

1. Write a `while` loop that lets the user enter a number. The number should be multiplied by 10 and the result assigned to a variable named `product`. The loop should iterate as long as `product` is less than 100.

2. Write a `while` loop that asks the user to enter two numbers. The numbers should be added and the sum displayed. The loop should ask the user if he or she wishes to perform the operation again. If so, the loop should repeat; otherwise, it should terminate.

3. Write a `for` loop that displays the following set of numbers:

   0, 10, 20, 30, 40, 50 . . . 1000

4. Design a loop that asks the user to enter a number. The loop should iterate 10 times and keep a running total of the numbers entered.

5. Write a `for` loop that calculates the total of the following series of numbers:

   $$\frac{1}{30} + \frac{2}{29} + \frac{3}{28} + \ldots \frac{30}{1}$$

6. Write a set of nested loops that displays 10 rows of '#' characters. There should be 15 '#' characters in each row.

7. Convert the `while` loop in the following code to a `do-while` loop:

```
int x = 1;
while (x > 0)
{
    cout << "Enter a number: ";
    cin >> x;
}
```

Programming Exercises

1. **Bug Collector**
   A bug collector collects bugs every day for seven days. Write a program that keeps a running total of the number of bugs collected during the seven days. The loop should ask for the number of bugs collected for each day, and when the loop is finished, the program should display the total number of bugs collected.

2. **Calories Burned**
   Running on a particular treadmill, you burn 3.9 calories per minute. Write a program that uses a loop to display the number of calories burned after 10, 15, 20, 25, and 30 minutes.

   VideoNote

   Solving the Calories
   Burned Problem

3. **Ocean Levels**
   Assuming the ocean's level is currently rising at about 1.5 millimeters per year, write a program that displays a table showing the number of millimeters that the ocean will rise each year for the next 25 years.

4. **Budget Analysis**
   Write a program that asks the user to enter the amount that he or she has budgeted for a month. A loop should then prompt the user to enter each

of his or her expenses for the month and keep a running total. When the loop finishes, the program should display the amount that the user is over or under budget.

5. **Distance Traveled**
The distance a vehicle travels can be calculated as follows:

   Distance = Speed × Time

   For example, if a train travels 40 miles per hour for three hours, the distance traveled is 120 miles. Write a program that asks the user for the speed of a vehicle (in miles per hour) and the number of hours it has traveled. It should then use a loop to display the distance the vehicle has traveled for each hour of that time period. Here is an example of the output:

   ```
   What is the speed of the vehicle in mph? 40 [Enter]
   How many hours has it traveled? 3 [Enter]

   Hour      Distance Traveled
   1         40
   2         80
   3         120
   ```

6. **Average Rainfall**
Write a program that uses nested loops to collect data and calculate the average rainfall over a period of years. The program should first ask for the number of years. The outer loop will iterate once for each year. The inner loop will iterate twelve times, once for each month. Each iteration of the inner loop will ask the user for the inches of rainfall for that month. After all iterations, the program should display the number of months, the total inches of rainfall, and the average rainfall per month for the entire period.

7. **Centigrade to Fahrenheit Table**
Write a program that displays a table of the centigrade temperatures 0 through 20 and their Fahrenheit equivalents. The formula for converting a temperature from centigrade to Fahrenheit is

$$F = \frac{9}{5} C + 32$$

where F is the Fahrenheit temperature and C is the centigrade temperature. Your program must use a loop to display the table.

8. **Pennies for Pay**
Write a program that calculates the amount of money a person would earn over a period of time if his or her salary is one penny the first day, two pennies the second day, and continues to double each day. The program should ask the user for the number of days. Display a table showing what the salary was for each day, and then show the total pay at the end of the period. The output should be displayed in a dollar amount, not the number of pennies.

9. **Square Display**
Write a program that asks the user for a positive integer no greater than 15. The program should then display a square on the screen using the character X. The

number entered by the user will be the length of each side of the square. For example, if the user enters 5, the program should display the following:

```
XXXXX
XXXXX
XXXXX
XXXXX
XXXXX
```

If the user enters 8, the program should display the following:

```
XXXXXXXX
XXXXXXXX
XXXXXXXX
XXXXXXXX
XXXXXXXX
XXXXXXXX
XXXXXXXX
XXXXXXXX
```

10. **Pattern Displays**

Write a program that uses a loop to display Pattern A as follows, followed by another loop that displays Pattern B.

Pattern A	Pattern B
+	++++++++++
++	+++++++++
+++	++++++++
++++	+++++++
+++++	++++++
++++++	+++++
+++++++	++++
++++++++	+++
+++++++++	++
++++++++++	+

5 Functions

TOPICS

5.1 Introduction to Functions

CONCEPT: A function is a group of statements that exist within a program for the purpose of performing a specific task.

In Chapter 2 you saw a simple algorithm for calculating an employee's pay (Program 2-10). In the program, the number of hours worked is multiplied by an hourly pay rate. A more realistic payroll algorithm, however, would do much more than this. In a real-world application, the overall task of calculating an employee's pay would consist of several subtasks, such as the following:

- Getting the employee's hourly pay rate
- Getting the number of hours worked
- Calculating the employee's gross pay
- Calculating overtime pay
- Calculating withholdings for taxes and benefits
- Calculating the net pay
- Printing the paycheck

Most programs perform tasks that are large enough to be broken down into several subtasks. For this reason, programmers usually break down their programs into small manageable pieces known as functions. A *function* is a group of statements that exist within a program for the purpose of performing a specific task. Instead of writing a large program as one long sequence of statements, it can be written as several small functions, each one performing a specific part of the task. These small functions can then be executed in the desired order to perform the overall task.

This approach is sometimes called *divide and conquer* because a large task is divided into several smaller tasks that are easily performed. Figure 5-1 illustrates this idea by comparing two programs: one that performs a task with a long sequence of statements in the main function, and another that divides the task into smaller tasks, each of which is performed by a separate function.

Figure 5-1 Using functions to divide and conquer a large task

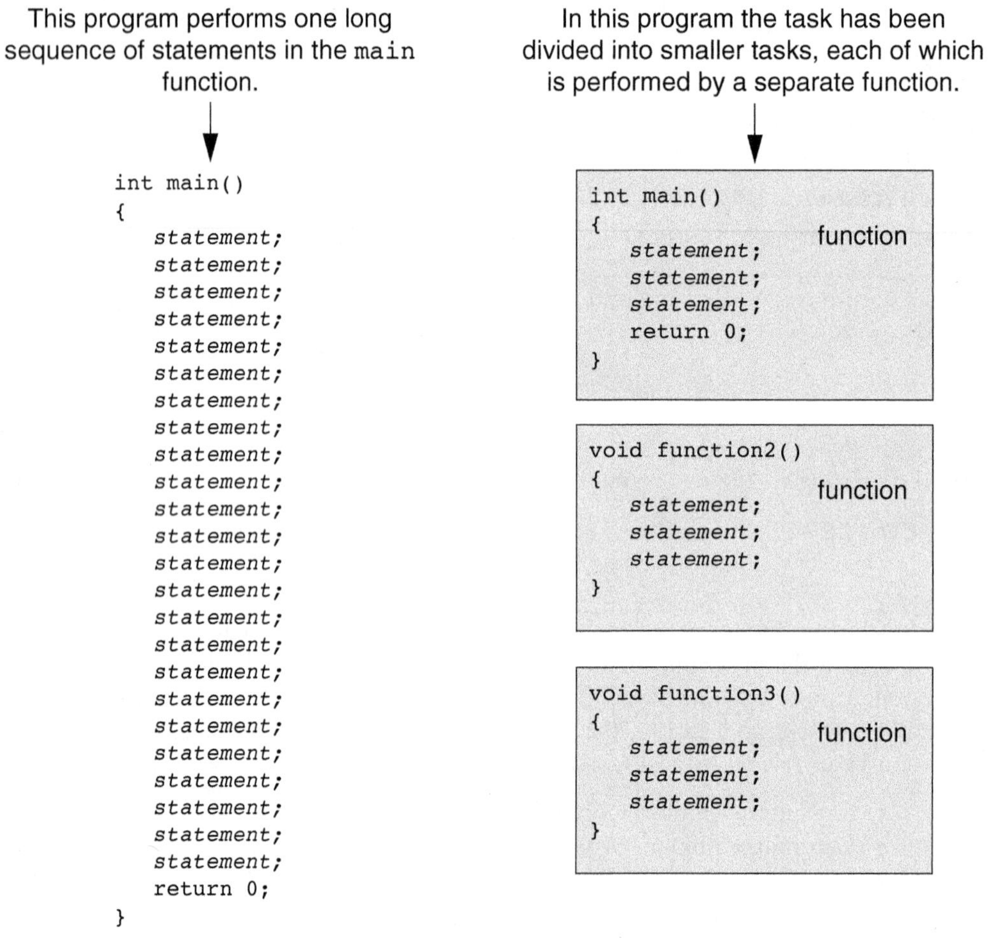

This program performs one long sequence of statements in the main function.

```
int main()
{
    statement;
    statement;
    statement;
    statement;
    statement;
    statement;
    statement;
    statement;
    statement;
    statement;
    statement;
    statement;
    statement;
    statement;
    statement;
    statement;
    statement;
    statement;
    statement;
    statement;
    statement;
    statement;
    return 0;
}
```

In this program the task has been divided into smaller tasks, each of which is performed by a separate function.

```
int main()
{                        function
    statement;
    statement;
    statement;
    return 0;
}
```

```
void function2()
{                        function
    statement;
    statement;
    statement;
}
```

```
void function3()
{                        function
    statement;
    statement;
    statement;
}
```

When using functions in a program, you generally isolate each task within the program in its own function. For example, a realistic pay calculating program might have the following functions:

- A function that gets the employee's hourly pay rate
- A function that gets the number of hours worked
- A function that calculates the employee's gross pay

- A function that calculates the overtime pay
- A function that calculates the withholdings for taxes and benefits
- A function that calculates the net pay
- A function that prints the paycheck

A program that has been written with each task in its own function is called a *modularized program.*

In general terms, a program that is broken into smaller units of code, such as functions, is known as a *modularized program.* Modularization tends to simplify code. If a specific task is performed in several places in a program, a function can be written once to perform that task and then be executed any time it is needed. This benefit of using functions is known as *code reuse* because you are writing the code to perform a task once and then reusing it each time you need to perform the task.

void Functions and Value-Returning Functions

In this chapter you will learn to write two types of functions: void functions and value-returning functions. When you call a *void function*, it simply executes the statements it contains and then terminates. When you call a *value-returning function*, it executes the statements that it contains and then it returns a value to the statement that called it. The pow function that you saw in Chapter 2 is an example of a value-returning function. The first type of function that you will learn to write is the void function.

5.2 void Functions

CONCEPT: A **void** function performs a task and then terminates. It does not return a value to the statement that called it.

To create a function you write its definition. A function definition has two parts: a header and a body. The *function header*, which appears at the beginning of a function definition, lists several important things about the function, including the function's name. The *function body* is a collection of statements that are performed when the function is executed. These statements are enclosed inside a set of curly braces. Here is an example of a function definition:

```
void displayMessage()
{
    cout << "This is the displayMessage function." << endl;
}
```

The Function Header

Using the previously shown function definition, Figure 5-2 points out the different parts of the function header, which is the first line.

Figure 5-2 Parts of the function header

```
Return        Function
type          name        Parentheses

void displayMessage()
{
    cout << "This is the displayMessage function." << endl;
}
```

Let's take a closer look at the parts identified in the figure:

- **Return type**—Recall our previous discussion of void and value-returning functions. When the key word void appears here, it means that the function is a void function and does not return a value. As you will see later in this chapter, a value-returning function lists a data type here.
- **Function name**—You should give each function a descriptive name. In general, the same rules that apply to variable names also apply to function names. The function in this example is named displayMessage, so we can easily guess what the function does: it displays a message.
- **Parentheses**—In the header, the function name is always followed by a set of parentheses. As you will see later in this chapter, you sometimes write declarations inside the parentheses, but for now, the parentheses will be empty.

> **NOTE:** The function header is never terminated with a semicolon.

The Function Body

Beginning at the line after the function header, one or more statements will appear inside a set of curly braces ({ }). These statements are the function's body and are performed any time the function is executed.

When you write a function definition, Visual Studio automatically indents the statements in the function body. The indentation is not required, but it makes the code easier to read and debug. By indenting the statements in the body of the function, you visually set them apart from the surrounding code. This allows you to tell at a glance what part of the program is part of the function.

Calling a Function

A function executes when it is called. When a function is called, the program branches to that function and executes the statements in its body. Here is an example of a statement that calls the displayMessage function we previously examined:

```
displayMessage();
```

The statement is simply the name of the function followed by a set of parentheses. Because it is a complete statement, it is terminated with a semicolon. Program 5-1 shows a complete program that uses the displayMessage function.

Program 5-1   (`SimpleFunction.cpp`)

```cpp
 1 #include <iostream>
 2 using namespace std;
 3
 4 // Definition of the displayMessage function
 5 void displayMessage()
 6 {
 7    cout << "This is the displayMessage function." << endl;
 8 }
 9
10 // Definition of the main function
11 int main()
12 {
13    cout << "This is the main function." << endl;
14    displayMessage();
15    cout << "Back in the main function." << endl;
16    return 0;
17 }
```

Program Output

```
This is the main function.
This is the displayMessage function.
Back in the main function.
```

Let's step through this program. When the program runs, it begins executing in the main function, which starts in line 11. Line 13 displays *This is the main function.*, and then line 14 calls the `displayMessage` function. As shown in Figure 5-3, the program jumps to the `displayMessage` function and executes the statements in its body. Only one statement is in the body of the `displayMessage` function, which is line 7. This statement displays *This is the displayMessage function.*, and then the function ends.

Figure 5-3 Calling the `displayMessage` function

The program jumps to the `displayMessage` function and executes the statements in its body.

```cpp
#include <iostream>
using namespace std;

// Definition of the displayMessage function
void displayMessage()
{
    cout << "This is the displayMessage function." << endl;
}

// Definition of the main function
int main()
{
    cout << "This is the main function." << endl;
    displayMessage();
    cout << "Back in the main function." << endl;
    return 0;
}
```

As shown in Figure 5-4, the program jumps back to the part of the program that called the `displayMessage` function and resumes execution from that point. In this case, the program resumes execution at line 15, which displays *Back in the main function*. The main function ends at line 17.

Figure 5-4 The `displayMessage` function returns

When the `displayMessage` function ends, the program returns to the part of the program that called it, and resumes execution at that point.

```
#include <iostream>
using namespace std;

// Definition of the displayMessage function
void displayMessage()
{
    cout << "This is the displayMessage function." << endl;
}

// Definition of the main function
int main()
{
    cout << "This is the main function." << endl;
    displayMessage();
    cout << "Back in the main function." << endl;
    return 0;
}
```

When a function is called, some operations are performed "behind the scenes" so the system will know where the program should return after the function ends. First, the system saves the memory address of the location where it should return. This is typically the statement that appears immediately after the function call. This memory location is known as the *return point*. Then, the system jumps to the function and executes the statements in its body. When the function ends, the system jumps back to the return point and resumes execution.

NOTE: When a program calls a function, programmers commonly say that the *control* of the program transfers to that function. This simply means that the function takes control of the program's execution.

Function Prototypes

Before the compiler encounters a call to a particular function, it must already know the function's return type, the number of parameters it uses, and the type of each parameter. (You will learn how to use parameters in the next section.)

One way of ensuring that the compiler has this information is to place the function definition before all calls to that function. This was the approach taken in Program 5-1. A more common technique, however, is to write a function prototype near the top of the program. A *function prototype* is a statement that declares the existence of a function, but does not define the function. It is a way of telling the compiler that a particular function exists in the program and that its definition appears at a later point. The function prototype for the displayMessage function in Program 5-1 would look like this:

```
void displayMessage();
```

The prototype looks similar to the function header, except a semicolon is at the end. Program 5-2 shows how a function prototype is typically used. In this program, the prototype for the displayMessage function appears in line 5. The definition of the main function appears next, in lines 8 through 14, and then the definition of the displayMessage function appears in lines 17 through 20.

Program 5-2   **(FunctionPrototype.cpp)**

```
 1 #include <iostream>
 2 using namespace std;
 3
 4 // Function prototype
 5 void displayMessage();
 6
 7 // Definition of the main function
 8 int main()
 9 {
10    cout << "This is the main function." << endl;
11    displayMessage();
12    cout << "Back in the main function." << endl;
13    return 0;
14 }
15
16 // Definition of the displayMessage function
17 void displayMessage()
18 {
19    cout << "This is the displayMessage function." << endl;
20 }
```

Program Output

```
This is the main function.
This is the displayMessage function.
Back in the main function.
```

 NOTE: You must place either the function definition or the function prototype ahead of all calls to the function. Otherwise the program will not compile.

Top-Down Design

In this section, we have discussed and demonstrated how functions work. You've seen how the program jumps to a function when it is called and returns to the part of the program that called the function when the function ends. It is important to understand these mechanical aspects of functions.

Just as important as understanding how functions work is understanding how to use functions to modularize a program. Programmers commonly use a technique known as *top-down design* to break down an algorithm into functions. The process of top-down design is performed in the following manner:

- The overall task that the program is to perform is broken down into a series of subtasks.
- Each of the subtasks is examined to determine whether it can be further broken down into more subtasks. This step is repeated until no more subtasks can be identified.
- Once all the subtasks have been identified, they are written in code.

This process is called top-down design because the programmer begins by looking at the topmost level of tasks that must be performed, and then breaks down those tasks into lower levels of subtasks.

NOTE: The top-down design process is sometimes called *stepwise refinement*.

Checkpoint

5.1. What is the difference between a void function and a value-returning function?

5.2. What two parts does a function definition have?

5.3. What does the phrase "calling a function" mean?

5.4. When a void function is executing, what happens when the end of the function is reached?

5.5. Describe the steps involved in the top-down design process.

5.3 Local Variables

CONCEPT: A local variable is a variable that is declared inside a function. A local variable cannot be accessed by statements that are outside the function. Different functions can have local variables with the same names because the functions cannot see each other's local variables.

A variable that is declared inside a function is called a *local variable*. A local variable belongs to the function in which it is declared, and only statements inside that function can access the variable. (The term *local* is meant to indicate that the variable can be used only locally, within the function in which it is declared.) An error will occur if a statement in one function tries to access a local variable that belongs to another function. For example, look at the following code:

```
// This program has an error!
#include <iostream>
#include <string>
using namespace std;

// Function prototype
void getName();

// Definition of main function
int main()
{
    getName();
    cout << "Hello " << name << endl;
}

// Definition of getName function
void getName()
{
    string name;
    cout << "Enter your first name: ";
    cin >> name;
}
```

This will cause an error because name is not accessible to the main function.

name is local to the getName function.

First, look at the getName function, and notice that the name object is declared in inside the getName function. Because it is declared inside the getName function, it is local to that function. The getName function prompts the user to enter his or her name, and the cin statement stores the user's input in the name object.

Now look at the main function. It calls the getName function, and then the cout statement tries to access the name object. This causes a compiler error because the name object is local to the getName function, and statements in the main function cannot access it.

Scope and Local Variables

Programmers commonly use the term *scope* to describe the part of a program in which a variable may be accessed. A variable is visible only to statements inside the variable's scope.

A local variable's scope begins at the variable's declaration and ends at the end of the function in which the variable is declared. The variable cannot be accessed by statements that are outside this region. This means that a local variable cannot be accessed by code that is outside the function or inside the function but before the variable's declaration. For example, look at the following code. It has an error because the cin statement tries to store a value in the age variable, but the statement is outside the variable's scope. Moving the variable declaration to a line before the cin statement will fix this error.

```
void getAge()
{
    cout << "Enter your age: ";
    cin >> age;
    int age;
}
```

This statement will cause an error because the age variable has not been declared yet.

Duplicate Variable Names

You cannot have two variables with the same name in the same scope. For example, look at the following function:

```
void getTwoAges()
{
   int age;
   cout << "Enter your age: ";
   cin >> age;

   int age;              This will cause an error because
   cout << "Enter your pet's age: ";    the age variable has already
   cin >> age;           been declared.
}
```

This `getTwoAges` function declares two local variables named age. The second variable declaration will cause an error because a variable named age has already been declared in the function. Renaming one of the variables will fix this error.

TIP: You cannot have two variables with the same name in the same function because the compiler would not know which variable to use when a statement tries to access one of them. All variables that exist within the same scope must have unique names.

Although you cannot have two local variables with the same name in the same function, it is okay for a local variable in one function to have the same name as a local variable in a different function. For example, suppose a program has two functions: `getPersonAge` and `getPetAge`. It would be legal for both functions to have a local variable named age.

 Checkpoint

5.6. What is a local variable? How is access to a local variable restricted?

5.7. What is a variable's scope?

5.8. Is it permissible to have more than one variable with the same name in the same scope? Why or why not?

5.9. Is it permissible for a local variable in one function to have the same name as a local variable in a different function?

 5.4 **Passing Arguments to Functions**

CONCEPT: An argument is any piece of data that is passed into a function when the function is called. A parameter is a variable that receives an argument that is passed into a function.

Sometimes it is necessary to send one or more pieces of data into a function when you call the function. Pieces of data that are sent into a function are known as *arguments*. The function can use its arguments in calculations or other operations.

If you want a function to receive arguments when it is called, you must equip the function with one or more parameter variables. A *parameter variable*, often simply called a *parameter*, is a special variable that is assigned the value of an argument when a function is called. Here is an example of a function that has a parameter variable:

```cpp
void showDouble(int number)
{
    int result = number * 2;
    cout << result << endl;
}
```

This function's name is showDouble. Its purpose is to accept an integer as an argument and display the value of that integer doubled. Look at the function header and notice the words int number that appear inside the parentheses. This is the declaration of a parameter variable. The parameter variable's name is number, and its data type is int. The purpose of this variable is to receive an int argument when the function is called. Program 5-3 demonstrates the function in a complete program.

Program 5-3   (PassArgument.cpp)

```cpp
 1 #include <iostream>
 2 using namespace std;
 3
 4 // Function prototype
 5 void doubleNumber(int);
 6
 7 // Definition of the main function
 8 int main()
 9 {
10    doubleNumber(4);
11    return 0;
12 }
13
14 // Definition of the doubleNumber function
15 void doubleNumber(int number)
16 {
17    int result = number *2;
18    cout << result << endl;
19 }
```

Program Output

8

First, notice the function prototype for doubleNumber in line 5:

```cpp
void doubleNumber(int);
```

In the function prototype, it is not necessary to list the name of the parameter variable inside the parentheses. Only its data type is required. This function prototype could optionally have been written as:

```
void doubleNumber(int number);
```

However, the compiler ignores the name of the parameter variable in the function prototype.

When this program runs, the main function will begin executing. The statement in line 10 calls the doubleNumber function. Notice that the number 4 appears inside the parentheses. This is an argument that is being passed to the doubleNumber function. When this statement executes, the doubleNumber function will be called with the value 4 copied into the number parameter variable. This is shown in Figure 5-5.

Figure 5-5 The argument 4 is copied into the number parameter variable

```
int main()
{
    doubleNumber(4)
    return 0;                   The argument 4 is copied into
}                               the number parameter variable.

void doubleNumber(int number)
{
    int result = number * 2;
    cout << result << endl;
}
```

Let's step through the doubleNumber function. As we do, remember that the number parameter variable will be assigned the value that was passed to it as an argument. In this program, that number is 4.

Line 17 declares a local variable named result and initializes the result variable with the value of the expression number * 2. Because the number parameter is assigned the value 4, this statement assigns 8 to result. Line 18 displays the result variable.

You can also pass the contents of a variable as an argument. For example, look at Program 5-4. The main function declares an int variable named value in line 10. Line 12 prompts the user to enter a number, and line 13 reads the user's input into the value variable. Notice that in line 14 value is passed as an argument to the doubleNumber function, which causes the value variable's contents to be copied into the number parameter variable. This is shown in Figure 5-6.

Program 5-4   (PassVariable.cpp)

```
 1 #include <iostream>
 2 using namespace std;
 3
 4 // Function prototype
 5 void doubleNumber(int);
 6
```

```
 7 // Definition of the main function
 8 int main()
 9 {
10    int value;
11
12    cout << "Enter a value and I will double it: ";
13    cin >> value;
14    doubleNumber(value);
15    return 0;
16 }
17
18 // Definition of the doubleNumber function
19 void doubleNumber(int number)
20 {
21    int result = number *2;
22    cout << result << endl;
23 }
```

Program Output with Input Shown in Bold

```
Enter a value and I will double it: 5 [Enter]
10
```

Figure 5-6 The value variable is passed into the number parameter variable

```
int main()
{
   int value;

   cout << "Enter a value and I will double it: ";
   cin >> value;
   doubleNumber(value);        The contents of the value
   return 0;            5       variable are assigned to the
}                               number parameter variable.

void doubleNumber(int number)
{
   int result = number * 2;
   cout << result << endl;
}
```

WARNING! When passing a variable as an argument, simply write the variable name inside the parentheses of the function call. Do not write the data type of the argument variable in the function call. For example, the following function call will cause an error:

```
doubleNumber(int x);      // Error!
```

The function call should appear as

```
doubleNumber(x);           // Correct
```

> **NOTE:** If you pass an argument whose type is not the same as the parameter's type, the argument will be promoted or demoted automatically. For instance, the argument in the following function call would be truncated, causing the value 4 to be passed to num:
>
> ```
> doubleNumber(4.7);
> ```
>
> It is worth mentioning that the compiler will warn you that this function call could result in a possible loss of data. However, the program will still be compiled and will execute.

Parameter Variable Scope

Earlier in this chapter, you learned that a variable's scope is the part of the program in which the variable may be accessed. A variable is visible only to statements inside the variable's scope. A parameter variable's scope is the function in which the parameter is used. All the statements inside the function can access the parameter variable, but no statement outside the function can access it.

Passing Multiple Arguments

Often it is useful to write functions that can accept multiple arguments. Program 5-5 shows a function named showSum that accepts two arguments. The function adds the two arguments and displays their sum.

Program 5-5   (TwoArgs.cpp)

```
 1 #include <iostream>
 2 using namespace std;
 3
 4 // Function prototype
 5 void showSum(int, int);
 6
 7 // Definition of the main function
 8 int main()
 9 {
10    cout << "The sum of 12 and 45 is:" << endl;
11    showSum(12, 45);
12    return 0;
13 }
14
15 // Definition of the showSum function
16 void showSum(int num1, int num2)
17 {
18    int result = num1 + num2;
19    cout << result << endl;
20 }
```

Program Output

```
The sum of 12 and 45 is:
57
```

Notice in line 16 that two parameter variables, num1 and num2, are declared inside the parentheses in the showSum function header. This is often referred to as a *parameter list*. Also notice that a comma separates the declarations. Also notice in line 5 that the function prototype shows the data type for each parameter.

The statement in line 11 calls the showSum function and passes two arguments: 12 and 45. The arguments are passed into the parameter variables in the order that they appear in the function call. In other words, the first argument is passed into the first parameter variable, and the second argument is passed into the second parameter variable. So, this statement causes 12 to be passed into the num1 parameter and 45 to be passed into the num2 parameter, as shown in Figure 5-7.

Figure 5-7 Two arguments passed into two parameters

```cpp
int main()
{
    cout << "The sum of 12 and 45 is:" << endl;
    showSum(12, 45);
    return 0;
}

void showSum(int num1, int num2)
{
    int result = num1 + num2;
    cout << result << endl;
}
```

Suppose we were to reverse the order in which the arguments are listed in the function call, as shown here:

```cpp
showSum(45, 12);
```

This would cause 45 to be passed into the num1 parameter and 12 to be passed into the num2 parameter. The following code snippet shows one more example. This time we are passing variables as arguments.

```cpp
int value1 = 2;
int value2 = 3;
showSum(value1, value2);
```

When the showSum function executes as a result of this code, the num1 parameter will contain 2, and the num2 parameter will contain 3.

NOTE: In a function header, you have to write the data type for each parameter variable that is declared in a parameter list. For example, a compiler error would occur if the parameter list for the showSum function were written as shown here:

```cpp
void showSum(int num1, num2) // Error!
```

A data type for both the num1 and num2 parameter variables must be listed, as shown here:

```cpp
void showSum(int num1, int num2)
```

Passing Arguments by Value

All of the example programs that you have looked at so far pass arguments by value. Arguments and parameter variables are separate items in memory. When an argument is *passed by value*, only a copy of the argument's value is passed into the parameter variable. If the contents of the parameter variable are changed inside the function, it has no effect on the argument in the calling part of the program. For example, look at Program 5-6.

Program 5-6   (PassByValue.cpp)

```cpp
 1 #include <iostream>
 2 using namespace std;
 3
 4 // Function Prototype
 5 void changeMe(int);
 6
 7 int main()
 8 {
 9    int number = 99;
10
11    // Display the value in number.
12    cout << "In main, number is " << number << endl;
13
14    // Call changeMe, passing the value in number
15    // as an argument.
16    changeMe(number);
17
18    // Display the value in number again.
19    cout << "Now back in main again." << endl;
20    cout << "The number variable is " << number << endl;
21    return 0;
22 }
23
24 // Definition of the changeMe function
25 void changeMe(int myValue)
26 {
27    // Change the value of myValue to 0.
28    myValue = 0;
29
30    // Display the value in myValue.
31    cout << "In changeMe, the value is " << myValue << endl;
32 }
```

Program Output

```
In main, number is 99
In changeMe, the value is 0
Now back in main again.
The number variable is 12
```

The `main` function declares a local variable named `number` in line 9 and initializes it to the value 99. As a result, the `cout` statement in line 12 displays "In main, number is 99." The `number` variable's value is then passed as an argument to the `changeMe` function in line 16. This means that in the `changeMe` function, the value 99 will be copied into the `myValue` parameter variable.

Inside the `changeMe` function, in line 28, the `myValue` parameter variable is set to 0. As a result, the `cout` statement in line 31 displays "In changeMe, the value is 0." The function ends, and control of the program returns to the `main` function. The next statements to execute are the `cout` statements in lines 19 and 20. The statement in line 20 displays "The number variable is 99." Even though the `myValue` parameter variable was changed in the `changeMe` function, the argument (the `number` variable in `main`) was not modified.

Passing an argument is a way that one function can communicate with another function. When the argument is passed by value, the communication channel works in only one direction: the calling function can communicate with the called function. The called function, however, cannot use the argument to communicate with the calling function.

Passing Arguments by Reference

Passing an argument *by reference* means that the argument is passed into a special type of parameter known as a *reference variable*. When a reference variable is used as a parameter in a function, it allows the function to modify the argument in the calling part of the program.

A reference variable acts as an alias for the variable that was passed into it as an argument. It is called a reference variable because it references the other variable. Anything that you do to the reference variable is actually done to the variable it references. Reference variables are useful for establishing two-way communication between functions.

When a function calls another function and passes a variable by reference, communication between the functions can take place in the following ways:

- The calling function can communicate with the called function by passing an argument.
- The called function can communicate with the calling function by modifying the value of the argument via the reference variable.

Reference variables are declared like regular variables, except you place an ampersand (`&`) in front of the name. Program 5-7 shows an example. In the program, an `int` argument is passed by reference to the `setToZero` function. The `setToZero` function sets its parameter variable to 0, which also sets the original variable that was passed as an argument to 0.

Program 5-7   (PassByReference.cpp)

```
1 #include <iostream>
2 using namespace std;
3
4 // Function prototype
```

```
 5 void setToZero(int &);
 6
 7 int main()
 8 {
 9    int value = 99;
10    cout << "The value is " << value << endl;
11    setToZero(value);
12    cout << "Now the value is " << value << endl;
13    return 0;
14 }
15
16 // Definition of the setToZero function
17 void setToZero(int &num)
18 {
19    num = 0;
20 }
```

Program Output

```
The value is 99
Now the value is 0
```

 Checkpoint

5.10. What are the pieces of data that are passed into a function called?

5.11. What are the variables that receive pieces of data in a function called?

5.12. Typically, what is a parameter variable's scope?

5.13. Explain the difference between passing by value and passing by reference.

 5.5 Global Variables and Global Constants

CONCEPT: Global variables and global constants are accessible to all the functions in a program.

Global Variables

A *global variable* is a variable that is visible to every function in the program. A global variable's scope is the entire program, so all the functions in the program can access a global variable. To declare a global variable or constant in a C++ program, you write the declaration outside all functions and above the definitions of the functions. As a result, all the functions in the program have access to the variable or constant. Program 5-8 shows two functions, main and anotherFunction, that access the same global variable, num.

Program 5-8   (`GlobalVariable.cpp`)

```
 1 #include <iostream>
 2 using namespace std;
 3
 4 // Function prototype
 5 void anotherFunction();
 6
 7 // Global variable declaration
 8 int num = 2;
 9
10 // Definition of the main function
11 int main()
12 {
13     cout << "In main, num is " << num << endl;
14     anotherFunction();
15     cout << "Back in main, num is " << num << endl;
16     return 0;
17 }
18
19 // Definition of anotherFunction
20 void anotherFunction()
21 {
22     cout << "In anotherFunction, num is " << num << endl;
23     num = 50;
24     cout << "But, it is now changed to " << num << endl;
25 }
```

Program Output

```
In main, num is 2
In anotherFunction, num is 2
But, it is now changed to 50
Back in main, num is 50
```

Line 8 declares an `int` variable named `num`. Because the declaration does not appear inside a function, the number variable is a global variable. All the functions that are defined in the program have access to the variable.

Although you will see some programs that require global variables in Part 2 of this book, you should be very careful hen using them. The reasons are as follows:

- Global variables make debugging difficult. Any statement in a program can change the value of a global variable. If you find that the wrong value is being stored in a global variable, you have to track down every statement that accesses it to determine where the bad value is coming from. In a program with thousands of lines of code, this can be difficult.
- Functions that use global variables are usually dependent on those variables. If you want to use such a function in a different program, most likely you will have to redesign it so it does not rely on the global variable.

- Global variables make a program hard to understand. A global variable can be modified by any statement in the program. If you are to understand any part of the program that uses a global variable, you have to be aware of all the other parts of the program that access the global variable.

When possible, you should declare variables locally and pass them as arguments to the functions that need to access them.

Global Constants

A *global constant* is a named constant that is available to every function in the program. Because a global constant's value cannot be changed during the program's execution, you do not have to worry about many of the potential hazards that are associated with the use of global variables.

Global constants are typically used to represent unchanging values that are needed throughout a program. For example, suppose a banking program uses a named constant to represent an interest rate. If the interest rate is used in several functions, it is easier to create a global constant, rather than a local named constant in each function. This also simplifies maintenance. If the interest rate changes, only the declaration of the global constant has to be changed, instead of several local declarations.

In the Spotlight:
Using Global Constants and Reference Parameters

Marilyn works for Integrated Systems, Inc., a software company that has a reputation for providing excellent fringe benefits. One of its benefits is a quarterly bonus that is paid to all employees. Another benefit is a retirement plan for each employee. The company contributes 5 percent of each employee's gross pay and bonuses to his or her retirement plan. Marilyn wants to design a program that will calculate the company's contribution to an employee's retirement account for a year. She wants the program to show the amount of contribution for the employee's gross pay and for the bonuses separately.

Here is an outline of the actions that the program will perform:

1. Get the employee's annual gross pay.
2. Get the amount of bonuses paid to the employee.
3. Calculate and display the contribution for the gross pay.
4. Calculate and display the contribution for the bonuses.

Program 5-9 shows the program's code.

Program 5-9   (Contributions.cpp)

```
1 #include <iostream>
2 using namespace std;
3
4 // Function prototypes
```

```cpp
 5 void getGrossPay(double &);
 6 void getBonuses(double &);
 7 void showGrossPayContrib(double);
 8 void showBonusContrib(double);
 9
10 // Global variable declaration
11 double CONTRIBUTION_RATE = 0.05;
12
13 // Definition of the main function
14 int main()
15 {
16    // Variables
17    double annualGrossPay, // To hold the annual gross pay
18           totalBonuses;   // To hold the total bonuses
19
20    // Get the annual gross pay.
21    getGrossPay(annualGrossPay);
22
23    // Get the total of the bonuses.
24    getBonuses(totalBonuses);
25
26    // Display the contribution for the gross pay.
27    showGrossPayContrib(annualGrossPay);
28
29    // Display the contribution for the bonuses.
30    showBonusContrib(totalBonuses);
31    return 0;
32 }
33
34 // The getGrossPay function gets the user's
35 // annual gross pay and assigns it to the
36 // grossPay reference parameter.
37 void getGrossPay(double &grossPay)
38 {
39    cout << "Enter the annual gross pay: ";
40    cin >> grossPay;
41 }
42
43 // The getBonuses function gets the amount
44 // of bonuses and assigns it to the bonuses
45 // reference parameter.
46 void getBonuses(double &bonuses)
47 {
48    cout << "Enter the amount of bonuses: ";
49    cin >> bonuses;
50 }
51
52 // The showGrossPayContrib function accepts
53 // the gross pay as an argument and displays
54 // the retirement contribution for gross pay.
55 void showGrossPayContrib(double grossPay)
56 {
57    double contrib = grossPay * CONTRIBUTION_RATE;
58    cout << "Contribution for the gross pay: $"
59         << contrib << endl;
```

```
60 }
61
62 // The showBonusContrib function accepts
63 // the bonus amount as an argument and displays
64 // the retirement contribution for bonuses.
65 void showBonusContrib(double bonuses)
66 {
67     double contrib = bonuses * CONTRIBUTION_RATE;
68     cout << "Contribution for bonuses: $"
69          << contrib << endl;
70 }
```

Program Output with Input Shown in Bold

Enter the annual gross pay: **80000 [Enter]**
Enter the amount of bonuses: **20000 [Enter]**
Contribution for the gross pay: $4000
Contribution for bonuses: $1000

A global constant named CONTRIBUTION_RATE is declared in line 11 and initialized with the value 0.05. The constant is used in the calculation in line 57 (in the showGrossPayContrib function) and again in line 67 (in the showBonusContrib function). Marilyn decided to use this global constant to represent the 5 percent contribution rate for two reasons:

- It makes the program easier to read. When you look at the calculations in lines 57 and 67, it is apparent what is happening.
- Occasionally the contribution rate changes. When this happens, it will be easy to update the program by changing the declaration statement in line 11.

 Checkpoint

5.14. What is the scope of a global variable?

5.15. Give one good reason why you should not use global variables in a program.

5.16. What is a global constant? Is it permissible to use global constants in a program?

 ## 5.6 Value-Returning Functions

CONCEPT: A value-returning function is a function that returns a value to the part of the program that called it.

A value-returning function is like a void function in the following ways:

- It contains a group of statements that performs a specific task.
- When you want to execute the function, you call it.

When a value-returning function finishes, however, it returns a value to the statement that called it. The value that is returned from a function can be used like any other value: It can be assigned to a variable, displayed on the screen, used in a mathematical expression (if it is a number), and so on.

The pow function, which you have already seen, is an example of a value-returning function. Here is an example:

```
double x;
x = pow(4.0, 2.0);
```

The second line in this code calls the pow function, passing 4.0 and 2.0 as arguments. The function calculates the value of 4.0 raised to the power of 2.0 and returns that value. The value, which is 16.0, is assigned to the x variable by the = operator.

Writing Your Own Value-Returning Functions

You write a value-returning function in the same way that you write a void function, with two exceptions:

- You must specify a data type for a value-returning function. The value that is returned from the function must be of the specified data type.
- A value-returning function must have a return statement. The return statement causes a value to be returned from the function.

Here is the general format of a value-returning function definition in C++:

```
DataType FunctionName(ParameterList)
{
    statement;
    statement;
    etc.
    return expression;
}
```

- *DataType* is the data type of the value that the function returns. We commonly call this the function's *return type*. For example, if the function returns an integer, the word *int* will appear here. If the function returns a *double* value, then the word *double* will appear here.
- *FunctionName* is the name of the function.
- *ParameterList* is an optional parameter list. If the function does not accept arguments, then an empty set of parentheses will appear.

One of the statements inside the function must be a return statement, which takes the following form:

```
return expression;
```

The value of the *expression* that follows the key word return will be sent back to the statement that called the function. This can be any value, variable, or expression that has a value (such as a math expression). The value that is returned must be of the same data type as that specified in the function header, or a compiler error will occur.

Here is an example of a value-returning function:

```
int sum(int num1, int num2)
{
    return num1 + num2;
}
```

Figure 5-8 illustrates the various parts of the function header. Notice that the function returns an int, the function's name is sum, and the function has two int parameters, named num1 and num2.

Figure 5-8 Parts of the function header

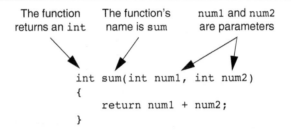

The purpose of this function is to accept two int values as arguments and return their sum. Notice that the return statement returns the value of the expression num1 + num2. When the return statement executes, the function ends its execution and sends the value of num1 + num2 back to the part of the program that called the function.

Let's look at a complete program that demonstrates the sum function.

Program 5-10   (**ValueReturn.cpp**)

```
 1 #include <iostream>
 2 using namespace std;
 3
 4 // Function prototypes
 5 int sum(int, int);
 6
 7 // Definition of the main function
 8 int main()
 9 {
10    // Variables
11    int userAge,        // The user's age
12        friendAge,      // A friend's age
13        combinedAge;    // The combined age
14
15    // Get the user's age.
16    cout << "What is your age? ";
17    cin >> userAge;
18
19    // Get a friend's age.
20    cout << "What is your friend's age? ";
21    cin >> friendAge;
```

```
22
23    // Get the combined age.
24    combinedAge = sum(userAge, friendAge);
25
26    // Display the combined age.
27    cout << "Your combined age is "
28        << combinedAge << " years." << endl;
29    return 0;
30 }
31
32 // The sum function accepts two int
33 // arguments and returns their sum.
34 int sum(int num1, int num2)
35 {
36     return num1 + num2;
37 }
```

Program Output with Input Shown in Bold

What is your age? **23 [Enter]**
What is your friend's age? **25 [Enter]**
Your combined age is 48 years.

In lines 16 and 17 the user is prompted to enter his or her age, and the input is assigned to the userAge variable. In lines 20 and 21 the user is prompted to enter a friend's age, and the input is assigned to the friendAge variable. Line 24 calls the sum function, passing the userAge and friendAge variables as arguments. The sum of the two variables is returned from the function and assigned to the combinedAge variable. In lines 27 and 28 the value of the combinedAge variable is displayed.

Let's assume the userAge variable is set to the value 23 and the friendAge variable is set to the value 25. Figure 5-9 shows how the arguments are passed to the function and how a value is returned from the function.

Figure 5-9 Arguments passed to sum and a value returned

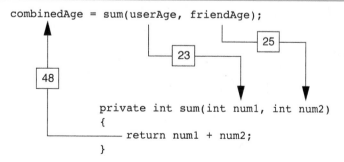

When you call a value-returning function, you usually want to do something meaningful with the value it returns. In line 24 of Program 5-10, the value that is returned from the sum function is assigned to a variable. This is commonly how return values are used, but you can do many other things with them. For example, the following code shows a math expression that uses a call to the sum function:

```
int x = 10, y = 15;
double average;
average = sum(x, y) / 2.0;
```

In the last statement, the sum function is called with x and y as its arguments. The function's return value, which is 25, is divided by 2.0. The result, 12.5, is assigned to average. Here is another example:

```
int x = 10, y = 15;
cout << "The sum is " + sum(x, y) << endl;
```

This code uses cout to display the sum function's return value on the screen. The message *"The sum is 25"* will be displayed. Remember, a value-returning function returns a value of a specific data type. You can use the function's return value anywhere that you can use a regular value of the same data type. This means that anywhere an int value can be used, a call to an int value-returning function can be used. Likewise, anywhere a double value can be used, a call to a double value-returning function can be used. The same is true for any other data type.

In the Spotlight:
Writing Value-Returning Functions

Your friend Michael runs a catering company. Some of the ingredients that his recipes require are measured in cups. When he goes to the grocery store to buy those ingredients, however, they are sold only by the fluid ounce. He has asked you to write a simple program that converts cups to fluid ounces.

You design the following algorithm:

1. *Display an introductory screen that explains what the program does.*
2. *Get the number of cups.*
3. *Convert the number of cups to fluid ounces, and display the result.*

This algorithm lists the top level of tasks that the program needs to perform and becomes the basis of the program's main function. In addition to main, you decide to break down the program into the following functions:

- showIntro—This function will display a message on the screen that explains what the program does.
- getCups—This function will prompt the user to enter the number of cups and then returns that value as a double.
- cupsToOunces—This function will accept the number of cups as an argument and then return equivalent number of fluid ounces as a double.

Program 5-11 shows the code for the program.

Program 5-11   **(CupsToOunces.cpp)**

```cpp
 1 #include <iostream>
 2 using namespace std;
 3
 4 // Function prototypes
 5 void showIntro();
 6 double getCups();
 7 double cupsToOunces(double);
 8
 9 int main()
10 {
11    // Variables for the cups and ounces.
12    double cups, ounces;
13
14    // Display an intro screen.
15    showIntro();
16
17    // Get the number of cups.
18    cups = getCups();
19
20    // Convert cups to fluid ounces.
21    ounces = cupsToOunces(cups);
22
23    // Display the number of ounces.
24    cout << cups << " cups equals "
25         << ounces << " ounces.\n";
26
27    return 0;
28 }
29
30 // The showIntro function displays an intro screen.
31 void showIntro()
32 {
33    cout << "This program converts measurements" << endl
34         << "in cups to fluid ounces. For your" << endl
35         << "reference the formula is:" << endl
36         << "    1 cup = 8 fluid ounces" << endl << endl;
37 }
38
39 // The getCups function prompts the user to enter
40 // the number of cups and then returns that value
41 // as a double.
42 double getCups()
43 {
44    double numCups;
45
46    cout << "Enter the number of cups: ";
47    cin >> numCups;
48    return numCups;
49 }
50
51 // The cupsToOunces function accepts a number of
52 // cups as an argument and returns the equivalent
```

```
53 // number of fluid ounces as a double.
54 double cupsToOunces(double numCups)
55 {
56     return numCups * 8.0;
57 }
```

Program Output with Input Shown in Bold

```
This program converts measurements
in cups to fluid ounces. For your
reference the formula is:
    1 cup = 8 fluid ounces
Enter the number of cups: 2 [Enter]
    2 cups equals 16 ounces.
```

bool Functions

A bool function returns either true or false. You can use a bool function to test a condition and then return either true or false to indicate whether the condition exists. bool functions are useful for simplifying complex conditions that are tested in decision and repetition structures.

For example, suppose you are writing a program that will ask the user to enter a number and then determine whether that number is even or odd. The following code shows how you can make that determination. Assume number is an int variable containing the number entered by the user.

```
if (number % 2 == 0)
{
    cout << "The number is even." << endl;
}
else
{
    cout << "The number is odd." << endl;
}
```

The meaning of the bool expression being tested by this if-else statement isn't clear, so let's take a closer look at it:

```
number % 2 == 0
```

This expression uses the % operator, which was introduced in Chapter 2. Recall that the % operator divides two integers and returns the remainder of the division. So, this code is saying, "If the remainder of number divided by 2 is equal to 0, then display a message indicating the number is even, or else display a message indicating the number is odd."

Because dividing an even number by 2 will always give a remainder of 0, this logic will work. The code would be easier to understand, however, if you could somehow rewrite it to say, "If the number is even, then display a message indicating it is even, or else display a message indicating it is odd." As it turns out, this can be done with a bool function. In this example, you could write a bool function named isEven that accepts an int as an argument and returns true if the number is even, or false otherwise. Here is an example how the isEven function might be written:

```cpp
bool isEven(int number)
{
    // Local variable to hold true or false
    bool numberIsEven;

    // Determine whether the number is even.
    if (number % 2 == 0)
    {
        numberIsEven = true;
    }
    else
    {
        numberIsEven = false;
    }

    // Return the result.
    return numberIsEven;
}
```

Then you can rewrite the previously shown if-else statement so it calls the isEven function to determine whether number is even:

```cpp
if (isEven(number))
{
    cout << "The number is even." << endl;
}
else
{
    cout << "The number is odd." << endl;
}
```

Not only is this logic easier to understand, but now you have a function that you can call in the program anytime you need to test a number to determine whether it is even.

Returning a String from a Function

So far you've seen examples of functions that return numbers and Boolean values. You can write functions that return any type of data. Program 5-12 shows an example that uses a string-returning function.

Program 5-12   (ReturnString.cpp)

```cpp
1 #include <iostream>
2 #include <string>
3 using namespace std;
4
5 // Function prototype
```

```
 6 string fullName(string, string, string);
 7
 8 // The main function
 9 int main()
10 {
11    // String objects
12    string first,      // To hold the first name
13           middle,     // To hold the middle name
14           last,       // To hold the last name
15           full;       // To hold the full name
16
17    // Get the user's first name.
18    cout << "Enter your first name: ";
19    cin >> first;
20
21    // Get the user's middle name.
22    cout << "Enter your middle name: ";
23    cin >> middle;
24
25    // Get the user's last name.
26    cout << "Enter your last name: ";
27    cin >> last;
28
29    // Get the user's full name.
30    full = fullName(first, middle, last);
31
32    // Display the user's full name.
33    cout << "Your full name is " << full << endl;
34    return 0;
35 }
36
37 // The showIntro function displays an intro screen.
38 string fullName(string first, string middle, string last)
39 {
40    return first + " " + middle + " " + last;
41 }
```

Program Output with Input Shown in Bold

```
Enter your first name: Sarah [Enter]
Enter your middle name: Lynn [Enter]
Enter your last name: MacEwen [Enter]
Your full name is Sarah Lynn MacEwen
```

Lines 38 through 41 define a function named fullName. Notice the following things about the function:

- Its return type is string.
- It accepts has three string parameters: first, middle, and last. When we call the function, we pass a first name, a middle name, and a last name as arguments.
- In line 40 it returns a string that is the concatenation of the first, middle, and last parameters, with spaces inserted between each.

Checkpoint

5.17. What is a value-returning function? How is it used?

5.18. What is returned by a bool function?

5.19. Can a function be written to return any type of data?

 ## 5.7 Calling string Class Member Functions

CONCEPT: A member function is a special function that operates on an object.

Recall from Chapter 2 that string objects are created from the standard library's string class. Objects that are created from a class are much more versatile than simple variables. For example, objects that are created from a class usually have built-in functions that are known as member functions. A *member function* is a function that operates on a specific object's data. You call a member function in a slightly different manner than a regular function. Here is the general format:

```
objectName.functionName(arguments)
```

In the general format, *objectName* is the name of the object that you are using to call the member function, *functionName* is the name of the member function, and *arguments* are arguments (if any) that you are passing to the function.

For example, if you want to know the length of the string that is stored in a string object, you can call the object's length member function. Here is an example of how to use it.

```
string state = "Texas";
int size;
size = state.length();
```

The first statement creates a string object named state, initialized with the string "Texas". The second statement declares an int variable named size. The third statement calls the state object's length member function, which returns the length of the string in the state object. The value that is returned from the member function is assigned to the size variable. After this code executes, the size variable will hold the value 5.

Another string member function that you will use quite a bit in the second part of this book is the c_str() member function. The c_str() member function returns the value of a string object formatted as a null terminated string. A *null-terminated string* is stored in memory with a byte that is set to the numeric value 0 at the end of the string. This is a particular format that is required by the App Game Kit library. You will see several examples of this member function used later in the book.

Review Questions

Multiple Choice

1. In general terms, a program that is broken into smaller units of code, such as functions, is known as a(n) _____.
   a. object-oriented program
   b. modularized program
   c. procedural program
   d. function-driven program

2. Writing the code to perform a task once and then reusing it each time you need to perform the task is a benefit of using functions called _____.
   a. code reuse
   b. the single use philosophy
   c. function recycling
   d. code reprocessing

3. When you call a(n) _____, it simply executes the statements it contains then terminates.
   a. intrinsic function
   b. empty function
   c. logical function
   d. void function

4. The _____, which appears at the beginning of a function definition, lists several important things about the function, including the function's name.
   a. function title
   b. function description
   c. function header
   d. function declaration

5. The _____ is a collection of statements enclosed inside a set of curly braces that are performed when the function is executed.
   a. function body
   b. function designation
   c. function code
   d. function classification

6. A statement, usually appearing near the top of the program, which declares the existence of a function, but does not define the function is a _____.
   a. function predefinition
   b. function prototype
   c. function initialization
   d. function disclosure

7. The _____ is the memory address that is saved by the system when a function is called and is the location the system should return to after a function ends.
   a. calling address
   b. function address
   c. return point
   d. come back position

8. Programmers commonly use a technique known as _____ to break down an algorithm into functions.
   a. prototyping
   b. function modeling
   c. algorithm division
   d. top-down design

9. Pieces of data that are sent into a function are known as _____.
   a. arguments
   b. references
   c. function variables
   d. data entries

10. A(n) _____ is a special variable that receives an argument when a function is called.
    a. reference variable
    b. argument variable
    c. parameter variable
    d. function variable

11. When an argument is _____, only a copy of the argument's value is passed into the parameter variable.
    a. a named constant
    b. passed by association
    c. passed by reference
    d. passed by value

12. When you want a function to be able to change the value of a variable that is passed to it as an argument, the variable must be _____.
    a. passed by reference
    b. a local variable
    c. passed by value
    d. a named constant

13. A _____ is a special type of parameter variable that is useful for establishing two-way communication between functions.
    a. communication variable
    b. reference parameter
    c. function parameter
    d. global variable

14. A function's _____ is the type of value that the function returns.
    a. data type
    b. return type
    c. value type
    d. function type

True or False

1. Dividing a large problem into several smaller problems that are easily solved is sometimes called divide and conquer.

2. Calling a function and defining a function mean the same thing.

3. A function prototype declares the existence of a function, but does not define the function.

4. A value-returning function must contain a `return` statement.

5. A statement in one function can access a local variable in another function.

6. You cannot have two variables with the same name in the same scope.

7. It is permissible to have local variables with the same name declared in separate functions.

8. Functions are not allowed to accept multiple arguments.

9. When an argument is passed by reference, the function can modify the argument in the calling part of the program.

10. Passing an argument by value is a means of establishing two-way communication between functions.

11. A Boolean function returns either `yes` or `no`.

Short Answer

1. What do you call a function that executes the statements it contains and then returns a value back to the statement that called it?

2. What is another name for the top-down design process?

3. What is a parameter list?

4. How is a value-returning function like a `void` function? How is it different?

5. When a function is executing, what happens when the end of the function is reached?

6. What is a local variable? What statements are able to access a local variable?

7. Where does a local variable's scope begin and end?

8. What is the difference between passing an argument by value and passing it by reference?

Algorithm Workbench

1. Examine the following function header, then write an example call to the function.

   ```
   private void showValue()
   ```

2. The following statement calls a function named `showHalf`. The `showHalf` function displays a value that is half that of the argument. Write the function.

   ```
   showHalf(50);
   ```

3. Write the function header for a function named `showRetailPrice`. The function should include parameter variables for a wholesale price and a markup percentage.

4. Examine the following function header, then write an example call to the function.

   ```
   private void resetValue(int &value)
   ```

5. A program contains the following value-returning function.

```
private int square(int value)
{
    return value * value;
}
```

Write a statement that passes the value 10 as an argument to this function and assigns its return value to the variable result.

Programming Exercises

1. **Retail Price Calculator**
   Write a program that lets the user enter an item's wholesale cost and its markup percentage. It should then display the item's retail price. For example:
   - If an item's wholesale cost is 5.00 and its markup percentage is 100 percent, then the item's retail price is 10.00.
   - If an item's wholesale cost is 5.00 and its markup percentage is 50 percent, then the item's retail price is 7.50.

   The program should have a function named calculateRetail that receives the wholesale cost and the markup percentage as arguments and returns the retail price of the item.

2. **Celsius Temperature Table**
   The formula for converting a temperature from Fahrenheit to Celsius is

   $$C = \frac{5}{9}(F - 32)$$

   where F is the Fahrenheit temperature and C is the Celsius temperature. Write a function named celsius that accepts a Fahrenheit temperature as an argument. The function should return the temperature, converted to Celsius. Demonstrate the function by calling it in a loop that displays a table of the Fahrenheit temperatures 0 through 20 and their Celsius equivalents.

3. **Falling Distance**
   When an object is falling because of gravity, the following formula can be used to determine the distance the object falls in a specific time period:

   $$d = \frac{1}{2}\, gt^2$$

   The variables in the formula are as follows: d is the distance in meters, g is 9.8, and t is the amount of time in seconds that the object has been falling. Write a program that allows the user to enter the amount of time that an object has fallen and then displays the distance that the object fell. The program should have a function named fallingDistance. The fallingDistance function should accept an object's falling time (in seconds) as an argument. The function should return in meters the distance that the object has fallen during that time interval.

4. **Kinetic Energy**
   In physics, an object that is in motion is said to have kinetic energy. The following formula can be used to determine a moving object's kinetic energy:

   $$KE = \frac{1}{2}\, mv^2$$

In the formula *KE* is the kinetic energy, *m* is the object's mass in kilograms, and *v* is the object's velocity in meters per second. Write a program that allows the user to enter an object's mass and velocity and then displays the object's kinetic energy. The program should have a function named `kineticEnergy` that accepts an object's mass (in kilograms) and velocity (in meters per second) as arguments. The function should return the amount of kinetic energy that the object has.

5. **Calories from Fat and Carbohydrates**

   A nutritionist who works for a fitness club helps members by evaluating their diets. As part of her evaluation, she asks members for the number of fat grams and carbohydrate grams that they consumed in a day. Then, she calculates the number of calories that result from the fat, using the following formula:

   $$\text{Calories from Fat} = \text{Fat Grams} \times 9$$

   Next, she calculates the number of calories that result from the carbohydrates, using the following formula:

   $$\text{Calories from Carbs} = \text{Carb Grams} \times 4$$

   Write a program that will make these calculations. In the program, you should have the following functions:

   - `fatCalories`—This function should accept a number of fat grams as an argument and return the number of calories from that amount of fat.
   - `carbCalories`—This function should accept a number of carbohydrate grams as an argument and return the number of calories from that amount of carbohydrates.

6. **Hospital Charges**

   Write a program that calculates the total cost of a hospital stay. The daily base charge is $350. The hospital also charges for medication, surgical fees, lab fees, and physical rehab. The program should accept the following input:

   - The number of days spent in the hospital
   - The amount of medication charges
   - The amount of surgical charges
   - The amount of lab fees
   - The amount of physical rehabilitation charges

   Create and use the following value-returning functions in the application:

   - `calcStayCharges`—Calculates and returns the base charges for the hospital stay. This is computed as $350 times the number of days in the hospital.
   - `calcMiscCharges`—Calculates and returns the total of the medication, surgical, lab, and physical rehabilitation charges.
   - `calcTotalCharges`—Calculates and returns the total charges.

7. **Present Value**

   Suppose you want to deposit a certain amount of money into a savings account and then leave it alone to draw interest for the next 10 years. At the end of 10 years you would like to have $10,000 in the account. How much do you need to deposit today to make that happen? You can use the following formula, which is known as the present value formula, to find out:

$$P = \frac{F}{(1 + r)^n}$$

The terms in the formula are as follows:

- P is the present value, or the amount that you need to deposit today.
- F is the future value that you want in the account. (In this case, F is $10,000.)
- r is the annual interest rate.
- n is the number of years that you plan to let the money sit in the account.

Write a function named `presentValue` that performs this calculation. The function should accept the future value, annual interest rate, and number of years as arguments. It should return the present value, which is the amount that you need to deposit today. Demonstrate the function in a program that lets the user experiment with different values for the formula's terms.

8. **Population**

In a population, the birthrate is the percentage increase of the population due to births, and the death rate is the percentage decrease of the population due to deaths. Write a program that displays the size of a population for any number of years. The program should ask for the following data:

The starting size of a population
The annual birthrate
The annual death rate
The number of years to display

Write a function that calculates the size of the population for a year. The formula is

$$N = P + BP - DP$$

where N is the new population size, P is the previous population size, B is the birthrate, and D is the death rate.

9. **Prime Numbers**

A prime number is a number that can be evenly divided by only itself and 1. For example, the number 5 is prime because it can be evenly divided by only 1 and 5. The number 6, however, is not prime because it can be evenly divided by 1, 2, 3, and 6. Write a `bool` function named `isPrime` that takes an integer as an argument and returns `true` if the argument is a prime number or `false` otherwise. Use the function in a program that lets the user enter a number and then displays a message indicating whether the number is prime.

> **TIP:** Recall that the `%` operator divides one number by another and returns the remainder of the division. In an expression such as `num1 % num2`, the `%` operator will return 0 if `num1` is evenly divisible by `num2`.

10. **Prime Number List**

This exercise assumes you have already written the `isPrime` function in Programming Exercise 9. Write another program that uses this function to display all the prime numbers from 1 through 100. The program should have a loop that calls the `isPrime` function.

6 Arrays

6.1 Array Basics

CONCEPT: An array allows you to store a group of items of the same data type together in memory. Processing a large number of items in an array is usually easier than processing a large number of items stored in separate variables.

In the programs you have written so far, you have used variables to store data in memory. The simplest way to store a value in memory is to store it in a variable. Variables work well in many situations, but they have limitations. For example, they can hold only one value at a time. Consider the following variable declaration:

```
int number = 99;
```

This statement declares an int variable named number, initialized with the value 99. Consider what happens if the following statement appears later in the program:

```
number = 5;
```

This statement assigns the value 5 to number, replacing the value 99 that was previously stored there. Because number is an ordinary variable, it can hold only one value at a time.

Because variables hold only a single value, they can be cumbersome in programs that process lists of data. For example, suppose you are asked to write a program that holds the names of 50 employees. Imagine declaring 50 variables to hold all those names:

```
string employee1;
string employee2;
string employee3;
```

and so on . . .

```
string employee50
```

Then, imagine writing the code to process all 50 names. For example, if you wanted to display the contents of the variables, you would write code such as this:

```
cout << employee1 << endl;   // Display employee 1
cout << employee2 << endl;   // Display employee 2
cout << employee3 << endl;   // Display employee 3
```

and so on . . .

```
cout << employee50 << endl;   // Display employee 50
```

As you can see, variables are not well suited for storing and processing lists of data. Each variable is a separate item that must be declared and individually processed.

Fortunately, you can use an array as an alternative to a group of variables. An **array** can hold a group of values that are all of the same data type. You can have an array of int values, an array of double values, or an array of string values, but you cannot store a mixture of data types in an array. Once you create an array, you can write simple and efficient code to process the values that are stored in it. Here is an example of how you can declare an int array:

```
int values[20];
```

Notice that this statement looks like a regular int variable declaration except for the number inside the brackets. The number inside the brackets is known as a *size declarator*. The size declarator specifies the number of values that the array can hold. This statement declares an array named values that can hold 20 integer values. The array size declarator must be a nonnegative integer. Here is another example:

```
double salesAmounts[7];
```

This statement declares an array named salesAmounts that can hold 7 double values. The following statement shows one more example. This statement declares an array that can hold 50 string values. The name of the array is names.

```
string names[50];
```

An array's size cannot be changed while the program is running. If you have written a program that uses an array and then find that you must change the array's size, you have to change the array's size declarator in the source code. Then you must recompile the program with the new size declarator. To make array sizes easier to maintain, it's a good idea to use named constants as array size declarators. Here is an example:

```
const int SIZE = 20;
int values[SIZE];
```

As you will see later in this chapter, many array processing techniques require you to refer to the array's size. When you use a named constant as an array's size declarator, you can use the constant to refer to the size of the array in your algorithms. If you ever need to modify the program so that the array is a different size, you only need to change the value of the named constant.

Array Elements and Subscripts

The storage locations in an array are known as *elements*. In memory, an array's elements are located in consecutive memory locations. Each element in an array is assigned a unique number known as a *subscript*. Subscripts are used to identify specific elements in an array. In C++, the first element is assigned the subscript 0, the second element is assigned the subscript 1, and so forth. For example, suppose we have the following declarations in a program:

```
const int SIZE = 5;
int numbers[SIZE];
```

As shown in Figure 6-1, the numbers array has five elements. The elements are assigned the subscripts 0 through 4. (Because subscript numbering starts at zero, the subscript of the last element in an array is one less than the total number of elements in the array.)

Figure 6-1 Array subscripts

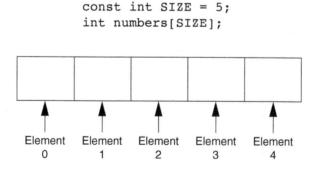

Assigning Values to Array Elements

You access the individual elements in an array by using their subscripts. For example, assuming numbers is the int array previously described, the following code assigns values to each of its five elements:

```
numbers[0] = 20;
numbers[1] = 30;
numbers[2] = 40;
numbers[3] = 50;
numbers[4] = 60;
```

This code assigns the value 20 to element 0, the value 30 to element 1, and so forth. Figure 6-2 shows the contents of the array after these statements execute.

 NOTE: The expression numbers[0] is pronounced "numbers sub zero."

Figure 6-2 Values assigned to each element

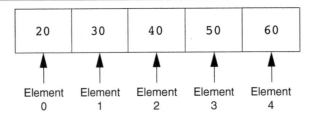

Inputting and Outputting Array Contents

You can read values from the keyboard and store them in an array element just as you can a regular variable. You can also output the contents of an array element. The code in Program 6-1 shows an array being used to store and display values entered by the user.

Program 6-1 (ArrayInputOutput.cpp)

```cpp
 1 #include <iostream>
 2 using namespace std;
 3
 4 int main()
 5 {
 6    const int SIZE = 3;    // Constant for array size
 7    int hours[SIZE];       // Array to hold hours
 8
 9    // Get the hours worked by employee 1.
10    cout << "Enter the hours worked by employee 1: ";
11    cin >> hours[0];
12
13    // Get the hours worked by employee 2.
14    cout << "Enter the hours worked by employee 2: ";
15    cin >> hours[1];
16
17    // Get the hours worked by employee 3.
18    cout << "Enter the hours worked by employee 3: ";
19    cin >> hours[2];
20
21    // Display the values in the array.
22    cout << "The hours you entered are:" << endl;
23    cout << hours[0] << endl;
24    cout << hours[1] << endl;
25    cout << hours[2] << endl;
26    return 0;
27 }
```

Program Output with Input Shown in Bold

```
Enter the hours worked by employee 1: 40 [Enter]
Enter the hours worked by employee 2: 20 [Enter]
Enter the hours worked by employee 3: 15 [Enter]
The hours you entered are:
40
20
15
```

Let's take a closer look at the program. A named constant, SIZE, is declared in line 6 and initialized with the value 3. Then, an int array named hours is declared in line 7. The SIZE constant is used as the array size declarator, so the hours array will have three elements. The cin statements in lines 11, 15, and 19 read values from the keyboard and store those values in the elements of the hours array. Then, the cout statements in lines 23 through 25 output the values stored in each array element.

In the sample running of the program, the user entered the values 40, 20, and 15, which were stored in the hours array. Figure 6-3 shows the contents of the array after these values are stored in it.

Figure 6-3 Contents of the hours array

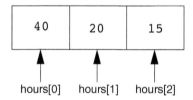

Array Initialization

When you create an array, you can optionally initialize it with a group of values. Here is an example:

```
const int SIZE = 5;
int numbersArray[SIZE] = { 10, 20, 30, 40, 50 };
```

The series of values inside the braces and separated with commas is called an *initialization list*. These values are stored in the array elements in the order they appear in the list. (The first value, 10, is stored in numbersArray[0], the second value, 20, is stored in numbersArray[1], and so forth).

When you provide an initialization list, the size declarator can be left out. The compiler will determine the size of the array from the number of items in the initialization list. Here is an example:

```
int numbersArray[] = { 10, 20, 30, 40, 50 };
```

In this example, the compiler will determine that the array should have five elements because five values appear in the initialization list.

Here are two separate examples that declare and initialize a string array named days. Each of these examples results in the same array:

```
// Example 1
const int SIZE = 7;
string days[SIZE] = { "Sunday", "Monday", "Tuesday",
                      "Wednesday", "Thursday",
                      "Friday","Saturday" };

// Example 2
const int SIZE = 7;
string days[] = { "Sunday", "Monday", "Tuesday",
                  "Wednesday", "Thursday",
                  "Friday","Saturday" };
```

Using a Loop to Step through an Array

You can store a number in an int variable and then use that variable as a subscript. This makes it possible to use a loop to step through an array, performing the same operation on each element. For example, look at the following code sample:

VideoNote

Accesing array elements with a loop

```
1   // Create an array to hold three integers.
2   const int SIZE = 3;
3   int myValues[SIZE];
4
5   // Assign 99 to each array element.
6   for (int index = 0; index < SIZE; index++)
7   {
8       myValues[index] = 99;
9   }
```

Line 3 creates an int array named myValues with three elements. The for loop that starts in line 6 uses an int variable named index as its counter. The index variable is initialized with the value 0 and is incremented after each loop iteration. The loop iterates as long as index is less than 3. Thus, the loop will iterate three times. As it iterates, the index variable will be assigned the values 0, 1, and 2.

Inside the loop, the statement in line 8 assigns the value 99 to an array element, using the index variable as the subscript. The following is what happens as the loop iterates.

- The first time the loop iterates, index will be set to 0, so 99 will be assigned to myValues[0].
- The second time the loop iterates, index will be set to 1, so 99 will be assigned to myValues[1].
- The third time the loop iterates, index will be set to 2, so 99 will be assigned to myValues [2].

NOTE: We should emphasize the fact that the loop shown in the previous code iterates as long as index *is less than* SIZE. Remember, the subscript of the last element in an array is one less than the size of the array. In this case, the subscript of the last element of the myValues array is 2, which is one less than SIZE. It would be an error to write the loop as shown in the following:

```
// Create an array to hold three integers.
const int SIZE = 3;
int myValues[SIZE];

// ERROR! This loop writes outside the array!
for (int index = 0; index <= SIZE; index++)
{
    myValues[index] = 99;
}
```

Can you spot the error in this code? The for loop iterates as long as index is less than or equal to SIZE. The last time the loop iterates, the index variable will be set to 3, and the statement inside the loop will try to assign the value 99 to myValues[3], which is a nonexistent element.

Program 6-2 shows a complete example, using two loops to process the contents of an array.

Program 6-2   (ArrayLoop.cpp)

```
 1 #include <iostream>
 2 using namespace std;
 3
 4 int main()
 5 {
 6     const int SIZE = 3;    // Constant for array size
 7     int hours[SIZE];       // Array to hold hours
 8
 9     // Get the hours for each employee.
10     for (int index = 0; index < SIZE; index++)
11     {
12         cout << "Enter the hours worked by employee "
13             << index + 1 << ": ";
14         cin >> hours[index];
15     }
16
17     // Display the values in the array.
18     cout << "The hours you entered are:" << endl;
19     for (int index = 0; index < SIZE; index++)
20     {
21         cout << hours[index] << endl;
22     }
23     return 0;
24 }
```

Program Output with Input Shown in Bold

```
Enter the hours worked by employee 1: 40 [Enter]
Enter the hours worked by employee 2: 20 [Enter]
Enter the hours worked by employee 3: 15 [Enter]
The hours you entered are:
40
20
15
```

Let's take a closer look at the first `for` loop, which appears in lines 10 through 15. Here is the first line of the loop:

```
for (int index = 0; index < SIZE; index++)
```

This specifies that the `index` variable will be initialized with the value 0 and will be incremented at the end of each iteration. The loop will iterate as long as `index` is less than `SIZE`. As a result, the `index` variable will be assigned the values 0 through 2 as the loop executes. Inside the loop, in line 14, the `index` variable is used as a subscript:

```
cin >> hours[index];
```

During the loop's first iteration, the `index` variable will be set to 0, so the user's input is stored in `hours[0]`. During the next iteration, the user's input is stored in `hours[1]`. Then, during the last iteration, the user's input is stored in `hours[2]`. Notice that the loop correctly starts and ends the `index` variable with valid subscript values (0 through 2).

The second `for` loop appears in lines 19 through 22. This loop also uses a variable named `index`, which takes on the values 0 through 2 as the loop iterates. The first time the loop iterates, the statement in line 21 displays the contents of `hours[0]`. The second time the loop iterates, the statement displays the contents of `hours[1]`. The third time the loop iterates, the statement displays the contents of `hours[2]`.

There is one last thing to point out about the program. Notice that the program output refers to the employees as "employee 1," "employee 2," and "employee 3." Here is the `cout` statement that appears inside the first `for` loop, in lines 12 and 13:

```
cout << "Enter the hours worked by employee "
     << index + 1 << ": ";
```

Notice that the statement uses the expression `index + 1` to display the employee number. What do you think would happen if we left out the `+ 1` part of the expression, and the statements were written like this?

```
cout << "Enter the hours worked by employee "
     << index << ": ";
```

Because the `index` variable is assigned the values 0, 1, and 2 as the loop runs, this statement would cause the program to refer to the employees as "employee 0," "employee 1," and "employee 2." Most people find it unnatural to start with 0 when counting people or things, so we used the expression `index + 1` to start the employee numbers at 1.

No Array Bounds Checking in C++

The C++ language does not perform *array bounds checking*, which means the C++ compiler does not check the values that you use as array subscripts to make sure they are valid. For example, look at the following code:

```cpp
// Create an array
const int SIZE = 5;
int numbers[SIZE];

// ERROR! The following statement uses an invalid
subscript!
numbers[5] = 99;
```

This code declares an array with five elements. The subscripts for the array's elements are 0 through 4. The last statement, however, attempts to assign a value to `numbers[5]`, a nonexistent element. If this code were part of a complete program, it would compile and execute. When the assignment statement executes, however, it will attempt to write the value 99 to an invalid location in memory. This is an error and will most likely cause the program to crash.

Watch for Off-by-One Errors

In working with arrays, a common type of mistake is the *off-by-one error*. This is an easy mistake to make because array subscripts start at 0 rather than 1. For example, look at the following code:

```cpp
// This code has an off-by-one error.
const int SIZE = 100;
int numbers[SIZE];

for (int index = 1; index <= SIZE; index++)
{
    numbers[index] = 0;
}
```

The intent of this code is to create an array of integers with 100 elements and store the value 0 in each element. However, this code has an off-by-one error. The loop uses the `index` variable as a subscript with the `numbers` array. During the loop's execution, the `index` variable takes on the values 1 through 100 when it should take on the values 0 through 99. As a result, the first element, which is at subscript 0, is skipped. In addition, the loop attempts to use 100 as a subscript during the last iteration. Because 100 is an invalid subscript, the program will write data beyond the array's boundaries.

Processing the Elements of an Array

Processing array elements is no different than processing other variables. In the previous programs, you saw how you can assign values to array elements, store input in array elements, and display the contents of array elements. The following *In the Spotlight* section shows how array elements can be used in math expressions.

In the Spotlight:
Using Array Elements in a Math Expression

Megan owns a small neighborhood coffee shop, and she has six employees who work as baristas (coffee bartenders). All the employees have the same hourly pay rate. Megan has asked you to design a program that will allow her to enter the number of hours worked by each employee and then display the amounts of all the employees' gross pay. You determine that the program should perform the following steps:

1. Get the hourly pay rate for all employees.
2. For each employee:
   Get the number of hours worked and store it in an array element.
3. For each array element:
   Use the value stored in the element to calculate an employee's gross pay.
   Display the amount of the gross pay.

Program 6-3 shows the code for the program.

Program 6-3   **(CoffeShopPayroll.cpp)**

```cpp
 1 #include <iostream>
 2 using namespace std;
 3
 4 int main()
 5 {
 6    const int SIZE = 6;      // Constant for array size
 7    int hours[SIZE];         // Array to hold employee's hours
 8    double payRate,          // To hold pay rate
 9           grossPay;         // To hold gross pay
10
11    // Get the hourly pay rate for all employees.
12    cout << "Enter the hourly pay rate: ";
13    cin >> payRate;
14
15    // Get the hours for each employee.
16    for (int index = 0; index < SIZE; index++)
17    {
18       cout << "Enter the hours worked by employee "
19            << index + 1 << ": ";
20       cin >> hours[index];
21    }
22
23    // Display each employee's gross pay.
24    cout << "Gross pay for each employee:" << endl;
25    for (int index = 0; index < SIZE; index++)
26    {
27       grossPay = hours[index] * payRate;
28       cout << "Employee " << index + 1
29            << ": $" << grossPay << endl;
30    }
31    return 0;
32 }
```

Program Output with Input Shown in Bold

```
Enter the hourly pay rate: 12.00 [Enter]
Enter the hours worked by employee 1: 10 [Enter]
Enter the hours worked by employee 2: 20 [Enter]
Enter the hours worked by employee 3: 15 [Enter]
Enter the hours worked by employee 4: 40 [Enter]
Enter the hours worked by employee 5: 20 [Enter]
Enter the hours worked by employee 6: 18 [Enter]
Gross pay for each employee:
Employee 1: $120
Employee 2: $240
Employee 3: $180
Employee 4: $480
Employee 5: $240
Employee 6: $216
```

NOTE: Suppose Megan's business increases, and she has to hire two additional baristas. This would require you to change the program so it processes 8 employees instead of 6. Because you used a named constant for the array size, this is a simple modification—you just have to change the statement in line 6 to read:

```
const int SIZE = 8;
```

Because the SIZE constant is used as the array size declarator in line 7, the size of the hours array will automatically become 8. Also, because you used the SIZE constant to control the loop iterations in lines 16 and 25, the loops will automatically iterate 8 times, once for each employee.

Imagine how much more difficult this modification would be if you had not used a named constant to specify the array size. You would have to change each individual statement in the program that refers to the array size. Not only would this require more work, but it would also open the possibility for errors. If you overlooked only one of the statements that refer to the array size, a bug would occur.

 Checkpoint

6.1. Can you store a mixture of data types in an array?

6.2. What is an array size declarator?

6.3. Can the size of an array be changed while the program is running?

6.4. What is an array element?

6.5. What is a subscript?

6.6. What is the first subscript in an array?

6.7. Look at the following code sample and answer questions a through d.

```cpp
const int SIZE = 7;
double numbers[SIZE];
```

   a. What is the name of the array that is being declared?
   b. What is the size of the array?
   c. What data type are the array elements?
   d. What is the subscript of the last element in the array?

6.8. What does "array bounds checking" mean?

6.9. What is an off-by-one error?

6.2 Sequentially Searching an Array

CONCEPT: The sequential search algorithm is a simple technique for finding an item in an array. It steps through the array, beginning at the first element, and compares each element to the item being searched for. The search stops when the item is found or the end of the array is reached.

Programs commonly need to search for data that is stored in an array. Various techniques known as *search algorithms* have been developed to locate a specific item in a larger collection of data, such as an array. This section shows you how to use the simplest of all search algorithms—the sequential search. The *sequential search algorithm* uses a loop to sequentially step through an array, starting with the first element. It compares each element with the value being searched for and stops when the value is found or the end of the array is encountered. If the value being searched for is not in the array, the algorithm unsuccessfully searches to the end of the array.

Figure 6-4 shows the general logic of the sequential search algorithm. Here is a summary of the data items in the figure:

- array is the array being searched.
- searchValue is the value that the algorithm is searching for.
- found is a bool variable that is used as a flag. Setting found to false indicates that searchValue has not been found. Setting found to true indicates that searchValue has been found.
- index is an int variable used to step through the elements of the array.

When the algorithm finishes, the found variable will be set to true if the searchValue was found in the array. When this is the case, the index variable will be set to the subscript of the element containing the searchValue. If the searchValue was not found in the array, found will be set to false. The following shows the C++ code for this logic:

```cpp
found = false;
index = 0;
while (found == false && index < SIZE)
```

```
        {
            if (array[index] == searchValue)
            {
                found = true;
            }
            else
            {
                index = index + 1;
            }
        }
```

Figure 6-4 Sequential search logic

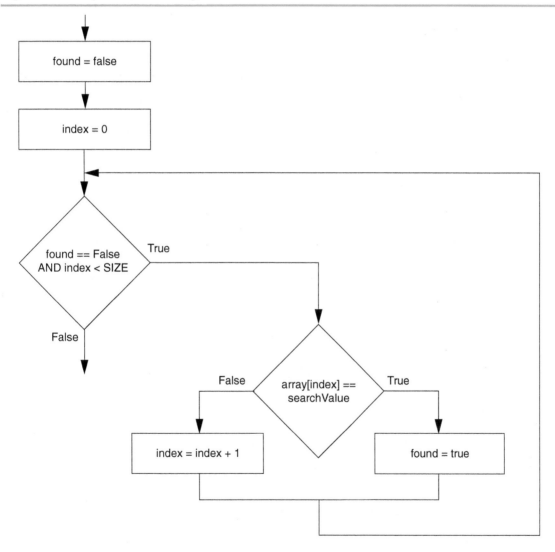

The code in Program 6-4 demonstrates how to implement the sequential search in a program. This program has an array that holds test scores. It sequentially searches the array for a score of 100. If a score of 100 is found, the program displays the test number.

Program 6-4   (SequentialSearch.cpp)

```cpp
 1 #include <iostream>
 2 using namespace std;
 3
 4 int main()
 5 {
 6    // Constant for the array size.
 7    const int SIZE = 10;
 8
 9    // Declare an array to hold test scores.
10    int scores[SIZE] = { 87, 75, 98, 100, 82,
11                         72, 88, 92, 60,  78 };
12
13    // Declare a Boolean variable to act as a flag.
14    bool found;
15
16    // Declare a variable to step through the array.
17    int index;
18
19    // The flag must initially be set to False.
20    found = false;
21
22    // Set the counter variable to 0.
23    index = 0;
24
25    // Step through the array searching for a
26    // score equal to 100.
27    while (found == false && index < SIZE)
28    {
29       if (scores[index] == 100)
30       {
31          found = true;
32       }
33       else
34       {
35          index = index + 1;
36       }
37    }
38
39    // Display the search results.
40    if (found)
41    {
42       cout << "you earned 100 on test number "
43            << (index + 1) << endl;
44    }
45    else
46    {
47       cout << "you did not earn 100 on any test." << endl;
48    }
49    return 0;
50 }
```

Program Output

```
You earned 100 on test number 4
```

Searching a String Array

Program 6-4 demonstrates how to use the sequential search algorithm to find a specific number in an int array. As shown in Program 6-5, you can also use the algorithm to find a string in a string array.

Program 6-5   (StringSearch.cpp)

```cpp
 1 #include <iostream>
 2 #include <string>
 3 using namespace std;
 4
 5 int main()
 6 {
 7    // Declare a constant for the array size.
 8    const int SIZE = 6;
 9
10    // Declare a string array initialized with values.
11    string cars[SIZE] = { "BMW", "Audi", "Lamborghini",
12                          "Mercedes", "Porsche", "Ferrari" };
13
14    // Declare a variable to hold the search value.
15    string searchValue;
16
17    // Declare a Boolean variable to act as a flag.
18    bool found;
19
20    // Declare a variable to step through the array.
21    int index;
22
23    // The flag must initially be set to False.
24    found = false;
25
26    // Set the counter variable to 0.
27    index = 0;
28
29    // Get the string to search for.
30    cout << "What car should I search for? ";
31    cin >> searchValue;
32
33    // Step through the array searching for
34    // the specified name.
35    while (found == false && index < SIZE)
36    {
37       if (cars[index] == searchValue)
38       {
39          found = true;
40       }
41       else
42       {
43          index = index + 1;
44       }
45    }
46
```

```
47      // Display the search results.
48      if (found)
49      {
50          cout << "That car was found in element "
51                  << index << endl;
52      }
53      else
54      {
55          cout << "That car was not found in the array." << endl;
56      }
57      return 0;
58 }
```

Program Output with Input Shown in Bold

```
What car should I search for? Mercedes [Enter]
That car was found in element 3
```

Program Output

```
What car should I search for? Fiat [Enter]
That car was not found in the array.
```

 Checkpoint

6.10. What is a search algorithm?

6.11. Which array element does the sequential search algorithm look at first?

6.12. What does the loop do in the sequential search algorithm? What happens when the value being searched for is found?

6.13. How many elements does the sequential search algorithm look at in the case that the search value is not found in the array?

 6.3 Processing the Contents of an Array

In this chapter you've seen several examples of how loops are used to step through the elements of an array. You can perform many operations on an array using a loop, and this section examines several such algorithms.

Copying an Array

If you need to copy the contents of one array to another, you have to assign the individual elements of the array that you are copying to the elements of the other array. Usually this is best done with a loop. For example, look at the following code:

```
const int SIZE = 5;
int firstArray[SIZE] = { 100, 200, 300, 400, 500 };
int secondArray[SIZE];
```

Suppose you wish to copy the values in `firstArray` to `secondArray`. The following code assigns each element of `firstArray` to the corresponding element in `secondArray`.

```
for (int index = 0; index < SIZE; index++)
{
    secondArray[index] = firstArray[index];
}
```

Comparing Arrays

You cannot use the == operator to compare two arrays and determine whether the arrays are equal. For example, the following code sample appears to compare two arrays, but in reality does not:

```
 1 const int SIZE = 5;
 2 int firstArray[SIZE]  = { 5, 10, 15, 20, 25 };
 3 int secondArray[SIZE] = { 5, 10, 15, 20, 25 };
 4
 5 if (firstArray == secondArray) // This is a mistake.
 6 {
 7     cout << "The arrays are the same." << endl;
 8 }
 9 else
10 {
11     cout << "The arrays are not the same." << endl;
12 }
```

When you use the == operator with two arrays, the operator compares the arrays' starting memory addresses, not the contents of the arrays. Because the `firstArray` and `secondArray` variables in this example are stored at different memory addresses, the result of the Boolean expression `firstArray == secondArray` is false, and the code reports that the arrays are not the same.

To compare the contents of two arrays, you must compare the individual elements of the two arrays. Program 6-6 shows an example.

Program 6-6   (`CompareArrays.cpp`)

```
1 #include <iostream>
2 using namespace std;
3
4 int main()
```

```
 5 {
 6     // Declare a constant for the array size.
 7     const int SIZE = 5;
 8
 9     // Declare and initialize two arrays.
10     int firstArray[SIZE]  = { 5, 10, 15, 20, 25 };
11     int secondArray[SIZE] = { 5, 10, 15, 20, 25 };
12
13     // Variables
14     bool arraysEqual = true; // Flag variable
15     int index = 0;           // To hold array subscripts
16
17     // Determine whether the elements contain the same data.
18     while (arraysEqual && index < SIZE)
19     {
20         if (firstArray[index] != secondArray[index])
21         {
22             arraysEqual = false;
23         }
24         index++;
25     }
26
27     // Display the results.
28     if (arraysEqual)
29     {
30         cout << "The arrays are equal." << endl;
31     }
32     else
33     {
34         cout << "The arrays are not equal." << endl;
35     }
36     return 0;
37 }
```

Program Output

```
The arrays are equal.
```

This program determines whether firstArray and secondArray (declared in lines 10 and 11) contain the same values. A bool flag variable, arraysEqual, declared and initialized to true, is declared in line 14. The arraysEqual variable is used to signal whether the arrays are equal. Another variable, index, is declared and initialized to 0 in line 15. The index variable is used in a loop to step through the arrays.

Then a while loop begins in line 18. The loop executes as long as arraysEqual is true and the index variable is less than SIZE. During each iteration, it compares a different set of corresponding elements in the arrays. When it finds two corresponding elements that have different values, the flag variable arraysEqual is set to false.

After the loop finishes, an `if` statement examines the `arraysEqual` variable in line 28. If the variable is `true`, then the arrays are equal, and a message indicating so is displayed in line 30. Otherwise, they are not equal, so a different message is displayed in line 34.

Totaling the Values in an Array

To calculate the total of the values in a numeric array, you use a loop with an accumulator variable. Recall from Chapter 4 that an accumulator is a variable that is used to accumulate the total of a series of numbers. First, the accumulator is initialized with 0. Then, the loop steps through the array, adding the value of each array element to the accumulator.

Program 6-7   **(TotalArray.cpp)**

```
 1 #include <iostream>
 2 using namespace std;
 3
 4 int main()
 5 {
 6    // Declare a constant for the array size.
 7    const int SIZE = 5;
 8
 9    // Create an int array.
10    int numbers[SIZE] = { 2, 4, 6, 8, 10 };
11
12    // Declare and initialize an accumulator variable.
13    int total = 0;
14
15    // Step through the array, adding each element to
16    // the accumulator.
17    for (int index = 0; index < SIZE; index++)
18    {
19       total += numbers[index];
20    }
21
22    // Display the total.
23    cout << "The total is " << total << endl;
24    return 0;
25 }
```

Program Output

```
The total is 30
```

Averaging the Values in an Array

The first step in calculating the average of all the values in a numeric array is to get the total of the values. The second step is to divide the total by the number of elements in the array. Program 6-8 shows an example.

Program 6-8   (AverageArray.cpp)

```cpp
 1 #include <iostream>
 2 using namespace std;
 3
 4 int main()
 5 {
 6     // Declare a constant for the array size.
 7     const int SIZE = 4;
 8
 9     // Declare an array.
10     double scores[SIZE] = { 92.5, 81.6, 65.7, 72.8 };
11
12     // Declare and initialize an accumulator variable.
13     double total = 0.0;
14
15     // Declare a variable to hold the average.
16     double average;
17
18     // Step through the array, adding each element to
19     // the accumulator.
20     for (int index = 0; index < SIZE; index++)
21     {
22         total += scores[index];
23     }
24
25     // Calculate the average.
26     average = total / SIZE;
27
28     // Display the average.
29     cout << "The average is " <<  average << endl;
30     return 0;
31 }
```

Program Output

```
The average is 78.15
```

The loop in lines 20 through 23 gets the sum of the array elements, and line 26 divides the sum by the size of the array. Notice that the calculation in line 26 is not inside the loop. This statement should only execute once, after the loop has finished its iterations.

Finding the Highest and Lowest Values in an Array

Some programming tasks require you to find the highest value in a set of data. Examples include programs that report the highest sales amount for a given time period, the highest test score in a set of test scores, the highest temperature for a given set of days, and so forth.

The algorithm for finding the highest value in an array works like this: You create a variable to hold the highest value (the following example names this variable highest). Then, you assign the value at element 0 to the highest variable. Next, you use a loop to step through the rest of the array elements, beginning at element 1. Each time the loop iterates, it compares an array element to the highest variable. If the array element is greater than the highest variable, then the value in the array element is assigned to the highest variable. When the loop finishes, the highest variable will contain the highest value in the array. The flowchart in Figure 6-5 illustrates this logic. Program 6-9 shows a simple demonstration of the algorithm.

Figure 6-5 Flowchart for finding the highest value in an array

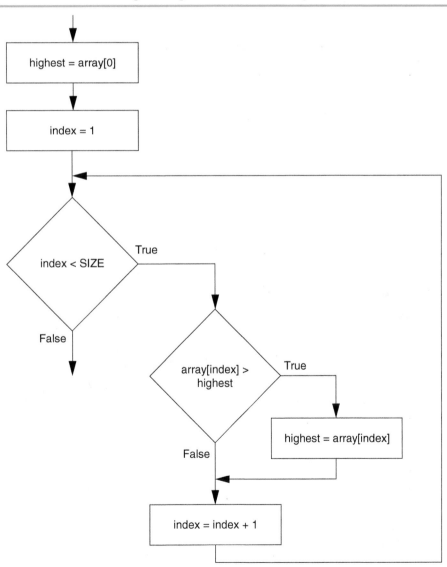

Program 6-9   (`HighestElement.cpp`)

```cpp
 1 #include <iostream>
 2 using namespace std;
 3
 4 int main()
 5 {
 6    // Declare a constant for the array size.
 7    const int SIZE = 5;
 8
 9    // Declare an array.
10    int numbers[SIZE] = { 8, 1, 12, 6, 2 };
11
12    // Declare a variable to hold the highest value, and
13    // initialize it with the first value in the array.
14    int highest = numbers[0];
15
16    // Step through the rest of the array, beginning at
17    // element 1. When a value greater than highest is found,
18    // assign that value to highest.
19    for (int index = 1; index < SIZE; index++)
20    {
21       if (numbers[index] > highest)
22       {
23          highest = numbers[index];
24       }
25    }
26
27    // Display the highest value.
28    cout << "The highest value is " << highest << endl;
29    return 0;
30 }
```

Program Output

```
The highest value is 12
```

In some programs you are more interested in finding the lowest value than the highest value in a set of data. For example, suppose you are writing a program that stores several players' golf scores in an array, and you need to find the best score. In golf, the lower the score the better, so you would need an algorithm that finds the lowest value in the array.

The algorithm for finding the lowest value in an array is very similar to the algorithm for finding the highest score. It works like this: You create a variable to hold the lowest value (the following example names this variable `lowest`). Then, you assign the value at element 0 to the `lowest` variable. Next, you use a loop to step through the rest of the array elements, beginning at element 1. Each time the loop iterates, it compares an array element to the `lowest` variable. If the array element is less than the `lowest` variable, then the value in the array element is assigned to the `lowest` variable. When the loop finishes, the `lowest` variable will contain the lowest

Figure 6-6 Flowchart for finding the lowest value in an array

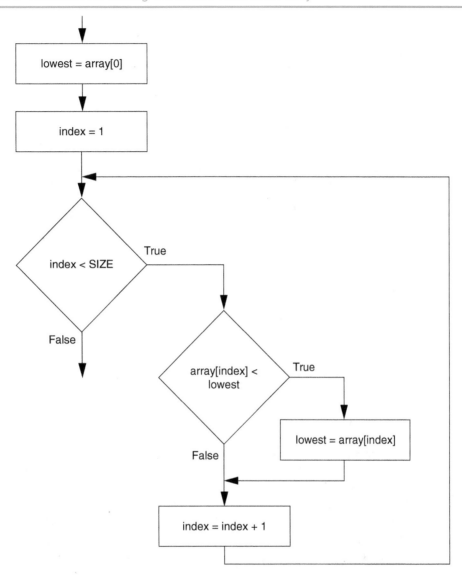

value in the array. The flowchart in Figure 6-6 illustrates this logic. Program 6-10 demonstrates this algorithm.

Program 6-10   (LowestElement.cpp)

```
1 #include <iostream>
2 using namespace std;
3
4 int main()
5 {
6    // Declare a constant for the array size.
7    const int SIZE = 5;
```

```
 8
 9      // Declare an array.
10      int numbers[SIZE] = { 8, 1, 12, 6, 2 };
11
12      // Declare a variable to hold the lowest value, and
13      // initialize it with the first value in the array.
14      int lowest = numbers[0];
15
16      // Step through the rest of the array, beginning at
17      // element 1. When a value less than lowest is found,
18      // assign that value to lowest.
19      for (int index = 1; index < SIZE; index++)
20      {
21         if (numbers[index] < lowest)
22         {
23            lowest = numbers[index];
24         }
25      }
26
27      // Display the lowest value.
28      cout << "The lowest value is " << lowest << endl;
29      return 0;
30 }
```

Program Output

```
The lowest value is 1
```

Passing an Array as an Argument to a Function

VideoNote

Passing an array to a function

You can pass an array as an argument to a function, which gives you the ability to modularize many of the operations that you perform on the array. Passing an array as an argument typically requires that you pass two arguments: (1) the array itself, and (2) an integer that specifies the number of elements in the array. The following code shows a function that has been written to accept an array as an argument:

```
void showArray(int array[], int size)
{
    for (int i = 0; i < size; i++)
    {
        cout << array[i] << " ";
    }
}
```

Notice that the parameter variable, array, is declared as an int array, without a size declarator. When we call this function, we must pass an int array to it as an argument. Let's assume that numbers is the name of an int array, and SIZE is a constant that specifies the size of the array. Here is a statement that calls the showArray function, passing the numbers array and SIZE as arguments:

```
showArray(numbers, SIZE);
```

Program 6-11 shows another example. This program has a function that accepts an int array as an argument. The function returns the total of the array's elements.

Program 6-11   (`ArrayArgument.cpp`)

```cpp
 1 #include <iostream>
 2 using namespace std;
 3
 4 // Function prototype
 5 int getTotal(int[], int );
 6
 7 int main()
 8 {
 9    // A constant for the array size
10    const int SIZE = 5;
11
12    // An array initialized with values
13    int numbers[SIZE] = { 2, 4, 6, 8, 10 };
14
15    // A variable to hold the sum of the elements
16    int sum;
17
18    // Get the sum of the elements.
19    sum = getTotal(numbers, SIZE);
20
21    // Display the sum of the array elements.
22    cout << "The sum of the array elements is "
23         << sum << endl;
24
25    return 0;
26 }
27
28 // The getTotal function accepts an Integer array, and the
29 // array's size as arguments. It returns the total of the
30 // array elements.
31 int getTotal(int arr[], int size)
32 {
33    // Accumulator, initialized to 0
34    int total = 0;
35
36    // Calculate the total of the array elements.
37    for (int index = 0; index < size; index++)
38    {
39       total = total + arr[index];
40    }
41
42    // Return the total.
43    return total;
44 }
```

Program Output

```
The sum of the array elements is 30
```

In the main function, an int array is declared in line 13 and initialized with five values. In line 19, the following statement calls the getTotal function and assigns its return value to the sum variable:

```
sum = getTotal(numbers, SIZE);
```

This statement passes two arguments to the getTotal function: the numbers array and the value of the SIZE constant. Here is the first line of the getTotal function, which appears in line 31:

```
int getTotal(int arr[], int size)
```

Notice that the function has the following two parameters:

- int arr[]—This parameter accepts an array of ints as an argument.
- int size—This parameter accepts an integer that specifies the number of elements in the array.

When the function is called in line 19, it passes the numbers array into the arr parameter and the value of the SIZE constant into the size parameter. This is shown in Figure 6-7. The function then calculates the total of the values in array and returns that value.

Figure 6-7 Passing arguments to the getTotal function

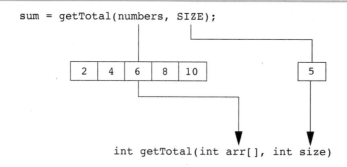

Partially Filled Arrays

Sometimes you need to store a series of items in an array, but you do not know the total number of items. As a result, you do not know the exact number of elements needed for the array. One solution is to make the array large enough to hold the largest possible number of items. This can lead to another problem, however. If the actual number of items stored in the array is less than the number of elements, the array will only be partially filled. When you process a partially filled array, you must process only the elements that contain valid data items.

A partially filled array is normally used with an accompanying integer variable that holds the number of items stored in the array. For example, suppose a program uses the following code to create an array named myNumbers with 100 elements and an int variable named count that will hold the number of items stored in the array:

```
const int SIZE = 100;
int myNumbers[SIZE];
int count = 0;
```

Each time we add an item to the array, we must increment count. The following code demonstrates:

```cpp
int number;

// Get a number from the user.
cout << "Enter a number or -1 to quit: ";
cin >> number;

// Add numbers to the myNumbers array until the user
// enters -1.
while (number != -1 && count < SIZE)
{
    // Increment count.
    count++;

    // Add the number to the array.
    myNumbers[count - 1] = number;

    // Get the next number
    cout << "Enter a number or -1 to quit: ";
    cin >> number;
}
```

Each iteration of this loop allows the user to enter a number to be stored in the array, or –1 to quit. The count variable is incremented and then used to calculate the subscript of the next available element in the array. When the user enters –1, or count exceeds 99, the loop stops. The following code displays all the valid items in the array:

```cpp
for (int index = 0; index < count; index++)
{
    cout << myNumbers[index] << endl;
}
```

Notice that this code uses count instead of the array size to determine where the array subscripts end.

Program 6-12 shows an example that uses a partially filled array.

Program 6-12   (**PartiallyFilledArray.cpp**)

```cpp
 1 #include <iostream>
 2 using namespace std;
 3
 4 int main()
 5 {
 6     // Declare a constant for the array size.
 7     const int SIZE = 100;
 8
 9     // Declare an array.
10     int values[SIZE];
11
```

```
12     // Declare a variable to hold the number of items
13     // that are actually stored in the array.
14     int count = 0;
15
16     // Declare a variable to hold the user's input.
17     int number;
18
19     // Prompt the user to enter a number. If the user enters
20     // -1 we will stop accepting input.
21     cout << "Enter a number or -1 to quit: ";
22     cin >> number;
23
24     // If the input is not -1 and the array is not
25     // full, process the input.
26     while (number != -1 && count < SIZE)
27     {
28        // Store the input in the array.
29        values[count] = number;
30
31        // Increment count.
32        count++;
33
34        // Prompt the user for the next number.
35        cout << "Enter a number or -1 to quit: ";
36        cin >> number;
37     }
38
39     // Display the values stored in the array.
40     cout < "Here are the numbers you entered:" << endl;
41     for (int index = 0; index < count; index++)
42     {
43        cout << values[index] << endl;
44     }
45     return 0;
46 }
```

Program Output with Input Shown in Bold

```
Enter a number or -1 to quit: 2 [Enter]
Enter a number or -1 to quit: 4 [Enter]
Enter a number or -1 to quit: 6 [Enter]
Enter a number or -1 to quit: -1 [Enter]
Here are the numbers you entered:
2
4
6
```

Let's examine the code in detail. Line 7 declares a constant, SIZE, initialized with the value 100. Line 10 declares an int array named values, using SIZE as the size declarator. As a result, the values array will have 100 elements. Line 14 declares an int variable named count, which will hold the number of items that are stored in the values array. Notice that count is initialized with 0 because no values are stored in the array. Line 17 declares an `int` variable named `number` that will hold values entered by the user.

Line 21 prompts the user to enter a number or –1 to quit. When the user enters –1, the program will stop reading input. Line 22 reads the user's input and stores it in the `number` variable. A `while` loop begins in line 26. The loop iterates as long as `number` is not –1 and `count` is less than the size of the array. Inside the loop, in line 29 the `numbers` variable is assigned to `values[count]`, and in line 32 the `count` variable is incremented. (Each time a number is assigned to an array element, the `count` variable is incremented. As a result, the `count` variable will hold the number of items that are stored in the array.) Then, line 35 prompts the user to enter another number (or –1 to quit), and line 36 reads the user's input into the `number` variable. The loop then starts over.

When the user enters –1, or `count` reaches the size of the array, the `while` loop stops. The `for` loop that begins in line 41 displays all the items that are stored in the array. Rather than stepping through all of the elements in the array, however, the loop steps through only the elements that contain values. Notice that the loop iterates as long as `index` is less than `count`. The loop will stop when the element containing the last valid value has been displayed, not when the end of the array has been reached.

In the Spotlight:
Processing an Array

Dr. LaClaire gives four exams during the semester in her chemistry class. At the end of the semester she drops each student's lowest test score before averaging the scores. She has asked you to write a program that will read a student's four test scores as input and calculate the average with the lowest score dropped. Here is the pseudocode algorithm that you developed:

> *Read the student's four test scores.*
> *Calculate the total of the scores.*
> *Find the lowest score.*
> *Subtract the lowest score from the total. This gives the adjusted total.*
> *Divide the adjusted total by 3. This is the average.*
> *Display the average.*

Program 6-13 shows the program, which is modularized. Rather than presenting the entire program at once, let's first examine the `main` function and then each additional function separately. Here is the first part of the program, including the `main` function:

Program 6-13   (main function)

```
1 #include <iostream>
2 using namespace std;
3
4 // Function prototypes
5 void getTestScores(double[], int);
```

```
 6 double getTotal(double[], int);
 7 double getLowest(double[], int);
 8
 9 int main()
10 {
11    const int SIZE = 4;         // Array size
12    double testScores[SIZE],    // Array of test scores
13           total,               // Total of the scores
14           lowestScore,         // Lowest test score
15           average;             // Average test score
16
17    // Get the test scores from the user.
18    getTestScores(testScores, SIZE);
19
20    // Get the total of the test scores.
21    total = getTotal(testScores, SIZE);
22
23    // Get the lowest test score.
24    lowestScore = getLowest(testScores, SIZE);
25
26    // Subtract the lowest score from the total.
27    total -= lowestScore;
28
29    // Calculate the average. Divide by 3 because
30    // the lowest test score was dropped.
31    average = total / (SIZE - 1);
32
33    // Display the average.
34    cout << "The average with the lowest score "
35         << "dropped is " << average << ".\n";
36
37    return 0;
38 }
39
```

Lines 11 through 15 define the following items:

- SIZE, an int constant that is used as an array size declarator
- testScores, a double array to hold the test scores
- total, a double variable that will hold the test score totals
- lowestScore, a double variable that will hold the lowest test score
- average, a double variable that will hold the average of the test scores

Line 18 calls the getTestScores function, passing the testScores array and the value of the SIZE constant as arguments. The function gets the test scores from the user and stores them in the array.

Line 21 calls the getTotal function, passing the testScores array and the value of the SIZE constant as arguments. The function returns the total of the values in the array. This value is assigned to the total variable.

Line 23 calls the getLowest function, passing the testScores array and the value of the SIZE constant as arguments. The function returns the lowest value in the array. This value is assigned to the lowestScore variable.

Line 27 subtracts the lowest test score from the total variable. Then, line 31 calculates the average by dividing total by SIZE − 1. (The program divides by SIZE − 1 because the lowest test score was dropped.) Lines 34 and 35 display the average.

The getTestScores function appears next, as shown here:

Program 6-13   **(getTestScores function)**

```
40 // The getTestScores function accepts an array and its size
41 // as arguments. It prompts the user to enter test scores,
42 // which are stored in the array.
43 void getTestScores(double scores[], int size)
44 {
45    // Get each test score.
46    for(int index = 0; index <= size - 1; index++)
47    {
48       cout << "Enter test score number "
49            << (index + 1) << ": ";
50       cin > scores[index];
51    }
52 }
53
```

The getTestScores function has two parameters:

- scores[]—A double array
- size—An int specifying the size of the array that is passed into the scores[] parameter

The purpose of this function is to get a student's test scores from the user and store them in the array that is passed as an argument into the scores[] parameter.

The getTotal function appears next, as shown here:

Program 6-13   **(getTotal function)**

```
54 // The getTotal function accepts a double array
55 // and its size as arguments. The sum of the array's
56 // elements is returned as a double.
57 double getTotal(double array[], int size)
58 {
59    double total = 0; // Accumulator
60
61    // Add each element to total.
62    for (int count = 0; count < size; count++)
63    {
64       total += array[count];
65    }
66
67    // Return the total.
68    return total;
69 }
70
```

The getTotal function has two parameters:

- array[ ]—A double array
- size—An int specifying the size of the array that is passed into the array[ ] parameter

This function returns the total of the values in the array that is passed as an argument into the array[ ] parameter.

The getLowest function appears next, as shown here:

Program 6-13 (getlowest function)

```
71  // The getLowest function accepts a double array and
72  // its size as arguments. The lowest value in the
73  // array is returned as a double.
74  double getLowest(double array[], int size)
75  {
76     double lowest;   // To hold the lowest value
77
78     // Get the first array's first element.
79     lowest = array[0];
80
81     // Step through the rest of the array. When a
82     // value less than lowest is found, assign it
83     // to lowest.
84     for (int count = 1; count < size; count++)
85     {
86        if (array[count] < lowest)
87        {
88             lowest = array[count];
89        }
90     }
91
92     // Return the lowest value.
93     return lowest;
94  }
```

The getLowest function has two parameters:

- array[ ]—A double array
- size—An int specifying the size of the array that is passed into the array[ ] parameter

This function returns the lowest value in the array that is passed as an argument into the array[ ] parameter. Here is an example of the program's output:

Program Output with Example Input Shown in Bold

```
Enter test score number 1: 92 [Enter]
Enter test score number 2: 67 [Enter]
Enter test score number 3: 75 [Enter]
Enter test score number 4: 88 [Enter]
The average with the lowest score dropped is 85
```

 **Checkpoint**

6.14. Briefly describe how you calculate the total of the values in an array.

6.15. Briefly describe how you get the average of the values in an array.

6.16. Describe the algorithm for finding the highest value in an array.

6.17. Describe the algorithm for finding the lowest value in an array.

6.18. How do you copy the contents of one array to another array?

6.4 Parallel Arrays

CONCEPT: By using the same subscript, you can establish relationships between data stored in two or more arrays.

Sometimes it is useful to store related data in two or more arrays. For example, assume you have designed a program with the following array declarations:

```
const int SIZE = 5;
string names[SIZE];
int idNumbers[SIZE];
```

The names array stores the names of five people, and the idNumbers array stores the ID numbers of the same five people. The data for each person is stored in the same relative location in each array. For instance, the first person's name is stored in names[0], and that same person's ID number is stored in idNumbers[0]. Figure 6-8 illustrates this. To

Figure 6-8 The names and idNumbers arrays

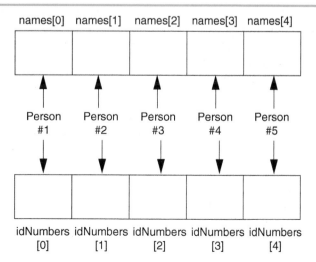

access the data, you use the same subscript with both arrays. For example, the loop in the following code displays each person's name and address:

```
for (int index = 0; index < SIZE; index++)
{
    cout << names[index] << endl;
    cout << addresses[index] << endl;
}
```

The names and idNumbers arrays are examples of parallel arrays. *Parallel arrays* are two or more arrays that hold related data, and the related elements in each array are accessed with a common subscript.

Program 6-14, another payroll program variation, demonstrates. It uses two arrays: one to store the hours worked by each employee (as ints), and another to store each employee's hourly pay rate (as doubles).

Program 6-14   (ParallelArrays.cpp)

```
 1 #include <iostream>
 2 using namespace std;
 3 int main()
 4 {
 5     const int NUM_EMPLOYEES = 3;   // Number of employees
 6     int hours[NUM_EMPLOYEES];      // Holds hours worked
 7     double payRate[NUM_EMPLOYEES]; // Holds pay rates
 8     double grossPay;               // Holds gross pay
 9
10     // Input the hours worked and the hourly pay rate.
11     cout << "Enter the hours worked by " << NUM_EMPLOYEES
12         << " employees and their" << endl;
13     cout << "hourly pay rates." << endl;
14
15     for (int index = 0; index < NUM_EMPLOYEES; index++)
16     {
17         cout << "Hours worked by employee #"
18             << index+1 << ": ";
19         cin >> hours[index];
20
21         cout << "Hourly pay rate for employee #"
22             << index+1 << ": ";
23         cin >> payRate[index];
24     }
25
26     // Display each employee's gross pay.
27     cout << "Gross pay for each employee:" << endl;
28     for (int index = 0; index < NUM_EMPLOYEES; index++)
29     {
30         grossPay = hours[index] * payRate[index];
31         cout << "Employee #" << index + 1
32             << ": $" << grossPay << endl;
33     }
34     return 0;
35 }
```

Program Output with Input Shown in Bold

```
Enter the hours worked by 3 employees and their
hourly pay rates.
Hours worked by employee #1: 15 [Enter]
Hourly pay rate for employee #1: 10.00 [Enter]
Hours worked by employee #2: 20 [Enter]
Hourly pay rate for employee #2: 12.00 [Enter]
Hours worked by employee #3: 40 [Enter]
Hourly pay rate for employee #3: 15.00 [Enter]
Here is the gross pay for each employee:
Employee #1: $150
Employee #2: $240
Employee #3: $600
```

 Checkpoint

6.19. How do you establish a relationship between the data stored in two parallel arrays?

6.20. A program uses two parallel arrays: names and creditScore. The names array holds customer names, and the creditScore array holds customer credit scores. If a particular customer's name is stored in names[82], where would that customer's credit score be stored?

6.5 Two-Dimensional Arrays

CONCEPT: A two-dimensional array is like several identical arrays put together. It is useful for storing multiple sets of data.

The arrays that you have studied so far are known as one-dimensional arrays. They are called *one dimensional* because they can hold only one set of data. Two-dimensional arrays, which are also called *2-D arrays,* can hold multiple sets of data. Think of a two-dimensional array as having rows and columns of elements, as shown in Figure 6-9.

Figure 6-9 A two-dimensional array

	Column 0	Column 1	Column 2	Column 3
Row 0				
Row 1				
Row 2				

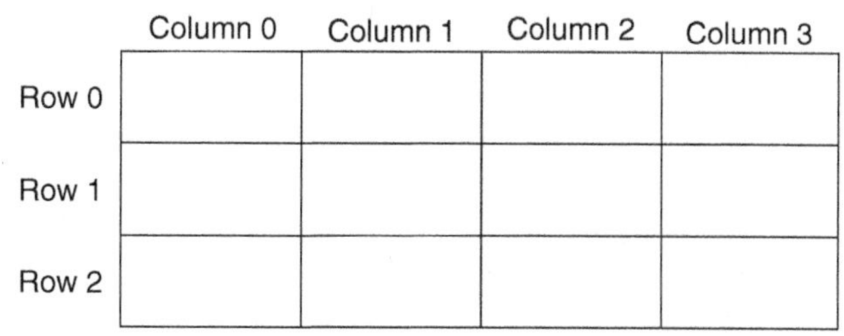

This figure shows a two-dimensional array having three rows and four columns. Notice that the rows are numbered 0, 1, and 2, and the columns are numbered 0, 1, 2, and 3. This creates a total of twelve elements in the array.

Two-dimensional arrays are useful for working with multiple sets of data. For example, suppose you are designing a grade-averaging program for a teacher. The teacher has six students, and each student takes five exams during the semester. One approach would be to create six one-dimensional arrays, one for each student. Each of these arrays would have five elements, one for each exam score. This approach would be cumbersome, however, because you would have to separately process each of the arrays. A better approach would be to use a two-dimensional array with six rows (one for each student) and five columns (one for each exam score), as shown in Figure 6-10.

Figure 6-10 Two-dimensional array with six rows and five columns

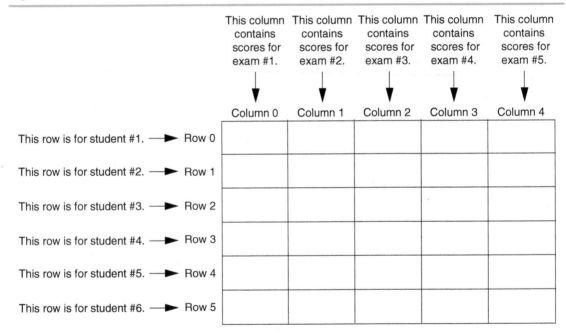

Declaring a Two-Dimensional Array

To declare a two-dimensional array, two size declarators are required: The first one is for the number of rows, and the second one is for the number of columns. The following code sample shows an example of how to declare a two-dimensional array:

```
int values[3][4];
```

This statement declares a two-dimensional integer array with three rows and four columns. The name of the array is `values`, and it has a total of twelve elements in the array. As with one-dimensional arrays, it is best to use named constants as the size declarators. Here is an example:

```
const int ROWS = 3;
const int COLS = 4;
int values[ROWS][COLS];
```

When processing the data in a two-dimensional array, each element has two subscripts: one for its row and another for its column. In the values array, the elements in row 0 are referenced as follows:

```
values[0][0]
values[0][1]
values[0][2]
values[0][3]
```

The elements in row 1 are as follows:

```
values[1][0]
values[1][1]
values[1][2]
values[1][3]
```

And the elements in row 2 are as follows:

```
values[2][0]
values[2][1]
values[2][2]
values[2][3]
```

Figure 6-11 illustrates the array with the subscripts shown for each element.

Figure 6-11 Array with subscripts shown for each element

	Column 0	Column 1	Column 2	Column 3
Row 0	values[0][0]	values[0][1]	values[0][2]	values[0][3]
Row 1	values[1][0]	values[1][1]	values[1][2]	values[1][3]
Row 2	values[2][0]	values[2][1]	values[2][2]	values[2][3]

Accessing the Elements in a Two-Dimensional Array

To access one of the elements in a two-dimensional array, you must use both subscripts. For example, the following statement assigns the number 95 to values[2][1]:

```
values[2][1] = 95;
```

Programs that process two-dimensional arrays commonly do so with nested loops. The code in Program 6-15 shows an example. It declares an array with three rows and four columns, prompts the user for values to store in each element, and then displays the values in each element.

Program 6-15 (`TwoDimensionalArray.cpp`)

```cpp
 1 #include <iostream>
 2 using namespace std;
 3
 4 // Function prototype
 5 int getTotal(int[], int );
 6
 7 int main()
 8 {
 9    // Create a 2D array
10    const int ROWS = 3;
11    const int COLS = 4;
12    int values[ROWS][COLS];
13
14    // Counter variables for rows and columns
15    int row, col;
16
17    // Get values to store in the array.
18    for (row = 0; row <= ROWS - 1; row++)
19    {
20       for (col = 0; col <= COLS - 1; col++)
21       {
22          cout << "Enter a number: ";
23          cin >> values[row][col];
24       }
25    }
26
27    // Display the values in the array.
28    cout << "Here are the values you entered." << endl;
29    for (row = 0; row <= ROWS - 1; row++)
30    {
31       for (col = 0; col <= COLS - 1; col++)
32       {
33          cout << values[row][col] << endl;
34       }
35    }
36
37    return 0;
38 }
```

Program Output

```
Enter a number: 1 [Enter]
Enter a number: 2 [Enter]
Enter a number: 3 [Enter]
Enter a number: 4 [Enter]
Enter a number: 5 [Enter]
Enter a number: 6 [Enter]
Enter a number: 7 [Enter]
Enter a number: 8 [Enter]
Enter a number: 9 [Enter]
```

```
Enter a number: 10 [Enter]
Enter a number: 11 [Enter]
Enter a number: 12 [Enter]
Here are the values you entered.
1
2
3
4
5
6
7
8
9
10
11
12
```

When initializing a two-dimensional array, it helps to enclose each row's initialization list in a set of braces. Here is an example:

```
const int ROWS = 3;
const int COLS = 2;
int values[ROWS][COLS] = { {8, 5}, {7, 9}, {6, 3} };
```

The same declaration could also be written as:

```
const int ROWS = 3;
const int COLS = 2;
int values[ROWS][COLS] = { {8, 5},
                           {7, 9},
                           {6, 3} };
```

In either case, the initial values are assigned to the values array in the following manner:

values[0][0] is set to 8
values[0][1] is set to 5
values[1][0] is set to 7
values[1][1] is set to 9
values[2][0] is set to 6
values[2][1] is set to 3

The extra braces that enclose each row's initialization list are optional. Both the following statements perform the same initialization:

```
const int ROWS = 3;
const int COLS = 2;
int values[ROWS][COLS] = {{8, 5}, {7, 9}, {6, 3}};
int values[ROWS][COLS] = {8, 5, 7, 9, 6, 3};
```

Because the extra braces visually separate each row, however, it's a good idea to use them.

Passing Two-Dimensional Arrays to Functions

Program 6-16 demonstrates passing a two-dimensional array to a function. When a two-dimensional array is passed to a function, the parameter type must contain a size declarator for the number of columns. Here is the header for the function showArray, from Program 6-16:

```cpp
void showArray(const int array[][COLS], int rows)
```

COLS is a global named constant that is set to 4. The function can accept any two-dimensional integer array, as long as it consists of four columns. In the program, the contents of two separate arrays are displayed by the function.

Program 6-16   (Pass2dArray.cpp)

```cpp
 1 #include <iostream>
 2 using namespace std;
 3
 4 // Global constants
 5 const int COLS = 4;        // Number of columns in each array
 6 const int ARR1_ROWS = 3;   // Number of rows in array1
 7 const int ARR2_ROWS = 4;   // Number of rows in array2
 8
 9 // Function prototype
10 void showArray(const int [][COLS], int);
11
12 int main()
13 {
14    // Declare and initialize two arrays.
15    int array1[ARR1_ROWS][COLS] = {{1, 2, 3, 4},
16                                   {5, 6, 7, 8},
17                                   {9, 10, 11, 12}};
18
19    int array2[ARR2_ROWS][COLS] = {{10, 20, 30, 40},
20                                   {50, 60, 70, 80},
21                                   {90, 100, 110, 120},
22                                   {130, 140, 150, 160}};
23
24    // Display the contents of array1.
25    cout << "The contents of array1 are:\n";
26    showArray(array1, ARR1_ROWS);
27
28    // Display the contents of array2.
29    cout << "The contents of array2 are:\n";
30    showArray(array2, ARR2_ROWS);
31    return 0;
32 }
33
34 // Function Definition for showArray
```

```
35 // The first argument is a two-dimensional int array with
36 // COLS columns. The second argument, rows, specifies the
37 // number of rows in the array. The function displays the
38 // array's contents.
39 void showArray(const int arr[][COLS], int rows)
40 {
41    for (int x = 0; x < rows; x++)
42    {
43       for (int y = 0; y < COLS; y++)
44       {
45          cout << arr[x][y] << "\t";
46       }
47       cout << endl;
48    }
49 }
```

Program Output

```
The contents of array1 are:
1          2          3          4
5          6          7          8
9          10         11         12
The contents of array2 are:
10         20         30         40
50         60         70         80
90         100        110        120
130        140        150        160
```

Checkpoint

6.21. How many rows and how many columns are in the following array?

```
int points[88][100];
```

6.22. Write a statement that assigns the value 100 to the very last element in the points array declared in Checkpoint 6.21

6.23. Write a declaration for a two-dimensional array initialized with the following table of data:

```
12      24      32      21      42
14      67      87      65      90
19      1       24      12      8
```

6.24. Write code with a set of nested loops that stores the value 99 in each element of the following info array.

```
const int ROWS = 100;
const int COLS = 50;
int info[ROWS][COLS];
```

6.6 Arrays of Three or More Dimensions

CONCEPT: To model data that occurs in multiple sets, most languages allow you to create arrays with multiple dimensions.

In the previous section you saw examples of two-dimensional arrays. You can also create arrays with three or more dimensions. Here is an example of a three-dimensional array declaration:

```
double seats[3][5][8];
```

You can think of this array as three sets of five rows, with each row containing eight elements. The array might be used to store the prices of seats in an auditorium, where eight seats are in a row, five rows in a section, and a total of three sections. Figure 6-12 illustrates the concept of a three-dimensional array as "pages" of two-dimensional arrays.

Figure 6-12 A three-dimensional array

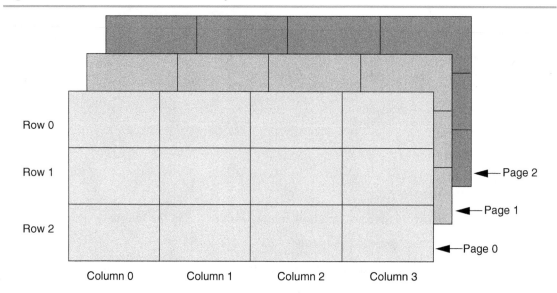

Arrays with more than three dimensions are difficult to visualize, but they can be useful in some programming problems. For example, in a factory warehouse where cases of widgets are stacked on pallets, an array with four dimensions could be used to store a part number for each widget. The four subscripts of each element could represent the pallet number, case number, row number, and column number of each widget. Similarly, an array with five dimensions could be used in the case of multiple warehouses.

 Checkpoint

6.25. A bookstore keeps books on 50 racks with 10 shelves each. Each shelf holds 25 books. Declare a 3-D `string` array to hold the names of all the books in the store. The array's three dimensions should represent the racks, shelves, and books in the store.

Review Questions

Multiple Choice

1. This appears in an array declaration and specifies the number of elements in the array:
   a. subscript.
   b. size declarator.
   c. array name.
   d. initialization value.

2. To make programs easier to maintain, many programmers use these to specify the size of an array:
   a. real numbers.
   b. string expressions.
   c. math expressions.
   d. named constants.

3. This is an individual storage location in an array:
   a. element.
   b. bin.
   c. cubbyhole.
   d. size declarator.

4. This is a number that identifies a storage location in an array:
   a. element.
   b. subscript.
   c. size declarator.
   d. identifier.

5. This is the first subscript in an array:
   a. –1.
   b. 1.
   c. 0.
   d. the size of the array minus one.

6. This is the last subscript in an array:
   a. –1.
   b. 99.
   c. 0.
   d. the size of the array minus one.

7. This algorithm uses a loop to step through each element of an array, starting with the first element, searching for a value:
   a. sequential search.
   b. step-by-step search.
   c. elemental search.
   d. binary search.

8. The C++ compiler does not do this:
   a. check the syntax of array declarations.
   b. allow the use of int arrays.

    c. array bounds checking.

    d. allow arrays of more than two dimensions.

9. This term describes two or more arrays that hold related data, and the related elements in each array are accessed with a common subscript:

    a. synchronous arrays.

    b. asynchronous arrays.

    c. parallel arrays.

    d. two-dimensional arrays.

10. You typically think of a two-dimensional array as containing

    a. lines and statements.

    b. chapters and pages.

    c. rows and columns.

    d. horizontal and vertical elements.

True or False

1. You can store a mixture of different data types in an array.

2. An array's size cannot be changed while the program is running.

3. An array's size declarator can be either a literal, a named constant, or a variable.

4. If you leave out the size declarator of an array definition, you do not have to include an initialization list.

5. C++ performs array bounds checking when the program is compiled

6. You can do many things with arrays, but you cannot pass one as an argument to a function.

7. A declaration for a two-dimensional array requires only one size declarator.

8. C++ allows you to create arrays with three or more dimensions.

Short Answer

1. What is an off-by-one error?

2. Look at the following code:

```
const int SIZE = 10;
int values[SIZE];
```

    a. How many elements does the array have?

    b. What is the subscript of the first element in the array?

    c. What is the subscript of the last element in the array?

3. Look at the following code:

```
const int SIZE = 3;
int numbers[SIZE] = { 1, 2, 3 };
```

    a. What value is stored in numbers[2]?

    b. What value is stored in numbers[0]?

4. A program uses two parallel arrays named customerNumbers and balances. The customerNumbers array holds customer numbers, and the balances array

holds customer account balances. If a particular customer's customer number is stored in `customerNumbers[187]`, where would that customer's account balance be stored?

5. Look at the following array declaration:

```
double sales[8][10];
```

a. How many rows does the array have?
b. How many columns does the array have?
c. How many elements does the array have?
d. Write a statement that stores a number in the last column of the last row in the array.

Algorithm Workbench

1. Write a declaration for a `string` array initialized with the following strings: `"Einstein"`, `"Newton"`, `"Copernicus"`, and `"Kepler"`.

2. Assume `numbers` is an `int` array with 20 elements. Write a `for` loop that displays each element of the array.

3. Assume the arrays `numberArray1` and `numberArray2` each have 100 elements. Write code that copies the values in `numberArray1` to `numberArray2`.

4. In a program you need to store the identification numbers of 10 employees (as `int`s) and their weekly gross pay (as `double`s).

a. Declare two arrays that may be used in parallel to store the 10 employee identification numbers and gross pay amounts.
b. Write a loop that uses these arrays to display each employee's identification number and weekly gross pay.

5. Declare a two-dimensional array of integers named `grades`. It should have 30 rows and 10 columns.

6. Write a function that accepts an `int` array as an argument and returns the total of the values in the array.

Programming Exercises

VideoNote
**Solving the Total
Sales problem**

1. **Total Sales**
Write a program that asks the user to enter a store's sales for each day of the week. The amounts should be stored in an array. Use a loop to calculate the total sales for the week and display the result.

2. **Largest/Smallest Array Values**
Write a program that lets the user enter 10 values into an array. The program should then display the largest and smallest values stored in the array.

3. **Rainfall Statistics**
Write a program that lets the user enter the total rainfall for each of 12 months into an array of `double`s. The program should calculate and display the total rainfall for the year, the average monthly rainfall, and the months with the highest and lowest amounts.

4. **Driver's License Exam**

The local driver's license office has asked you to create an application that grades the written portion of the driver's license exam. The exam has 20 multiple-choice questions. Here are the correct answers:

1. B	6. A	11. B	16. C
2. D	7. B	12. C	17. C
3. A	8. A	13. D	18. B
4. A	9. C	14. A	19. D
5. C	10. D	15. D	20. A

Your program should store these correct answers in an array. It should ask the user to enter the student's answers for each of the 20 questions, and the answers should be stored in another array. After the student's answers have been entered, the program should display a message indicating whether the student passed or failed the exam. (A student must correctly answer 15 of the 20 questions to pass the exam.) It should then display the total number of correctly answered questions, the total number of incorrectly answered questions, and a list showing the question numbers of the incorrectly answered questions.

5. **Days of Each Month**

Write a program that displays the number of days in each month. The program's output should be similar to this:

January has 31 days.
February has 28 days.
March has 31 days.
April has 30 days.
May has 31 days.
June has 30 days.
July has 31 days.
August has 31 days.
September has 30 days.
October has 31 days.
November has 30 days.
December has 31 days.

The program should have two parallel arrays: a 12-element `string` array that is initialized with the names of the months and a 12-element `int` array that is initialized with the number of days in each month. To produce the output specified, use a loop to step through the arrays getting the name of a month and the number of days in that month.

6. **Payroll**

Write a program that uses the following arrays:

- `empId`: an array of seven `int`s to hold employee identification numbers.
- The array should be initialized with the following numbers:

  ```
  658845 520125 895122 777541
  451277 302850 580489
  ```

- `hours`: an array of seven `int`s to hold the number of hours worked by each employee
- `payRate`: an array of seven `double`s to hold each employee's hourly pay rate
- `wages`: an array of seven `double`s to hold each employee's gross wages

The program should relate the data in each array through the subscripts. For example, the number in element 0 of the `hours` array should be the number of hours worked by the employee whose identification number is stored in element 0 of the `empId` array. That same employee's pay rate should be stored in element 0 of the `payRate` array.

The program should display each employee number and ask the user to enter that employee's hours and pay rate. It should then calculate the gross wages for that employee (hours times pay rate) and store them in the `wages` array. After the data has been entered for all the employees, the program should display each employee's identification number and gross wages.

7. **Tic-Tac-Toe Game**

Write a program that allows two players to play a game of tic-tac-toe. Use a two-dimensional `string` (or `char`) array with three rows and three columns as the game board. Each element of the array should be initialized with an asterisk (*). The program should run a loop that:

- Displays the contents of the board array.
- Allows player 1 to select a location on the board for an X. The program should ask the user to enter the row and column number.
- Allows player 2 to select a location on the board for an O. The program should ask the user to enter the row and column number.
- Determines whether a player has won, or a tie has occurred. If a player has won, the program should declare that player the winner and end. If a tie has occurred, the program should say so and end.

Player 1 wins when there are three Xs in a row on the game board. The Xs can appear in a row, in a column, or diagonally across the board. A tie occurs when all the locations on the board are full, but there is no winner.

Figure C-1 Red, green, and blue channels

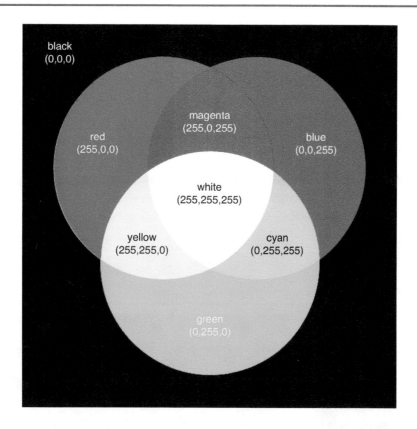

Figure C-2 Output of Program 7-4

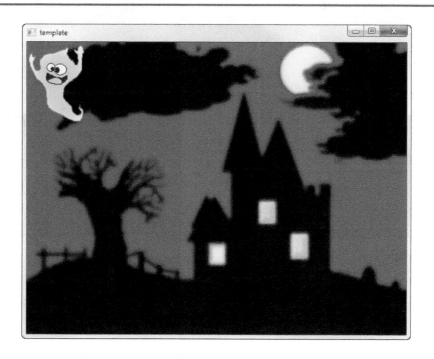

Figure C-3 The ghost.png image with its transparent background

Figure C-4 The Dog and Beach images

Figure C-5 Output of Program 7-7

Figure C-6 Ghost sprite with alpha value of 100

Figure C-7 Example output for Program 8-3

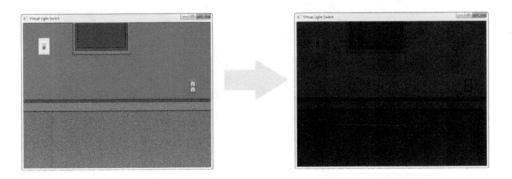

Figure C-8 Screens from the Bug Zapper game

Figure C-9 Vulture Trouble title screen and introductory screen

Figure C-10 Vulture Trouble main screen and summary screen

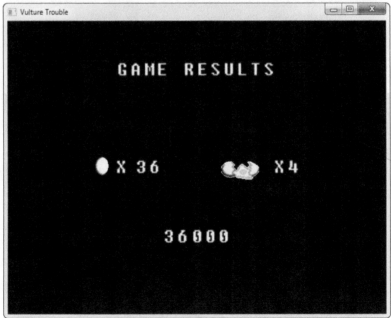

Figure C-11 A tile-based image

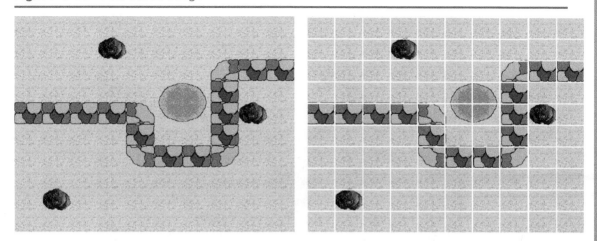

Figure C-12 Tiles

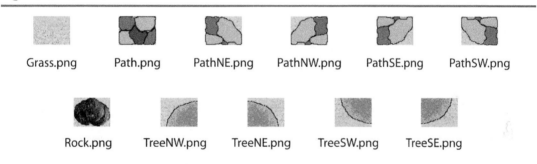

Grass.png Path.png PathNE.png PathNW.png PathSE.png PathSW.png

Rock.png TreeNW.png TreeNE.png TreeSW.png TreeSE.png

Figure C-13 Animated sprite frames for the Alec character (stored in Alec.png)

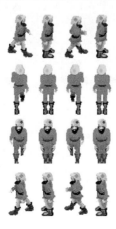

Figure C-14 Starting screen from Program 10-9

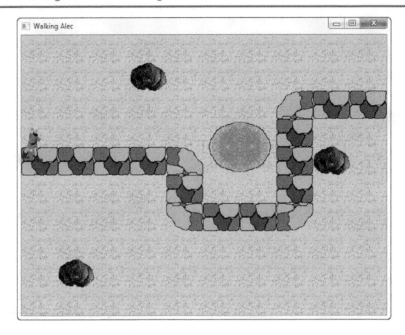

Figure C-15 The Balloon Target game

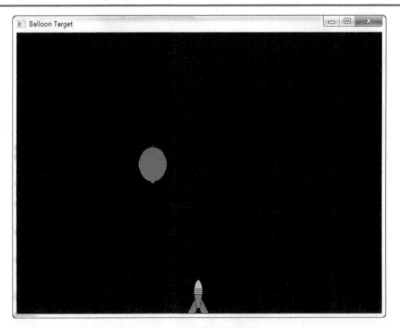

2

Introduction to Game Programming with C++ and App Game Kit

7 Using the App Game Kit with C++

TOPICS

7.1 The App Game Kit and the Structure of a Game Program

CONCEPT: The App Game Kit, or AGK, is a commercial programming tool that you can use to write games in C++. It provides a programming template that supports the typical structure of a game program.

In the previous chapters you learned to write simple programs using only the standard features of C++. The programs that you have written, until now, have displayed text output in a console window and read input from the keyboard. We mentioned in Chapter 1 that although C++ is a fast and efficient programming language, it does not have built-in features for writing graphical programs or games. In this chapter we will move beyond the standard features of C++. We will begin using the App Game Kit library, which allows you to write games and interactive graphical programs in C++.

The App Game Kit (or AGK, as it is commonly called) is a commercial programming environment that was developed by The Game Creators, a software company based in the United Kingdom. It is designed to create games for Windows, as well as a variety of smartphones and tablets. The AGK is available in two levels:

Tier 1: This product provides a programming language that is derived from BASIC and an integrated development environment.

Tier 2: This product provides everything in Tier 1, plus a C++ library that works with Microsoft Visual Studio.

255

In this book we will use the C++ library from the AGK Tier 2, along with Visual Studio 2010. The Game Creators provide a free trial version of AGK Tier 2 that is fully functional and is not time restricted. The difference between the trial version and the commercial version is that all programs developed with the trial version run with a watermark message displayed on the screen. See Appendix A for instructions on downloading and installing the AGK trial version.

The Structure of a Typical Game Program

Virtually all game programs are structured into the following three general phases:

- **Initialization**—The initialization phase occurs when the program starts. During initialization, the program loads the resources that it needs, such as graphic images and sound files, and gets things set up so the game can play.
- **Game Loop**—This is a loop that repeats continuously until the game is over. During each iteration of the loop, the program gets the latest input from the user, moves objects on the screen, plays sounds, and so forth. When the game is over, the loop stops.
- **Shutdown**—When the game is over, the program saves any data that must be kept (such as the user's score), and then the program ends.

Figure 7-1 illustrates these three program phases.

Figure 7-1 Typical game phases

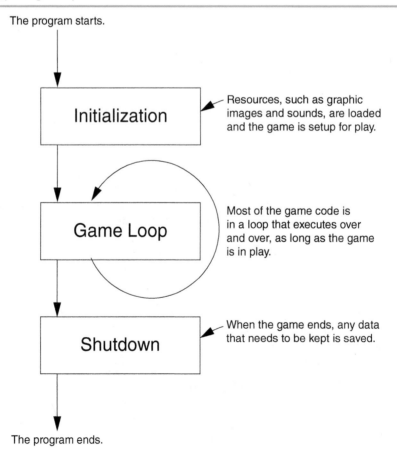

When you write a C++ program that uses the AGK, you work with a code template that is already set up for the three phases of a game program. A C++ program that uses the AGK looks quite different from the standard C++ programs that you are accustomed to writing, however.

For example, you learned in Chapter 2 that all C++ programs must have a function named main, and that the main function is the program's starting point. Although that is still true, you will not actually see the main function in any of your C++ programs that use the AGK. This is because graphics programming can be quite complex, and the AGK is designed to handle much of that complexity for you. As a result, the main function in an AGK program is hidden.

Instead, you will work primarily with three functions shown in the following program template:

```
1   // Includes, namespace and prototypes
2   #include "template.h"
3   using namespace AGK;
4   app App;
5
6   // Begin app, called once at the start
7   void app::Begin( void )
8   {
9   }
10
11  // Main loop, called every frame
12  void app::Loop ( void )
13  {
14  }
15
16  // Called when the app ends
17  void app::End ( void )
18  {
19  }
```

At this point, you do not need a deep understanding of the code in lines 2, 3, and 4, but here is a brief overview of those statements:

- The include directive in line 2 includes the contents of a file named template.h. The template.h file contains declarations and other code needed by the AGK library.
- The using namespace statement in line 3 declares that we are using the AGK namespace. You have already learned that when you write a program using the standard C++ library, you need to use the std namespace. Likewise, when you write a program using the AGK library, you need to use the AGK namespace.
- Line 4 declares an object named App that is used by the AGK to control the program.

The remaining code consists of three functions, named app::Begin, app::Loop, and app::End. You will spend most of your time writing code in these three functions, which correspond to the three phases of a game program. Here is a summary of each function:

- The **app::Begin** function is in lines 7 through 9. This function executes once, when the program starts. Its purpose is to perform initialization, such as loading graphical images and sounds, and to prepare the program when it first executes.
- The **app::Loop** function appears in lines 12 through 14. This function performs the game loop, and it does most of the work in an AGK program. After the app::Begin function has executed, the app::Loop function executes over and over until the program ends.
- The **app::End** function appears in lines 17 through 19. This function executes when the program ends. It performs any necessary shutdown operations, such as saving game data.

Figure 7-2 illustrates the sequence in which these functions execute.

Figure 7-2 Sequence of function execution in an AGK program

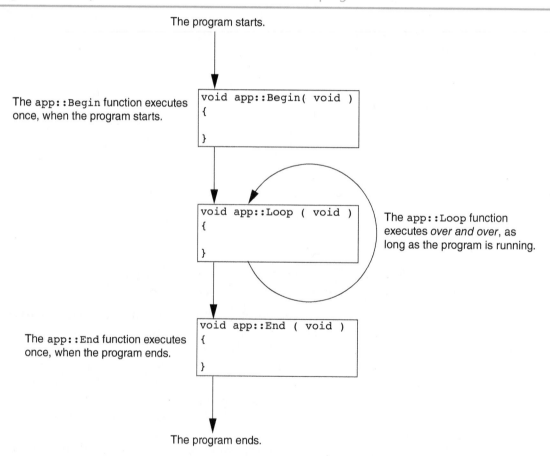

A metaphor for these three functions might go as follows: The app::Begin function is similar to a person getting ready to go to work, making sure they have everything they need. When they are ready, they head off for work and enter the app::Loop function.

This function is like the person working at a job where he or she completes many different tasks over and over until quitting time. Then, when the work is finished, the person enters the `app::End` function. In this function the person cleans up the work area and goes home.

Remember—The `app::Loop` Function Loops Automatically

Up to this chapter, you have been in control of the "flow" of each program that you have written. For example, if you want a group of statements to execute repeatedly in a standard C++ program, you have to write a loop that executes those statements. In the AGK template, however, the `app::Loop` function repeats automatically. Any statement or statements that you write inside the `app::Loop` function will execute over and over until the game is over or the user ends the program.

Creating an AGK Project for Visual C++

Once you have installed the AGK on your system, you will have a template C++ project that you can copy and then open in Visual Studio. You can then add your own code to the template project. The following tutorial leads you through the steps of copying the template project and opening it in Visual Studio.

Tutorial:

Copying the AGK Template Project and Opening It in Visual Studio

VideoNote

Copying the AGK Template Project and Opening It in Visual Studio

Step 1: Open Windows Explorer, and go to the folder where the AGK is installed. (If you followed the instructions in Appendix A, you installed the AGK in a folder named *AGK*, under *My Documents*. This is the location that we recommend.)

Inside the AGK folder, go to the IDE folder, and then go to the templates folder, as shown in Figure 7-3. Inside the templates folder, you should see the folders shown in Figure 7-4.

Figure 7-3 Go to the `AGK\IDE\templates` folder

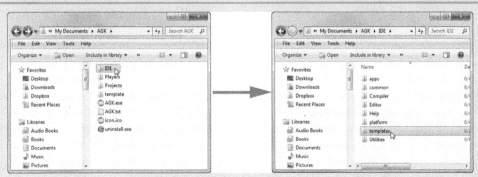

Figure 7-4 Contents of the AGK\IDE\templates folder

Step 2: As shown in Figure 7-4, one of the folders is *template_vs10*. This is the template for Visual Studio 2010, which is the version we are using in this book. Make a copy of this folder, as shown in Figure 7-5. (To copy the folder, right-click the *template_vs10* folder, then select *Copy* from the menu. Next, right-click anywhere inside the current folder, then select *Paste*.)

WARNING! You must paste the copy of the folder in the *templates* folder. If you paste it anywhere else on your system, the Visual Studio compiler will not be able to find many of the files that it needs to compile your project.

Figure 7-5 Make a copy of the template_vs10 folder

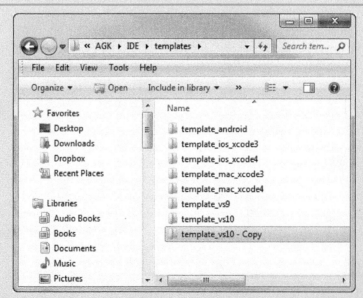

Step 3: As shown in Figure 7-6, rename the copy of the *template_vs10* folder that you just created. In the figure, we have renamed it as *MyFirstAGKProject*. (To rename the folder, right-click it, then select *Rename* from the menu.)

Figure 7-6 The folder renamed

Step 4: Go into the folder that you just renamed, and locate the file named *template.sln* (as shown in Figure 7-7). This is the Visual Studio solution file for the project. Double-click the file to open it in Visual Studio.

Figure 7-7 Double-click the template.sln file

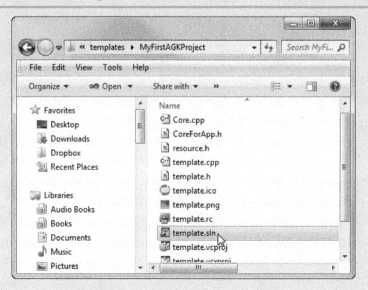

Step 5: In the Solution Explorer window in Visual Studio, open the App folder, and then double-click the template.cpp file to open it in the editor, as shown in Figure 7-8. This is the C++ file that contains the template AGK code that you will work with in each project you create.

Figure 7-8 Open the `template.cpp` file in the editor

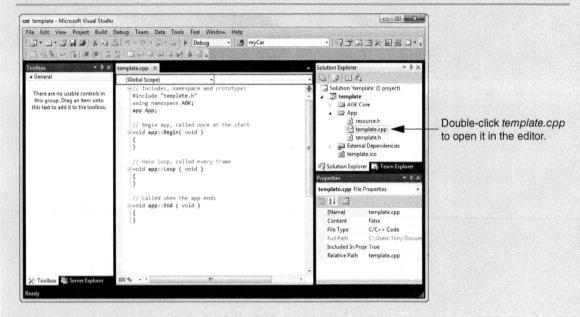

Double-click *template.cpp* to open it in the editor.

App Game Kit Online Documentation

We cover many aspects of AGK programming in this book, but we do not cover everything. You can find documentation for all the AGK function, as well as other topics, at `http://www.appgamekit.com/documentation`.

 Checkpoint

7.1. What is the App Game Kit?

7.2. Virtually all games are structured into what three general phases?

7.3. What three functions are already written in the AGK C++ template?

7.4. Which AGK template function performs the work of the game loop?

 7.2 The Screen Coordinate System

CONCEPT: A system of *X*- and *Y*-coordinates is used to identify the locations of pixels in a window.

When you run a program that you have created with the AGK, the output appears in a graphics window. The display area in the window is made up of tiny dots called *pixels*, and a *screen coordinate system* is used to identify the position of each pixel in the window.

Each pixel has an *X*-coordinate and a *Y*-coordinate. The *X*-coordinate identifies the pixel's horizontal position, and the *Y*-coordinate identifies its vertical position. The coordinates are usually written in the form (*X*, *Y*). For example, the coordinates of the pixel in the upper-left corner of the window are (0, 0). This means that its *X*-coordinate is 0 and its *Y*-coordinate is 0. The *X*-coordinates increase from left to right, and the *Y*-coordinates increase from top to bottom.

The AGK has two ways of handling screen coordinates. The default method uses a percentage-based coordinate system where the screen coordinates start in the upper-left corner at (0, 0) and end in the lower-right corner at (100, 100). This is shown in Figure 7-9. As you can see from the figure, the displayable area does not fill the entire window.

Figure 7-9 The percentage-based screen coordinate system

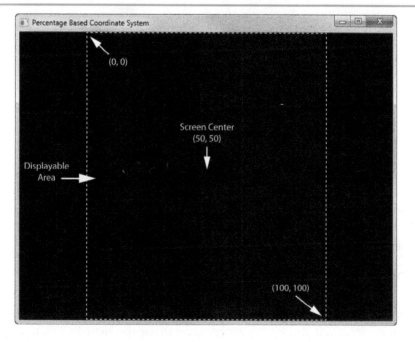

The second method, which we will use in this book, is called virtual resolution. It is somewhat easier to use than the percentage-based system because it is based on the screen size of the window. The default window that is displayed by an AGK program is 640 pixels wide and 480 pixels high. We say that the window has a *resolution* of 640 by 480. In a window that is 640 pixels wide by 480 pixels high, the coordinates of the pixel at the bottom-right corner of the screen are (639, 479). In the same window, the coordinates of the pixel in the center of the screen are (319, 239). Figure 7-10 shows some coordinates of a resolution-based system.

Figure 7-10 The resolution-based screen coordinate system

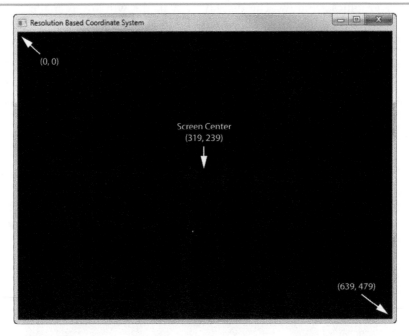

Notice that the pixels at the far right edge of the screen have an X-coordinate of 639, not 640. This is because coordinate numbering begins at 0 in the upper-left corner. Likewise, the pixels at the bottom edge of the screen have a Y-coordinate of 479, not 480.

NOTE: The screen coordinate system differs from the Cartesian coordinate system that you learned about in mathematics. In the Cartesian coordinate system, the Y-coordinates decrease as you move downward. In the screen coordinate system the Y-coordinates increase as you move downward, toward the bottom of the screen.

Setting the Virtual Resolution

As previously mentioned, an AGK program uses the percentage-based screen resolution by default. If you want your program to use the virtual resolution system (which we use in this book), you have to call the agk::SetVirtualResolution function. Here is the general format of how you call the function:

```
agk::SetVirtualResolution(width, height);
```

You pass two integer arguments to the function. The *width* argument sets the number of pixels wide that the screen will be, and the *height* argument sets the number of pixels high that the screen will be. The following statement sets the virtual resolution to 640 by 480:

```
agk::SetVirtualResolution(640, 480);
```

You call this function in your program's app::Begin function, as shown in line 14 of Program 7-1. Notice that we have declared two global constants for the screen's width and height, in lines 7 and 8.

Program 7-1   (`VirtualResolutionSetup`)

```
 1 // Includes, namespace and prototypes
 2 #include "template.h"
 3 using namespace AGK;
 4 app App;
 5
 6 // Constants for the screen resolution
 7 const int SCREEN_WIDTH = 640;
 8 const int SCREEN_HEIGHT = 480;
 9
10 // Begin app, called once at the start
11 void app::Begin( void )
12 {
13    // Set the virtual resolution.
14    agk::SetVirtualResolution(SCREEN_WIDTH, SCREEN_HEIGHT);
15 }
16
17 // Main loop, called every frame
18 void app::Loop ( void )
19 {
20 }
21
22 // Called when the app ends
23 void app::End ( void )
24 {
25 }
```

Checkpoint

7.5. What are the tiny dots that make up the display area of the screen?

7.6. What two coordinates identify a position in the AGK's output window?

7.7. The AGK uses what two methods of handling screen coordinates?

7.8. What are the coordinates of the upper-left corner of the AGK's output window?

7.9. In the percentage-based system, what are the coordinates of the position in the lower-right corner of the AGK's output window?

7.10. In the virtual resolution system, what are the coordinates of the position in the lower-right corner of the AGK's output window?

7.11. How are the screen coordinates different from the Cartesian coordinate system?

7.12. How do you switch to the virtual resolution system in an AGK C++ program?

7.3 Displaying Sprites

CONCEPT: A sprite is a graphic image that is displayed in a game.

Bitmap Images

Most of the programs that you will write with the AGK will display images that have been created with a graphics program such as Microsoft Paint or perhaps captured with a digital camera and stored on your computer's disk. When graphic images are stored on a computer's disk, they are commonly stored as bitmaps. The term *bitmap* refers to a set of data that describes every pixel in an image. When an image is saved on the computer's disk as a bitmap, it is saved in a file that contains data describing every pixel in the image.

If you use a digital camera, a scanner, or a graphics program like Microsoft Paint, you have probably created image files that end with extensions such as .png, .jpg, and .bmp. These are all different formats for saving a bitmap image in a file.

Sprites

Graphic images are used extensively in computer games. The graphics for the background scenery, the game characters, and practically everything else are images that are loaded from bitmap files. The graphic images that are displayed in a computer game are commonly known as *sprites*. The AGK provides many functions for creating and using sprites.

To create a sprite in an AGK program, you use the agk::CreateSprite function. Here is the general format that we will typically use:

```
agk::CreateSprite(SpriteIndex, ImageFile);
```

Here is a summary of the two arguments that you pass to the function:

- *SpriteIndex* is the sprite index, which is a number that identifies the sprite in your program. The sprite index can be an integer in the range of 1 through 4,294,967,295. Once the sprite is created, you will use its sprite index to identify it in subsequent operations.
- *ImageFile* is the name of the file that contains the image. This can be the name of any image file of the .png, .jpg, or .bmp file formats.

For example, suppose we have an image file named LadyBug.png that we want to use as a sprite. The following statement shows how we can create the sprite, and assign 1 as its sprite index:

```
agk::CreateSprite(1, "LadyBug.png");
```

When a sprite is created, its default position on the screen will be the upper-left corner, at the coordinates (0, 0).

The Location of a Program's Graphic Files

When an AGK program looks for an image file, it looks in the *My Documents > AGK > template* folder, as shown in Figure 7-11. Any graphic files that you want to use in your program should be stored in this folder.

Figure 7-11 Location of the *template* folder that holds your project's graphic files

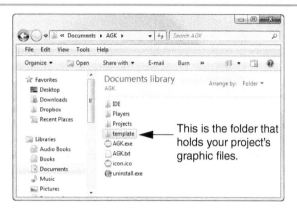

This is the folder that holds your project's graphic files.

NOTE: The *template* folder that holds your project's graphic files will be created the first time you load the template project in Visual Studio.

Understanding the Backbuffer and Syncing

Although the `agk::CreateSprite` function creates a sprite in memory, it does not display the sprite on the screen. This is because the AGK keeps a copy of the output screen, known as the *backbuffer*, in memory. When the AGK draws an image, it draws the image on the backbuffer instead of the actual screen. When you are ready for the contents of the backbuffer to be displayed on the actual screen, you call the `agk::Sync` function. (The word *sync* stands for synchronize. When you call the `agk::Sync` function, it synchronizes the screen with the backbuffer.)

You call the `agk::Sync` function in the `app::Loop` function. Calling the `agk::Sync` function is typically the last operation performed in `app::Loop`, after all other actions have taken place.

As an example, look at Program 7-2. This program creates a sprite, using a graphic file named *ghost.png*. (Before you run this program, you must copy *ghost.png* file to the *template* folder that is in the *AGK* folder.) When the program runs, it displays the screen shown in Figure 7-12. To end the program's execution, click the window's close button ( ).

VideoNote

The SpriteDemo Program

Program 7-2	**(SpriteDemo)**

```
1 // Includes, namespace and prototypes
2 #include "template.h"
3 using namespace AGK;
4 app App;
5
```

```
 6 // Constants for the screen resolution
 7 const int SCREEN_WIDTH = 640;
 8 const int SCREEN_HEIGHT = 480;
 9
10 // Constant for the sprite index
11 const int SPRITE_INDEX = 1;
12
13 // Begin app, called once at the start
14 void app::Begin( void )
15 {
16     // Set the virtual resolution.
17     agk::SetVirtualResolution(SCREEN_WIDTH, SCREEN_HEIGHT);
18
19     // Create the ghost sprite.
20     agk::CreateSprite(SPRITE_INDEX, "ghost.png");
21 }
22
23 // Main loop, called every frame
24 void app::Loop ( void )
25 {
26     // Display the screen.
27     agk::Sync();
28 }
29
30 // Called when the app ends
31 void app::End ( void )
32 {
33 }
```

Figure 7-12 Output of Program 7-2

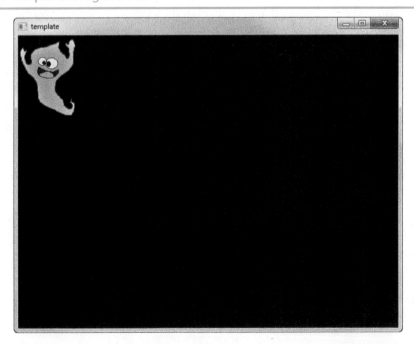

Let's take a closer look at the program. Lines 7 and 8 declare global constants for the screen's width and height. Line 11 declares the global constant SPRITE_INDEX, set to the value 1. We will use this constant as the ghost's sprite index.

Inside the app::Begin function, line 17 sets the virtual resolution. Line 20 creates a sprite with the index 1, using the graphic file *ghost.png*. (The program will look for this file in the *My Documents > AGK > template* folder.) The sprite will be positioned in the upper-left corner of the backbuffer.

After the app::Begin function finishes, the program executes the app::Loop function. Line 27 calls the agk::Sync function, which displays the backbuffer. This causes the ghost sprite to appear on the screen. The app::Loop function continues to execute repeatedly, but its only action is to display the ghost sprite.

NOTE: Simple programs such as this one do not usually perform any actions in the app::End function. The app::End function is typically used to save game data.

Using a Sprite as the Background

Most of the games and other programs that you develop with the AGK will display a bitmap image for the background. If you want to fill the entire background, it is best to use an image that is the same size as the window (which, by default, is 640 by 480 pixels). You simply create a sprite using the desired bitmap image, and it will fill the window when the agk::Sync function is called. Program 7-3 demonstrates by creating a sprite from a bitmap image that is 640 by 480 pixels in size. The program's output is shown in Figure 7-13.

Figure 7-13 Output of Program 7-3

If you study Program 7-3 carefully, you will notice that the only difference between it and Program 7-2 is the name of the graphic file that is being used to create the sprite in line 20. Program 7-3 uses a file named *beach.png* (which must be located in the *My Documents > AGK > template* folder).

Program 7-3   **(BeachBackground)**

```
 1 // Includes, namespace and prototypes
 2 #include "template.h"
 3 using namespace AGK;
 4 app App;
 5
 6 // Constants for the screen resolution
 7 const int SCREEN_WIDTH = 640;
 8 const int SCREEN_HEIGHT = 480;
 9
10 // Constant for the sprite index
11 const int SPRITE_INDEX = 1;
12
13 // Begin app, called once at the start
14 void app::Begin( void )
15 {
16    // Set the virtual resolution.
17    agk::SetVirtualResolution(SCREEN_WIDTH, SCREEN_HEIGHT);
18
19    // Create the beach sprite.
20    agk::CreateSprite(SPRITE_INDEX, "beach.png");
21 }
22
23 // Main loop, called every frame
24 void app::Loop ( void )
25 {
26    // Display the screen.
27    agk::Sync();
28 }
29
30 // Called when the app ends
31 void app::End ( void )
32 {
33 }
```

Displaying Multiple Sprites

Most of your AGK programs will have more than one sprite. When you create multiple sprites in the same program, each sprite must have a unique index. For example, Program 7-4 creates two sprites: the first is a haunted house image, used for the background, and the second is a ghost. Notice that in lines 11 and 12 we declare two global constants for the sprite indices. Then, in lines 21 and 24 we create the individual sprites. The program's output is shown in Figure 7-14. (This also appears as Figure C-2 in the book's color insert.)

Program 7-4   (HauntedHouse)

```
1 // Includes, namespace and prototypes
2 #include "template.h"
3 using namespace AGK;
4 app App;
5
6 // Constants for the screen resolution
7 const int SCREEN_WIDTH = 640;
8 const int SCREEN_HEIGHT = 480;
9
10 // Constants for the sprite indices
11 const int HOUSE_INDEX = 1;
12 const int GHOST_INDEX = 2;
13
14 // Begin app, called once at the start
15 void app::Begin( void )
16 {
17    // Set the virtual resolution.
18    agk::SetVirtualResolution(SCREEN_WIDTH, SCREEN_HEIGHT);
19
20    // Create the haunted house sprite for the background.
21    agk::CreateSprite(HOUSE_INDEX, "haunted_house.png");
22
23    // Create the ghost sprite.
24    agk::CreateSprite(GHOST_INDEX, "ghost.png");
25 }
26
27 // Main loop, called every frame
28 void app::Loop ( void )
29 {
30    // Display the screen.
31    agk::Sync();
32 }
33
34 // Called when the app ends
35 void app::End ( void )
36 {
37 }
```

NOTE: You can use the same image file for multiple sprites. For example, suppose you have an image file named Fish.png. The following code creates two sprites, both using the same image:

```
const int FISH1_INDEX = 1;
const int FISH2_INDEX = 2;
agk::CreateSprite(FISH1_INDEX, "Fish.png");
agk::CreateSprite(FISH2_INDEX, "Fish.png");
```

Figure 7-14 Output of Program 7-4

Sprite Depth

It is important to note that sprites are drawn on the screen in the order that they were created in the program. In Program 7-4, the sprite for the background image (the haunted house) was created first, and the sprite for the ghost was created second. When the screen is displayed, the background image is drawn first, and the ghost is drawn second. If we had reversed the order in which the sprites were created, the ghost would have been drawn first, and then the haunted house would have been drawn second. If this were the case, we would not see the ghost because the haunted house image would cover it.

In situations where you want to control the order in which sprites are displayed, regardless of the order in which they were created, you can use the agk::SetSpriteDepth function. Here is the function's general format:

```
agk::SetSpriteDepth(SpriteIndex, Depth);
```

In the general format, *SpriteIndex* is the index of the sprite that we are affecting, and *Depth* is an integer in the range of 0 through 1000. The lower the depth value, the closer to the screen the sprite will be positioned. For example, suppose you have two sprites: one with a depth of 0 and the other with a depth of 5. The sprite that has the depth of 0 will be closer to the screen, so any time the two sprites overlap, the one that has the depth of 0 will be drawn in front.

Program 7-5 demonstrates. In this program, the ghost sprite is created first (in line 21), and the haunted house sprite is created second (in line 24). To make sure that the ghost is drawn in front of the haunted house, we set the ghost sprite's depth to 0 (in line 28) and the haunted house sprite's depth to 1000 (in line 29). The output of the program is the same as previously shown in Figure 7-14.

Program 7-5   (`SpriteDepth`)

```
 1 // Includes, namespace and prototypes
 2 #include "template.h"
 3 using namespace AGK;
 4 app App;
 5
 6 // Constants for the screen resolution
 7 const int SCREEN_WIDTH = 640;
 8 const int SCREEN_HEIGHT = 480;
 9
10 // Constants for the sprite indices
11 const int HOUSE_INDEX = 1;
12 const int GHOST_INDEX = 2;
13
14 // Begin app, called once at the start
15 void app::Begin( void )
16 {
17    // Set the virtual resolution.
18    agk::SetVirtualResolution(SCREEN_WIDTH, SCREEN_HEIGHT);
19
20    // Create the ghost sprite.
21    agk::CreateSprite(GHOST_INDEX, "ghost.png");
22
23    // Create the haunted house sprite for the background.
24    agk::CreateSprite(HOUSE_INDEX, "haunted_house.png");
25
26    // Set the sprite depth values so the ghost is always
27    // drawn in front of the haunted house.
28    agk::SetSpriteDepth(GHOST_INDEX, 0);
29    agk::SetSpriteDepth(HOUSE_INDEX, 1000);
30 }
31
32 // Main loop, called every frame
33 void app::Loop ( void )
34 {
35    // Display the screen.
36    agk::Sync();
37 }
38
39 // Called when the app ends
40 void app::End ( void )
41 {
42 }
```

Setting a Sprite's Position

By default, a sprite is positioned in the upper-left corner of the screen. However, you can call the `agk::SetSpritePosition` function to move a sprite to a new position. Here is the function's general format:

```
agk::SetSpritePosition(SpriteIndex, X, Y);
```

In the general format, *SpriteIndex* is the index of the sprite that you are moving, *x* is an *X*-coordinate, and *y* is a *Y*-coordinate. The function will move the sprite so its upper-left corner is positioned at the specified *X*- and *Y*-coordinates. Program 7-6 demonstrates this function. The statement in line 31 positions the ghost sprite at the coordinate (200, 150). The program's output is shown in Figure 7-15.

NOTE: It should be mentioned that the agk::SetSpritePosition function expects the arguments for the *X*- and *Y*-coordinates to be of the float data type. This is because programs using the percentage-based coordinate systems can express coordinates as floating-point numbers. In this book, however, we are using the virtual coordinate system, and all the coordinates will be expressed as whole numbers.

Program 7-6   **(SpritePosition)**

```
 1 // Includes, namespace and prototypes
 2 #include "template.h"
 3 using namespace AGK;
 4 app App;
 5
 6 // Constants for the screen resolution
 7 const int SCREEN_WIDTH = 640;
 8 const int SCREEN_HEIGHT = 480;
 9
10 // Constants for the sprite indices
11 const int HOUSE_INDEX = 1;
12 const int GHOST_INDEX = 2;
13
14 // Constants for the ghost's position
15 const float GHOST_X = 200;
16 const float GHOST_Y = 150;
17
18 // Begin app, called once at the start
19 void app::Begin( void )
20 {
21     // Set the virtual resolution.
22     agk::SetVirtualResolution(SCREEN_WIDTH, SCREEN_HEIGHT);
23
24     // Create the haunted house sprite for the background.
25     agk::CreateSprite(HOUSE_INDEX, "haunted_house.png");
26
27     // Create the ghost sprite.
28     agk::CreateSprite(GHOST_INDEX, "ghost.png");
29
30     // Set the ghost's position.
31     agk::SetSpritePosition(GHOST_INDEX, GHOST_X, GHOST_Y);
32 }
33
34 // Main loop, called every frame
35 void app::Loop ( void )
```

```
36 {
37    // Display the screen.
38    agk::Sync();
39 }
40
41 // Called when the app ends
42 void app::End ( void )
43 {
44 }
```

Figure 7-15 Output of Program 7-6

You can also use the agk::SetSpriteX function to set a sprite's X-coordinate only and the agk::SetSpriteY function to set a sprite's Y-coordinate only. Here are the functions' general formats:

```
agk::SetSpriteX(SpriteIndex, X);
agk::SetSpriteY(SpriteIndex, Y);
```

In each of the general formats, *SpriteIndex* is the index of the sprite that you are moving. The *X* and *Y* arguments are X- and Y-coordinates. For example, assuming GHOST_INDEX is a valid sprite index, the following statement will move the sprite so its upper-left corner is at the X-coordinate 200. The sprite will not be moved along the Y-axis, however.

```
agk::SetSpriteX(GHOST_INDEX, 200);
```

Assuming GHOST_INDEX is a valid sprite index, the following statement will move the sprite so its upper-left corner is at the Y-coordinate 150. The sprite will not be moved along the X-axis, however.

```
agk::SetSpriteY(GHOST_INDEX, 150);
```

Getting a Sprite's *X*- and *Y*-Coordinates

You can get the current *X*- and *Y*-coordinates of any existing sprite by calling the `agk::GetSpriteX` and `agk::GetSpriteY` functions, passing the sprite index as an argument. The `agk::GetSpriteX` function returns the sprite's *X*-coordinate, as a `float`, and the `agk::GetSpriteY` function returns the sprite's *Y*-coordinate, also as a `float`.

For example, assume that `GHOST_INDEX` is a valid sprite index from the previously shown program. The following statements declare two variables: `spriteX` and `spriteY`. The `spriteX` variable is initialized with the value that is returned from the `agk::GetSpriteX` function, and the `spriteY` variable is initialized with the value that is returned from the `agk::GetSpriteY` function. As a result, the `spriteX` variable will hold the sprite's *X*-coordinate, and the `spriteY` variable will hold the sprite's *Y*-coordinate.

```
float spriteX = agk::GetSpriteX(GHOST_INDEX);
float spriteY = agk::GetSpriteY(GHOST_INDEX);
```

Getting the Width and Height of a Sprite

You can get the width of an existing sprite by calling the `agk::GetSpriteWidth` function, passing the sprite index as an argument. The function returns the width of the sprite as a `float`. Assuming that `SPRITE_INDEX` is a valid sprite index, the following statement shows an example.

```
float spriteWidth = agk::GetSpriteWidth(SPRITE_INDEX);
```

This statement declares a `float` variable named `spriteWidth`, initialized with the width of the sprite that is specified by `SPRITE_INDEX`.

You can get the height of an existing sprite by calling the `agk::GetSpriteHeight` function, passing the sprite index as an argument. The function returns the height of the sprite as a `float`. Assuming that `SPRITE_INDEX` is a valid sprite index, the following statement shows an example.

```
float spriteHeight = agk::GetSpriteHeight(SPRITE_INDEX);
```

This statement declares a `float` variable named `spriteHeight`, initialized with the height of the sprite that is specified by `SPRITE_INDEX`.

Scaling a Sprite

You can scale the size of an existing sprite by calling the `agk::SetSpriteScale` function. The function resizes the sprite by a multiple of its original size. Here is the general format of how you call the function:

```
agk::SetSpriteScale(SpriteIndex, Xscale, Yscale);
```

The *SpriteIndex* is the index of the sprite you want to scale. *Xscale* is the amount to scale the sprite in the *X* direction, and *Yscale* is the amount to scale the sprite in the *Y* direction. (Both *Xscale* and *Yscale* are `float` values.) For example, suppose `SPRITE_INDEX` is a valid sprite index, and you call the function in the following manner:

```
agk::SetSpriteScale(SPRITE_INDEX, 2, 2);
```

This function call will make the sprite twice as big in both the *X* and *Y* directions, as shown in Figure 7-16. Here is another example:

```
agk::SetSpriteScale(SPRITE_INDEX, 0.5, 0.5);
```

This function call will make the sprite smaller than its original size. In fact, it will make the sprite half as big in both the *X* and *Y* directions.

> **NOTE:** The `agk::SetSpriteScale` function scales the sprite from the top-left corner. The sprite's top-left corner will still be in the same location after the scaling is done.

Figure 7-16 A sprite shown at its original size, and scaled by 2 in the *X* and *Y* directions

Original Size

Scaled by 2 in both the
X and *Y* directions

Rotating a Sprite

You can use the `agk::SetSpriteAngle` function to rotate a sprite around its center point. A sprite can be rotated any angle from 0 degrees through 359 degrees. Here is the general format of how you call the function:

```
agk::SetSpriteAngle(SpriteIndex, Angle);
```

SpriteIndex is the index of the sprite that you want to rotate, and *Angle* is a floating-point value indicating the angle of rotation, in degrees. Assuming that SPRITE_INDEX is a valid sprite index, the following statement rotates the specified sprite 90 degrees:

```
agk::SetSpriteAngle(SPRITE_INDEX, 90);
```

You can determine the current rotation of a sprite with the `agk::GetSpriteAngle` function. You pass the function a sprite index as an argument, and it returns the number of degrees that the sprite has been rotated. Assuming that SPRITE_INDEX is a valid sprite index, the following statement shows an example:

```
float angle = agk::GetSpriteAngle(SPRITE_INDEX);
```

This statement declares a `float` variable named `angle`, initialized with the current rotation of the specified sprite.

> **NOTE:** If you prefer to work in radians instead of degrees, you can use the `agk::SetSpriteAngleRad` function to rotate a sprite. It works just like `agk::SetSpriteAngle`, but the angle is specified in radians. Then, you can use the `agk::GetSpriteAngleRad` function to get the sprite's current rotation in radians.

Flipping a Sprite

You can use the `agk::SetSpriteFlip` function to flip a sprite either horizontally or vertically. The function's general format is

```
agk::SetSpriteFlip(SpriteIndex, Horizontal, Vertical);
```

Here is a summary of the arguments:

- `SpriteIndex` is the index of the sprite that you want to flip.
- `Horizontal` is either 0 or 1. If 0, the sprite will not be flipped horizontally. If 1, the sprite will be flipped horizontally.
- `Vertical` is either 0 or 1. If 0, the sprite will not be flipped vertically. If 1, the sprite will be flipped vertically.

Assuming that `SPRITE_INDEX` is a valid sprite index, the following statement flips the specified sprite horizontally, but not vertically:

```
agk:: SetSpriteFlip(SPRITE_INDEX, 1, 0);
```

The following statement flips the specified sprite vertically, but not horizontally:

```
agk:: SetSpriteFlip(SPRITE_INDEX, 0, 1);
```

And, the following statement flips the specified sprite both horizontally and vertically:

```
agk:: SetSpriteFlip(SPRITE_INDEX, 1, 1);
```

Making a Sprite Visible or Invisible

You can make a sprite invisible or visible by calling the `agk::SetSpriteVisible` function. Here is the general format of how you call the function:

```
agk::SetSpriteVisible(SpriteIndex, Visible);
```

The `SpriteIndex` is the index of a sprite, and `Visible` is either 0 or 1. If you pass 0 for the `Visible` argument, the sprite will become invisible. If you pass 1 for the `Visible` argument, the sprite will become visible. Assuming `SPRITE_INDEX` is a valid sprite index, here is an example:

```
agk::SetSpriteVisible(SPRITE_INDEX, 0);
```

This function call will make the sprite invisible. To make it visible again, you would use the following function call:

```
agk::SetSpriteVisible(SPRITE_INDEX, 1);
```

Cloning a Sprite

A sprite clone is a copy of an existing sprite. When you clone a sprite, you are making a copy that is independent from the original sprite. The clone will be created at the same location as the original, and it will have the characteristics of the original sprite, such as size, rotation angle, and so on. If you manipulate the original sprite, (such as resize or flip it), it has no effect on the sprite's clones. The opposite is also true: if you manipulate a clone, it has no effect on the original sprite.

You clone a sprite by calling the `agk::CloneSprite` function. Here is the general format for calling the function:

```
agk::CloneSprite(SpriteIndex, DestinationSpriteIndex);
```

SpriteIndex is the number of the original sprite, and *DestinationSpriteIndex* is the number you want to assign to the clone. For example assume that `SPRITE_INDEX` is a valid sprite index. The following statement creates a clone of the sprite, assigning it the index specified by `CLONE_INDEX`:

```
agk::CloneSprite(SPRITE_INDEX, CLONE_INDEX);
```

The clone specified by `CLONE_INDEX` will have the same image, be of the same size and rotation, and be in the same location as the sprite specified by `SPRITE_INDEX`.

Transparent Backgrounds in Sprites

Most graphic images are rectangular. However, the contents of many of the graphic images that you will use to create sprites are not rectangular. For example, look at the image in Figure 7-17. The image is a circle, but it is saved in a black rectangle in the image file.

Figure 7-17 Circle image on a rectangular background

Let's say you are using this image to create a sprite in a game, perhaps as a ball that is moving around on the screen. You have another image that you will use as the game's background, and you want the ball to be displayed on top of the background image. You will probably want the black, rectangular area in the circle image to be invisible so only the ball is shown moving around the screen, on top of the background image.

Fortunately, images that are saved in the png format can have transparent backgrounds. For example, the ghost.png graphic shown in Figure 7-18 shows a checkerboard pattern to indicate the transparent region of the image. (This figure also appears as Figure C-3 in the book's color insert.) When you use a graphics editor to create a png image, you can specify that the image should have a transparent background, and then, when you load that image into an AGK program, its transparent background region will be invisible.

> **NOTE:** The specific steps for creating an image with a transparent background vary from one editor to another. On this book's companion Web site you will find a VideoNote that gives one example of how it is done.

Figure 7-18 The ghost.png image with its transparent background

Using Black to Create Transparent Backgrounds

Some of the simpler graphics editors do not support transparent backgrounds, even in png files. Microsoft Paint is an example. If you are using such an editor, you can still create sprites that are displayed with a transparent background in your AGK programs. The process requires extra steps, however, than those previously shown.

> **NOTE:** The steps following steps are necessary only if you are using a graphics editor that does not support transparency in .png files, such as Microsoft Paint.

First, in your graphics editor, use black as the background color. (The background must be pure black. A dark shade of gray will not work.) Then, in your AGK program, use the agk::LoadImage function to load the image into memory, using the following general format:

```
agk::LoadImage(ImageIndex, ImageFile, BlackToTransparent);
```

Here is a summary of the three arguments that you pass to the function:

- *ImageIndex* is the image index, which is a number that identifies the image in your program. The image index can be an integer in the range of 1 through 4,294,967,295. Once the image is loaded into memory, you will use its image index to identify it in subsequent operations. (Take note that the image index is not the same thing as a sprite index. The image index identifies an image only, not a sprite.)
- *ImageFile* is the name of the file that contains the image. This can be the name of any image file of the .png, .jpg, or .bmp file formats, however, only the .png format supports transparency.

- *BlackToTransparent* can be either 0 or 1. It must be 1 if you want the black pixels to become transparent. If 0 is used, the black pixels will be displayed.

The agk::LoadImage function does not create a sprite. It only loads the specified image into memory. To create a sprite from the loaded image, you use the agk::CreateSprite function, using the following general format:

```
agk::CreateSprite(SpriteIndex, ImageIndex);
```

Here is a summary of the two arguments that you pass to the function:

- *SpriteIndex* is the sprite index, which is a number that identifies the sprite in your program. The sprite index can be an integer in the range of 1 through 4,294,967,295. Once the sprite is created, you will use its sprite index to identify it in subsequent operations.
- *ImageIndex* is the image index of an image that you have previously loaded with the agk::LoadImage function.

Let's look at an example of how to do this. The image on the left of Figure 7-19 is in a file named Dog.png. Notice that the image's background is black. The image on the right is in a file named Beach.png. (The figure also appears as Figure C-4 in the book's color insert.) In Program 7-7 we will do the following:

- Create a sprite from the Beach.png image and display it.
- Load the Dog.png image with its black pixels transparent.
- Create a sprite from the dog image.
- Display the dog sprite over the beach sprite. Because the dog image's black pixels are transparent, it will look like the dog is at the beach. Figure 7-20 (which also appears as Figure C-5 in the book's color insert) shows the program's output.

Figure 7-19 The Dog and Beach images

Program 7-7   **(DogAtTheBeach)**

```cpp
 1 // Includes, namespace and prototypes
 2 #include "template.h"
 3 using namespace AGK;
 4 app App;
 5
 6 // Constants for the screen resolution
 7 const int SCREEN_WIDTH = 640;
 8 const int SCREEN_HEIGHT = 480;
 9
10 // Constants for the beach background
11 const int BEACH_SPRITE_INDEX = 1;
12
13 // Constants for the Dog image and sprite
14 const int DOG_IMAGE_INDEX = 1;
15 const int DOG_SPRITE_INDEX = 2;
16 const int BLACK_TRANSPARENT = 1;
17 const int DOG_X = 100;
18 const int DOG_Y = 240;
19
20 // Begin app, called once at the start
21 void app::Begin( void )
22 {
23    // Set the virtual resolution.
24    agk::SetVirtualResolution(SCREEN_WIDTH, SCREEN_HEIGHT);
25
26    // Create the beach sprite.
27    agk::CreateSprite(BEACH_SPRITE_INDEX, "Beach.png");
28
29    // Load the dog image with black pixels transparent.
30    agk::LoadImage(DOG_IMAGE_INDEX, "Dog.png",
31                   BLACK_TRANSPARENT);
32
33    // Create the dog sprite from the dog image.
34    agk::CreateSprite(DOG_SPRITE_INDEX, DOG_IMAGE_INDEX);
35
36    // Set the dog sprite's position.
37    agk::SetSpritePosition(DOG_SPRITE_INDEX, DOG_X, DOG_Y);
38 }
39
40 // Main loop, called every frame
41 void app::Loop ( void )
42 {
43    // Display the screen.
44    agk::Sync();
45 }
46
47 // Called when the app ends
48 void app::End ( void )
49 {
50 }
```

Figure 7-20 Output of Program 7-7

Let's take a closer look at the program. Here is a summary of the global constants:

- Lines 7 and 8 declare constants for the screen width and height.
- Line 11 declares a constant for the beach sprite's index, which is 1.
- Line 14 declares a constant for the dog image index, which is 1.
- Line 15 declares a constant for the dog sprite index, which is 2.
- Line 16 declares a constant to specify that black pixels are transparent. We will use this when we load the dog image.
- Lines 17 and 18 declare constants for the dog sprite's screen position.

Here is a summary of the app::Begin function:

- Line 24 sets the virtual resolution.
- Line 27 creates a sprite with the index 1, using the graphic file *Beach.png*. (The program will look for this file in the *My Documents > AGK > template* folder.)
- Lines 30 and 31 load the Dog.png image, assigning it the image index 1 and specifying that black pixels should be transparent.
- Line 34 creates a sprite from the dog image (image index 1) and assigns the sprite the sprite index 2.
- Line 37 positions the dog sprite at the coordinates (100, 240).

After the app::Begin function finishes, the program executes the app::Loop function. Line 44 calls the agk::Sync function, which displays the backbuffer.

Deleting Sprites

After a program is finished using a sprite, it can remove it with the `agk::DeleteSprite` function. You pass a sprite index as an argument to the function, and it removes that sprite from memory. Assuming `SPRITE_INDEX` is a valid sprite index, here is an example:

```
agk::DeleteSprite(SPRITE_INDEX);
```

This statement removes the sprite specified by `SPRITE_INDEX` from memory. Deleting unused sprites frees memory and can improve the program's performance. If a program has several sprites loaded and continues to run when those sprite are no longer needed, it's a good idea to delete them to increase system performance.

You can determine whether a sprite exists with the `agk::GetSpriteExists` function. Here is the general format:

```
agk::GetSpriteExists(SpriteIndex)
```

In the general format, `SpriteIndex` is the index of the sprite you are testing. If the sprite exists in memory, the function returns 1. Otherwise, it returns 0. The following code sample shows an example. It determines whether the sprite specified by `SPRITE_INDEX` exists. If so, it sets the sprite's location to (0, 0).

```
if ( agk::(GetSpriteExists(SPRITE_INDEX) == 1 )
{
    agk::SetSpritePosition(SPRITE_INDEX, 0, 0);
}
```

Organizing the Images in Your `template` Folder

VideoNote

Organizing the Images in your template Folder

As you develop more AGK projects, your *My Documents > AGK > template* folder will soon become cluttered with lots of image files. Fortunately, you can organize the image files in *My Documents > AGK > template* folder. You do this by creating a subfolder for each project in *My Documents > AGK > template* and then storing all the image files for that project in the subfolder. Of course, in your project's source code you must include the name of the subfolder in the image file's path. Let's look at an example of how we might do this with a project that uses the ghost and haunted house graphics shown previously in this chapter.

First, we will create a folder named *HauntedHouse* in the *My Documents > AGK > template* folder, as shown on the left in Figure 7-21. Then, in the *HauntedHouse* folder you will store the `haunted_house.png` and `ghost.png` graphic files, as shown on the right in Figure 7-21. Then, in Program 7-8 we load the images as sprites in lines 25 through 26 and lines 29 through 30. Notice that we use the path names `HauntedHouse/haunted_house.png` and `HauntedHouse/ghost.png` to load the images.

Program 7-8   **(ImageSubfolderDemo)**

```
1 // Includes, namespace and prototypes
2 #include "template.h"
3 using namespace AGK;
4 app App;
```

```
 5
 6 // Constants for the screen resolution
 7 const int SCREEN_WIDTH = 640;
 8 const int SCREEN_HEIGHT = 480;
 9
10 // Constants for the sprite indices
11 const int HOUSE_INDEX = 1;
12 const int GHOST_INDEX = 2;
13
14 // Constants for the ghost's position
15 const float GHOST_X = 200;
16 const float GHOST_Y = 150;
17
18 // Begin app, called once at the start
19 void app::Begin( void )
20 {
21    // Set the virtual resolution.
22    agk::SetVirtualResolution(SCREEN_WIDTH, SCREEN_HEIGHT);
23
24    // Create the haunted house sprite for the background.
25    agk::CreateSprite(HOUSE_INDEX,
26        "HauntedHouse/haunted_house.png");
27
28    // Create the ghost sprite.
29    agk::CreateSprite(GHOST_INDEX,
30        "HauntedHouse/ghost.png");
31
32    // Set the ghost's position.
33    agk::SetSpritePosition(GHOST_INDEX, GHOST_X, GHOST_Y);
34 }
35
36 // Main loop, called every frame
37 void app::Loop ( void )
38 {
39    // Display the screen.
40    agk::Sync();
41 }
42
43 // Called when the app ends
44 void app::End ( void )
45 {
46 }
```

NOTE: The *My Documents > AGK > template* folder is the base folder for all your AGK projects' media files. Your AGK projects will always look in this folder for resources such as image files. For this reason, any location that you specify for an image file in your AGK source code must be relative to the *My Documents > AGK > template* folder. You cannot specify a location that is not under the *My Documents > AGK > template* folder.

Figure 7-21 The *HauntedHouse* folder created under *My Documents > AGK > template*

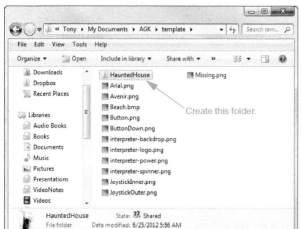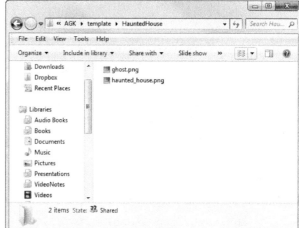

 Checkpoint

7.13. What is a bitmap?

7.14. What is a sprite?

7.15. What is a sprite index?

7.16. When you create a sprite, what is its default position on the screen?

7.17. What is the backbuffer?

7.18. What AGK function do you call to update the screen with the contents of the backbuffer?

7.19. You can have multiple sprites on the screen at one time. By default, in what order are sprites drawn on the screen?

7.20. How do you set a sprite's position on the screen? How do you get a sprite's current position?

7.21. How do you get a sprite's width and height? How do you scale a sprite so it is larger or smaller than its original size?

7.22. How do you rotate a sprite? How do you get a sprite's current angle of rotation?

7.23. How do you make a sprite invisible? If a sprite is already invisible, how do you make it visible?

 7.4 **Working in the Game Loop**

CONCEPT: Most of your program's work will be done in the app::Loop function, which is the game loop of an AGK application.

Now that you know the basics of creating and manipulating sprites, you can have some fun working in the app::Loop function. The important thing to remember about the app::Loop function is that it works like a loop. It begins executing after the app::Begin function finishes, and it automatically repeats until the user ends the program. Each iteration of the app::Loop function is called a *frame*.

Program 7-9 shows a simple example. When the program runs, it creates the ghost sprite that you have seen previously and displays it at the default coordinates of (0, 0). During each iteration of the app::Loop function, the sprite is rotated by 10 degrees. Figure 7-22 shows an example of the program's output during one frame of execution.

Program 7-9   **(SpinningSprite)**

```
1 // Includes, namespace and prototypes
2 #include "template.h"
3 using namespace AGK;
4 app App;
5
6 // Constants for the screen resolution
7 const int SCREEN_WIDTH = 640;
8 const int SCREEN_HEIGHT = 480;
9
10 // Constants for the sprite index
11 const int GHOST_INDEX = 1;
12
13 // Constant for the amount to rotate
14 const float ROTATION = 10;
15
16 // Begin app, called once at the start
17 void app::Begin( void )
18 {
19     // Set the virtual resolution.
20     agk::SetVirtualResolution(SCREEN_WIDTH, SCREEN_HEIGHT);
21
22     // Create the ghost sprite.
23     agk::CreateSprite(GHOST_INDEX, "ghost.png");
24 }
25
26 // Main loop, called every frame
27 void app::Loop ( void )
28 {
29     // Get the ghost's angle.
30     float ghostAngle = agk::GetSpriteAngle(GHOST_INDEX);
31
32     // Rotate the ghost.
33     agk::SetSpriteAngle(GHOST_INDEX, ghostAngle + ROTATION);
34
35     // Display the screen.
36     agk::Sync();
37 }
38
```

```
39 // Called when the app ends
40 void app::End ( void )
41 {
42 }
```

Figure 7-22 Screen capture of one frame from Program 7-9

Let's take a closer look at the program. First, we have the following global constants:

- In lines 7 and 8, the SCREEN_WIDTH and SCREEN_HEIGHT constants will be used to set the virtual resolution to 640 by 480 pixels.
- In line 11 the GHOST_INDEX constant is set to 1. This will be used as the sprite index for the ghost.
- Line 14 sets the ROTATION constant to 10. This is the amount by which the ghost sprite will be rotated during each frame.

The app::Begin function does the following:

- Line 20 sets the virtual resolution to 640 by 480 pixels.
- Line 23 creates the ghost sprite.

The app::Loop function does the following during each frame:

- Line 30 declares a float variable named ghostAngle. The variable is initialized with the value that is returned from the agk::GetSpriteAngle function. After this statement executes, the ghostAngle variable will hold the ghost sprite's current degrees of rotation. (If the sprite has not been rotated, the degrees of rotation will be 0).
- Line 33 calls the agk::SetSpriteAngle function to rotate the ghost sprite. Notice that the second argument is the expression ghostAngle + ROTATION. This specifies that the sprite's angle of rotation should be its current angle plus 10.
- Line 36 calls the agk::Sync function, which updates the screen.

Program 7-10 shows another simple example. When the program runs, it creates the ghost sprite and displays it at the coordinates (0, 150). During each iteration of the app::Loop function, the sprite is moved to the right by 10 pixels. When the sprite reaches the rightmost edge of the screen, it is moved back to its original position. Figure 7-23 shows an example of the program's output, during one frame of execution.

Program 7-10   (`LoopMoveSprite`)

```cpp
1 // Includes, namespace and prototypes
2 #include "template.h"
3 using namespace AGK;
4 app App;
5
6 // Constants for the screen resolution
7 const int SCREEN_WIDTH = 640;
8 const int SCREEN_HEIGHT = 480;
9
10 // Constants for the sprite index
11 const int GHOST_INDEX = 1;
12
13 // Constants for the ghost's starting position
14 const float GHOST_START_X = 0;
15 const float GHOST_START_Y = 150;
16
17 // Constant for the ghost's ending X coordinate
18 const float GHOST_END_X = 540;
19
20 // Constant for the amount to increment the
21 // ghost's X coordinate
22 const int INCREMENT = 10;
23
24 // Begin app, called once at the start
25 void app::Begin( void )
26 {
27     // Set the virtual resolution.
28     agk::SetVirtualResolution(SCREEN_WIDTH, SCREEN_HEIGHT);
29
30     // Create the ghost sprite.
31     agk::CreateSprite(GHOST_INDEX, "ghost.png");
32
33     // Set the ghost's position.
34     agk::SetSpritePosition(GHOST_INDEX,
35                 GHOST_START_X, GHOST_START_Y);
36 }
37
38 // Main loop, called every frame
39 void app::Loop( void )
40 {
41     // Get the ghost's current X coordinate.
42     float ghostX = agk::GetSpriteX(GHOST_INDEX);
43
44     if (ghostX < GHOST_END_X)
45     {
46         agk::SetSpriteX(GHOST_INDEX, ghostX + INCREMENT);
47     }
48     else
49     {
50         agk::SetSpriteX(GHOST_INDEX, GHOST_START_X);
51     }
52
53     // Display the screen.
```

```
54      agk::Sync();
55 }
56
57 // Called when the app ends
58 void app::End ( void )
59 {
60 }
```

Figure 7-23 Screen capture of one frame from Program 7-10

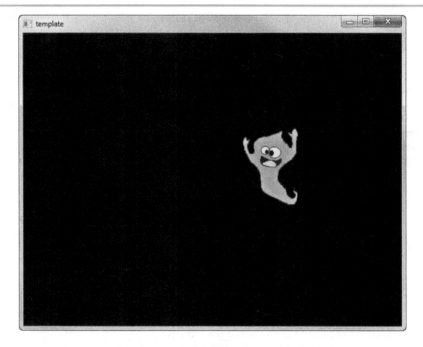

Let's take a closer look at the program. First, we have several global constants:

- In lines 7 and 8, the SCREEN_WIDTH and SCREEN_HEIGHT constants will be used to set the virtual resolution to 640 by 480 pixels.
- In line 11 the GHOST_INDEX constant is set to 1. This will be used as the sprite index for the ghost.
- In lines 14 and 15, the GHOST_START_X and GHOST_START_Y constants are set to 0 and 150, respectively. These will be used to set the ghost sprite's initial position.
- In line 18 the GHOST_END_X constant is set to 540. This is the ghost sprite's ending position on the screen. When the sprite's upper-left corner reaches this X-coordinate, the program will move the sprite back to its original position. (The sprite is 100 pixels wide, so it will be at the far right side of the screen when its upper-left corner is at 540.)
- Line 22 sets the INCREMENT constant to 10. This is the amount by which the ghost sprite will move across the screen during each frame.

The `app::Begin` function does the following:

- Line 28 sets the virtual resolution to 640 by 480 pixels.
- Line 31 creates the ghost sprite.
- Lines 34 and 35 position the ghost sprite at the coordinates (0, 150).

The `app::Loop` function does the following during each frame:

- Line 42 declares a `float` variable named `ghostX`. The variable is initialized with the value that is returned from the `agk::GetSpriteX` function. After this statement executes, the `ghostX` variable will hold the ghost sprite's current X-coordinate.
- The `if` statement that begins in line 44 determines whether `ghostX` is less than `GHOST_END_X` (which is 540). If this is true, then the ghost has not reached the right edge of the screen, so line 46 moves the sprite right by 10 pixels. If `ghostX` is not less than `GHOST_END_X`, then the sprite has reached the right edge of the screen, and line 50 moves the sprite back to its original X position, which is 0.
- Line 54 calls the `agk::Sync` function, which updates the screen.

Changing the Sync Rate

The *sync rate*, or *frame rate*, is the number of times per second that `app::Loop` function is executing. By default, the function executes approximately 60 times per second. Recall that each iteration of the `app::Loop` function is called a frame. If the function is executing 60 times per second, we say that the program has a sync rate of 60 *frames per second*.

Sometimes you might want to change the sync rate. For example, in Program 7-9 the ghost sprite moves very quickly across the screen, and you might want to slow the program down so you can see the ghost more easily. To slow the program down, you decrease its sync rate. You use the `agk::SetSyncRate` function to specify a sync rate. Here is the function's general format:

```
agk::SetSyncRate(FramesPerSecond, Mode);
```

Here is a summary of the function's arguments in the general format:

- *FramesPerSecond* is a `float` specifying the maximum number of frames per second for the program. While the program is running, it will attempt to execute the `app::Loop` function this many times per second. (We say *attempt* because the program might be busy doing so much work that it cannot fully achieve the specified frame rate.)
- *Mode* is an `int` that can be either 0 or 1. When the *Mode* is 0, the program uses the CPU less between frames and requires less power. This can be important for programs that run on mobile devices. When the *Mode* is 1, the program will use the CPU more intensively and consume more power, but the sync rate will be more accurate.

For example, if we want the ghost to move more slowly in Program 7-9, and we aren't particularly concerned with CPU usage, we might add the following global constants:

```
const float FRAMES_PER_SECOND = 5;
const int REFRESH_MODE = 1;
```

Then, we might add the following statement to the `app::Begin` function:

```
agk::SetSyncRate(FRAMES_PER_SECOND, REFRESH_MODE);
```

This will slow the program's sync rate to five frames per second, which is much slower than the default 60 frames per second.

Game State

A game can be in different states while it is running. For example, suppose you are playing a game in which you are driving a car on a racetrack. At any given moment, the game can be in one of several possible states, including the following:

- You are driving the car in the correct direction on the track.
- You are driving the car in the wrong direction on the track.
- You have crashed the car.

As your programs become more sophisticated, you will usually find that the game loop must determine the state that the game is in, and then act accordingly. For example, suppose we want to enhance Program 7-10 so that the ghost moves back and forth across the screen. When the ghost reaches one side of the screen, it reverses directions and goes toward the opposite side of the screen. When it reaches that side of the screen, it reverses direction again. At any moment, the program can be in one of the following states:

- The ghost is moving to the right
- The ghost is moving to the left

In the game loop, the program has to determine which of these states the program is in and then determine whether the sprite has reached the edge of the screen that it is moving toward. If the sprite has not reached the edge of the screen, it must keep moving in its current direction. Otherwise, the sprite must reverse its direction. The following pseudocode shows the program's logic:

```
If the ghost is moving to the right
    If the ghost has not reached the right edge of the screen
        Move the ghost right 10 pixels
    Else
        Reverse the ghost's direction
    End If
Else
    If the ghost has not reached the left edge of the screen
        Move the ghost left 10 pixels
    Else
        Reverse the ghost's direction
    End If
End If
```

Program 7-11 shows actual code that implements this logic. Figure 7-24 illustrates how the program runs.

Program 7-11 (GameState)

```
1  // Includes, namespace and prototypes
2  #include "template.h"
3  using namespace AGK;
4  app App;
```

```
 5
 6  // Global constants for screen resolution
 7  const int   SCREEN_WIDTH = 640;  // Screen width
 8  const int   SCREEN_HEIGHT = 480; // Screen height
 9
10  // Global constants for the ghost sprite
11  const int   GHOST_INDEX = 1;      // Ghost sprite index
12  const float GHOST_START_X = 0;    // Ghost's starting X
13  const float GHOST_START_Y = 150;  // Ghost's starting Y
14  const float GHOST_END_X = 540;    // Ghost's ending X
15  const int   INCREMENT = 10;       // Amount to move the ghost
16
17  // Global constants for the game state
18  const int   MOVING_RIGHT = 0;
19  const int   MOVING_LEFT  = 1;
20
21  // Global variable for game state
22  int g_gameState = MOVING_RIGHT;
23
24  // Begin app, called once at the start
25  void app::Begin( void )
26  {
27      // Set the virtual resolution.
28      agk::SetVirtualResolution(SCREEN_WIDTH, SCREEN_HEIGHT);
29
30      // Create the ghost sprite.
31      agk::CreateSprite(GHOST_INDEX, "ghost.png");
32
33      // Set the ghost's position.
34      agk::SetSpritePosition(GHOST_INDEX,
35                  GHOST_START_X, GHOST_START_Y);
36  }
37
38  // Main loop, called every frame
39  void app::Loop( void )
40  {
41      // Get the ghost's current X coordinate.
42      float ghostX = agk::GetSpriteX(GHOST_INDEX);
43
44      // Is the sprite moving to the right side of the screen?
45      if (g_gameState == MOVING_RIGHT)
46      {
47          // The sprite is moving right. Has it reached the
48          // edge of the screen?
49          if (ghostX < GHOST_END_X)
50          {
51              // Not at the edge yet, so keep moving right.
52              agk::SetSpriteX(GHOST_INDEX, ghostX + INCREMENT);
53          }
54          else
55          {
56              // The sprite is at the right edge of the screen.
57              // Change the game state to reverse directions.
58              g_gameState = MOVING_LEFT;
59          }
60      }
```

```
61    else
62    {
63        // The sprite is moving to the left.
64        // Has it reached the edge of the screen?
65        if (ghostX > GHOST_START_X)
66        {
67            // Not at the edge yet, so keep moving left.
68            agk::SetSpriteX(GHOST_INDEX, ghostX - INCREMENT);
69        }
70        else
71        {
72            // The sprite is at the left edge of the screen.
73            // Change the game state to reverse directions.
74            g_gameState = MOVING_RIGHT;
75        }
76    }
77
78    // Display the screen.
79    agk::Sync();
80 }
81
82 // Called when the app ends
83 void app::End ( void )
84 {
85 }
```

Figure 7-24 The moving sprite from Program 7-11

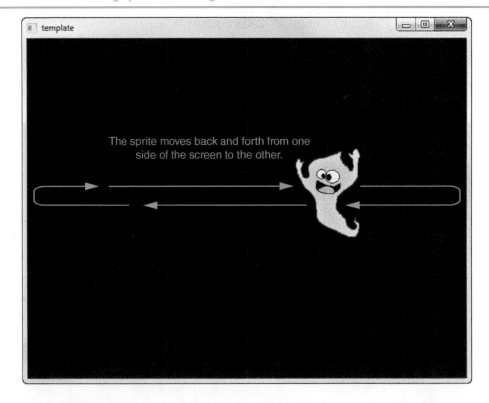

Let's take a closer look at the program. First, we have the global constant declaration for the screen resolution and various properties of the sprite:

- In lines 7 and 8, the SCREEN_WIDTH and SCREEN_HEIGHT constants will be used to set the virtual resolution to 640 by 480 pixels.
- In line 11 the GHOST_INDEX constant is set to 1. This will be used as the sprite index for the ghost.
- In lines 12 and 13, the GHOST_START_X and GHOST_START_Y constants are set to 0 and 150, respectively. These will be used to set the ghost sprite's initial position.
- In line 14 the GHOST_END_X constant is set to 540. This is the ghost sprite's ending position on the screen. When the sprite's upper-left corner reaches this X-coordinate, the program will move the sprite back to its original position. (The sprite is 100 pixels wide, so it will be at the far right side of the screen when its upper-left corner is at 540.)
- Line 15 sets the INCREMENT constant to 10. This is the amount by which the ghost sprite will move across the screen during each frame.

Next we have the following global constant declarations that will be used to indicate which state the program is in:

- Line 18 declares the int constant MOVING_RIGHT, set to the value 0.
- Line 19 declares the int constant MOVING_LEFT, set to the value 1.

Then we declare the following global declaration:

- Line 22 declares the global int variable g_gameState, initialized to the value MOVING_RIGHT.

The global variable g_gameState will be used to indicate which state the program is in. When the sprite is moving to the right, this variable will be set to the value MOVING_RIGHT. When the sprite is moving to the left, this variable will be set to the value MOVING_LEFT. Any time the program needs to know what state it is in, it can examine the contents of this variable. (Note that we have started the name of the variable with the g_ prefix to indicate that it is a global variable. This is not required, but it is a convention that we will use in this book. When you are reading the code, the g_ prefix serves as a reminder that the variable is global.)

The app::Begin function does the following:

- Line 28 sets the virtual resolution to 640 by 480 pixels.
- Line 31 creates the ghost sprite.
- Lines 34 and 35 position the ghost sprite at the coordinates (0, 150).

The app::Loop function does the following:

- Line 42 declares a float variable named ghostX. The variable is initialized with the value that is returned from the agk::GetSpriteX function. After this statement executes, the ghostX variable will hold the ghost sprite's current X-coordinate.
- The logic that was previously shown as pseudocode is implemented in the set of nested if statements that begins in line 45:
  - The if statement in line 45 determines whether g_gameState is equal to MOVING_RIGHT. If so, then the sprite is moving to the right, and the if statement

in line 49 determines whether the sprite has not reached the right edge of the screen. If this is the case, the statement in line 52 moves the sprite to the right 10 pixels. However, if the sprite has reached the right edge of the screen, line 58 assigns MOVING_LEFT to the g_gameState variable to indicate that the sprite is now moving to the left. (This changes the game state.)

- When the if statement in line 45 executes, if the g_gameState variable is set to MOVING_LEFT, the program will jump to the else clause in line 61. Then, the if statement in line 65 determines whether the sprite has not reached the left edge of the screen. If this is the case, the statement in line 68 moves the sprite to the left 10 pixels. However, if the sprite has reached the left edge of the screen, line 74 assigns MOVING_RIGHT to the g_gameState variable, to indicate that the sprite is now moving to the right. (This changes the game state.)

- Line 79 calls the agk::Sync function, which updates the screen.

WARNING! It should be mentioned that, whenever possible, the use of global variables should be avoided, or at least kept to a minimum. Recall that Chapter 6 discussed the potential problems that global variables can cause. In some situations, however, a global variable can be justified if there is simply no better way to accomplish the required task. This is the case with Program 7-10.

Checkpoint

7.24. What is a frame?

7.25. What is the sync rate (or frame rate)?

7.26. How do you change the default sync rate in an AGK program?

7.27. In your own words, what is meant by "game state"?

7.5 Working with Colors and Transparency

CONCEPT: The AGK uses the RGB (red, green, and blue) system to specify colors for pixels. The pixels of images that are stored in .png files also have a fourth component, known as the alpha channel, that specifies transparency.

The RGB Color System

The AGK uses the *RGB color system* to define colors. In the RGB color system, all colors are created by mixing various shades of red, green, and blue. For example, in the RGB system, if you mix bright red, bright green, and no blue, you get yellow. If you mix bright red, bright blue, and no green, you get purple. White is created by mixing all three colors at their maximum brightness, and black is created when there is no red, green, or blue.

In programming, we commonly refer to the red, green, and blue components of a color as *color channels*. When you define a color, you specify a value in the range of 0 through 255 for each of the color channels. The higher the number for a channel, the brighter that color component will be. For a quick demonstration of how these channels work, we can use the agk::SetClearColor function and the agk::ClearScreen function. The agk::SetClearColor function specifies a background color that will fill the screen when the agk::ClearScreen function is called. Here is the general format of how you call the agk::SetClearColor function:

```
agk::SetClearColor(Red, Green, Blue);
```

In the general format, the *Red*, *Green*, and *Blue* arguments are values for the red, green, and blue color channels. For example, the following statement calls the function and specifies 255 for the red channel, 0 for the green channel, and 127 for the blue channel:

```
agk::SetClearColor(255, 0, 127);
```

The color that is created by these channel values will be the combination of bright red, no green, and medium-intensity blue. The result will be a color in the purple or magenta family. Here is another example:

```
agk::SetClearColor(255, 0, 0);
```

This statement specifies 255 for red, 0 for green, and 0 for blue. These values specify a bright red color. Here is another example:

```
agk::SetClearColor(255, 255, 255);
```

This statement specifies 255 for red, 255 for green, and 255 for blue. These values result in the color white. Figure C-1 (which is located in this book's color insert) shows how various red, green, and blue channel values create cyan, magenta, white, and black.

Once you have set the background color, you can call the agk::ClearScreen function to clear the screen and fill it with the specified color. Here is the function's general format:

```
agk::ClearScreen();
```

Applying Colors and Transparency to Sprites

Although image files have their own colors, you can apply a color to an existing sprite, giving it a tint. For example, if you can give a sprite a red tint by setting its red color channel. You can set the individual red, green, and blue color channels with the following functions:

```
agk::SetSpriteColorRed(SpriteIndex, RedChannel);
agk::SetSpriteColorGreen(SpriteIndex, GreenChannel);
agk::SetSpriteColorBlue(SpriteIndex, BlueChannel);
```

In each of the functions, the *SpriteIndex* is the index of a sprite. The *RedChannel*, *GreenChannel*, and *BlueChannel* arguments are integers in the range of 0 through 255, specifying a value for the sprite's red channel, green channel, or blue channel.

For example, assuming SPRITE_INDEX is a valid sprite index, the following statement sets the sprite's red channel to 200, giving it a red tint:

```
agk::SetSpriteColorRed(SPRITE_INDEX, 200);
```

The following statements set the sprite's red, green, and blue channels to 50, 100, and 200, respectively:

```
agk::SetSpriteColorRed(SPRITE_INDEX, 50);
agk::SetSpriteColorGreen(SPRITE_INDEX, 100);
agk::SetSpriteColorBlue(SPRITE_INDEX, 200);
```

Sprites also have an alpha value, which specifies the sprite's transparency. A sprite's alpha value is an integer in the range of 0 through 255. If a sprite's alpha value is set to 255 (which is the default value), then the sprite is completely opaque, and you cannot see through it. An alpha value of 0 makes a sprite completely invisible. Alpha values between 0 and 255 will make the sprite semitransparent. You can use the agk::SetSpriteColorAlpha to set a sprite's alpha value. Here is the function's general format:

```
agk::SetSpriteColorAlpha(SpriteIndex, Alpha);
```

In the general format, *SpriteIndex* is the index of a sprite, and *Alpha* is an integer in the range of 0 through 255, specifying the sprite's transparency. For example, assuming SPRITE_INDEX is a valid sprite index, the following statements demonstrate the function:

```
agk::SetSpriteColorAlpha(SPRITE_INDEX, 100); // Semitransparent
agk::SetSpriteColorAlpha(SPRITE_INDEX, 0);   // Invisible
agk::SetSpriteColorAlpha(SPRITE_INDEX, 255); // Opaque
```

Figure 7-25 shows an example of a semitransparent sprite. The ghost sprite in the figure has an alpha value of 100. (This also appears as Figure C-6 in the book's color insert.)

Figure 7-25 Ghost sprite with alpha value of 100

You can use the `agk::SetSpriteColor` function to set all of a sprite's color channels, including its alpha value, with one function call. Here is the general format:

```
agk::SetSpriteColor(SpriteIndex, Red, Green, Blue, Alpha);
```

In the general format, *SpriteIndex* is the index of a sprite. The *Red*, *Green*, and *Blue*, and *Alpha* arguments are integers in the range of 0 through 255, specifying a value for the sprite's red, green, and blue channels, and the sprite's alpha value. Assuming SPRITE_INDEX is a valid sprite index, the following statement demonstrates the function:

```
agk::SetSpriteColorAlpha(SPRITE_INDEX, 50, 25, 200, 100);
```

In this example, the sprite's red, green and blue channels are set to 50, 25, and 200, respectively. Its alpha value is set to 100.

Getting a Sprite's Color and Alpha Values

You can get a sprite's red, green, blue, and alpha values with the following functions:

```
agk::GetSpriteColorRed(SpriteIndex);
agk::GetSpriteColorGreen(SpriteIndex);
agk::GetSpriteColorBlue(SpriteIndex);
agk::GetSpriteColorAlpha(SpriteIndex);
```

In each of the general formats, *SpriteIndex* is the index of a sprite. The functions return the specified sprite's red, green, blue, and alpha values. For example, assuming SPRITE_INDEX is a valid sprite index, the following code demonstrates each function call:

```
// Declare variables to hold the sprite's color attributes.
int red, green, blue, alpha;
// Get the sprite's color attributes.
red = agk::GetSpriteColorRed(SPRITE_INDEX);
green = agk::GetSpriteColorGreen(SPRITE_INDEX);
blue = agk::GetSpriteColorBlue(SPRITE_INDEX);
alpha = agk::GetSpriteColorAlpha(SPRITE_INDEX);
```

After this code executes, the variables `red`, `green`, `blue`, and `alpha` will contain the sprite's red, green, blue, and alpha values.

Checkpoint

7.28. What three color channels does the RGB system use to generate colors?

7.29. What color is specified by each of the following statements?
```
agk::SetClearColor(0, 0, 255);
agk::SetClearColor(255, 0, 0);
agk::SetClearColor(0, 255, 0);
agk::SetClearColor(255, 255, 255);
agk::SetClearColor(0, 0, 0);
```

7.30. What happens when you apply a color to a sprite?

7.31. What is a sprite's alpha value? What are the valid values for a sprite's alpha value?

7.6 Displaying Text in the AGK Window

CONCEPT: You can use the `agk::Print` and `agk::PrintC` functions to display text in the AGK window.

Most of your AGK programs will use sprites to display graphics, but in some situations you might want to display text. The AGK provides two functions for displaying text in the AGK window. These functions are `agk::Print` and `agk::Printc`.

The `agk::Print` function prints a line of output in the AGK window, followed by a newline. This is similar to using `endl` with a `cout` statement in standard C++. After the `agk::Print` function executes, the output of a subsequent to the function will appear on the next line in the window.

The three different general formats for the `agk::Print` function are shown here:

```
agk::Print(IntValue);
agk::Print(FloatValue);
agk::Print(String);
```

In the first general format, `IntValue` is an integer value that is displayed. In the second general format, `FloatValue` is a `float` value that is displayed. In the third general format, `String` is a string that is displayed. Program 7-12 demonstrates each of these functions. The program's output is shown in Figure 7-26.

Program 7-12 (PrintDemo)

```
1  // Includes, namespace and prototypes
2  #include "template.h"
3  using namespace AGK;
4  app App;
5
6  // Constants for the screen resolution
7  const int SCREEN_WIDTH = 640;
8  const int SCREEN_HEIGHT = 480;
9
10 // Begin app, called once at the start
11 void app::Begin( void )
12 {
13     // Set the virtual resolution.
14     agk::SetVirtualResolution(SCREEN_WIDTH, SCREEN_HEIGHT);
15 }
16
17 // Main loop, called every frame
18 void app::Loop ( void )
19 {
20     // Declare variables
21     int iNum = 1;
```

```
22     float fNum = 99.5;
23
24     // Display some values.
25     agk::Print("This demonstrates the agk::Print function.");
26     agk::Print("Here are an int and a float:");
27     agk::Print(iNum);
28     agk::Print(fNum);
29
30     // Display the screen.
31     agk::Sync();
32 }
33
34 // Called when the app ends
35 void app::End ( void )
36 {
37 }
```

Figure 7-26 Output of Program 7-12

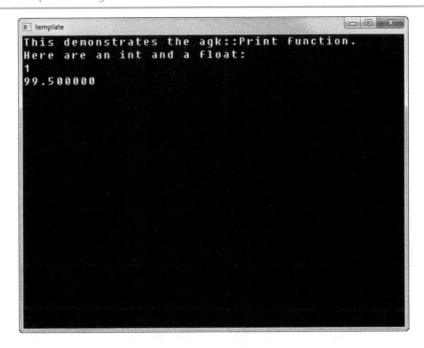

The agk::PrintC function prints a line of output in the AGK window without an ending newline. The output of any subsequent call to agk::PrintC or agk::Print will follow immediately, on the same line. Here are the general formats of the agk::PrintC function:

```
agk::PrintC(IntValue);
agk::PrintC(FloatValue);
agk::PrintC(String);
```

In the first general format, *IntValue* is an integer value that is displayed. In the second general format, *FloatValue* is a float value that is displayed. In the third general format, *String* is a string that is displayed. Program 7-13 demonstrates each of these functions. The program's output is shown in Figure 7-27.

Program 7-13   **(PrintCDemo)**

```
 1 // Includes, namespace and prototypes
 2 #include "template.h"
 3 using namespace AGK;
 4 app App;
 5
 6 // Constants for the screen resolution
 7 const int SCREEN_WIDTH = 640;
 8 const int SCREEN_HEIGHT = 480;
 9
10 // Begin app, called once at the start
11 void app::Begin( void )
12 {
13     // Set the virtual resolution.
14     agk::SetVirtualResolution(SCREEN_WIDTH, SCREEN_HEIGHT);
15 }
16
17 // Main loop, called every frame
18 void app::Loop ( void )
19 {
20     // Declare variables
21     int iNum = 1;
22     float fNum = 99.5;
23
24     // Display some values.
25     agk::PrintC("Here are an int and a float:");
26     agk::PrintC(iNum);
27     agk::PrintC(fNum);
28
29     // Display the screen.
30     agk::Sync();
31 }
32
33 // Called when the app ends
34 void app::End ( void )
35 {
36 }
```

In this program, line 25 prints the string "Here are an int and a float:". Then, line 26 prints the value of the iNum variable, which is 1. Notice that the output of line 26 appears immediately after the output of line 25. Then, line 27 prints the value of the fNum variable, which is 99.5. Notice that the output of line 27 appears immediately after the output of line 26.

Figure 7-27 Output of Program 7-13

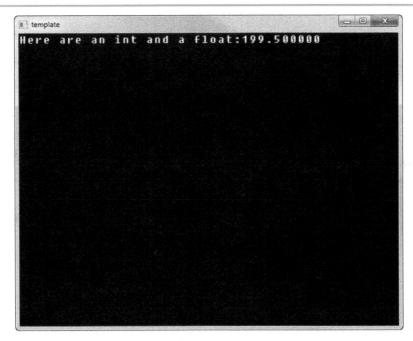

Printing string Objects

In Programs 7-12 and 7-13 you saw string literals being printed in the AGK window. You can declare string objects in your AGK programs, but you cannot pass a string object directly to the agk::Print or agk::PrintC functions. Instead, you must call a member function named c_str that is built into the string object. Functions that are built into objects are known as *member functions*. The c_str member function converts the contents of a string object to a format that is compatible with the agk::Print and agk::PrintC functions. This is the general format of the c_str member function:

```
StringObject.c_str()
```

In the general format, *StringObject* is the name of the string object that you are converting. The function returns a string that can be passed directly to agk::Print or agk::PrintC. Program 7-14 demonstrates how this is done. Figure 7-28 shows the program's output.

Program 7-14   **(AGKPrintString)**

```
1 // Includes, namespace and prototypes
2 #include <string>      // Needed for string objects
3 #include "template.h"
4 using namespace AGK;
5 using namespace std;    // Needed for string objects
6 app App;
```

```
 7
 8 // Constants for the screen resolution
 9 const int SCREEN_WIDTH = 640;
10 const int SCREEN_HEIGHT = 480;
11
12 // Begin app, called once at the start
13 void app::Begin( void )
14 {
15    // Set the virtual resolution.
16    agk::SetVirtualResolution(SCREEN_WIDTH, SCREEN_HEIGHT);
17 }
18
19 // Main loop, called every frame
20 void app::Loop ( void )
21 {
22    // Declare a string object.
23    string str = "This is a test.";
24
25    // Display the string object.
26    agk::Print(str.c_str());
27
28    // Display the screen.
29    agk::Sync();
30 }
31
32 // Called when the app ends
33 void app::End ( void )
34 {
35 }
```

Figure 7-28 Output of Program 7-14

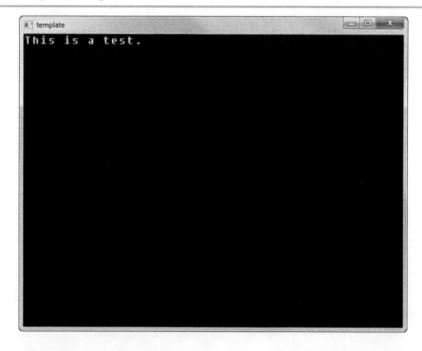

Let's take a closer look at the program.

- Line 2 includes the `string` header file, which is required for any program using `string` objects.
- The `using namespace std;` statement in line 5 is also required for `string` objects because the `string` class is part of the C++ standard library.
- Inside the `app::Loop` function, in line 23 we declare a `string` object named `str`, initialized with the string `"This is a test."`
- Line 26 calls the `str` object's `c_str()` member function, and the value that is returned from the function is passed to the `agk::Print` function. As a result, the value of the `str` object is displayed.
- Line 29 calls the `agk::Sync` function to update the screen.

Displaying a Title in the Window's Title Bar

In an AGK program, the `agk::SetWindowTitle` function displays text in the window's title bar, which appears at the top of the window. This helps you to customize the appearance of the window. Here is the general format of how you call the function:

```
agk::SetWindowTitle(String)
```

In the general format *String* is the string that you want to appear in the window's title bar. Here is an example:

```
agk::SetWindowTitle("My AGK Program");
```

This causes the text `"My AGK Program"` to appear in the window's title bar, as shown in Figure 7-29.

Figure 7-29 The window title set

 Checkpoint

7.32. What is the difference between the `agk::Print` and `agk::PrintC` functions?

7.33. How do you print the contents of a string object with the `agk::Print` and `agk::PrintC` functions?

7.34. How do you display text in the output window's title bar?

 7.7 **Generating Random Numbers**

CONCEPT: Random numbers are used in many applications, including games. The AGK provides a function named **agk::Random** that generates random numbers.

The AGK provides a function named `agk::Random` that generates random numbers. Random numbers are useful for lots of different programming tasks. The following are a few examples:

- Random numbers are commonly used in games. For example, computer games that let the player roll dice use random numbers to represent the values of the dice. Games that show cards being drawn from a shuffled deck use random numbers to represent the face values of the cards.
- Random numbers are useful in simulation programs. In some simulations, the computer must randomly decide how a person, animal, insect, or other living being will behave. Formulas can be constructed in which a random number is used to determine various actions and events that take place in the program.
- Random numbers are useful in statistical programs that must randomly select data for analysis.
- Random numbers are commonly used in computer security to encrypt sensitive data.

The `agk::Random` function can be called in the following general format:

```
agk::Random()
```

In this general format, the function returns a random number in the range of 0 through 65,535. For example, after the following statement executes, the `number` variable will be assigned a value in the range of 0 through 65,535:

```
int number;
number = agk::Random();
```

If you want to specify a range for the random number, you can call the function using the following general format:

```
agk::Random(From, To)
```

In this general format the *From* argument is the lowest possible value to return and *To* is the highest possible value to return. The function will return a random number within the range of these two values. For example, after the following code executes, the `number` variable will be assigned a random value in the range of 1 through 10:

```
int number;
number = agk::Random(1, 10);
```

The following code sample shows another example: positioning a sprite at a random location on the screen. Assume the constants `SCREEN_WIDTH` and `SCREEN_HEIGHT` have been set to the width and height of the AGK window and that `SPRITE_INDEX` is a valid sprite index.

```
1  // Declare variables for the sprite's X- and Y-coordinates.
2  int spriteX, spriteY;
3
4  // Get random values for the X- and Y-coordinates.
5  spriteX = agk::Random(0, SCREEN_WIDTH);
6  spriteY = agk::Random(0, SCREEN_HEIGHT);
7
8  // Set the sprite's position.
9  agk::SetSpritePosition(SPRITE_INDEX, spriteX, spriteY);
```

Let's take a closer look at the code:

- Line 2 declares two `int` variables: `spriteX` and `spriteY`. These variables will be used to hold the sprite's *X*- and *Y*-coordinates.
- Line 5 gets a random number in the range of 0 through `SCREEN_WIDTH` and assigns it to the `spriteX` variable.
- Line 6 gets a random number in the range of 0 through `SCREEN_HEIGHT` and assigns it to the `spriteY` variable.
- Line 9 sets the sprite that is specified by `SPRITE_INDEX` to the coordinates held in the `spriteX` and `spriteY` variables.

The following *In the Spotlight* section shows how this is done in a complete program.

In the Spotlight:
Using Random Numbers to Position
a Sprite and Set its Transparency

Program 7-15 displays the haunted house sprite as the background image, and during each frame, it displays the ghost sprite at a random location. The ghost's alpha value is also randomly generated during each frame (within the range of 50 through 255). As a result, the ghost will appear to jump around to random locations on the screen, with varying levels of transparency. The program's sync rate is slowed to five frames per second to make the ghost easier to see. Figure 7-30 shows the ghost as it appears in various frames.

Program 7-15   **(RandomPositionAndAlpha)**

```
 1 // Includes, namespace and prototypes
 2 #include "template.h"
 3 using namespace AGK;
 4 app App;
 5
 6 // Constants for the screen resolution
 7 const int SCREEN_WIDTH = 640;
 8 const int SCREEN_HEIGHT = 480;
 9
10 // Constants for the frame rate and refresh mode.
11 const float FRAME_RATE = 5;
12 const int REFRESH_MODE = 1;
13
14 // Constants for the sprite indices
15 const int HOUSE_INDEX = 1;
16 const int GHOST_INDEX = 2;
17
18 // Constants for the ghost's minimum and maximum alpha.
19 const int MIN_ALPHA = 50;
20 const int MAX_ALPHA = 255;
21
22 // Begin app, called once at the start
```

```
23 void app::Begin( void )
24 {
25    // Set the virtual resolution.
26    agk::SetVirtualResolution(SCREEN_WIDTH, SCREEN_HEIGHT);
27
28    // Create the haunted house sprite for the background.
29    agk::CreateSprite(HOUSE_INDEX,
30          "HauntedHouse/haunted_house.png");
31
32    // Create the ghost sprite.
33    agk::CreateSprite(GHOST_INDEX,
34          "HauntedHouse/ghost.png");
35
36    // Set the frame rate.
37    agk::SetSyncRate(FRAME_RATE, REFRESH_MODE);
38 }
39
40 // Main loop, called every frame
41 void app::Loop ( void )
42 {
43    // Variables for the ghost's location and alpha value
44    int ghostX, ghostY, ghostAlpha;
45
46    // Get random coordinates.
47    ghostX = agk::Random(0, SCREEN_WIDTH);
48    ghostY = agk::Random(0, SCREEN_HEIGHT);
49
50    // Get a random value for the ghost's alpha.
51    ghostAlpha = agk::Random(MIN_ALPHA, MAX_ALPHA);
52
53    // Set the ghost's position.
54    agk::SetSpritePosition(GHOST_INDEX, ghostX, ghostY);
55
56    // Set the ghost's alpha value.
57    agk::SetSpriteColorAlpha(GHOST_INDEX, ghostAlpha);
58
59    // Display the screen.
60    agk::Sync();
61 }
62
63 // Called when the app ends
64 void app::End ( void )
65 {
66 }
```

Let's take a closer look at the program. Here is a summary of the global constants:

- Lines 7 and 8 declare constants for the screen size.
- Line 11 declares a constant for that will be used to change the program's sync rate. This constant specifies a sync rate of five frames per second.
- Line 12 declares a constant specifying a refresh mode of 1. Recall that the refresh mode 1 causes the program to use more CPU power, but more accurately refreshes the screen at the specified number of frames per second.

Figure 7-30 Three frames of output of Program 7-15

- Lines 15 and 16 declare constants for the sprite indices.
- Lines 19 and 20 declare constants that specify the minimum and maximum alpha values for the ghost sprite.

Here is a description of the `app::Begin` function:

- Line 26 sets the virtual resolution.
- Lines 29 and 30 create the haunted house sprite.
- Lines 33 and 34 create the ghost sprite.
- Line 37 sets the sync rate to five frames per second. This will cause the program to update the screen slowly enough to see the ghost between frames.

Here is a description of the `app::Loop` function:

- Line 44 declares the `ghostX` variable, which will hold the ghost's X-coordinate, the `ghostY` variable, which will hold the ghost's Y-coordinate, and the `ghostAlpha` variable, which will hold the ghost's alpha value.
- Line 47 gets a random number between 0 and the width of the screen and assigns the number to the `ghostX` variable.
- Line 48 gets a random number between 0 and the height of the screen and assigns the number to the `ghostY` variable.
- Line 51 gets a random number between 50 and 255 and assigns the number to the `ghostAlpha` variable.
- Line 54 sets the ghost sprite's position to the coordinates specified by the `ghostX` and `ghostY` variables.
- Line 57 sets the ghost sprite's alpha value to the number stored in the `ghostAlpha` variable.
- Line 60 updates the screen.

Checkpoint

7.35. After this statement executes, what value will be stored in the number variable?

```
int number = agk::Random();
```

7.36. After this statement executes, what value will be stored in the number variable?

```
int number = agk::Random(0, 100);
```

Review Questions

Multiple Choice

1. This is a loop that repeats continuously, until the game is over:
   a. Initialization loop.
   b. Game loop.
   c. Player's loop.
   d. AGK Loop.

2. In the AGK C++ template, this function executes once, when the program starts:
   a. `app::Begin`.
   b. `app::Loop`.
   c. `app::End`.
   d. `app::Start`.

3. In the AGK C++ template, this function performs the game loop:
   a. `app::Begin`.
   b. `app::Loop`.
   c. `app::End`.
   d. `app::GameLoop`.

4. In the AGK C++ template, this function executes when the program ends:
   a. `app::Begin`.
   b. `app::Loop`.
   c. `app::End`.
   d. `app::Shutdown`.

5. These are the tiny dots that make up the display area of the screen:
   a. display points.
   b. pixels.
   c. backlights.
   d. display elements.

6. This is used to identify a specific position within the AGK's output window:
   a. coordinate system.
   b. position locator.
   c. position sensor.
   d. memory address.

7. This is the AGK's default method of handling screen coordinates:
   a. planar.
   b. virtual resolution.
   c. percentage-based.
   d. memory mapped.

8. This is the default size of the AGK output window:
   a. 1024 by 768.
   b. 100 by 100.
   c. 640 by 480.
   d. 2048 by 1536.

9. You call this function in an AGK program to use the virtual resolution system:
   a. agk::SetVirtualResolution.
   b. agk::VirtualResolution.
   c. agk::Resolution.
   d. Nothing. Virtual resolution is used by default.

10. This is a set of data that describes every pixel in an image:
    a. pixel dataset.
    b. display database.
    c. bitmap.
    d. pixelmap.

11. A graphic image displayed in a game program is usually called this:
    a. pixie.
    b. sprite.
    c. elf.
    d. troll.

12. This is a copy of the output screen that the AGK keeps in memory:
    a. backbuffer.
    b. backcopy.
    c. backup screen.
    d. screen clone.

13. This function updates the screen:
    a. agk::UpdateScreen.
    b. agk::DrawScreen.
    c. agk::Sync.
    d. agk::SyncScreen.

14. Each iteration of the app::Loop function is:
    a. one millisecond long.
    b. one CPU clock cycle.
    c. one frame.
    d. one second long.

15. In the AGK, colors are generated by combining these color channels:
    a. red, green, and yellow.
    b. cyan, magenta, and yellow.
    c. red, orange, yellow, green, blue, indigo, and violet.
    d. red, green, and blue.

16. A sprite's transparency is specified by this:
    a. the sprite's alpha value.
    b. the sprite's name.
    c. the value of the sprite's RGB channels added together.
    d. the program's sync rate.

True or False

1. In the AGK C++ template, the app::Begin function works as the program's game loop.

2. The app::Loop function does not loop automatically. It is meant to be called from a while loop.

3. By default, the AGK uses the virtual resolution system for its output window.

4. The default size of the AGK output window in virtual resolution is 100 by 100.

5. A sprite index must be in the range of 0 through 255.

6. A sprite with a depth of 0 will be drawn before a sprite with a depth of 100.

7. You can specify a value in the range of 0 through 255 for an RGB color channel.

Short Answer

1. What three general phases are virtually all game programs structured into?

2. What is the game loop in a game program?

3. What are the three functions that are already provided in the AGK C++ template? How do they relate to the three phases of a game program?

4. What is a pixel?

5. What is the default resolution of the AGK's output window when virtual resolution is used?

6. What is the default resolution of the AGK's output window when virtual resolution is used?

7. What is a bitmap?

8. What is a sprite?

9. What is the backbuffer?

10. How does sprite depth affect the order in which sprites are drawn?

11. What are the three color channels in the RGB system?

12. What color would result from the RGB color channels (0, 0, 255)?

13. What is an alpha value? What happens if you set a sprite's alpha value to 0? What happens if you set a sprite's alpha value to 255? What happens if you set a sprite's alpha value to 50?

Algorithm Workbench

1. Assume the file goldfish.png is in your *My Documents > AGK > template* folder. Write a statement that creates a sprite using this image file, with the sprite index 1.

2. Assume SPRITE_INDEX is a valid sprite index. Write a statement that makes the sprite twice its current size.

3. Assume SPRITE_INDEX is a valid sprite index. Write a statement that rotates the sprite 45 degrees.

4. Assume SPRITE_INDEX is a valid sprite index. Write a statement that positions the sprite's upper-left corner at the coordinates 100, 50.

5. Assume SPRITE_INDEX is a valid sprite index. Write code that displays the sprite's *X*- and *Y*-coordinates in the output window.

6. Assume SPRITE_INDEX is a valid sprite index. Write code that displays the sprite's width and height in the output window.

7. Write code that clears the output window to green.

8. Assume SPRITE_INDEX is a valid sprite index. Write code that sets the sprite's alpha value to 50.

9. Assume SPRITE_INDEX is a valid sprite index. Write code that applies a red tint to the sprite.

Programming Exercises

1. **Random Screen Colors**
   Write an AGK program that repeatedly clears the screen to a random color as long as the program is running. (Generate random numbers for each of the clear color's RGB channels.)

VideoNote

Solving the Moving Ball Problem

2. **Moving Ball**
   In the sample media that you can download from this book's Web site, you will find a ball image. Write an AGK program that makes a sprite from the ball image and makes the ball move up and down on the screen, from the bottom of the window to the top, and back again.

3. **Fish**
   In the sample media that you can download from this book's Web site, you will find a fish image and an undersea background. Write an AGK program that displays the undersea background and makes the fish move back and forth across the screen.

4. **School of Fish**
   Modify the program that you created for Programming Exercise 3 so it has three fish sprites, each moving back and forth across the screen. Use the same image file for each fish sprite.

5. **Fish Swimming in Opposite Directions**
   Write a program similar to the one that you wrote for Programming Exercise 3, except this one should have two fish moving in opposite directions. Use the same image file for each fish sprite.

6. **Growing and Shrinking Ghost**

   Write a program that displays the ghost shown earlier in this chapter (available in the book's sample media collection) first at its normal size. Then the ghost should then grow to twice its size, and then to four times its size. Next, the ghost should shrink back down to twice its size, and then shrink back down to its normal size. This pattern of growing and shrinking should repeat as long as the program is running.

7. **Random Falling Ball**

   In the sample media that you can download from this book's Web site, you will find a ball image. Write a program that displays the ball at a random location and then makes the ball move down to the bottom of the screen. When the ball reaches the bottom of the screen, it should start these actions over again, appearing at another random location, and then moving to the bottom of the screen.

8. **Two Random Falling Balls**

   Modify the program that you wrote for Programming Exercise 7 so it has two balls that appear at random locations and fall to the bottom of the screen.

9. **Embarrassed Ghost**

   Use the ghost and haunted house images shown in this chapter (available in the book's sample media collection) in a program that makes the ghost appear with an increasingly red tint. At first, the ghost should be displayed normally, but as the program runs, you should increase the value of the ghost's red color channel a small amount until it has reached its maximum value. Then, you should decrease the ghost's red color channel a small amount until it has reached 0. This pattern of becoming more red, and then less red should repeat as long as the program is running.

10. **Fading Ghost**

    Use the ghost and haunted house images shown in this chapter (available in the book's sample media collection) in a program that makes the ghost fade in and out. At first, the ghost should be completely transparent, but as the program runs, it should fade in until it is completely opaque. Then, the ghost should start fading out until it is completely transparent. This pattern of fading in and out should repeat as long as the program is running.

8 Input, Animation, and Sound

8.1 The Mouse

CONCEPT: The AGK provides functions that you can use to work with the mouse. These functions allow you to track the mouse pointer's location on the screen and determine when the user is pressing one or more of the mouse buttons.

VideoNote

Working with the Mouse

Getting the Mouse Coordinates

You can call the `agk::GetRawMouseX` and `agk::GetRawMouseY` functions to get the current coordinates of the mouse pointer. The following code shows an example. Assume that x and y are `float` variables.

```
x = agk::GetRawMouseX();
y = agk::GetRawMouseY();
```

After this code executes, x will contain the mouse pointer's X-coordinate, and y will contain the mouse pointer's Y-coordinate. Program 8-1 demonstrates how these functions work. The program uses the `app::Loop` function to continually get the mouse pointer's coordinates (lines 32 and 33) and sets the sprite's position to that location (line 37). This is shown in Figure 8-1. As the user moves the mouse pointer, the sprite moves with it.

Program 8-1 (Sprite Mouse)

```
1  // This program demonstrates how to get
2  // the mouse pointer's location.
3
4  // Includes, namespace and prototypes
5  #include "template.h"
6  using namespace AGK;
7  app App;
8
9  // Constants
10 const int SCREEN_WIDTH    = 640;
11 const int SCREEN_HEIGHT   = 480;
12 const int SPRITE_INDEX    = 1;
13
14 // Variables to hold the mouse pointer's
15 // X- and Y-coordinates.
16 float g_mouseX, g_mouseY;
17
18 // Begin app, called once at the start
19 void app::Begin( void )
20 {
21    // Set the virtual resolution, window title, and
22    // create the sprite.
23    agk::SetVirtualResolution(SCREEN_WIDTH, SCREEN_HEIGHT);
24    agk::SetWindowTitle("Sprite Mouse");
25    agk::CreateSprite(SPRITE_INDEX, "mouse.png");
26 }
27
28 // Main loop, called every frame
29 void app::Loop ( void )
30 {
31    // Get the mouse pointer's location.
32    g_mouseX = agk::GetRawMouseX();
33    g_mouseY = agk::GetRawMouseY();
34
35    // Set the sprite's position to the mouse
36    // pointer's location.
37    agk::SetSpritePosition(SPRITE_INDEX, g_mouseX, g_mouseY);
38
39    // Refresh the screen.
40    agk::Sync();
41 }
42
43 // Called when the app ends
44 void app::End ( void )
45 {
46 }
```

Figure 8-1 Example output of Program 8-1

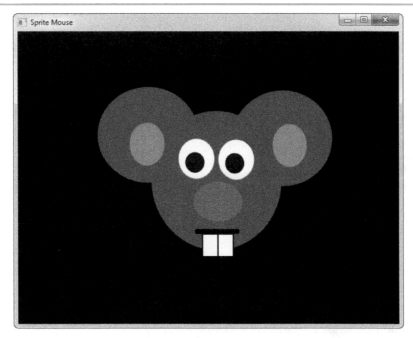

Showing and Hiding the Mouse

By default, the mouse pointer is visible when an AGK program is running. You can control the mouse pointer's visibility, however, with the `agk::SetRawMouseVisible` function. Here is the general format of how you call the function.

```
agk::SetRawMouseVisible(Visible);
```

The function accepts an integer value as an argument. The value 0 will hide the mouse pointer, and the value 1 will show the mouse pointer. When you call the function and pass the value 0 as an argument, the mouse pointer becomes invisible within the program's window. (When the user moves the mouse pointer outside the program's window, it becomes visible again.) When the mouse is hidden, it is still active within the program's window. For example, you can still call `agk::GetRawMouseX` and `agk::GetRawMouseY` to get its position. To make the mouse pointer visible again, you call the `agk::SetRawMouseVisible` function and pass the value 1 as an argument.

Detecting Mouse Input

The AGK provides several functions to determine if a mouse button has been pressed, released, or held down.

The `agk::GetRawMouseLeftPressed` and `agk::GetRawMouseLeftPressed` functions can be used to determine when the user presses the left or right mouse button. The functions return a value of 1 when the mouse button is pressed; otherwise, they return a value of 0.

Program 8-2 demonstrates the `GetRawMouseLeftPressed` and `GetRawMouseRightPressed` functions. The program draws a mouse sprite when the left mouse button is pressed, and if the right mouse button is pressed it draws a cat sprite.

Program 8-2 (Mouse Presses)

```
1 // This program demonstrates pressing
2 // the left or right mouse buttons.
3
4 // Includes, namespace and prototypes
5 #include "template.h"
6 using namespace AGK;
7 app App;
8
9 // Begin app, called once at the start
10 void app::Begin( void )
11 {
12    // Set the window title and the virtual resolution.
13    agk::SetWindowTitle("Mouse Presses");
14    agk::SetVirtualResolution(agk::GetDeviceWidth(),
15                              agk::GetDeviceHeight());
16 }
17
18 // Main loop, called every frame
19 void app::Loop ( void )
20 {
21    // Determine if the left mouse button was pressed.
22    if(agk::GetRawMouseLeftPressed())
23    {
24       // Create a sprite using the "mouse.png" image, and
25       // set its position to the current mouse coordinates.
26       agk::SetSpritePosition(agk::CreateSprite("mouse.png"),
27                              agk::GetRawMouseX(),
28                              agk::GetRawMouseY());
29    }
30
31    // Determine if the right mouse button was pressed.
32    if(agk::GetRawMouseRightPressed())
33    {
34       // Create a sprite using the "cat.png" image, and
35       // set its position to the current mouse coordinates.
36       agk::SetSpritePosition(agk::CreateSprite("cat.png"),
37                              agk::GetRawMouseX(),
38                              agk::GetRawMouseY());
39    }
40
41    // Refresh the screen.
42    agk::Sync();
43 }
44
45 // Called when the app ends
46 void app::End ( void )
47 {
48 }
```

Figure 8-2 Example output of Program 8-2

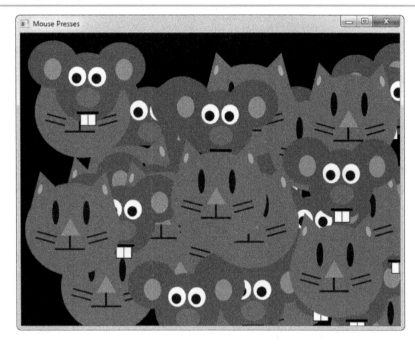

The agk::GetRawMouseLeftReleased and agk::GetRawMouseRightReleased functions can be used to determine when the user releases the left or right mouse button. The functions return 1 when the mouse button is released; otherwise, they return a value of 0.

The agk::GetRawMouseLeftState and agk::GetRawMouseRightState functions can be used to determine when the left or right mouse button is being held down. The functions return 1 while the button is held down; otherwise, they return a value of 0.

Determining If the Mouse Has Hit a Sprite With the agk::GetSpriteHit Function

You may want to determine when the user has clicked on a sprite and then perform some action in response. Earlier we introduced the functions for detecting mouse input, but how do we know when the mouse pointer is actually overlapping a sprite? The following pseudocode shows the logic for checking the position of the mouse pointer and the position of the sprite to see if they overlap:

```
Let x equal the X-coordinate of the mouse pointer.
Let y equal the Y-coordinate of the mouse pointer.

Let x1 equal the upper-left X-coordinate of the sprite.
Let y1 equal the upper-left Y-coordinate of the sprite.

Let x2 equal the lower-right X-coordinate of the sprite.
Let y2 equal the lower-right Y-coordinate of the sprite.

If x is greater than or equal to x1 and y is greater than or equal
to y1 and x is less than or equal to x2 and y is less than or equal
to y2, then the mouse pointer is overlapping the sprite.
```

Figure 8-3 illustrates the method of determining if a single point is overlapping a sprite's bounding box.

Figure 8-3 Single point bounding box collision test

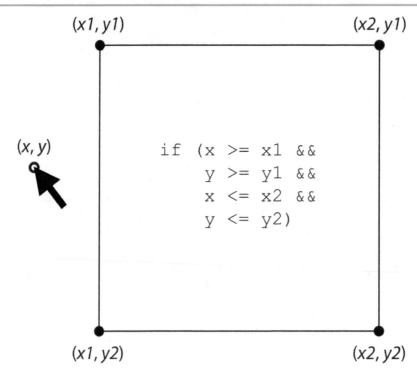

Fortunately, the AGK provides a function, named `agk::GetSpriteHit` that performs this logic for you. It determines if a single point has hit a sprite and returns the index number of the sprite if it does. Here is the general format of the function:

```
agk::GetSpriteHit(x, y)
```

`x` is the *X*-coordinate of the point, and `y` is the *Y*-coordinate of the point. If the specified *XY*-coordinate is overlapping a sprite, the function will return the index number of the sprite; otherwise, the function returns 0.

Putting It All Together

The `agk::GetRawMouseLeftPressed` or `agk::GetRawMouseRightPressed` functions can be used along with the `agk::GetSpriteHit` function to determine if the user has clicked on a sprite. Program 8-3 demonstrates using these functions. Figure 8-4 shows an example of the program's output (this figure is also shown as Figure C-7 in the book's color insert).

Program 8-3   **(Virtual Light Switch)**

```
1 // This program demonstrates a virtual light switch.
2
3 // Includes, namespace and prototypes
4 #include "template.h"
```

```
 5 using namespace AGK;
 6 app App;
 7
 8 // Constants
 9 const int SCREEN_WIDTH  = 640;
10 const int SCREEN_HEIGHT = 480;
11
12 const int ROOM    = 1;
13 const int SWITCH  = 2;
14 const int ON      = 1;
15 const int OFF     = 2;
16
17 // Global variable for the light switch state.
18 bool g_lightOn = true;
19
20 // Begin app, called once at the start
21 void app::Begin( void )
22 {
23    // Set the window title.
24    agk::SetWindowTitle("Virtual Light Switch");
25
26    // Set the virtual resolution.
27    agk::SetVirtualResolution(SCREEN_WIDTH, SCREEN_HEIGHT);
28
29    // Load the images.
30    agk::LoadImage(ON, "light_switch_on.png");
31    agk::LoadImage(OFF, "light_switch_off.png");
32
33    // Create the sprites.
34    agk::CreateSprite(ROOM, "room.png");
35    agk::CreateSprite(SWITCH, ON);
36    agk::SetSpriteScale(SWITCH, 0.15f, 0.15f);
37    agk::SetSpritePosition(SWITCH, 50, 50);
38 }
39
40 // Main loop, called every frame
41 void app::Loop ( void )
42 {
43    // Determine if the left mouse button was pressed.
44    if(agk::GetRawMouseLeftPressed())
45    {
46       // Get the mouse coordinates.
47       float mouseX = agk::GetRawMouseX();
48       float mouseY = agk::GetRawMouseY();
49
50       // Determine if the mouse hit the sprite.
51       if (agk::GetSpriteHit(mouseX, mouseY) == SWITCH)
52       {
53          // Determine if the light is already on.
54          if(g_lightOn)
55          {
56             // Turn the light switch off.
57             agk::SetSpriteColor(ROOM, 64, 64, 64, 255);
58             agk::SetSpriteColor(SWITCH, 64, 64, 64, 255);
59             agk::SetSpriteImage(SWITCH, OFF);
```

```
60
61                g_lightOn = false;    // Set the state to false.
62            }
63            else
64            {
65                // Turn the light switch on.
66                agk::SetSpriteColor(ROOM, 255, 255, 255, 255);
67                agk::SetSpriteColor(SWITCH, 255, 255, 255, 255);
68                agk::SetSpriteImage(SWITCH, ON);
69
70                g_lightOn = true; // Set the state to true.
71            }
72        }
73    }
74
75    // Refresh the screen.
76    agk::Sync();
77 }
78
79 // Called when the app ends
80 void app::End ( void )
81 {
82 }
```

Figure 8-4 Example output for Program 8-3

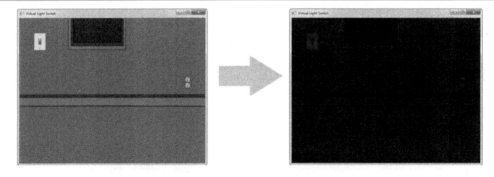

Checkpoint

8.1. What two functions are used to get the coordinates of the mouse pointer?

8.2. Briefly describe each of the functions for detecting mouse input.

8.3. How can you determine whether or not the mouse pointer is over a sprite?

8.2 Virtual Buttons

CONCEPT: The AGK allows you to create up to 12 virtual buttons on the screen. Virtual buttons can be used to determine when the user clicks on them with the mouse.

Adding a Virtual Button to the Screen

A virtual button is an image of a button that you can display in your AGK program. The user may click the button with the mouse. You can have up to 12 virtual buttons in an AGK program. To add a virtual button, call the `agk::AddVirtualButton` function. Here is the general format of the function:

```
agk::AddVirtualButton(Index, X, Y, Size);
```

This function accepts four arguments. The first argument, `Index`, sets the index number that will be used to identify the virtual button, the value used for the index should be an integer in the range of 1 through 12. The second argument, `X`, is a floating-point value that sets the X-coordinate where the button will appear on the screen and is based on the center of the virtual button. The third argument, `Y`, is a floating-point value that sets the Y-coordinate where the button will appear on the screen and is based on the center of the virtual button. The fourth argument, `Size`, is a floating point value that sets the diameter of the button. Figure 8-5 illustrates how the size of the virtual button is determined based on diameter.

Figure 8-5 The size of a virtual button is based on the diameter of a circle

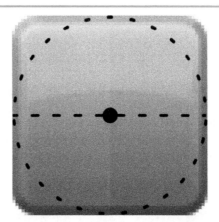

Changing a Virtual Button's Position on the Screen

If at any time you need to change the position of a virtual button, you can do so by calling the `agk::SetVirtualButtonPosition` function and passing the index number of the virtual button and the new X and Y values as arguments. For example, the following statement positions a virtual button with an index value of 1 centered at the screen coordinates (120, 120):

```
agk::SetVirtualButtonPosition(1, 120, 120);
```

Changing the Size of a Virtual Button

If you find you need to change the size of a virtual button you added to the screen earlier, you can call the `agk::SetVirtualButtonSize` function passing the index number of the button and a floating-point value containing the new size as arguments. For example, the following statement changes the size of a virtual button with index number 1 to a diameter of 50.

```
agk::SetVirtualButtonSize(1, 50);
```

Displaying Text on a Virtual Button

It is possible to display text on top of a virtual button. Displaying text on a virtual button can help the user determine what the button will do. If you want to display text on a virtual button, call the `agk::SetVirtualButtonText` function passing the index number of the button and a string containing the text you want to display as arguments. For example, the following statement causes the text "OK" to be displayed on a virtual button with an index number of 1.

```
Agk::SetVirtualButtonText(1, "OK");
```

Changing the Color of a Virtual Button

Occasionally you might want to add a little variety to the virtual buttons in an application. One way you can do this is by changing their color. To change the color of a virtual button you have added to the screen, call the `agk::SetVirtualButtonColor` function. Here is the general format of how you call the function.

```
agk::SetVirtualButtonColor(Index, Red, Green, Blue);
```

The first argument is the index number of the virtual button whose color you want to change. The remaining arguments are for the red, green, and blue color channels. You pass a value from 0 to 255 for each of these arguments. The 0 means that the color channel will have no intensity, and 255 means that the color channel will be displayed at full intensity. For example, the following statement changes the color of a button with the index number 1 to the color yellow.

```
agk::SetVirtualButtonColor(1, 255, 255, 0);
```

Changing the Transparency of a Virtual Button

A virtual button can be displayed with varying alpha transparency values. This might be a good idea when you want your button to become transparent when not in use and then become completely opaque when the mouse cursor rolls over it. You can change the alpha value of a virtual button by calling the `agk::SetVirtualButtonAlpha` function. Here is the general format of how you call the function.

```
agk::SetVirtualButtonAlpha(Index, Alpha);
```

The first argument is the index number of the virtual button whose alpha value you want to change. The second argument is an integer ranging from 0, which is completely transparent to 255 and will cause the button to be completely solid or opaque. The following statement sets the alpha value of virtual button 1 to 255.

```
agk::SetVirtualButtonAlpha(1, 255);
```

Showing and Hiding a Virtual Button

In some instances, you might want to hide the virtual buttons in an application until they are needed. If you want to hide a virtual button or show a previously hidden virtual button, you can call the `agk::SetVirtualButtonVisible` function. Here is the general format of how you call the function:

```
agk::SetVirtualButtonVisible(Index, Visible);
```

The first argument is the index number of the virtual button whose visibility you want to set. The second argument sets the visibility. Passing a value of 0 (false) will hide the virtual button, and passing a value of 1 (true) will show the virtual button. The following example hides a virtual button with an index number of 1.

```
agk::SetVirtualButtonVisible(1, 0);
```

Enabling or Disabling a Virtual Button

In some situations you may or may not want a button to be active in an application. For instance, if the purpose of a virtual button is to load a previously saved game, then the button should only be active if the game data exists. Or if you have a virtual button that throws a dart in a game, when the player runs out of darts, the button should be disabled. Maybe your game has a virtual button that should become active when the player has collected enough items, and so forth. You can make a virtual button active or inactive by calling the `agk::SetVirtualButtonActive` function. Here is the general format of how you call the function:

```
agk::SetVirtualButtonActive(Index, Active);
```

The first argument is the index number of the virtual button you want to set. The second argument sets the button as either active or inactive. A value of 0 (false) will disable the button making it inactive, whereas a value of 1 (true) will cause the button to become active. The following statement disables a virtual button with an index number of 1.

```
agk::SetVirtualButtonActive(1, 0);
```

Changing a Virtual Button's Images

A virtual button uses two images: one image for when the button is up and another image for when the button is down. The AGK provides a set of default images for a virtual button (which are stored in your *My Documents* > *AGK* > *template* folder), but you can change these images to anything that suits your needs or matches the theme of your game.

To set the images for a virtual button, you must first load the images you want to use. Next, set the image for when the button is up with the `agk::SetVirtualButtonUp` function. You set the image for when the button is down with the `agk::SetVirtualButtonDown` function. Both functions accept two arguments: The first argument is the index number of the virtual button you want to change, and the second argument is the index number of the image you want to use. For example, look at the following statements:

```
1 agk::LoadImage(1, "myButtonUp.png");
2 agk::LoadImage(2, "myButtonDown.png");
3
4 agk::SetVirtualButtonImageUp(1, 1);
5 agk::SetVirtualButtonImageDown(1, 2);
```

The first two statements (in lines 1 and 2) load the images, and the last two statements (lines 4 and 5) set the virtual button to use those images. Notice that index numbers are used to identify the virtual button and to set the image.

As you have learned, the AGK provides many ways to customize how virtual buttons look and behave. This kind of customization is great for developing unique games and applications. Next we will take a look at a program that responds to virtual button presses.

Responding to the Virtual Button Presses

Responding to the virtual button presses is very similar to how we responded to mouse button presses earlier in the chapter. Just like the mouse, three different functions are used for determining when the user has pressed a virtual button. The agk::GetVirtualButtonPressed function returns 1 (true) when the user initially presses the button, then it returns 0 (false). The agk::GetVirtualButtonState returns 1 (true) as long as the button is held down, and otherwise it returns 0 (false). The agk::GetVirtualButtonReleased function returns 1 (true) as soon as the button is released, then it returns 0 (false). All three functions accept a single argument: the index number of the virtual button you want to check. In the following statements, each type of function is called, and the return value is stored in a variable. These variables could be used later in a program, along with an if statement to perform an action.

```
int pressed = agk::GetVirtualButtonPressed(1);
int down = agk::GetVirtualButtonState(1);
int released = agk::GetVirtualButtonReleased(1);
```

Program 8-4 demonstrates how to add virtual buttons to an application and how to respond when a virtual button is pressed. Figure 8-6 shows the program's output.

Program 8-4 (Virtual Buttons)

```
1 // This program demonstrates virtual buttons.
2
3 // Includes, namespace and prototypes
4 #include "template.h"
5 using namespace AGK;
6 app App;
7
8 // Constants
```

```
 9 const int SCREEN_WIDTH       = 640;
10 const int SCREEN_HEIGHT      = 480;
11 const int SPRITE_INDEX       = 1;
12 const int SHOW_BUTTON_INDEX = 1;
13 const int HIDE_BUTTON_INDEX = 2;
14 const float BUTTON_SIZE      = 100.0;
15
16 // Begin app, called once at the start
17 void app::Begin( void )
18 {
19     // Set the window title.
20     agk::SetWindowTitle("Virtual Buttons");
21
22     // Set the virtual resolution.
23     agk::SetVirtualResolution(SCREEN_WIDTH, SCREEN_HEIGHT);
24
25     // Create the sprite.
26     agk::CreateSprite(SPRITE_INDEX, "frog.png");
27
28     // Calculate the position of the sprite.
29     float spriteWidth = agk::GetSpriteWidth(SPRITE_INDEX);
30     float spriteX = SCREEN_WIDTH / 2 - spriteWidth / 2;
31     float spriteY = 0.0;
32
33     // Set the position of the sprite.
34     agk::SetSpritePosition(SPRITE_INDEX, spriteX, spriteY);
35
36     // Calculate the position of the virtual "show" button.
37     float showButtonX = SCREEN_WIDTH / 2 - BUTTON_SIZE;
38     float showButtonY = SCREEN_HEIGHT - BUTTON_SIZE;
39
40     // Calculate the position of the virtual "hide" button.
41     float hideButtonX = SCREEN_WIDTH / 2 + BUTTON_SIZE;
42     float hideButtonY = SCREEN_HEIGHT - BUTTON_SIZE;
43
44     // Add the virtual buttons.
45     agk::AddVirtualButton(SHOW_BUTTON_INDEX, showButtonX,
46                           showButtonY, BUTTON_SIZE);
47     agk::AddVirtualButton(HIDE_BUTTON_INDEX, hideButtonX,
48                           hideButtonY, BUTTON_SIZE);
49
50     // Set the text of the virtual buttons.
51     agk::SetVirtualButtonText(SHOW_BUTTON_INDEX, "Show");
52     agk::SetVirtualButtonText(HIDE_BUTTON_INDEX, "Hide");
53 }
54
55 // Main loop, called every frame
56 void app::Loop ( void )
57 {
58     // Determine if the virtual "show" button was pressed.
59     if(agk::GetVirtualButtonPressed(SHOW_BUTTON_INDEX))
60     {
61        // Show the sprite.
62        agk::SetSpriteVisible(SPRITE_INDEX, 1);
63     }
```

```
64
65    // Determine if the virtual "hide" button was pressed.
66    if(agk::GetVirtualButtonPressed(HIDE_BUTTON_INDEX))
67    {
68        // Hide the sprite.
69        agk::SetSpriteVisible(SPRITE_INDEX, 0);
70    }
71
72    // Refresh the screen.
73    agk::Sync();
74 }
75
76 // Called when the app ends
77 void app::End ( void )
78 {
79 }
```

Figure 8-6 Example Output of Program 8-4

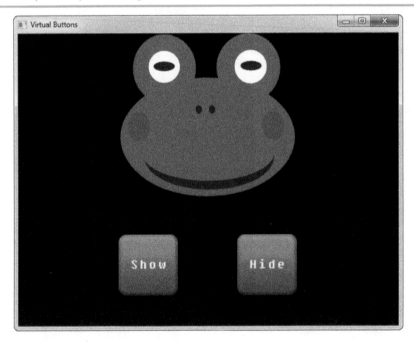

Checkpoint

8.4. How is the size of a virtual button determined? Is it possible to change this value?

8.5. Is there a limit to the number of virtual buttons you can create, and if so, what is it?

8.6. How can you determine if a virtual button is being held down?

8.3 Virtual Joysticks

CONCEPT: The AGK provides up to four virtual joysticks that you can you use to control sprites or other items in a game. Virtual joysticks are controlled using the mouse or other pointing device.

Adding Virtual Joysticks

VideoNote

Working with Virtual Joysticks

A *virtual joystick* is a simulated joystick that you can display in your program and that the user can interact with. You add a virtual joystick to the screen with the agk::AddVirtualJoystick function. Here is the general format of the function:

```
agk::AddVirtualJoystick(Index, X, Y, Size);
```

The function accepts four arguments. The first argument is the index number you want to assign the joystick. It can be a number from 1 to 4. The second and third arguments are floating-point values for the X- and Y-coordinates for the center of the joystick on the screen. The fourth argument, *Size*, is a floating-point value that sets the diameter of the joystick. Figure 8-7 illustrates how the size of the virtual joystick is determined based on diameter, which is similar to a virtual button.

Figure 8-7 The size of a virtual joystick is based on the diameter of a circle

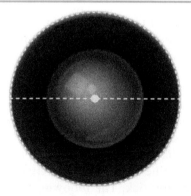

The following code adds a virtual joystick with an index number of 1 to the top-left corner of the screen using a size of 50:

```
agk::AddVirtualJoystick(1, 50, 50, 50);
```

Setting the Position of a Virtual Joystick

If you ever want to move the virtual joystick after it has been added to the screen, you can do so with the agk::SetVirtualJoystickPosition function. Here is the format of how you call the function:

```
agk::SetVirtualJoystickPosition(Index, X, Y)
```

The function takes three arguments; first is an integer value containing the index number for the virtual joystick whose position you want to change. The second and third arguments are floating-point values for the *X*- and *Y*-coordinates of the new location. The following statement positions a virtual joystick with an index number of 1 to be centered at the screen position (100, 100):

```
agk::SetVirtualJoystickPosition(1, 100, 100);
```

Setting the Size of a Virtual Joystick

There may be times when you want to resize a virtual joystick after it has been added to the screen. You can change the size of a virtual joystick you have previously created by calling the `agk::SetVirtualJoystickSize` function. Here is the general format of the function:

```
agk::SetVirtualJoystickSize(Index, Size);
```

The function accepts two arguments. The first argument is an integer containing the index number of the virtual joystick whose size you want to change, and the second argument is a floating-point value containing the new size of the virtual joystick. For example, the following statement sets the size of a virtual joystick with an index number of 1 to 200:

```
agk::SetVirtualJoystickSize(1, 200);
```

Setting Transparency of a Virtual Joystick

You can change the alpha transparency of a virtual joystick that you have added to your program by calling the `agk::SetVirtualJoystickAlpha` function. Here is the general format of how you call the function:

```
agk::SetVirtualJoystickAlpha(Index, Alpha1, Alpha2);
```

The function accepts three arguments. The first argument is an integer value containing the index number of the virtual joystick whose transparency you want to change. The second argument, *Alpha1*, is an integer value that should be between 0 and 255 for the alpha value of the outer part of the joystick. The third argument, *Alpha2*, is an integer value that should be between 0 and 25 for the alpha value of the inner part of the joystick. The following statement changes the transparency of a virtual joystick with an index number of 1 so that the outer part of the joystick is completely transparent, whereas the inner part of the virtual joystick is completely opaque.

```
agk::SetVirtualJoystickAlpha(1, 0, 255);
```

Setting a Virtual Joystick as Active or Inactive

You can disable a virtual joystick so that it no longer responds to input by the mouse pointer or enable it again by calling the `agk::SetVirtualJoystickActive` function. Here is the general format of the function:

```
agk::SetVirtualJoystickActive(Index, Active);
```

The function accepts two arguments. The first argument is an integer containing the index number of the virtual joystick that you want to enable or disable. The second argument is an integer value that will enable or disable the virtual joystick's ability to receive input. A value of 1 (true) enables the joystick to receive input, whereas a value of 0 (false) will disable the joystick and prevent it from receiving input. The following statement sets a virtual joystick with an index value of 1 to be inactive.

```
agk::SetVirtualJoystickActive(1, 0);
```

Setting the Visibility of a Virtual Joystick

There may be times when you want to hide a virtual joystick in your program and then show it again. You can do this by calling the `agk::SetVirtualJoystickVisible` function. Keep in mind that even though a virtual joystick may be hidden, it can still accept input, so it might be a good idea to make a joystick inactive before it is hidden and then enable it again when it is shown. Here is the general format of how you call the function:

```
agk::SetVirtualJoystickVisible(Index, Visible);
```

The function accepts two arguments. The first argument is an integer containing the index number for the virtual joystick whose visibility you want to set. The second argument is an integer value of either 0 or 1. A value of 0 (false) will hide the virtual joystick and a value of 1 (true) will show the virtual joystick. The following code segment disables and then hides a virtual joystick with an index number of 1.

```
agk::SetVirtualJoystickActive(1, 0);
agk::SetVirtualJoystickVisible(1, 0);
```

Changing a Virtual Joystick's Images

Like a virtual button, a virtual joystick uses two images: One image for the outer part of the joystick and another image for the inner part of the joystick. The AGK provides a set of default images for a virtual joystick, but you can easily change the images.

To set the inner and outer images used by a virtual joystick, you must first load the images you want to use with the `agk::LoadImage` function. You set the image for the outer part of the virtual joystick with the `agk::SetVirtualJoystickImageOuter` function. You set the image for the inner part of the joystick with the `agk::SetVirtualJoystickImageInner` function. Both functions accept two arguments: the first argument is the index number of the virtual button you want to change, and the second argument is the index number of the image you want to use. For example, look at the following statements:

```
1 agk::LoadImage(1, "myOuterJoystickImage.png");
2 agk::LoadImage(2, "myInnerJoystickImage.png");
3
4 agk::SetVirtualJoystickImageOuter(1, 1);
5 agk::SetVirtualJoystickImageInner(1, 2);
```

The first two statements (in lines 1 and 2) load the images, and the last two statements (lines 4 and 5) set the virtual joystick to use image 1 for the outer image and image 2 for the inner image. If, for any reason, you want to return the joystick to its default images, you can call the functions and pass 0 as the index number. The following statements return the virtual joystick whose images were changed earlier to use the default images.

```
agk::SetVirtualJoystickImageOuter(0, 1);
agk::SetVirtualJoystickImageInner(0, 2);
```

Notice in the preceding statements that we still must specify the index numbers for the inner and outer joystick images.

Determining If a Virtual Joystick Exists

You can call the `agk::GetVirtualJoystickExists` function to determine whether a virtual joystick exists. When you call the function, you pass the index number, in the range of 1 through 4, of the virtual joystick you want to check. The function returns a value of 1 (true) if a virtual joystick exists with the specified index number, and it returns 0 (false) otherwise. For example, the following statement determines if a virtual joystick with an index number of 1 exists. It calls the function passing a value of 1 for the argument and then assigns the return value of the function to an integer variable named `virtualJoystickExists`:

```
int virtualJoystickExists = agk::GetVirtualJoystickExists(1);
```

Deleting an Existing Virtual Joystick

You can delete a virtual joystick and remove it from the screen by calling the `agk::DeleteVirtualJoystick` function passing the index number of the virtual joystick you want to delete as an argument. It is a good idea to check if the joystick exists and then delete it. The following code segment determines if a virtual joystick with an index number of 2 exists and then, if it does, deletes it:

```
if(agk::GetVirtualJoystickExists(2))
{
    agk::DeleteVirtualJoystick(2);
}
```

Setting the Virtual Joystick Dead Zone

You can customize the sensitivity of all virtual joysticks that you might add to the screen by calling the `agk::SetVirtualJoystickDeadZone` function. The *dead zone* is an area around the virtual joystick's center that affects how far you have to move the joystick before it registers input. You can totally disable a virtual joystick by setting the dead zone value to 1 or allow the joystick to be extremely sensitive by setting the dead zone to 0. The default setting for all virtual joysticks is 0.15. The following statement sets the dead zone for all virtual joysticks to a value of 0.05:

```
agk::SetVirtualJoystickDeadZone(0.05);
```

Getting Virtual Joystick Input

You can get the input of a virtual joystick along the *X*- and *Y*-axes with the `agk::GetVirtualJoystickX` and `agkGetVirtualJoystickY` functions. The `agk::GetVirtualJoystickX` function returns input along the *X*-axis. It will return a floating-point value of –1.0 if the joystick is moved to the far left, and it will return a floating-point value of 1.0 if the joystick is moved to the far right. If the joystick is not receiving input (or input is within the dead zone), the function returns a value of 0. The same is true for the `agk::GetVirtualJoystickY` function, except this function returns input along the *Y*-axis. The function will return a floating-point value of –1.0 if the joystick is moved all the way up and 1.0 if the joystick is moved all the way down. The function returns a value of 0 if the joystick is within the dead zone or is not receiving input. You call each of these functions, passing the index number of the virtual joystick whose input you want to receive as an argument. The following code segment stores the input of a joystick with an index number of 1 in two floating-point variables named `joystickX` and `joystickY`:

```
float joystickX = agk::GetVirtualJoystickX(1);
float joystickY = agk::GetVirtualJoystickY(1);
```

Program 8-5 demonstrates how to use a virtual joystick to move a sprite around the screen.

Program 8-5　　(Virtual Joystick)

```
1 // This program demonstrates a virtual joystick.
2
3 // Includes, namespace and prototypes
4 #include "template.h"
5 using namespace AGK;
6 app App;
7
8 // Constants
9 const int SCREEN_WIDTH  = 640;
10 const int SCREEN_HEIGHT = 480;
11 const int SPRITE_INDEX  = 1;
12 const int JOY_INDEX     = 1;
13 const float JOY_SIZE    = 100.0;
14
15 // Begin app, called once at the start
16 void app::Begin( void )
17 {
18     // Set the window title.
19     agk::SetWindowTitle("Virtual Joystick");
```

```
20
21    // Set the virtual resolution.
22    agk::SetVirtualResolution(SCREEN_WIDTH, SCREEN_HEIGHT);
23
24    // Create the sprite.
25    agk::CreateSprite(SPRITE_INDEX, "fish.png");
26
27    // Calculate the position of the virtual joystick.
28    float joyX = SCREEN_WIDTH / 2;
29    float joyY = SCREEN_HEIGHT - JOY_SIZE / 2;
30
31    // Add the virtual joystick.
32    agk::AddVirtualJoystick(JOY_INDEX, joyX, joyY, JOY_SIZE);
33 }
34
35 // Main loop, called every frame
36 void app::Loop ( void )
37 {
38    // Get the joystick input.
39    float joystickX = agk::GetVirtualJoystickX(JOY_INDEX);
40    float joystickY = agk::GetVirtualJoystickY(JOY_INDEX);
41
42    // Get the sprite position.
43    float spriteX = agk::GetSpriteX(SPRITE_INDEX);
44    float spriteY = agk::GetSpriteY(SPRITE_INDEX);
45
46    // Calculate how far the sprite will move.
47    float moveX = spriteX + joystickX;
48    float moveY = spriteY + joystickY;
49
50    // Set the sprite position.
51    agk::SetSpritePosition(SPRITE_INDEX, moveX, moveY);
52
53    // Refresh the screen.
54    agk::Sync();
55 }
56
57 // Called when the app ends
58 void app::End ( void )
59 {
60 }
```

The program starts by storing the sprite and virtual joystick index numbers, the screen size, and the size of the virtual joystick in named constants in lines 9 through 13.

First, we set up our virtual joystick and sprite in the app::Begin function in lines 16 through 33. Lines 28 and 29 set the position of the virtual joystick to be centered horizontally and to appear at the bottom of the screen. This is done by setting the X value of the joystick to the center of the screen, which we store in the variable joyX. We calculate the Y value of the joystick to the height of the screen minus half the size of the joystick. Keep in mind when you position a virtual joystick or a virtual button that the *X* and *Y* values are located in the center and not the upper-left corner, as is the default for sprites.

In line 32 we add the virtual joystick to the screen by supplying the index number, JOY_INDEX, the calculated *X* and *Y* values, joyX and joyY, and the size of the joystick, JOY_SIZE, to the agk::AddVirtualJoystick function.

Now that our virtual joystick has been added to the screen and our sprite has been created, we can enter the game loop, which is defined in the app::Loop function in lines 36 through 55.

To make our sprite move, one of the things we need to know is how far the sprite needs to be moved. The distance that the sprite will move along the *X*- and *Y*-axes needs to be stored once each frame by getting the virtual joystick input. In lines 39 and 40 we declare two floating-point variables named joystickX and joystickY. These variables are assigned the return values of the agk::GetVirtualJoystickX and agk::GetJoystickY functions. The purpose of these variables is to store the input of the joystick when it is moved left or right along the *X*-axis and up or down along the *Y*-axis. We will use these values later in the program to move the sprite to a new location on the screen.

The next thing we need to know is the location of the sprite. We need to store the *X* and *Y* values of the sprite so that we can calculate its new position using the values we stored earlier for the virtual joystick input. In lines 43 and 44, we store the *X* and *Y* values of the sprite, as they are in the current frame. The location of the sprite along the *X*-axis is stored in the floating-point variable spriteX, and the location of the sprite along the *Y*-axis is stored in the floating-point variable spriteY. These values will be used together with the joystick input stored in the joystickX and joystickY variables to move the sprite.

Now that we have the current location of the sprite and the distance we want to move, we can calculate the new position of the sprite. In lines 47 and 48 we declare two floating-point variables, moveX and moveY. The value of the moveX variable is calculated by adding the value of the joystickX variable to the spriteX variable, and the value of the moveY variable is calculated by adding the value of the joystickY variable to the spriteY variable. Remember that the joystickX and joystickY variables are assigned values based on the joystick input, which can range anywhere from −1.0 to 1.0, so if the joystick is moved left or up, the joystickX or joystickY variables will contain a negative value. Adding a negative value to the sprite's current location along the *X*- or *Y*-axes will cause it to move left or up. On the other hand, if the joystick is moved right or down, the joystickX or joystickY variables will contain a positive value, and the sprite's location along the *X*- or *Y*-axis will increase moving it right or down. This is because the values we add to the sprite's current position will be positive.

The last thing to do before we update the screen is to actually move the sprite to a new location. We do this in line 51 by calling the agk::SetSpritePosition function and passing it the moveX and moveY values that we calculated earlier by adding the joystick input to the sprite's current position. When the screen is updated, the sprite will appear to move to the new position. Figure 8-8 shows example output from Program 8-5.

Figure 8-8 Example output for Program 8-5

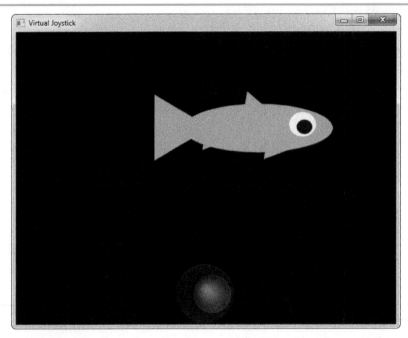

 Checkpoint

8.7. How do you control a virtual joystick?

8.8. What does the term *dead zone* refer to?

8.9. Is it possible to change the images used by a virtual joystick, and if so, how is it done?

8.4 The Keyboard

CONCEPT: The AGK provides functions that let you know whether certain keys are being pressed on the keyboard. Many games and animation programs allow the user to control objects on the screen with such keys.

VideoNote
Working with the Keyboard

Games commonly allow the player to use keys on the keyboard to control objects on the screen. For example, the up, down, left, and right arrow keys are typically used to move objects. Also, other keys such as the spacebar and Enter key are sometimes used to perform actions.

Moving Objects with the Keyboard Arrow Keys

In the previous section we introduced the virtual joystick, and in Program 8-5 we demonstrated how to use input from a virtual joystick to move a sprite around the screen. That program could easily be modified to use the arrow keys on the keyboard as input to move the sprite. Take a look at Program 8-6:

Program 8-6   (Direction Keys)

```
1  // This program demonstrates direction keys.
2
3  // Includes, namespace and prototypes
4  #include "template.h"
5  using namespace AGK;
6  app App;
7
8  // Constants
9  const int SCREEN_WIDTH    = 640;
10 const int SCREEN_HEIGHT   = 480;
11 const int SPRITE_INDEX    = 1;
12
13 // Begin app, called once at the start
14 void app::Begin( void )
15 {
16    // Set the window title.
17    agk::SetWindowTitle("Direction Keys");
18
19    // Set the virtual resolution.
20    agk::SetVirtualResolution(SCREEN_WIDTH, SCREEN_HEIGHT);
21
22    // Create the sprite.
23    agk::CreateSprite(SPRITE_INDEX, "fish.png");
24 }
25
26 // Main loop, called every frame
27 void app::Loop ( void )
28 {
29    // Get the direction as input from the keyboard.
30    float directionX = agk::GetDirectionX();
31    float directionY = agk::GetDirectionY();
32
33    // Get the sprite position.
34    float spriteX = agk::GetSpriteX(SPRITE_INDEX);
35    float spriteY = agk::GetSpriteY(SPRITE_INDEX);
36
37    // Calculate how far the sprite will move.
38    float moveX = spriteX + directionX;
39    float moveY = spriteY + directionY;
40
41    // Set the sprite position.
42    agk::SetSpritePosition(SPRITE_INDEX, moveX, moveY);
43
44    // Refresh the screen.
45    agk::Sync();
46 }
47
48 // Called when the app ends
49 void app::End ( void )
50 {
51 }
```

Program 8-6 has the same output as Program 8-5 (except for the virtual joystick).

Most of this program remains unchanged except for the removal of the code to create the virtual joystick and the way we are getting input in lines 30 and 31. Program 8-6 uses the agk::GetDirectionX and agk::GetDirectionY functions to move the sprite along the X- and Y-axes.

These functions are very similar to how the virtual joystick input functions worked, as they return a value ranging from −0.9 to 0.9, depending on the arrow key that is pressed. They return a value of 0 when no key is pressed. When the agk::GetDirectionX function is called in line 30, it returns a positive or negative value, depending on whether the right or left arrow key is being pressed. Similarly, when the agk::GetDirectionY function is called in line 31, it returns a positive or negative value, depending on whether the down arrow key or up arrow key is being pressed. As was shown in Program 8-6, these values are then used in a calculation that sets the new position of the sprite for each frame, making it appear to move.

> **NOTE:** The agk::GetDirectionX and agk::GetDirectionY functions can be used to get input from a device that has an accelerometer, but when no accelerometer is available, they simulate its behavior and make the task of moving sprites around with the arrow keys very easy to accomplish.

Responding to Specific Key Presses

Responding the specific key presses on the keyboard is very similar to how we responded to virtual button presses earlier in the chapter. Just like a virtual button, three different functions are used for determining when the user has pressed a specific key on the keyboard. The agk::GetRawKeyPressed function returns 1 (true) when the user initially presses the specified key, then it returns 0 (false). The agk::GetRawKeyboardState returns 1 (true) as long as the specified key is held down, and otherwise it returns 0 (false). The agk::GetRawKeyReleased function returns 1 (true) as soon as the specified key is released, then it returns 0 (false). All three functions accept a single argument: an integer value in the range of 0 through 255 representing the key code for the specific key you want to check.

Many of the common key codes are defined by the AGK. Table 8-1 lists a few of them.

Table 8-1 Key codes defined by the AGK

Name	Key
AGK_KEY_UP	Up Arrow Key
AGK_KEY_DOWN	Down Arrow Key
AGK_KEY_LEFT	Left Arrow Key
AGK_KEY_RIGHT	Right Arrow Key
AGK_KEY_SPACE	Spacebar Key
AGK_KEY_TAB	Tab Key
AGK_KEY_ENTER	Enter Key

In the following statements, each type of function is called with the `AGK_KEY_TAB` value passed as an argument, and the return value is stored in a variable. These variables could be used later in a program, along with an `if` statement to perform an action when the user presses the Tab key on the keyboard.

```
int tabPressed = agk::GetRawKeyPressed(AGK_KEY_TAB);
int tabDown = agk::GetRawKeyboardState(AGK_KEY_TAB);
int tabReleased = agk::GetRawKeyReleased(AGK_KEY_TAB);
```

Determining the Last Key That Was Pressed

You can determine the last key that was pressed by calling the `agk::GetRawLastKey` function. The function returns the key code for the last key that was pressed. You can compare this value to one of the defined key codes provided by the AGK as a way to detect input for specific keys. Program 8-7 demonstrates this idea.

Program 8-7   **(Last Key Pressed)**

```
1  // This program demonstrates detecting the
2  // last key that was pressed on the keyboard.
3
4  // Includes, namespace and prototypes
5  #include "template.h"
6  using namespace AGK;
7  app App;
8
9  // Constants
10 const int SCREEN_WIDTH    = 640;
11 const int SCREEN_HEIGHT   = 480;
12
13 // Begin app, called once at the start
14 void app::Begin( void )
15 {
16    // Set the window title.
17    agk::SetWindowTitle("Last Key Pressed");
18
19    // Set the virtual resolution.
20    agk::SetVirtualResolution(SCREEN_WIDTH, SCREEN_HEIGHT);
21 }
22
23 // Main loop, called every frame
24 void app::Loop ( void )
25 {
26    // Get the key code of the last key that was pressed.
27    int keycode = agk::GetRawLastKey();
28
29    // Determine which message to display.
30    switch(keycode)
31    {
32       case AGK_KEY_SPACE:
33          agk::Print("You pressed the spacebar.");
34          break;
```

```
35
36        case AGK_KEY_ENTER:
37            agk::Print("You pressed the enter key.");
38            break;
39
40        default:
41            agk::Print("Press the spacebar or enter key.");
42            break;
43    }
44
45    // Refresh the screen.
46    agk::Sync();
47 }
48
49 // Called when the app ends
50 void app::End ( void )
51 {
52 }
```

In line 27 we declare an integer variable named `keycode` and use it to store the value returned by the `agk::GetRawLastKey` function.

In lines 30 through 43 we have a `switch` statement that displays a message to the user based on the last key that was pressed. If the spacebar or enter keys are pressed, a message is displayed to the user indicating that those keys were pressed. If any other key is pressed, a message is displayed for the user to press either the spacebar or the enter key.

 Checkpoint

8.10. Briefly describe the method used to move a sprite with the arrow keys.

8.11. Is it possible to determine when a specific key on the keyboard is pressed, and if so how do you determine its value?

8.12. What function could you use to keep track of the keys pressed during a game?

 8.5 Animation

CONCEPT: You can create a simple animation by displaying a sequence of images one after the other. This can be done by manually loading and displaying separate images or via a texture atlas, which contains all the animation frames in a single image.

Perhaps you've seen simple animations created with flip books. The first page in a flip book shows an image. The next page shows a nearly identical image, but with a slight change. Following this pattern, each page in the book is slightly different from the previous page. When you flip rapidly through the pages, the illusion of movement is created. This type of animation is often called *cel animation*. The term *cel* is an abbreviation of the world *celluloid*, which was the material onto which animators once painted the individual images of cartoons.

You can create simple cel animations by displaying a sequence of images, one after the other, in the same location on the screen. If the images are similar except for slight changes and are displayed in the correct order, the illusion of movement can be created.

For example, look at the sequence of eight images shown in Figure 8-9. Each image shows a cartoon person in a different position. When the images are viewed one after the other, the person appears to be walking.

Figure 8-9 Cel animation images

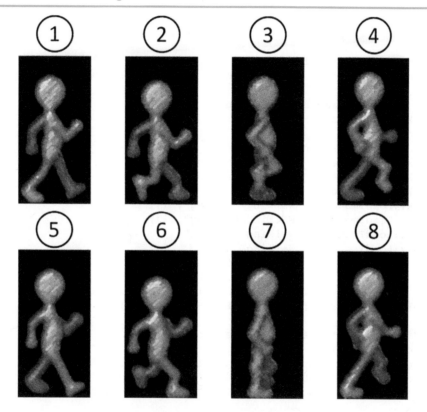

The eight images shown in Figure 8-9 are named WalkingMan1.png, WalkingMan2.png, and so forth. Each image is considered a frame in the animation sequence. Program 8-8 loads these images and then displays them one after the other. After the last image is displayed, the program starts over with the first image.

Program 8-8   **(CelAnimation)**

```
1 // This program demonstrates cel animation.
2
3 // Includes, namespace and prototypes
4 #include "template.h"
5 using namespace AGK;
6 app App;
7
8 // Constants
```

```
 9 const int SCREEN_WIDTH   = 640;
10 const int SCREEN_HEIGHT  = 480;
11 const int FIRST_IMAGE    = 1;
12 const int LAST_IMAGE     = 8;
13 const int SPRITE_INDEX   = 1;
14 const float FPS          = 8;
15 const int MODE           = 0;
16
17 // Begin app, called once at the start
18 void app::Begin( void )
19 {
20    // Set the window title.
21    agk::SetWindowTitle("Cel Animation");
22
23    // Set the virtual resolution.
24    agk::SetVirtualResolution(SCREEN_WIDTH, SCREEN_HEIGHT);
25
26    // Set the frame rate and mode.
27    agk::SetSyncRate(FPS, MODE);
28
29    // Load the walking man images.
30    agk::LoadImage(1, "WalkingMan1.png", 1);
31    agk::LoadImage(2, "WalkingMan2.png", 1);
32    agk::LoadImage(3, "WalkingMan3.png", 1);
33    agk::LoadImage(4, "WalkingMan4.png", 1);
34    agk::LoadImage(5, "WalkingMan5.png", 1);
35    agk::LoadImage(6, "WalkingMan6.png", 1);
36    agk::LoadImage(7, "WalkingMan7.png", 1);
37    agk::LoadImage(8, "WalkingMan8.png", 1);
38
39    // Create the sprite using the first frame of animation.
40    agk::CreateSprite(SPRITE_INDEX, FIRST_IMAGE);
41
42    // Calculate the sprite's position.
43    float spriteWidth = agk::GetSpriteWidth(SPRITE_INDEX);
44    float spriteHeight = agk::GetSpriteHeight(SPRITE_INDEX);
45    float spriteX = SCREEN_WIDTH / 2 - spriteWidth / 2;
46    float spriteY = SCREEN_HEIGHT / 2 - spriteHeight / 2;
47
48    // Set the sprite's position.
49    agk::SetSpritePosition(SPRITE_INDEX, spriteX, spriteY);
50 }
51
52 // Main loop, called every frame
53 void app::Loop ( void )
54 {
55    // Get the sprite's image number.
56    int currentImage = agk::GetSpriteImageID(SPRITE_INDEX);
57
58    // Update the sprite's image number.
59    if (currentImage == LAST_IMAGE)
60    {
61      currentImage = FIRST_IMAGE;
62    }
63    else
```

```
64      {
65          currentImage++;
66      }
67
68      // Set the sprite's image number.
69      agk::SetSpriteImage(SPRITE_INDEX, currentImage);
70
71      // Refresh the screen.
72      agk::Sync();
73  }
74
75  // Called when the app ends
76  void app::End ( void )
77  {
78  }
```

The following global constants are declared in lines 9 through 15:

- The SCREEN_WIDTH and SCREEN_HEIGHT constants are declared in lines 9 and 10 and initialized with the values 640 and 480. We will use these constants to set the virtual resolution of the screen.
- Lines 11 and 12 declare the FIRST_IMAGE constant (initialized with 1) and the LAST_IMAGE constant (initialized with 8). These are the image numbers that we will use for the first and last images in the animation sequence.
- The SPRITE_INDEX constant is declared in line 13 and initialized with the value 1. This value will be used to reference the sprite that will display the images that make up the animation sequence.
- Lines 14 and 15 declare the FPS and MODE constants. The FPS constant is initialized with the value 8. We will use this constant to set the number of frames per second that the app::Loop function will iterate. We chose 8, a low value, because we want the animation to run somewhat slowly. (If we use the default value, the cartoon man will appear to be running instead of walking!) The MODE constant is initialized with a value of 0. This is the default value, which will cause the game loop to sleep between frames, but a value of 1, which uses a continuous loop, could have been used as well. We will use these constants to set the rate that the frames of animation will be drawn to the screen and define the behavior of the game loop between frames.

The app::Begin function is defined in lines 18 through 50:

- In line 21 we set the window title to *"Cel Animation"*. This is the text that will appear in the window's title bar during execution of the program.
- In line 24 we set the virtual resolution using the constants SCREEN_WIDTH and SCREEN_HEIGHT that we initialized earlier in the program.
- In line 27 we set the frame rate and the game loop mode using the constants FPS and MODE.
- In lines 30 through 37 we load each of the eight images that will be used for the animation sequence. These statements store each image in memory so that we can retrieve any of the images at a later time by using its image number.

- In line 40 we create the sprite we will use to display the animation on the screen. The sprite is created using the SPRITE_INDEX and FIRST_IMAGE constants. This will create a sprite that will use the first frame of animation as its image, so when the program begins, the sprite will display the image for the very first frame of animation.
- In lines 43 through 46 we calculate the position where we would like to display the sprite on the screen. The sprite's width and height are stored in the spriteWidth and spriteHeight variables in lines 43 and 44. These values are based on the width and height of the image that is currently being used by the sprite (which is the image for the first frame of animation). In lines 45 and 46 the sprite's width and height are used along with the SCREEN_WIDTH and SCREEN_HEIGHT constants to calculate the center of the screen and then center the sprite accordingly.
- In line 49 we set the sprite's position. When the program executes, the sprite will appear centered on the screen.

The app::Loop function is defined in lines 53 through 73:

- In line 56 we declare a variable named currentImage and initialize it with the image number of the image that is currently being used by the sprite.
- An if statement in lines 59 through 66 determines whether the currentImage is equal to LAST_IMAGE. If so, we reset currentImage to FIRST_IMAGE in line 61.
- Line 69 sets the sprite's image to currentImage. In line 72, we update the game loop.

The app::End function in lines 76 through 78 contains no code.

Simplifying Animation with Texture Atlases

VideoNote

Working with Texture Atlases

Although Program 8-8 illustrates the fundamental idea behind cel animation, the AGK provides a simpler way to achieve the same results. Instead of having separate image files for the frames in an animation sequence stored on your disk, you can have one image file that contains all the images. Such a file is known as a *texture atlas*. Figure 8-10 shows an example of a texture atlas containing all the images for the walking man animation we looked at previously.

Figure 8-10 A texture atlas

The images in a texture atlas are organized in rows and columns. The texture atlas shown in Figure 8-10 has one row and eight columns. When this texture atlas is used to create an animation, the images are displayed from left to right. This means the image (or frame) in the first column is displayed, then the image (or frame) in the second column is displayed, and so forth.

The AGK can calculate the positions of each image in a texture atlas by using the width and height of each frame. For example, the entire texture atlas shown in Figure 8-10 is 1024 pixels wide by 256 pixels high. There are eight columns in the texture atlas, so each column is 128 pixels wide. The first 128 by 256 block contains the first image, the second 128 by 256 block contains the second image, and so forth.

Figure 8-11 shows another example of a texture atlas. This one has two rows and four columns. Each image in the texture atlas occupies an area that is 240 pixels wide by 240 pixels high. The entire texture atlas is 960 pixels wide by 480 pixels high.

Figure 8-11 A texture atlas with two rows and four columns

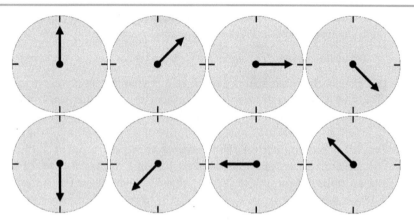

When a texture atlas containing multiple rows is used to create an animation, the images in the first row are displayed from left to right, then the images in the second row are displayed from left to right, and so forth.

This is consistent with the internal numbering system that the AGK uses to identify the images in a texture atlas. The images are numbered, starting at 1, from left to right. If the texture atlas contains multiple rows, the numbering continues from one row to the next. For example, in the texture atlas shown in Figure 8-11, the images in the first row would be numbered 1, 2, 3, and 4, and the images in the second row would be numbered 5, 6, 7, and 8.

Playing Sprite Animations with the AGK

To play an animation using the images in a texture atlas, first must you load the image containing the texture atlas, create a sprite, and then set up the animation frames that will be used by the sprite. To set up the animation, you call the agk::SetSpriteAnimation function. Here is the general format of how you call the function:

```
agk::SetSpriteAnimation(SpriteIndex, FrameWidth,
                    FrameHeight, FrameCount);
```

SpriteIndex is the sprite index number you will use for the animated sprite; *FrameWidth* is the width, in pixels, of a single frame of animation; *FrameHeight* is the height, in pixels, of a single frame of animation; and *FrameCount* is the total number of frames that make up the animation sequence. Here is an example that loads a texture atlas, creates a sprite, and then sets up sprite to use the animation sequence stored in the texture atlas:

```
1   agk::LoadImage(1, "animation.png");
2   agk::CreateSprite(1, 1);
3   agk::SetSpriteAnimation(1, 128, 256, 8);
```

The first statement loads the texture atlas stored in the animation.png file. The second statement creates a sprite specifying the texture atlas as its image. The third statement sets up the animation for the sprite. It is made up of eight frames of animation, where each frame is 128 pixels wide by 256 pixels high.

Once a sprite has been set up for animation, it may be played by calling the agk::PlaySprite function. Here is the general format of how you call the function:

```
agk::PlaySprite(SpriteIndex, Fps, Loop, FromFrame, ToFrame);
```

SpriteIndex is the integer index number of the sprite you want to play the animation for, and it is the only required argument for the function. If you don't need to do a lot of customization for your animation, the calling the function with only the sprite index will work fine. *Fps* is an optional float argument that sets the frames per second of the animation. The value of the *Fps* argument applies to the frame rate of the animation only and does not change the frame rate of the game loop. *Loop* is an optional integer argument that sets whether or not the animation will loop. If the *Loop* value is set to 0 (false), the animation to play once and then stop, whereas a value of 1 (true) will loop the animation. *FromFrame* is an optional integer argument that sets the first frame of animation, and *ToFrame* is an optional integer argument that sets the last frame of animation.

To demonstrate, look at Program 8-9. This program loads the clock texture atlas shown in Figure 8-11 and plays the animation.

Program 8-9   (Clock Texture Atlas)

```
1  // This program demonstrates using a texture atlas
2  // to display an animated clock.
3
4  // Includes, namespace and prototypes
5  #include "template.h"
6  using namespace AGK;
7  app App;
8
9  // Constants
10 const int SCREEN_WIDTH  = 640;
11 const int SCREEN_HEIGHT = 480;
12 const int IMAGE_INDEX   = 1;
13 const int FRAME_WIDTH   = 240;
14 const int FRAME_HEIGHT  = 240;
```

```
15 const int FRAME_COUNT   = 8;
16 const int SPRITE_INDEX  = 1;
17 const float SPRITE_X = SCREEN_WIDTH / 2 - FRAME_WIDTH / 2;
18 const float SPRITE_Y = SCREEN_HEIGHT / 2 - FRAME_HEIGHT / 2;
19
20 // Begin app, called once at the start
21 void app::Begin( void )
22 {
23    // Set the window title.
24    agk::SetWindowTitle("Clock Texture Atlas");
25
26    // Set the virtual resolution.
27    agk::SetVirtualResolution(SCREEN_WIDTH, SCREEN_HEIGHT);
28
29    // Load the texture atlas.
30    agk::LoadImage(IMAGE_INDEX, "ClockTextureAtlas.png");
31
32    // Create the sprite using the texture atlas as the image.
33    agk::CreateSprite(SPRITE_INDEX, IMAGE_INDEX);
34
35    // Set the sprite animation.
36    agk::SetSpriteAnimation(SPRITE_INDEX, FRAME_WIDTH,
37                            FRAME_HEIGHT, FRAME_COUNT);
38
39    // Set the sprite's position.
40    agk::SetSpritePosition(SPRITE_INDEX, SPRITE_X, SPRITE_Y);
41
42    // Play the clock animation.
43    agk::PlaySprite(SPRITE_INDEX);
44 }
45
46 // Main loop, called every frame
47 void app::Loop ( void )
48 {
49    // Refresh the screen.
50    agk::Sync();
51 }
52
53 // Called when the app ends
54 void app::End ( void )
55 {
56 }
```

Stopping and Resuming an Animated Sprite

You can stop an animated sprite with the agk::StopSprite function. You can resume animation for a sprite with the agk::ResumeSprite function. Both functions accept a sprite index number as their only argument. When animation for a sprite is stopped, the frame where the animation was stopped is persevered, and the sprite will begin the animation sequence right where it left off when the animation sequence is resumed.

The following example calls the agk::StopSprite function to stop a sprite's animation sequence and then calls the agk::ResumeSprite function to resume the animation.

```
agk::StopSprite(1);
agk::ResumeSprite(1);
```

 Checkpoint

8.13. What is a texture atlas?

8.14. What AGK function do you call to set up a sprite for animation?

8.15. What AGK function do you call to play a sprite's animation?

 8.6 Music and Sound

CONCEPT: The AGK lets you play audio files that have been saved in the MP3 and WAV formats. The library provides numerous functions for working with these audio files.

VideoNote

Working with Music and Sound

Sound effects are important in games, as they are often used to signal events like colliding objects, selecting items, completing part of a game, and gaining extra power. Background music also plays an important role in games. It can create a particular mood, for example, by making the game seem silly and whimsical or dark and mysterious.

The AGK allows you to play sound from audio files that are stored in the WAV and MP3 formats. In the AGK, audio that is saved in the WAV format is classified as sound, and audio that is saved in the MP3 format is classified as music. There are two sets of functions for loading and playing audio: one for sound files and one for music files.

Loading a Sound File

Audio files that are saved in the WAV format are considered sound files by the AGK. To use a sound file, first you must load it into memory. Then you can play the sound file and perform other operations with it.

You load a sound file into memory by calling the agk::LoadSound function. There are several versions of this function, but the version we will use accepts two arguments: an index number and filename for the sound you want to load. The following shows the general format of how you call the function:

```
agk::LoadSound(SoundNumber, Filename);
```

The following code shows an example that loads a sound from the file *mySound.wav* and assigns it an index value of 1:

```
agk::LoadSound(1, "mySound.wav");
```

In this example, we have specified only the filename, without a path. Audio files must be placed in the same folder as image files for the program to find them.

Playing a Sound

Once you have loaded a sound file into memory, you can play it with the agk::PlaySound function. Here is the general format of how you call the function:

```
agk::PlaySound(SoundNumber);
```

SoundNumber is the index number of the sound that you want to play. For example, the following statement plays a sound with an index number of 1.

```
agk::PlaySound(1);
```

When you call the agk::PlaySound function, the specified sound will be played. Program 8-10 shows a simple example that plays a sound. Program 8-11 shows a more elaborate example that lets the user play a guitar, a drum, and a horn by clicking them with the mouse.

Program 8-10   **(Play Sound)**

```
1  // This program loads a sound file and plays it.
2
3  // Includes, namespace and prototypes
4  #include "template.h"
5  using namespace AGK;
6  app App;
7
8  // Begin app, called once at the start
9  void app::Begin( void )
10 {
11     // Set the window title.
12     agk::SetWindowTitle("Play Sound");
13
14     // Set the virtual resolution.
15     agk::SetVirtualResolution(640, 480);
16
17     // Load the sound file sparkle.wav as
18     // sound number 1.
19     agk::LoadSound(1, "sparkle.wav");
20
21     // Play sound number 1.
22     agk::PlaySound(1);
23 }
24
25 // Main loop, called every frame
26 void app::Loop ( void )
27 {
28     // Refresh the screen.
29     agk::Sync();
30 }
31
32 // Called when the app ends
33 void app::End ( void )
34 {
35 }
```

Program 8-11   (Sprite Sounds)

```
1 // This program demonstrates playing sounds
2 // when a sprite is clicked by the mouse.
3
4 // Includes, namespace and prototypes
5 #include "template.h"
6 using namespace AGK;
7 app App;
8
9 // Constants
10 const int SCREEN_WIDTH  = 640;
11 const int SCREEN_HEIGHT = 480;
12 const int GUITAR_SPRITE = 1;
13 const int DRUM_SPRITE   = 2;
14 const int HORN_SPRITE   = 3;
15 const int GUITAR_SOUND  = 1;
16 const int DRUM_SOUND    = 2;
17 const int HORN_SOUND    = 3;
18
19 // Begin app, called once at the start
20 void app::Begin( void )
21 {
22    // Set the window title.
23    agk::SetWindowTitle("Sprite Sounds");
24
25    // Set the virtual resolution.
26    agk::SetVirtualResolution(SCREEN_WIDTH, SCREEN_HEIGHT);
27
28    // Load the sounds.
29    agk::LoadSound(GUITAR_SOUND, "guitar.wav");
30    agk::LoadSound(DRUM_SOUND, "drum.wav");
31    agk::LoadSound(HORN_SOUND, "horn.wav");
32
33    // Create the sprites.
34    agk::CreateSprite(GUITAR_SPRITE, "guitar.png");
35    agk::CreateSprite(DRUM_SPRITE, "drum.png");
36    agk::CreateSprite(HORN_SPRITE, "horn.png");
37
38    // Position the sprites.
39    agk::SetSpritePosition(GUITAR_SPRITE, 0.0, 0.0);
40    agk::SetSpritePosition(DRUM_SPRITE, 200.0, 200.0);
41    agk::SetSpritePosition(HORN_SPRITE, 300.0, 300.0);
42 }
43
44 // Main loop, called every frame
45 void app::Loop ( void )
46 {
47    // Get the mouse coordinates.
48    float mouseX = agk::GetRawMouseX();
49    float mouseY = agk::GetRawMouseY();
50
51    // Determine if the left mouse button was pressed.
52    if(agk::GetRawMouseLeftPressed())
```

```
53    {
54        // Get the index number of the sprite that the mouse
55        // is pointing at.
56        int spriteIndex = agk::GetSpriteHit(mouseX, mouseY);
57
58        // Determine if the sound is already playing.
59        if(agk::GetSoundsPlaying(spriteIndex))
60        {
61            // Stop the sound.
62            agk::StopSound(spriteIndex);
63        }
64        else
65        {
66            // Play the sound.
67            agk::PlaySound(spriteIndex);
68        }
69    }
70
71    // Refresh the screen.
72    agk::Sync();
73 }
74
75 // Called when the app ends
76 void app::End ( void )
77 {
78 }
```

Figure 8-12 Example output for Program 8-11

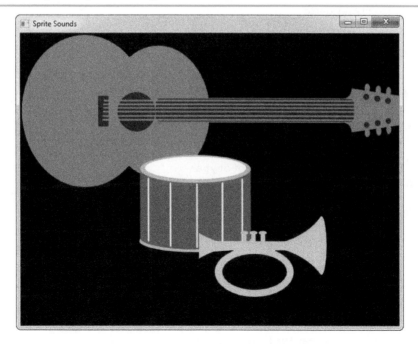

Music Files

Music files are files that are saved in the MP3 format. The AGK provides many of the same operations for music files as sound files. Let's take a closer look at some of the things you can do with music files.

Loading a Music File

Before you can use a music file, you have to load it into memory by calling the `agk::LoadMusic` function. Here is the general format of how you call the function:

```
agk::LoadMusic(MusicNumber, Filename);
```

MusicNumber is an integer number that you are assigning to the music. This can be an integer in the range of 1 through 50. You will use the music number to identify the music when you want to play it or perform other operations with it. *Filename* is the name of the music file that you would like to load into the program's memory. For example, the following statement loads the file *myMusic.mp3* as music number 1.

```
agk::LoadMusic(1, "myMusic.mp3");
```

Playing Music

Once you have loaded a music file into memory, you can play it with the `agk::PlayMusic` function. Only one music file may be played at any one time. Here is the general format of how you call the function:

```
agk::PlayMusic(MusicNumber);
```

MusicNumber is the number of the music that you want to play. For example, the following statement plays music number 1:

```
agk::PlayMusic(1);
```

Program 8-12 demonstrates playing three different music files when the user clicks on three different virtual buttons.

Program 8-12 (Play Music)

```
 1 // This program demonstrates playing music
 2 // when a virtual button is clicked by the mouse.
 3
 4 // Includes, namespace and prototypes
 5 #include "template.h"
 6 using namespace AGK;
 7 app App;
 8
 9 // Begin app, called once at the start
10 void app::Begin( void )
11 {
12     // Set the window title.
13     agk::SetWindowTitle("Music Player");
14
15     // Set the virtual resolution.
16     agk::SetVirtualResolution(640, 480);
17
```

```
18      // Load the music files.
19      agk::LoadMusic(1, "MusicA.mp3");
20      agk::LoadMusic(2, "MusicB.mp3");
21      agk::LoadMusic(3, "MusicC.mp3");
22
23      // Add the virtual buttons.
24      agk::AddVirtualButton(1, 220, 240, 100);
25      agk::AddVirtualButton(2, 320, 240, 100);
26      agk::AddVirtualButton(3, 420, 240, 100);
27
28      // Set the text for the virtual buttons.
29      agk::SetVirtualButtonText(1, "1");
30      agk::SetVirtualButtonText(2, "2");
31      agk::SetVirtualButtonText(3, "3");
32   }
33
34   // Main loop, called every frame
35   void app::Loop ( void )
36   {
37      // If button 1 was pressed, play music 1.
38      if(agk::GetVirtualButtonPressed(1))
39      {
40         agk::PlayMusic(1);
41      }
42
43      // If button 2 was pressed, play music 2.
44      if(agk::GetVirtualButtonPressed(2))
45      {
46         agk::PlayMusic(2);
47      }
48
49      // If button 3 was pressed, play music 3.
50      if(agk::GetVirtualButtonPressed(3))
51      {
52         agk::PlayMusic(3);
53      }
54
55      // Refresh the screen.
56      agk::Sync();
57   }
58
59   // Called when the app ends
60   void app::End ( void )
61   {
62   }
```

8.7 The Bug Zapper Game

In this section we will look at a simple game that incorporates many of the topics that we have discussed in this chapter. The Bug Zapper game displays an animated sprite of a bug. The user zaps the bug by clicking it with the mouse. When this happens, a new bug appears at a random location on the screen. The game will run for 10 seconds before ending. The object of the game is to zap as many bugs as possible within the allotted time. When the game ends, a screen displays the number of bugs that were zapped.

In the Spotlight:
The Bug Zapper Game

Figure 8-13 shows some screens from the game (this is also shown as Figure C-8 in the book's color insert). The intro screen shown in the top-left is displayed when the game begins. The user presses a key on the keyboard, and a screen similar to the one in the top-right is displayed. The user zaps as many bugs as possible until time runs out. Then the bottom screen is displayed, showing the number of bugs that were zapped.

Figure 8-13 Screens from the Bug Zapper game

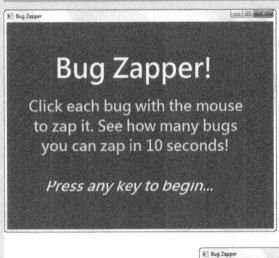
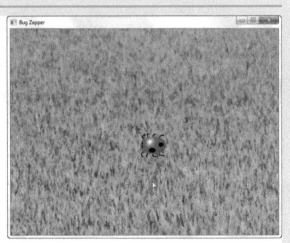

To determine when 10 seconds has elapsed, the program will use two AGK functions: `agk::ResetTimer` and `agk::Timer`. The AGK has a timer that measures the number of seconds that have elapsed since the program started or since the last time the timer was reset. The `agk::ResetTimer` function resets the timer. Its general format is shown here:

```
agk::ResetTimer();
```

The `agk::Timer` function returns the value of the timer. When you call the `agk::Timer` function, it returns either the number of seconds since the program started or since the last time that the timer was restarted. Its general format is shown here:

```
agk::Timer();
```

Program 8-13 shows the code for the game, but rather than showing all the code at once, we will show sections of it, with a description following each section. Lines 1 through 11 are shown first. These lines contain the initial code and a set of function prototypes in lines 7 through 11.

Program 8-13   (**BugZapper** *partial listing*)

```
 1 // Includes, namespace and prototypes
 2 #include "template.h"
 3 using namespace AGK;
 4 app App;
 5
 6 // Function prototypes
 7 void generateNewBug();
 8 void displayIntro();
 9 void hideIntro();
10 void playGame();
11 void closingScreen();
12
```

Lines 13 through 41 are shown next. These statements contain the program's global declarations.

Program 8-13   (**BugZapper** *partial listing*)

```
13 // Constants for the screen resolution
14 const int SCREEN_WIDTH = 640;
15 const int SCREEN_HEIGHT = 480;
16
17 // Constants for sprites
18 const int INTRO_INDEX = 1;
19 const int GRASS_INDEX = 2;
20 const int BUG_INDEX   = 3;
21
22 // Constant for the sound file
23 const int BOINK_SOUND = 1;
24
25 // Constants for animation
26 const int FRAME_WIDTH = 64;
27 const int FRAME_HEIGHT = 64;
28 const int FRAME_COUNT = 2;
29
30 // Constant for game time
31 const int MAX_TIME = 10;
32
33 // Constants for the possible game states.
34 const int GAME_JUST_STARTED = 0;
35 const int GAME_IN_PLAY      = 1;
36 const int GAME_OVER         = 3;
37
38 // Global counter for the number of bugs zapped.
```

```
39 int g_bugsZapped = 0;
40 int g_gameState = GAME_JUST_STARTED;
41
```

Here is a summary of the global declarations:

- Lines 14 and 15 declare constants for the screen sizes.
- Lines 18 through 20 declare the INTRO_INDEX, GRASS_INDEX and BUG_INDEX constants that will be used as sprite indices.
- Line 23 declares a constant named BOINK_INDEX that will be used as a sound index.
- Lines 26 through 28 declare the FRAME_WIDTH, FRAME_HEIGHT, and FRAME_COUNT constants that are used in the lady bug animation.
- Line 31 declares the const MAX_TIME that is set to the number of seconds that the game should run.
- Lines 34 through 36 declare the constants GAME_JUST_STARTED, GAME_IN_PLAY, and GAME_OVER. These constants will represent the three states of the game.
- Line 39 declares the global variable g_bugsZapped, initialized with 0. This variable will be used to keep count of the number of bugs that are zapped.
- Line 40 declares the global variable g_gameState, initialized with the constant GAME_JUST_STARTED. Throughout the running of the program, this variable will always be assigned one of the constants declared in lines 34 through 36 to indicate the current game state.

The app::Begin function is shown next.

Program 8-13   (BugZapper *partial listing*)

```
42 // Begin app, called once at the start
43 void app::Begin( void )
44 {
45     // Set the virtual resolution.
46     agk::SetVirtualResolution(SCREEN_WIDTH, SCREEN_HEIGHT);
47
48     // Set the text in the window title bar.
49     agk::SetWindowTitle("Bug Zapper");
50
51     // Create the background sprite.
52     agk::CreateSprite(GRASS_INDEX, "BugZapper/Grass.png");
53
54     // Create the bug sprite.
55     agk::CreateSprite(BUG_INDEX, "BugZapper/Bug.png");
56
57     // Create the intro screen sprite.
58     agk::CreateSprite(INTRO_INDEX, "BugZapper/Intro.png");
59
60     // Load the sound file.
61     agk::LoadSound(BOINK_SOUND, "BugZapper/Boink.wav");
62
63     // Randomly position the bug.
64     generateNewBug();
```

```
65
66      // Set the sprite animation
67      agk::SetSpriteAnimation(BUG_INDEX, FRAME_WIDTH,
68                   FRAME_HEIGHT, FRAME_COUNT);
69
70      // Play the bug animation.
71      agk::PlaySprite(BUG_INDEX);
72 }
```

Here is a summary of the function:

- Line 46 sets the virtual resolution.
- Line 49 sets the text in the window's title bar.
- Line 52 creates a sprite that will be used as the game's background image. The sprite is an image of grass that fills the entire screen.
- Line 55 creates the bug sprite.
- Line 58 creates the sprite that is displayed as the game's intro screen.
- Line 61 loads the sound file that will be played each time the user zaps a bug.
- Line 64 calls a function named `generateNewBug`. This function, which is defined in lines 121 through 133, positions the bug sprite at a random location.
- Lines 67 and 68 call the `agk::SetSpriteAnimation` function to setup the animation of the bug.
- Line 71 calls the `agk::PlaySprite` function to start the bug animation.

The `app::Loop` function appears in lines 75 through 112.

Program 8-13   (**BugZapper** *partial listing*)

```
74 // Main loop, called every frame
75 void app::Loop ( void )
76 {
77     // Determine the game state and
78     // act accordingly.
79     switch (g_gameState)
80     {
81     case GAME_JUST_STARTED:
82         // Display the intro screen.
83         displayIntro();
84
85         // Check for a key press.
86         if (agk::GetRawLastKey())
87         {
88             // Hide the intro screen
89             hideIntro();
90
91             // Change the game state.
92             g_gameState = GAME_IN_PLAY;
93
94             // Reset the timer.
95             agk::ResetTimer();
96         }
```

```
 97          break;
 98
 99     case GAME_IN_PLAY:
100          // Engage in game play.
101          playGame();
102          break;
103
104     case GAME_OVER:
105          // Display the closing screen.
106          closingScreen();
107          break;
108     };
109
110     // Update the screen.
111     agk::Sync();
112 }
113
114 // Called when the app ends
115 void app::End ( void )
116 {
117 }
118
```

Most of the code in this function is in a switch statement that determines the state of the game and then acts accordingly. The g_gameState variable can be set to one of the following constants:

- GAME_JUST_STARTED, which indicates that the game just started, and the intro screen should be displayed.
- GAME_IN_PLAY, which indicates that the intro screen has been dismissed, and the game is in play. In this state, the user has 10 seconds to zap as many bugs as possible.
- GAME_OVER, which indicates that the 10 seconds have ended, and the game is over.

The switch statement tests the g_gameState variable and works as follows:

- If g_gameState is equal to GAME_JUST_STARTED, the program jumps to the case statement in line 81. Line 83 calls the displayIntro function, which displays the intro screen. The if statement in line 86 determines if the user has pressed a key on the keyboard. It does this by testing the value that is returned from the agk::GetRawLastKey function. The function returns a nonzero value if the user has pressed a key, or zero otherwise. The if statement will treat a nonzero value as true, so if the user has pressed a key, the program branches to line 89, which calls the hideIntro function. The hideIntro function hides the intro screen and makes the grass and bug visible. Then, line 92 assigns GAME_IN_PLAY to g_gameState to indicate that the game is now in play. Line 95 resets the timer.
- If g_gameState is equal to GAME_IN_PLAY, the program jumps to the case statement in line 99. Line 101 calls the playGame function, which handles all the game action.
- If g_gameState is equal to GAME_OVER, the program jumps to the case statement in line 104. Line 106 calls the closingScreen function, which displays the game's closing screen reporting the number of bugs that were zapped.

After the switch statement, line 111 calls the agk::Sync function to update the screen.

The generateNewBug function is shown next, in lines 121 through 133.

Program 8-13   (BugZapper *partial listing*)

```
119 // The generateNewBug function generates a new bug at
120 // random location.
121 void generateNewBug()
122 {
123     // Get the bug's width and height.
124     int bugWidth = agk::GetSpriteWidth(BUG_INDEX);
125     int bugHeight = agk::GetSpriteHeight(BUG_INDEX);
126
127     // Generate a new location.
128     int x = agk::Random(0, SCREEN_WIDTH - bugWidth);
129     int y = agk::Random(0, SCREEN_HEIGHT - bugHeight);
130
131     // Put the bug at that location.
132     agk::SetSpritePosition(BUG_INDEX, x, y);
133 }
134
```

Lines 124 and 125 get the bug sprite's width and height and assign those values to the local variables bugWidth and bugHeight. We use these values in lines 128 and 129 to generate random numbers for the bug sprite's *X*- and *Y*-coordinates. Line 132 positions the bug sprite at the new coordinates.

The displayIntro function is shown next, in lines 137 through 145.

Program 8-13   (BugZapper *partial listing*)

```
135 // The displayIntro function hides the grass and the
136 // bug sprite and makes the intro screen visible.
137 void displayIntro()
138 {
139     // Make the grass and bug invisible.
140     agk::SetSpriteVisible(GRASS_INDEX, 0);
141     agk::SetSpriteVisible(BUG_INDEX, 0);
142
143     // Make the intro screen visible.
144     agk::SetSpriteVisible(INTRO_INDEX, 1);
145 }
146
```

The displayIntro function simply hides the grass and bug sprites (in lines 140 and 141) and makes the intro screen sprite visible (in line 144).

The hideIntro function is shown next, in lines 149 through 154.

Program 8-13   (**BugZapper** *partial listing*)

```
147  // The hideIntro function hides the intro screen
148  // and makes the grass and bug visible.
149  void hideIntro()
150  {
151      agk::SetSpriteVisible(INTRO_INDEX, 0);
152      agk::SetSpriteVisible(BUG_INDEX, 1);
153      agk::SetSpriteVisible(GRASS_INDEX, 1);
154  }
155
```

The hideIntro function simply hides the intro screen sprite (in line 151) and makes the grass and bug sprites visible (in lines 152 and 153).

The playGame function is shown next, in lines 157 through 191.

Program 8-13   (**BugZapper** *partial listing*)

```
156  // The playGame function processes a frame of game play.
157  void playGame()
158  {
159          // Variables for mouse coordinates
160      float mouseX, mouseY;
161
162      // Do we still have time left?
163      if (agk::Timer() < MAX_TIME)
164      {
165          // Determine if the left mouse button was pressed.
166          if(agk::GetRawMouseLeftPressed())
167          {
168              // Get the mouse pointer location.
169              mouseX = agk::GetRawMouseX();
170              mouseY = agk::GetRawMouseY();
171
172              // Check to see if the bug was hit.
173              if (agk::GetSpriteHit(mouseX, mouseY) == BUG_INDEX)
174              {
175                  // Play the boink sound.
176                  agk::PlaySound(BOINK_SOUND);
177
178                  // Update the count.
179                  g_bugsZapped++;
180
181                  // Generate a new bug.
182                  generateNewBug();
183              }
184          }
185      }
```

```
186     else
187     {
188         // Time is up, game over.
189         g_gameState = GAME_OVER;
190     }
191 }
192
```

The `playGame` function handles all the game action while the user is zapping bugs. It also monitors the timer to determine when the game is over. Here is a summary of the function's code:

- Line 160 declares two local variables, `mouseX` and `mouseY`, to hold the coordinates of the mouse pointer.
- The `if` statement in line 163 gets the amount of time that the program has been running (since it was last reset) and determines if this is less than `MAX_TIME`. If so, the game is still in play, and the program branches to line 166. Line 166 is another `if` statement. It determines whether the left mouse button was clicked. If so, the program branches to line 169. Lines 169 and 170 get the mouse pointer's coordinates and assigns them to the `mouseX` and `mouseY` variables. Then the `if` statement in line 170 determines whether the mouse was clicked on the bug sprite. If so, line 176 plays a sound, line 179 adds one to the `g_bugsZapped` variable, and line 182 calls the `generateNewBug` function to reposition the bug at a new, random location.
- If the `if` statement in line 163 determines that that the game's play time is over, then line 189 assigns the constant `GAME_OVER` to the `g_gameState` variable.

The `closingScreen` function is shown next, in lines 194 through 203.

Program 8-13   (**BugZapper** *partial listing*)

```
193 // The closingScreen function displays the closing screen.
194 void closingScreen()
195 {
196     // Hide the bug and the grass.
197     agk::SetSpriteVisible(GRASS_INDEX, 0);
198     agk::SetSpriteVisible(BUG_INDEX, 0);
199
200     // Display the results.
201     agk::PrintC("Number of bugs zapped: ");
202     agk::Print(g_bugsZapped);
203 }
```

Lines 197 and 198 make the grass and bug sprites invisible. Then, lines 201 and 202 display a message reporting the number of bugs that have been zapped.

Review Questions

Multiple Choice

1. These functions return the mouse pointer's *X*- and *Y*-coordinates.
   a. `agk::GetMouseX` and `agk::GetMouseY`
   b. `agk::GetRawMouseX` and `agk::GetRawMouseY`
   c. `agk::MouseX` and `agk::MouseY`
   d. `agk::GetXMouse` and `agk::GetYMouse`

2. This function makes the mouse pointer visible or invisible.
   a. `agk::SetMouseVisible`
   b. `agk::SetMouseInvisible`
   c. `agk::SetRawMouseVisible`
   d. `agk::ShowMouse`

3. These functions can be used to determine whether the left or right mouse button is being pressed.
   a. `agk::GetRawMouseLeftPressed` and `agk::GetRawMouseRightPressed`
   b. `agk::GetMouseLeftPressed` and `agk::GetMouseRightPressed`
   c. `agk::GetLeftPressed` and `agk::GetRightPressed`
   d. `agk::GetMouseLeft` and `agk::GetMouseRight`

4. This function determines if the user clicked on a sprite with the mouse.
   a. `agk::MouseSpriteHit`
   b. `agk::GetSpriteClicked`
   c. `agk::GetSpriteHit`
   d. `agk::GetMouseClicked`

5. When you set a virtual button's position, you set it by the button's _____.
   a. upper-left corner
   b. center point
   c. lower-right corner
   d. lower-left corner

6. This function returns 1 (true) as long as the button is held down, and otherwise it returns 0 (false).
   a. `agk::GetVirtualButtonPressed`
   b. `agk::GetVirtualButtonState`
   c. `agk::GetVirtualButtonReleased`
   d. `agk::GetVirtualButtonRawData`

7. This is an area around a virtual joystick's center that affects how far you have to move the joystick before it registers input:
   a. dead zone.
   b. home position.
   c. center point.
   d. sensitivity zone.

8. You use this function to determine whether the left or right arrow keys have been pressed on the keyboard.
   a. `agk::GetArrowKey`
   b. `agk::GetLeftRightArrow`
   c. `agk::GetDirectionY`
   d. `agk::GetDirectionX`

9. You use this function to determine the last key that was pressed on the keyboard.
   a. `agk::GetRawLastKey`
   b. `agk::GetKey`
   c. `agk::GetLastKey`
   d. `agk::KeyPressed`

10. This is an image file containing all the images used in an animation.
    a. Sprite array
    b. Texture atlas
    c. Image sheet
    d. Animation matrix

True or False

1. By default, the mouse pointer is invisible when an AGK program is running.

2. A virtual button is positioned by its upper-left corner.

3. You can change the color of a virtual button.

4. You can change the images that are used to display a virtual button.

5. You can have an unlimited number of virtual buttons in an AGK program.

6. You can have four virtual joysticks in an AGK program.

7. You can totally disable a virtual joystick by setting the dead zone value to 0.

8. Files that are stored in the `.wav` format are considered music files.

Short Answer

1. Using the AGK, how do you tell if the user has clicked on a sprite using the mouse?

2. What is a virtual button?

3. How can you determine if a virtual button is being held down?

4. What is a virtual joystick?

5. How do you adjust the sensitivity of a virtual joystick?

6. What is the default dead zone value of a virtual joystick?

7. How do you know if a virtual joystick is being moved to the left? How do you know if it is being moved to the right?

8. What is cel animation?

9. MP3 files are considered what kind of file?

Algorithm Workbench

1. Write code that gets the mouse pointer's coordinates and assigns those values to variables named mouseX and mouseY.

2. Write a statement that makes the mouse pointer invisible.

3. Write a statement that adds a virtual button to the program. The virtual button's index should be 1, its size should be 50 pixels, and its coordinates should be (400, 100).

4. Write a statement that deactivates the virtual button with the index 1.

5. Suppose you have two image files that you want to use for a virtual button, instead of the default images provided by the AGK. The image files are named custom_button_up.png and custom_button_down.png. Write code that sets these image files as the images for the virtual button with the index 1.

6. Write a statement that adds a virtual joystick with an index number of 1 to the top-left corner of the screen using a size of 75.

7. Write a statement that sets all virtual joystick dead zones to 0.5.

8. Write code that determines whether the last key that was pressed was the space-bar and, if so, displays a message.

9. You have an image file named animation.png that contains all the images for an animation. Each frame in the file is 128 pixels wide and 246 pixels high. Write the code to load the image file, and then play the animation sequence.

10. Write code that loads and plays the sound file roar.wav.

Programming Exercises

1. **Mouse Rollover**
Write a program that displays an image. When the user moves the mouse pointer over the image, it should change to a second image. The second image should remain displayed as long as the mouse pointer is over it. When the user moves the mouse pointer away from the second image, it should change back to the first image.

2. **Coin Toss**
Write a program that simulates the tossing of a coin. The program should wait for the user to press a key and then generate a random number in the range of 0 through 1. If the number is 0, the program should display the image of a coin with heads facing up. If the number is 1, the program should display the image of a coin with tails facing up. (You can create your own coin images or use the ones provided in the book's online resources, downloadable from www.pearsonhighered.com/gaddis.)

3. **Make Your Head Spin**

   Have a friend use a digital camera to take photos of your head from different angles. (For example, your left profile, your face, your right profile, the back of your head, etc.) Copy the photos to your computer, and put them together as a texture atlas. Then write a program that creates an animation that shows your head spinning.

4. **Lunar Lander, Part 1**

   The book's online resources (downloadable from www.pearsonhighered.com/gaddis) provide images of a spacecraft and a background drawing of the moon's surface. Write a program that initially displays the spacecraft on the moon's surface. When the user presses the spacebar, the spacecraft should slowly lift off the surface and continue to lift as long as the spacebar is held down. When the user releases the spacebar, the spacecraft should slowly descend back down toward the surface and stop when it reaches the surface.

5. **Lunar Lander, Part 2**

   Enhance the lunar lander program (see Programming Exercise 4) so the user can press the left or right arrow keys, along with the spacebar, to slowly guide the spacecraft to the left or right. If the spacebar is not pressed, however, the left and right arrow keys should have no effect.

6. **Lunar Lander, Part 3**

   Enhance the lunar lander program (see Programming Exercises 4 and 5) so the spacecraft initially appears on one side of the screen, and a landing pad appears on the opposite side. The user should try to fly the spacecraft and guide it so that it lands on the landing pad. If the spacecraft successfully lands on the landing pad, display a message congratulating the user.

7. **Change for a Dollar Game**

   The book's online resources (downloadable from www.pearsonhighered.com/gaddis) provide images of a penny, a nickel, a dime, and a quarter. Create a game that displays each of these images, plus another image showing the text "Count Change". The game should let the user click on any of the coins, in any order. To win the game, the user must click on the coins that, when added together, equal exactly one dollar. When the user clicks the "Count Change" image the program should show the amount of money that the user clicked. If the amount equals one dollar, the program should indicate that the user won the game.

8. **Rock, Paper, Scissors Game**

   Write a program that lets the user play the game of Rock, Paper, Scissors against the computer. The program should work as follows.
   (1) When the program begins, a random number in the range of 0 through 2 is generated. If the number is 0, then the computer has chosen rock. If the number is 1, then the computer has chosen paper. If the number is 2, then the computer has chosen scissors. (Don't display the computer's choice yet.)
   (2) To make his or her selection, the user clicks an image on the screen. (You can find images for this game included in the book's online resources at www.pearsonhighered.com/gaddis.)

(3) The computer's choice is displayed.

(4) A winner is selected according to the following rules:

- If one player chooses rock and the other player chooses scissors, then rock wins. (The rock smashes the scissors.)
- If one player chooses scissors and the other player chooses paper, then scissors wins. (Scissors cuts paper.)
- If one player chooses paper and the other player chooses rock, then paper wins. (Paper wraps rock.)
- If both players make the same choice, the game is a tie.

CHAPTER 6

Text, Collisions, and the Vulture Trouble Game

TOPICS

9.1 Text Objects

CONCEPT: You can create text objects to display messages and information. Text objects have properties such as position, size, and color.

VideoNote

Working with Text Objects

So far we have used the `agk::Print` and `agk::PrintC` functions to display text on the screen. These functions work well for displaying simple messages, but they don't allow you to change the position of the text or perform other operations. With the AGK you can create text objects that you can use to display custom text anywhere on the screen. A text object is similar to a sprite. It has an index number that identifies it in code. Instead of an image, however, a text object contains a string of characters that you can place anywhere on the screen. You can change many properties of a text object such as its position, color, and size. In this section we will take a look at some of the basics of working with text objects.

Creating a Text Object

Before you can display text using a text object, you must create it. You can create a text object by calling the `agk::CreateText` function. Creating a text object is very similar to the way we have created other resources such sprites or images. Here is the general format of how you call the function:

```
agk::CreateText(TextIndex, String);
```

TextIndex is an integer index that that will be used to identify the text object. *String* is a string value containing the text you want to display. For example, the following statement creates a text object with an index number of 1 and sets its *String* argument to display the text *"GAME OVER"*:

```
agk::CreateText(1, "GAME OVER");
```

Deleting a Text Object

If you are finished using a text object and would like to remove it from memory, then you can call the agk::DeleteText function. Here is the general format of how you call the function:

```
agk::DeleteText(TextIndex);
```

TextIndex is the index number of the text object that you want to delete. For example, the following statement deletes a text object with an index number of 1:

```
agk::DeleteText(1);
```

Determining If a Text Object Exists

If you need to make sure that a text object exists before you perform operations on it, you can use the agk::GetTextExists function. Here is the general format of how you call the function:

```
agk::GetTextExists(TextIndex)
```

TextIndex is the index number of the text object whose existence you want to check. The function returns an integer value of 0 (false) if the specified text object does not exist or 1 (true) if the text object does exist. For example, the following if statement calls the agk::GetTextExists function and uses its return value to determine whether a text object with an index number of 1 exists. If the text object exists, then it is deleted:

```
If (agk::GetTextExists(1))
{
    agk::DeleteText(1);
}
```

Setting the Size of a Text Object

By default the size of a text object is set to 4 units (which is approximately 4 pixels in our 640 by 480 virtual resolution), but you can easily change the size of a text object to any value. You do this by calling the agk::SetTextSize function. Here is the general format of how you call the function:

```
agk::SetTextSize(TextIndex, Size);
```

TextIndex is the index number of the text object whose size you want to change. *Size* is a floating-point value that will set the height of the text object. The width of the text object is calculated internally by the AGK. The following statement sets the size of a text object with an index number of 1 to 16 units.

```
agk::SetTextSize(1, 16);
```

Getting the Size of a Text Object

You can get the size of a text object by calling the agk::GetTextSize function. Here is the general format of how you call the function:

```
agk::GetTextSize(TextIndex)
```

TextIndex is the index number of the text object whose size you want to get. The function returns a floating-point value for the size of the text object specified by the index number. The following statement gets the size of a text object with an index number of 1 and stores the return value in the floating-point variable named textSize:

```
float textSize = agk::GetTextSize(1);
```

Setting the Position of a Text Object

Text objects are positioned in the top-left corner of the screen by default. After you have created a text object, you can change its position by calling the agk::SetTextPosition function. Here is the general format of how you call the function:

```
agk::SetTextPosition(TextIndex, X, Y)
```

TextIndex is the index number of the text object whose position you want to change. The remaining arguments, *X* and *Y*, are floating-point values for the *X*- and *Y*-coordinates that you want to move the text object to. For example, the following statement changes the position of a text object with an index number of 1 so that its top-left corner appears 10 units across and 10 units down from the top-left corner of the screen:

```
agk::SetTextPosition(1, 10, 10);
```

Setting the *X*-Coordinate of a Text Object

Sometimes you may only want to move a text object left or right across the screen. You can do this by calling the agk::SetTextX function. Here is the general format of how you call the function:

```
agk::SetTextX(TextIndex, X)
```

TextIndex is the index number of the text object you want to change. The second argument, *X*, is a floating-point value specifying the *X*-coordinate you want to move the text object to. For example, the following statement sets the *X*-coordinate of a text object with an index number of 1 to 100 units along the *X*-axis:

```
agk::SetTextX(1, 100);
```

Getting the *X*-Coordinate of a Text Object

You can get the value of a text object's *X*-coordinate by calling the agk::GetTextX function and passing the index number of the text object you want to get the value of the *X*-coordinate for. The function returns a floating-point value. For example, the following statement gets the *X*-coordinate of a text object with an index number of 1 and stores it in a floating-point variable named textX:

```
float textX = agk::GetTextX(1);
```

Setting the *Y*-Coordinate of a Text Object

You can change the vertical position of a text object by calling the `agk::SetTextY` function and passing the index number of the text object you want to change followed by the value of the new *Y*-coordinate. For example, the following statement sets the *Y*-coordinate of a text object with an index number of 1 to 100:

```
agk::SetTextY(1, 100);
```

Getting the *Y*-Coordinate of a Text Object

You can get the value of a text object's *Y*-coordinate by calling the `agk::GetTextY` function and passing the index number of the text object you want to get the value of the *Y*-coordinate for. The function returns a floating-point value. For example, the following statement gets the *Y*-coordinate of a text object with an index number of 1 and stores it in a floating-point variable named `textY`:

```
float textY = agk::GetTextY(1);
```

Now that we have covered several properties of text objects, it is a good time to look at a program that uses these functions to create text objects and set some of their properties. Program 9-1 demonstrates setting the size and position of several text objects.

Program 9-1   (Text Sizes)

```
 1 // This program demonstrates setting the
 2 // size and position of several text objects.
 3
 4 // Includes, namespace and prototypes
 5 #include "template.h"
 6 using namespace AGK;
 7 app App;
 8
 9 // Constants for the screen resolution
10 const int SCREEN_WIDTH  = 640;
11 const int SCREEN_HEIGHT = 480;
12
13 // Constants for the text object index numbers
14 const int TEXT_A = 1;
15 const int TEXT_B = 2;
16 const int TEXT_C = 3;
17 const int TEXT_D = 4;
18 const int TEXT_E = 5;
19 const int TEXT_F = 6;
20
21 // Constants for the text object sizes
22 const float SIZE_A = 12;
23 const float SIZE_B = 16;
24 const float SIZE_C = 24;
25 const float SIZE_D = 36;
26 const float SIZE_E = 48;
27 const float SIZE_F = 72;
```

```
28
29 // Begin app, called once at the start
30 void app::Begin( void )
31 {
32     // Set the virtual resolution.
33     agk::SetVirtualResolution(SCREEN_WIDTH, SCREEN_HEIGHT);
34
35     // Set the window title.
36     agk::SetWindowTitle("Text Sizes");
37
38     // Create the text objects.
39     agk::CreateText(TEXT_A, "Text Size 12");
40     agk::CreateText(TEXT_B, "Text Size 16");
41     agk::CreateText(TEXT_C, "Text Size 24");
42     agk::CreateText(TEXT_D, "Text Size 36");
43     agk::CreateText(TEXT_E, "Text Size 48");
44     agk::CreateText(TEXT_F, "Text Size 72");
45
46     // Set the size of each text object.
47     agk::SetTextSize(TEXT_A, SIZE_A);
48     agk::SetTextSize(TEXT_B, SIZE_B);
49     agk::SetTextSize(TEXT_C, SIZE_C);
50     agk::SetTextSize(TEXT_D, SIZE_D);
51     agk::SetTextSize(TEXT_E, SIZE_E);
52     agk::SetTextSize(TEXT_F, SIZE_F);
53
54     // Variables to hold XY-coordinates, initialized to 0.
55     float x = 0;
56     float y = 0;
57
58     // Set the position of text object A.
59     agk::SetTextPosition(TEXT_A, x, y);
60
61     // Increment the Y-coordinate with
62     // the size of text object A.
63     y += SIZE_A;
64
65     // Set the position of text object B.
66     agk::SetTextPosition(TEXT_B, x, y);
67
68     // Increment the Y-coordinate with
69     // the size of text object B.
70     y += SIZE_B;
71
72     // Set the position of text object C.
73     agk::SetTextPosition(TEXT_C, x, y);
74
75     // Increment the Y-coordinate with
76     // the size of text object C.
77     y += SIZE_C;
78
79     // Set the position of text object D.
80     agk::SetTextPosition(TEXT_D, x, y);
81
```

```
82     // Increment the Y-coordinate with
83     // the size of text object D.
84     y += SIZE_D;
85
86     // Set the position of text object E.
87     agk::SetTextPosition(TEXT_E, x, y);
88
89     // Increment the Y-coordinate with
90     // the size of text object E.
91     y += SIZE_E;
92
93     // Set the position of text object F.
94     agk::SetTextPosition(TEXT_F, x, y);
95  }
96
97  // Main loop, called every frame
98  void app::Loop ( void )
99  {
100     // Refresh the screen.
101     agk::Sync();
102  }
103
104  // Called when the app ends
105  void app::End ( void )
106  {
107  }
```

The following global constants are declared in lines 14 through 27:

- The TEXT_A, TEXT_B, TEXT_C, TEXT_D, TEXT_E, and TEXT_F constants are declared in lines 14 through 19. These constants will be used for the index numbers of each type of text object. TEXT_A contains the index number for the text object that will have the smallest size. TEXT_F contains the index number for the text object that will have the largest size.
- Lines 22 through 27 declare the SIZE_A, SIZE_B, SIZE_C, SIZE_D, SIZE_E, and SIZE_F constants. These constants represent the values we will use to set the size of each text object. Each of the constants contains a value for the size it will set. SIZE_A represents the smallest size, which is the value 12. SIZE_F represents the largest size, which is the value 72.

The app::Begin function appears in lines 30 through 95:

- In lines 39 through 44 we create each of the text objects. Notice that the string value for each text object specifies its size. The string "Text Size 12" belongs to the TEXT_A text object. The string "Text Size 72" belongs to the TEXT_F text object.
- In lines 47 through 52 we set the size of each text object. TEXT_A is set to use SIZE_A. TEXT_B is set to use SIZE_B, and so on.
- In lines 55 and 56 we declare two floating-point variables: x and y. These variables will be used to store the X- and Y-coordinates we will use to position each

text object. These variables are initialized with the value 0. This will represent the position of the top-left corner of the screen.

- In lines 59 through 94 we set the position of each text object. The position of `TEXT_A` is set to the top-left corner of the screen. In line 63 the y variable is incremented by the `SIZE_A` constant. This will move the position of the next text object down by the value of the `SIZE_A` constant. This pattern is repeated for the remaining text objects, with each text object's y value being incremented by the size of the previous text object.

Inside the `app::Loop` function, in line 101 the `agk::Sync` function is called to refresh the screen.

In Figure 9-1 you can see the output of Program 9-1. Notice how the vertical spacing increases as the size of each text object increases.

Figure 9-1 Output of Program 9-1

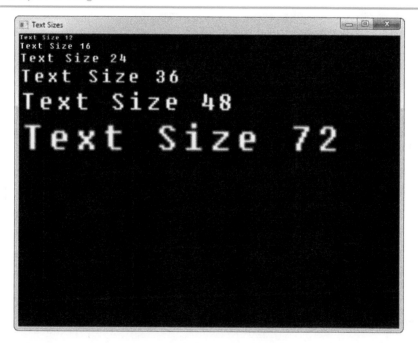

Setting the Alignment of a Text Object

The alignment of a text object is set to its top-left corner (left-aligned) by default. You can change the alignment of a text object by calling the `agk::SetTextAlignment` function passing the index number of the text object you want to change the alignment for and an integer value, *Mode*, indicating the type of alignment you want to use for the text object. A value of 0 will set the alignment to left. A value of 1 sets the alignment to center, and a value of 2 sets the alignment to right.

Figure 9-2 illustrates each type of alignment. Program 9-2 demonstrates the three different types of text alignment.

Figure 9-2 Different alignments of a text object

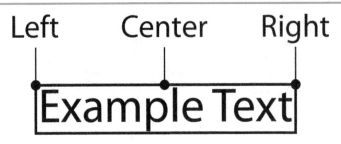

Program 9-2 (Text Alignment)

```
 1 // This program demonstrates text alignment.
 2 #include "template.h"
 3 using namespace AGK;
 4 app App;
 5
 6 // Constants for the screen resolution
 7 const int SCREEN_WIDTH  = 640;
 8 const int SCREEN_HEIGHT = 480;
 9
10 // Constants for the text objects
11 const int LEFT_TEXT     = 1;
12 const int CENTER_TEXT   = 2;
13 const int RIGHT_TEXT    = 3;
14
15 const int ALIGN_LEFT    = 0;
16 const int ALIGN_CENTER  = 1;
17 const int ALIGN_RIGHT   = 2;
18
19 const float TEXT_SIZE   = 16;
20
21 const float CENTER_X = SCREEN_WIDTH / 2;
22 const float CENTER_Y = SCREEN_HEIGHT / 2;
23
24 // Begin app, called once at the start
25 void app::Begin( void )
26 {
27    // Set the virtual screen resolution.
28    agk::SetVirtualResolution(SCREEN_WIDTH, SCREEN_HEIGHT);
29
30    // Set the window title.
31    agk::SetWindowTitle("Text Alignment");
32
33    // Create the text objects.
34    agk::CreateText(LEFT_TEXT, "Left-aligned");
35    agk::CreateText(CENTER_TEXT, "Center-aligned");
36    agk::CreateText(RIGHT_TEXT, "Right-aligned");
37
```

```
38     // Set the size of each text object.
39     agk::SetTextSize(LEFT_TEXT, TEXT_SIZE);
40     agk::SetTextSize(CENTER_TEXT, TEXT_SIZE);
41     agk::SetTextSize(RIGHT_TEXT, TEXT_SIZE);
42
43     // Set the alignment of each text object.
44     agk::SetTextAlignment(LEFT_TEXT, ALIGN_LEFT);
45     agk::SetTextAlignment(CENTER_TEXT, ALIGN_CENTER);
46     agk::SetTextAlignment(RIGHT_TEXT, ALIGN_RIGHT);
47
48     // Set the position of each text object.
49     agk::SetTextPosition(LEFT_TEXT, CENTER_X, CENTER_Y - 40);
50     agk::SetTextPosition(CENTER_TEXT, CENTER_X, CENTER_Y);
51     agk::SetTextPosition(RIGHT_TEXT, CENTER_X, CENTER_Y + 40);
52 }
53
54 // Main loop, called every frame
55 void app::Loop ( void )
56 {
57     // Refresh the screen.
58     agk::Sync();
59 }
60
61 // Called when the app ends
62 void app::End ( void )
63 {
64 }
```

The following global constants are declared in lines 11 through 22:

- The LEFT_TEXT, CENTER_TEXT, and RIGHT_TEXT constants are declared in lines 11 through 13. These constants will be used for the index numbers of each type of text object. LEFT_TEXT is the index number for the text object that will be left-aligned. CENTER_TEXT is the index number for the text object that will be center-aligned, and RIGHT_TEXT is the index number for the text object that will be right-aligned.

- Lines 15 through 17 declare the ALIGN_LEFT, ALIGN_CENTER, and ALIGN_RIGHT constants. These constants represent the values we will use to set the alignment of each text object. Each of the constants contains the value for the mode it will set. ALIGN_LEFT, which has a value of 0, will set the text object to be left-aligned, ALIGN_CENTER, which has a value of 1, will set the text object to be center-aligned, and ALIGN_RIGHT, which has a value of 2, will set the text object to be right-aligned.

- Line 19 declares the floating-point constant TEXT_SIZE initialized with the value 16. This value will be used to set the size of each text object.

- Lines 21 and 22 declare the CENTER_X and CENTER_Y constants. These are floating-point values for *XY*-coordinates for the center of the screen. CENTER_X is initialized with half the value of SCREEN_WIDTH, and CENTER_Y is initialized with half the value of SCREEN_HEIGHT. We will use these constants to set the position of each text object.

The app::Begin function appears in lines 25 through 52:

- In lines 34 through 36 we create each of the text objects. Notice that the string value for each text object specifies its alignment. The string "Left-aligned" belongs to the LEFT_TEXT text object. The string "Center-aligned" belongs to the CENTER_TEXT text object. The string "Right-aligned" belongs to the RIGHT_TEXT text object.
- In lines 39 through 41 we set the size of each text object with the TEXT_SIZE constant.
- In lines 44 through 46 we set the alignment for each text object. The LEFT_TEXT text object has its alignment set using the ALIGN_LEFT value, which is the default. The CENTER_TEXT text object is set to be center-aligned because its alignment mode is set using the ALIGN_CENTER value. RIGHT_TEXT is set to be right-aligned because its alignment mode is set using the ALIGN_RIGHT value.
- In lines 49 through 51 we set the position of each text object. To show how the alignment mode affects the position of each text object, each text object is set using the same value for the X-coordinate. The LEFT_TEXT object will appear left-aligned, the CENTER_TEXT object will appear center-aligned, and the RIGHT_TEXT object will appear right-aligned.

Inside the app::Loop function, in line 58 the agk::Sync function is called to refresh the screen.

In Figure 9-3 you can see how the alignment affects the position of the text. Although each text object has the same X-coordinate value, the text appears differently. Left-aligned text has its origin in the top-left corner. Center-aligned text has its origin in the top-center. Right-aligned text has its origin in the top-right corner.

Figure 9-3 Output of Program 9-2

Changing the Spacing between Letters in a Text Object

You can change the spacing between letters in a text object by calling the
agk::SetTextSpacing function. Here is the general format of how you call the function:

```
agk::SetTextSpacing(TextIndex, Spacing);
```

TextIndex is the integer index of the text object whose spacing you want to change.
Spacing is a floating-point value that indicates the amount of spacing between each letter in the text object. If you specify a positive value, then the spacing will increase. If
you specify a negative value, then the spacing will decrease, and the letters will appear
closer together. A value of zero displays the text object using the default spacing.

Program 9-3 demonstrates letter spacing with three different text objects. Figure 9-4
shows the program's output.

Program 9-3   **(Text Spacing)**

```
1  // This program demonstrates text spacing.
2  #include "template.h"
3  using namespace AGK;
4  app App;
5
6  // Constants for the screen resolution
7  const int SCREEN_WIDTH  = 640;
8  const int SCREEN_HEIGHT = 480;
9
10 // Constants for the text objects
11 const int TEXT_A  = 1;
12 const int TEXT_B  = 2;
13 const int TEXT_C  = 3;
14
15 const int ALIGN_CENTER  = 1;
16 const float TEXT_SIZE    = 16;
17
18 const float CENTER_X = SCREEN_WIDTH / 2;
19 const float CENTER_Y = SCREEN_HEIGHT / 2;
20
21 // Begin app, called once at the start
22 void app::Begin( void )
23 {
24    // Set the virtual screen resolution.
25    agk::SetVirtualResolution(SCREEN_WIDTH, SCREEN_HEIGHT);
26
27    // Set the window title.
28    agk::SetWindowTitle("Text Spacing");
29
30    // Create the text objects.
31    agk::CreateText(TEXT_A, "Default Spacing");
32    agk::CreateText(TEXT_B, "Ten Unit Spacing");
33    agk::CreateText(TEXT_C, "Twenty Unit Spacing");
34
35    // Set the size of each text object.
36    agk::SetTextSize(TEXT_A, TEXT_SIZE);
37    agk::SetTextSize(TEXT_B, TEXT_SIZE);
```

```
38        agk::SetTextSize(TEXT_C, TEXT_SIZE);
39
40        // Set the alignment of each text object.
41        agk::SetTextAlignment(TEXT_A, ALIGN_CENTER);
42        agk::SetTextAlignment(TEXT_B, ALIGN_CENTER);
43        agk::SetTextAlignment(TEXT_C, ALIGN_CENTER);
44
45        // Set the spacing of each text object.
46        agk::SetTextSpacing(TEXT_A, 0);
47        agk::SetTextSpacing(TEXT_B, 10);
48        agk::SetTextSpacing(TEXT_C, 20);
49
50        // Set the position of each text object.
51        agk::SetTextPosition(TEXT_A, CENTER_X, CENTER_Y - 40);
52        agk::SetTextPosition(TEXT_B, CENTER_X, CENTER_Y);
53        agk::SetTextPosition(TEXT_C, CENTER_X, CENTER_Y + 40);
54 }
55
56 // Main loop, called every frame
57 void app::Loop ( void )
58 {
59        // Refresh the screen.
60        agk::Sync();
61 }
62
63 // Called when the app ends
64 void app::End ( void )
65 {
66 }
```

The following global constants are declared in lines 11 through 19:

- The TEXT_A, TEXT_B, and TEXT_C constants are declared in lines 11 through 13. These constants will be used for the index numbers of each type of text object. TEXT_A is the index number for the text object that will use default spacing. TEXT_B is the index number for the text object that will be spaced 10 units between each letter, and TEXT_C is the index number for the text object that will be spaced 20 units between each letter.
- Line 15 declares the ALIGN_CENTER constant. This constant represents the value we will use to set the alignment of each text object to be center-aligned.
- Line 16 declares the floating-point constant TEXT_SIZE initialized with the value 16. This value will be used to set the size of each text object.
- Lines 18 and 19 declare the CENTER_X and CENTER_Y constants. These are floating-point values for the XY-coordinates of the center of the screen. CENTER_X is initialized with half the value of SCREEN_WIDTH. CENTER_Y is initialized with half the value of SCREEN_HEIGHT. We will use these constants to set the position of each text object.

The app::Begin function appears in lines 22 through 54:

- In lines 31 through 33 we create each of the text objects. Notice that the string value for each text object describes the spacing it will use. The string "Default Spacing" belongs to the TEXT_A text object. The string "Ten Unit Spacing" belongs to the TEXT_B text object. The string "Twenty Unit Spacing" belongs to the TEXT_C text object.

- In lines 36 through 38 we set the size of each text object with the TEXT_SIZE constant.
- In lines 41 through 43 we set the alignment for each text object by using the ALIGN_CENTER value.
- In lines 46 through 48 we set the spacing of each text object. TEXT_A is set to use default spacing. TEXT_B is set to use 10 units of spacing. TEXT_C is set to use 20 units of spacing.
- In lines 51 through 53 we set the position of each text object. The position of each text object is set using the same value for the X-coordinate. The Y-coordinate of each text object is modified so that each text object appears in its own vertical space. If we were to use the same Y-coordinate, the text objects would overlap.

In the app::Loop function, line 60 calls the agk::Sync function is called to refresh the screen.

Figure 9-4 Output of Program 9-3

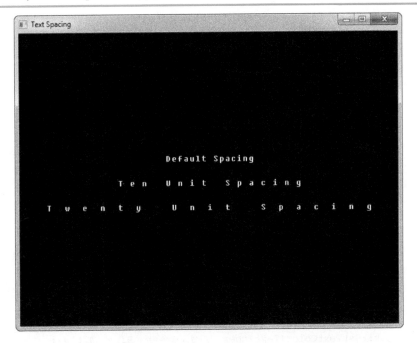

Setting the String Value of a Text Object

If you want to change the string value that was initially set for a text object to a different value, you can call the agk::SetTextString function. Here is the general format of how you call the function:

```
agk::SetTextString(TextIndex, String);
```

This function is similar to the agk::CreateTextFunction, but in this case the *TextIndex* argument is for an existing text object. *String* contains the string of characters you want to display. For example, the following statement changes the string value of a text object with an index number of 1 to *"GAME START"*:

```
agk::SetTextString(1, "GAME START");
```

Getting the Total Width of a Text Object

You can get the total width of a text object by calling the `agk::GetTextTotalWidth` function and passing the index number of the text object whose total width you want to get. The function returns a floating-point value for the total width of the text object. For example, the following statement stores the total width of a text object with an index number of 1 in a floating-point variable named `textTotalWidth`:

```
float textTotalWidth = agk::GetTextTotalWidth(1);
```

Getting the Total Height of a Text Object

You can get the total height of a text object by calling the `agk::GetTextTotalHeight` function and passing the index number of the text object whose total height you want to get. The function returns a floating-point value for the total height of the text object. For example, the following statement stores the total height of a text object with an index number of 1 in a floating-point variable named `textTotalHeight`:

```
float textTotalHeight = agk::GetTextTotalHeight(1);
```

Showing or Hiding a Text Object

In some instances you might want to hide the text objects in an application until they are needed. If you want to hide a text object or show a previously hidden text object, you can call the `agk::SetTextVisible` function. Here the general format of how you call the function:

```
agk::SetTextVisible(TextIndex, Visible);
```

The first argument, `TextIndex`, is the integer index of the text object whose visibility you want to set. The second argument, `Visible`, is an integer value that sets the visibility. Passing a value of 0 (false) will hide the text object, and passing a value of 1 (true) will show the text object. The following example hides a text object with an index number of 1.

```
agk::SetVirtualButtonVisible(1, 0);
```

Changing the Color of a Text Object

You can call the `agk::SetTextColor` function to change the color and transparency of a text object. Here is the general format of how you call the function:

```
agk::SetTextColor(TextIndex, Red, Green, Blue, Alpha);
```

The first argument is the index number of the text object whose color you want to change. The next three arguments are for the red, green, and blue color channels. You pass a value from 0 to 255 for each of these arguments. A 0 means that the color channel will have no intensity and 255 means that the color channel will be displayed at full intensity. The final argument, `Alpha`, is an optional argument that is set to 255 by default. If you want to specify a value for this argument, it must be an integer ranging from 0, which is completely transparent, to 255 which would draw the text object completely solid or opaque. For example, the following statement changes the color of a text object with an index number of 1 to the color yellow. It does not specify the optional `Alpha` argument.

```
agk::SetTextColor(1, 255, 255, 0);
```

Detecting Collisions with a Text Object

You can detect if a single point is within the bounds of a text object's bounding box by using the agk::GetTextHitTest function. Here is the general format of the function:

```
agk::GetTextHitTest(TextIndex, X, Y)
```

TextIndex is an integer value containing the index number of the text object you want to check for a collision. The remaining arguments, *X* and *Y*, are floating-point values for the *X*- and *Y*-coordinates of the point that you want to check. The function returns an integer value of 1 (true) if the point is within the text object's bounding box. Otherwise, the function returns 0 (false).

Program 9-4 demonstrates detecting a collision between a text object and the mouse pointer. Figure 9-5 shows the program's output.

Program 9-4   (Text Object Collision)

```
 1  // This program demonstrates collision detection
 2  // with a text object and the mouse pointer.
 3
 4  // Includes, namespace and prototypes
 5  #include "template.h"
 6  using namespace AGK;
 7  app App;
 8
 9  // Constants for the screen resolution
10  const int SCREEN_WIDTH  = 640;
11  const int SCREEN_HEIGHT = 480;
12
13  // Constant for the text object index number.
14  const int TEXT = 1;
15
16  // Constant for the text object size.
17  const float TEXT_SIZE = 16;
18
19  // Constant for the text object alignment.
20  const int ALIGN_CENTER = 1;
21
22  // Constants for the center of the screen.
23  const float CENTER_X = SCREEN_WIDTH / 2;
24  const float CENTER_Y = SCREEN_HEIGHT / 2;
25
26  // Begin app, called once at the start
27  void app::Begin( void )
28  {
29      // Set the virtual resolution.
30      agk::SetVirtualResolution(SCREEN_WIDTH, SCREEN_HEIGHT);
31
32      // Set the window title.
33      agk::SetWindowTitle("Text Object Collision");
34
35      // Create the text object.
36      agk::CreateText(TEXT, "");
37
```

```
38      // Set the size of the text object.
39      agk::SetTextSize(TEXT, TEXT_SIZE);
40
41      // Set the alignment of the text object.
42      agk::SetTextAlignment(TEXT, ALIGN_CENTER);
43
44      // Set the position of the text object.
45      agk::SetTextPosition(TEXT, CENTER_X, CENTER_Y);
46 }
47
48 // Main loop, called every frame
49 void app::Loop ( void )
50 {
51      // Get the mouse coordinates.
52      float mouseX = agk::GetRawMouseX();
53      float mouseY = agk::GetRawMouseY();
54
55      // Determine if the mouse pointer has hit the text object.
56      if (agk::GetTextHitTest(TEXT, mouseX, mouseY))
57      {
58          agk::SetTextString(TEXT, "Ouch! You hit me.");
59      }
60      else
61      {
62          agk::SetTextString(TEXT, "I am a text object.");
63      }
64
65      // Refresh the screen.
66      agk::Sync();
67 }
68
69 // Called when the app ends
70 void app::End ( void )
71 {
72 }
```

The following global constants are declared in lines 14 through 24:

- The TEXT constant is declared in line 14 and initialized with the value 1. This is the constant we will use as the index number to identify the text object.
- Line 17 declares the floating-point constant TEXT_SIZE initialized with the value 16. This value will be used to set the size of the text object.
- Line 20 declares the ALIGN_CENTER constant. This constant represents the value we will use to set the alignment of the text object to be center-aligned.
- Lines 23 and 24 declare the CENTER_X and CENTER_Y constants. These are floating-point values for the XY-coordinates of the center of the screen. CENTER_X is initialized with half the value of SCREEN_WIDTH. CENTER_Y is initialized with half the value of SCREEN_HEIGHT. We will use these constants to set the position of the text object to the center of the screen.

The app::Begin function appears in lines 27 through 46:

- In line 36 we create the text object. Notice that the string value is an empty string. An empty string is being used as the initialization value of the text object because it will be changed when the program runs, so its value is not important.

- In line 39 we set the size of the text object with the TEXT_SIZE constant.
- In line 42 we set the alignment of the text object by using the ALIGN_CENTER value.
- In line 45 we set the position of the text object by using the CENTER_X and CENTER_Y constants we declared earlier. This will center the text on the screen.

The app::Loop function appears in lines 49 through 67:

- In lines 52 and 53 we declare two floating-point variables: mouseX and mouseY. The mouseX variable in line 52 is initialized with the return value of the agk::GetRawMouseX function. The mouseY variable in line 53 is initialized with the return value of the agk::GetRawMouseY function. These variables will be updated during each frame of the program's game loop. During the game loop, the mouseX and mouseY variables will store the updated coordinates of the mouse pointer, which we will use as the point for the collision detection with the text object.
- In line 56 we have an if statement that checks the return value of the agk::GetTextHitTest function. If the function returns true, then we execute the statement in line 58, otherwise we execute the statement In line 62.
- In line 58 the agk::SetTextString function is called. It changes the text object's string to "*Ouch! You hit me.*"
- In line 62 the agk::SetTextString function is called. It sets the text object's string to "*I am a text object.*"
- In line 66 the agk::Sync function is called. When this statement executes, it will update the screen and display any changes that were made.

Figure 9-5 Output of Program 9-4

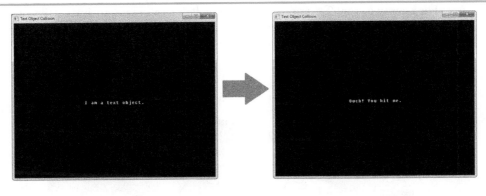

Checkpoint

9.1. What advantage does a text object have over the agk::Print or agk::PrintC functions when displaying text in a game or other application?

9.2. How can you change the string displayed by a text object after it has been created?

9.3. How can you determine if a text object exists?

9.4. Is it possible to change the size of a text object? If so, how is it accomplished?

9.5. Briefly describe the effect on text spacing if a negative value is used.

9.6. Consider a situation where you only need to move a text object left or right. What function could you use to do this?

9.7. What function do you call to change the color of a text object?

9.8. Is it possible to detect collisions with text objects? If so, what function do you call?

9.2 Sprite Collision Detection

CONCEPT: A collision between sprites occurs when one sprite's bounding box comes in contact with another sprite's bounding box. Collisions between sprites can be detected.

VideoNote

Sprite Collision Detection

When a sprite is displayed on the screen, it is displayed within a rectangle that is known as the sprite's *bounding box*. The bounding box is the size, in pixels, of the sprite's image file. If the image file is saved with transparency, then the bounding box will not be visible, but if the image is created with a black background color as the transparency, then you can clearly see the bounding box. This is illustrated in Figure 9-6.

> **NOTE:** A sprite's bounding box will be the size, in pixels, of the sprite's image file. For example, suppose you use Microsoft Paint to create an image file that is 64 pixels wide by 96 pixels high. If a sprite uses this image, the sprite's bounding box will be 64 pixels wide by 64 pixels high.

Figure 9-6 A sprite displayed inside its bounding box

When one sprite's bounding box comes in contact with another sprite's bounding box, it is said that the two sprites have *collided*. In games, sprite collisions are usually an important part of the game play. For this reason, it is important that you can detect collisions between sprites in your programs.

The AGK provides a function called `agk::GetSpriteCollision` that determines whether two sprites have collided. You pass two sprite index numbers as arguments, and the function returns 1 (true) if the bounding boxes of the two sprites are overlapping or 0 (false) otherwise. The following code shows an example; it determines whether the sprite referenced by index number 1 and the sprite referenced by index number 2 have collided, and if so, it hides both sprites:

```
if (agk::GetSpriteCollision(1, 2))
{
    agk::SetSpriteVisible(1, 0);
    agk::SetSpriteVisible(2, 0);
}
```

Program 9-5 shows a complete example that detects sprite collisions. When the program runs, it displays the two bowling ball sprites shown in Figure 9-7. The sprites move toward each other until a collision is detected. When that happens, they are reset back to their original positions.

Program 9-5   **(Sprite Collision)**

```
1 // This program demonstrates how sprite
2 // collisions can be detected.
3
4 // Includes, namespace and prototypes
5 #include "template.h"
6 using namespace AGK;
7 app App;
8
9 // Constants for the screen resolution
10 const int SCREEN_WIDTH  = 640;
11 const int SCREEN_HEIGHT = 480;
12
13 // Constant for the image index numbers.
14 const int BALL1_IMAGE = 1;
15 const int BALL2_IMAGE = 2;
16
17 // Constant for the sprite index numbers.
18 const int BALL1_SPRITE = 1;
19 const int BALL2_SPRITE = 2;
20
21 // Constant for ball 1's initial X position.
22 const float BALL1_X = 0;
23
24 // Constant for ball 2's initial Y position.
25 const float BALL2_X = 511;
26
27 // Constant for the Y position of both sprites.
28 const float BALL_Y = 175;
29
30 // Constant for the distance to move each frame.
31 const float DISTANCE = 1;
32
```

```
33 // Begin app, called once at the start
34 void app::Begin( void )
35 {
36    // Set the virtual resolution.
37    agk::SetVirtualResolution(SCREEN_WIDTH, SCREEN_HEIGHT);
38
39    // Set the window title.
40    agk::SetWindowTitle("Sprite Collision");
41
42    // Load the images.
43    agk::LoadImage(BALL1_IMAGE, "BowlingBall1.png");
44    agk::LoadImage(BALL2_IMAGE, "BowlingBall2.png");
45
46    // Create the sprites.
47    agk::CreateSprite(BALL1_SPRITE, BALL1_IMAGE);
48    agk::CreateSprite(BALL2_SPRITE, BALL2_IMAGE);
49
50    // Set the position of each sprite.
51    agk::SetSpritePosition(BALL1_SPRITE, BALL1_X, BALL_Y);
52    agk::SetSpritePosition(BALL2_SPRITE, BALL2_X, BALL_Y);
53 }
54
55 // Main loop, called every frame
56 void app::Loop ( void )
57 {
58    // Get the X-coordinate of each sprite.
59    float ball1x = agk::GetSpriteX(BALL1_SPRITE);
60    float ball2x = agk::GetSpriteX(BALL2_SPRITE);
61
62    // Determine if the two sprites have collided.
63    if (agk::GetSpriteCollision(BALL1_SPRITE, BALL2_SPRITE))
64    {
65       // Reset the sprites to their original locations.
66       agk::SetSpriteX(BALL1_SPRITE, BALL1_X);
67       agk::SetSpriteX(BALL2_SPRITE, BALL2_X);
68    }
69    else
70    {
71       // Move ball 1 to the right.
72       agk::SetSpriteX(BALL1_SPRITE, ball1x + DISTANCE);
73
74       // Move ball 2 to the left.
75       agk::SetSpriteX(BALL2_SPRITE, ball2x - DISTANCE);
76    }
77
78    // Refresh the screen.
79    agk::Sync();
80 }
81
82 // Called when the app ends
83 void app::End ( void )
84 {
85 }
```

The following global constants are declared in lines 14 through 31:

- Lines 14 through 19 declare constants for the bowling ball image index numbers and sprite index numbers.
- Lines 22 and 25 declare constants for ball 1's initial X-coordinate and ball 2's initial X-coordinate. Line 28 declares a constant that will be used for both balls' Y-coordinates.
- Line 31 declares a constant for the distance that each ball will move during an iteration of the game loop.

The `app::Begin` function appears in lines 34 through 53:

- In lines 43 and 44 we load the image that will be used by the sprites.
- In lines 47 and 48 we create the sprites that will display the bowling ball images.
- In lines 51 and 52 we set the position of each sprite to the default location.

The `app::Loop` function appears in lines 56 through 80:

- Lines 59 and 60 declare variables to store the X-coordinate of ball 1 and ball 2.
- In line 63 we use an `if` statement to determine if ball 1 has collided with ball 2.
- If a collision occurs, the code in lines 66 and 67 will reset the balls to their default X-coordinates.
- Line 72 moves ball 1 to the right by adding the value of the DISTANCE constant to the value of its X-coordinate.
- Line 75 moves ball 2 to the left by subtracting the value of the DISTANCE constant from the value of its X-coordinate.
- Line 79 calls the `agk::Sync` function to refresh the screen.

Figure 9-7 Sprites displayed by Program 9-5

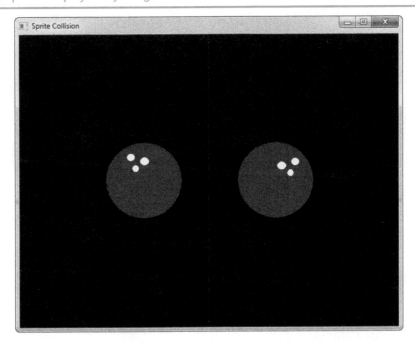

In the Spotlight:
The PizzaBot Game

Program 9-6 is called PizzaBot because the main character is a pizza-eating robot! Figure 9-8 shows the texture atlas that we will use to create an animated sprite for the robot. The image is saved in a file named `Robot.png`. Notice that the texture atlas has one row and three columns.

When the program runs, the robot will appear in the lower-right corner of the screen. The slice of pizza shown on the left in Figure 9-9 will also appear, in a random location. This image is saved in a file named `Pizza.png`. The object of the game is to use the arrow keys to move the robot to the slice of pizza. When the robot collides with the slice of pizza, the Yum! image shown on the right in Figure 9-9 will appear in place of the pizza. It is saved in a file named `Yum.png`.

Program 9-6   **(PizzaBot)**

```
 1  // This program lets the user chase randomly generated
 2  // pizza slices with a robot. It demonstrates collision
 3  // detection with sprites.
 4
 5  // Includes, namespace and prototypes
 6  #include "template.h"
 7  using namespace AGK;
 8  app App;
 9
10  // Constants for the screen resolution
11  const int SCREEN_WIDTH  = 640;
12  const int SCREEN_HEIGHT = 480;
13
14  // Constants for images
15  const int ROBOT_IMAGE = 1;
16  const int PIZZA_IMAGE = 2;
17  const int YUM_IMAGE   = 3;
18
19  // Constants for sprites
20  const int ROBOT_SPRITE = 1;
21  const int PIZZA_SPRITE = 2;
22  const int YUM_SPRITE   = 3;
23
24  // Constants for animation
25  const int FRAME_WIDTH   = 128;
26  const int FRAME_HEIGHT  = 128;
27  const int FRAME_COUNT   = 3;
28  const float FRAMES_PER_SECOND = 3;
29
30  // Constant for the amount to move the robot
31  const float ROBOT_MOVE = 4;
32
33  // Constants for the robot's initial XY values.
34  const float ROBOT_X = 0;
```

```
35 const float ROBOT_Y = SCREEN_HEIGHT - FRAME_HEIGHT;
36
37 // Constant for the sleep time.
38 const int HALF_SECOND = 500;
39
40 // Constants for showing and hiding sprites.
41 const int HIDE = 0;
42 const int SHOW = 1;
43
44 // Function prototypes
45 void updateRobot();
46 void detectCollision();
47 void showYum();
48 void generatePizza();
49
50 // Begin app, called once at the start
51 void app::Begin( void )
52 {
53     // Set the virtual resolution.
54     agk::SetVirtualResolution(SCREEN_WIDTH, SCREEN_HEIGHT);
55
56     // Set the window title.
57     agk::SetWindowTitle("PizzaBot");
58
59     // Load the Images.
60     agk::LoadImage(ROBOT_IMAGE, "PizzaBot/Robot.png");
61     agk::LoadImage(PIZZA_IMAGE, "PizzaBot/Pizza.png");
62     agk::LoadImage(YUM_IMAGE, "PizzaBot/Yum.png");
63
64     // Create the sprites.
65     agk::CreateSprite(ROBOT_SPRITE, ROBOT_IMAGE);
66     agk::CreateSprite(PIZZA_SPRITE, PIZZA_IMAGE);
67     agk::CreateSprite(YUM_SPRITE, YUM_IMAGE);
68
69     // Set the sprite animation sequence for the robot.
70     agk::SetSpriteAnimation(ROBOT_SPRITE, FRAME_WIDTH,
71                             FRAME_HEIGHT, FRAME_COUNT);
72
73     // Set the position of the robot sprite.
74     agk::SetSpritePosition(ROBOT_SPRITE, ROBOT_X, ROBOT_Y);
75
76     // Play the robot sprite animation.
77     agk::PlaySprite(ROBOT_SPRITE, FRAMES_PER_SECOND);
78
79     // Generate a slice of pizza.
80     generatePizza();
81 }
82
83 // Main loop, called every frame
84 void app::Loop ( void )
85 {
86     // Update the robot's position.
87     updateRobot();
88
```

```
 89     // Check for a collision between
 90     // the robot and the pizza.
 91     detectcollision();
 92
 93     // Refresh the screen.
 94     agk::Sync();
 95 }
 96
 97 // Called when the app ends
 98 void app::End ( void )
 99 {
100 }
101
102 // The update function moves the robot if the user
103 // is pressing an arrow key.
104 void updateRobot()
105 {
106     // Store the robot's X-and Y-coordinates.
107     float robotX = agk::GetSpriteX(ROBOT_SPRITE);
108     float robotY = agk::GetSpriteY(ROBOT_SPRITE);
109
110     // Determine if the user is pressing the down arrow key,
111     // and if so move the robot down.
112     if (agk::GetRawKeyState(AGK_KEY_DOWN))
113         robotY += ROBOT_MOVE;
114
115     // Determine if the user is pressing the up arrow key,
116     // and if so, move the robot up.
117     if (agk::GetRawKeyState(AGK_KEY_UP))
118         robotY -= ROBOT_MOVE;
119
120     // Determine if the user is pressing the left arrow key,
121     // and if so, move the robot left.
122     if (agk::GetRawKeyState(AGK_KEY_LEFT))
123         robotX -= ROBOT_MOVE;
124
125     // Determine if the user is pressing the right arrow key,
126     // and if so, move the robot up.
127     if (agk::GetRawKeyState(AGK_KEY_RIGHT))
128         robotX += ROBOT_MOVE;
129
130     // Update the robot's position.
131     agk::SetSpritePosition(ROBOT_SPRITE, robotX, robotY);
132 }
133
134 // The generatePizza function generates a new slice of
135 // pizza at a random location.
136 void generatePizza()
137 {
138     // Store the width and height of the pizza sprite.
139     float width = agk::GetSpriteWidth(PIZZA_SPRITE);
140     float height = agk::GetSpriteHeight(PIZZA_SPRITE);
141
```

```
142      // Calculate the maximum XY values for the
143      // random position of the pizza sprite.
144      float maxX = SCREEN_WIDTH - width;
145      float maxY = SCREEN_HEIGHT - height;
146
147      // Generate and store the random XY-
148      // coordinates of the pizza.
149      float x = (float)(agk::Random(0, (int)maxX));
150      float y = (float)(agk::Random(0, (int)maxY));
151
152      // Hide the Yum! sprite.
153      agk::SetSpriteVisible(YUM_SPRITE, HIDE);
154
155      // Set the new position of the pizza and Yum! sprites.
156      agk::SetSpritePosition(PIZZA_SPRITE, x, y);
157      agk::SetSpritePosition(YUM_SPRITE, x, y);
158
159      // Show the pizza sprite.
160      agk::SetSpriteVisible(PIZZA_SPRITE, SHOW);
161 }
162
163 // The showYum function momentarily displays the Yum!
164 // sprite in place of the pizza sprite.
165 void showYum()
166 {
167      // Hide the pizza sprite.
168      agk::SetSpriteVisible(PIZZA_SPRITE, HIDE);
169
170      // Show the Yum! sprite.
171      agk::SetSpriteVisible(YUM_SPRITE, SHOW);
172
173      // Refresh the screen, so we can see the changes.
174      agk::Sync();
175
176      // Wait for half a second.
177      agk::Sleep(HALF_SECOND);
178 }
179
180 // The detectCollision function determines whether the
181 // robot has collided with the pizza. If so, a new slice
182 // of pizza is generated.
183 void detectCollision()
184 {
185      // Determine if the robot has collided with the pizza.
186      if (agk::GetSpriteCollision(ROBOT_SPRITE, PIZZA_SPRITE))
187      {
188          // Hide the pizza and show the Yum! sprite.
189          showYum();
190
191          // Hide the Yum! sprite and show the pizza.
192          generatePizza();
193      }
194 }
```

Figure 9-8 Robot texture atlas

Figure 9-8 Robot texture atlas

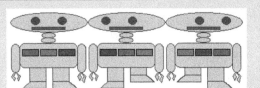

Figure 9-9 The pizza and Yum! images

The sprite displaying the Yum! image will appear only briefly, and then disappear. After that, another slice of pizza will be randomly placed on the screen.

Let's review each part of the program.

Global Constants

Several global constants are declared in lines 11 through 42, summarized here:

- Lines 11 and 12 declare SCREEN_WIDTH and SCREEN_HEIGHT to represent the virtual resolution of the screen.
- Lines 15 through 17 declare ROBOT_IMAGE, PIZZA_IMAGE, and YUM_IMAGE to represent the robot, pizza, and Yum! image index numbers.
- Lines 20 through 22 declare ROBOT_SPRITE, PIZZA_SPRITE, and YUM_SPRITE to represent the robot, pizza, and Yum! sprite index numbers.
- Lines 25 through 28 declare FRAME_WIDTH, FRAME_HEIGHT, FRAME_COUNT, and FRAMES_PER_SECOND to represent the animation values of the robot texture atlas.
- Line 31 declares ROBOT_MOVE, which holds the amount by which the robot will move when the user presses an arrow key.
- Lines 34 and 35 declare ROBOT_X and ROBOT_Y to represent the robot's starting X and Y screen coordinates.
- Line 38 declares HALF_SECOND, which represents the number of milliseconds the application will sleep after displaying the Yum! sprite.
- Lines 41 and 42 declare HIDE and SHOW, which represent the values used to hide and show the pizza and Yum! sprites.

The `app::Begin` Function

The `app::Begin` function is defined in lines 51 through 81. It sets the virtual resolution in line 54. The window title is set in line 57. In lines 60 through 62, we load the robot, pizza, and Yum! images. In lines 65 through 67, we create the robot, pizza, and Yum! sprites. The animation is set for the robot sprite in lines 70 and 71. In line 74, we set the position of the robot sprite to the bottom-left portion of the screen. In line 77, we play the robot sprite's animation. Finally, in line 80, we call the `generatePizza` function.

The `app::Loop` Function

The `app::Loop` function is defined in lines 84 through 95. It calls the `updateRobot` function in line 87. This function determines whether an arrow key has been pressed and, if so, updates the robot's position accordingly. Then, we call the `detectCollision` function in line 91. This function determines whether the robot has collided with the pizza. If so, it displays the Yum! sprite for a brief instant and then generates a new slice of pizza at a random location. Line 94 calls the `agk::Sync` function to refresh the screen.

The `updateRobot` Function

The updateRobot function is defined in lines 104 through 132. Its purpose is to determine whether the user is pressing an arrow key and update the robot's position accordingly. The statements in lines 107 and 108 get the robot sprite's current *X* and *Y* screen coordinates and assigns those values to the `robotX` and `robotY` variables.

The `if` statements that appear in lines 112 through 128 check each of the keyboard's arrow keys. If any of them are being pressed, the `robotX` and `robotY` variables are adjusted accordingly.

The `agk::SetSpritePosition` function is called in line 131. This function sets the robot's new position using the `robotX` and `robotY` variables.

The `generatePizza` Function

The generatePizza function is defined in lines 136 through 161. Its purpose is to display the pizza sprite at a random location on the screen. Lines 139 and 140 get the width and height of the pizza sprite and assign those values to the local `width` and `height` variables. Lines 144 and 145 calculate the maximum *X*- and *Y*-coordinates that we can use, to make sure the pizza sprite doesn't get placed somewhere off-screen, and assign those values to the local `maxX` and `maxY` variables. Then, lines 149 and 150 generate random values for the local variables x and y. Line 153 hides the Yum! sprite (by setting its visibility using the `HIDE` constant). The local x and y values are used to set the new position of the pizza and Yum! sprites in lines 156 and 157. Line 160 shows the pizza sprite (by setting its visibility using the `SHOW` constant).

The `showYum` Function

The showYum function is defined in lines 165 through 178. Its purpose is to display the Yum! sprite in place of the pizza sprite. (This occurs when the robot collides with the pizza.) Line 168 hides the pizza sprite. Line 171 shows the Yum! sprite. Line 174 immediately refreshes the screen by calling the `agk::Sync` function. This line of code is important because if we wait until the screen is refreshed in the `app::Loop` function (in line 94), the changes will not show. In line 177 we call the `agk::Sleep` function passing the `HALF_SECOND` constant we defined earlier as an argument. This will pause the program's execution for half of a second, allowing the Yum! sprite to be shown for a brief instant. The Yum! sprite will be hidden when the `generatePizza` function is called (in line 192).

The `detectCollision` Function

The detectCollision function is defined in lines 183 through 194. Its purpose is to determine whether the robot sprite has collided with the pizza sprite. The `if` statement in line 186 calls the `agk::GetSpriteCollision` function to make this determination. If the sprites have collided, the `showYum` function is called (line 189) to display the Yum! sprite, and then the `generatePizza` function is called in line 192 to show the pizza sprite at a new location.

Checkpoint

9.9. What is a sprite's bounding box?

9.10. What constitutes a sprite collision?

9.11. How do you detect a collision between two sprites?

 9.3 Simulating Falling Objects

CONCEPT: When an object in the real world falls to Earth, its speed increases as it falls. If you want to write a program that realistically simulates falling objects, you will need to incorporate this acceleration into your program.

VideoNote

Simulating Falling Objects

Game programmers often need to simulate moving objects, and in many cases the objects must move realistically. For example, suppose you are writing a program that shows an object falling toward the ground. You could design a loop that merely moves the object down the screen's Y-axis the same amount each time the loop iterates. The resulting animation would not be realistic, however, because in the world, objects do not fall at a steady speed.

Designing programs that simulate realistic motion requires some knowledge of simple physics. In this section, we will discuss the motion of an object that is falling toward Earth because of gravity. Then we will look at how that motion can be reasonably simulated in a computer program.

NOTE: If you're thinking, "Wait a minute, I didn't sign up to learn physics. I want to learn programming!"—then relax. You don't need to master physics to program realistic motion. Understanding a little about the physics of gravity and free fall, however, will go a long way toward helping you understand the code that we will write later.

Gravity is a force that attracts objects to one another. The more massive the objects are, the greater the gravitational attraction between them. For example, Earth is so massive that its gravitational pull keeps us from floating off into space. When an apple falls from a tree, it falls because it is attracted to Earth by gravity.

If you watch an object fall from a considerable height, such as the top of a building, you will notice that the object's speed increases as it falls. The object's increase in speed is known as *acceleration*. When an object falls in a vacuum (where there are no air molecules to slow it down), its speed increases at a rate of 9.8 meters per second, *each second*. Did you get that? For each second that an object falls, its speed increases by an additional 9.8 meters per second.

For example, suppose a construction worker is building a skyscraper, and he accidently drops a brick from the top of the building. If we forget about the fact that the air will slow the brick down a small amount, we can calculate how fast the brick will be traveling each second as it plummets to the ground:

- At one second the brick is falling at a speed of 9.8 meters per second.
- At two seconds the brick is falling at a speed of 19.6 meters per second.
- At three seconds the brick is falling at a speed of 29.4 meters per second.
- At four seconds the brick is falling at a speed of 39.2 meters per second.
- And so forth.

This is illustrated in Figure 9-10.

Figure 9-10 Speed of a falling brick at various time intervals (not drawn to scale)

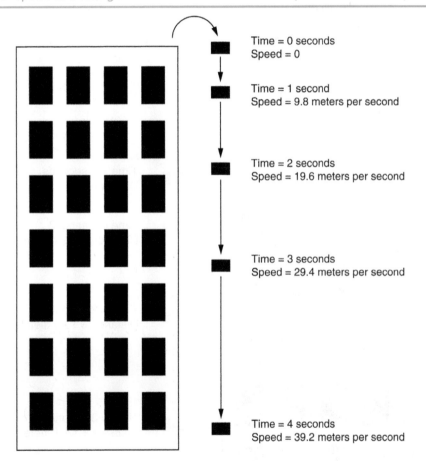

If this is interesting enough to make you want to read a physics book, you will see the acceleration rate of a falling object written as 9.8 m/s^2 (which is pronounced "9.8 meters per second squared"). The letter g is commonly used to represent the acceleration rate of a falling object in formulas.

Now let's talk about the distance that an object falls over time. When an object is moving, two factors determine the distance the object moves: the object's speed and the amount of time the object is moving. For example, a ball that is moving at a constant speed of 12 meters per second will travel a distance of 24 meters in two seconds. By constant speed, we mean that the ball is not speeding up or slowing down; it is moving steadily at 12 meters per second. However, a falling object does not move at a constant speed. A falling object speeds up as it falls. As a result, a falling object travels downward an increasingly greater distance each second that it falls. We can use the following formula to calculate the distance that a falling object falls:

$$d = \frac{1}{2}gt^2$$

In this formula, d is the distance, g is 9.8, and t is the number of seconds that the object has been falling. Going back to the brick example, we can use the formula to calculate the following distances:

- At one second the brick is falling at a speed of 4.9 meters.
- At two seconds the brick is falling at a speed of 19.6 meters.
- At three seconds the brick is falling at a speed of 44.1 meters.
- At four seconds the brick is falling at a speed of 78.4 meters.
- And so forth.

This is illustrated in Figure 9-11.

Figure 9-11 A falling brick's distance at various time intervals (not drawn to scale)

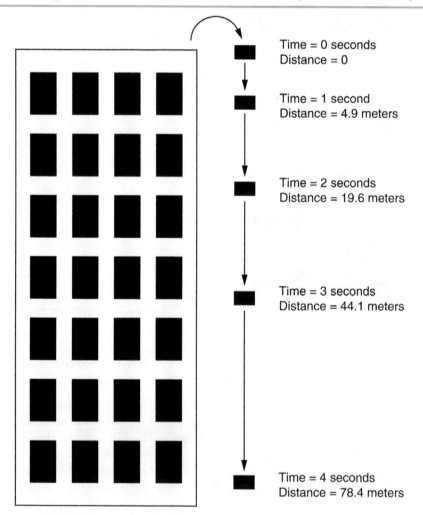

So how do you simulate the behavior of falling objects in a program? After all, a computer screen is measured in pixels, not meters. Because of this, the formula for calculating the distance that a falling object moves on the screen will have to be "tweaked."

First, you have to decide how accurate the simulation must be. If your program will be used for scientific research, it will need to be accurate. If you are creating a game, however, accuracy is probably not essential. That's the case with the Vulture Trouble game that is presented later in this chapter. We want to display eggs that are falling realistically, but also we want the falling motion to work for the game and the game player. If the eggs fall too fast, then the player might get frustrated because the game is too difficult. Likewise, if the eggs fall too slowly, then the game will not be challenging enough.

Program 9-7 shows how we can approximate the motion of a falling object, at a speed that is slow enough to easily observe, yet fast enough to seem realistic. When the program runs, it displays the ball sprite shown in Figure 9-12 falling from the top of the screen to the bottom. To achieve the falling motion, we have used the value 0.98 as the gravitational acceleration and the default screen refresh rate of 60 frames per second.

Program 9-7   **(Free Fall)**

```
1 // This program simulates a falling ball.
2
3 // Includes, namespace and prototypes
4 #include "template.h"
5 using namespace AGK;
6 app App;
7
8 // Global Constants
9 const int SCREEN_WIDTH   = 640;
10 const int SCREEN_HEIGHT  = 480;
11 const int BALL_IMAGE     = 1;
12 const int BALL_SPRITE    = 1;
13 const float ACCELERATION = 0.98;
14
15 // Global variables
16 float g_time     = 0;
17 float g_distance = 0;
18
19 // Begin app, called once at the start
20 void app::Begin( void )
21 {
22    // Set the virtual resolution.
23    agk::SetVirtualResolution(SCREEN_WIDTH, SCREEN_HEIGHT);
24
25    // Set the window title.
26    agk::SetWindowTitle("Free Fall");
27
28    // Load the ball image.
29    agk::LoadImage(BALL_IMAGE, "ball.png");
30
```

```
31      // Create the ball sprite.
32      agk::CreateSprite(BALL_SPRITE, BALL_IMAGE);
33
34      // Set the starting position of the ball sprite.
35      agk::SetSpriteX(BALL_SPRITE, SCREEN_WIDTH / 2 -
36          agk::GetSpriteWidth(BALL_SPRITE) / 2);
37  }
38
39  // Main loop, called every frame
40  void app::Loop ( void )
41  {
42      // Get the Y-coordinate of the ball sprite.
43      float y = agk::GetSpriteY(BALL_SPRITE);
44
45      // If the ball is above the bottom of the screen,
46      // then update its position.
47      if (y < SCREEN_HEIGHT - agk::GetSpriteHeight(BALL_SPRITE))
48      {
49          // Calculate the object's distance using the
50          // distance formula.
51          g_distance = 0.5 * ACCELERATION * g_time * g_time;
52
53          // Set the Y-coordinate of the ball sprite to
54          // the distance.
55          y = g_distance;
56
57          // Increment time.
58          g_time++;
59      }
60      // Else, set the Y-coordinate of the ball sprite at
61      // the bottom of the screen.
62      else
63      {
64          y = SCREEN_HEIGHT - agk::GetSpriteHeight(BALL_SPRITE);
65      }
66
67      // Update the Y-coordinate of the ball sprite.
68      agk::SetSpriteY(BALL_SPRITE, y);
69
70      // Refresh the screen.
71      agk::Sync();
72  }
73
74  // Called when the app ends
75  void app::End ( void )
76  {
77  }
```

The following global constants are declared in lines 9 through 13:

- The SCREEN_WIDTH and SCREEN_HEIGHT constants are declared in lines 9 and 10. These constants are used to set the virtual resolution of the screen.
- Line 11 declares the BALL_IMAGE constant. This constant represents the index number we will use to reference the ball image.

Figure 9-12 Ball sprite from Program 9-7

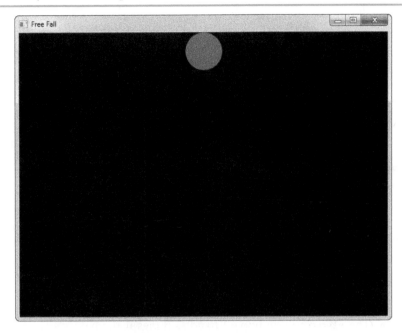

- Line 12 declares the BALL_SPRITE constant. This constant represents the index number we will use to reference the ball sprite.
- Line 13 declares the floating-point ACCELERATION constant, initialized with the value 0.98. We will use this value for gravitational acceleration. If you're wondering how we decided to use the value 0.98, we used the trial-and-error method. When we tried the value 9.8, it produced motion that was so fast the ball could barely be seen. So, we knew that we needed to scale down the acceleration value. Next, we tried the value 0.98, and we were happy with the results.

The following global variables are declared in lines 16 and 17:

- Line 16 declares the g_time global variable, initialized with the value 0. This variable will keep a count of the game loop's iterations. We will use it as the time value in the distance calculation.
- Line 17 declares the g_distance global variable, initialized with the value 0. This variable will hold the distance that the ball sprite falls during each iteration of the game loop.

The app::Begin function appears in lines 20 through 37:

- In line 23 we set the virtual resolution using the SCREEN_WIDTH and SCREEN_HEIGHT constants.
- In line 26 we set the window title so that when the program runs, it displays the string "Free Fall" in the window's title bar.
- In line 29 we load the ball.png image, using the BALL_IMAGE constant as the image index number.
- In line 32 we create the ball sprite, using the BALL_SPRITE constant as the sprite index number and the BALL_IMAGE constant for the image index number.

- In lines 35 through 36 we set the ball sprite to its starting position. In this program, we want the ball to start at the top of the screen and to be centered along the *X*-axis. Because the *Y*-coordinate is already set to 0 by default, we only need to set the *X*-coordinate. The expression SCREEN_WIDTH / 2 - agk::GetSpriteWidth(BALL_SPRITE) / 2 calculates the center of the screen along the *X*-axis and then subtracts half the width of the ball sprite. This will position the ball exactly where we want it to be when the program starts.

The app::Loop function appears in lines 40 through 72:

- In line 43, we declare a local floating-point variable named y. The y variable will update as the loop iterates, storing the most recent value for the ball sprite's *Y*-coordinate.
- The if statement in line 47 determines whether the ball sprite's *Y*-coordinate is less than the expression SCREEN_HEIGHT - agk::GetSpriteHeight(BALL_SPRITE). This expression calculates the bottom edge of the screen minus the height of the ball sprite. If the expression is true, then the ball sprite is above the bottom of the screen, and the ball will continue to fall. In that case, line 51 uses the distance formula you saw earlier to calculate the distance that ball has fallen down the screen. Then, line 55 sets the y variable to this distance. Line 58 increments the time variable.
- The else clause in line 62 handles things if the ball has reached the bottom of the screen. If that is the case, the y variable is set to the expression SCREEN_HEIGHT - agk::GetSpriteHeight(BALL_SPRITE). This makes the ball stop falling, and the ball remains at the bottom of the screen.
- The agk::Sync function appears in line 71 and refreshes the screen once for each iteration of the game loop.

Simulating Motion in Two Directions

In the previous example, we simulated a ball that was moving in one direction: straight down. But what about situations in which an object is moving in two directions simultaneously? For example, when a baseball pitcher throws the ball toward the catcher, the baseball is moving in two directions simultaneously:

- It is moving horizontally, toward the catcher, because the pitcher threw it in that direction.
- It is moving vertically, toward the ground, because gravity is pulling it down.

To simulate this type of motion, we need to update the falling object's position along both the *X*- and *Y*-axes. Program 9-8 shows an example.

Program 9-8 (Dual Motion)

```
1 // This program simulates a ball that is falling
2 // and moving horizontally.
3
4 // Includes, namespace and prototypes
5 #include "template.h"
6 using namespace AGK;
7 app App;
```

```
 8
 9 // Constants
10 const int SCREEN_WIDTH    = 640;
11 const int SCREEN_HEIGHT   = 480;
12 const int BALL_IMAGE      = 1;
13 const int BALL_SPRITE     = 1;
14 const float X_MOVEMENT    = 10.0;
15 const float ACCELERATION  = 0.98;
16
17 // Global variables
18 float g_time     = 0;
19 float g_distance = 0;
20
21 // Begin app, called once at the start
22 void app::Begin( void )
23 {
24    // Set the virtual resolution.
25    agk::SetVirtualResolution(SCREEN_WIDTH, SCREEN_HEIGHT);
26
27    // Set the window title.
28    agk::SetWindowTitle("Dual Motion");
29
30    // Load the ball image.
31    agk::LoadImage(BALL_IMAGE, "ball.png");
32
33    // Create the ball sprite.
34    agk::CreateSprite(BALL_SPRITE, BALL_IMAGE);
35
36    // Set the starting position of the ball sprite.
37    agk::SetSpriteX(BALL_SPRITE, SCREEN_WIDTH -
38         agk::GetSpriteWidth(BALL_SPRITE));
39 }
40
41 // Main loop, called every frame
42 void app::Loop ( void )
43 {
44    // Get the XY-coordinates of the ball sprite.
45    float y = agk::GetSpriteY(BALL_SPRITE);
46    float x = agk::GetSpriteX(BALL_SPRITE);
47
48    // If the ball is above the bottom of the screen,
49    // then update its position.
50    if (y < SCREEN_HEIGHT - agk::GetSpriteHeight(BALL_SPRITE))
51    {
52
53       // Set the X-coordinate of the ball sprite so
54       // that it will move to the left.
55       x -= X_MOVEMENT;
56
57       // Calculate the object's distance using the
58       // distance formula.
59       g_distance = 0.5 * ACCELERATION * g_time * g_time;
60
61       // Set the Y-coordinate of the ball sprite to
62       // the distance.
63       y = g_distance;
```

```
64
65        // Increment time.
66        g_time++;
67    }
68    // Else, set the Y-coordinate of the ball sprite at
69    // the bottom of the screen.
70    else
71    {
72        y = SCREEN_HEIGHT - agk::GetSpriteHeight(BALL_SPRITE);
73    }
74
75    // Update the XY-coordinates of the ball sprite.
76    agk::SetSpritePosition(BALL_SPRITE, x, y);
77
78    // Refresh the screen.
79    agk::Sync();
80 }
81
82 // Called when the app ends
83 void app::End ( void )
84 {
85 }
```

In this program, a ball is initially positioned in the upper-right corner of the screen. As the ball accelerates toward the bottom of the screen, it also moves to the left along the X-axis at a constant speed. The resulting animation looks like the ball was not merely dropped, but also given a slight kick toward the left side of the screen. In Figure 9-13 we have captured four different frames from the program's output and superimposed them so you can see the ball's path as it falls.

Figure 9-13 Four frames captured from Program 9-8's output

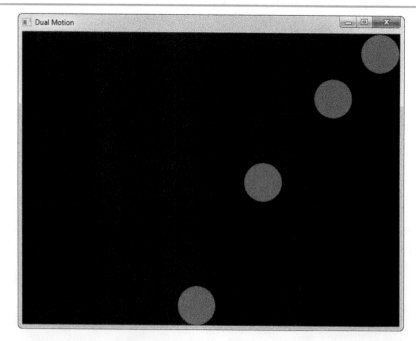

This program's code is very similar to Program 9-7. We have declared a constant named x_MOVEMENT, initialized with the value 10. This is the distance that the ball will move along the *X*-axis each time the loop iterates.

Inside the game loop we subtract the value of the x_MOVEMENT constant from the x variable in line 55, and we assign the value of the distance variable to the y variable in line 63. As a result, the ball moves to the left 10 pixels and accelerates down toward the bottom of the screen each time the game loop iterates.

NOTE: If you have downloaded the book's sample programs from www.pearsonhighered.com/gaddis, you will find an additional program named DropTheBall that provides a more in-depth example of horizontal and vertical motion.

 Checkpoint

9.12. When gravity causes an object to fall in a vacuum toward Earth, does the object fall at a steady speed, or does its speed increase as it falls?

9.13. If gravity is causing an object to fall in a vacuum toward Earth, how far will the object have fallen after 10 seconds?

 ## 9.4 The Vulture Trouble Game

In this section, we will demonstrate the Vulture Trouble game. In the game, a greedy vulture has stolen eggs from a farmer's henhouse. The vulture realizes he's been caught and is dropping the eggs one by one. The player's objective is to use a basket to catch as many eggs as possible. If the player does not catch an egg, it hits the ground and breaks.

The top screen shown in Figure 9-14 shows the game's title screen, which is displayed when the program starts. The bottom screen is the introductory screen that is displayed after the user presses the Enter key. The introductory screen gives the user instructions for playing the game. The top screen shown in Figure 9-15 shows the game's main screen, which appears next. The vulture is an animated sprite that moves back and forth across the screen. The egg that is dropped from the vulture, as well as the basket that appears at the bottom of the screen, are also sprites. The player uses the left and right arrow keys to move the basket sprite and, hopefully, catch the eggs as they fall. The vulture has stolen a total of 40 eggs.

When the game begins, a row of 40 mini-eggs appears across the top of the screen. This serves as an indicator of the number of eggs left. Each time the vulture drops an egg, one of the mini-eggs is removed from the top of the screen. The program keeps count of the number of eggs that the player catches, as well as the number of broken eggs. After the last egg has been dropped, a summary screen like the one shown at the bottom of Figure 9-15 appears.

Figure 9-16 shows all the images that we will use in the game. Here is a summary of each:

- The farm.png image will serve as the background for the game.
- The vulture.png image contains the texture atlas we will use to create an animated sprite for the flying vulture.

- The egg.png image shows an egg.
- The basket.png image shows the basket that the player will use to catch eggs.
- The hitBasket.png image will be displayed briefly when an egg hits the basket.
- The brokenEgg.png image will be displayed briefly when an egg hits the ground.

Figure 9-14 Vulture Trouble title screen and introductory screen

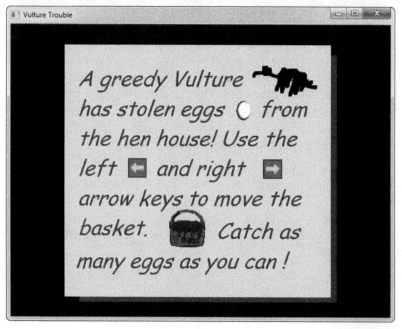

Figure 9-15 Vulture Trouble main screen and summary screen

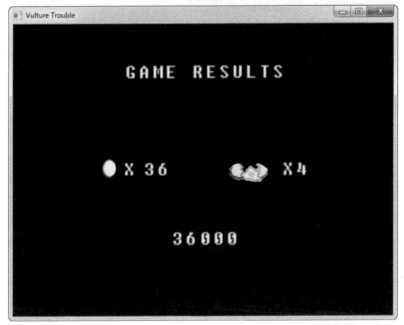

Now let's look at the game's code in Program 9-9. Rather than presenting all the code at once, we will show a section at a time, discussing each part. The first part of the program shows the global constant declarations and global variables.

Figure 9-16 Images used in the Vulture Trouble game

Program 9-9   (**VultureTrouble**, *partial listing*)

```
 1 // This program demonstrates the Vulture Trouble Game.
 2
 3 // Includes, namespace and prototypes
 4 #include "template.h"
 5 using namespace AGK;
 6 app App;
 7
 8 // Constants for the screen resolution
 9 const int SCREEN_WIDTH  = 640;
10 const int SCREEN_HEIGHT = 480;
11
12 // Constants for images
13 const int TITLE_SCREEN_IMAGE  = 1;
14 const int INTRO_SCREEN_IMAGE  = 2;
15 const int EGG_IMAGE           = 3;
16 const int BROKEN_EGG_IMAGE    = 4;
17 const int FARM_IMAGE          = 5;
18 const int BASKET_IMAGE        = 6;
19 const int HIT_BASKET_IMAGE    = 7;
20 const int VULTURE_IMAGE       = 8;
21
22 // Constants for sprites
23 const int TITLE_SCREEN_SPRITE = 1;
24 const int INTRO_SCREEN_SPRITE = 2;
25 const int EGG_SPRITE          = 3;
26 const int BROKEN_EGG_SPRITE   = 4;
27 const int FARM_SPRITE         = 5;
```

```
28 const int BASKET_SPRITE      = 6;
29 const int HIT_BASKET_SPRITE  = 7;
30 const int VULTURE_SPRITE     = 8;
31
32 // Constants for animation
33 const int FRAME_WIDTH         = 120;
34 const int FRAME_HEIGHT        = 110;
35 const int FRAME_COUNT         = 8;
36 const float FRAMES_PER_SECOND = 8;
37
38 // Constants for the sounds
39 const int POP_SOUND           = 1;
40 const int CLAP_SOUND          = 2;
41 const int TYPE_SOUND          = 3;
42 const int COMPLETE_SOUND      = 4;
43 const int PERFECT_SCORE_SOUND = 5;
44
45 // Constants for the music
46 const int INTRO_MUSIC = 1;
47 const int MAIN_MUSIC  = 2;
48
49 // Constants for text
50 const int GAME_OVER_TEXT          = 1;
51 const int GAME_RESULTS_TEXT       = 2;
52 const int EGGS_CAUGHT_TEXT        = 3;
53 const int EGGS_MISSED_TEXT        = 4;
54 const int TOTAL_SCORE_TEXT        = 5;
55 const int CAUGHT_MULTIPLIER_TEXT  = 6;
56 const int MISSED_MULTIPLIER_TEXT  = 7;
57 const int PERFECT_SCORE_TEXT      = 8;
58 const float TEXT_SIZE             = 36;
59
60 // Constants for the possible game states
61 const int GAME_STARTED    = 1;
62 const int INTRO_STARTED   = 2;
63 const int GAME_IN_PLAY    = 3;
64 const int GAME_OVER       = 4;
65 const int SUMMARY_STARTED = 5;
66
67 // Other constants
68 const int SCORE_MULTIPLIER  = 1000;
69 const int MAX_EGGS          = 40;
70 const int EGG_CLONE         = 100;
71 const int HIDE              = 0;
72 const int SHOW              = 1;
73 const int LOOP              = 1;
74 const int NO                = 0;
75 const int YES               = 1;
76 const float ACCELERATION    = 0.008f;
77 const float MIN_X           = 0;
78 const float MAX_X           = SCREEN_WIDTH;
79 const float BASKET_MOVE     = 4;
80 const float VULTURE_MOVE    = 2;
81 const float INTRO_TIMER     = 5;
82 const float SUMMARY_TIMER   = 5;
83 const float GAME_OVER_TIMER = 4;
84
```

```
 85 // Global variables
 86 int g_eggs           = MAX_EGGS;
 87 int g_time           = 0;
 88 int g_eggsCaught     = 0;
 89 int g_eggsMissed     = 0;
 90 int g_totalScore     = 0;
 91 int g_summaryComplete = NO;
 92 int g_gameState      = GAME_STARTED;
 93
 94 // Function prototypes
 95 void displayTitleScreen();
 96 void hideTitleScreen();
 97 void displayIntroScreen();
 98 void hideIntroScreen();
 99 void playGame();
100 void hideGame();
101 void moveBasket();
102 void moveVulture();
103 void moveEgg();
104 void checkCollisions();
105 void showHitBasket();
106 void showBrokenEgg();
107 void resetEgg();
108 void displayGameOverScreen();
109 void hideGameOverScreen();
110 void displaySummaryScreen();
111 void hideSummaryScreen();
112
```

Here is a summary of the constant declarations:

- Lines 9 and 10 declare constants for the virtual resolution.
- Lines 13 through 20 declare constants for the image index numbers that we will use.
- Lines 23 through 30 declare constants for the sprite index numbers that we will use.
- Lines 33 through 36 declare constants that we will use for the animated vulture sprite.
- Lines 39 through 43 declare constants for the sound index numbers that we will use.
- Lines 46 and 47 declare constants for the music index numbers that we use will use.
- Lines 50 through 57 declare constants for the text object index numbers that we will use.
- Line 58 declares a constant for the size of the text objects.
- Lines 61 through 65 declare constants for the game states we will use.
- Lines 68 through 83 declare these other constants:
  - SCORE_MULTIPLIER is the value that each egg that is caught will be multiplied by when tallying the score.
  - MAX_EGGS is the total number of eggs that the vulture has stolen.
  - EGG_CLONE is the starting index number for the mini-egg sprites.
  - HIDE is the value we will use when hiding a sprite.
  - SHOW is the value we will use when showing a sprite.
  - LOOP is the value we will use when lopping music.
  - NO is the value we will use for false.
  - YES is the value we will use for true.
  - ACCELERATION is the value we will use for the acceleration of a dropped egg.

- MIN_X is the value we will use for the left-edge of the screen while moving the vulture sprite.
- MAX_X is the value we will use for the right-edge of the screen while moving the vulture sprite.
- BASKET_MOVE is the value we will use when moving the basket.
- VULTURE_MOVE is the value we will use when moving the vulture.
- INTRO_TIMER is the value we will use when displaying the introduction screen.
- SUMMARY_TIMER is the value we will use when displaying the summary screen.
- GAME_OVER_TIMER is the value we will use when displaying the game over text.

Here is a summary of the global variable declarations In lines 86 through 92:

- g_eggs is a global variable initialized with the value of the MAX_EGGS constant. This variable will keep track of the number of eggs left in play during the game.
- g_time is a global variable initialized with the value 0. This variable will keep track of the time in which one of the eggs is falling.
- g_eggsCaught is a global variable initialized with the value 0. This variable will keep track of the number of eggs that are caught in the basket.
- g_eggsMissed is a global variable initialized with the value 0. This variable will keep track of the number of eggs that are missed, hit the ground, and are broken.
- g_totalScore is a global variable initialized with the value 0. This variable will keep track of the total score when the game is finished.
- g_gameSummaryComplete is a global variable initialized with value of the NO constant. This variable acts as a flag. It keeps track of whether or not the summary is complete.
- g_gameState is a global variable initialized with the value of the GAME_STARTED constant. This variable will keep track of the game state as the game is played.

Lines 95 through 111 hold the function prototypes, and then the app::Begin function is shown:

Program 9-9   (**VultureTrouble,** *continued*)

```
113 // Begin app, called once at the start
114 void app::Begin( void )
115 {
116     // Set the virtual screen resolution.
117     agk::SetVirtualResolution(SCREEN_WIDTH, SCREEN_HEIGHT);
118
119     // Set the window title.
120     agk::SetWindowTitle("Vulture Trouble");
121
122     // Load the images.
123     agk::LoadImage(TITLE_SCREEN_IMAGE, "titleScreen.png");
124     agk::LoadImage(INTRO_SCREEN_IMAGE, "intro.png");
125     agk::LoadImage(EGG_IMAGE, "egg.png");
126     agk::LoadImage(BROKEN_EGG_IMAGE, "brokenEgg.png");
127     agk::LoadImage(FARM_IMAGE, "farm.png");
128     agk::LoadImage(BASKET_IMAGE, "basket.png");
129     agk::LoadImage(HIT_BASKET_IMAGE, "hitBasket.png");
130     agk::LoadImage(VULTURE_IMAGE, "vulture.png");
131
132     // Create the sprites.
```

```
133   agk::CreateSprite(TITLE_SCREEN_SPRITE,
134       TITLE_SCREEN_IMAGE);
135   agk::CreateSprite(INTRO_SCREEN_SPRITE,
136       INTRO_SCREEN_IMAGE);
137   agk::CreateSprite(FARM_SPRITE, FARM_IMAGE);
138   agk::CreateSprite(EGG_SPRITE, EGG_IMAGE);
139   agk::CreateSprite(VULTURE_SPRITE, VULTURE_IMAGE);
140   agk::CreateSprite(BASKET_SPRITE, BASKET_IMAGE);
141   agk::CreateSprite(BROKEN_EGG_SPRITE, BROKEN_EGG_IMAGE);
142   agk::CreateSprite(HIT_BASKET_SPRITE, HIT_BASKET_IMAGE);
143
144   // Load the sounds.
145   agk::LoadSound(POP_SOUND, "pop.wav");
146   agk::LoadSound(CLAP_SOUND, "clap.wav");
147   agk::LoadSound(TYPE_SOUND, "type.wav");
148   agk::LoadSound(COMPLETE_SOUND, "complete.wav");
149   agk::LoadSound(PERFECT_SCORE_SOUND,"vulturePerfect.wav");
150
151   // Load the music.
152   agk::LoadMusic(INTRO_MUSIC, "vultureTrouble.mp3");
153   agk::LoadMusic(MAIN_MUSIC, "vultureLevel.mp3");
154
155   // Set up the vulture animation sequence.
156   agk::SetSpriteAnimation(VULTURE_SPRITE, FRAME_WIDTH,
157       FRAME_HEIGHT, FRAME_COUNT);
158
159   // Set the X-coordinate of the vulture sprite.
160   float vultureX = SCREEN_WIDTH / 2 -
161       agk::GetSpriteWidth(VULTURE_SPRITE) / 2;
162
163   // Set the Y-coordinate of the vulture sprite.
164   float vultureY = 0;
165
166   // Set the starting position of the vulture sprite.
167   agk::SetSpritePosition(VULTURE_SPRITE, vultureX,
168       vultureY);
169
170   // Set the X-coordinate of the basket sprite.
171   float basketX = SCREEN_WIDTH / 2 -
172       agk::GetSpriteWidth(BASKET_SPRITE) / 2;
173
174   // Set the Y-coordinate of the basket sprite.
175   float basketY = SCREEN_HEIGHT -
176       agk::GetSpriteHeight(BASKET_SPRITE);
177
178   // Set the starting position of the basket sprite.
179   agk::SetSpritePosition(BASKET_SPRITE, basketX,
180       basketY);
181
182   // Set the X-coordinate of the egg sprite.
183   float eggX = vultureX;
184
185   // Set the Y-coordinate of the egg sprite.
186   float eggY = vultureY +
187       agk::GetSpriteHeight(EGG_SPRITE) * 1.5;
188
```

```
189        // Set the starting position of the egg sprite.
190        agk::SetSpritePosition(EGG_SPRITE, eggX, eggY);
191
192        // Hide the sprites.
193        agk::SetSpriteVisible(TITLE_SCREEN_SPRITE, HIDE);
194        agk::SetSpriteVisible(INTRO_SCREEN_IMAGE, HIDE);
195        agk::SetSpriteVisible(EGG_SPRITE, HIDE);
196        agk::SetSpriteVisible(BROKEN_EGG_SPRITE, HIDE);
197        agk::SetSpriteVisible(FARM_SPRITE, HIDE);
198        agk::SetSpriteVisible(BASKET_SPRITE, HIDE);
199        agk::SetSpriteVisible(HIT_BASKET_SPRITE, HIDE);
200        agk::SetSpriteVisible(VULTURE_SPRITE, HIDE);
201
202        // Generate the row of mini-eggs clones.
203        for(int count = 0; count < MAX_EGGS; count++)
204        {
205            // Store the sprite index number of the
206            // mini-egg sprite.
207            int clone = EGG_CLONE + count;
208
209            // Set the scale of the mini-egg sprite.
210            float scale = 0.5;
211
212            // Clone the mini-egg sprite.
213            agk::CloneSprite(clone, EGG_SPRITE);
214
215            // Set the scale of the mini-egg sprite.
216            agk::SetSpriteScale(clone, scale, scale);
217
218            // Set the X-coordinate of the mini-egg sprite.
219            float x = agk::GetSpriteWidth(clone) * count;
220
221            // Set the Y-coordinate of the mini-egg sprite.
222            float y = 0;
223
224            // Set the position of the mini-egg sprite.
225            agk::SetSpritePosition(clone, x, y);
226        }
227
228        // Create the text objects.
229        agk::CreateText(GAME_OVER_TEXT, "GAME OVER");
230        agk::CreateText(GAME_RESULTS_TEXT, "GAME RESULTS");
231        agk::CreateText(EGGS_CAUGHT_TEXT, "0");
232        agk::CreateText(EGGS_MISSED_TEXT, "0");
233        agk::CreateText(CAUGHT_MULTIPLIER_TEXT, " X ");
234        agk::CreateText(MISSED_MULTIPLIER_TEXT, " X ");
235        agk::CreateText(TOTAL_SCORE_TEXT, "0");
236        agk::CreateText(PERFECT_SCORE_TEXT, "PERFECT SCORE!");
237
238        // Set the size of the text objects.
239        agk::SetTextSize(GAME_OVER_TEXT, TEXT_SIZE);
240        agk::SetTextSize(GAME_RESULTS_TEXT, TEXT_SIZE);
241        agk::SetTextSize(EGGS_CAUGHT_TEXT, TEXT_SIZE);
242        agk::SetTextSize(EGGS_MISSED_TEXT, TEXT_SIZE);
243        agk::SetTextSize(CAUGHT_MULTIPLIER_TEXT, TEXT_SIZE);
244        agk::SetTextSize(MISSED_MULTIPLIER_TEXT, TEXT_SIZE);
```

```
245    agk::SetTextSize(TOTAL_SCORE_TEXT, TEXT_SIZE);
246    agk::SetTextSize(PERFECT_SCORE_TEXT, TEXT_SIZE);
247
248    // Set the X-coordinate of the game over text object.
249    float gameOverTextX = SCREEN_WIDTH / 2 -
250        agk::GetTextTotalWidth(GAME_OVER_TEXT) / 2;
251
252    // Set the Y-coordinate of the game over text object.
253    float gameOverTextY = SCREEN_HEIGHT / 2 -
254        agk::GetTextTotalHeight(GAME_OVER_TEXT) / 2;
255
256    // Set the position of the game over text object.
257    agk::SetTextPosition(GAME_OVER_TEXT, gameOverTextX,
258        gameOverTextY);
259
260    // Set the X-coordinate of the game results text object.
261    float gameResultsTextX = SCREEN_WIDTH / 2 -
262        agk::GetTextTotalWidth(GAME_RESULTS_TEXT) / 2;
263
264    // Set the Y-coordinate of the game results text object.
265    float gameResultsTextY = SCREEN_HEIGHT / 6 -
266        agk::GetTextTotalHeight(GAME_RESULTS_TEXT) / 2;
267
268    // Set the position of the game results text object.
269    agk::SetTextPosition(GAME_RESULTS_TEXT,
270        gameResultsTextX, gameResultsTextY);
271
272    // Set the X-coordinate of the eggs caught
273    // multiplier text object.
274    float caughtMultiplierTextX = SCREEN_WIDTH / 4;
275
276    // Set the Y-coordinate of the eggs caught
277    // multiplier text object.
278    float caughtMultiplierTextY = SCREEN_HEIGHT / 2 -
279        agk::GetTextTotalHeight(CAUGHT_MULTIPLIER_TEXT)/ 2;
280
281    // Set the position of the eggs caught
282    // multiplier text object.
283    agk::SetTextPosition(CAUGHT_MULTIPLIER_TEXT,
284        caughtMultiplierTextX, caughtMultiplierTextY);
285
286    // Set the X-coordinate of the eggs caught text object.
287    float eggsCaughtTextX = caughtMultiplierTextX +
288        agk::GetTextTotalWidth(EGGS_CAUGHT_TEXT) * 3;
289
290    // Set the Y-coordinate of the eggs caught text object.
291    float eggsCaughtTextY = SCREEN_HEIGHT / 2 -
292        agk::GetTextTotalHeight(EGGS_CAUGHT_TEXT) / 2;
293
294    // Set the position of the eggs caught text object.
295    agk::SetTextPosition(EGGS_CAUGHT_TEXT, eggsCaughtTextX,
296        eggsCaughtTextY);
297
298    // Set the X-coordinate of the eggs missed
299    // multiplier text object.
```

```
300    float missedMultiplierTextX = SCREEN_WIDTH -
301        SCREEN_WIDTH / 3;
302
303    // Set the Y-coordinate of the eggs missed
304    // multiplier text object.
305    float missedMultiplierTextY = SCREEN_HEIGHT / 2 -
306        agk::GetTextTotalHeight(MISSED_MULTIPLIER_TEXT) /
307        2;
308
309    // Set the position of the eggs missed
310    // multiplier text object.
311    agk::SetTextPosition(MISSED_MULTIPLIER_TEXT,
312        missedMultiplierTextX, missedMultiplierTextY);
313
314    // Set the X-coordinate of the eggs missed text object.
315    float eggsMissedTextX = missedMultiplierTextX +
316        agk::GetTextTotalWidth(EGGS_MISSED_TEXT) * 3;
317
318    // Set the Y-coordinate of the eggs missed text object.
319    float eggsMissedTextY = SCREEN_HEIGHT / 2 -
320        agk::GetTextTotalHeight(EGGS_MISSED_TEXT) / 2;
321
322    // Set the position of the eggs missed text object.
323    agk::SetTextPosition(EGGS_MISSED_TEXT, eggsMissedTextX,
324        eggsMissedTextY);
325
326    // Set the X-coordinate of the total score text object.
327    float totalScoreTextX = SCREEN_WIDTH / 2 -
328        agk::GetTextTotalWidth(TOTAL_SCORE_TEXT) / 2;
329
330    // Set the Y-coordinate of the total score text object.
331    float totalScoreTextY = SCREEN_HEIGHT -
332        agk::GetTextTotalHeight(TOTAL_SCORE_TEXT) * 4;
333
334    // Set the position of the total score text object.
335    agk::SetTextPosition(TOTAL_SCORE_TEXT, totalScoreTextX,
336        totalScoreTextY);
337
338    // Set the X-coordinate of the perfect score text object.
339    float perfectScoreTextX = SCREEN_WIDTH / 2 -
340        agk::GetTextTotalWidth(PERFECT_SCORE_TEXT) / 2;
341
342    // Set the Y-coordinate of the perfect score text object.
343    float perfectScoreTextY = SCREEN_HEIGHT -
344        agk::GetTextTotalHeight(TOTAL_SCORE_TEXT) * 2;
345
346    // Set the position of the perfect score text object.
347    agk::SetTextPosition(PERFECT_SCORE_TEXT,perfectScoreTextX,
348        perfectScoreTextY);
349
350    // Hide the text objects.
351    agk::SetTextVisible(GAME_OVER_TEXT, HIDE);
352    agk::SetTextVisible(GAME_RESULTS_TEXT, HIDE);
353    agk::SetTextVisible(EGGS_CAUGHT_TEXT, HIDE);
354    agk::SetTextVisible(EGGS_MISSED_TEXT, HIDE);
355    agk::SetTextVisible(CAUGHT_MULTIPLIER_TEXT, HIDE);
```

```
356    agk::SetTextVisible(MISSED_MULTIPLIER_TEXT, HIDE);
357    agk::SetTextVisible(TOTAL_SCORE_TEXT, HIDE);
358    agk::SetTextVisible(PERFECT_SCORE_TEXT, HIDE);
359 }
360
```

This function does a lot of work! First we set the virtual resolution and the window title. We load the images (lines 123 through 130), create the sprites (lines 133 through 142), and load the sounds and music (lines 145 through 153). Then, in lines 156 and 157 we set up the animation sequence for the vulture. Next, in lines 160 through 190, we set the starting positions of the vulture, egg, and basket sprites. Then, in lines 193 through 200, we hide the sprites. In lines 203 through 226 we step through a for loop and create the mini-egg sprites, as shown in Figure 9-17. Then, we create the text objects, set their sizes, and set the initial position of each one in lines 229 through 348. After this is done, we hide the text objects.

Figure 9-17 Row of mini-egg sprites at the top of the screen

Next is the app::Loop Function:

Program 9-9   (**VultureTrouble**, *continued*)

```
361 // Main loop, called every frame
362 void app::Loop ( void )
363 {
364    // This switch statement determines the game state.
365    switch(g_gameState)
366    {
367        // The game has just started.
368        case GAME_STARTED:
369
370            // Display the title screen.
371            displayTitleScreen();
372
373            // If the user presses the enter key,
374            // hide the title screen and change
375            // the game state to intro started.
376            if (agk::GetRawKeyPressed(AGK_KEY_ENTER))
377                hideTitleScreen();
378            break;
379
380        // The intro has just started.
381        case INTRO_STARTED:
382
383            // Display the instructions to the user.
384            displayIntroScreen();
```

```
385
386                // When the time has expired, hide
387                // the instructions and change the
388                // game state to in play.
389                if (agk::Timer() >= INTRO_TIMER)
390                   hideIntroScreen();
391                break;
392
393          // The game is in play.
394          case GAME_IN_PLAY:
395
396                // Play the game.
397                playGame();
398
399                // When the number of eggs in play
400                // reaches zero, hide the game and
401                // change the game state to game over.
402                if (g_eggs <= 0)
403                   hideGame();
404                break;
405
406          // The game is over.
407          case GAME_OVER:
408
409                // Display the game over screen.
410                displayGameOverScreen();
411
412                // When the time has expired, hide
413                // the game over screen and change the
414                // game state to summary started.
415                if (agk::Timer() >= GAME_OVER_TIMER)
416                   hideGameOverScreen();
417                break;
418
419          // The summary has started.
420          case SUMMARY_STARTED:
421
422                // Display the summary screen.
423                displaySummaryScreen();
424
425                // When the time has expired, hide
426                // the summary screen and change the
427                // game state to game started.
428                if (agk::Timer() >= SUMMARY_TIMER)
429                   hideSummaryScreen();
430                break;
431    }
432
433    // Refresh the screen.
434    agk::Sync();
435 }
436
437 // Called when the app ends
438 void app::End ( void )
439 {
440 }
441
```

As you know by now, the app:Loop function is the game loop. It is where all the action takes place, frame by frame, in our game. The Vulture Trouble game displays several screens while the program is running, and a great way to handle the transitions from one screen to the next is by using game states. Here is a summary of the game loop and each of its states:

- The GAME_STARTED state is the initial state of the game. It displays the title screen and plays the music until the enter key is pressed. When the enter key is pressed, we move onto the next state.
- The INTRO_STARTED state is the second state of the game. It displays the introduction screen for a short amount of time. When the timer has expired, then the game state changes to its third state.
- The GAME_IN_PLAY state is the third and most important state of the game. This is where the actual game takes place, and we move the basket while the vulture flies back and forth across the screen dropping eggs. Once the vulture has dropped all its eggs, and we have been given a chance to either catch or miss them, the game state changes.
- The GAME_OVER state is the fourth state of the game. During this state of the game we simply display the text *GAME OVER* in the center of the screen. When the timer is up, we change states.
- The SUMMARY_STARTED state is the fifth state of the game. This is where we tally up the player's score. Once the score has been tallied and the timer expires, we reset the game and return to the first state. This creates a loop, so the game is never really over. This provides the player an opportunity to play the game as many times as they wish, without having to restart the application.

The app::End function appears in lines 438 through 440 and contains no code.

Next is the displayTitleScreen function:

Program 9-9 (**VultureTrouble**, *continued*)

```
442  // The displayTitleScreen function plays the
443  // intro music and displays the title screen.
444  void displayTitleScreen()
445  {
446      // If the title screen is not visible, display it.
447      if (!agk::GetSpriteVisible(TITLE_SCREEN_SPRITE))
448          agk::SetSpriteVisible(TITLE_SCREEN_SPRITE, SHOW);
449
450      // If the intro music is not playing, play it.
451      if (!agk::GetMusicPlaying())
452          agk::PlayMusic(INTRO_MUSIC, LOOP, INTRO_MUSIC,
453              INTRO_MUSIC);
454  }
455
```

This function displays the title screen and plays the intro music. It contains if statements that determine if the title screen sprite is visible and if the intro music is playing. If the title screen is hidden, then the program displays it. If the intro music is not playing, then the program plays it. Notice that the intro music is played so that it will loop, and it will be the only music that is played.

Next, is the `hideTitleScreen` function:

Program 9-9   (**VultureTrouble**, *continued*)

```
456 // The hideTitleScreen function hides the title screen
457 // and changes the game state to intro started.
458 void hideTitleScreen()
459 {
460     // Hide the title screen.
461     agk::SetSpriteVisible(TITLE_SCREEN_SPRITE, HIDE);
462
463     // Reset the game timer.
464     agk::ResetTimer();
465
466     // Change the game state.
467     g_gameState = INTRO_STARTED;
468 }
469
```

This function hides the title screen, resets the game timer, and changes the game state to `INTRO_STARTED`.

Next, is the `displayIntroScreen` function:

Program 9-9   (**VultureTrouble**, *continued*)

```
470 // The displayIntroScreen function displays an
471 // intro screen with instructions for how to
472 // play the game.
473 void displayIntroScreen()
474 {
475     // If the intro screen is not visible, display it.
476     if (!agk::GetSpriteVisible(INTRO_SCREEN_SPRITE))
477       agk::SetSpriteVisible(INTRO_SCREEN_SPRITE, SHOW);
478
479     // If the main music is not playing, play it.
480     if (agk::GetMusicPlaying() != MAIN_MUSIC)
481       agk::PlayMusic(MAIN_MUSIC, LOOP, MAIN_MUSIC,
482           MAIN_MUSIC);
483 }
484
```

This function is called when the game state changes to `INTRO_STARTED`. It contains `if` statements that determine if the introduction screen is visible and if the main music is playing. If the introduction screen is hidden, then the program displays it. If the main music is not playing, then the program plays it. Notice that the main music is played so that it will loop, and it will be the only music that is played.

Next is the hideIntroScreen function:

Program 9-9   (**VultureTrouble**, *continued*)

```
485 // The hideIntroScreen function hides the intro screen
486 // shows the game sprites, and changes the game state
487 // to game in play.
488 void hideIntroScreen()
489 {
490    // Hide the intro screen.
491    agk::SetSpriteVisible(INTRO_SCREEN_IMAGE, HIDE);
492
493    // Show the farm, basket, egg, and vulture sprites.
494    agk::SetSpriteVisible(FARM_SPRITE, SHOW);
495    agk::SetSpriteVisible(BASKET_SPRITE, SHOW);
496    agk::SetSpriteVisible(VULTURE_SPRITE, SHOW);
497    agk::SetSpriteVisible(EGG_SPRITE, SHOW);
498
499    // Show the row of mini-egg sprites.
500    for(int count = 0; count < MAX_EGGS; count++)
501    {
502       int clone = EGG_CLONE + count;
503       agk::SetSpriteVisible(clone, YES);
504    }
505
506    // Change the game state.
507    g_gameState = GAME_IN_PLAY;
508 }
509
```

This function hides the introduction screen. It shows the farm, basket, egg, and vulture sprites. It also steps through a for loop that shows all the mini-egg sprites. After these operations are complete, the game state is changed to GAME_IN_PLAY.

Next is the playGame function:

Program 9-9   (**VultureTrouble**, *continued*)

```
510 // The playGame function processes a frame of game play.
511 void playGame()
512 {
513    // Move the basket.
514    moveBasket();
515
516    // Move the vulture.
517    moveVulture();
518
519    // Move the egg.
520    moveEgg();
521
522    // Check for collisions.
523    checkCollisions();
524 }
525
```

This function is the heart of the game. It calls the moveBasket function to update the position of the basket sprite when it is moved by the player. It calls the moveVulture function, which is responsible for moving the vulture back and forth across the top of the screen. It calls the moveEgg function that updates the position of the egg as it falls. Finally, it calls the checkCollisions function. This function is responsible for determining if the egg has hit the basket and was caught, or if the egg has hit the ground and was broken. This function is called until there are no more eggs left.

Next is the hideGame function:

Program 9-9　　　(**VultureTrouble**, *continued*)

```
526 // The hideGame function stops the game's main music
527 // and hides the sprites. It changes the game state
528 // to game over.
529 void hideGame()
530 {
531     // Stop the music.
532     agk::StopMusic();
533
534     // Hide the farm, basket, egg, and vulture sprites.
535     agk::SetSpriteVisible(FARM_SPRITE, HIDE);
536     agk::SetSpriteVisible(BASKET_SPRITE, HIDE);
537     agk::SetSpriteVisible(VULTURE_SPRITE, HIDE);
538     agk::SetSpriteVisible(EGG_SPRITE, HIDE);
539
540     // Reset the game timer.
541     agk::ResetTimer();
542
543     // Change the game State.
544     g_gameState = GAME_OVER;
545 }
546
```

This function is called after no more eggs are left. It stops the main music and hides the farm, basket, egg, and vulture sprites. It resets the timer and changes the game state to GAME_OVER.

Next is the moveBasket function:

Program 9-9　　　(**VultureTrouble**, *continued*)

```
547 // The moveBasket function moves the basket sprite back
548 // and forth along the X-axis according to user input.
549 void moveBasket()
550 {
551     // Get the X-coordinate of the basket sprite.
552     float x = agk::GetSpriteX(BASKET_SPRITE);
553
554     // Get the width of the basket sprite.
555     float width = agk::GetSpriteWidth(BASKET_SPRITE);
```

```
556
557     // Store the minimum value that the X-coordinate of
558     // the basket sprite can reach without going beyond
559     // the left edge of the screen.
560     float minimumX = MIN_X;
561
562     // Store the maximum value that the X-coordinate of
563     // the basket sprite can reach without going beyond
564     // the right edge of the screen.
565     float maximumX = MAX_X - width;
566
567     // Determine if the keyboard's left arrow key is
568     // being held down.
569     if (agk::GetRawKeyState(AGK_KEY_LEFT))
570     {
571        // If the X-coordinate of the basket sprite
572        // has reached the left edge of the screen,
573        // it can go no further.
574        if (x <= minimumX)
575           x = minimumX;
576
577        // Otherwise, move to the left.
578        else
579           x -= BASKET_MOVE;
580     }
581
582     // Determine if the keyboard's right arrow key is
583     // being held down.
584     if (agk::GetRawKeyState(AGK_KEY_RIGHT))
585     {
586        // If the X-coordinate of the basket sprite
587        // has reached the right edge of the screen,
588        // it can go no further.
589        if (x >= maximumX)
590           x = maximumX;
591
592        // Otherwise, move to the right.
593        else
594           x += BASKET_MOVE;
595     }
596
597     // Update the basket sprite's X-coordinate.
598     agk::SetSpriteX(BASKET_SPRITE, x);
599  }
600
```

This function moves the basket back and forth along the bottom of the screen. It gets the current X-coordinate of the basket, determines if the basket is within the limits of the screen, and moves the basket left or right, depending on whether the user presses the left or right arrow key. Finally, it sets the position of the basket sprite, which will update its position.

Next is the moveVulture function:

Program 9-9   (`VultureTrouble`, *continued*)

```
601  // The moveVulture function moves the vulture sprite back
602  // and forth along the X-axis based on location and angle.
603  void moveVulture()
604  {
605     // If the vulture animation is not playing, play it.
606     if (!agk::GetSpritePlaying(VULTURE_SPRITE))
607        agk::PlaySprite(VULTURE_SPRITE, FRAMES_PER_SECOND);
608
609     // Get the X-coordinate of the vulture sprite.
610     float x = agk::GetSpriteX(VULTURE_SPRITE);
611
612     // Get the width of the vulture sprite.
613     float width = agk::GetSpriteWidth(VULTURE_SPRITE);
614
615     // Store the minimum value that the X-coordinate of
616     // the vulture sprite can reach without going beyond
617     // the left edge of the screen.
618     float minimumX = MIN_X;
619
620     // Store the maximum value that the X-coordinate of
621     // the vulture sprite can reach without going beyond
622     // the right edge of the screen.
623     float maximumX = MAX_X - width;
624
625     // If the X-coordinate of the vulture sprite
626     // has reached the left edge of the screen,
627     // it can go no further.
628     if (x <= minimumX)
629     {
630        // Flip the sprite vertically and set its angle to
631        // 180 degrees. This will make the sprite turn and
632        // face right.
633        agk::SetSpriteFlip(VULTURE_SPRITE, NO, YES);
634        agk::SetSpriteAngle(VULTURE_SPRITE, 180.0f);
635     }
636
637     // If the X-coordinate of the vulture sprite
638     // has reached the right edge of the screen,
639     // it can go no further.
640     if (x >= maximumX)
641     {
642        // Do not flip the sprite, just set the angle
643        // to 0 degrees.
644        // This will make the sprite turn and face left.
645        agk::SetSpriteFlip(VULTURE_SPRITE, NO, NO);
646        agk::SetSpriteAngle(VULTURE_SPRITE, 0.0f);
647     }
648
649     // If the vulture sprite is facing right, move right.
650     if (agk::GetSpriteAngle(VULTURE_SPRITE) == 180.0f)
651        x += VULTURE_MOVE;
652
653     // Otherwise, the vulture sprite is facing left,
```

```
654       // so move left.
655       else
656          x -= VULTURE_MOVE;
657
658       // Update the vulture sprite's X-coordinate.
659       agk::SetSpriteX(VULTURE_SPRITE, x);
660 }
661
```

This function moves the vulture sprite back and forth across the top of the screen. It stores the vulture's current X-coordinate and then determines if the vulture needs to be rotated, so that it will appear to be flying in the other direction when it reaches the edges of the screen. Finally, it sets the X-coordinate of the vulture sprite, which will update its position.

Next is the moveEgg function:

Program 9-9   (**VultureTrouble**, *continued*)

```
662 // The moveEgg function moves the egg sprite both
663 // down the screen and across the screen.
664 void moveEgg()
665 {
666     // Get the egg sprite's XY-coordinates.
667     float eggX = agk::GetSpriteX(VULTURE_SPRITE);
668     float eggY = agk::GetSpriteY(EGG_SPRITE);
669
670     // Create a variable to hold the falling distance.
671     float distance;
672
673     // Set the egg's X position so it is below
674     // the vulture's beak. This will depend on
675     // the vulture's angle.
676     if(agk::GetSpriteAngle(VULTURE_SPRITE) == 180.0f)
677     {
678        eggX = agk::GetSpriteX(VULTURE_SPRITE) +
679               agk::GetSpriteWidth(VULTURE_SPRITE) -
680               agk::GetSpriteWidth(EGG_SPRITE);
681     }
682
683     // Calculate the falling distance.
684     distance = 0.5 * ACCELERATION * g_time * g_time;
685
686     // Update the egg sprite's Y-coordinate.
687     eggY += distance;
688
689     // Update the egg sprite's position.
690     agk::SetSpritePosition(EGG_SPRITE, eggX, eggY);
691
692     // Increment the falling time.
693     g_time++;
694 }
695
```

The moveEgg function updates the position of the egg while it is in the vulture's beak and also while it is falling toward the ground, as illustrated in Figure 9-18. The Y-coordinate of the egg is determined by the free fall distance formula.

Figure 9-18 An egg moving horizontally and vertically

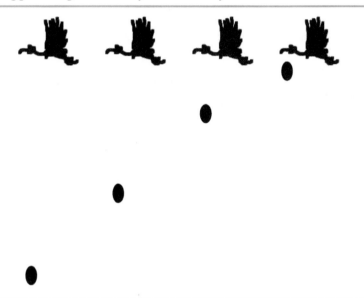

Next is the checkCollisions function:

Program 9-9   (**VultureTrouble**, *continued*)

```
696 // The checkCollisions function checks for a collision
697 // between the egg and the basket or the ground.
698 void checkCollisions()
699 {
700     // Get the Y-coordinate for the bottom of the egg sprite.
701     float eggBottom = agk::GetSpriteY(EGG_SPRITE) +
702                       agk::GetSpriteHeight(EGG_SPRITE);
703
704     // Determine if the egg has hit the basket.
705     if (agk::GetSpriteCollision(EGG_SPRITE, BASKET_SPRITE))
706     {
707         // Increment the number of eggs caught.
708         g_eggsCaught++;
709
710         // Decrement the number of eggs in play.
711         g_eggs--;
712
713         // Show the hit basket effect.
714         showHitBasket();
715
716         // Reset the egg.
717         resetEgg();
```

```
718
719        // Reset the falling time.
720        g_time = 0;
721    }
722
723    // The egg has missed the basket and hit the ground.
724    else if (eggBottom >= SCREEN_HEIGHT)
725    {
726        // Increment the number of eggs missed.
727        g_eggsMissed++;
728
729        // Decrement the number of eggs in play.
730        g_eggs--;
731
732        // Show the broken egg effect.
733        showBrokenEgg();
734
735        // Reset the egg.
736        resetEgg();
737
738        // Reset the falling time.
739        g_time = 0;
740    }
741 }
742
```

This function determines whether the egg has hit the basket or has hit the ground. First we get the *Y*-coordinate for the bottom of the egg. Then we check for a collision with the basket. If the egg collides with the basket, then we know it has been caught, but if the bottom of the egg is greater than or equal to the ground, then we know the egg has been missed. If an egg is caught, we call the showHitBasket function, which will display an image and play a sound indicating that the egg has been caught. We also increment the number of eggs caught. If an egg has been missed, however, we call the showBrokenEgg function, which will display an image and play a sound indicating that the egg was missed and has been broken. We also increment the number of eggs missed. Notice that in both cases, whether the egg is caught in the basket or is missed and breaks on the ground, we decrement the number of eggs left in the game, we reset the time variable needed to calculate the free fall distance, and we reset the egg to appear in the vulture's beak.

Next is the showHitBasket function:

Program 9-9   (**VultureTrouble**, *continued*)

```
743 // The showHitBasket function displays the hit
744 // basket effect and plays the pop sound.
745 void showHitBasket()
746 {
747     // Set the hit basket sprite to the same
748     // position as the basket sprite.
```

```
749    agk::SetSpritePosition(HIT_BASKET_SPRITE,
750        agk::GetSpriteX(BASKET_SPRITE),
751        agk::GetSpriteY(BASKET_SPRITE));
752
753    // Show the hit basket sprite.
754    agk::SetSpriteVisible(HIT_BASKET_SPRITE, SHOW);
755
756    // Play the pop sound.
757    agk::PlaySound(POP_SOUND);
758
759    // Refresh the screen now, so we can see the changes.
760    agk::Sync();
761
762    // Wait for 1/10 of a second.
763    agk::Sleep(100);
764
765    // Hide the hit basket sprite.
766    agk::SetSpriteVisible(HIT_BASKET_SPRITE, HIDE);
767 }
768
```

This function is called when the egg collides with the basket. It shows the hit basket sprite as shown in Figure 9-19, and plays a sound indicating that the user has caught an egg in the basket. Notice that in line 760 we call the agk::Sync function. This is so we can update the screen to show the effects. After we update the screen, we sleep for an instant and then hide the sprite.

Figure 9-19 The hit basket sprite displayed

Next is the showBrokenEgg function:

Program 9-9   (**VultureTrouble**, *continued*)

```
769 // The showBrokenEgg function displays the broken
770 // egg effect and plays the clap sound.
771 void showBrokenEgg()
772 {
773    // Set the broken egg sprite's position.
774    agk::SetSpritePosition(BROKEN_EGG_SPRITE,
775        agk::GetSpriteX(EGG_SPRITE),
776        agk::GetSpriteY(EGG_SPRITE) -
777        agk::GetSpriteHeight(EGG_SPRITE) / 2);
778
```

```
779    // Show the broken egg sprite.
780    agk::SetSpriteVisible(BROKEN_EGG_SPRITE, SHOW);
781
782    // Play the clap sound.
783    agk::PlaySound(CLAP_SOUND);
784
785    // Refresh the screen now, so we can see the changes.
786    agk::Sync();
787
788    // Wait for 1/10 of a second.
789    agk::Sleep(100);
790
791    // Hide the broken egg sprite.
792    agk::SetSpriteVisible(BROKEN_EGG_SPRITE, HIDE);
793 }
794
```

This function is called when the egg collides with the ground. It shows the broken egg sprite, as shown in Figure 9-20, and plays a sound indicating that the user has missed an egg and it has broken on the ground. Notice that in line 786 we call the agk::Sync function. This is so we can update the screen to show the effects. After we update the screen, we sleep for an instant and then hide the sprite.

Figure 9-20 The broken egg sprite displayed

Next is the resetEgg function:

Program 9-9 (**VultureTrouble**, *continued*)

```
795 // The resetEgg function resets the egg after it has
796 // either been caught in the basket or hit the ground.
797 void resetEgg()
798 {
799    // Hide the current mini-egg sprite clone.
800    agk::SetSpriteVisible(EGG_CLONE + g_eggs, HIDE);
801
802    // Reset the egg sprite's position.
803    agk::SetSpriteY(EGG_SPRITE,
804        agk::GetSpriteY(VULTURE_SPRITE) +
805        agk::GetSpriteHeight(EGG_SPRITE) * 1.5);
806 }
807
```

This function is called when the egg collides with either the basket or the ground. It hides one of the mini-eggs and resets the eggs position so that it appears in the vulture's beak, as shown in Figure 9-21.

Figure 9-21 Egg positioned below the vulture's beak

Next, is the `displayGameOverScreen` Function:

Program 9-9   (**VultureTrouble,** *continued*)

```
808 // The displayGameOverScreen function displays the
809 // game over text and plays the complete sound.
810 void displayGameOverScreen()
811 {
812    // Display the game over text.
813    agk::SetTextVisible(GAME_OVER_TEXT, SHOW);
814
815    // If the complete sound is not playing, play it.
816    if (!agk::GetSoundsPlaying(COMPLETE_SOUND))
817      agk::PlaySound(COMPLETE_SOUND);
818 }
819
```

This function displays the game over screen. It shows the game over text object and plays the game complete sound. It contains an `if` statement that determines if the sound is not playing, to play it. This screen is displayed for a short while, and when the timer expires, it is hidden.

Next is the `hideGameOverScreen` function:

Program 9-9   (**VultureTrouble,** *continued*)

```
820 // The hideGameOverScreen function prepares the
821 // game for the summary screen.
822 void hideGameOverScreen()
823 {
824    // Hide the game over text.
825    agk::SetTextVisible(GAME_OVER_TEXT, HIDE);
826
827    // Stop the complete sound.
828    agk::StopSound(COMPLETE_SOUND);
829
830    // Reset the timer.
831    agk::ResetTimer();
832
833   // Change the game state.
834    g_gameState = SUMMARY_STARTED;
835 }
836
```

This function is called when the timer expires for the game over screen. It hides the game over text object, stops the game complete sound, resets the timer, and changes the game state to SUMMARY_STARTED.

Next is the displaySummaryScreen function:

Program 9-9   (**VultureTrouble**, *continued*)

```
837  // The displaySummaryScreen function displays a
838  // summary of the player's performance, including
839  // points earned.
840  // Each egg caught earns 1000 points.
841  void displaySummaryScreen()
842  {
843      // Determine if the summary is complete.
844      if (g_summaryComplete == NO)
845      {
846          // Update the string of the eggs caught text object.
847          agk::SetTextString(EGGS_CAUGHT_TEXT,
848              agk::Str(g_eggsCaught));
849
850          // Update the X-coordinate of the eggs caught text
851          // object.
852          agk::SetTextX(EGGS_CAUGHT_TEXT,
853              agk::GetTextX(CAUGHT_MULTIPLIER_TEXT) +
854              agk::GetTextTotalWidth(CAUGHT_MULTIPLIER_TEXT)
855              / 2 +
856              agk::GetTextTotalWidth(EGGS_CAUGHT_TEXT) / 2);
857
858          // Set the egg sprite position inline with the text.
859          agk::SetSpritePosition(EGG_SPRITE,
860              agk::GetTextX(CAUGHT_MULTIPLIER_TEXT) -
861              agk::GetSpriteWidth(EGG_SPRITE) / 2,
862              agk::GetTextY(EGGS_CAUGHT_TEXT));
863
864          // Update the string of the eggs missed text object.
865          agk::SetTextString(EGGS_MISSED_TEXT,
866              agk::Str(g_eggsMissed));
867
868          // Update the X-coordinate of the eggs missed text
869          // object.
870          agk::SetTextX(EGGS_MISSED_TEXT,
871              agk::GetTextX(MISSED_MULTIPLIER_TEXT) +
872              agk::GetTextTotalWidth(MISSED_MULTIPLIER_TEXT)
873              / 2 +
874              agk::GetTextTotalWidth(EGGS_MISSED_TEXT) / 2);
875
876          // Set the broken egg sprite position inline
877          // with the text.
878          agk::SetSpritePosition(BROKEN_EGG_SPRITE,
879              agk::GetTextX(MISSED_MULTIPLIER_TEXT) -
880              agk::GetSpriteWidth(BROKEN_EGG_SPRITE),
881              agk::GetTextY(EGGS_MISSED_TEXT));
882
```

```
883        // Show the egg and broken egg sprites.
884        agk::SetSpriteVisible(EGG_SPRITE, SHOW);
885        agk::SetSpriteVisible(BROKEN_EGG_SPRITE, SHOW);
886
887        // Show the text objects.
888        agk::SetTextVisible(GAME_RESULTS_TEXT, SHOW);
889        agk::SetTextVisible(EGGS_CAUGHT_TEXT, SHOW);
890        agk::SetTextVisible(EGGS_MISSED_TEXT, SHOW);
891        agk::SetTextVisible(CAUGHT_MULTIPLIER_TEXT, SHOW);
892        agk::SetTextVisible(MISSED_MULTIPLIER_TEXT, SHOW);
893        agk::SetTextVisible(TOTAL_SCORE_TEXT, SHOW);
894
895        // Tally up the total score.
896        for(int i = 0; i <= g_eggsCaught; i++)
897        {
898           // Update the string of the total score
899           // text object.
900           agk::SetTextString(TOTAL_SCORE_TEXT,
901              agk::Str(i * SCORE_MULTIPLIER));
902
903           // Update the X-coordinate of the total
904           // score text object.
905           agk::SetTextX(TOTAL_SCORE_TEXT,
906              SCREEN_WIDTH / 2 -
907              agk::GetTextTotalWidth(TOTAL_SCORE_TEXT) /
908              2);
909
910           // Play the type sound.
911           agk::PlaySound(TYPE_SOUND);
912
913           // Wait for 1/10 of a second.
914           agk::Sleep(100);
915
916           // Refresh the screen now, so we can see the
917           // changes.
918           agk::Sync();
919        }
920
921        // If no eggs were broken, display a special message.
922        if (g_eggsCaught == MAX_EGGS)
923        {
924           // Display the perfect score text object.
925           agk::SetTextVisible(PERFECT_SCORE_TEXT, SHOW);
926
927           // Play the perfect score sound.
928           agk::PlaySound(PERFECT_SCORE_SOUND);
929
930           // Wait for 1/10 of a second.
931           agk::Sleep(100);
932
933           // Refresh the screen now, so we can see the
934           // changes.
935           agk::Sync();
936        }
937
```

```
938        // After we tally the score and exit the loop,
939        // the summary is complete.
940        g_summaryComplete = YES;
941
942        // Reset the timer.
943        agk::ResetTimer();
944     }
945 }
946
```

This function displays the results of the game to the user. It shows the text objects, updates their positions, and then tallies the player's score based on how many eggs were caught during the game. Notice that the agk::Sync function is called to update the screen. If the user had a perfect score and caught all the eggs, a special message appears and a sound is played. When the tally is complete, the g_summaryComplete variable is set to YES. The timer is reset, and the screen is displayed until the timer expires.

Next is the hideSummaryScreen function:

Program 9-9   (**VultureTrouble,** *continued*)

```
947 // The hideSummaryScreen hides the summary screen
948 // and changes the game state to when the game
949 // started.
950 void hideSummaryScreen()
951 {
952     // Hide the text.
953     agk::SetTextVisible(GAME_OVER_TEXT, HIDE);
954     agk::SetTextVisible(GAME_RESULTS_TEXT, HIDE);
955     agk::SetTextVisible(EGGS_CAUGHT_TEXT, HIDE);
956     agk::SetTextVisible(EGGS_MISSED_TEXT, HIDE);
957     agk::SetTextVisible(CAUGHT_MULTIPLIER_TEXT, HIDE);
958     agk::SetTextVisible(MISSED_MULTIPLIER_TEXT, HIDE);
959     agk::SetTextVisible(TOTAL_SCORE_TEXT, HIDE);
960     agk::SetTextVisible(PERFECT_SCORE_TEXT, HIDE);
961
962     // Hide the sprites.
963     agk::SetSpriteVisible(EGG_SPRITE, HIDE);
964     agk::SetSpriteVisible(BROKEN_EGG_SPRITE, HIDE);
965
966     // Reset X-coordinate of the vulture sprite to the
967     // starting value.
968     float vultureX = SCREEN_WIDTH / 2 -
969         agk::GetSpriteWidth(VULTURE_SPRITE) / 2;
970
971     // Reset Y-coordinate of the vulture sprite to the
972     // starting value.
973     float vultureY = 0;
974
975     // Reset the vulture sprite to the starting position.
976     agk::SetSpritePosition(VULTURE_SPRITE, vultureX,
977         vultureY);
978
```

```
979    // Reset X-coordinate of the basket sprite to the
980    // starting value.
981    float basketX = SCREEN_WIDTH / 2 -
982         agk::GetSpriteWidth(BASKET_SPRITE) / 2;
983
984    // Reset Y-coordinate of the basket sprite to the
985    // starting value.
986    float basketY = SCREEN_HEIGHT -
987         agk::GetSpriteHeight(BASKET_SPRITE);
988
989    // Reset the basket sprite to the starting position.
990    agk::SetSpritePosition(BASKET_SPRITE, basketX, basketY);
991
992    // Reset X-coordinate of the egg sprite to the
993    // starting value.
994    float eggX = vultureX;
995
996    // Reset Y-coordinate of the egg sprite to the
997    // starting value.
998    float eggY = vultureY +
999         agk::GetSpriteHeight(EGG_SPRITE) * 1.5f;
1000
1001   // Reset the egg sprite to the starting position.
1002   agk::SetSpritePosition(EGG_SPRITE, eggX, eggY);
1003
1004   // Reset the timer.
1005   agk::ResetTimer();
1006
1007   // Reset the global variables.
1008   g_summaryComplete = NO;
1009   g_eggs = MAX_EGGS;
1010   g_eggsMissed = 0;
1011   g_eggsCaught = 0;
1012
1013   // Reset the game state.
1014   g_gameState = GAME_STARTED;
1015 }
```

This function hides the text objects and sprites and resets the global variables, so that the game may be played again. It sets the game state to GAME_STARTED, and the game starts all over again.

Review Questions

Multiple Choice

1. The _____ function returns the size of a text object.
    a. agk::GetSize
    b. agk::TextSize
    c. agk::TotalTextSize
    d. agk::GetTextSize

2. When _____ overlap, a sprite collision occurs.
   a. two sprites
   b. bounding boxes
   c. several particles
   d. two copies of the same sprite

3. Without considering the effects of air resistance, suppose a boy drops a marble off the top of a building. The marble's speed will _____.
   a. increase as it falls
   b. be the same all the way down
   c. decrease as it falls
   d. alternatively decrease and increase

4. Which one of the following is the default alignment for text objects?
   a. Left
   b. Right
   c. Center
   d. Bottom

5. If you specify a negative value when setting the spacing of a text object, the spacing between letters will _____.
   a. increase
   b. not change
   c. decrease
   d. double

6. What function can be used to detect a collision between a text object and a single point?
   a. `agk::TextHit`
   b. `agk::TextCollidePoint`
   c. `agk::GetTextCollision`
   d. `agk::GetTextHitTest`

7. You can change the vertical position of a text object by calling the _____ function.
   a. `agk::ChangeTextY`
   b. `agk::SetTextY`
   c. `agk::MoveTextY`
   d. `agk::SetTextVertical`

8. Which one of the following functions will show or hide a text object?
   a. `agk::SetTextVisible`
   b. `agk::ShowText`
   c. `agk::HideText`
   d. `agk::SetTextSize`

9. If you want to simulate a falling object, you must change the value of the _____.
   a. gravity
   b. Y-coordinate
   c. acceleration
   d. X-coordinate

10. Which one of the following is an optional argument when setting the color of a text object?
    a. `Red`
    b. `Green`
    c. `Blue`
    d. `Alpha`

True or False

1. By default, the size of a text object is set to 16.

2. When gravity causes an object to fall toward Earth, the object's speed increases as it falls.

3. You can set a text object's size and color, but not its position.

4. You call the `agk::GetSpritesHit` function to determine if two sprites have collided.

5. When setting the spacing of a text object, If you specify a positive value, then the spacing will increase.

6. Even if a sprite uses an image that has been saved with transparency, the bounding box will always be visible.

7. You can detect collisions between two text objects with the `agk::GetTextCollision` function.

8. Once a text object has been created, its string value can never be changed.

Short Answer

1. Suppose gravity is causing an object to fall in a vacuum, toward Earth. At three seconds, what is the object's speed?

2. What is a sprite's bounding box?

3. How do you simulate an object that is moving both horizontally and vertically?

4. What function can you call to determine the total width of a text object?

5. When a text object is created, what two values must be passes as arguments?

Algorithm Workbench

1. Write code that sets the size of a text object to twice its current value.

2. Write a statement that determines if a sprite that has an index number of 1 has collided with a sprite that has an index number of 4.

3. Write a statement that sets the color of a text object with an index number of 5 to yellow.

4. Write a statement that determines if a sprite that has an index number of 3 has collided with a sprite that has an index number of 4. If so, hide both sprites.

5. Write a statement that determines if a text object with an index number of 1 exists. If it does, set the alignment of the text object to right-aligned.

Programming Exercises

1. **Randomly Moving Bowling Balls**
   The *Sprite Collision* program shown earlier in this chapter (see Program 9-5) shows two bowling balls that initially appear on opposite sides of the screen. The balls move toward each other, and when they collide, they are repositioned back at their original locations, and the animation repeats. Modify the program so that the bowling balls move in random directions. If a ball reaches the edge of the screen, it should change directions. If the bowling balls collide, they should be repositioned back at their random locations.

2. **Vulture Trouble Modification**
   Modify the Vulture Trouble game (see Program 9-9) so that the gravitational acceleration increases a slight amount for each egg that drops. This will make the game more challenging because the eggs will fall faster and faster as play continues.

3. **Catch the Boulder Game**
   Design and create a game named Catch the Boulder. The object of the game is to catch falling boulders in a cart that can be moved back and forth on a railroad track. Figure 9-22 shows an example of the game's screen. In many ways the game can be patterned after the Vulture Trouble game presented in this chapter. This book's online resources (downloadable from www.pearsonhighered.com/gaddis) provide several images that you can use to create the game.

Figure 9-22 Sample screen from Catch the Boulder

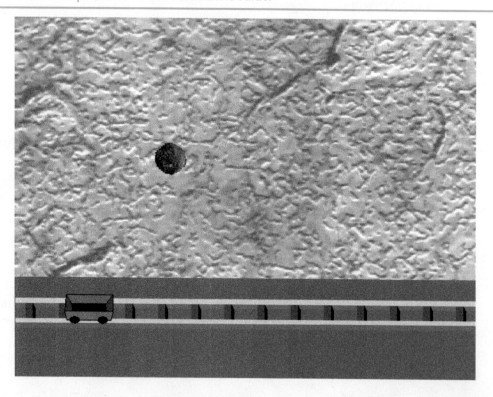

4. **Balloon Ace Game**

   Design and create a game named Balloon Ace. Figure 9-23 shows an example of a screen from the game. When the game runs, the user will control the movement of an airplane. Yellow and green balloons will randomly appear from the right edge of the screen and move toward the left edge of the screen. This will give the appearance that the plane is flying toward the balloons. The object of the game is to pop the green balloons by colliding into them with the plane and to avoid the yellow balloons. At the end of the game the program should award points to the user for the number of green balloons popped and the number of yellow balloons avoided. The book's online resources (downloadable from www.pearsonhighered.com/gaddis) provide several images that you can use to create the game.

Figure 9-23 Sample screen from Balloon Ace

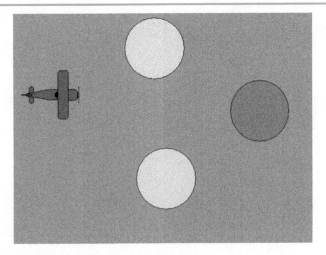

5. **Invisible Pizza Modification**

   Modify the PizzaBot game (see Program 9-6) so the slice of pizza is shown on the screen for a half second, and then becomes invisible. The user must then guide the robot to the invisible slice of pizza.

10 Using Files and Arrays with the AGK

10.1 File Input and Output

CONCEPT: When a program needs to save data for later use, it writes the data in a file. The data can be read from the file later.

The data that is stored in variables in RAM disappears once the program stops running. If a program is to retain data between the times it runs, it must have a way of saving it. Data is saved in a file, which is usually stored on a computer's disk. Once the data is saved in a file, it will remain there after the program stops running. Data that is stored in a file can be retrieved and used later.

Most of the commercial software packages that you use store data in files. Here are a few examples:

- **Games:** Many computer games keep data stored in files. For example, some games keep a list of player names with their scores stored in a file. Some games also allow you to save your current game status in a file so you can quit the game and then resume playing it without having to start from the beginning.
- **Word Processors:** Word processing programs are used to write letters, memos, reports, and other documents. The documents can then be saved in files so they can be edited and printed.
- **Image Editors:** Image editing programs are used to draw graphics and edit images such as the ones that you take with a digital camera. The images that you create or edit with an image editor are saved in files.

- **Spreadsheets:** Spreadsheet programs are used to work with numerical data. Numbers and mathematical formulas can be inserted into the rows and columns of the spreadsheet. The spreadsheet can then be saved in a file for later use.
- **Web Browsers:** Sometimes when you visit a Web page, the browser stores a small file known as a cookie on your computer. Typically, cookies contain information about the browsing session, such the contents of a shopping cart.

Programs that are used in daily business operations rely extensively on files. Payroll programs keep employee data in files, inventory programs keep data about a company's products in files, accounting systems keep data about a company's financial operations in files, and so forth.

Programmers usually refer to the process of saving data in a file as "writing data" to the file. When a piece of data is written to a file, it is copied from a variable in RAM to the file. This is illustrated in Figure 10-1. The term *output file* is used to describe a file to which data is written. It is called an output file because the program stores output in it.

Figure 10-1 Writing data to a file

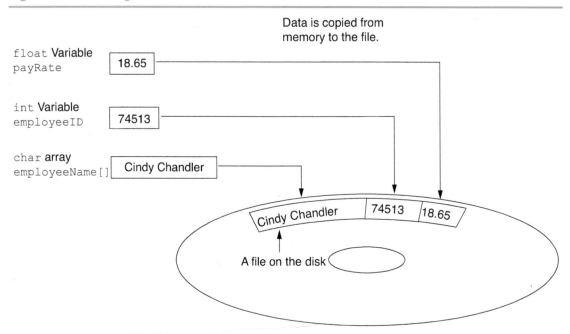

The process of retrieving data from a file is known as "reading data" from the file. When a piece of data is read from a file, it is copied from the file into a variable in RAM, as shown in Figure 10-2. The term *input file* is used to describe a file from which data is read. It is called an input file because the program gets input from the file.

In this section, we will discuss writing data to files and reading data from files. Three steps must always be taken when a file is used by a program:

1. **Open the file**—Opening a file creates a connection between the file and the program. Opening an output file creates the file on the disk and allows the program to write data to it. Opening an input file allows the program to read data from the file.

Figure 10-2 Reading data from a file

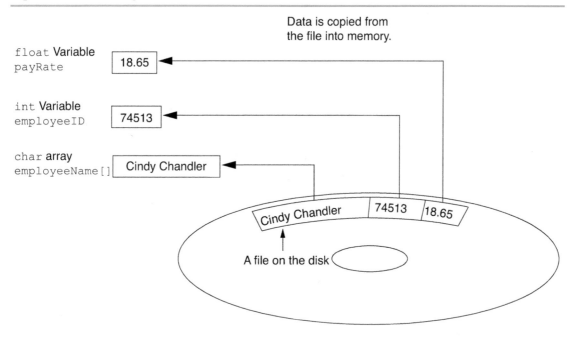

2. **Process the file**—In this step, data is either written to the file (if it is an output file) or read from the file (if it is an input file).
3. **Close the file**—When the program is finished using the file, the file must be closed. Closing a file disconnects the file from the program.

File Names

Most computer users are accustomed to the fact that a file is identified by a file name. For example, when you create a document with a word processor and then save the document in a file, you have to specify a file name. When you use a utility such as Windows Explorer to examine the contents of your disk, you see a list of file names. Figure 10-3 shows how three files named cat.jpg, notes.txt, and resume.doc might be represented in Windows Explorer.

Figure 10-3 Three files

Each operating system has its own rules for naming files. Many systems, including Windows, support the use of file name extensions, which are short sequences of characters that appear at the end of a file name, preceded by a period (which is known as a "dot"). For example, the file names shown in Figure 10-3 have the extensions .jpg, .txt, and .doc. The extension usually indicates the type of data stored in the file. For example, the .jpg extension usually indicates that the file contains a graphic image that is compressed according to the JPEG image standard. The .txt extension usually indicates that the file contains text. The .doc extension usually indicates that the file contains a Microsoft Word document. In this book, we will use the .dat extension with all the files we create in our programs. The .dat extension simply stands for "data."

File Numbers

When you use the AGK to open a file, you assign a file number to the file. A *file number* is an integer that you use to identify the file in subsequent operations. (Just as a sprite index identifies a sprite, a file number identifies a file.)

Opening an Output File

To open an output file with the AGK, you use the `agk::OpenToWrite` function. Here is the general format for calling the function:

```
agk::OpenToWrite( FileNumber, FileName );
```

`FileNumber` is the integer file number that you are assigning to the file, and `FileName` is a string specifying the name of the file. Here is an example:

```
agk::OpenToWrite( 1, "GameData.dat" );
```

After this statement executes, a file named GameData.dat will be opened as an output file, which means that we will be able to write data to the file. The file number 1 will be assigned to the file. Most of the time you will want to declare a constant for the file number, as follows:

```
const int OUTPUT_FILE = 1;
agk::OpenToWrite( OUTPUT_FILE, "GameData.dat" );
```

Declaring a constant for the file number will make the code easier to read and maintain.

Opening an output file actually creates the file on the disk.

Appending Data to an Existing File

Calling the `agk::OpenToWrite` function creates the specified file if it does not exist. By default, if the file already exists, its contents will be erased. You can change this behavior by specifying an optional third argument to the `agk::OpenToWrite` function. Here is the general format:

```
agk::OpenToWrite( FileNumber, FileName, AppendMode);
```

`FileNumber` is the integer file number that you are assigning to the file. `FileName` is a string specifying the name of the file. `AppendMode` is an integer (either 0 or 1). If `AppendMode` is 0, the specified file's contents will be erased if the file already exists. If `AppendMode` is 1, the specified file's contents will be preserved if the file already exists, and any new data will be appended to the file's existing contents. Here is an example that opens a file, preserving its existing contents:

```
const int OUTPUT_FILE = 1;
const int APPEND_MODE = 1;
agk::OpenToWrite( OUTPUT_FILE, "GameData.dat", APPEND_MODE );
```

After this code executes, any data that is written to the GameData.dat file will be appended to the file's existing contents. If the file does not exist, it will be created.

 NOTE: The files that an AGK program creates are located in the *My Documents > AGK > template* folder.

Writing Data to an Output File

Once a file has been opened with the `agk::OpenToWrite` function, you can write data to it. The AGK provides the following functions for writing data to files: `agk::WriteInteger`, `agk::WriteFloat`, `agk::WriteString`, and `agk::WriteLine`. We will look at each function.

The `agk::WriteInteger` Function

The `agk::WriteInteger` function writes an `int` value to a file. This is the general format:

```
agk::WriteInteger( FileNumber, Value );
```

FileNumber is the file number of a file that is open for writing, and *Value* is an `int` value. The function will write the integer *value* to the specified file. The following code shows an example. Assume that `OUTPUT_FILE` is the file number for an open output file and `myData` is an `int` variable.

```
agk::WriteInteger( OUTPUT_FILE, myData );
```

The `agk::WriteFloat` Function

The `agk::WriteFloat` function writes a `float` value to a file. This is the general format:

```
agk::WriteFloat( FileNumber, Value );
```

FileNumber is the file number of a file that is open for writing, and *Value* is a `float` value. The function will write the `float` value to the specified file. The following code shows an example. Assume that `OUTPUT_FILE` is the file number for an open output file and `myData` is a `float` variable.

```
agk::WriteFloat( OUTPUT_FILE, myData );
```

The `agk::WriteString` Function

The `agk::WriteString` function writes a null-terminated string to a file. A *null-terminated string* is a string that is followed by a byte that is set to the numeric value 0. This is the general format:

```
agk::WriteString( FileNumber, String );
```

FileNumber is the file number of a file that is open for writing, and *String* is a string literal, or the value of a `string` object that has been returned from the `c_str` member function. The `agk::WriteString` function will write the string to the specified file. Here is an example that writes a string literal to a file:

```
agk::WriteString( OUTPUT_FILE, "Activity Log" );
```

The following code shows another example. Assume that OUTPUT_FILE is the file number for an open output file, and name is a string object.

```
agk::WriteString( OUTPUT_FILE, name.c_str() );
```

The `agk::WriteLine` Function

The `agk::WriteLine` function writes a string to a file and ends the string with a newline character. This is the general format:

```
agk::WriteLine ( FileNumber, String );
```

FileNumber is the file number of a file that is open for writing, and *String* is a string literal, or the value of a string object that has been returned from the c_str member function. The `agk::WriteLine` function will write the string to the specified file, followed by a newline character. Here is an example that writes a string literal to a file:

```
agk::WriteString( OUTPUT_FILE, "Activity Log" );
```

Closing an Output File

Once a program is finished writing data to a file, it should use the `agk::CloseFile` function to close the file. Closing a file disconnects the program from the file and frees the file number so it can be used with another file. Here is the general format of the `agk::CloseFile` function:

```
agk::CloseFile(FileNumber);
```

FileNumber is the file number of a file that is currently open. After the `agk::CloseFile` function executes, the file associated with that file number will be closed. The following statement shows an example. Assume that OUTPUT_FILE is a constant that specifies the file number of an open file.

```
agk::CloseFile(OUTPUT_FILE);
```

Opening an Input File

To open an input file with the AGK, use the `agk::OpenToRead` function. Here is the general format for calling the function:

```
agk::OpenToRead( FileNumber, FileName );
```

FileNumber is the integer file number that you are assigning to the file. *FileName* is a string specifying the name of the file. The following code shows an example. Assume that INPUT_FILE is a constant that has been declared to specify the file number.

```
agk::OpenToRead( INPUT_FILE, "GameData.dat" );
```

After this statement executes, a file named GameData.dat will be opened as an input file. This means that we will be able to read data from the file. The file number specified by the INPUT_FILE constant will be assigned to the file.

When opening an input file, the file must exist in the *My Documents > AGK > template* folder, or the `agk::OpenToRead` function will fail. You can use the `agk::GetFileExists` function to make sure the file exists before attempting to open it, as shown here:

```
// Constant for the file number
const int INPUT_FILE = 1;

// If the GameData.dat file exists, open it.
if ( agk::GetFileExists("GameData.dat") )
{
    agk::OpenToRead( INPUT_FILE, "GameData.dat" );
}
```

> **NOTE:** A file must be located in the *My Documents > AGK > template* folder to be opened by an AGK program.

Reading Data from an Input File

Once a file has been opened with the `agk::OpenToRead` function, you can read data from it. The AGK provides several functions for reading data from files. We will discuss four of the most useful functions: `agk::ReadInteger`, `agk::ReadFloat`, `agk::ReadString`, and `agk::ReadLine`.

The `agk::ReadInteger` Function

The `agk::ReadInteger` function is a value-returning function. You pass the file number of a file that is open for reading as an argument. The function reads a value from the file and returns that value as an `int`. The following code shows an example. Assume that `INPUT_FILE` is the file number for an open input file and `myData` is an `int` variable.

```
myData = agk::ReadInteger( INPUT_FILE );
```

The `agk::ReadFloat` Function

The `agk::ReadFloat` function is a value-returning function. You pass the file number of a file that is open for reading as an argument. The function reads a value from the file and returns that value as a `float`. The following code shows an example. Assume that `INPUT_FILE` is the file number for an open input file and `myData` is a `float` variable.

```
myData = agk::ReadFloat( INPUT_FILE );
```

The `agk::ReadString` Function

The `agk::ReadString` function is a value-returning function. You pass the file number of a file that is open for reading as an argument. The function reads a null-terminated string from the file and returns that string. (Any string that was written to the file with the `agk::WriteString` function can be read from the file with the `agk::ReadString` function.) The following code shows an example. Assume that INPUT_FILE is the file number for an open input file, and str is a string object.

```
str = agk::ReadString(INPUT_FILE);
```

After this statement executes, a string will be read from the file specified by INPUT_FILE. The string will be assigned to the str object.

The agk::ReadLine Function

The agk::ReadLine function is a value-returning function. You pass the file number of a file that is open for reading as an argument. The function reads a string that is terminated with a newline character from the file and returns that string. (Any string that was written to the file with the agk::WriteLine function can be read from the file with the agk::ReadLine function.) The following code shows an example. Assume that INPUT_FILE is the file number for an open input file, and str is a string object.

```
str = agk::ReadLine(INPUT_FILE);
```

After this statement executes, a string will be read from the file specified by INPUT_FILE. The string will be assigned to the str object.

Closing an Output File

Once a program is finished reading data from a file, it should use the agk::CloseFile function to close the file. As previously mentioned, closing a file disconnects the program from the file and frees the file number so it can be used with another file. The following statement shows an example. Assume that INPUT_FILE is a constant that specifies the file number of an open file.

```
agk::CloseFile(INPUT_FILE);
```

Determining If a File Is Open

In some circumstances you might need to determine if a file is opened before performing operations with the file. This can be done with the agk::FileIsOpen function. You pass a file number as an argument to agk::FileIsOpen, and it returns 1 (true) if the file is open or 0 (false) if the file is not open. Here is an example:

```
if ( agk::FileIsOpen(INPUT_FILE) )
{
    // Code here reads from the file.
}
else
{
    agk::Print("Error: The file is not open.");
}
```

You can use the agk::FileIsOpen function to test both input and output files.

Let's look at an example program that writes data to a file. The following *In the Spotlight* section shows how a game can save its highest score in a file.

In the Spotlight:
Saving a Game's High Score

VideoNote

**Saving a Game's
High Score**

Many games keep track of the highest score that has been earned in the game. When a player beats the current high score, he or she is usually congratulated, and their score replaces the old high score. This provides motivation for the player to continue playing the game to beat the current high score.

A game that keeps track of the high score usually works something like this: A file is kept on the disk that contains the highest score achieved so far. When the player has finished the game, the program reads the file to get the high score. If the player's score is greater than the high score, the player is congratulated, and then the player's score is written to the file. The first time the game is played, the file will not exist. In that case, the file is created, and the player's score is written to it.

To demonstrate this, Program 10-1 shows a modified version of the Bug Zapper game that was presented in Chapter 8. Recall that the Bug Zapper game displays an animated sprite of a bug. The user zaps the bug by clicking it with the mouse. When this happens, a new bug appears at a random location on the screen. The game will run for 10 seconds before ending. The object of the game is to zap as many bugs as possible within the allotted time. When the game ends, a screen displays the user's score, which is the number of bugs that were zapped. This modified version of the game keeps the high score in a file named BugZapperHighScore.dat. Each time the user beats the high score, he or she is congratulated with the screen shown in Figure 10-4, and then the user's score is written to the BugZapperHighScore.dat file, replacing the value previously stored there.

Because we discussed the original Bug Zapper game in detail in Chapter 8, we will discuss only the modifications that were made in this version. First, we've added a new state that the game can be in. Line 38 declares a constant named CHECK_FOR_HIGH_SCORE. This constant represents the state that the game is in immediately after the 10 seconds of game play has expired, but before the closing screen is displayed. Notice that in line 200 (which executes as soon as we determine that 10 seconds has passed), we assign CHECK_FOR_HIGH_SCORE to the g_gameState variable.

Inside the app::Loop function, the switch statement jumps to line 111 when the g_gameState variable is set to CHECK_FOR_HIGH_SCORE. Line 113 calls the checkForHighScore function. The checkForHighScore function is defined in lines 226 through 256. Inside the function, the if statement in line 230 determines if the BugZapperHighScore.dat file exists. If it does, lines 233 and 234 open the file for reading, line 237 reads an integer from the file (the high score) and assigns it to the g_prevHighScore variable, and line 240 closes the file. If the BugZapperHighScore.dat file does not exist, line 244 assigns 0 to the g_prevHighScore variable. (The BugZapperHighScore.dat file will not exist the first time the program runs.) Next, the if statement in line 249 determines if the current score is higher than the high score that was read from the file. If so, we have a new high score, and line 251 calls the newHighScore function. Then, line 255 sets the g_gameState variable to GAME_OVER.

The newHighScore function is defined in lines 260 through 272. This function simply writes the current score to the BugZapperHighScore.dat file. Lines 264 and 265 open the file for writing (erasing its contents if the file already exists), line 268 writes the value of the g_bugsZapped variable to the file, and line 271 closes the file.

Program 10-1 (BugZapperVersion2)

```
 1 // Includes, namespace and prototypes
 2 #include "template.h"
 3 using namespace AGK;
 4 app App;
 5
 6 // Function prototypes
 7 void generateNewBug();
 8 void displayIntro();
 9 void hideIntro();
10 void playGame();
11 void checkForHighScore();
12 void newHighScore();
13 void closingScreen();
14
15 // Constants for the screen resolution
16 const int SCREEN_WIDTH  = 640;
17 const int SCREEN_HEIGHT = 480;
18
19 // Constants for sprites
20 const int INTRO_INDEX = 1;
21 const int GRASS_INDEX = 2;
22 const int BUG_INDEX   = 3;
23
24 // Constant for the sound file
25 const int BOINK_SOUND = 1;
26
27 // Constants for animation
28 const int FRAME_WIDTH  = 64;
29 const int FRAME_HEIGHT = 64;
30 const int FRAME_COUNT  = 2;
31
32 // Constant for game time
33 const int MAX_TIME = 10;
34
35 // Constants for the possible game states.
36 const int GAME_JUST_STARTED    = 0;
37 const int GAME_IN_PLAY         = 1;
38 const int CHECK_FOR_HIGH_SCORE = 2;
39 const int GAME_OVER            = 3;
40
41 // Constant for the high score file number
42 const int HIGH_SCORE_FILE = 1;
43
44 // Global variables
45 int g_bugsZapped = 0;          // Counter for bugs zapped
46 int g_prevHighScore = 0;       // Previous high score
```

```
47 int g_gameState = GAME_JUST_STARTED;  // Game state
48
49 // Begin app, called once at the start
50 void app::Begin( void )
51 {
52    // Set the virtual resolution.
53    agk::SetVirtualResolution(SCREEN_WIDTH, SCREEN_HEIGHT);
54
55    // Set the text in the window title bar.
56    agk::SetWindowTitle("Bug Zapper");
57
58    // Create the background sprite.
59    agk::CreateSprite(GRASS_INDEX, "BugZapper/Grass.png");
60
61    // Create the bug sprite.
62    agk::CreateSprite(BUG_INDEX, "BugZapper/Bug.png");
63
64    // Create the intro screen sprite.
65    agk::CreateSprite(INTRO_INDEX, "BugZapper/Intro.png");
66
67    // Load the sound file.
68    agk::LoadSound(BOINK_SOUND, "BugZapper/Boink.wav");
69
70    // Randomly position the bug.
71    generateNewBug();
72
73    // Set the sprite animation
74    agk::SetSpriteAnimation(BUG_INDEX, FRAME_WIDTH,
75                            FRAME_HEIGHT, FRAME_COUNT);
76
77    // Play the bug animation.
78    agk::PlaySprite(BUG_INDEX);
79 }
80
81 // Main loop, called every frame
82 void app::Loop ( void )
83 {
84    // Determine the game state and
85    // act accordingly.
86    switch (g_gameState)
87    {
88    case GAME_JUST_STARTED:
89       // Display the intro screen.
90       displayIntro();
91
92       // Check for a key press.
93       if (agk::GetRawLastKey())
94       {
95          // Hide the intro screen
96          hideIntro();
97
98          // Change the game state.
99          g_gameState = GAME_IN_PLAY;
100
```

```
101                   // Reset the timer.
102                   agk::ResetTimer();
103            }
104         break;
105
106     case GAME_IN_PLAY:
107         // Engage in game play.
108         playGame();
109         break;
110
111     case CHECK_FOR_HIGH_SCORE:
112         // Get the high score so far.
113         checkForHighScore();
114
115     case GAME_OVER:
116         // Display the closing screen.
117         closingScreen();
118         break;
119     };
120
121     // Update the screen.
122     agk::Sync();
123 }
124
125 // Called when the app ends
126 void app::End ( void )
127 {
128 }
129
130 // The generateNewBug function generates a new bug at
131 // random location.
132 void generateNewBug()
133 {
134     // Get the bug's width and height.
135     int bugWidth = agk::GetSpriteWidth(BUG_INDEX);
136     int bugHeight = agk::GetSpriteHeight(BUG_INDEX);
137
138     // Generate a new location.
139     int x = agk::Random(0, SCREEN_WIDTH - bugWidth);
140     int y = agk::Random(0, SCREEN_HEIGHT - bugHeight);
141
142     // Put the bug at that location.
143     agk::SetSpritePosition(BUG_INDEX, x, y);
144 }
145
146 // The displayIntro function hides the grass and the
147 // bug sprite, and makes the intro screen visible.
148 void displayIntro()
149 {
150     // Make the grass and bug invisible.
151     agk::SetSpriteVisible(GRASS_INDEX, 0);
152     agk::SetSpriteVisible(BUG_INDEX, 0);
153
154     // Make the intro screen visible.
155     agk::SetSpriteVisible(INTRO_INDEX, 1);
156 }
```

```
157
158 // The hideIntro function hides the intro screen
159 // and makes the grass and bug visible.
160 void hideIntro()
161 {
162     agk::SetSpriteVisible(INTRO_INDEX, 0);
163     agk::SetSpriteVisible(BUG_INDEX, 1);
164     agk::SetSpriteVisible(GRASS_INDEX, 1);
165 }
166
167 // The playGame function processes a frame of game play.
168 void playGame()
169 {
170     // Variables for mouse coordinates
171     float mouseX, mouseY;
172
173     // Do we still have time left?
174     if (agk::Timer() < MAX_TIME)
175     {
176         // Determine if the left mouse button was pressed.
177         if(agk::GetRawMouseLeftPressed())
178         {
179             // Get the mouse pointer location.
180             mouseX = agk::GetRawMouseX();
181             mouseY = agk::GetRawMouseY();
182
183             // Check to see if the bug was hit.
184             if (agk::GetSpriteHit(mouseX, mouseY) == BUG_INDEX)
185             {
186                 // Play the boink sound.
187                 agk::PlaySound(BOINK_SOUND);
188
189                 // Update the count.
190                 g_bugsZapped++;
191
192                 // Generate a new bug.
193                 generateNewBug();
194             }
195         }
196     }
197     else
198     {
199         // Time is up, check for a high score.
200         g_gameState = CHECK_FOR_HIGH_SCORE;
201     }
202 }
203
204 // The closingScreen function displays the closing screen.
205 void closingScreen()
206 {
207     // Hide the bug and the grass.
208     agk::SetSpriteVisible(GRASS_INDEX, 0);
209     agk::SetSpriteVisible(BUG_INDEX, 0);
210
211     // Display the results.
212     agk::PrintC("Number of bugs zapped: ");
```

```
213        agk::Print(g_bugsZapped);
214
215        if (g_bugsZapped > g_prevHighScore)
216        {
217            // Congratulate the user.
218            agk::Print("Congratulations!");
219            agk::Print("You set a new high score!");
220        }
221 }
222
223 // The checkForHighScore function reads the high score from
224 // the BugZapperHighScore.dat file and determines whether
225 // the user's score is the new high score.
226 void checkForHighScore()
227 {
228     // If the BugZapperHighScore.dat file exists, open it
229     // and read its value. Otherwise, set highScore to 0.
230     if (agk::GetFileExists("BugZapperHighScore.dat"))
231     {
232         // Open the file.
233         agk::OpenToRead(HIGH_SCORE_FILE,
234                         "BugZapperHighScore.dat");
235
236         // Read the high score.
237         g_prevHighScore = agk::ReadInteger(HIGH_SCORE_FILE);
238
239         // Close the file.
240         agk::CloseFile(HIGH_SCORE_FILE);
241     }
242     else
243     {
244         g_prevHighScore = 0;
245     }
246
247     // If this is the new high score, write it to
248     // the file.
249     if (g_bugsZapped > g_prevHighScore)
250     {
251         newHighScore();
252     }
253
254     // Change the game state to end the game.
255     g_gameState = GAME_OVER;
256 }
257
258 // The newHighScore function writes the current score to
259 // the BugZapperHighScore.dat
260 void newHighScore()
261 {
262     // Open the BugZapperHighScore.dat file for writing.
263     // If the file already exists, this will replace it.
264     agk::OpenToWrite(HIGH_SCORE_FILE,
265                      "BugZapperHighScore.dat");
266
```

```
267       // Write the current score to the file.
268       agk::WriteInteger(HIGH_SCORE_FILE, g_bugsZapped);
269
270       // Close the file.
271       agk::CloseFile(HIGH_SCORE_FILE);
272 }
```

Figure 10-4 Closing screen with high score message

To prevent a program from reading beyond the end of a file, the AGK provides a

In the Spotlight:

Detecting the End of a File

Quite often, a program must read the contents of a file without knowing the number of items that are stored in the file. This presents a problem if you want to write a program that processes all the items in the file, regardless of how many there are. You can write a loop that reads all the items in a file, or in an AGK program you can write code in the app::Loop function that repeatedly reads items from a file, but an error will occur if the program attempts to read beyond the last item in the file.

To prevent a program from reading beyond the end of a file, the AGK provides a function named agk::FileEOF. You pass a file number to the agk::FileEOF function, and it returns 1 (true) if the last item in the file has been read. If there are more items to read from the file, the function returns 0 (false). The following code shows how you use the agk::FileEOF function to determine whether the end of the file has not been reached. Assume INPUT_FILE a file number.

```
if (!agk::FileEOF(INPUT_FILE))
{
    // Read an item from the file and process it.
}
```

To demonstrate how this technique works, we will look at Programs 10-2 and 10-3. Program 10-2 generates a set of random color values (as integers) and writes them to a file. Then, Program 10-3 reads each set of color values from the file. Each time Program 10-3 reads a set of color values from the file, it clears the screen to the specified color. The program reads color values from the file until it encounters the end of the file.

Program 10-2   (`WriteRandomColors`)

```
1  // Includes, namespace and prototypes
2  #include "template.h"
3  using namespace AGK;
4  app App;
5
6  // Constants for the screen resolution
7  const int SCREEN_WIDTH = 640;
8  const int SCREEN_HEIGHT = 480;
9
10 // Constant for the file number
11 const int OUTPUT_FILE = 1;
12
13 // Constant for the number of colors
14 const int MAX_COLORS = 10;
15
16 // Global variable to count the colors
17 int g_numColors = 0;
18
19 // Begin app, called once at the start
20 void app::Begin( void )
21 {
22     // Set the virtual resolution.
23     agk::SetVirtualResolution(SCREEN_WIDTH, SCREEN_HEIGHT);
24
25     // Open the output file.
26     agk::OpenToWrite(OUTPUT_FILE, "Colors.dat");
27 }
28
29 // Main loop, called every frame
30 void app::Loop ( void )
31 {
32     // Variables to hold color channel values
33     int red, green, blue;
34
35     if (g_numColors < MAX_COLORS)
36     {
37         // Generate random color values
38         red = agk::Random(0, 255);
39         green = agk::Random(0, 255);
40         blue = agk::Random(0, 255);
41
42         // Write the color values to the file.
43         agk::WriteInteger(OUTPUT_FILE, red);
44         agk::WriteInteger(OUTPUT_FILE, green);
45         agk::WriteInteger(OUTPUT_FILE, blue);
46
47         // Increment the color counter.
48         g_numColors++;
49     }
50     else
51     {
52         agk::Print("Finished!");
53     }
```

```
54
55      // Update the screen.
56      agk::Sync();
57 }
58
59 // Called when the app ends
60 void app::End ( void )
61 {
62      // Close the file.
63      agk::CloseFile(OUTPUT_FILE);
64 }
```

Let's take a closer look at Program 10-2. Lines 7 and 8 declare the usual constants that we will use to set the virtual resolution. Line 11 declares an `int` constant named `OUTPUT_FILE`, set to 1, which we will use as a file number. Line 14 declares an `int` constant named `MAX_COLORS`, set to 10, which we will use as the number of colors to generate and save to the file. Line 17 declares a global `int` variable named `g_numColors`, initialized with 0, which we will use to count the number of colors that are written to the file.

Inside the `app::Begin` function, line 23 sets the virtual resolution, and line 26 opens a file named Colors.dat for writing. Inside the `app::Loop` function, line 33 declares the local `int` variables `red`, `green`, and `blue`. These variables will be assigned the random numbers that we generate for each color's red, green, and blue channels.

The `if` statement that begins in line 35 determines whether we have written the maximum number of colors yet. If not, lines 38 through 40 generate three random integers in the range of 0 through 255 and assign them to the `red`, `green`, and `blue` variables. Then, lines 43 through 45 write the values to the file. Line 48 increments the `g_numColors` variable.

If the maximum number of colors has been written, the program jumps to the `else` clause in line 50, and line 52 prints "Finished!" on the screen. Line 56 calls the `agk::Sync` function to update the screen. Inside the `app::End` function, line 63 closes the file.

Next, we look at Program 10-3, which opens the Colors.dat file and reads the values from it.

Program 10-3   (ReadRandomColors)

```
 1 // Includes, namespace and prototypes
 2 #include "template.h"
 3 using namespace AGK;
 4 app App;
 5
 6 // Constants for the screen resolution, refresh rate,
 7 // and refresh mode
 8 const int SCREEN_WIDTH = 640;
 9 const int SCREEN_HEIGHT = 480;
10 const int REFRESH_RATE = 1;
11 const int REFRESH_MODE = 0;
```

```
12
13 // Constant for the file number
14 const int INPUT_FILE = 1;
15
16 // Begin app, called once at the start
17 void app::Begin( void )
18 {
19     // Set the virtual resolution.
20     agk::SetVirtualResolution(SCREEN_WIDTH, SCREEN_HEIGHT);
21
22     // Set the sync rate.
23     agk::SetSyncRate(REFRESH_RATE, REFRESH_MODE);
24
25     // Open the output file.
26     agk::OpenToRead(INPUT_FILE, "Colors.dat");
27 }
28
29 // Main loop, called every frame
30 void app::Loop ( void )
31 {
32     // Variables to hold color channel values
33     int red, green, blue;
34
35     // If not at the end of the file, read the next
36     // set of color values and clear the screen to
37     // that color.
38     if (!agk::FileEOF(INPUT_FILE))
39     {
40         // Generate random color values
41         red = agk::ReadInteger(INPUT_FILE);
42         green = agk::ReadInteger(INPUT_FILE);
43         blue = agk::ReadInteger(INPUT_FILE);
44
45         // Set the screen's clear color.
46         agk::SetClearColor(red, green, blue);
47
48         // Clear the screen.
49         agk::ClearScreen();
50     }
51     else
52     {
53         agk::Print("Finished!");
54     }
55
56     // Update the screen.
57     agk::Sync();
58 }
59
60 // Called when the app ends
61 void app::End ( void )
62 {
63     // Close the file.
64     agk::CloseFile(INPUT_FILE);
65 }
```

Let's take a closer look at Program 10-3. Lines 8 and 9 declare the constants that we will use to set the virtual resolution. Line 10 declares an int constant named REFRESH_RATE, set to 1, which we will use to set the sync rate to 1 frame per second. Line 11 declares an int constant named REFRESH_MODE, set to 0, which we will use to set the refresh mode. (Recall that the refresh mode 0 is the most energy efficient mode.) Line 14 declares an int constant named INPUT_FILE, set to 1, which we will use as a file number.

Inside the app::Begin function, line 20 sets the virtual resolution, line 23 sets the sync rate to 1 frame per second, and line 26 opens a file named Colors.dat for writing. Inside the app::Loop function, line 33 declares the local int variables red, green, and blue. These variables will be assigned the color values that are read from the file.

The if statement that begins in line 38 determines whether or not we have reached the end of the file. If we have not, lines 41 through 43 read three integers from the file and assign them to the red, green, and blue variables. Then, line 46 uses these values to set the screen's clear color. Line 49 clears the screen to the current color.

If the maximum number of colors has been written, the program jumps to the else clause in line 51, and line 53 prints "Finished!" on the screen. Line 57 calls the agk::Sync function to update the screen. Inside the app::End function, line 64 closes the file.

In the Spotlight:
Writing a Log File

Sometimes, for debugging purposes, it is helpful to for a program to keep a log of its activity in a file. Each time the program performs an operation, it writes a line of information to a file describing what it just did. Such a file, known as a *log file*, usually contains pure text so it can be opened in a text editor such as Notepad.

In an AGK program, you use the agk::WriteString and agk::WriteLine functions to write pure text to a file. These functions simply write a string to an open file. Recall that the agk::WriteLine function writes a newline character after the string, which starts a new line in the file when viewed in a text editor.

If you want to write the contents of an integer or floating-point value to a file as text, you must use the agk::Str function to convert the value to a string. Here is the general format of the function:

```
agk::Str(NumericValue)
```

In the general format, *NumericValue* is an integer or a floating-point numeric value. The function returns that value as a string. For example, assume that number is an int or a float variable and that OUTPUT_FILE is the file number of a file that is opened for writing. The following statement writes the contents of the number variable, as text, to the file:

```
agk::WriteString( agk::Str(number) );
```

You can also use the agk::WriteLine function if you want the value to appear on its own line in the file:

```
agk::WriteLine( agk::Str(number) );
```

Program 10-4 shows a demonstration of how a log file can be kept by a program. This is a modified version of the DirectionKeys project that was shown in Chapter 8. Recall that the program displays a fish sprite (shown in Figure 10-5) that can be moved around the screen with the arrow keys. Each time the user presses an arrow key, the program records the amount of movement in a log file.

Program 10-4 **(DirectionKeysLog)**

```
1  // Includes, namespace and prototypes
2  #include "template.h"
3  using namespace AGK;
4  app App;
5
6  // Constants
7  const int SCREEN_WIDTH  = 640;  // Screen width
8  const int SCREEN_HEIGHT = 480;  // Screen height
9  const int SPRITE_INDEX  = 1;    // Sprite index
10 const int OUTPUT_FILE   = 1;    // File number
11
12 // Begin app, called once at the start
13 void app::Begin( void )
14 {
15     // Set the window title.
16     agk::SetWindowTitle("Direction Keys");
17
18     // Set the virtual resolution.
19     agk::SetVirtualResolution(SCREEN_WIDTH, SCREEN_HEIGHT);
20
21     // Create the sprite.
22     agk::CreateSprite(SPRITE_INDEX, "fish.png");
23
24     // Open the activity log file.
25     agk::OpenToWrite(OUTPUT_FILE, "ActivityLog.txt");
26 }
27
28 // Main loop, called every frame
29 void app::Loop ( void )
30 {
31     // Get the direction as input from the keyboard.
32     float directionX = agk::GetDirectionX();
33     float directionY = agk::GetDirectionY();
34
35     // Log any movement along the X-axis.
36     if (directionX != 0)
37     {
38         agk::WriteString(OUTPUT_FILE, "X movement: ");
39         agk::WriteLine(OUTPUT_FILE, agk::Str(directionX));
40     }
```

```
41
42     // Log any movement along the Y-axis.
43     if (directionY != 0)
44     {
45         agk::WriteString(OUTPUT_FILE, "Y movement: ");
46         agk::WriteLine(OUTPUT_FILE, agk::Str(directionY));
47     }
48
49     // Get the sprite position.
50     float spriteX = agk::GetSpriteX(SPRITE_INDEX);
51     float spriteY = agk::GetSpriteY(SPRITE_INDEX);
52
53     // Calculate how far the sprite will move.
54     float moveX = spriteX + directionX;
55     float moveY = spriteY + directionY;
56
57     // Set the sprite position.
58     agk::SetSpritePosition(SPRITE_INDEX, moveX, moveY);
59
60     // Refresh the screen.
61     agk::Sync();
62 }
63
64 // Called when the app ends
65 void app::End ( void )
66 {
67     // Close the activity log file.
68     agk::CloseFile(OUTPUT_FILE);
69 }
```

Figure 10-5 Output of Program 10-4

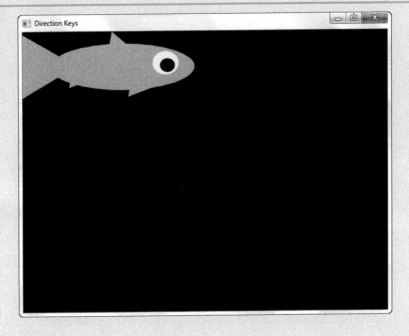

Let's take a closer look at Program 10-4. Lines 7 and 8 declare the usual constants that we will use to set the virtual resolution. Line 9 declares an int constant named SPRITE_INDEX, set to 1, which we will use as a sprite index, and line 10 declares an int constant named OUTPUT_FILE, set to 1, which we will use as a file number.

Inside the app::Begin function, line 16 sets the window's title bar text, and line 19 sets the virtual resolution. Line 22 creates the fish sprite, and line 25 opens the ActivityLog.txt file for writing.

Inside the app::Loop function, lines 32 and 33 call the agk::GetDirectionX and agk::GetDirectionY functions to determine whether the arrow keys are being pressed. The values returned from these functions are assigned to the directionX and directionY variables.

The if statement in line 36 determines whether the left or right arrow was pressed. (Recall that the agk::GetDirectionX function returns 0 if neither the left or right arrow is being pressed. If one of these keys is being pressed, it returns negative or a positive number.) If the left or right arrow key is being pressed, line 38 writes the string "X movement:", and then line 39 writes the value of the directionX variable, converted to a string. Notice that line 39 uses the agk::WriteLine function, which writes a string to the file, followed by a newline character to end the line.

The if statement in line 43 determines whether the up or down arrow was pressed. (Recall that the agk::GetDirectionY function returns 0 if neither the up or down arrow is being pressed. If one of these keys is being pressed, it returns negative or a positive number.) If the up or down arrow key is being pressed, line 45 writes the string "Y movement:", and then line 46 writes the value of the directionY variable, converted to a string. Line 46 uses the agk::WriteLine function, which writes a string to the file, followed by a newline character to end the line.

The rest of the app::Loop function calculates the fish sprite's new position and moves it to that location. In the app::End function, line 68 closes the file.

Figure 10-6 shows an example of the ActivityLog.txt file, opened in Notepad.

Figure 10-6 Example activity log generated by Program 10-4

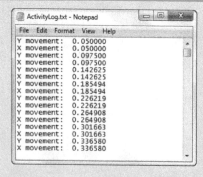

Checkpoint

10.1. What is an input file? What is an output file?

10.2. What three steps are always taken when a file is used by a program?

10.3. How are files identified on a computer disk?

10.4. How are files identified in an AGK program?

10.5. What AGK function do you use to perform the following?

- Open a file for writing
- Open a file for reading
- Write an integer to a file
- Write a floating-point number to a file
- Write a null-terminated string to a file
- Write a string, followed by a newline, to a file
- Read an integer from a file
- Read a floating-point number from a file
- Read a null-terminated string from a file
- Read a newline-terminated string from a file
- Close a file

10.6. What is the difference between append mode 0 and append mode 1 when opening an output file?

10.7. Describe the `agk::FileEOF` function.

10.2 Using Arrays in an AGK Program

CONCEPT: Arrays can be used for a variety of tasks in a game, such as simulating a card deck, keeping a list of sprites, or creating a tile-based screen.

In Chapter 6 you learned how to use arrays in a standard C++ program. Arrays are also useful in AGK programs to hold sets of data such as sprite numbers, image numbers, and other items. In this section we will look at examples in which an array is used to represent a deck of cards. We will also look at a programming technique known as tile mapping, in which a two-dimensional array is used to construct a game's background imagery.

In the Spotlight:

Using an Array as a Deck of Cards

VideoNote

Using an Array as a Deck of Cards

Card games are very popular, and in many ways, a deck of cards is similar to an array. To demonstrate this, we will look at an AGK program that creates a set of poker card sprites and uses an `int` array to hold the sprite indices. When the program runs, it initially appears as shown in Figure 10-7. The image of a card backface is shown to represent the deck of cards. Each time the user clicks the virtual button that appears in the lower-right corner, a card is dealt from the deck and appears faceup. The program has a total of 9 card sprites, and when all 9 cards have been dealt from the deck, the screen appears as shown in Figure 10-8.

Figure 10-7 Initial screen of the DealCards program

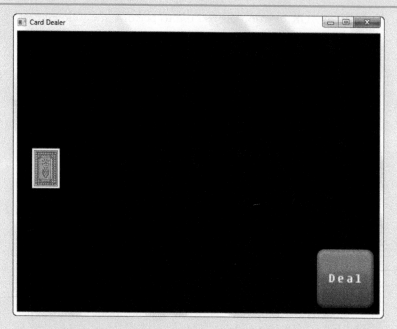

Figure 10-8 Screen after all cards are dealt

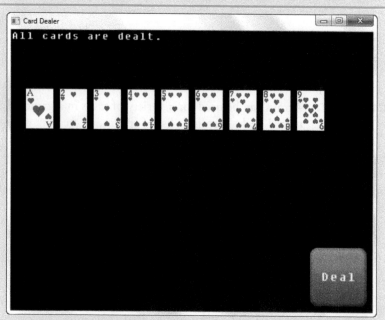

Program 10-5   (DealCards)

```
1 // Includes, namespace and prototypes
2 #include "template.h"
3 #include <string>       // Needed for string class
4 using namespace std;    // Needed for string class
```

```
 5  using namespace AGK;
 6  app App;
 7
 8  // Function prototype
 9  void createCardSprites();
10
11  // Constants for the screen resolution
12  const int SCREEN_WIDTH  = 640;   // Screen width
13  const int SCREEN_HEIGHT = 480;   // Screen height
14
15  // Constants for the virtual button
16  const int   BUTTON_INDEX = 1;
17  const int   BUTTON_SIZE  = 100;
18  const float BUTTON_X     = 580;
19  const float BUTTON_Y     = 420;
20
21  // Constants for card sprite numbers
22  const int HEARTS_ACE = 1;
23  const int HEARTS_2   = 2;
24  const int HEARTS_3   = 3;
25  const int HEARTS_4   = 4;
26  const int HEARTS_5   = 5;
27  const int HEARTS_6   = 6;
28  const int HEARTS_7   = 7;
29  const int HEARTS_8   = 8;
30  const int HEARTS_9   = 9;
31  const int BACKFACE   = 10;
32
33  // Constants for card screen placement
34  const float STARTING_X    = 25;
35  const float CARD_Y        = 100;
36  const float CARD_DISTANCE = 10;
37  const float BACKFACE_X    = 25;
38  const float BACKFACE_Y    = 200;
39
40  // Constant for the number of cards
41  const int NUM_CARDS = 9;
42
43  // Array holding the card sprite numbers.
44  int g_cardSprites[NUM_CARDS] = { HEARTS_ACE, HEARTS_2,
45      HEARTS_3, HEARTS_4, HEARTS_5, HEARTS_6, HEARTS_7,
46      HEARTS_8, HEARTS_9 };
47
48  // Array holding the names of the card image files
49  string g_imageFiles[NUM_CARDS] = { "Cards/Ace_hearts.png",
50              "Cards/2_hearts.png", "Cards/3_hearts.png",
51              "Cards/4_hearts.png", "Cards/5_hearts.png",
52              "Cards/6_hearts.png", "Cards/7_hearts.png",
53              "Cards/8_hearts.png", "Cards/9_hearts.png" };
54
55  // Variable to hold the number of cards dealt
56  int g_cardsDealt = 0;
57
58  // Variable to hold each card's X-coordinate
59  float g_cardX = STARTING_X;
```

```
60
61   // Begin app, called once at the start
62   void app::Begin( void )
63   {
64       // Set the window title.
65       agk::SetWindowTitle("Card Dealer");
66
67       // Set the virtual resolution.
68       agk::SetVirtualResolution(SCREEN_WIDTH, SCREEN_HEIGHT);
69
70       // Add the virtual button.
71       agk::AddVirtualButton(BUTTON_INDEX, BUTTON_X, BUTTON_Y, BUTTON_SIZE);
72       agk::SetVirtualButtonText(BUTTON_INDEX, "Deal");
73
74       // Create the backface card sprite.
75       agk::CreateSprite(BACKFACE, "Cards/Backface_Red.png");
76
77       // Position the backface card sprite.
78       agk::SetSpritePosition(BACKFACE, BACKFACE_X, BACKFACE_Y);
79
80       // Create the card sprites.
81       createCardSprites();
82   }
83
84   // Main loop, called every frame
85   void app::Loop ( void )
86   {
87       // Variables for the card location
88       float cardX, cardY;
89
90       // Are cards left to be dealt?
91       if (g_cardsDealt < NUM_CARDS)
92       {
93           // Check for a button press.
94           if (agk::GetVirtualButtonPressed(BUTTON_INDEX))
95           {
96               // Position the card sprite that is being dealt.
97               agk::SetSpritePosition(g_cardSprites[g_cardsDealt],
98                                      g_cardX, CARD_Y);
99
100              // Make the card sprite visible.
101              agk::SetSpriteVisible(g_cardSprites[g_cardsDealt], 1);
102
103              // Calculate the next card's X-coordinate.
104              g_cardX += agk::GetSpriteWidth(g_cardSprites[g_cardsDealt]) +
105                         CARD_DISTANCE;
106
107              // Increment the number of cards dealt.
108              g_cardsDealt++;
109          }
110      }
111      else
112      {
113          // All cards are dealt. Print a message and hide
```

```
114            // the backface card.
115            agk::Print("All cards are dealt.");
116            agk::SetSpriteVisible(BACKFACE, 0);
117        }
118
119        // Refresh the screen.
120        agk::Sync();
121    }
122
123    // Called when the app ends
124    void app::End ( void )
125    {
126    }
127
128    // The createCardSprites function creates the card sprites
129    // and makes them invisible.
130    void createCardSprites()
131    {
132        for (int count = 0; count < NUM_CARDS; count++)
133        {
134            // Create the next card sprite.
135            agk::CreateSprite(g_cardSprites[count],
136                              g_imageFiles[count].c_str());
137
138            // Make the sprite invisible.
139            agk::SetSpriteVisible(g_cardSprites[count], 0);
140        }
141    }
```

Let's take a closer look at the program. First, notice that in line 3 we have an include directive for the string header file, and in line 4 we have the using namespace std; statement. These are necessary because we are going to have a string array containing the names of the card image files.

Here is a summary of the global constants:

- Lines 12 and 13 declare constants for the screen resolution.
- Lines 16 through 19 declare constants for the virtual button.
- Lines 22 through 31 declare constants for the card sprite indices.
- Lines 34 through 38 declare the following constants that are related to the location of the cards on the screen:
  - The STARTING_X constant specifies the X-coordinate of the first card that is dealt from the deck.
  - The CARD_Y constant specifies the Y-coordinate for each card that is dealt from the deck.
  - The CARD_DISTANCE constant specifies the distance between cards, in pixels.
  - The BACKFACE_X and BACKFACE_Y constants specify the X- and Y-coordinates of the card backface.
- Line 41 declares the NUM_CARDS constant that specifies the number of cards we will have.

Lines 44 through 46 declare an int array named g_cardSprites that is initialized with all the sprite indices for the cards:

```
int g_cardSprites[NUM_CARDS] = { HEARTS_ACE, HEARTS_2,
    HEARTS_3, HEARTS_4, HEARTS_5, HEARTS_6, HEARTS_7,
    HEARTS_8, HEARTS_9 };
```

Lines 49 through 53 declare a string array named g_imageFiles that is initialized with the names of the image files for the cards:

```
string g_imageFiles[NUM_CARDS] = { "Cards/Ace_hearts.png",
                "Cards/2_hearts.png", "Cards/3_hearts.png",
                "Cards/4_hearts.png", "Cards/5_hearts.png",
                "Cards/6_hearts.png", "Cards/7_hearts.png",
                "Cards/8_hearts.png", "Cards/9_hearts.png" };
```

Note that a parallel relationship exists between the g_cardSprites array and the g_imageFiles array. Recall from Chapter 6 that parallel arrays are two or more arrays that hold related data, and the related elements in each array are accessed with a common subscript. In this case, element 0 of the g_cardSprites array holds the sprite index for the ace of hearts card, and element 0 of the g_imageFiles array holds the name of the image file for the ace of hearts card. This parallel relationship exists for all the corresponding elements of the two arrays.

Line 56 declares an int variable named g_cardsDealt, initialized with the value 0. This variable will keep count of the number of cards that have been dealt.

Line 59 declares a float variable named g_cardX, initialized with the value of the STARTING_X constant. The g_cardX variable holds the X-coordinate of the next card that will be dealt.

The app::Begin function appears in lines 62 through 82. Here is a summary of its code:

- Line 65 sets the text for the window's title bar.
- Line 68 sets the virtual resolution.
- Line 71 adds the virtual button, and line 72 displays the string "Deal" on the button.
- Line 75 creates the sprite for the card backface, and line 78 positions the backface on the screen.
- Line 81 calls the createCardSprites function, which creates the card sprites and then hides them. (The definition of the createCardSprites function appears in lines 130 through 141.)

The app::Loop function appears in lines 85 through 121. Here is a summary of its code:

- Line 88 declares the cardX and cardY variables that will hold the X- and Y-coordinates of the cards as they are displayed on the screen.
- The if statement in line 91 determines whether the number of cards dealt is less than the number of cards. If so, cards are still left in the deck, and the following actions take place:
  - Line 94 determines whether the virtual button is being clicked. If so, the following actions take place:
    - Lines 97 and 98 position the next card sprite on the screen.
    - Line 101 makes the card sprite visible.

- Lines 104 and 105 calculate the next card's X-coordinate.
- Line 108 increments the g_cardsDealt variable, which holds the number of cards dealt.
- If all the cards have been dealt, the program jumps to the else clause in line 111. Line 115 displays the message "All cards are dealt." Line 116 makes the card backface invisible.
- Line 120 updates the screen.

The createCardSprites function appears in lines 130 through 141. The for loop that starts in line 132 creates all the card sprites, using the elements of the g_cardSprites array as the sprite indices and the elements of the g_imageFiles array as the names of the corresponding image files. After each sprite is created, the statement in line 139 makes it invisible.

Figure 10-9 shows how the first element of the array holds the index of the ace of hearts sprite, the second element holds the index of the two of hearts sprite, and so on.

Figure 10-9 The g_cardSprites array

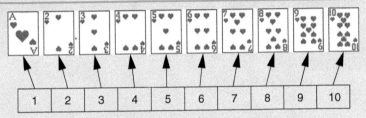

The g_cardSprites array

In the Spotlight:
Shuffling an Array

In Program 10-5, the card sprite numbers were stored in the g_cardSprites array in the following order: ace of hearts, two of hearts, three of hearts, and so forth. When the cards were dealt from the deck, they were displayed on the screen in the order that their sprite numbers were stored in the array. If you want to write a card game program, however, you will probably want a shuffled deck, instead of one in which the cards are arranged in order.

To *shuffle* an array means to randomly rearrange its contents. Program 10-6 shows a modified version of the DealCards program, in which we have added a function that shuffles the contents of the g_cardSprites array. The shuffle function is called just after the card sprites are created, so when the user clicks the virtual button to deal the cards, they are displayed in random order. Figure 10-10 shows an example.

Figure 10-10 Cards dealt in random order

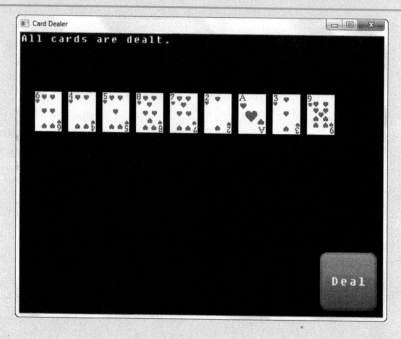

Program 10-6 (ShuffleCards)

```
1 // Includes, namespace and prototypes
2 #include "template.h"
3 #include <string>        // Needed for string class
4 using namespace std;     // Needed for string class
5 using namespace AGK;
6 app App;
7
8 // Function prototypes
9 void createCardSprites();
10 void shuffle();
11 void swap(int &, int &);
12
13 // Constants for the screen resolution
14 const int SCREEN_WIDTH  = 640;  // Screen width
15 const int SCREEN_HEIGHT = 480;  // Screen height
16
17 // Constants for the virtual button
18 const int   BUTTON_INDEX = 1;
19 const int   BUTTON_SIZE  = 100;
20 const float BUTTON_X     = 580;
21 const float BUTTON_Y     = 420;
22
23 // Constants for card sprite numbers
24 const int HEARTS_ACE = 1;
25 const int HEARTS_2   = 2;
26 const int HEARTS_3   = 3;
```

```
27 const int HEARTS_4    = 4;
28 const int HEARTS_5    = 5;
29 const int HEARTS_6    = 6;
30 const int HEARTS_7    = 7;
31 const int HEARTS_8    = 8;
32 const int HEARTS_9    = 9;
33 const int BACKFACE    = 10;
34
35 // Constants for card screen placement
36 const float STARTING_X    = 25;
37 const float CARD_Y        = 100;
38 const float CARD_DISTANCE = 10;
39 const float BACKFACE_X    = 25;
40 const float BACKFACE_Y    = 200;
41
42 // Constant for the number of cards
43 const int NUM_CARDS = 9;
44
45 // Array holding the card sprite numbers.
46 int g_cardSprites[NUM_CARDS] = { HEARTS_ACE, HEARTS_2,
47     HEARTS_3, HEARTS_4, HEARTS_5, HEARTS_6, HEARTS_7,
48     HEARTS_8, HEARTS_9 };
49
50 // Array holding the names of the card image files
51 string g_imageFiles[NUM_CARDS] = { "Cards/Ace_hearts.png",
52              "Cards/2_hearts.png", "Cards/3_hearts.png",
53              "Cards/4_hearts.png", "Cards/5_hearts.png",
54              "Cards/6_hearts.png", "Cards/7_hearts.png",
55              "Cards/8_hearts.png", "Cards/9_hearts.png" };
56
57 // Variable to hold the number of cards dealt
58 int g_cardsDealt = 0;
59
60 // Variable to hold each card's X-coordinate
61 float g_cardX = STARTING_X;
62
63 // Begin app, called once at the start
64 void app::Begin( void )
65 {
66     // Set the window title.
67     agk::SetWindowTitle("Card Dealer");
68
69     // Set the virtual resolution.
70     agk::SetVirtualResolution(SCREEN_WIDTH, SCREEN_HEIGHT);
71
72     // Add the virtual button.
73     agk::AddVirtualButton(BUTTON_INDEX, BUTTON_X, BUTTON_Y, BUTTON_SIZE);
74     agk::SetVirtualButtonText(BUTTON_INDEX, "Deal");
75
76     // Create the backface card sprite.
77     agk::CreateSprite(BACKFACE, "Cards/Backface_Red.png");
78
79     // Position the backface card sprite.
80     agk::SetSpritePosition(BACKFACE, BACKFACE_X, BACKFACE_Y);
```

```
 81
 82     // Create the card sprites.
 83     createCardSprites();
 84
 85     // Shuffle the card sprites.
 86     shuffle();
 87 }
 88
 89 // Main loop, called every frame
 90 void app::Loop ( void )
 91 {
 92     // Variables for the card location
 93     float cardX, cardY;
 94
 95     // Are cards left to be dealt?
 96     if (g_cardsDealt < NUM_CARDS)
 97     {
 98         // Check for a button press.
 99         if (agk::GetVirtualButtonPressed(BUTTON_INDEX))
100         {
101             // Position the card sprite that is being dealt.
102             agk::SetSpritePosition(g_cardSprites[g_cardsDealt],
103                                     g_cardX, CARD_Y);
104
105             // Make the card sprite visible.
106             agk::SetSpriteVisible(g_cardSprites[g_cardsDealt], 1);
107
108             // Calculate the next card's X-coordinate.
109             g_cardX += agk::GetSpriteWidth(g_cardSprites[g_cardsDealt]) +
110                     CARD_DISTANCE;
111
112             // Increment the number of cards dealt.
113             g_cardsDealt++;
114         }
115     }
116     else
117     {
118         // All cards are dealt. Print a message and hide
119         // the backface card.
120         agk::Print("All cards are dealt.");
121         agk::SetSpriteVisible(BACKFACE, 0);
122     }
123
124     // Refresh the screen.
125     agk::Sync();
126 }
127
128 // Called when the app ends
129 void app::End ( void )
130 {
131 }
132
133 // The createCardSprites function creates the card sprites
134 // and makes them invisible.
135 void createCardSprites()
```

```
136 {
137     for (int count = 0; count < NUM_CARDS; count++)
138     {
139         // Create the next card sprite.
140         agk::CreateSprite(g_cardSprites[count],
141                           g_imageFiles[count].c_str());
142
143         // Make the sprite invisible.
144         agk::SetSpriteVisible(g_cardSprites[count], 0);
145     }
146 }
147
148 // The shuffle function shuffles the elements of the
149 // g_cardSprites array randomly.
150 void shuffle()
151 {
152     // Variable to hold a random subscript
153     int randomSub;
154
155     // Step through the array, swapping each element with
156     // a random subscript.
157     for (int index = 0; index < NUM_CARDS; index++)
158     {
159         // Get a random subscript.
160         randomSub = agk::Random(0, NUM_CARDS - 1);
161
162         // Swap two elements.
163         swap(g_cardSprites[index], g_cardSprites[randomSub]);
164     }
165 }
166
167 // The swap function accepts two int arguments, passed
168 // by reference. The function swaps the contents of the
169 // two arguments.
170 void swap(int &a, int &b)
171 {
172     // Assign a to temp.
173     int temp = a;
174
175     // Assign b to a.
176     a = b;
177
178     // Assign temp to b.
179     b = temp;
180 }
```

Inside the app::Begin function, in line 86, we call the shuffle function, which is defined in lines 150 through 165. Before we look at the code, let's take a look at the general logic used to shuffle the array's contents. The algorithm works like this:

For each element in the array:
Randomly select another element
Swap the contents of this element with the randomly selected element

Now let's look at the code. Line 153 declares a local int variable named randomSub, which will hold a randomly generated subscript. The loop that begins in line 157 iterates once for each element in the array. (Inside the loop, the index variable will be assigned the values 0 through NUM_CARDS - 1.) Line 160 generates a random number in the range of 0 through NUM_CARDS - 1 and assigns the number to randomNum. Then line 163 calls the swap function, passing numbers[index] and numbers[randomNum] as arguments. These arguments are passed by reference, and after the function call is complete, the contents of the two array elements will be swapped.

Swapping Array Elements

Before we look at the code for the swap function, let's briefly discuss the process of swapping two items in computer memory. Assume we have the following variable declarations:

```
int a = 1;
int b = 9;
```

Suppose we want to swap the values in these variables so variable a contains 9 and variable b contains 1. At first, you might think that we only need to assign the variables to each other, like this:

```
// ERROR! This does NOT swap the variables.
a = b;
b = a;
```

To understand why this doesn't work, let's step through the code. The first statement is a = b;. This causes the value 9 to be assigned to a. But, what happens to the value 1 that was previously stored in a? Remember, when you assign a new value to a variable, the new value replaces any value that was previously stored in the variable. So the old value, 1, will be thrown away. Then the next statement is b = a;. Because variable a contains 9, this assigns 9 to b. After these statements execute, both variables a and b will contain the value 9.

To successfully swap the contents of two variables, we need a third variable to serve as a temporary storage location:

```
int temp;
```

Then we can perform the following steps to swap the values in variables a and b:

- Assign the value of a to temp.
- Assign the value of b to a.
- Assign the value of temp to b.

Now let's look at the code for the swap function, which appears in lines 170 through 180. The function has two reference parameters, a and b. It is critical that these parameters be reference variables because the function will need to change the values of the arguments that are passed into them. Line 173 assigns the value of a to the local variable temp, line 176 assigns the value of b to a, and line 179 assigns the value of temp to b. After these steps have been performed, the arguments that were passed into a and b will be swapped.

Sorting an Array

Many programming tasks require that the data in an array be sorted in some order. If an array is sorted in *ascending order*, it means the values in the array are stored from lowest to highest. If the values are sorted in *descending order*, they are stored from highest to lowest. To sort the data in an array, the programmer must use an appropriate sorting algorithm. A *sorting algorithm* is a technique for stepping through an array and rearranging its contents in some order. In this chapter, we will examine the *selection sort algorithm*.

The selection sort algorithm works like this: The smallest value in the array is located and moved to element 0. Then, the next smallest value is located and moved to element 1. This process continues until all the elements have been placed in their proper order. Let's see how the selection sort works when arranging the elements of the array in Figure 10-11.

Figure 10-11 Values in an array

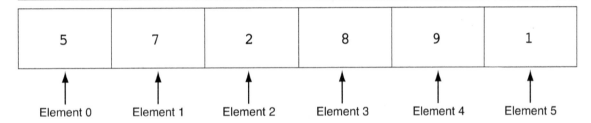

The selection sort scans the array, starting at element 0, and locates the element with the smallest value. Then the contents of this element are swapped with the contents of element 0. In this example, the 1 stored in element 5 is swapped with the 5 stored in element 0. After the swap, the array appears as shown in Figure 10-12.

Figure 10-12 Values in the array after the first swap

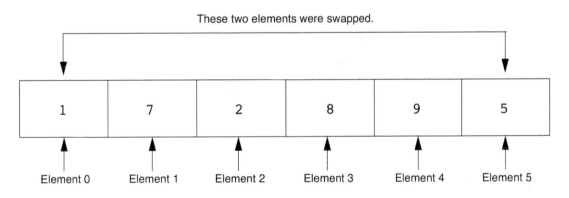

Then, the algorithm repeats the process, but because element 0 already contains the smallest value in the array, it can be left out of the procedure. This time, the algorithm begins the scan at element 1. In this example, the value in element 2 is swapped with the value in element 1. Then the array appears as shown in Figure 10-13.

Figure 10-13 Values in the array after the second swap

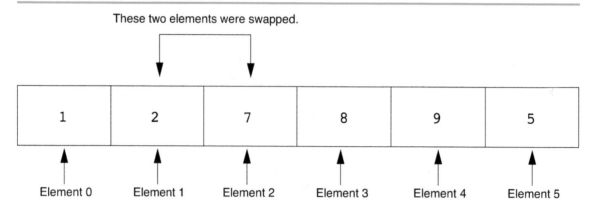

Once again the process is repeated, but this time the scan begins at element 2. The algorithm will find that element 5 contains the next smallest value. This element's value is swapped with that of element 2, causing the array to appear as shown in Figure 10-14.

Figure 10-14 Values in the array after the third swap

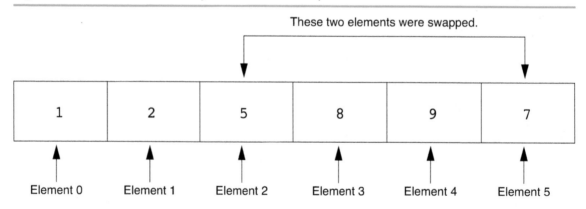

Next, the scanning begins at element 3. Its value is swapped with that of element 5, causing the array to appear as shown in Figure 10-15.

Figure 10-15 Values in the array after the fourth swap

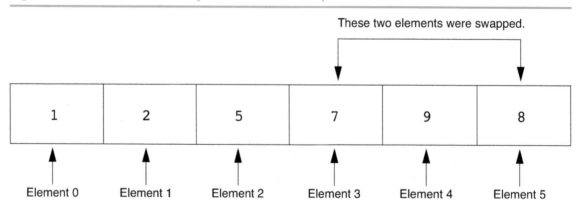

At this point only two elements are left to sort. The algorithm finds that the value in element 5 is smaller than that of element 4, so the two are swapped. This puts the array in its final arrangement, as shown in Figure 10-16.

Figure 10-16 Values in the array after the fifth swap

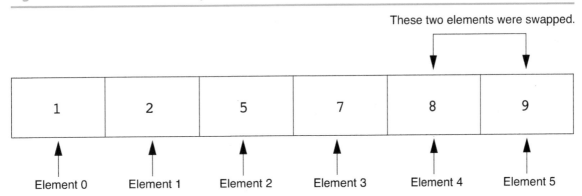

Program 10-7 shows a demonstration of the selection sort algorithm using the simulated deck of cards that you saw in Programs 10-5 and 10-6. This program has two virtual buttons: one that sorts the cards and displays them, and another that shuffles the cards and displays them. Figure 10-17 shows an example of the program's output. The screen on the left shows the cards after they have been sorted, and the screen on the right shows the cards after they have been shuffled.

Figure 10-17 The cards sorted and shuffled

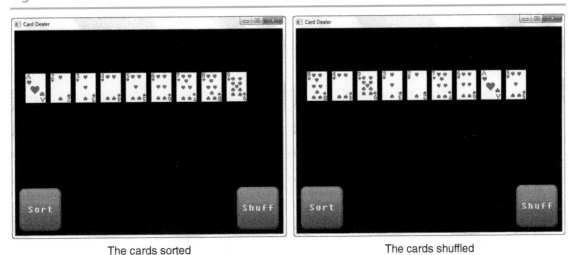

The cards sorted   The cards shuffled

Program 10-7   (SortAndShuffle)

```
1 // Includes, namespace and prototypes
2 #include "template.h"
3 #include <string>      // Needed for string class
4 using namespace std;   // Needed for string class
5 using namespace AGK;
```

```
 6 app App;
 7
 8 // Function prototypes
 9 void createCardSprites();
10 void shuffle();
11 void selectionSort();
12 void swap(int &, int &);
13 void displayCards();
14
15 // Constants for the screen resolution
16 const int SCREEN_WIDTH  = 640;
17 const int SCREEN_HEIGHT = 480;
18
19 // Constants for the virtual buttons
20 const int    BUTTON_SIZE  = 100;
21
22 const int    SORT_BUTTON_INDEX = 1;
23 const float SORT_BUTTON_X      = 60;
24 const float SORT_BUTTON_Y      = 420;
25
26 const int    SHUFFLE_BUTTON_INDEX = 2;
27 const float SHUFFLE_BUTTON_X      = 580;
28 const float SHUFFLE_BUTTON_Y      = 420;
29
30 // Constants for card sprite numbers
31 const int HEARTS_ACE = 1;
32 const int HEARTS_2   = 2;
33 const int HEARTS_3   = 3;
34 const int HEARTS_4   = 4;
35 const int HEARTS_5   = 5;
36 const int HEARTS_6   = 6;
37 const int HEARTS_7   = 7;
38 const int HEARTS_8   = 8;
39 const int HEARTS_9   = 9;
40 const int BACKFACE   = 10;
41
42 // Constants for card screen placement
43 const float STARTING_X    = 25;
44 const float CARD_Y        = 100;
45 const float CARD_DISTANCE = 10;
46
47 // Constant for the number of cards
48 const int NUM_CARDS = 9;
49
50 // Array holding the card sprite numbers.
51 int g_cardSprites[NUM_CARDS] = { HEARTS_ACE, HEARTS_2,
52      HEARTS_3, HEARTS_4, HEARTS_5, HEARTS_6, HEARTS_7,
53      HEARTS_8, HEARTS_9 };
54
55 // Array holding the names of the card image files
56 string g_imageFiles[NUM_CARDS] = { "Cards/Ace_hearts.png",
57               "Cards/2_hearts.png", "Cards/3_hearts.png",
58               "Cards/4_hearts.png", "Cards/5_hearts.png",
59               "Cards/6_hearts.png", "Cards/7_hearts.png",
60               "Cards/8_hearts.png", "Cards/9_hearts.png" };
```

```
61
62  // Begin app, called once at the start
63  void app::Begin( void )
64  {
65      // Set the window title.
66      agk::SetWindowTitle("Card Dealer");
67
68      // Set the virtual resolution.
69      agk::SetVirtualResolution(SCREEN_WIDTH, SCREEN_HEIGHT);
70
71      // Add the virtual sort button.
72      agk::AddVirtualButton(SORT_BUTTON_INDEX, SORT_BUTTON_X,
73                            SORT_BUTTON_Y, BUTTON_SIZE);
74      agk::SetVirtualButtonText(SORT_BUTTON_INDEX, "Sort");
75
76      // Add the virtual shuffle button.
77      agk::AddVirtualButton(SHUFFLE_BUTTON_INDEX, SHUFFLE_BUTTON_X,
78                            SHUFFLE_BUTTON_Y, BUTTON_SIZE);
79      agk::SetVirtualButtonText(SHUFFLE_BUTTON_INDEX, "Shuff");
80
81      // Create the card sprites.
82      createCardSprites();
83  }
84
85  // Main loop, called every frame
86  void app::Loop ( void )
87  {
88      // Check for the shuffle button.
89      if (agk::GetVirtualButtonPressed(SHUFFLE_BUTTON_INDEX))
90      {
91          // Shuffle the card sprites.
92          shuffle();
93
94          // Display the cards.
95          displayCards();
96      }
97
98      // Check for the sort button.
99      if (agk::GetVirtualButtonPressed(SORT_BUTTON_INDEX))
100     {
101         // Shuffle the card sprites.
102         selectionSort();
103
104         // Display the cards.
105         displayCards();
106     }
107
108     // Refresh the screen.
109     agk::Sync();
110 }
111
112 // Called when the app ends
113 void app::End ( void )
114 {
115 }
```

```
116
117  // The createCardSprites function creates the card sprites
118  // and makes them invisible.
119  void createCardSprites()
120  {
121      for (int count = 0; count < NUM_CARDS; count++)
122      {
123          // Create the next card sprite.
124          agk::CreateSprite(g_cardSprites[count],
125                            g_imageFiles[count].c_str());
126
127          // Make the sprite invisible.
128          agk::SetSpriteVisible(g_cardSprites[count], 0);
129      }
130  }
131
132  // The shuffle function shuffles the elements of the
133  // g_cardSprites array randomly.
134  void shuffle()
135  {
136      // Variable to hold a random subscript
137      int randomSub;
138
139      // Step through the array, swapping each element with
140      // a random subscript.
141      for (int index = 0; index < NUM_CARDS; index++)
142      {
143          // Get a random subscript.
144          randomSub = agk::Random(0, NUM_CARDS - 1);
145
146          // Swap two elements.
147          swap(g_cardSprites[index], g_cardSprites[randomSub]);
148      }
149  }
150
151  // The selectionSort function sorts the g_cardSprites array
152  // in ascending order.
153  void selectionSort()
154  {
155      int startScan; // Starting position of the scan
156      int index;     // To hold a subscript value
157      int minIndex;  // Element with smallest value in the scan
158      int minValue;  // The smallest value found in the scan
159
160      // The outer loop iterates once for each element in the
161      // g_cardSprites array. The startScan variable marks the position
162      // where the scan should begin.
163      for (startScan = 0; startScan < (NUM_CARDS - 1); startScan++)
164      {
165          // Assume the first element in the scannable area
166          // is the smallest value.
167          minIndex = startScan;
168          minValue = g_cardSprites[startScan];
169
170          // Scan the array starting at the 2nd element in the
```

```
171            // scannable area. We are looking for the smallest
172            // value in the scannable area.
173            for(index = startScan + 1; index < NUM_CARDS; index++)
174            {
175                if (g_cardSprites[index] < minValue)
176                {
177                    minValue = g_cardSprites[index];
178                    minIndex = index;
179                }
180            }
181
182            // Swap the element with the smallest value
183            // with the first element in the scannable area.
184            swap( g_cardSprites[minIndex], g_cardSprites[startScan] );
185        }
186 }
187
188 // The swap function accepts two int arguments, passed
189 // by reference. The function swaps the contents of the
190 // two arguments.
191 void swap(int &a, int &b)
192 {
193     // Assign a to temp.
194     int temp = a;
195
196     // Assign b to a.
197     a = b;
198
199     // Assign temp to b.
200     b = temp;
201 }
202
203 // The displayCards function displays the card sprites
204 // in the order that their sprite numbers appear in
205 // the g_cardSprites array.
206 void displayCards()
207 {
208     // Variable to hold each card's X-coordinate
209     float cardX = STARTING_X;
210
211     for (int index = 0; index < NUM_CARDS; index++)
212     {
213         // Position this card sprite.
214         agk::SetSpritePosition(g_cardSprites[index],
215                               cardX, CARD_Y);
216
217         // Make the card sprite visible.
218         agk::SetSpriteVisible(g_cardSprites[index], 1);
219
220         // Calculate the next card's X-coordinate.
221         cardX += agk::GetSpriteWidth(g_cardSprites[index]) +
222                                     CARD_DISTANCE;
223     }
224 }
```

NOTE: You can modify the selectionSort function so it sorts the array in descending order by changing the less-than operator in line 175 to a greater-than operator, as shown here:

```
if (g_cardSprites[index] > maxValue)
```

Notice that we have also changed the name of the minValue variable to maxValue, which is more appropriate for a descending order sort. You would need to make this change throughout the function.

10.3 Tile Maps

CONCEPT: Tiles are small rectangular images that are commonly used to construct the background imagery in a game. A tile map is a two-dimensional array that specifies tiles and their locations on the screen.

VideoNote

Tile Maps

Tiles are small rectangular images that can be put together to form a larger image. In the early days of video games, computers had much less memory and much lower processing speeds than they do today. Game developers commonly used tiles to construct the background imagery in games. Breaking a large image down into many smaller ones was more memory efficient, and processing the smaller images was faster. Many game programmers today still prefer to use tiles. In this section, we will discuss how two-dimensional arrays are used to map the locations of tiles on the screen.

For example, the image on the left in Figure 10-18 shows a screen from a game (this also appears as Figure C-11 in the book's color insert). We are looking down on the scene, which is a grass field with a stone path that leads around a tree and some rocks. The image on the right shows how the image is actually constructed of small tiles. This particular scene has 10 rows and 10 columns of tiles, for a total of 100 tiles. In this example, the entire screen is 640 pixels wide by 480 pixels high. So each tile is 64 pixels wide by 48 pixels high.

Figure 10-18 A tile-based image

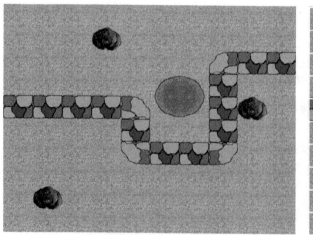
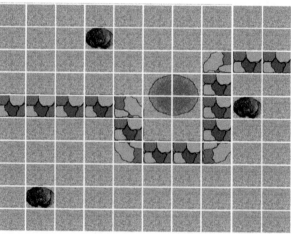

Although a total of 100 tiles are in the image, many of them are duplicates. The entire image is actually constructed of only 11 tiles, which are shown in Figure 10-19 (this also appears as Figure C-12 in the book's color insert). One tile is used for the grass, five tiles for different sections of the path, one tile for the rocks, and four tiles for the different sections of the tree.

Figure 10-19 Tiles

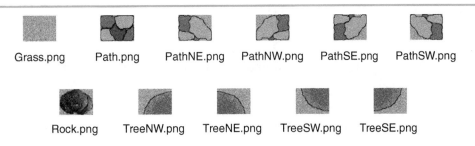

Grass.png   Path.png   PathNE.png   PathNW.png   PathSE.png   PathSW.png

Rock.png   TreeNW.png   TreeNE.png   TreeSW.png   TreeSE.png

> **NOTE:** The letters NE, NW, SE, and SW in the tile names stand for northeast, northwest, southeast, and southwest.

Let's look at the steps we would take to construct the image shown in Figure 10-18 from the tiles shown in Figure 10-19. As usual we declare constants for the image indices, as shown here:

```
// Constants for the image indices
const int GRASS  = 1;
const int PATH   = 2;
const int PATHNE = 3;
const int PATHNW = 4;
const int PATHSE = 5;
const int PATHSW = 6;
const int TREENW = 7;
const int TREENE = 8;
const int TREESW = 9;
const int TREESE = 10;
const int ROCK   = 11;
```

We use these image indices when we load the tile images, as shown in the following function:

```
void loadTiles()
{
    agk::LoadImage(GRASS,  "Alec/Grass.png");
    agk::LoadImage(PATH,   "Alec/Path.png");
    agk::LoadImage(PATHNE, "Alec/PathNE.png");
    agk::LoadImage(PATHNW, "Alec/PathNW.png");
    agk::LoadImage(PATHSE, "Alec/PathSE.png");
    agk::LoadImage(PATHSW, "Alec/PathSW.png");
    agk::LoadImage(TREENE, "Alec/TreeNE.png");
```

```
    agk::LoadImage(TREENW,  "Alec/TreeNW.png");
    agk::LoadImage(TREESE,  "Alec/TreeSE.png");
    agk::LoadImage(TREESW,  "Alec/TreeSW.png");
    agk::LoadImage(ROCK,    "Alec/Rock.png");
}
```

We will also declare constants for the tile image sizes, as shown here:

```
// Constants for the tile image sizes
const int TILE_WIDTH  = 64;
const int TILE_HEIGHT = 48;
```

Then we create a two-dimensional int array to serve as the tile map. A *tile map* is an array that maps the location of each tile on the screen. In this example, the image is constructed using 10 rows of tiles, with each row containing 10 tiles. As a result, our tile map will be an array with 10 rows and 10 columns. Here are the constants that we will use as the array size declarators:

```
// Constants for the tile map size declarators
const int TILE_ROWS = 10;
const int TILE_COLS = 10;
```

Each element of the tile map array will hold the image number for a tile. For example, the element at subscript [0][0] will hold the image number for the first tile in the first row. (This is the tile in the upper-left corner of the screen.) The element at subscript [0][1] will hold the image number for the second tile in the first row. This continues until the last element in the array, at subscript [9][9], which will hold the image number for the tenth tile in the 10th row (the tile in the lower-right corner). The following code shows how we would declare and initialize the array:

```
int g_tileMap[TILE_ROWS][TILE_COLS] =
{ {GRASS, GRASS, GRASS, GRASS, GRASS,  GRASS, GRASS, GRASS,  GRASS, GRASS},
  {GRASS, GRASS, GRASS, ROCK,  GRASS,  GRASS, GRASS, GRASS,  GRASS, GRASS},
  {GRASS, GRASS, GRASS, GRASS, GRASS,  GRASS, GRASS, PATHNW, PATH,  PATH },
  {GRASS, GRASS, GRASS, GRASS, GRASS,  TREENW, TREENE, PATH,  GRASS, GRASS},
  {PATH,  PATH,  PATH,  PATH,  PATHNE, TREESW, TREESE, PATH,  ROCK,  GRASS},
  {GRASS, GRASS, GRASS, GRASS, PATH,   GRASS, GRASS, PATH,   GRASS, GRASS},
  {GRASS, GRASS, GRASS, GRASS, PATHSW, PATH,  PATH,  PATHSE, GRASS, GRASS},
  {GRASS, GRASS, GRASS, GRASS, GRASS,  GRASS, GRASS, GRASS,  GRASS, GRASS},
  {GRASS, ROCK,  GRASS, GRASS, GRASS,  GRASS, GRASS, GRASS,  GRASS, GRASS},
  {GRASS, GRASS, GRASS, GRASS, GRASS,  GRASS, GRASS, GRASS,  GRASS, GRASS}
};
```

To display the tiles we will write a function such as shown in the following code. This is obviously not a complete program, but we have provided line numbers so we can discuss each part of the code.

```
1 // The displayTiles function displays the tiles, as
2 // specified by the tile map.
3 void displayTiles()
4 {
```

```
 5     // Variables for the tile coordinates
 6     float x = 0, y = 0;
 7
 8     // Variable to temporarily hold a sprite index
 9     int spriteIndex;
10
11     // Display all the tiles specified in the map.
12     for (int r = 0; r < TILE_ROWS; r++)
13     {
14         // Set x to 0.
15         x = 0;
16
17         // Display all the tiles in this row.
18         for (int c = 0; c < TILE_COLS; c++)
19         {
20             // Create a sprite for this tile.
21             spriteIndex = agk::CreateSprite(g_tileMap[r][c]);
22
23             // Set the tile's position.
24             agk::SetSpritePosition(spriteIndex, x, y);
25
26             // Update the X-coordinate for the next tile.
27             x += TILE_WIDTH;
28         }
29
30         // Increase y for the next row.
31         y += TILE_HEIGHT;
32     }
33 }
```

In line 6 we declare two local float variables named x and y. These variables will hold the coordinates for each tile that we display. The for loop in lines 12 through 28 displays each row of tiles. Inside the loop, in line 15, we set x to 0 because the X-coordinate of the first tile in each row is 0. Then the nested for loop that appears in lines 18 through 28 displays each of the tiles in the row. When this loop iterates, line 21 creates a sprite, using the tile image specified in the g_tileMap array, line 24 sets the sprite's position, and line 27 increases the value of x for the next tile. After this loop finishes all its iterations, a complete row of tiles will have been displayed. Then line 31 increases the y variable for the next row.

The code in Program 10-8 demonstrates how this works in a complete program. When you execute this program, it will display the image previously shown on the left of Figure 10-18.

Program 10-8   (TileDemo)

```
1 // Includes, namespace and prototypes
2 #include "template.h"
3 using namespace AGK;
4 app App;
```

```
 5
 6 // Function prototypes
 7 void loadTiles();
 8 void displayTiles();
 9
10 // Constants for the screen resolution
11 const int SCREEN_WIDTH  = 640;
12 const int SCREEN_HEIGHT = 480;
13
14 // Constants for the image indices
15 const int GRASS  = 1;
16 const int PATH   = 2;
17 const int PATHNE = 3;
18 const int PATHNW = 4;
19 const int PATHSE = 5;
20 const int PATHSW = 6;
21 const int TREENW = 7;
22 const int TREENE = 8;
23 const int TREESW = 9;
24 const int TREESE = 10;
25 const int ROCK   = 11;
26
27 // Constants for the tile image sizes
28 const int TILE_WIDTH  = 64;
29 const int TILE_HEIGHT = 48;
30
31 // Constants for the tile map size declarators
32 const int TILE_ROWS = 10;
33 const int TILE_COLS = 10;
34
35 // The tile map
36 int g_tileMap[TILE_ROWS][TILE_COLS] =
37 { {GRASS, GRASS, GRASS, GRASS, GRASS,  GRASS,  GRASS,  GRASS,  GRASS,  GRASS},
38   {GRASS, GRASS, GRASS, ROCK,  GRASS,  GRASS,  GRASS,  GRASS,  GRASS,  GRASS},
39   {GRASS, GRASS, GRASS, GRASS, GRASS,  GRASS,  GRASS,  PATHNW, PATH,   PATH },
40   {GRASS, GRASS, GRASS, GRASS, GRASS,  TREENW, TREENE, PATH,   GRASS,  GRASS},
41   {PATH,  PATH,  PATH,  PATH,  PATHNE, TREESW, TREESE, PATH,   ROCK,   GRASS},
42   {GRASS, GRASS, GRASS, GRASS, PATH,   GRASS,  GRASS,  PATH,   GRASS,  GRASS},
43   {GRASS, GRASS, GRASS, GRASS, PATHSW, PATH,   PATH,   PATHSE, GRASS,  GRASS},
44   {GRASS, GRASS, GRASS, GRASS, GRASS,  GRASS,  GRASS,  GRASS,  GRASS,  GRASS},
45   {GRASS, ROCK,  GRASS, GRASS, GRASS,  GRASS,  GRASS,  GRASS,  GRASS,  GRASS},
46   {GRASS, GRASS, GRASS, GRASS, GRASS,  GRASS,  GRASS,  GRASS,  GRASS,  GRASS}
47 };
48
49 // Begin app, called once at the start
50 void app::Begin( void )
51 {
52    // Set the window title.
53    agk::SetWindowTitle("Walking Alec");
54
55    // Set the virtual resolution.
56    agk::SetVirtualResolution(SCREEN_WIDTH, SCREEN_HEIGHT);
57
58    // Load the tile images.
59    loadTiles();
```

```
60
61     // Create the tile sprites and display them.
62     displayTiles();
63 }
64
65 // Main loop, called every frame
66 void app::Loop ( void )
67 {
68     // Refresh the screen.
69     agk::Sync();
70 }
71
72 // Called when the app ends
73 void app::End ( void )
74 {
75 }
76
77 // The loadTiles function loads the images that will be
78 // used for tiles.
79 void loadTiles()
80 {
81     agk::LoadImage(GRASS,   "Alec/Grass.png");
82     agk::LoadImage(PATH,    "Alec/Path.png");
83     agk::LoadImage(PATHNE, "Alec/PathNE.png");
84     agk::LoadImage(PATHNW, "Alec/PathNW.png");
85     agk::LoadImage(PATHSE, "Alec/PathSE.png");
86     agk::LoadImage(PATHSW, "Alec/PathSW.png");
87     agk::LoadImage(TREENE, "Alec/TreeNE.png");
88     agk::LoadImage(TREENW, "Alec/TreeNW.png");
89     agk::LoadImage(TREESE, "Alec/TreeSE.png");
90     agk::LoadImage(TREESW, "Alec/TreeSW.png");
91     agk::LoadImage(ROCK,    "Alec/Rock.png");
92 }
93
94 // The displayTiles function displays the tiles, as
95 // specified by the tile map.
96 void displayTiles()
97 {
98     // Variables for the tile coordinates
99     float x = 0, y = 0;
100
101     // Variable to temporarily hold a sprite index
102     int spriteIndex;
103
104     // Display all the tiles specified in the map.
105     for (int r = 0; r < TILE_ROWS; r++)
106     {
107         // Set x to 0.
108         x = 0;
109
110         // Display all the tiles in this row.
111         for (int c = 0; c < TILE_COLS; c++)
112         {
113             // Create a sprite for this tile.
114             spriteIndex = agk::CreateSprite(g_tileMap[r][c]);
```

```
115
116             // Set the tile's position.
117             agk::SetSpritePosition(spriteIndex, x, y);
118
119             // Update the X-coordinate for the next tile.
120             x += TILE_WIDTH;
121          }
122
123       // Increase y for the next row.
124       y += TILE_HEIGHT;
125    }
126 }
```

Now that we've demonstrated the basic technique for displaying a set of tiles using a tile map, let's add some action. Program 10-9 displays the same set of tiles as Program 10-8 and also displays a sprite of a character that we've named Alec. When you run the program, you can use the arrow keys to make Alec walk around the screen.

Program 10-9   (WalkingAlec)

```
 1 // Includes, namespace and prototypes
 2 #include "template.h"
 3 using namespace AGK;
 4 app App;
 5
 6 // Function prototypes
 7 void loadTiles();
 8 void displayTiles();
 9 void updateAlecX(float);
10 void updateAlecY(float);
11
12 // Constants for the screen resolution
13 const int SCREEN_WIDTH  = 640;
14 const int SCREEN_HEIGHT = 480;
15
16 // Constants for the image numbers
17 const int GRASS  = 1;
18 const int PATH   = 2;
19 const int PATHNE = 3;
20 const int PATHNW = 4;
21 const int PATHSE = 5;
22 const int PATHSW = 6;
23 const int TREENW = 7;
24 const int TREENE = 8;
25 const int TREESW = 9;
26 const int TREESE = 10;
27 const int ROCK   = 11;
28
29 // Constants for the tile image sizes
30 const int TILE_WIDTH  = 64;
31 const int TILE_HEIGHT = 48;
```

```
32
33 // Constants for the tile map size declarators
34 const int TILE_ROWS = 10;
35 const int TILE_COLS = 10;
36
37 // Constants for the Alec sprite sheet
38 const int ALEC_IMAGE        = 12;  // Texture atlas image index
39 const int ALEC_SPRITE       = 100; // Alec's sprite index
40 const int ALEC_FRAME_WIDTH  = 40;  // Alec's frame width
41 const int ALEC_FRAME_HEIGHT = 75;  // Alec's frame height
42 const int ALEC_FRAME_COUNT  = 16;  // Alec's frame count
43 const int EAST_START        = 1;   // First frame for going east
44 const int EAST_END          = 4;   // Last frame for going east
45 const int NORTH_START       = 5;   // First frame for going north
46 const int NORTH_END         = 8;   // Last frame for going north
47 const int SOUTH_START       = 9;   // First frame for going south
48 const int SOUTH_END         = 12;  // Last frame for going south
49 const int WEST_START        = 13;  // First frame for going west
50 const int WEST_END          = 16;  // Last frame for going west
51 const int ALEC_FPS          = 5;   // Alec's frames per second
52 const int ANIMATION_LOOP    = 1;   // To make Alec loop
53 const float ALEC_STARTING_X = 0;   // Alec's starting X-coordinate
54 const float ALEC_STARTING_Y = 150; // Alec's starting Y-coordinate
55
56 // Constants for Alec's direction
57 const int NORTH  = 1;
58 const int SOUTH = 2;
59 const int EAST  = 3;
60 const int WEST  = 4;
61
62 // The tile map
63 int g_tileMap[TILE_ROWS][TILE_COLS] =
64 { {GRASS, GRASS, GRASS, GRASS, GRASS,  GRASS,  GRASS,  GRASS,   GRASS,  GRASS},
65   {GRASS, GRASS, GRASS, ROCK,  GRASS,  GRASS,  GRASS,  GRASS,   GRASS,  GRASS},
66   {GRASS, GRASS, GRASS, GRASS, GRASS,  GRASS,  GRASS,  PATHNW, PATH,   PATH },
67   {GRASS, GRASS, GRASS, GRASS, GRASS,  TREENW, TREENE, PATH,    GRASS,  GRASS},
68   {PATH,  PATH,  PATH,  PATH,  PATHNE, TREESW, TREESE, PATH,    ROCK,   GRASS},
69   {GRASS, GRASS, GRASS, GRASS, PATH,   GRASS,  GRASS,  PATH,    GRASS,  GRASS},
70   {GRASS, GRASS, GRASS, GRASS, PATHSW, PATH,   PATH,   PATHSE, GRASS,  GRASS},
71   {GRASS, GRASS, GRASS, GRASS, GRASS,  GRASS,  GRASS,  GRASS,   GRASS,  GRASS},
72   {GRASS, ROCK,  GRASS, GRASS, GRASS,  GRASS,  GRASS,  GRASS,   GRASS,  GRASS},
73   {GRASS, GRASS, GRASS, GRASS, GRASS,  GRASS,  GRASS,  GRASS,   GRASS,  GRASS}
74 };
75
76 // Variable for Alec's direction
77 int g_alecDirection = EAST;
78
79 // Begin app, called once at the start
80 void app::Begin( void )
81 {
82    // Set the window title.
83    agk::SetWindowTitle("Walking Alec");
84
85    // Set the virtual resolution.
86    agk::SetVirtualResolution(SCREEN_WIDTH, SCREEN_HEIGHT);
```

```
 87
 88      // Load the texture atlas.
 89      agk::LoadImage(ALEC_IMAGE, "Alec/Alec.png");
 90
 91      // Create the sprite using the texture atlas as the image.
 92      agk::CreateSprite(ALEC_SPRITE, ALEC_IMAGE);
 93
 94      // Make sure Alec is displayed on top of the tile sprites.
 95      agk::SetSpriteDepth(ALEC_SPRITE, 0);
 96
 97      // Set Alec's starting position.
 98      agk::SetSpritePosition(ALEC_SPRITE, ALEC_STARTING_X,
 99                             ALEC_STARTING_Y);
100
101      // Set the sprite animation.
102      agk::SetSpriteAnimation(ALEC_SPRITE, ALEC_FRAME_WIDTH,
103                             ALEC_FRAME_HEIGHT, ALEC_FRAME_COUNT);
104
105      // Load the tile images.
106      loadTiles();
107
108      // Create the tile sprites and display them.
109      displayTiles();
110 }
111
112 // Main loop, called every frame
113 void app::Loop ( void )
114 {
115      // Get the state of the direction keys.
116      float directionX = agk::GetDirectionX();
117      float directionY = agk::GetDirectionY();
118
119      // If the right or left arrow keys are pressed,
120      // update Alec's X-coordinate.
121      if (directionX != 0)
122      {
123         updateAlecX(directionX);
124      }
125
126      // If the up or down arrow keys are pressed,
127      // update Alec's Y-coordinate.
128      if (directionY != 0)
129      {
130         updateAlecY(directionY);
131      }
132
133      // Refresh the screen.
134      agk::Sync();
135 }
136
137 // Called when the app ends
138 void app::End ( void )
139 {
140 }
141
```

```
142 // The loadTiles function loads the images that will be
143 // used for tiles.
144 void loadTiles()
145 {
146    agk::LoadImage(GRASS,  "Alec/Grass.png");
147    agk::LoadImage(PATH,   "Alec/Path.png");
148    agk::LoadImage(PATHNE, "Alec/PathNE.png");
149    agk::LoadImage(PATHNW, "Alec/PathNW.png");
150    agk::LoadImage(PATHSE, "Alec/PathSE.png");
151    agk::LoadImage(PATHSW, "Alec/PathSW.png");
152    agk::LoadImage(TREENE, "Alec/TreeNE.png");
153    agk::LoadImage(TREENW, "Alec/TreeNW.png");
154    agk::LoadImage(TREESE, "Alec/TreeSE.png");
155    agk::LoadImage(TREESW, "Alec/TreeSW.png");
156    agk::LoadImage(ROCK,   "Alec/Rock.png");
157 }
158
159 // The displayTiles function displays the tiles, as
160 // specified by the tile map.
161 void displayTiles()
162 {
163    // Variables for the tile coordinates
164    float x = 0, y = 0;
165
166    // Variable to temporarily hold a sprite index
167    int spriteIndex;
168
169    // Display all the tiles specified in the map.
170    for (int r = 0; r < TILE_ROWS; r++)
171    {
172       // Set x to 0.
173       x = 0;
174
175       // Display all the tiles in this row.
176       for (int c = 0; c < TILE_COLS; c++)
177       {
178          // Create a sprite for this tile.
179          spriteIndex = agk::CreateSprite(g_tileMap[r][c]);
180
181          // Set the tile's position.
182          agk::SetSpritePosition(spriteIndex, x, y);
183
184          // Update the X-coordinate for the next tile.
185          x += TILE_WIDTH;
186       }
187
188       // Increase y for the next row.
189       y += TILE_HEIGHT;
190    }
191 }
192
193 // The updateAlecX function turns Alec either east or west,
194 // depending on which arrow key is being pressed, and moves
195 // him to his new X-coordinate.
196 void updateAlecX(float directionX)
```

```
197 {
198     float alecX,    // Alec's current X position
199           newX;      // Alec's new X-coordinate
200
201     // Get Alec's X-coordinate
202     alecX = agk::GetSpriteX(ALEC_SPRITE);
203
204     // Which key was pressed? Right or left?
205     if (directionX > 0)
206     {
207         // Turn Alec east
208         agk::PlaySprite(ALEC_SPRITE, ALEC_FPS,
209                         ANIMATION_LOOP,
210                         EAST_START, EAST_END);
211
212         // Save Alec's current direction.
213         g_alecDirection = EAST;
214
215         // Calculate Alec's new X-coordinate.
216         newX = alecX + 1;
217     }
218     else if (directionX < 0)
219     {
220         // Turn Alec west
221         agk::PlaySprite(ALEC_SPRITE, ALEC_FPS,
222                         ANIMATION_LOOP,
223                         WEST_START, WEST_END);
224
225         // Save Alec's current direction.
226         g_alecDirection = WEST;
227
228         // Calculate Alec's new X-coordinate
229         newX = alecX - 1;
230     }
231
232     // Move Alec
233     agk::SetSpriteX(ALEC_SPRITE, newX);
234 }
235
236 // The updateAlecY function turns Alec either north or south,
237 // depending on which arrow key is being pressed, and moves
238 // him to his new Y-coordinate.
239 void updateAlecY(float directionY)
240 {
241     float alecY,    // Alec's current Y position
242           newY;      // Alec's new Y-coordinate
243
244     // Get Alec's Y-coordinate
245     alecY = agk::GetSpriteY(ALEC_SPRITE);
246
247     // Which key was pressed? Up or down?
248     if (directionY < 0)
249     {
250         // Turn Alec north
251         agk::PlaySprite(ALEC_SPRITE, ALEC_FPS,
252                         ANIMATION_LOOP,
253                         NORTH_START, NORTH_END);
```

```
254
255        // Save Alec's current direction.
256        g_alecDirection = NORTH;
257
258        // Calculate Alec's new Y-coordinate.
259        newY = alecY - 1;
260    }
261    else if (directionY > 0)
262    {
263        // Turn Alec south
264        agk::PlaySprite(ALEC_SPRITE, ALEC_FPS,
265                        ANIMATION_LOOP,
266                        SOUTH_START, SOUTH_END);
267
268        // Save Alec's current direction.
269        g_alecDirection = SOUTH;
270
271        // Calculate Alec's new Y-coordinate.
272        newY = alecY + 1;
273    }
274
275    // Move Alec
276    agk::SetSpriteY(ALEC_SPRITE, newY);
277 }
```

The Alec character is an animated sprite, created from the Alec.png texture atlas shown in Figure 10-20 (this also appears as Figure C-13 in the book's color insert). When you press the *Right* arrow key, the program uses the four frames in the top row (frames 1 through 4) to make Alec face east as he walks. When you press the *Up* arrow key, the program uses the four frames in the second row (frames 5 through 8) to make Alec face north as he walks. When you press the *Down* arrow key, the program uses the four frames in the third row (frames 9 through 12) to make Alec face south as he walks. When you press the *Left* arrow key, the program uses the four frames in the fourth row (frames 13 through 16) to make Alec face west as he walks.

Figure 10-20 Animated sprite frames for the Alec character (stored in Alec.png)

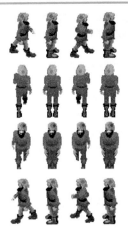

Figure 10-21 shows the screen that is displayed when you start the program, with Alec positioned on the stone pathway (this also appears as Figure C-14 in the book's color insert).

Figure 10-21 Starting screen from Program 10-9

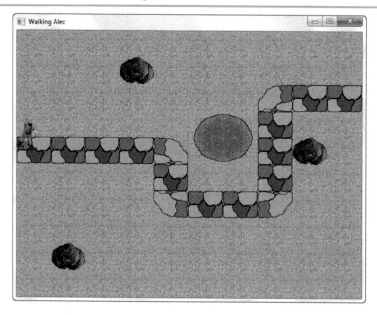

Let's analyze the program. Lines 17 through 27 declare the constants that we will use as image numbers for the tiles. Lines 30 and 31 declare constants for the tile image width and height. Lines 34 and 35 declare constants for the numbers of tile rows and columns that we will display. (These constants will be used as size declarators for the two-dimensional tile map array.)

Lines 38 through 54 declare the following constants that are used for the Alec character's animated sprite:

```
37   // Constants for the Alec sprite sheet
38   const int ALEC_IMAGE        = 12;  // Texture atlas image index
39   const int ALEC_SPRITE       = 100; // Alec's sprite index
40   const int ALEC_FRAME_WIDTH  = 40;  // Alec's frame width
41   const int ALEC_FRAME_HEIGHT = 75;  // Alec's frame height
42   const int ALEC_FRAME_COUNT  = 16;  // Alec's frame count
43   const int EAST_START        = 1;   // First frame for going east
44   const int EAST_END          = 4;   // Last frame for going east
45   const int NORTH_START       = 5;   // First frame for going north
46   const int NORTH_END         = 8;   // Last frame for going north
47   const int SOUTH_START       = 9;   // First frame for going south
48   const int SOUTH_END         = 12;  // Last frame for going south
49   const int WEST_START        = 13;  // First frame for going west
50   const int WEST_END          = 16;  // Last frame for going west
51   const int ALEC_FPS          = 5;   // Alec's frames per second
52   const int ANIMATION_LOOP    = 1;   // To make Alec loop
53   const float ALEC_STARTING_X = 0;   // Alec's starting X-coordinate
54   const float ALEC_STARTING_Y = 150; // Alec's starting Y-coordinate
```

- Line 38: ALEC_IMAGE is the image index that we will use for the texture atlas that contains the animation frames for the Alec character.
- Line 39: ALEC_SPRITE is the sprite index for the Alec character.
- Lines 40 and 41: ALEC_FRAME_WIDTH and ALEC_FRAME_HEIGHT are the width and height of each frame in the texture atlas.
- Line 42: ALEC_FRAME_COUNT is the number of frames in the texture atlas.
- Lines 43 and 44: EAST_START is the frame number for Alec's first east-facing frame, and EAST_END is the frame number for Alec's last east-facing frame.
- Lines 45 and 46: NORTH_START is the frame number for Alec's first north-facing frame, and NORTH_END is the frame number for Alec's last north-facing frame.
- Lines 47 and 48: SOUTH_START is the frame number for Alec's first south-facing frame, and SOUTH_END is the frame number for Alec's last south-facing frame.
- Lines 49 and 50: WEST_START is the frame number for Alec's first west-facing frame, and WEST_END is the frame number for Alec's last west-facing frame.
- Line 51: ALEC_FPS specifies the frames per second for the animation.
- Line 52: ANIMATION_LOOP specifies that the Alec animation sequence should loop.
- Lines 53 and 54: ALEC_STARTING_X and ALEC_STARTING_Y specify the starting X- and Y-coordinates for the Alec sprite.

Lines 57 through 60 declare the constants NORTH, SOUTH, EAST, and WEST, initialized with the values 1, 2, 3, and 4, respectively. We will use these constants to indicate the direction that Alec is facing.

In lines 63 through 74 we declare the g_tileMap array and initialize it with image index constants for the tiles.

Inside the app::Begin function, we set the text for the window's title bar in line 83, and we set the virtual resolution in line 86. In line 89 we load the Alec.png file as an image. This file contains the texture map for the Alec character.

In line 92 we create the Alec sprite, using the texture map as its image. In line 95 we set the Alec sprite's depth to 0 to ensure that it is displayed on top of the tile images. In lines 98 and 99 we set the Alec sprite's position. In lines 102 through 103 we call the agk::SetSpriteAnimation function to specify the frame width, frame height, and frame count in the texture atlas.

Line 106 calls the loadTiles function, to load the image tiles, and line 109 calls the displayTiles function to display the tiles.

Inside the app::Loop function, line 116 declares a local variable, directionX, initialized with the value returned from the agk::GetDirectionX function. Line 117 declares a local variable, directionY, initialized with the value returned from the agk::GetDirectionY function. Recall from Chapter 8 that the agk::GetDirectionX function returns a nonzero value if either the left or right arrow key is being pressed, and the agk::GetDirectionY function returns a nonzero value if either the up or down arrow key is being pressed.

The if statement in line 121 determines whether the directionX variable is not zero. If this is the case, then either the left or right arrow key was pressed, so line 123 calls the updateAlecX function, passing directionX as an argument. The updateAlecX function, which is defined in lines 196 through 234, determines which arrow key is bring pressed and updates Alec accordingly.

The `if` statement in line 128 determines whether the `directionY` variable is not zero. If this is the case, then either the up or down arrow key was pressed, so line 130 calls the `updateAlecY` function, passing `directionY` as an argument. The `updateAlecY` function, which is defined in lines 239 through 277, determines which arrow key is bring pressed and updates Alec accordingly.

Line 134 calls the `agk::Sync` function to update the screen.

The `loadTiles` function, in lines 144 through 157, and the `displayTiles` function, in lines 161 through 191, are the same as in Program 10-8.

The `updateAlecX` function is defined in lines 196 through 234. The function has a parameter variable named `directionX`. When this function is called, the value that is returned from `agk::GetDirectionX` is passed as an argument. Line 198 declares a local variable named `alecX`, which is used to hold Alec's current X-coordinate. Line 199 declares a local variable named `newX` that will hold Alec's new X-coordinate. Line 202 gets Alec's current X-coordinate. The `if` statement in line 205 determines whether `directionX` is greater than 0. If this is the case, then the right arrow key is pressed. Lines 208 through 210 start Alec's east-facing animation, line 213 saves Alec's new direction to the `g_alecDirection` variable, and line 216 calculates Alec's new X-coordinate by adding 1 to the sprite's current X-coordinate. Otherwise, the `else if` clause in line 218 determines whether `directionX` is less than 0. If this is the case, then the left arrow key is pressed, and lines 221 through 223 start Alec's west-facing animation. Line 226 saves Alec's new direction to the `g_alecDirection` variable, and line 229 calculates Alec's new X-coordinate by subtracting 1 from the sprite's current X-coordinate. Line 233 moves the Alec sprite.

The `updateAlecY` function is defined in lines 239 through 273. The function has a parameter variable named `directionY`. When this function is called, the value that is returned from `agk::GetDirectionY` is passed as an argument. Line 241 declares a local variable named `alecY`, which is used to hold Alec's current Y-coordinate. Line 242 declares a local variable named `newY` that will hold Alec's new Y-coordinate. Line 245 gets Alec's current Y-coordinate. The `if` statement in line 248 determines whether `directionY` is less than 0. If this is the case, then the up arrow key is pressed. Lines 251 through 253 start Alec's north-facing animation, line 256 saves Alec's new direction to the `g_alecDirection` variable, and line 259 calculates Alec's new Y-coordinate by subtracting 1 from the sprite's current Y-coordinate. Otherwise, the `else if` clause in line 261 determines whether `directionY` is less than 0. If this is the case, then the down arrow key is pressed, and lines 264 through 266 start Alec's south-facing animation. Line 269 saves Alec's new direction to the `g_alecDirection` variable, and line 272 calculates Alec's new Y-coordinate by adding 1 to the sprite's current Y-coordinate. Line 276 moves the Alec sprite.

Encountering Obstacles

In Program 10-10, the user can make the Alec character walk anywhere on the screen on top of the background tiles. This includes the rock tiles and the tiles that make up the tree. To make the program more realistic, we should treat the rocks and the tree as obstacles and prevent Alec from walking on those tiles.

To achieve this, we will create an array to hold the sprite indices of the tiles that we consider obstacles. Then, when we move Alec around on the screen, we will check for collisions with any of those sprites. If Alec collides with an obstacle sprite, we will prevent him from moving on top of that sprite. Program 10-10 demonstrates how this is done.

Program 10-10   (Obstacles.cpp)

```
 1 // Includes, namespace and prototypes
 2 #include "template.h"
 3 using namespace AGK;
 4 app App;
 5
 6 // Function prototypes
 7 void loadTiles();
 8 void displayTiles();
 9 void addObstacle(int);
10 void updateAlecX(float);
11 void updateAlecY(float);
12 void checkForCollision();
13
14 // Constants for the screen resolution
15 const int SCREEN_WIDTH  = 640;
16 const int SCREEN_HEIGHT = 480;
17
18 // Constants for the image numbers
19 const int GRASS  = 1;
20 const int PATH   = 2;
21 const int PATHNE = 3;
22 const int PATHNW = 4;
23 const int PATHSE = 5;
24 const int PATHSW = 6;
25 const int TREENW = 7;
26 const int TREENE = 8;
27 const int TREESW = 9;
28 const int TREESE = 10;
29 const int ROCK   = 11;
30
31 // Constants for the tile image sizes
32 const int TILE_WIDTH  = 64;
33 const int TILE_HEIGHT = 48;
34
35 // Constants for the tile map size declarators
36 const int TILE_ROWS = 10;
37 const int TILE_COLS = 10;
38
39 // Constants for the Alec sprite sheet
40 const int ALEC_IMAGE        = 12;  // Texture atlas image index
41 const int ALEC_SPRITE       = 100; // Alec's sprite index
42 const int ALEC_FRAME_WIDTH  = 40;  // Alec's frame width
43 const int ALEC_FRAME_HEIGHT = 75;  // Alec's frame height
44 const int ALEC_FRAME_COUNT  = 16;  // Alec's frame count
45 const int EAST_START        = 1;   // First frame for going east
46 const int EAST_END          = 4;   // Last frame for going east
47 const int NORTH_START       = 5;   // First frame for going north
48 const int NORTH_END         = 8;   // Last frame for going north
```

```
49 const int SOUTH_START    = 9;    // First frame for going south
50 const int SOUTH_END      = 12;   // Last frame for going south
51 const int WEST_START     = 13;   // First frame for going west
52 const int WEST_END       = 16;   // Last frame for going west
53 const int ALEC_FPS       = 5;    // Alec's frames per second
54 const int ANIMATION_LOOP = 1;    // To make Alec loop
55 const float ALEC_STARTING_X = 0;   // Alec's starting X-coordinate
56 const float ALEC_STARTING_Y = 150; // Alec's starting Y-coordinate
57
58 // Constants for Alec's direction
59 const int NORTH = 1;
60 const int SOUTH = 2;
61 const int EAST  = 3;
62 const int WEST  = 4;
63
64 // Constant for the maximum number of obstacles
65 const int MAX_OBSTACLES = 7;
66
67 // Constant for the collision sound index
68 const int COLLISION_SOUND = 1;
69
70 // The tile map
71 int g_tileMap[TILE_ROWS][TILE_COLS] =
72 { {GRASS, GRASS, GRASS, GRASS, GRASS,  GRASS,  GRASS,  GRASS,  GRASS,  GRASS},
73   {GRASS, GRASS, GRASS, ROCK,  GRASS,  GRASS,  GRASS,  GRASS,  GRASS,  GRASS},
74   {GRASS, GRASS, GRASS, GRASS, GRASS,  GRASS,  GRASS,  PATHNW, PATH,   PATH },
75   {GRASS, GRASS, GRASS, GRASS, GRASS,  TREENW, TREENE, PATH,   GRASS,  GRASS},
76   {PATH,  PATH,  PATH,  PATH,  PATHNE, TREESW, TREESE, PATH,   ROCK,   GRASS},
77   {GRASS, GRASS, GRASS, GRASS, PATH,   GRASS,  GRASS,  PATH,   GRASS,  GRASS},
78   {GRASS, GRASS, GRASS, GRASS, PATHSW, PATH,   PATH,   PATHSE, GRASS,  GRASS},
79   {GRASS, GRASS, GRASS, GRASS, GRASS,  GRASS,  GRASS,  GRASS,  GRASS,  GRASS},
80   {GRASS, ROCK,  GRASS, GRASS, GRASS,  GRASS,  GRASS,  GRASS,  GRASS,  GRASS},
81   {GRASS, GRASS, GRASS, GRASS, GRASS,  GRASS,  GRASS,  GRASS,  GRASS,  GRASS}
82 };
83
84 // Obstacle array
85 int g_obstacles[MAX_OBSTACLES];
86
87 // Variable for Alec's direction
88 int g_alecDirection = EAST;
89
90 // Begin app, called once at the start
91 void app::Begin( void )
92 {
93    // Set the window title.
94    agk::SetWindowTitle("Walking Alec");
95
96    // Set the virtual resolution.
97    agk::SetVirtualResolution(SCREEN_WIDTH, SCREEN_HEIGHT);
98
99    // Load the collision sound.
100   agk::LoadSound(COLLISION_SOUND, "Alec/boink.wav");
101
102   // Load the texture atlas.
103   agk::LoadImage(ALEC_IMAGE, "Alec/Alec.png");
104
```

```
105     // Create the sprite using the texture atlas as the image.
106     agk::CreateSprite(ALEC_SPRITE, ALEC_IMAGE);
107
108     // Make sure Alec is displayed on top of the tile sprites.
109     agk::SetSpriteDepth(ALEC_SPRITE, 0);
110
111     // Set Alec's starting position.
112     agk::SetSpritePosition(ALEC_SPRITE, ALEC_STARTING_X,
113                         ALEC_STARTING_Y);
114
115     // Set the sprite animation.
116     agk::SetSpriteAnimation(ALEC_SPRITE, ALEC_FRAME_WIDTH,
117                         ALEC_FRAME_HEIGHT, ALEC_FRAME_COUNT);
118
119     // Load the tile images.
120     loadTiles();
121
122     // Create the tile sprites and display them.
123     displayTiles();
124 }
125
126 // Main loop, called every frame
127 void app::Loop ( void )
128 {
129     // Get the state of the direction keys.
130     float directionX = agk::GetDirectionX();
131     float directionY = agk::GetDirectionY();
132
133     // If the right or left arrow keys are pressed,
134     // update Alec's position.
135     if (directionX != 0)
136     {
137        // Update Alec's X-coordinate.
138        updateAlecX(directionX);
139
140        // Check for any collisions.
141        checkForCollision();
142     }
143
144     // If the up or down arrow keys are pressed,
145     // update Alec's position.
146     if (directionY != 0)
147     {
148        // Update Alec's Y-coordinate
149        updateAlecY(directionY);
150
151        // Check for any collisions.
152        checkForCollision();
153     }
154
155     // Refresh the screen.
156     agk::Sync();
157 }
158
159 // Called when the app ends
160 void app::End ( void )
```

```
161 {
162 }
163
164 // The loadTiles function loads the images that will be
165 // used for tiles.
166 void loadTiles()
167 {
168     agk::LoadImage(GRASS,   "Alec/Grass.png");
169     agk::LoadImage(PATH,    "Alec/Path.png");
170     agk::LoadImage(PATHNE,  "Alec/PathNE.png");
171     agk::LoadImage(PATHNW,  "Alec/PathNW.png");
172     agk::LoadImage(PATHSE,  "Alec/PathSE.png");
173     agk::LoadImage(PATHSW,  "Alec/PathSW.png");
174     agk::LoadImage(TREENE,  "Alec/TreeNE.png");
175     agk::LoadImage(TREENW,  "Alec/TreeNW.png");
176     agk::LoadImage(TREESE,  "Alec/TreeSE.png");
177     agk::LoadImage(TREESW,  "Alec/TreeSW.png");
178     agk::LoadImage(ROCK,    "Alec/Rock.png");
179 }
180
181 // The displayTiles function displays the tiles, as
182 // specified by the tile map.
183 void displayTiles()
184 {
185     // Variables for the tile coordinates
186     float x = 0, y = 0;
187
188     // Variable to temporarily hold a sprite index
189     int spriteIndex;
190
191     // Variable to be an obstacle counter
192     int obstacleCounter = 0;
193
194     // Display all the tiles specified in the map.
195     for (int r = 0; r < TILE_ROWS; r++)
196     {
197         // Set x to 0.
198         x = 0;
199
200         // Display all the tiles in this row.
201         for (int c = 0; c < TILE_COLS; c++)
202         {
203             // Create a sprite for this tile.
204             spriteIndex = agk::CreateSprite(g_tileMap[r][c]);
205
206             // If this is an obstacle, add it to the
207             // obstacle array.
208             if (g_tileMap[r][c] > PATHSW)
209             {
210                 // Add it to the array.
211                 g_obstacles[obstacleCounter] = spriteIndex;
212
213                 // Update the obstacle counter.
214                 obstacleCounter++;
215             }
```

```
216
217              // Set the tile's position.
218              agk::SetSpritePosition(spriteIndex, x, y);
219
220              // Update the X-coordinate for the next tile.
221              x += TILE_WIDTH;
222          }
223
224          // Increase y for the next row.
225          y += TILE_HEIGHT;
226      }
227  }
228
229  // The updateAlecX function turns Alec either east or west,
230  // depending on which arrow key is being pressed, and moves
231  // him to his new X-coordinate.
232  void updateAlecX(float directionX)
233  {
234      float alecX,    // Alec's current X position
235            newX;     // Alec's new X-coordinate
236
237      // Get Alec's X-coordinate
238      alecX = agk::GetSpriteX(ALEC_SPRITE);
239
240      // Which key was pressed? Right or left?
241      if (directionX > 0)
242      {
243          // Turn Alec east
244          agk::PlaySprite(ALEC_SPRITE, ALEC_FPS,
245                          ANIMATION_LOOP,
246                          EAST_START, EAST_END);
247
248          // Save Alec's current direction.
249          g_alecDirection = EAST;
250
251          // Calculate Alec's new X-coordinate.
252          newX = alecX + 1;
253      }
254      else if (directionX < 0)
255      {
256          // Turn Alec west
257          agk::PlaySprite(ALEC_SPRITE, ALEC_FPS,
258                          ANIMATION_LOOP,
259                          WEST_START, WEST_END);
260
261          // Save Alec's current direction.
262          g_alecDirection = WEST;
263
264          // Calculate Alec's new X-coordinate
265          newX = alecX - 1;
266      }
267
268      // Move Alec
269      agk::SetSpriteX(ALEC_SPRITE, newX);
270  }
```

```
271
272  // The updateAlecY function turns Alec either north or south,
273  // depending on which arrow key is being pressed, and moves
274  // him to his new Y-coordinate.
275  void updateAlecY(float directionY)
276  {
277      float alecY,    // Alec's current Y position
278            newY;     // Alec's new Y-coordinate
279
280      // Get Alec's Y-coordinate
281      alecY = agk::GetSpriteY(ALEC_SPRITE);
282
283      // Which key was pressed? Up or down?
284      if (directionY < 0)
285      {
286          // Turn Alec north
287          agk::PlaySprite(ALEC_SPRITE, ALEC_FPS,
288                          ANIMATION_LOOP,
289                          NORTH_START, NORTH_END);
290
291          // Save Alec's current direction.
292          g_alecDirection = NORTH;
293
294          // Calculate Alec's new Y-coordinate.
295          newY = alecY - 1;
296      }
297      else if (directionY > 0)
298      {
299          // Turn Alec south
300          agk::PlaySprite(ALEC_SPRITE, ALEC_FPS,
301                          ANIMATION_LOOP,
302                          SOUTH_START, SOUTH_END);
303
304          // Save Alec's current direction.
305          g_alecDirection = SOUTH;
306
307          // Calculate Alec's new Y-coordinate.
308          newY = alecY + 1;
309      }
310
311      // Move Alec
312      agk::SetSpriteY(ALEC_SPRITE, newY);
313  }
314
315  // The checkForCollision function determines whether Alec
316  // has collided with an obstacle. If Alec has collided
317  // with an obstacle, it moves his position in the opposite
318  // direction one pixel.
319  void checkForCollision()
320  {
321      // Get Alec's position.
322      float x = agk::GetSpriteX(ALEC_SPRITE);
323      float y = agk::GetSpriteY(ALEC_SPRITE);
324
325      // Step through the obstacles array checking for
```

```
326     // a collision.
327     for (int index = 0; index < MAX_OBSTACLES; index++)
328     {
329        if (agk::GetSpriteCollision(ALEC_SPRITE, g_obstacles[index]))
330        {
331           // Play the collision sound.
332           agk::PlaySound(COLLISION_SOUND);
333
334           // Move Alec one pixel in the direction opposite
335           // that which he is facing.
336           switch (g_alecDirection)
337           {
338           case NORTH:
339              y++;
340              break;
341
342           case SOUTH:
343              y--;
344              break;
345
346           case EAST:
347              x--;
348              break;
349
350           case WEST:
351              x++;
352              break;
353           }
354
355           // Move Alec.
356           agk::SetSpritePosition(ALEC_SPRITE, x, y);
357        }
358     }
359 }
```

Program 10-10 works in many ways like Program 10-9, but we need to look at the differences. First, let's look at the new constants that are declared:

- Line 65 declares an int constant named MAX_OBSTACLES, which specifies the number of obstacles that appear in the game. We set this constant to the value 7 because we have a total of 7 obstacle tiles in the tile map. This constant will be used as the size declarator for the array that holds the obstacle sprite numbers

- Line 68 declares an int constant named COLLISION_SOUND, which specifies the sound index for a sound that we will play when Alec collides with an obstacle.

In line 85 we declare an int array named g_obstacles. This is the array that will hold the sprite indices of the obstacle sprites. The sprite numbers of the obstacles are added to the array in the displayTiles function. In the displayTiles function, in line 192, we have declared a local variable named obstacleCounter, initialized with 0. This variable will be used to keep count of the obstacles as we add them to the g_obstacles array. The for loop that appears in lines 201 through 222 steps through each element of the g_tileMap array, creating and displaying all the tile sprites. We have added the if statement that appears in lines 208 through 215. The if statement starts like this:

```
if (g_tileMap[r][c] > PATHSW)
```

To understand how this works, look at the constants declared in lines 19 through 29 for the tile image indices:

```
19   const int GRASS  = 1;
20   const int PATH   = 2;
21   const int PATHNE = 3;
22   const int PATHNW = 4;
23   const int PATHSE = 5;
24   const int PATHSW = 6;
25   const int TREENW = 7;
26   const int TREENE = 8;
27   const int TREESW = 9;
28   const int TREESE = 10;
29   const int ROCK   = 11;
```

The constants that represent the obstacles are TREENW, TREENE, TREESW, TREESE, and ROCK. Notice that the values of all of these constants are greater than the value of the PATHSW constant. The if statement in line 208 determines whether a value in the array represents an obstacle. If so, it means the sprite that was just created is an obstacle, so line 211 adds the sprite index to the g_obstacles array, and line 214 increments the obstacleCounter variable. When the displayTiles function finishes, the g_obstacles array will contain the sprite indices of all the obstacle sprites.

The app::Begin function is the same as previously shown in Program 10-9, except for the new statement in line 100 that loads a sound file. We will play this sound each time Alec collides with an obstacle sprite.

In the app::Loop function, notice that we call a function named checkForCollision in lines 141 and 152. The checkForCollision function determines whether Alec has collided with an obstacle. If so, it moves him back one pixel, thus preventing him from walking over it.

The checkForCollision function appears in lines 319 through 359. The statements in lines 322 and 323 get the Alec sprite's X- and Y-coordinates and stores those values in the local variables x and y. Then, the for loop that starts in line 327 steps through the g_obstacles array, checking to see if the Alec sprite has collided with any obstacles. It does this with the if statement in line 329. If a collision has occurred, line 332 plays the collision sound, and the switch statement in line 336 executes. The switch statement tests the value of the g_alecDirection variable and then branches to the appropriate case statement to increase or decrease either the x or y variable (to move Alec backward by one pixel). The statement in line 356 sets the Alec sprite's position.

When you run this program, you will be able to move Alec up to, but not over, any of the rocks or the tree.

 **Checkpoint**

10.8. What are tiles?

10.9. What is a tile map?

10.10. Suppose you are writing a tile-based game that uses a screen 640 pixels wide by 480 pixels high. The tiles that you want to use for the background are 80 pixels wide by 80 pixels high. How many rows and columns will the tile map have?

Review Questions

Multiple Choice

1. A file that data is written to is known as a(n) _____.
   a. input file
   b. output file
   c. sequential access file
   d. binary file

2. A file that data is read from is known as a(n) _____.
   a. input file
   b. output file
   c. sequential access file
   d. binary file

3. Before a file can be used by a program, it must be _____.
   a. formatted
   b. encrypted
   c. closed
   d. opened

4. When a program is finished using a file, it should _____.
   a. erase the file
   b. open the file
   c. close the file
   d. encrypt the file

5. You use _____ to open an output file.
   a. `agk::OpenToWrite`
   b. `agk::OpenToRead`
   c. `agk::OpenOutput`
   d. `agk::Open`

6. You use _____ to open an input file.
   a. `agk::OpenToWrite`
   b. `agk::OpenToRead`
   c. `agk::OpenInput`
   d. `agk::Open`

7. You use _____ to write an integer value to a file.
   a. agk::WriteInteger
   b. agk::WriteInt
   c. agk::IntegerOut
   d. agk::WriteFile

8. You use _____ to write a null-terminated string to a file.
   a. agk::WriteNullString
   b. agk::WriteStr
   c. agk::WriteLine
   d. agk::WriteString

9. You use _____ to write a string, followed by a newline, to a file.
   a. agk::WriteNullString
   b. agk::WriteStr
   c. agk::WriteLine
   d. agk::WriteString

10. _____ returns 1 (true) if the end of the specified file has been reached.
    a. agk::FileEOF
    b. agk::FileEnd
    c. agk::EndOfFile
    d. agk::EndReached

11. Small rectangular images that can be put together to form a larger image are called _____.
    a. tiles
    b. maps
    c. components
    d. elements

12. A _____ is a two-dimensional array that specifies the locations of tiles on the screen.
    a. tile locator
    b. tile specifier
    c. tile bank
    d. tile map

True or False

1. The agk::OpenToWrite function will fail if the specified file already exists.

2. When an input file is opened, the read position is set to the last item in the file.

3. You use the same AGK function to close input files and output files.

4. The process of opening a file is only necessary with input files. Output files are automatically opened when data is written to them.

5. When a file that already exists is opened for writing in append mode 0, the file's existing contents are erased.

Short Answer

1. Describe the three steps that must be taken when a file is used by a program.

2. Why should a program close a file when it's finished using it?

3. What is the purpose of the `agk::FileEOF` function?

4. If an existing file is opened for writing in append mode 0, what happens to the file's existing contents?

5. If an existing file is opened for writing in append mode 1, what happens to the file's existing contents?

6. How can you determine whether a file is open in an AGK program?

Algorithm Workbench

1. Write an AGK program that does the following:
   - In the `app::Begin` function, opens an output file with the name NumberList.dat
   - In the `app::Loop` function writes the numbers 1 through 100 to the file
   - In the `app::End` function closes the file

2. Write an AGK program that does the following:
   - In the `app::Begin` function, opens the NumberList.dat file that was created by the program created in question 1
   - In the `app::Loop` function, reads all the numbers from the file
   - In the `app::End` function closes the file

3. Modify the program that you created in question 2 so it adds all the numbers read from the file and displays their total.

4. Suppose you have the images shown in Figure 10-22 to use as tiles in a program. In the program you declare the following constants for image numbers:

```
const int GRASS  = 1;
const int PATH   = 2;
const int PATHNE = 3;
const int PATHNW = 4;
const int PATHSE = 5;
const int PATHSW = 6;
```

Figure 10-22 Tile images

Grass.bmp   Path.bmp   PathNE.bmp   PathNW.bmp   PathSE.bmp   PathSW.bmp

In the same program you load the images using the following statements:

```
agk::LoadImage(GRASS,  "Grass.bmp");
agk::LoadImage(PATH,   "Path.bmp");
agk::LoadImage(PATHNE, "PathNE.bmp");
agk::LoadImage(PATHNW, "PathNW.bmp");
agk::LoadImage(PATHSE, "PathSE.bmp");
agk::LoadImage(PATHSW, "PathSW.bmp");
```

Write the declaration for a tile map that you would use to display the image shown in Figure 10-23. Assume that the program uses a virtual resolution of 640 by 480, and each of the tiles is 64 pixels wide by 48 pixels high.

Figure 10-23 Tile-based screen

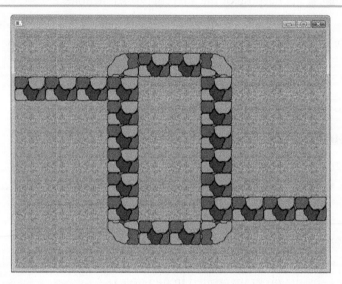

Programming Exercises

VideoNote
Solving the Bug Zapper Bonus Time Problem

1. **Bug Zapper Bonus Time**
   Modify the Bug Zapper game so it reads the high score file when the program begins. If the user beats the high score while the game is playing, the user should immediately get an extra three seconds of play time.

2. **Log File**
   Modify the Obstacle program shown in this chapter so it writes data to a log file describing the movements of the Alec character. For example, the program should make an entry in the log file each time Alec changes direction and each time Alec collides with an obstacle.

3. **ESP Game**
   Create a game that can test your ESP abilities. In the book's online resources (located at www.pearsonhighered.com/gaddis), you will find images for cards with a triangle, a square, and a circle, as well as a facedown card image. The game should work this way:
   Three cards are shown facedown. Internally, the program should randomly select values for each card (one triangle, one square, and one circle). The user should be instructed to use the mouse to select which card is the triangle. The selected card should then be revealed.
   Repeat this 10 times, and then display the number of times the user correctly identified the triangle card.

4. **Matching Card Game**

   For this game you will use six of the poker card images provided in the book's online resources (available at www.pearsonhighered.com/gaddis) to create a deck of 12 cards. There should two of each symbol in the deck. For example, there might be two queen of hearts cards, two ace of spades cards, two jack of diamonds cards, and so forth.

   This game is designed for two players. When the game begins, the cards should be shuffled, and then all the cards should be shown facedown. Each player takes turns picking two cards, with the objective of finding two cards that match. If the two cards match, the player gets points, and those two cards are removed from the game. If the two cards don't match, the computer turns them back over, and the next player takes a turn. The game ends when all the matching cards have been selected, and the player with the highest score wins.

5. **Domination Card Game**

   This is a card game where the user plays against the computer. Create a deck of at least 20 cards in which the cards are numbered 1 through 20. When the game begins, the deck is shuffled. Then half the deck is given to the user, and the other half is given to the computer, with no card values showing. At this point in the game, you might want to display the two players' cards as two separate facedown decks, one on the left side of the screen and the other on the right side.

   During each turn, one card from the user and one card from the computer are turned over. The player with the highest value gets to keep both cards, which are placed back at the bottom of that player's deck. The game is won when one player has all the cards. (As an alternative, you can design the game to end after a specified number of turns. The player with the highest value set of cards wins.)

6. **Coins and Snakes**

   In this chapter, you saw Program 10-10, which lets the user move the Alec character around a tile-based screen. Use the same tile images to create a similar game that has at least 10 rocks placed around the screen. Some of the rocks should turn into a coin when Alec comes in contact with them, and some of the rocks should turn into a snake. When a rock turns into a coin, the player earns one point, and when a rock turns into a snake, the player loses one point. When all the coins or all the snakes have been uncovered, the game ends. The object of the game is to have at least one point when the game ends. (You will find coin and snake images in the book's online resources at www.pearsonhighered.com/gaddis.)

11 Object-Oriented Programming

TOPICS

11.1 Procedural and Object-Oriented Programming

CONCEPT: Procedural programming is a method of writing software. It is a programming practice centered on the procedures or actions that take place in a program. Object-oriented programming is centered on objects. Objects are created from abstract data types that encapsulate data and functions together.

Primarily two methods of programming are in use today: procedural and object oriented. The earliest programming languages were procedural, meaning a program was made of one or more procedures. A *procedure* is simply a function that performs a specific task such as gathering input from the user, performing calculations, reading or writing files, or displaying output. The programs that you have written so far have been procedural in nature.

Procedures typically operate on data items that are separate from the procedures. In a procedural program, the data items are commonly passed from one procedure to another. As you might imagine, the focus of procedural programming is on the creation of procedures that operate on the program's data. The separation of data and the code that operates on the data can lead to problems, however, as the program becomes larger and more complex.

For example, suppose you are part of a programming team that has developed a game. When the program was initially designed, it kept several sprite indices in int variables. Your job was to design several functions that accept those variables as arguments and perform operations with them. The software has been operating successfully for some

507

time, but your team has been asked to update it by adding several new features. During the revision process, the senior programmer informs you that the sprite indices will no longer be stored in variables. Instead, they will be stored in an int array. This means that you will have to modify all the functions that you have designed so they accept and work with an int array instead of the variables. Making these extensive modifications is not only a great deal of work, but it also opens the opportunity for errors to appear in your code.

Whereas procedural programming is centered on creating functions, *object-oriented programming* (OOP) is centered on creating objects. An *object* is a software entity that contains fields and methods. An object's *fields* are simply variables, arrays, or other data structures that are stored in the object. An object's *methods* are functions that perform operations on the object's data. The object is, conceptually, a self-contained unit consisting of data (fields) and functions (methods). This is illustrated in Figure 11-1.

OOP addresses the problem of code/data separation through encapsulation and data hiding. *Encapsulation* refers to combining data and code into a single object. *Data hiding* refers to an object's ability to hide its fields from code that is outside the object. Only the object's methods may then directly access and make changes to the object's fields. An object typically hides its fields, but allows outside code to access its methods. As shown in Figure 11-2, the object's methods provide programming statements outside the object with indirect access to the object's fields.

Figure 11-1 An object contains data and functions

Figure 11-2 Code outside the object interacts with the object's methods

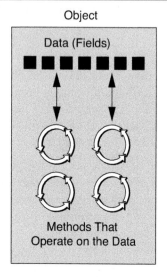

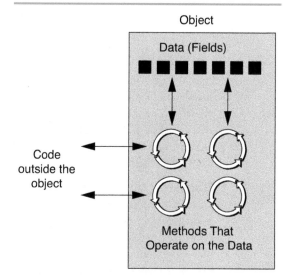

When an object's fields are hidden from outside code and access to those fields is restricted to the object's methods, the fields are protected from accidental corruption. In addition, the programming code outside the object does not need to know about the format or internal structure of the object's fields. The code only needs to interact with the object's methods. When a programmer changes the structure of an object's internal data, he or she also modifies the object's methods so they may properly operate on the data. The way in which outside code interacts with the methods, however, does not change.

Object Reusability

In addition to solving the problems of code/data separation, the use of OOP has also been encouraged by the trend of *object reusability*. An object is not a stand-alone program, but is used by programs that need its service. For example, Sharon is a programmer who has developed an object for rendering 3-D images. She is a math whiz and knows a lot about computer graphics, so her object is coded to perform all the necessary 3-D mathematical operations and handle the computer's video hardware. Tom, who is writing a program for an architectural firm, needs his application to display 3-D images of buildings. Because he is working under a tight deadline and does not possess a great deal of knowledge about computer graphics, he can use Sharon's object to perform the 3-D rendering (for a small fee, of course!).

An Everyday Example of an Object

Think of your alarm clock as an object. It has the following fields:

- The current second (a value in the range of 0–59)
- The current minute (a value in the range of 0–59)
- The current hour (a value in the range of 1–12)
- The time the alarm is set for (a valid hour and minute)
- Whether the alarm is on or off ("on" or "off")

As you can see, the fields are merely data values that define the *state* that the alarm clock is currently in. You, the user of the alarm clock object, cannot directly manipulate these fields because they are *private*. To change a field's value, you must use one of the object's methods. Here are some of the alarm clock object's methods:

- Set time
- Set alarm time
- Turn alarm on
- Turn alarm off

Each method manipulates one or more of the fields. For example, the "Set time" method allows you to set the alarm clock's time. You activate the method by pressing a button on the clock. By using another button, you can activate the "Set alarm time" method.

In addition, another button allows you to execute the "Turn alarm on" and "Turn alarm off" methods. Notice that all these methods can be activated by you, who are outside the alarm clock. Methods that can be accessed by entities outside the object are known as *public methods*.

OOP Terminology

OOP programmers commonly use the term *fields* to describe the items of data that are stored in an object and the term *methods* to describe the procedures that operate on an object's data. C++ programmers often refer to fields as *member variables* and refer to methods as *member functions*. These are the terms that we will use because they are commonly used in C++.

 Checkpoint

11.1. What is an object?

11.2. What is encapsulation?

11.3. Why is an object's internal data usually hidden from outside code?

11.4. What are public methods?

11.2 Classes and Objects

CONCEPT: A class is code that specifies the fields and methods for a particular type of object.

Let's discuss how objects are created in software. Before an object can be created, it must be designed by a programmer. The programmer determines the member variables and member functions that are necessary and then creates a *class*. A class is code that specifies the member variables and member functions that a particular type of object has. Think of a class as a "blueprint" that may be used to create objects. It serves a similar purpose as the blueprint for a house. The blueprint itself is not a house, but is a detailed description of a house. When we use the blueprint to build an actual house, we could say we are building an instance of the house described by the blueprint. If we so desire, we can build several identical houses from the same blueprint. Each house is a separate instance of the house described by the blueprint. This idea is illustrated in Figure 11-3.

Figure 11-3 A blueprint and houses built from the blueprint

Blueprint that describes a house.

Instances of the house described by the blueprint.

Another way of thinking about the difference between a class and an object is to think of the difference between a cookie cutter and a cookie. A cookie cutter itself is not a cookie, but it describes a cookie. The cookie cutter can be used to make several cookies, as shown in Figure 11-4. Think of a class as a cookie cutter and the objects created from the class as cookies.

Figure 11-4 The cookie cutter metaphor

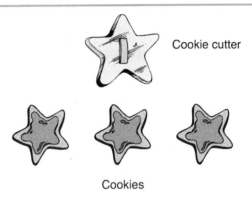

Cookie cutter

Cookies

Think of a class as a cookie cutter and objects as the cookies.

So, a class is not an object, but a description of an object. When the program is running, it can use the class to create, in memory, as many objects of a specific type as needed. Each object that is created from a class is called an *instance* of the class.

For example, Jessica is a game programmer. She is developing a game in which the user moves a hero sprite around the screen. During game play, the program automatically moves an enemy sprite around the screen. The user must make sure the hero sprite does not come in contact with the enemy sprite.

Although the hero and enemy sprites are separate elements in the game, all sprites have the same characteristics. For example, all sprites have a sprite index, an X-coordinate, a Y-coordinate, and an alpha value. Jessica decides that she can write a Sprite class that specifies member variables to hold a sprite's data and member functions that perform operations on a sprite. The Sprite class is not an object, but a blueprint from which objects may be created.

Jessica's program will then use the Sprite class to create a hero object in memory. The hero object is an instance of the Sprite class, and it stores data specific to the hero sprite. When the program needs to manipulate the hero sprite, it calls the hero object's member functions. The program will also use the Sprite class to create an enemy object in memory. The enemy object is also an instance of the Sprite class, and it stores data specific to the enemy sprite. When the program needs to manipulate the enemy sprite, it calls the enemy object's member functions. Figure 11-5 illustrates the idea that the hero object and the enemy object are both instances of the Sprite class.

Figure 11-5 The hero and enemy objects are instances of the Sprite class

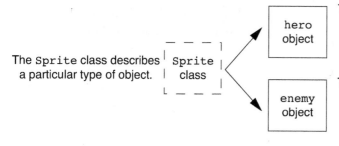

The Sprite class describes a particular type of object.

hero object

The hero object is an instance of the Sprite class. It has the member variables and member functions described by the Sprite class.

enemy object

The enemy object is an instance of the Sprite class. It has the member variables and member functions described by the Sprite class.

Class Declarations

To create a class, you first write the *class declaration*. This is the general format that we will use to write a class definition in C++:

```
class ClassName
{
private:

    Member variables go here.

public:

    Member function declarations go here.

};
```

The first line is known as the *class header*. It starts with the key word class, followed by the name of the class. The same rules for naming variables apply to naming classes. Many programmers follow the convention of beginning class names with an uppercase letter. This serves as a visual reminder that the name is that of a class, not a variable.

Following the class header is an opening curly brace. On the line after the opening curly brace we write the key word private followed by a colon. This marks the beginning of the class's *private section*. We typically declare all the class's member variables (fields) in the private section. As a result, those member variables can be accessed only by the class's member functions.

After the private section we write the key word public, followed by a colon. This marks the beginning of the class's *public section*. Any class members that are declared in the public section can be accessed by code that is outside the class. This is where we typically declare the class's member functions. Declaring member functions in the public section makes them available to code outside the class.

At the end of the class definition is a closing curly brace, followed by a semicolon. Don't forget to write the semicolon, or an error will occur when you compile the code.

NOTE: You normally don't write a semicolon after a closing brace, but C++ requires that you write a semicolon after a class's closing brace. Forgetting to do so is a common mistake and will prevent your code from compiling.

Mutators and Accessors

By declaring a class's member variables private and providing access to those variables through public member functions, you ensure that the object owning those member variables is in control of all changes being made to them. A member function that stores a value in a member variable or changes the value of a member variable in some other way is known as a *mutator function*. A member function that gets a value from a class's member variable but does not change it is known as an *accessor function*.

Constructors

Classes usually have a special member function known as a constructor. A *constructor* is automatically executed when an object of the class is created. A constructor is used to initialize the object's member variables with starting values and perform any startup operations. These member functions are called "constructors" because they help construct an object. A constructor will always have the same name as the class that it belongs to.

Destructors

Classes sometimes have a special member function known as a destructor. A destructor is automatically called when an object of the class is destroyed. In the same way that constructors set things up when an object is created, destructors perform shutdown procedures when the object is destroyed. Destructors always have the same name as the class, preceded by a tilde character (~).

Designing a Sprite Class

Let's look at an example of a class that you can use in your AGK programs. When designing a game as an object-oriented program, you will want to make objects for all the major elements in the game. Sprites are excellent candidates to become objects. Earlier in this chapter we mentioned that all sprites have the same characteristics. For example, all sprites have a sprite index, an X-coordinate, a Y-coordinate, an alpha value, and so on. In addition, all sprites support the same set of operations, such as setting the position, hiding, showing, and so forth. Because all sprites have so much in common, we can create a Sprite class, and then each time we need a sprite in our program, use the class to create an object.

We will examine a simple Sprite class that provides the basic operations needed to create and work with a sprite. The class will have the following private member variables:

- spriteIndex—An int variable will hold the sprite's index.
- imageFile—A string object to hold the name of the sprite's image file.

The class also has the following public member functions:

- Constructor—Initializes the member variables.
- createSprite—Creates the sprite in the AGK window.
- setPosition—Sets the sprite's position to a specific set of XY-coordinates.
- setX—Sets the sprite's X-coordinate only.
- setY—Sets the sprite's Y-coordinate only.

- getSpriteIndex—Returns the index for the sprite.
- getX—Returns the sprite's current X-coordinate.
- getY—Returns the sprite's current Y-coordinate.
- Destructor—Deletes the sprite from memory.

Program 11-1 shows a partial listing for the program that demonstrates the class. The Sprite class declaration is shown in lines 8 through 30.

Let's look at the actual code for the Sprite class. We will write the class in an AGK template.cpp program, after the include directives and other code that appears at the top of the program, but before the app::Begin function. Program 11-1 is a partial listing for the program, showing only lines 1 through 32. The Sprite class declaration begins in line 8.

Program 11-1 (**SpriteClassDemo1**, *partial listing*)

```
 1 // Includes, namespace and prototypes
 2 #include "template.h"
 3 #include <string>        // Needed for the string class
 4 using namespace std;     // Needed for the string class
 5 using namespace AGK;
 6 app App;
 7
 8 class Sprite
 9 {
10 private:
11     int spriteIndex;    // The sprite index
12     string imageFile;   // The name of the image file
13 public:
14     // Constructor
15     Sprite(int, string);
16
17     // Mutators
18     void createSprite();
19     void setPosition(float, float);
20     void setX(float);
21     void setY(float);
22
23     // Accessors
24     int getSpriteIndex() const;
25     string getImageFile() const;
26     float getX() const;
27     float getY() const;
28
29     // Destructor
30     ~Sprite();
31 };
32
```

Let's step through the code. First, notice that we have an include directive for the string header file in line 3, and the using namespace std; statement in line 4. These are necessary because we are using string objects in the program.

The `Sprite` class definition appears in lines 8 through 31. Notice that the name of the class begins with an uppercase letter. As previously mentioned, this serves as a visual reminder that `Sprite` is a class.

The class's private section begins in line 10. In lines 11 and 12 we declare the `spriteIndex` and `imageFile` member variables. As previously mentioned, these variables will hold the sprite's index and the name of the image file to use when the sprite is created on the screen. Because these member variables are declared in the `Sprite` class's private section, they can be accessed only by functions that are members of the `Sprite` class.

We declare the member functions in the class's public section, which begins in line 13. Notice that the member function declarations look just like function prototypes, except that they appear inside the class declaration. Here is a summary of the member function declarations:

- In line 15 we declare the constructor. Notice that the constructor's name is the same as the class—`Sprite`. Also notice that there is no return type—not even `void`. This is because constructors are not executed by explicit function calls and cannot return a value.
- In line 18 we declare a `void` member function named `createSprite`. The function creates the sprite in the AGK output window, at the default position of (0, 0).
- In line 19 we declare a `void` member function named `setPosition`. The function accepts two `float` arguments. These arguments are the *X*- and *Y*-coordinates where the sprite will be positioned.
- In line 20 we declare a `void` member function named `setX`. The function accepts a `float` argument for the sprite's *X*-coordinate.
- In line 21 we declare a `void` member function named `setY`. The function accepts a `float` argument for the sprite's *Y*-coordinate.
- In line 24 we declare an `int` member function named `getSpriteIndex`. The function returns the sprite's index.
- In line 25 we declare an `string` member function named `getImageFile`. The function returns the name of the sprite's image file.
- In line 26 we declare a `float` member function named `getX`. The function returns the sprite's *X*-coordinate.
- In line 27 we declare a `float` member function named `getY`. The function returns the sprite's *Y*-coordinate.
- In line 30 we declare the destructor. Notice that the destructor's name is the same as the class, with a tilde character (~) at the beginning. Also notice that there is no return type. Like constructors, destructors are not executed by explicit function calls and cannot return a value.

NOTE: Perhaps you noticed that the word `const` appears at the end of the function headers in lines 24 through 27. This specifies that these functions do not change any data stored in the calling object. In any of these functions, if you inadvertently write code that changes the calling object's data, the compiler will generate an error. It is good programming practice to mark all accessor functions as `const`.

Defining Member Functions

In lines 15 through 30 of the Sprite class we declared 10 member functions. Those declarations alone do nothing. They simply inform the compiler that those functions are members of the class. Now we must write the definitions of those member functions. The definition of the constructor is shown in lines 36 through 40, as follows.

Program 11-1   (**SpriteClassDemo1**, *continued*)

```
33 // The Sprite class constructor accepts as arguments
34 // the sprite index and the name of the image file,
35 // and initializes the member variables.
36 Sprite::Sprite(int index, string filename)
37 {
38    spriteIndex = index;
39    imageFile = filename;
40 }
41
```

The function header appears in line 36. Notice that the function name starts with Sprite::. This indicates that the function is not a regular function, but a member of the Sprite class. Following that, the word Sprite is the name of the function. Because this is a constructor, it has the same name as the class that it belongs to. Inside the parentheses are two parameters, index and filename. The constructor header is illustrated in Figure 11-6.

Figure 11-6 Constructor function header

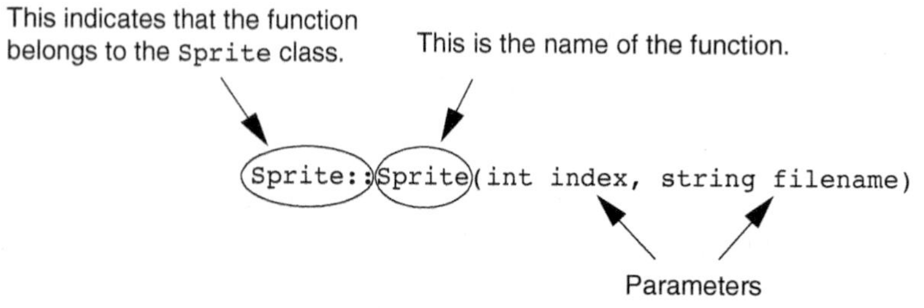

This indicates that the function belongs to the Sprite class.

This is the name of the function.

Sprite::Sprite(int index, string filename)

Parameters

The purpose of the constructor is to initialize the two private member variables, spriteIndex and imageFile with the values that are passed as arguments to the constructor. The argument passed into index is assigned to spriteIndex, and the argument passed into filename is assigned to imageFile.

The definition of the createSprite member function is shown in lines 43 through 51, as follows:

Program 11-1   (**SpriteClassDemo1**, *continued*)

```
42 // The Sprite::createSprite member function
43 void Sprite::createSprite()
44 {
45    // If the sprite does not already exist,
```

```
46      // then create it.
47      if (!agk::GetSpriteExists(spriteIndex))
48      {
49          agk::CreateSprite(spriteIndex, imageFile.c_str());
50      }
51 }
52
```

The function header appears in line 43. Once again, notice that the function name is prefixed with `Sprite::` to indicate that it is a member of the `Sprite` class. The purpose of this function is to create the sprite on the screen. The `if` statement in line 47 determines whether the sprite already exists. If it does not exist, line 49 calls the `agk::CreateSprite` function to create it.

Recall that when you call the `agk::CreateSprite` function, you pass the sprite index and the name of the image file as arguments. In line 49 we pass the following arguments to the `agk::CreateSprite` function:

- For the first argument, we pass the `spriteIndex` member variable. This assigns the value of `spriteIndex` as the sprite's index.
- For the second argument, we call the `imageFile` object's `c_str` member function. This is necessary because you cannot pass a `string` object directly to the `agk::CreateSprite` function. The `string` object's `c_str` member function returns the object's contents formatted in a way that is compatible with the `agk::CreateSprite` function. (You might recall from Chapter 7 that you have to use the `c_str` member function to print the contents of a `string` object with the `agk::Print` and `agk::PrintC` functions.)

The definition of the `setPosition` member function is shown in lines 55 through 58, as follows:

Program 11-1   (**SpriteClassDemo1**, *continued*)

```
53 // The Sprite::setPosition member function sets the
54 // sprite's position.
55 void Sprite::setPosition(float x, float y)
56 {
57     agk::SetSpritePosition(spriteIndex, x, y);
58 }
59
```

The purpose of the `setPosition` member function is to set the sprite's position. When you call this function, you pass two arguments: an *X*- and a *Y*-coordinate. Line 57 calls the `agk::SetSpritePosition` function, passing the sprite index and the *XY*-coordinates as arguments.

The definition of the `setX` member function is shown in lines 62 through 65, as follows:

Program 11-1 (**SpriteClassDemo1**, *continued*)

```
60 // The Sprite::setX member function sets the
61 // sprite's X-coordinate.
62 void Sprite::setX(float x)
63 {
64    agk::SetSpriteX(spriteIndex, x);
65 }
66
```

The purpose of the setX member function is to set the sprite's X-coordinate only. When you call this function, you pass an X-coordinate as an argument, and line 64 calls the agk::SetSpriteX function, passing the sprite index and the X-coordinate as arguments.

The definition of the setY member function is shown in lines 69 through 72, as follows:

Program 11-1 (**SpriteClassDemo1**, *continued*)

```
67 // The Sprite::setY member function sets the
68 // sprite's Y-coordinate.
69 void Sprite::setY(float y)
70 {
71    agk::SetSpriteY(spriteIndex, y);
72 }
73
```

The purpose of the setY member function is to set the sprite's Y-coordinate only. When you call this function, you pass a Y-coordinate as an argument, and line 71 calls the agk::SetSpriteY function, passing the sprite index and the Y-coordinate as arguments.

The definition of the getSpriteIndex member function is shown in lines 76 through 79, as follows:

Program 11-1 (**SpriteClassDemo1**, *continued*)

```
74 // The Sprite::getSpriteIndex member function
75 // returns the sprite's index.
76 int Sprite::getSpriteIndex() const
77 {
78    return spriteIndex;
79 }
80
```

The purpose of the getSpriteIndex member function is to return the sprite's index. The getSpriteIndex member function is an accessor that returns the value of the spriteIndex member variable. Notice that the word const appears at the end of the function header in line 76. As previously mentioned, this specifies that the function does not modify the object's state. It merely returns a value from the object.

The definition of the getImageFile member function is shown in lines 84 through 87, as follows:

Program 11-1   (**SpriteClassDemo1**, *continued*)

```
81 // The Sprite::getImageFile member function
82 // returns the name of the image file used to
83 // create this sprite.
84 string Sprite::getImageFile() const
85 {
86     return imageFile;
87 }
88
```

The purpose of the getImageFile member function is to return the name of the sprite's image file. The getSpriteIndex member function is an accessor that returns the value of the imageFile member variable. (As previously mentioned, the word const at the end of the function header specifies that the function does not modify the object's state. It merely returns a value from the object.)

The definition of the getX member function is shown in lines 91 through 94, as follows:

Program 11-1   (**SpriteClassDemo1**, *continued*)

```
89 // The Sprite::getX member function returns the
90 // sprite's X-coordinate.
91 float Sprite::getX() const
92 {
93     return agk::GetSpriteX(spriteIndex);
94 }
95
```

The purpose of the getX member function is to return the sprite's X-coordinate. In line 93, the agk::GetSpriteX function is called to get the sprite's X-coordinate, and that value is returned from the getX member function. (As previously mentioned, the word const at the end of the function header specifies that the function does not modify the object's state. It merely returns a value from the object.)

The definition of the getY member function is shown in lines 98 through 101, as follows:

Program 11-1   (**SpriteClassDemo1**, *continued*)

```
 96 // The Sprite::getY member function returns the
 97 // sprite's Y-coordinate.
 98 float Sprite::getY() const
 99 {
100     return agk::GetSpriteY(spriteIndex);
101 }
102
```

The purpose of the getY member function is to return the sprite's Y-coordinate. In line 100, the agk::GetSpriteX function is called to get the sprite's Y-coordinate, and that value is returned from the getY member function. (As previously mentioned, the word const at the end of the function header specifies that the function does not modify the object's state. It merely returns a value from the object.)

The class destructor is shown next, in lines 105 through 108. When an instance of this class is destroyed, the destructor deletes the sprite from memory.

Program 11-1   (**SpriteClassDemo1**, *continued*)

```
103 // The Sprite class destructor deletes the
104 // sprite from memory.
105 Sprite::~Sprite()
106 {
107     agk::DeleteSprite(spriteIndex);
108 }
109
```

Now, let's look at the rest of the program, which uses the Sprite class to create and display a spaceship sprite. Lines 110 through 144 are shown here:

Program 11-1   (**SpriteClassDemo1**, *continued*)

```
110 // Constants for the screen resolution
111 const int SCREEN_WIDTH = 640;
112 const int SCREEN_HEIGHT = 480;
113
114 // Constants related to the sprite.
115 const int SPACESHIP_INDEX = 1;
116 const float SPACESHIP_X = 215;
117 const float SPACESHIP_Y = 212;
118
119 Sprite spaceship(SPACESHIP_INDEX, "Space/spaceship.png");
120
121 // Begin app, called once at the start
122 void app::Begin( void )
123 {
124     // Set the virtual resolution.
125     agk::SetVirtualResolution(SCREEN_WIDTH, SCREEN_HEIGHT);
126
127     // Create the sprite on the screen.
128     spaceship.createSprite();
129
130     // Position the sprite.
131     spaceship.setPosition(SPACESHIP_X, SPACESHIP_Y);
132 }
133
134 // Main loop, called every frame
135 void app::Loop ( void )
```

```
136 {
137     // Display the screen.
138     agk::Sync();
139 }
140
141 // Called when the app ends
142 void app::End ( void )
143 {
144 }
```

Lines 111 and 112 declare global constants for the screen resolution, and lines 115 through 117 declare global constants for the sprite's index, X-coordinate, and Y-coordinate.

Line 119 creates an object from the Sprite class. Here is the statement that creates the object:

```
Sprite spaceship(SPACESHIP_INDEX, "Space/spaceship.png");
```

Think of this statement as being similar to a variable declaration. Instead of a variable, however, we are declaring an object of the Sprite class. The object's name is spaceship. The items that appear inside the parentheses are arguments we are passing to the class constructor (previously shown in lines 36 through 40). After this statement executes, an object that is an instance of the Sprite class will exist in memory, and the object's name will be spaceship. That object's index member variable will be assigned the value 1 (the value of the SPACESHIP_INDEX constant), and the object's imageFile member variable will be assigned the string "Space/spaceship.png". This is illustrated in Figure 11-7. Note that because the object is declared globally, it will be available to all the functions in the program.

Figure 11-7 An instance of the Sprite class

spaceship is a Sprite object

index	1
imageFile	"Space/spaceship.png"

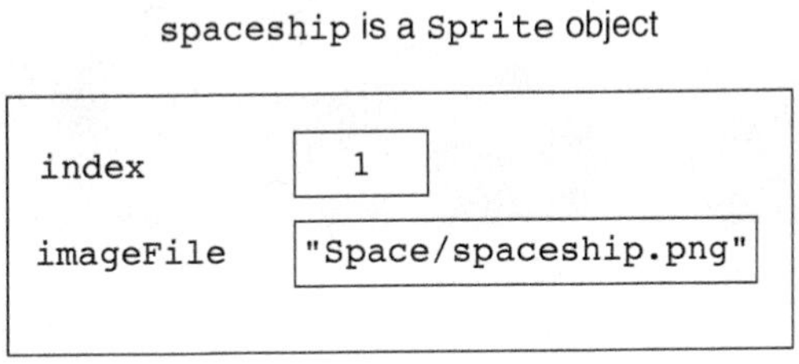

Next is the app::Begin function, shown in lines 122 through 132. Line 125 sets the virtual resolution. Line 128, shown here, appears next:

```
spaceship.createSprite();
```

The statement is written in *dot notation*. It's called dot notation because programmers refer to the period as a "dot." On the left side of the dot is the name of an object. On the right side of the dot is the name of the member function we are calling. When this statement executes, the createSprite member function will be called to operate on the spaceship object. Recall that the createSprite member function (previously shown in lines 43 through 51) creates the sprite on the screen.

Next, in line 131, we call the `setPosition` member function on the `spaceship` object, passing the constants `SPACESHIP_X` and `SPACESHIP_Y` as arguments:

```
spaceship.setPosition(SPACESHIP_X, SPACESHIP_Y);
```

The values of the constants `SPACESHIP_X` and `SPACESHIP_Y` are 215 and 212, respectively. After this statement executes, the sprite will be located at the coordinates (215, 212).

Next is the `app::Loop` function that simply calls the `agk::Sync` function in line 138 to update the screen. The program's output is shown in Figure 11-8.

> **NOTE:** To run this program, you will need to create a folder named *Space* in your *My Documents > AGK > template* folder and then copy the image file `spaceship.png` into the *Space* folder.

Figure 11-8 Output of Program 11-1

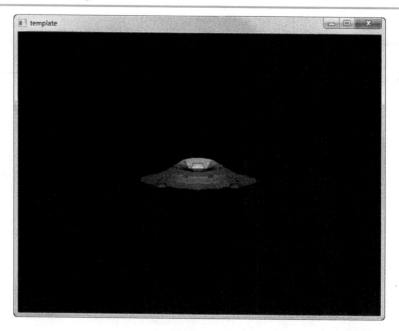

Creating Multiple Objects From the Same Class

You can create several objects from the same class in a program. Each object has its own set of member variables. For example, look at Program 11-2, which creates three spaceship sprites, each of which is an instance of the `Sprite` class. The spaceship sprites are placed at different positions on the screen. (To save space, we have left out lines 32 through 109, which contain the definitions of the `Sprite` class's member functions. The function definitions are the same as those shown in Program 11-1.)

Program 11-2   (MultipleObjects)

```
1 // Includes, namespace and prototypes
2 #include "template.h"
3 #include <string>        // Needed for the string class
```

```
 4 using namespace std;    // Needed for the string class
 5 using namespace AGK;
 6 app App;
 7
 8 class Sprite
 9 {
10 private:
11     int spriteIndex;  // The sprite index
12     string imageFile; // The name of the image file
13 public:
14     // Constructor
15     Sprite(int, string);
16
17     // Mutators
18     void createSprite();
19     void setPosition(float, float);
20     void setX(float);
21     void setY(float);
22
23     // Accessors
24     int getSpriteIndex() const;
25     string getImageFile() const;
26     float getX() const;
27     float getY() const;
28
29     // Destructor
30     ~Sprite();
31 };
```

Lines 32 through 109 are not shown. They are the same as was shown in Program 11-1.

```
110 // Constants for the screen resolution
111 const int SCREEN_WIDTH = 640;
112 const int SCREEN_HEIGHT = 480;
113
114 // Constants for the sprite indices
115 const int SPACESHIP1_INDEX = 1;
116 const int SPACESHIP2_INDEX = 2;
117 const int SPACESHIP3_INDEX = 3;
118
119 // Constants for the sprite positions
120 const float SPACESHIP1_X = 0;
121 const float SPACESHIP1_Y = 0;
122
123 const float SPACESHIP2_X = 215;
124 const float SPACESHIP2_Y = 212;
125
126 const float SPACESHIP3_X = 430;
127 const float SPACESHIP3_Y = 424;
128
129 Sprite spaceship1(SPACESHIP1_INDEX, "Space/spaceship.png");
130 Sprite spaceship2(SPACESHIP2_INDEX, "Space/spaceship.png");
131 Sprite spaceship3(SPACESHIP3_INDEX, "Space/spaceship.png");
132
133 // Begin app, called once at the start
134 void app::Begin( void )
```

```
135 {
136     // Set the virtual resolution.
137     agk::SetVirtualResolution(SCREEN_WIDTH, SCREEN_HEIGHT);
138
139     // Create the sprites on the screen.
140     spaceship1.createSprite();
141     spaceship2.createSprite();
142     spaceship3.createSprite();
143
144     // Position the sprite.
145     spaceship1.setPosition(SPACESHIP1_X, SPACESHIP1_Y);
146     spaceship2.setPosition(SPACESHIP2_X, SPACESHIP2_Y);
147     spaceship3.setPosition(SPACESHIP3_X, SPACESHIP3_Y);
148 }
149
150 // Main loop, called every frame
151 void app::Loop ( void )
152 {
153     // Display the screen.
154     agk::Sync();
155 }
156
157 // Called when the app ends
158 void app::End ( void )
159 {
160 }
```

In lines 115 through 117 we declare constants for the three sprite indices. In lines 120 through 127 we declare constants for the three sprite's *XY*-coordinates. Then, in lines 129 through 131 we declare three Sprite objects, named spaceship1, spaceship2, and spaceship3:

- Line 129 declares the spaceship1 object. We pass the SPACESHIP1_INDEX constant (which is set to the value 1) as the sprite index and "Space/spaceship.png" as the name of the image file.
- Line 130 declares the spaceship2 object. We pass the SPACESHIP2_INDEX constant (which is set to the value 2) as the sprite index and "Space/spaceship.png" as the name of the image file.
- Line 131 declares the spaceship3 object. We pass the SPACESHIP3_INDEX constant (which is set to the value 3) as the sprite index and "Space/spaceship.png" as the name of the image file.

Figure 11-9 illustrates the state of these three objects, showing the values of each object's index and imageFile member variable.

Figure 11-9 The spaceship1, spaceship2, and spaceship3 objects

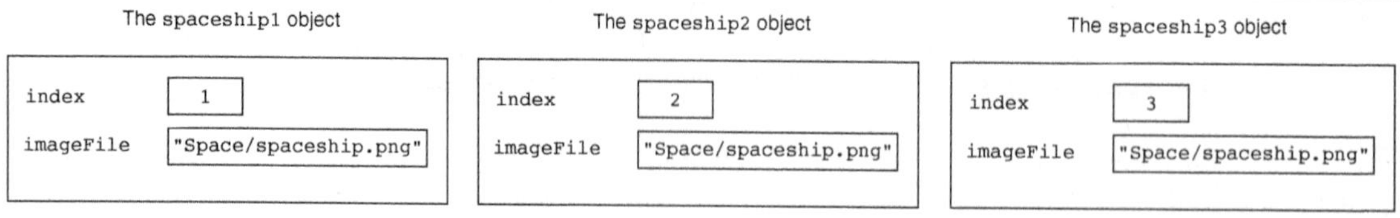

The spaceship1 object	The spaceship2 object	The spaceship3 object
index `1`	index `2`	index `3`
imageFile `"Space/spaceship.png"`	imageFile `"Space/spaceship.png"`	imageFile `"Space/spaceship.png"`

Next is the `app::Begin` function, shown in lines 134 through 148. Line 137 sets the virtual resolution. Line 140 through 142, shown here, appears next:

```
spaceship1.createSprite();
spaceship2.createSprite();
spaceship3.createSprite();
```

These statements call each object's `createSprite` member function, which creates the sprites on the screen. Then, lines 145 through 147 call each object's `setPosition` member function, passing the constants that were previously created for the X- and Y-coordinates:

```
spaceship1.setPosition(SPACESHIP1_X, SPACESHIP1_Y);
spaceship2.setPosition(SPACESHIP2_X, SPACESHIP2_Y);
spaceship3.setPosition(SPACESHIP3_X, SPACESHIP3_Y);
```

After these statements execute, the `spaceship1` object's sprite will be positioned at (0,0), the `spaceship2` object's sprite will be positioned at (215, 212), and the `spaceship3` object's sprite will be positioned at (430, 424).

Next is the `app::Loop` function that simply calls the `agk::Sync` function in line 154 to update the screen. The program's output is shown in Figure 11-10.

Figure 11-10 Output of Program 11-2

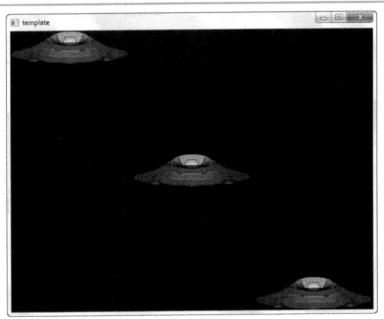

Overloaded Constructors and Member Functions

Sometimes you need different ways to perform the same operations in a class. For example, the `Sprite` class that was previously shown in Programs 11-1 and 11-2 requires that you pass a sprite index and an image file name as arguments to the constructor. Suppose that in some situations, you need to create an instance of the `Sprite` class without providing these arguments. For example, the sprite index might be calculated by the program, or the image file name might be selected by the program from several potential file names just before the sprite is created.

Fortunately, you can have more than one constructor in a class. When a class has multiple constructors, we say that the constructor is *overloaded*. When a class has overloaded constructors, each of the constructors must have a different parameter list. Here is an example of two overloaded Sprite class constructors:

```
// Constructor #1
Sprite::Sprite()
{
    spriteIndex = 1;
    imageFile = "";
}

// Constructor #2
Sprite::Sprite(int index, string filename)
{
    spriteIndex = index;
    imageFile = filename;
}
```

The first constructor accepts no arguments. It simply assigns the number 1 to the spriteIndex member variable, and it assigns an empty string ("") to the imageFile member variable. You would use this constructor any time you wanted to create an instance of the Sprite class, but you were not ready to assign a sprite index or specify an image file.

The second constructor is the same one that you saw in Programs 11-1 and 11-2. It has two parameters: an int named index and a string named filename. These parameters are assigned to the object's member variables. You would use this version of the constructor when you know the sprite number and image file name at the time the object is created.

> **NOTE:** A constructor that accepts no arguments is known as the class's *default constructor*. A constructor that accepts arguments is known as a *parameterized* constructor.

Regular member functions can be overloaded too. For example, here are two overloaded versions of the Sprite class's createSprite member function:

```
// Version #1 of the createSprite member function
void Sprite::createSprite()
{
    // If the sprite does not already exist,
    // then create it.
    if (!agk::GetSpriteExists(spriteIndex))
    {
        agk::CreateSprite(spriteIndex, imageFile.c_str());
    }
}
```

```
// Version #2 of the createSprite member function
void Sprite::createSprite(int index, string filename)
{
    // Set the member variables.
    spriteIndex = index;
    imageFile = filename;

    // If the sprite does not already exist,
    // then create it.
    if (!agk::GetSpriteExists(spriteIndex))
    {
        agk::CreateSprite(spriteIndex, imageFile.c_str());
    }
}
```

The first version of the member function is the same as you previously saw in Programs 11-1 and 11-2. It accepts no arguments and creates the sprite using the existing values of the spriteIndex and imageFile member variables. You would use this version of the member function whenever the object already contains, in its member variables, the desired sprite index and the image file name. (This would be the case when the object was created with constructor #2).

The second one, however, has two parameters: an int named index, and a string named filename. These parameters are assigned to the object's member variables, and then the sprite is created using those values. You would use this version of the function whenever the desired sprite index and image file name have not been assigned to the object's member variables. (This would be the case when the object was created with constructor #1).

When an overloaded constructor or member function is called, the compiler must determine which of the overloaded constructors or member functions we intended to call. The process of matching a function call with the correct function is known as *binding*. When an overloaded constructor or function is being called, the compiler uses the function's name and parameter list to determine to which function to bind the call. For example, if no arguments are passed to the createSprite member function, the version of the function with no parameters is called. Likewise, when an int and a string are passed as arguments to the createSprite function, the version with int and string parameters is called.

> **NOTE:** When a class has a constructor that accepts no arguments, that constructor is referred to as the *default constructor*.

The compiler uses a function's signature to distinguish it from other functions of the same name. A function's *signature* consists of the function's name and the data types of the function's parameters, in the order that they appear. For example, here are the signatures of the createSprite functions that were previously shown:

```
Sprite::createSprite()
Sprite::createSprite(int, string)
```

Note that the function's return type is *not* part of the signature. For this reason, you cannot overload functions by giving them different return types.

Program 11-3 demonstrates the Sprite class with the overloaded constructors and overloaded createSprite member functions that we just discussed. This program is very similar to Program 11-2, except that it uses the Sprite class's default constructor (with no arguments) to create the three Sprite objects. Then, in the app::Begin function, it uses the createSprite member function that accepts an index and an image file name as arguments. The program's output is the same as that of Program 11-2, which was previously shown in Figure 11-10.

Program 11-3 (Overloaded)

```
 1 // Includes, namespace and prototypes
 2 #include "template.h"
 3 #include <string>        // Needed for the string class
 4 using namespace std;     // Needed for the string class
 5 using namespace AGK;
 6 app App;
 7
 8 class Sprite
 9 {
10 private:
11     int spriteIndex;     // The sprite index
12     string imageFile;    // The name of the image file
13 public:
14     // Constructors
15     Sprite();
16     Sprite(int, string);
17
18     // Mutators
19     void createSprite();
20     void createSprite(int, string);
21     void setPosition(float, float);
22     void setX(float);
23     void setY(float);
24
25     // Accessors
26     int getSpriteIndex() const;
27     string getImageFile() const;
28     float getX() const;
29     float getY() const;
30
31     // Destructor
32     ~Sprite();
33 };
34
35 // This is the default constructor for the Sprite
36 // class. It sets index to 1 and imageFile to
37 // an empty string.
38 Sprite::Sprite()
39 {
40     spriteIndex = 1;
41     imageFile = "";
42 }
43
```

```
44 // This Sprite class constructor accepts as arguments
45 // the sprite index and the name of the image file,
46 // and initializes the member variables.
47 Sprite::Sprite(int index, string filename)
48 {
49    spriteIndex = index;
50    imageFile = filename;
51 }
52
53 // The Sprite::createSprite member function
54 void Sprite::createSprite()
55 {
56    // If the sprite does not already exist,
57    // then create it.
58    if (!agk::GetSpriteExists(spriteIndex))
59    {
60       agk::CreateSprite(spriteIndex, imageFile.c_str());
61    }
62 }
63
64 // The Sprite::createSprite member function
65 void Sprite::createSprite(int index, string filename)
66 {
67    // Set the member variables.
68    spriteIndex = index;
69    imageFile = filename;
70
71    // If the sprite does not already exist,
72    // then create it.
73    if (!agk::GetSpriteExists(spriteIndex))
74    {
75       agk::CreateSprite(spriteIndex, imageFile.c_str());
76    }
77 }
78
79 // The Sprite::setPosition member function sets the
80 // sprite's position.
81 void Sprite::setPosition(float x, float y)
82 {
83    agk::SetSpritePosition(spriteIndex, x, y);
84 }
85
86 // The Sprite::setX member function sets the
87 // sprite's X-coordinate.
88 void Sprite::setX(float x)
89 {
90    agk::SetSpriteX(spriteIndex, x);
91 }
92
93 // The Sprite::setY member function sets the
94 // sprite's Y-coordinate.
95 void Sprite::setY(float y)
96 {
97    agk::SetSpriteY(spriteIndex, y);
98 }
```

```
 99
100 // The Sprite::getSpriteIndex member function
101 // returns the sprite's index.
102 int Sprite::getSpriteIndex() const
103 {
104     return spriteIndex;
105 }
106
107 // The Sprite::getImageFile member function
108 // returns the name of the image file used to
109 // create this sprite.
110 string Sprite::getImageFile() const
111 {
112     return imageFile;
113 }
114
115 // The Sprite::getX member function returns the
116 // sprite's X-coordinate.
117 float Sprite::getX() const
118 {
119     return agk::GetSpriteX(spriteIndex);
120 }
121
122 // The Sprite::getY member function returns the
123 // sprite's Y-coordinate.
124 float Sprite::getY() const
125 {
126     return agk::GetSpriteY(spriteIndex);
127 }
128
129 // The Sprite class destructor deletes the
130 // sprite from memory.
131 Sprite::~Sprite()
132 {
133     agk::DeleteSprite(spriteIndex);
134 }
135
136 // Constants for the screen resolution
137 const int SCREEN_WIDTH = 640;
138 const int SCREEN_HEIGHT = 480;
139
140 // Constants for the sprite indices
141 const int SPACESHIP1_INDEX = 1;
142 const int SPACESHIP2_INDEX = 2;
143 const int SPACESHIP3_INDEX = 3;
144
145 // Constants for the sprite positions
146 const float SPACESHIP1_X = 0;
147 const float SPACESHIP1_Y = 0;
148
149 const float SPACESHIP2_X = 215;
150 const float SPACESHIP2_Y = 212;
151
152 const float SPACESHIP3_X = 430;
153 const float SPACESHIP3_Y = 424;
```

```
154
155  // Declare three Sprite objects.
156  Sprite spaceship1;
157  Sprite spaceship2;
158  Sprite spaceship3;
159
160  // Begin app, called once at the start
161  void app::Begin( void )
162  {
163      // Set the virtual resolution.
164      agk::SetVirtualResolution(SCREEN_WIDTH, SCREEN_HEIGHT);
165
166      // Create the sprites on the screen.
167      spaceship1.createSprite(SPACESHIP1_INDEX, "Space/spaceship.png");
168      spaceship2.createSprite(SPACESHIP2_INDEX, "Space/spaceship.png");
169      spaceship3.createSprite(SPACESHIP3_INDEX, "Space/spaceship.png");
170
171      // Position the sprite.
172      spaceship1.setPosition(SPACESHIP1_X, SPACESHIP1_Y);
173      spaceship2.setPosition(SPACESHIP2_X, SPACESHIP2_Y);
174      spaceship3.setPosition(SPACESHIP3_X, SPACESHIP3_Y);
175  }
176
177  // Main loop, called every frame
178  void app::Loop ( void )
179  {
180      // Display the screen.
181      agk::Sync();
182  }
183
184  // Called when the app ends
185  void app::End ( void )
186  {
187  }
```

Inside the Sprite class, notice the following:

- The two overloaded constructors are declared in lines 15 and 16.
- The two overloaded createSprite member functions are declared in lines 19 and 20.

After the class definition, the overloaded constructors are defined in lines 38 through 42 and 47 through 51. The overloaded createSprite member functions are defined in lines 54 through 62 and lines 65 through 77.

In lines 156 through 158, we declare three Sprite objects named spaceship1, spaceship2, and spaceship3. Notice that no arguments are passed to the constructor (in fact, there aren't even any parentheses following the object names). This causes the default constructor, which is defined in lines 38 through 42, to execute. As a result, each object's spriteIndex member variable will be set to 1, and each object's imageFile member variable will be set to an empty string ("").

Inside the `app::Begin` function, lines 167 through 169, shown here, call each object's createSprite member function:

```
spaceship1.createSprite(SPACESHIP1_INDEX, "Space/spaceship.png");
spaceship2.createSprite(SPACESHIP2_INDEX, "Space/spaceship.png");
spaceship3.createSprite(SPACESHIP3_INDEX, "Space/spaceship.png");
```

In each of these statements we are passing an int and a string as arguments. As a result, the version of the createSprite function that appears in lines 65 through 77 will be called.

Creating Arrays of Objects

As with any other data type in C++, you can define arrays of class objects. For example, the following creates an array of Sprite objects:

```
const int ARRAY_SIZE = 5;
Sprite mysprites[ARRAY_SIZE];
```

This code creates an array of five Sprite objects. The name of the array is mysprites, and the default constructor is called for each object in the array. Program 11-4 declares such an array and demonstrates how to process its elements. (To save space, we have left out lines 34 through 135, which contain the definitions of the Sprite class's member functions. The function definitions are the same as those shown in Program 11-3.) The program's output is shown in Figure 11-11.

Program 11-4   (ObjectArray)

```
 1 // Includes, namespace and prototypes
 2 #include "template.h"
 3 #include <string>        // Needed for the string class
 4 using namespace std;     // Needed for the string class
 5 using namespace AGK;
 6 app App;
 7
 8 class Sprite
 9 {
10 private:
11    int spriteIndex;  // The sprite index
12    string imageFile; // The name of the image file
13 public:
14    // Constructors
15    Sprite();
16    Sprite(int, string);
17
18    // Mutators
19    void createSprite();
20    void createSprite(int, string);
21    void setPosition(float, float);
22    void setX(float);
23    void setY(float);
24
```

```
25      // Accessors
26      int getSpriteIndex() const;
27      string getImageFile() const;
28      float getX() const;
29      float getY() const;
30
31      // Destructor
32      ~Sprite();
33 };
```

Lines 34 through 135 are not shown. They are the same as was shown in Program 11-3.

```
136 // Constants for the screen resolution
137 const int SCREEN_WIDTH = 640;
138 const int SCREEN_HEIGHT = 480;
139
140 // Constants for the sprite positions
141 const float STARTING_X = 0;
142 const float STARTING_Y = 0;
143
144 // Declare an array of 5 Sprite objects.
145 const int ARRAY_SIZE = 5;
146 Sprite mysprites[ARRAY_SIZE];
147
148 // Begin app, called once at the start
149 void app::Begin( void )
150 {
151     // Set the virtual resolution.
152     agk::SetVirtualResolution(SCREEN_WIDTH, SCREEN_HEIGHT);
153
154     // Create the sprites on the screen, in a column
155     // along the left edge of the window.
156     for (int i = 0; i < ARRAY_SIZE; i++)
157     {
158         mysprites[i].createSprite(i + 1, "Space/spaceship.png");
159     }
160
161     // Position the sprite.
162     for (int i = 0; i < ARRAY_SIZE; i++)
163     {
164         mysprites[i].setPosition(STARTING_X, STARTING_Y + i * 100);
165     }
166 }
167
168 // Main loop, called every frame
169 void app::Loop ( void )
170 {
171     // Display the screen.
172     agk::Sync();
173 }
174
175 // Called when the app ends
176 void app::End ( void )
177 {
178 }
```

Figure 11-11 Output of Program 11-4

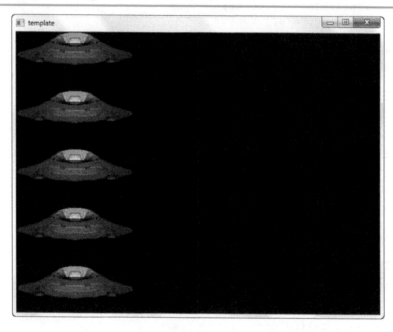

The STARTING_X and STARTING_Y constants, declared in lines 141 and 142, are used as the XY-coordinates of the first sprite that is displayed. We will calculate the coordinates of the remaining sprites, using these values.

The following statements in lines 145 and 146 create an array of five Sprite objects. The name of the array is mysprites, and the default constructor is called for each object:

```
const int ARRAY_SIZE = 5;
Sprite mysprites[ARRAY_SIZE];
```

Then, in the app::Begin function, the following loop appears in lines 156 through 159:

```
for (int i = 0; i < ARRAY_SIZE; i++)
{
    mysprites[i].createSprite(i + 1, "Space/spaceship.png");
}
```

This loop steps through each element of the mysprites array. Inside the loop, the element's createSprite member function is called. The value of the expression i + 1 is passed as the sprite's index. As a result, the five sprites will have the indices 1 through 5. The string "Space/spaceship.png" is passed as the image file name for each element.

Next, the following loop appears in lines 162 through 165:

```
for (int i = 0; i < ARRAY_SIZE; i++)
{
    mysprites[i].setPosition(STARTING_X, STARTING_Y + i * 100);
}
```

This loop also steps through each element of the mysprites array. Inside the loop, the element's setPosition member function is called to position the element on the screen.

The constant STARTING_X (which is set to 0) is passed as the *X*-coordinate for each element. The value of the expression STARTING_Y + i * 100 is passed as the *Y*-coordinate. As a result, the sprites are displayed in a column along the left edge of the window.

Passing Objects as Arguments to Functions

Objects can be passed as arguments to functions just like regular variables. When you pass an object by value, only a copy of the object is passed into the function. If you want the function to be able to modify the object, you must pass it by reference. Program 11-5 shows an example. In this program we have written a void function named placeSprite. The placeSprite function accepts a Sprite object by reference. It then sets the object's position to a random value. (As with previous programs, we have left out lines 34 through 135, which contain the definitions of the Sprite class's member functions. The function definitions are the same as those shown in Program 11-3.)

Program 11-5   **(PassObject)**

```
 1 // Includes, namespace and prototypes
 2 #include "template.h"
 3 #include <string>      // Needed for the string class
 4 using namespace std;   // Needed for the string class
 5 using namespace AGK;
 6 app App;
 7
 8 class Sprite
 9 {
10 private:
11    int spriteIndex;  // The sprite index
12    string imageFile; // The name of the image file
13 public:
14    // Constructors
15    Sprite();
16    Sprite(int, string);
17
18    // Mutators
19    void createSprite();
20    void createSprite(int, string);
21    void setPosition(float, float);
22    void setX(float);
23    void setY(float);
24
25    // Accessors
26    int getSpriteIndex() const;
27    string getImageFile() const;
28    float getX() const;
29    float getY() const;
30
31    // Destructor
32    ~Sprite();
33 };
```

Lines 34 through 135 are not shown. They are the same as was shown in Program 11-3.

```
136 // Function prototype for the placeSprite function
137 void placeSprite(Sprite &);
```

```
138
139 // Constants for the screen resolution
140 const int SCREEN_WIDTH = 640;
141 const int SCREEN_HEIGHT = 480;
142
143 // Constants for the sprite index
144 const int SPRITE_INDEX = 1;
145
146 // Declare an instance of the Sprite class
147 Sprite spaceship(SPRITE_INDEX, "Space/spaceship.png");
148
149 // Begin app, called once at the start
150 void app::Begin( void )
151 {
152     // Set the virtual resolution.
153     agk::SetVirtualResolution(SCREEN_WIDTH, SCREEN_HEIGHT);
154
155     // Create the sprite on the screen.
156     spaceship.createSprite();
157
158     // Place the sprite at a random location.
159     placeSprite(spaceship);
160 }
161
162 // Main loop, called every frame
163 void app::Loop ( void )
164 {
165     // Display the screen.
166     agk::Sync();
167 }
168
169 // Called when the app ends
170 void app::End ( void )
171 {
172 }
173
174 // The placeSprite function accepts a Sprite object as
175 // an argument, and it places that sprite at a random
176 // location on the screen.
177 void placeSprite(Sprite &sprite)
178 {
179     // Get random XY-coordinates for the sprite.
180     int x = agk::Random(0, SCREEN_WIDTH - 210);
181     int y = agk::Random(0, SCREEN_HEIGHT - 56);
182
183     // Position the sprite.
184     sprite.setPosition(x, y);
185 }
```

Note that the function prototype for the placeSprite function, in line 137, is written after the declaration of the Sprite class. This is necessary because the placeSprite function accepts a Sprite object as an argument. The compiler must be aware of the Sprite class's existence before it can process the prototype or the definition of the placeSprite function.

Also note that in line 180, we get a random number in the range of 0 through SCREEN_WIDTH - 210, and in line 181 we get a random number in the range of 0 through SCREEN_HEIGHT - 56. This is because the spaceship.png image is 210 pixels wide and 56 pixels high, and by using these calculations, we make sure the sprite is never positioned offscreen.

Checkpoint

11.5. You hear someone make the following comment: "A blueprint is a design for a house. A carpenter can use the blueprint to build the house. If the carpenter wishes, he or she can build several identical houses from the same blueprint." Think of this as a metaphor for classes and objects. Does the blueprint represent a class, or does it represent an object?

11.6. In this chapter we use the metaphor of a cookie cutter and cookies that are made from the cookie cutter to describe classes and objects. In this metaphor, are objects the cookie cutter, or the cookies?

11.7. An object's private members are accessible by what code?

11.8. Are a class's member variables typically declared in the class's public section or the class's private section?

11.9. Are a class's member functions typically declared in the class's public section or the class's private section?

11.10. What is an accessor? What is a mutator?

11.11. What is a constructor?

11.12. What is a parameterized constructor? What is a default constructor?

11.13. What are overloaded member functions?

11.14. What is a destructor?

11.3 Inheritance

CONCEPT: Inheritance allows a new class to extend an existing class. The new class inherits the members of the class it extends.

Generalization and Specialization

In the real world you can find many objects that are specialized versions of other more general objects. For example, the term *insect* describes a very general type of creature with numerous characteristics. Because grasshoppers and bumblebees are insects, they have all the general characteristics of an insect. In addition, they have special characteristics of their own. For example, the grasshopper has its jumping ability, and the bumblebee has its stinger. Grasshoppers and bumblebees are specialized versions of an insect. This is illustrated in Figure 11-12.

Figure 11-12 Bumblebees and grasshoppers are specialized versions of an insect

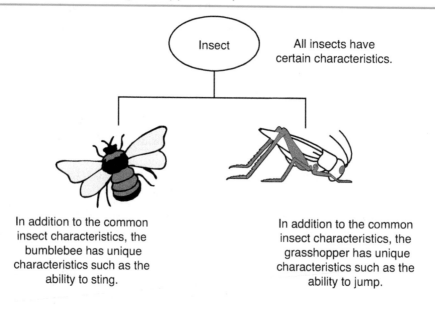

All insects have certain characteristics.

In addition to the common insect characteristics, the bumblebee has unique characteristics such as the ability to sting.

In addition to the common insect characteristics, the grasshopper has unique characteristics such as the ability to jump.

Inheritance and the "Is-a" Relationship

When one object is a specialized version of another object, an "is-a" relationship exists between them. For example, a grasshopper is an insect. Here are a few other examples of the is-a relationship:

- A poodle is a dog.
- A car is a vehicle.
- A flower is a plant.
- A rectangle is a shape.
- A football player is an athlete.

When an is-a relationship exists between objects, it means that the specialized object has all the characteristics of the general object, plus additional characteristics that make it special. In object-oriented programming, inheritance is used to create an is-a relationship among classes. This allows you to extend the capabilities of a class by creating another class that is a specialized version of the first one.

Inheritance involves a base class and a derived class. The *base class* is the general class, and the *derived class* is the specialized class. You can think of the derived class as an extended version of the base class. The derived class inherits members from the base class without any of them having to be rewritten. Furthermore, new members may be added to the derived class, and that is what makes it a specialized version of the base class.

Let's look at an example of inheritance. In the previous section we demonstrated a simple `Sprite` class that provides the basic operations needed to create and work with a sprite. In this section we will examine a `MoveableSprite` class that is derived from the `Sprite` class. The `MoveableSprite` class will give the ability to move the sprite on the screen.

When we derive the `MoveableSprite` class from the `Sprite` class, the `MoveableSprite` class will inherit all the members of the `Sprite` class. So, when we declare the

MoveableSprite class, we only specify the members that are new to the MoveableSprite class. We will have the following member variable in the MoveableSprite class:

- distance—This int variable will hold the sprite's moving distance. This is the number of pixels that the sprite is to move each time it is moved.

The MoveableSprite class will also have the following public member functions:

- Constructor—A parameterized constructor that accepts as arguments the sprite index number, the image file name, and the sprite's moving distance.
- setDistance—This member function accepts an argument for the sprite's moving distance and assigns it to the distance member variable.
- getDistance—This member function returns the sprite's moving distance.
- moveUp—This member function moves the sprite up.
- moveDown—This member function moves the sprite down.
- moveLeft—This member function moves the sprite to the left.
- moveRight—This member function moves the sprite to the right.

Program 11-6 demonstrates the MoveableSprite class. When this program is compiled and executed, it displays the spaceship sprite on the screen. You can use the arrow keys on the keyboard to move the spaceship up, down, left, or right. To save space, we will not show lines 1 through 135 of the program. These lines contain the include directives, other initial code, and the Sprite class code, which is the same as was shown in Program 11-5.

The declaration for the MoveableSprite class begins in line 137.

Program 11-6   (**MoveableSpriteDemo**, *partial listing*)

```
136 // MoveableSprite declaration
137 class MoveableSprite : public Sprite
138 {
139 private:
140    int distance;
141 public:
142    // Constructors
143    MoveableSprite();
144    MoveableSprite(int, string, int);
145
146    // Mutators and accessors
147    void setDistance(int);
148    int getDistance() const;
149
150    // Functions to move the sprite
151    void moveUp();
152    void moveDown();
153    void moveLeft();
154    void moveRight();
155 };
156
```

The only new notation in this class declaration appears in line 137. After the name of the class, MoveableSprite, a colon appears, followed by public Sprite. This indicates that the

MoveableSprite class is derived from the Sprite class. (The MoveableSprite class is the derived class, and the Sprite class is the base class.) Figure 11-13 illustrates this notation.

Figure 11-13 Inheritance notation in the class header

The class being declared (the derived class)

The colon indicates that this class is derived from another class.

```
class MoveableSprite : public Sprite
{
private:
    int distance;              The base class
public:
    // Constructors
    MoveableSprite();
    MoveableSprite(int, string, int);
```

and so forth...

 WARNING! When writing the class header for a derived class, don't forget the word *public* that appears after the colon. If you leave out the word *public*, the class will compile, but it will not be able to access any of the base class members.

The MoveableSprite class has two overloaded constructors, shown here:

Program 11-6   (**MoveableSpriteDemo**, *continued*)

```
157 // Default constructor
158 MoveableSprite::MoveableSprite() : Sprite()
159 {
160    distance = 0;
161 }
162
163 // This constructor accepts arguments for the sprite
164 // index, image file name, and distance to move.
165 MoveableSprite::MoveableSprite(int index, string filename,
166                int dist) : Sprite(index, filename)
167 {
168    distance = dist;
169 }
170
```

The default constructor, defined in lines 158 through 161, sets the distance member variable to 0. Notice the notation : Sprite that appears at the end of line 158. This is an explicit call to the Sprite class's constructor. This indicates that the Sprite class's default constructor will be executed first, then the MoveableSprite constructor will execute.

The second constructor, which appears in lines 165 through 169, accepts arguments for the sprite index, the image file name, and the sprite's moving distance. Notice the following that appears at the end of line 166:

    : Sprite(index, filename)

This is an explicit call to the Sprite class constructor. This executes the parameterized Sprite class constructor, passing the values of index and filename as arguments. After the parameterized Sprite class constructor executes, the MoveableSprite class constructor executes. In line 168, it assigns the value of the dist parameter to the distance member variable.

The setDistance member function is defined in lines 173 through 176.

Program 11-6   (**MoveableSpriteDemo**, *continued*)

```
171 // The setDistance member function sets
172 // the moving distance.
173 void MoveableSprite::setDistance(int dist)
174 {
175    distance = dist;
176 }
177
```

The getDistance member function is defined in lines 180 through 183.

Program 11-6   (**MoveableSpriteDemo**, *continued*)

```
178 // The getDistance member function returns the
179 // sprite's moving distance.
180 int MoveableSprite::getDistance() const
181 {
182    return distance;
183 }
184
```

The moveUp member function is defined in lines 186 through 197.

Program 11-6   (**MoveableSpriteDemo**, *continued*)

```
185 // The moveUp member function moves the sprite up.
186 void MoveableSprite::moveUp()
187 {
188    // Get the sprite's current coordinates.
189    int x = getX();
190    int y = getY();
191
192    // Decrease y.
193    y -= distance;
194
195    // Move the sprite to its new location.
196    setY(y);
197 }
198
```

Lines 189 and 190 call the Sprite class's getX and getY member functions to get the sprite's current XY-coordinates. Those values are assigned to the local variables x and y.

Line 193 decreases the value of y by the value of the distance member variable. Line 196 calls the Sprite class's setY function to position the sprite at its new location.

The moveDown member function is defined in lines 200 through 211, as follows:

Program 11-6 (MoveableSpriteDemo, *continued*)

```
199 // The moveDown member function moves the sprite down.
200 void MoveableSprite::moveDown()
201 {
202     // Get the sprite's current coordinates.
203     int x = getX();
204     int y = getY();
205
206     // Increase y.
207     y += distance;
208
209     // Move the sprite to its new location.
210     setY(y);
211 }
212
```

Lines 203 and 204 call the Sprite class's getX and getY member functions to get the sprite's current *XY*-coordinates. Those values are assigned to the local variables x and y. Line 207 increases the value of y by the value of the distance member variable. Line 210 calls the Sprite class's setY function to position the sprite at its new location.

The moveLeft member function is defined in lines 214 through 225, as follows:

Program 11-6 (MoveableSpriteDemo, *continued*)

```
213 // The moveLeft member function moves the sprite left.
214 void MoveableSprite::moveLeft()
215 {
216     // Get the sprite's current coordinates.
217     int x = getX();
218     int y = getY();
219
220     // Decrease x.
221     x -= distance;
222
223     // Move the sprite to its new location.
224     setX(x);
225 }
226
```

Lines 217 and 218 call the Sprite class's getX and getY member functions to get the sprite's current *XY*-coordinates. Those values are assigned to the local variables x and y. Line 221 decreases the value of x by the value of the distance member variable. Line 224 calls the Sprite class's setX function to position the sprite at its new location.

The moveRight member function is defined in lines 228 through 239, as follows:

Program 11-6   (MoveableSpriteDemo, *continued*)

```
227 // The moveRight member function moves the sprite right.
228 void MoveableSprite::moveRight()
229 {
230    // Get the sprite's current coordinates.
231    int x = getX();
232    int y = getY();
233
234    // Increase x.
235    x += distance;
236
237    // Move the sprite to its new location.
238    setX(x);
239 }
240
```

Lines 231 and 232 call the Sprite class's getX and getY member functions to get the sprite's current XY-coordinates. Those values are assigned to the local variables x and y. Line 235 increases the value of x by the value of the distance member variable. Line 238 calls the Sprite class's setX function to position the sprite at its new location.

The remaining lines of the program are shown here:

Program 11-6   (MoveableSpriteDemo, *continued*)

```
241 // Function prototype for the updateSprite function
242 void updateSprite(MoveableSprite &);
243
244 // Constants for the screen resolution
245 const int SCREEN_WIDTH = 640;
246 const int SCREEN_HEIGHT = 480;
247
248 // Constant for the sprite index
249 const int SPRITE_INDEX = 1;
250
251 // Constant for the moving distance
252 const int MOVING_DISTANCE = 10;
253
254 // Declare an instance of the MoveableSprite class
255 MoveableSprite spaceship(SPRITE_INDEX,
256    "Space/spaceship.png", MOVING_DISTANCE);
257
258 // Begin app, called once at the start
259 void app::Begin( void )
260 {
261    // Set the virtual resolution.
262    agk::SetVirtualResolution(SCREEN_WIDTH, SCREEN_HEIGHT);
263
264    // Create the sprite on the screen.
265    spaceship.createSprite();
```

```
266
267     // Position the sprite at the center of the screen.
268     spaceship.setPosition(SCREEN_WIDTH / 2 - 105,
269                           SCREEN_HEIGHT / 2 - 26);
270 }
271
272 // Main loop, called every frame
273 void app::Loop ( void )
274 {
275     // Update the sprite position.
276     updateSprite(spaceship);
277
278     // Display the screen.
279     agk::Sync();
280 }
281
282 // Called when the app ends
283 void app::End ( void )
284 {
285 }
286
287 // The updateSprite function checks for arrow key
288 // presses and moves the argument accordingly.
289 void updateSprite(MoveableSprite &sprite)
290 {
291     // Get the direction as input from the keyboard.
292     float directionX = agk::GetDirectionX();
293     float directionY = agk::GetDirectionY();
294
295     // Check for left/right arrow keys.
296     if (directionX < 0)
297     {
298         sprite.moveLeft();
299     }
300     else if (directionX > 0)
301     {
302         sprite.moveRight();
303     }
304
305     // Check for up/down arrow keys.
306     if (directionY < 0)
307     {
308         sprite.moveUp();
309     }
310     else if (directionY > 0)
311     {
312         sprite.moveDown();
313     }
314 }
```

Here is a summary of the code:

- Line 242 is the function prototype for a function named updateSprite. (The function definition appears in lines 289 through 314.)
- Lines 245 and 246 declare constants for the screen width and height.
- Line 249 declares a constant for the sprite index.
- Line 252 declares a constant for the moving distance.

- Lines 255 and 256 declare an instance of the MoveableSprite class named spaceship. This statement calls the class's parameterized constructor, passing arguments for the sprite index, the image file name, and the moving distance.

Here is a summary of the app::Begin function:

- Line 262 sets the virtual resolution.
- Line 265 calls the spaceship object's createSprite member function (inherited from the Sprite class), which creates the sprite on the screen.
- Lines 268 and 269 set the sprite's position to the middle of the screen.

Here is a summary of the app::Loop function:

- Line 276 calls the updateSprite function, passing the spaceship object as an argument. The updateSprite function definition is shown in lines 289 through 313.
- Line 279 calls the agk::Sync function to update the screen.

Here is a summary of the updateSprite function:

- Line 292 calls the agk::GetDirectionX function. Recall from Chapter 8 that this function returns a positive number if the right arrow key is being pressed, a negative number if the left arrow key is being pressed, or 0 is neither key is being pressed. The value that is returned is assigned to the directionX variable.
- Line 293 calls the agk::GetDirectionY function. Recall from Chapter 8 that this function returns a positive number if the down arrow key is being pressed, a negative number if the up arrow key is being pressed, or 0 is neither key is being pressed. The value that is returned is assigned to the directionY variable.
- The if-else statements that appear in lines 296 through 313 determine whether one of the arrow keys is being pressed, and if so, call the spaceship object's appropriate member function.

When the program runs, the screen shown in Figure 11-14 appears. When the user presses any of the arrow keys, the spaceship sprite moves accordingly.

Figure 11-14 Output of Program 11-6

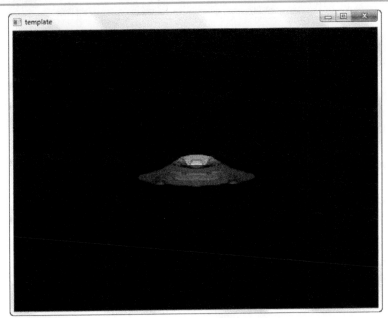

In the Spotlight:

An Object-Oriented Game: Balloon Target

VideoNote
The Balloon Target Game

In this section we will examine an object-oriented game program named Balloon Target. Figure 11-15 shows a screen from the game (this also appears as Figure C-15 in the book's color insert). In the game, a balloon moves repeatedly across the screen, from the left to the right. Each time the balloon starts at the left side of the screen, its speed randomly changes. A dart is positioned at the bottom of the screen. When the user presses the spacebar, the dart is launched. The object of the game is to hit the balloon as many times as possible with the dart.

Figure 11-15 The Balloon Target game

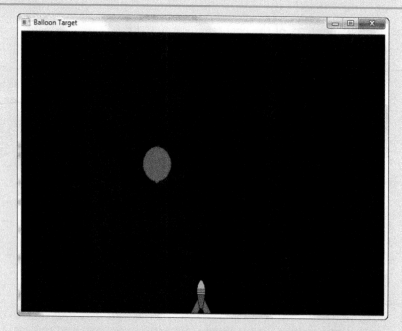

Program 11-7 shows the code. In the program, we create instances of the MoveableSprite class to represent the balloon and the dart. The MoveableSprite class is exactly as it was presented in Program 11-6, so we will not show its code again. However, we have added two member functions to the Sprite class: getSpriteHeight and getSpriteWidth. These member functions return the height and width of the sprite, respectively. The following shows the first part of the program, including the updated Sprite class declaration. The declarations for the getSpriteHeight and getSpriteWidth functions appear in lines 30 and 31.

Program 11-7   (**BalloonTarget**, *partial listing*)

```
1 // Includes, namespace and prototypes
2 #include "template.h"
3 #include <string>        // Needed for the string class
4 using namespace std;     // Needed for the string class
```

```
 5 using namespace AGK;
 6 app App;
 7
 8 class Sprite
 9 {
10 private:
11     int spriteIndex;   // The sprite index
12     string imageFile; // The name of the image file
13 public:
14     // Constructors
15     Sprite();
16     Sprite(int, string);
17
18     // Mutators
19     void createSprite();
20     void createSprite(int, string);
21     void setPosition(float, float);
22     void setX(float);
23     void setY(float);
24
25     // Accessors
26     int getSpriteIndex() const;
27     string getImageFile() const;
28     float getX() const;
29     float getY() const;
30     float getSpriteHeight() const;
31     float getSpriteWidth() const;
32
33     // Destructor
34     ~Sprite();
35 };
```

The definitions for the getSpriteHeight and getSpriteWidth functions appear in lines 133 through 143, as shown here. All the other Sprite class member functions are the same as shown earlier in this chapter, so we will not repeat their code here.

Program 11-7   (**BalloonTarget**, *continued*)

```
131 // The getSpriteHeight member function returns
132 // the sprite's height.
133 float Sprite::getSpriteHeight() const
134 {
135     return agk::GetSpriteHeight(spriteIndex);
136 }
137
138 // The getSpriteWidth member function returns
139 // the sprite's height.
140 float Sprite::getSpriteWidth() const
141 {
142     return agk::GetSpriteWidth(spriteIndex);
143 }
```

Next, we will skip to lines 257 through 262, where we have function prototypes for the various functions that we have written to modularize the program.

Program 11-7   (**BalloonTarget**, *continued*)

```
257 // Function prototypes
258 void restartDart();
259 void restartBalloon();
260 void moveBalloon();
261 void moveDart();
262 void checkForCollision();
263
```

Starting at line 265, we have global constant and variable declarations:

Program 11-7   (**BalloonTarget**, *continued*)

```
264 // Constants for the screen resolution
265 const int SCREEN_WIDTH = 640;
266 const int SCREEN_HEIGHT = 480;
267
268 // Constants for sprites and sound
269 const int BALLOON_INDEX    = 1;  // Balloon sprite index
270 const int DART_INDEX       = 2;  // Dart sprite index
271 const int DART_DIST        = 10; // Dart moving distance
272 const int MAX_BALLOON_DIST = 14; // Maximum balloon distance
273 const int LASER_SOUND      = 1;  // Sound number
274
275 // Variable to indicate whether the dart has been launched
276 bool g_dartLaunched = false;
277
```

Lines 265 and 266 declare constants for the screen width and height. Here is a summary of the other declarations in this section of code:

- BALLOON_INDEX and DART_INDEX will be used as sprite indices.
- DART_DIST is the dart sprite's moving distance.
- MAX_BALLOON_DIST is used to calculate the maximum moving distance for the balloon sprite. The greater the balloon's moving distance, the faster it moves across the screen.
- LASER_SOUND will be used as a sound number.
- g_dartLaunched is a bool variable that will indicate the state of the dart sprite. When this variable is set to true, it means the dart has been launched and is currently in motion. When it is set to false, the dart has not been launched.

Program 11-7   (**BalloonTarget**, *continued*)

```
278 // Create MoveableSprite objects for the balloon and dart.
279 MoveableSprite balloon(BALLOON_INDEX,
280                 "BalloonTarget/balloon.png", 0);
```

```
281
282  MoveableSprite dart(DART_INDEX,
283               "BalloonTarget/dart.png", DART_DIST);
284
```

In lines 279 and 280 we declare a `MoveableSprite` object named `balloon`. This object will represent the balloon. We pass the `BALLOON_INDEX` constant as the sprite index, the string `"balloon.png"` as the image file name, and 0 as the argument for the moving distance. At this point, the value that we pass for the balloon's moving distance is unimportant because it will soon be set to a random value.

In lines 282 and 283 we create a `MoveableSprite` object named `dart`. This object will represent the dart. We pass the `DART_INDEX` constant as the sprite index, the string `"dart.png"` as the image file name, and `DART_DIST` as the argument for the moving distance.

The `app::Begin` function is shown next:

Program 11-7   (**BalloonTarget**, *continued*)

```
285  // Begin app, called once at the start
286  void app::Begin( void )
287  {
288      // Set the virtual resolution.
289      agk::SetVirtualResolution(SCREEN_WIDTH, SCREEN_HEIGHT);
290
291      // Set the text in the window title bar.
292      agk::SetWindowTitle("Balloon Target");
293
294      // Load the laser sound.
295      agk::LoadSound(LASER_SOUND, "BalloonTarget/laser.wav");
296
297      // Create the balloon and dart sprites on the screen.
298      balloon.createSprite();
299      dart.createSprite();
300
301      // Position the dart and balloon.
302      restartDart();
303      restartBalloon();
304  }
305
```

Line 289 sets the virtual resolution, and line 292 sets the text for the window's title bar. Line 295 loads the `laser.wav` sound file, which will be played when the dart pops a balloon. Line 298 calls the balloon object's `createSprite` member function to create the balloon sprite on the screen, and line 299 calls the dart object's `createSprite` member function to create the dart sprite on the screen.

In line 302 we call the `restartDart` function, which horizontally centers the dart at the bottom of the screen. In line 303 we call the `restartBalloon` function, which positions the balloon at a random location along the screen's left edge and sets the balloon's moving distance to a random value.

The app::Loop function is shown next:

Program 11-7   (**BalloonTarget,** *continued*)

```
306 // Main loop, called every frame
307 void app::Loop ( void )
308 {
309     // Move the balloon.
310     moveBalloon();
311
312     // Determine whether the spacebar is being pressed.
313     if (agk::GetRawKeyState(AGK_KEY_SPACE))
314     {
315         g_dartLaunched = true;
316     }
317
318     // If the dart is launched, move it.
319     if (g_dartLaunched)
320     {
321         moveDart();
322     }
323
324     // Check for collisions.
325     checkForCollision();
326
327     // Display the screen.
328     agk::Sync();
329 }
330
331 // Called when the app ends
332 void app::End ( void )
333 {
334 }
335
```

Line 310 calls the moveBalloon function, which moves the balloon toward the screen's right edge. If the balloon is at the edge of the screen, it is restarted.

The if statement in line 313 determines whether the user is pressing the spacebar. If so, the g_dartLaunched variable is set to true to indicate that the dart has been launched.

The if statement in line 319 determines whether the g_dartLaunched variable is set to true. If so, the moveDart function is called in line 321, which moves the dart up the screen. If the dart is at the top of the screen, it is reset, and g_dartLaunched is set to false.

Line 324 calls the checkForCollision function, which determines whether the dart and the balloon have collided. If so, the laser sound is played, both the balloon and the dart are reset, and the g_dartLaunched variable is set to false.

Line 328 updates the screen.

The definition of the `restartBalloon` function is shown in lines 338 through 358, as follows.

Program 11-7   (**BalloonTarget**, *continued*)

```
336 // The restartBalloon function restarts the balloon along
337 // the left edge of the screen, with a random moving distance.
338 void restartBalloon()
339 {
340     // We want to keep the balloon in the top
341     // two-thirds of the screen. Calculate the
342     // greatest Y-coordinate for the balloon.
343     int maxY = SCREEN_HEIGHT * 0.66;
344
345     // Get a random value for the Y-coordinate.
346     int y = agk::Random(0, maxY);
347
348     // Display the balloon at its new location
349     // along the left edge of the screen.
350     balloon.setPosition( 0, y );
351
352     // Generate a random value for the balloon's
353     // moving distance.
354     int dist = agk::Random(1, MAX_BALLOON_DIST);
355
356     // Set the balloon's moving distance.
357     balloon.setDistance(dist);
358 }
359
```

When we reposition the balloon, we want it to appear somewhere in the top two-thirds of the screen. The statement in line 343 calculates the maximum Y-coordinate for the balloon and assigns it to the local variable maxY. Line 346 gets a random number in the range of 0 through maxY and assigns that value to the local variable y. Line 350 displays the balloon at its new position. (We always want the balloon to appear at the left edge of the screen, so 0 is always passed as the X-coordinate in this statement.)

Line 354 gets a random value for the balloon's moving distance. The MAX_BALLOON_DIST constant is set to 14, so this statement will get a random number in the range of 1 through 14. Line 357 uses this value to set the moving distance.

The definition of the `restartDart` function is shown in lines 362 through 375, as follows.

Program 11-7   (**BalloonTarget**, *continued*)

```
360 // The restartDart function repositions the dart sprite
361 // at the bottom center of the screen.
362 void restartDart()
```

```
363 {
364     // Calculate the dart's X-coordinate so it is
365     // centered horizontally on the screen.
366     int x = ( SCREEN_WIDTH / 2 ) -
367             (dart.getSpriteWidth()  / 2);
368
369     // Set the dart's Y-coordinate so it is at the
370     // bottom of the screen.
371     int y = SCREEN_HEIGHT - dart.getSpriteHeight();
372
373     // Position the dart at its new location.
374     dart.setPosition( x, y );
375 }
376
```

We want to display the dart sprite horizontally centered at the bottom of the screen. In lines 366 and 367 we calculate the X-coordinate, and in line 371 we calculate the Y-coordinate. In line 374 we call the setPosition member function to display the dart at these coordinates.

The definition of the moveBalloon function is shown in lines 380 through 390, as follows.

Program 11-7 (BalloonTarget, *continued*)

```
377 // The moveBalloon function moves the balloon to the
378 // right. If it is at the right edge of the screen,
379 // it restarts the balloon.
380 void moveBalloon()
381 {
382     if (balloon.getX() < SCREEN_WIDTH)
383     {
384         balloon.moveRight();
385     }
386     else
387     {
388         restartBalloon();
389     }
390 }
391
```

The if statement in line 382 determines whether the balloon sprite is at the right edge of the screen. If the balloon sprite has not reached the screen's right edge, line 384 calls the balloon object's moveRight member function. Otherwise, line 388 calls the restartBalloon function to restart the balloon sprite at the left side of the screen.

The definition of the moveDart function is shown in lines 397 through 415, as follows.

Program 11-7   **(BalloonTarget,** *continued***)**

```
392 // The moveDart function updates the dart's position.
393 // If the dart has been launched, it is moved up.
394 // If the dart has reached the top of the screen,
395 // it is restarted, and the dartLaunched flag is
396 // set to false.
397 void moveDart()
398 {
399     // If the dart has been launched, move it up.
400     if (g_dartLaunched)
401     {
402         dart.moveUp();
403     }
404
405     // If the dart has reached the top of the screen,
406     // restart it.
407     if ( dart.getY() < 0 )
408     {
409         // Restart the dart.
410         restartDart();
411
412         // Reset the dartLaunched flag.
413         g_dartLaunched = false;
414     }
415 }
416
```

The `if` statement in line 400 tests the `g_dartLaunched` variable. If it is `true`, then the dart has been launched, so line 402 moves the dart up. The `if` statement in line 407 determines whether the dart has reached the top of the screen. If it has, line 410 calls `restartDart` to reposition the dart, and line 413 sets the `g_dartLaunched` variable to `false`.

The definition of the `checkForCollision` function is shown in lines 421 through 439, as follows.

Program 11-7   **(BalloonTarget,** *continued***)**

```
418 // The checkForCollision function determines whether
419 // the dart and the balloon have collided. If so, a
420 // laser sound is played, and the objects are reset.
421 void checkForCollision()
422 {
423     // Determine whether the dart and the balloon
424     // have collided.
425     if ( agk::GetSpriteCollision( dart.getSpriteIndex(),
426                     balloon.getSpriteIndex() ) )
427     {
428         // Play the laser sound.
429         agk::PlaySound(LASER_SOUND);
```

```
430
431        // Restart the balloon.
432        restartBalloon();
433
434        // Restart the dart.
435        restartDart();
436
437        // Reset the g_dartLaunched flag.
438        g_dartLaunched = false;
439    }
440 }
```

The if statement that begins in line 425 determines whether the dart and the balloon sprites have collided. If the sprites have collided, line 429 plays the laser sound. Line 432 calls restartBalloon to restart the balloon at the left side of the screen, and line 435 calls the restartDart function to restart the dart at the bottom of the screen. Line 438 sets g_dartLaunched to false.

 Checkpoint

11.15. In this section we discussed base classes and derived classes. Which is the general class, and which is the specialized class?

11.16. What does it mean to say there is an is-a relationship between two objects?

11.17. What does a derived class inherit from its base class?

11.18. Look at the following code, which is the first line of a class declaration. What is the name of the base class? What is the name of the derived class?

```
class Canary : public Bird
```

11.19. Can a derived class have a member function with the same name as base class member function?

Review Questions

Multiple Choice

1. This programming practice is centered on creating functions that are separate from the data that they work on:
   a. modular programming.
   b. procedural programming.
   c. functional programming.
   d. object-oriented programming.

2. This programming practice is centered on creating objects:
   a. object-centric programming.
   b. objective programming.
   c. procedural programming.
   d. object-oriented programming.

3. This is a member of a class that holds data:
   a. method, or member function.
   b. instance.
   c. field, or member variable.
   d. constructor.

4. A class's member variables are commonly declared in this section of a class.
   a. Private
   b. Public
   c. Read Only
   d. Hidden

5. This is a member function that gets a value from a class's member variable but does not change it:
   a. retriever.
   b. constructor.
   c. mutator.
   d. accessor.

6. This is a member function that stores a value in a member variable or changes the value of a member variable in some other way:
   a. modifier.
   b. constructor.
   c. mutator.
   d. accessor.

7. This is a member function that is automatically called when an object is created:
   a. accessor.
   b. constructor.
   c. setter.
   d. mutator.

8. In an inheritance relationship, this is the general class:
   a. derived class.
   b. base class.
   c. slave class.
   d. child class.

9. In an inheritance relationship, this is the specialized class:
   a. base class.
   b. master class.
   c. derived class.
   d. parent class.

10. If a derived class constructor does not explicitly call a base class constructor, this base class constructor will be automatically called.
    a. Default constructor
    b. The first parameterized constructor
    c. None. Nothing will happen.
    d. None. An error will occur.

True or False

1. The base class inherits member variables and member functions from the derived class.

2. The practice of procedural programming is centered on the creation of objects.

3. Object reusability has been a factor in the increased use of object-oriented programming.

4. It is a common practice in object-oriented programming to make all of a class's member variables public.

5. If a derived class constructor does not explicitly call a base class constructor, none of the base class's constructors will be called.

Short Answer

1. What is encapsulation?

2. Why is an object's internal data usually hidden from outside code?

3. What is the difference between a class and an instance of a class?

4. The following statement calls an object's member function. What is the name of the member function? What is the name of the object?

   ```
   wallet.getDollar();
   ```

5. What is a destructor?

6. What is a constructor?

7. What is an is-a relationship between classes?

8. What does a derived class inherit from its base class?

9. Look at the following class header. What is the name of the base class? What is the name of the derived class?

   ```
   class Tiger : public Felis
   ```

10. Which executes first, the derived class constructor or the base class constructor?

Algorithm Workbench

1. Suppose myCar is the name of an object, and go is the name of a member function. (The go function does not take any arguments.) Write a statement that uses the myCar object to call the member function.

2. Look at the following partial class definition, and then respond to the questions that follow it:

```
class Point
{
private:
    int x;
    in y;


    };
```

a. Write a constructor for this class. The constructor should accept an argument for each of the member variables.

b. Write accessor and mutator member functions for each member variable.

3. Write the class header for a `Poodle` class. The class should be derived from the `Dog` class.

Programming Exercises

VideoNote

Solving the Coin Class Problem

1. **Coin Class**

Write a program with a class named `Coin` that can simulate the tossing of a coin. When an object of the class is created, it should display the image of a coin that is faceup. The class should have a member function named `toss` that randomly determines whether the coin is faceup or facedown and displays the appropriate coin image. (You can create your own coin images or use the ones provided in the book's online resources, downloadable from www.pearsonhighered.com/gaddis.)

In the program, create a `Coin` object. Each time the user presses the spacebar, the program should simulate the tossing of the coin.

2. **Dice Simulator**

Write a program with a class named `Die` that can simulate the rolling of a die. The class should have a member function named `toss` that randomly determines which side of the die is facing up (a value in the range of 1 through 6). When the `toss` member function is called, it should display an image of die side that is facing up. (You can create your own die images or use the ones provided in the book's online resources, downloadable from www.pearsonhighered.com/gaddis.)

In the program, create two `Die` objects to simulate a pair of dice. Each time the user presses the spacebar, the program should simulate the rolling of the dice.

3. **PointKeeper Class**

Modify the Balloon Target game so it reports the number of points earned by the user. (Each balloon that is popped earns 1 point.) To keep track of the points, you will write a `PointKeeper` class that has one member variable named `points`. This member variable will hold the number of points earned by the user. The class will also have a constructor and the appropriate mutator and accessor functions.

In the Balloon Target game, create an instance of the `PointKeeper` class. Each time the user pops a balloon, the program should update the `PointKeeper` object. At the end of the game, the program should report the number of points earned.

4. **Floating Asteroids, Part 1**

Write a program that creates an array of at least five MoveableSprite objects. Each of the objects in the array should display an image of an asteroid. (You can create your own image, or use the one provided in the book's online resources at www.pearsonhighered.com/gaddis.)

As the program runs, the asteroids should slowly move across the screen, from right to left. When each asteroid reaches screen's the left edge, it should be repositioned at a random location along the screen's right edge.

5. **Floating Asteroids, Part 2**

Modify the program that you wrote for Programming Exercise 4 to include a spaceship that the user can control with the arrow keys. As the program runs, the user should maneuver the spaceship to avoid colliding with any of the floating asteroids. If the spaceship collides with an asteroid, play an appropriate sound and then regenerate the spaceship at a random location. In the program, create a MoveableSprite object to represent the spaceship.

6. **Object-Oriented Catch the Boulder Game**

In Chapter 9, Programming Exercise 3 asks you to design and create a game named Catch the Boulder. The object of the game is to catch falling boulders in a cart that can be moved back and forth on a railroad track. Create an object-oriented version of the game. The program should create objects to represent the boulders and the cart.

Downloading and Installing the Required Software

To use this text you will need the following software and files:

- Microsoft Visual C++ 2010
- The AGK (App Game Kit)
- Sample Source Code, Media Files, and Game Case Studies

This appendix serves as a guide for installing these items.

> **NOTE:** To see a video demonstrating the software installation, go to the book's companion Web site at www.pearsonhighered.com/gaddis.

Step 1: **Install Microsoft Visual C++ 2010.** When purchased new, this book includes Visual Studio 2010 Express Edition on a DVD. This DVD provides a suite of software development tools. You will need to insert the DVD and install Visual C++ 2010 Express Edition.

The setup program is very simple. Follow the instructions in the next few screens, and in a few minutes Visual C++ 2010 Express Edition will be installed on your system. You can now continue to Step 2, Download and Install the AGK.

If You Do Not Have the Microsoft DVD

If your book does not have the Visual Studio 2010 Express Edition DVD, you can download and install Visual C++ 2010 Express Edition from the following Microsoft Web site:

www.microsoft.com/express/download

Scroll down the Web page until you see the download area for Visual C++ 2010 Express Edition, as shown in Figure A-1. Click the download link.

Figure A-1 Visual Studio 2010 Express Edition download page

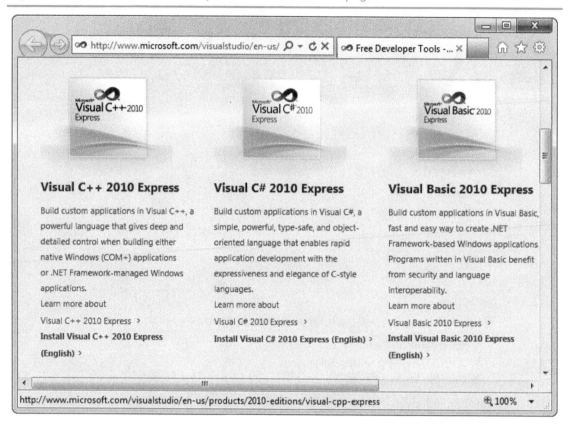

Next you should see a *File Download* dialog box. Depending on the browser you are using, it will be similar to that shown in Figure A-2.

Figure A-2 File Download dialog box

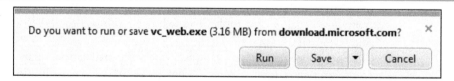

Click *Run*. At this point you will probably see another dialog asking for permission to run the program. Click *Continue* in that dialog box. Some files will be downloaded to your system, and then the installation will begin.

The installation is very simple. Follow the instructions in the next few screens. The time required to install the software will depend on the speed of your Internet connection. Once the installation is complete, you can proceed to Step 2, Download and Install the AGK.

Step 2:   **Download and Install the AGK.** To download and install the AGK trial directly from The Game Creators Web site, go to the following address:

http://files.thegamecreators.com/agk/AppGameKitTrial.zip

Next you should see the AGK trial *File Download* dialog box, as shown in Figure A-3.

Figure A-3 AGK trial download dialog box

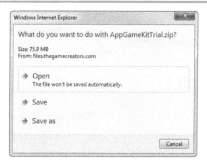

Click *Open*. The download process will begin. This may take some time, depending on the speed of your Internet connection. When the download is complete, a window will appear containing the *AppGameKitTrial.exe* file. *Run* the file. If you are prompted for permission to continue, click *Yes*.

When the setup program executes, you will see the screen shown in Figure A-4. Click the *Next* button to continue with the setup. On the next screen you will choose the location where the AGK trial will be installed. Because of the way C++ programs are developed with the AGK, we advise that you do not install the AGK in its default location. Instead, you will install it under *My Documents*, in a folder named *AGK*. Click the *Browse* button, as shown in Figure A-5.

Figure A-4 AGK trial setup

Figure A-5 Choose Install Location dialog

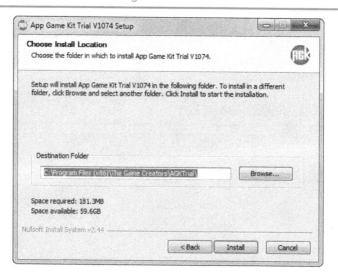

The *Browse For Folder* dialog appears as shown in Figure A-6. Select *My Documents*. Click the *Make New Folder* button. Name the new folder *AGK*. When you have finished naming the folder, click *OK*.

Figure A-6 Browse for Folder Dialog

The installation program returns to the previous window, as illustrated in Figure A-7. Notice that the installation path has changed. Click the *Install* button to begin installing the AGK trial in the specified location.

The installation will take a few minutes. When it is finished, you will see a screen similar to the one in Figure A-8. Uncheck the *Launch AGK Trial* checkbox and click *Finish*. The AGK trial has now been installed on your system.

Figure A-7 Destination Path for AGK Installation

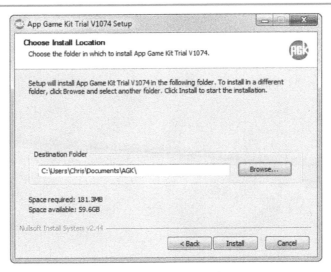

Figure A-8 AGK Trial Installation Complete

Step 3: **Download the Sample Source Code, Media Files, and Game Case Studies.**
The last step is to download the sample source code for the examples shown in the book, sample media files, and game case studies. Go to www. pearsonhighered.com/gaddis, and click the image of this book's cover. This will take you to the book's online resource page, where you can download the supplementary files.

After downloading and installing the required software and files, you are ready to begin working through this book.

Index

Credits

Figure 1.1a © IKO | Shutterstock, Figure 1.1b © feng Yu | Shutterstock, Figure 1.1c © Nikita Rogul | Shutterstock, Figure 1.1d © Chiyacat | Shutterstock, Figure 1.1e © Eikostas | Shutterstock, Figure 1.1f © tkemot | Shutterstock, Figure 1.1g © Vitaly Korovin | Shutterstock, Figure 1.1h © Lusoimages | Shutterstock, Figure 1.1i © jocic | Shutterstock, Figure 1.1j © Marina7 | Shutterstock, Figure 1.1k © Peter Guess | Shutterstock, Figure 1.1l © Aquila | Shutterstock, Figure 1.2 © US Army Center of Military History, Figure 1.3 © Ronstik | Shutterstock, Figure 1.4 © Garsya | Shutterstock, Figures 1.19–1.34 © Microsoft Visual C++® 2010 Express screenshots copyright © 2010 by Microsoft Corporation. Reprinted with permission, Figures A.4–A.8 © Reprinted with permission of The Game Creators Ltd.

ORGANIZATIONAL BEHAVIOR

A Strategic Approach

SECOND EDITION

Michael A. Hitt

Texas A&M University

C. Chet Miller

Wake Forest University

Adrienne Colella

Tulane University

WILEY

John Wiley & Sons, Inc.

VICE PRESIDENT & PUBLISHER	George Hoffman
PROJECT EDITOR	Joan Kalkut
EXECUTIVE MARKETING MANAGER	Amy Scholz
ASSISTANT MARKETING MANAGER	Carly DeCandia
PRODUCTION MANAGER	Dorothy Sinclair
SENIOR PRODUCTION EDITOR	Sandra Dumas
SENIOR DESIGNER	Kevin Murphy
COVER DESIGNER	Nancy Field
MEDIA EDITOR	Allison Morris
PHOTO DEPARTMENT MANAGER	Jennifer MacMillan
PRODUCTION MANAGEMENT SERVICES	Suzanne Ingrao
PROGRAM ASSISTANT	Carissa Marker Doshi
MEDIA ASSISTANT	Elena Santa Maria

This book was typeset in 10/12 Times Ten Roman at Aptara®, Inc. and printed and bound by R. R. Donnelley/Jefferson City. The cover was printed by R. R. Donnelley/Jefferson City.

The paper in this book was manufactured by a mill whose forest management programs include sustained yield harvesting of its timberlands. Sustained yield harvesting principles ensure that the number of trees cut each year does not exceed the amount of new growth.

This book is printed on acid-free paper. ∞

Hitt, Michael, A., Miller, C., Chet, Colella, Adrienne
Organizational Behavior: A Strategic Approach, Second Edition

ISBN 13   978-0470-08697-1

Printed in the United States of America.

10 9 8 7 6 5 4 3 2

Why WileyPLUS for Management?

WileyPLUS helps today's students succeed in the classroom using resources relevant to their everyday lives and to the workplace that will help make them globally competitive. With the complete e-book plus a variety of interactive tools, WileyPLUS makes teaching, learning, and retaining the material easier, more relevant, and more exciting than ever.

"I wish all my classes had WileyPLUS linked to their textbooks so I could study better in all my classes"

— Student David Delgado, Texas A&M University-Corpus Christi

⊕ *Instructors using WileyPLUS easily choose all of the resources they need to effectively design and deliver their course with maximum impact and minimum preparation time. Conveniently organized and highly integrated resources include the Instructor's Manual, Test Bank, PowerPoint slides, Cases, Videos, and more.*

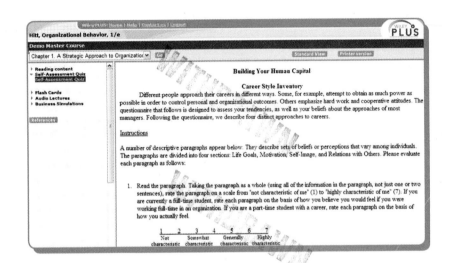

⊕ **WileyPLUS links students directly from homework assignments to specific portions of the online text for the contextual help they need—when they need it.**

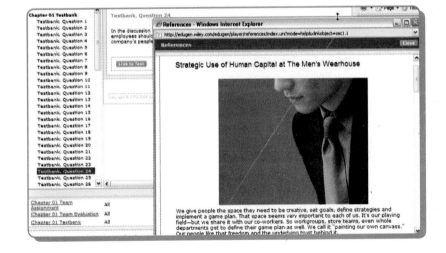

WILEY
PLUS
www.wileyplus.com

See—and Try WileyPLUS in action!
Details and Demo: www.wileyplus.com

WileyPLUS combines robust course management tools with the complete online text and all of the interactive teaching and learning resources you and your students need in one easy to use system.

"WileyPLUS definitely increased my interest for my course, contributed a lot to my performance on the exams, and improved my grades."

– Student Pardha Saradhi Vishnumolakala
University of Houston Clearlake

⊕ Up-to-date and relevant video clips, tutorials, simulations, interactive demonstration problems, and cases involve students as interested participants. With various ways to learn, retain, and apply the material they have read about or learned in lectures, students build the skill and confidence it takes to perform better.

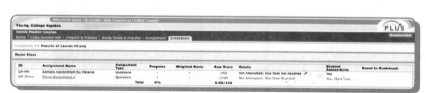

⊕ Instructors can easily and immediately asses their students' progress—individually, or by class—using the online gradebook and assessment tools contained in WileyPLUS.

"I enjoyed using WileyPLUS because I learned a lot, and performed very well!"

– Student David Villarreal
St. Phillips College

WILEY PLUS ⊕

www.wileyplus.com

To my life partner, Frankie. Thank you for all of your love and support.

—MICHAEL

To my best friend, Laura. As the song says, you are still the one.

—CHET

To my husband, Angelo. You make life a grand adventure.
Thank you for everything.

—ADRIENNE

ABOUT THE AUTHORS

Michael A. Hitt
Texas A & M University

Michael A. Hitt is a Distinguished Professor and holds the Joe B. Foster Chair in Business Leadership at Texas A & M University. He received his Ph.D. from the University of Colorado. He has authored over 250 publications in the form of books and scholarly journal articles. He has served on the editorial review boards of multiple journals including *Academy of Management Journal, Academy of Management Review, Academy of Management Executive, Journal of Applied Psychology, Journal of Management, Journal of World Business,* and *Journal of Applied Behavioral Sciences.* Furthermore, he has served as Consulting Editor (1988–90) and Editor (1991–1993) of the *Academy of Management Journal.* He is currently the co-editor of the *Strategic Management Journal.* He is a Past President of the Academy of Management and current president of the Strategic Management Society. He received the 1996 Award for Outstanding Academic Contributions to Competitiveness and the 1999 Award for Outstanding Intellectual Contributions to Competitiveness Research from the American Society for Competitiveness. He is a Fellow in the Academy of Management and in the Strategic Management Society. He received an honorary doctorate (Doctor Honoris Causa) from the Universidad Carlos III de Madrid. He is a member of the Academy of Management Journals Hall of Fame and received awards for the best articles published in the *Academy of Management Executive* (1999), *Academy of Management Journal* (2000), and *Journal of Management* (2006). He received the Irwin Outstanding Educator Award and the Distinguished Service Award from the Academy of Management.

C. Chet Miller
Wake Forest University

Since working as a shift manager and subsequently completing his graduate studies, Dr. Miller has taught full-time at Baylor University, Cornell University, and Wake Forest University. At Baylor, he served as Director of the Center for Executive Education. At Wake Forest, he has served as an area coordinator, an associate dean, and a program director. He is an active member of the Academy of Management and the Strategic Management Society, having served in such roles as associate editor for *Academy of Management Journal* and panel member for the Strategic Management Society Best Conference Paper Award. Awards and honors include the Outstanding Young Researcher Award (from Baylor University), teaching awards from Duke University and Wake Forest University, and designation as the Farr Fellow in Leadership at Wake Forest.

Dr. Miller has worked with a number of managers and executives. Through management development programs, he has contributed to the development of individuals from such organizations as ABB, Bank of America, Krispy Kreme, La Farge, Red Hat, State Farm Insurance, Texas Special Olympics, and the United States Postal Service. His focus has been change management, strategic visioning, and high-commitment/high-involvement approaches to managing people.

Dr. Miller's published research focuses on the functioning of management teams, the design of organizational structures and management systems, and the design of strategic decision processes. His publications have appeared in several outlets, including *Organization Science, Academy of Management Journal, Strategic Management Journal, Academy of Management Executive, Journal of Organizational Behavior,* and *Journal of Behavioral Decision Making.*

Adrienne Colella
Tulane University

Adrienne Colella is a Professor and the Freeman Chair in Doctoral Studies and Research in the A.B. Freeman School of Business at Tulane University. Professor Colella has also been a faculty member at Rutgers University and Texas A&M University. She received her Ph.D. in Industrial/Organizational Psychology from the Ohio State University. She is a Fellow of the Society for Industrial and Organizational Psychology (SIOP) and the American Psychological Association.

Professor Colella is an active member of both the Academy of Management and the Society for Industrial Organizational Psychology (SIOP, Division 14 of the APA). She has served in many roles such as an elected member of the SIOP Executive Committee and the Executive Committee of the HR Division. She serves (or has served) on the editorial boards of *Personnel Psychology, Journal of Applied Psychology, Academy of Management Journal, Journal of Organizational Behavior, Human Resource Management Review, Human Performance,* the SIOP Frontiers Series, *Journal of Management,* and *Human Resource Management.*

Dr. Colella's research focuses on treatment issues regarding persons with disabilities in the workplace and workplace accommodation. Dr. Colella has also published on the topics of organizational entry, newcomer socialization, goal setting, utility analysis, and biographical data testing. Her research appears in the *Journal of Applied Psychology, Personnel Psychology, Academy of Management Journal, Academy of Management Review, Research in Personnel and Human Resource Management, Human Resource Management Review, Journal of Applied Social Psychology,* and the *Journal of Occupational Rehabilitation,* among other places. She is the editor of a SIOP Frontiers Series book on the psychology of workplace discrimination. Her research has been funded by a number of grants and contracts from the New Jersey Developmental Disabilities Council, the Army Research Institute, the Navy Personnel R&D Center, Rutgers University, and Texas A&M University.

BRIEF CONTENTS

CONTENTS

PREFACE

"The best leaders know where all the great companies start.
It's the people . . . !"

—Fast Company

The quote above from the cover of Fast Company seems intuitive, thus everyone knows that people are the primary base for success in all organizations, don't they? Unfortunately, they do not appear to know it. A number of managers seem to give "lip service" to the importance of people but act differently, according to Jeff Pfeffer, a noted professor at Stanford's graduate school of business. Yet, there are a few who appear to act as if people are critical. For example, Brad Anderson, CEO of Best Buy, has suggested that the strength of his company is based on the intelligence, insight, and creativity of the company's frontline employees. To win the challenging battles with its competitors, Anderson believes that Best Buy must select the best people, train them effectively, and give them the best tools to serve their customers.[1]

Purpose

We wrote this book for several reasons. First, we wanted to communicate in an effective way the knowledge of managing people in organizations. The book presents up-to-date concepts of organizational behavior in a lively and easy-to-read manner. The book is based on classic and cutting-edge research on the primary topic of each chapter. Second, we wanted to emphasize the importance of people to the success of organizations. We do so by taking a strategic approach, communicating how managing people is critical to implementing an organization's strategy, gaining an advantage over competitors, and ensuring positive organizational performance. This approach helps students to better understand the relevance of managing people, allowing the student to integrate these concepts with knowledge gained in other core business courses. To emphasize the importance of people, we use the term human capital. People are important assets to organizations; application of their knowledge and skills is necessary for organizations to accomplish their goals.

New to the Second Edition

A number of changes have been made to enrich the content of the book. Almost all extended examples, opening cases and insert materials have been changed or

---

[1] Breen, B. 2005. The clear leader. *Fast Company,* March:65.

updated to the present (except for classic examples such as the one on military decisions in the U.S. civil war in chapter 10). These changes in our real-world application materials help to maintain the current fit with managerial practice in the book. Several of the major changes to the core content are as follows:

- New materials added on *positive organizational behavior* (Chapter 1)
- New discussion of *faultlines,* a new area of focus in group diversity research (Chapter 2)
- New information added on national culture from the GLOBE research (Chapter 3)
- A new section added on *social learning theory* (Chapter 4)
- Enriched exploration of *equity and organizational justice added* (Chapter 6)
- A second model of stress was added along with new materials on *work-family conflict and balance* (Chapter 7)
- New materials on *servant leadership* and *leader-member exchange* included (Chapter 8)
- Major enrichment of the discussions on *conflict* and *personality* (Chapter 12)
- New sections added on negotiations and on *dispositional trust* (Chapter 12)
- New discussions of *individual* and or*ganizational learning* were inserted (Chapters 4 and 14, respectively)
- New focus on *personal* and *organizational values (and fit)* added (Chapter 13)
- Enriched discussions of *expectancy theory of motivation* (Chapter 6), *organizational communications* (e.g., rumors and gossip, technology, media norms and communication climate) (Chapter 9), *coping with stress* (Chapter 7), *managing expatriate employees* (Chapter 3), the *'Glass Border'* (Chapter 3), *job satisfaction* and *organizational commitment* (Chapter 5) and *virtual teams* and team *diversity* (Chapter 11).

Approximately 400 new references were added to update the materials in the text to ensure accurate and current descriptions of the most recent research and practices in organizations. While making important revisions, we maintained all of the basic OB content which students and instructors found to be valuable in the first edition. Also, we added several new or enriched personal assessments (Building Your Human Capital) and team exercises.

Although we have made many changes in our efforts to keep the book fresh and to engage in continuous improvement, we have maintained much of the original structure and core content. Thus, we maintained the quality content and user-friendly approach appreciated by the many first-edition users.

Value Provided by this Book

Managing organizational behavior (OB) involves acquiring, developing, managing, and applying the knowledge, skills, and abilities of people. A strategic approach to OB rests on the premise that people are the foundation for any firm's competitive advantage. Providing exceptionally high quality products and services, excellent customer service, best-in-class cost structure, and other advantages are based on the capabilities of the firm's people, its human capital. If organized and managed effectively, the knowledge and skills of the people in the firm are the basis for gaining an advantage over competitors and achieving long-term financial success.

Individual, interpersonal, and organizational characteristics determine the behavior and ultimately the value of an organization's people. Factors such as an individual's technical skills, personality characteristics, personal values, ability to learn, and ability to be self-managing are important bases for the development of organizational capabilities. At the interpersonal level, factors such as quality of leadership, communication within and between groups, and conflict within and between groups are noteworthy in the organization's ability to build important capabilities and apply them to achieve its goals. Finally, at the organizational level, the culture and policies of the firm are also among the most important factors, as they influence whether the talents and positive predispositions of individuals are effectively used. Thus, managing human capital is critical for an organization to beat its competition and to perform effectively.

This book explains how to effectively manage behavior in organizations. Additionally, we emphasize how effective behavioral management relates to organizational performance. We link the specific behavioral topic(s) emphasized in each chapter to organizational strategy and performance through explicit but concise discussions. We also provide short cases and examples to highlight the relationships.

Therefore, we emphasize the importance of managing organizational behavior and its effect on the outcomes of the organization. This is highly significant because a number of organizations routinely mismanage their workforce. For example, some organizations routinely implement major reductions in the workforce (layoffs, downsizing) whenever they experience performance problems. How does an organization increase its effectiveness by laying off thousands of its employees? The answer is that it rarely does so.[2] This action reduces costs but it also results in losses of significant human capital and valuable knowledge. These firms then suffer from diminished capabilities and their performance decreases further. Research shows that firms increasing their workforce during economic downturns enjoy much stronger performance when the economy improves.[3] These firms have the capabilities to take advantage of the improving economy whereas firms that downsized must rebuild their capabilities and are less able to compete effectively. The firms listed annually in Fortune's "100 Best Companies to Work for" are consistently among the highest performers in their industries (e.g., Starbucks, Whole Foods Market, Marriott, American Express).

Concluding Remarks

The knowledge learned from a course in organizational behavior is important for managers at all levels: top executives, middle managers, and lower-level managers. While top executives may understand the strategic importance of managing human capital, middle and lower-level managers must also understand the linkage between managing behavior effectively and the organization's ability to formulate and

---

[2] Krishnan, H, Hitt, M.A. & Park, D. 2007. Acquisition premiums, subsequent workplace reductions and post-acquisition performance, *Journal of Management Studies*, 44: 709–732; Nixon, R.D., Hitt, M.A., Lee, H. & Jeong, E. 2004. Market reactions to announcements of corporate downsizing actions and implementation strategies. *Strategic Management Journal*, 25: 1121–1129.

[3] Greer, C.R. & Ireland, T.C. 1992. Organizational and financial correlates of a 'contrarian' human resource investment strategy. *Academy of Management Journal*. 35: 956–984.

implement its strategy. Managers do not focus solely on individual behavior. They also manage interpersonal, team, inter-group, and inter-organizational relationships. Some refer to these relationships as "social capital." The essence of managing organizational behavior is the development and use of human capital and social capital.

Jack Welch, former CEO of GE, suggested that he and his management team used management concepts that energized armies of people allowing them to dream, dare, reach, and stretch their talents in order to do things they never thought possible. This book presents concepts that will help students to gain the knowledge needed to effectively manage behavior in organizations. This, in turn, helps in the implementation of the organization's strategy, affects the organization's productivity, allows the organization to gain advantages over its competitors, and therefore contributes to the organization's overall performance.

MAH
CCM
AJC

FOCUS AND PEDAGOGY

The book explains and covers all organizational behavior topics, based on the most current research available. Unlike other OB texts, it uses the lens of an organization's strategy as a guide. Some examples of this strategic approach include.

Exploring Behavior in Action

Each chapter opens with a case, grounding the chapter in a real world context. Some of the companies featured include Men's Wearhouse, McDonalds, W. L. Gore & Associates, Starbucks, and FedEx.

6

WORK MOTIVATION

On January 1, 1958, Wilbert and Genevieve Gore founded a small company to develop applications of polytetrafluoroethylene (PTFE). Wilbert, a chemist and research scientist, tended to the technical work while Genevieve handled accounting and other business matters.

Wilbert Gore initially focused on applications in the emerging computer industry, where PTFE's insulation characteristics were potentially useful in cables and circuit boards. After solving a number of technical issues, he and his company

EXPLORING BEHAVIOR IN ACTION
Work Motivation at W.L. Gore & Associates

succeeded with cable and wire products. Some of these products eventually landed on the moon as part of the technology used in the Apollo space program. More recently, they have been incorporated into the U.S. space shuttle program. Moving beyond cables and wires, Gore has created a number of leading products for a number of industries. Best known among consumers for waterproof Gore-Tex fabrics, the company also places products in industries such as aerospace, automotive, chemical processing, computing, telecommunications, environmental protection, medical/healthcare, pharmaceutical, biotechnology, and textiles.

Having previously experienced bureaucratic roadblocks in highly structured

organizations, Wilbert Gore designed a different kind of company to support the work with PTFE. Using the term *lattice* structure to signify an emphasis on informal communication and fluid work networks, he set up a company that focused on equality among people as well as freedom for those people to pursue their own ideas and projects. To a significant degree, individuals were and still are expected to define their own jobs within areas that interest them. Assigned sponsors help both new and existing Gore personnel with job definition.

Formal leadership assignments are less common at Gore than in more structured companies. Instead of formal

assignments, Gore looks for individuals who have attracted "followers" for their ideas and projects. Thomas Malone, a professor at Massachusetts Institute of Technology, has studied the company and summarizes the approach as follows: "The way you become a [leader] is by finding people who want to work for you. . . . In a certain sense, you're elected rather than appointed. It's a democratic structure inside a business organization."

Culturally, four principles govern the behavior of individuals within W.L. Gore & Associates:

• The ability to make one's own commitments and keep them

The Strategic Importance of **Personality, Intelligence, Attitudes, and Emotions**

The discussion of personality testing in *Exploring Organizational Behavior in Action* illustrates how important it is for organizations to select the right individuals. Everyone has individual differences that cannot be easily changed. As Herb Kelleher mentioned above, organizations can train people to do only so much; there are individual differences in people that are not easily influenced. In this chapter we explore three such differences: personality, intelligence, and emotions. We also explore another individual difference: attitudes that can be more easily affected by one's organizational experience. All of these human attributes influence organizational effectiveness by influencing associates' performance, work attitudes, motivation, willingness to stay in the organization, and ability to work together in a high-involvement environment.

In Chapter 1, we stated that an important part of high-involvement work systems was that organizations engage in selective hiring, illustrating the importance of hiring people with the right set of attributes. A great deal of research has been done that has shown that certain traits, such as conscientiousness[1] and intelligence,[2] are related to associate performance. Associates' traits have also been linked to how likely they will be to engage in counterproductive work behavior, such as being frequently absent or stealing.[3] In addition to traits directly affecting performance, the degree to which associates' traits fit the work environment and culture is also linked with how satisfied and committed associates are to their organization[4] and how likely they will be to remain in the organization.[5] Furthermore, the attributes of top leaders in the organization have a direct impact on organizational functioning by relating to the group dynamics among top decision

makers[6] and the strategic decisions they make.[7] Thus, the individual traits and attitudes of everyone in the organization can have an important impact on the functioning of that organization.

Because personalities have such important effects on behavior in organizations, care must be taken in adding new people. For a manufacturing firm emphasizing stable, efficient operations as it competes on the basis of low cost, hiring newcomers who are serious, conscientious, and emotionally stable is logical. For a manufacturing firm competing on the basis of frequent process and product innovations, hiring newcomers who embrace change and are inquisitive is important. Furthermore, as you will learn in this chapter, it is critical to hire associates who fit the characteristics of the particular jobs they will hold. Inside the same firm, personalities suitable for the tasks required in sales may be less suitable for the tasks involved in research and development. Although personality, intelligence, attitudes, and emotions are not perfect predictors of job performance and should never be used alone in selection decisions, they are important.

In this chapter, we open with a discussion of fundamentals of personality, including its origins and the degree to which it changes over time. Building on this foundation, we examine a major personality framework that has emerged as the most useful for understanding workplace behaviors. Next, we discuss several cognitive and motive-based characteristics of personality not explicitly included in the major framework. Next, we examine intelligence, another individual difference that has become a controversial topic in employee selection. We then move on to an exploration of attitudes, including attitude development and change as well as several important types of workplace attitudes. Finally, we address emotions and their role in organizations.

KNOWLEDGE OBJECTIVES

After reading this chapter, you should be able to:

1. Define *personality* and explain the basic nature of personality traits.

2. Describe the Big Five personality traits, with particular emphasis on the relationship with job performance, success on teams, and job satisfaction.

145

The Strategic Importance of . . .

Links the issues in the opening case to the organizational behavior topic of the chapter. The issues are discussed in light of their importance to organization strategy and ultimately how they affect the organization's performance.

"*The Strategic Importance of . . .* and *The Strategic Lens* are appropriate 'bookends' for the chapter; they set up how decision making is strategic and reinforce that at the end of the chapter."

(Pam Roffol-Dobies, University of Missouri Kansas City)

Experiencing Strategic Organizational Behavior

These two sections in each chapter apply the key concepts in the chapter. Real-world case situations are used including such topics as women, work and stereotypes; Google and high quality associates; Coca Cola's new fizz; extreme jobs; Google and high quality associates; and communication at J. Crew. These discussions highlight their connection to the organization's strategy and performance.

> "The *Experiencing Strategic OB* section is also useful since it provides a conceptual view of the changing approach to OB. I like the idea that it walks the students through a situation and then summarizes the prospects for acting successfully."
>
> **(Marian Schultz, University of West Florida)**

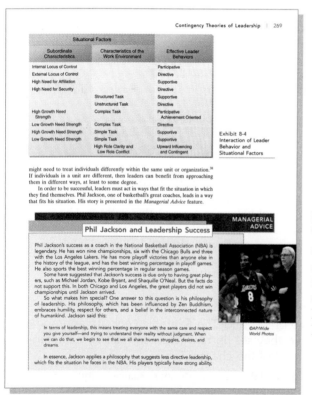

> "After reading the *Experiencing Strategic OB* section on the football league, I also found that the example was an excellent choice. My classroom includes both traditional and nontraditional students, ranging in age from 20–72 and I think it is important to provide a variety of examples that everyone can relate to in the course."
>
> **(Marilyn Wesner, George Washington University)**

Managerial Advice

These sections provide advice for future managers and make a connection to the organization's strategy and performance. Examples of Managerial Advice include managers over the edge; Phil Jackson's leadership success; surfing for applicants on MySpace and Facebook; managing virtual teams; finding a fit at Home Depot; "green" policies and practices.

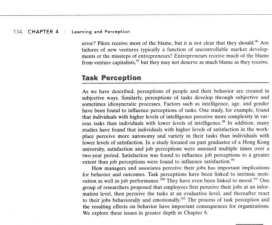

134 CHAPTER 4 | Learning and Perception

error? Pilots receive most of the blame, but it is not clear that they should.[96] Are failures of new ventures typically a function of uncontrollable market developments or the missteps of entrepreneurs? Entrepreneurs receive much of the blame from venture capitalists,[97] but they may not deserve as much blame as they receive.

Task Perception

As we have described, perceptions of people and their behavior are created in subjective ways. Similarly, perceptions of tasks develop through subjective and sometimes idiosyncratic processes. Factors such as intelligence, age, and gender have been found to influence perceptions of tasks. One study, for example, found that individuals with higher levels of intelligence perceive more complexity in various tasks than individuals with lower levels of intelligence.[98] In addition, many studies have found that individuals with higher levels of satisfaction in the workplace perceive more autonomy and variety in their tasks than individuals with lower levels of satisfaction. In a study focused on past graduates of a Hong Kong university, satisfaction and job perceptions were assessed multiple times over a two-year period. Satisfaction was found to influence job perceptions to a greater extent than job perceptions were found to influence satisfaction.[99]

How managers and associates perceive their jobs has important implications for behavior and outcomes. Task perceptions have been linked to intrinsic motivation as well as job performance.[100] They have even been linked to mood.[101] One group of researchers proposed that employees first perceive their jobs at an information level, then perceive the tasks at an evaluative level, and thereafter react to their jobs behaviorally and emotionally.[102] The process of task perception and the resulting effects on behavior have important consequences for organizations. We explore these issues in greater depth in Chapter 6.

The Strategic Lens

Organizations compete on the basis of their resources. The strongest organizations usually win the competitive battles if their managers develop effective strategies and implement them well. To be competitive, managers use the organization's resources to create capabilities to act.[103] A critical component of these capabilities is knowledge. In fact, Bill Breen of Fast Company suggests that "Companies compete with their brains as well as their brawn. Organizations today must not only outgun and outhustle competitors, they must also outthink them. Companies win with ideas."[104]

Given the importance of knowledge in gaining a competitive advantage, learning is critical to organizational success. Managers and associates must continuously learn if they are to stay ahead of the competition. Perception is a key component of learning. It is particularly important to top executives, as they must carefully and thoroughly analyze their organization's external environment, with special emphasis on competitors. If they do not perceive their environment correctly, these executives may formulate ineffective strategies and cause the organization to lose its competitive advantage. Understanding the concepts of learning and perception, then, is absolutely essential to the effective operation of an organization.

Critical Thinking Questions

1. How does the knowledge held by managers and associates affect the performance of an organization?

2. What are some important ways in which associates can learn and thereby enhance their stock of knowledge? What role does perception play in the learning process?

3. What are the connections between learning, perception, and organizational strategies?

The Strategic Lens

The Strategic Lens section concludes each chapter. The section explains the topic of the chapter through the lens of organizational strategy. Highlighted is the critical contribution of the chapter's concepts to the organization's achievement of its goals. The Strategic Lens concludes with *Critical Thinking Questions* that are designed to emphasize the student's knowledge of the OB topic, its effects on the organization's strategy, and its effects on organizational functioning.

Building Your Human Capital

To help students better know themselves and develop needed skills in organizational behavior, a personal assessment instrument is included in each chapter. This includes information on scoring and interpreting the results. Examples include approaches to difficult learning situations, assessing your needs as well as your creativity, managing with power and tolerating change.

> "The *Building Your Human Capital* segment is unique. Students need to recognize the importance of the topics for developing their personal skills. This section does a good job in forwarding that idea."
>
> **(Ceasar Douglas, Florida State Universtiy)**

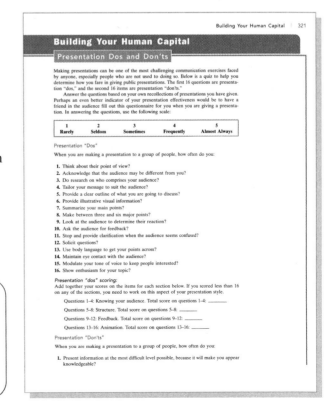

Building Your Human Capital | 321

Building Your Human Capital

Presentation Dos and Don'ts

Making presentations can be one of the most challenging communication exercises faced by anyone, especially people who are not used to doing so. Below is a quiz to help you determine how you fare in giving public presentations. The first 16 questions are presentation "dos," and the second 16 items are presentation "don'ts."

Answer the questions based on your own recollections of presentations you have given. Perhaps an even better indicator of your presentation effectiveness would be to have a friend in the audience fill out this questionnaire for you when you are giving a presentation. In answering the questions, use the following scale:

1	2	3	4	5
Rarely	Seldom	Sometimes	Frequently	Almost Always

Presentation "Dos"

When you are making a presentation to a group of people, how often do you:

1. Think about their point of view?
2. Acknowledge that the audience may be different from you?
3. Do research on who comprises your audience?
4. Tailor your message to suit the audience?
5. Provide a clear outline of what you are going to discuss?
6. Provide illustrative visual information?
7. Summarize your main points?
8. Make between three and six major points?
9. Look at the audience to determine their reaction?
10. Ask the audience for feedback?
11. Stop and provide clarification when the audience seems confused?
12. Solicit questions?
13. Use body language to get your points across?
14. Maintain eye contact with the audience?
15. Modulate your tone of voice to keep people interested?
16. Show enthusiasm for your topic?

Presentation "dos" scoring:
Add together your scores on the items for each section below. If you scored less than 16 on any of the sections, you need to work on this aspect of your presentation style.

Questions 1–4: Knowing your audience. Total score on questions 1–4: _____
Questions 5–8: Structure. Total score on questions 5–8: _____
Questions 9–12: Feedback. Total score on questions 9–12: _____
Questions 13–16: Animation. Total score on questions 13–16: _____

Presentation "Don'ts"

When you are making a presentation to a group of people, how often do you:

1. Present information at the most difficult level possible, because it will make you appear knowledgeable?

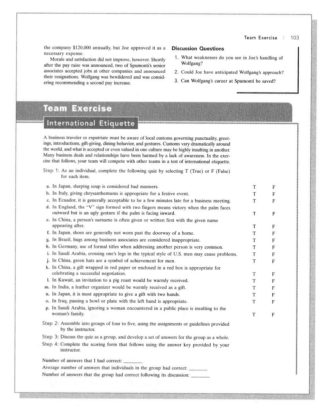

A Strategic Organizational Behavior Moment
The applied, hypothetical case at the end of each chapter gives students an opportunity to apply the knowledge they have gained throughout the chapter. Each case concludes with questions. Teaching suggestions are included in the instructor's resources.

> "The case was a good illustration of what life as a manger is like and it lends itself to a discussion of what might keep a manager from being highly involved."
>
> **(Deborah Butler, Georgia State University)**

Team Exercise
These experiential exercises expand the student's learning through activities and engage students in team building skills. Teaching suggestions are included in the instructor's resources.

> "The Exercise at the end of the chapter seemed like a great way to get students involved and to help them understand the material."
>
> **(Sharon Purkiss, California State University at Fullerton)**

SUPPLEMENTS

Instructor's Resource Guide

prepared by David Fearon at Central Connecticut State University

The Instructor's Resource Guide includes an Introduction with sample syllabi; Chapter Outlines; Chapter Objectives; Teaching Notes on how to integrate and assign special features within the text; and suggested answers for all quiz and test questions found in the text. The Instructor's Resource Guide also includes additional discussion questions and assignments that relate specifically to the cases, as well as case notes, self-assessments, and team exercises. The Instructor's Resource Guide can be accessed on the Instructor portion of the Hitt Web Site at http://www.wiley.com/college/hitt.

Test Bank

prepared by Melinda Blackman of California State University, Fullerton

This robust Test Bank consists of true/false (approx. 60 per chapter), multiple choice (approx. 60 per chapter), short answer (approx. 25 per chapter), and essay questions (approx. 5 per chapter). Further, it is specifically designed so questions will vary in degree of difficulty, ranging from straightforward recall to more challenging questions to ensure student mastery of all key concepts and topics. The organization of test questions also offer instructors the most flexibility when designing their exams. A **Computerized Test Bank** provides even more flexibility and customization options to instructors. The Computerized Test Bank requires a PC running Windows. This electronic version of the Test Bank includes all the questions from the Test Bank within a test-generating program that allows instructors to customize their exams and also to add their own test questions in addition to what is already available. Both the Test Bank and Computerized Test Bank are available for viewing and download on the Instructor portion of the Hitt Web site at http://www.wiley.com/college/hitt.

Power Point Presentations

prepared by Ralph Braithwaite of University of Hartford

These PowerPoint Presentations provide another visual enhancement and learning aid for students, as well as additional talking points for instructors. Each chapter's set of interactive PowerPoint slides includes lecture notes to accompany each slide. Each presentation includes roughly 30 slides with illustrations, animations, and related web links interspersed appropriately. The PowerPoint Presentations can be accessed on the Instructor portion of the Hitt Web Site at http://www.wiley.com/college/hitt.

Lecture Notes

prepared by Karen Markel of Oakland University

Lecture Notes provide an outline of the chapter overview and knowledge objectives, highlighting the key topics/concepts presented within each chapter. Power-Point slides have been integrated, where relevant, and the lecture notes reference to instructors when it's best to show the class each slide within a particular chapter's PowerPoint Presentation.

Web Quizzes

prepared by Melinda Blackman of California State University, Fullerton

Online quizzes with questions varying in level of difficulty have been designed to help students evaluate their individual comprehension of the key concepts and topics presented within each chapter. These web quizzes are available at http://www.wiley.com/college/hitt. Each chapter's quiz includes 10 questions, including true/false and multiple choice questions. These review questions, developed by the Test Bank author, Melinda Blackman, have been created to provide the most effective and efficient testing system for students as they prepare for quizzes and exams. Within this system, students have the opportunity to "practice" responding to the types of questions they'll be expected to address on a quiz or exam.

Pre- and Post-Lecture Quizzes

prepared by Karen Markel of Oakland University

The Pre- and Post-Lecture Quizzes can be found exclusively in *WileyPLUS*. These quizzes consist of multiple choice and true/false questions which vary in level of detail and difficulty while focusing on a particular chapter's key terms and concepts. This resource allows instructors to quickly and easily evaluate their students' progress by monitoring their comprehension of the material both before and after each lecture.

The pre-lecture quiz questions enable instructors to gauge their students' comprehension of a particular chapter's content so they can best determine what to focus on in their lecture.

The post-lecture quiz questions are intended to be homework or review questions that instructors can assign to students after covering a particular chapter. The questions typically provide hints, solutions or explanations to the students, as well as page references.

Personal Response System (PRS)

prepared by Melinda Blackman of California State University, Fullerton

Personal Response System or "Clicker" questions have been designed for each chapter to spark additional in-class discussion and debate. These questions consist of both questions from the Test Bank and the web quizzes. For more information on PRS content, please contact your local Wiley sales representative.

mp3 Download Mini-Lectures

prepared by Sandi Zeljko at Eastern Unversity

These mini-lectures, one for each chapter, cover the main concepts and key points of each chapter in more of a conversational manner. Each 5-minute audio file is a perfect tool for student review and students can download these mp3 files from WileyPLUS to their computers or personal mp3 players.

Organizational Behavior Lecture Launcher Video

Nineteen video clips from the Films for the Humanities, ranging from 2–10 minutes in length tied to the major topics in organizational behavior are available. These video clips, available on both VHS and DVD, provide an excellent starting point for lectures. An instructor's manual for using the lecture launcher is available on the Instructor's portion of the Hitt Web site. For more information on the OB Lecture Launcher, please contact your local Wiley sales representative

Art Imitates Life: Using Movies and Music in Organizational Behavior

prepared by Robert L. Holbrook, Ohio University

Interested in integrating pop culture into your OB course? Looking for ways of integrating the humanities (movies and music) into your classroom? Dr. Holbrook provides innovative teaching ideas for integrating these ideas into your classroom experience. This instructor's supplement is available on the Instructor's portion of the Hitt Web site. Please contact your local Wiley sales representative for additional information on OB video resources.

Business Extra Select Online Courseware system

www.wiley.com/college/bxs

This program provides instructors with millions of content resources from an extensive database of cases, journals, periodicals, newspapers, and supplemental readings. This courseware system lends itself extremely well to the integration of real-world content within organizational behavior to enable instructors to convey the relevance of the course content to their students.

Companion Web site

The text's Web site at **www.wiley.com/college/hitt** contains a myriad of resources and links to aid both teaching and learning, including the web quizzes described above.

WileyPLUS

WileyPLUS provides an integrated suite of teaching and learning resources, along with a complete online version of the text, in one easy-to-use web site. WileyPLUS will help you create class presentations, create assignments, automate the assigning and grading of homework or quizzes, track your students' progress, and administer your course, Also includes MP3 chapter downloads of the key chapter topics, team exercises and team evaluation tools, experiential exercises, pre- and post-lecture quizzes, student self assessments, flashcards of key terms and more! For more information, go to www.wiley.com/college/wileyplus.com.

ACKNOWLEDGMENTS

We thank the many people who helped us develop this book. We owe a debt of gratitude to the following people who reviewed this book through its development and revision, providing us with helpful feedback.

Thanks to those professors who provided valuable feedback for the second edition.

Fred Blass, *Florida State University*
H. Michael Boyd, *Bentley College*
Marie Dasborough, *University of Miami*
Molly Kern, *Baruch College*
Lorianne Mitchell, *East Tennessee State University*
Ron Piccolo, *University of Central Florida*
David Radosevich, *Montclair State University*
Joe Rode, *Miami University of Ohio*
Daniel Sherman, *University of Alabama—Huntsville*
John Stark, *California State University—Bakersfield*

Thanks to those professors who reviewed the book in its first edition and helped us hone its approach and focus.

Syed Ahmed, *Florida International University*
Johnny Austin, *Chapman University*
Rick Bartlet, *Columbus State Community College*
Melinda Blackman, *California State University—Fullerton*
Regina Bento, *University of Baltimore*
Ralph Brathwaite, *University of Hartford*
David Bush, *Villanova University*
Mark Butler, *San Diego State University*
Steve Buuck, *Concordia University*
Jay Caulfield, *Marquette University*
William Clark, *Leeward Community College*
Michelle Duffy, *University of Kentucky*
Michael Ensby, *Clarkson University*
Cassandra Fenyk, *Centenary College*
Meltem Ferendeci-Ozgodek, *Bilkent University*
Dean Frear, *Wilkes University*
Sharon Gardner, *College of New Jersey*
James Gelatt, *University of Maryland-University College*
John George, *Liberty University*
Lucy Gilson, *University of Connecticut-Storrs*
Mary Giovannini, *Truman State University*

Yezdi Godiwalla, *University of Wisconsin-Whitewater*
Elaine Guertler, *Lees-McRae College*
Carol Harvey, *Assumption College*
David Hennessy, *Mt. Mercy College*
Kenny Holt, *Union University*
Janice Jackson, *Western New England College*
Paul Jacques, *Western Carolina University*
William Judge, *University of Tennessee-Knoxville*
Barbara Kelley, *St. Joseph's University*
Robert Ledman, *Morehouse College*
James Maddox, *Friends University*
Bill Mellan, *Florida Sothern College*
Edward Miles, *Georgia State University*
Atul Mitra, *University of Northern Iowa*
Christine O'Connor, *University of Ballarad*
Regina O'Neill, *Suffolk University*
Laura Paglis, *Univwersity of Evansville*
Chris Poulson, *California State Polytechinal University—Pomana*
Sharon Purkiss, *California State University-Fullerton*
William Reisel, *St. John's University*
Pam Roffol-Dobies, *University of Missouri—Kansas City*
Sammie Robinson, *Illinoise Wesleyan Universtiy*
Bob Roller, *Letourneau University*
Sophie Romack, *John Carroll Universtiy*
William Rudd, *Boise State College*
Joel Rudin, *Rowan University*
Jane Schmidt-Wilk, *Maharishi University of Management*
Mel Schnake, *Valdosta State University*
Holly Schroth, *University of Califorr;ia-Berkeley*
Randy Sleeth, *Virginia Commonwealth University*
Shane Spiller, *Morehead State University*
John Stark, *California State University—Bakersfield*
Robert Steel, *University of Michigan-Dearborn*
David Tansik, *University of Arizona*
Tom Thompson, *University of Maryland-University*
Edward Tomlinson, *John Carroll University*
Tony Urban, *Rutgers University-Camden*
Fred Ware, *Valdosta State University*
Joseph Wright, *Portland Community College*

We also greatly appreciate the guidance and support we received from the
excellent Wiley team consisting of Don Fowley, Joan Kalkut, Carissa Marker,
Cindy Rhoads, Amy Scholtz, Carly DeCandia, Sandra Dumas, Suzanne Ingrao,
Kevin Murphy, Nancy Field and Jennifer Macmillian. We also acknowledge and
thank former members of the editorial team who made contributions to this
edition to include, Jayme Heffler, Kim Mortimer and Jennifer Conklin. Our colleagues at Texas A&M University, Wake Forest University and Tulane University have also provided valuable support by providing intellectual input through

discussions and debates. There are many people over the years that have contributed to our own intellectual growth and development and led us to write this book. For all of your help and support, we thank you. Finally, we owe a debt of gratitude to our many students from whom we have learned and to the students who have used this text and provided feedback directly to us and through their instructors. Thank you.

MAH
CCM
AC

Whole Foods, Whole People

WHOLE FOODS MARKET is the largest natural food retailer in the world. With operations located primarily in the U.S., Whole Foods sells natural and organic food products that include produce, meat, poultry, seafood, grocery products, baked and prepared goods, many drinks such as beer and wine, cheese, floral products, and pet products. The origin of the company dates to 1978 when John Mackey and his girlfriend used $45,000 in borrowed funds to start a small natural food store then named SaferWay. The store was located in Austin, Texas. John and his girlfriend lived in the space over the store (without a shower) because they were "kicked out" of their apartment for storing food products in it.

In 1980, John Mackey developed a partnership with Craig Weller and Mark Skiles, merging SaferWay with Weller's and Skiles's Clarksville Natural Grocer to create the Whole Foods Market. Its first store opened in 1980 with 12,500 square feet and 19 employees. This was a very large health food store relative to others at that time. There was a devastating flood in Austin within a year of its opening and the store was heavily damaged. Much of its inventory was ruined and its equipment was damaged. The total losses were approximately $400,000 and the company had no insurance. Interestingly, customers and neighbors helped the staff of the store to repair and clean up the damage. Creditors, vendors, and investors all partnered to help the store reopen only 28 days after the flood. With their assistance, Whole Foods survived this devastating natural disaster.

Whole Foods started to expand in 1984 when it opened its first store outside of Austin. The new store was located in Houston followed by another store in Dallas and one in New Orleans. It also began acquiring other companies that sold natural foods, which helped to increase its expansion into new areas of the United States. In 2007, it expanded into international markets by opening its first Whole Foods branded store in London, England. (In 2004, it acquired a small natural foods company in the UK, Fresh & Wild, but did not use the Whole Foods brand until opening its new store in London.) It now has more than 54,000 employees in about 270 stores with annual sales of $5.6 billion. Thus, Whole Foods has become a major business enterprise and the most successful natural and organic food retailer in the world.

Managing Human Capital

Whole Foods Market has done a number of things right, thereby achieving considerable success. Yet, many people believe that one of the best things it has done is to implement an effective people management system. Each Whole Foods store employs approximately 40 to as many as 650 associates. All of the associates are organized into self-directed teams; associates are referred to as team members. Each of the teams is responsible for a specific product or service area (e.g., prepared foods, meats and poultry, customer service). Team members report to a team leader who then works with store management, referred to as store team leaders. The team members are a critically important part of the Whole Foods operation. Individuals are carefully selected and trained to be highly knowledgeable in their product areas, to offer friendly service, and to make critical decisions related to the types and quality of products offered to the public. Thus, they operate much differently than most "employees" in retail grocery outlets. These team members work together with their team leader to make a number of decisions with regard to their specific areas and they also contribute to store level decisions as well. In fact, many of the team members are attracted to Whole Foods because of the discretion they have in making decisions regarding product lines and so on. Of course, there are other attractions such as the compensation. For example, the company's stock option program involves employees at all levels. In fact, 94 percent of the stock options offered by the company have been presented to non-executive members, including front-line team members. The company pays competitive wages and pays for the full cost of health insurance for full-time associates. Actually, all of the benefit options are voted on by the associates in the company. Current programs include options for dental, vision, disability, and life insurance in addition to the full medical coverage for full-time associates.

Whole Foods follows a democratic model in the selection of new associates. For example, potential new team members can apply for any one of the 13 teams that operate in most Whole Foods Markets. Current team members participate in the interview process and actually vote on whether to offer a job to prospective colleagues. A candidate is generally given a four-week trial period if s/he is felt to have potential. At the end of that trial period, team members vote on whether to offer a permanent job to the candidate. The candidate must receive a two-thirds majority positive vote from the department team members in order to be hired.

Teams also receive bonuses if they perform exceptionally well. They set goals relative to prior performance and must achieve those goals to attain a bonus. Exceptionally high performing teams may earn up to $2 an hour more than their current wage base.

The top management of Whole Foods believes that the best philosophy is to build a shared identity with all team members. They do so by involving them in decisions and encouraging their participation at all levels in the business. They empower employees to make decisions and even allow them to participate in the decision of the benefit options as noted above. All team members have access to full information on the company. It is referred to as Whole Foods' open-book policy. In this open-book policy, team members have access to the firm's financial records, which include compensation information for all associates and even the top management team and the CEO. Therefore, the firm operates with full transparency regarding its associates. This approach emphasizes the company's core values of collaboration and decentralization. The company attracts people who share those core values and tries to reward a highly engaged and productive workforce.

The company also limits the pay of top executives to no more than 19 times the lowest paid associate in the firm. While this amount has been increased over time in order to maintain competitive compensation for managers, it is still well below industry averages for top management team members. And, in recent times, John Mackey, the CEO, announced that he no longer will accept a salary above $1 annually nor the stock options provided to him. Thus, his salary was reduced from $1 million to $1 per year. The money saved from his salary is donated to a fund to help needy associates.

The outcomes of this unique system for managing human capital have been impressive. For example, Whole Foods' voluntary turnover is much lower than the industry average. The industry average is almost 90 percent annually, but Whole Foods' data show that it has a voluntary turnover rate of approximately 27 percent. In addition, Whole Foods was ranked #5 in the top 100 best companies to work for by *Fortune* magazine in 2007. It has been on the top 100 best companies to work for list for the last 10 years and its ranking has steadily improved to its highest mark in 2007.

In addition to its flat organization structure and decentralized decision making, the company believes that each employee should feel a stake in the success of the company. In fact, this is communicated in its "Declaration of Interdependence." The Declaration of Interdependence suggests that the company has five core values. They are listed in Table 1.

The company attempts to support team member excellence and happiness through its empowering work environment in which team members work together to create the results. In such an environment, they try to create a motivated work team that achieves the highest possible productivity. There is an emphasis on individuals taking responsibility for their success and failure and see both as opportunities for personal

Table 1
Whole Foods' Declaration of Interdependence (Five Core Values)
1. Selling the highest quality natural and organic food products available.
2. Satisfying and delighting customers.
3. Supporting team member excellence and happiness.
4. Creating wealth through profits and growth.
5. Caring about communities and the environment.

and organizational growth. The company develops self-directed work teams and gives them significant decision-making authority to resolve problems and build a department and product line that satisfy and delight the customers. The company believes in providing open and timely information and in being highly transparent in all of its operations. It also focuses on achieving progress by continuously allowing associates to apply their collective creativity and intellectual capabilities to build a highly competitive and successful organization. Finally, they emphasize a shared fate among all stakeholders. This is why there are no entitlements even to top managers. They assume that everybody works together to achieve success.

Social and Community Responsibilities

Whole Foods Market takes pride in being a responsible member of its community and of society. For example, it emphasizes the importance of sustainable agriculture. In particular, the firm tries to support organic farmers, growers, and the environment by a commitment to using sustainable agriculture and expanding the market for organic products. In this regard, the Whole Foods Market launched a program to loan approximately $10 million annually to help independent local producers around the country to expand. It holds seminars and teaches producers how to move their products onto grocery shelves and how to command and receive premium prices for their products. These seminars and related activities have been quite popular. As an example, its first seminar held in Colorado in 2007 attracted 130 growers, which was almost twice as many as expected. Overall, the Whole Foods Market does business with more than 2,400 independent growers.

Whole Foods Market also supports its local communities in other ways. For example, the company promotes active involvement in local communities by giving a minimum of 5 percent of its profits each year to a variety of community and nonprofit organizations. These actions encourage philanthropy and outreach in the communities that Whole Foods serves.

Whole Foods Market also tries to promote positive environmental practices. The company emphasizes the importance of recycling and reusing products and reducing waste wherever possible. Furthermore, Whole Foods was the first retailer to build a supermarket that met environmental standards of the Leadership in Energy and Environmental Design Green Building Rating System (LEED). It was the largest corporate purchaser of wind credits in the history of the U.S. when it purchased enough to offset 100 percent of its total electricity use in 2006. Finally, Whole Foods announced a new initiative a few years ago to create an animal compassion standard that emphasizes the firm's belief in the needs of an animal. They developed standards for each of the species that are used for foods and sold through their supermarkets.

Very few, if any, major corporations, including competing supermarket chains, have established programs that rival those of the Whole Foods Market to meet social and community responsibilities.

Some Bumps in the Road

While the Whole Foods Market has been a highly successful company, it still has experienced some problems along the way. Obviously, it has produced a concept that has been imitated by other natural foods companies and a number of competing supermarkets as well. In general, Whole Foods has been able to maintain its competitive advantage and market leadership, partly by being the first to the market and with its practices which continue to generate a strong reputation and a positive company image. Yet, a number of firms have developed competing products and are making headway in selling organic foods, even including some regular large supermarket chains. In order to maintain its leadership and to continue to command a premium price, Whole Foods Market must continuously differentiate its products and its image so that people will buy from it rather than from competitors.

The top management of the Whole Foods Market has been strongly opposed to unionization. The belief is that the company pays workers well, treats them with dignity and respect, and that a union is likely to interfere in its relationship with associates. John Mackey, the CEO of the company, suggests that it is a campaign to "love the worker, not a union." Yet, the first union for Whole Foods was voted in at its Madison, Wisconsin store. The vote was 65 to 54 in favor of organizing a union by the Madison associates. When this vote was announced, Mr. Mackey referred to it as a sad day in the history of the company. He suggested that the associates had made a mistake and believed that they would eventually realize the error of their ways. However, the Whole Foods Market executives have been able to fend off union efforts at other stores.

Another recent problem became evident when it was announced that John Mackey had, for a few years, posted on a Yahoo! financial message board anonymous online critiques of competitors and self-congratulating statements about the Whole Foods Market. These comments were made using a pseudonym so no one knew that he was the CEO of Whole Foods. This action was strongly criticized by analysts and others and several questioned the ethics of his actions. Given that Whole Foods has emphasized its ethical approach to business and suggested that it conducts fair and open operations, such actions could be potentially harmful to the Whole Foods Market image and reputation. In fact, the company launched an investigation of his actions. In addition, the Securities and Exchange Commission (SEC) investigated some of the postings to Internet chat rooms by Mr. Mackey in which he used a pseudonym. The concern was that he may have released information that should not have been provided to the market. The Whole Foods' Board completed its investigation and reaffirmed its support for John Mackey. Stakeholders will have to await the outcome of the SEC investigation to determine if there has been much harm done to the Whole Foods Market image.

Firm Performance and the Future

Whole Foods Market has performed well over the past several years, sustaining significant growth in sales and profits. Its stock price has also generally performed well. However, for the last couple of years, analysts have argued that the stock is overvalued. This is partly because they do not believe that Whole Foods can sustain the growth rate and returns that it has achieved in recent years. Undoubtedly, being able to maintain the growth rate will be difficult as the competition in its natural and organic foods grows and as the number of markets and opportunities narrows, particularly in the U.S. Likely, in order to sustain its growth, Whole Foods Market will have to expand with additional operations overseas.

John Mackey, the CEO, has stated on several occasions that he does not make decisions on the basis of Wall Street's reactions. He argues that investors should not invest in his stock for the short term. Rather, they should look for long-term value increases because he will make decisions in the best interest of the share-holders for the long term. Perhaps this approach will provide better returns over time, but only time will tell. Clearly, Whole Foods Market has been a very positive force in dealing with its associates through its highly unique means of managing human capital. It also has built a strong positive reputation and differentiated its products in the eyes of consumers. Yet, there are some "chinks in its armor," particularly with the competition, the potential unionization, and with the CEO's recent actions that some have questioned as unethical. While the future likely remains bright, further evaluation will be needed to determine if there will be continued growth and positive returns for all stakeholders of the Whole Foods Market.

Source: Whole Foods Market logo used with permission.

References

1. 100 best companies to work for: Whole Foods Market snapshot. 2007. CNNmoney.com. http://money.cnn.com, June 13.

2. Declaration of interdependence. 2007. Whole Foods Market website, http://www.wholefoodsmarket.com, April 29.

3. P.J. Erickson & L. Gratton. 2007. What it means to work here. *Harvard Business Review,* March: 85(3): 104–112.

4. J.P. Fried. 2007. At Whole Foods, a welcome sign for immigrants seeking jobs. *New York Times.* http://www.nytimes.com, April 29.

5. S. Hammer & T. McNicol. 2007. Low-cow compensation. *Business 2.0,* May: 62.

6. M. Hogan. 2007. Whole Foods: A little too rich? *BusinessWeek,* http://www.businessweek.com, July 21.

7. P. Huetlin. 2007. Flagship Whole Foods opens in London. *BusinessWeek,* http://www.businessweek.com, July 5.

8. L. Hunt. 2005. Whole Foods Market, Inc. http://www.marketbusting.com/casestudies, March 30.

9. D. Kesmodel & J. Eig. 2007. Unraveling rahodeb: A grocer's brash style takes unhealthy turn. *Wall Street Journal Online,* http://online.wsj.com, July 30.

10. N.S. Koehn & K. Miller. 2007. John Mackey and Whole Foods Market. *Harvard Business School Case #9-807-111,* May 14.

11. J. Mackey. 2007. I no longer want to work for money. *Fast Company,* http://www.fastcompany.com, February.

12. A. Nathans. 2003. Love the worker, not the union, a store says as some organize. *New York Times,* http://www.nytimes.com, May 24.

13. Our core values, Whole Foods Market website, http://www.wholefoodsmarket.com, April 29.

14. K. Richardson & D. Kesmodel. 2007. Why Whole Foods investors may want to shop around. *Wall Street Journal Online,* http://online.wsj.com, November 23.

15. C. Rohwedder. 2007. Whole Foods opens new front. *Wall Street Journal Online,* http://online.wsj.com, June 6.

16. J. Sonnenfeld. 2007. What's rotten at Whole Foods. *Business-Week,* http://www.businessweek.com, July 17.

17. S. Thurm. 2007. Whole Foods CEO serves up heated word for FTC. *Wall Street Journal Online,* http://online.swj.com, June 27.

18. Welcome to Whole Foods Market. Whole Foods Market website, http://www.wholefoodsmarket.com, April 29.

19. J.E. Wells & T. Haglock. 2005. Whole Foods Market, Inc. *Harvard Business School Case #9-705-476,* June 9.

20. Whole Foods closes buyout of Wild Oats. 2007. *New York Times,* http://www.nytimes.com, August 29.

21. Whole Foods Market soars to #5 spot on *Fortune's "100 Best Companies to Work For" list.* Whole Foods Market website, http://www.wholefoodsmarket.com, January 9.

22. Whole Foods Market. 2007. *Wikipedia,* http://www.wikipedia.com, September 2.

23. Whole Foods promotes local buying. 2007. *New York Times,* http://www.nytimes.com, April 29.

Whole Foods Case Discussion Questions

Chapter 1

1. Describe how Whole Foods uses human capital as a source of competitive advantage.

2. Identify the aspects of high involvement management contained in Whole Foods' approach to managing its associates.

Chapter 2

1. Compared to other companies in the service sector, is Whole Foods more or less likely to experience discrimination problems? Explain your answer.

2. How could Whole Foods' democratic model of selection interfere with the development or continuance of a diverse workforce? What should it do to prevent difficulties?

Chapter 3

1. How do you think that globalization will affect Whole Foods over time? Please explain several ways it could affect the company operations.

2. In what ways can national culture affect the management of human capital? Will Whole Foods have to adapt its democratic approach to selecting new team members or the benefits it provides to its associates as it expands further into international markets?

Chapter 4

1. To what extent do you think that training and associate learning would be more important for Whole Foods compared to other grocery stores?

2. What type of perceptual problems on the part of associates and the public may have resulted from the scandal regarding John Mackey's blog activities?

Chapter 5

1. Given the nature of Whole Foods' jobs and the way in which associates are selected, what type of personality traits would be important for Whole Foods' associates to possess?

2. Compared to the industry average, Whole Foods has a low turnover rate and is consistently ranked as a great place to work. Why do you think Whole Foods' associates are so satisfied and committed to the organization?

Chapter 6

1. Are Whole Foods' team members likely to experience problems with procedural and/or distributive justice? Explain.

2. Which of the major motivational practices are emphasized by Whole Foods in its management system? Finding meaningful rewards? Tying rewards to performance? Designing enriched jobs? Providing feedback? Clarifying expectations and goals? All of these?

Chapter 7

1. Based on the demand-control and effort-reward models of stress, are Whole Foods' team members likely to experience a great deal of stress? Executives?

2. Does Whole Foods need a wellness program? Why/why not?

Chapter 8

1. Is John Mackey a transformational leader? Why/why not?

2. Based on contingency theories of leadership, what approach to leadership seems best for Whole Foods' team leaders?

Chapter 9

1. Whole Foods' open-book policy allows all associates to have full access to all information about the company and its executives. Would this degree of open communication work as well in other companies? Why or why not? What impact do you think this degree of transparency has on the attitudes and behavior of Whole Foods' associates?

2. What ethical issues arise from John Mackey's use of a pseudonym to post opinions, information, and critiques on blog sites?

Chapter 10

1. What decision styles does John Mackey appear to use? Do these fit his situation?

2. Which group decision-making pitfalls appear most likely within Whole Foods' teams, and which decision-making techniques would you recommend to counter those pitfalls?

Chapter 11

1. What policies and procedures does Whole Foods enact that allow it to develop successful associate teams?

2. What impact do you think that the process of allowing team members to vote on hiring new members has on the dynamics and performance of the Whole Foods teams?

Chapter 12

1. Whole Foods' "Declaration of Interdependence" states that two of the company's core values are "creating wealth through profits and growth" and "caring about our communities and the environment." Often, these two values are in conflict for many companies. How does Whole Foods resolve this conflict?

2. Whole Foods has been opposed to the unionization of its associates. However, associates in a Madison, Wisconsin store recently voted to become unionized. What type of conflicts or power struggles may have led this to occur?

Chapter 13

1. Analyze effects of the democratic approach to store operations and hiring new associates on store performance.

2. What does the transparency on company financial data and associate and managers' compensation communicate about Whole Foods' culture? How does the Declaration of Interdependence reflect aspects of Whole Foods' culture?

Chapter 14

1. Analyze how Whole Foods has managed change over the years since it started.

2. Whole Foods now faces a significant amount of competition. How should it respond to the changes in the competitive landscape of its industry? What future challenges do you envision for Whole Foods' market?

PART I THE STRATEGIC LENS

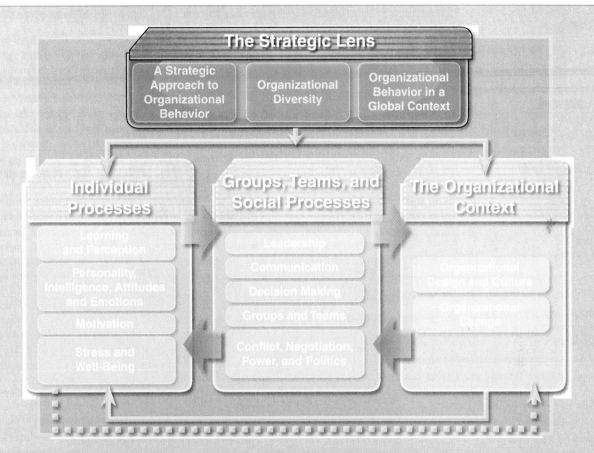

This book describes the rich and important concepts that make up the field of organizational behavior. We have based the book on cutting-edge research as well as current practices in organizations. Beyond this, the book is unique in presenting these concepts through a *strategic lens*. That is, in each chapter, we explain the strategic importance of the primary concepts presented in the chapter. Our discussions emphasize how managers can use knowledge of these concepts to improve organizational performance.

In Part I, we develop and explain the strategic lens for organizational behavior. To begin, we describe in **Chapter 1** the concept of competitive advantage and how behavior in an organization affects the organization's ability to gain and maintain an advantage over its competitors. Gaining and maintaining a competitive advantage is critical for organizations to perform at high levels and provide returns to their stakeholders (including owners). We emphasize the importance and management of human capital for high perform-ance and describe the high-involvement organization and how to manage associates to achieve it.

Chapter 2 examines the critical topic of organizational diversity. Given the demographic diversity in the United States, all organizations' workforces are likely to become increasingly diverse. Thus, it is important to understand diversity and how to manage it effectively. Also, it is important to recognize that diversity can be managed to gain a competitive advantage. This chapter explains how.

Chapter 3 discusses managing organizations in a global environment. International markets offer more opportunities but also are likely to present greater challenges than domestic markets. Understanding the complexities of managing in international markets is a necessity. It is especially important to understand how to manage in the face of diverse cultures and varying types of institutional environments.

The three chapters of Part I provide the setting for exploring the topics covered in the chapters that follow.

1

A STRATEGIC APPROACH TO ORGANIZATIONAL BEHAVIOR

"We give people the space they need to be creative, set goals, define strategies, and implement a game plan. That space is very important to each of us. It's our playing field—but we share it with our co-workers. So workgroups, store teams, even whole departments get to define their game plan as well. We call it "painting our own canvas." Our people like that freedom and the underlying trust behind it."

PhotoDisc, Inc./Getty Images

EXPLORING BEHAVIOR IN ACTION

Strategic Use of Human Capital at The Men's Wearhouse

George Zimmer, founder and chief executive officer (CEO) of The Men's Wearhouse, frequently uses words such as these to describe his firm's philosophy on the people who carry out day-to-day work. Under this philosophy, individuals are given substantial discretion in choosing work methods and goals. Training is both quantitatively and qualitatively greater at The Men's Wearhouse than at the vast majority of retailers. Such training provides the base for effective use of discretion by individuals. Reward systems that value individual and team productivity help to encourage the type of behavior that is desired. Responsibility and accountability complement the system.

The base for the system of discretion and accountability is a core set of workplace beliefs, including the following:

1. Work should be fulfilling.
2. Workplaces should be fearless and energized.
3. Work and family life should be balanced.
4. Leaders should serve followers.

5. Employees should be treated like customers.
6. People should not be afraid to make mistakes.

The Men's Wearhouse has been successful with its approach. Compared with most major retailers, it has experienced lower turnover, higher satisfaction, and stronger motivation among employees. As a testament to its philosophy, the company was listed on *Fortune* magazine's list of the "100 Best Companies to Work For" in 2005, 2006, and 2007 and has received an Optimas award from *Workforce* magazine in recognition of its positive management practices. Financial outcomes have also been positive over the years. Net income and return on total invested capital have been superior to industry averages for men's tailored clothing and comparable to or better than those of many other industries in which returns are usually higher. Sales and positive returns continued to grow in recent years (e.g., 2006–2007). For example, its net profits increased by 60 percent in the fourth quarter of 2006 compared to the same quarter in 2005.

Despite the intuitive appeal of many of its practices, many analysts have been surprised by the success of The Men's Wearhouse, for two reasons. First, the company operates in an industry where financial success is uncommon, for several industry reasons. For example, the industry has low barriers to entry (new firms easily enter and compete in the market), customers and suppliers have too many choices for any one specialty retailer to have much market power, and firms in the industry are highly competitive (rivalries among firms often produce harmful price wars). Second, retailers typically do not have access to workers who are among the elite of the U.S. labor force. Charlie Bresler, a top executive at The Men's Wearhouse, commented, "The retail worker in the United States is somebody who often came from a dysfunctional home, like a lot of us . . . somebody who didn't do well in school."

With the success of The Men's Wearhouse, we might expect frequent attempts to imitate its practices, but this has not been the case. Instead, confronted with the difficult industry conditions described above, managers in many retailing firms have attempted to minimize costs through low compensation and little training. Confronted with a labor pool deemed substandard, they have implemented supervision and surveillance systems designed to tightly control employees. Bresler again sheds light on this segment of the labor market:

Most people who are executives or managers in retail . . . look at human beings who work [for them] and see people who are supposed to do tasks [but] don't do them very well. . . . What the typical retailer sees are . . . people who are stuck there and if they could get a better job, they would.

Managers at The Men's Wearhouse respond differently to the same industry and applicant pool than other retailers. In part, they respond on the basis of an ideology based on the notion that every human being has significant value and should be treated accordingly. Eric Anderson, director of training, put it this way: "We happen to sell men's clothing, but by recognizing what is really important—the people—we have a different paradigm than many other businesses." There is more to the story, however, than a simple ideology about valuing people. The leadership of the company firmly believes that valuing people is crucial for business success. They believe they get more out of their employees by providing them power and autonomy, and the results seem to support this belief. Bresler best summarizes the reasons why: "[Our people] treat customers better partly because . . . they don't feel put down by the corporation. That energy . . . sells more products. . . . That's how you build a retail business, from our point of view."

Sources: M. Cianciolo, "Tailoring Growth at Men's Wearhouse: Fool by the Numbers," *The Motley Fool,* www.fool.com, May 23 2007; "Men's Wearhouse Shares Soar," Boston.com, www.boston.com, Mar. 8, 2007; "Fortune 100 Best Companies to Work For 2007, CNNMoney.com, money.cnn.com, Jan. 22, 2007; V.D. Infante, "Optimas 2001—Managing Change: Men's Wearhouse: Tailored for Any Change That Retail Brings," *Workforce* 80, no. 3 (2001): 48–49; R. Levering and M. Moskowitz, "The 100 Best Companies to Work For" *Fortune,* Jan. 24, 2005, 61–71; C.A. O'Reilly and J. Pfeffer, *Hidden Value: How Great Companies Achieve Extraordinary Results with Ordinary People* (Boston: Harvard Business School Press, 2000); G. Zimmer, "Building Community through Shared Values, Goals, and Experiences," 2005, at http://www.menswearhouse.com/home_page/common_threads; G. Zimmer, "Our Philosophy," 2005, at http://www.menswearhouse.com/home_page/common_threads.

After reading this chapter, you should be able to:

1. Define organizational behavior and explain the strategic approach to OB.

2. Provide a formal definition of *organization*.

3. Describe the nature of human capital.

4. Discuss the conditions under which human capital is a source of competitive advantage for an organization.

5. Describe positive organizational behavior and explain how it can contribute to associates' productivity.

6. Explain the five characteristics of high-involvement management and the importance of this approach to management.

The Men's Wearhouse case shows the powerful difference that a firm's human capital can make. Faced with less-than-favorable industry characteristics and a labor pool that many find unattractive, the company has succeeded in part by paying careful attention to human behavior. Any firm can sell men's clothing, but it requires special management to effectively embrace and use to advantage the complexities and subtleties of human behavior. From the motivational and leadership practices of managers to the internal dynamics of employee-based teams to the values that provide the base for the organization's culture, successful firms develop approaches that unleash the potential of their people (human capital).

In today's competitive world, the ability to understand, appreciate, and effectively leverage human capital is critical in all industries. A strategic approach to organizational behavior is focused on these issues. In this chapter, we introduce the concept of organizational behavior and explain how to view it through a strategic lens.

To introduce the strategic approach to organizational behavior, or (OB), we address several issues. First, we define organizational behavior and discuss its strategic importance. Next, we explore the notion of human capital, addressing questions about its role in organizations. We then discuss the circumstances in which human capital most likely contributes to a competitive advantage for an organization. A discussion of high-involvement management follows. This form of management is helpful in developing and using human capital and is becoming increasingly important as firms search for ways to maximize the potential of all of their people (managers and nonmanagers). In the final section of the chapter, we describe the model and plan for the concepts explained in this book.

Basic Elements of Strategic Organizational Behavior

Important resources for businesses and other types of organizations include technologies, distribution systems, financial assets, patents, and the knowledge and skills of people. **Organizational behavior** involves the actions of individuals and groups in an organizational context. **Managing organizational behavior** focuses on acquiring, developing, and applying the knowledge and skills of people. The **strategic OB approach** rests on the premise that people are the foundation of an organization's competitive advantages. An organization might have exceptionally high-quality products and services, excellent customer service, best-in-class cost structure, or some other advantage, but all of these are outcomes of the capabilities of the organization's people—its human capital. If organized and managed effectively, the knowledge and skills of the people in the organization drive sustainable competitive advantage and long-term financial success.[1] Thus, the strategic approach to OB involves organizing and managing the people's knowledge and skills effectively to implement the organization's strategy and gain a competitive advantage.

Individual, interpersonal, and organizational factors determine the behavior and the ultimate value of an organization's people; these factors are shown in Exhibit 1-1. For individuals, factors such as the ability to learn, the ability to be self-managing, technical skills, personality characteristics, and personal values are important. These elements represent or are related to important capabilities. At the interpersonal level, factors such as quality of leadership, communication within

organizational behavior
The actions of individuals and groups in an organizational context.

managing organizational behavior
Actions focused on acquiring, developing, and applying the knowledge and skills of people.

strategic OB approach
An approach that involved organizing and managing people's knowledge and skills effectively to implement the organization's strategy and gain a competitive advantage.

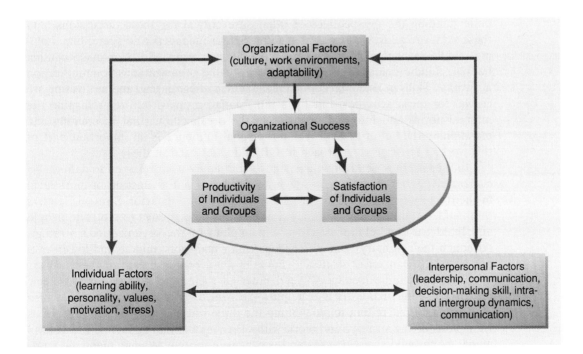

Exhibit 1-1 Factors and Outcomes of a Strategic Approach to Organizational Behavior

and between groups, and conflict within and between groups are noteworthy. These elements influence the degree to which the capabilities of individuals are unleashed and fully utilized within an organization. Finally, at the organizational level, the culture and policies of the organization are among the most important factors, as they influence whether the talents and positive predispositions of individuals are effectively leveraged to create positive outcomes.

The factors discussed above interact to produce the outcomes of productivity, satisfaction, and organizational success. *Productivity* refers to the output of individuals and groups, whereas *satisfaction* relates to the feelings that individuals and groups have about their work and the workplace. *Organizational success* is defined in terms of competitive advantage and ultimately financial performance (success). In essence, then, a strategic approach to organizational behavior requires understanding how individual, interpersonal, and organizational factors influence the behavior and value of an organization's people, where value is reflected in productivity, satisfaction, and ultimately the organization's competitive advantages and financial success.

The Importance of Using a Strategic Lens

Studying organizational behavior with a strategic lens is valuable for managers and aspiring managers at all levels of the organization, as well as for the workers who complete the basic tasks. For example, effective senior managers spend much of their time talking with insiders and outsiders about vision, strategy, and other major issues crucial to the direction of the organization.[2] Senior leaders make the strategic decisions for the firm.[3] Skills in conceptualizing, communicating, and understanding the perspectives of others are critical for these discussions, and these skills are addressed by strategic OB. Senior managers also spend time helping middle managers to define and redefine their roles and to manage conflict because middle managers are often central to the organization's communication networks.[4] Skills in listening, conflict management, negotiating, and motivating are crucial for these activities. Finally, senior managers invest effort in shaping the internal norms and informal practices of the organization (that is, creating and maintaining the culture). Skill in interpersonal influence is an important part of this work. The strategic approach to OB addresses each of these issues.

In recent times, senior managers have commonly been referred to as *strategic leaders.*[5] However, exercising strategic leadership is not a function of one's level in the organization; rather, it is a matter of focus and behavior. Strategic leaders think and act strategically, and they use the skills noted above to motivate people and build trusting relationships to help implement the organization's strategy. Although their primary tasks differ from senior managers, middle and lower-level managers also can act as strategic leaders in the accomplishment of their tasks.[6]

Effective middle managers spend much of their time championing strategic ideas with senior managers and helping the firm to remain adaptive.[7] They also play an important role in implementing the organization's strategy. They serve as champions of the strategy and work with other middle managers and lower-level managers to build the processes and set them in motion to implement the strategy. Skills in networking, communicating, and influencing are important for these aspects of their work. Middle managers also spend time processing data and information for use by individuals at all levels of the firm, requiring skills in analysis and communication. When delivering the strategic initiatives to lower-level managers, skills in communicating, motivating, understanding values, and managing stress are among the most important. A strategic approach to OB addresses each of these aspects of managerial work.

Effective lower-level managers spend a great deal of their time coaching the firm's **associates**—our term for the workers who carry out the basic tasks.[8] Skills in teaching, listening, understanding personalities, and managing stress are among the most important for performing these activities. Lower-level managers also remove obstacles for associates and deal with personal problems that affect their work. Skills in negotiating and influencing others are critical for removing obstacles, whereas skills in counseling and understanding personalities are important for dealing with personal problems. Finally, lower-level managers expend effort to design jobs, team structures, and reward systems. Skills in analysis, negotiating, and group dynamics are among the most important for these activities. The strategic approach to OB addresses each of these aspects of managerial work.

> **associates**
> The workers who carry out the basic tasks.

Lower-level managers will be more effective when they understand the organization's strategy and how their work and that of their associates fit into the strategy. Much of what they do is required to implement the strategy. It is also helpful to get these managers to take a longer-term view. If they do not take a strategic approach, many of these managers are likely to focus on short-term problems. In fact, they may emphasize resolving problems without examining how they can prevent them in the future. Taking a strategic approach enables them to use their skills to prevent problems, implement the strategy effectively, and complete their current tasks efficiently while remaining focused on the future.

Despite the relevance of formal study in OB, some people believe that managers can be successful solely on the basis of common sense. If this were true, fewer organizations would have difficulty unleashing the potential of people, and there would be less dissatisfaction and unhappiness with jobs. Also, if this were true, absenteeism and turnover rates would be lower. The truth is that fully leveraging the capabilities of people involves subtleties and complexities that are difficult to grasp and manage. Common sense cannot be the only basis of action for managers. Effective managers understand that deep knowledge about people and organizations is the true source of their success.

Without meaningful working knowledge of OB, managers' efforts to be successful resemble those of the drunkard and his keys. According to this classic story, the drunkard dropped his keys by the car but could not find them because it was very dark there. So, instead of bringing light to the appropriate area, he looked under a nearby streetlight where he could see better![9]

Managers in today's fast-paced organizations cannot afford to adopt the drunkard's approach when working with associates and each other. They must avoid looking for answers where it is easiest to see. Managers are often unsuccessful when they fail to develop the insights and skills necessary for working with others effectively.

In closing our discussion regarding the importance of understanding organizational behavior, we focus on the findings of two research studies. In both studies, the investigators examined the impact of formal business education on skills in information gathering, quantitative analysis, and dealing with people.[10] Significantly, they found that business education had positive effects on these important skills, including the interpersonal skills of leadership and helping others to grow. These findings suggest that understanding a strategic approach to OB can add value to our managerial knowledge and skills. There is no substitute for experience, but formal study can be very helpful in providing important insights and guidance.

Foundations of a Strategic Approach to Organizational Behavior

Insights from several disciplines inform our understanding of OB. The field builds on behavioral science disciplines, including psychology, social psychology, sociology, economics, and cultural anthropology. A strategic approach to OB, however, differs from these disciplines in two important ways. First, it integrates knowledge from all of these areas to understand behavior in organizations. It does not address organizational phenomena from the limited perspective of any one discipline. Second, it focuses on behaviors and processes that help to create competitive advantages and financial success. Unlike basic social science disciplines, where the goal is often to simply understand human and group behavior, the goal of the strategic OB approach is to improve the outcomes of organizations.

One might ask the following questions: Can taking courses in psychology, social psychology, sociology, economics, and cultural anthropology provide the knowledge needed to be an effective manager or to successfully accept the responsibility of working as a key member of an organization? Is it necessary to take a course in organizational behavior?

Acquiring knowledge directly from other disciplines can inform the study of organizational behavior. Knowledge from other disciplines, however, is not a substitute for the unique understanding and insights that can be gained from studying OB from a strategic perspective. As noted earlier, a strategic approach to OB *integrates* useful concepts from other disciplines while emphasizing their application in organizations.

Gaining an effective working knowledge of organizational behavior helps those who want to become successful managers. The following points summarize this important field of study:

1. There are complexities and subtleties involved in fully leveraging the capabilities of people. Common sense alone does not equip the manager with sufficient understanding of these complexities and subtleties.

2. Managers must avoid the allure of seeking simple answers to resolve organizational issues. A working knowledge of OB helps managers gain the confidence required to empower associates and work with them to find creative solutions to problems that arise. The complexity of organizational life challenges people to perform at high levels to contribute to organizational success and to achieve personal growth.

3. The strategic approach to OB integrates important behavioral science knowledge within an organizational setting and emphasizes application. This knowledge cannot be obtained from information derived independently from other specialized fields (psychology, economics, and the like).

Definition of an Organization

As we have already emphasized, OB is focused on organizations and what happens inside them. This is important, because organizations play an important role in modern society. Several commentators from Harvard University expressed it this way: "Modern societies are not market economies; they are organizational economies in which companies are the chief actors in creating value and advancing economic progress."[11] But what is an organization? Below we provide a formal definition of this term.

Although it is sometimes difficult to define the term *organization* precisely, most people agree that an organization is characterized by these features:[12]

- Network of individuals
- System
- Coordinated activities
- Division of labor
- Goal orientation
- Continuity over time, regardless of change in individual membership

Thus, we define an **organization** as a collection of individuals, whose members may change over time, forming a coordinated system of specialized activities for the purpose of achieving certain goals over some extended period of time.

organization
A collection of individuals forming a coordinated system of specialized activities for the purpose of achieving certain goals over some extended period of time.

One prominent type of organization is the business organization, such as Intel, Microsoft, or Procter & Gamble. There are other important types of organizations as well. Public-sector organizations, for example, have a major presence in most countries. Although we focus primarily on business firms in this book, the strategic approach to OB applies to the public sector as well as the not-for-profit sector. For example, we can discuss motivating associates in the context of business firms, but motivating people is important in all types of organizations. Some organizations may have more motivational problems than others, but the knowledge of how to motivate workers is critical for managers in all types of situations.

EXPERIENCING STRATEGIC ORGANIZATIONAL BEHAVIOR

Creating Innovation: Leading and Managing the Human Capital to Achieve Creativity

BusinessWeek ranked Apple as the most innovative company for 2007. How has Apple achieved this lofty status? The following statement by Apple CEO, Steve Jobs explains, "Innovation has nothing to do with how many R&D dollars you have. When Apple came up with the Mac, IBM was spending at least 100 times more on R&D. It's not about money. It's about the people you have, how they're led, and how much you get it." In the early 1990s, Apple redesigned its workplace for the R&D associates, providing them both with private offices and also common areas where they could gather and share ideas, engage in teamwork, and generally discuss their research. A former manager at Apple notes that Apple's success is based on empowering its associates, delegating authority and responsibility down in the organization, and allowing the people a lot of freedom.

The results are obvious. *BusinessWeek* describes Apple as the creative king. For example, to launch the iPod, Apple's immensely successful portable music

player, it integrated seven different innovations. It was able to create these innovations because of the innovation culture created at Apple and the high-quality scientists and engineers it has attracted to the company. Apple managers encourage and nurture a sense of community in which a passion for creative designs and innovation exists. Apple's designs have been described as more elegant, functional for customers, and effective than those developed by competitors. In short, Apple sets the standard in design.

Other companies are learning the importance of human capital in innovation and how it is managed. For example, Genentech allows its researchers and scientists to publish the results of their research in academic journals. This seems rather a small issue, but it is important for career status and opportunities for these scientists, and such publication has been disallowed at most pharmaceutical companies to guard their research "secrets." Yet, Genentech's policy allows it to compete with Harvard and Stanford for the best scientific researchers. These leading scientists attracted to Genentech has made it one of the innovation leaders in its industry.

Likewise, IBM has major innovation programs but also emphasizes the innovation of all of its associates. In 2006, IBM had an InnovationJam in which it brought together 150,000 IBM associates, customers, and supply partners to identify where IBM should focus its creative energies for the next-generation products and services. And, IBM CEO Samuel J. Palmisano funded the 10 best ideas that emerged from this process.

Apple and other innovative companies are the stars today and in the future. For example, Apple recently unveiled its new iPhone. Many believe that it may change the standard in the wireless communications industry. Thus, Apple's passion for innovation and the power of its human capital portends a very bright future for the company.

Sources: R. Enderle, "Apple's Competitive Advantage," *TechNewsWorld*, www.technewsworld.com/story, Mar. 8, 2004; J. McGregor, "The 25 Most Innovative Companies," *BusinessWeek*, May 14, 2007, pp. 52–62; A. Hesseldahl, "Apple's iPhone Rings a Lot of Bells," *BusinessWeek.com*, www.businessweek.com, Jan. 11, 2007; J. Scanton, "Apple Sets the Design Standard," *BusinessWeek.com*, www.businessweek.com, Jan. 8, 2007; J. McGregor, M. Amdt, R. Berner, I. Rowley, K. Hall, G. Edmondson, S. Hamm, M. Ihlwan and A. Reinhardt, "The World's Most Innovative Companies," *BusinessWeek.com*, www.businessweek.com, Apr. 24, 2006; "Apple's R&D Investment—Too Low or Too High?," *Noise Between Stations*, www.noisebetweenstations.com/personal/weblogs, June 16, 2007; B. Helm, "Apple's Other Legacy: Top Designers," *BusinessWeek.com*, www.businessweek.com, Sept. 6, 2005; J. Markoff, "Where the Cubicle is Dead," *New York Times*, www.nytimes.com/gst, Apr. 25, 1993.

As explained in the *Experiencing Strategic Organizational Behavior* feature, Apple has achieved significant success because of its innovations. In turn, Apple's innovations are due to the quality associates working in design, its innovation culture, and the way managers lead by empowering the associates to be creative and develop innovations. Apple's strategic leaders are willing to take risks and they nurture the innovation culture. But it also requires strategic leadership to implement Apple's innovation strategy throughout the company. As noted in the quote by Apple CEO Steven Jobs, the base of Apple's innovation is its human capital. Other companies, such as Genentech and IBM, similarly emphasize the importance of attracting, holding, and leading effectively high-quality human capital.

The Role of Human Capital in Creating Competitive Advantage

We have already noted the importance of human capital and competitive advantage to strategic OB. We now examine these concepts more closely.

The Nature of Human Capital

An organization's resource base includes both tangible and intangible resources. Property, factories, equipment, and inventory are examples of tangible resources. Historically, these types of resources have been the primary means of production and competition.[13] This is less true today because intangible resources have become critically important for organizations to successfully compete in the global economy. Intangible resources, including the reputation of the organization, trust between managers and associates, knowledge and skills of associates, organizational culture, brand name, and relationships with customers and suppliers, are the organization's nonphysical economic assets that provide value.[14] Such assets are often deeply rooted in a company's history and experiences, for they tend to develop through day-to-day actions and accumulate over time.[15] On a comparative basis, it is more difficult to quantify the value of intangible resources than that of tangible resources, but intangible resources are increasing in importance nonetheless.

Human capital is a critical intangible resource. As a successful business executive recently stated, "Burn down my buildings and give me my people, and we will rebuild the company in a year. But leave my buildings and take away my people . . . and I'll have a real problem."[16] As we highlighted in the opening case, **human capital** is the sum of the skills, knowledge, and general attributes of the people in an organization.[17] It represents capacity for today's work and potential for tomorrow's work. Human capital encompasses not only easily observed skills, such as those associated with operating machinery or selling products, but also the skills, knowledge, and capabilities of managers and associates for learning, communicating, motivating, building trust, and effectively working on teams. It also includes basic values, beliefs, and attitudes.

> **human capital**
> The sum of the skills, knowledge, and general attributes of the people in an organization.

Human capital does not depreciate in value as it is used. Contrast this with tangible resources—for example, manufacturing equipment—whose productive capacity or value declines with use. In economic terms, we can say that human capital does not suffer from the law of diminishing returns. In fact, increasing returns are associated with applications of knowledge because knowledge tends to expand with use.[18] In other words, we learn more as we apply knowledge. Knowledge, then, is "infinitely expansible" and grows more valuable as it is shared and used over time.[19]

Knowledge has become a critical resource for many firms.[20] Knowledge plays a key role in gaining and sustaining an advantage over competitors. Firms that have greater knowledge about their customers, markets, technologies, competitors, and themselves can use this knowledge to gain a competitive advantage. Because most knowledge in organizations is held by the managers and associates, it is important to acquire and hold a highly knowledgeable workforce to perform well.[21] Because of the importance of knowledge and human capital, firms need to invest in continuous development of its human capital. The goal is to enhance organizational learning and build the knowledge and skills in the firm. In short, firms try to acquire and enrich their human capital.[22]

The importance of human capital and knowledge is explained in the *Experiencing Strategic Organizational Behavior* on innovation. Apple largely is able to be a leader in innovation because of its high-quality human capital and the manner in which it empowers its associates working in design. These associates developed and designed the highly successful iPod and the new iPhone for which major sales are forecasted. The same is true for Genentech, which has been able to recruit some of the best scientists and engineers to work in its R&D laboratories.

The Concept of Competitive Advantage

competitive advantage
An advantage enjoyed by an organization that can perform some aspect of its work better than competitors or in a way that competitors cannot duplicate, such that it offers products/ services that are more valuable to customers.

A **competitive advantage** results when an organization can perform some aspect of its work better than competitors or when it can perform the work in a way that competitors cannot duplicate.[23] By performing the work differently from and better than competitors, the organization offers products/services that are more valuable for the customers.[24] For example, Apple developed and marketed the iPod, which took significant market share from Sony's previously highly successful Walkman MP3 players. Its new iPhone is predicted to do the same in the wireless communications market. As noted by the statement by Steven Jobs, CEO of Apple, the primary difference in Apple's ability to create innovation is its people and how they are led.

Human Capital as a Source of Competitive Advantage

Although human capital is crucial for competitive advantage, not all organizations have the people resources needed for success. The degree to which human capital is useful for creating true competitive advantage is determined by its value, rareness, and imitability.[25]

VALUE

In a general sense, the value of human capital can be defined as the extent to which individuals are capable of handling the basic work of an organization. Lawyers with poor legal training do not add value to a law firm because they cannot provide high-quality legal services. Similarly, individuals with poor skills in painting and caulking do not add value to a house-painting company.

human capital value
The extent to which individuals are capable of producing work that supports an organization's strategy for competing in the marketplace.

More directly, **human capital value** can be defined as the extent to which individuals are capable of producing work that supports an organization's strategy for competing in the marketplace.[26] In general, business firms emphasize one of two basic strategies. The first involves creating low-cost products or services for the customer while maintaining acceptable or good quality.[27] Buyers at the Closeout Division of Consolidated Stores, Inc., for example, scour the country to purchase low-cost goods. Their ability to find such goods through manufacturers' overruns and discontinued styles is crucial to the success of Closeout, the largest U.S. retailer of closeout merchandise. The buyers' skills allow the division to sell goods at below-discount prices.[28] The second strategy involves differentiating products or services from those of competitors on the basis of special features or superior quality and charging higher prices for the higher-value goods.[29] Ralph Lauren designers, for example, create special features for which customers are willing to pay a premium.[30]

Human capital plays an important role in the development and implementation of these strategies. For example, top managers are generally highly valuable resources for the firm. Their human capital as perceived by investors coupled with the strategic decisions that they make affect the investors' decisions of whether to invest in the firm.[31] Yet, most senior managers' knowledge and skills become obsolete very quickly because of the rapidly changing competitive landscape. Thus these managers must invest time and effort to continuously enrich their capabilities in order to maintain their value to the firm.[32] Overall, managers must expend considerable effort to acquire quality human capital and demonstrate to the firm's external constituencies its value.[33]

RARENESS

Human capital rareness is the extent to which the skills and talents of an organization's people are unique in the industry.[34] In some cases, individuals with rare skills are hired into the organization. Corporate lawyers with relatively rare abilities to reduce the tensions of disgruntled consumers, programmers with the unusual ability to produce thousands of lines of code per day with few errors, and house painters who are exceptionally gifted can be hired from the outside. In other cases, individuals develop rare skills inside the organization. Training and mentoring programs assist in these efforts.

> **human capital rareness**
> The extent to which the skills and talents of an organization's people are unique in the industry.

Sales associates at Nordstrom, an upscale retailer, have several qualities that are relatively rare in the retailing industry. First, they tend to be highly educated. Nordstrom explicitly targets college graduates for its entry-level positions. College graduates are willing to accept these positions because of their interest in retailing as a career, because managers are commonly drawn from the ranks of successful salespeople, and because Nordstrom's strong incentive-based compensation system provides financial rewards that are much higher than the industry average. Second, sales associates at Nordstrom have both the willingness and the ability to provide "heroic service." This type of service at times extends to delivering merchandise to the homes of customers, changing customers' flat tires, and paying for customers' parking. Nordstrom's culture, which is based on shared values that support exceptional customer service, is an important driver of heroic service. Some believe that Nordstrom's culture is more important to the company's performance than are its strategy and structure and even its compensation system.[35]

IMITABILITY

Human capital imitability is the extent to which the skills and talents of an organization's people can be copied by other organizations.[36] A competing retailer, for example, could target college graduates and use a promotion and compensation system similar to Nordstrom's. If many retailers followed this approach, some of the skills and talents at Nordstrom would become more common in the industry.

> **human capital imitability**
> The extent to which the skills and talents of an organization's people can be copied by other organizations.

The least imitable skills and talents are usually those that are complex and learned inside a particular organization. Typically, these skills involve *tacit knowledge*,[37] a type of knowledge that people have but cannot articulate. Automobile designers at BMW, the German car manufacturer, cannot tell us exactly how they arrive at effective body designs. They can describe the basic process of styling with clay models and with CAS (computer-aided styling), but they cannot fully explain why some curves added to the auto body are positive while others are not. They just know. They have a feel for what is right.[38] As a result, those firms that manage their knowledge effectively can make their skills and capabilities difficult to imitate by competitors.[39]

The culture of an organization represents shared values, which in turn partially determine the skills and behaviors that associates and managers are expected to have.[40] In some cases, organizational culture promotes difficult-to-imitate skills and behavior. Southwest Airlines, for example, is thought to have a culture that encourages people to display spirit and positive attitudes that are valuable, rare, and difficult to duplicate at other airlines. Spirit and attitude result from complex interactions among people that are challenging to observe and virtually impossible to precisely describe. Associates and managers know the spirit and attitude are there. They cannot, however, fully explain how they work to create value for customers.[41]

OVERALL POTENTIAL FOR COMPETITIVE ADVANTAGE

For human capital to be the basis for sustainable competitive advantage, it must satisfy all three conditions discussed earlier: it must be valuable for executing an organization's strategy, it must be rare in the industry, and it must be difficult to imitate. An organization that hires individuals with valuable but common skills does not have a basis for competitive advantage, because any organization can easily acquire those same skills. As shown in Exhibit 1-2, the human capital in such an organization can contribute only to competitive parity; that is, it can make the organization only as good as other organizations but not better. An organization that hires individuals with valuable and rare skills, or an organization that hires individuals with valuable skills and then helps them to develop additional rare skills, has the foundation for competitive advantage, but perhaps only in the short run. The organization may not have the foundation for long-term competitive advantage because other organizations may be able to copy what the organization has done. For long-term advantage through people, an organization needs human capital that is valuable, rare, and difficult to imitate.[42]

Although the value, rareness, and low imitability of skills and talents are crucial for competitive advantage, alone they are not enough. These three factors determine the potential of human capital. To translate that potential into actual advantage, an organization must leverage its human capital effectively.[43] An organization may have highly talented, uniquely skilled associates and managers, but if

Exhibit 1-2
Human Capital and
Competitive Advantage

Source: Adapted from
J. Barney and P. Wright,
"On Becoming a Strategic
Partner," *Human Resource
Management* 37 (1999):
31–46.

Are human resources in the firm . . .

Valuable?	Rare?	Difficult to Imitate?	Supported by Effective Management?	Competitive Implications	Performance
No	—	—	↕	Competitive Disadvantage	Below normal
Yes	No	—		Competitive Parity	Normal
Yes	Yes	No		Temporary Competitive Advantage	Above normal
Yes	Yes	Yes		Sustained Competitive Advantage	Above normal

these individuals are not motivated or are not given proper support resources, they will not make a positive difference. Thus, sustainable competitive advantage through people depends not only on the skills and talents of those people, but also on how they are treated and deployed.[44] In the next section, we discuss a general approach for effectively developing and leveraging human capital. As a prelude, we explore an important issue related to labor markets in the *Managerial Advice* feature.

MANAGERIAL ADVICE

Labor Markets for Human Capital: Shortages of Skilled Labor Can Retard Growth in Emerging Economies

Human capital is a global resource and important for firms from all over the world, especially those wanting to compete in global markets. Yet, there is a global shortage of qualified managers. This shortage is exacerbated in growing emerging economies such as China and India.

China's economy has been growing rapidly compared to most economies around the world. This growth demands talented human resources. And China has an abundance of workers but not those with high levels of skills. In particular, China will need 75,000 additional managers with international experience over the period 2006–2016, but it only had about 5,000 such managers in 2006. Furthermore, while China has the largest number of college graduates in the world, many of them do not have the knowledge and skills to operate effectively in foreign multinational firms.

India and China have over 40 percent of the world's labor supply but many of them are unskilled laborers. Out of its 600,000 engineering graduates each year, about 160,000 have adequate skills to work in foreign multinational firms. Likewise, India enjoys about 3 million college graduates each year but it faces a shortage of professionals in the IT industry by 2010. In both countries, the number of expatriates employed by local and multinational firms operating there has increased. In fact, firms are drawing talented associates from other Asian countries and from Hong Kong, causing them to deal with shortages of talented labor. This shortage of human capital could retard the growth of emerging economies over time.

To overcome this problem, Wipro, a major technology outsourcer based in India, places a heavy emphasis on training and building associates' and managers' skills. Wipro can train up to 5,500 at a given time. Yet even with such training, deficiencies in the educational system of the country may produce too few qualified candidates over time to help them become more competitive, especially in global markets. Both India and China must invest heavily in upgrading their secondary and higher educational systems. Additional firms operating in these countries must invest heavily in training programs to enrich the skills and capabilities of their managers and technical professionals in particular.

Sources: "China's Looming Talent Shortage," *McKinseyQuarterly.com*, www.mckinseyquarterly.com/article, June 16, 2007.; "Shortage of Top Executives Bites," *KERALANEXT.com*, www.keralanext.com/news, May 5, 2007; G. Dhungama, "Brains Outflow," *The Standard*, www.thestandard.com.hk/news, Dec. 18, 2006; J. Ribeiro, "Wipro Chief: India Staff Shortage No Big Deal," *CIO*, www.cio.com/article, Oct. 18, 2006; J. Johnson, R. McGregor, "Are India and China Up to the Job?" *FT.com*, www.ft.com, July 19, 2006; R. Ecke, "Speaking Freely: Success in Training China's Managers," *ATimes.com*, www.atimes.com, June 16, 2007.

As suggested in the *Managerial Advice,* China and India are facing a major shortage of skilled managers and engineers. Because of the critical nature of human capital to gaining and maintaining competitive advantages, the countries and companies operating in them must invest heavily to upgrade their talents or face declining economic opportunities in future years. Because of the growth of China's and India's economies, there is significant competition for quality human capital. These battles for human capital have produced higher turnover for firms, thereby increasing their costs and reducing their talent pools. The challenge of acquiring and maintaining a workforce with the needed knowledge and skills exists for all firms operating in these countries, domestic and foreign.

The previous arguments and research underscore the strategic value of human capital.[45] Because of the potential value of human capital to an organization, the way it is managed is critical. We next discuss a new focus referred to as *positive organizational behavior.*

Positive Organizational Behavior

positive organizational behavior
nurtures individual's greatest strengths and helps people use them to their and the organization's advantage.

Positive organizational behavior grew out of positive organizational psychology, which developed to avoid focusing on trying to "fix" what was wrong with people. Rather, **positive organizational behavior** focuses on nurturing individuals' greatest strengths and helping people use them to their and the organization's advantage.[46] Positive OB suggests that people will likely perform best when they have self-confidence, are optimistic (hope), and are resilient.

People are healthier and more productive if they have a strong self-efficacy with regard to the work that they are doing. Thus managers should try to build associates' self-efficacy for the tasks assigned to them. Yet, we know from research that the effects of self-efficacy are perhaps more important on average in the United States than in many other countries.[47] In addition to the self-efficacy of individual associates, recent research suggests the importance of the efficacy of teams' performance. To the extent that a team believes that it can accomplish its assigned tasks, the team's performance is likely to be higher.[48]

Individuals who are managed in a positive manner and who take a personally positive approach to outperform the other candidates often are healthier mentally and physically. These people are likely to have a positive self-concept, lead life with a purpose, and have quality relationships with other people. Such people tend to be healthier, happier, and more productive and thus usually experience less stress on the job.[49] As such, managers should help their associates to develop positive emotions in themselves and others. It helps them to develop the means and implement them so as to achieve success within the organization.[50]

Providing leadership that encourages and nurtures positive emotions often requires the application of *emotional intelligence (EI).* Persons with strong EI have self-awareness, possess good social skills, display empathy, have strong motivation, and regulate their own behavior without the oversight of others (discussed in more depth in Chapter 8).[51] Leaders using EQ build trusting relationships with their associates, exhibit optimism, and build associates' efficacy by providing the training needed and empowering them to complete the task without direct oversight.[52] The leadership approach using positive OB resembles *high-involvement management,* which we discuss next.

High-Involvement Management

High-involvement management requires that senior, middle, and lower-level managers all recognize human capital as the organization's most important resource. Sometimes referred to as high-performance management or high-commitment management, the **high-involvement management** approach involves carefully selecting and training associates and giving them significant decision-making power, information, and incentive compensation.[53] Combining decision power with important tactical and strategic information provides associates with the ability to make or influence decisions about how to complete tasks in ways that create value for the organization. Associates are closer to the day-to-day activities than are others in the organization, and empowering them through high-involvement management allows them to use their unique knowledge and skills.[54] In general, empowerment can increase the likelihood that associates will provide maximum effort in their work, including a willingness to (1) work hard to serve the organization's best interests, (2) take on different tasks and gain skills needed to work in multiple capacities, and (3) work using their intellect as well as their hands.[55]

> **high-involvement management**
> involves carefully selecting and training associates and giving them significant decision-making power, information, and incentive compensation.

Key Characteristics of High-Involvement Management

Five key characteristics of high-involvement management have been identified. We summarize these characteristics in Exhibit 1-3 and examine them further in the following discussion.

SELECTIVE HIRING

Sound selection systems are the first crucial characteristic of the high-involvement approach. Without selecting the right people, an organization cannot expect delegated authority and information to be used properly. Efforts to generate a large pool of applicants and to assess applicants through rigorous evaluations, including multiple rounds of interviews with managers and peers, are important in the selection process.[56] These efforts help to identify the most promising candidates while promoting the development of commitment on the part of the individuals chosen. Individuals selected in the course of thorough processes often respect the integrity of the organization.

Another important part of the selection process involves examining applicants' fit with the organization's culture and mission; selecting new hires solely on the basis of technical skills is a mistake. In situations where most or all of the required technical skills can be taught by the organization, it is quite acceptable to pay less attention to existing skills and more attention to cultural fit (along with the person's ability to learn the needed skills).[57] This is the approach taken by The Men's Wearhouse. A number of studies show the impact of cultural fit on satisfaction, intent to leave the organization, and job performance.[58] For example, a study of newly hired auditors in the largest accounting firms in the United States found that lack of fit with the organizational culture caused dissatisfaction and lower commitment among these auditors.[59] Furthermore, work context can affect the creative output of individuals so that individuals wishing to use their creative capabilities are attracted to organizations with cultures that promote the expression of creativity in work.[60]

Exhibit 1-3	Dimensions of High-Involvement Management
Aspect	**Description**
Selective Hiring	Large pools of applicants are built through advertising, word of mouth, and internal recommendations. Applicants are evaluated rigorously using multiple interviews, tests, and other selection tools. Applicants are selected on the basis of not only skills but also of fit with culture and mission.
Extensive Training	New associates and managers are thoroughly trained for job skills through dedicated training exercises as well as on-the-job training. They also participate in structured discussions of culture and mission. Existing associates and managers are expected or required to enhance their skills each year through in-house or outside training and development. Often, existing associates and managers are rotated into different jobs for the purpose of acquiring additional skills.
Decision Power	Associates are given authority to make decisions affecting their work and performance. Associates handle only those issues about which they have proper knowledge. Lower-level managers shift from closely supervising work to coaching associates. In addition to having authority to make certain decisions, associates participate in decisions made by lower-level and even middle managers.
Information Sharing	Associates are given information concerning a broad variety of operational and strategic issues. Information is provided through bulletin boards, company intranets, meetings, posted performance displays, and newsletters.
Incentive Compensation	Associates are compensated partly on the basis of performance. Individual performance, team performance, and business performance all may be considered.

EXTENSIVE TRAINING

Training is the second vital component of high-involvement management. Without proper training, new hires cannot be expected to perform adequately. And even when new hires are well trained for a position, it is important to help them build skills and capabilities beyond those needed in their present position. Furthermore, socialization into the norms of the organization is an important part of initial training. For existing associates, ongoing training in the latest tools and techniques is crucial.

Although valid calculations of return on investment for training are difficult to make, several studies reinforce the value of training. One study involving 143 *Fortune* 1000 companies reported that training significantly affected productivity, competitiveness, and employee satisfaction. (Training included job skills, social skills, quality/statistical analysis, and cross-training in different jobs.)[61]

DECISION POWER

The third key dimension of high-involvement management is decision-making power—providing associates with the authority to make some important decisions while inviting them to influence other decisions. For example, in a mass-production firm, such as Dell Computer, a single associate might have the authority to stop an entire production line to diagnose and address a quality problem. The associate might also have the authority, in conjunction with co-workers, to contact a supplier about quality problems, to schedule vacation time, and to discipline co-workers behaving in inappropriate ways. Beyond this decision-making authority, an associate might have significant input to capital expenditure decisions, such as a decision to replace an aging piece of equipment.

In many cases, decision power is given to teams of associates. In fact, self-managed or self-directed teams are a central part of most high-involvement systems.[62] With regard to our mass-production example, such a team might include the individuals working on a particular production line, or it might include individuals who complete similar tasks in one part of a production line. The tellers in a particular branch bank can operate as a team, the nurses in a particular hospital unit on a particular shift could be a team, and junior brokers in an investment banking firm might act as a formal team in a particular area.

Many studies of decision-making power have been conducted over the years. In general, these studies support giving associates bounded authority and influence. The study of *Fortune* 1000 firms discussed earlier assessed the impact of associates' holding significant decision power. As with training, the executives in the 143 firms reported a positive effect on productivity, competitiveness, and employee satisfaction.[63] Another recent study of empowering associates found that it enhanced knowledge sharing within and the efficacy of teams that in turn increased performance.[64]

INFORMATION SHARING

The fourth characteristic of high-involvement management is information sharing. In order for associates to make effective decisions and provide useful inputs to decisions made by managers, they must be properly informed. Examples of information that could be shared include the firm's operating results and business plan, costs of materials, costs of turnover and absenteeism, potential technologies for implementation, competitors' initiatives, and results and roadblocks in supplier negotiations. At AES, a Virginia-based power company, so much information had been shared with associates that the Securities and Exchange Commission (SEC) identified every employee of the firm as an *insider* for stock-trading purposes. This was unusual; typically, only those at the top of a firm have enough information to be considered insiders by the SEC.

INCENTIVE COMPENSATION

The fifth and final dimension of high-involvement management is incentive compensation. This type of compensation can take many forms, including the following:

- Individual piece-rate systems, where associates are compensated based on the amount produced or sold
- Individual incentive systems, where associates receive bonuses based on short- or long-term performance
- Knowledge or skill-based pay, where associates are paid based on the amount of knowledge or number of skills they acquire
- Profit sharing, where associates earn bonuses based on company profits
- Gain sharing, where associates share in a portion of savings generated from employee suggestions for improvement

In the study of *Fortune* 1000 firms mentioned earlier, executives indicated that incentive pay positively affected productivity and competitiveness.[65]

Evidence for the Effectiveness of High-Involvement Management

Considering the five aspects of high-involvement management as a coherent system, research evidence supports the effectiveness of the approach. One study, for example, found this approach to have a positive effect on the performance of steel mini-mills.[66] In this study, 30 U.S. mini-mills were classified as having a control orientation or a commitment orientation. Under the control orientation, employees were forced to comply with detailed rules, had little decision-making authority or influence, received limited training and information, and had no incentive compensation. Under the commitment orientation, which closely resembled the high-involvement approach described above, employees had strong training; information on quality, costs, productivity, and usage rates of materials; incentive pay; the authority to make decisions regarding workflow scheduling and new equipment; and input into strategic decisions. The mills with commitment systems had lower rates of unused materials, higher productivity, and lower associate turnover.

PhotoDisc, Inc./Getty Images

In another study, 62 automobile plants around the world were classified as using traditional mass production or flexible production.[67] Under the traditional mass-production system, employees did not participate in empowered teams, whereas employees under the flexible approach participated in such teams. Companies that used the flexible system also offered employees more cross-training in different jobs and opportunities for incentive compensation. Furthermore, these companies displayed fewer symbols of higher status for managers (no reserved parking, no separate eating areas, and so on). The plants with flexible production had 47.4 percent fewer defects and 42.9 percent greater productivity than those with traditional production systems.

In a third study, firms were drawn from many different industries, ranging from biotechnology to business services.[68] Firms placing strong value on their people had a 79 percent probability of surviving for five years after the initial public offering (IPO), whereas firms placing low value on their people had a 60 percent probability of surviving five years.

Demands on Managers

When a high-involvement approach has all of the characteristics identified above, associates are fully and properly empowered. High-involvement managers place significant value on empowerment because empowered associates have the tools and support required to create value for the organization. But managers implementing high-involvement approaches must take specific and calculated actions to promote empowerment. We turn now to a discussion of the demands a high-involvement approach places on managers.

Because they believe strongly in empowering associates, high-involvement managers constantly seek to identify situations in which responsibility can be delegated. The intent is to move decision making to the lowest level in the organization where associates have the information and knowledge required to make an effective decision. Managing through encouragement and commitment rather than fear and threats, high-involvement managers respect and value each associate's skills and knowledge. In addition, effective managers understand that cultural differences in a diverse workforce challenge them to empower people in ways that are consistent with their uniqueness as individuals. Listening carefully to associates and asking questions of them in a genuine attempt to understand their perspectives demonstrates managerial respect and facilitates attempts to be culturally sensitive. People who feel respected for who they are as well as for their skills and knowledge are willing to act in a prudent and forthright manner in completing their assigned work. Over time, empowered, respected associates become confident in their ability and willingness to help create value for the organization.

Trust between managers and associates is critical in a high-involvement organization. Managers must trust associates not to abuse their decision power. For their part, associates must trust managers not to punish them for mistakes when they are trying to do the right thing for the organization. Furthermore, research has shown that trust between associates and those formally responsible for their behavior has a positive effect on the organization's financial performance.[69] Thus, effective managers invest effort in building and maintaining trust. In so doing, they dramatically increase their credibility with associates.[70] Confident in their abilities as well as their associates' abilities, high-involvement managers recognize that they don't have all the knowledge necessary for the organization to be successful. As a result, they work with their peers and associates to find solutions when problems arise.[71]

High-involvement managers think continuously about how human capital can be used as the foundation for competitive advantage. Is there another way to use our people's skills and knowledge to further reduce costs or to more crisply differentiate the products we produce? How can the creativity of our empowered associates be used to create more value for the organization? How can we use information our associates gather through their work with people outside our organization (such as customers and suppliers) to make certain we are currently doing things that will allow us to shape the competitive advantages needed to be successful tomorrow? Finding answers to these questions and others that are unique to a particular organization can lead to long-term success.

As suggested in the *Experiencing Strategic Organizational Behavior* feature, firms use their core strengths to provide value to customers. And core strengths are commonly based on human capital. A prime example is Microsoft. Its core strength is software development and the managers and associates in Microsoft are prominent in developing new software to meet customers' needs. While Microsoft does not exhibit all of the characteristics of a high-involvement organization, it empowers its associates with considerable authority to determine their work projects, schedule, and where they will complete most of their work. Microsoft's CEO claims that the company has hired more top talent in this area over the last 20 years than any other company. The freedom it provides the software developers and their compensation packages are designed to retain their services for Microsoft for the long term.

Building, Maintaining, and Exploiting Core Strengths: The Power of Human Capital

Most successful companies have core strengths that they leverage to create more value for their customers than competitors can do. By leveraging core strengths, they achieve a competitive advantage. Apple (discussed in an earlier *Experiencing Strategic Organizational Behavior* segment) has a core strength in designing attractive, innovative, and functional consumer electronics products. It builds and leverages its core strength through strong human capital. Similarly, Ideo's core strength is its capability to design innovative products for others. It has a particular process it uses that focuses on innovation from the outside in emphasizing customers' needs that has been highly successful. But it has been successful primarily because of the highly regarded managers and associates it attracts and retains on the staff.

Microsoft's core strength is in the development of software. It excels in developing innovative software that provides value to its customers. It does so largely through high-quality human capital in software development. Steve Ballmer, CEO of Microsoft, argues that people drive business success and that no company has higher-quality computer software talent in the last 20 years than Microsoft. Managers at Microsoft suggest that the ideas that lead to better software come from human capital. They believe that organizations succeed by empowering people to use their expertise and information to exploit opportunities.

An employee in software development at Microsoft explains that the company provides a nurturing environment for its associates, which enhances their productivity. He suggests that Microsoft empowers associates with significant control over their work, schedule, and work environment. They decide what training is needed and when they desire to receive it. They largely decide the projects on which they will work and the timing of their accomplishment. Goals are established cooperatively with managers. There are no timecards, no requisition forms, no authorization sheets required. They can even choose what times they are to work and where they do their work (e.g., at the office or at home).

Microsoft has been criticized, primarily because of its market power (i.e., monopolistic practices). But, many associates see the company and its executives as exhibiting highly ethical practices. In fact, ethical practices are emphasized even in the regular performance reviews. Microsoft has won a number of awards related to its "associate-friendly" policies and practices. It has won awards for the company's commitment to diversity and for its flexible work arrangements. For example, it received the Working Families Innovation Award Employer of the Year in 2004. These awards suggest that it has a number of successful policies and practices in managing its associates. It pays off in the development of innovative software packages that create value for Microsoft's customers.

Sources: "Working at Microsoft," www.qbrundage.com, June 16 2007; "Company Profile—Microsoft Corporation," About.com, jobsearchtech.about.com, June 16, 2007; "Work–Life Balance," Microsoft Corporation, www.wherewomenwanttowork.com, June 16, 2007; "People Make the Difference," Microsoft Corporation, www.microsoft.com, May 28, 2007; A. Tan, "Ballmer: Innovation Takes Time," *BusinessWeek*, www.businessweek.com, May 23, 2007; M. Witzel, "Sustain Your Company's Heart," *Financial Times*, www.ft.com, Aug. 23, 2005; S. Morrison, "Sharp Focus Gives Design Group the Edge," *Financial Times*, www.ft.com, Feb. 17, 2005.

Organization of the Book

Our objective in this book is to provide managers, aspiring managers, and even individual contributors with the knowledge they need to perform effectively in organizations, especially in today's high-involvement organizations. Essentially, the book offers readers a working knowledge of OB and its strategic importance. The book has 14 chapters divided into four parts. The titles of the parts and the topics of the chapters are presented in Exhibit 1-4, which graphically depicts the model for the book.

As suggested in the exhibit, the strategic approach to OB emphasizes how to manage behavior in organizations to achieve a competitive advantage. The book unfolds in a logical sequence. In Part I, The Strategic Lens, we explain the

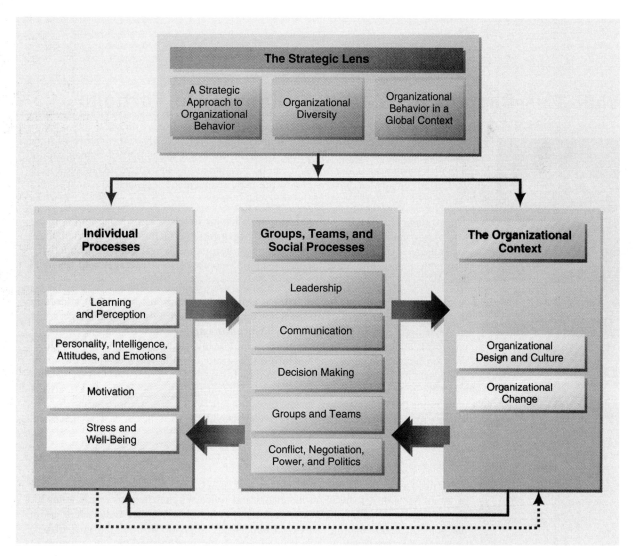

Exhibit 1-4 Managing Organizational Behavior for Competitive Advantage

strategic approach to OB (Chapter 1) and then discuss the importance of managing diversity in organizations (Chapter 2) and describe how organizations must operate in a global context (Chapter 3). In Part II, Individual Processes, we turn to the individual as the foundation of an organization's human capital, focusing on the development of a sound understanding of individuals and how they affect each other and the organization's success. Topics considered include learning and perception (Chapter 4), personality (Chapter 5), motivation (Chapter 6), and stress (Chapter 7). In Part III, Groups, Teams, and Social Processes, we examine the effects of interpersonal processes on individual and organizational outcomes. Specific interpersonal processes include leadership (Chapter 8), communication (Chapter 9), decision making (Chapter 10), group dynamics (Chapter 11), and conflict (Chapter 12). Finally, in Part IV, The Organizational Context, we examine several organization-level processes and phenomena. Using insights from the book's first three parts, we study organizational design and culture (Chapter 13) and organizational change (Chapter 14). Overall, the book takes you on an exciting journey through managerial opportunities and problems related to behavior in organizations.

What This Chapter Adds to Your Knowledge Portfolio

In this chapter, we have examined the importance of strategic OB to the success of individuals and organizations. In addition, we have discussed the nature of human capital and the circumstances under which it can be the source of competitive advantage for an organization. Finally, we have explored the high-involvement approach to management. To summarize, we have covered the following points:

- The strategic approach to organizational behavior involves knowledge and application of how individual, interpersonal, and organizational factors influence the behavior and value of an organization's people, where value is reflected in productivity, satisfaction, and ultimately the organization's competitive advantages and financial success.

- A strategic approach to organizational behavior is important because it addresses key issues for managers at all levels of the organization. For senior managers, the strategic approach to OB provides guidance for activities such as shaping the internal norms and practices of the organization. For middle managers, it provides guidance on matters such as implementing the strategic initiatives designed by senior managers. For lower-level managers, taking a strategic approach to OB helps with coaching and negotiating, among other important activities necessary to effectively implement the organization's strategy. Managers who lack an appreciation for the subject matter of organizational behavior are likely to experience less-successful careers.

- A strategic approach to organizational behavior builds on knowledge from the behavioral sciences. It differs from these fields, however, in two important ways. First, it integrates knowledge from these fields, rather than taking the narrow view of any one of them. Second, it focuses on behaviors and processes that help to create competitive advantages and financial success for the organization. Other fields often adopt the goal of understanding individual and group behavior without the goal of also understanding how such knowledge can contribute to enhancing the performance of organizations.

- An organization is formally defined as a collection of individuals, whose members may change over time, formed into a coordinated system of specialized activities for the purpose of achieving certain goals over some extended period of time.

- Human capital is an intangible resource of the organization. It represents capacity for today's work and potential for tomorrow's work. It includes the skills, knowledge, capabilities, values, beliefs, and attitudes of the people in the organization. Human capital is important because in the current global economy, an organization's ability to create something of value for customers comes largely from the know-how and intellect embodied in its people rather than from machinery and other tangible assets.

- Human capital can be a source of competitive advantage for an organization when it has *value* (it is relevant for the organization's strategy), *rareness* (skills and knowledge are possessed by relatively few outside the organization), and *low imitability* (other organizations cannot easily duplicate the skills and knowledge). These three characteristics set the stage for gaining an advantage. For human capital to be a source of competitive advantage, it must be managed effectively.

- Positive organizational behavior focuses on nurturing individuals' greatest strengths and helping people use them to their and the organization's advantage. Positive OB suggests that people will likely perform best when they have self-confidence, are optimistic (hope), and are resilient. People are healthier and more productive if they have a strong self-efficacy with regard to the work that they are doing. Individuals who are managed in a positive manner and who take a personally positive approach to outperform the other candidates often are healthier mentally and physically.

- High-involvement management is an important method for developing and leveraging human capital. This approach has five key components: (1) selective hiring, (2) extensive training, (3) decision power, (4) information sharing, and (5) incentive compensation. Collectively, these five aspects of high-involvement management yield empowered workers.

- The effectiveness of high-involvement management is supported by strong evidence. In studies of the steel, automobile, and semiconductor industries, among many others, high-involvement management has been found to positively affect productivity, satisfaction, financial success, and competitiveness.

Back to the Knowledge Objectives

1. What is organizational behavior? Why is it important for managers and aspiring managers to study OB using a strategic approach? Can the study of a field such as psychology substitute for a strategic approach to organizational behavior? Why or why not?

2. What makes an organization an organization? What are the defining characteristics?

3. What is human capital? Be specific.

4. How does human capital provide the basis for competitive advantage?

5. What is positive organizational behavior and how can it contribute to associates' productivity?

6. What are the five characteristics of high-involvement management? What evidence exists to support the effectiveness of this approach?

Key Terms

organizational behavior,
   p. 5
managing organizational
   behavior, p. 5
strategic OB approach,
   p. 5
associates, p. 7

organization, p. 9
human capital, p. 11
competitive advantage,
   p. 12
human capital value, p. 12
human capital rareness,
   p. 13

human capital imitability,
   p. 13
positive organizational
   behavior, p. 16
high-involvement
   management, p. 17

Building Your Human Capital

Career Style Inventory

Different people approach their careers in different ways. Some, for example, attempt to obtain as much power as possible in order to control personal and organizational outcomes. Others emphasize hard work and cooperative attitudes. The questionnaire that follows is designed to assess your tendencies, as well as your beliefs about the approaches of most managers. Following the questionnaire, we describe four distinct approaches to careers, some of which are more useful in high-involvement organizations than others.

Instructions

A number of descriptive paragraphs appear below. They describe sets of beliefs or perceptions that vary among individuals. The paragraphs are divided into four sections: Life Goals, Motivation, Self-Image, and Relations with Others. Please evaluate each paragraph as follows:

1. Read the paragraph. Taking the paragraph as a whole (using all of the information in the paragraph, not just one or two sentences), rate the paragraph on a scale from "not characteristic of me" (1) to "highly characteristic of me" (7). If you are currently a full-time student, rate each paragraph on the basis of how you believe you would feel if you were working full-time in an organization. If you are a part-time student with a career, rate each paragraph on the basis of how you actually feel.

1	2	3	4	5	6	7
Not characteristic of me		Somewhat characteristic of me		Generally characteristic of me		Highly characteristic of me

2. In addition, rate each paragraph in terms of the way you would *like* to be, regardless of how you are now. Rate each on a scale from "would not like to be like this" (1) to "would very strongly like to be like this" (7).

1	2	3	4	5	6	7
I would not like to be like this		I would somewhat like to be like this		I would generally like to be like this		I would very strongly like to be like this

3. Finally, rate each paragraph in terms of how descriptive it is of most managers, from "not at all characteristic of most managers" (1) to "very characteristic of most

managers" (7). In providing this assessment, think about managers with whom you have worked, managers you have read about or heard about, and managers you have seen in videos.

1	2	3	4	5	6	7
Not at all characteristic of most managers		Somewhat characteristic of most managers		Generally characteristic of most managers		Very characteristic of most managers

Questionnaire

Please be as honest, realistic, and candid as possible in your self-evaluations. Try to accurately describe yourself, not represent what you think others might want you to say or believe. Generally, individuals do not have high scores on every question.

A. Life Goals

1. I equate my personal success in life with the development and success of the organization for which I work. I enjoy a sense of belonging, responsibility, and loyalty to an organization. If it were best for my organization, I would be satisfied with my career if I progressed no higher than a junior or middle management level.

How characteristic is this of you (1–7)?_____

How much would you like to be like this (1–7)?_____

How characteristic is this of most managers (1–7)?_____

2. I have two major goals in life: to do my job well and to be committed to my family. I believe strongly in the work ethic and want to succeed by skillfully and creatively accomplishing goals and tasks. I also want to be a good family person. Work and family are equally important.

How characteristic is this of you (1–7)?_____

How much would you like to be like this (1–7)?_____

How characteristic is this of most managers (1–7)?_____

3. My goal in life is to acquire power and prestige; success for me means being involved in a number of successful, diverse enterprises. I generally experience life and work as a jungle; like it or not, it's a dog-eat-dog world, and there will always be winners and losers. I want to be one of the winners.

How characteristic is this of you (1–7)?_____

How much would you like to be like this (1–7)?_____

How characteristic is this of most managers (1–7)?_____

4. I tend to view life and work as an important game. I see my work, my relations with others, and my career in terms of options and possibilities as if they were part of a strategic game that I am playing. My main goal in life is to be a winner at this game while helping others to succeed as well.

How characteristic is this of you (1–7)?_____

How much would you like to be like this (1–7)?_____

How characteristic is this of most managers (1–7)?_____

B. Motivation

1. My interest in work is in the process of building something. I am motivated by problems that need to be solved; the challenge of work itself or the creation of a quality product gets me excited. I would prefer to miss a deadline rather than do something halfway—quality is more important to me than quantity.

> How characteristic is this of you (1–7)?_____
>
> How much would you like to be like this (1–7)?_____
>
> How characteristic is this of most managers (1–7)?_____

2. I like to take risks and am fascinated by new methods, techniques, and approaches. I want to motivate myself and others by pushing everyone to the limit. My interest is in challenge, or competitive activity, where I can prove myself to be a winner. The greatest sense of exhilaration for me comes from managing a team of people and gaining victories. When work is no longer challenging, I feel bored and slightly depressed.

> How characteristic is this of you (1–7)?_____
>
> How much would you like to be like this (1–7)?_____
>
> How characteristic is this of most managers (1–7)?_____

3. I like to control things and to acquire power. I want to succeed by climbing the corporate ladder, acquiring positions of greater power and responsibility. I want to use this power to gain prestige, visibility, and financial success and to be able to make decisions that affect many other people. Being good at "politics" is essential to this success.

> How characteristic is this of you (1–7)?_____
>
> How much would you like to be like this (1–7)?_____
>
> How characteristic is this of most managers (1–7)?_____

4. My interest in work is to derive a sense of belonging from organizational membership and to have good relations with others. I am concerned about the feelings of people with whom I work, and I am committed to maintaining the integrity of my organization. As long as the organization rewards my efforts, I am willing to let my commitment to my organization take precedence over my own narrow self-interest.

> How characteristic is this of you (1–7)?_____
>
> How much would you like to be like this (1–7)?_____
>
> How characteristic is this of most managers (1–7)?_____

C. Self-Image

1. I am competitive and innovative. My speech and my thinking are dynamic and come in quick flashes. I like to emphasize my strengths and don't like to feel out of control. I have trouble realizing and living within my limitations. I pride myself on being fair with others; I have very few prejudices. I like to have limitless options to succeed; my biggest fears are being trapped or being labeled as a loser.

> How characteristic is this of you (1–7)?_____
>
> How much would you like to be like this (1–7)?_____
>
> How characteristic is this of most managers (1–7)?_____

2. My identity depends on being part of a stable, noteworthy organization. I see myself as a trustworthy, responsible, and reasonable person who can get along with almost anyone. I'm concerned about making a good impression on others and representing the organization well. I may not have as much toughness, aggressiveness, and risk-taking skills as some, but I make substantial contributions to my organization.

> How characteristic is this of you (1–7)?_____
>
> How much would you like to be like this (1–7)?_____
>
> How characteristic is this of most managers (1–7)?_____

3. My sense of self-worth is based on my assessment of my skills, abilities, self-discipline, and self-reliance. I tend to be quiet, sincere, and practical. I like to stay with a project from conception to completion.

How characteristic is this of you (1–7)?_____

How much would you like to be like this (1–7)?_____

How characteristic is this of most managers (1–7)?_____

4. I tend to be brighter, more courageous, and stronger than most of the people with whom I work. I see myself as bold, innovative, and entrepreneurial. I can be exceptionally creative at times, particularly in seeing entrepreneurial possibilities and opportunities. I am willing to take major risks in order to succeed and willing to be secretive if it will further my own goals.

How characteristic is this of you (1–7)?_____

How much would you like to be like this (1–7)?_____

How characteristic is this of most managers (1–7)?_____

D. Relations with Others

1. I tend to dominate other people because my ideas are better. I generally don't like to work closely and cooperate with others, I would rather have other people working for me, following my directions. I don't think anyone has ever really helped me freely; either I controlled and directed them, or they were expecting me to do something for them in return.

How characteristic is this of you (1–7)?_____

How much would you like to be like this (1–7)?_____

How characteristic is this of most managers (1–7)?_____

2. My relations with others are generally good. I value highly those people who are trustworthy, who are committed to this organization, and who act with integrity in the things that they do. In my part of the organization, I attempt to sustain an atmosphere of cooperation, mild excitement, and mutuality. I get "turned off" by others in the organization who are out for themselves, who show no respect for others, or who get so involved with their own little problems that they lose sight of the "big picture."

How characteristic is this of you (1–7)?_____

How much would you like to be like this (1–7)?_____

How characteristic is this of most managers (1–7)?_____

3. At times, I am tough and dominating, but I don't think I am destructive. I tend to classify other people as winners and losers. I evaluate almost everyone in terms of what they can do for the team. I encourage people to share their knowledge with others, trying to get a work atmosphere that is both exciting and productive. I am impatient with those who are slower and more cautious, and I don't like to see weakness in others.

How characteristic is this of you (1–7)?_____

How much would you like to be like this (1–7)?_____

How characteristic is this of most managers (1–7)?_____

4. My relations with others are generally determined by the work that we do. I feel more comfortable working in a small group or on a project with a defined and understandable structure. I tend to evaluate others (both peers and managers) in terms of whether they help or hinder me in doing a craftsmanlike job. I do not compete against other people as I do against my own standards of quality.

How characteristic is this of you (1–7)?_____

How much would you like to be like this (1–7)?_____

How characteristic is this of most managers (1–7)?_____

When you have evaluated each paragraph, follow the instructions below and "score" the questionnaire.

Scoring Key for Career Style Inventory

To calculate scores for each of the four primary career orientations, add up your scores for individual paragraphs as shown below. For example, to obtain your "characteristic of me" score for the orientation known as "craftsperson," add your "characteristic of me" scores for paragraph 2 under Life Goals, paragraph 1 under Motivation, paragraph 3 under Self-Image, and paragraph 4 under Relations with Others.

Scores can range from 4 to 28. A score of 23 or higher can be considered high. A score of 9 or lower can be considered low.

	Characteristic of me	Would like to be like this	Characteristic of most managers
Craftsperson Orientation			
Life Goals—Paragraph 2	_____	_____	_____
Motivation—Paragraph 1	_____	_____	_____
Self-Image—Paragraph 3	_____	_____	_____
Relations with Others—Paragraph 4	_____	_____	_____
TOTAL scores for Craftsperson	_____	_____	_____
Company Orientation			
Life Goals—Paragraph 1	_____	_____	_____
Motivation—Paragraph 4	_____	_____	_____
Self-Image—Paragraph 2	_____	_____	_____
Relations with Others—Paragraph 2	_____	_____	_____
TOTAL scores for Company Man/Woman	_____	_____	_____
Jungle Fighter Orientation			
Life Goals—Paragraph 3	_____	_____	_____
Motivation—Paragraph 3	_____	_____	_____
Self-Image—Paragraph 4	_____	_____	_____
Relations with Others—Paragraph 1	_____	_____	_____
TOTAL scores for Jungle Fighter	_____	_____	_____
Strategic Game Orientation			
Life Goals—Paragraph 4	_____	_____	_____
Motivation—Paragraph 2	_____	_____	_____
Self-Image—Paragraph 1	_____	_____	_____
Relations with Others—Paragraph 3	_____	_____	_____
TOTAL scores for Gamesman/Gameswoman	_____	_____	_____

Descriptions of the Four Primary Career Orientations

- The *Craftsperson,* as the name implies, holds traditional values, including a strong work ethic, respect for people, concern for quality, and thrift. When talking about work, such a person tends to show an interest in specific projects that have a defined structure. He or she sees others, peers as well as managers, in terms of whether they help or hinder the completion of work in a craftsmanlike way.

The virtues of craftspersons are admired by almost everyone. In high-involvement organizations, craftspersons are valuable because they respect people and work hard and smart. On the downside, they can become overly absorbed in perfecting their projects, which can slow them down and harm their leadership on a broader stage.

- The *Jungle Fighter* lusts for power. He or she experiences life and work as a jungle where "eat or be eaten" is the rule and the winners destroy the losers. A major part of his or her psychic resources is budgeted for a personal department of defense. Jungle fighters tend to see their peers as either accomplices or enemies and their associates as objects to be used.

  There are two types of jungle fighters: lions and foxes. The lions are the conquerors who, when successful, may build an empire. The foxes make their nests in the corporate hierarchy and move ahead by stealth and politicking. The most gifted foxes rise rapidly by making use of their entrepreneurial skills. In high-involvement organizations, jungle fighters can cause many problems. They tend not to value people. Leveraging human capital may take place, but only in limited ways for the purpose of self-gain.

- The *Company Man or Woman* bases personal identity on being part of a protective organization. He or she can be fearful and submissive, seeking security even more than success. These are not positive attributes for high-involvement organizations. On the other hand, the company man or woman is concerned with the human side of the company, interested in the feelings of people, and committed to maintaining corporate integrity. The most creative company men and women sustain an atmosphere of cooperation and stimulation, but they tend to lack the daring to lead in competitive and innovative organizations.

- The *Strategic Gamesman or Gameswoman* sees business life in general, and his or her career in particular, in terms of options and possibilities, as if he or she were playing a game. Such a person likes to take calculated risks and is drawn to new techniques and methods. The contest is invigorating, and he or she communicates enthusiasm, energizing peers and associates like the quarterback on a football team. Unlike the jungle fighter, the gamesman or gameswoman competes not to build an empire or to pile up riches, but to gain the exhilaration of victory. The main goal is to be known as a winner, along with the rest of the team.

  The character of a strategic gamesman or gameswoman, which might seem to be a collection of near paradoxes, is very useful in a high-involvement organization. Such a person is cooperative but competitive, detached and playful but compulsively driven to succeed, a team player but a would-be superstar, a team leader but often a rebel against bureaucratic hierarchy, fair and unprejudiced but contemptuous of weakness, tough and dominating but not destructive. Balancing these issues is important in a team-oriented organization, where associates and managers at all levels are expected to work together for personal and organizational success.

Source: Adapted from *Experiences in Management and Organizational Behavior*, 4th ed. (New York: John Wiley & Sons, 1996). Original instrument developed by Roy J. Lewicki.

A Strategic Organizational Behavior Moment

All in a Day's Work

After earning a business degree with a major in marketing, Ann Wood went to work for Norwich Enterprises as a research analyst in the Consumer Products Division. While working, she also attended graduate school at night, receiving her MBA in three years. Within a year of reaching that milestone, Ann was promoted to manager of market research. Ann became assistant director of marketing after another three years. After a stay of slightly less than 24 months in that position, Ann was appointed director of marketing for the Consumer Products Division. In this new role, she leads many more people than in her previous roles—85 in total across three different groups: market research, marketing strategy and administration, and advertising and public relations.

Ann felt good this morning, ready to continue working on several important projects that Anil Mathur, Norwich's executive vice president for marketing, had assigned to her. Ann felt that she was on a fast track to further career success and wanted to continue performing well. With continuing success, she expected an appointment in Norwich's international business operations in the near future. Ann was pleased about this prospect, as international experience was becoming a prerequisite at Norwich for senior-level managerial positions—her ultimate goal. Several problems, however, were brought to her attention on what she thought was going to be a good day at the office.

As Ann was entering the building, Joe Jackson, the current manager of the market research group, stopped her in the hall and complained that the company's intranet had been down about half of the night. This technical problem had prevented timely access to data from a central server, resulting in a delay in the completion of an important market analysis. Ann thought that immediately jumping in to help with the analysis would be useful in dealing with this matter. She had promised Anil that the analysis would be available to him and other upper-level managers this morning. Now it would have to be finished on a special priority basis, delaying work on other important projects.

Joe also told Ann that two of his analysts had submitted their resignations over the last 24 hours. Ann asked, "Why are we having so much trouble with turnover?" The manager responded, "The market is tight for smart analysts who understand our product lines. We've been having problems hiring anyone with the skills we need, much less people who have any loyalty. Maybe we should offer higher starting salaries and more attractive stock options if we expect to have much hope of keeping the people we need." Ann asked Joe to develop a concrete proposal about what could be done to reduce turnover, promising to work with him to resolve the issue.

Just as she reached her office, Ann's phone rang. It was Brooke Carpenter, the manager of market strategy and administration. "I'm glad you're here, Ann. I need to talk to you now. I'm on my way." As Brooke came through the door, Ann could tell that he was quite upset. He explained that two of his people had discovered through searches on the Internet that the average pay for their type of work was 7 percent higher than what they were currently earning. Sharing this information with co-workers had created an unpleasant environment in which people were concentrating on pay instead of focusing on tasks to be completed. Ann had a conference call coming in a few minutes, stopping her from dealing with the matter further, but she asked Brooke to set up a time when the two of them could meet with his people to talk about their concerns.

After her conference call, Ann spent the rest of her morning dealing with e-mails that were primarily related to dissatisfaction with her department's work. Most of these concerned the delays that other Norwich units were experiencing in receiving outputs from her department. The problem was complicated by the inability to retain workers.

Ann had just returned from lunch when her phone rang. "Ann, it's Brooke. Can you meet with us at 2:30 this afternoon? I know that this is short notice, but we really do need to talk with my people." Although the time was inconvenient, given that Anil expected his analysis today, Ann knew that dealing with issues concerning Brooke's associates was also important. Plus, she believed that Anil's report was about to be finished by the research group, taking that immediate problem off her plate.

The meeting with Brooke and his people lasted almost an hour. Not surprisingly, other concerns surfaced during the conversation. Ann thought to herself that this was to be expected. Her managerial experience indicated that complaints about pay often masked concerns about other issues. She learned that people weren't satisfied with the technology made available to them to do their work or Norwich's commitment to training and development. Young and eager to advance, Brooke's associates wanted assurances from Ann that Norwich would spend more money and time to develop their skills. Ann agreed to the importance of skill development—both for associates and for Norwich. She said that she would examine the matter and provide feedback to them. "It may take some time, but my commitment to you is that I'll work hard to make this happen. While I can't promise much about the pay structure overnight, I'll also investigate this matter to become more informed. Brooke and I will work on this together so you can have direct access to what is going on." Ann wanted to deal with these issues, knowing that their resolution had the potential to help both associates and the company reach their goals.

Ann then spent a couple of hours dealing with still more e-mail messages, a few phone calls, and other requests that reached her desk during the day. Anil received the report he needed and seemed to be satisfied. Although she had been busy, Ann felt good as she left for home around 8:30 that night. Nothing came easily, she thought.

Discussion Questions

1. Describe the people-related problems or issues Ann Wood faced during the day. Did she handle these effectively? If not, what do you believe she should have done?

2. Is Ann Wood a high-involvement manager? If so, provide evidence. If not, how well do you think she'll perform in her new job as head of marketing?

3. Assume that Ann Wood wants her managers and associates to be the foundation for her department's competitive advantages. Use the framework summarized in Exhibit 1-2 (in the chapter text) to assess the degree to which Ann's people are a source of competitive advantage at this point in time.

Team Exercise

McDonald's: A High-Involvement Organization?

One experience most people in North America and Europe have shared is that of dining in the hamburger establishment known as McDonald's. In fact, someone has claimed that thirtieth-century archeologists may dig into the ruins of our present civilization and conclude that twenty-first-century religion was devoted to the worship of golden arches.

Your group, Fastalk Consultants, is known as the shrewdest, most insightful, and most overpaid management consulting firm in the country. You have been hired by the president of McDonald's to make recommendations for improving the motivation and performance of personnel in their franchise operations. Let us assume that the key activities in franchise operations are food preparation, order-taking and dealing with customers, and routine clean-up operations.

Recently, the president of McDonald's has come to suspect that his company's competitors, such as Burger King, Wendy's, Jack in the Box, Dunkin' Donuts, various pizza establishments, and others, are making heavy inroads into McDonald's market. He has hired a separate market research firm to investigate and compare the relative merits of the sandwiches, french fries, and drinks served by McDonald's and the competitors and has asked the market research firm to assess the advertising campaigns of the competitors. Hence, you will not be concerned with marketing issues, except as they may affect employee behavior. The president wants you to look into the organization of the franchises to determine their strengths and weaknesses. He is very interested in how the restaurants score with respect to high-involvement management and the impact on McDonald's of the use or nonuse of this approach.

The president has established an unusual contract with you. He wants you and your colleagues in the firm to make recommendations based on your observations as customers. He does not want you to do a complete analysis with interviews, surveys, or behind-the-scenes observations.

Steps

1. Assemble into groups of four to five. Each group will act as a separate Fastalk consulting team.
2. Think about your past visits to McDonald's. What did you see and experience? How was the food prepared and served? What was the process? Did the employees seem to be happy with their work? Did they seem to be well trained and well suited for the work? Did the supervisor act as a coach or a superior? Your instructor may ask you to visit a McDonald's in preparation for this exercise and/or to research the organization via the Internet or school library.
3. Assess McDonald's on each dimension of high-involvement management.
4. Develop recommendations for the president of McDonald's.
5. Reassemble as a class. Discuss your group's assessments and recommendations with the rest of the class, and listen to other groups' assessments. Do you still assess McDonald's in the same way after hearing from your colleagues in the class?
6. The instructor will present additional points for consideration.

Source: Adapted from *Experiences in Management and Organizational Behavior*, 4th ed. (New York: John Wiley & Sons, 1996). Original version developed by D.T. Hall and F.S. Hall.

Endnotes

1. Beyester, J.R. & Economy, P. 2007. *The SAIC solution.* Hoboken, NJ: John Wiley & Sons; Barney, J.B. 2002. *Gaining and sustaining competitive advantage* (2nd ed.). Upper Saddle River, NJ: Prentice-Hall; Barney, J.B. 1991. Firm resources and sustained competitive advantage. *Journal of Management,* 17: 99–120; Hitt, M.A., & Ireland, R.D. 2002. The essence of strategic leadership: Managing human and social capital. *Journal of Leadership and Organizational Studies,* 9: 3–14; Moses, B. 2001. It's about passion. *Across the Board,* May/June: 56–58.

2. Kor, Y.Y. 2006. Direct and interaction effects of top management team and board compositions on R&D investment strategy. *Strategic Management Journal,* 27: 1081–1099; Heifetz, R.A., & Laurie, D.L. 1997. The work of the leader. *Harvard Business Review,* 75(1): 124–134; Ireland, R.D., & Hitt, M.A. 1999. Achieving and maintaining strategic competitiveness in the 21st century: The role of strategic leadership. *Academy of Management Executives,* 13(1): 43–57; Kotter, J.P. 1990. What effective general managers really do. *Harvard Business Review,* 77(2): 145–159.

3. Elbanna, S., & Child, J. 2007. Influences on strategic decision effectiveness: Development and test of an integrative model. *Strategic Management Journal,* 28: 431–453.

4. Pappas, J.M., & Woolridge, B. 2007. Middle managers divergent strategic activity: An investigation of multiple measures of network centrality. *Journal of Management Studies,* 44: 323–341.

5. Finklestein, S., Hambrick, D.C., & Cannella, A.A. 2008. *Strategic leadership: Top executives and their effects on organizations,* New York: Oxford University Press.

6. Hitt, M.A., Black, S., & Porter, L. 2008. *Management.* Upper Saddle River, NJ: Prentice Hall.

7. Pappas & Woolridge. Middle managers divergent strategic activity; Huy, Q.N. 2001. In praise of middle managers. *Harvard Business Review,* 76(8): 73–79; Sethi, D. 1999. Leading from the middle. *Human Resource Planning,* 22(3): 9–10.

8. Manz, C., & Neck, C.P. 2007. *Mastering self leadership.* Upper Saddle River, NJ: Prentice Hall.

9. Faris, G.F. 1969. The drunkard's search in behavioral science. *Personnel Administration,* 32(1): 11–18.

10. Boyatzis, R.E., Baker, A., Leonard, L., Rhee, K., & Thompson, L. 1995. Will it make a difference? Assessing a value-added, outcome-oriented, competency-based professional program. In R.E. Boyatzis, S.S. Cowan, & D.A. Kolb (Eds.), *Innovation in professional education: Steps on a journey from teaching to learning.* San Francisco: Jossey-Bass; Kretovics, M.A. 1999. Assessing the MBA: What do our students learn? *The Journal of Management Development,* 18: 125–136.

11. Ghoshal, S., Bartlett, C.A., & Moran, P. 1999. A new manifesto for management. *Sloan Management Review,* 40(3): 9–20.

12. Etzioni, A. 1964. *Modern organizations.* Englewood Cliffs, NJ: Prentice-Hall.

13. Dess, G.G., & Picken, J.C. 1999. *Beyond productivity: How leading companies achieve superior performance by leveraging their human capital.* New York: AMACOM.

14. Dickson, G.W., & DeSanctis, G. 2001. *Information technology and the future enterprise.* Upper Saddle River, NJ: Prentice-Hall; Nelson, R.R., & Winter, S.G. 1982. *The evolutionary theory of economic change.* Cambridge, MA: Belknap Press.

15. Hitt, M.A., Ireland, R.D., & Hoskisson, R.E. 2007. *Strategic management: Competitiveness and globalization.* Cincinnati, OH: South-Western College Publishing.

16. Nelson, M.C. 2000. Facing the future: Intellectual capital of our workforce. *Vital Speeches of the Day,* December 15: 138–143.

17. Dess & Picken, *Beyond productivity;* Hitt, Ireland, & Hoskisson, *Strategic management.*

18. Day, J.D., & Wendler, J.C. 1998. The new economics of the organization. *The McKinsey Quarterly,* 1998 (1): 4–17.

19. Dess & Picken, *Beyond productivity.*

20. McGee, J., & Thomas, H. 2007, Knowledge as a lens on the jigsaw puzzle of strategy. *Management Decision,* 45: 539–563.

21. Felin, T., & Hesterly, W.S. 2007. The knowledge-based view, nested heterogeneity, and new value creation: Philosophical considerations on the locus of knowledge. *Academy of Management Review,* 22: 195–218; Thornhill, S. 2006. Knowledge, innovation and firm performance in high- and low-technology regimes. *Journal of Business Venturing,* 21: 687–703.

22. Salk, J., & Lyles, M.A. 2007. Gratitude, nostalgia and what now? Knowledge acquisition and learning a decade later. *Journal of International Business Studies,* 38: 19–26; Gupta, A.K., Smith, K.G., & Shalley, C.E. 2006. The interplay between exploration and exploitation. *Academy of Management Journal,* 49: 693–706.

23. Porter, M.E. 1980. *Competitive strategy.* New York: Free Press; Porter, M.E. 1985. *Competitive advantage.* New York: Free Press.

24. Sirmon, D.G., Hitt, M.A., & Ireland, R.D. 2007. Managing firm resources in dynamic environments to create value: Looking inside the black box. *Academy of Management Review,* 32: 273–292.

25. Our discussion of the value, rare, and nonimitable terms draws significantly from: Barney, J.B., & Wright, P.M. 1998. On becoming a strategic partner: The role of human resources in gaining competitive advantage. *Human Resource Management,* 37: 31–46.

26. Barney, J.B., & Clark, D.N. 2007. *Resource-based theory: Creating and sustaining competitive advantage.* New York: Oxford University Press; Barney, Firm resources and sustained competitive advantage; Barney & Wright, On becoming a strategic partner; Lepak, D.P., & Snell, S.A. 1999. The human resource architecture: Toward a theory of human capital allocation and development. *Academy of Management Review,* 24: 31–48.

27. Porter, *Competitive strategy.*

28. Hitt, Ireland, & Hoskisson, *Strategic management.*

29. Porter, *Competitive strategy.*

30. Hitt, Ireland, & Hoskisson, *Strategic management.*

31. Higgins, M.C., & Gulati, R. 2006. Stacking the deck: The effects of top management backgrounds on investor decisions. *Strategic Management Journal,* 27: 1–25.

32. Henderson, A.D., Miller, D., & Hambrick, D.C. 2006. How quickly do CEOs become obsolete? Industry dynamism, CEO tenure, and company performance. *Strategic Management Journal,* 27: 447–460.

33. Ployhart, R.E. 2006. Staffing in the 21st century: New challenges and strategic opportunities. *Journal of Management,* 32: 868–897.

34. Newbert, S.L. 2007. Empirical assessments of the resource-based view of the firm: An assessment and suggestions for future research. *Strategic Management Journal*, 28: 121–146; Barney & Wright, On becoming a strategic partner; Lepak & Snell, The human resource architecture.

35. Pfeffer, J. 1994. *Competitive advantage through people: Unleashing the power of the work force*. Boston: Harvard Business School Press.

36. Barney & Wright, On becoming a strategic partner.

37. Ibid.

38. Bangle, C. 2001. The ultimate creativity machine: How BMW turns art into profit. *Harvard Business Review*, 79(1): 47–55.

39. Bogner, W.C., & Bansal, P. 2007. Knowledge management as the basis of sustained high performance. *Journal of Management Studies*, 44: 165–188.

40. Tsui, A.S., Wang, H., & Xin, K.R. 2006. Organizational culture in China: An analysis of culture dimensions and culture types. *Management and Organization Review*, 2: 345–376.

41. Pfeffer, *Competitive advantage*.

42. Barney & Wright, On becoming a strategic partner.

43. Sirmon, Hitt, & Ireland, Managing firm resources in dynamic environments to create value.

44. Bowman, C., & Swart, J. 2007. Whose human capital? The challenge of value capture when capital is embedded. *Journal of Management Studies*, 44: 488–505.

45. Collins, C.J., & Smith, K.G. 2006. Knowledge exchange and combination: The role of human resource practices in the performance of high-technology firms. *Academy of Management Journal*, 544–560; Reed, K.K., Lubatkin, M., & Srinivasan, N. 2006. Proposing and testing an intellectual capital-based view of the firm. *Journal of Management Studies*, 43: 867–893.

46. Luthans, F. 2002. The need for and meaning of positive organizational behavior. *Journal of Organizational Behavior*, 23: 695–706.

47. Luthans, F. 2006. The impact of efficacy on work attitudes across cultures. *Journal of World Business*, 41: 121–132.

48. Gibson, C.B., & Earley, P.C. 2007. Collective cognition in action: Accumulation, interaction, examination, and accommodation in the development and operation of group efficacy beliefs in the workplaces. *Academy of Management Review*, 32: 438–458.

49. Quick, J.C., Macik-Frey, M., & Cooper, C.L. 2007. Managerial dimensions of organizational slack. *Journal of Management Studies*, 44: 189–205.

50. Fineman, S. 2006. On being positive: Concerns and counterpoints. *Academy of Management Review*, 31: 270–291.

51. Goleman, D. 2004. What makes a leader? *Harvard Business Review*, 82 (January): 82–91.

52. McKee, A., & Massimillian, D. 2006. Resonant leadership: A new kind of leadership for the digital age. *Journal of Business Strategy*, 27(5): 45–49.

53. The five aspects of high-commitment management that are used in this book are the most commonly mentioned aspects. See, for example, the following: Arthur, J.B. 1994. Effects of human resource systems on manufacturing performance and turnover. *Academy of Management Journal*, 37: 670–687; Becker, B., & Gerhart, B. 1996. The impact of human resource management on organizational performance: Progress and prospects. *Academy of Management Journal*, 39: 779–801; Guthrie, J.P. 2001. High-involvement work practices, turnover, and productivity: Evidence from New Zealand. *Academy of*

Management Journal, 44: 180–190; MacDuffie, J.P. 1995. Human resource bundles and manufacturing performance: Organizational logic and flexible production systems in the world auto industry. *Industrial and Labor Relations Review*, 48: 197–221; Pfeffer, The human equation; Pfeffer, J., & Veiga, J.F. 1999. Putting people first for organizational success. *Academy of Management Executive*, 13(2): 37–48.

54. Zatzick, C.D., & Iverson, R.D. 2006. High-involvement management and workforce reduction: Competitive advantage or disadvantage. *Academy of Management Journal*, 49: 999–1015.

55. Baron, J.N., & Kreps, D.M. 1999. *Strategic human resources: Frameworks for general managers*. New York: John Wiley & Sons.

56. Ployhart, Staffing in the 21st century; Pfeffer, *The human equation;* Pfeffer & Veiga, Putting people first for organizational success.

57. Ibid.

58. Erdogan, B., Liden, R.C., & Kraimer, M.L. 2006. Justice and leader-member exchange: The moderating role of organizational culture, *Academy of Management Journal*, 49: 395–406.

59. O'Reilly, C.A., Chatman, J., & Caldwell, D.F. 1991. People and organizational culture: A profile comparison approach to assessing person-organization fit. *Academy of Management Journal*, 34: 487–516.

60. Perry-Smith, J.E. 2006. Social yet creative: The role of social relationships in facilitating individual creativity. *Academy of Management Journal*, 49: 85–101.

61. Lawler, E.E., Mohrman, S.A., & Benson, G. 2001. *Organizing for high performance: Employee involvement, TQM, reengineering, and knowledge management in the Fortune 1000*. San Francisco: Jossey-Bass.

62. Manz & Neck, *Mastering self leadership;* Pfeffer, *The human equation;* Pfeffer & Veiga, Putting people first for organizational success.

63. Lawler, Mohrman, & Benson, *Organizing for high performance*.

64. Srivastava, A., Bartol, K.M., & Locke, E.A., 2006. Empowering leadership in management teams: Effects on knowledge sharing, efficacy and performance. *Academy of Management Journal*, 49: 1239–1251.

65. Lawler, Mohrman, & Benson, *Organizing for high performance*.

66. Arthur, Effects of human resource systems on manufacturing performance and turnover.

67. MacDuffie, Human resource bundles and manufacturing performance.

68. Welbourne, T.M., & Andrews, A.O. 1996. Predicting the performance of initial public offerings: Should human resource management be in the equation? *Academy of Management Journal*, 39: 891–919.

69. Davis, J.H., Schoorman, F.D., Mayer, R.C., & Tan, H.H. 2000. The trusted general manager and business unit performance: Empirical evidence of a competitive advantage. *Strategic Management Journal*, 21: 563–576; Mayer, R.C., Davis, J.H., & Schoorman, F.D. 1995. An integrative model of organizational trust. *Academy of Management Review*, 20: 709–734.

70. Peters, T. 2001. Leadership rule #3: Leadership is confusing as hell. *Fast Company*, March: 124–140.

71. Guaspari, J. 2001. How to? Who cares! *Across the Board*, May/June: 75–76.

2

ORGANIZATIONAL DIVERSITY

Melissa Kelley had a rich background in firefighting. Early in life, she learned from her grandfather, who worked as a firefighter. In college, she learned through coursework as a fire-science major. After college, she spent five years learning and honing her skills as a firefighter with the California Department of Forestry.

Armed with her experiences and passion for the work, she joined the Los Angeles Fire Department in 2001. Although aware of possible discrimination and harassment against women in the department, she did not hesitate to join when presented with the opportunity. In her words, "I was willing to overlook that . . . the dirty jokes, the porn, the . . . mentality. . . . I just wanted to be part of the team." To her, only two simple rules applied: "Do not touch me. Do not hurt me on purpose."

league left, but for several weeks following the incident he clucked like a chicken whenever she was present.

During a routine training exercise later in her career, the second rule came into sharp focus. While the rule probably was not violated explicitly, it is relevant nonetheless to the events that occurred. Following a fire call, Ms. Kelley engaged in the "Humiliator" drill, a drill that involves lifting and positioning a heavy ladder, climbing the ladder with a large saw, and using the saw to cut through metal bars in a window. Although she had previously demonstrated the abilities needed for the drill, on that particular day she dropped the ladder onto her head, resulting in her helmet becoming stuck between two of its rungs. She immediately felt pain and could not lift her arm to free herself, saying in a later interview: "In my head I'm

©AP/Wide World Photos

EXPLORING BEHAVIOR IN ACTION

Diversity in the Los Angeles Fire Department

According to media accounts, the first of her rules was violated early in her career with the LAFD. Soon after joining the department, a male colleague entered her bed at the firehouse. He then attempted to kiss and touch her. She resisted and the col-

thinking, I'm dying. My arm is messed up. My back is hurting. My legs are going to give out if I don't get this ladder off me." She continued to struggle with the ladder while showing obvious signs of pain. One colleague apparently tried to help but was stopped. Others

reportedly cursed at the struggling firefighter. In the end, Ms. Kelley was taken to a local hospital where multiple injuries were discovered. She subsequently had to be reassigned as a dispatcher. In reflecting on the events of that day, she summed up the situation this way: "Those were my teammates. They would help a dog pinned under a ladder. But they wouldn't help me."

Ms. Kelley's experiences are not unique. Alicia Mathis, a captain who joined the LAFD in 1989, also reports being approached in bed at a firehouse. She recently filed a complaint with the California Department of Fair Employment and Housing. Ruthie Bernal recently settled a lawsuit related to sexual advances that were followed by harsh treatment when the advances were rejected. Interestingly, Ms. Bernal reports that such advances and subsequent harsh treatment occurred in three different situations involving three different firefighters. Beyond sexual advances, other inappropriate acts have been reported, including mouthwash bottles being filled with inappropriate substances, unflattering female training experiences being captured on video and circulated among male colleagues, sexual materials being delivered, and disproportionately difficult training/testing being applied. In a recent survey released by the City Controller, 80 percent of women reported discrimination as an issue.

Beyond gender-based problems, race also has played a role in the Los Angeles Fire Department. In a racially charged incident that took place a few years ago, an African American firefighter ate dog food that had been put into his spaghetti at a firehouse. The nature of this incident remains a matter of controversy, as some claim it was harmless horseplay. Even so, because of a history of racial discrimination and harassment, it sparked outrage and a lawsuit. In the survey mentioned just above, 87 percent of African Americans reported discrimination as an issue. Hispanics have also reported problems.

The overall effects of these gender and racial issues have been significant. Beyond the loss of talented individuals and the reduced opportunity to attract talented women and minorities, the LAFD has had to pay millions of dollars to settle lawsuits. Job satisfaction also has been affected for some individuals of both genders and all races. Additionally, turmoil at the top of the organization has been significant as multiple fire chiefs have been fired because of the discrimination and harassment. Has the ultimate mission of the organization been compromised? The mission is to "preserve life and property, promote public safety and foster economic growth. . . ." Given the loss of talent, reduced satisfaction for some, and turmoil at the top, the effective pursuit of the mission has not been helped.

The news is not all bad, however. City and fire department officials have taken steps to remedy the situation. Surveys designed to stay abreast of the problems have been conducted, as noted earlier. Events such as "Black History Month Recruitment Exposition and Family Carnival" have been held. A new fire chief committed to a positive culture has been hired. The first female African American fire captain has been installed. In addition to these steps, the majority of white males have continued to be a positive force in the organization.

Sources: S. Banks, "Firehouse Culture an Ordeal for Women," *Los Angeles Times*, Dec. 3, 2006, p. A.1; S. Glover, "Rising Star Caught in Turmoil at the LAFD," *Los Angeles Times*, Feb. 12, 2007, B.1; D. Hernandez, "Bringing Diversity to the Force," *Los Angeles Times*, Feb. 6, 2006, B.4; J. Kandel, "Hostile Acts," *The IRE Journal* 29, no. 4 (2006): 22; LAFD, "Core Values," 2007, at http://www.joinlafd.org/CoreValues.htm; L. Richardson, "Audit Faults Fire Dept.," *Los Angeles Times*, Jan. 27, 2006, p. B.4; L. Richardson, "L.A. Fire Captain Alleges Gender Bias," *Los Angeles Times*, Sept. 28, 2006, p. B.4.

The Strategic Importance of Organizational Diversity

As the LAFD case shows, negative reactions to diversity can have harmful effects on an organization. These reactions, including discrimination and harassment of various forms, often lead to lawsuits, turnover, reduced satisfaction, and performance issues. In the most effective organizations, associates and managers understand the value of diversity. Moreover, associates and managers cannot escape diverse workgroups and organizations. Differences in gender, race, functional background, and so on are all around us. The United States is a particularly diverse country with respect to race and ethnicity, and current demographic trends indicate that its population will become even more diverse.

LAFD's legal troubles, financial settlement costs, and public embarrassment have led to renewed efforts to change the culture. The changing nature of the fire-fighter's job, where 80 percent of fire calls no longer involve structural or brush fires, probably has helped in this process.[1] Many organizations, however, have not needed public embarrassment or changing jobs to motivate diversity efforts. Many organizations, particularly large ones, have voluntarily adopted diversity management programs aimed at recruiting, retaining, and motivating high-quality associates from all demographic backgrounds. Most *Fortune* 500 companies, for example, have diversity management programs.[2] In a recent survey, over 79 percent of human resource managers at *Fortune* 1000 companies said they believed that successfully managing diversity improves their organizations.[3]

Diversity, if properly managed, can help a business build competitive advantage. For example, hiring and retaining managers and associates from various ethnicities can help an organization better understand and serve an existing diverse customer base. Diversity among associates also might help the organization attract additional customers from various ethnic groups. Diverse backgrounds and experiences incorporated into a work team or task force can help the organization more effectively handle an array of complex and challenging problems. Kevin Johnson, Co-President of Platforms and Services at Microsoft, puts it this way: ". . . we must recognize, respect, and leverage the different perspectives our employees bring to the marketplace as strengths. Doing so will ensure that we will be more competitive in the global marketplace, will be seen as an employer of choice, and will be more creative and innovative in developing products, services, and solutions for our customers."[4]

In the case of nonprofit organizations or governmental units such as the Los Angeles Fire Department, diversity can help build a form of competitive advantage. For instance, hiring and retaining managers and associates from both genders and multiple ethnic groups could help a nonprofit organization better understand its actual and potential client base as well as its actual and potential donors. Thus, the organization might be able to attract resources that would have gone to another nonprofit organization or that would have been withheld from donation. In the case of the Los Angeles Fire Department, diverse captains, firefighters, and paramedics could better communicate with and predict the behavior of the diverse citizenry of Los Angeles. This would enable the department to better serve the city. It also would position it to receive more resources from the city and state and would increase its likelihood of being chosen over other organizations for additional duties in the Los Angeles area.

Many individuals feel most comfortable interacting and working with people who are similar to them on a variety of dimensions (such as age, race, ethnic background, education, functional area, values, and personality).[5] They must, however, learn to work with all others in an organization to achieve common goals. In a truly inclusive workplace, everyone feels valued and all associates are motivated and committed to the mission of the organization. Such outcomes are consistent with a high-involvement work environment and can help organizations achieve competitive advantage.

We begin this chapter by defining organizational diversity and distinguishing it from other concepts, such as affirmative action. Next, we describe the forces in a changing world that have made diversity such a crucial concern. We then discuss possible benefits of effective diversity management, followed by roadblocks to such management and to the development of an inclusive workplace. We conclude the chapter with a discussion of what can be done to successfully manage a diverse organization.

KNOWLEDGE OBJECTIVES

After reading this chapter, you should be able to:

1. Define *organizational diversity* and distinguish between affirmative action and diversity management.

2. Distinguish among multicultural, plural, and monolithic organizations.

3. Describe the demographic characteristics of the U.S. population and explain their implications for the composition of the workplace.

4. Discuss general changes occurring in the United States that are increasing the importance of managing diversity effectively.

5. Understand why successfully managing diversity is extremely important for high-involvement work organizations.

6. Discuss the various roadblocks to effectively managing a diverse workforce.

7. Describe how organizations can successfully manage diversity.

 ## Diversity Defined

Diversity can be defined as a characteristic of a group of people where differences exist on one or more relevant dimensions such as gender.[6] Notice that diversity is a *group* characteristic, not an individual characteristic. Thus, it is inappropriate to refer to an individual as "diverse." If the group is predominantly male, the presence of a woman will make the group more diverse. However, if the group is predominantly female, the presence of a particular woman will make the group more homogeneous and less diverse.

In practice, diversity is often defined in terms of particular dimensions, most commonly gender, race, and ethnicity. Other important dimensions also exist.[7] These include age, religion, social class, sexual orientation, personality, functional experience (e.g., finance, marketing, accounting), and geographical background (e.g., background in the Canadian province of Ontario versus the province of Saskatchewan).[8] Any characteristic that would influence a person's identity or the way he or she approaches problems and views the world can be important to consider when defining diversity.[9] Two diversity scholars put it this way: "the effects of diversity can result from any attribute that people use to tell themselves that another person is different."[10] Visible attributes (e.g., race, gender, ethnicity),[11] attributes directly related to job performance (e.g., education and functional experience),[12] and rare attributes[13] are the most likely to be seen as important. Examples of how some large organizations define diversity appear below:

> Texas Instruments: "Diversity is 'all the ways in which we differ.' This includes the obvious differences such as race, gender, age, disability and more subtle differences such as education, sexual orientation, religious affiliation, work styles and thoughts or ideas."[14]

> Microsoft: "[Diversity] means not only having a workforce balanced by race, ethnic origin, gender, sexual orientation, and gender identity and expression, but also having a workforce that embraces differences in approaches, insights, ability, and experience."[15]

> Bank of America: "Our commitment to diversity is . . . about creating an environment in which all associates can fulfill their potential without artificial barriers, and in which the team is made stronger by the diverse backgrounds, experiences and perspectives of individuals."[16]

Affirmative action programs (AAPs) differ from diversity management programs. This important distinction should be noted before proceeding. AAPs are specific measures an organization takes to remedy and/or prevent discrimination. The key idea is to ensure fair representation of women and racial and ethnic

diversity
A characteristic of a group of people where differences exist on one or more relevant dimensions such as gender.

minorities in the workplace. In the United States, federal contractors (with 50 or more employees or government contracts over $50,000) are required to have AAPs. Other organizations may voluntarily adopt an AAP or may be court-ordered to adopt a program to remedy discriminatory practices. Central features of AAPs include a utilization analysis, which indicates the proportion of women and minorities hired and occupying various positions; goals and timetables for remedying underutilization of women and minorities; specific recruiting practices aimed at recruiting women and minorities (for example, recruiting at traditionally African American universities); and provision of developmental opportunities.[17] AAPs do not require that specific hiring quotas be implemented (which may be illegal) or that standards for selection and promotion be lowered. Also, AAPs usually provide temporary action; once women and minorities are appropriately represented in an organization, the AAP (with the exception of monitoring) is no longer necessary.

In contrast, diversity management programs are put in place to improve organizational performance. Because of their different goals, these programs differ from AAPs in several ways,[18] as summarized in Exhibit 2-1. Diversity management programs address diversity on many dimensions. They are often meant to change the organizational culture to be more inclusive and to enable and empower all associates. In addition, they focus on developing people's ability to work together.

Exhibit 2-1	Differences between Affirmative Action Programs and Diversity Management Programs	
	Affirmative Action	Diversity Management
Purpose	To prevent and/or remedy discrimination	To create an inclusive work environment where all associates are empowered to perform their best
Assimilation	Assumes individuals will individually assimilate into the organization; individuals will adapt	Assumes that managers and the organizations will change (i.e., culture, policies, and systems foster an all-inclusive work environment)
Focus	Recruitment, mobility, and retention	Creating an environment that allows all associates to reach their full potential
Cause of Diversity Problems	Does not address the cause of problems	Attempts to uncover the root causes of diversity problems
Target	Individuals identified as disadvantaged (usually racial and ethnic minorities, women, people with disabilities)	All associates
Time Frame	Temporary, until there is appropriate representation of disadvantaged groups	Ongoing, permanent changes

Sources: Adapted from R.R. Thomas, Jr., "Managing Diversity: A Conceptual Framework," in S.E. Jackson et al. (Eds.), *Diversity in the Workplace* (New York: Guilford Press, 1992), pp. 306–317. Society for Human Resource Management, "How Is a Diversity Initiative Different from My Affirmative Action Plan?," 2004, at http://www.shrm.org/diversity.

When diversity is managed successfully, a multicultural organization is the result.[19] A **multicultural organization** is one in which the organizational culture fosters and values differences. People of all gender, ethnic, racial, and cultural backgrounds are integrated and represented at all levels and positions in the organization. Because of the effective management of diversity, there is little intergroup conflict. Very few organizations in the United States or elsewhere are truly multicultural organizations; most organizations are either plural or monolithic.

> **multicultural organization**
> An organization in which the organizational culture values differences.

Plural organizations have diverse workforces and take steps to be inclusive and respectful of people from different backgrounds. However, diversity is tolerated rather than valued and fostered. Whereas multicultural organizations take special actions to make the environment inclusive and to ensure that all members feel valued, plural organizations focus on the law and on avoiding blatant discrimination.[20] Furthermore, people of various backgrounds may not be integrated throughout the levels and jobs of the organization, as they are in multicultural organizations. For example, even though a company may employ a large number of women, most of them may be in secretarial jobs. Plural organizations may also have human resource management policies and business practices that exclude minority members, often unintentionally. For example, many companies reward people for being self-promoters; that is, people who brag about themselves and make their achievements known are noticed and promoted, even though their achievements may not be as strong as those who do not self-promote. However, self-promoting behavior may be quite unnatural for people from cultural backgrounds where modesty and concern for the group are dominant values, such as the Japanese and Chinese cultures.[21] Finally, we would expect more intergroup conflict in plural organizations than in multicultural organizations because diversity is not proactively managed.

> **plural organization**
> An organization that has a diverse workforce and takes steps to be inclusive and respectful of differences, but where diversity is tolerated rather than truly valued.

Finally, **monolithic organizations** are homogeneous. These organizations tend to have extreme occupational segregation, with minority group members holding low-status jobs. Monolithic organizations actively discourage diversity; thus, anyone who is different from the majority receives heavy pressure to conform. Most U.S. organizations have moved away from a monolithic model because changes in the external environment and the workforce have required them to do so.[22] In the next section, we describe what these changes have been.

> **monolithic organization**
> An organization that is homogeneous.

Forces of Change

Over the past 20 years, several important changes in the United States and in many other countries have focused more attention on diversity, and these trends are expected to continue. The most important changes are (1) shifts in population demographics, (2) increasing importance of the service economy, (3) the globalization of business, and (4) new management methods that require teamwork.

Changing Population Demographics

Over the past ten years, more than one-third of people entering the U.S. workforce have been members of racial or ethnic minority groups.[23] Moreover, the proportion of racial and ethnic minorities in the workforce is expected to increase indefinitely. The situation is similar in some European countries.[24]

Exhibit 2-2	Projected U.S. Population Demographics			
Percentage by Race or Hispanic Origin	**2000**	**2010**	**2030**	**2050**
White, alone	81.0	79.3	75.8	72.1
Black, alone	12.7	13.1	13.9	14.6
Asian, alone	3.8	4.6	6.2	8.0
Other, or more than one	2.5	3.0	4.1	5.3
Hispanic origin (all races)	12.6	15.5	20.1	24.4
White (not Hispanic origin)	69.4	65.1	57.5	50.1
Percentage by Age	**2000**	**2010**	**2030**	**2050**
0–4	6.8	6.9	6.7	6.7
5–19	21.7	20.0	19.5	19.3
20–44	36.9	33.8	31.6	31.2
45–64	22.1	26.2	22.6	22.2
65–84	10.9	11.0	17.0	15.7
85+	1.5	2.0	2.6	5.0
Percentage by Sex	**2000**	**2010**	**2030**	**2050**
Male	49.1	49.1	49.1	49.2
Female	50.9	50.9	50.9	50.8

Source: U.S. Census Bureau, "U.S. Interim Projections by Age, Sex, Race, and Hispanic Origin," 2004. http://census.gov/ipc/usinterimproj/.

Exhibit 2-2 provides data on trends that affect the workforce in the United States. It shows, for example, that non-Hispanic white people are expected to decrease as a percentage of the overall population, moving from almost 70 percent to only 50 percent by 2050 (note that most Hispanics are racially white). The percentage of the population from Hispanic origins (any race) is expected to almost double, from just under 13 percent to almost 25 percent. The Asian American population is also expected to grow, from approximately 4 percent to 8 percent of the overall population. The expansion of the Hispanic American and Asian American populations is due in part to immigration. The percentage of black Americans (some of whom are of Hispanic origin) is expected to grow at a more moderate rate, from approximately 13 percent to almost 15 percent of the population. Clearly, increasing racial and ethnic diversity is a reality in the United States.

Exhibit 2-2 also shows a trend related to the continued aging of the U.S. population. The decade between 2000 and 2010 will see a growth spurt in the group made up of people aged 45 through 64. This spurt reflects the aging of the post–World War II baby boom generation—people born between 1946 and 1964. A major U.S. labor shortage is expected between 2015 and 2025 as members of the baby boom generation retire.[25] Thus, it will be even more important for organizations to be able to attract and retain talented associates. Another aspect of the aging population also will likely influence the composition of the labor force. The proportion of people 65 and older is expected to grow from about 12.4 percent to almost 21 percent of the population. If people work beyond the traditional retirement age of 65 due to improved health and the Age Discrimination Act (which protects people 40 and older from discrimination such as being forced to retire), the workforce will continue to age.

Finally, Exhibit 2-2 indicates that the proportion of men and women in the population is likely to remain stable. While women make up 50.9 percent of the population, approximately 48 percent of the labor force is female.[26] This number has grown from 40 percent in 1975 and is expected to increase slightly over the next decade,[27] indicating that proportionally more women than men will be entering the workforce. About 73 percent of mothers work, and about 60 percent of mothers who work have children under the age of three.[28] In contrast, less than 50 percent of mothers worked in 1975. The number of combined hours per week that married couples with children work increased from 55 in 1969 to 66 in 2000.[29] These trends create a need for policies that take family issues into consideration and that deal with the differing issues of workers who have children versus those who do not have children.

Increase in the Service Economy

The U.S. Bureau of Labor Statistics has predicted that the number of service-producing jobs (including those in transportation, utility, communications, wholesale and retail trade, finance, insurance, real estate, and government) will grow by approximately 17 percent between 2004 and 2014.[30] Service jobs are projected to make up more than 78 percent of all jobs in the United States by 2014.[31] Importantly, a service-based economy depends on high-quality interactions between people, whether between beauticians and their clients, home health-care workers and their patients, or human resource managers and their corporate associates. Because diversity within these and other customer groups is increasing, the service economy demands greater understanding and appreciation of diversity.[32]

The Global Economy

Globalization of the business world is an accelerating trend, gaining momentum from the increasing ease of communication, the opening of new markets, and growth in the number of multinational firms. In 2006, the United States exported $1,437 billion in goods and services and imported $2,202 billion in goods and services.[33] Since 2003, the export figure has increased by more than 40 percent in nominal dollars, while the import figure has increased by 45 percent.[34] Most of the largest companies in the world (for example, GE, Exxon, and Toyota) are the largest owners, worldwide, of foreign assets.[35] These same companies employ millions of workers outside of their home countries. Also, many of these companies require workers in their home countries to work with people from other parts of the world. Finally, many companies now conduct worldwide searches for managers and executives, so that the world serves as the labor market.

©AP/Wide World Photos

The continuing growth of globalization indicates that people will be working with others from different countries and cultures at an ever-increasing rate. Furthermore, many U.S. associates will work outside the United States with people who speak different languages, are accustomed to different business practices, and have different worldviews. As globalization increases, the need for successful diversity management also increases. You will read more about global issues in Chapter 3.

Requirements for Teamwork

Organizations that wish to succeed must respond to increasing globalization, rapidly changing technology and knowledge, and increasing demands for meaningfulness of associates' work. To meet these goals, many organizations are adopting strategies that rely strongly on teamwork. The Malcolm Baldrige National Quality Award has also focused attention on teamwork. It recognizes companies for the outstanding quality of their products. Teamwork is one way to provide better-quality goods and services, because people are more likely to become engaged and committed to the goals of the organization when they are members of strong teams. Whole Foods Market provides an example. At this very successful U.S.-based international provider of organic foods, everyone is assigned to a small, self-directed team.[36]

Teamwork requires that individuals work well together. Having diverse teams may allow for synergistic effects, where the variety of team experiences, attitudes, and viewpoints leads to better team performance.[37] However, to realize these positive effects, diversity must be managed effectively. Teams are discussed in more detail in Chapter 11.

Diversity Management and High-Involvement Organizations

High-involvement organizations expect their associates to respect, learn from, and help one another. They also recognize that associates must be committed to the organization in order to use training, information, and decision power in appropriate ways. Managing diversity effectively is important in the achievement of these aims. Individuals, groups, organizations, and even society as a whole can benefit.

Individual Outcomes

Associates' perceptions of the extent to which they are valued and supported by their organization have a strong effect on their commitment to the organization and their job involvement and satisfaction.[38] In the case of associates who are different from those around them, a positive, inclusive climate for diversity is necessary for full engagement in the work.[39] Research has found that women, racial and ethnic minority group members, and people with disabilities have less positive attitudes toward their organizations, jobs, and careers when they feel that their organizations have poor climates for diversity.[40] In addition, when an organization encourages and supports diversity, individuals are less likely to feel discriminated against and to be treated unfairly. When people feel they have been treated unfairly, they react negatively by withdrawing, performing poorly, retaliating, or filing lawsuits.[41]

Consider the case of a person whose religion forbids alcohol use, requires prayer at certain times of the day, and considers sexual jokes and materials offensive. This person, though, works in an environment where many deals are made over drinks in the local bar, where co-workers tease him because of his daily prayers, and where office walls are covered with risqué pictures. It is likely that this person feels uncomfortable in the office and devalued by his co-workers, leading to dissatisfaction and low commitment to his associates and the organization. Furthermore, he may avoid uncomfortable social activities where important information is exchanged and work accomplished, thus hurting his job performance. A work environment and culture that are sensitive, respectful, and accepting of this person's beliefs would likely result in a more committed, satisfied, and higher-performing associate.

With respect to individuals who are in the majority, diversity management programs must be sensitive to their needs as well. Otherwise, the ideals of diversity management will not be met and outcomes for some individuals will be less positive than they should be. In the United States, white men are often in the majority in a given organizational situation. For them, diversity management can be threatening. One study showed that white men placed less value on efforts to promote diversity.[42] Another study showed that white men perceived injustice when laid off in disproportionate numbers in the face of active diversity management, but did not perceive injustice in the face of disproportionate layoffs in situations without active diversity management.[43] To ensure commitment, satisfaction, and strong performance among those in a majority group, organizational leaders must (1) carefully build and communicate the case for diversity by citing the forces of change discussed earlier and (2) ensure fair decision processes and fair outcomes for all.

Organizations that create, encourage, and support diversity make all associates feel valued and provide them with opportunities to reach their full potential and be truly engaged in their work. This is a necessary condition of high-involvement work environments. To put it another way, creating and successfully managing diversity is a necessary condition for achieving a high-involvement work environment.

Group Outcomes

Diversity should have positive effects on the outcomes of organizational groups, particularly on decision-making, creative, or complex tasks.[44] This is because individual group members have different ideas, viewpoints, and knowledge to contribute, resulting in a wider variety of ideas and alternatives being considered.[45] Individuals who are different in terms of age, gender, race, ethnicity, functional background, and education often think about issues differently.[46]

For example, have you ever wondered why phones have rounded edges instead of sharp corners and why there is often a raised dot on the "5" key? One reason is that design groups at AT&T include people who have disabilities, including visual impairments. Rounded corners are less dangerous for people who cannot see the phone, and a raised dot on the "5" key allows people who cannot see to orient their fingers on the keypad. Ohmny Romero, who has worked as a manager in AT&T's technical division and is visually impaired, stated that AT&T

associates with disabilities become involved in developing new technologies because they want to "give back" to their community.[47] As a result, everyone has less dangerous phones and keypads that can be used when it is difficult to see. These innovations might never have come about if AT&T design teams had not included members with disabilities and respected their inputs.

In spite of its potential benefits, diversity has been described as a "mixed blessing" in terms of outcomes for organizational groups.[48] Indeed, research has produced mixed results, with some studies showing positive effects but other studies failing to show such effects.[49] There are two issues to consider in interpreting these research outcomes. First, faultlines can be present in situations characterized by diversity. *Faultlines* occur when two or more dimensions of diversity are correlated. For example, if all/most of the young people on a cross-functional task force represent marketing while all/most of the older individuals represent product engineering, then a faultline is said to exist. Faultlines merge multiple identities (e.g., young and marketing focused) to produce barriers to effective collaboration within a group. Research on this phenomenon is relatively new, but has produced findings suggesting poor group outcomes.[50]

Second, problems can develop in all situations characterized by some level of diversity. People often label group members who are different from themselves as "out-group members" and like them less,[51] leading to difficulties in group problem solving and decision making. Diverse organizational groups are more likely to experience personal conflict, problems in communication, and conflict among subgroups.[52]

In light of the above issues, the goal becomes one of facilitating the positive effects of diversity while eradicating the potentially negative effects. One way of harnessing the positive potential of group diversity, while avoiding the negative, is to establish a common identity for the group and to focus on common goals.[53] Richard Hackman, a leading researcher and consultant in the area of teams, has pointed out the importance of common goals for a team, as well as the importance of coaching for team problems.[54] Furthermore, when a company has a positive diversity culture, the problems associated with group diversity are much less likely to occur.[55] An organization that implements effective diversity programs, philosophies, and practices tends to avoid the problems associated with diversity, allowing it to yield the benefits that can be so important.[56] We develop these ideas later in this chapter.

Organizational Outcomes

As discussed above, diversity can lead to more satisfied, motivated, and committed associates who perform more effectively at their individual tasks. Properly managed, diversity can also lead to better-performing and more innovative groups. Therefore, diversity, through its effects on individual and group outcomes, is likely to affect the bottom-line performance of the organization.[57]

Despite the importance of the issue, little systematic research has been conducted that explicitly examines whether the diversity of an organization's workforce is tied to bottom-line performance. One exception is a study that examined the effect of racial and ethnic diversity in the banking industry. Diversity was positively related to the productivity, return on equity, and market performance of banks, but only when the bank had a corporate strategy that reflected growth. The positive relationship between diversity and firm performance was not found in banks that were pursuing a downsizing strategy. In these banks, greater diversity tended to result in poorer performance.[58]

Another exception is a large-scale study commissioned by business executives and conducted by researchers at MIT's Sloan School of Management, Harvard Business School, the Wharton School, Rutgers University, the University of Illinois, and the University of California at Berkeley.[59] This research examined the impact of demographic diversity on various aspects of firm performance in several *Fortune* 500 companies. Diversity was found to have no straightforward effects on performance. The researchers concluded that organizations need to manage diversity more effectively, especially because of the potential benefits that diversity offers. That is, diversity alone does not guarantee good corporate performance. It's what the company does with diversity that matters!

In addition to diversity in the workforce, diversity among those leading an organization might have effects. During the past decade or so, the business press has called for an increase in the demographic diversity of boards of directors and upper-echelon management teams.[60] Indeed, the number of women and racial/ethnic minority group members on corporate boards and in top executive positions has been consistently increasing.[61]

This trend appears to make good sense. A recent study of *Fortune* 500 firms found that the companies with the highest representation of women in top positions strongly outperformed those with the poorest representation of women in terms of return on equity and return to shareholders.[62] Other studies have found that the demographic diversity of boards of directors (in terms of race, gender, and age) is positively related to firm performance.[63] Thus, demographic diversity on boards can have a direct positive impact on the organization. One reason for this effect is that women and minorities who actually make it to the top may be better performers and better connected than typical board members.[64] Thus, including them on boards of directors usually increases the quality and talent of the board; the same is usually true for the upper-echelon management team. Another reason for positive outcomes is that by having demographically diverse boards and management teams, companies are sending positive social signals that attract both associates and potential shareholders.[65]

Other types of diversity on boards of directors and upper-echelon management teams also might be beneficial to the firm's bottom-line performance. Research suggests that diversity in functional areas, educational background, social/professional networks, and length of service can have positive effects on firm performance through better decision making.[66] Again, the diversity must be managed properly for benefits to appear.

Societal and Moral Outcomes

In order to have a society based on fairness and justice, U.S. federal laws prohibit employers from discriminating against applicants or employees on the basis of age, gender, race, color, national origin, religion, or disability. Discrimination is an expensive proposition for companies. Some recent awards to plaintiffs resulting from either out-of-court settlements or court cases include the following:

- Ford Motor Company paid out $10.5 million for age discrimination and $8 million for sex discrimination.
- Coca-Cola paid out $192.5 million for race discrimination.
- Texaco paid out $176 million for race discrimination.

Exhibit 2-3	Federal Laws Preventing Employment Discrimination	
Law	**Employers Covered**	**Who Is Protected**
Title VII of the 1964 Civil Rights Act, Civil Rights Act of 1991	Private employers, state and local governments, education institutions, employment agencies, and labor unions with 15 or more individuals	Everyone based on race, color, religion, sex, or national origin
Equal Pay Act of 1963	Virtually all employers	Men and women who perform substantially equal work
Age Discrimination in Employment Act of 1967	Private employers, state and local governments, education institutions, employment agencies, and labor unions with 20 or more individuals	Individuals who are 40 years old or older
Title I of the Americans with Disabilities Act of 1990	Private employers, state and local governments, education institutions, employment agencies, and labor unions with 15 or more individuals	Individuals who are qualified and have a disability

Source: U.S. Equal Employment Opportunity Commission, 2002, http://www.eeoc.gov/facts/qanda.html.

- CalPERS paid out $250 million for age discrimination.
- Shoneys paid out $132.5 million for race discrimination.
- Rent-a-Center paid out $47 million for sex discrimination.
- Information Agency and Voice of America paid out $508 million for sex discrimination.

Apart from these direct costs, firms suffer other losses when suits are filed against them, including legal costs, bad publicity, possible boycotts, and a reduction in the number of job applicants. One study found that stock prices increased for companies that won awards for affirmative action and diversity initiatives, whereas they fell for companies that experienced negative publicity because of discrimination cases.[67] Exhibit 2-3 summarizes applicable federal laws. Individual states may also have laws that protect people from discrimination based on additional characteristics, such as sexual orientation and marital status.

Companies that manage diversity well do not discriminate, and their associates are less likely to sue for discrimination. Managing diversity means more than just avoiding discrimination, however. In addition to legal reasons for diversity, there are also moral reasons.

The goal of most diversity programs is to foster a sense of inclusiveness and provide all individuals with equal opportunity—an important cultural value in the United States and in many other countries.

The *Experiencing Strategic Organizational Behavior* feature shows that prevailing ideologies are different in France versus the United States. Although both countries pride themselves on equality and inclusiveness, they take very different approaches to encourage these ideals. In the United States, differences across groups are highlighted and even celebrated, and laws are used to help in the advancement of minority and disadvantaged groups. In France, differences are downplayed as unimportant and there is limited affirmative action to promote the advancement of minority groups. Britain takes the middle road by recognizing differences but with limited affirmative action to promote fair outcomes in society.[68]

EXPERIENCING STRATEGIC ORGANIZATIONAL BEHAVIOR

Inclusiveness: The Case of France

In November 2005, riots broke out in the suburbs of Paris. Hundreds of people were injured and more than 80 buildings were damaged. Many automobiles were destroyed. A state of emergency was declared by the government. What caused the rioting? Deep seated frustration by minority groups over employment opportunities, living conditions and general treatment by French society.

In some ways, the rioting was surprising. French society is built on the principles of liberty, equality, and fraternity. There is an official ideology of colorblind decision making. Officially, there are no religious or ethnic enclaves. But individuals of African and Middle-eastern descent, most of them Muslim, do exist in enclaves, and they experience discrimination in profound ways.

Richard Passmore/ Stone/Getty Images

A recent study highlights the problems faced by minority citizens in France. It suggests that a job applicant with an African-sounding name is three times less likely to be offered an interview than a candidate with a French-sounding name. When the daughter of Sri-Lankan immigrants sent out résumés following graduation from an engineering school, she received no interview offers. At a job fair, she observed a recruiter throwing her résumé in the garbage without taking the time to properly look it over. Other common experiences highlight the problems faced by members of minority groups. In one case, an individual of Algerian descent was repeatedly passed over for promotion in favor of less-experienced candidates who were ethnic French.

To many observers, the problems faced by minority groups begin with the French establishment's approach to promoting equality. In the official French approach, color and ethnicity are simply ignored as irrelevant. It is, in fact, illegal to collect and report data on race and ethnicity. Furthermore, there are no affirmative action laws. Such laws are perceived as reverse discrimination. In 2006, there was an effort to create a bill that would require companies to hide or delete ethnic-identifying information from résumés prior to their evaluation. The bill was defeated.

Recognizing the talent in growing minority communities and the need to effectively understand and interact with an increasingly diverse customer base both at home and abroad, individual companies have begun their own diversity initiatives. Peugeot, an automaker, and AXA, an insurance company, have begun to use anonymous résumés. Peugeot and Total, the oil company, have begun sending representatives to job fairs in disadvantaged neighborhoods. Peugeot and cosmetics company L'Oreal have begun sending managers to high schools to provide advice on résumés and behavior during interviews. These initiatives are making a difference, and could be the start of a grassroots effort that results in a more inclusive society.

Sources: A. Cowell, "What Britain Can Tell France about Rioters," *New York Times*, Nov. 20, 2005, p. 4.4; J. Farouky, "The Many Faces of Europe," *Time International* 169, no. 9 (2007): 16–20; P. Ford, "More French Firms Diversify," *Christian Science Monitor*, Nov. 29, 2005, p. 1; T. Nguyen, "Lessons from France," *Colorlines* 9, no. 1 (2006): 8–9; M. Valla, "France Seeks Path to Workplace Diversity," *Wall Street Journal*, Jan. 3, 2007, A.2.

Roadblocks to Diversity

In the preceding section, we focused on the potential benefits of creating and managing diversity in organizations. Organizations working to institute effective diversity management programs face a number of obstacles, however. In this section, we consider the roadblocks to creating an inclusive workplace.

Prejudice and Discrimination

prejudice
Unfair negative attitudes we hold about people who belong to social or cultural groups other than our own.

discrimination
Behavior that results in unequal treatment of individuals based on group membership.

modern racism
Subtle forms of discrimination that occur despite people knowing it is wrong to be prejudiced against other racial groups and despite believing they are not racist.

Prejudice refers to unfair negative attitudes we hold about people who belong to social or cultural groups other than our own. Racism, sexism, and homophobia are all examples of prejudice. Prejudice influences how we evaluate other groups ("Arabs are bad," "People with disabilities are to be pitied") and can also lead to emotional reactions, such as hate, fear, disgust, contempt, and anxiety. Unfair **discrimination** is behavior that results in unequal treatment of individuals based on group membership. Examples of discrimination include paying a woman less than a man to do the same work, assigning people with disabilities easier jobs than others, and not promoting Asian Americans to leadership positions.

Prejudice and discrimination do not have to be overt or obvious. Consider racism as an example. Overt prejudice and discrimination toward racial minorities have been on the decline in the United States since passage of the 1964 Civil Rights Act.[69] Whites have become more accepting of residential integration and interracial marriage over the past several decades, for example.[70] However, prejudice and discrimination still exist in more subtle forms, a phenomenon often referred to as *modern racism*.[71] In general, **modern racism** occurs when people know that it is wrong to be prejudiced against other racial groups and believe themselves not to be racists. However, deep-seated, perhaps unconscious, prejudice still exists in these people, conflicting with their belief that racism is wrong.

People who are modern racists do not make racial slurs or openly treat someone of another race poorly. However, they may discriminate when they have an opportunity to do so, and then attribute their discriminatory behavior to another cause (such as poor performance) or hide their discriminatory behavior. In some cases, the discrimination is unintentional.

A recent study demonstrates modern racism in action.[72] Participants were asked to evaluate candidates for a university peer counseling position. White participants evaluated either a black or a white candidate. The qualifications of the candidates were varied, so that sometimes the candidates had very good qualifications, sometimes they had very bad qualifications, and sometimes qualifications were ambiguous and less obviously good or bad. The white evaluators showed no discriminatory behavior toward black candidates who had either very good or very bad qualifications. These candidates were chosen (or rejected) as frequently as white candidates with similar credentials. However, when qualifications were ambiguous and it was not obvious what hiring decision was appropriate, the evaluators discriminated a

PhotoDisc, Inc./Getty Images

great deal against black candidates. When qualifications were ambiguous, black candidates were chosen only 45 percent of the time, whereas white candidates with ambiguous qualifications were chosen 76 percent of the time.

Most research and discussion concerning modern racism has focused on whites' attitudes toward and treatment of blacks. However, evidence reveals that the same dynamics occur with non-Hispanic white behavior toward Hispanics, men's behavior toward women, nondisabled individuals' behavior toward people with disabilities, and heterosexuals' behavior toward homosexuals.[73] Further, minority group members may hold negative attitudes toward majority group members, and one minority group may hold negative attitudes toward another. Regardless of the source, prejudice and discrimination can prevent people from working effectively, getting along with one another, and reaping the benefits that can be derived from a diverse workforce.

Prejudice and discrimination can serve as barriers to effectively managing diversity, leading to stress, poor performance, feelings of injustice, and poor organizational commitment on the part of its victims.[74] In addition to preventing an organization from becoming a high-involvement workplace, prejudice and discrimination, as discussed above, can also be costly in terms of lawsuits and poor public relations. The Los Angeles Fire Department has experienced this firsthand. Thus, diversity management programs must eliminate prejudice and discrimination before they can be effective and foster a high-involvement work environment.

Stereotyping

A **stereotype** is a generalized set of beliefs about the characteristics of a group of individuals. Stereotypes are unrealistically rigid, often negative, and frequently based on factual errors.[88] When individuals engage in stereotyping, they believe that all or most members of a group have certain characteristics or traits. Thus, when we meet a member of that group, we assume that the person possesses those traits.

> **stereotype**
> A generalized set of beliefs about the characteristics of a group of individuals.

The problem with stereotypes is, of course, that they ignore the fact that the individuals within any group vary significantly. We can always find examples of someone who fits our stereotype; alternatively, we can just as easily find examples of people who do not fit the stereotype. For example, a common stereotype is that black people are poor.[75] However, the overwhelming majority of black people are middle class (just as are the majority of white people). It is statistically easier to find a middle-class black person than a poor one—and yet the stereotype persists.

Stereotyping is particularly difficult to stop for several reasons. First, stereotypes are very difficult to dispel. When we meet someone who has characteristics that are incongruent with our stereotypes (a smart athlete, a rich black person, a socially skilled accountant, or a sensitive white male), we ignore the discrepancy, distort the disconfirming information, see the individual as an exception to the rule, or simply forget the disconfirming information.[76] Thus, disconfirming information is not as likely as it should be to change stereotypes.

Second, stereotypes guide what information we look for, process, and remember.[77] For example, suppose I believe that all accountants are socially inept. When I meet an accountant, I will look for information that confirms my stereotype. If the accountant is alone at a party, I will assume he or she is antisocial. I will remember instances of when the accountant was quiet and nervous around people. I may also actually "remember" seeing the accountant acting like a nerd, even

Exhibit 2-4	Common Stereotypes Applied to Various Groups of People	
Women	**People with Disabilities**	**White Men**
Dependent	Quiet	Responsible for society's problems
Passive	Helpless	Competitive
Uncompetitive	Hypersensitive	Intelligent
Unconfident	Bitter	Aggressive
Unambitious	Benevolent	Ignorant
Warm	Inferior	Racist
Expressive	Depressed	Arrogant
Black People	**Japanese Men**	**Jewish People**
Athletes	Meticulous	Rich
Underqualified	Studious	Miserly
Poor	Workaholics	Well-educated
Good dancers	Racist	Family-oriented
Unmotivated	Unemotional	Cliquish
Violent	Defer to authority	Status conscious
Funny	Unaggressive	Good at business
Athletes	**Accountants**	**Arab People**
Dumb	Smart	Terrorists
Strong	Nerdy	Extremely religious
Sexist	Unsociable	Extremely sexist
Macho	Good at math	Rich
Male	Bad dressers	Hate Americans
Uneducated	Quiet	Jealous of Americans
Greedy	Dishonest	Don't value human life

Sources: M.E. Heilman, "Sex Bias in Work Settings: The Lack of Fit Model," in B.M. Staw and L.L. Cummings (Eds.), *Research in Organizational Behavior,* Vol. 5 (Greenwich, CT: JAI Press, 1983), pp. 269–298; C.S. Fichten and R. Amsel, "Trait Attributions about College Students with a Physical Disability: Circumplex Analysis and Methodological Issues," *Journal of Applied Social Psychology* 16 (1986): 410–427; Reprinted with permission of the publisher. From *Cultural Diversity in Organizations: Theory, Research and Practice,* © 1993 by T.H. Cox, Jr., Berrett-Koehler Publishers, Inc., San Francisco, CA. All rights reserved. www.bkconnection.com.

if I actually did not. Thus, my stereotype is guiding how I process all information about this person based on his or her membership in the accountant group.

Third, stereotypes seem to be an enduring human quality; we all hold stereotypes.[78] Stereotyping is so prevalent in part because it allows us to simplify the information that we deal with on a day-to-day basis.[79] Another reason is that it allows us to have a sense of predictability. That is, if we know a person's group membership (such as race, occupation, or gender), we also believe we have additional information about that person based on our stereotype for that group. Thus, the stereotype provides us with information about other people that enables us to predict their behavior and know how to respond to them. The comedian Dave Chappelle provides an amusing example of this in a skit in which he plays a fortuneteller. Instead of relying on mystic powers, he relies on his stereotypes. Given the race and gender of a phone-in caller, fortuneteller Chappelle can identify all sorts of information about the person's life (like whether the person is calling from prison or is on drugs).

Because stereotypes can drive behavior and lead to unrealistic or false assumptions about members of other groups, they can have very detrimental effects on interpersonal relations. Stereotypes can also have direct effects on individuals' careers by causing unfair treatment. In essence, when we rely on stereotypes to make judgments about an individual, rather than obtaining factual information, we are engaging in faulty decision making that causes harm. Exhibit 2-4 lists some common stereotypes for select groups.

The *Experiencing Strategic Organizational Behavior* feature shows that many individuals continue to stereotype women, and to harm their outcomes. Over time, changes in how women are viewed might be aided by examples of success and ambition among women leaders. Anne Mulcahy, CEO of Xerox, and Meg Whitman, former CEO of eBay, are examples. Mulcahy has been instrumental in turning around a company that was near death only a few years ago.[80] Whitman helped to build eBay from a very small company to one in which millions of people do more than $50 billion in business annually. Her vision for eBay was ambitious and included changing consumers' current emphasis on buying at retail stores. Although competition and market dynamics have cooled the company's growth to some degree, eBay continues to be strong.[81]

EXPERIENCING STRATEGIC ORGANIZATIONAL BEHAVIOR

Women, Work, and Stereotypes

Over the past three decades, women in western, industrialized nations have achieved a great deal in workplace acceptance, respect, and advancement. In fields as diverse as accounting, risk management, general management, and police work, women have made substantial progress. For example, chief financial officers, polled a few years ago by America's Community Bankers, reported substantial increases in the number of women managers in their banks. *Women in Business* recently reported that the percentage of women holding supervisory roles had increased from 20 percent to almost 50 percent in a recent 30-year period. *Fortune* 500 firms reported a few years ago that women in officer positions had increased from 2 percent to more than 10 percent.

Comstock/
Getty Images

With this advancement, it would seem that stereotypes characterizing women as submissive, frivolous, indecisive, and uncommitted to the workplace have been eliminated. Problems still exist, however. Consider the language used in major media outlets to describe some businesswomen. Carly Fiorina, former chief executive officer of Hewlett-Packard, has been characterized as being "as comfortable with power as any woman could be." A former chief executive at Mattel, Jill Barad—who admittedly had some problems—was slighted with the following dismissive statement: "She should have stuck to marketing, rather than worrying her pretty little head about running the company." Darla Moore, who contributed $25 million to the University of South Carolina School of Business, was characterized as a "babe in business." This type of language may help to keep gender stereotypes alive. Stereotypical language and images routinely found in such places as television commercials, radio ads, and travel brochures may also contribute.

Further evidence that gender stereotypes are not dead comes from the financial sector. According to Sheila McFinney, an organizational psychologist familiar with Wall Street, "Stereotypes about women's abilities run rampant in the financial industry. A lot of men in management feel that women don't have the stomach for selling on Wall Street." In support of this statement, a number of Wall Street firms have been forced to settle major harassment and discrimination claims with thousands of current and former women associates. Interestingly, women are more prevalent in finance than in many other functional areas.

Finally, evidence that suggests ongoing stereotypes comes from a 2007 survey conducted by *Elle* magazine in conjunction with MSNBC.com. Sixty-thousand respondents from a variety of occupations and industries answered questions about women and men as leaders. Approximately half of them indicated that women and men have differing abilities, with women being less able than men. Women, however, were given high marks for supportive environments.

Sources: "Women Accountants Advance in Management Ranks," *Community Banker* 10, no. 4 (2001): 52; J. Anderson, "Six Women at Dresdner File Bias Suit," *New York Times,* Jan. 10, 2006, C.1; C. Daily and D.R. Dalton, "Coverage of Women at the Top: The Press Has a Long Way to Go," *Columbia Journalism Review* 39, no. 2 (2000): 58–59; M.K. Haben, "Shattering the Glass Ceiling," *Executive Speeches* 15, no. 5 (2001): 4–10; M-L. Kamberg, "A Woman's Touch," *Women in Business* 57, no. 4 (2005): 14–17; M. Ligos, "Nightmare on Wall Street," *Sales and Marketing Management* 152, no. 2 (2000): 66–76; E. Tahmincioglu, "Men Rule—At Least in Workplace Attitudes," 2007, at http://www.msnbc.msn.com/id/17345308/.

Differences in Social Identity

Everyone's personal self-identity is based in part on his or her membership in various social groups.[82] This aspect of self-identity is referred to as social identity. **Social identity** is defined as a person's knowledge that he belongs to certain social groups, where belonging to those groups has emotional significance.[83] In describing yourself, you might respond with a statement such as "I am a Catholic," "I am Jewish," "I am a member of my sorority," "I am of Puerto Rican descent," "I am an African American," or "I am a Republican." Such a statement describes an aspect of your social identity structure. Exhibit 2-5 provides examples of overall structures.

Having a social identity different from that of the majority can be very difficult, for several reasons. First, a person's social identity becomes more salient, or noticeable, when the person is in the minority on an important dimension. Accordingly, racial and ethnic minorities are much more likely to state that their membership in a racial or ethnic group is an important part of their self-concept.[84] For example, in one study, researchers asked people, "Tell me about yourself."[85] Only one out of every 100 white people mentioned that she was white. However, one in six black respondents mentioned his race, and one in seven Hispanic respondents mentioned ethnicity. Also, many women remark that they are more conscious of being female when they are in a work environment that is all male than when they are in a mixed-gender group. When a person's minority social identity becomes salient, the person is made more aware that he or she is different from the majority of people in the situation.

social identity
A person's knowledge that he belongs to certain social groups, where belonging to those groups has emotional significance.

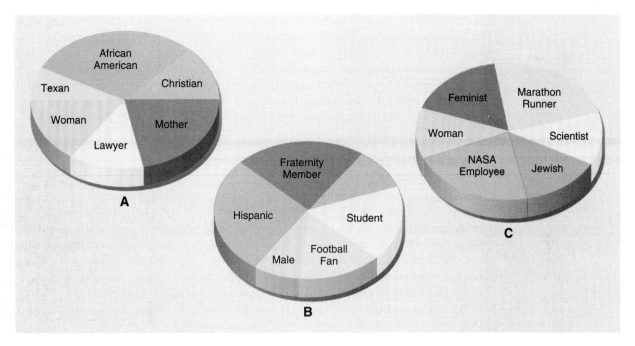

Exhibit 2-5   Sample Social-Identity Structures

Second, having a social identity different from that of the majority may make people feel they have to behave in ways that are unnatural for them in certain contexts. Feeling that they are acting out a false role will in turn lead to stress and dissatisfaction.[86] For example, women operating in an all-male environment may try to act more like men in order to fit in and meet others' expectations.[87] In discussing being an African American in a predominantly white business world, Kenneth I. Chenault, CEO of American Express, says that he had to learn how to become comfortable dealing with multiple cultures with different expectations. He states, "I learned very early on how to move between both worlds and develop a level of comfort and confidence no matter what world I'm operating in."[88] Clearly, if you belong to the majority group, you do not have to learn how to act in different worlds.

A third issue resulting from differences in social identities is that often minority group members fear losing this social identity.[89] Social identity is often a source of pride and honor.[90] Thus, being forced to "check their identity at the gate" creates a sense of loss and discomfort for many people.

A final issue related to differences in social identities concerns the fact that people often evaluate others based on their membership in social groups. People tend to favor members of their own groups because their group membership is often tied to feelings of high self-esteem.[91] We think people who belong to our own group must somehow be better than those who do not belong. In other words, we tend to categorize people according to in-group and out-group membership,[92] and we tend to favor members of our own group—the in-group—and disfavor those whom we have categorized as belonging to an out-group. We often exaggerate the positive attributes of our own group and the negative aspects of the out-group. Furthermore, we are more likely to have stereotypes regarding out-group members and to ignore differences among out-group members.[93] So, for example, members of the legal department, who have strong identities as lawyers, may view other associates who are not lawyers as being similar, less savvy, and peripheral to the success of the company. In contrast, the lawyers are more likely to see other lawyers as individuals, and think they are smarter and are central to the company's success. In conclusion, social identity dynamics can be a roadblock to successful diversity management because they foster forming in-groups and out-groups and can lead to stress and dissatisfaction among those with minority identities.

Power Differentials

Power is not equally distributed among the individuals and groups in an organization. Individuals gain power in many ways—by having expert knowledge or a powerful formal position, by controlling valuable rewards or important resources, or by being irreplaceable, for example.[94] In some organizations that rely on selling, the individuals in the sales and marketing departments have most of the power, whereas the individuals in the human resources and accounting departments have less power. An executive secretary controlling those who are allowed to meet with and speak to the CEO also has power. In essence, this secretary controls everyone's communication with top management.

On the other hand, people are also awarded or deprived of power and status for reasons that have nothing to do with work life. On a societal level, groups of people have what is called *ascribed* status and power. **Ascribed status** is status and power that is assigned by cultural norms and depends on group membership.[95] In other words, societal culture defines who has power and who does not. In North America, women, racial and ethnic minorities, and people with disabilities, among other groups, are traditionally perceived to be of lower status than white men.[96] Thus, members of these groups have traditionally had less power in the workplace than white men. When such power differentials exist, they can prevent an organization from developing an inclusive workplace for at least two reasons.

First, research has shown that high-status individuals speak more and use stronger influence tactics than members of low-status groups.[97] Thus, low-status individuals may not have a chance to contribute as much to group problem-solving tasks. When people do not feel free to speak up, a major benefit of diversity is lost because different ideas and viewpoints are not presented. This phenomenon also causes problems because it perpetuates status differentials and may lead to frustration and dissatisfaction among people who do not feel free to speak up.

Second, people belonging to groups with different amounts of power and status may avoid interacting with one another and may form cliques with members of their own groups.[98] High-status groups may downgrade, ignore, or harass members of low-status groups. Associates in low-status groups may stay away from high-status associates in order to avoid rejection or humiliation. This tendency to form cliques undermines diversity efforts by setting the stage for increased conflict among groups.

Poor Structural Integration

You may have heard phrases such as "pink-collar ghetto" and "glass ceiling." These phrases refer to the tendency for women and members of racial and ethnic minority groups to be "stuck" in certain occupations or at certain levels in an organization. Recall from the earlier part of this chapter that one criterion for

ascribed status
Status and power that is assigned by cultural norms and depends on group membership.

Company A
Poorly Integrated

Functional Area

Level	Finance	Marketing	HR	Sales	Average across functions
Top Management	0%	0%	2%	0%	.5%
Mid Management	0%	1%	10%	2%	3.25%
Supervisor	0%	5%	15%	5%	6.25%
Staff	25%	25%	40%	26%	29%
Line Worker	60%	65%	80%	75%	70%

Company B
Well Integrated

Functional Area

Level	Finance	Marketing	HR	Sales	Average across functions
Top Management	35%	35%	35%	35%	35%
Mid Management	35%	35%	35%	35%	35%
Supervisor	35%	35%	35%	35%	35%
Staff	35%	35%	35%	35%	35%
Line Worker	35%	35%	35%	35%	35%

The numbers in each cell represent the percentage of people in each job level and functional area who are female and/or racial and ethnic minority group members.

The total percentage of employees for both companies who are female and/or a racial ethnic minority is 35%.

Exhibit 2-6 Examples of Poorly Integrated and Well-Integrated Organizations

having a truly multicultural organization is that people from traditionally under-represented groups appear at all levels and in all occupations. Exhibit 2-6 illustrates a well-integrated organization and a poorly integrated organization.

Note in the figure that 35 percent of the employees in both Company A and Company B are either female and/or a member of a racial minority group. So if we look only at the total number of employees, then we might conclude that both companies are equally well integrated. Such a conclusion would be erroneous, however.

In Company A, on average across functional areas, only .5 percent of top management jobs are held by women or minorities. At the same time, on average across functional areas, 70 percent of the lowest-level jobs are held by women and minorities. These figures indicate that women and minorities are extremely under-represented in high-level positions and overrepresented in low-level (low-status, low-power, and low-pay) positions. Furthermore, in Company A, women and racial minorities are severely underrepresented in the areas of finance, marketing, and sales. Coca-Cola was sued by African Americans because it resembled Company A (to some degree) despite having talented people in the minority group. The company settled in 2000 for $192.5 million.[101]

Contrast these patterns with those in Company B. In that company, women and minorities are represented in all areas in proportion to their total representation in the company. Company B illustrates the ideal distribution for an inclusive organization—which occurs infrequently.

Data compiled in 2003 by the Equal Employment Opportunity Commission suggest that U.S. companies look more like Company A than Company B.[102] White males made up about 37 percent of the workforce in private industry but held about 56 percent of the executive and managerial jobs. In contrast, they only held about 13 percent of lower-level clerical jobs and 21 percent of service jobs. White women, who made up almost 33 percent of the workforce, held almost 55 percent of clerical jobs. Black people (both men and women) made up almost 14 percent of the workforce but held less than 7 percent of executive and managerial jobs. Black women were overrepresented in clerical and service jobs, and black men were overrepresented in operations and laborer jobs. This pattern held true for most other minority groups as well.

Why are social groups so unequally distributed across occupations and job levels? Many explanations have been offered, with discrimination being a common one. Lack of skills on the part of groups holding lower-level positions is also cited frequently. Whatever the reason, poor integration of women and minorities in organizations can present several roadblocks to creating a multicultural environment.

- Poor integration creates power and status differentials, which then become associated with gender or race.
- Poor integration fosters negative stereotypes.
- Where integration is poor overall, women and minorities who do reach higher levels may have token status. That is, since they may be the only persons of their race or gender in that type of job, they will be considered an exception.[103]
- Where integration is poor, most women and minorities may feel that it is impossible for them to rise to the top.

Communication Problems

Communication can be a roadblock to establishing an effective diversity environment. One potential communication problem arises when not everyone speaks the same language fluently. Associates who are less fluent in the dominant language may refrain from contributing to conversations. Furthermore, groups may form among those who speak the same language, excluding those who do not speak that language. Finally, many misunderstandings may occur because of language differences. For example, U.S. college students often complain that having teachers who are not fluent in English makes it difficult for them to understand class lectures.

Another communication problem arises because different cultures have different norms about what is appropriate. For example, African Americans and Hispanics tend to prefer verbal communication to written communication,[99] whereas Anglo Americans and Asian Americans prefer written communication. African Americans, Hispanics, and Asians are less likely than Anglo Americans to feel they can speak freely during meetings.[100] Common areas of communication disagreement among cultures include the following:

- Willingness to openly disagree
- The importance of maintaining "face," or dignity
- The way agreement is defined
- The amount of time devoted to establishing personal relationships
- Willingness to speak assertively
- Mode of communication (written, verbal)
- Personal space and nonverbal communication

While communication differences exist for people from different backgrounds, it is important not to stereotype. Some individuals from a particular background will not share the communication preferences often associated with that background.

Effectively Creating and Managing Diversity

Organizations face many roadblocks to creating multicultural environments, but these roadblocks are not insurmountable. In this section, we discuss some strategies for effectively creating and managing diversity.

Most large companies and many small companies have in recent years instituted some type of diversity management plan. These plans have varied in effectiveness, from being very successful at creating a diverse, inclusive, and productive workplace to having no effect or to actually having negative effects. Because so many diversity programs have been instituted, there is substantial knowledge about what works and what does not work. In the late 1990s, the U.S. Department of Commerce set out to study 600 firms that had been cited for having excellent diversity climates.[104] The study revealed several criteria for success, including commitment by the organization's leaders, integration of the program with the organization's strategic plan, and involvement of all associates.

Commitment of the Organization's Leaders

The first criterion for having an effective diversity program is genuine commitment from the organization's upper-level leadership. Insincere support of diversity is damaging. Leaders must take ownership of diversity initiatives and effectively communicate the vision that inclusiveness is important. Actions that corporate leaders have initiated to ensure that the message comes across include the following:

- High-ranking leaders send relevant communications through multiple channels, such as intranet postings, policy statements, formal newsletters, meetings, speeches, and training programs.
- One high-ranking leader personally leads all diversity efforts. He holds town meetings and eats lunch in the cafeteria to talk about diversity.
- Multiple high-ranking executives sponsor employee councils devoted to fostering cross-cultural communication. The councils are all-inclusive— anyone who wants to join can do so. Therefore, anyone can "have the ears" of executives on diversity issues.
- Managers at all levels are held accountable for advancing diversity initiatives.

The *Managerial Advice* feature focuses on ideas that managers can use to promote positive work environments. The actions recommended are valuable for associates but are most important for managers because they have the strongest effects on the organization's culture.

MANAGERIAL ADVICE

Promoting a Positive Diversity Environment

Banana Stock/ PictureQuest

Robin Ely, Debra Meyerson, and Martin Davidson are professors at Harvard University, Stanford University, and the University of Virginia, respectively. In conjunction with the human development and organizational learning professionals at Learning as Leadership, they have developed several principles designed to ensure that members of various social identity groups do not become trapped in low quality workplace relationships. These principles are designed to encourage engagement and learning. The principles are perhaps best applied in the context of individuals experiencing uncomfortable events that are open to interpretation, such as when the member of a minority group is told by a someone from the majority that she is being too aggressive, or when a man is told by a woman that he is acting as his grandfather might have acted. The principles are listed below:

a. *Pause to short circuit the emotion and reflect.* Individuals who have experienced an uncomfortable event should take a few moments to identify their feelings and consider a range of responses.

b. *Connect with others in ways that affirm the importance of relationships.* Individuals who have experienced an uncomfortable event should reach out to those who have caused the difficulty, thereby valuing relationships.

c. *Question interpretations and explore blind spots.* Individuals who have experienced an uncomfortable event should engage in self-questioning as well as the questioning of others. They should be open to the interpretations that others have of the situation, while realizing that their own interpretations might be correct.

d. *Obtain genuine support that doesn't necessarily validate initial points of view but, rather, helps in gaining broader perspective.* Individuals who have experienced an uncomfortable event should seek input from those who will challenge their initial points of view on the situation.

e. *Shift the mindset.* Individuals who have experienced an uncomfortable event should be open to the idea that both parties might need to change to some degree.

Sources: R.J. Ely, D.E. Meyerson, and M.N. Davidson, "Rethinking Political Correctness," *Harvard Business Review* 84 (September 2006); Learning as Leadership, "Research," 2007, at http://www.learnaslead.com/index.php.

Integration with the Strategic Plan

The second criterion for effective diversity management requires that diversity be linked to the organization's strategic plan. That is, it is necessary to be clear about the ways in which diversity can contribute to the strategic goals, directions, and plans of the organization. The organization must develop ways of defining and measuring diversity effectiveness and then use these measures in the strategic planning process. Common measures of diversity effectiveness focus on:

- Increased market share and new customer bases
- External awards for diversity efforts

- Associates' attrition rate
- Associates' work satisfaction
- Associates' and managers' satisfaction with the workplace climate

Another tactic for elevating diversity to the strategic level involves making it a core value and part of the formal mission statement of the organization. Many organizations that truly value diversity express this as a core value and include their beliefs in a mission statement. These statements go beyond the common catchphrase that "We are an affirmative action employer." For example, one of six principles in Starbucks' mission statement is: "Embrace diversity as an essential component in the way we do business." Another is: "Provide a great work environment and treat each other with respect and dignity."[105]

Associate Involvement

The third criterion for effective diversity management calls for the involvement of all associates. Diversity programs can produce suspicion or feelings of unfairness in some associates, particularly if they misinterpret the program's purpose. Some individuals may feel they are excluded from the program, whereas others may feel that it infringes on benefits they are currently enjoying. It is important for diversity programs to address the needs of both majority group members and minority group members. Organizations can use many methods to obtain input from associates. Some of these include:

- Discussion groups made up of all types of associates who help in developing, implementing, and evaluating the program
- Employee satisfaction surveys
- Cultural diversity audits, which help the company studying the diversity culture and environment of the organization
- Informal employee feedback hotlines where associates can provide unsolicited feedback

Another common way of involving associates in diversity programs is to develop and support *affinity groups*—groups that share common interests and serve as a mechanism for the ideas and concerns of associates to be heard by managers. Affinity groups are also good sources of feedback about the effectiveness of diversity initiatives. Finally, these groups can provide networking opportunities, career support, and emotional support to their members. Ford Motor Company has the following affinity groups: Ford-Employee African American Ancestry Network; Ford Asian Indian Association; Ford Chinese Association; Ford Finance Network; Ford Gay, Lesbian or Bisexual Employees; Ford Hispanic Network Group; Professional Women's Network; Ford's Parenting Network; Women in Finance; Ford Interfaith Network; Middle Eastern Community @ Ford Motor Company; and Ford Employees Dealing with Disabilities.[106]

Finally, another way of involving all associates is through training. Training programs often include an explanation of the business necessity for effectively managing diversity, along with empathy training, cross-cultural knowledge instruction, and exercises to help associates avoid stereotyping and engaging in offensive or prejudicial treatment of others. To create a truly inclusive environment, diversity programs also need to teach people how to value and respect diversity rather than just tolerate it.

Denny's, the U.S. restaurant chain, is an example of a company that has implemented the three aspects of diversity management discussed here. Following lawsuits and settlements in the 1990s, Jim Anderson became the CEO in 1996 and drove true commitment to diversity. Anderson himself was committed to building what Roosevelt Thomas, an expert on corporate diversity, terms a *diversity-mature* organization in which the mission and vision of the company includes a diversity management component.

To fully integrate the management of diversity into its mission, Denny's requires all managers and associates to participate in diversity training sessions. In addition, they are held accountable for their behavior. Associates who engage in inappropriate behavior are put on notice and must indicate how they will change their behavior in the future. Those who do not change their behavior are terminated. More blatant transgressions, such as racial slurs, result in immediate termination.

Overall, companies such Denny's use diversity initiatives in at least seven different areas:[107]

1. Recruiting (e.g., diverse recruiting teams, minority job fairs)

2. Retention (e.g., affinity groups, onsite child care)

3. Development (e.g., mentoring programs, leadership development programs)

4. External partnerships (e.g., minority supplier programs, community outreach)

5. Communication (e.g., addresses by high-ranking leaders, newsletters)

6. Training (e.g., awareness training, team building)

7. Staffing and infrastructure (e.g., dedicated diversity staffs, executive diversity councils).

The Strategic Lens

Organizational diversity, when managed effectively, has many benefits for organizations. In general, effectively managed diversity programs contribute to an organization's ability to achieve and maintain a competitive advantage. Diversity in teams at all levels can be helpful in solving complex problems because heterogeneous teams integrate multiple perspectives. This benefit applies to the upper-echelon management team as well as to project teams, such as new product development teams, much lower in the organization. Not only can the diversity help resolve complex problems, but it also better mirrors U.S. society. Thus, it signals to potential associates and potential customers that the organization understands and effectively uses diversity. As a result, the organization has a larger pool of candidates for potential associates from which it can select the best. In addition, the organization is likely to have a larger potential market because of its understanding of the products and services desired by a diverse marketplace. Having a diverse organization that reflects the demographic composition of U.S. society is smart business.[108]

Critical Thinking Questions

1. How does organizational diversity contribute to an organization's competitive advantage?

2. What actions are required to create diversity in an organization, particularly in one that has homogeneous membership at present?

3. How does diversity in an organization affect its strategy?

What This Chapter Adds to Your Knowledge Portfolio

In this chapter we discussed the importance of diversity to organizations and the need to effectively manage diversity. We also discussed the forces of change that have made diversity a primary concern of many organizations, and we described some of the more common roadblocks to successfully managing diversity. Finally, we discussed the essential components of an effective diversity program. To summarize, we made the following points:

- Organizational diversity refers to differences among the individuals in an organization. Important differences are those that are personally important to people and affect the way in which they perceive the world. Common dimensions of diversity include race, ethnicity, gender, disability, functional area, sexual orientation, and parenthood.

- Diversity programs are aimed at developing inclusive work cultures, which are important in high-involvement work environments. Affirmative action programs are aimed at making sure there is fair representation or numbers of various groups within jobs and organizations. Affirmative action programs can be legally mandated or voluntarily adopted.

- Multicultural organizations have diverse associates and are inclusive of all associates. Plural organizations have reasonably diverse associates and tolerate diversity. Monolithic organizations are homogeneous and do not tolerate diversity.

- The U.S. population is getting older and more diverse in terms of race and ethnicity. Other changes that are occurring in the environment include an increasing service economy, increasing globalization, and increasing need for teamwork. These changes make management of diversity more important today than ever.

- Successfully managing diversity is important because it can lead to more committed, better satisfied, better-performing employees, attraction of the best talent, better group decision making, and potentially better financial performance for the organization. Effectively managing diversity also ensures that the moral principle that everyone be treated fairly will be upheld. Furthermore, effective diversity management can result in fewer lawsuits for discrimination.

- Discrimination, prejudice, stereotyping, differing social identities, power differentials poor structural integration, and communication concerns, have a negative impact on managing a diverse workforce.

- Organizations that successfully manage diversity have senior managers who fully support diversity initiatives, tie their diversity plans to the overall strategic goals of the organization, and ensure involvement from all associates through a variety of mechanisms.

Back to the Knowledge Objectives

1. What is organizational diversity, and how does diversity management differ from affirmative action? Do these kinds of programs have anything in common?

2. Distinguish between multicultural, plural, and monolithic organizations. How might these organizations differ in the types of policies they use? For example, how would they differ in terms of staffing practices?

3. What trends can be seen in the demographic characteristics of the U.S. population? What are the implications of these trends for organizational diversity?

4. What other changes are occurring in the environment that contribute to the importance of managing diversity effectively? Why do these changes have this effect?

5. Why is successfully managing diversity important to high-involvement work organizations? Give specific examples.

6. What problems do discrimination, prejudice, and stereotyping create in an organization attempting to manage a diverse workforce?

7. How do social identities, power differentials, and poor structural integration affect the successful management of diversity?

8. What does a diversity program need in order to be effective? How would you determine whether your diversity program was effective?

Thinking about Ethics

1. Suppose that an organization has discriminated in the past. Should it now simply stop its discriminatory practices, or should it also take specific actions to increase its diversity by targeting, hiring, and promoting minorities ahead of non-minorities? Discuss.

2. Should all managers and associates in an organization be required to undergo diversity training regardless of their desire to do so? Why or why not?

3. Are there any circumstances in which it is appropriate to discriminate against a particular class of people (such as women)? If so, explain the circumstances. If not, explain why.

4. Women are not a minority in the population but represent a minority in the U.S. workforce, particularly in some occupations. Why has this occurred in U.S. society (or your home country, if applicable)?

5. Should all cultures and modes of conduct be tolerated, even if they conflict with the values of the organization? Why or why not?

6. What percentage of the organization's budget should be invested in building and maintaining an effective diversity management program? How should this percentage compare with other major budget items?

Key Terms

Diversity, p. 39
Multicultural organization, p. 41
Plural organization, p. 41

Monolithic organization, p. 41
Prejudice, p. 50
Discrimination, p. 50

Modern racism, p. 50
Stereotype, p. 51
Social identity, p. 54
Ascribed status, p. 56

Building Your Human Capital

What's Your DQ (Diversity Quotient)?

How well do you handle diversity? Your ability to be flexible, work with many different types of people, and deal with ambiguous situations will be crucial to a successful career in the twenty-first century. The following assessment will allow you to determine whether you have had the experience necessary to help in successfully navigating a diverse work environment.

Use the following scale to answer the questions below:

1 point = never	3 points = three or four times
2 points = once or twice	4 points = four or more times

In the last month, how often did you . . .?

1. See a foreign movie.
2. Speak a language other than your first language.
3. Visit an art or history museum.
4. Have a conversation with someone who was of a different race.
5. Have a conversation with someone who was from a different country.
6. Attend a social event where at least half of the people differed from you in race or ethnic background.
7. Visit a church that was of a religion different from yours.
8. Visit a place where people spoke a language different from your first language.
9. Do something you've never done before.
10. Attend a cultural event (art show, concert).
11. Eat ethnic food.
12. Visit a foreign country.
13. Watch a program about world (non-U.S.) history.
14. Read a book about another culture.
15. Watch a movie or TV show about another culture.
16. Attend a social event where you didn't know anyone.
17. Read a book written by a foreign author.
18. Listen to music from a different culture.
19. Attend an event where you were in a minority based on any demographic characteristic (age, gender, race, ethnicity, religion, sexual orientation).
20. Learn something new about a country or culture other than your own.
21. Study a different language.
22. Attend an event about a different culture (an ethnic festival, a concert by musicians from a different culture, a student meeting of an ethnic group).
23. Have a conversation with someone from a different social class.
24. Develop a friendship with someone from a different background.
25. Discuss world affairs with someone who disagreed with you.

Scoring: Add up your total points for the 25 questions. Scoring can range from 25 to 100

25–39: Your current environment is rather homogeneous. You can increase your DQ by making a concerted effort to reach out to people who are different from you, attend events that expose you to different cultures, and learn about people and cultures that differ from yours. Your score may be low because you live in an area where there is little diversity in people or cultural events. You will need to go out of your way to gain exposure to different cultures.

40–59: Your current environment could be more diverse than it currently is. You can increase your DQ by making a concerted effort to reach out to people who are different from you, attend events that expose you to different cultures, and learn about people and cultures that differ from yours.

60–79: Your environment is fairly culturally diverse. Look more closely at your scores for each question and determine whether there are any areas in which you can broaden your horizons even further. Perhaps, for example, you read and watch materials that expose you to different cultures but do not personally interact frequently with people who are different from you. If that is the case, join a club where you are likely to meet people different from yourself.

80–100: Your environment is quite culturally diverse. You experience a great deal of cultural variety, which should help prepare you for working in a culturally diverse work environment.

A Strategic Organizational Behavior Moment

Project "Blow Up"

Big State University (BSU) is proud of the success of its international executive MBA (EMBA) program. The program is designed to bring together promising middle- and higher-level managers from around the globe for an exceptional learning experience. BSU's EMBA program has been ranked very highly by the business press. Alumni praise the program for its excellent faculty, networking opportunities, and exposure to colleagues from around the world. Students in the program can either attend weekend classes on BSU's campus or participate through distance-learning technology from campuses around the world.

One of the defining features of the program is the first-year team project. Students are randomly assigned to five-member teams. Each team has a faculty advisor, and each must develop a business plan for a startup company. A major part of the business plan involves developing a marketing strategy. The teams begin the project during orientation week and finish at the end of the next summer. Each team must turn in a written report and a business plan and make an hour-long presentation to the other students and faculty as well as several executives from well-respected multinational companies. Students must earn a passing grade on the project to graduate from the program. The project is also a good way of meeting and impressing important executives in the business community.

The A-Team consists of five people, who did not know each other before the project began. They are:

- **Rebecca**—A 27-year-old marketing manager for a large, high-end Italian fashion company. Rebecca is a white female of Italian descent who was born and raised in New York City. Rebecca earned her bachelor's degree in business at the University of Virginia's McIntire Business School when she was 22. She speaks English, Italian, and Spanish fluently. She speaks a little German and Japanese as well. Rebecca is single. Her job involves analyzing worldwide markets and traveling to the 136 stores around the world that carry her company's clothes. She hopes the EMBA from BSU will help her to be promoted to an executive position.

- **Aran**—The 52-year-old founder and CEO of an Egyptian management consulting firm. His firm employs 12 people who consult with local companies on issues involving information systems. Aran is an Egyptian male who is a fairly devout Muslim. He earned his business degree 25 years ago at the American University in Cairo. He speaks English and Arabic fluently. Aran is married with two adult children. He is attending BSU's program because he wants to retire from his consulting firm and become an in-house IS consultant to a large multinational firm.

- **Katie**—A 30-year-old financial analyst at a large Wall Street firm. At present, Katie's job requires little travel, but she works long hours as a financial analyst. Katie is an American female who does not consider herself to have any strong ethnic roots. She earned her business degree two years ago from New York University. Before going to college, she worked as a bank teller on Long Island. She was concerned about her lack of progress and went back to college to get a degree. She now wants to further her education to open up even more opportunities. Katie speaks only English. She is married but has no children. However, she cares for her elderly mother, who lives nearby in New Jersey.

- **Cameron**—A 23-year-old Internet entrepreneur who heads his own small but successful company. He is the youngest student BSU has ever accepted. He was something of a child prodigy, graduating from Georgia Tech at the age of 19 with a degree in computer science. Cameron is a single, African American male who has lived all over the United States. His company is based in Austin, Texas. He speaks only English. He is attending BSU's program because, though confident of his technical expertise, he would like to learn more about business, since he is planning to expand his company.

- **Pranarisha**—A 31-year-old manager for a nongovernmental organization (NGO) that provides support to poverty-stricken areas of Thailand. Pranarisha's job is to coordinate efforts from a variety of worldwide charitable organizations. She speaks four languages fluently; however, she is not fluent in English. She graduated from the most prestigious university in Thailand. She is married with a four-year-old son and is a devout Buddhist. She is attending BSU's program at the request of her organization, so she can help to make the organization more efficient.

The A-Team was doomed almost as soon as the project began. The team's first task was to decide how roles would be allocated to individuals on the team.

Aran: Before we begin, we need to decide what everyone will be doing on this project, how we will divide and coordinate the work. Since I have the most experience, I should serve in the executive function. I'll assign and oversee everyone's work. I will also give the presentation at the end of the project, since I know how to talk to important people. Cameron will be in charge of analyzing the financial feasibility of our project, developing the marketing plan, and evaluating the technical operations. The girls will assist him in . . .

Rebecca (Interrupting): Hold on a minute! First, we are not girls! Second, Cameron, Katie, and I decided last night over beers at happy hour that I should handle the marketing plan, Cameron the technical aspects, and Katie the financial aspects. You can serve as the coordinator, since you're not going to be attending class on campus—you can keep track of everything when we submit electronic reports.

Cameron: Yeah—your role would be to just make sure everyone is on the same page, but we'd individually decide how to conduct our own projects.

Aran: This team needs a leader and I . . .

Cameron and Katie (in unison): Who says?

Rebecca: We're all responsible adults, and since the three of us are most accustomed to the western way of doing business—which as we all know focuses on *individual empowerment*—then we'll get the most out of the project doing it our way.

Aran: You are all young and inexperienced. What do you know about the business world?

Katie: I know a lot more about finance than you.

Rebecca: Get with the twenty-first century. Just because we're women doesn't mean . . .

Cameron: He isn't just ragging on women. He's ragging on me, too.

Katie: Yeah, but at least he gave you a real job. You're a guy—"Boy Wonder."

Cameron: What kind of crack was that? After all, you two didn't start your own company. You're a number cruncher, and Rebecca sells dresses, and . . .

Rebecca: I think we need to stop this right now, and the four of us need to decide once and for all who is doing what!

Katie: Four of us? Wasn't our team supposed to have five people? Where's that other woman? The one from Vietnam? Parisa? Prana? Whatever her name is?

At this point, Professor Bowell, the group's advisor, walks in and tells them that the team is to be disbanded. Pranarisha had walked out of the group meeting (without anyone noticing) and informed Dr. Bowell that she just couldn't take it any longer. She had come here to learn how to run an organization more efficiently and how to work with businesspeople. However, she was so disheartened by the way the group was acting, she was going to quit the program. This was the first time in over 10 years that Dr. Bowell had heard of anyone quitting the program in the first week because of the behavior of the members of her team. The advisor just didn't see any way that this group of individuals could get their act together to become a functioning team.

Discussion Questions

1. What happened with the A-Team? Why did the group process break down? What dimensions of diversity were responsible for the conflict?

2. Describe which barriers to effectively managing diversity were present in this situation.

3. What could have been done to manage the group process better?

Team Exercise

What Is It Like to Be Different?

One reason people have a difficult time dealing with diversity in others or understanding why it is important to value and respect diversity is that most people spend most of their lives in environments where everyone is similar to them on important dimensions. Many people have seldom been in a situation in which they felt they didn't belong or didn't know the "rules." The purpose of this exercise is to have you experience such a situation and open up a dialogue with others about what it feels like to be different and what you can personally learn from this experience to become better at managing diversity in the future.

Step 1: Choose an event that you would not normally attend and at which you will likely be in the minority on some important dimension. Attend the event.

- You can go with a friend who would normally attend the event, but not one that will also be in a minority.
- Make sure you pick a place where you will be safe and where you are sure you will be welcomed, or at least tolerated. You may want to check with your instructor about your choice.
- Do not call particular attention to yourself. Just observe what is going on and how you feel.

Some of you may find it easy to have a minority experience, since you are a minority group member in your everyday life. Others may have a more difficult time. Here are some examples of events to consider attending:

- A religious service for a religion totally different from your own.
- A sorority or fraternity party where the race of members is mostly different from your own.
- A political rally where the politics are different from your own.

Step 2: After attending the event, write down your answers to the following questions:

1. How did you feel being in a minority situation? Did different aspects of your self-identity become salient? Do you think others who are in minority situations feel as you did?
2. What did you learn about the group you visited? Do you feel differently about this group now?
3. What did people do that made you feel welcome? What did people do that made you feel self-conscious?
4. Could you be an effective team member in this group? How would your differences with group members impact on your ability to function in this group?
5. What did you learn about managing diversity from this exercise?

Step 3: Discuss the results of the exercise in a group as assigned by the Instructor.

Endnotes

1. Bamattre, W. (former LAFD Fire Chief), as reported in Richardson, L. 2006. Audit faults fire department. *Los Angeles Times,* January 27, B.4.
2. See, for example, Ball, P., Monaco, G., Schmeling, J., Schartz, H., Blanck, P. 2005. Disability as diversity in *Fortune* 100 companies. *Behavioral Sciences and Law,* 23: 97–121; Jolna, K.A. 2003. Beyond race and gender? Doctoral Dissertation. Atlanta, GA: Emory University; Society of Human Resources Management. 1997. *SHRM survey of diversity of programs.* Alexandria, VA: Society for Human Resources Management.
3. Campbell, T. 2003. Diversity in depth. *HRMagazine,* 48(3): 152.
4. Johnson, K. 2007. Kevin Johnson, Diversity Executive Workgroup Sponsor, on executive commitment. At http://www.microsoft.com/about/diversity/exec.mspx.
5. Schneider, B., Goldstein, H.W., & Smith, D.B. 1995. The ASA framework: An update. *Personnel Psychology,* 48: 747–773.
6. Ely, R.J., & Thomas, D.A. 2001. Cultural diversity at work: The effects of diversity perspectives on work group processes and outcomes. *Administrative Science Quarterly,* 46: 229–274.
7. See, for example, Kochan, T., Bezrukova, K., Ely, R., Jackson, S., Joshi, S., Jehn, K., Leonard, J., Levine, D., & Thomas, D. 2003. The effects of diversity on business performance: Report of the diversity research network. *Human Resource Management,* 42: 3–21.
8. For additional commentary on the various dimensions, see the following: Ball, C., & Haque, A. 2003. Diversity in religious practice: Implications of Islamic values in the public

workplace. *Public Personnel Management,* 32: 315–328; Bantel, K.A., & Jackson, S.E. 1989. Top management and innovations in banking: Does the composition of the top team make a difference? *Strategic Management Journal,* 10: 107–124; Barsade, S.G., Ward, A.J., Turner, J.D.F., & Sonnenfeld, J.A. 2000. To your heart's content: A model of affective diversity in top management teams. *Administrative Science Quarterly,* 45: 802–837; Cummings, J.N. 2004. Work groups, structural diversity, and knowledge sharing in a global organization. *Management Science,* 50: 352–365; Ely, R.J., & Thomas, D.A. 2001. Cultural diversity at work: The effects of diversity perspectives on work group processes and outcomes. *Administrative Science Quarterly,* 46: 229–274; Kochan, Bezrukova, Ely, Jackson, Joshi, Jehn, Leonard, Levine, & Thomas, The effects of diversity on business performance; Richard, O.C., Ford, D., & Ismail, K. 2006. Exploring the performance effects of visible attribute diversity: The moderating role of span of control and organizational life cycle. *International Journal of Human Resource Management,* 17: 2091–2109.

9. Konrad, A.M. 2003. Special issue introduction: Defining the domain of workplace diversity scholarship. *Group and Organization Management,* 28: 4–18.

10. Williams, K.Y., & O'Reilly, C.A. 1998. Demography and diversity in organizations: A review of 40 years of research. In L.L. Cummings & B.M. Staw (Eds.), *Research in Organizational Behavior,* 20: 77–140. Greenwich, CT: JAI Press, p. 81.

11. Ibid.

12. See, for example, Jehn, K.A., Northcraft, G.B., & Neale, M.A. Why differences make a difference: A field study of diversity, conflict, and performance in groups. *Administrative Science Quarterly,* 44: 741–763.

13. Kanter, R.M. 1977. *Men and women of the corporation.* New York: Basic Books.

14. Texas Instruments. 2007. Diversity overview. At http://www.ti.com/corp/docs/company/citizen/diversity/index.shtml.

15. Microsoft. 2007. Message from Claudette Whiting. At http://www.microsoft.com/about/diversity/fromoffice.mspx?pf=true.

16. Bank of America. 2007. Fact Sheets. At http://careers.bankofamerica.com/learnmore/factsheets.asp.

17. United States Department of Labor. 2002. Facts on Executive Order 11246—Affirmative Action. At www.dol.gov/esa/regs/compliance/ofccp/aa.htm.

18. Thomas, R.R., Jr. 1992. Managing diversity: A conceptual framework. In S.E. Jackson & Associates (Eds.), *Diversity in the workplace.* New York: Guilford Press, pp. 306–317.

19. Cox, T.H., Jr. 1993. *Cultural diversity in organizations: Theory, research, and practice.* San Francisco, CA: Berrett-Koehler Publishers.

20. Gilbert, J.A., & Ivancevich, J.M. 2000. Valuing diversity: A tale of two organizations. *Academy of Management Review,* 14: 93–106.

21. Farh, J.L., Dobbins, G.H., & Cheng, B. 1991. Cultural relativity in action: A comparison of self-ratings made by Chinese and U.S. workers. *Personnel Psychology,* 44: 129–147.

22. Cox, *Cultural diversity in organizations.*

23. See, for example, Campbell, T. 2003. Diversity in depth. *HRMagazine,* 48(3): 152.

24. Farouky, J. 2007. The many faces of Europe. *Time International,* 169 (9): 16–20.

25. United States Department of Labor. 2000. Working in the 21st century. At http://www.bls.gov/opub/home.htm.

26. United States Equal Employment Opportunity Commission. 2003. Occupational employment in private industry by race/ethnic group/sex, and by industry. At http://www.eeoc.gov/stats/jobpat/2003/national.html.

27. United States Department of Labor, Working in the 21st century.

28. Ibid.

29. Ibid.

30. Bureau of Labor Statistics. 2005. Economic and employment projections. At http://www.bls.gov/news.release/ecopro.toc.htm.

31. Ibid.

32. See, for example, Jackson, S.E., & Alvarez, E.B. 1992. Working through diversity as a strategic imperative. In S.E. Jackson & Associates (Eds.), *Diversity in the workplace,* pp. 13–29.

33. U.S. Department of Commerce. 2007. FT900: U.S. International trade in goods and services. At http://www.census. gov/foreign-trade/Press-Release/current_press_release/press.html#current.

34. Ibid.

35. Hitt, M.A., Ireland, D.I., & Hoskisson. 2007. *Strategic management: Competitiveness and globalization* (7th ed.). Stamford, CT: Thompson Learning.

36. Whole Foods Market. 2007. Our core values. At http://www.wholefoodsmarket.com/company/corevalues.html.

37. Cox, T.H., & Blake, S. 1991. Managing cultural diversity: Implications for organizational competitiveness. *Academy of Management Executive,* 5(3) 45–56; Jackson & Alvarez, Working through diversity as a strategic imperative.

38. Eisenberger, R., Huntington, R., Hutchison, S., & Sowa, D. 1986. Perceived organizational support. *Journal of Applied Psychology,* 71: 500–507; Eisenberger, R., Fasolo, P., & Davis-LaMastro, V. 1990. Perceived organizational support and employee diligence, commitment, and innovation. *Journal of Applied Psychology,* 75: 51–59.

39. Cox, *Cultural diversity in organizations.*

40. Hicks-Clarke, D., & Iles, P. 2000. Climate for diversity and its effects on career and organizational perceptions. *Personnel Review,* 29: 324–347.

41. For research on these outcomes, see: Colquitt, J.A., Conlon, D.E., Wesson, M.J., Porter, C.O.L.H., & Ng, K.Y. 2001. Justice at the millennium: A meta-analytic review of 25 years of organizational justice research. *Journal of Applied Psychology.* 86: 425–445; Goldman, B.M. 2001. Toward an understanding of employment discrimination claiming by terminated workers: Integration of organizational justice and social information processing theories. *Personnel Psychology,* 54: 361–386; Goldman, B.M. 2003. The application of referent cognitions theory to legal-claiming by terminated workers: The role of organizational justice and anger. *Journal of Management,* 29: 705–728; Skarlicki, D.P., & Folger, R. 2003. Broadening our understanding of organizational retaliatory behavior. In R.W. Griffin & A.M. O'Leary-Kelly (Eds.), *The darkside of organizational behavior.* San Francisco, CA: Jossey-Bass, pp. 373–402.

42. Kossek, E.E., & Zonia, S.C. 1993. Assessing diversity climate: A field-study of reactions to employer efforts to promote diversity. *Journal of Organizational Behavior,* 14: 61–81.

43. Mollica, K.A. 2003. The influence of diversity context on white men's and racial minorities' reactions to disproportionate group harm. *Journal of Social Psychology,* 143: 415–431.

44. Jehn, Northcraft, & Neale, Why differences make a difference: A field study of diversity, conflict, and performance in groups.

45. Bantel, K.A., & Jackson, S.E. 1989. Top management and innovations in banking: Does the composition of the top team make a difference? *Strategic Management Journal,* 10: 107–124; Jackson, S.E. (1992). Consequences of group composition for the interpersonal dynamics of strategic issue processing. *Advances in Strategic Management,* 8: 345–382.

46. For research related to these dimensions, see: Hambrick, D.C., Cho, S.T., & Chen, M.J. 1996. The influence of top management team heterogeneity on firm's competitive moves. *Administrative Science Quarterly,* 41: 659–684; Jackson, S.E., May, K., & Whitney, K. 1995. Diversity in decision making teams. In R.A. Guzzo & E. Salas (Eds.), *Team effectiveness and decision making in organizations.* San Francisco, CA: Jossey-Bass, pp. 204–261; Jehn, Northcraft, & Neale, Why differences make such a difference: A field study of diversity, conflict, and performance in groups; Wood, W. 1987. Meta-analysis of sex differences in group performance. *Psychological Bulletin,* 102: 53–71; Zajac, E.J., Golden, B.R., & Shortell, S.M. 1991. New organizational forms for enhancing innovation: The case of internal corporate joint ventures. *Management Science,* 37: 170–184.

47. Grensing-Phophal, L. 2002. Reaching for diversity: What minority workers hope to get from diversity programs is what all employees want in the workplace. *HRMagazine,* 47 (5): 52–56.

48. Williams & O'Reilly, Demography and diversity in organizations.

49. Van Knippenberg, D., & Schippers, M.C. 2007. Work group diversity. *Annual Review of Psychology,* 58: 515–541.

50. See, for example, Li, J.T., & Hambrick, D.C. 2005. Factional groups: A new vantage on demographic faultlines, conflict, and disintegration in work teams. *Academy of Management Journal,* 48: 794–813; Molleman, E. Diversity in demographic characteristics, abilities and personality traits: Do faultlines affect team functioning? *Group Decision and Negotiation,* 14: 173–193; Rico, R., Molleman, E., Sanchez-Manzanares, M., & Van der Vegt, G.S. 2007. The effects of diversity faultlines and team task autonomy on decision quality and social integration. *Journal of Management,* 33: 111–132; Sawyer, J.E., Houlette, M.A., & Yeagley, E.L. 2006. Decision performance and diversity structure: Comparing faultlines in convergent, crosscut, and racially homogeneous groups. *Organizational Behavior and Human Decision Processes,* 99: 1–15.

51. Williams & O'Reilly, Demography and diversity in organizations.

52. See, for example, Richard, O.C., Kochan, T.A., & McMillan-Capehart. 2002. The impact of visible diversity on organizational effectiveness: Disclosing the contents in Pandora's black box. *Journal of Business and Management,* 8: 265–291; Pelled, L.H. 1996. Demographic diversity, conflict, and work group outcomes: An intervening process theory. *Organization Science,* 7: 615–631.

53. Williams & O'Reilly, Demography and diversity in organizations.

54. Hackman, J.R. 2002. *Leading teams: Setting the stage for great performances.* Boston, MA: Harvard Business School Press.

55. Richard, Kochan, & McMillan-Capehart, The impact of visible diversity on organizational effectiveness.

56. Ibid.

57. Cox, *Cultural diversity in organizations;* Cox & Blake, Managing cultural diversity.

58. Richard, O.C. 2000. Racial diversity, business strategy, and firm performance: A resource based view. *Academy of Management Journal,* 43: 164–177.

59. Kochan, T., Bezrukova, K., Ely, R., Jackson, S., Joshi, A., Jehn, K. Leonard, J., Levine, D., & Thomas, D. 2003. The effects of diversity on business performance: Report of the Diversity Research Network. *Human Resource Management,* 42: 3–21.

60. See, for example, Fletcher, A.A. 2000. Business and race: Only halfway there. *Fortune,* 141 (5): 76–77.

61. See, for example, Westphal, J., & Zajac, E. 1997. Defections from the inner circle: Social exchange, reciprocity and the diffusion of board independence in U.S. corporations. *Administrative Science Quarterly,* 42: 161–183.

62. Sellers, P. 2004. By the numbers: Women and profits. *Fortune,* at http://www.fortune.com/fortune/subs/article/0,15114,582783,00.html.

63. Siciliano, J.I. 1996. The relationship of board member diversity to organizational performance. *Journal of Business Ethics,* 15: 1313–1320.

64. Hillman, A.J., Cannella, A.A., Jr., & Harris, I.C. 2002. Women and racial minorities in the boardroom: How do directors differ? *Journal of Management,* 28: 747–763.

65. Ibid.

66. Bantel, & Jackson, Top management and innovations in banking; Hambrick, Cho, & Chen, The influence of top management team heterogeneity on firm's competitive moves.

67. Wright, P., Ferris, S.P., & Kroll, M. 1995. Competitiveness through management of diversity: Effects on stock price evaluation. *Academy of Management Journal,* 38: 272–287.

68. Cowell, A. 2005. What Britain can tell France about rioters. *The New York Times,* November 20, 4.4.

69. Dovidio, J.F., Gaertner, S.L., Kawakami, K., & Hodson, G. 2002. Why can't we just get along? Interpersonal biases and interracial distrust. *Cultural Diversity and Ethnic Minority Psychology,* 8: 88–102.

70. Bobo, L.D. 2001. Racial attitudes and relations at the close of the twentieth century. In N.J. Smelser, W.J. Wilson, & F. Mitchell (Eds.), *Racial trends and their consequences (Vol. 1).* Washington, DC: National Academic Press, pp. 264–301.

71. McConahay, J.B. 1986. Modern racism, ambivalence, and the modern racism scale. In J.F. Dovidio & S.L. Gaertner (Eds.), *Prejudice, discrimination, and racism.* Orlando, FL: Academic Press, pp. 91–125.

72. Dovidio, J.F., & Gaertner, S.L. 2000. Aversive racism and selection decisions: 1989 and 1999. *Psychological Science,* 11: 319–323

73. For example research, see: Cleveland, J.N., Vescio, T.K., & Barnes-Farrell, J.L. 2005. Gender discrimination in organizations. In R.L. Dipboye, & A. Colella (Eds.), *Discrimination at work: The psychological and organizational bases.* Mahwah, NJ: Lawrence Erlbaum; Colella, A., & Varma, A. 2001. The impact of subordinate disability on leader-member exchange dynamics. *Academy of Management Journal,* 44: 304–315; Dovidio, J.F., Gaertner, S.L., Anastasio, P.A., & Sanitaso, R. 1992. Cognitive and motivational bases of bias: The implications of aversive racism for attitudes towards Hispanics. In S. Knouse, P. Rosenfeld, & A. Culbertson (Eds.). *Hispanics in the workplace.* Newbury Park, CA: Sage, pp. 75–106; Hebl, M.R., Bigazzi Foster, J., & Dovidio, J.F. 2002. Formal and interpersonal discrimination: A field study of bias toward

homosexual applicants. *Personality and Social Psychology Bulletin,* 28: 815–825.

74. R.L. Dipboye & A. Colella 2005. The dilemmas of workplace discrimination. In R.L. Dipboye & A. Colella (Eds.), *Discrimination at work: The psychological and organizational bases.* Mahwah, NJ: Lawrence Erlbaum. pp. 425–462.

75. Cox, *Cultural diversity in organizations.*

76. Crocker, J., Fiske, S.T., & Taylor, S.E. 1984. Schematic bases of belief change. In J.R. Eiser (Ed.), *Attitudinal judgment.* New York: Springer-Verlag, pp. 197–226; Weber, R., & Crocker, J. 1983. Cognitive processes in the revision of stereotypic beliefs. *Journal of Personality and Social Psychology,* 45: 961–977.

77. von Heppel, W., Sekaquaptewa, D., & Vargas, P. 1995. On the role of encoding processes in stereotype maintenance. In M.P. Zanna (Ed.), *Advances in experimental social psychology*, Vol. 27. San Diego, CA: Academic Press, pp. 177–254.

78. Fiske, S.T. 1998. Stereotyping, prejudice, and discrimination. In D.T. Gilbert, S.T. Fiske, & G. Lindzey (Eds.), *The handbook of social psychology, Vol. 2* (4th ed.). New York: McGraw-Hill, pp. 357–411.

79. Cox, *Cultural diversity in organizations.*

80. Helft, M. 2007. Xerox's strategy pays off with a new search venture. *The New York Times,* February 9, C.3; Maney, K. 2006. Mulcahy traces steps of Xerox's comeback. *USA Today,* September 21, 4B.

81. Ireland, R.D., Hoskisson, R.E., & Hitt, M.A. 2006. *Understanding business strategy.* Mason, OH: South-western Publishing; Stone, B. 2007. eBay beats the estimates for 4th-quarter earnings. *New York Times,* January 25, C.3; Vara, V. 2007. eBay's strong earnings, outlook help to quiet critics, for now. *Wall Street Journal,* January 25, A.3.

82. Brewer, M.B., & Miller, N. 1984. Beyond the contact hypothesis: Theoretical perspectives on desegregation. In N. Miller & M.B. Brewer (Eds.), *Groups in contact.* San Diego, CA: Academic Press, pp. 281–302; Tajfel, H. 1978. *Differentiation between social groups: Studies in the social psychology of intergroup relations.* San Diego, CA: Academic Press; Ashforth, B., & Mael, F. 1989. Social identity theory and the organization. *Academy of Management Review,* 14: 20–39.

83. Abrams, D., & Hogg, M.A. 1990. An introductory to the social identity approach. In D. Abrams & M.A. Hogg (Eds.), *Social identity theory: Constructive and critical advances.* New York: Springer-Verlag, pp. 1–9.

84. Cox, *Cultural diversity in organizations.*

85. McGuire, W.J., McGuire, C.V., Child, P., & Fujioka, T. 1978. Salience of ethnicity in the spontaneous self-concept as a function of one's ethnic distinctiveness in the social environment. *Journal of Personality and Social Psychology,* 36: 511–520.

86. Cox, *Cultural diversity in organizations.*

87. Ely, R.J. 1994. The effects of organizational demographics and social identity on relationships among professional women. *Administrative Science Quarterly,* 39: 203–239.

88. Cited in Slay, H.S. 2003. Spanning two worlds: Social identity and emergent African American leaders. *Journal of Leadership and Organizational Studies,* 9: 56–66.

89. Cox, *Cultural diversity in organizations.*

90. Abrams & Hogg, An introductory to the social identity approach.

91. Turner, J.C. 1975. Social comparison and social identity: Some prospects for intergroup behavior. *European Journal of Social Psychology,* 5: 5–34.

92. Hogg, M.A., & Terry, D.J. 2000. Social identity and self-categorization processes in organizational contexts. *Academy of Management Review,* 25: 121–140.

93. Ibid.

94. French, J.R.P., & Raven, B. 1959. The bases of social power. In D. Cartwright (Ed.), *Social power.* Ann Arbor: University of Michigan, Institute for Social Research, pp. 150–167; Pfeffer, J., & Salancik, G.R. 1978. *The external control of organizations: A resource dependence view.* New York: Harper and Row.

95. Sidananius, J., & Pratto, F. 1999. *Social dominance.* Cambridge, UK: Cambridge University Press.

96. Ibid.

97. Kalkhoff, W., & Barnum, C. 2000. The effects of status-organizing and social identity processes on patterns of social influence. *Social Psychology Quarterly,* 63: 95–115.

98. Konard, A.M. 2003. Special issue introduction: Defining the domain of workplace diversity scholarship. *Group and Organizational Management,* 28: 4–18.

99. Winters, M.F. 2003. Globalization presents both opportunities and challenges for diversity. At http://search.shrm.org/search?q= cache:8b6YiQjDjFoJ:www.shrm.org/diversity/library_published/ nonIC/CMS_012382.asp+++globalization+challenges+ diversity&access=p&output=xml_no_dtd&ie=UTF-8&lr=& client=shrm_frontend&num=10&site=&proxystylesheet =shrm_frontend&oe=ISO-8859-1.

100. Ibid.

101. For additional details, see Deogun, N. Coke was told in '95 of need for diversity. *Wall Street Journal,* May 20, A.3; McKay, B. 2000. Coke settles bias suit for $192.5 million. *Wall Street Journal,* November 17, A.3.

102. United States Equal Employment Opportunity Commission, Occupational employment in private industry by race/ethnic group/sex, and by industry.

103. Kanter, *Men and women of the corporation.*

104. U.S. Department of Commerce and Vice President Al Gore's National Partnership for Reinventing Government Benchmarking Study. 1998. Best practices in achieving workplace diversity. Washington, DC: U.S. Department of Commerce.

105. Starbucks. 2007. Starbucks mission statement. At http://www. starbucks.com/aboutus/environment.asp.

106. Ford Motor Company. 2007. Valuing diversity. At http://www. mycareer.ford.com/ONTHETEAM.ASP?CID=15.

107. Jayne, M.E.A., & Dipboye, R.L. 2004. Leveraging diversity to improve business performance: Research findings and recommendations for organizations. *Human Resource Management,* 43: 409–424.

108. Cox, T.H. 2001. *Creating the multicultural organization: A strategy for capturing the power of diversity.* San Francisco: Jossey-Bass.

3

ORGANIZATIONAL BEHAVIOR IN A GLOBAL CONTEXT

In 1948, brothers Richard and Maurice McDonald opened the first McDonald's restaurant in San Bernardino, California. Over the next decade, hundreds of McDonald's restaurants were built alongside the new interstate highway systems in the United States. McDonald's was one of the first restaurants to make fast food available to the newly mobile American population. In 1967, McDonald's decided to go international and opened its first restaurant outside the United States in Richmond, British Columbia.

Agence France Presse/Getty Images

EXPLORING BEHAVIOR IN ACTION
McDonald's Thinks Globally and Acts Locally

Today there are over 31,000 McDonald's restaurants in almost 120 countries. It is interesting to learn how McDonald's adapted to the cultural differences in the various international locations of its restaurants.

Trying to maintain a global brand is difficult because of the different cultural expectations experienced across different countries. It is important to maintain a positive reputation for the company and the quality of its products. So, McDonald's needed to build a global reputation of the quality and efficiency of its products and service

while simultaneously meeting consumer expectations across different cultures. McDonald's has developed and maintained a competitive advantage because the company has taken steps to know, understand, and service customer needs without compromising its core strengths (fast, easy, clean meals for families to enjoy). An example of how McDonald's adapted was when McDonald's dispensed with its most prominent ingredient (beef) in order to respect and serve its Indian customers. Many Indians do not eat beef or any meat at all, so McDonald's

managers knew it was necessary to adapt the company's offering while maintaining its core brand values. The menu has evolved and local creations are made, like the McPuff and the McVeggie. Today, 70 percent of the menu in India has been altered to meet the customer needs and desires. In Europe, McDonald's introduced a menu featuring salads, fruit, and the option of substituting carrots for Happy Meals for French fries, a menu modification made to appeal to health-conscious consumers. Recently, these same menu items were offered in the

United States as well. So, while the menu may be different in some ways, the McDonald's experience around the world is consistent by offering quality, great service, cleanliness, and value.

It is equally important to develop a culturally appropriate strategy for a new international location. Innovation is successful when it is culturally appropriate. In Brazil, McDonald's changed its marketing tactics and now caters to the afternoon meal rather than to a lunch meal. This change was made because Brazilians prefer their main meal at midday, often eating at a leisurely pace with business associates. Another marketing initiative was to cater to Brazilians on Sunday. McDonald's identified that many Brazilians employed cooks for their homes but most of these cooks had Sunday off. So McDonald's realigned its ads and began marketing "enjoying McDonald's on the cook's day off." In doing so, McDonald's found a niche for Sunday evening meals in Brazil.

There are many abroad who are concerned about having companies like McDonald's expand their restaurants globally. Some cultural connoisseurs feel that the world is becoming too Americanized and McDonald's is one of the largest culprits. In addition, they are fearful that western food chains are undermining local cuisine. There is no doubt that McDonald's does provide some common menu items across its many restaurants: A Big Mac is a Big Mac no mater where you are. But McDonald's has done more to accommodate cultural differences in its restaurants than many other companies. In Berlin, patrons can enjoy a beer with their cheeseburgers and fries. In Rome, the floor on which locals and tourists order and then rest their feet while dining is cobble-stoned. Replicas of Roman statues, walls made of Italian marble, and frescoes of city views of Rome enhance the dining atmosphere. Customers also eat fresh Italian gelato, as opposed to ordinary ice cream. McDonald's is regularly adapting its restaurants and marketing tactics to reflect cultural, architectural, and regional differences within each country. Even in the United States, McDonald's is adapting locally. In Maine, where there are many fresh seafood restaurants, McDonald's now offers lobster rolls. Even in Michigan, customers can purchase Halal McNuggets, chicken that is processed under strict religious supervision in order to cater to the 150,000 Muslims who live in the Detroit area. The McDonald's Corporation will continue to incorporate local culture and, at the same time, maintain core values of providing "fast, clean, and easy meals for families to enjoy together." Thus McDonald's is an example of a company that thinks globally and acts locally.

Sources: Nini Bhan and Brad Nemer, "Brand Magic in India," *BusinessWeek,* May 8, 2006, www.businessweek.com; Roy Barnes, "Why McDonald's Enhances Travel and Cultural Experiences," Associated Content, 2007, www.associatedcontent. com; The Corporation, Online Extra: "McDonald's: The Rise and Stall," *BusinessWeek,* Mar. 3, 2003, www.businessweek. com; Conrad P. Kottak, 2003, McDonald's in Brazil: Culturally Appropriate Marketing, *Ethnographic Solutions,* www.ethnographic-solutions. com; David Kiley, "Brands Abroad Under Fire," *BusinessWeek,* Jan. 5, 2005, www.businessweek.com; Andy Greenberg, "Is China More Globalized Than the U.S.?," *NYU Journalism,* Nov. 24, 2006, www.journalism.nyu.edu; Beth Carney, 2005, "In Europe, the Fat Is in the Fire," *BusinessWeek,* Feb. 8, 2005, www.businessweek.com.

The Strategic Importance of Organizational Behavior in a Global Context

The *Exploring Behavior in Action* discussion of McDonald's shows us how one firm operates on the world stage and emphasizes the importance of cross-cultural knowledge and skills. Because of substantial competition and differing cultural expectations across the many countries in which McDonald's has restaurants, the company has strong needs for efficiency and flexibility in resource use. McDonald's has developed a global reputation for providing clean restaurants and fast and easy meals for value-conscious families. From these strategic locations, the firm develops, produces, sells, and supports its products for the world marketplace. To be successful, however, this firm must be especially attentive to local cultural values and desired foods. McDonald's always provides some consistent products on its menu regardless of location (e.g., the Big Mac) but it also provides menu items adapted to the local cultural tastes (such as vegetable meals in India and gelato in Italy). Obviously, McDonald's has trained its managers to be sensitive to local culture and yet to take advantage of global efficiencies. Actions such as those used by McDonald's to take advantage of the different international markets opened due to globalization have led to higher overall firm performance.[1]

To create cost advantages, to pursue growth, or to spread risk across different markets, many firms have adopted strategies that call for investment in foreign countries. Such involvement can take many forms, including the creation of company-owned manufacturing or back-office facilities, company-owned marketing and sales units, and/or alliances with companies based in a particular foreign country. In all cases, effectively handling cross-country cultural differences is crucial. Executing competitive strategies would be impossible without an understanding of how these differences affect day-to-day relationships among associates and managers, as well as relationships with external parties (such as suppliers and customers).

One of the most famous examples of a corporate failure to fully appreciate the importance of cultural differences is Walt Disney Company's attempt to execute a strategy involving efficient operations and exceptional customer service in its theme park just outside Paris.[2] American leaders of the Euro Disney project failed to understand some European workplace norms that produced a less friendly approach to guests in the park. Disney leaders also failed to anticipate the uproar over grooming and dress requirements for associates, including "appropriate undergarments," and they did not recognize the potential for conflict between individuals of different nationalities. One of the 1,000 associates and lower-level managers who departed in the first nine weeks of Euro Disney's operation commented, "I don't think [non-European supervisors] realized what Europeans were like." Concerning the park, a critic expressed the feelings of the French elite: "A horror made of cardboard, plastic, and appalling colors; a construction of hardened chewing gum and idiotic folklore taken straight out of comic books written for obese Americans."[3] Failure to fully appreciate and respond to cultural differences helped to create a disastrous early period for Euro Disney. Its performance suffered, but having learned several hard lessons, the company has improved its practices in the park and increased its performance as well.

Because of the importance of globalization and the related diversity and ethical issues it poses, we present examples and applications involving firms operating in multiple countries throughout the book. In this chapter, we discuss these issues in depth. We open the chapter with a discussion of globalization, addressing the opportunities and challenges that globalization has for nations and firms. Next, we discuss the ways in which associates and managers can deal with international issues and the pitfalls to avoid in these activities. A discussion of high-involvement management follows, with a focus on how this management approach can be tailored to different countries or regions of the world. Finally, we describe ethical issues frequently confronted by firms with substantial international involvement.

KNOWLEDGE OBJECTIVES

After reading this chapter, you should be able to:

1. Define *globalization* and discuss the forces that influence this phenomenon.

2. Discuss three types of international involvement by associates and managers and describe problems that can arise with each.

3. Explain how international involvement by associates and managers varies across firms.

4. Describe high-involvement management in the international arena, emphasizing the adaptation of this management approach to different cultures.

5. Identify and explain the key ethical issues in international business.

Forces of Globalization

In a global economy, products, services, people, technologies, and financial capital move relatively freely across national borders.[4] Tariffs, currency laws, travel restrictions, immigration restrictions, and other barriers to these international flows become less difficult to manage. Essentially, a global economy provides firms with a unified world market in which to sell products and services, as well as a unified world market for acquiring the resources needed to create those products and services.

Globalization, the trend toward a more global economy, has increased substantially since 1980. Direct foreign investment by firms based in developed countries increased from an average of 6.4 percent of home-country gross domestic product (GDP) in 1980 to an average of 19.0 percent of GDP in 1999.[5] Direct foreign investment made in developed countries, mostly by firms based in other developed countries, increased from 4.7 percent of receiving-country GDP in 1980 to 14.5 percent of GDP in 1999. While several developed countries suffered a recession early in the twenty-first century, there were healthy increases in direct foreign investments made by them and by others in their countries in the period of 2000–2005.[6] These investments represent increased interest in producing goods and services in foreign countries. Exporting goods and services into other countries increased 69 percent from 1980 to 1990 and 83 percent from 1990 to 2000. And, the growth continued as exports of goods and services continued to increase at an average rate of 10 percent per year for the period of 2000–2005.[7] Interestingly, in recent years, significant amounts of foreign investment has been focused on emerging-economy countries such as China and India. Furthermore, these emerging economies have been making major foreign investments in other countries, exceeding $1 trillion in 2004.[8] The results of globalization are evident in the fact that major multinational firms obtain almost 55 percent of their sales from outside their home country and almost 50 percent of their assets and associates reside outside of their home country.[9] Clearly, goods and services flowed across borders in record amounts at the end of the twentieth century and early in the twenty-first century, with firms such as Toyota leading the way.

Many national leaders promote globalization as a means for economic growth inside their countries as well as in the world as a whole. Most economists agree that a highly global economy would be beneficial for most countries. Goods, services, and the resources needed to produce them freely flowing across borders likely would reduce the costs of doing business, resulting in economic stimulation.[10] It has been estimated that genuine free trade in manufactured goods among the United States, Europe, and Japan (that is, trade with no tariffs) would result in a 5 to 10 percent annual increase in the economic output of these three areas. Genuine free trade in services would increase economic output by an additional 15 to 20 percent.[11]

Despite the potential economic benefits, officials in a number of nations have expressed concerns about globalization's long-term effects on societal culture.[12] **Culture** involves shared values and taken-for-granted assumptions about how to act and think.[13] Many fear that unique cultures around the world will disappear over time if the world becomes one unified market for goods and services. They argue that cultural distinctiveness—indeed what makes a country special—will disappear as similar products and services are sold worldwide.[14] Individuals with these concerns took notice when a Taiwanese Little League baseball team playing in the

globalization
The trend toward a unified global economy where national borders mean relatively little.

culture
Shared values and taken-for-granted assumptions that govern acceptable behavior and thought patterns in a country and that give a country much of its uniqueness.

United States was comforted by a McDonald's restaurant because it reminded them of home.[15] In developing nations, there are also concerns over labor exploitation and natural resource depletion. In wealthy nations, there are concerns over the export of jobs to low-wage countries and the possibility that wealthy nations ultimately will need to lower their wage structures in order to compete in a truly global economy.[16]

From the perspective of an individual company, there are many reasons to consider substantial international involvement (see Exhibit 3-1). First, a firm may want to expand sales efforts across borders in order to sustain growth. Opportunities for growth may have been exhausted in the home country (for example, if the market is saturated), but owners, business analysts, and the media often demand continuing sales and profit growth. Second, a firm may be able to reduce its business risk by selling its products and services in a number of different countries. By diversifying its sales across a number of regions of the world, a company may be able to offset bad economic times when they occur in one part of the world with good economic times in other parts of the world. Third, a firm may enjoy greater economies of scale by expanding its markets internationally. This applies most often to manufacturing firms. Hyundai, for example, could not develop operations with efficient scale by serving only the domestic South Korean automobile market.[17] To achieve a reasonable cost structure, the firm needed to build and sell more automobiles than the South Korean market could handle. The larger volume of automobiles manufactured and sold allows them to obtain quantity discounts on raw materials purchased and to spread their fixed costs across more autos, thereby reducing their cost per unit (increasing their profit margins). Fourth, when locating units internationally, a firm may enjoy location advantages such as low labor costs or specialized expertise.[18]

Clearly, globalization and the value to be gained from participating in international markets is changing the competitive landscape for many firms, regardless of their home base.[19] Even many smaller and younger firms are now participating in international markets. The openness of markets and advancing technology (and lower costs of this technology) provide opportunities for young and small firms as well as for older, larger, and established firms.[20] These opportunities in international markets have been prompted by changes in many countries'

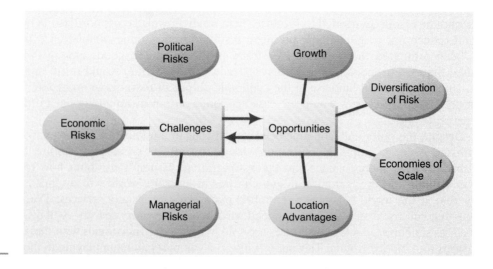

Exhibit 3-1
Opportunities and
Challenges for Firms
with International
Involvement

institutional environments. For example, several emerging-economy countries have reduced regulations to allow more foreign firms to enter their markets (e.g., China and India). In this way, their economies have grown larger and their firms have learned new capabilities, allowing them to compete more effectively in their home markets and abroad. Thus, the countries' institutional environments affect home and foreign country firms' strategies.[21] Institutional environments contribute to the opportunities and challenges depicted in Exhibit 3-1.

These powerful forces encourage many firms to expand into international markets, but there are substantial risks. These risks can be classified as political, economic, and managerial.[22]

- *Political risks* relate to instability in national governments, the threat of civil or international war, and the threat of state-sponsored terrorism. These risks create uncertainty, and they can result in destruction of assets and disruption of resource flows. One of the most difficult situations occurs when a government nationalizes an industry, meaning that it takes over the assets of private companies, often with little or no compensation provided to the firms.

- *Economic risks* relate to fluctuations in the value of foreign currencies and the possibility of sudden economic contraction in some countries. When a foreign country's currency declines in value relative to the home country's currency, assets and earnings in that foreign country are worth less, and exporting to that country becomes more difficult, as exported goods cost more there.

- *Managerial risks* relate to the difficulties inherent in managing the complex resource flows required by most international firms. Tariffs, logistics, and language issues can become a significant challenge as a firm does business in an increasing number of countries. Radically new marketing programs and distribution networks may be needed as firms enter new countries. Some executives and managers are better at managing these complexities than are others.

 # The Globalization Experience for Associates and Managers

For individual associates and managers, international exposure or experience can occur in several ways, which we discuss below. In each case, opportunities for personal learning, growth, and advancement are substantial. Several pitfalls, however, must be avoided.

Internationally Focused Jobs

An individual may work directly on international issues as part of her day-to-day job. Although dealing with finance issues, accounting concerns, information technology tasks, and so on can be challenging in a purely domestic context, adding an international dimension usually creates situations with significant complexity.

Individuals who thrive on challenge are well suited to these environments. At Dow Chemical, for example, international finance activities are often demanding because of the firm's exposure to fluctuations in the value of many different countries' currencies. With manufacturing facilities in dozens of countries and sales in well over 100 countries, Dow faces substantial currency risk.

Associates and managers who hold internationally focused jobs are often members of geographically dispersed teams. Many of these teams complete work related to new marketing programs, new product development projects, and other nonroutine initiatives. Other teams focus on routine issues, such as product flow from central manufacturing facilities. In many cases, associates and managers working on geographically dispersed teams have different working and decision styles because of cultural differences. Some prefer starting meetings with social rather than business topics, others prefer an autocratic rather than an egalitarian team leader, and still others prefer indirect to direct confrontations. To facilitate their work, team members use a complex set of tools to communicate, including electronic mail, Internet chat rooms, company intranets, teleconferencing, video-conferencing, and perhaps occasional face-to-face meetings.[23] Individuals complete team-related tasks around the clock as they live and work in different time zones, creating additional coordination challenges.

virtual electronic teams
Teams that rely heavily on electronically mediated communication rather than face-to-face meetings as the means to coordinate work.

Because international teams largely rely on electronically mediated communication to coordinate and accomplish their work, they are often referred to as **virtual electronic teams.**[24] Although virtual teams are efficient, a virtual world with little face-to-face communication combined with substantial cross-cultural differences sets the stage for misperceptions and misunderstandings. Small disagreements can escalate quickly, and trust can be strained. A recent study showed that virtual teams with substantial cross-cultural differences often exhibit lower trust than virtual teams with more cross-cultural similarities.[25] Low trust, suggesting little confidence that others will maintain their promises, be honest, and not engage in negative politics, is harmful to the team's efforts. Researchers have discovered several potential negative outcomes for virtual teams with low trust, including unwillingness to cooperate, poor conflict resolution, few or no goals established, poor risk mitigation, and lack of adjustment to the virtual format for work.[26] Although trust is important for any group, it is particularly important for virtual teams because of the propensity for misunderstanding as well as the absence of traditional direct supervision.[27]

swift trust
A phenomenon where trust develops rapidly based on positive, reciprocated task-related communications.

The initial communications of a virtual cross-cultural team may be particularly important in the development of trust. When early communication is task focused, positive, and reciprocated (i.e., questions and inputs do not go unanswered), a phenomenon known as **swift trust** can occur.[28] Swift trust occurs when individuals who have little or no history of working together, but who have a clear task to accomplish, quickly develop trust in one another based on interpersonal communication. Although social communication (i.e., friendly, non-task-related) can help to maintain this trust, task-related exchanges that facilitate the team's progress are critical.

In the face of possible trust issues, it is important for managers to help team members identify with the team. According to identity theory, when an individual identifies with a team, he feels connected to it, and he takes very seriously his role as a team member. Failure to identify with the team often results in withholding of effort on team projects, a common problem.[29] Steps can be taken to increase the chances that an individual will identify with the international team. First, it is important to provide training in international negotiating and conflict resolution.[30] Techniques that are sensitive to cultural differences and focused on collaborative

| Exhibit 3-2 | Learning about a Counterpart's Culture |

- Don't attempt to identify another's culture too quickly. Common cues (name, physical appearance, language, accent, and location) may be unreliable. In a global economy and multicultural societies, some people are shaped by more than one culture.

- Beware of the Western bias toward taking actions. In Arab, Asian, and Latin groups, thinking and talking can shape relationships more than actions.

- Try to avoid the tendency to formulate simple perceptions of others' cultural values. Most cultures are highly complex, involving many dimensions.

- Don't assume that your values are the best for the organization. For example, U.S. culture is individualistic and this is often assumed to be productive. While individual competition and pride can be positive to some degree, cultural values in India and China emphasize the importance of family, friends, and social relationships, making associates in these countries highly loyal to the organizations for which they work, and this is positive as well. Loyalty to the organization is less common among U.S. associates.

- Recognize that norms for interactions involving outsiders may differ from those for interactions between compatriots. Trust is especially important in some cultures and greatly affects interactions with others.

- Be careful about making assumptions regarding cultural values and expected behaviors based on the published dimensions of a person's national culture. Different ages, genders, and even geographic regions may cause differences within a country.

Source: Based on work in M. Javidan & R.J. House, 2001. Cultural acumen for the global manager. *Organizational Dynamics,* 29(4): 289–305; C.J. Robertson, J.A. Al-Khatib, M. Al-Habib, & D. Lanoue, 2001. Beliefs about work in the Middle East and the convergence versus divergence of values. *Journal of World Business,* 36(3): 223–244; S.E. Weiss, 1994. Reprinted from Negotiating with "Romans" (part 2) by S.E. Weiss, *MIT Sloan Management Review,* 35 (3), pp. 85–99, by permission of publisher. Copyright © 1994 by Massachusetts Institute of Technology. All rights reserved.

outcomes work best. Exhibit 3-2 provides specific ideas on how managers can be sensitive to cultural differences. Second, it is important to have team members jointly develop a unified vision.[31] The shared experience of discussing the future of the team, its goals and aspirations, can draw people together. Finally, it is helpful for team members to spend some time in face-to-face meetings, especially early in a team's life.[32] Face-to-face meetings increase the chances that team members will identify personal similarities, and these similarities contribute to understanding and cooperation.[33] Absent face-to-face interactions, videoconferencing provides richer communication than Internet chat rooms and teleconferencing because of the value of seeing each other. In one study, members of international teams reported that it was even helpful to have photographs of teammates posted in the workplace.[34]

Although research on the role of personal characteristics is not conclusive, several characteristics appear to play important roles in the success of cross-cultural virtual teams.[35] Individuals who value diversity, flexibility, and autonomy may offer more positive contributions to both the task and social aspects of the team. A general disposition to trust, a significant degree of trustworthiness, relational skills (involving the ability to work with others who possess different knowledge), and skills for communicating through electronic means are also important to success in virtual teams.

Foreign Job Assignments

Individuals may accept foreign job assignments that entail dealing directly with the complexities of operating in a foreign culture. These people are referred to as **expatriates,** or "expats" for short. Foreign experience can be exciting because of the new and different work situations that are encountered. The opportunity outside of work to learn about and live in a different culture can also be valuable. Many companies indicate that international experience results in faster promotions and makes associates more attractive to other companies because of the enhanced knowledge and capabilities they develop. In addition to the knowledge gained by expatriates, they also provide a means of transferring knowledge from the home company to foreign subsidiaries. In other words, expatriates carry with them the knowledge of the industry, technology, and firm.[36] Using expatriate managers also can facilitate coordination between the home office and foreign subsidiaries.[37]

Petroleum engineers, management consultants, operations managers, sales managers, and information technology project managers are among the common candidates for international assignments. According to a recent relocation trends survey from GMAC Global Relocation Services, international assignments are commonly made to fill skill gaps in foreign units, to launch new units, to facilitate technology transfer to another country, and to help build management expertise in a foreign unit.[38]

International assignments, however, should be treated with caution. Many things can go wrong, resulting in poor job performance and an early return to the home country.[39] **Culture shock** is a key factor in failure. This stress reaction can affect an individual who faces changes in and uncertainty over what is acceptable behavior.[40] Some behaviors that are acceptable in the home country may not be acceptable in the new country, and vice versa. For example, in many cultures, one of the hands (either the left or the right, depending on the culture) is considered dirty and should not be used in certain situations. This can be difficult for an American or European to remember. In addition, simple limitations such as an inability to acquire favorite foods, read road signs, and communicate easily often cause stress.

Beyond the associate's or manager's experience of culture shock, a spouse may also experience stress. Research suggests that spousal inability to adjust to the new setting is a significant cause of premature departure from a foreign assignment.[41] One study suggested that spousal adjustment occurs on three dimensions: (1) effectiveness in building relationships with individuals from the host country, (2) effectiveness in adjusting to local culture in general, and (3) effectiveness in developing a feeling of being at home in the foreign country.[42] This same study showed that spouses who spoke the language of the host country adjusted much more effectively. Spouses with very

expatriate
An individual who leaves his or her home country to live and work in a foreign land.

culture shock
A stress reaction involving difficulties coping with the requirements of life in a new country.

Digital Vision

young children also fared better because that spouse will likely spend a great deal of time engaged in the same activities as before the move—child care in the home. Familiar activities make the adjustment easier.

Individuals exposed to **ethnocentrism** in foreign assignments can also experience stress. Ethnocentrism is the belief that one's culture is superior to others, and it can lead to discrimination and even hostility.[43] In some cases, discrimination is subtle and even unintentional. It nonetheless can harm an expatriate's ability to adjust.

A number of remedies have been proposed to reduce or eliminate expatriate stress. In most cases, these remedies include screening and training before departure, training and social support after arrival in the country, and support for the individual returning to the home country.

Predeparture activities set the stage for success. Such activities include favoring for selection those individuals who have personal characteristics associated with success in foreign assignments. Although there are no simple relationships between personal characteristics and success in foreign posts, associates and managers who possess strong interpersonal skills, are flexible, and are emotionally stable often adapt effectively as expatriates.[44] Even so, predeparture training often plays a more important role than do personal characteristics.

Training can take many forms; a firm may provide books and CDs or arrange for role playing and language training, for example.[45] An expert on training for expatriates has offered the following advice.[46]

> ethnocentrism
> The belief that one's culture is better than others.

- *Train the entire family, if there is one.* If the spouse or children are unhappy, the expatriate assignment is more likely to be unsuccessful.

- *Conduct the predeparture orientation one to two months prior to departure.* The associate or manager and the family can forget information provided earlier than that, and if the orientation occurs too close to departure, the individuals may be too preoccupied to retain training information. Activities such as packing and closing up a home must be handled and will occupy family members in the days immediately prior to moving.

- *Include in the training key cultural information.* The Aperian Global consulting firm provides training for associates selected for expatriate assignments. The firm recommends providing side-by-side cultural comparisons of the home and host cultures, an explanation of the challenges that will likely be faced and when, lifestyle information related to such areas as tipping and gift-giving, and personal job plans for the jobholder, with an emphasis on cultural issues that help the expatriate to thrive in the new environment.[47]

- *Concentrate on conversational language training.* The ability to converse with individuals is more important than the ability to fully understand grammar or to write the foreign language.

- *Be prepared to convince busy families of the need for training.* Families with little foreign experience may not recognize the value of predeparture training.

After arrival, additional training may be useful, especially if little training was provided before departure. Language training may continue, and initial cultural exposure may bring new questions and issues. Host-country social support is also important, particularly in the early months. Individuals familiar with the country may assist in showing newcomers the area, running errands, identifying appropriate schools, and establishing local bank accounts.[48]

Finally, reintegration into the home country should be carefully managed following an international assignment. Research suggests that many associates and managers returning from foreign assignments leave their companies in the first year or two.[49] Old social and political networks may not be intact; information technology may have changed; and key leaders with whom important relationships existed may have departed. Each of these factors can influence the decision to leave. Career planning and sponsors inside the company can help in understanding the new landscape.

Although participation by women appears to be increasing,[50] women historically have not had as many opportunities for expatriate assignments as men. Managers must be sensitive to this deficit because they need to develop and effectively utilize all of the organization's human capital. As explained in the *Experiencing Strategic Organizational Behavior* feature, there are several reasons for the development of this **glass border.** By not providing women with international assignments, they are failing to develop women's knowledge and capabilities for higher-level jobs. As a result, these organizations may not be able to exploit strategic opportunities in international markets because of a shortage of human capital. And interestingly, recent research suggests that women are often more effective in expatriate roles because they tend to be flexible and develop a more empowering identity in order to be effective in a variety of situations.[51] While the plight of women executives is largely a global phenomenon, the segment suggests that Asian firms particularly may not be using their female human capital effectively. Companies that utilize all of their human capital effectively are more likely to gain a competitive advantage.

glass border
The unseen but strong discriminatory barrier that blocks many women from opportunities for international assignments.

EXPERIENCING STRATEGIC ORGANIZATIONAL BEHAVIOR

Are Asian Women Breaking the Glass Border?

China Tourism Press/The Image Bank/ Getty Images

There are many women who experience barriers preventing them from reaching career aspirations. For international women, these barriers may be even stronger. For example, women in Asian countries often experience these barriers because of cultural values and traditions. For many Asian women, marriage and male chauvinism are primary reasons they are unable to reach career potentials. Asian countries should be concerned about this problem because of the need for more human capital and because they are not fully utilizing the human capital available.

With the population rapidly aging and most able-bodied men already employed because of strong economies, especially in China, Asian companies may need more women associates. They will need to develop and effectively utilize all of the organization's human capital. The current situation has led Korean companies to adopt global business practices that include rewarding performance regardless of seniority or gender.

It remains problematic in many Asian cultures to have a woman in charge. Even though women have been a part of the workforce for a long time, for the most part their roles have been limited to staff entry-level positions and lower-level positions in manufacturing; rarely are they found in managerial or executive positions. A glass border (which is an unseen and strong discriminatory barrier) exists that blocks women from accessing many managerial and executive-level positions. It is important to note that many Asian companies are still family owned, with the men in the family in higher-level positions than the women. In addition, Asian companies often are unwilling to support having the female as the expatriate while her husband remains at his job in the home country. Another major problem is the lack of day-care facilities. Not only are there not enough facilities, but they are commonly open only until 5 P.M. and do not normally accept children under three years of age. In addition, in some Asian cultures, men rarely help to care for the children, thereby requiring women who work outside the home to rely on female relatives for babysitting. Finally, patriarchal attitudes are difficult to change, especially at the office. Many clients still ask to replace women consultants with men and some bankers continue to require female CEOs to obtain loan guarantees from their husbands.

The situation is beginning to change. In 1986, just 1.6 percent of Korean executives were women. In 1999, they accounted for 7 percent of executive positions in Korea. In Japan, changes are occurring as well. For example, Nissan declared that by 2007, it would triple the number of female managers to 5 percent of the company's total number of managers. In addition, Matsushita Electric Industrial Co. said it boosted the number of female managers by 170 percent in 2006. Companies operating in the Asia-Pacific region said they assigned 16 times more women expatriates to this region than in 2001, according to Mercer Human Resource Consulting. But even with some companies taking new initiatives to increase the number of female executives, many Asian women continue to experience barriers to many managerial roles.

Even though there is an increase in the number of female nonexecutives, the change in the number becoming executive directors has been small. Recent figures have shown that only 3.7 percent of executive directors of FTSE 100 companies are women. To overcome this problem, Asian companies must promote on the basis of merit and ignore gender in the workplace. Asian women must continue to work hard to break these barriers and overcome glass borders.

Sources: Hiroko Tashiro and Ian Rowley, "Japan: The Glass Ceiling Stays Put," *BusinessWeek*, May 2, 2005, www.businessweek.com; William Barnes, "Women Executives Poised to Enter the Maelstrom," *Financial Times*, Oct. 26, 2006, www.ft.com; Jane Croft, "Women Encouraged to Aim for Board Posts," *Financial Times*, June 28, 2005, www.ft.com; Toddi Gutner, "The Rose-Colored Glass Ceiling," *Keep Media*, Sept. 2, 2002, www.keepmedia.com; Moon Ihlwan, "Cracking Korea Inc.'s Glass Ceiling," *BusinessWeek*, Nov. 26, 2001, www.businessweek.com.

Foreign Nationals as Colleagues

Beyond gaining international exposure and experience through a job focused on international work or through a foreign assignment, an associate or manager can gain international experience in other ways. For example, associates and managers may work in a domestic unit with people from other countries or may report to a manager/executive who has relocated from another country. In the United States, H-1B visas allow skilled foreign professionals to live and work in the country for up to six years. L1 visas allow workers in foreign-based multinational companies to be transferred to the United States. Finally, J1 visas allow foreign students to fill seasonal jobs in U.S. resort areas, including jobs as waiters, lifeguards, fast-food cooks, and supermarket clerks. In fact, in recent years the demand for foreign skilled workers has been growing in many countries, including the United States.[52]

With hundreds of thousands of visas approved each year, an individual born in the United States and working in a domestic company may therefore work alongside a foreign national. U.S.-based associates and managers at Microsoft, for example, often work with foreign nationals. An associate recently observed, "I am surrounded every day by people from many diverse cultural and ethnic backgrounds, each contributing their unique ideas and talents so that people around the world can realize their full potential."[53] True to its multicultural profile, Microsoft supports a number of international worker groups, including Brazilian, Chinese, Filipino, Hellenic, Indian, Korean, Malaysian, Pakistani, Singaporean, and Taiwanese groups.[54]

Working side by side with individuals from other countries can indeed be a rich and rewarding experience, but problems sometimes develop. As already noted, individuals from different countries often have different values and different ways of thinking—and even different norms for behavior in business meetings. Although differences in values and thought patterns can be a source of creativity and insight, they also can create friction. Preferences for different working styles and decision styles can be particularly troublesome. Even outside of the workplace, in business schools teams of culturally diverse individuals experience problems on occasion.[55]

A key aspect of culture affecting cross-cultural working relationships is the issue of high versus low context.[56] In **high-context cultures,** such as Japan and South Korea, individuals value personal relationships, prefer to develop agreements on the basis of trust, and favor slow, ritualistic negotiations.[57] Understanding others and understanding particular messages depend in large part on contextual cues, such as the other person's job, schooling, and nationality. Being familiar with a person's background and current station in life is crucial, although directly asking about these things could be insulting. In **low-context cultures,** such as the United States and Germany, individuals value performance and expertise, prefer to develop agreements that are formal and perhaps legalistic, and engage in efficient negotiations.[58] Understanding others in general and understanding particular messages depend on targeted questioning. Written and spoken words are crucial; contextual cues tend to carry less meaning.

A related aspect of culture is monochronic versus polychronic time.[59] Individuals with a **monochronic time orientation** prefer to do one task or activity in a given time period. They dislike multitasking; they prefer not to divert attention from a planned task because of an interruption; and they usually are prompt, schedule-driven, and time focused.[60] North Americans and Northern Europeans are usually viewed as relatively monochronic. In contrast, individuals with a **polychronic time orientation** are comfortable engaging in more than one task at a time and are not troubled by interruptions.[61] For these individuals, time is less of a guiding force, and plans are flexible. Latin Americans and Southern Europeans are often polychronic. Individuals from much of South and Southeast Asia are also polychronic, but many Japanese do not fit this pattern.

Understandably, individuals from high-context cultures can have difficulty working with people from low-context cultures. A high-context individual may not understand or appreciate the direct questioning and task orientation of a low-context individual. As a result, the high-context individual can experience hurt feelings, causing him or her to struggle in a low-context culture. In the same way, a low-context person can be frustrated with the pace and focus of a high-context culture. Similarly, monochronic individuals might clash with people who are more polychronic. People who are driven by schedules and who do not appreciate interruptions often are frustrated by the more relaxed view of time held by polychronic

---

high-context cultures
A type of culture where individuals use contextual cues to understand people and their communications and where individuals value trust and personal relationships.

low-context cultures
A type of culture where individuals rely on direct questioning to understand people and their communications and where individuals value efficiency and performance.

monochronic time orientation
A preference for focusing on one task per unit of time and completing that task in a timely fashion.

polychronic time orientation
A willingness to juggle multiple tasks per unit of time and to have interruptions and an unwillingness to be driven by time.

people. To alleviate these cross-cultural difficulties, training in cultural differences is crucial in order to build managers' cultural intelligence. **Cultural intelligence** helps people understand others' behavior, with the ability to separate those aspects that are universally human from those that are unique to the person and those that are based in culture. It allows managers to understand and respond effectively to people from different cultures.[62]

> **cultural intelligence**
> The ability to separate the aspects of behavior that are based in culture as opposed to unique to the individual or all humans in general.

Opportunities for International Participation

Associates' and managers' opportunities for international experiences differ across firms. Purely domestic firms offer few opportunities beyond perhaps working with foreign nationals who have been hired. Firms that have expanded beyond the main domestic base through exporting offer more opportunities, because some individuals are needed for internationally focused work, such as international accounting, and a few are needed to staff foreign sales offices. Firms that have more substantial commitments to foreign operations usually offer still more opportunities for international work, but the degree to which this is true varies by type of strategy. As shown in Exhibit 3-3, we can classify firms with substantial commitments to foreign operations as multidomestic, global, or transnational.

Exhibit 3-3	International Approaches and Related Organizational Characteristics		
	Multidomestic	**Global**	**Transnational**
Local responsiveness			
Local production	High	Low	Medium
Local R&D	High	Low	Medium
Local product modification	High	Low	Medium/High
Local adaptation of marketing	High	Low/Medium	Medium/High
Organizational design			
Delegation of power to local units	High	Low	Medium/Low
Inter-unit resource flows between and among local units	Low	Low/Medium	High
International resource flows from and/or controlled by corporate headquarters	Low	High	Low/Medium
International participation			
Opportunities for associates and managers	Low	High	High

Source: Information in this exhibit is based on A. Harzing, "An Empirical Analysis and Extension of the Bartlett and Ghoshal Typology of Multinational Companies," *Journal of International Business Studies* 31(2000): 101–120.

Multidomestic Firms

multidomestic strategy
A strategy by which a firm tailors its products and services to the needs of each country or region in which it operates and gives a great deal of power to the managers and associates in those countries or regions.

Firms that use a **multidomestic strategy** tailor their products and services for various countries or regions of the world.[63] When customer tastes and requirements vary substantially across countries, a firm must be responsive to the differences. Tastes often vary, for example, in consumer packaged goods. Unilever, the British/Dutch provider of detergents, soaps, shampoos, and other consumer products, is a prime example of a consumer goods company that offers different versions of its products in various parts of the world.[64] It produces, for example, approximately 20 brands of black tea in order to meet the different tastes of individuals in different countries.

Firms such as Unilever tend to transfer power from the corporate headquarters to units based in various countries or homogeneous regions of the world (that is, local units).[65] These units typically are self-contained—they conduct their own research and development, produce their own products and services, and market and distribute in their own ways. This approach is expensive because geographically based units do not share resources or help one another as much as in firms using other international strategies. Yet, it may be important to allow autonomy when the subsidiary is a long distance from the home office, especially when that distance entails major differences in culture and institutional environments. In these cases, the subsidiary needs to develop a strategy that fits its competitive environment and the home office is less likely to be of help in doing so.[66]

Among firms with substantial foreign commitments, multidomestic firms provide fewer opportunities for associates, lower-level managers, and mid-level managers to participate in international activities. Individuals tend to work in their home countries and do not interact with people located in other geographical locations. Individuals in each unit are focused on their unit's country or homogeneous set of countries (region). Interunit learning, interunit transfers of people, and interunit coordination are rare in firms using a multidomestic strategy.

David Young-Wolff/PhotoEdit

Global Firms

global strategy
A strategy by which a firm provides standard products and services to all parts of the world while maintaining a strong degree of central control in the home country.

Firms following a **global strategy** offer standardized products and services in the countries in which they are active.[67] When cost pressures demand efficient use of resources and when tailoring to local tastes is not necessary, a firm must do all it can to manage its resources efficiently. It is costly to develop, produce, and market substantially different versions of the same basic product or service across different countries. For example, Microsoft does not significantly tailor the functionality of Windows for different countries. Nor does Cemex, the world's third largest cement company, tailor its cement for different countries. While the firm sells almost 100 million metric tons of cement annually across four major regions of the world, the firm provides the same product in all countries where it operates.

Cemex exhibits many features typical of global firms.[68] First, key decisions related to (1) products and services, (2) research and development, and (3) methods for serving each country are often made at corporate headquarters in Monterrey, Mexico. (Recall that, in contrast, firms using the multidomestic strategy make key decisions locally.) Second, country-based and regionally based units do not have a full complement of resources covering all of the major functions (production, marketing, sales, finance, research and development, human resources). For example, Cemex has operations in more than 50 countries but only has manufacturing operations in select parts of the world. A great deal of manufacturing also takes place in the home country of Mexico, and the product is then exported to other countries. By not having manufacturing plants located in and dedicated to each country or even each region, and by having large-scale manufacturing facilities in select locations, Cemex efficiently uses its resources. Cemex also focuses significant attention on global coordination. With units depending on decisions and resources controlled by the home country as well as resources from other countries, coordinating a global flow of information and resources is crucial. One means of growth for Cemex has been by acquisition. Fortunately, the strong global coordination used by the firm helps to rapidly integrate major acquisitions.

Compared with firms following a multidomestic strategy, firms using the global strategy provide more opportunities for associates and managers to participate in international activities. For example, many individuals in the home country and in foreign units must coordinate effectively to ensure a smooth flow of worldwide resources. Thus, many jobs are internationally oriented. In addition, there are often a large number of expatriate assignments. Global firms treat the world as a unified market and frequently transfer people across borders. Thus, in any given unit, there may be a significant number of foreign nationals. As noted earlier, expatriates learn and transfer knowledge across borders. Yet, to achieve the most learning at the team level requires the firm to consciously manage the flow of knowledge across the organization.[69]

Transnational Firms

Firms using a **transnational strategy** attempt to achieve both local responsiveness and global efficiency.[70] In industries where both of these criteria are important for success, a careful integration of multidomestic and global approaches may work best. Thus, a transnational strategy calls for more tailoring to individual countries than is typically found in global firms but generally less tailoring than in multidomestic firms.

Such an approach also requires the deployment of more resources in a given country than is typical in the global firm but fewer resources in each country than is typical in the multidomestic firm. Finally, the approach calls for less central direction from the corporate headquarters than the global strategy but more central coordination than the multidomestic strategy. In a transnational firm, interdependent geographical units must work closely together to facilitate interunit resource flows and learning. In the multidomestic firm, these flows are trivial. In the global firm, they are largely controlled by corporate headquarters.

Ogilvy & Mather Worldwide, a U.S.-based advertising subsidiary of WPP, a worldwide marketing communications group, uses a transnational strategy.[71] At one time, the firm employed a strategy that most closely resembled a multidomestic approach. Ogilvy & Mather tailored the advertising it produced to different

transnational strategy
A strategy by which a firm tailors its products and services to some degree to meet the needs of different countries or regions of the world but also seeks some degree of standardization in order to keep costs reasonably low.

areas of the world based on local customs, expressions, sensibilities, and norms for humor. To support this strategy, it had strong, self-contained local units. Clients, however, began to object to costs, and because many of these clients were becoming global firms, they wanted a more unified message spread around the world through advertising. Ogilvy & Mather began to pursue global efficiency and local responsiveness simultaneously. It refers to itself as "the most local of internationals and the most international of the locals." It has almost 500 offices in 160 cities across the globe.[72]

To prevent local units from reinventing largely the same advertising campaign (in other words, unnecessarily tailoring campaigns to the local market), Ogilvy & Mather implemented international teams that were assigned to service major accounts.[73] These teams create ad campaigns and send them to local units for implementation. One recent team is called Ogilvy*Action,* designed to provide a full range of brand activation services to customers on a global basis.[74] Local units pursue local accounts and have complete control over them but are constrained in their ability to pursue and oversee international work.

Overall, individual associates and managers have many opportunities for international exposure and experiences in firms using a transnational approach. Geographically based units are highly interdependent because they must exchange resources, and they often must coordinate these resource exchanges for their benefit as well. Rich personal networks and formal coordination mechanisms such as international work teams are developed to handle the interdependence. International meetings and travel are very important, and foreign assignments are common. Interestingly, the location of the headquarters for these firms is less important and some move their headquarters unit from their traditional home country when they adopt the transnational strategy. Normally, these moves are designed to respond to external stakeholders such as shareholders and financial markets.[75]

High-Involvement Management in the International Context

High-involvement management provides associates with decision power and the information they need to use that power effectively. As discussed in Chapter 1, firms that adopt this approach often perform better than other firms. Although most evidence supporting the effectiveness of the high-involvement approach has been collected from domestic units of North American firms,[76] sound evidence has come from other countries as well. One study, for example, focused on automobile plants worldwide;[77] another, on a variety of firms in New Zealand;[78] and a third, on firms in 11 different countries.[79] A recent study in China suggested that such practices enhanced short-term associates' feelings of competence and increased their commitment to the organization.[80]

Although available evidence is supportive of high-involvement management, caution must be taken when implementing this approach in different cultures. Modifying the approach to fit local circumstances is crucial. In this section, we discuss several dimensions of national culture that should be considered. The dimensions are drawn from the GLOBE (Global Leadership and Organizational Behavior Effectiveness) research program, which involves a number of researchers studying issues related to organizational behavior in 61 countries.[81]

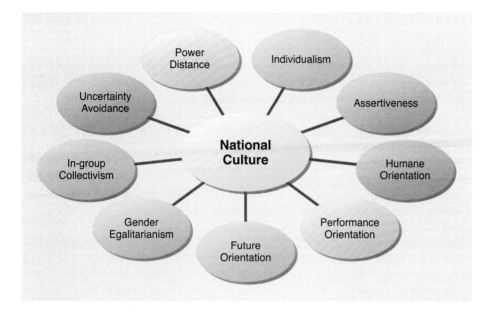

Exhibit 3-4
Dimensions of National
Culture

Dimensions of National Culture

As shown in Exhibit 3-4, the GLOBE project uses nine dimensions of national culture. Four of these dimensions have been used by many other researchers over the years. These four dimensions were originally developed by the Dutch social scientist Geert Hofstede[82] and they are listed first.

1. *Uncertainty avoidance* is the degree to which members of a society wish to avoid unpredictable lives. It is focused on a society's desire for orderliness through formal procedures and rules as well as through strong norms that govern behavior. Countries with high scores do not value free spirits. Such countries include Austria and Germany. Countries with lower scores include Russia and Hungary. The United States has a midrange score.

2. *Power distance* is the degree to which members of a society expect power to be unequally distributed. This dimension corresponds to expectations for strong autocratic leadership rather than more egalitarian leadership. Strong central governments and centralized decision structures in work organizations are frequently found in countries with high scores. For example, Russia scores high on this dimension. Alternatively, Denmark and the Netherlands have low scores on power distance.

3. *Individualism* is the degree to which members of society are comfortable focusing on personal goals and being rewarded for personal efforts and outcomes. In individualistic cultures, personal outcomes are valued. Countries scoring high on individualism include Italy and Germany. Countries scoring low on this dimension include Japan, Singapore, and South Korea.

4. *Assertiveness* is the degree to which members of society are aggressive and confrontational. In his original work, Hofstede labeled this aspect of culture "masculinity." Examples of countries with high scores on this dimension are

the United States, Austria, and Germany. Examples of countries with low scores are Sweden and Kuwait.

5. *In-group collectivism* indicates how much members of society take pride in the groups and organizations to which they belong, including the family. China and India have high scores on this dimension in the GLOBE research.

6. *Gender egalitarianism* refers to equal opportunities for women and men. Sweden and Denmark score high on this dimension.

7. *Future orientation* is the degree to which members of the society value long-term planning and investing in the future. Denmark and the Netherlands are among those scoring high on this dimension.

8. *Performance orientation* is the degree to which members of society appreciate and reward improvement and excellence in schoolwork, athletics, and work life. The United States, Taiwan, Hong Kong, and Singapore have high performance orientations.

9. *Humane orientation* is the degree to which members of society value generous, caring, altruistic behavior. Countries scoring high on this dimension include the Philippines and Malaysia.

Exhibit 3-5 compares India, Germany, and the United States on all nine culture dimensions.

Exhibit 3-5	National Culture in India, Germany, and the United States		
Culture Dimension	India	Germany	United States
Uncertainty avoidance	Medium	High	Medium
Power distance	Medium/High	Medium	Medium/Low
Individualism	Medium	High	Medium
Assertiveness	Low/Medium	High	High
In-group collectivism	High	Low/Medium	Medium/Low
Gender egalitarianism	Low	Medium/Low	Medium
Future orientation	Medium	Medium	Medium
Performance orientation	Medium	Medium	High
Humane orientation	High/Medium	Low	Medium

Source: Based on the GLOBE Project.

Research has shown that national culture affects major business practices.[83] For example, decisions to enter particular international markets are affected by the cultural dimensions of the targeted country.[84] In particular, the cultural distance between a firm's home country and the country targeted for entry has a major impact. *Cultural distance* refers to the extent of the differences in culture between countries.[85] Therefore, managers must pay careful attention to culture in designing and implementing management practices in each country.

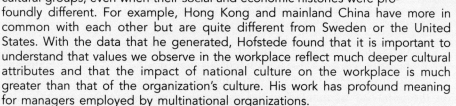

Managing Diverse Cultures

Geert Hofstede pioneered the study of culture in the workplace and conducted research to examine global variations in the psychology of work and of organizations, which affected international human resource management. While working at IBM in 1968, he noticed that although the company had a strong company culture, there were variations in cultural values among the employees of IBM subsidiaries around the world. Between 1968 and 1972, he surveyed over 116,000 employees. His survey responses from over 40 countries showed general similarities within cultural groups, even when their social and economic histories were profoundly different. For example, Hong Kong and mainland China have more in common with each other but are quite different from Sweden or the United States. With the data that he generated, Hofstede found that it is important to understand that values we observe in the workplace reflect much deeper cultural attributes and that the impact of national culture on the workplace is much greater than that of the organization's culture. His work has profound meaning for managers employed by multinational organizations.

Managers and top executives of companies seeking to expand globally need to recognize the complexities of cross-border collaboration. Difficulty in managing people is magnified when even small differences in perceptions and expectations occur, making collaboration difficult. An example of where cultural differences caused problems was the merger between the U.S. pharmaceutical company Upjohn and the Swedish firm Pharmacia. It quickly became apparent that the two cultures seemed incompatible when the Americans could not understand why the Swedes took a holiday during the entire month of August and the Swedes could not understand why Americans banned serving alcohol at lunch. These small disagreements eventually escalated into more serious problems. The problems occurred because of behavior differences such as the Swedes' gradualist style of management through consensus, which clashed with the U.S. management style, which focuses on getting results and decisive action. Eventually the problems were resolved, but the integration could have been much smoother had the cultural differences been understood and better managed. Pfizer eventually bought the Pharmacia company.

Another example of cross-cultural problems occurred in the merger between Daimler and Chrysler. Some experts believed that the merger had substantial potential because of the different but complementary capabilities possessed by the two firms. However, that potential was not realized partly because of national cultural differences between Germans and Americans. The Germans in Daimler disliked Chrysler managers' unstructured approach while American Chrysler managers found the German Daimler managers too rigid and formal. The culture clash disallowed effective integration of the two firms and their respective associates. Thus, the original integration plan was changed in order to create a separate Chrysler and Mercedes Benz division within the Daimler-Chrysler Corporation. Many Chrysler managers left the organization and the potential synergy between the two firms was never realized. The company has never recovered from the merger and eventually the CEO resigned because of the poor performance.

Managers may need to utilize different concepts and methods for different times and places. Managers need to be aware of the local cultures' values, social ideals, and their workplace behavior and attitudes. Multinational companies engaging in cross-border mergers can be successful when they have managers who possess "cultural intelligence," the ability to understand and effectively manage different values and expectations existing in different parts of the world. The key to collaborating across borders is to ensure goodwill on both sides through genuine tolerance and understanding.

Sources: Morgan Witzel, "Geert Hofstede: The Quantifier of Culture," *Financial Times*, Aug. 25, 2003, www.ft.com; Andy McCue, "Culture Clashes Harm Offshoring," *BusinessWeek*, July 17, 2006, www.businessweek.com; George Walden, "How England Got Its National Character," *Bloomberg*, Dec. 18, 2006, www.bloomberg.com; Morgen Witzel, "The Power of Difference," *Financial Times*, Nov. 8, 2006, www.ft.com; Roberto Foa, "United in a World of Difference," *Financial Times*, Oct. 14, 2004, www.ft.com; M.A. Hitt, R.S. Harrison, & R.D. Ireland, *Mergers and Acquisitions: A Guide to Creating Value for Stakeholders,* New York: Oxford University Press, 2001; G.R. Carroll, & J.R. Harrison, "Come Together? The Organizational Dynamics of Post-Merger Cultural Integration," *Simulation Modelling Practice and Theory* 10 (2002): 349–368.

In the *Experiencing Strategic Organizational Behavior* feature, we learn of the pioneering work of Geert Hofstede to identify the universal dimensions of national culture. He also discovered that national culture had a stronger effect on the behavior of managers and associates than did organizational culture. Hofstede's work also suggested the need to understand and manage diverse cultures. This need is highlighted in the problems experienced in the mergers between Pharmacia and Upjohn and between Daimler Benz and Chrysler, in which the managers of the respective firms were not understanding and tolerant of the cultural attributes that differed from their own. In fact, DaimlerChrysler has suffered significantly because of these problems. A large number of Chrysler managers left the firm after the merger. As such, the firm lost a substantial amount of human capital and knowledge. Thus, part of the value of Chrysler, some of its complementary capabilities, was lost with the high turnover of many key managers. With increasing globalization, understanding and managing diverse cultures has become a critical managerial attribute for competitive success in international markets.

National Culture and High-Involvement Management

High-involvement management must be implemented in accordance with a country's cultural characteristics. Although not every individual from a country will possess all of the cultural characteristics associated with that country, many people will share these traits. In the next section, we discuss how information sharing and decision power can be adapted to different levels of power distance, uncertainty avoidance, individualism, and assertiveness.[86]

INFORMATION SHARING

A firm's leaders must share tactical and strategic information if empowered individuals and teams are to make high-quality decisions. In cultures high in uncertainty avoidance, associates must have information to clarify issues and provide basic direction. If they lack such information, anxiety and poor performance can result. Where uncertainty avoidance is low, associates need less information of this kind. Rather, increasing information that encourages new ideas and ways of thinking can be useful. In cultures where assertiveness is high, associates want information that clearly and directly helps them to perform well, and they will desire continuous information on how they are performing. Where assertiveness is low, associates do not want information that is exclusively focused on performance and bottom-line business goals. Instead, they want information on improving soft processes such as teamwork. Similarly, associates in individualistic cultures desire information that relates to their individual jobs and responsibilities; they are less interested in information on team, department, and company issues. Associates in collectivistic cultures tend to have the opposite needs. Finally, associates in high-power-distance cultures do not expect to receive a great deal of information and probably will not know what to do with it if they receive it. For these individuals, careful training in information use is required, and relapses can occur. In low-power-distance cultures, associates expect information and put it to use when it is received. Thus, cultural attributes have effects on the type and amount of information shared and the knowledge learned in organizations.[87]

DECISION POWER AND INDIVIDUAL AUTONOMY

Some high-involvement systems give a great deal of decision power to individual associates rather than to teams. In cultures characterized by high uncertainty avoidance, such autonomy can cause stress because it is associated with less direction from above as well as less support from peers. To avoid stress, clear boundaries must be set for how the autonomy is used, and managers must be available to provide direction at all times. In cultures with low uncertainty avoidance, associates do not need direction and are generally able to tolerate uncertainty regarding the boundaries to their authority. In high-assertiveness cultures, associates are likely to use autonomy creatively to achieve task success. In low-assertiveness cultures, associates may channel too much of their autonomy into work on soft issues such as relationships and social networks. Managers must guard against excesses in this regard. For countries characterized by an individualistic culture, associates appreciate autonomy provided to individuals rather than to teams and emphasize individual goals. Because of this focus, managers may need to explicitly channel associates' attention to any required group or team tasks. In countries characterized by a collectivistic culture, associates are unlikely to be motivated by individual autonomy. Managers may wish to emphasize autonomy at the team level in such cultures. Finally, in cultures characterized by high power distance, autonomy may be difficult to implement. Associates expect a great deal of direction from managers. In this situation, managers may want to provide small increases in autonomy over time, so that associates can grow accustomed to having discretion. Managers may want to maintain a fairly strong role even in the long run. In cultures characterized by low power distance, associates welcome autonomy from managers and can channel their efforts to be more innovative.[88]

DECISION POWER AND SELF-MANAGING TEAMS

In cultures with high uncertainty avoidance, associates need clear boundaries for self-managing teams, and managers must be readily available for mentoring and coaching.[89] In cultures with low uncertainty avoidance, teams can define their own roles. In countries characterized by high assertiveness, teams tend to be task focused. For low-assertiveness cultures, associates often devote a great deal of time to soft issues such as team dynamics. Managers must monitor the time focused on such issues. In cultures characterized by individualism, managers must pay particular attention to team training for associates and to the design of team-based reward systems. In contrast, in cultures characterized by collectivism, managers are in a more favorable situation because associates naturally are drawn to teamwork. Finally, in cultures characterized by high power distance, associates may have difficulties using their decision power if their manager is too visible. Managers must be less visible and resist the temptation to offer a great deal of assistance to the team. Where power distance is low, associates work in a natural way with the manager as an equal or as a coach rather than a supervisor.

AES, a U.S.-based power-generation company, is known for its high-involvement management system. Associates enjoy tremendous freedom to make decisions individually and in teams. Firing vendors for safety violations, expending funds from capital budgets, and making key decisions about important day-to-day work issues have been common among associates since implementation of the system. With careful selection and training, and with access to key information, AES associates typically are able to use their freedom wisely.

As AES began to grow and establish operations in several countries, many analysts and reporters questioned whether its high-involvement system and underlying values could be applied in an international context. AES leaders, however, remained committed to the system they had created. Yet they realized that some modifications might be needed for a particular country. Although the core of the approach was preserved, some aspects were altered to fit the local culture.

When entering Nigeria, for example, AES responded appropriately to the prevailing culture. Norman Bell, the lead on the Nigerian project, and his AES colleagues encountered high power distance and high individualism as they began to work in Nigeria. Taken together, these cultural features forced Bell to initially adopt a more autocratic management system. Bell needed time to delegate decision power to associates, and teams needed particular attention for training and team-based reward systems.

In Hungary, China, Ireland, and elsewhere, AES has used the same basic approach: high-involvement management built on the company's core values with sensitivity to local cultural differences.[90] Thus, executives and managers at AES effectively used the high-involvement approach on a global basis while modifying the approach based on cultural differences. The high-involvement approach facilitated the global strategy used by AES. Therefore, it helped top managers to implement the firm's strategy.

Ethics in the International Context

international ethics
Principles of proper conduct focused on issues such as corruption, exploitation of labor, and environmental impact.

A critically important issue in globalization and international business is ethics. The *American Heritage Dictionary* defines ethics as "principle[s] of right or good conduct; a system of moral principles and values." Implicit in this definition is the idea that ethical conduct can be different in different cultures. After all, what one society deems "right or good conduct" may be quite unacceptable to another.[91] Thus, **international ethics** are complex.

Corruption is often considered to be the misuse of power for private gain.[92] Three issues are prominent in discussions of proper conduct in developed nations: (1) corruption, (2) exploitation of labor, and (3) environmental impact.[93] For corruption, the chief issue involves bribing foreign public officials in order to win business. Many developed nations have taken steps to fight corruption because it creates uncertainty and results in a reduction of merit-based decision making. The United States, for example, passed the Foreign Corrupt Practices Act in 1977 to prevent U.S. managers from bribing foreign officials. (See Exhibit 3-6 for a recent ranking of countries based on corruption.) Exploitation of labor involves the

Exhibit 3-6		Absence of Corruption in Select Countries	
Rank	**Country**	**Rank**	**Country**
1	Iceland	137	Indonesia
2	Finland	137	Iraq
2	New Zealand	137	Liberia
4	Denmark	137	Uzbekestan
5	Singapore	144	Kenya
6	Sweden	144	Pakistan
7	Switzerland	144	Paraquay
8	Norway	144	Democratic Republic of Congo
9	Australia	144	Somalia
10	Austria	144	Sudan
11	Netherlands	144	Tajikistan
11	United Kingdom	151	Angola
13	Luxembourg	152	Cote d' Ivoire
14	Canada	152	Equatorial Guinea
15	Hong Kong (part of China)	152	Nigeria
16	Germany	155	Turkmenistan
17	United States	155	Myanmar
18	France	155	Haiti
19	Belgium	158	Bangladesh
19	Ireland	158	Chad

Source: Rankings are drawn from Transparency International's Corruption Perception's Index 2005 for 159 countries. (www.transparency.org). Scores are based on the perceptions of the degree of corruption as seen by business people and country analysts. The score ranges from 10 (highly clean) and 0 (highly corrupt).

employment of children, the forced use of prison labor, unreasonably low wages, and poor working conditions. In one well-known example involving a line of clothing produced for Wal-Mart, Chinese women were working 84 hours per week in dangerous conditions while living in monitored dormitories with 12 persons to a room.[94] Americans and others were outraged. Finally, environmental impact relates to pollution and overuse of scarce resources. From global warming to clear cutting of forests, the concerns are many. In the United States, many Americans have become more sensitive to the environment because of the recent obvious effects of global warming.

The economic development of countries with higher levels of corruption tends to suffer. For example, countries with high corruption index scores as shown in Exhibit 3-6 often receive less direct investment from foreign firms. Additionally, the foreign investment in these countries more commonly comes from firms based in other countries with greater corruption.[95] Thus, corruption harms the country and its citizens.

MANAGERIAL ADVICE

Caux Round Table Principles for Business

© Ingrid H. Shafer, Ph.D.

Business leaders from Japan, Europe, and North America formed the Caux Round Table 1986 to promote moral values in business (Caux is a city in Switzerland where the group holds meetings). The principles they developed are based on two ideals: *kyosei* and human dignity. *Kyosei*, a Japanese concept, means "living and working together for the common good, enabling cooperation and mutual prosperity to exist with healthy and fair competition." Human dignity involves respect for the value of each person and the avoidance of treating a person as a means to fulfill someone else's desires. The seven specific principles the executives promote are listed below, as drawn from their web site (*http://www.cauxroundtable.org*).

1. *The Responsibilities of Business.* The value of a business to society is the wealth and employment it creates and the marketable products and services it provides to consumers at a reasonable price commensurate with quality. To create such value, a business must maintain its economic health and viability, but survival is not a sufficient goal. Businesses have a role to play in improving the lives of all of their customers, associates, and shareholders by sharing with them the wealth they have created. Suppliers and competitors as well should expect businesses to honor their obligations in a spirit of honesty and fairness. As responsible citizens of the local, national, regional, and global communities in which they operate, businesses have a part in shaping the future of those communities.

2. *The Economic and Social Impact of Business.* Businesses established in foreign countries to develop, produce, or sell should also contribute to the social advancement of those countries by creating productive employment and helping to raise the purchasing power of their citizens. Businesses also should contribute to human rights, education, welfare, and vitalization of the countries in which they operate.

   Businesses should contribute to economic and social development not only in the countries in which they operate, but also in the world community at large, through effective and prudent use of resources, free and fair competition, and emphasis upon innovation in technology, production methods, marketing, and communications.

3. *Business Behavior.* While accepting the legitimacy of trade secrets, businesses should recognize that sincerity, candor, truthfulness, the keeping of promises, and transparency contribute not only to their own credibility and stability but also to the smoothness and efficiency of business transactions, particularly on the international level.

4. *Respect for Rules.* To avoid trade frictions and to promote freer trade, equal conditions for competition, and fair and equitable treatment for all participants, businesses should respect international and domestic rules. In addition, they should recognize that some behavior, although legal, can still have adverse consequences.

5. *Support for Multilateral Trade.* Businesses should support the multilateral trade systems of the General Agreement in Tariffs and Trade (GATT) World Trade Organization (WTO), and similar international agreements. They should cooperate in efforts to promote the progressive and judicious liberalization of trade and to relax those domestic measures that unreasonably hinder global commerce, while giving respect to national policy objectives.

6. *Respect for the Environment.* A business should protect and, where possible, improve the environment, promote sustainable development, and prevent the wasteful use of natural resources.

7. *Avoidance of Illicit Operations.* A business should not participate in or condone bribery, money laundering, or other corrupt practices: indeed, it should seek cooperation with others to eliminate them. It should not trade in arms or other materials used for terrorist activities, drug traffic, or other organized crime.

Sources: Caux Round Table, "Principles for Business," 2007, at http://www.cauxroundtable.org; P. Carlson and M.S. Blodgett, "International Ethics Standards for Business: NAFTA, CAUX Principles and Corporate Code of Ethics," *Review of Business* 18, no. 3 (1997): 20–23.

The United Nations, the World Bank, the International Labor Organization, the World Trade Organization, and the Organization for Economic Co-operation and Development are among many organizations that advocate a unified set of global ethical standards to govern labor practices and general issues related to international business. As shown in the *Managerial Advice* feature, business leaders from Japan, Europe, and North America in the Caux Round Table have developed a list of expectations for companies engaging in international business. These ethical standards are intended to govern what strategies managers select and how they implement those strategies in dealings with others, both within and outside their organizations.

The Strategic Lens

Organizations large and small must develop strategies to compete in the global economy. For some organizations, strategies leading to direct investment in foreign operations are valuable for growth, lower costs, and better management of the organization's risk. For other organizations, just selling goods and services in other countries is sufficient to meet their goals. For still other firms, particularly small ones, participation in international markets may be limited, but competition from foreign firms in their domestic markets can require competitive responses. In all cases, understanding other cultures and effectively managing cross-cultural activities and contexts are crucial. Without insight and sensitivity to other cultures, senior managers are unlikely to formulate effective strategies. Without appreciation for other cultures, associates and mid- and lower-level managers can also fail in their efforts to implement carefully developed strategic plans. Furthermore, managers must prepare associates to work in international environments. This preparation often requires training and international assignments. Managers must also develop all of the organization's human capital—including women, who often have not had as many opportunities for expatriate assignments as men—and must ensure that the organization has the capabilities to take advantage of and exploit opportunities in international markets when they are identified. Many organizations operate or sell their products in foreign markets. Thus, managers and associates must understand cultural diversity and use this knowledge to their advantage in managing it.

Critical Thinking Questions

1. Given the complexity and challenges in operating in foreign countries, why do organizations enter international markets?

2. How can understanding and managing cultural diversity among associates contribute positively to an organization's performance?

3. How can being knowledgeable of diverse cultures enhance an individual's professional career?

What This Chapter Adds to Your Knowledge Portfolio

In this chapter, we have defined globalization and discussed the forces that influence it. We have also discussed three types of international involvement on the part of associates and managers: internationally focused jobs, foreign job assignments, and working with foreign nationals in the home country. After describing differing opportunities for international involvement, we have explored dimensions of culture from the GLOBE project and examined the implications of cultural differences for high-involvement management. Finally, we have briefly discussed international ethics. More specifically, we have covered the following points:

- Globalization is the trend toward a global economy whereby products, services, people, technologies, and financial capital move relatively freely across national borders. Globalization increased dramatically in the last 20 years of the twentieth century.

- Globalization presents opportunities and challenges for nations. The principal opportunity is for economic growth. Challenges include the possible loss of a nation's cultural uniqueness as uniform goods and services become commonplace throughout the world. For developing nations, additional challenges include the protection of labor from exploitation and natural resources from depletion. For wealthy nations, additional challenges include prevention of job loss to lower-wage countries and preservation of high-level wage structures at home.

- Globalization presents opportunities and challenges for organizations. Opportunities include growth, risk reduction through diversification, greater economies of scale, and location advantages (for example, moving into an area with a particularly talented labor pool). Challenges include political risk (instability of national governments, threat of war, and threat of state-sponsored terrorism), economic risk (fluctuation in the value of foreign currencies and the possibility of sudden economic contraction in some countries), and managerial risk (difficulties inherent in managing the complex resource flows required in a global or transnational firm).

- Individuals can be involved in the international domain through internationally focused jobs. Such individuals work from their home countries but focus on international issues as part of their day-to-day work. Membership in one or more virtual teams is often part of the job. Members of a virtual team coordinate their activities mainly through videoconferencing, teleconferencing, chat rooms, and e-mail. Having some face-to-face meetings and taking steps to ensure that individuals identify with the team facilitate team success.

- Individuals can also be involved in the international domain through foreign job assignments. These individuals are known as expatriates, and they often are on a fast track for advancement. In their new countries, expatriates may experience culture shock, a stress reaction caused by a foreign situation. Failure of a spouse to adjust and strong ethnocentrism in the host country are two additional factors leading to stress for expats. Careful screening of candidates for foreign assignments and rich cultural training can reduce stress and improve chances for success.

- Individuals can be involved in the international domain by working alongside foreign nationals. This is often exciting and rewarding, but cultural differences must be appreciated and accommodated, particularly those differences related to low versus high context and monochronic versus polychronic time.

- Some executives and managers choose a multidomestic strategy for their firm's international activities. This strategy, involving tailoring products and services for different countries or regions, tends to be used when local preferences vary substantially. Because country-based or regionally based units are focused on their own local domains, associates and managers have limited opportunities for international exposure and experience.

- Some executives and managers choose a global strategy for their firm's international activities. This strategy, involving standardized products and services for world markets, tends to be emphasized when needs for global efficiency are strong. Country-based or regionally based units are not self-contained, independent, or exclusively focused on local markets. Instead, at a minimum, each unit interacts frequently and intensively with the home country, and probably with some units located in other countries. Global firms offer associates and managers many more opportunities for international involvement than do multidomestic firms.

- Some executives and managers choose a transnational strategy for their firm's international activities. This strategy balances needs for local responsiveness and global efficiency through a complex network of highly interdependent local units. Associates and managers enjoy many opportunities for international involvement in transnational firms.

- National cultures differ in many ways. Four dimensions have proven to be particularly useful in analyzing these differences: uncertainty avoidance, power distance, individualism, and assertiveness. Organizational behavior researchers have proposed five other dimensions: in-group collectivism, gender egalitarianism, future orientation, performance orientation, and humane orientation.

- High-involvement management must be adapted to differences in national culture. Two aspects of this management approach, information sharing and decision power, are particularly important for adaptation.

- Many groups, including the World Trade Organization, have developed guidelines for ethics in the international context. Key issues for developed countries include (1) corruption, (2) exploitation of children, and (3) environmental impact.

Back to the Knowledge Objectives

1. What is globalization?

2. What are the three types of international involvement available to associates and managers? What problems can be encountered with each type?

3. How do opportunities for international involvement differ in firms emphasizing multidomestic, global, and transnational strategies? Which type of firm would you prefer to join and why?

4. What are the key dimensions of national culture that influence the success of high-involvement management? How should high-involvement management be adapted to differences in culture?

5. What are several international standards for ethical behavior by businesses (refer to the Caux Principles)? Briefly discuss each one.

Thinking about Ethics

1. Some have argued that globalization is a negative process because it can destroy national cultures. Do senior managers in global firms have a responsibility to prevent such damage? Or is their primary responsibility to maximize profits for their shareholders?

2. The members of cross-cultural virtual teams are prone to misperceptions and misunderstandings due to the lack of rich face-to-face communication. Under these circumstances, should a manager terminate an individual who has been a source of interpersonal problems in the context of such a team? Explain your answer.

3. A hard-working and generally effective associate has shown little appreciation for the cultural diversity in his unit. In fact, he has expressed some minor hostility toward several foreign nationals in the workplace. Also, he has not taken cross-cultural training seriously. How should the manager respond?

4. An experienced expatriate has hired underage labor at a cheap rate in order to save money. How should her firm respond to this situation?

Key Terms

globalization, p. 75
culture, p. 75
virtual electronic teams,
   p. 78
swift trust, p. 78
expatriate, p. 80
culture shock, p. 80
ethnocentrism, p. 81

glass border, p. 82
high-context cultures, p. 84
low-context cultures,
   p. 84
monochronic time
   orientation, p. 84
polychronic time
   orientation, p. 84

cultural intelligence, p. 85
multidomestic strategy,
   p. 86
global strategy, p. 86
transnational strategy,
   p. 87
international ethics, p. 94

Building Your Human Capital

Assessment of Openness for International Work

In this age of globalization, it is important to clearly understand your own feelings about international teams and assignments. In the following installment of *Building Your Human Capital,* we present an assessment of openness for international work. The assessment measures specific attitudes and behaviors thought to be associated with this type of openness.

Instructions

In the following assessment, you will read 24 statements. After carefully reading each statement, use the accompanying rating scale to indicate how the statement applies to you. Rate yourself as honestly as possible.

	Never				Often
1. I eat at a variety of ethnic restaurants.	1	2	3	4	5
2. I attend foreign films.	1	2	3	4	5
3. I read magazines that address world events.	1	2	3	4	5
4. I follow world news on television or the Internet.	1	2	3	4	5
5. I attend ethnic festivals.	1	2	3	4	5
6. I visit art galleries and/or museums.	1	2	3	4	5
7. I attend the theater, concerts, ballet, etc.	1	2	3	4	5
8. I travel widely within my own country.	1	2	3	4	5

	Strongly Disagree				Strongly Agree
9. I would host a foreign exchange student.	1	2	3	4	5
10. I have extensively studied a foreign language.	1	2	3	4	5
11. I am fluent in another language.	1	2	3	4	5
12. I have spent substantial time in another part of the world.					
13. I visited another part of the world by the age of 18.	1	2	3	4	5
14. My friends' career goals, interests, and education are diverse.	1	2	3	4	5
15. My friends' ethnic backgrounds are diverse.	1	2	3	4	5
16. My friends' religious affiliations are diverse.					
17. My friends' first languages are diverse.	1	2	3	4	5
18. I have moved or been relocated substantial distances.	1	2	3	4	5
19. I hope the company I work for (or will work for) will send me on an assignment to another part of the world.	1	2	3	4	5
20. Foreign language skills should be taught in elementary school.	1	2	3	4	5
21. Traveling the world is a priority in my life.	1	2	3	4	5
22. A year-long assignment in another part of the world would be a fantastic opportunity for me and/or my family.	1	2	3	4	5
23. Other cultures fascinate me.	1	2	3	4	5
24. If I took a vacation in another part of the world, I would prefer to stay in a small, locally owned hotel rather than a global chain.	1	2	3	4	5

Scoring Key for Openness to International Work

Four aspects of openness to international work have been assessed. To create scores for each of the four, combine your responses as follows:

Extent of participation in cross-cultural activities: Item 1 + Item 2 + Item 3 + Item 4 + Item 5 + Item 6 + Item 7 + Item 8
Participation scores can range from 8 to 40. Scores of 32 and above may be considered high, while scores of 16 and below may be considered low.

Extent to which international attitudes are held: Item 9 + Item 19 + Item 20 + Item 21 + Item 22 + Item 23 + Item 24
Attitude scores can range from 7 to 35. Scores of 28 and above may be considered high, while scores of 14 and below may be considered low.

Extent of international activities: Item 10 + Item 11 + Item 12 + Item 13 + Item 18
Activity scores can range from 5 to 25. Scores of 20 and above may be considered high, while scores of 10 and below may be considered low.

Degree of comfort with cross-cultural diversity: Item 14 + Item 15 + Item 16 + Item 17
Diversity scores can range from 4 to 20. Scores of 16 and above may be considered high, while scores of 8 and below may be considered low.

High scores on two or more aspects of openness, with no low scores on any aspects, suggest strong interest in and aptitude for international work.

Source: Based on P.M. Caligiuri, R.R. Jacobs, and J.L. Farr, "The Attitudinal and Behavioral Openness Scale: Scale Development and Construct Validation," *International Journal of Intercultural Relations* 24 (2000): 27–46.

A Strategic Organizational Behavior Moment

Managing in a Foreign Land

Spumonti, Inc. is a small manufacturer of furniture. The company was founded in 1983 by Joe Spumonti, who had been employed as a cabinetmaker in a large firm before he decided to open his own shop in the town of Colorado Springs. He soon found that some of his customers were interested in special furniture that could be built to complement their cabinets. Joe found their requests easy to accommodate. In fact, it wasn't long before their requests for custom furniture increased to the point that Joe no longer had time to build cabinets.

Joe visited a banker, obtained a loan, and opened a larger shop. He hired several craftspeople, purchased more equipment, and obtained exclusive rights to manufacture a special line of furniture. By 1993, the business had grown considerably. He then expanded the shop by purchasing adjoining buildings and converting them into production facilities. Because of the high noise level, he also opened a sales and administrative office several blocks away, in the more exclusive downtown business district.

Morale was very good among all associates. The workers often commented on Joe Spumonti's dynamic enthusiasm, as he shared his dreams and aspirations with them and made them feel like members of a big but close-knit family. Associates viewed the future with optimism and anticipated the growth of the company along with associated growth in their own responsibilities. Although their pay was competitive with other local businesses, it was not exceptional. Still, associates and others in the community viewed jobs with Spumonti as prestigious and desirable. The training, open sharing of information, and individual autonomy were noteworthy.

By 2005, business volume had grown to the extent that Joe found it necessary to hire a chief operating officer (COO) and to incorporate the business. Although incorporation posed no problem, the COO did. Joe wanted someone well acquainted with modern management techniques who could monitor internal operations and help computerize many of the procedures. Although he preferred to promote one of his loyal associates, none of them seemed interested in management at that time. Ultimately he hired Wolfgang Schmidt, a visa holder from Germany who had recently completed his MBA at a German university. Joe thought Wolfgang was the most qualified among the applicants, especially with his experience in his family's furniture company in Germany.

Almost immediately after Wolfgang was hired, Joe began to spend most of his time on strategic planning and outside relationship development. Joe had neglected these functions for a long time and felt they demanded his immediate attention. Wolfgang did not object to being left on his own because he was enthusiastic about his duties. It was his first leadership opportunity.

Wolfgang was more conservative in his approach than Joe had been. He did not like to leave things to chance or to the gut feel of the associates, so he tried to intervene in many decisions the associates previously had been making for themselves. It wasn't that Wolfgang didn't trust the associates; rather, he simply felt the need to be in control. Nonetheless, his approach was not popular.

Dissatisfaction soon spread to most associates in the shop, who began to complain about lack of opportunity, noise, and low pay. Morale was now poor, and productivity was low among all associates. Absenteeism increased, and several longtime associates expressed their intention of finding other jobs. Wolfgang's approach had not been successful, but he attributed its failure to the lack of employee openness to new management methods. He suggested to Joe that they give a pay raise to all associates "across the board" to improve their morale and reestablish their commitment. The pay raise would cost the company $120,000 annually, but Joe approved it as a necessary expense.

Morale and satisfaction did not improve, however. Shortly after the pay raise was announced, two of Spumonti's senior associates accepted jobs at other companies and announced their resignations. Wolfgang was bewildered and was considering recommending a second pay increase.

Discussion Questions

1. What weaknesses do you see in Joe's handling of Wolfgang?

2. Could Joe have anticipated Wolfgang's approach?

3. Can Wolfgang's career at Spumonti be saved?

Team Exercise

International Etiquette

A business traveler or expatriate must be aware of local customs governing punctuality, greetings, introductions, gift-giving, dining behavior, and gestures. Customs vary dramatically around the world, and what is accepted or even valued in one culture may be highly insulting in another. Many business deals and relationships have been harmed by a lack of awareness. In the exercise that follows, your team will compete with other teams in a test of international etiquette.

Step 1: As an individual, complete the following quiz by selecting T (True) or F (False) for each item.

a.	In Japan, slurping soup is considered bad manners.	T	F
b.	In Italy, giving chrysanthemums is appropriate for a festive event.	T	F
c.	In Ecuador, it is generally acceptable to be a few minutes late for a business meeting.	T	F
d.	In England, the "V" sign formed with two fingers means victory when the palm faces outward but is an ugly gesture if the palm is facing inward.	T	F
e.	In China, a person's surname is often given or written first with the given name appearing after.	T	F
f.	In Japan, shoes are generally not worn past the doorway of a home.	T	F
g.	In Brazil, hugs among business associates are considered inappropriate.	T	F
h.	In Germany, use of formal titles when addressing another person is very common.	T	F
i.	In Saudi Arabia, crossing one's legs in the typical style of U.S. men may cause problems.	T	F
j.	In China, green hats are a symbol of achievement for men.	T	F
k.	In China, a gift wrapped in red paper or enclosed in a red box is appropriate for celebrating a successful negotiation.	T	F
l.	In Kuwait, an invitation to a pig roast would be warmly received.	T	F
m.	In India, a leather organizer would be warmly received as a gift.	T	F
n.	In Japan, it is most appropriate to give a gift with two hands.	T	F
o.	In Iraq, passing a bowl or plate with the left hand is appropriate.	T	F
p.	In Saudi Arabia, ignoring a woman encountered in a public place is insulting to the woman's family.	T	F

Step 2: Assemble into groups of four to five, using the assignments or guidelines provided by the instructor.

Step 3: Discuss the quiz as a group, and develop a set of answers for the group as a whole.

Step 4: Complete the scoring form that follows using the answer key provided by your instructor.

Number of answers that I had correct: _____

Average number of answers that individuals in the group had correct: _____

Number of answers that the group had correct following its discussion: _____

International mastery: 13–15 correct
International competence: 9–12 correct
International deficiency: 5–8 correct
International danger: 1–4 correct

Step 5: Designate a spokesperson to report your group's overall score and to explain the logic or information used by the group in arriving at wrong answers.

Endnotes

1. Makino, S., Isobe, T., & Chan, C.M. 2005. Does country matter? *Strategic Management Journal,* 25: 1027–1043.

2. Loveman, G., Schlesinger, L., & Anthony, R. 1993. *Euro Disney: The first 100 days.* Boston: Harvard Business School Publishing.

3. Ibid.

4. Hitt, M.A., Ireland, R.D., & Hoskisson, R.E. 2007. *Strategic management: Competitiveness and globalization* (7th ed.). Cincinnati, OH: South-Western College Publishing.

5. Hejazi, W., & Pauly, P. 2003. Motivations for FDI and domestic capital formation. *Journal of International Business Studies,* 34: 282–289.

6. Ibid; UNTAD. 2006. World Investment Report, New York, U.S.A.

7. World Trade Organization. 2006. International Trade Statistics. Geneva, Switzerland; World Trade Organization. 2003. International Trade Statistics. Geneva, Switzerland.

8. Mathews, J.A., 2006. Dragon multinationals: New players in 21st century globalization. *Asia Pacific Journal of Management,* 23: 5–27.

9. World Investment Report, 2005. Transnational corporations and the internationalization of R&D. Geneva, Switzerland: United Nations Conference on Trade and Development (UNTAD).

10. Dollar, D. 1992. Outward-oriented developing economies really do grow more rapidly. *Economic Development and Cultural Change,* 40: 523–544; Frankel, J., & Romer, D. 1999. Does trade cause growth? *American Economic Review,* 89: 379–399.

11. Hitt, Ireland, & Hoskisson, *Strategic management.*

12. For a discussion of this issue, see Asgary, N., & Walle, A.H. The cultural impact of globalization: Economic activity and social change. *Cross Cultural Management,* 9(3): 58–75; Holton, R. 2000. Globalization's cultural consequences. *The Annals of the American Academy of Political and Social Science,* 570: 140–152; Zhelezniak, O. 2003. Japanese culture and globalization. *Far Eastern Affairs,* 31(2): 114–120.

13. Hall, E.T. 1976. *Beyond culture.* New York: Anchor Books–Doubleday.

14. Sheth, J.N. 2006. Clash of cultures or fusion of cultures? Implications for international business. *Journal of International Management,* 12: 218–221;

15. Asgary & Walle, The cultural impact of globalization.

16. Friedman, T.L. 2005. *The world is flat.* New York: Farrar, Straus and Giroux.

17. Hitt, Ireland & Hoskisson, *Strategic management.*

18. Ibid.; Hitt, M.A., Tihanyi, L., Miller, T., & Connelly, B. 2006. International diversification: Antecedents, outcomes and moderators. *Journal of Management,* 32: 831–867.

19. Meyer, K. 2006. Globalfocusing: From domestic conglomerates to global specialists. *Journal of Management Studies,* 43: 1109–1144.

20. Sapienza, H.J., Autio, E., George, G., & Zahra, S. 2006. A capabilities perspective on the effects of early internationalization on firm survival and growth. *Academy of Management Review,* 31: 914–933.

21. Hitt, M.A., Franklin, V., & Zhu, H. 2006. Culture, institutions and international strategy. *Journal of International Management,* 12: 222–234.

22. Hitt, Ireland, & Hoskisson, *Strategic management.*

23. Shapiro, D.L., Furst, S.A., Spreitzer, G.M., & Von Glinow, M.A. 2002. Transnational teams in the electronic age: Are team identity and high performance at risk? *Journal of Organizational Behavior,* 23: 455–467.

24. Cohen, S.G., & Gibson, C.B. 2003. In the beginning: Introduction and framework. In C.B. Gibson & S.G. Cohen (Eds.), *Virtual teams that work: Creating conditions for virtual team effectiveness.* San Francisco: Jossey-Bass.

25. Gibson, C.B., & Manuel, J.A. 2003. Building trust: Effective multicultural communication processes in virtual teams. In Gibson & Cohen (Eds.), *Virtual teams that work.*

26. Shin, Y. 2004. A person-environment fit model for virtual organizations. *Journal of Management,* 30: 725–743. Also see: Grabowski, M., & Roberts, K.H. 1999. Risk mitigation in virtual organizations. *Organization Science,* 10: 704–721; Jarvenpaa, S.L., & Leidner, D.E. 1999. Communication and trust in global virtual teams. *Organization Science,* 10: 791–815; Kasper-Fuehrer, E.C., & Ashkanasy, N.M. 2001. Communicating trustworthiness and building trust in interorganizational virtual organizations. *Journal of Management,* 27: 235–254; Raghuram, S., Garud, R., Wiesenfeld, B., & Gupta, V. 2001. Factors contributing to virtual work adjustment. *Journal of Management,* 27: 383–405.

27. Shin, A person–environment fit model for virtual organizations.

28. Jarvenpaa & Leidner, Communication and trust in global virtual teams.

29. Blackburn, R.S., Furst, S.A., & Rosen, B. 2003. Building a winning virtual team: KSAs, selection, training, and evaluation. In Gibson & Cohen (Eds.), *Virtual teams that work;* Shapiro, Furst, Spreitzer, & Von Glinow, Transnational teams in the electronic age.

30. Weiss, S.E. 1994. Negotiating with "Romans"—Part 2. *Sloan Management Review,* 35(3): 85–99.

31. Blackburn, Furst & Rosen, Building a winning virtual team.

32. Shapiro, Furst, Spreitzer, & Von Glinow, Transnational teams in the electronic age.

33. Cramton, C.D., & Webber, S.S. 2002. *The impact of virtual design on the processes and effectiveness of information technology work teams.* Fairfax, VA: George Washington University.

34. Blackburn, Furst & Rosen, Building a winning virtual team.

35. Shin, A person-environment fit model for virtual organizations.

36. Li, S. & Scullion, H. 2006. Bridging the distance: Managing cross-border knowledge holders. *Asia Pacific Journal of Management,* 23: 71–92.

37. GMAC Global Relocation Services. 2003. Global relocation trends: 2002 Survey Report. Warren, NJ.

38. Tan, D. & Mahoney, J. T. 2006. Why a multinational firm chooses expatriates: Integrating resource-based, agency and transaction costs perspectives. *Journal of Management Studies,* 43: 457–484.

39. Andreason, A.W. 2003. Direct and indirect forms of in-country support for expatriates and their families as a means of reducing premature returns and improving job performance. *International Journal of Management,* 20: 548–555; McCall, M.W., & Hollenbeck, G.P. 2002. Global fatalities: When international executives derail. *Ivey Business Journal,* 66(5): 74–78.

40. Black, J.S., & Gregersen, H.B. 1991. The other half of the picture: Antecedents of spouse cross-cultural adjustment. *Journal of International Business Studies,* 3: 461–478; Sims, R.H., & Schraeder, M. 2004. An examination of salient factors affecting expatriate culture shock. *Journal of Business and Management,* 10: 73–87.

41. See, for example: Andreason, Direct and indirect forms of in-country support for expatriates and their families as a means of reducing premature returns and improving job performance; Tung, R. Selection and training procedures of U.S., European, and Japanese multinationals. *California Management Review,* 25(1): 57–71.

42. Shaffer, M.A., & Harrison, D.A. 2001. Forgotten partners of international assignments: Development and test of a model of spouse adjustment. *Journal of Applied Psychology,* 86: 238–254.

43. Gouttefarde, C. 1992. Host national culture shock: What management can do. *European Management Review,* 92(4): 1–3.

44. Andreason, Direct and indirect forms of in-country support for expatriates and their families as a means of reducing premature returns and improving job performance; Caligiuri, P.M. 2002. The big five personality characteristics as predictors of expatriate's desire to terminate the assignment and supervisor-rated performance. *Personnel Psychology,* 53: 67–98; McCall & Hollenbeck, Global fatalities; Sims & Schraeder, An examination of salient factors affecting expatriate culture shock.

45. For one important summary of research on the usefulness of training, see Black, J.S., & Mendenhall, M. Cross-cultural training effectiveness: A review and a theoretical framework for future research. *Academy of Management Review,* 15: 113–136.

46. Frazee, V. 1999. Culture and language training: Send your expats prepared for success. *Workforce,* 4(2): 6–11.

47. Aperian Global, 2007. Global assignment services. http://www.aperianglobal.com/practice_areas_global_assignment_services.asp.

48. Sims & Schraeder, An examination of salient factors affecting expatriate culture shock.

49. Black, J.S., & Gregersen, H. 1999. The right way to manage expatriates. *Harvard Business Review,* 77(2): 52–63; Paik, Y., Segaud, B., & Malinowski, C. 2002. How to improve repatriation management: Are motivations and expectations congruent between the company and expatriates? *International Journal of Manpower,* 23: 635–648; Stroh, L., Gregersen, H., & Black, S. 1998. Closing the gap: Expectations versus reality among repatriates. *Journal of World Business,* 33: 111–124.

50. Fisher, C.M. 2002. Increase in female expatriates raises dual-career concerns. *Benefits & Compensation International,* 32(1): 73.

51. Janssens, M., Cappellen, T. & Zanoni, P. 2006. Successful female expatriates as agents: Positioning oneself through gender, hierarchy and culture. *Journal of World Business,* 41: 133–148.

52. Farrell, D., Laboissiere, M.A., & Rosenfeld, J. 2006. Sizing the emerging global labor market: Rational behavior from both companies and countries can help it work. *Academy of Management Perspectives,* 20 (4): 23–34.

53. Anonymous. 2003. College careers: Pride in diversity. http://www.microsoft.com/college/diversity/jose.asp.

54. Microsoft Corporations. 2007. Pride in diversity: Diversity & employee groups. http://members.microsoft.com/careers/mslife/diversepride/employeegroups.mspx.

55. Tomlinson, F., & Egan, S. 2002. Organizational sensemaking in a culturally diverse setting: Limits to the "valuing diversity" discourse. *Management Learning,* 33: 79–98.

56. Hall, *Beyond culture.*

57. Fitzgerald, M. 2007. Can you ace this test? A new exam forces managers to prove their mettle. *Fast Company,* February: 27.

58. Munter, M. 1993. Cross-cultural communication for managers. *Business Horizons,* 36(3): 69–78.

59. Hall, E.T. 1983. *The dance of life: The other dimension of time.* New York: Anchor Books.

60. Bluedorn, A.C., Felker, C., & Lane, P.M. 1992. How many things do you like to do at once? An introduction to monochromic and polychromic time. *Academy of Management Executive,* 6(4): 17–26; Wessel, R. 2003. Is there time to slow down? As the world speeds up, how cultures define the elastic nature of time may affect our environmental health. *Christian Science Monitor,* January 9: 13.

61. Bluedorn, Felker & Lane. 1992. How many things do you like to do at once? Wessel, Is there time to slow down?

62. Earley, P.C., & Ang, S. 2003. *Cultural intelligence: Individual interactions across cultures.* Stanford, CA: Stanford University Press.

63. Bartlett, C.A., & Ghoshal, S. 1998. *Managing across borders: The transnational solution* (2nd ed.). Boston: Harvard Business School Press; Harzing, A. 2000. An empirical analysis and extension of the Bartlett and Ghoshal typology of multinational companies. *Journal of International Business Studies,* 31: 101–120; Hitt, Ireland, & Hoskisson, *Strategic management.*

64. Unilever N.V./Unilever PLC. 2007. About Unilever. http://www.unilever.com/ourcompany/aboutunilever/introducingunilever/asp.

65. Li, L. 2005. Is regional strategy more effective than global strategy in the U.S. service industries? *Management International Review,* 45: 37–57; Harzing, An empirical analysis and extension of the Bartlett and Ghoshal typology of multinational companies.

66. Harzing, A.-W., & Nooderhaven, N. 2006. Geographical distance and the role and management of subsidiaries: The case of subsidiaries down-under. *Asia Pacific Journal of Management,* 23: 167–185.

67. Bartlett & Ghoshal, Managing across borders: The transnational solution; Harzing, An empirical analysis and extension of the Bartlett and Ghoshal typology of multinational companies; Hitt, Ireland, & Hoskisson, *Strategic management.*

68. This is Cemex. 2007. Cemex web site. http://www.cemex.com/tc/tc_lp.asp, January; Anonymous. 2001. Business: The Cemex way. *The Economist,* 359(8226): 75–76.

69. Zellmer-Bruhn, M., & Gibson, C. 2006. Multinational organization context: Implications for team learning and performance. *Academy of Management Journal,* 49: 501–518.

70. Bartlett & Ghoshal, Managing across borders: The transnational solution; Harzing, An empirical analysis and extension of the Bartlett and Ghoshal typology of multinational companies; Hitt, Ireland, & Hoskisson, *Strategic management.*

71. Ibarra, H., & Sackley, N. 1995. *Charlotte Beers at Ogilvy & Mather Worldwide.* Boston: Harvard Business School Publishing.

72. Ogilvy & Mather. 2007. Company information. http://www.ogilvy.com/company.

73. Bentley, S. 1997. Big agencies profit from global tactics. *Marketing Week,* 19(43): 25–26.

74. Ogilvy & Mather. 2007. Ogilvy introduces Ogilvy*Action*. http://www.ogilvy.com.

75. Birkinshaw, J., Braunerhjelm, P., & Holm, U. 2006. Why some multinational corporations relocate their headquarters overseas. *Strategic Management Journal,* 27: 681–700.

76. See, for example, Zatzick, C.D., & Iverson, R.D. 2006. High-involvement and workforce reduction: Competitive advantage or disadvantage? *Academy of Management Journal,* 49: 999–1015.

77. MacDuffie, J.P. 1995. Human resource bundles and manufacturing performance: Organizational logic and flexible production systems. *Industrial and Labor Relations Review,* 48: 197–221.

78. Guthrie, J.P. 2001. High-involvement work practices, turnover, and productivity: Evidence from New Zealand. *Academy of Management Journal,* 44: 180–190.

79. Black, B. 1999. National culture and high commitment management. *Employee Management,* 21: 389–404.

80. Huang, X., Shi, K., Zhang, Z., & Cheung, Y.L. 2006. The impact of participative leadership behavior on psychological empowerment and organizational commitment in Chinese state-owned enterprises: The moderating role of organizational tenure. *Asia Pacific Journal of Management,* 23: 345–367.

81. House, R., Javidan, M., Hanges, P., & Dorfman, P. 2002. Understanding cultures and implicit leadership theories across the globe: An introduction to project GLOBE. *Journal of World Business,* 37: 3–10; Javidan, M., & House, R.J. 2001. Cultural acumen for the global manager: Lessons from Project GLOBE. *Organizational Dynamics,* 29: 289–305.

82. Hofstede, G. 1984. *Culture's consequences: International differences in work-related values* (abridged edition). Beverly Hills, CA: Sage Publications.

83. Leung. K., Bhagat, R.S., Buchan, N.R., Erez, M., & Gibson, C.B. 2005. Culture and international business: Recent advances and their implications for future research. *Journal of International Business Studies,* 36: 357–378.

84. Rothaermel, F.T., Kotha, S., & Steensma, H.K. 2006. International market entry by U.S. Internet firms: An empirical analysis of country risk, national culture and market size. *Journal of Management,* 32: 56–82.

85. Zaheer, S., & Zaheer, A. 2006. Trust across borders. *Journal of International Business Studies,* 37: 21–29.

86. This discussion draws substantially from the work of Randolph and Sashkin, Can organizational empowerment work in multinational settings?

87. Michailova, S., & Hutchings, K. 2006. National cultural influences on knowledge sharing: A comparison of China and Russia. *Journal of Management Studies,* 43: 383–405; Wong, A., & Tjosvold, D. 2006. Collectivist values for learning in organizational relationships in China: The role of trust and vertical coordination. *Asia Pacific Journal of Management,* 23: 299–317.

88. van der Vegt, G.S., van de Vliert, E., & Huang, X. 2005. Location-level links between diversity and innovative climate depend on national power distance. *Academy of Management Journal,* 48: 1171–1182.

89. Newburry, W., & Yakova, N. 2006. Standardization preferences: A function of national culture, work interdependence and local embeddedness. *Journal of International Business Studies,* 37: 44–60.

90. Hamilton, M.M. 2003. AES's new power structure: Struggling utility overhauls corporate (lack of) structure. *The Washington Post,* June 2, E1; McMillan, J. & Dosunmu, A. 2002. *Nigeria.* Palo Alto, CA: Stanford Graduate School of Business; O'Reilly, C.A. & Pfeffer, J. 2000. *Hidden value: How great companies achieve extraordinary results with ordinary people.* Boston: Harvard Business School Press; Paine, L.S. & Mavrinac, S. 1995, *AES honeycomb.* Boston: Harvard Business School Publishing.

91. Thorne, L., & Saunders, S.B. 2002. The socio-cultural embeddedness of individuals' ethical reasoning in organizations (cross-cultural ethics). *Journal of Business Ethics,* 35: 1–13.

92. Rodriguez, P., Siegel, D.S., Hillman, A., & Eden, L. 2006. Three lenses on the multinational enterprise: Politics, corruption, and corporate social responsibility. *Journal of International Business Studies,* 37: 733–746.

93. Davids, M. 1999. Global standards, local problems. *The Journal of Business Strategy,* 20: 38–43.

94. Ibid.

95. Cuervo-Cazurra, A. 2006. Who cares about corruption? *Journal of International Business Studies,* 37: 807–822.

PART II INDIVIDUAL PROCESSES

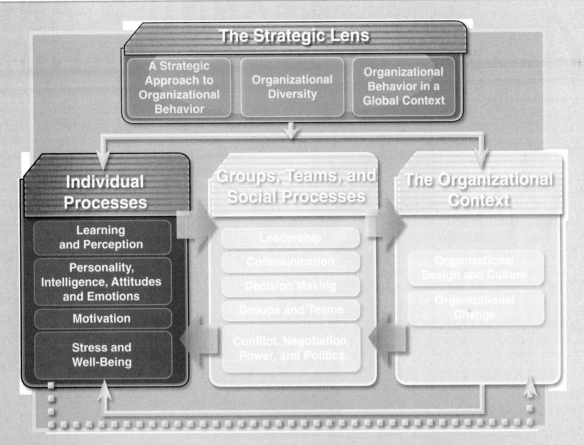

The chapters in Part I provided the strategic lens that is central to discussions throughout the book and they explained how organizational diversity and the global environment affect all organizations. In Part II, we explore important concepts related to individual-level processes in organizations.

Chapter 4 explains the concepts of learning and perception. Through individual learning, associates gain the knowledge and skills they need to perform their jobs in organizations. Individual learning contributes to the value of an organization's human capital and provides the base for organizational learning, both of which are critical for organizations to capture a competitive advantage.

Chapter 5 focuses on personality, intelligence, attitudes, and emotions. Managers in organizations need to understand how each of these human characteristics affects individual behavior. Personality and intelligence are an important determinant of a person's behavior and performance and cannot be easily changed. Thus, organizations must learn how to select associates with desirable personalities and intelligence levels to maximize the value of their human capital. However, attitudes and emotions can and do vary. Attitudes and emotions affect behavior, and managers can have a significant effect on individuals' behavior by taking actions that affect their attitudes and emotions.

Chapter 6 examines a fundamental concept in organizational behavior: motivation. Individuals can be motivated in various ways and by various factors. Because individual motivation is highly critical to individual and organizational productivity, understanding how to motivate is vital to effective management.

Chapter 7 deals with stress and well-being, critical issues in today's workplace. While some stress can be functional, much of the stress individuals experience can have negative effects on their productivity and health. When managers understand the causes and consequences of stress, they can attempt to manage it to reduce dysfunctional outcomes.

4

LEARNING AND PERCEPTION

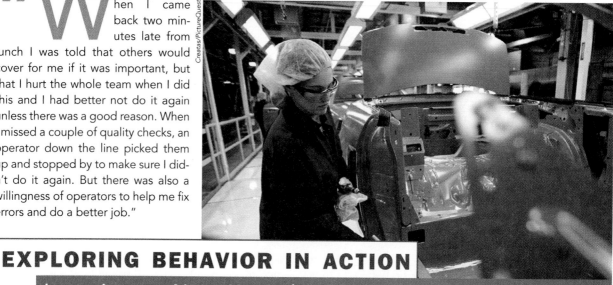

Creatas/PictureQuest

"**W**hen I came back two minutes late from lunch I was told that others would cover for me if it was important, but that I hurt the whole team when I did this and I had better not do it again unless there was a good reason. When I missed a couple of quality checks, an operator down the line picked them up and stopped by to make sure I didn't do it again. But there was also a willingness of operators to help me fix errors and do a better job."

EXPLORING BEHAVIOR IN ACTION

Learning at New United Motor Manufacturing, Inc.

Jamie Hresko, an associate at New United Motor Manufacturing, Inc., or NUMMI, the joint venture between Toyota and General Motors, made these remarks when discussing his experiences as a newcomer. As he pointed out, while his peers helped correct his errors, they also delivered mild reprimands and generally showed disapproval whenever he acted in ways that harmed the ability of the organization to assemble quality automobiles in a cost-effective manner. The mildly negative feedback reduced the likelihood that he would display these undesirable behaviors again.

New associates learn the norms and culture of NUMMI largely from their peers. Peers create consequences for various actions, thereby shaping future behavior by showing what is and is not acceptable. Managers play an important role as well, but the emphasis on associate empowerment means less frequent inputs from managers on a day-to-day basis. As Hresko put it, "Most days I never saw a supervisor, but I was always called on any violation."

Interestingly, Hresko was actually a high-level manager from another part of General Motors. He had heard about the positive culture and organization at NUMMI and wanted to investigate for himself. Rather than ask for the usual plant tour, he asked NUMMI leaders to allow him to enter the workforce undercover. Once working at NUMMI, he tested the system by purposely returning from lunch a few minutes late, failing to complete some quality checks, building a buffer of extra parts for his workstation so he could rest when he so chose, and stacking parts on the floor to make his life easier (but causing a safety problem). In all cases, peers whose energy and enthusiasm had been unleashed by empowerment and trust delivered swift consequences for behavior that harmed the organization's mission.

The situation was far different before the plant's conversion to a high-involvement Toyota-GM operation. An associate at the old plant reported the following:

> But you know, they made us build cars that way. One day I found a bolt missing. I called the supe over and he said, "What's the matter with you boy, you goin' to buy it [the car]? Move it!" Then when the plant failed they blamed us.

This associate acted in a manner that he considered proper. He reported a problem with the manufacturing process, but his behavior was ridiculed by a GM supervisor. The associate learned that his manager did not value identification of problems. The same associate also had learned that his peers would not react negatively to a lack of concern for quality, returning late from lunch, or taking unauthorized breaks. In fact, many of his peers approved of those behaviors. The learning that occurred at the old plant was no less powerful than the learning at NUMMI, but the learning at the old plant was harmful to the goal of assembling quality cars at a reasonable cost.

Beyond different experiences in routine work behaviors, the old plant and the NUMMI organization also differed in another important way. At NUMMI, as at all facilities using the Toyota Production System, associates and lower-level managers were expected to continuously improve their own work processes by trying new approaches and learning from the resulting successes and failures. Associates were taught the scientific method, where they examined a situation, formulated a hypothesis about how a new approach was likely to affect efficiency and quality, and tested their hypothesis to learn from experience. This type of learning is often more complex than learning existing rules and norms, because the outcomes are uncertain.

In addition to this unique on-the-job training, new NUMMI associates (or team members, as they are called) go through a formal four-week program called "Foundations in Training" where they take classes on the Toyota production system, team building, union–management relations, and safety. Thus, they begin by not only understanding the production process, but also learning the importance of teamwork at NUMMI.

NUMMI's unique approach to training among automobile manufacturers has certainly paid off. The joint venture plant consistently leads the industry in terms of labor hours per vehicle, union–management relations, and being awarded the J.D. Powers award for the last several years.

Sources: P. Adler, "Time and Motion Regained," *Harvard Business Review* 71 (Jan.–Feb. 1993), 97–108; N. Chetnik, "Inside NUMMI," *San Jose Mercury News,* Feb. 9, 1987; M. Nauman, "New United Motor Manufacturing Inc. to Mark 20 Years in Fremont, Calif.," *Knight Ridder Tribune Business News,* Feb. 11, 2004, p. 1; C.A. O'Reilly and J. Pfeffer, *Hidden Value: How Great Companies Achieve Extraordinary Results with Ordinary People* (Boston: Harvard Business School Press, 2000); S. Spear and K. Bowen, "Decoding the DNA of the Toyota Production System," *Harvard Business Review* 77 (Sept.–Oct. 1999), 96–106; P. Waurzyniak, "Lean at NUMMI," *Manufacturing Engineering* 135 (no. 3, 2005) at http://www.sme.org.; http://www.nummi. com. Accessed March 12, 2007.

The Strategic Importance of Learning and Perception

At NUMMI, we see the importance of learning processes. These processes help to maintain NUMMI's high-involvement system and culture. An associate who violates the trust placed in her by the system quickly experiences negative consequences from other associates. As a result of peer pressure, she is less likely to exhibit such behavior in the future. Conversely, an associate who meets expectations experiences positive consequences from peers and managers and is likely to repeat the positive behaviors in the future. This is the essence of simple learning. Behavior that is punished is less likely to occur in the future, whereas behavior that is positively reinforced is more likely to be repeated. Although these relationships may seem straightforward, there are complexities involved even in simple learning situations. These complexities are discussed in this chapter.

Simple learning can enhance an organization's productivity, quality, and competitive success. In the NUMMI case, the organization was able to produce a higher-quality automobile at a lower cost than other comparable U.S. auto manufacturing plants. The comparison with the old GM plant showed why NUMMI is more competitive and likely to sell more autos over time.

At a second level, learning processes help NUMMI with its need for continuous improvement. Experimentation is crucial to NUMMI's ongoing improvement but would be useless if associates and managers could not learn effectively from their attempts to try new ways of doing things. Unfortunately, as discussed later, this kind of learning can be difficult in some situations.

To be competitive in the dynamic twenty-first century, an organization must have associates and managers who can effectively learn and grow. Continuous learning based on trying new things plays a critical role in an organization's capability to gain and sustain a competitive advantage. Organizations can improve only when their human capital is enriched through learning. Their human capital must be better and produce more value for customers than their competitors to gain an advantage in the marketplace and to maintain that advantage.[1] Thus, managers need to develop the means for associates and all managers to continuously improve their knowledge and skills.

To open this chapter, we explore the fundamentals of learning, including contingencies of reinforcement and various schedules of reinforcement. From there, we apply learning principles to the training of newcomers and the purposeful modification of existing associates' behavior. We focus on specific conditions helpful to learning, the use of behavior modification, simulations, and how people can learn from failure. Next, we move to a discussion of perception. Accurately perceiving characteristics of people, attributes of tasks, and the nature of cause-and-effect relationships is critical to properly assessing and learning from experiences. Several mental biases, however, can interfere with accurate perceptions.

KNOWLEDGE OBJECTIVES

After reading this chapter, you should be able to:

1. Describe the effects on learning of positive reinforcement, negative reinforcement, punishment, and extinction.

2. Discuss continuous and intermittent schedules of reinforcement.

3. Explain how principles of learning can be used to train newcomers as well as to modify the behavior of existing associates.

4. Describe the conditions under which adults learn, in addition to rewards and punishments.

5. Describe some specific methods that organizations use to train associates.

6. Discuss learning from failure.

7. Identify typical problems in accurately perceiving others and solutions to these problems.

8. Explain the complexities of causal attributions and task perception.

Fundamental Learning Principles

When individuals first enter an organization, they bring with them their own unique experiences, perceptions, and ways of behaving. These patterns of behavior have developed because they have helped these individuals cope with the world around them. However, associates introduced to a new organization or to new tasks may need to learn new behaviors that will make them effective in the new situation. Associates and managers must therefore be acquainted with the principles and processes that govern learning.

In the field of organizational behavior, **learning** refers to relatively permanent changes in human capabilities that occur as a result of experience rather than a natural growth process.[2] These capabilities are related to specific learning outcomes, such as new behaviors, verbal information, intellectual skills, motor skills, attitudes, and cognitive strategies. Both parts of this definition are important. First, learning takes place only when changes in capabilities occur. Ultimately, these changes should result in changed behavior since true learning represents adaptation to circumstances, and this must be reflected in behavior. Furthermore, this change should be relatively permanent until a new response is learned to the given situation. Second, learning is driven by experience with a particular situation. An associate may gain insights into a situation by thoughtfully trying different approaches to see what happens, by randomly trying different actions in a trial-and-error process, or by carefully observing others' actions. In all cases, however, the associate has gained experience in the situation—experience that affects behavior when the situation occurs again. Change in one's capabilities due to a natural growth process (e.g., gaining muscle strength) is not learning.

> **learning**
> A process through which individuals change their behavior based on positive or negative experiences in a situation.

Operant Conditioning and Social Learning Theory

Most behavior exhibited by associates and managers is intentional in the sense that a given behavior is designed to bring about a positive consequence or avoid a negative consequence. Some associates shake hands when they see each other in the morning because it feels good and expresses respect or affection. Other associates apply the brakes on a forklift to avoid an accident. Managers may not develop close social relationships with their organization's associates in order to avoid the complications that can result. All of these behaviors have been learned.

Operant conditioning theory and social learning theory both can be used to explain learning. Both are reinforcement theories based on the idea that behavior is a function of its consequences.[3] **Operant conditioning theory** traces its roots at least back to a famous set of experiments involving cats, dogs, and other animals in the late 1800s.[4] The goal of the experiments was to show that animals learn from the consequences of their behavior in a very straightforward way—that presentation of a reward, such as food, conditions an animal to repeat the rewarded behavior in the same or similar situations. In later years, researchers such as B. F. Skinner emphasized this same conditioning in people.[5] These researchers, known as *behaviorists,* adopted the position that higher mental processes typically ascribed to human beings are irrelevant for behavior because all human learning is the result of simple conditioning, just as in cats, rats, dogs, and monkeys. In other words, people do not need to think to learn.

> **operant conditioning theory**
> An explanation for consequence-based learning that assumes learning results from simple conditioning and that higher mental functioning is irrelevant.

While operant conditioning explains a great deal of human learning, later scientists argued that people can learn in other ways. The most prominent of these theories is social learning theory. **Social learning theory,** developed by psychologist Albert Bandura, rejects the idea that higher mental processes are nonexistent or irrelevant in humans.[6] This theory emphasizes that humans can observe others in a situation and learn from what they see. Thus, humans do not need to directly experience a particular situation to develop some understanding of the behaviors that are rewarded in that situation.

> **social learning theory**
> An explanation for consequence-based learning that acknowledges the higher mental functioning of human beings and the role such functioning can play in learning.

Contingencies of Reinforcement

The basic elements of learning include:

- The situation (sometimes referred to as the stimulus situation)
- The behavioral response of the associate or manager to the situation
- The consequence(s) of the response for the associate or manager

These elements interact to form contingencies of reinforcement. These contingencies, explained below, describe different types of consequences that can follow behavioral responses.

POSITIVE AND NEGATIVE REINFORCEMENT

As shown in Exhibit 4-1, when the consequences of a behavior are positive in a particular situation, individuals are likely to repeat that behavior when the situation occurs again. The introduction of positive consequences, such as peer approval for an associate's correction of quality problems, increases the likelihood of that behavior being repeated in similar settings. This is called **positive reinforcement.** Similarly, when a particular behavior in a given situation results in the removal of previous negative consequences, the likelihood of repeating the behavior in similar settings will probably increase. Thus, the removal of negative consequences is called **negative reinforcement.** If working harder and smarter removes the frown from a manager's face, an associate may attempt to work harder and smarter.

PUNISHMENT

When behavior results in the introduction of a negative consequence, individuals are less likely to repeat the behavior. This is called **punishment.** Punishment differs from negative reinforcement in that an undesirable consequence is introduced rather than removed. Punishment reduces the likelihood of a behavior, whereas negative reinforcement increases the likelihood. An associate who is reprimanded by peers for returning a few minutes late from lunch experiences punishment,

positive reinforcement
A reinforcement contingency in which a behavior is followed by a positive consequence, thereby increasing the likelihood that the behavior will be repeated in the same or similar situations.

negative reinforcement
A reinforcement contingency in which a behavior is followed by the withdrawal of a previously encountered negative consequence, thereby increasing the likelihood that the behavior will be repeated in the same or similar situations.

punishment
A reinforcement contingency in which a behavior is followed by a negative consequence, thereby reducing the likelihood that the behavior will be repeated in the same or similar situations.

Exhibit 4-1
Effects of Reinforcing
Consequences on
Learning New
Behaviors

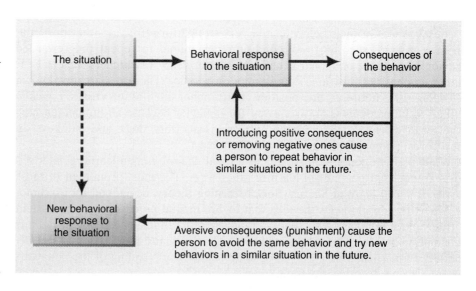

as does an associate whose manager assigns him less preferred work hours in response to tardiness.

Punishment must be used judiciously in organizations because it can create a backlash both among those punished and among those who witness the punishment.[7] It is imperative that when punishment is doled out it be made contingent upon associates engaging in negative behavior.[8] Several examples illustrate this problem. At the *Providence Journal,* a newspaper organization in the northeastern United States, senior management reprimanded two individuals and suspended a third for an editorial cartoon that seemed to poke fun at the publisher. Union officials and many union members believed the punishments were too harsh, resulting in ill will at a time when relations were already strained.[9] At Fireman's Fund, the leadership of a Tampa office terminated an associate who had "dangerous and violent propensities." Although termination was probably a reasonable response, the result was far from reasonable; the terminated individual returned intending to harm former co-workers, illustrating the complexity of managing punishment.[10] At the IRS, some managers failed to discipline associates for tardiness, extended lunches, and so forth in a consistent manner, resulting in numerous problems.[11]

What constitutes an appropriate use of punishment in an organization? When associates exhibit minor counterproductive behaviors, such as rudeness to a peer or a lunch that lasts a few minutes too long, punishment involving a verbal reprimand can be delivered informally by peers or a manager. For more serious behaviors, such as intentional and repeated loafing or consistently leaving the workplace early, a more formal process should be used. Based on requirements set by the National Labor Relations Act, Union Carbide has successfully used the following formal process when dealing with problems as they unfold over time: (1) the problem is discussed informally, and the associate is reminded of expectations; (2) the associate receives one or more written reminders; (3) the associate is suspended for one day, with pay, and asked to consider his future with the organization; and (4) the associate is terminated.[12]

Whether they are imposing minor informal punishment or major formal punishment, associates and managers should follow several guidelines:

- Deliver the punishment as quickly as possible following the undesirable behavior.
- Direct the punishment at specific behaviors that have been made clear to the recipient.
- Deliver the punishment in an objective, impersonal fashion.
- Listen to the offending party's explanation before taking action.

The problems at Korean Air discussed in the following *Managerial Advice* feature were caused at least in part by the overuse of punishment. Clearly, as the case illustrates, the use of punishment at this airline played a role in the crash. Being struck by a person above you in the organization is a particularly difficult situation, even for those in an authoritarian culture. Such an approach is inappropriate in a high-involvement organization. In complex situations, associates and managers need the input of others to avoid making possibly serious errors such as those leading to the Korean Air crash. The changes implemented by the new president of the airline and the director of flight operations have helped to resolve the problem. Because Korean culture respects traditional authority, changing the culture at this airline was difficult.[13] Yet the changes were important for the airline to compete in a global marketplace.

MANAGERIAL ADVICE

Punishment Taken Too Far

Kim Kulish/ Corbis Images

At 1:00 A.M. on August 6, 1997, the pilots of a Korean Air 747 prepared to land at the Guam airport. Because the airport's glide slope guidance system had been turned off for maintenance and because the airport's radio beacon was located in a nonstandard position, the landing was more difficult than usual. A rainstorm further complicated the situation. Under these conditions, the captain needed frank and timely advice from a fully informed and empowered co-pilot and flight engineer. Sadly, no such advice was given by the intimidated subordinates. The resulting crash claimed 228 lives.

The suboptimal cockpit climate on board the aircraft that morning seems to have been caused in part by Korean Air's authoritarian culture, which included heavy-handed punishment delivered by captains for unwanted subordinate input and mistakes. Park Jae Hyun, a former captain with the airline and then a flight inspector with the Ministry of Transportation, believed that teamwork in the cockpit was nearly impossible in the existing "obey or else" environment, where co-pilots "couldn't express themselves if they found something wrong with the captain's piloting skills." This environment was perhaps most clearly evident during training. An American working as a pilot for the airline reported, "I've seen a captain punch a co-pilot . . . for a mistake and the co-pilot just said, 'Oh, sorry, sorry.'" Another American reports being hit as well, but as an outsider he did not accept the abuse and said to the captain, "Do it again and I'll break your arm."

Korean officials, American officials, and many others believed change was necessary to prevent additional accidents and to generally improve the organization. Following another crash and the forced resignations of key leaders in the late 1990s, new leaders inside Korean Air took actions to change the authoritarian, punishment-oriented culture. Yi Taek Shim, the new president, vowed that cultural and technological problems would be addressed whatever the cost. Koh Myung Joon, who became the new director of flight operations, sought captains for training duty who had "the right temperament," meaning they would not use inappropriate, heavy-handed punishment but rather would focus on positive reinforcement for desired behavior. These leaders clearly had useful insights. Korean Air has had an excellent safety record in the twenty-first century, and crucial relationships with partner airlines have been strengthened.

Consistent with actions and outcomes at Korean Air, Francis Friedman of Time & Place Strategies in New York has said that individuals in positions of authority should not "get into a kick-the-dog mentality." Even Simon Kukes, a Russian who achieved notoriety as CEO of Tyumen Oil, has suggested that managers should not "yell, scream, and try to find someone to punish." This is interesting advice, given the general authoritarian culture in Russia.

Sources: "Korean Air Is Restructuring Its Flight Operations Division," *Aviation Week & Space Technology* 152, no. 21 (2000): 21; "Cargo Airline of the Year: Korean Air Cargo," *Air Transport World* 40, no. 2 (2000): 30–31; W.M. Carley and A. Pasztor, "Pilot Error: Korean Air Confronts Dismal Safety Record Rooted in Its Culture," *Wall Street Journal,* July 7, 1999; Z. Coleman and M. Song, "Inquiry Blames Cockpit Crew for KAL Crash," *Wall Street Journal,* June 6, 2001; P.M. Perry, "Cage the Rage," *Warehousing Management* 8, no. 2 (2001): 37–40; P. Starobin, "The Oilman as Teacher," *BusinessWeek,* June 25, 2001; G. Thomas, "Korean Air CEO Vows 'No More Excuses,'" *Aviation Week & Space Technology* 153, no. 1 (2000): 48; G. Thomas, "The Yin and Yang of Korean Air," *Air Transport World* 39, no. 10 (2002): 26–29.

EXTINCTION

Because punishment can be a difficult process to manage, organizations may instead desire to extinguish dysfunctional behavior by removing its reinforcing consequences. This procedure is called **extinction.** It is difficult to use extinction, however, unless a manager has full control over all reinforcing consequences. For instance, an associate may be consistently late to work because he prefers to avoid morning rush-hour traffic or likes to sleep late. Missing the rush hour and sleeping late are both activities that offer rewarding consequences for being late to work. Associates and managers desiring to extinguish this behavior are unlikely to be able to remove these reinforcing consequences.

The reinforcing consequences of some dysfunctional work behaviors, however, may be completely removable. For example, an associate may have developed a habit of regularly visiting the manager's office to complain about her co-workers. Most of the complaints are trivial, and the manager wishes to extinguish this practice. However, the fact that the manager has appeared to be attentive and understanding is a positive, reinforcing consequence. The manager may therefore extinguish the behavior by refusing to listen whenever this associate complains about her co-workers. (During a useful conversation with the associate, the manager would, of course, be attentive; only the dysfunctional behavior should be extinguished.) To use extinction, then, managers must recognize the reinforcing consequences of a behavior, and these consequences must be controllable.

Extinction is supposedly used to eliminate dysfunctional behavior. However, this phenomenon can also result in unintended consequences by extinguishing desirable behavior. In a study of hospital employees, some researchers found that when managers failed to provide feedback for good performance (a reward), employees performed more poorly and became unsatisfied with their jobs.[14]

extinction
A reinforcement contingency in which a behavior is followed by the absence of a previously encountered positive consequence, thereby reducing the likelihood that the behavior will be repeated in the same or similar situations.

Schedules of Reinforcement

Positive and negative reinforcement are powerful tools in many situations. To fully leverage these two tools, it is important to understand schedules of reinforcement.[15] These schedules determine how often reinforcement is given for desired behavior. Reinforcement does not necessarily need to follow every instance of a positive behavior.

The simplest schedule is **continuous reinforcement,** whereby reward occurs after each instance of a particular behavior or set of behaviors. This schedule tends to produce reasonably high rates of the rewarded behavior because it is relatively easy for an individual to understand the connection between a behavior and its positive consequences.[16] Behavior in organizations, however, often is not reinforced on a continuous schedule, for several reasons. First, once initial learning has occurred through training and/or coaching, continuous reinforcement is not required to maintain learned behavior. Second, in today's organizations, both managers and associates are presumed to be self-managing, at least to some degree. Thus, they do not need continuous reinforcement of positive actions.

Intermittent reinforcement, then, is often used to maintain learned behavior. Schedules can vary by rewarding responses only after a specified number of correct behaviors have occurred or after a specified amount of time has passed. The four most common intermittent schedules found in organizations are as follows:

continuous reinforcement
A reinforcement schedule in which a reward occurs after each instance of a behavior or set of behaviors.

intermittent reinforcement
A reinforcement schedule in which a reward does not occur after each instance of a behavior or set of behaviors.

1. *Fixed interval.* With this schedule, a reinforcement becomes available only after a fixed period of time has passed since previous reinforcement. For

example, an associate at an airport car rental counter might receive a dollar and praise for saying "May I help you?" rather than using the grammatically incorrect "Can I help you?" Because the manager delivering the reinforcement has a limited amount of money and time to devote to this bonus plan, he might listen from his back office for the proper greeting only after two hours have passed since his last delivery of reinforcement. Upon hearing the greeting after the two-hour interval, the manager would provide the next reinforcement. A fixed-interval schedule like this one can make the desired behavior more resistant to extinction than the continuous schedule because the associate is not accustomed to being reinforced for every instance of the desired behavior. However, it can also yield lower probabilities of the desired behavior immediately after reinforcement has occurred because the person may realize that no additional reinforcement is possible for a period of time. Moreover, it can yield generally low probabilities of the desired behavior if the fixed interval is too long for the situation.[17] Overall, this schedule of reinforcement tends to be the least effective.

2. *Variable interval.* With this second schedule, a reinforcement becomes available after a variable period of time has passed since previous reinforcement. In our car rental example, the manager might listen for and reward the desired greeting one hour after the previous reinforcement, and then again after one half hour, and then again after three hours. This schedule can produce a consistently high rate of the desired behavior because the associate does not know when reinforcement might be given next. If, however, the average time between reinforcements becomes too great, the variable-interval schedule can lose its effectiveness.[18]

3. *Fixed ratio.* With this third reinforcement schedule, a reinforcer is introduced after the desired behavior has occurred a fixed number of times. In our car rental example, the manager might listen closely to all of the greetings used by a given associate and reward the desired greeting every third time it is used. In industrial settings, managers may create piece-rate incentive systems whereby individual production workers are paid, for example, $5.00 after producing every fifth piece. Although the fixed-ratio schedule can produce a reasonably high rate of desired behavior, it can also result in a short period immediately following reinforcement when the desired behavior does not occur.[19] Such outcomes occur because associates and managers relax following reinforcement, knowing they are starting over.

4. *Variable ratio.* With our final schedule, a reinforcement is introduced after the desired behavior has occurred a variable number of times. The manager of our car rental counter may listen closely all day to the greetings but, because of money and time constraints, reward only the first desired greeting, the fifth, the eight, the fifteenth, the seventeenth, and so on. This schedule of reinforcement tends to produce consistently high rates of desired behavior and tends to make extinction less likely than under the other schedules.[20] The variable-ratio schedule is very common in many areas of life, including sports: baseball and softball players are reinforced on this schedule in their hitting, basketball players in their shot making, anglers in their fishing, and gamblers in their slot machine activities. In business organizations, salespersons are perhaps more subject to this schedule than others, with a variable number of sales contacts occurring between actual sales.

Exhibit 4-2 summarizes various schedules of reinforcement.

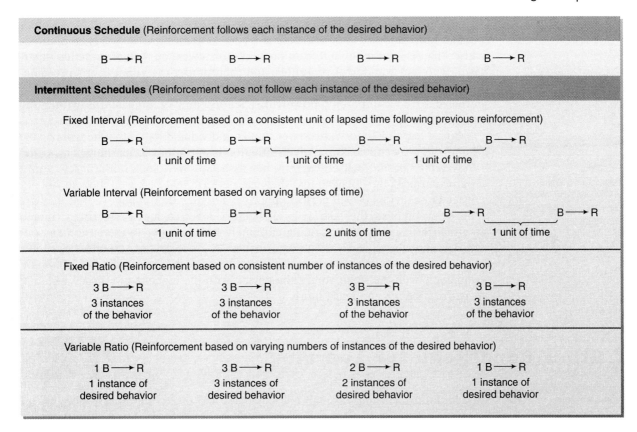

Exhibit 4-2 Schedules of Reinforcement

Social Learning Theory

Although the principles of operant conditioning explain a great deal of learning that takes place, people also learn in other ways. *Social learning theory,* and later, *social cognitive theory,* argue that in addition to learning through direct reinforcement, people can also learn by anticipating consequences of their behavior and by modeling others.[21] In other words, learning occurs through the mental processing of information.[22]

According to these approaches to learning, one way that associates can learn is through symbolization and forethought.[23] People have the ability to symbolize events and to anticipate consequences. This means that rather than having to directly experience possible consequences of one's behavior, a person can try out various scenarios in his or her mind to determine what potential consequences may result from a particular behavior. For example, if a manager has to make a decision about whether to open a new branch office, she can rely on past experience to come up with symbolic representation of the problem and then anticipate what outcomes may occur if she decides to open the new office.

According to Social Learning Theory, people also learn by observing others. Rather than having to experience consequences first hand, associates can observe the behavior of others and the results of that behavior.[24] When results are positive, then associates will model the behavior demonstrated by the other person. For example, if an associate is trying to learn how to give presentations, rather than try out many different presentation styles, he may observe his supervisor, who is a wonderful presenter, and then model the supervisor's presentation style. Associates are most likely to model the behavior of people they perceive to be competent, powerful, friendly, and of high status within the organization.[25]

Social learning theory also states that an individual's belief that he will be able to perform a specific task in a given situation is important to learning. This belief is referred to as one's **self-efficacy.**[26] When associates have high self-efficacy toward a particular task, they believe that they can perform that task well. People will not engage in behaviors or will perform poorly when they do not believe that they are able to accomplish the task at a satisfactory level. Athletes are often trained to visualize themselves performing extremely well in order to increase their self-efficacy, and consequently their performance. A great deal of research has shown that self-efficacy increases performance and learning, beyond ability.[27] If there are two people with the same ability, the person with the higher self-efficacy will tend to perform better and learn more.

self-efficacy
An individual's belief that he or she will be able to perform a specific task in a given situation.

Other Conditions for Learning

In addition to learning through consequences and observing others, more recent research has noted that the following conditions help facilitate adult learning:[28]

- *Associates need to know why they are learning what they are learning.* People become more motivated to learn when they understand why what they are learning is important.[29] For example, in order to successfully train associates to engage in safe behaviors, they must first understand what constitutes safe behavior and then understand the consequences of not engaging in these behaviors.[30] In order for associates to know why they are learning what they are learning, they must be provided with specific learning objectives.[31] Also, allowing associates to either directly or vicariously experience the negative effects of *not* learning may help them understand why learning the material is important.[32] We discuss learning from failure in more detail later in this chapter.

- *Associates need to use their own experiences as the basis for learning.* Many teaching and learning experts believe that people learn best when they can tie newly learned material to their past experiences, take an active role in their own learning, and are able to reflect on their learning experiences.[33] According to the *experiential learning* perspective, it is imperative for learning to include active experimentation and reflective observation.[34] This is why many MBA programs include team exercises to teach teamwork skills. Rather than just reading about the importance of teamwork and how to achieve it, students actually experience their lessons and later are asked to reflect upon what they have learned.

- *Associates need to practice what they have learned.* Practicing means repetitively demonstrating performance stated in the learning objectives. Overlearning due to constant practice improves the likelihood that associates will engage in newly learned behaviors once they leave the learning situation.[35] Overlearning means that performing the new behavior takes little conscious thought, so that the performance becomes automatic.

- *Associates need feedback.* A great deal of research has been conducted on the effects of feedback on learning.[36] Feedback can facilitate learning by providing associates with information about what they should be learning and it can also act as a reward. Feedback is most conducive to learning when associates are comfortably familiar with the material to be learned or when the material is relatively simple.[37]

Training and Enhancing the Performance of Associates

The learning concepts discussed thus far have been successfully used over the years to train newcomers as well as to improve the performance of existing associates. To achieve positive results when training a newcomer, managers often reinforce individuals as they move closer to the desired set of behaviors. The following steps capture the most important elements in the process:

1. Determine the new behaviors to be learned.

2. For more complex behavior, break the new behavior down into smaller, logically arranged segments.

3. Demonstrate desired behaviors to the trainee. Research indicates that modeling appropriate behaviors is very useful.[38] Research also indicates that unless the key behaviors are distinctive and meaningful, the trainee is not likely to remember them on the job.[39]

4. Have the trainee practice the new behaviors in the presence of the trainer.

5. Make reinforcement contingent on approximations of desired behavior. At the outset, mild reinforcement can be given for a good start. As the training continues, reinforcement should be given only as progress is made. Reinforcement should be immediate, and over time behavior should be reinforced only if it comes closer to the ultimate desired behavior.[40]

In newcomer training, managers in many organizations use this approach. Trilogy, a software firm based in Austin, Texas, uses positive reinforcement as new hires work through successively more difficult assignments in a boot camp that lasts several months.[41] E.L. Harvey & Sons, a refuse collector based in Westborough, Massachusetts, has used positive reinforcement as well as mild punishment in its training and orientation program for new drivers.[42] Dallas-based Greyhound Bus Company has used positive reinforcement and mild punishment as drivers master proper city, rural, and mountain driving techniques. As one recent trainee stated, "You're not going to be perfect the first time. Some things you'll get used to doing. I'll get better."[43]

Organizations use numerous methods to train employees.[44] On-the-job training methods include orientation programs, organizational socialization experiences, apprenticeship training, coaching, formal mentoring, job rotation, career development activities, and technology-based training. Off-site training methods include instructor-led classrooms, videoconferencing, corporate universities and institutes, and virtual-reality simulators. Learning can also take place informally through trial-and-error, informal mentoring relationships, interactions with co-workers, or from learning from one's mistakes. We highlight three learning methods below: OB Mod, simulation learning, and learning from failure.

OB Mod

To improve the performance of existing associates on ongoing tasks, organizations must be concerned not only with developing good habits but also with breaking bad ones. As an aid in this process, a formal procedure known as *organizational behavior modification,* or **OB Mod,** is often used.[45] The basic goal of OB Mod, which some refer to as *performance management,* is to improve task performance through positive reinforcement of desirable behaviors and elimination of reinforcements that support undesirable behaviors.[46] Its value lies in the specific, detailed steps that it offers.

As shown in Exhibit 4-3, the OB Mod framework can be represented as a simple flowchart. In the initial steps, managers determine desirable and undesirable behaviors and assess the extent to which individuals are currently exhibiting those behaviors. Desirable behaviors may be as simple as using a production machine or answering the telephone in a different way. In the next step, the functional analysis, managers determine reinforcers that can be used to increase the frequency of desired behavior (for example, praise, preferential work arrangements, time off) and reinforcers that must be eliminated to extinguish undesirable behaviors (for example, social approval from co-workers for loafing). Next, managers apply the knowledge they have gained concerning reinforcers in an effort to alter behavior in a fruitful way. If successful in this step, they can develop an appropriate reinforcement schedule for the future. Finally, the impact of modified behaviors on job performance indicators, such as units produced per day, is assessed.

Research has been generally supportive of OB Mod. One study found that PIGS (positive, immediate, graphic, and specific) feedback, coupled with social reinforcement for desired behavior (for example, praise, attention, compliments), improved the delivery of quality service by tellers in a bank.[47] Another study found that feedback coupled with social reinforcement and time off helped overcome significant performance problems among municipal workers.[48] In Russia, a study determined that feedback and social reinforcement improved the quality of fabric produced by textile workers.[49] Overall, research has found an average performance gain of 17 percent when OB Mod was explicitly used.[50]

OB Mod research reveals that performance improvements tend to be greater in manufacturing organizations (33 percent on average) than in service organizations (13 percent on average).[51] This difference across types of organizations highlights a weakness of the OB Mod approach. For jobs that are complex and nonroutine, such as those found in some service organizations (for example, accounting firms, law firms, and hospitals), OB Mod tends to be less effective. In complex jobs, where excellent performance in core job areas (successful audits, effective surgical procedures) is based on deep, rich knowledge and on skills that can take months or years to develop, short-term interventions based on the simple principles of operant conditioning and social learning may not

OB Mod
A formal procedure focused on improving task performance through positive reinforcement of desired behaviors and extinction of undesired behaviors.

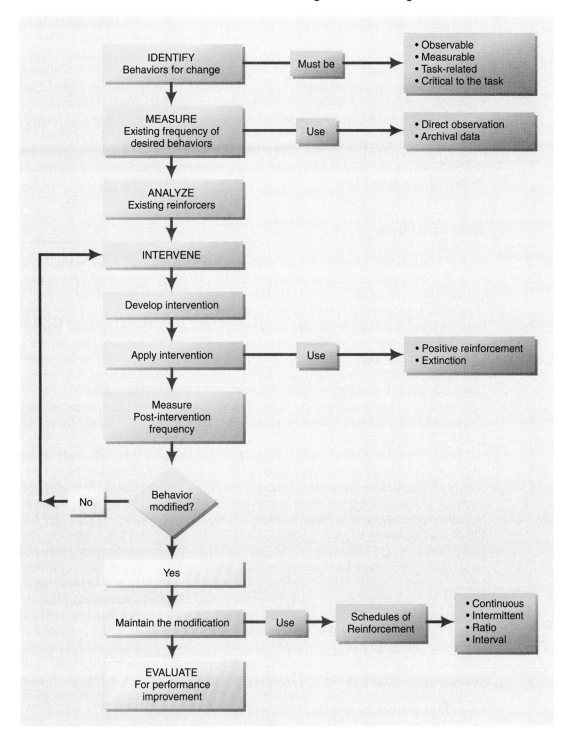

Exhibit 4-3   Shaping Behavior Through OB Modification

Source: Adapted from Luthans and Stajkovic, "Reinforce for Performance: The Need to Go Beyond Pay and Even Rewards," *Academy of Management Executive* 13(2): 49–57.

yield particularly strong performance gains.[52] For organizations seeking to develop their human capital for competitive advantage, this limitation must be considered.

OB Mod research also reveals another important fact: performance feedback coupled with social reinforcements can be as effective as feedback coupled with monetary reinforcers.[53] In the studies of bank tellers, municipal workers, and Russian textile workers, for example, no monetary reinforcement was involved. For managers and organizations, this is very important. Although managers, as part of high-involvement management, should provide fair financial compensation overall, they do not necessarily need to spend significant amounts of money to improve performance.

Simulations

In some situations, an associate or manager may take a particular action with unclear consequences.[54] This happens when the effects of an action combine with the effects of other factors in unpredictable ways. Suppose, for example, that a team leader brings pizza to celebrate a week of high productivity. The team members express appreciation and appear generally pleased with the gesture, but the appreciation is not overwhelming. The team leader may conclude that having a pizza party is not worth the trouble. She may be correct, or she may be incorrect, because other factors may have contributed to the situation. At the time of the pizza party, a key member of the team was out caring for a sick parent. In addition, rumors circulated among the team members that the new plant controller did not embrace high-involvement management. Did these two factors affect the team's reaction to the pizza?

In this example, the team leader could discuss the situation with team members in order to better understand their reactions. Other situations may be so complex that discussions with team members may not be adequate. Consider the complex situation facing the general manager at a Canadian curling club. He plans to increase the annual membership fee to enhance profits. As shown in Exhibit 4-4, the annual fee does influence profits, but the effects are not clear. On the one hand, increasing the annual fee has a positive effect on revenue from membership fees because members who stay are paying more, and this in turn has a positive effect on profits. On the other hand, increasing the annual fee puts upward pressure on the cancellation rate among members and therefore downward pressure on the total number of club members. As the number of club members declines, revenue is lost, which reduces profits. What actual effect, then, will an increase in the membership fee have? Is the overall effect positive or negative? Perhaps an increase up to a point results in more revenue from the members who stay than is lost from the members who leave. But where is the point at which total revenue begins to decline? A further complication is that factors other than membership fee influence revenues and costs and profits.

In situations where a complex system of variables exists and we have some understanding of how the variables affect one another, a **simulation** may be a useful tool for understanding the effects of a potential action. A simulation mimics the real system but allows us to take one action at a time to understand its effects. In our curling club example, the relationships among the variables shown in Exhibit 4-4 could be developed into a simulation. If the manager of the club wanted to change the annual fee to affect profits, he could implement various increases in this fee within the simulation to observe the effects.

simulation
A representation of a real system that allows associates and managers to try various actions and receive feedback on the consequences of those actions.

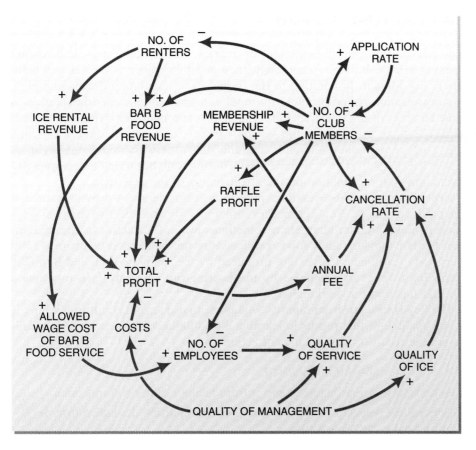

Exhibit 4-4   Causal Relationships at a Sports Club

Note: A "+" between two variables indicates a direct, noninverse relationship. When the variable at the start of an arrow exhibits an increase, there is upward pressure on the variable at the end of that arrow. When the variable at the start exhibits a decrease, there is downward pressure on the variable at the end. A "−" between two variables indicates an inverse relationship. When the variable at the start of an arrow exhibits an increase, there is downward pressure on the variable at the end of that arrow. When the variable at the start exhibits a decrease, there is upward pressure on the variable at the end.

Source: Reprinted by permission, R.D. Hall, "A Corporate System Model of a Sports Club: Using Simulation as an Aid to Policy Making in a Crisis," *Management Science*, 29(1): 52–64, 1983, the Institute for Operations Research and the Management Sciences (INFORMS), 901 Elkridge Landing Road, Suite 400, Linthicum, Maryland 21090-2909 USA.

Although simulations are important and useful, they typically represent simplified models of reality. For this reason, and because some situations are too complex to be accurately represented in simulations, some organizations prefer to substitute or augment simulations with formal experimentation in the real world.[55] The idea is to have associates and managers try different approaches, even though some will no doubt fail to discover which approach seems to work best under particular conditions. Such experimentation has often been used in the development of technology for new products,[56] and it has also been used in areas such as setting the strategic direction of the organization.[57] Bank of America is one of many organizations that regularly conducts experiments.[58] It has a number of branches specifically designated for testing new ideas in décor, kiosks, service procedures, and so on.

Learning from Failure

High-involvement firms often attempt to leverage their human capital in ways that will enhance innovation.[59] Accordingly, they often empower associates and managers to experiment. In addition to the formal experimentation discussed earlier, these organizations often promote informal and smaller-scale experimentation in almost all areas of organizational life, ranging from a manager trying a new leadership style to an associate on the assembly line trying a new method of machine setup. Such experimentation yields learning that otherwise would not occur. A manager's leadership style may have been working well, but trying a new style will provide him with information on the effectiveness of the new style.

Experimentation, however, does not always result in success; by its nature, it often produces failure. New approaches sometimes are less effective than old ways of doing things. New product ideas sometimes are not attractive in the marketplace. Gerber Singles (adult foods produced by the baby food company), Life-Savers Soda (carbonated beverages produced by the candy maker), and Ben-Gay Aspirin (pain relievers produced by the heating-rub company) are reasonable ideas that failed in the marketplace.[60]

The key is to learn from failure.[61] A failure that does not result in learning is a mistake; a failure that results in learning is an intelligent failure. Intelligent failures are the result of certain kinds of actions:[62]

- Actions are thoughtfully planned.
- Actions have a reasonable chance of producing a successful outcome.
- Actions are typically modest in scale, to avoid putting the entire firm or substantial parts of it at risk.
- Actions are executed and evaluated in a speedy fashion, since delayed feedback makes learning more difficult.
- Actions are limited to domains that are familiar enough to allow proper understanding of the effects of the actions.

Firms serious about experimentation and intelligent failure create cultures that protect and nurture associates and managers willing to take calculated risks and try new things.[63] Such cultures have visible examples of individuals who have been promoted even after having failed in trying a new approach. Such cultures also have stories of associates who have been rewarded for trying something new even though it did not work out. At IDEO, a product design firm based in Palo Alto, California, the culture is built on the idea that designers should "fail often to succeed sooner."[64] At 3-M, the global giant based in St. Paul, Minnesota, the culture is built on the idea that thoughtful failure should not be a source of shame.[65]

Learning from failure, OB Mod, and simulations are just three ways in which organizations can train associates. Many organizations, such as the Ritz-Carlton Hotel Company, use multiple methods as evidenced in the *Experiencing Strategic Organizational Behavior* feature on the next page. The Ritz-Carlton provides an excellent example of the strategic importance of training and continuous employee learning. Although the Ritz-Carlton Hotel Company spends much more on associate training than its competitors, the company sees payoff from its training on all important indicators. Customer satisfaction is higher and associates work harder and turn over less frequently at the Ritz-Carlton than they do at other hotels. This superb performance has led the Ritz-Carlton to win almost every prestigious business and training award, while making it an exceptionally successful company.

"We Are Ladies and Gentlemen Serving Ladies and Gentlemen"

This credo of the Ritz-Carlton Hotel Associates may seem simple. However, in order to enact it, associates must go through constant training of a quality that led *Training* magazine to name the Ritz-Carlton the number-one company for employee training and development in 2007. The Ritz-Carlton is known for its exemplary service, which has been recognized by two Malcolm Baldrige National Quality Awards and consistently high rankings in travel periodicals of the world's greatest hotels. The Ritz-Carlton has 64 hotels worldwide, with at least 30 other projects underway; 32,000 associates work for the company.

Keith Bedford/The New York Times/Redux Pictures

All Ritz-Carlton associates are expected to go for what the company calls the "wow" factor by not only meeting guests' needs but also anticipating them. If you order your favorite drink at a Ritz-Carlton in Hong Kong, the bartender at the Ritz-Carlton in New Orleans will know what you want when you sit down at his bar. Special room requests, such as M&Ms in the minibar, will be met each time someone visits a Ritz-Carlton without the guest ever having to ask for the favor. Special software makes such anticipatory service doable. However, this type of service could never be carried out without exceptional associate service performance.

In order to reach this performance level, all associates go through constant training throughout their careers with the Ritz-Carlton. It all begins with a two-day orientation session taught by master trainers. However, training does not stop there. New associates go through at least 310 hours of training in their first year, where they are personally paired with a departmental trainer. They receive a training certification, much like mastercraftsmen, when they can demonstrate mastery of their job. Reviews take place on days 21 and 365.

New employees are not the only associates who receive constant training. All Ritz-Carlton associates are trained continuously. Methods of training include:

- Daily meetings where all employees give and receive feedback on what has been done right and what has been done wrong. Time is also spent discussing one of the Ritz-Carlton's 12 service values.

- On-the-job training by mentors and training directors.

- Classroom training delivery.

- Good performance is clearly rewarded either monetarily or by verbal praise. Ritz-Carlton Associates are almost twice as likely as other hotel associates to report that they receive constructive feedback and are clearly rewarded.

Unlike many other companies, the Ritz-Carlton also devotes a great deal of time to evaluating their training programs, using knowledge tests, performance appraisals, associate and guest surveys, and quantitative service quality measures. Their training programs are responsible for the fact that the Ritz-Carlton sets industry standards for the total revenue per hours worked, employee satisfaction, low turnover rates, and customer satisfaction. In fact, the Ritz-Carlton training methods are so successful that the company began the Leadership Center, which provides training to associates, mostly senior managers, from other companies.

Sources: http://corporate.ritzcarlton.com. Anonymous, "Ritz-Carlton: Redefining Elegance (No. 1 of the Training Top 125)," *Training Magazine*, Mar. 1, 2007 at http://www.trainingmag.com; Lampton, B., "My Pleasure," *ExpertMagazine.com*, Dec. 1, 2003 at http://www.expertmagazine. com; The Ritz-Carlton Hotel Company, L.L.C., "Application Summary for the Malcolm Baldrige National Quality Award," 2000 at http://corporate.ritzcarlton.com.

Perception

As we have shown in the preceding sections, associates and managers who can effectively learn from experience, and help others to do so, contribute positively to an organization's human capital and therefore contribute positively to its capacity to develop sustainable competitive advantage. To further develop the story of learning, we now turn to issues of **perception.** If an associate or manager does not perceive people, tasks, and events accurately, learning from experience is difficult. If an associate or manager does not perceive the world accurately, he will base his behavior on inaccurate perceptions of the world rather than on reality.

Associates and managers are constantly exposed to a variety of sensory inputs that influence their perceptions. Sensory inputs refer to things that are heard, seen, smelled, tasted, and touched. These inputs are processed in the mind and organized to form concepts pertaining to what has been sensed or experienced. For instance, an associate in a catering firm may sense a common item such as a loaf of bread. He touches it, squeezes it, smells it, looks at its shape and color, and tastes it. His mind processes all of the sensory inputs, and he forms ideas and attitudes about that loaf of bread and the bakery that produced it. He may determine that the bread is fresh or stale, good or bad, worth the price or not, and subsequently decide whether products of this particular bakery are to be used. These are his perceptions of the bread and of the producer.

Perception comprises three basic stages:[66]

1. *Sensing various characteristics of a person, task, or event.* This stage consists of using the senses (touch, sight, smell, and so on) to obtain data. Some data in the environment, however, cannot be detected by the sensory organs. For example, operators of the Three Mile Island nuclear facility, which almost melted down in the 1970s, could not sense that a relief valve was stuck open in the nuclear core because they could not see it and the instrument panel indicated that it was closed.[67] Some data, though accessible, are not sensed. Engineers and managers with NASA and Morton Thiokol failed to sense certain features of their booster rockets when considering whether to launch the ill-fated *Challenger* shuttle in the 1980s.[68]

2. *Selecting from the data those facts that will be used to form the perception.* An individual does not necessarily use all of the data that she senses. At times, a person may be overloaded by information and unable to use all of it. For example, U.S. Defense Department officials dealt with overwhelming amounts of data from various sources with regard to the events of September 11 and the conflict in Iraq. At other times, a person may purposely exclude information that is inconsistent with her other existing perceptions. A manager who firmly believes an associate is a weak performer, for example, may discount and ultimately exclude information suggesting otherwise.[69] Accurate perception, however, requires the use of all relevant information.

3. *Organizing the selected data into useful concepts pertaining to the object or person.* An individual must order and sort data in a way that is useful in establishing approaches to dealing with the world. We now explore this aspect of perception in discussing perceptions of people.

Perceptions of People

Shortcomings in the ability to sense the full range of data, to select appropriate data for further processing, and to organize the data into useful information can lead to inaccurate perceptions about people.[70] These erroneous perceptions in turn can interfere with learning how to best interact with a person and can lead to poor decisions and actions toward the person. Effective associates and managers are able to develop complete and accurate perceptions of the various people with whom they interact—customers, sales representatives, peers, and so on. An effective manager, for example, knows when a sales representative is sincere, when an associate has truly achieved superior performance, and when another manager is dependable. These accurate perceptions are crucial to a firm's human capital that contributes to competitive advantage. Next, we discuss several factors that influence the process of perceiving other people. These factors are shown in Exhibit 4-5.

THE NATURE OF THE PERCEIVER

The perception process is influenced by several factors related to the nature of the perceiver. Impaired hearing or sight and temporary conditions such as those induced by alcohol or prescribed medications can, of course, affect perception. Beyond those challenges, the most important factors are the perceiver's familiarity with the other person, the perceiver's existing feelings about the other person, and the emotional state of the perceiver.

Getty Images News

Familiarity with the person is important. On the one hand, an individual may have more accurate perceptions of people with whom she has had a substantial history. Over time, the individual has had many opportunities to observe those people. On the other hand, an individual may pay more attention to newcomers, making extra efforts to notice and process data about them.

If an individual has put a great deal of effort over time into properly understanding certain people, she probably has developed accurate perceptions of their

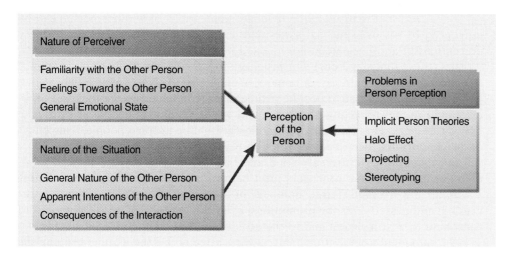

Nature of Perceiver		
Familiarity with the Other Person		
Feelings Toward the Other Person		
General Emotional State		

Nature of the Situation		
General Nature of the Other Person		
Apparent Intentions of the Other Person		
Consequences of the Interaction		

Perception of the Person

Problems in Person Perception		
Implicit Person Theories		
Halo Effect		
Projecting		
Stereotyping		

Exhibit 4-5   Person Perception

characteristics and abilities. If, however, those characteristics and abilities change, or if the people act in ways that are not consistent with their longstanding characteristics and abilities, the perceiving individual may not accurately interpret the new characteristics or behaviors. In this case, the perceiver may be too focused on existing beliefs about the friends and associates to accurately interpret new characteristics or behaviors. A manager who has had an excellent, trusting relationship with an associate over many years may thus disregard evidence of lying or poor performance because it does not fit preexisting conceptions of the person.[71]

An individual's feelings about another person also may affect the perception process. If the individual generally has positive feelings toward a particular person, he may view the person's actions through a favorable lens and thus may interpret those actions more positively than is warranted. In contrast, if the individual generally has negative feelings toward a particular person, he may view the person's actions through an unfavorable lens and thus interpret those actions more negatively than is warranted.

Research conducted at a large multinational firm provides evidence for these commonsense effects. In this research, 344 middle managers were rated by 272 superiors, 470 peers, and 608 associates. The feelings of the 1,350 raters were assessed through measures of admiration, respect, and liking. Raters who had positive feelings toward a particular ratee consistently rated his or her performance more leniently than they should have. Raters who had negative feelings rated performance too severely.[72]

An individual's emotional state may also affect perceptions of others. If the individual is happy and excited, she may perceive others as more exuberant and cheerful than they really are. If the individual is sad and depressed, she may perceive others as more unhappy than they really are or even as more sinister than they really are. For example, in one study, several women judged photographs of faces after they had played a frightening game called "Murder." Those women perceived the faces to be more menacing than did women who had not played the game.[73]

THE NATURE OF THE SITUATION

Factors present in a situation can affect whether an associate or manager senses important information, and these factors can influence whether this information is used in perceptions. Relevant factors are numerous and varied. Three of them are discussed here: obvious characteristics of the other person, the other person's apparent intentions, and the consequences of interactions with the person.

As previously discussed, an individual's perceptions of another person can be influenced by his own internal states and emotions. In addition, the individual's perceptions of another person are affected by that person's most obvious characteristics (those that stand out). For instance, the perceiver is likely to notice things that are intense, bright, noisy, or in motion. He is also likely to notice highly attractive and highly unattractive people, people dressed in expensive clothes and those dressed in clothes reflecting poor taste, and bright, intelligent people or extremely dull-witted ones. He is less likely to notice normal or average people. This effect on perceptions has been demonstrated in research.[74]

In organizations, extremely good and bad performers may be noticed more than average associates. Managers must be aware of this tendency because most associates are average. Large numbers of associates may go unnoticed, unrewarded, and passed over for promotions, even though they have the potential to contribute to a firm's goals and to the achievement of competitive advantage.

An individual's perceptions may also be affected by the assumed intentions behind another person's actions. If, for example, assumed intentions are undesirable

from the perceiver's point of view, the other person may be see
or hostile.[75]

Finally, an individual may be affected by the consequences of
tion with another person. If the consequences are basically positive
likely to perceive the other person favorably. If, however, the resu
tion are negative, the individual is more likely to view the other pe

In one study, a researcher's accomplice was the only member
to fail on the assigned task. The study included two conditions. I
the accomplice's failure prevented the other members from receiv
the task. This accomplice was perceived unfavorably (as less
dependable, and less likable). In a second condition, the other m
payment despite the accomplice's failure. This accomplice was see
competent, dependable, and likable, even though the actual level
was the same as the first accomplice's.[76]

PROBLEMS IN PERSON PERCEPTION

The preceding discussion shows that perceiving others accurately can be challenging. In fact, some of the most noteworthy conflicts in organizations have been the result of misperceiving others. In a well-known example involving Apple Computer, a mid-level manager in charge of distribution misperceived the character and motives of a manager in charge of one of the manufacturing operations, resulting in a battle that was unnecessarily protracted.[77] The distribution manager almost resigned her job with the organization before realizing the other manager was not committed to dismantling the existing distribution function. Because perceptions influence how associates and managers behave toward one another, it is important to strengthen our understanding of the perceptual process so that our perceptions of others reflect reality.

The perceptual process is influenced by factors associated with both the perceiver and the general situation. The problems that prevent the formation of accurate perceptions arise from factors that can be ordered into four general problem groups: implicit personality theories, halo effect, projecting, and stereotyping.

*Peter Marshall/Taxi/
Getty Images*

People hold **implicit person theories,**[78] which are personal theories about what personality traits and abilities occur together and how these attributes are manifested in behavior. For example, if an associate notices that her colleague's office is brightly decorated and messy, she may infer that this associate will be very talkative and outgoing because her implicit personality theory states that messiness and extraversion go together.[79] One type of implicit personality theory that individuals hold concerns whether people believe that personality traits and abilities are fixed and unchangeable in people.[80] Those who believe that people cannot change are called *entity theorists,* while those who believe that people's attributes such as skills and abilities can change and develop are called *incremental theorists.* Recent research has shown that managers who hold an entity theorist perspective are less likely to help and coach their subordinates because they believe that their behavior is unchangeable.[81]

The **halo effect** occurs when a person makes a general assessment of another person (such as "good" or "bad"), and then uses this general impression to interpret

implicit person theories
Personal theories about what personality traits and abilities occur together and how these attributes are manifested in behavior.

halo effect
A perception problem in which an individual assesses a person positively or negatively in all situations based on an existing general assessment of the person.

thing that the person does, regardless of whether the general impression curately portrays the behavior.[82] With regard to the halo effect, if a person is perceived as generally "good," a manager or associate will tend to view the person in a positive way in any circumstance or on any evaluative measure. Thus, if Marianne is perceived as being a generally "good" person, she may be seen as an active, positive force in the organization's culture even if she is actually neutral in promoting a positive culture. If Ted is perceived as being a "bad" person, he may be considered insolent and cunning even if he does not truly exhibit those particular negative traits. In the many studies of this phenomenon, halo error has been found in ratings given to job candidates, teachers, ice skaters, and others.[83]

Assuming that most other people have the same values and beliefs as we do is known as **projecting.** For example, a production manager may think that lathe operators should always check with her on important decisions. The production manager may also believe that the lathe operators prefer this checking to making their own decisions. This may be an inaccurate perception, however, and the lathe operators may complain about the need to check with the manager. Obviously, falsely believing that other persons share our beliefs can lead to ineffective behavior. Specific problems include overestimating consensus, undervaluing objective assessments, and undervaluing those with opposing views.[84]

As already noted in Chapter 3, when an individual has preconceived ideas or perceptions about a certain group of people, **stereotyping** can occur. When the individual meets someone who is obviously a member of a particular group, he may perceive that person as having the general characteristics attributed to the group rather than perceiving the person as an individual with a unique set of characteristics.[85] For example, a manager may perceive union members (a group) to be strong, assertive troublemakers. When she meets John, a union member, she perceives him to be a troublemaker simply because he is a union member. This type of perceptual problem is commonly found among managers who deal ineffectively with union leaders, associates who deal ineffectively with members of the other gender, and associates who deal ineffectively with members of other ethnic groups.

To fully leverage its human assets, an organization must have associates and managers who respect one other and appreciate the unique characteristics of each person. Stereotyping can interfere with these outcomes. Effective, productive interactions require accurate perceptions of people, and stereotypes are frequently incorrect, for two reasons. First, the stereotyped characteristics of a group may simply be wrong. Erroneous stereotypes may result from a number of factors, such as fear of a group and contact with only a select subset of a group. Obviously, when the stereotype itself is inaccurate, applying the stereotype to an individual can only result in error. Second, even if stereotyped characteristics of a group are generally correct, any given individual within the group is unlikely to have all, or even most, of the characteristics attributed to the group.

The following *Experiencing Strategic Organizational Behavior* feature suggests that physical attractiveness plays an inordinate role in the decisions that get made about associates, such as whom to hire, fire, or promote. Such bias, while usually not illegal, is strategically unsound for organizations. Bias of this type means that organizations are making less-than-optimal decisions about how to use their human capital.[86] Furthermore, such unfair treatment can be demoralizing, stressful, and lead associates to perform at less-than-optimal levels.[87] In some cases, such as the L'Oreal and Christine Craft cases, such treatment can lead to discrimination charges due to sex discrimination when men and women are held to different attractiveness standards.[88] As discussed in Chapter 2, such cases are extremely costly for organizations, not to mention the individuals involved.

---

rojecting
A perception problem in which an individual assumes that others share his or her values and beliefs.

stereotyping
A perception problem in which an individual has preconceived ideas about a group and assumes that all members of that group share the same characteristics.

"Beauty Is Only Skin Deep"—Or Is It?

In 1981, Christine Craft was fired from her anchorwoman job at KMBC-TV Channel 9, an ABC-affiliate channel in Kansas City, because she was "too old, too unattractive, and wouldn't defer to men."

Elysa Yanowitz was fired by L'Oreal USA, Inc. for not firing a Macy's saleswoman who was "not good looking enough". A company executive said "Get me somebody hot" for the job."

Annette McConnell, a sales company employee who weighed 300 pounds, was told by a manager that "they were going to lay me off because people don't like buying from fat people."

A large-scale study of factors influencing recruiters' assessments of MBA job applicants found that attractiveness was more strongly related to hiring recommendations than GPA, business experience, and major.

©AP/Wide
World Photos

Research has consistently found that attractive people are more successful at work in terms of hiring, promotions, and salary. The attractiveness bias is a well-documented phenomenon in terms of how people get evaluated at work. It appears that we have a bias favoring people who are good looking and a negative bias against those who are not. Perceptual errors account, in part, for this "what is beautiful is good" effect.

One reason people perceive attractive people to be more suitable for jobs is that attractive people are perceived to be smarter, more confident, and more likeable than less attractive people. A common implicit person theory is that physically attractive people also have a host of other very positive attributes, even in light of examples that prove this not to be the case.

The bias against unattractive people is especially bad when those people are blamed for their unattractiveness, such as in the case of obesity. It seems as if projection is at play here, whereby people project their fears of becoming unattractive onto the person they perceive as unattractive and, thus, ascribe to him negative traits such as being lazy.

As described in Chapter 3, there are several laws that protect people from discrimination based on other characteristics that could lead to perceptual biases, for example, sex, race, and disability. However, there are no federal laws protecting people from discrimination due to unattractiveness. Thus, perceptual errors regarding unattractiveness are particularly problematic because they lead to unfair treatment and to organizations making bad judgments about the qualifications of associates.

Sources: E. Tahmincioglu, "It's Not Easy for Obese Workers," MSNBC.com (Jan. 26, 2007) at http://www.msnbc.msn,com; "L'Oreal to Ask S.C. to Review Ruling on the Firing of Unattractive Worker," *Metropolitan New Enterprise* (Apr. 14, 2003) at http://www.metnews.com; T. Birk, "Christine Craft," The Museum of Broadcast Communications, at http://www.museum.tv/archives/etv/C/htmlC/craftchrist/craftchrist.htm; W.R. Corbett, "The Ugly Truth About Appearance Discrimination and the Beauty of Our Employment Discrimination Law, *Duke Journal of Gender Law and Policy*, 14(2007): 153–175; S. Rynes, & B. Gerhart, "Interviewer Assessments of Applicant 'Fit': An Exploratory Investigation," *Personnel Psychology*, 43(1990): 13–35; R.L. Dipboye, "Looking the Part: Bias against the Physically Unattractive as a Discrimination Issue," in R.L. Dipboye & A. Colella (Eds.), *Discrimination at Work: The Psychological and Organizational Bases*, Mahwah, NJ: Lawrence Erlbaum Associates (2005): 281–301.

Self-Perception

It is widely recognized that perceptions of others have important consequences, but an individual's perception of self may have important consequences as well. Individuals who perceive themselves as highly competent are likely to try new approaches to tasks and perhaps be more productive than their peers. Self-confidence is a powerful force. In an examination of lower-level managers, self-perceptions of competence were found to play a significant role in task performance.[89]

Attributions of Causality

As individuals consider the behavior of others, they will perceive that actions have various causes. Different people, however, may see the same behavior as being caused by different factors. For example, suppose two people observe someone busily working at a task. Both may conclude that he is being positively reinforced for the task, but they may disagree about the nature of the reinforcement. One of the observers may believe that the person is making diligent efforts "because the boss is looking and smiling," whereas the other observer may believe the efforts are caused by the satisfaction inherent in doing the task. The process of deciding what caused the behavior is known as *attribution*.[90]

INTERNAL–EXTERNAL ATTRIBUTION

A person's behavior is often interpreted as having been caused by either internal factors (such as personality, attitudes, and abilities) or external factors (such as organizational resources, luck, and uncontrollable influences). When making these internal–external attributions, we depend to a great extent on our perceptions of the consistency, consensus, and distinctiveness associated with the behavior.

- *Consistency* is the extent to which the same person behaves in the same manner in the same situation over time (he returns from lunch late every day).
- *Consensus* is the degree to which other people in the same situation behave in the same manner (everyone returns from lunch late).
- *Distinctiveness* is the degree to which the same person tends to behave differently in other situations (he returns from lunch late every day but does not come to work late in the morning or leave work early at night).[91]

As shown in Exhibit 4-6, when we see a person's behavior as high in consistency, low in consensus, and low in distinctiveness, we tend to attribute that behavior to internal factors. If the behavior is low in consistency, high in consensus, and high in distinctiveness, we tend to attribute the behavior to external factors. If the behavior is perceived as having a mixed profile (such as high in consistency and high in distinctiveness with consensus being neutral), we often are biased toward internal attributions.

Studies have highlighted many situations in which internal and external attributions play major roles in attitudes and behavior. For example, one study suggests that unemployment counselors and their clients are influenced by these attributions in contrasting ways. On the one hand, unemployed persons are at the greatest risk for mental depression when they believe their situation is caused by uncontrollable external factors. The less control we perceive ourselves to have over events, the more likely we are to become despondent. On the other hand, a counselor is more likely to help an unemployed person if she sees that the

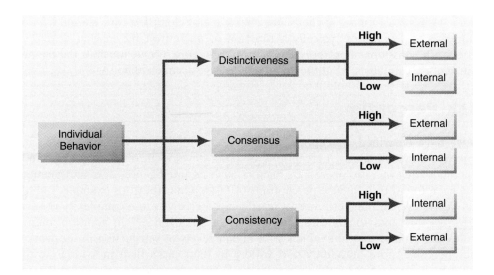

Exhibit 4-6
Attribution Theory

unemployment is caused by uncontrollable external factors. If the counselor has attributed the cause of a client's unemployment to an internal factor (such as poor attitude or low motivation), she is less likely to be helpful.[92] Interestingly, researchers suggest that, in general, observers tend to overestimate the impact of internal causes on other people's behavior and underestimate the effect of external causes. This general tendency is called the **fundamental attribution error.**[93]

fundamental attribution error
A perception problem in which an individual is too likely to attribute the behavior of others to internal rather than external causes.

ATTRIBUTIONS OF SUCCESS AND FAILURE

Monitoring and responding to poor performance are important tasks for managers and, in high-involvement organizations, for associates as well. To respond appropriately, managers must accurately assess the cause of any poor performance they observe. If they are unable to accurately identify the cause, individuals could suffer or benefit unjustly. Unfortunately, several troublesome attributional tendencies play a role.

First, the fundamental attribution error has an effect, although it may be minor. This error causes managers to attribute the behavior of others to internal factors. Thus, an individual's poor performance may be externally caused, but a manager may attribute it to internal causes. For example, equity fund managers who perform poorly are often subjected to unfair criticism from those above them in the firm. Although skill is involved, fund-manager performance is often determined by uncontrollable factors.

Second, the **self-serving bias** plays a role, and it often has a significant effect. This bias works as follows. We have a strong tendency to attribute our own successes to internal factors (a high level of skill or hard work) and our own failures to external causes (a difficult task or bad luck). Conversely, we tend to attribute someone else's success to external factors and someone else's failures to internal factors.

self-serving bias
A perception problem in which an individual is too likely to attribute the failure of others to internal causes and the successes of others to external causes, whereas the same individual will be too likely to attribute his own failure to external causes and his own successes to internal causes.

The fundamental attribution error and the self-serving bias work together to produce a significant bias toward assessments of internal causation for poor performance.[94] This bias means that managers and others make evaluation errors more often than they should. Was the Three Mile Island nuclear disaster in the late 1970s a function of several unforeseeable events coming together unexpectedly or a function of simple operator error? Operators received much of the blame, but it is not clear that they deserved it.[95] Are crashes of large planes—those not caused by sabotage or weather—typically a function of complex technologies that occasionally produce subtle problems, or are they a function of simple pilot error? Pilots receive most of the blame, but it is not clear that they should.[96] Are failures of new ventures typically a function of uncontrollable market developments or the missteps of entrepreneurs? Entrepreneurs receive much of the blame from venture capitalists,[97] but they may not deserve as much blame as they receive.

Task Perception

As we have described, perceptions of people and their behavior are created in subjective ways. Similarly, perceptions of tasks develop through subjective and sometimes idiosyncratic processes. Factors such as intelligence, age, and gender have been found to influence perceptions of tasks. One study, for example, found that individuals with higher levels of intelligence perceive more complexity in various tasks than individuals with lower levels of intelligence.[98] In addition, many studies have found that individuals with higher levels of satisfaction in the workplace perceive more autonomy and variety in their tasks than individuals with lower levels of satisfaction. In a study focused on past graduates of a Hong Kong university, satisfaction and job perceptions were assessed multiple times over a two-year period. Satisfaction was found to influence job perceptions to a greater extent than job perceptions were found to influence satisfaction.[99]

How managers and associates perceive their jobs has important implications for behavior and outcomes. Task perceptions have been linked to intrinsic motivation as well as job performance.[100] They have even been linked to mood.[101] One group of researchers proposed that employees first perceive their jobs at an information level, then perceive the tasks at an evaluative level, and thereafter react to their jobs behaviorally and emotionally.[102] The process of task perception and the resulting effects on behavior have important consequences for organizations. We explore these issues in greater depth in Chapter 6.

The Strategic Lens

Organizations compete on the basis of their resources. The strongest organizations usually win the competitive battles if their managers develop effective strategies and implement them well. To be competitive, managers use the organization's resources to create capabilities to act.[103] A critical component of these capabilities is knowledge. In fact, Bill Breen of *Fast Company* suggests that "Companies compete with their brains as well as their brawn. Organizations today must not only outgun and outhustle competitors, they must also outthink them. Companies win with ideas."[104]

Given the importance of knowledge in gaining a competitive advantage, learning is critical to organizational success. Managers and associates must continuously learn if they are to stay ahead of the competition. Perception is a key component of learning. It is particularly important to top executives, as they must carefully and thoroughly analyze their organization's external environment, with special emphasis on competitors. If they do not perceive their environment correctly, these executives may formulate ineffective strategies and cause the organization to lose its competitive advantage. Understanding the concepts of learning and perception, then, is absolutely essential to the effective operation of an organization.

Critical Thinking Questions

1. How does the knowledge held by managers and associates affect the performance of an organization?

2. What are some important ways in which associates can learn and thereby enhance their stock of knowledge? What role does perception play in the learning process?

3. What are the connections between learning, perception, and organizational strategies?

What This Chapter Adds to Your Knowledge Portfolio

In this chapter, we have discussed basic learning principles and described how they can be used in effectively training and developing associates and managers. We have discussed problems that can occur in complex learning situations and how these problems can be avoided. Finally, we have seen many problems associated with perception processes. For individuals to function as effectively as possible, these perception issues must be understood and managed. At a more detailed level, we have covered the following points:

* Learning is the process by which we acquire new behaviors from experience. Operant conditioning theory and social learning theory are important explanations for how learning from experience works in practice. Learning new behaviors involves three basic elements: the situation, the behavioral response to the situation, and the consequences of that response for the person.

* Positive reinforcement involves the presentation of positive consequences for a behavior, such as praise for working hard, which increases the probability of an individual repeating the behavior in similar settings. Negative reinforcement is the removal of a negative consequence following a behavior, such as taking an employee off probation, which also increases the probability of an individual repeating the behavior. Punishment involves the presentation of negative consequences, such as a reduction in pay, which reduces the probability of repeating a behavior. Extinction refers to the removal of all reinforcing consequences, which can be effective in eliminating undesired behaviors.

* Various schedules of reinforcement exist for learning, including continuous reinforcement and several types of intermittent schedules. Although continuous schedules are rare in organizational settings, several applications of intermittent schedules can be found. Strategic use of reinforcement schedules helps in effectively shaping the behavior of newcomers and modifying the behavior of current associates and managers.

* In addition to direct reinforcement or punishment, individuals also learn by anticipating potential outcomes associated with certain behaviors and by modeling similar or important others.

* Self-efficacy is an important condition for learning to occur. Other important conditions are that people know why they are learning what they are learning, that they can tie the material to be learned to their own previous experiences, that they have the opportunity to practice, and that they receive feedback.

* People learn through many formal and informal mechanisms in organizations. Three examples are OB MOD programs, simulations, and learning from failure.

* Perception refers to the way people view the world around them. It is the process of receiving sensory inputs and organizing these inputs into useful ideas and concepts. The process consists of three stages: sensing, selecting, and organizing.

* Person perception is influenced by several factors associated with the nature of the perceiver, including the perceiver's familiarity with the person, feelings toward the person, and general emotional state. Situational factors influencing person perception include the general nature of the other person, that person's apparent intentions, and the anticipated or actual consequences of the interaction between perceiver and perceived.

* Four general perceptual problems are implicit person theories, halo effect, projecting, and stereotyping. Implicit person theories are individuals' beliefs about the nature of human personality and attributes that can influence how they perceive other people. Halo effect is similar but involves having a general impression of a person and allowing it to affect perceptions of all other aspects of the person. Projecting is the tendency to believe that other people have characteristics like our own. Stereotyping

occurs when we have generalized perceptions about a group that we apply to an individual who belongs to that group.

- Attribution refers to the process by which individuals interpret the causes of behavior. Whether behavior is seen as resulting from internal or external forces is influenced by three factors: distinctiveness, consistency, and consensus. Beyond these factors, there is a general tendency to attribute someone else's failures to internal causes.

Back to the Knowledge Objectives

1. Explain the difference between negative reinforcement and punishment. Give examples of how each process might be used by managers with their associates.

2. What are four intermittent schedules of reinforcement? Give an example of how each schedule might be used by managers with their associates.

3. Explain how an instructor might effectively apply OB Mod in the classroom.

4. What can an organization do to promote learning from failure?

5. What can organizations do to train people to deal with complex and novel problems?

6. What are implicit person theories and the halo effect? How can an individual overcome a tendency to make these mistakes?

7. Give an example of a situation in which you attributed someone's behavior to internal or external factors. What influenced the attribution?

Thinking about Ethics

1. Should associates be punished for making mistakes? If so, for what types of mistakes should they be punished? Are there mistakes for which they should not be punished? If so, what are they?

2. Should all associates be given the opportunity to learn new skills? If not, explain. Should some associates have greater learning opportunities than others? If so, when should this occur?

3. Are there circumstances when it is acceptable to use perceptual stereotypes of others? Explain why or why not.

4. Are accurate perceptions always necessary? In what situations (if any) is it less important to ensure that perceptions are accurate?

5. You are a manager of a unit with 15 associates. These associates have varying levels of education (high school to college educated) and varying levels of skills and motivation. In your organization, associates receive higher pay for acquiring new and valuable skills. How would you decide to whom you would give learning opportunities and to whom you would not provide such opportunities?

Key Terms

learning, p. 111
operant conditioning
   theory, p. 111

social learning theory, p. 111
positive reinforcement,
   p. 112

negative reinforcement,
   p. 112
punishment, p. 112

Building Your Human Capital

Assessment of Approaches Used to Handle Difficult Learning Situations

Associates and managers often face difficulties in learning from experience. When there is little opportunity to learn from experience and when experience is unclear, individuals at all levels in an organization may draw the wrong conclusions. Interestingly, individuals vary in how they handle these situations. Some are prone to contemplate major issues alone. Others tend to discuss major issues with others. Both approaches can be useful, but extremes in either direction may be risky. In this installment of *Building Your Human Capital,* we present an assessment tool focused on approaches to handling difficult learning situations.

Instructions

In this assessment, you will read 12 phrases that describe people. Use the rating scale below to indicate how accurately each phrase describes *you*. Rate yourself as you generally are now, not as you wish to be in the future, and rate yourself as you honestly see yourself. Keep in mind that very few people have extreme scores on all or even most of the items (a "1" or a "5" is an extreme score); most people have midrange scores for many of the items. Read each item carefully, and then circle the number that corresponds to your choice from the rating scale.

1	2	3	4	5
Not at all like me	Somewhat unlike me	Neither like nor unlike me	Somewhat like me	Very much like me

1. Spend time reflecting on things.	1	2	3	4	5
2. Enjoy spending time by myself.	1	2	3	4	5
3. Live in a world of my own.	1	2	3	4	5
4. Enjoy my privacy.	1	2	3	4	5
5. Don't mind eating alone.	1	2	3	4	5
6. Can't stand being alone.	1	2	3	4	5
7. Do things at my own pace.	1	2	3	4	5
8. Enjoy contemplation.	1	2	3	4	5
9. Prefer to be alone.	1	2	3	4	5
10. Have point of view all my own.	1	2	3	4	5
11. Don't like to ponder over things.	1	2	3	4	5
12. Want to be left alone.	1	2	3	4	5

Scoring Key for Approaches to Handling Difficult Learning Situations
To create your score, combine your responses to the items as follows:

Private reflection = (Item 1 + Item 2 + Item 3 + Item 4 + Item 5 + Item 7 + Item 8 + Item 9 + Item 10 + Item 12) + (12 − (Item 6 + Item 11))

Scores can range from 12 to 60. Scores of 50 and above may be considered high, while scores of 22 and below may be considered low. Other scores are moderate. High scores suggest that a person prefers to spend time alone considering major issues (high private reflection). Such a person spends quality quiet time considering the possibilities. Low scores suggest that a person prefers to talk through problems with others (low private reflection). This type of person spends time exchanging information and viewpoints with others.

Additional Task

Think of a time when you faced a major problem with no clear answer. Did you handle the situation mostly by thinking alone, mostly by consulting with others, or with a mix of these two approaches? How effective was your approach? Explain.

Source of the Assessment Tool: International Personality Item Pool (2001). A Scientific Collaboration for the Development of Advanced Measures of Personality Traits and Other Individual Differences (http://ipip.ori.org/).

A Strategic Organizational Behavior Moment

It's Just a Matter of Timing

Teresa Alvarez ate dinner slowly and without enthusiasm. Mike, her husband of only a few months, had learned that Teresa's "blue funks" were usually caused by her job. He knew that it was best to let her work out the problem alone. He excused himself and went to watch TV. Teresa poked at her dinner, but the large knot in her stomach kept her from eating much.

She had been very excited when Vegas Brown had approached her about managing his small interior decorating firm. At the time, she was a loan officer for a local bank and knew Vegas through his financial dealings with the bank. As Vegas explained to her, his biggest problem was in managing the firm's financial assets, mostly because the firm was undercapitalized. It was not a severe problem, he assured her. "Mostly," he had said, "it's a cash flow problem. We have to be sure that the customers pay their accounts in time to pay our creditors. With your experience, you should be able to ensure a timely cash flow."

Teresa thought this was a good opportunity to build her managerial skills, since she had never had full responsibility for a company. It also meant a substantial raise in salary. After exploring the opportunity with Mike, she accepted the job.

During her first week with Vegas, she discovered that the financial problems were much more severe than he had led her to believe. The firm's checking account was overdrawn by about $40,000. There was a substantial list of creditors, mostly companies that sold furniture and carpeting to the firm on short-term credit. She was astonished that this financial position did not seem to bother Vegas.

"All you have to do, Teresa, is collect enough money each day to cover the checks we have written to our cred-itors. As you'll see, I'm the best sales rep in the business, so we have lots of money coming in. It's just a matter of timing. With you here, we should turn this problem around in short order."

Teresa, despite her misgivings, put substantial effort into the new job. She worked late almost every day and began to realize that it was more than simple cash-flow timing. For example, if the carpet layers made an error or if the furniture came in damaged, the customer would refuse to pay. This would mean that the customer's complaint must be serviced. However, the carpet layers disliked correcting service complaints, and furniture reorders might take several weeks.

Thus, Teresa personally began to examine all customer orders at crucial points in the process. Eventually this minimized problems with new orders, but there remained a large number of old orders still awaiting corrections.

Teresa also arranged a priority system for paying creditors that eased some financial pressures in the short run and that would allow old, noncritical debts to be repaid when old customer accounts were repaid. After six months, the day arrived when the checking account had a zero balance, which was substantial progress. A few weeks later, it actually had a $9,000 positive balance. During all this time Teresa had made a point of concealing the financial status from Vegas. But with the $9,000 positive balance, she felt elated and told Vegas.

Vegas was ecstatic, said she had done a remarkable job, and gave her an immediate raise. Then it was Teresa's turn to be ecstatic. She had turned a pressure-packed job into one of promise. The future looked exciting, and the financial pressures had developed into financial opportunities. But that was last week.

This morning Vegas came into Teresa's office and asked her to write him a check for $30,000. Vegas said everything was looking so good that he was buying a new home for his family ($30,000 was the down payment). Teresa objected violently. "But this will overdraw our account by $21,000 again. I just got us out of one hole, and you want to put us back in. Either you delay the home purchase or I quit. I'm not going to go through all the late nights and all the pressure again because of some stupid personal decision you make. Can't you see what it means for the business to have money in the bank?"

"No, I can't!" Vegas said sternly. "I don't want to have money in the bank. It doesn't do me any good there. I'll just go out and keep selling our services, and the money will come in like always. You've proved to me that it's just a matter of timing. Quit if you want, but I'm going to buy the house. It's still my company, and I'll do what I want."

Discussion Questions

1. What did Teresa learn?

2. Other than quitting, what can Teresa do to resolve the problem? What learning and perception factors should she consider as she analyzes the situation?

3. If you were an outside consultant to the firm, could you recommend solutions that might not occur to Teresa or Vegas? What would they be?

Team Exercise

Best Bet for Training

Management development programs are expensive. When organizations are determining which of several managers to send to these programs, they must evaluate each person. Some of the criteria considered might be whether the manager has the ability to learn, whether the manager and the organization will benefit, and whether a manager is moving into or has recently moved into a new position. The purpose of this exercise is to evaluate three potential candidates for developmental training, thus gaining insight into the process.

The exercise should take about 20 minutes to complete and an additional 15 to 20 minutes to discuss. The steps are as follows.

1. Read the following case about *High Tech International*.
2. Assemble into groups of four.
3. List the criteria you should consider for determining which of the three managers to send to the training program.
4. Choose the manager to send using the criteria developed in step 3.
5. Reassemble. Discuss your group's choice with the rest of the class, and listen to other groups' choices and criteria. Do you still prefer your group's choice? Why or why not?
6. The instructor will present additional points for consideration.

High Tech International

High Tech International has reserved one training slot every other year in an off-site leadership-development program. The program emphasizes personal and professional assessment and requires six days of residency to complete. High Tech's vice president for human resources must choose the manager to attend the next available program, which is to be run in three months. The cost of the program is high, including a tuition fee of $7,500, round-trip airfare, and lodging. The challenge is to choose the individual who has the greatest capacity to learn from the assessment and apply that learning back in the organization. Because of prior commitments and ongoing projects, the list of nominees has been narrowed to three:

- Gerry is slated for a major promotion in four months from regional sales manager to vice president for marketing. Her division has run smoothly during the past three years. Anticipating the move upward, she has asked for training to increase her managerial skills. Gerry is to be married in two months.

- John was a supervisor over a portion of a production process for two years before being promoted one year ago to manager of the entire process. His unit has been under stress for the past eight months due to the implementation of new technology and a consequent decline in productivity and morale. No new technological changes are planned in John's unit for at least another year.

- Bill has been considered a "fast-tracker" by his colleagues in the organization. He came to the company four years ago, at the age of 37, as a vice president for foreign operations. Historically, this position has been the stepping stone for division president. In the past year, Bill has displayed less energy and enthusiasm for the work. Eight months ago Bill and his wife separated, and two months ago he was hospitalized temporarily with a mild heart problem. For one month twice a year Bill has to travel abroad. His next trip will be in four months.

Endnotes

1. Hitt, M.A., Bierman, L., Shimizu, K., & Kochhar, R. 2001. Direct and moderating effects of human capital on strategy and performance in professional service firms: A resource-based perspective. *Academy of Management Journal,* 44: 13–28; Sirmon, D.G., Hitt, M.A., & Ireland, R.D. 2006. Managing resources in dynamic environments to create value: Looking inside the black box. *Academy of Management Review,* in press.

2. Gange, R.M., & Medsker, K.L. 1996. *The conditions of learning.* Fort Worth, TX: Harcourt-Brace.

3. Luthans, F., & Stajkovic, A.D. 1999. Reinforce for performance: The need to go beyond pay and even performance. *Academy of Management Executive,* 13(2): 49–57.

4. Thorndike, E.L. 1898. Animal intelligence. *Psychological Review,* 2: all of issue 8; Thorndike, E.L. 1911. *Animal intelligence: Experimental studies.* New York: Macmillan.

5. Hull, C.L. 1943. *Principles of behavior.* New York: D. Appleton Century; Skinner, B.F. 1969. *Contingencies of reinforcement: A theoretical analysis.* Englewood Cliffs, NJ: Prentice-Hall.

6. Bandura, A. 1996. *Social foundations of thought and action: A social cognitive theory.* Englewood Cliffs, NJ: Prentice-Hall; Kreitner, R., & Luthans, F. 1984. A social learning theory approach to behavioral management: Radical behaviorists "mellowing out." *Organizational Dynamics,* 13(2): 47–65.

7. Podsakoff, P.M., Bommer, W.H., Podsakoff, N.P., & MacKenzie. 2005. Relationships between leader reward behavior and punishment behavior and subordinate attitudes, perceptions, and behaviors: A meta-analytic review of existing and new research. *Organizational Behavior and Human Decision Processes,* 99: 113–142.

8. Trevino, L.K., 1992. The social effects of punishment in organizations: A justice perspective. *Academy of Management Review,* 17: 647–676.

9. Strupp, J. 2000. No providence in Rhode Island. *Editor and Publisher,* 133(11): 6–8.

10. Friedman, S. 1994. Allstate faces suit over Fireman's Fund Shooting. *National Underwriter,* 98(39): 3.

11. Guffey, C.J., & Helms, M.M. 2001. Effective employee discipline: A case of the Internal Revenue Service. *Public Personnel Management,* 30: 111–127.

12. Ibid.

13. Hitt, M.A., Lee, H., & Yucel, E. 2002. The importance of social capital to the management of multinational enterprises: Relational networks among Asian and western firms. *Asia Pacific Journal of Management,* 19: 353–372.

14. Hinkin, T.R., & Schreisheim, C.A. 2004. "If you don't hear from me you know you are doing fine": The effects of management nonresponse to employee performance. *Cornell Hotel and Restaurant Administration Quarterly,* 45: 362–373.

15. Latham, G.P., & Huber, V. 1992. Schedules of reinforcement: Lessons from the past and issues for the future. *Journal of Organizational Behavior Management,* 12(1): 125–149.

16. Scott, W.E., & Podsakoff, P.M. 1985. *Behavioral principles in the practice of management.* New York: John Wiley & Sons.

17. Ibid.

18. Ibid.

19. Ibid.

20. Ibid.

21. Bandura, A. 1986. *Social foundations of thought and action.* Englewood Cliffs, NJ: Prentice-Hall; Bandura, A. 2001. Social cognitive theory: An agentic perspective. *Annual Review of Psychology,* 52: 1–26.

22. Stadjkovic, A.D., Luthans, F., & Slocum, J.W. Jr. 1998. Social cognitive theory and self-efficacy: Going beyond traditional motivational and behavioral approaches. *Organizational Dynamics,* 26: 62–74.

23. Ibid.

24. Bandura, A. 1986. *Social foundations of thought and action.* Englewood Cliffs, NJ: Prentice Hall.

25. Wexley, K.N, & Latham, G.P. 2002. *Developing and training human resources in organizations* (3rd Ed.). Upper Saddle River, NJ: Prentice Hall.

26. Bandura, A. 1997. *Self-efficacy: The exercise of self-control.* New York: W.H. Freeman.

27. Judge, T.A., & Bono, J.E. 2001. Relationship of core self-evaluations traits, self-esteem, generalized self-efficacy, locus of control and emotional stability with job satisfaction and job performance: A meta-analysis. *Journal of Applied Psychology,* 86: 80–93; Stajkovic, A.D., & Luthans, F. 1998. Social cognitive

theory and work-related performance: A meta-analysis. *Psychological Bulletin,* 124: 240–261.

28. Noe, R.A. 1999. *Employee training and development.* Boston: Irwin McGraw-Hill.

29. Colquitt, J., Lepine, J., & Noe, R.A. 2000. Toward an integrative theory of training motivation: A meta-analytic pat analysis of 20 years of research. *Journal of Applied Psychology,* 85: 678–707.

30. Burke, M.J., Bradley, J., & Bowers, H.N. 2003. Health and safety programs. In J.E. Edwards, J. Scott, & N.S. Raju (Eds.), *The human resources-evaluation handbook.* Thousand Oaks, CA: Sage, pp. 429–446.

31. Noe, R.A. 1999. *Employee training and development.* Boston: Irwin McGraw-Hill.

32. Burke, M.J., Holman, D., & Birdi, K. 2006. A walk on the safe side: The implications of learning theory for developing effective safety and health training. In G.P. Hodgkinson, & J.K. Ford (Eds.), *International review of industrial and organizational psychology, volume 21.* Hoboken, NJ: John Wiley & Sons, pp. 1–44.

33. Weill, S., & McGill, I. 1989. *Making sense of experiential learning.* Buckingham, UK: SRHE/OU Press.

34. Kolb, D.A. 1984. *Experiential learning: Experience as the source of learning and development.* Englewood Cliffs, NJ: Prentice-Hall.

35. Ford, J.K., Smith, E.M., Weissbein, D.A., Gully, S.M., & Salas, E. 1998. Relationships of goal orientation, metacognitive memory, and practice strategies with learning outcomes and transfer. *Journal of Applied Psychology,* 83: 218–233.

36. Kluger, A.N., & DeNisi, A.S. 1996. The effects of feedback interventions on performance: Historical review, a meta-analysis and a preliminary feedback intervention theory. *Psychological Bulletin,* 119:254–284.

37. Ibid.

38. Bandura, A. 1977. *Social learning theory.* Englewood Cliffs, NJ: Prentice-Hall.

39. Mann, R.B., & Decker, P.J. 1984. The effect of key behavior distinctiveness on generalization and recall in behavior modeling training. *Academy of Management Journal,* 27: 900–910.

40. Sidman, M. 1962. Operant techniques. In A.J. Bachrach (Ed.), *Experimental foundations of clinical psychology.* New York: Basic Books.

41. Tichy, N.M. 2001. No ordinary boot camp. *Harvard Business Review,* 79(4): 63–70.

42. Fickes, M. 2000. Taking driver training to new levels. *Waste Age,* 31(4): 238–248.

43. Robertson, G. 2001. Steering true: Greyhound's training is weeding-out process. *Richmond Times-Dispatch,* May 14: B1, B3.

44. Wexley, K.N., & Latham, G.P. 2002. *Developing and training human resources in organizations* (3rd Ed.). Upper Saddle River, NJ: Prentice-Hall.

45. Luthans, F., & Kreitner, R. 1975. *Organizational behavior modification.* Glenview, IL: Scott & Foresman; Luthans, F., & Kreitner, R. 1985. *Organizational behavior modification and beyond.* Glenview, IL: Scott & Foresman.

46. Frederiksen, L.W. 1982. *Handbook of organizational behavior management.* New York: John Wiley & Sons.

47. Luthans, F., & Davis, E. 1991. Improving the delivery of quality service: Behavioral management techniques. *Leadership and Organization Development Journal,* 12(2): 3–6.

48. Nordstrom, R., Hall, R.V., Lorenzi, P., & Delquadri, J. 1988. Organizational behavior modification in the public sector. *Journal of Organizational Behavior Management,* 9(2): 91–112.

49. Welsh, D.H.B., Luthans, F., & Sommer, S.M. 1993. Managing Russian factory workers: The impact of U.S.-based behavioral and participatory techniques. *Academy of Management Journal,* 36: 58–79; Welsh, D.H.B., Luthans, F., & Sommer, S.M. 1993. Organizational behavior modification goes to Russia: Replicating an experimental analysis across cultures and tasks. *Journal of Organizational Behavior Management,* 13(2): 15–35.

50. Stajkovic, A.D., & Luthans, F. 1997. A meta-analysis of the effects of organizational behavior modification on task performance, 1975–95. *Academy of Management Journal,* 5: 1122–1149.

51. Ibid.

52. Schneier, C.J. 1974. Behavior modification in management. *Academy of Management Journal,* 17: 528–548.

53. Stajkovic, A.D., & Luthans, F. 1997. A meta-analysis of the effects of organizational behavior modification on task performance, 1975–95. *Academy of Management Journal,* 5: 1122–1149.

54. Levitt, B., & March, J.G. 1988. Organizational learning. *Annual Review of Sociology,* 14: 319–340.

55. Thomke, S. 2001. Enlightened experimentation: The new imperative for innovation. *Harvard Business Review,* 79(2): 66–75.

56. Thomke, S.H. 1998. Managing experimentation in the design of new products. *Management Science,* 44: 743–762.

57. Nicholls-Nixon, C.L., Cooper, A.C., & Woo, C.Y. 2000. Strategic experimentation: Understanding change and performance in new ventures. *Journal of Business Venturing,* 15: 493–521.

58. Thomke, S. 2003. R&D comes to service: Bank of America's pathbreaking experiments. *Harvard Business Review,* 81(4): 70–79.

59. Pfeffer, J. 1998. *The human equation.* Boston: Harvard Business School Press.

60. Master, M. 2001. Spectacular failures. *Across the Board,* 38(2): 20–26.

61. McGrath, G. 1999. Falling forward: Real options reasoning and entrepreneurial failure. *Academy of Management,* 24: 13–30; Sitkin, S.B. 1992. Learning through failure: The strategy of small losses. *Research in Organizational Behavior,* 14: 231–266.

62. Sitkin, Learning through failure.

63. Shimizu, K., & Hitt, M.A. 2004. Strategic flexibility: Managerial capability to reverse poor strategic decisions. *Academy of Management Executive,* in press.

64. Thomke, Enlightened experimentation.

65. Ibid.

66. Robinson, H. 1994. *Perception.* New York: Routledge.

67. Perrow, C. 1984. *Normal accidents: Living with high-risk technologies.* New York: Basic Books.

68. Tufte, E.R. 1997. *Visual and statistical thinking: Displays of evidence for making decisions.* Cheshire, CT: Graphics Press.

69. Einhorn, H.J., & Hogarth, R.M. 1978. Confidence in judgment: Persistence in the illusion of validity. *Psychological Review,* 85: 395–416; Wason, P.C. 1960. On the failure to eliminate hypotheses in a conceptual task. *Quarterly Journal of Experimental Psychology,* 20: 273–283.

70. Bierhoff, H-W. 1989. *Person perception.* New York: Springer-Verlag; Heil, J. 1983. *Perception and cognition.* Berkeley: University of California Press.

71. Jacobs, R., & Kozlowski, S.W.J. 1985. A closer look at halo error in performance ratings. *Academy of Management Journal,* 28: 201–212.

72. Tsui, A.S., & Barry, B. 1986. Interpersonal affect and rating errors. *Academy of Management Journal,* 29: 586–599.

73. Murray, H.A. 1933. The effects of fear upon estimates of the maliciousness of other personalities. *Journal of Social Psychology,* 4: 310–329.

74. See, for example, Assor, A., Aronoff, J., & Messe, L.A. 1986. An experimental test of defensive processes in impression formation. *Journal of Personality and Social Psychology,* 50: 644–650.

75. Berkowitz, L. 1960. Repeated frustrations and expectations in hostility arousal. *Journal of Abnormal and Social Psychology,* 60: 422–429.

76. Jones, E.E., & deCharms, R. 1957. Changes in social perception as a function of the personal relevance of behavior. *Sociometry,* 20: 75–85.

77. Jick, T., & Gentile, M. 1995. Donna Dubinsky and Apple Computer, Inc. (Part A). Boston: Harvard Business School Publishing.

78. Mehl, M.R., Gosling, S.D., & Pennebaker, J.W. 2006. Personality in its natural habitat: Manifestations and implicit folk theories of personality in daily life. *Journal of Personality and Social Psychology,* 90: 862–877.

79. Gosling, S.D., Ko, S.J., Mannarelli, T., & Morris, M.E. 2002. A room with a cue: Personality judgments based on offices and bedrooms. *Journal of Personality and Social Psychology,* 82: 379–398.

80. Dweck, C.S. 1999. *Self-theories: Their role in motivation, personality, and development.* Philadelphia, PA: Psychology Press.

81. Heslin, P.A., Vandewalle, D., & Latham, G.P. 2006. Keen to help: Managers' implicit person theories and their subsequent employee coaching. *Personnel Psychology,* 59: 871–902.

82. Guilford, J.P. Psychometric methods.

83. Becker, B.E., & Cardy, R.L. 1986. Influence of halo error on appraisal effectiveness: A conceptual and empirical reconsideration. *Journal of Applied Psychology,* 71: 662–671; Jacobs, R., & Kozlowski, S.W.J. 1985. A closer look at halo error in performance ratings. *Academy of Management Journal,* 28: 201–212; Nisbett, R.D., & Wilson, T.D. 1977. The halo effect: Evidence for unconscious alteration of judgments. *Journal of Personality and Social Psychology,* 35: 250–256; Solomon, A.L., & Lance, C.E. 1997. Examination of the relationship between true halo and halo error in performance ratings. *Journal of Applied Psychology,* 82: 665–674.

84. Gross, R.L., & Brodt, S.E. 2001. How assumptions of consensus undermine decision making. *Sloan Management Review,* 42(2): 86–94.

85. See, for example, Finkelstein, L.M., & Burke, M.J. 1998. Age stereotyping at work: The role of rater and contextual factors on evaluation of job applicants. *Journal of General Psychology,* 125: 317–345.

86. Dipboye, R.L., & Colella, A. 2005. *Discrimination at work: The psychological and organizational bases.* Mahwah, NJ: Lawrence Erlbaum Associates.

87. Ibid.

88. Corbett, W.R. 2007. The ugly truth about appearance discrimination and the beauty of our employment discrimination law. *Duke Journal of Gender Law and Policy,* 14: 153–175.

89. McEnrue, M.P. 1984. Perceived competence as a moderator of the relationship between role clarity and job performance: A test of two hypotheses. *Organizational Behavior and Human Performance,* 34: 379–386.

90. Heider, F. 1958. *The psychology of interpersonal relations.* New York: John Wiley & Sons.

91. Kelley, H.H., & Michela, J. 1981. Attribution theory and research. *Annual Review of Psychology,* 31: 457–501.

92. Young, R.A. 1986. Counseling the unemployed: Attributional issues. *Journal of Counseling and Development,* 64: 374–377.

93. Harvey, J.H., & Weary, G. 1984. Current issues in attribution theory and research. *Annual Review of Psychology,* 35: 428–432.

94. Mitchell, T.R., & Green, S.G. 1983. Leadership and poor performance: An attributional analysis. In J.R. Hackman, E.E. Lawler, & L.W. Porter (Eds.), *Perspectives on behavior in organizations.* New York: McGraw-Hill.

95. Perrow, *Normal accidents: Living with high risk technologies.*

96. Brooks, R. 2000. Regulators point to pilot error in crash of FedEx cargo plane. *Wall Street Journal,* July 26, B.10.

97. Ruhnka, J.C., & Feldman, H.D. 1992. The "Living Dead" phenomenon in venture capital investments. *Journal of Business Venturing,* 7: 137–155.

98. Ganzach, Y., & Pazy, A. 2001. Within-occupation sources of variance in incumbent perception of complexity. *Journal of Occupational and Organizational Psychology,* 74: 95–108.

99. Wong, C., Hui, C., & Law, K.S. 1998. A longitudinal study of the perception–job satisfaction relationship: A test of the three alternative specifications. *Journal of Occupational and Organizational Psychology,* 71: 127–146.

100. Hackman, J.R., Oldham, G., Janson, R., & Purdy, K. 1975. A new strategy of job enrichment. *California Management Review,* 17(4): 57–71.

101. Saavedra, R., & Kwun, S.K. 2000. Affective states in job characteristic theory. *Journal of Organizational Behavior,* 21 (Special Issue): 131–146.

102. Slusher, E.A., & Griffin, R.W. 1985. Comparison processes in task perceptions, evaluations, and reactions. *Journal of Business Research,* 13: 287–299.

103. Simon, D., Hitt, M.A., & Ireland, D. 2007. Managing resources in dynamic environments to create value. *Academy of Management Review,* 32:273–292.

104. Breen, B. 2004. Hidden asset. *Fast Company,* March:93.

PERSONALITY, INTELLIGENCE, ATTITUDES, AND EMOTIONS

5

Answer "true" or "false" to the following questions:

It's maddening when the court lets guilty criminals go free.

Slow people irritate me.

I can easily cheer up and forget my problems.

I am tidy.

I am not polite when I don't want to be.

I would like the job of a racecar driver.

Paul Figura/Getty Images

EXPLORING BEHAVIOR IN ACTION

I Know She's Smart and Accomplished . . . But Does She Have "Personality"?

My teachers were unfair to me in school.

I like to meet new people.

The way you answer these questions, or similar items, could determine whether you get the job or not. These questions are examples of the types of questions found on personality tests commonly used to hire people

for jobs. A recent survey found that over 30 percent of employers use some form of personality test to hire employees. Another survey found that 29 percent of adults aged 18 to 24 took a personality test in the past two years in order to be considered for a job. One of the largest testing companies, Unicru (now a part of Kronos), tested over 11 million candi-

dates in one year for companies like Universal Studios. Personality testing has taken the employment field by storm. Employers are no longer relying only on stellar resumes and amazing experience, they also care about whether an applicant has the right temperament to carry out the job and fit in with the organization. "Although personality-based testing has been around for years, it's now in the spotlight" said Bill Byham, CEO of Development Dimensions International, a consulting firm that is a leader in the personality testing field.

So, what are the right answers? That depends on what the employer is looking for. Common things that employers look for are conscientiousness, ability to handle stress, ability to get along with others, potential leadership, problem-solving style, and service orientation. Different employers look for different personality profiles, and often it depends on the job being sought.

For example, Karen Schoch, who hires employees for Women & Infants Hospital of Rhode Island, states, "A person must be qualified to do the job, but they also require the right personality. We're a hospital that puts a premium on patient care, and we want people who can deliver the concept." Thus, she looks for people who have a blend of compassion, diplomacy, energy, and self-confidence.

Harbor Group LLC, a Houston financial advisory firm, examines dominance, influence, steadiness, and conscientiousness to predict how its associates will handle stress. David Hanson, a founding principal at First Harbor, states "Stress can result in lower productivity, increased absenteeism, tardiness, and high employee turnover." Thus, it is important for his company to identify how people deal with stress so that they can develop ways to counteract the effects of stress.

Southwest Airlines, a company well known for its relaxed, fun culture, takes creating a relaxed, warm environment on its flights seriously. To accomplish this goal, Southwest Airlines carefully screens job applicants to ensure that only individuals with personalities and attitudes consistent with the desired culture are hired. Libby Sartain, former vice president of the People Department at Southwest, put it this way: "If we hire people who don't have the right attitude, disposition, and behavioral characteristics to fit into our culture, we will start to change that culture." Herb Kelleher, chair of the company's board of directors and former CEO, has said, "We look for attitudes; people with a sense of humor who don't take themselves too seriously. We'll train you on whatever it is you have to do, but the one thing Southwest cannot change in people is inherent attitudes." Thus, Southwest tests people for kindness and creativity.

These four organizations all have different cultures and work environments. Therefore, they all look for different personality traits in new employees. The extent to which the personality of associates fits with an organization's culture has been found to have a positive impact on both associates and the organization, and personality testing is one way to make sure that employees have the right disposition to mesh with the organization's culture. This emphasis on cultural fit is found in many high-involvement organizations, where identifying and selecting individuals who complement a carefully developed and maintained culture is a highly important task. One example of a company that has used personality testing to directly impact its bottom line is Outback Steakhouse. Personality testing helped Outback to identify applicants who would fit the firm's needs. Better hiring decisions resulted in growth in revenues and higher profits over time. As a result, associate turnover was reduced by 50 percent, decreasing the company's recruitment and training costs by millions of dollars.

Sources: A.E. Cha, "Employers Relying on Personality Tests to Screen Applicants," *Washington Post,* Mar. 27, 2005, p. A01; A. Overholt, "True or False: You're Hiring the Right People," *Fast Company,* Issue 55, Jan. 2002, p. 110; S.B. Fink, Getting Personal: 10 Reasons to Test Personality Before Hiring," *Training,* Issue 43, Nov. 2006, p. 16; V. Knight, "Personality Tests as Hiring Tools," *Wall Street Journal (Eastern Edition),* Mar. 15, 2006, p. B3A; B. Dattner, "Snake Oil or Science? That's the Raging Debate on Personality Testing," *Workforce Management,* Issue 83 (10), Oct. 2004, p. 90, accessed at www.workforce3.com, Mar. 2007; E. Frauenheim, "The (Would Be) King of HR Software," *Workforce Management,* Issue 85 (15), Aug. 14, 2006, pp. 34–39, accessed at www.workforce3.com, Mar. 2007; www.kronos.com, accessed Mar. 2007; K. Brooker, "The Chairman of the Board Looks Back," *Fortune* 143, no. 11 (2001): 62–76; R. Chang, "Turning into Organizational Performance," *Training and Development* 55, no. 5 (2001): 104–111; K. Ellis, "Libby Sartain," *Training* 38, no. 1 (2001): 46–50; L. Ellis, "Customer Loyalty," *Executive Excellence* 18, no. 7 (2001): 13–14; K. Freiberg, & J. Freiberg, *Nuts!: Southwest Airlines' Crazy Recipe for Business and Personal Success* (Austin, TX: Bard Press, 1996); K. Freiberg, & J. Freiberg, "Southwest Can Find Another Pilot," *Wall Street Journal (Eastern Edition),* Mar. 26, 2001, p. A22; H. Lancaster, "Herb Kelleher Has One Main Strategy: Treat Employees Well," *Wall Street Journal (Eastern Edition),* Aug. 31, 1999, p. B1; S.F. Gale, "Three Companies Cut Turnover with Tests," *Workforce* 81, no. 4 (2002): 66–69.

The Strategic Importance of

Personality, Intelligence, Attitudes, and Emotions

The discussion of personality testing in *Exploring Organizational Behavior in Action* illustrates how important it is for organizations to select the right individuals. Everyone has individual differences that cannot be easily changed. As Herb Kelleher mentioned above, organizations can train people to do only so much; there are individual differences in people that are not easily influenced. In this chapter we explore three such differences: personality, intelligence, and emotions. We also explore another individual difference: attitudes that can be more easily affected by one's organizational experience. All of these human attributes influence organizational effectiveness by influencing associates' performance, work attitudes, motivation, willingness to stay in the organization, and ability to work together in a high-involvement environment.

In Chapter 1, we stated that an important part of high-involvement work systems was that organizations engage in selective hiring, illustrating the importance of hiring people with the right set of attributes. A great deal of research has been done that has shown that certain traits, such as conscientiousness[1] and intelligence,[2] are related to associate performance. Associates' traits have also been linked to how likely they will be to engage in counterproductive work behavior, such as being frequently absent or stealing.[3] In addition to traits directly affecting performance, the degree to which associates' traits fit the work environment and culture is also linked with how satisfied and committed associates are to their organization[4] and how likely they will be to remain in the organization.[5] Furthermore, the attributes of top leaders in the organization have a direct impact on organizational functioning by relating to the group dynamics among top decision

makers[6] and the strategic decisions they make.[7] Thus, the individual traits and attitudes of everyone in the organization can have an important impact on the functioning of that organization.

Because personalities have such important effects on behavior in organizations, care must be taken in adding new people. For a manufacturing firm emphasizing stable, efficient operations as it competes on the basis of low cost, hiring newcomers who are serious, conscientious, and emotionally stable is logical. For a manufacturing firm competing on the basis of frequent process and product innovations, hiring newcomers who embrace change and are inquisitive is important. Furthermore, as you will learn in this chapter, it is critical to hire associates who fit the characteristics of the particular jobs they will hold. Inside the same firm, personalities suitable for the tasks required in sales may be less suitable for the tasks involved in research and development. Although personality, intelligence, attitudes, and emotions are not perfect predictors of job performance and should never be used alone in selection decisions, they are important.

In this chapter, we open with a discussion of fundamentals of personality, including its origins and the degree to which it changes over time. Building on this foundation, we examine a major personality framework that has emerged as the most useful for understanding workplace behaviors. Next, we discuss several cognitive and motive-based characteristics of personality not explicitly included in the major framework. Next, we examine intelligence, another individual difference that has become a controversial topic in employee selection. We then move on to an exploration of attitudes, including attitude development and change as well as several important types of workplace attitudes. Finally, we address emotions and their role in organizations.

KNOWLEDGE OBJECTIVES

After reading this chapter, you should be able to:

1. Define *personality* and explain the basic nature of personality traits.

2. Describe the Big Five personality traits, with particular emphasis on the relationship with job performance, success on teams, and job satisfaction.

3. Discuss specific cognitive and motivational concepts of personality, including locus of control and achievement motivation.

4. Define *intelligence* and describe its role in the workplace.

5. Define an *attitude* and describe how attitudes are formed and how they can be changed.

6. Discuss the role of emotions in organizational behavior.

Fundamentals of Personality

The term *personality* may be used in several ways. One common use—or, rather, misuse—of the word is in describing the popularity of our classmates or colleagues. We may think that Hank has a pleasant personality or that Susan is highly personable. In your high school yearbook, someone was probably listed with the title of Mr. or Ms. Personality. When *personality* is used in this way, it means that person is popular or well liked. This meaning has little value, however, in understanding or predicting behavior. To know that some people are popular does not enable us to have a rich understanding of them, nor does it improve our ability to interact with them.

For our purposes, personality describes a person's most striking or dominant characteristics—jolly, shy, domineering, assertive, and so on. This meaning of *personality* is more useful because a set of rich characteristics tells us much about the behavior we can expect a person to exhibit and can serve as a guide in our interactions with her.

personality
A stable set of characteristics representing internal properties of an individual, which are reflected in behavioral tendencies across a variety of situations.

More formally, **personality** is a stable set of characteristics representing the internal properties of an individual, which are reflected in behavioral tendencies across a variety of situations.[8] These characteristics are often referred to as *traits* and have names such as dominance, assertiveness, and neuroticism. More important than the names of personality traits, however, is the meaning given to them by psychologists. The traditional meaning of personality traits rests on three basic beliefs:

1. Personality traits are individual psychological characteristics that are relatively enduring—for example, if one is introverted or shy, he or she will likely remain so for a long period of time.

2. Personality traits are major determinants of one's behavior—for example, an introverted person will be withdrawn and exhibit nonassertive behavior.

3. Personality traits influence one's behavior across a wide variety of situations—an introverted person will be withdrawn and nonassertive at a party, in class, in sports activities, and at work.

Some researchers and managers have criticized these traditional beliefs about personality traits, believing instead that personality can undergo basic changes. They believe, for example, that shy people can become more assertive and outgoing. Furthermore, by examining our own behaviors, we may learn that sometimes we behave differently from situation to situation. Our behavior at a party, for example, may be different from our behavior at work.

Still, we often can observe consistencies in a person's behavior across situations. For example, many people at various levels of Scott Paper saw Al Dunlap act in hardhearted ways and exhibit outbursts of temper when he served this company as CEO. Many individuals at Sunbeam, where he next filled the CEO role, observed the same behaviors. Apparently, family members also experienced similar treatment. When Dunlap was fired by the board of directors at Sunbeam, his only child said, "I laughed like hell. I'm glad he fell on his . . .."[9] His sister said, "He got exactly what he deserved."[10]

Determinants of Personality Development

To properly understand personality, it is important to examine how it develops. Both heredity and environment play important roles in the development of personality.

HEREDITY

From basic biology, we know that parents provide genes to their children. Genes in turn determine height, hair color, eye color, size of hands, and other basic physical characteristics. Similarly, genes seem to influence personality, as demonstrated in three different types of studies.

The first type of study involves examinations of identical twins. Identical twins have identical genes and should therefore have similar personalities if genes play an important role. Moreover, if genes influence personality, identical twins separated at birth should have similar adult personalities even though they have had different childhood and adolescent experiences. This is precisely the case, as has been found in a number of studies.[11] Consider identical twins Oskar and Jack, who were parented by different people. Oskar was raised in Germany by his Roman Catholic maternal grandmother, whereas Jack was raised outside of Germany by his Jewish father. As adults, however, both of the brothers were domineering, prone to anger, and absentminded.[12]

The second type of study involves assessments of newborns. Because newborns have had little exposure to the world, the temperaments they exhibit—including their activity levels, adaptability, sensitivity to stimulation, and general disposition—are probably determined to a large degree by genetics. If newborn temperament in turn predicts personality later in life, a link between genes and personality is suggested. Several studies have provided evidence for this relationship. In one such study, newborns ranging in age from 8 to 12 weeks were tracked into adult life. Temperament in the early weeks of life was found to predict personality later in life.[13]

The third type of study supporting genetic effects focuses directly on genes. In several studies, researchers have identified distinct genes thought to influence personality. Gene D_4DR serves as a useful example. This gene carries the recipe for a protein known as *dopamine receptor,* which controls the amount of dopamine in the brain. Dopamine is crucial because it seems to affect initiative and adventure seeking. Individuals with a long version of the gene, where a key sequence of DNA repeats itself six or more times, are more likely to be adventure-seeking than individuals with a short version of the gene.[14]

Although genes clearly play an important role in personality, we must be careful not to overemphasize their effects. Researchers typically believe that 50 percent of adult personality is genetically

Ebby May/Stone/Getty Images

determined. Furthermore, we should not conclude that a single magical gene controls a particular aspect of personality. The best information currently available suggests that combinations of genes influence individual personality traits.[15] For example, gene D_4DR plays an important role in how much adventure a person desires, but other genes also affect this trait.

ENVIRONMENT

Beyond genes, the environment a person experiences as a child plays an important role in personality. In other words, what a child is exposed to and how she is treated influence the type of person she becomes. Warm, nurturing, and supportive households are more likely to produce well-adjusted, outgoing individuals.[16] Socioeconomic circumstances of the household may also play a role, with favorable circumstances being associated with value systems that promote hard work, ambition, and self-control.[17] Events and experiences outside the home can also affect personality. Schools, churches, and athletic teams are important places for lessons that shape personality.

Although research suggests that personality is reasonably stable in the adult years,[18] events and experiences later in life can affect personality. Reports have described, for example, how a heart attack survivor reaches deep inside to change himself. In addition, some psychological theories suggest that change may occur over time. One theory proposes a model of personality that includes possible transitions at various points in life, including infancy, early childhood, late childhood, the teenage years, early adulthood, middle adulthood, and late adulthood, for instance.[19] The specific changes that might occur are less important than the fact that change is possible.

The Big Five Personality Traits

For managers and associates to effectively use personality traits in predicting behavior, they must work with a concise set of traits. But thousands of traits can be used to describe a person. Which traits are most useful? Which correspond to the most meaningful behavioral tendencies in the workplace? These questions have puzzled researchers for many years. Fortunately, a consensus among personality experts has emerged to focus on five traits. These traits, collectively known as the Big Five, include extraversion, conscientiousness, agreeableness, emotional stability, and openness to experience, as shown in Exhibit 5-1.

EXTRAVERSION

extraversion
The degree to which an individual is outgoing and derives energy from being around other people.

The **extraversion** trait was an important area of study for many well-known psychologists in the early-to-middle portion of the twentieth century, including Carl Jung, Hans Eysenck, and Raymond Cattell. For Jung and many of his contemporaries, this aspect of personality was considered the most important driver of behavior. Extraversion is the degree to which a person is outgoing and derives energy from being around other people. In more specific terms, it is the degree to which a person (1) enjoys being around other people, (2) is warm to others, (3) speaks up in group settings, (4) maintains a vigorous pace, (5) likes excitement, and (6) is cheerful.[20] Herb Kelleher of Southwest Airlines clearly fits this mold, as does Terry Semel, current CEO of Yahoo![21]

Modern research has shown that people scoring high on this dimension, known as *extraverts,* tend to have a modest but measurable performance advantage over

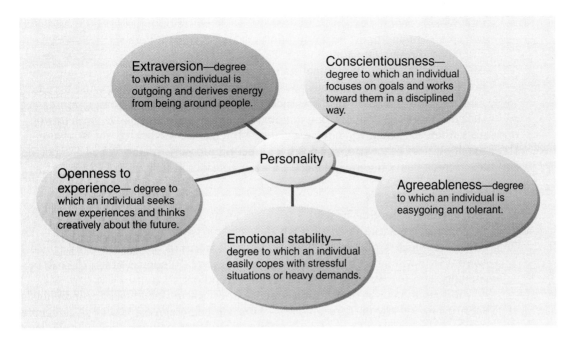

Exhibit 5.1   The Big Five Personality Traits

introverts in occupations requiring a high level of interaction with other people.[22] Specific occupations where extraverts have been found to perform particularly well include sales and management. In contrast, *introverts,* who do not score high on extraversion, tend to do particularly well in occupations such as accounting, engineering, and information technology, where more solitary work is frequently required. For any occupation where teams are central, or in a high-involvement organization where teams are emphasized, extraverts may also have a slight edge, as teams involve face-to-face interaction, group decision making, and navigation of interpersonal dynamics.[23] A team with a very high percentage of extraverts as members, however, may function poorly, for too many team members may be more interested in talking than in listening. Finally, research suggests that extraversion is related to job satisfaction, with extraverts exhibiting slightly more satisfaction regardless of the specific conditions of the job situation.[24]

CONSCIENTIOUSNESS

The **conscientiousness** trait has played a central role in personality research over the past 10 to 15 years. Many current personality researchers believe this dimension of personality has the greatest effect of all personality dimensions on a host of outcomes in the workplace. Conscientiousness is the degree to which a person focuses on goals and works toward them in a disciplined way. In specific terms, it is the degree to which a person (1) feels capable, (2) is organized, (3) is reliable, (4) possesses a drive for success, (5) focuses on completing tasks, and (6) thinks before acting.[25]

Research has shown that individuals scoring high on conscientiousness have a performance edge in most occupations and tend to perform well on teams.[26] This is to be expected because irresponsible, impulsive, low-achievement-striving

conscientiousness
The degree to which an individual focuses on goals and works toward them in a disciplined way.

individuals generally are at a disadvantage in activities both inside and outside the workplace. In an important study, hundreds of individuals were tracked from early childhood through late adulthood.[27] Their success was assessed in terms of job satisfaction in midlife, occupational status in midlife, and annual income in late adulthood. Conscientiousness, which was fairly stable over the participants' lifetimes, positively affected each of these success measures. This is the reason companies such as Microsoft, Bain & Company, and Goldman Sachs emphasize conscientiousness when searching for new associates.[28] Interestingly, research shows that conscientiousness has a stronger positive effect on job performance when the person also scores high on agreeableness, the trait considered next.[29]

AGREEABLENESS

The **agreeableness** trait has also received a great deal of attention in recent years. Agreeableness is the degree to which a person is easygoing and tolerant—the degree to which a person (1) believes in the honesty of others, (2) is straightforward, (3) is willing to help others, (4) tends to yield under conflict, (5) exhibits humility, and (6) is sensitive to the feelings of others.[30]

Research has not shown a consistent pattern of job outcomes for individuals scoring high or low on agreeableness. After all, being agreeable and disagreeable can be valuable at different times in the same job. A manager, for example, may need to discipline an associate in the morning but behave very agreeably toward union officials in the afternoon. A salesperson may need to be tough in negotiations on one day but treat a long–standing customer with gracious deference on the next day.

Agreeable individuals do, however, seem to be consistently effective in teamwork.[31] They are positive for interpersonal dynamics, as they are sensitive to the feelings of others and often try to ensure the participation and success of all team members. Teams with many members who are agreeable have been found to perform well.[32] Having an extremely high percentage of very agreeable team members, however, may be associated with too little debate on important issues. When teams must make important decisions and solve nonroutine problems, having some individuals with lower scores on agreeableness may be an advantage.

EMOTIONAL STABILITY

The trait of **emotional stability** relates to how a person copes with stressful situations or heavy demands. Specific features of this trait include the degree to which a person (1) is relaxed, (2) is slow to feel anger, (3) rarely becomes discouraged, (4) rarely becomes embarrassed, (5) resists unhealthy urges associated with addictions, and (6) handles crises well.[33] Research has shown that emotionally stable individuals tend to have an edge in task performance across a large number of occupations.[34] This is reasonable, for stable individuals are less likely to exhibit characteristics that may interfere with performance, such as being anxious, hostile, and insecure. Similarly, emotionally stable individuals seem to have modest but measurable advantages as team members.[35] Several studies reveal that teams perform more effectively when composed of members scoring high on this trait.[36] Finally, research shows that emotional stability is positively linked to job satisfaction, independent of the specific conditions of the job situation.[37]

OPENNESS TO EXPERIENCE

The **openness** trait is the degree to which a person seeks new experiences and thinks creatively about the future. More specifically, openness is the degree to which a person (1) has a vivid imagination, (2) has an appreciation for art and

agreeableness
The degree to which an individual is easygoing and tolerant.

emotional stability
The degree to which an individual easily handles stressful situations and heavy demands.

openness to experience
The degree to which an individual seeks new experiences and thinks creatively about the future.

beauty, (3) values and respects emotions in himself and others, (4) prefers variety to routine, (5) has broad intellectual curiosity, and (6) is open to reexamining closely held values.[38] Research suggests that both individuals scoring high and individuals scoring low on openness can perform well in a variety of occupations and can function well on teams.[39] Those who score high on this dimension of personality, however, are probably more effective at particular tasks calling for vision and creativity, such as the creative aspects of advertising, the creative aspects of marketing, and many aspects of working in the arts. At W.L. Gore and Associates, maker of world–renowned Gore-Tex products (such as sealants and fabrics), strong openness is valued for many aspects of engineering, sales, and marketing because the company has been successful through innovation and wants to keep its culture of creativity, discovery, and initiative.[40] Individuals with lower openness scores may be more effective in jobs calling for strong adherence to rules, such as piloting airplanes and accounting.

The Big Five as a Tool for Selecting New Associates and Managers

Given the links between important competencies and specific personality traits, it is not surprising that personality assessment can play a role in hiring decisions. Although no single tool should be used as the basis for hiring new associates and managers, personality assessment can be a useful part of a portfolio of tools that includes structured interviews and skills evaluations. In recent reviews of available tools, Big Five assessments have been shown to provide useful predictions of future job performance.[43] It is important, however, to develop a detailed understanding of how personality traits predict performance in a specific situation. Such understanding requires that the general information just discussed be supplemented by (1) an in-depth analysis of the requirements of a particular job in a particular organization and (2) an in-depth determination of which traits support performance in that particular job. In some cases, only certain aspects of a trait may be important in a specific situation. For example, being slow to anger and not prone to frustration may be crucial aspects of emotional stability for particular jobs, whereas being relaxed may be much less important for these jobs. Call center operator positions call for this particular combination of characteristics. They have to respond positively to customers, even when customers are rude or hostile.[44]

The Big Five and High-Involvement Management

We now turn to competencies that are important for high-involvement management. Combinations of several Big Five traits likely provide a foundation for important competencies. Although research connecting the Big Five to these competencies has not been extensive, the evidence to date suggests important linkages.

Recall that high-involvement management focuses on developing associates so that substantial authority can be delegated to them. Available research suggests that managers' competencies in developing, delegating, and motivating are enhanced by high extraversion, high conscientiousness, and high emotional stability.[41] This

Exhibit 5-2	The Big Five and High-Involvement Management		
Competencies	Description	Big Five Traits*	

For Managers

Competencies	Description	Big Five Traits*
Delegating to others	Patience in providing information and support when empowering others, but also the ability to confront individuals when there is a problem	E+ C+ A– ES+ O+
Developing others	Interest in sharing information, ability to coach and train, and interest in helping others plan careers	E+ (C+) A++ ES+ (O+)
Motivating others	Ability to bring out the best in other people, desire to recognize contributions of others, and in general an interest in others	E++ C+ (A+) ES+

For Associates

Competencies	Description	Big Five Traits*
Decision-making skills	Careful consideration of important inputs, little putting off of decisions, and no tendency to change mind repeatedly	E+ C++ A– ES+ O+
Self-development	Use of all available resources for improvement, interest in feedback, and lack of defensiveness	E+ C++ A+ ES+ (O–)
Self-management	Little procrastination, effective time management, and a focus on targets	E+ C+ (A–)
Teamwork	Willingness to subordinate personal interests for the team, ability to follow or lead depending on the needs of the team, and commitment to building team spirit	E+ C+ A++ ES+ O+

* Entries in the exhibit are defined as follows: E = extraversion, C = conscientiousness, A = agreeableness, ES = emotional stability (many researchers define this using a reverse scale and use the label "need for stability" or "neuroticism"), and O = openness to experience. A "+" indicates that higher scores on the trait appear to promote the listed competency. A "++" indicates that higher scores on a trait appear to have very significant effects on the listed competency. Similarly, a "–" indicates that low levels of a trait appear to promote the listed competency. Parentheses are used in cases where some aspects of a trait are associated with the listed competency but the overall trait is not. For example, only the first and fourth aspects of conscientiousness (feels capable and possesses a drive for success) have been found to be associated with the competency for developing others.

Source: Adapted from P.J. Howard and J.M. Howard, *The Owner's Manual for Personality at Work* (Austin, TX: Bard Press, 2001).

research is summarized in Exhibit 5-2 and is consistent with our earlier discussion, which pointed out that conscientious, emotionally stable individuals have advantages in many situations and that extraverts have a slight advantage in situations requiring a high level of interaction with people.

As might be expected, available research also indicates that these same characteristics provide advantages to associates in high-involvement organizations. For associates, competencies in self-development, decision making, self-management, and teamwork are crucial. Conscientious, emotionally stable individuals are likely to work at these competencies, and being an extravert may present a slight advantage.[42] Agreeableness and openness do not appear to have consistent effects on the competencies discussed here.

Cognitive and Motivational Properties of Personality

We turn next to several cognitive and motivational concepts that have received attention as separate and important properties related to personality. They are defined as follows (see Exhibit 5-3):

- *Cognitive properties*—properties of individuals' perceptual and thought processes that affect how they typically process information
- *Motivational properties*—stable differences in individuals that energize and maintain overt behaviors

COGNITIVE CONCEPTS

Differences in how people use their intellectual capabilities may result in vastly different perceptions and judgments. Personality concepts that focus on cognitive processes help us to understand these differences. Three such concepts are locus of control, authoritarianism, and self-monitoring.

The personality concept of **locus of control** refers to a person's tendency to attribute the cause or control of events either to herself or to factors in the external environment. People who tend to believe that they have control over events are said to have an "internal" locus of control. Those who consistently believe that

locus of control
The degree to which an individual attributes control of events to self or external factors.

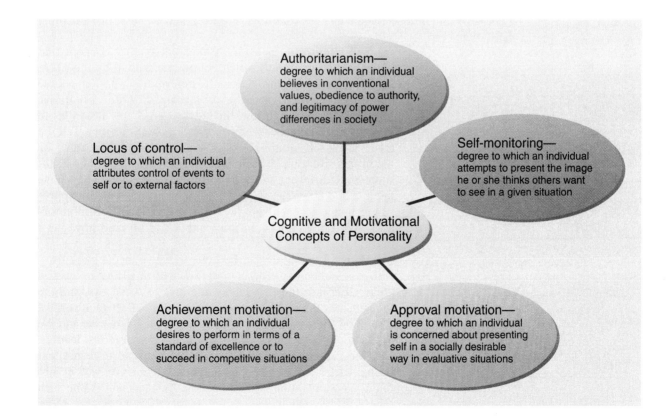

Exhibit 5-3   Cognitive and Motivational Concepts of Personality

events are controlled by outside forces in the environment have an "external" locus of control.[45]

Internals believe they can control what happens to them. This often leads them to engage in work and leisure activities requiring greater skill[46] and to be less conforming to group influences.[47] Internals, then, tend to think they can be successful if they simply work hard enough, and this belief may be reflected in their work habits, especially on difficult tasks. They also tend to exhibit a greater sense of well-being, a finding that holds worldwide.[48] *Externals* believe that what happens to them is more a matter of luck or fate, and they see little connection between their own behavior and success or failure. They are more conforming and may therefore be less argumentative and easier to supervise. Structured tasks and plenty of supervision suit them well. Overall, associates with an internal locus of control experience more positive work outcomes than people with an external locus of control, including higher motivation and less job stress.[49]

The original research on **authoritarianism** began as an effort to identify people who might be susceptible to anti-Semitic ideologies. Over time, the concept evolved into its present meaning—the extent to which a person believes in conventional values, obedience to authority, and the legitimacy of power and status differences in society.[50] Authoritarianism has been extensively researched. Individuals who score high on this concept tend to believe that status and the use of power in organizations are proper. They are submissive to people in power and aggressive toward those who break rules.[51] Furthermore, they may be more willing to accept unethical behavior in others when those others are in powerful or high-status positions.[52] Such people tend to adjust readily to rules and regulations and emerge as leaders in situations requiring a great deal of control by the manager.

authoritarianism
The degree to which an individual believes in conventional values, obedience to authority, and legitimacy of power differences in society.

self-monitoring
The degree to which an individual attempts to present the image he or she thinks others want to see in a given situation.

Self-monitoring is an important personality concept that describes the degree to which people are guided by their true selves in decisions and actions. It determines whether people are fully consistent in behavior across different situations. Low self-monitors follow the advice given by Polonius to Laertes in Shakespeare's *Hamlet*:[53] "To thine own self be true." Low self-monitors ask, "Who am I, and how can I be me in this situation?"[54] In contrast, high self-monitors present somewhat different faces in different situations. They have been called chameleon-like, as they try to present the appropriate image to each separate audience.[55] High self-monitors ask, "Who does this situation want me to be, and how can I be that person?"[56]

High self-monitors can be quite effective in the workplace, with a tendency to outperform low self-monitors in several areas.[57] Because they are highly attentive to social cues and the thoughts of others, they are sometimes more effective at conflict resolution. Because they are attentive to social dynamics and the expectations of others, they frequently emerge as leaders. Because they are more likely to use interpersonal strategies that fit the desires of other people, they tend to perform well in jobs requiring cooperation and interaction. Management is one such job, and research indicates that high self-monitors are more effective managers. In one study, MBA graduates were tracked for five years after graduation. Those MBAs who were high self-monitors received more managerial promotions.[58]

Fabian Cevallos/Corbis Sygma

MOTIVATIONAL CONCEPTS

Motivational concepts of personality are reflected more in a person's basic needs than in his or her thought processes. Two important concepts in this category are achievement motivation and approval motivation.

Achievement motivation is commonly referred to as the need for achievement (or *n-Ach*). It is an important determinant of aspiration, effort, and persistence in situations where performance will be evaluated according to some standard of excellence.[59] Thus, need for achievement is the strength of a person's desire to perform in terms of a standard of excellence or to succeed in competitive situations. Unlike most conceptualizations of personality traits, need for achievement has been related to particular situations. That is, it is activated only in situations of expected excellence or competition. The interaction of personality and the immediate environment is obvious in this theory, and it affects the strength of motivation.

Persons with a high need for achievement set their goals and tend to accept responsibility for both success and failure. They dislike goals that are either extremely difficult or easy, tending to prefer goals of moderate difficulty. They also need feedback regarding their performance. People with a high need for achievement are also less likely to procrastinate than people with a low need for achievement.[60]

This personality characteristic is often misinterpreted. For example, some may think that need for achievement is related to desire for power and control. High need achievers, however, tend to focus on task excellence rather than on power.

Approval motivation is another important motive-based personality concept. Researchers have noted the tendency for some people to present themselves in socially desirable ways when they are in evaluative situations. Such people are highly concerned about the approval of others. Approval motivation is also related to conformity and "going along to get along."[61]

Ironically, the assessment of one's own personality is an evaluative situation, and persons high in approval motivation tend to respond to personality tests in socially desirable ways. In other words, such people will try to convey positive impressions of themselves. Such tendencies lead individuals to "fake" their answers to personality questionnaires according to the perceived desirability of the responses. Many questionnaires contain "lie" scales and sets of items to detect this social approval bias. Such precautions are especially important when personality tests are used to select, promote, or identify persons for important organizational purposes.

> **achievement motivation**
> The degree to which an individual desires to perform in terms of a standard of excellence or to succeed in competitive situations.

> **approval motivation**
> The degree to which an individual is concerned about presenting him- or herself in a socially desirable way in evaluative situations.

Some Cautionary and Concluding Remarks

Personality characteristics may change to some degree, and situational forces may at times overwhelm the forces of personality. People can adjust to their situations, particularly those who are high self-monitors. An introverted person may be somewhat sociable in a sales meeting, and a person with an external locus of control may on occasion accept personal responsibility for his failure. Furthermore, some people can be trained or developed in jobs that seem to conflict with their personalities. Fit between an individual's personality and the job does, however, convey some advantages. Overall, the purpose of measuring personality is to know that some people may fit a given job situation better than others. For those who fit less well, we may want to provide extra help, training, or counseling before making the decision to steer them toward another position or type of work. We also note that personality testing in organizations should focus only on "normal" personality characteristics. According to the Americans with Disabilities Act (1990), it is illegal to screen out potential employees based on the results of personality tests designed to measure psychological disabilities (e.g., depression or extreme anxiety).

The information on personality and performance presented in this chapter has been developed largely from research in the United States and Canada. Research in Europe is reasonably consistent,[62] but other parts of the world have been studied less. Great care must be taken in applying the results of U.S.- and Canadian-based research to other regions of the world.

In conclusion, determining the personality and behavioral attributes of higher performers in an organization can help a firm to improve its performance over time, as suggested in the *Experiencing Strategic Organizational Behavior* feature. Patricia Harris, Vice President of McDonald's Corporation, USA and Global Chief Diversity Officer, exemplifies such a high performer whose personality fits the organization's strategies and goals.

EXPERIENCING STRATEGIC ORGANIZATIONAL BEHAVIOR

"I Have Ketchup in My Veins"

Nathan Mandell Photography

Patricia Harris uses the above phrase to describe her commitment and fit with the McDonald's Corporation. Ms. Harris, currently a Vice President of McDonald's Corporation, USA and the Global Chief Diversity Officer, began her career with the company over 30 years ago. She started at McDonald's in 1976 in a secretarial position and soon began rising through the ranks, while attending college part-time and raising a family. Many of Ms. Harris's positions have been in human resource management and she is often attributed in making McDonald's a current leader and early forerunner in promoting employee diversity, leading the company to win the coveted Equal Employment Opportunity Commission's "Freedom to Compete Award" in 2006.

Several attributes of Patricia Harris have led to her phenomenal career. First of all, she is high on conscientiousness. Ms. Harris's colleagues describe her as "driven" and she has often "stepped out of her comfort zone" to take on new job challenges. She is also goal driven to develop diversity processes and programs to help build McDonald's business all over the world. While being extremely performance-focused, Ms. Harris also displays agreeableness by serving as a mentor to many other McDonald's associates and crediting her own mentors and team members when asked about her success. Her high need for achievement came through when, early in her career, she told her boss and mentor: "I want your job!" Ms. Harris also has a strong internal locus of control because she focuses on making her environment and the company's a better place to work. Finally, she demonstrates a great deal of intelligence in dealing with her job. In addition to a temperament that makes her very well suited for her career, she also possesses the knowledge and intelligence that have helped make McDonald's a leader in diversity. Rich Floersch, executive vice president in charge of human relations, states: "She's very well informed, a true student of diversity. She is good at analyzing U.S. diversity principles and applying them in an international market. She's also a good listener who understands the business and culture very well."

Patricia Harris would probably be a success anywhere she worked—yet her true passion for McDonald's and its diversity initiatives seems to set her apart from most other executives. In 1985, when Ms. Harris was first asked to become an affirmative action manager, she was apprehensive about taking the job because affirmative action was not a popular issue at the time. She overcame her apprehension and started on her path to dealing with diversity issues. She states that "this job truly became my passion. It's who I am, both personally and professionally." By working on diversity issues, Ms. Harris was able to realize not only her professional goals, but her personal goals of helping women and minorities. Ray Kroc, the founder of McDonald's, stated that "None of us is as good as all of us," focusing on the importance of inclusion and ownership by all employees. This value permeates McDonald's corporate vision and also coincides with the personal vision of Patricia Harris. Thus, not only is she extremely competent at her job, she is also passionate about her job and her organization. Patricia Harris exemplifies what happens when an individual's traits, abilities, and passion line up with the vision of the organization.

Sources: A. Pomeroy, Dec. 2006. "She's Still Lovin' It," *HRMagazine*, pp. 58–61; anonymous staff writer, "An Interview with Pat Harris, Vice President Diversity Initiatives with McDonald's Corporation," http://www.wmploymwntguide.com/careeradvice/Leading_teh_Way-in_Diversity.html, accessed Apr. 18, 2007; J. Lawn, July 2006, "Shattered Glass and Personal Journeys," *FoodManagement*, http://www.food-management.com/article/13670; anonymous, Apr. 11, 2005, "Ray Kroc: Founder's Philosophies Remain at the Heart of McDonald's Success," *Nation's Restaurant News*, http://findarticles.com/p/articles/mi_m3190/is_15_39/ai_n13649039.

Intelligence

In the preceding section, we saw how important personality is to organizational behavior and achieving a high-involvement workplace. There is another stable individual difference that can greatly affect organizational behavior, particularly job performance. This trait is *cognitive ability,* more commonly referred to as **intelligence.** Intelligence refers to the ability to develop and understand concepts, particularly more complex and abstract concepts.[63] Despite its importance, intelligence as an aspect of human ability has been somewhat controversial. Some psychologists and organizational behavior researchers do not believe that a meaningful general intelligence factor exists. Instead, they believe that many different types of intelligence exist and that most of us have strong intelligence in one or more areas. These areas might include the following:[64]

intelligence
General mental ability used in complex information processing.

- *Number aptitude*—the ability to handle mathematics
- *Verbal comprehension*—the ability to understand written and spoken words
- *Perceptual speed*—the ability to process visual data quickly
- *Spatial visualization*—the ability to imagine a different physical configuration—for example, to imagine how a room would look with the furniture rearranged
- *Deductive reasoning*—the ability to draw a conclusion or make a choice that logically follows from existing assumptions and data
- *Inductive reasoning*—the ability to identify, after observing specific cases or instances, the general rules that govern a process or that explain an outcome—for example, to identify the general factors that play a role in a successful product launch after observing one product launch in a single company
- *Memory*—the ability to store and recall previous experiences

Most psychologists and organizational behavior researchers who have extensively studied **intelligence** believe, however, that a single unifying intelligence factor exists, a factor that blends together all of the areas from above. They also

Exhibit 5-4	Intelligence and Success
Job	**Effects of Intelligence**
Military Jobs*	*Percentage of Success in Training Attributable to General Intelligence*
Nuclear weapons specialist	77%
Air crew operations specialist	70%
Weather specialist	69%
Intelligence specialist	67%
Fireman	60%
Dental assistant	55%
Security police	54%
Vehicle maintenance	49%
General maintenance	28%
Civilian Jobs**	*Degree to which General Intelligence Predicts Job Performance (0 to 1 scale)*
Sales	.61
Technical assistant	.54
Manager	.53
Skilled trades and craft workers	.46
Protective professions workers	.42
Industrial workers	.37
Vehicle operator	.28
Sales clerk	.27

* *Source:* M.J. Ree and J.A. Earles, *Differential Validity of a Differential Aptitude Test,* AFHRL-TR-89–59 (San Antonio, TX: Brooks Air Force Base, 1990).

** *Source:* J.E. Hunter and R.F. Hunter, "Validity and Utility of Alternative Predictors of Job Performance," *Psychological Bulletin* 96 (1984): 72–98.

believe that general intelligence has meaningful effects on success in the workplace. Existing evidence points to the fact that general intelligence is an important determinant of workplace performance and career success.[65] This is particularly true for jobs and career paths that require complex information processing, as opposed to simple manual labor. Exhibit 5-4 illustrates the strong connection between intelligence and success for complex jobs.

Although the use of intelligence tests is intended to help organizations select the best human capital, as explained in the *Experiencing Strategic Organizational Behavior* feature on page 159, their use is controversial. It is controversial because some question the ability of these tests to accurately capture a person's true level of intelligence. Also, there can be legal problems with intelligence tests if they result in adverse impact. However, if a test accurately reflects individual intelligence, it can help managers select higher-quality associates. The superior human capital in the organization will then lead to higher productivity and the ability to gain an advantage over competitors. A competitive advantage in turn usually produces higher profits for the organization.[66]

Intelligence and Intelligence Testing in the National Football League

Each spring, representatives of National Football League teams join a large group of college football players in Indianapolis, Indiana. They are in town to participate in the so-called draft combine, where the players are given the opportunity to demonstrate their football skills. After showing their speed, strength, and agility, the players hope to be selected by a team early in the draft process and to command a large salary. For some, success at the combine is critical to being chosen by a team. For others, success is important because the combine plays a role in determining the amount of signing bonuses and other financial incentives.

Talented football players work to achieve the best physical condition they can in anticipation of the important evaluations. They focus on the upcoming medical examinations, weightlifting assessments, 40-yard dashes, vertical- and broad-jump tests, and tackling dummy tests. They may be less focused on another key feature of the draft combine—the intelligence test. The practice of testing general intelligence has been a fixture of the NFL since the early 1970s. The test that is used by all teams, the Wonderlic Personnel Test, has 50 questions and a time limit of 12 minutes in its basic version.

*Tom Hauck/
Getty Images*

Teams place different levels of importance on the intelligence test. The Green Bay Packers, for example, historically have not put a great deal of emphasis on it. "The Wonderlic has never been a big part of what we do here," said former Green Bay general manager and current consultant Ron Wolf. "To me, it's [just] a signal. If it's low, you better find out why it's low, and if the guy is a good football player, you better satisfy your curiosity." The Cincinnati Bengals, in contrast, have generally taken the test very seriously, in part "because it is the only test of its kind given to college players." In Atlanta, former head coach Dan Reeves showed his faith in the intelligence-testing process by choosing a linebacker who was equal in every way to another linebacker, except for higher intelligence scores. In New York, intelligence and personality testing has been taken to an extreme for the NFL. The Giants organization has used a test with nearly 400 questions. The late Giants manager, George Young, stated, "Going into a draft without some form of psychological testing on the prospects is like going into a gunfight with a knife."

Can a player be too smart? According to some, the answer is yes. "I've been around some players who are too smart to be good football players," said Ralph Cindrich, a linebacker in the NFL many years ago. Many others have the opinion that high intelligence scores are indicative of a player who will not play within the system but will want to improvise too much on the field and argue with coaches too much off of the field. There isn't much evidence, however, to support this argument. Many successful quarterbacks, for example, have had high scores. Super Bowl winner Tom Brady of the New England Patriots scored well above average, as did the New York Giants' Eli Manning.

Quarterbacks score higher on the test than players in several other positions but do not score the highest. Average scores for various positions are shown below, along with scores from the business world for comparison. A score of 20 correct out of 50 is considered average and equates to approximately 100 on a standard IQ test. Any score of 15 (the lowest score shown below) or above represents reasonable intelligence.

Offensive tackles—26   Safeties—19
Centers—25   Wide receivers—17
Quarterbacks—24   Fullbacks—17

Chemists—31	Salespersons—24
Programmers—29	Bank tellers—17
News reporters—26	Security guards—17
Halfbacks—16	Warehouse workers—15

Many players become tense over the NFL intelligence test. What types of questions are causing the anxiety? A sample of the easier questions follows (to learn more, go to www.wonderlic.com):

1. The 11th month of the year is: (a) October, (b) May, (c) November, (d) February.

2. Severe is opposite of: (a) harsh, (b) stern, (c) tender, (d) rigid, (e) unyielding.

3. In the following set of words, which word is different from the others? (a) sing, (b) call, (c) chatter, (d) hear, (e) speak.

4. A dealer bought some televisions for $3,500. He sold them for $5,500, making $50 on each television. How many televisions were involved?

5. Lemon candies sell at 3 for 15 cents. How much will 1½ dozen cost?

6. Which number in the following group of numbers represents the smallest amount? (a) 6, (b) .7, (c) 9, (d) 36, (e) .31, (f) 5.

7. Look at the following row of numbers. What number should come next? 73 66 59 52 45 38.

8. A plane travels 75 feet in ¼ second. At this speed, how many feet will it travel in 5 seconds?

9. A skirt requires 2⅓ yards of material. How many skirts can be cut from 42 yards?

10. ENLARGE, AGGRANDIZE. Do these words: (a) have similar meanings, (b) have contradictory meanings, (c) mean neither the same nor the opposite?

11. Three individuals form a partnership and agree to divide the profits equally. X invests $4,500, Y invests $3,500, Z invests $2,000. If the profits are $2,400, how much less does X receive than if profits were divided in proportion to the amount invested?

Sources: D. Dillon, "Testing, Testing: Taking the Wonderlic," *Sporting News.com*, Feb. 23, 2001, at www.sportingnews.com/voices/dennis_dillon/20010223.html; K. Kragthorpe, "Is Curtis Too Smart for NFL?" *Utah Online*, Apr. 23, 2003, at www.sltrib.com/2003/Apr/04232003/Sports/50504.asp; J. Litke, "Smarter Is Better in the NFL, Usually: But Not Too Smart to Be Good Football Players," *National Post (Canada)*, May 1, 2003, p. S2; J. Magee, "NFL Employs the Wonderlic Test to Probe the Minds of Draft Prospects," *SignOnSanDiego.com*, Apr. 20, 2003, at www.signonsandiego.com/sports/nfl/magee/200304209999–ls20nflcol.html; J. Merron, "Taking Your Wonderlics," *ESPN Page 2*, Feb. 2, 2002, at www.espn.go.com/page2/s/closer/020228.html; T. Silverstein, "What's His Wonderlic? NFL Uses Time-Honored IQ Test as Measuring Stick for Rookies," *Milwaukee Journal Sentinel*, Apr. 18, 2001, p. C1; A. Barra, "Do These NFL Scores Count for Anything?" *Wall Street Journal (Eastern Edition)*, Apr. 25, 2006, p. D.6.

Attitudes

It is sometimes difficult to distinguish between an individual's personality and attitudes. The behavior of Southwest associates and managers described in the opening case, for example, might be interpreted by some as based primarily on attitudes rather than personality, whereas others might believe that personality plays a larger role. Regardless, managers are concerned about the attitudes of associates because they can be major causes of work behaviors. Positive attitudes frequently lead to productive efforts, whereas negative attitudes often produce poor work habits.

An **attitude** is defined as a persistent mental state of readiness to feel and behave in a favorable or unfavorable way toward a specific person, object, or idea. Close examination of this definition reveals three important conclusions. First, attitudes are reasonably stable. Unless people have strong reasons to change their attitudes, they will persist or remain the same. People who like jazz music today will probably like it tomorrow, unless important reasons occur to change their musical preferences.

Second, attitudes are directed toward some object, person, or idea; that is, we may have an attitude toward our job, our supervisor, or an idea the college instructor presented. If the attitude concerns the job (for example, if a person dislikes monotonous work), then the attitude is specifically directed toward that job. We cannot extend that negative job attitude to an attitude toward jazz music.

Third, an attitude toward an object or person relates to an individual's behavior toward that object or person. In this sense, attitudes may influence our actions. For example, if an individual likes jazz music (an attitude), he may go to a jazz club (a behavior) or buy a jazz CD (a behavior). If an associate dislikes her work (an attitude), she may avoid coming to work (absenteeism behavior) or exert very little effort on the job (poor productivity behavior). People tend to behave in ways that are consistent with their feelings. Therefore, to change an unproductive worker into a productive one, it may be necessary to deal with that worker's attitudes.

As illustrated in Exhibit 5-5, our behavior toward an object, person, or idea is influenced by our attitudes. In turn, our attitudes are constantly developing and changing as a result of our behaviors. It is important to recognize that our behaviors are also influenced by other factors, such as motivational forces and situational factors. We therefore can understand why behaviors are not always predictable from attitudes. For example, we may have a strong positive attitude about a close friend. But we might reject an opportunity to go to a movie with that friend if we are preparing for a difficult exam to be given tomorrow. Thus, attitudes include behavioral tendencies and intentions, but our actual behaviors are also influenced by other factors.

attitude
A persistent tendency to feel and behave in a favorable or unfavorable way toward a specific person, object, or idea.

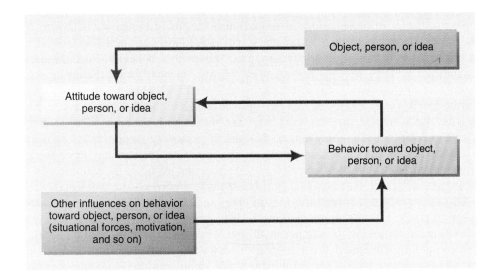

Exhibit 5-5
Influence of Attitudes on Behavior

Attitude Formation

Understanding how attitudes are formed is the first step in learning how to apply attitude concepts to organizational problems. This understanding can be developed by examining the three essential elements of an attitude, which are (1) cognitive, (2) affective, and (3) behavioral.[67]

- The *cognitive* element of an attitude consists of the facts we have gathered and considered about the object, person, or idea. Before we can have feelings about something, we must first be aware of it and think about its complexities.
- The *affective* element of an attitude refers to the feelings one has about the object or person. Such feelings are frequently expressed as like or dislike of the object or person and the degree to which one holds these feelings. For example, an employee may love the job, like it, dislike it, or hate it.
- Finally, most attitudes contain a *behavioral* element, which is the individual's intention to act in certain ways toward the object of the attitude. As previously explained, how we behave toward people may depend largely on whether we like or dislike them based on what we know about them.

The formation of attitudes may be quite complex. In the following discussion, we examine some ways in which attitudes are formed.

LEARNING

Attitudes can be formed through the learning process.[68] As explained in the previous chapter, when people interact with others or behave in particular ways toward an object, they often experience rewards or punishments. For example, if you touch a cactus plant, you may experience pain. As you experience the outcomes of such behavior, you begin to develop feelings about the objects of that behavior. Thus, if someone were to ask you how you felt about cactus plants, you might reply, "I don't like them—they can hurt." Of course, attitudes can also develop from watching others experience rewards and punishments. A person may not touch the cactus herself, but a negative attitude toward cacti could develop after she watches a friend experience pain.

SELF-PERCEPTION

People may form attitudes based on simple observations of their own behaviors.[69] This is called the *self-perception effect,* and it works as follows. An individual engages in a particular behavior without thinking much about that behavior. Furthermore, no significant positive rewards are involved. Having engaged in the behavior, the person then diagnoses his actions, asking himself what the behavior suggests about his attitudes. In many instances, this person will conclude that he must have had a positive attitude toward the behavior. Why else would he have done what he did? For example, an individual may join co-workers in requesting an on-site cafeteria at work, doing so without much thought. Up to that point, the person may have had a relatively neutral attitude about a cafeteria. After having joined in the request, however, he may conclude that he has a positive attitude toward on-site cafeterias.

Influencing people through the foot-in-the-door technique is based on the self-perception effect. This technique involves asking a person for a small favor (foot-in-the-door) and later asking for a larger favor that is consistent with the initial request. After completing the small favor with little thought, the target often concludes that she has a positive view toward whatever was done, and therefore she is more likely to perform the larger favor. In one study of the foot-in-the-door technique,

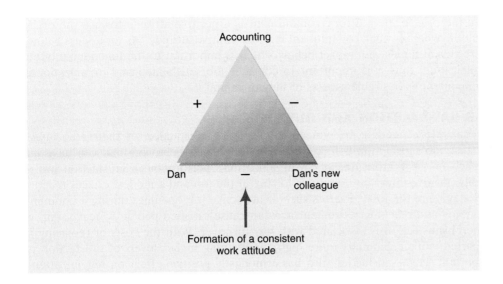

Accounting

+   −

Dan   −   Dan's new
                           colleague

Formation of a consistent
work attitude

Exhibit 5-6
Formation of
Consistent Attitudes

researchers went door-to-door asking individuals to sign a petition for safer driving.[70] The request was small and noncontroversial; thus, most people signed the petition without much thought. Weeks later, colleagues of the researchers visited these same people and asked them to put a large, unattractive sign in their yards that read "Drive Carefully." These same colleagues also approached other homeowners who had not been asked for the initial small favor. Fifty-five percent of the individuals who had signed the petition agreed to put an ugly sign in their yards, whereas only 17 percent of those who had not been asked to sign the petition agreed to the yard sign.

NEED FOR CONSISTENCY

A major concept associated with attitude formation is consistency.[71] Two well-known theories in social psychology, *balance theory* and *congruity theory,* are important to an understanding of attitude consistency. The basic notion is that people prefer that their attitudes be consistent with one another (in balance or congruent). If we have a specific attitude toward an object or person, we tend to form other consistent attitudes toward related objects or persons.

A simple example of attitude formation based on consistency appears in Exhibit 5-6. Dan is a young accounting graduate. He is impressed with accounting theory and thinks that accountants should work with data to arrive at important conclusions for management. Obviously, he has a positive attitude toward accounting, as illustrated by the plus sign between Dan and accounting in the exhibit. Now suppose that Dan's new job requires him to work with someone who dislikes accounting (represented by the minus sign between the new colleague and accounting). In this case, Dan may form a negative attitude toward the person in order to have a consistent set of attitudes. Dan likes accounting and may have a negative attitude toward those who do not.

Two Important Attitudes in the Workplace

The two most thoroughly examined attitudes in strategic OB are job satisfaction and organizational commitment. Job satisfaction is a broad attitude related to the job. A high level of satisfaction represents a positive attitude toward the job, while a low level of satisfaction represents a negative attitude. Organizational commitment, as defined here, is a broad attitude toward the organization as a whole. It represents how strongly an individual identifies with and values being associated with the organization. Strong commitment is a positive attitude toward the organization, whereas weak commitment is a less positive attitude. As we discuss below, these two attitudes can impact behavior that is important to the functioning of an organization; thus it is important to consider job satisfaction and organizational commitment as desirable aspects of human capital.[72]

JOB SATISFACTION AND OUTCOMES

Organizations need to be concerned with the satisfaction of their associates, because job satisfaction is linked to many important behaviors that can have an impact on the bottom line of an organization's performance. Satisfaction has a highly positive effect on intentions to stay in the job and a modest effect on actually staying in the job.[73] Factors such as attractive job openings during a booming economy and reaching retirement age can cause satisfied people to leave, but in general satisfaction is associated with low turnover. With the costs of replacing a departed worker generally quite high, maintaining higher levels of satisfaction is important. High satisfaction also has a modestly positive effect on regular attendance at work.[74] Factors such as a very liberal sick-leave policy can, however, cause even highly satisfied associates and managers to miss work time. Satisfaction also has a moderately strong relationship with motivation.[75]

Job satisfaction has a reasonably straightforward relationship with intention to stay, actually staying, absenteeism, and motivation. In contrast, the specific form of the relationship between satisfaction and job performance has been the subject of a great deal of controversy. Many managers and researchers believe that high satisfaction produces strong performance. This idea seems reasonable, for a positive attitude should indeed result in strong effort and accountability. Other managers and researchers, however, believe that it is strong performance that causes workers to be satisfied with their jobs. For this second group of investigators, a positive attitude does not cause strong performance but strong performance does cause a positive attitude. Still others believe that satisfaction and performance are not related or are only weakly related. For this last group, factors other than attitudes, such as skills and incentive systems, are believed to have much stronger effects on job performance.

A recent study has helped to put these differences of opinion into perspective.[76] In this study, all previously published research on satisfaction and performance was synthesized using modern quantitative and qualitative techniques. The study concluded with an integrative model suggesting that all three of the groups mentioned above are correct to some degree. High satisfaction causes strong performance, strong performance also causes high satisfaction, and the relationship between the two is weaker in some situations. On this last point, low conscientiousness and the existence of simple work are examples of factors that may cause the relationship to be weaker. Individuals who have positive attitudes toward the job but who are lower in conscientiousness may not necessarily work hard, which weakens the effects of job satisfaction on performance. In addition, strong performance at simple work does not necessarily result in strong satisfaction, which weakens the effects of performance on satisfaction. For engineers, managers, and others with complex jobs, performance and satisfaction have a reasonably strong connection.

ORGANIZATIONAL COMMITMENT AND OUTCOMES IN THE WORKPLACE

Similar to satisfaction, commitment has important effects on intentions to stay in the job and modest effects on actually staying in the job and attending work regularly.[77] Commitment also is significantly related to motivation. Interestingly, length of employment plays a role in the relationship between commitment and staying in the job. A high level of organizational commitment tends to be more important in decisions to stay for associates and managers who have worked in their jobs for less time.[78] For longer-term employees, simple inertia and habit may prevent departures independent of the level of commitment to the organization. Commitment also has positive effects on job performance, but the effects are somewhat small.[79] This linkage to performance appears to be stronger for managers and professionals. Although the relationship between commitment and regular job performance is not extremely strong, organizational commitment does have a very strong relationship with discretionary organizational citizenship behaviors, such as helping others and taking on voluntary assignments.[80]

CAUSES OF JOB SATISFACTION AND ORGANIZATIONAL COMMITMENT

Given that job satisfaction and organizational commitment can impact on many important organizational behaviors, it is imperative that organizations understand what makes their associates satisfied and committed. A recent survey[81] found that less than one-half of workers say that they are satisfied with their jobs, and that 62 percent of workers under the age of 25 are satisfied. In this survey, respondents said that they were most dissatisfied with their performance review process, workload, work/life balance, communication channels, and potential for future growth.

Many of the same factors that lead to job satisfaction also lead to organizational commitment. These factors include:

- Role ambiguity[82]
- Supervision/leadership[83]
- Pay and benefits[84]
- Nature of the job[85]
- Organization climate[86]
- Stress[87]
- Perceptions of fair treatment[88]

Although these factors have all been linked to satisfaction and commitment, the relationships are not always so simple. For example, in order to best understand whether someone will be satisfied with a given dimension of her work, you need to consider her comparison standard. People compare desirable facets of their work with what they expect to receive or what they think they should receive.[89] So, while one person may be very satisfied with earning $100,000 per year, another person may find this amount unsatisfactory because she was expecting to earn more.

Another complication arises when we consider that associates may be committed to their organization for different reasons. There are three general reasons why people are committed to their organizations.[90] **Affective commitment** is usually what we think of when we talk about organizational commitment because it means someone has strong positive attitudes toward the organization. **Normative commitment** means that someone is committed to the organization because he feels he should be. Someone who stays with their organization because he does not want to let his co-workers down is normatively committed. Finally, associates may experience **continuance commitment**, which means that they are committed to the organization because they do not have any better opportunities. Different

affective commitment
Organizational commitment due to one's strong positive attitudes toward the organization.

normative commitment
Organizational commitment due to feelings of obligation.

continuance commitment
Organizational commitment due to lack of better opportunities.

factors affect different types of commitment.[91] For example, benefits may affect continuance commitment, for example, only when a person is committed to an organization because her retirement plan will not transfer to another organization. On the other hand, benefits may not influence how positive one feels about the organization, so that benefits would be unrelated to affective commitment.

One other thing to note about the factors affecting satisfaction and commitment is that the presence of high-involvement management is particularly important. Individuals usually have positive experiences working with this management approach, and thus strong satisfaction and commitment is likely to develop through the learning mechanism of attitude formation. As part of high-involvement management, individuals are selected for organizations in which their values fit, they are well trained, they are encouraged to think for themselves, and they are treated fairly (e.g., receive equitable compensation).

Finally, satisfaction and commitment are not totally dependent on situational factors; personality also can play a role. Some individuals have a propensity to be satisfied and committed, whereas others are less likely to exhibit positive attitudes, no matter the actual situation in which they work.[92] In addition to one's personality disposition, emotions can also affect job attitudes. Thus, we discuss emotions in the workplace later in this chapter.

Attitude Change

Personality characteristics are believed to be rather stable, as we have seen, but attitudes are more susceptible to change. Social forces, such as peer pressure or changes in society, act on existing attitudes, so that over time attitudes may change, often in unpredictable ways. In addition, in many organizations, managers find they need to be active in changing employee attitudes. Although it is preferable for associates to have positive attitudes toward the job, the manager, and the organization, many do not. When the object of the attitude cannot be changed (for example, when a job cannot be redesigned), managers must work directly on attitudes. In such cases, it is necessary to develop a systematic approach to change attitudes in favorable directions. We discuss two relevant techniques next.

PERSUASIVE COMMUNICATION

Most of us experience daily attempts by others to persuade us to change our attitudes. Television, radio, and Internet advertisements are common forms of such persuasive communication. Political campaigns are another form. Occasionally, a person who is virtually unknown at the beginning of a political campaign (such as Bill Clinton) can win an election by virtue of extensive advertising and face-to-face communication.

The persuasive communication approach to attitude change consists of four elements:[93]

1. *Communicator*—the person who holds a particular attitude and wants to convince others to share that attitude

2. *Message*—the content designed to induce the change in others' attitudes

3. *Situation*—the surroundings in which the message is presented

4. *Target*—the person whose attitude the communicator wants to change

Several qualities of the communicator affect attitude change in the target. First, the communicator's overall credibility has an important effect on the target's response to the persuasion attempt. Research shows that people give more weight to persuasive messages from people they respect.[94] It is more difficult to reject messages that disagree with our attitudes when the communicator has high credibility.

Second, people are more likely to change their attitudes when they trust the intentions of the communicator. If we perceive that the communicator has something to gain from the attitude change, we are likely to distrust his or her intentions. But if we believe the communicator is more objective and less self-serving, we will trust his or her intentions and be more likely to change our attitudes. Individuals who argue against their own self-interests are effective at persuasion.[95]

Third, if people like the communicator or perceive that person to be similar to them in interests or goals, they are more likely to be persuaded.[96] This is one reason that movie stars, athletes, and other famous people are used for television ads. These people are widely liked and have characteristics that we perceive ourselves to have (correctly or incorrectly) or would like to have.

Finally, if the communicator is attractive, people have a stronger tendency to be persuaded. The effects of attractiveness have been discussed in studies of job seeking and political elections. The most notable example is the U.S. presidential election of 1960. By many accounts, Richard Nixon had equal, if not superior, command of the issues in the presidential debates that year, but the more handsome John Kennedy received higher ratings from the viewing public and won the election.[97]

The message involved in the communication can also influence attitude change. One of the most important dimensions of message content is fear arousal. Messages that arouse fear often produce more attitude change.[98] For example, a smoker who is told that smoking is linked to heart disease may change his attitude toward smoking. The actual amount of fear produced by the message also seems to play a role. If the smoker is told that smoking makes teeth turn yellow, rather than being told of a link to heart disease, the fear is weaker, and the resulting attitude change also is likely to be weaker.

Greater fear usually induces larger changes in attitudes, but not always. Three factors beyond amount of fear play a role:[99] (1) the probability that negative consequences will actually occur if no change in behavior is made, (2) the perceived effect of changing behavior, and (3) the perceived ability to change behavior. Returning to our smoker, even if the message regarding smoking risk arouses a great deal of fear, he still may not alter his attitude if he does not believe that he is likely to develop heart disease, if he has been smoking for so many years that he does not believe that quitting now will help the situation, or if he does not believe he can stop smoking.

So far, we have discussed how the communicator and the message affect attitude change. In general, each affects the degree to which the target believes the attitude should be changed. Frequently, however, people are motivated by factors outside of the actual persuasion attempt. Such factors may be found in the situation in which persuasion is attempted. We can see a good example of this when a person is publicly reprimanded. If you have ever been present when a peer has been publicly chastised by an instructor, you may have been offended by the action. Instead of changing your attitude about the student or the student's skills, you may have changed your attitude about the instructor. Other situational factors include the reactions of those around you. Do they smile or nod their heads in approval when the communicator presents her message? Such behaviors encourage attitude change, whereas disapproving behavior may influence you to not change your attitudes.

Finally, characteristics of the target also influence the success of persuasion. For example, people differ in their personalities, their perceptions, and the way they learn. Some are more rigid and less willing to change their attitudes—even when most others believe that they are wrong. Locus of control and other characteristics also influence attitudes. People with high self-esteem are more likely to believe that their attitudes are correct and they are less likely to change them. Therefore, it is difficult to predict precisely how different people will respond, even to the same persuasive communication. The effective manager is prepared for this uncertainty.

COGNITIVE DISSONANCE

cognitive dissonance
An uneasy feeling produced when a person behaves in a manner inconsistent with an existing attitude.

Another way in which attitudes can change involves **cognitive dissonance.** Like balance and congruity theories, discussed earlier in this chapter, dissonance theory deals with consistency.[100] In this case, the focus is usually on consistency between attitudes and behaviors—or, more accurately, inconsistency between attitudes and behaviors. For example, a manager may have a strong positive attitude toward incentive compensation, which involves paying people on the basis of their performance. This manager, however, may refuse workers' requests for such a compensation scheme. By refusing, she has created an inconsistency between an attitude and a behavior. If certain conditions are met, as explained below, this inconsistency will create an uneasy feeling (dissonance) that causes the manager to change her positive attitude.

What are the key conditions that lead to dissonance and the changing of an attitude? There are three.[101] First, the behavior must be substantially inconsistent with the attitude rather than just mildly inconsistent. Second, the inconsistent behavior must cause harm or have negative consequences for others. If no harmful or negative consequences are involved, the individual exhibiting the inconsistent behavior can more easily move on without giving much consideration to the inconsistency. Third, the inconsistent behavior must be voluntary and not forced, or at least the person must perceive it that way.

In our example, the manager's behavior satisfies the first two conditions. It was substantially inconsistent with her attitude, and it had negative consequences for the workers who wanted incentive pay. We have no way of knowing whether the third condition was met because we do not know whether someone higher in the organization ordered the manager to refuse the requests for incentive compensation or whether a union agreement prohibited such a compensation scheme. If the manager's behavior was not forced by a higher-level manager or an agreement, dissonance is more likely to occur, leading to a change of the manager's attitude toward incentive pay from positive to negative.

If an executive had wanted to change this manager's attitude toward incentive pay, he could have gently suggested that such pay not be used. If the manager acted on this suggestion, she may have experienced dissonance and changed the attitude because her behavior was at least partly voluntary. She was not required to act in a manner inconsistent with her attitude, but she did so anyway. To eliminate the uneasy feeling associated with the inconsistent behavior, she may convince herself that she does not like incentive pay as much as she previously thought.

Emotions

During a sales force team meeting, Chad became frustrated with Bob's, the team leader's, presentation. He felt that Bob was ignoring the needs of his unit. In a pique of anger, Chad yelled out that Bob was hiding something from everyone and being dishonest. Bob's reaction to Chad's outburst was to slam his fist on the table and tell him to be quiet or leave. Next door, in the same company, Susan had just learned that her team had won a coveted account. She jumped with joy and was all smiles when she ran down the hall to tell her teammates. Everyone she passed grinned and felt better when they saw Susan running past their desks.

Chad, Bob, and Susan are all displaying their emotions at work. Despite the common norms that associates should hide their emotions when they are at work,[102] people are emotional beings and emotions play a big role in everyday organizational behavior. Indeed, organizational scholars have recently begun studying the role emotions play at work[103] and organizations have become more concerned with the emotions of their employees. For example, Douglas Conant, CEO of Campbell Soup, says that in his company care is taken to make sure that employees focus their emotions on their jobs, so that employees "fall in love with (the) company's agenda."[104]

Emotions are complex reactions that have both a physical and mental component. These reactions include anger, happiness, anxiety, pride, contentment, and guilt. Emotional reactions include a subjective feeling accompanied by changes in bodily functioning such as increased heart rate or blood pressure.[105] Emotions can play a part in organizational functioning in several ways. First, associates' emotions can directly affect their behavior. For example, angry associates may engage in workplace violence[106] or happy employees may be more likely to help other people on the job.[107] Another way in which emotions come into play at work is when the nature of the job calls for associates to display emotions that they might not actually be feeling. For example, on a rocky airplane ride, flight attendants have to appear calm, cool, and collected, while reassuring passengers that everything is okay. However, these flight attendants may have to do this while hiding their own fear and panic. This dynamic is called *emotional labor*. Finally, both business scholars and organizations have become concerned with what has been termed *emotional intelligence*. We turn now to discussions of these three roles that emotions play in organizational behavior.

emotions
Complex subjective reactions that have both a physical and mental component.

Direct Effects of Emotions on Behavior

Emotions can have several direct causal effects on behavior. The relationship between emotions and other important behaviors, such as job performance, is less clear. While it would seem most likely that positive emotion would always lead to high performance, this is not always the case. In some instances, negative emotions, such as anger, can serve as a motivator. Research on creativity demonstrates this point. Some researchers have found that positive emotions increase creativity,[108] while others have found that negative emotions lead to greater creativity.[109] Positive emotions should lead to greater creativity because when people feel good they are more likely to be active and inquisitive. On the other hand, negative emotions, such as fear, can serve as a signal that something is amiss, leading people to

Exhibit 5-7	**The Direct Effects of Emotion**

Positive Emotions Influence:

Social activity

Altruism and helping behavior

Effective conflict resolution

Job Satisfaction

Motivation

Organizational Citizenship Behavior

Negative Emotions Influence:

Aggression against coworkers

Aggression towards the organization

Workplace Deviance

Job Dissatisfaction

Decision Making

Negotiation Outcomes

Sources: S. Lyubomirsky, L. King, & E. Deiner, 2005. The Benefits of Frequent Positive Affect: Does Happiness Lead to Success? *Psychological Bulletin*, 131: 803–855; T.A. Judge, B.A. Scott, & R. Ilies, 2006. Hostility, Job Attitudes, and Workplace Deviance: Test of a Multilevel Model. *Journal of Applied Psychology*, 91: 126–138; M.S. Hershcovis, N. Turner, J. Barling, K.A. Arnols, K.E. Dupre, M. Inness, M.M. LeBlanc, & N. Sivanathan, 2007. Predicting Workplace Aggression: A Meta-analysis. *Journal of Applied Psychology*, 92; 228–238; A.P. Brief, H.M. Weiss, 2002. Organizational Behavior: Affect in the Workplace. In S.T. Fiske (Ed.), *Annual Review of Psychology*, vol 53: 279–307. Palo Alto, CA; Annual Reviews.

search for creative solutions to solve the problem. Indeed, a recent study found that people were most creative when they were experiencing emotional ambivalence, that is, both positive and negative emotions at the same time.[110]

The direct effects of emotions can be either beneficial or harmful to organizational effectiveness. The impact of these emotions, whether negative or positive, is even greater when one considers the phenomenon of **emotional contagion.** Emotional contagion occurs when emotions experienced by one or a few members of a work group spread to other members.[111] One recent study found that leaders' emotions were particularly important in influencing the emotions of followers.[112] This study indicated that charismatic leaders have a positive influence on organizational effectiveness because they are able to induce positive emotions in their followers. Thus, angry and anxious leaders are likely to develop followers who are angry and anxious, whereas leaders who are happy and passionate about their work are likely to develop followers who experience the same emotions. Exhibit 5-7 summarizes the direct effects of emotions.

emotional contagion Phenomenon where emotions experienced by one or a few members of a work group spread to other members.

Emotional Labor

Many service and sales jobs require that individuals display certain emotions, regardless of what they are really experiencing. For example, flight attendants are expected to be warm and cordial, call center employees are expected to keep their cool when customers are hostile toward them, and sales associates are expected to be enthusiastic about the product they are selling, no matter what they actually feel. The process whereby associates must display emotions that are contrary to what they are feeling is termed **emotional labor.**[113] Organizations often indicate to employees what emotions they must express and under what circumstances. When these required emotions, or display rules, are contrary to what associates are actually feeling, they can experience stress, emotional exhaustion, and burnout.[114] Emotional labor does not always lead to overstressed employees. When associates actually come to feel the emotions they are required to display, they can experience positive outcomes such as greater job satisfaction.[115]

Even when associates may not feel the emotions they are required to express, several factors can influence whether this acting will have a negative outcome on associates' well being. First, the manner in which supervisors enforce display rules can influence whether emotional labor is harmful to associates.[116] When supervisors are quite demanding, associates will become more exhausted. Another factor that influences the effects of emotional labor is the self-identities of associates.[117] When associates have a strong self-identity as a service worker or a caregiver then they will be less likely to experience negative effects from emotional labor. For example, a hospice care worker may feel tired and frustrated, but behave in a caring and nurturing manner with her patients. If the care worker has a strong self-identity as a caregiver, she will experience less exhaustion from her emotional labor. Finally, when associates have networks of supportive people and caring mentors, the negative effects of emotional labor will be mitigated.[118]

Emotional Intelligence

Are some people just better dealing with emotions, theirs and others, than are other people? The last 10 years has seen an explosion in what has been termed the concept of **emotional intelligence** in both the study and practice of management. The best-accepted definition of emotional intelligence (EI) is that it is the ability to

- Accurately appraise one's own and others' emotions.
- Effectively regulate one's own and others' emotions.
- Use emotion to motivate, plan, and achieve.[119]

A person displaying high emotional intelligence can accurately determine his or her own emotions and the effect those emotions will have on others, then go on to regulate the emotions to achieve one's goals.

Emotional intelligence has been linked to career success, leadership effectiveness, managerial performance, and performance in sales jobs.[120] It also is the subject of many management development programs, popular books,[121] and articles that may at times inflate the value of emotional intelligence relative to cognitive intelligence.[122] The specific abilities generally associated with emotional intelligence are discussed in more detail in the following *Managerial Advice* box.

While emotional intelligence is quite a popular concept right now, it is not without its critics.[123] One major criticism is that emotional intelligence is not intelligence at all, but rather a conglomeration of specific social skills and personality traits. Another criticism is that sometimes emotional intelligence is so broadly defined that it is meaningless. Nonetheless, the basic abilities that make up emotional intelligence are important influences on organizational behavior, whether they form one construct called emotional intelligence or are simply considered alone.

emotional labor
The process whereby associates must display emotions that are contrary to what they are feeling.

emotional intelligence
The ability to accurately appraise one's own and others' emotions, effectively regulate one's own and others' emotions, and use emotion to motivate, plan, and achieve.

MANAGERIAL ADVICE

The Characteristics of High EI

Getty Images

As mentioned above, there is a debate over what exactly emotional intelligence is. However, whichever stance one takes, certain characteristics are effective in determining career success, leadership effectiveness, and performance in many types of jobs. These characteristics are:

- *Self-awareness.* Associates with high self-awareness understand how their feelings, beliefs, and behaviors affect themselves and others. For example, a supervisor knows that her reaction to a valuable (and otherwise high-performing) associate's chronic lateness and excuses is one of anger, but she realizes that if she displays this anger, it will cause the associate to withdraw even further.

- *Self-regulation.* Self-regulation is the ability to control one's emotions. The supervisor may feel like yelling at the associate or being punitive in making work assignments; however, if she is high in self-regulation, she will choose her words and actions carefully. She will behave in a manner that will more likely encourage the associate to come to work on time rather than make the associate withdraw even more.

- *Motivation or drive.* This characteristic is the same as achievement motivation, discussed previously in this chapter, and drive, discussed above under trait theories. Associates with high EI want to achieve for achievement's sake alone. They always want to do things better and seek out feedback about their progress. They are passionate about their work.

- *Empathy.* Effective empathy means thoughtfully considering others' feelings when making decisions and weighting those feelings appropriately, along with other factors. Consider again our example of the supervisor dealing with the tardy associate. Suppose she knows that the associate is frequently late because he is treated poorly by the work group. The supervisor can display empathy by acknowledging this situation and can act on it by attempting to change work arrangements rather than punishing the associate for being late. Thus, she can remove an obstacle for the associate and perhaps retain an associate who performs well and comes to work on time.

- *Social skill.* Social skill refers to the ability to build effective relationships with the goal of moving people toward a desired outcome. Socially skilled associates know how to build bonds between people. Often, leaders who appear to be socializing with co-workers are actually working to build relationships and exercise their influence in a positive manner.

There are many management consultants who have developed programs to teach associates and managers these skills. However, developing a strong EI is a lifelong process that should be practiced with passion. Take time out to listen carefully to what others are saying. Notice the impact that your behavior has on others. Be cautious in your responses—choose your words carefully. Develop meaningful relationships with people. To quote Daniel Goleman, the author of the influential book *Emotional Intelligence:* "building one's emotional intelligence cannot—will not—happen without sincere desire and concerted effort."

Source: D. Goleman, "What Makes a Leader?" *Harvard Business Review*, Jan. 2004: 82–91; D. Goleman, 1995, *Emotional Intelligence*, New York: Bantam; S. Fineman, "Appreciating Emotion at Work: Paradigm Tensions," *International Journal of Work Organisation and Emotion*, 1: 4–19.

The Strategic Lens

Understanding personality, intelligence, attitudes, and emotions enables managers to more effectively manage the behavior of their associates. Selecting new associates based on personality and intelligence can have an impact on organizational performance, as demonstrated by Outback Steakhouse and the National Football League. Hiring associates that fit its culture in turn enables an organization to better implement its strategy, as illustrated by the success of Patricia Harris at McDonald's. Organizations can further increase existing associates' organizational fit, performance, and tenure, by creating work environments that lead to positive attitudes and emotionally healthy environments. Furthermore, from the examples presented throughout the chapter and summarized above, we can see how knowledge of personality, intelligence, attitudes, and emotions allows executives to more effectively implement their strategies through management of behavior in their organizations.

Critical Thinking Questions

1. Specifically, how can you use knowledge of personality, attitudes, intelligence, and emotions to make better hiring decisions?

2. If top executives wanted to implement a strategy that emphasized innovation and new products, how could they use knowledge of personality, attitudes, and emotions to affect the organization's culture in ways to enhance innovation?

3. How could a manager use knowledge about personality and attitudes to form a high-performance work team?

What This Chapter Adds to Your Knowledge Portfolio

In this chapter, we have discussed personality in some detail. We have seen how personality develops and how important it is in the workplace. We have also discussed intelligence. If an organization is to be successful, its associates and managers must understand the effects of personality and intelligence and be prepared to act on this knowledge. Moving beyond enduring traits and mental ability, we have examined attitude formation and change. Without insights into attitudes, associates and managers alike would miss important clues about how a person will act in the workplace. Finally, we have briefly examined emotions and their various roles in behavior and organizational life. More specifically, we have made the following points:

- Personality is a stable set of characteristics representing the internal properties of an individual. These characteristics, or traits, are relatively enduring, are major determinants of behavior, and influence behavior across a wide variety of situations.

- Determinants of personality include heredity and environment. Three types of studies have demonstrated the effects of heredity: (1) investigations of identical twins, (2) assessments of newborns and their behavior later in life, and (3) direct examinations of genes. Studies of environmental effects have emphasized childhood experiences as important forces in personality development.

- There are many aspects of personality. Five traits, however, have emerged as particularly important in the workplace. These traits, collectively known as the Big Five, are extraversion, conscientiousness, agreeableness, emotional stability, and openness to experience.

- Extraversion (the degree to which a person is outgoing and derives energy from being around people) tends to affect overall job performance, success in team interactions, and job satisfaction. For performance, fit with the job is important, as extraverts have at least modest advantages in occupations calling for a high level of interaction with other people, whereas introverts appear to have advantages in occupations calling for more solitary work.

- Conscientiousness (the degree to which a person focuses on goals and works toward them in a disciplined way) also affects job performance, success as a team member, and job satisfaction. Higher levels of conscientiousness tend to be positive for these outcomes.

- Agreeableness (the degree to which a person is easygoing and tolerant) does not have simple, easily specified effects on individual job performance but does appear to contribute positively to successful interactions on a team.

- Emotional stability (the degree to which a person handles stressful, high-demand situations with ease) affects job performance, success as a team member, and job satisfaction. Higher levels of emotional stability tend to be positive.

- Openness to experience (the degree to which a person seeks new experiences and thinks creatively about the future) does not have simple links to overall job performance, success at teamwork, or job satisfaction, but individuals scoring higher on this aspect of personality do appear to have an edge in specific tasks calling for vision and creativity.

- The Big Five personality traits may play a role in high-involvement management. Certain combinations of these traits seem to provide a foundation for the competencies needed by managers and associates. Absent these trait combinations, individuals may still be effective in high-involvement systems, but they may need to work a little harder.

- A Big Five assessment can be useful in selecting new associates and managers but must be combined with other tools, such as structured interviews and evaluations of the specific job skills needed for a particular job.

- Beyond the Big Five, several cognitive and motivational personality concepts are important in the workplace. Cognitive concepts correspond to perceptual and thought processes and include locus of control, authoritarianism, and self-monitoring. Motivational concepts correspond to needs in individuals that are directly involved in energizing and maintaining overt behaviors. They include achievement motivation and approval motivation.

- There are many areas of intelligence, including number aptitude, verbal comprehension, and perceptual speed. Most psychologists who have extensively studied intelligence believe these various areas combine to form a single meaningful intelligence factor. This general intelligence factor has been found to predict workplace outcomes.

- An attitude is a persistent mental state of readiness to feel and behave in favorable or unfavorable ways toward a specific person, object, or idea. Attitudes consist of a cognitive element, an affective element, and a behavioral element.

- Attitudes may be learned as a result of direct experience with an object, person, or idea. Unfavorable experiences are likely to lead to unfavorable attitudes, and favorable experiences to favorable attitudes. Attitudes may also form as the result of self-perception, where an individual behaves in a certain way and then concludes he has an attitude that matches the behavior. Finally, attitudes may form on the basis of a need for consistency. We tend to form attitudes that are consistent with our existing attitudes.

- Job satisfaction and organizational commitment are two of the most important workplace attitudes. Job satisfaction is a favorable or unfavorable view of the job, whereas organizational commitment corresponds to how strongly an individual identifies with and values being associated with the organization. Both of these attitudes affect intentions to stay in the job, actual decisions to stay, and absenteeism. They are also related to job performance, though not as strongly as some other factors.

- Attitudes may change through exposure to persuasive communications or cognitive dissonance. Persuasive communication consists of four important elements: the communicator, message, situation, and target. Dissonance refers to inconsistencies between attitude and behavior. Under certain conditions, a behavior that is inconsistent with an existing attitude causes the attitude to change. Key conditions include (1) the behavior being substantially inconsistent with the attitude, (2) the behavior causing harm or being negative for someone, and (3) the behavior being voluntary.

- Emotions are the subjective reactions associates experience that contain both a psychological and physiological component. Emotions can influence organizational behavior directly, as the basis of emotional labor, or through associates' emotional intelligence.

Back to the Knowledge Objectives

1. What is meant by the term *personality*? What key beliefs do psychologists traditionally hold about personality traits?

2. What are the Big Five traits, and how do they influence behavior and performance in the workplace? Give an example of someone you know whose personality did not fit the job he or she had. This could be a person in an organization in which you worked, or it could be a person from a school club or civic organization. What was the outcome? If you had been the individual's manager, how would you have attempted to improve the situation?

3. Describe a situation in which a manager's or a friend's locus of control, authoritarianism, self-monitoring, need for achievement, or approval motivation had an impact on your life.

4. What is intelligence, and what is its effect in the workplace?

5. How are attitudes similar to and different from personality? How do attitudes form? How can managers change attitudes in the workplace? Assume that the target of the attitude cannot be changed (that is, the job, boss, technology, and so on cannot be changed). Be sure to address both persuasive communication and dissonance.

6. What is the relationship between emotions and attitudes? Describe the emotions displayed by a past or current boss and explain how those emotions affected your job.

Thinking about Ethics

1. Is it appropriate for an organization to use personality tests to screen applicants for jobs? Should organizations reject applicants whose personalities do not fit a particular profile, ignoring the applicants' performance on previous jobs, their capabilities, and their motivation?

2. Should organizations use intelligence tests to screen applicants even though the accuracy of such tests is questioned by some? Why or why not?

3. Are there right and wrong values? How should values be used to manage the behavior of associates in organizations?

4. Can knowledge of personality, attitudes, and values be used inappropriately? If so, how?

5. Is it appropriate to change people's attitudes? If so, how can a person's attitudes be changed without altering that person's values?

Key Terms

personality, p. 146
extraversion, p. 148
conscientiousness, p. 149
agreeableness, p. 150
emotional stability, p. 150
openness to experience,
   p. 150
locus of control, p. 153
authoritarianism, p. 154

self-monitoring, p. 154
achievement motivation,
   p. 155
approval motivation, p. 155
intelligence, p. 157
attitude, p. 161
affective commitment, p. 165
normative commitment,
   p. 165

continuance commitment,
   p. 165
cognitive dissonance, p. 168
emotions, p. 169
emotional contagion, p. 170
emotional labor, p. 171
emotional intelligence,
   p. 171

Building Your Human Capital

Big Five Personality Assessment

Different people have different personalities, and these personalities can affect outcomes in the workplace. Understanding your own personality can help you to understand how and why you behave as you do. In this installment of *Building Your Human Capital*, we present an assessment tool for the Big Five.

Instructions

In this assessment, you will read 50 phrases that describe people. Use the rating scale below to indicate how accurately each phrase describes you. Rate yourself as you generally are now, not as you wish to be in the future; and rate yourself as you honestly see yourself. Keep in mind that very few people have extreme scores on all or even most of the items (a "1" or a "5" is an extreme score); most people have midrange scores for many of the items. Read each item carefully, and then circle the number that corresponds to your choice from the rating scale.

1	2	3	4	5
Not at all like me	Somewhat unlike me	Neither like nor unlike me	Somewhat like me	Very much like me

1. Am the life of the party.	1	2	3	4	5
2. Feel little concern for others.	1	2	3	4	5
3. Am always prepared.	1	2	3	4	5
4. Get stressed out easily.	1	2	3	4	5
5. Have a rich vocabulary.	1	2	3	4	5
6. Don't talk a lot.	1	2	3	4	5
7. Am interested in people.	1	2	3	4	5
8. Leave my belongings around.	1	2	3	4	5
9. Am relaxed most of the time.	1	2	3	4	5
10. Have difficulty understanding abstract ideas.	1	2	3	4	5
11. Feel comfortable around people.	1	2	3	4	5
12. Insult people.	1	2	3	4	5
13. Pay attention to details.	1	2	3	4	5
14. Worry about things.	1	2	3	4	5
15. Have a vivid imagination.	1	2	3	4	5

16. Keep in the background.	1	2	3	4	5
17. Sympathize with others' feelings.	1	2	3	4	5
18. Make a mess of things.	1	2	3	4	5
19. Seldom feel blue.	1	2	3	4	5
20. Am not interested in abstract ideas.	1	2	3	4	5
21. Start conversations.	1	2	3	4	5
22. Am not interested in other people's problems.	1	2	3	4	5
23. Get chores done right away.	1	2	3	4	5
24. Am easily disturbed.	1	2	3	4	5
25. Have excellent ideas.	1	2	3	4	5
26. Have little to say.	1	2	3	4	5
27. Have a soft heart.	1	2	3	4	5
28. Often forget to put things back in their proper place.	1	2	3	4	5
29. Get easily upset.	1	2	3	4	5
30. Do not have a good imagination.	1	2	3	4	5
31. Talk to a lot of different people at parties.	1	2	3	4	5
32. Am not really interested in others.	1	2	3	4	5
33. Like order.	1	2	3	4	5
34. Change my mood a lot.	1	2	3	4	5
35. Am quick to understand things.	1	2	3	4	5
36. Don't like to draw attention to myself.	1	2	3	4	5
37. Take time out for others.	1	2	3	4	5
38. Shirk my duties.	1	2	3	4	5
39. Have frequent mood swings.	1	2	3	4	5
40. Use difficult words.	1	2	3	4	5
41. Don't mind being the center of attention.	1	2	3	4	5
42. Feel others' emotions.	1	2	3	4	5
43. Follow a schedule.	1	2	3	4	5
44. Get irritated easily.	1	2	3	4	5
45. Spend time reflecting on things.	1	2	3	4	5
46. Am quiet around strangers.	1	2	3	4	5
47. Make people feel at ease.	1	2	3	4	5
48. Am exact in my work.	1	2	3	4	5
49. Often feel blue.	1	2	3	4	5
50. Am full of ideas.	1	2	3	4	5

Scoring Key

To determine your scores, combine your responses to the items above as follows:

Extraversion = (Item 1 + Item 11 + Item 21 + Item 31 + Item 41) + (30 − (Item 6 + Item 16 + Item 26 + Item 36 + Item 46))

Conscientiousness = (Item 3 + Item 13 + Item 23 + Item 33 + Item 43 + Item 48) + (24 − (Item 8 + Item 18 + Item 28 + Item 38))

Agreeableness = (Item 7 + Item 17 + Item 27 + Item 37 + Item 42 + Item 47) + (24 − (Item 2 + Item 12 + Item 22 + Item 32))

Emotional stability = (Item 9 + Item 19) + (48 − (Item 4 + Item 14 + Item 24 + Item 29 + Item 34 + Item 39 + Item 44 + Item 49))

Openness to experience = (Item 5 + Item 15 + Item 25 + Item 35 + Item 40 + Item 45 + Item 50) + (18 − (Item 10 + Item 20 + Item 30))

Scores for each trait can range from 10 to 50. Scores of 40 and above may be considered high, while scores of 20 and below may be considered low.

Source: International Personality Item Pool. (2001). A Scientific Collaboration for the Development of Advanced Measures of Personality Traits and Other Individual Differences (http://ipip.ori.org/).

A Strategic Organizational Behavior Moment

Whatever Is Necessary!

Marian could feel the rage surge from deep within her. Even though she was usually in control of her behavior, it was not easy to control her internal emotions. She could sense her rapid pulse and knew that her face was flushed. But she knew that her emotional reaction to the report would soon subside in the solitary confines of her executive office. She would be free to think about the problem and make a decision about solving it.

Marian had joined the bank eight months ago as manager in charge of the consumer loan sections. There were eight loan sections in all, and her duties were both interesting and challenging. But for some reason there had been a trend in the past six months of decreasing loan volume and increasing payment delinquency. The month-end report to which she reacted showed that the past month was the worst in both categories in several years.

Vince Stoddard, the president, had been impressed by her credentials and aggressiveness when he hired her. Marian had been in the business for 10 years and was the head loan officer for one of the bank's competitors. Her reputation for aggressive pursuit of business goals was almost legendary among local bankers. She was active in the credit association and worked long, hard hours. Vince believed that she was the ideal person for the position.

When he hired her, he had said, "Marian, you're right for the job, but I know it won't be easy for you. Dave Kattar, who heads one of the loan sections, also wanted the job. In fact, had you turned down our offer, it would have been Dave's. He is well liked around here, and I also respect him. I don't think you'll have any problems working with him, but don't push him too hard at first. Let him get used to you, and I think you'll find him to be quite an asset."

But Dave was nothing but a "pain in the neck" for Marian. She sensed his resentment from the first day she came to work. Although he never said anything negative, his aggravating way of ending most conversations with her was, "Okay, Boss Lady. Whatever you want is what we'll do."

When loan volume turned down shortly after her arrival, she called a staff meeting with all of the section heads. As she began to explain that volume was off, she thought she noticed several of the section heads look over to Dave. Because she saw Dave only out of the corner of her eye, she couldn't be certain, but she thought he winked at the other heads. That action immediately angered her—and she felt her face flush. The meeting accomplished little, but each section head promised that the next month would be better.

In fact, the next month was worse, and each subsequent month followed that pattern. Staff meetings were now more frequent, and Marian was more prone to explode angrily with threats of what would happen if they didn't improve. So far she had not followed through on any threats, but she thought that "now" might be the time.

To consolidate her position, she had talked the situation over with Vince, and he had said rather coolly, "Whatever you think is necessary." He hadn't been very friendly toward her for several weeks, and she was worried about that also.

"So," Marian thought to herself, "I wonder what will happen if I fire Dave. If I get him out of here, will the others shape up? On the other hand, Vince might not support me. But maybe he's just waiting for me to take charge. It might even get me back in good graces with him."

Discussion Questions

1. What role did personality play in the situation at the bank? Which of the Big Five personality traits most clearly influenced Marian and Dave? Which of the cognitive and motivational aspects of personality played a role?

2. Working within the bounds of her personality, what should Marian have done when trouble first seemed to be brewing? How could she have maintained Dave's job satisfaction and commitment?

3. How should Marian proceed now that the situation has become very difficult?

Team Exercise

Experiencing Emotional Labor

Have you ever been forced to smile at someone who was annoying you? Have you ever had to be calm when you felt very afraid? If so, you have probably engaged in emotional labor. The purpose of this exercise is to examine how emotional labor can affect us in different ways and the factors that impact the toll that emotional labor can take on us.

Steps

1. At the beginning of class, assemble into teams of six to eight people.
2. During the next 30 minutes of class, each individual will be required to follow emotional display rules for one of the following emotions:
   a. Happiness
   b. Anger
   c. Compassion and caring
   d. Fear
   Assign the display rules so that at least one person is displaying each emotion.
3. Each person is to display his or her assigned emotion during the next 30 minutes of class lecture or activity—*no matter what he or she actually feels!*
4. At the end of the 30 minutes (or when instructed by your teacher), re-form into groups and address the following questions:
   a. How difficult was it for you to display your assigned emotion? Was your assigned emotion different from how you actually felt? Did your felt emotions begin to change to coincide with your displayed emotion?
   b. To what extent did the type of emotion required (e.g., happiness versus anger) influence your reaction to this exercise?
   c. How much longer could you have continued displaying your assigned emotion? Why?
5. Appoint a spokesperson to present the group's conclusions to the entire class.

Source: Adapted from *Experiences in Management and Organizational Behavior,* 4th ed. (New York: John Wiley & Sons, 1997).

Endnotes

1. Barrick, M.R., & Mount, M.K. 1991. The Big Five personality dimensions and performance: A meta-analysis. *Personnel Psychology,* 44: 1–26.
2. Hough, L.M., Oswald, F.L., & Ployhart, R.E. 2001. Determinants, detection, and amelioration of adverse impact in personnel selection procedures: Issues, evidence and lessons learned. *International Journal of Selection and Assessment,* 9: 152–194; Schmidt, F.L., & Hunter, J.E. 1998. The validity and utility of selection methods in personnel psychology: Practical and theoretical implications of 85 years of research findings. *Psychological Bulletin,* 124: 262–274.
3. Marcus, B., Lee, K., & Ashton, M.C. 2007. Personality dimensions explaining relationships between integrity tests and counterproductive behavior: Big Five, or one in addition? *Personnel Psychology,* 60: 1–35.
4. Kristof-Brown, A.L., Zimmerman, R.D., & Johnson, E.C. Consequences of individuals' fit at work: A meta-analysis of person-job, person-organization, person-group, and person-supervisor fit. *Personnel Psychology,* 58: 281–342; Arthur, W., Bell, S.T., Villado, A.J., & Doverspike, D. The use of person-organization fit in employment decision making: An assessment of its criterion related validity. *Journal of Applied Psychology,* 91: 786–801.
5. McCulloch, M.C., & Turban, D.B. 2007. Using person-organization fit to select employees for high turnover jobs. *International Journal of Selection and Assessment,* 15: 63.

6. Peterson, R.S., Smith, D.B., & Martorana, P.V. 2003. The impact of chief executive officer personality on top management team dynamics: One mechanism by which leadership affects organizational performance. *Journal of Applied Psychology,* 88: 795–808.

7. Miller, D., & Toulouse, J-M. 1986. Chief executive personality and corporate strategy and structure in small firms. *Organizational Science,* 32: 1389–1410.

8. Eysenck, H.J., Arnold, W.J., & Meili, R. 1975. *Encyclopedia of psychology (Vol. 2).* London: Fontana/Collins; Fontana, D. 2000. *Personality in the workplace.* London: Macmillan Press; Howard, P.J., & Howard, J.M. 2001. *The owner's manual for personality at work.* Austin, TX: Bard Press.

9. Byrne, J.A. 1998. How Al Dunlap self-destructed. *Business-Week,* July 6, 58–64.

10. Ibid.

11. See, for example, Bouchard, T.J., Lykken, D.T., McGue, M., Segal, N.L., & Tellegen, A. 1990. Sources of human psychological differences: The Minnesota study of twins reared apart. *Science,* 250: 223–228; Shields, J. 1962. *Monozygotic twins.* London: Oxford University Press.

12. Ibid.

13. Chess, S., & Thomas, A. 1987. *Know your child: An authoritative guide for today's parents.* New York: Basic Books.

14. Hamer, D., & Copeland, P. 1998. *Living with your genes.* New York: Doubleday; Ridely, M. 1999. *Genome: The autobiography of a species in 23 chapters.* New York: HarperCollins.

15. Ridely, M. 1999. *Genome: The autobiography of a species in 23 chapters.* New York: HarperCollins.

16. Friedman, H.S., & Schustack, M.W. 1999. *Personality: Classic theories and modern research.* Boston: Allyn and Bacon.

17. McCandless, B. 1969. *Children: behavior and development.* London: Holt, Rinehart, & Winston.

18. Costa, P.T., & McCrae, R.B. 1993. Set like plaster: Evidence for the stability of adult personality. In T. Heatherton and J. Weimberger (Eds.), *Can personality change?* Washington, DC: American Psychology Association.

19. Erikson, E. 1987. *A way of looking at things: Selected papers from 1930 to 1980.* New York: W.W. Norton.

20. Costa, P.T., & McCrae, R.R. 1992. *NEO PI-R: Professional manual.* Odessa, FL: Psychological Assessment Resources.

21. Silkos, R. 2006. When Terry met Jerry, Yahoo! *New York Times,* January 29. Accessed at www.nytimes.com/2006/01/29/business/yourmoney/29yahoo.html.

22. Barrick, M.R., & Mount, M.K. 1991. The Big Five personality dimensions and performance: A meta-analysis. *Personnel Psychology,* 44: 1–26; Barrick, M.R., Mount, M.K., & Judge, T.A. 2001. Personality and performance at the beginning of the new millennium: What do we know and where do we go next? *International Journal of Selection and Assessment,* 9: 9–30; Hurtz, G.M., & Donovan, J.J. 2000. Personality and job performance: The Big Five revisited. *Journal of Applied Psychology,* 85: 869–879; Mount, M.K., Barrick, M.R., & Strauss, G.L. 1998. Five-factor model of personality and performance in jobs involving interpersonal interactions. *Human Performance,* 11: 145–165.

23. de Jong, R.D., Bouhuys, S.A., & Barnhoorn, J.C. 1999. Personality, self-efficacy, and functioning in management teams: A contribution to validation. *International Journal of Selection and Assessment,* 7: 46–49.

24. Judge, T.A., Heller, D., & Mount, M.K. 2002. Five-factor model of personality and job satisfaction: A meta-analysis. *Journal of Applied Psychology,* 87: 530–541.

25. Costa, P.T., & McCrae, R.R. 1992. *NEO P-R: Professional manual.* Odessa, FL: Psychological Assessment Resources.

26. Barrick, M.R., & Mount, M.K. 1991. The Big Five personality dimensions and performance: A meta-analysis. *Personnel Psychology,* 44: 1–26; Barrick, M.R., Mount, M.K., & Judge, T.A. 2001. Personality and performance at the beginning of the new millennium: What do we know and where do we go next? *International Journal of Selection and Assessment,* 9: 9–30.

27. Judge, T.A., Higgins, C.A., Thoresen, C., & Barrick, M.R. 1999. The Big Five personality traits, general mental ability, and career success across the life span. *Personnel Psychology,* 52: 621–652.

28. Bain & Company, 2007. Springboard: People. www.bain.com/bainweb/Join_Bain/people_places.asp; Goldman Sachs Group, Inc. 2007. Our people. www2.goldmansachs.com/careers/inside_goldman_sachs/our_people/index.html; Microsoft. 2007. Meet Our People. http://members.microsoft.com/careers/mslife/meetpeople/default.aspx.

29. Witt, L.A., Burke, L.A., Barrick, M. R., & Mount, M.K. 2002. The interactive effects of conscientiousness and agreeableness on job performance. *Journal of Applied Psychology,* 87: 164–169.

30. Costa, P.T., & McCrae, R.R. 1992. *NEO P-R: Professional manual.* Odessa, FL: Psychological Assessment Resources.

31. Barrick, M.R., Mount, M.K., & Judge, T.A. 2001. Personality and performance at the beginning of the new millennium: What do we know and where do we go next? *International Journal of Selection and Assessment,* 9: 9–30.

32. Kichuk, S.L., & Weisner, W.H. 1997. The Big Five personality factors and team performance: Implications for selecting successful product design teams, *Journal of Engineering and Technology Management,* 14: 195–221; Neuman, G.A., Wagner, S.H., & Christiansen, N.D. 1999. The relationship between work-team personality composition and the job performance of teams. *Group and Organization Management,* 24: 28–45; Neuman, G.A., & Wright, J. 1999. Team effectiveness: beyond skills and cognitive ability. *Journal of Applied Psychology,* 84: 376–389.

33. Costa, P.T., & McCrae, R.R. 1992. *NEO P-R: Professional manual.* Odessa, FL: Psychological Assessment Resources.

34. Barrick, M.R., & Mount, M.K. 1991. The Big Five personality dimensions and performance: A meta-analysis. *Personnel Psychology,* 44: 1–26.

35. Barrick, M.R., Mount, M.K., & Judge, T.A. 2001. Personality and performance at the beginning of the new millennium: What do we know and where do we go next? *International Journal of Selection and Assessment,* 9: 9–30.

36. Kichuk, S.L., & Weisner, W.H. 1997. The Big Five personality factors and team performance: Implications for selecting successful product design teams, *Journal of Engineering and Technology Management,* 14: 195–221; Thomas, P., Moore, K.S., & Scott, K.S. 1996. The relationship between self-efficacy for participating in self-managed work groups and the Big Five personality dimensions. *Journal of Organizational Behavior,* 17: 349–363.

37. Judge, T.A., Heller, D., & Mount, M.K. 2002. Five-factor model of personality and job satisfaction: A meta-analysis. *Journal of Applied Psychology,* 87: 530–541.

38. Costa, P.T., & McCrae, R.R. 1992. *NEO P-R: Professional manual.* Odessa, FL: Psychological Assessment Resources.

39. Barrick, M.R., Mount, M.K., & Judge, T.A. 2001. Personality and performance at the beginning of the new millennium: What do we know and where do we go next? *International Journal of Selection and Assessment,* 9: 9–30.

40. W.L. Gore & Associates. 2007. Careers: North America. www.gore.com/careers/north_america_careers.html.

41. Howard, P.J., & Howard, J.M. 2001. *The owner's manual for personality at work.* Austin, TX: Bard Press.

42. Ibid.

43. Hough, L.M., Oswald, F.L., & Ployhart, R.E. 2001. Determinants, detection, and amelioration of adverse impact in personnel selection procedures: Issues, evidence and lessons learned. *International Journal of Selection and Assessment,* 9: 152–194; Schmidt, F.L., & Hunter, J.E. 1998. The validity and utility of selection methods in personnel psychology: Practical and theoretical implications of 85 years of research findings. *Psychological Bulletin,* 124: 262–274; Tett, R.P., Jackson, D.N., & Rothstein, M. 1991. Personality measures as predictors of job performance. *Personnel Psychology,* 44: 703–742.

44. Wilk, S.L. & Moynihan, L.M. 2005. Display rule regulators: The relationship between supervisors and worker emotional exhaustion. *Journal of Applied Psychology,* 90: 917–927.

45. Spector, P.E. 1982. Behavior in organizations as a function of employee's locus of control. *Psychological Bulletin,* 91: 482–497.

46. Kabanoff, B., & O'Brien, G.E. 1980. Work and leisure: A task-attributes analysis. *Journal of Applied Psychology,* 65: 596–609.

47. Spector, P.E. 1982. Behavior in organizations as a function of employee's locus of control. *Psychological Bulletin,* 91: 482–497.

48. Spector, P.E., Cooper, C.L., Sanchez, J.I., O'Driscoll, M., Sparks, K., Bernin, P., Bussing, A., Dewe, P., Hart, P., Lu, L., Miller, K., De Moraes, L. R., Ostrognay, G.M., Pagon, M., Pitariu, H.D., Poelmans, S.A.Y., Radhakrishnan, P., Russinova, V., Salamatov, V., Salgado, J.F., Shima, S., Siu, O., Stora, J.B., Teichmann, M., Theorell, T., Vlerick, P., Westman, M., Widerszal-Bazyl, M., Wong, P.T., & Yu, S. 2002. Locus of control and well-being at work: How generalizable are western findings? *Academy of Management Journal,* 45: 453–466.

49. Ng, T.W.H., Sorensen, K.L., & Eby, L.T. 2006. Locus of control at work: A meta-analysis. *Journal of Organizational Behavior,* 27: 1057–1087.

50. Blass, T. 1977. *Personality variables in behavior.* Hillsdale, NJ: Lawrence Erlbaum Associates.

51. Altmeyer, B. 1998. The other "authoritarian personality." In M.P. Zanna (Ed.), *Advances in experimental social psychology (Volume 30).* San Diego: Academic Press, pp. 47–92.

52. Son Hing, L.S., Bobocel, D.R., Zanna, M.P., and McBride, M.V. 2007. Authoritarian dynamics and unethical decision making: High social dominance orientation leaders and high right-wing authoritarian followers. *Journal of Personality and Social Psychology,* 92: 67–81.

53. Mehra, A., Kilduff, M., & Brass, D.J. 2001. The social networks of high and low self-monitors: Implications for workplace performance. *Administrative Science Quarterly,* 46: 121–146.

54. Snyder, M. 1979. Self-monitoring processes. *Advances in Experimental Social Psychology,* 12: 85–128.

55. Mehra, A., Kilduff, M., & Brass, D.J. 2001. The social networks of high and low self-monitors: Implications for workplace performance. *Administrative Science Quarterly,* 46: 121–146.

56. Snyder, M. 1979. Self-monitoring processes. *Advances in Experimental Social Psychology,* 12: 85–128.

57. Day, D.V., Schleicher, D.J., Unckless, A.L., & Hiller, N.J. 2002. Self-monitoring personality at work: A meta-analytic investigation of construct validity. *Journal of Applied Psychology,* 87: 390–401.

58. Kilduff, M., & Day, D.V. 1994. Do chameleons get ahead? The effects of self monitoring on managerial careers. *Academy of Management Journal,* 37: 1047–1060.

59. Blass, T. 1977. *Personality variables in behavior.* Hillsdale, NJ: Lawrence Erlbaum Associates.

60. Steel, P. 2007. The nature of procrastination: A meta-analytic and theoretical review of quintessential self-regulatory failure. *Psychological Bulletin,* 133: 65–94.

61. Blass, T. 1977. *Personality variables in behavior.* Hillsdale, NJ: Lawrence Erlbaum Associates.

62. See, for example, Salgado, J.F. 1997. The five factor model of personality and job performance in the European Community. *Journal of Applied Psychology,* 82: 30–43.

63. Locke, E.A. 2005. Why emotional intelligence is an invalid concept. *Journal of Organizational Behavior,* 26: 425–431.

64. Dunnette, M.D. 1976. Aptitudes, abilities, and skills. In M.D. Dunnette (Ed.), *Handbook of industrial and organizational psychology.* Chicago: Rand McNally.

65. Hunter, J.E., & Hunter, R.F. 1984. Validity and utility of alternative predictors of job performance. *Psychological Bulletin,* 96: 72–98; Hunter, J.E., & Schmidt, F.L. 1996. Intelligence and job performance: Economic and social implications. *Psychology, Public Policy, and Law,* 2: 447–472; Salgado, J.F., & Anderson, N. 2002. Cognitive and GMA testing in the European Community: Issues and evidence. *Human Performance,* 15: 75–96; Schmidt, F.L. 2002. The role of general cognitive ability and job performance: Why there cannot be a debate. *Human Performance,* 15: 187–210; Schmidt, F.L., & Hunter, J.E. 1998. The validity and utility of selection methods in personnel psychology: Practical and theoretical implications of 85 years of research findings. *Psychological Bulletin,* 124: 262–274.

66. Simon, D.G., Hitt, M.A., & Ireland, R.D. 2006. Managing firm resources in dynamic environments to create value: Looking inside the black box. *Academy of Management Review,* in press.

67. Katz, D., & Stotland, E. 1959. Preliminary statement to a theory of attitude structure and change. In S. Kock (Ed.), *Psychology: A study of science* (3rd ed.). New York: McGraw-Hill.

68. Petty, R.E., & Cacioppo, J.T. 1981. *Attitudes and persuasion: Classic and contemporary approaches.* Dubuque, IA: Wm. C. Brown.

69. Bem, D.J. 1972. Self-perception theory. In L. Berkowitz (Ed.), *Advances in experimental social psychology (Vol. 6).* New York: Academic Press.

70. Freedman, J.L., & Fraser, S.C. 1966. Compliance without pressure: The foot-in-the-door technique. *Journal of Personality and Social Psychology,* 4: 195–202.

71. Heider, F. 1958. *The psychology of interpersonal relations.* New York: John Wiley & Sons; Osgood, C.E., & Tannenbaum, P.H. The principle of congruity in the prediction of attitude change. *Psychological Review,* 62: 42–55.

72. Holtom, B.C., Mitchell, T.R., & Lee, T.W. 2006. Increasing human and social capital by applying embeddedness theory. *Organizational Dynamics,* 35: 316–331.

73. Mitchell, T.R., Holtom, B.C., Lee, T.W., Sablynski, C.J., & Erez, M. 2001. Why people stay: Using job embeddedness to predict voluntary turnover. *Academy of Management Journal,* 44: 1102–1121; Tett, R.P., & Meyer, J.P. 1993. Job satisfaction, organizational commitment, turnover intention, and turnover: Path analyses based on meta-analytic findings. *Personnel Psychology,* 46: 259–293.

74. Scott, K.D., & Taylor, G.S. 1985. An examination of conflicting findings on the relationship between job satisfaction and absenteeism: A meta-analysis. *Academy of Management Journal,* 28: 599–612.

75. Kinicki, A.J., McKee-Ryan, F.M., Schriesheim, C.A., & Carson, K.P. 2002. Assessing the construct validity of the Job Descriptive Index: A review and meta-analysis. *Journal of Applied Psychology,* 87: 14–32.

76. Judge, T.A., Thoresen, C.J., Bono, J.E., & Patton, G.K. 2001. The job satisfaction-job performance relationship: A qualitative and quantitative review. *Psychological Bulletin,* 127: 376–407.

77. Gellatly, I.R., Meyer, J.P., & Luchak, A.A. 2006. Combined effects of the three commitment components on focal and discretionary behaviors: A test of Meyer and Herscovitch's propositions. *Journal of Vocational Behavior,* 69: 331–345; Meyer, J.P., Stanley, D.J., Herscovitch, L., & Topolnytsky, L. 2002. Affective, continuance, and normative commitment to the organization: A meta-analysis of antecedents, correlates and consequences. *Journal of Vocational Behavior,* 61: 20–52.

78. Wright, T.A., & Bonett, D.G. 2002. The moderating effect of employee tenure on the relation between organizational commitment and job performance: A meta-analysis. *Journal of Applied Psychology,* 87: 1183–1190.

79. Riketta, M. 2002. Attitudinal organizational commitment and job performance. *Journal of Organizational Behavior,* 23: 257–266.

80. Gellatly, I.R., Meyer, J.P., & Luchak, A.A. 2006. Combined effects of the three commitment components on focal and discretionary behaviors: A test of Meyer and Herscovitch's propositions. *Journal of Vocational Behavior,* 69: 331–345.

81. Anonymous, 2007. Job satisfaction declines, especially among newest workforce entrants. *HR Focus,* April, 84(4): 8; http://www.conference-board.com.

82. Meyer, J.P., Stanley, D.J., Herscovitch, L., & Topolnytsky, L. 2002. Affective, continuance, and normative commitment to the organization: A meta-analysis of antecedents, correlates and consequences. *Journal of Vocational Behavior,* 61: 20–52; Kalbers, L.P., & Cenker, W.J. 2007. Organizational commitment and auditors in public accounting. *Managerial Auditing Journal,* 22: 354–375.

83. Vandenberghe, C., Bentein, K., & Stinglhamber, F. 2004. Affective commitment to the organization, supervisor, and work group: Antecedents and outcomes. *Journal of Vocational Behavior,* 64: 47–71.

84. Ford, M.T., Heinen, B.A., & Langkamer, K.L. 2007. Work and family satisfaction and conflict: A meta-analysis of cross-domain relations. *Journal of Applied Psychology,* 92: 57–106.

85. Meyer, J.P., Stanley, D.J., Herscovitch, L., & Topolnytsky, L. 2002. Affective, continuance, and normative commitment to the organization: A meta-analysis of antecedents, correlates and consequences. *Journal of Vocational Behavior,* 61: 20–52.

86. Schulte, M., Ostroff, C., & Kinicki, A.J. 2006. Organizational climate and psychological climate perceptions: A cross-level study of climate-satisfaction relationships. *Journal of Occupational and Organizational Psychology,* 79: 645–671.

87. Podsakoff, N.P., LePine, J.A., & LePine, M.A. 2007. Differential challenge stressor-hindrance relationships with job attitudes, turnover intentions, and withdrawal behavior: A meta-analysis. *Journal of Applied Psychology,* 92: 438–454.

88. Colquitt et al. Justice meta-analysis.

89. Locke. *Handbook of I/O.*

90. Meyer, J.P., & Allen, N.J. 1997. *Commitment in the workplace: Theory, research, and application.* Thousand Oaks, CA: Sage.

91. Meyer, J.P., Stanley, D.J., Herscovitch, L., & Topolnytsky, L. 2002. Affective, continuance, and normative commitment to the organization: A meta-analysis of antecedents, correlates and consequences. *Journal of Vocational Behavior,* 61: 20–52.

92. Ilies, R., Arvey, R.D., & Bouchard, T.J. 2006. Darwinism, behavioral genetics, and organizational behavior: A review and agenda for future research. *Journal of Organizational Behavior,* 27: 121–141.

93. Deaux, K., Dane, F.C., Wrightsman, L.S., & Sigelman, C.K. 1993. *Social psychology in the 90s.* Pacific Grove, CA: Brooks/Cole.

94. Aronson, E., Turner, J., & Carlsmith, J. 1963. Communicator credibility and communication discrepancy. *Journal of Abnormal and Social Psychology,* 67: 31–36; Hovland, C., Janis, I., & Kelley, H.H. 1953. *Communication and persuasion.* New Haven, CT: Yale University Press.

95. Eagly, A.H., Chaiken, S., & Wood, W. 1981. An attributional analysis of persuasion. In J. Harvey, W.J. Ickes, & R.F. Kidd (Eds.), *New directions in attribution research (Vol. 3).* Hillsdale, NJ: Lawrence Erlbaum Associates; Walster, E., Aronson, E., & Abrahams, D. 1966. On increasing the persuasiveness of a low prestige communicator. *Journal of Experimental Social Psychology,* 2: 325–342.

96. Berscheid, E. 1966. Opinion change and communicator–communicatee similarity and dissimilarity. *Journal of Personality and Social Psychology,* 4: 670–680.

97. McGinniss, J. 1969. *The selling of the president, 1968.* New York: Trident Press.

98. Leventhal, H. 1970. Findings and theory in the study of fear communications. In L. Berkowitz (Ed.), *Advances in experimental social psychology (Vol. 5).* New York: Academic Press.

99. Rogers, R.W. 1983. Cognitive and physiological processes in fear appeals and attitude change: A revised theory of protection motivation. In J. Cacioppo, & R. Petty (Eds.), *Social psychophysiology.* New York: Guilford Press; Maddux, J.E., & Rogers, R.W. 1983. Protection motivation and self-efficacy: A revised theory of fear appeals and attitude change. *Journal of Experimental Social Psychology,* 19: 469–479.

100. Festinger, L.A. 1957. *A theory of cognitive dissonance.* Stanford, CA: Stanford University Press.

101. Deaux, K., Dane, F.C., Wrightsman, L.S., & Sigelman, C.K. 1993. *Social psychology in the 90s.* Pacific Grove, CA: Brooks/Cole.

102. Johnson, P.R., & Indvik, J. 1999. Organizational benefits of having emotionally intelligent managers and employees. *Journal of Workplace Learning,* 11: 84–90.

103. Fisher, C.D., & Ashkanasy, N.M. 2000. The emerging role of emotions in work life: An introduction. *Journal of Organizational Behavior,* 21: 123–129.

104. Hymowitz, C. 2006. Business is personal, so managers need to harness emotions. *Wall Street Journal,* November 13 (eastern edition): p. B.1.

105. Lazarus, R.S., & Lazarus, A.D. 1994. *Passion and reason: Making sense of emotions.* New York: Oxford University Press.

106. Hershcovis, M.S., Turner, N., Barling, J., Arnols, K.A., Dupre, K.E., Inness, M., LeBlanc, M.M., & Sivanathan, N. 2007. Predicting workplace aggression: A meta-analysis. *Journal of Applied Psychology,* 92: 228–238.

107. George, J.M. & Brief, A.P. 1992. Feeling good—doing good: A conceptual analysis of mood at work—organizational spontaneity. *Psychological Bulletin,* 112: 310–329.

108. Isen, A.M., Daubman, K.A., & Nowicki, G.P. 1987. Positive affect facilitates creative problem solving. *Journal of Personality and Social Psychology,* 52: 1122–1131.

109. George, J.M., & Zhou, J. 2002. Understanding when bad moods foster creativity and good ones don't: The role of context and clarity of feelings. *Journal of Applied Psychology,* 87: 687–697.

110. Ting Fong, C. 2006. The effects of emotional ambivalence on creativity. *Academy of Management Journal,* 49: 1016–1030.

111. Barsade, S. 2002. The ripple effect: Emotional contagion and its influence on group behavior. *Administrative Science Quarterly,* 47: 644–675; Hatfield, E., Cacioppo, J.T., & Rapson, R.L. 1994. *Emotional contagion.* Cambridge, England: Cambridge University Press.

112. Bono, J.E., & Ilies, R. 2006. Charisma, positive emotions and mood contagion. *The Leadership Quarterly,* 17(4): 317–334.

113. Hochschild, A.R. 1983. *The managed heart: Commercialization of human feeling.* Berkeley, CA: University of California Press; Ashforth, B.E., & Humphrey, R.H. 1993. Emotional labor in service roles: The influence of identity. *Academy of Management Review,* 18: 88–115.

114. Cropanzano, R., Weiss, H. M., & Elias, S. M. 2004. The impact of display rules and emotional labor on psychological well-being at work. In P.L. Perrewé, & D.C. Ganster (Eds.), *Research in occupational stress and well-being (Vol. 3).* Amsterdam: Elsevier, pp. 45–89; Schaubroeck, J., & Jones, J.R. 2000. Antecedents of workplace emotional labor dimensions and moderators of their effects on physical symptoms. *Journal of Organizational Behavior,* 21: 163–183.

115. Zapf, D., & Holz, M. On the positive effect and negative effects of emotion work in organizations. *European Journal of Work and Organizational Psychology,* 15: 1–26.

116. Wilk, S.L., & Moynihan, L.M. 2005. Display rule "regulators": The relationship between supervisors and worker emotional exhaustion. *Journal of Applied Psychology,* 915–927.

117. Wilk, S.L., & Moynihan, L.M. 2005. Display rule "regulators": The relationship between supervisors and worker emotional exhaustion. *Journal of Applied Psychology,* 915–927; Ashforth, B.E., & Humphrey, R.H. 1993. Emotional labor in service roles: The influence of identity. *Academy of Management Review,* 18: 88–115.

118. Bozionelos, N. 2006. Mentoring and expressive network resources: Their relationship with career success and emotional exhaustion among Hellenes employees involved in emotion work. *Journal of Human Resource Management,* 17: 36–378.

119. Salovey, P., & Mayer, J. 1990. Emotional intelligence. *Imagination, Cognition, and Personality,* 9: 185–211.

120. Kerr, R., Garvin, J., Heaton, N., & Boyle, E. 2006. Emotional intelligence and leadership effectiveness. *Leadership and Organizational Development Journal,* 27: 265–279; Cote, S., & Miners, C.T.H. 2006. Emotional intelligence, cognitive intelligence, and job performance. *Administrative Science Quarterly,* 51: 1–28; Semadar, A., Robins, G., & Ferris, G.R. Comparing the validity of multiple social effectiveness constructs in the prediction of managerial job performance. *Journal of Organizational Behavior,* 27: 443–461. Rozell, E.J., Pettijohn, C.E., & Parker, R.S. 2006. *Journal of Marketing Theory and Practice,* 14: 113–125; Rooy, D.L., & Viswasvaran, C. 2004. Emotional intelligence: A meta-analytic investigation of predictive validity and nomonological net. *Journal of Vocational Behavior,* 65: 71–95.

121. Goleman, D. 1995. *Emotional intelligence.* New York: Bantam.

122. Locke, E.A. 2005. Why emotional intelligence is an invalid concept. *Journal of Organizational Behavior,* 26: 425–443.

123. Locke, E.A. 2005. Why emotional intelligence is an invalid concept. *Journal of Organizational Behavior,* 26: 425–431; Murphy, K.R. (editor) 2006. *A critique of emotional intelligence: What are the problems and how can they be fixed?* Mahwah, NJ: Lawrence Erlbaum Associates; Fineman, S. 2005. Appreciating emotion at work: Paradigm tensions. *International Journal of Work Organisation and Emotion,* 1: 4–19.

6

WORK MOTIVATION

On January 1, 1958, Wilbert and Genevieve Gore founded a small company to develop applications of polytetrafluoroethylene (PTFE). Wilbert, a chemist and research scientist, tended to the technical work while Genevieve handled accounting and other business matters.

Wilbert Gore initially focused on applications in the emerging computer industry, where PTFE's insulation characteristics were potentially useful in cables and circuit boards. After solving a number of technical issues, he and his company

Tyler Stableford/Stone/Getty Images

EXPLORING BEHAVIOR IN ACTION
Work Motivation at W.L. Gore & Associates

succeeded with cable and wire products. Some of these products eventually landed on the moon as part of the technology used in the Apollo space program. More recently, they have been incorporated into the U.S. space shuttle program. Moving beyond cables and wires, Gore has created a number of leading products for a number of industries. Best known among consumers for waterproof Gore-Tex fabrics, the company also places products in industries such as aerospace, automotive, chemical processing, computing, telecommunications, environmental protection, medical/healthcare, pharmaceutical, biotechnology, and textiles.

Having previously experienced bureaucratic roadblocks in highly structured

organizations, Wilbert Gore designed a different kind of company to support the work with PTFE. Using the term *lattice structure* to signify an emphasis on informal communication and fluid work networks, he set up a company that focused on equality among people as well as freedom for those people to pursue their own ideas and projects. To a significant degree, individuals were and still are expected to define their own jobs within areas that interest them. Assigned sponsors help both new and existing Gore personnel with job definition.

Formal leadership assignments are less common at Gore than in more structured companies. Instead of formal

assignments, Gore looks for individuals who have attracted "followers" for their ideas and projects. Thomas Malone, a professor at Massachusetts Institute of Technology, has studied the company and summarizes the approach as follows: "The way you become a [leader] is by finding people who want to work for you. . . . In a certain sense, you're elected rather than appointed. It's a democratic structure inside a business organization."

Culturally, four principles govern the behavior of individuals within W.L. Gore & Associates:

- The ability to make one's own commitments and keep them

- Freedom to encourage, help, and allow other associates to grow in knowledge, skill, and scope of responsibility
- Consultation with others before undertaking actions that could impact the reputation of the company
- Fairness to each other and everyone with whom contact is made

These structural and cultural features of the company set the stage for personal fulfillment and growth. The official Gore web site puts it this way: "Everyone can quickly earn the credibility to define and drive projects. Sponsors help associates chart a course in the organization that will offer personal fulfillment while maximizing their contribution to the enterprise." Current CEO Terri Kelly said this: "We work hard at maximizing individual potential . . . and cultivating an environment where creativity can flourish. . . . A fundamental belief in our people and their abilities continues to be the key to our success, even as we expand globally."

Of course, Gore is not for everyone. Individuals who work at the company must tolerate a certain amount of ambiguity and must thrive in autonomous settings. Moreover, they must value personal growth in the workplace. While many or even most individuals desire personal growth, some do not. Through rigorous selection procedures, Gore tends to find the right people. The result is a highly motivated and effective workforce.

The emphasis on fairness also affects motivation and effectiveness. In many companies, pay systems promote dysfunctional internal competition and jealousy. At W.L. Gore & Associates, the pay system tends to promote a sense of equity and justice. A key aspect of the system is the sponsor. Each individual at Gore has a sponsor, either a peer or a leader, who is responsible for ensuring fair pay. The sponsor collects information on contributions and achievements from an individual's peers and leaders and then shares this information with a compensation committee. Overall, Gore's approach can be summarized as follows: "Unlike companies which base an employee's pay on the evaluations of one or two people—or supervisors' opinions alone—Gore involves many [people] in the process. Our goal: internal fairness and external competitiveness."

Recognition and success have resulted from Gore's practices. For example, W.L. Gore & Associates is a top company in the latest *Fortune* list of the "Best 100 Companies to Work For." It has also been listed as a top company for which to work in German, Italian, and British rankings, and indeed in rankings for the entire European Union. It has received awards for many technological breakthroughs. Financially, the privately held company has enjoyed consistently strong performance.

Going forward, the company seems poised for continued success. Although challenged by growth as it moves from 7,000 employees to 10,000 or more, the company seems intent on maintaining its current structure and culture.

Sources: D. Anfuso, "Core Values Shape W.L. Gore's Innovative Culture," *Workforce*, 78 no. 3 (1999): 48–53; A. Deutschman, "The Fabric of Creativity," *Fast Company*, no. 89 (2004): 54–59; Gore & Associates, "Compensation," 2007, at http://www.gore.com/en_xx/careers/benefits/compensation.html; Gore & Associates, "Corporate Culture," 2007, at http://www.gore.com/en_xx/aboutus/culture/index.html; Gore & Associates, "Fast Facts," 2007, at http://www.gore.com/en_xx/aboutus/fastfacts/index.html; P. Kriger, "Power of the Individual," *Workforce Management* 85, no. 4 (2006): 1–7; F. Shipper and C.C. Manz, "W.L. Gore & Associates, Inc.," Pinnacle Management Strategy Case Base (1993); M. Weinreb, "Power to the People," *Sales and Marketing Management* 155, no. 4 (2003): 30–35.

The Strategic Importance of Work Motivation

Formulating strategies that can deliver competitive advantage is not easy. Senior managers working with other individuals engage in countless conversations, meetings, experiments, and analyses in order to create or modify company strategies. Implementing strategies and engaging in the day-to-day behaviors that help to create competitive advantage also are not easy tasks. Hard work is involved. Managers and associates must be willing to deliver strong efforts if a firm is to succeed.[1]

With strong efforts being so important, work motivation is a crucial topic in any discussion of organizational behavior. People must be motivated if they are to effectively engage in the behaviors and practices that bring advantage and success to a firm.

It is important to note that different strategies require different types of people and behavior, and therefore different approaches to motivation. W.L. Gore has adopted a general strategy of differentiation based on innovation and creativity. Differentiating in this way requires people who can think differently, experiment in smart ways, accept responsibility, and appreciate the learning that accompanies failed efforts. The strategy also requires people who want to be challenged and grow in the workplace. To fully motivate such people, resources for trying new ideas must be made available, including time. Opportunities to develop new skills and polish old ones are important. Recognition for successes and pats on the back for strong efforts that unexpectedly did not bear fruit also might be useful. Pay, while important, often takes a backseat.

There are many ways to motivate people. Hence, there is no simple answer to the question of what managers should do to increase and sustain their associates' motivation. A great deal is known, however, about how people are motivated. In this chapter, we describe the major theories of work motivation and the practices that are most likely to increase and sustain strong efforts. We begin by formally defining what is meant by *motivation*. Next, we describe fundamental theories of work motivation, including both content and process theories. To synthesize these theories, we close the main body of the chapter by distilling useful management practices.

After reading this chapter, you should be able to:

1. Define *work motivation* and explain why it is important to organizational success.

2. Discuss how managers can use Maslow's need hierarchy and ERG theory to motivate associates.

3. Describe how need for achievement, need for affiliation, and need for power relate to work motivation and performance.

4. Explain how Herzberg's two-factor theory of motivation has influenced current management practice.

5. Discuss the application of expectancy theory to motivation.

6. Understand equity theory and procedural justice, and discuss how fairness judgments influence work motivation.

7. Explain how goal-setting theory can be used to motivate associates.

8. Describe how jobs can be enriched and how job enrichment can enhance motivation.

9. Based on all major theories of work motivation, describe specific actions that can be taken to increase and sustain employee motivation.

What Is Motivation?

Man and machine . . . work in close harmony to achieve more than either could alone. Machines bring precision and capacity. They make our lives easier, perfect our processes, and in many ways, enrich our quality of life. But people possess something that machines don't—human spirit and inspiration. Our people work continuously at setting goals and tracking results for ongoing improvement as an overall business. They are an inspiration and their goals and accomplishments have won Branch-Smith Printing recognition on the highest of levels.[2]

This quotation from Branch-Smith Printing, a 2002 recipient of the Malcolm Baldrige National Quality Award, gets at the heart of motivation: it is the spirit and inspiration that leads people to apply their human capital to meet the goals of the organization. In Chapter 1, we discussed the strategic importance of human capital to the success of a firm. However, human capital alone is not enough to ensure behaviors that support organizational performance. Associates must translate their human capital into actions that result in performance important to the achievement of organizational goals. Motivation is the process through which this translation takes place.

Consider the following example. A manager has three assistants reporting to her. They have similar levels of experience and education. However, they have different levels of ability for the tasks at hand, and they perform at different levels. It is interesting that the person with the least ability has outperformed his counterparts. How can a person with less ability outperform individuals who have greater abilities? The answer may be that he is more motivated to apply his abilities than the others. The two other assistants are approximately equal to one another in their motivation to perform, judging by the fact that they work equally hard, and yet one of these assistants outperforms the other. How can this be when they are equally motivated? The answer may lie in their different ability levels. Thus, we can see that a person's level of performance is a function (*f*) of both ability and motivation:

$$\text{Performance} = f(\text{Ability} \times \text{Motivation})$$

Now consider another scenario. Two salespersons are equally motivated and have the same ability, yet one of them outperforms the other. How can we explain this, if performance is a function of ability and motivation? In this case, the better performer has a more lucrative sales territory than the other salesperson. Thus, environmental factors can also play a role in performance.

This brings us to our definition of work motivation. We know from the preceding discussion that ability and certain environmental factors exert influences on performance that are separate from the effects of motivation. **Motivation,** then, refers to forces coming from within a person that account for the willful direction, intensity, and persistence of the person's efforts toward achieving specific goals, where achievement is not due solely to ability or to environmental factors.[3] Several prominent theories offer explanations of motivation. Most of the theories can be separated into two groups: those concerned largely with content and those concerned largely with process. In the next two sections, we consider theories in each of these two groups.

motivation
Forces coming from within a person that account for the willful direction, intensity, and persistence of the person's efforts toward achieving specific goals, where achievement is not due solely to ability or to environmental factors.

Content Theories of Motivation

Content theories of motivation generally focus on identifying the specific factors that motivate people. These theories are, for the most part, straightforward. Four important content theories of motivation are Maslow's need hierarchy, Alderfer's ERG theory, McClelland's need theory, and Herzberg's two-factor theory.

Hierarchy of Needs Theory

hierarchy of needs theory
Maslow's theory that suggests people are motivated by their desire to satisfy specific needs, and that needs are arranged in a hierarchy with physiological needs at the bottom and self-actualization needs at the top. People must satisfy needs at lower levels before being motivated by needs at higher levels.

One of the most popular motivation theories, frequently referred to as the **hierarchy of needs theory,** was proposed in the 1940s by Abraham Maslow.[4] According to Maslow, people are motivated by their desire to satisfy specific needs. Maslow arranged these needs in hierarchical order, with physiological needs at the bottom, followed by safety needs, social and belongingness needs, esteem needs, and, at the top, self-actualization needs. In general, lower-level needs must be substantially met before higher-level needs become important. Below, we look at each level and its theoretical implications in organizational settings.

1. *Physiological needs.* Physiological needs include basic survival needs—for water, food, air, and shelter. Most people must largely satisfy these needs before they become concerned with other, higher-order needs. Money is one organizational award that is potentially related to these needs, to the extent that it provides for food and shelter.

2. *Safety needs.* The second level of Maslow's hierarchy concerns individuals' needs to be safe and secure in their environment. These needs include the need for protection from physical or psychological harm. People at this level might consider their jobs as security factors and as a way to keep what they have acquired. These managers and associates might be expected to engage in low-risk job behaviors, such as following rules, preserving the status quo, and making career decisions based on security concerns.

3. *Social and belongingness needs.* Social needs involve interaction with and acceptance by other people. These needs include the desire for affection, affiliation, friendship, and love. Theoretically, people who reach this level have primarily satisfied physiological and safety needs and are now concerned with establishing satisfying relationships with other people. Although a great deal of satisfaction may come from family relationships, a job usually offers an additional source of relationships. Managers and associates at this level may thus seek supportive co-worker and peer-group relationships.

4. *Esteem needs.* Esteem needs relate to feelings of self-respect and self-worth, along with respect and esteem from peers. The desire for recognition, achievement, status, and power fits in this category. People at this level may be responsive to organizational recognition and awards programs and derive pleasure from having articles about them published in the company newsletter. Money and financial rewards may also help satisfy esteem needs, because they provide signals of people's "worth" to the organization.

5. *Self-actualization needs.* A person's need for self-actualization represents her desire to fulfill her potential, maximizing the use of her skills and abilities. People at the self-actualization level are less likely to respond to the types of rewards described for the first four levels. They accept their own achievements and seek new opportunities to use their unique skills and talents. They often are highly motivated by work assignments that challenge these skills, and they might even reject common rewards (salary increase, promotion) that could distract them from using their primary skills. Only a few people are assumed to reach this level.

As mentioned, these needs are arranged in hierarchical order, with physiological needs the lowest and self-actualization the highest. According to Maslow's theory, each need is prepotent over all higher-level needs until it has been satisfied. A *prepotent* need is one that predominates over other needs. For example, a person at the social and belongingness level will be most concerned with rewards provided by meaningful relationships and will not be so concerned with esteem-related rewards, such as public recognition or large bonuses. It follows that a satisfied need is no longer a motivator. For example, after a person's social needs are met, she will no longer be concerned with developing and maintaining relationships but will instead be motivated to seek esteem-related rewards. The need hierarchy theory is supposed to apply to all normal, healthy people in a similar way.

Digital Vision

The need hierarchy theory has not been well supported by empirical research.[5] Research has indicated that a two-level hierarchy of lower-order and higher-order needs may exist, but it has not found much support for the five specific need categories proposed by Maslow. One reason for this finding may be the context of the studies. Most people in the United States, where the studies typically have been done, have satisfied their basic needs and are faced with a complex system of means to satisfy their higher-order ones. It may be difficult for researchers to separate the needs these people experience into the five specific categories proposed by Maslow.

In addition, the idea of prepotency has been questioned.[6] Some researchers have noted that several needs may be important at the same time. For example, a person can simultaneously have strong social, esteem, and self-actualization needs. Even Maslow's clinical studies showed that the idea of prepotency is not relevant for all individuals.[7]

A final problem with the need hierarchy theory involves a practical concern. It is difficult to determine the present need level for each associate and the exact rewards that would help satisfy that associate's specific needs. For example, a person's concern with being popular with co-workers may be related to either social and belongingness needs or esteem needs (or to both). Being popular can mean that one is liked, but it can also mean that one has high status in the group. If a manager is attempting to diagnose the meaning behind a person's desire to be popular, she could make an erroneous judgment. As another example, money can be used to meet both physiological and esteem needs, but it may not have the desired effect in all cases where esteem is the key issue. In general, it is challenging for managers to apply the need hierarchy to motivate associates.

Although the need hierarchy theory has many weaknesses, it is historically important because it focused attention on people's esteem and self-actualization needs. Previously, behaviorism had been the dominant approach to understanding human motivation. As you may recall, behaviorism proposes that people's behaviors are motivated solely by extrinsic rewards. The need hierarchy, in contrast, suggests that the behavior of many people is motivated by needs reflecting a human desire to be recognized and to grow as an individual. Beyond its historical significance, the need hierarchy also continues to guide some research in fields such as humanistic psychology.[8]

ERG Theory

ERG theory
Alderfer's theory that suggests people are motivated by three hierarchically ordered types of needs: existence needs (E), relatedness needs (R), and growth needs (G). A person may work on all three needs at the same time, although satisfying lower order needs often takes place before a person is strongly motivated by higher level needs.

ERG theory, developed by Clayton Alderfer, is similar to Maslow's need hierarchy theory in that it also proposes need categories.[9] However, it includes only three categories: existence needs (E), relatedness needs (R), and growth needs (G). The relationship of these categories to those of Maslow's need hierarchy theory is shown in Exhibit 6-1. As you can see in the exhibit, existence needs are similar to Maslow's physiological and safety needs, relatedness needs are similar to Maslow's social and belongingness needs, and growth needs are similar to Maslow's needs for esteem and self-actualization. Growth needs are particularly important in an organization such as W.L. Gore & Associates.

ERG theory differs from Maslow's theory in two important ways. First, the notion of prepotency is not fixed in ERG theory. A person's existence needs do not necessarily have to be satisfied before she can become concerned about her relationships with others or about using her personal capabilities. Her desire to meet the existence needs may be stronger than her desire to meet the two other types of needs, but the other needs may still be important. The need hierarchy theory proposes that the hierarchy is fixed and that physiological needs must be largely satisfied before other needs become important.

Second, even when a need is satisfied, it may remain the dominant motivator if the next need in the hierarchy cannot be satisfied. For instance, if a person has satisfied his relatedness needs but is frustrated in trying to satisfy his growth needs, his desire for relatedness needs again becomes strong (recall that a satisfied need is no longer a motivator in the need hierarchy theory). Alderfer called this the *frustration-regression process*.[10] Thus, it is possible that a need may never cease to be a motivator. An associate who has many friends and is very well liked may continue to seek friends and social approval if frustrated in satisfying growth needs. Understanding this is important for managers because it may provide them with the reasons for a person's behavior.

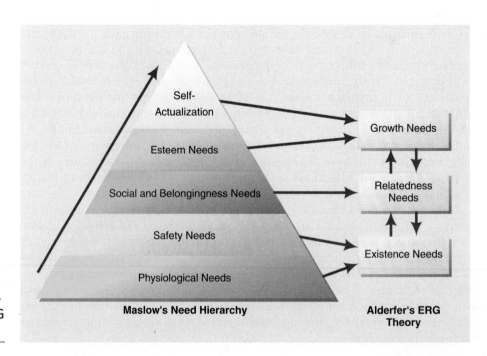

Exhibit 6-1
Maslow's Need Hierarchy and Alderfer's ERG Theory Compared

ERG theory has more research support than Maslow's hierarchy of needs. For example, some research has found evidence for the meaningfulness of the three categories of needs.[11] Support has also been found for several of Alderfer's basic propositions, such as the concept that a satisfied need may remain a motivator.[12] Indeed, relatedness and growth needs have been found to increase as they are satisfied. In other words, the more they are satisfied, the more they are desired. However, more research on ERG theory is necessary to test its usefulness under different conditions. In general, ERG theory may be viewed as a refinement of the need hierarchy theory.[13]

Theory of Achievement, Affiliation, and Power

A third theory, largely developed by David McClelland, also uses need classifications and focuses on the needs for achievement, affiliation, and power. Some have referred to these as learned needs because they are influenced by cultural background and can be acquired over time.[14] The three needs are also viewed as independent, meaning a person can be high or low on any one or all three needs. Although all three needs are important, the need for achievement has received the most attention from researchers because of its prominent organizational effects.[15]

NEED FOR ACHIEVEMENT

Need for achievement, first discussed in Chapter 5, was originally defined by McClelland and his colleagues as a "desire to perform well against a standard of excellence."[16] People with a high need for achievement feel good about themselves when surpassing a standard that is meaningful to them. Further, people with a high need for achievement prefer to set their own goals rather than to have no goals or to accept the goals set for them by others. Specifically:

> need for achievement
> The need to perform well against a standard of excellence.

- They tend to set goals of moderate difficulty that are achievable.
- They like to solve problems rather than leave the results to chance. They are more interested in achieving the goal than in the formal rewards they may receive, although they recognize the value of their inputs and tend to earn good incomes.
- They prefer situations in which they receive regular, concrete feedback on their performance.[17]
- They are positive thinkers who find workable solutions to life's hurdles and challenges.[18]
- They assume strong personal responsibility for their work.

Some consider the achievement motive to be a component of self-actualization.[19] Consistent with this belief, people high on need for achievement tend to do well in challenging jobs but do less well in boring or routine jobs. In a recent study of sales and sales support personnel, those individuals with high achievement needs had positive outcomes only when occupying more demanding, technically orientated roles.[20] Related to this finding, people who aspire to be entrepreneurs frequently have a high need for achievement.[21] Also, managers who have high achievement needs tend to manage differently relative to those who have lower achievement needs because of a more pronounced goal orientation.[22]

Although need for achievement is thought to be a relatively stable characteristic in adults, it is possible to train adults to increase their need for achievement. This training includes the following steps:[23]

1. Teach people how to think like persons with a high need for achievement. This includes teaching people how to imagine the achievement of desired goals and mentally rehearse the steps necessary to reach those goals.

2. Teach and encourage people to set challenging but realistic work-related goals.

3. Give people concrete feedback about themselves and their performance. Ensure that people are knowledgeable about their behavior and its outcomes.

4. Create *esprit de corps*.

In organizations such as W.L. Gore & Associates, people with high achievement needs are generally positive. Such people, however, can react negatively to the ambiguity found in these organizations. Without reasonably clear pathways to success, high achievement needs can go unmet in any given time period.

NEED FOR AFFILIATION

need for affiliation
The need to be liked and to stay on good terms with most other people.

People with a high **need for affiliation** have a strong desire to be liked and to stay on good terms with most other people. Affiliative people tend not to make good managers. They are more concerned with initiating and maintaining personal relationships than with focusing on the task at hand. In one study, managers of product development units were assessed. Those with high needs for affiliation were seen as less influential and as having less influential units. They also had units with weaker innovation profiles.[24]

Need for affiliation is a particularly important consideration in today's world where working from home as virtual contributors is common. At Microsoft, about 14 percent of the U.S. workforce works from home at least two days per week, and the percentage is expected to grow to 17 percent by 2009. At IBM, 42 percent of the workforce works from home, on the road, or at a client location. Significant percentages of people work virtually at Sun Microsystems, Convergys, and many other companies.

Without daily contact with other associates or managers, individuals with strong affiliation needs might have difficulty developing strong relations and assessing how well they are liked. They may be particularly prone to feelings of isolation and dissatisfaction. To combat these and other issues, companies that rely heavily on virtual contributors have introduced a host of technologies and practices. To ensure satisfied and productive workers, they generally have provided key technologies that help people stay connected, such as laptops, Internet access, and a personal digital assistant. Many companies also support instant messaging and provide sophisticated collaboration software. Companies such as Sun Microsystems, Ernst & Young, and Deloitte & Touche designate office and conference space for associates who occasionally stop in. Also, some managers insist on face-to-face team meetings every now and then.[25]

NEED FOR POWER

need for power
The desire to influence people and events.

The **need for power** can be defined as the desire to influence people and events. According to McClelland, there are two types of need for power: one that is directed toward the good of the organization (*institutional power*) and one that is directed toward the self (*personal power*).[26] People high in the need for institutional power want to influence others for altruistic reasons—they are concerned about the functioning of the organization and have a desire to serve others. They are also more controlled in their exercise of power. In contrast, those high in the need for personal power desire to influence others for their own personal gain. They are more impulsive in exercising power, show little concern for other people, and are focused on obtaining symbols of prestige and status (such as big offices).

Research has shown that a high need for institutional power is critical for high-performing managers. People with a high need for institutional power are particularly good at increasing morale, creating clear expectations, and influencing others to work for the good of the organization. Need for institutional power seems to be more important than need for achievement in creating managerial success,[27] although blending both is perhaps better than having one or the other.

As discussed in the *Managerial Advice* feature on page 193, the Hay Group has conducted a great deal of research on managers' needs. Its consultants apply this work in the firm's well-regarded global consulting practice. Importantly, Hay research shows that a strong need for achievement can create problems. Such problems, however, are less likely to occur when a strong achievement need is blended and balanced with a significant need for institutional power and perhaps also with some level of need for affiliation.

MANAGERIAL ADVICE

Managers Over the Edge

The Hay Group, an internationally renowned consulting firm, studies managers' needs for achievement, affiliation, and power. Through its McClelland Center, it continues the work that David McClelland began many years ago.

In a recent report, the organization identified changes in the needs of tens of thousands of managers, most of them from the United States. In terms of average strength, need for achievement exhibited a substantial increase from the mid-1980s through 2005, with most of the increase occurring after 1995. Moreover, it became by far the strongest need. Need for affiliation exhibited little change during the key time period, but slipped from the strongest to the second-strongest need. Need for power weakened and then strengthened over the time period. Overall, the average strength of this need exhibited little net change, ending the time period close to where it began. In terms of rank, it settled into a distant third place.

While increased need for achievement among managers implies many positive behaviors and outcomes, very high levels of this need can create problems for two reasons. First, a strong achievement need in a manager can set the stage for coercive tendencies, particularly when this need is paired with relatively weak needs for affiliation and institutional power. These coercive tendencies result from the manager wanting to achieve at any cost while having limited needs to be liked and to build engaged associates. Hay Research on IBM managers showed these tendencies in action. High need-for-achievement managers with lower needs for affiliation and institutional power produced inferior work climates through less delegation, less effort in connecting associates' work to the overall strategy and mission of the organization, more command-and-control behaviors, and more instances of taking over work that should be done by others.

David P. Hall/ Masterfile

Second, a strong achievement need can set the stage for shortcuts and illicit actions, all in the name of achievement. Again, this is of most concern when high need for achievement is paired with relatively weak needs for affiliation and institutional power. Hay researchers cite Jeffery Skilling as a relevant example. Skilling has been sentenced to prison for his role in the fall of Enron.

Scott Spreier, a senior consultant with The Hay Group, Mary Fontaine, a vice-president at Hay, and Ruth Malloy, director of research at Hay's McClelland Center, recently provided a set of guidelines designed to help high-achievement managers avoid problems.

- *Understand needs.* Without explicitly understanding their own personal needs in the workplace, managers cannot manage those needs. Understanding needs can be accomplished by simply thinking about valued activities and outcomes or by using available assessment tools (one popular tool will be presented in this chapter's installment of *Building Your Human Capital*).
- *Manage needs.* Having gained awareness of their needs, managers can take actions to handle them effectively. A manager with quite a strong achievement need might ask a trusted colleague to monitor his behavior for coercion. Such a manager might also seek training focused on the benefits of delegation and an empowered workforce. Finally, she might channel some of the need for achievement into non-work pursuits (e.g., competitive golf).

Sources: Hay Group, "About Hay Group," 2007, at http://www.haygroup.com/ww/About/Index.asp?id=495; Hay Group, "A Recent Rise in Achievement Drive among Today's Executives," 2006, at http://www.haygroup.com/ww/Media/index.asp; Hay Group, "The McClelland Center Fact Sheet," 2002, at http://www.haygroup.com/wwResearch/Detail.asp?PageID=703; S.W. Spreier, M.H. Fontaine, & R.L. Malloy, "Leadership Run Amok: The Destructive Potential of Overachievers," *Harvard Business Review* 84, no. 6 (2006): 72–82.

Two-Factor Theory

two-factor theory
Herzberg's motivation theory that suggests job satisfaction and dissatisfaction are not opposite ends of the same continuum but are independent states, and that different factors affect satisfaction and dissatisfaction.

The **two-factor theory** (sometimes called the *dual-factor theory*) is based on the work of Frederick Herzberg.[28] It has some similarities to the other need theories, but it focuses more on the rewards or outcomes of performance that satisfy individuals' needs. The two-factor theory emphasizes two sets of rewards or outcomes—those related to job satisfaction and those related to job dissatisfaction. This theory of motivation suggests that satisfaction and dissatisfaction are not opposite ends of the same continuum but are independent states. In other words, the opposite of high job satisfaction is not high job dissatisfaction; rather, it is low job satisfaction. Likewise, the opposite of high dissatisfaction is low dissatisfaction. It follows that the job factors leading to satisfaction are different from those leading to dissatisfaction, and vice versa. Furthermore, receiving excess quantities of a factor thought to decrease dissatisfaction will not produce satisfaction, nor will increasing satisfaction factors overcome dissatisfaction.

motivators
Job factors that can influence job satisfaction but not dissatisfaction.

The factors related to job satisfaction have been called *satisfiers,* or **motivators.** These are factors that, when increased, will lead to greater levels of satisfaction. They include:

- Achievement
- Recognition

- Responsibility
- Opportunity for advancement or promotion
- Challenging work
- Potential for personal growth

The factors related to dissatisfaction have been called *dissatisfiers,* or **hygienes.** When these factors are deficient, dissatisfaction will increase. However, providing greater amounts of these factors will not lead to satisfaction—only to less dissatisfaction. Hygiene factors include:

hygienes
Job factors that can influence job dissatisfaction but not satisfaction.

- Pay
- Technical supervision
- Working conditions
- Company policies, administration, and procedures
- Interpersonal relationships with peers, supervisors, and subordinates
- Status
- Security

Research has not generally supported Herzberg's two-factor theory.[29] One criticism is that the theory is method-bound—meaning that support can be found for the theory only when Herzberg's particular methodology is used. Researchers using different methodologies to test the theory have not found support. A second criticism is that the theory confuses job satisfaction and motivation. As discussed in the previous chapter, job satisfaction does not always lead to increased motivation. Happy associates are not always motivated associates. The causal path can also go the other way—with motivation, and consequently performance, influencing satisfaction—or there may be no relationship at all. A third criticism is that motivators and hygienes may not be uniquely different. For example, some factors, such as pay, can affect both satisfaction and dissatisfaction. Pay can help satisfy basic food and shelter needs (hygiene), but it can also provide recognition (motivator).

Despite the criticisms of two-factor theory, managers tend to find it appealing. Indeed, Herzberg's 1965 *Harvard Business Review* article on this theory was reprinted in a recent *Harvard Business Review* volume (January 2003), indicating that these ideas continue to be popular with managers. At a practical level, the theory is easy to understand and apply. To motivate associates, managers should provide jobs that include potential for achievement and responsibility. They should also try to maintain the hygiene factors at an appropriate level to prevent dissatisfaction. Thus, managers can motivate associates by manipulating job-content factors and can prevent associate dissatisfaction by manipulating the job context or environment.

Perhaps the most important managerial conclusion is that organizations should not expect high productivity in jobs that are weak in motivators, no matter how much they invest in hygienes. Simply providing good working conditions and pay may not result in consistently high performance. Thus, managers now give much more attention to how jobs are designed. Indeed, Herzberg's work helped launch the current focus on enriched jobs that emphasize responsibility, variety, and autonomy. This focus is consistent with high-involvement management, a key theme of our book.

Conclusions Regarding Content Theories

The four content theories we have just discussed address the factors that affect motivation. These factors include associates' needs and the various job and contextual attributes that might help them meet these needs. All four theories are popular among managers because each has an intuitive logic and is easy to understand. Although research support for the theories has not been strong overall, the theories have been useful in developing specific managerial practices that increase motivation and performance. Further, these theories can be integrated with process theories, discussed next.

Process Theories of Motivation

Whereas content theories emphasize the *factors* that motivate, process theories are concerned with the *process* by which such factors interact to produce motivation. One of the weaknesses of content theories is the assumption that motivation can be explained by only one or two factors, such as a given need or the content of a job. As we have seen, human motivation is much more complex than that. In most cases, several conditions interact to produce motivated behavior. Process theories take this complexity into account. Process theories generally focus on the cognitive processes in which people engage to influence the direction, intensity, and persistence of their behavior. Three important process theories of motivation are expectancy theory, equity theory, and goal-setting theory.

Expectancy Theory

expectancy theory
Vroom's theory that suggests motivation is a function of an individual's expectancy that a given amount of effort will lead to a particular level of performance, instrumentality judgments that indicate performance will lead to certain outcomes, and the valences of outcomes.

expectancy
The subjective probability that a given amount of effort will lead to a particular level of performance.

instrumentality
Perceived connections between performance and outcomes.

The first process theory to recognize the effects of multiple, complex sources of motivation was Victor Vroom's **expectancy theory.**[30] Expectancy theory suggests that managers and associates consider three factors in deciding whether to exert effort.

First, they consider the probability that a given amount of effort will lead to a particular level of performance. For example, an associate might consider the probability that working on a report for an extra four hours will lead to a significant improvement in that report. This probability is referred to as an **expectancy.**

The second factor individuals consider is the perceived connection between a particular level of performance and important outcomes. For example, the associate cited above would consider the potential outcomes of a better report. She may believe there is a strong positive connection between a better report and (1) praise from her supervisor and (2) interesting future assignments. In other words, she may perceive that good performance makes these outcomes very likely. She may also believe that there is a weak positive connection between a better report and an increase in pay, meaning she believes that good performance makes this outcome only slightly more likely to occur. Overall, she is interested in the effects of good performance on three outcomes. Each perceived connection between performance and an outcome is referred to as an **instrumentality.**

The third factor is the importance of each anticipated outcome. In our example, the associate may believe that more praise from her boss, better assignments, and an increase in pay would bring her a great deal of satisfaction. As a result, these outcomes have high valence. **Valence** is defined as the value placed on an outcome.

In essence, expectancy theory suggests that people are rational when deciding whether to expend a given level of effort. The following equation formally states how people implement expectancy theory:

$$MF = E \times \Sigma \ (I \times V)$$

where:

MF = Motivational force.

E = Expectancy, or the subjective probability that a given level of effort will lead to a particular level of performance. It can range from 0 to +1. Further, the expectancy of interest usually corresponds to the probability that strong effort will result in good performance.[31] Thus, an expectancy of zero means that an individual thinks there is no chance that strong effort will lead to good performance. An expectancy of one means that an individual thinks it is certain that strong effort will lead to good performance. For a given person in a given situation, self-esteem, previous experience with the task, and availability of help from a manager can influence this subjective probability.[32]

I = Instrumentality, or the perceived connection between a particular level of performance and an outcome. Instrumentality can range from −1 to +1, because it is possible for a performance level to make an outcome less likely as well as make an outcome more likely. For example, an instrumentality of −.8 indicates that an individual expects performing at a particular level would make an outcome very unlikely (e.g., praise from co-workers might be unlikely due to jealousy).

V = Valence, or the value associated with an outcome. Valence can be negative or positive, because some outcomes may be undesirable while others are desirable.

Exhibit 6-2 illustrates the expectancy theory process.

As an example, consider a car salesman who is considering the possibility of selling 15 automobiles next month. Would he attempt to sell that many cars? Assume that our salesman believes there is a .7 probability that strong effort would result in the desired performance. Also, assume that he perceives the following connections between performance and four key outcomes: +.9 for a $1,000 bonus, +.8 for strong praise from his managers, +.9 for high intrinsic satisfaction, and −.7 for meaningful praise from co-workers.[33] Finally, assume valences for these outcomes of 5, 3, 4, and

> **Valence**
> Value associated with an outcome.

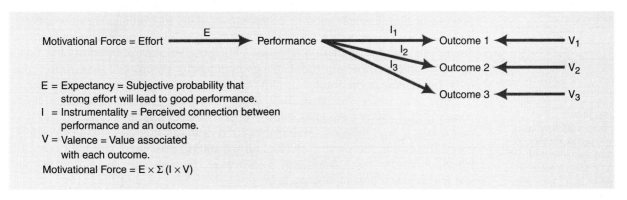

Exhibit 6-2 Expectancy Theory

1 (on a scale from 1 to 5, where 1 means not valued at all and 5 means highly valued). Based on these beliefs and perceptions, our salesman probably would be motivated to attempt to sell the automobiles. He believes there is a good chance that his strong effort would result in success (expectancy of .7), and he perceives strong positive connections between performance and three valued outcomes (instrumentalities of .9, .8, and .9) while perceiving a strong negative connection to a nonvalued outcome (−.7) (he perceives that success probably would yield no praise, and perhaps even scorn, from co-workers but he does not care).

Research has generally been supportive of expectancy theory.[34] Criticisms, however, have been expressed concerning how the components of expectancy theory are measured, how they should be combined, and the impact of individual differences. For example, it has been shown that all three components of expectancy theory predict motivation better when they are considered together than when any one component is examined alone. However, the three components do not appear to have equal strength in affecting motivation. That is, the desirability of outcomes may be the most important element in the equation. Not surprisingly, valence seems to be most important.[35] Another issue results from consideration of individual differences. For example, people who have high consideration of others are less likely to engage in the rational, outcome-maximizing decision-making processes underlying expectancy theory.[36] Although subsequent research has led to revised versions of Vroom's original model, the basic components remain the same.[37]

Expectancy theory has clear implications for managers. In order to increase motivation, managers can do one or more of the following:

- Heighten expectancy by increasing associates' beliefs that strong effort will lead to higher levels of performance.
- Increase instrumentalities by clearly linking high performance to outcomes.
- Increase valence by providing outcomes that are highly valued.

We discuss specific procedures later in this chapter.

Equity Theory

The notion of fairness and justice has been of concern to human beings throughout written history and undoubtedly before that as well. Thus, it should not be surprising that people's perception of how fairly they are being treated influences their motivation to perform tasks. The study of organizational justice has been popular in recent years,[38] and its popularity is likely to continue with the increasing incidence of corporate scandals (such as those involving Enron and Arthur Andersen) and discrimination lawsuits.[39] Further, the concept of equity has taken on added importance with the demands by minority groups and women for equitable treatment on the job.[40]

The basic model for using the fairness concept to explain human motivation comes from J. Stacey Adams's **equity theory.**[41] According to this theory, motivation is based on a person's assessment of the ratio of outcomes she receives (e.g., pay, status) for inputs on the job (e.g., effort, ability) compared with the same ratio for a comparison other, frequently a co-worker. Thus, in assessing equity, the person makes the following comparison:

equity theory
A theory that suggests motivation is based on a person's assessment of the ratio of outcomes she receives (e.g., pay, status) for inputs on the job (e.g., effort, ability) compared to the same ratio for a comparison other.

$$\frac{\text{My Outcomes}}{\text{My Inputs}} \quad \text{vs.} \quad \frac{\text{Other's Outcomes}}{\text{Other's Inputs}}$$

After making the comparison, the person forms equity perceptions. Based on the perceptions of equity or the lack of it, people make *choices* about the action to take (e.g., how much effort to exert to perform the task). Equity exists when the person's ratio of outcomes to inputs is equal to that of the other person, and inequity exists when the ratios are not equal. Inequity may result, for example, when one person is paid more than the other for the same inputs or when one person provides less input for the same pay. Note that an individual may compare his outcome–input ratio to the average ratio of several other people, but often the comparison is to one other person.

When individuals perceive inequity, they can reduce it in several ways. Consider the following tactics (pay is the focus here, but other inputs can affect perceptions of inequity):

- *Increasing or decreasing inputs.* Underpaid associates could decrease their effort, whereas overpaid associates could increase their effort to resolve inequity. This reaction to inequity demonstrates how equity perceptions can influence motivation.

- *Changing their outcomes.* If underpaid associates convince their supervisor to increase their pay, inequity is resolved. It is less likely, but possible, that overpaid workers would seek a salary reduction. However, they may seek to reduce or give up other outcomes, such as not taking interesting assignments or taking a less desirable office.

- *Distorting perceptions of their inputs and outcomes.* If it is not possible to actually change inputs or outcomes, inequitably paid associates may distort their perceptions of the situation. One common erroneous perception by underpaid workers is that their jobs offer many psychological benefits. Overpaid workers often believe they are working much harder than they actually are.

- *Distorting perceptions of the inputs or outcomes of the referent other.* This is similar to distorting perceptions of one's own inputs and outcomes to resolve inequity. For example, if an associate feels she is underpaid compared to her co-worker, she can reason that the co-worker really does stay late more often or has a degree from a better school and thereby the co-worker has higher inputs.

- *Changing the referent other.* If an associate perceives inequity in comparison to one co-worker, it may be easiest to find a co-worker who compares more favorably.

- *Leaving the organization.* In cases where inequity is resistant to other forms of resolution, associates may be motivated to resign from the organization and seek a more equitable situation elsewhere.

Research generally suggests that inequity is an important concept.[42] For example, some individuals have been found to respond to overpayment by increasing their effort and performance.[43] When these individuals believe they are being paid more than they deserve, they increase their inputs to bring them into balance with outcomes. In general, different individuals have been found to react differently to inequity. *Sensitives* are individuals who pay a great deal of attention to outcome–input ratios and are motivated to resolve any inequity, whether the inequity is favorable or unfavorable to them. *Benevolents* are tolerant of inequity that is unfavorable but are not comfortable with inequity that favors them. *Entitleds* do not tolerate unfavorable inequity but are comfortable with inequity that favors them.[44] In the overall population, many people exhibit behavior that seems consistent with the entitleds.

Professional athletes provide interesting case studies for the inequity concept, as indicated by frequent headlines telling us that some "star" is upset about his compensation. These highly paid athletes evidently feel that their outcome–input ratios—their salaries compared with their contributions to their teams—do not measure up to those of similar athletes in the same sport. In 2001, Alex Rodriguez, a young and talented professional baseball player, agreed to a 10-year, $252 million contract to play for the Texas Rangers. Even in the era of exceptional salaries for professional sports figures, this amount seemed almost outrageous. The contract provided Rodriguez, known as A-Rod to his fans, $25.2 million annually. However, that is not all. If by chance anyone in professional baseball negotiated a higher salary in the 10 years of his contract, A-Rod would be given that figure plus $1. In other words, his contract guaranteed that he would be the highest-paid professional baseball player for a decade.[45] Yet, partly because of this very high compensation level, he was traded to the New York Yankees, where he has had both good times and bad.[46]

Perceptions of inequity have several important effects in the workplace.[47] For example, research has found that feelings of inequity can lead to negative employee behaviors such as theft.[48] On the positive side, feelings of equity frequently lead to outcome satisfaction and job satisfaction, organizational commitment, and organizational citizenship behaviors. *Organizational citizenship behavior* refers to an associate's willingness to engage in organizationally important behaviors that go beyond prescribed job duties, such as helping co-workers with their work or expending extra effort to bring positive publicity to the organization.

distributive justice
The degree to which people think outcomes are fair.

procedural justice
The degree to which people think the procedures used to determine outcomes are fair.

Perceptions of inequity often are defined in terms of **distributive justice,** a form of justice that relates to perceptions of fairness in outcomes. Another type of justice is also important, however. **Procedural justice** is the degree to which procedures used to determine outcomes seem fair.[49] Research shows that when outcomes are unfavorable, people are likely to be concerned with the fairness used in determining those outcomes.[50] People will be less likely to have negative reactions to unfavorable or questionable outcomes when they perceive that procedures used to arrive at the outcomes are fair. Procedures based on the following rules are more likely to be perceived as fair:[51]

- People should feel that they have a voice in the decision process. For example, good performance appraisal systems allow associates to provide input into the evaluation process.
- Procedures should be applied consistently. For example, the same criteria should be used to decide on everyone's pay increase.
- Procedures should be free from bias.
- Procedures should be based on accurate information.
- A mechanism should be in place for correcting faulty outcome decisions. Such mechanisms sometimes involve formal grievance procedures.
- Procedures should conform to the prevailing ethical code.
- People should be treated with respect.
- People should be given reasons for the decisions. For example, survivors of a layoff are much more likely to remain motivated if the reasons for the layoff are explained.[52]

Overall, equity and procedural justice concepts can help managers understand associates' reactions to decisions about rewards. As discussed earlier, individuals at W.L. Gore & Associates have already mastered the use of equity and procedural justice.

Goal-Setting Theory

Goal-setting theory, developed by Edwin Locke, posits that goals enhance human performance because they direct attention and affect effort and persistence.[53] Given the nature of human beings, individuals are likely to be committed to the achievement of goals after they have been set and to exert effort toward goal attainment.[54] Indeed, goals serve as reference points that energize behavior.[55] The positive effects of goals on work motivation is one of the strongest findings in research on organizational behavior. Goal setting has been found to increase the motivation of associates in a multitude of jobs, such as air traffic controllers, truck drivers, faculty researchers, marine recruits, managers, social workers, nurses, research and development workers, truck maintenance workers, and weightlifters.[56] To effectively set goals for associates, managers should address several factors, including goal difficulty, goal specificity, goal commitment, participation in goal setting, and feedback.

goal-setting theory
A theory that suggests challenging and specific goals increase human performance because they affect attention, effort, and persistence.

- *Goal difficulty.* How difficult should the performance goal be? Should the goal be easy, moderately difficult, or very difficult to achieve?
- *Goal specificity.* How specific should the expected outcome be (e.g., number of parts assembled), or can goals be more loosely defined (do your best)?
- *Goal commitment.* What will make associates commit to goals?
- *Participation in setting goals.* How important is it for associates to have input in selecting the goals and levels of performance to be achieved? If important, how should they be involved?
- *Feedback.* To what extent should associates be informed of their progress as they work toward the performance goals?

GOAL DIFFICULTY

From the perspective of expectancy theory and achievement motivation theory, we might expect that associates exert the maximum effort at work when their performance goals are set at moderate levels of difficulty (i.e., somewhat difficult but achievable). Goals that are too difficult may be rejected by associates because the expectancy is low (strong effort would not lead to goal attainment). A number of researchers, however, have found that associates exert more effort when they have goals that are difficult to a significant degree. This has been found to be true of engineers and scientists, loggers, and many experimental subjects working on a variety of tasks in laboratory settings.[57] Thus, it seems that goals should be as difficult as possible, but not unreasonable. Stretch goals that are extremely difficult can be quite demotivating.

GOAL SPECIFICITY

Performance goals can be explicitly stated, clear in meaning, and specific in terms of quantity or quality of performance. For example, a goal might be to "generate twenty-seven pages of edited copy with an error rate of less than one error per ten pages in each work period" or "make twelve new customer contacts each month." The nature of some tasks, however, makes it difficult to clearly determine and state the exact performance levels that should be achieved. In such cases, a performance goal can be stated only in vague terms, such as "do your best" or "increase sales during the month."

Many studies have shown that specific goals lead to better performance than do vague goals, such as "do your very best."[58] If a goal is to act as a motivator, it must establish a specific target toward which people can direct their effort. Managers are likely to find this aspect of setting goals to be challenging because many jobs involve activities that are difficult to specify. For example, it may be difficult for a manager to be specific about an engineer's goals; yet the manager must make the attempt, or the engineer's motivation could be adversely affected.

GOAL COMMITMENT

In general, associates must accept and be committed to reaching externally set goals for these goals to be motivating. A great deal of research has been conducted on the factors that influence people's commitment to externally set goals. Expectancy theory provides a useful framework for organizing these factors: people will be committed to goals that (1) carry a reasonable expectation of being attained and (2) are viewed as desirable to attain.[59] A summary of the factors that can affect goal commitment is presented in Exhibit 6-3.

PARTICIPATION IN SETTING GOALS

A practical question for a manager, especially during performance counseling sessions with associates, is, "Should I set performance goals for the associate on the basis of my own knowledge and judgment of her abilities, or should I allow the associate to provide input and have some degree of control over them?" Importantly, associates who participate in setting a goal rather than having it dictated to them might be more satisfied with the goal and be more committed to it, resulting in stronger performance.[60] While some researchers have failed to find a relationship between participation in goal setting and performance,[61] others have found that performance is better when associates participate in setting goals.[62] Also, as discussed earlier, individuals with high achievement needs tend to dislike assigned goals.

Exhibit 6-3	Factors Affecting Goal Commitment

Factors Increasing the Desirability of Attaining a Given Goal

1. The goal is set by in conjunction with an appropriate authority figure.
2. The goal fosters a sense of self-achievement and potential for development.
3. The goal is set by or in conjunction with someone who is trustworthy.
4. The goal is set by or in conjunction with someone who is supportive and promotes self-efficacy.
5. Peers are committed to the goal.
6. The goal assigner, if there is one, provides a rationale for the goal.
7. The goal provides a challenge to prove oneself and meets ego needs.
8. The goal is public.

Factors Increasing the Perceived Ability of Attaining a Given Goal

1. There is high self-efficacy on the task.
2. There are successful role models.
3. The task is not impossibly difficult.
4. Expectancy for success is high.
5. There is competition with others.

Source: Based on E.A. Locke, & G.P. Latham, *A Theory of Goal Setting and Task Motivation* (Englewood Cliffs, NJ: Prentice-Hall, 1990).

FEEDBACK

The motivational effect of providing feedback to associates about their progress toward performance goals is well established. In fact, feedback on performance, even in the absence of established goals, is likely to have a positive effect on motivation.[63] However, feedback is especially important when performance goals exist and when they are relatively difficult to achieve. In this case, feedback permits an associate to gauge his actual progress toward the goal and make corresponding adjustments in his efforts. Such adjustments are unlikely in the absence of feedback. Thus, the presence of both goals and feedback exerts a positive influence on employee motivation.

Conclusions Regarding Process Theories

Expectancy theory, equity theory, and goal-setting theory emphasize the processes that occur in motivation. Expectancy theory focuses on people as rational decision makers: "If I exert a given amount of effort, how likely is it that my performance will result in outcomes I value?" The manager's job in this case is to develop situations in which associates have high expectancies and strong performance is rewarded. Equity theory focuses more on people's general feelings about how fairly they are being treated. This theory suggests that managers must take into account how associates are comparing themselves with others in the organization; a manager's treatment of one individual can influence the motivation of others. Finally, goal-setting theory suggests that managers can motivate associates by setting or helping to set goals.

In the *Experiencing Strategic Organizational Behavior* feature on pages 203–204, the importance of associates' motivation is emphasized. The owners of Visible Changes, the McCormacks, ensure challenging goals for their associates and then pay them handsome bonuses for meeting those goals. They also focus on expectancies held by associates, and use a variety of meaningful rewards. Finally, they support associates' growth needs through an education program, and they allow associates to participate in decisions. As a result, associates earn well above the industry average, and turnover is exceptionally low. The associates' high motivation and strong performance have made Visible Changes a top performer in its industry. Thus, Visible Changes is an industry leader both in methods of motivating associates and in company performance.

EXPERIENCING STRATEGIC ORGANIZATIONAL BEHAVIOR

Making Visible Changes

Imagine a grand ballroom filled with people in black ties and ball gowns. The room hushes as the award ceremony begins. A young woman in a red dress steps up on stage to receive her award: a $40,000 bonus. The woman is 25-year-old Lara Hadad, whose total pay package, including her bonus, will be almost a quarter of a million dollars. Lara is joining other colleagues who together are receiving 11 cars, a trip to Greece, and part of $8.7 million in bonuses.

Interestingly, Lara doesn't work for a large multinational firm. She is a hair stylist with Visible Changes hair salons. Visible Changes is an innovator in the hair salon industry. The company was started in 1977 in Houston, Texas. At the time, hairdressing was considered a risky business, and the McCormacks—the entrepreneurs who started the firm—had a difficult time convincing mall owners and bankers to support their project. However, the McCormacks implemented a management philosophy that has made them leaders in their field. Visible Changes has been recognized in *Inc.* magazine's list of the fastest growing companies in

Digital Vision

the United States. Furthermore, in an occupation plagued by high turnover and employment problems, Visible Changes associates have a low turnover rate and high satisfaction. The firm currently has 16 locations in major Texas malls with a total of over 700 associates. And each salon averages over $2 million in annual sales—well above the industry average.

How did the McCormacks build such a high-performance climate? Most of their success has been due to the way they motivate their employees.

- They provide well-defined career paths, and the performance standards required to move from one level to another are well-known by stylists. For example, to move from a senior cutter to a master cutter (with an associated increase in pay and potential bonuses), a stylist must increase the total number of haircuts given from 7,000 to 14,000, be requested by 65 percent of his clients, and complete additional education. Training and encouragement help to establish positive expectancies for these performance levels.

- They provide valued rewards and benefits showing employees that they are a part of the company "family" and that the company cares about them. For example, they have a profit-sharing plan whereby the company makes yearly contributions to associates' accounts. Associates are fully vested after 7 years, and the average person has about $100,000 in her account after 10 years. Such a plan is highly unusual in the hair salon industry. Furthermore, in addition to bonuses, employees are rewarded with cars, public recognition ceremonies, and travel to interesting locations. The "manager of the year" receives a one-carat diamond and the use of the company Mercedes. If she wins three times consecutively, she gets to keep the car! All these perks are based on meeting and exceeding clear performance standards.

- They set specific, challenging goals for each time period and reward people for achieving them. The average stylist at Visible Changes makes about $30,000 per year, with some earning six-figure incomes. The industry average is below $18,500. Beginning stylists are guaranteed $7 per hour; however, they are free to make as much as they can in commissions and bonuses. Commissions and bonuses are based on the number of requests by customers, amount of products sold, and general performance of the stylist.

- They provide support for their stylists to help them build their client base. For example, they provide brochures, business cards, and coupons.

- They avoid layoffs of associates.

- They engage associates in a variety of organizational decisions.

The McCormacks have been industry pioneers in the ways they motivate and provide support to their associates. Thus, their company is an industry leader. Other salons are copying their methods by introducing such things as better benefits packages and profit-sharing plans. We might say that the McCormacks have made significant Visible Changes.

Sources: D. Lauk, "Up Close: Local Company Puts Employees First," 11 News (Houston, Texas), Apr. 14, 2003, at http://www.khou.com; I. MacMillan and R.G. McGrath, *The Entrepreneurial Mindset: Strategies for Continuously Creating Opportunity in an Age of Uncertainty* (Cambridge, MA: Harvard Business School Press, 2000); Visible Changes, "Careers," 2007, at http://www.visiblechanges.com/Careers.aspx; Visible Changes, "Stylist," 2007, at http://www.visiblechanges.com/Stylist.aspx.

Motivating Associates: An Integration of Motivation Theories

Viewed as a set, the various motivation theories may suggest that motivation is highly complex and even confusing. That is not actually the case, however. Motivating associates and junior managers can be undertaken in a reasonably straightforward and meaningful way. While there are no foolproof approaches, there are sound tactics to employ. Exhibit 6-4 identifies connections between the various motivation theories and five categories of motivation practices that managers can use. As shown in the exhibit, multiple theories have similar implications for managers. We discuss these implications in the remainder of the chapter.

Find Meaningful Individual Rewards

All of the content theories suggest that individuals vary in what they find motivating. Furthermore, expectancy theory implies that individuals assign different valences to outcomes. This means that by tailoring individual rewards to individual needs and desires, companies can create a competitive advantage in attracting and motivating associates. One area in which this is obvious is the provision of benefits. An unmarried 28-year-old associate with no children likely

Exhibit 6-4	Motivation Practices Resulting from Motivation Theories				
	Motivation Practices				
Motivation Theories	Find Meaningful Individual Rewards	Tie Rewards to Performance	Redesign Jobs	Provide Feedback	Clarify Expectations and Goals
Need Hierarchies Maslow ERG	X		X	X	
McClelland's Needs	X	X	X	X	X
Herzberg's Two-Factor Theory			X		
Expectancy Theory	X	X		X	X
Equity Theory	X	X		X	X
Goal-Setting Theory		X		X	X

Note: The fact that there is no X in a particular cell indicates that the theory has nothing specific to say about the practice, not that the theory says the practice is ineffective.

places different values on various retirement and insurance plans relative to a 50-year-old associate with three children in college, for example.

One mistake that managers often make when trying to determine what motivates individual associates involves placing too much emphasis on extrinsic rewards (e.g., pay increases, bonuses, pay level, job security, job titles) while under-emphasizing intrinsic rewards (e.g., satisfaction based on exciting and challenging work, feelings of accomplishment).[64] Indeed, a recent survey of a random sample of U.S. adults indicated that they ranked "important work" as the most important aspect of their jobs. Pay was ranked third. When, however, these same people were asked what motivates "other people," 75 percent responded that pay was the primary motivator of others.[65] Apparently, most people feel that they are motivated by outcomes that meet higher-order growth or achievement needs, but they think others are primarily motivated by money as a way to meet physiological and security needs.

Some research has shown that if a person receives extrinsic rewards for performing an intrinsically satisfying task, he may attribute the performance to external forces, with a resulting reduction in his intrinsic interest in the job.[66] This suggests that relying too heavily on extrinsic rewards can cause people to lose any natural interest they have in performing their jobs. However, this position has been challenged by some researchers who argue that in work situations, extrinsic rewards are necessary for motivation on any kind of task. Despite the mixed research,[67] it is clear that managers must be concerned with both extrinsic and intrinsic rewards and not overemphasize either, striving instead for an appropriate balance between the two (keeping in mind that the appropriate balance differs across different people or types of people).

Individuals may vary in what they find motivating based on their position in the organization. People in different jobs and at different levels may have different concerns. Indeed, when *Harvard Business Review* asked a dozen top leaders to state their most important thoughts on motivating people, Liu Chuanzhi, chairman of the Legend Group of Beijing, noted that a leader must establish different incentives for people at different levels in the organization.[68] He divided his organization into three groups and provided appropriate incentives for each group:

- The company's executives wanted a sense of ownership in the company, so the company gave all of its executives stock, an unusual practice in Chinese state-owned organizations. They also wanted recognition, so they were given opportunities to speak to the media.

- Mid-level managers wanted to become senior-level managers. The major incentives applied to this group involved opportunities to display and develop their knowledge, skills, and abilities, so they would be in a better position to achieve promotions within the company.

- Associates wanted outcomes that would provide a sense of stability and security. Thus, based on their performance, they received predictable bonuses. Furthermore, they were allowed to participate in decisions regarding how bonuses were allotted.

Tie Rewards to Performance

A basic characteristic of high-involvement management involves tying rewards to performance. The importance of this tactic is supported by many theories concerning human motivation and learning. One of the basic principles of operant conditioning (Chapter 4) is that rewards should be tied directly to performance to encourage the desired behavior. This basic proposition is reflected in the process theories of motivation as well. Expectancy theory proposes that motivation is a function of the perceived connections between performance and outcomes. To the extent that people have experience with performance leading to rewards, they will develop stronger instrumentalities.

Equity theory suggests that performance in the recent past (an input) should play a role in rewards (outcomes). In addition, justice research indicates that linking performance and rewards should result in greater motivation because the reward decisions will be viewed as more ethical and unbiased as people are rewarded based on their achievement and contribution. Finally, goal-setting theory suggests that providing rewards for the achievement of goals can help associates accept and become committed to those goals, although external rewards are not necessarily required for goals to affect motivation.[69]

Although tying rewards to performance may seem obvious and simple, managers often find it to be challenging. One reason for this problem is that performance is sometimes difficult to measure.[70] How does one evaluate the work of an R&D professional whose job entails developing and testing many new ideas, most of which will not result in usable products? What if an individual is highly interdependent with others? Can his individual contributions be clearly assessed? Further, some managers may supervise too many employees to closely observe and easily evaluate the contributions of all of them. If one cannot measure or evaluate performance accurately, then one cannot link performance to rewards. To partially address these issues, managers can have their direct reports undertake self-assessments and generate peer assessments. These tactics coupled with managers' knowledge of performance are often very helpful.

Another problem with tying rewards to performance is that managers may have little flexibility with rewards, particularly financial rewards. For example, a manager may be able to give an average raise of only 3 percent to her employees. If the bottom third of performers are given 2 percent increases, to adjust for the cost of living, this means the best performers can receive only 4 percent increases. Associates are not likely to see this small differential as being commensurate with performance differences. Such a small differential can produce low instrumentalities or perceptions of inequity.

Such problems with flexibility underscore the importance of nonfinancial rewards. Although managers may be restricted in how they can distribute financial rewards, they often can be more creative in assigning other types of rewards based on performance. For example, high-performing associates can be given job assignments that allow them to develop new skills, or they can be given credits toward payment of tuition at a local university. In 2001, the Society for Human Resource Management surveyed its members and developed a list of over 150 creative rewards that companies offer their associates. These included the services of an ergonomics consultant, sophisticated office chairs, textbook money, funding to attend conferences in exotic locations, allowing pets at work, concierge services, free dinners, and flexible work hours.

To think more deeply about tying financial rewards to performance, consider the case of Susan. Susan supervises 10 customer call-center representatives. One of her associates, Angelo, clearly outperforms the others. Angelo's customer satisfaction ratings are much higher than those of the others, he handles the most calls, and there have been no complaints against him. Susan is highly pleased with Angelo's performance, especially because he has been on the job for only one month. Susan's worst performer is Jessica, who has the lowest customer service rating, handles an average number of calls, and has been the target of several customer complaints about rudeness. Jessica has worked in the unit for the past three years, which is a long tenure for a customer service representative. It's time to assign pay increases, and Susan's boss told her that her budget for salaries would be only 4 percent. This means that her employees can receive, on average, only a 4 percent raise. Susan is considering an 8 percent increase for Angelo and no increase for Jessica. However, when she begins to assign pay increases, she has a change of heart. She realizes that if she gives Angelo an 8 percent increase and gives no pay increase to Jessica, Angelo will receive more overall pay than Jessica, who has been on the job much longer. Susan doesn't want to alienate Jessica because it is difficult to retain people on the job (and Jessica has a tendency to react quite negatively to bad news). In the end, Susan gives Angelo a 5 percent pay increase and Jessica a 3 percent pay increase. Three months later, Susan notices that Angelo's customer service rating has decreased and that he is handling fewer calls. Jessica's performance hasn't improved either. In fact, the number of complaints against her has increased.[71]

Susan's dilemma illustrates several common pitfalls in tying financial rewards to performance.

One problem is that Susan didn't differentiate more between Angelo's and Jessica's pay increases because of her fear that Jessica would become angry. This is a common reaction of managers when distributing financial rewards. Too often, managers are overly focused on superficial harmony, and they mistakenly distribute rewards equally or nearly equally rather than equitably based on performance. Monica Barron, a management consultant from AMR research, has stated, "You should make your best performers role models and say to others 'Here's what you can do to get one of these checks.'"[72]

A second problem was that Susan really wanted to reward performance, but instead she ended up rewarding tenure. Jessica received a larger pay increase because she had remained with the organization and in the job for a relatively long time. If Susan was asked whether mediocre, or even poor, performers should be rewarded for remaining on the job, she would probably answer "No." This might not have happened if Susan had clearly established what performance she expected from associates and how that performance would be rewarded.

A third problem was Susan's dilemma of having only a 4 percent pay increase budget. Her situation reflects the current state for many companies. Indeed, Robert Heneman, a compensation expert from Ohio State University, has said that managers "need a 7 percent or 8 percent [compensation increase] just to catch anybody's attention."[73] Thus, the amount of money Susan had for rewards limited her flexibility.

Beyond the simple amount of money available, how the money is used also can make a difference. A frequent issue is too much emphasis placed on merit pay increases (i.e., year-to-year pay increases). With such a focus, rewards provided for good performance in any given year are maintained in an associate's pay regardless of future performance. In addition, such an approach is often inflexible in dealing with economic downturns (because higher levels of pay are locked in for some individuals who are no longer performing among the best). Finally, the approach constrains managers from being able to provide a wide distribution of rewards. There are more creative ways to provide merit-based pay, including profit sharing and bonuses.

Redesign Jobs

Job redesign is viewed as a way to make jobs more intrinsically meaningful to people and thus more likely to satisfy higher-order needs. Job redesign generally takes one of two forms: job enlargement or job enrichment.

JOB ENLARGEMENT

Job enlargement involves adding tasks with similar complexity to the current tasks. The added tasks offer more variety and often require the use of different skills. However, the additional tasks are not of greater complexity and therefore offer little opportunity for personal growth. Some refer to this practice as *horizontal job loading*.

An example of job enlargement involves giving a data entry specialist the additional task of filing correspondence. In this case, a different skill is utilized, but filing is no more complex than routine data entry. Even so, by providing variety, job enlargement may prevent boredom in simple tasks. However, the effects may be only temporary because the tasks do not offer more challenges or opportunities for personal growth. Overall, research has shown that the effects of job enlargement are mixed. Some studies have found that job enlargement produces positive results, whereas others have not.[74] Individuals with lower growth needs may benefit the most.

> **job enlargement**
> The process of making a job more motivating by adding tasks that are similar in complexity relative to the current tasks.

JOB ENRICHMENT

For our purposes, **job enrichment** can be differentiated from job enlargement by the complexity of tasks added to the job. Job enrichment is frequently referred to as *vertical job loading*. In enriched jobs, workers have greater responsibility for accomplishing assigned tasks; it may be said that they become "managers" of their own jobs. The concept of job enrichment was popularized by Herzberg's two-factor concept of motivation, which emphasizes responsibility, achievement, and the work itself as motivators. The concept of job enrichment also is consistent with McClelland's notion of developing a strong need for achievement and with Maslow's and Alderfer's ideas about meeting higher-order needs.

> **job enrichment**
> The process of making a job more motivating by increasing responsibility.

Many organizations, including AT&T, Corning, IBM, and Procter & Gamble, have implemented job enrichment programs. Usually, job enrichment involves adding tasks formerly handled at levels higher in the hierarchy. Boeing, for example, has implemented job enrichment by using work teams, empowering employees to work on their own ideas, and providing continuous learning opportunities. Because job enrichment involves giving associates greater control over their work, expanded job duties, and greater decision power, job enrichment is an integral part of high-involvement management.

Numerous studies have found positive results from job enrichment using outcome variables such as job satisfaction, commitment to the organization, and performance.[75] However, job enrichment programs are not always successful. To be effective, such programs must be carefully planned, implemented, and communicated to associates and must also take into account individual differences.[76]

Julio Etchart/Alamy

Interestingly, many individuals who are currently entering the workforce may embrace enriched jobs to a greater degree than some others have. These individuals are members of Generation Y, those born between 1981 and 1993. According to Deloitte Consulting, members of Generation Y love challenges in the workplace, appreciate the opportunity to be flexible and explore new ideas, and want to make a difference.[77]

The work of two researchers, Richard Hackman and Greg Oldham, has been very influential in specifying how to enrich jobs so that the motivating potential of the jobs is increased. They identified five job characteristics important in the design of jobs: skill variety, task identity, task significance, autonomy, and feedback.[78]

- *Skill variety* refers to the degree to which associates utilize a broad array of skills in doing their jobs.
- *Task identity* is the extent to which job performance results in an identifiable piece of work. Contrast the situation in which an assembly line worker's entire job is screwing bolts into one piece of metal versus the situation in which that associate is responsible for turning out an entire dashboard assembly.
- *Task significance* is the extent to which a job has an impact on the organization. It is important because people need to see how the work they do contributes to the functioning of the organization.
- *Autonomy* means that the associate has the independence to schedule his or her own work and influence the procedures with which it is carried out.
- *Feedback* involves obtaining accurate information about performance.

Hackman and Oldham propose that these five characteristics affect three psychological states: feeling of the work's meaningfulness, feeling of responsibility for the work done, and knowledge of results of personal performance on the job. Skill variety, task identity, and task significance affect the feeling of meaningfulness. Feeling of responsibility is affected by autonomy, and knowledge of results is affected by feedback. The following formula combines these factors to compute a motivating potential score (MPS) for a given job.[79]

$$MPS = \frac{(\text{Skill variety} + \text{Task identity} + \text{Task Significance}) \times \text{Autonomy} \times \text{Feedback}}{3}$$

Research has been generally supportive of the Hackman and Oldham model, finding that associates' perceptions of task characteristics relate to intrinsic motivation and performance.[80] However, several factors have been found to influence whether employees are motivated by enriched jobs. The most heavily researched factor is growth need strength.[81] People with high growth need strength tend to be more motivated by enriched jobs than those with low growth need strength. Perceptions of job characteristics have also been found to relate to job satisfaction and growth satisfaction.[82] On the negative side, however, enriched jobs, which require more skill variety, responsibility, and control, can also be more stressful to certain associates.[83]

As discussed in the *Experiencing Strategic Organizational Behavior* feature, there are steps managers can take to ensure that the demands of enriched jobs are successfully handled. When managers provide a proper setting and resources, associates interested in growth and challenge usually rise to the occasion.

EXPERIENCING STRATEGIC ORGANIZATIONAL BEHAVIOR

Connecting People in the Workplace

Enriched jobs have the potential to be highly motivating and rewarding. Such jobs, however, place significant demands on jobholders. To ensure success in dealing with these demands, individuals must rely on one another. In a recent report, Deloitte Research, an arm of Deloitte & Touche, put it this way: "Work has always been done through relationships. But as jobs become more complex, people increasingly depend on one another, whether it's to design software, lead a call center, or sell a service."

To facilitate connections among people, Deloitte recommends a number of tactics:

Michael Goldman/ Masterfile

- *Design physical space that fosters connections.* Proximity and layout matter. Being located far away from others who have relevant knowledge and insight can be particularly harmful to those with complex jobs. A lack of face-to-face interactions, the richest type, can be harmful to those who have such jobs. Also, an absence of dedicated areas for collaborative discussions as well as areas for quiet contemplation can be detrimental.

- *Build an organizational cushion of time and space.* Overly busy associates and managers often do not have the time to consult with others. With today's leaner organizations and stretched people, connecting to other people in rich ways can be difficult. Yet, those connections can improve productivity and quality in the long run, particularly for those who have complex jobs.

- *Cultivate communities.* Without a sense of community, associates and managers may not seek out those who have relevant knowledge and insight. Communities revolve around shared interests and goals, and they foster a sense of shared identity and belonging.

- *Stimulate rich networks of high-quality relationships.* Many associates and managers have limited informal networks of colleagues. Without a rich network that stretches across departments, divisions, and hierarchical levels, individuals are blocked from key sources of information and problem solving. In some organizations, explicit mapping of informal networks is carried out and those with deficient networks are counseled on how to improve.

- *Provide collaboration tools.* A lack of interactive, real-time collaborative technologies can be a roadblock for some types of jobs. Tools such as shared whiteboards and interactive decision-support systems can be quite useful. Wikis are also becoming useful (these involve open-access information sites whose core content can be edited by anyone at any time).

Sources: R. Athey, "It's 2008: Do You Know Where Your Talent Is?—Part 1" (New York: Deloitte & Touche USA, 2004); R. Athey, "It's 2008: Do You Know Where Your Talent Is?—Part 2" (New York: Deloitte & Touche USA, 2007); C. Mamberto, "Instant Messaging Invades the Office," *Wall Street Journal*, July 24, 2007, B.1; D. Fichter, "The Many Forms of E-Collaboration," *Online*, July–Aug. 2005, pp. 48–50.

Provide Feedback

Feedback is critical to motivation from a variety of perspectives. Those high in need for achievement seek it, it is necessary for development of expectancies and instrumentalities, it can influence perceptions of fairness by providing explanations for decisions, and it enhances the goal-setting process. A great deal of research has been conducted on the effects of performance feedback. A review of this research resulted in the following implications for making feedback effective:[84]

- Feedback is most effective when provided in conjunction with goals.
- Feedback should be repeated and provided at regular intervals. Robert Eckert, chairman and CEO of Mattel, states this succinctly: "People can't and won't do much for you if no one in the organization knows what's going on, what you expect of them. . . . And talking to them once a quarter is not enough."[85]
- Feedback should contain information about how associates can improve their performance. It is not enough to tell people whether they did well or poorly; performance strategies and plans must also be part of the message.
- Feedback should come from a credible source. The person giving the feedback should have the authority to do so and should also have sufficient knowledge of the recipient's performance.
- Feedback should focus on the performance, not on the person. In other words, feedback should always refer specifically to a performance measure, as in "Your performance is poor because you missed your quota by 10 percent," not "Your performance is poor because you are not a very good salesperson."

Clarify Expectations and Goals

The importance of goal setting to associates' motivation is made explicit in goal-setting theory. However, goal setting is also important from other motivational perspectives. Goal setting can be used to strengthen the relationships important in expectancy theory. For example, because goals help people analyze and plan performance, their effort-performance expectancies may be enhanced. Also, higher goals may be associated with higher outcome valences. Furthermore, goal setting is an important part of need for achievement because people high in this characteristic tend to set moderately difficult and reachable goals for themselves.

Many organizations have adopted goal setting, for two reasons. One is the motivating potential of goals; the other is that goals often can serve to align individual motives with organizational goals. One formal management program that aims to align motives and goals is referred to as management by objectives (MBO). Throughout the organization, individuals meet with their managers to agree on expectations for the upcoming time period.

The Strategic Lens

Associates' motivation is very important in all types of organizations. In general, associates who have greater motivation perform at higher levels and this helps to implement the organization's strategy. When the associates achieve their goals, the strategy is implemented. When the strategy is implemented effectively, the organization achieves higher performance. This result was evident in the case of W.L. Gore and later in the example of Visible Changes. The goals of associates at Visible Changes related to the strategic goal of the organization to provide high-quality service to its customers.

As part of motivation and performance, individuals must work with others to achieve success on interdependent tasks. Karl Malone, a former professional basketball player, experienced firsthand the disappointment that can occur when colleagues are unwilling to work together. He moved from the Utah Jazz to the Los Angeles Lakers in order to have a better chance to be on a championship team. He gave up a great deal of money as well as status as the sole star on a team in order to move, and he was highly motivated to perform well for the Lakers.[86] The Lakers, however, failed to play effectively as a team, and as a result they failed to win the championship. For organizations to achieve their goals and enjoy strong performance, associates and managers must be motivated not only to perform their individual tasks well but also to coordinate their activities with others in the organization to ensure that the organization's strategy is well implemented and success is ensured.

Critical Thinking Questions

1. Assume that you are managing a talented but unmotivated associate. Also assume that organizational resources needed for the job are generally sufficient. What factors would you consider first in attempting to motivate the associate? Why those factors?

2. A number of theories of motivation suggest that different rewards might be important to different people. How difficult is it to reward people differently for performing the same or similar work?

3. How will your individual motivation affect your career opportunities?

What This Chapter Adds to Your Knowledge Portfolio

In this chapter, we have discussed work motivation in some detail. We have defined motivation, discussed both content and process theories of motivation, and described how these theories can be integrated and translated into managerial practice. More specifically, we have made the following points:

- Motivation refers to forces coming from within a person that account for the willful direction, intensity, and persistence of the person's efforts toward achieving specific goals, where achievement is not due solely to ability or to environmental demands.

- Content theories of motivation generally are concerned with identifying the specific factors (such as needs, hygienes, or motivators) that motivate people. They tend to be somewhat simplistic and are easily understood by managers. The basic implications of these theories suggest that managers must take individual needs into account when trying to decipher what motivates associates.

- Maslow's need hierarchy includes five levels of needs: physiological, safety, social and belongingness, esteem, and self-actualization. These needs are arranged in prepotent hierarchical order. Prepotency refers to the concept that a lower-order need, until satisfied, is dominant in motivating a person's behavior. Once a need is satisfied, the next higher need becomes the active source of motivation. Research has not been very supportive of Maslow's theory; however, this theory has served as the basis for other theories and practices that have received empirical support.

- ERG theory is similar to Maslow's hierarchy but does not consider prepotency to be relevant. The three needs in ERG theory are existence, relatedness, and growth. A person may work on all three needs at the same time, although satisfying lower order needs often takes place before a person is strongly motivated by higher level needs.

- Achievement, affiliation, and power needs are the focus of McClelland's theory. Practitioners have given the most attention to the need for achievement. People with a high need for achievement like to establish their own goals and prefer moderately difficult ones. They seek feedback on their achievements and tend to be positive thinkers. However, the need that most distinguishes effective managers from non-managers is the need for institutionalized power.

- Herzberg's two-factor theory identifies two types of organizational rewards: those related to satisfaction (motivators) and those related to dissatisfaction (hygienes). It also raises the issue of intrinsic and extrinsic rewards. One important application of this theory, job enrichment, is widely practiced today.

- Whereas content theories emphasize the factors that motivate, process theories are concerned with the process by which such factors interact to produce motivation. They generally are more complex than content theories and offer substantial insights and understanding. Their application frequently results in highly motivated behaviors.

- Expectancy theory suggests that motivation is affected by several factors acting together. This theory emphasizes associates' perceptions of the relationship between effort and performance (expectancy), the linkage between performance and rewards (instrumentalities), and anticipated satisfaction with rewards (valence). Managers can influence employee motivation by affecting one of these areas but can have greater impact by affecting more than one.

- Equity theory considers the human reaction to fairness. According to this theory, a person compares her outcome–input ratio with that of another person, often a co-worker, to determine whether the relationship is equitable. An inequitable situation causes an individual to alter inputs or outcomes, distort his or her perception of inputs or outcomes, change the source of comparison, or leave the organization. Associates' perceptions of procedural justice can also influence how they react to perceived inequities.

- Goal-setting theory is concerned with several issues that arise in the process of setting performance goals for employees, including goal difficulty, goal specificity, goal commitment, associates' participation, and feedback. Generally, goals should be difficult but realistic and specific. Participation and feedback are also useful for increasing the effectiveness of goals in influencing motivation.

- Motivation theories support the use of several managerial practices to increase associates' motivation: (1) find meaningful individual rewards; (2) tie rewards to performance; (3) redesign jobs through enlargement or enrichment; (4) provide feedback; and (5) clarify expectations and goals.

Back to the Knowledge Objectives

1. What do we mean by work motivation, and how does it relate to performance? Why is individual work motivation important to organizational success?

2. What assumptions do Maslow's need hierarchy and ERG theory make about human motivation? How can managers use these theories to motivate associates?

3. How do need for achievement, need for affiliation, and need for power differ? How do these needs relate to work performance and motivation? How would you distinguish McClelland's notion of needs from those of other content theorists?

4. What does Herzberg's two-factor theory of motivation say about human motivation? How has it influenced current management practice?

5. What does expectancy theory suggest about people and motivation at work? When does expectancy theory best explain motivation? What implications does this theory have for managers?

6. What do equity theory and ideas from procedural justice suggest about motivation? How do fairness judgments influence work motivation, and how can managers ensure that associates perceive judgments as having been made fairly.

7. What are the basic tenets of goal-setting theory? What should a manager keep in mind when engaging in goal setting with his associates?

8. How does job enrichment affect associates' motivation to perform? To make sure job enrichment has the desired effects, what should the organization consider?

9. Considering the various theories of motivation, what can managers do to increase motivation?

Thinking about Ethics

1. Is there anything wrong with providing no pay increase to a person whose performance is average or below average? What are the implications of this action?

2. If the rewards provided are equitable, must the process used in providing them be fair? Why or why not?

3. Suppose a manager has provided what she believes is an equitable reward to an associate but he does not believe it is fair. What are the manager's responsibilities to the associate?

4. Is it appropriate for managers to set higher goals for some associates and lower goals for others performing the same job? Why or why not?

5. Is it acceptable to terminate an associate for being openly critical of managers? What effect will such actions probably have on other associates?

6. Can senior managers terminate whistleblowers who report what they believe to be wrongdoing by managers? Would the termination be acceptable if the whistleblowers truly believed that the managers were in the wrong but, in fact, the managers' actions had been judged as appropriate by independent external observers?

Key Terms

motivation, p. 187
hierarchy of needs theory, p. 188
ERG theory, p. 190
need for achievement, p. 191
need for affiliation, p. 192

need for power, p. 192
two-factor theory, p. 194
motivators, p. 194
hygienes, p. 195
expectancy theory, p. 196
expectancy, p. 196
instrumentality, p. 196

valence, p. 197
equity theory, p. 198
distributive justice, p. 200
procedural justice, p. 200
goal-setting theory, p. 201
job enlargement, p. 209
job enrichment, p. 209

Building Your Human Capital

Assessing Your Needs

Look at the picture below for 60 seconds. *Turn the picture over or close your book* and take 15 to 20 minutes to write a story about what you see happening in the picture. Your story should be at least one to two pages in length and it should address the following issues:

1. Who are the people in the picture? What is their relationship?
2. What is currently taking place in the picture? What are the people doing?
3. What took place in the hour preceding the taking of the picture?
4. What will take place in the hour following the taking of the picture?

Comstock Images

This exercise is based on a tool, the Thematic Apperception Test, used by McClelland and associates to assess people's needs for achievement, affiliation, and power. The Hay Group and other leading consulting and development firms continue to use this type of tool. To determine where you fall on the three needs, do the following:

1. Give yourself one point for need for achievement every time one of the following themes appears in your story:
   - Your story involves a work or competitive situation.
   - Feedback is being given or received.
   - Goals or standards are being discussed.
   - Someone is taking responsibility for his or her work.
   - Someone is expressing pride over his or her own accomplishments or those of another person.
2. Give yourself one point for need for affiliation every time one of the following themes appears in your story:
   - The relationship between the characters is personal.
   - Help is being given or received.

- Encouragement, comfort, empathy, or affection is being given or received.
- Someone is expressing a desire to be close to the other person.
- The characters are engaged in or talking about social activities.

3. Give yourself one point for need for power every time one of the following themes appears in your story:
   - The relationship between the characters is hierarchical. Someone has more status than the others.
   - Someone is trying to get someone else to do something.
   - Someone is attempting to get others to work together.
   - Someone is concerned about reaching organizational goals.
   - Someone is evoking rules, policies, or regulations.

Add up your points for each of the needs, and answer the following questions.

1. What is your dominant need? That is, in which category did you have the most points? What does this suggest about you?
2. Does this assessment seem valid to you? Why or why not?
3. If you are not as high on need for achievement as you thought you would be, what can you do to increase it?

Sources: D.C. McClelland et al., "A Scoring Manual for the Achievement Motive," in J.W. Atkinson (Ed.), *Motives in Fantasy, Action and Society* (New York: Van Nostrand, 1958); C.D. Morgan and H.A. Murray, "A Method for Investigating Fantasies: The Thematic Apperception Test," *Archives of Neurology and Psychiatry* 34 (1935): 289–306.

A Strategic Organizational Behavior Moment

The Motivation of a Rhodes Scholar

Frances Mead, compensation director for Puma Corporation, was pleased because she had just hired an individual whom she considered to be highly qualified to fill the position of benefits administrator. Dan Coggin was an extremely bright fellow. He had graduated summa cum laude with a B.S. degree in finance from the University of Chicago. He had then traveled to England for a year of study as a Rhodes Scholar. After returning from England, he had worked for a large bank in the investments area for a year. He had then accepted the position of benefits administrator in the corporate personnel department at Puma, headquartered in Salt Lake City, Utah.

Dan felt good about his new job. He would be well paid and have a position of some status. Most importantly, the job was located in Utah. Dan had always enjoyed the outdoors, and he liked to backpack, camp, and do some mountain climbing. Salt Lake City was the perfect location for him.

He arrived on the job happy and ready to tackle his new responsibilities. Dan's financial background aided him greatly in his new job, where he was responsible for the development and administration of the pension plan, life and health insurance packages, employee stock purchase plan, and other employee benefit programs. Within a month, Dan had learned all of the program provisions and had things working smoothly. Frances was satisfied with her selection for benefits administrator. In fact, she expected Dan to move up in the department ranks rapidly. Dan was enjoying himself, particularly his opportunities to get into the mountains. His only concern was that he did not seem to have enough time to enjoy his outdoor activities. After six months, he had his job mastered. He was quite talented, and the job did not present a strong challenge to him.

Frances recognized Dan's talents and wanted him to evaluate Puma's complete benefits package for the purpose of making needed changes. Frances believed that Puma's benefits package was outdated and needed to be revised. With Dan's abilities, Frances thought new programs could be designed without the help of costly outside consultants.

She held several discussions with Dan, encouraging him to evaluate the total benefits package. However, at the end of a year on the job, Dan had accomplished little in the way of evaluation. He seemed to be constantly thinking of and discussing his outdoor activities. Frances became concerned about his seeming lack of commitment to the job.

In the ensuing months, Dan's performance began to slack off. He had had the current programs running smoothly shortly after his arrival, but complaints from employees regarding errors and time delays in insurance claims and stock purchases began to increase. Also, he was making no progress in the evaluation of the benefit package and thus no progress in the design of new benefit programs. In addition, he began to call in sick occasionally. Interestingly, he seemed to be sick on Friday or Monday, allowing for a three-day weekend.

It was obvious that Dan had the ability to perform the job and even more challenging tasks. However, Frances was becoming concerned and thought that she would have to take some action.

Discussion Questions

1. Using ERG theory, explain the reasons for the situation described in the case.

2. Using expectancy theory, explain the reasons for the situation.

3. Using the integration framework found in the last major section of the chapter, describe what actions Frances should and should not take.

Team Exercise

Workplace Needs and Gender

Do women and men have similar needs in the workplace? Do they exhibit similar levels of need for achievement, need for affiliation, and need for power? In this exercise, you will have the opportunity to address these questions.

Steps

1. As an individual, think about women's and men's achievement, affiliation, and power needs. On average, do women and men exhibit similar levels of these needs? Spend five minutes on this step.

2. Assemble into groups of four or five. Each group should consist of both women and men (two or three of each). Spend 15 minutes completing the next steps.

3. Decide as a group whether:
   a. Women and men exhibit similar levels of the need for achievement.
   b. Women and men exhibit similar levels of the need for affiliation.
   c. Women and men exhibit similar levels of the need for institutional power.
   d. Women and men exhibit similar levels of the need for personal power.

4. Identify the reasons for your group's beliefs.

5. Appoint a spokesperson to present the group's ideas to the class.

Endnotes

1. Hitt, M.A., Ireland, R.D., & Hoskisson, R.E. 2007. *Strategic management: Competitiveness and globalization* (7th ed.). Cincinnati, OH: South-Western.

2. Branch-Smith Printing. 2007. Accomplishments & Quality Awards. At http://www.branchsmith.com/bsaawards.html.

3. Kanfer, R. 1995. Motivation. In N. Nicholson (Ed.), *Encyclopedic dictionary of organizational behavior*. Cambridge, MA: Blackwell Publishing, pp. 330–336.

4. Maslow, A.H. 1943. A theory of human motivation. *Psychological Review,* 50: 370–396; Maslow, A.H. 1954. *Motivation and personality*. New York: Harper.

5. Wahba, M.A., & Bridwell, L.G. 1976. Maslow reconsidered: A review of the research on the need hierarchy theory. *Organizational Behavior and Human Performance,* 15: 212–225; Kanfer, R. 1990. Motivation theory and industrial and organizational psychology. In M.D. Dunnette & L. Hough (Eds.),

Handbook of industrial and organizational psychology (Vol. 1). Palo Alto, CA: Consulting Psychologists Press, pp. 75–170.

6. Ibid.

7. Ibid.

8. See, for example, Laas, I. 2006. Self-actualization and society: A new application for an old theory. *Journal of Humanistic Psychology,* 46: 77–91; Zalenski, R.J., & Raspa, R. 2006. Maslow's hierarchy of needs: A framework for achieving human potential in hospice. *Journal of Palliative Medicine,* 9: 1120–1127.

9. Alderfer, C.P. 1972. *Existence, relatedness and growth human needs in organizational settings.* New York: The Free Press.

10. Ibid.

11. See, for example, Wanous, J.P., & Zwany, A. 1977. A cross-sectional test of need hierarchy theory. *Organizational Behavior and Human Performance,* 16: 78–97.

12. See, for example, Alderfer, C.P., Kaplan, R.E., & Smith, K.K. 1974. The effect of variations in relatedness need satisfaction on relatedness desires. *Administrative Science Quarterly,* 19: 507–532.

13. Arnolds, C.A., & Boshoff, C. 2002. Compensation, esteem valence and job performance: An empirical assessment of Alderfer's ERG theory. *International Journal of Human Resource Management,* 13: 697–719.

14. McClelland, D.C. 1966. That urge to achieve. *Think,* 32: 19–23.

15. McClelland, D.C. 1961. *The achieving society.* Princeton, NJ: Van-Nostrand.

16. McClelland, D.C., Atkinson, J.W., Clark, R.A., & Lowell, E.L. 1953. *The achievement motive.* New York: Appleton-Century-Crofts.

17. McClelland, That urge to achieve.

18. Korn, E.R., & Pratt, G.J. 1986. Reaching for success in new ways. *Management World,* 15 (7): 6–10.

19. Hershey, P., & Blanchard, K.H. 1972. *Management and organizational behavior.* New York, NY: Prentice-Hall.

20. Eisenberger, R., Jones, J.R., Stinglhamber, F., Shanock, L., & Randall, A.T. 2005. Flow experiences at work: For high achievers alone? *Journal of Organizational Behavior,* 26: 755–775.

21. See Shaver, K.G. 1995. The entrepreneurial personality myth. *Business and Economic Review,* 41 (3): 20–23.

22. Hall, J. 1976. To achieve or not: The manager's choice. *California Management Review,* 18: 5–18.

23. McClelland, D.C. 1965. Toward a theory of motivation acquisition. *American Psychologist,* 20: 321–333; Steers, R.M. 1981. *An introduction to organizational behavior.* Glenview, IL: Scott, Foresman, & Co.

24. Frischer, J. 1993. Empowering management in new product development units. *Journal of Product Innovation Management,* 10: 393–401.

25. Material related to virtual workers was drawn from: King, R. 2007. Working from home: It's in the details. *BusinessWeek,* special report at http://www.businessweek.com/technology/content/feb2007/tc20070212_457307.htm.

26. McClelland, D.C. 1975. *Power: The inner experiences.* New York: Irvington; McClelland, D.C., & Burnham, D.H. 1976. Power is the great motivator. *Harvard Business Review,* 54 (2): 100–110 (reprinted in 1995 and in 2003).

27. McClelland & Burnham, Power is the great motivator.

28. Herzberg, F., Mausner, B., & Synderman, B. 1959. *The motivation to work.* New York: John Wiley & Sons; Herzberg, F. 1966. *Work and the nature of man.* Cleveland: World Publishing.

29. House, R., & Wigdor, L. 1967. Herzberg's dual-factor theory of job satisfaction and motivation: A review of the empirical evidence and a criticism. *Personnel Psychology,* 20: 369–380; Dunnette, M.D., Campbell, J., & Hakel, M. 1967. Factors contributing to job dissatisfaction in six occupational groups. *Organizational Behavior and Human Performance,* 2: 143–174.

30. Vroom, V.H. 1964. *Work and motivation.* New York: John Wiley & Sons.

31. See, for example, Ferris, K.R. 1977. A test of the expectancy theory of motivation in an accounting environment. *The Accounting Review,* 52: 605–615; Reinharth, L., & Wahba, M.A. 1975. Expectancy theory as a predictor of work motivation, effort expenditure, and job performance. *Academy of Management Journal,* 18: 520–537.

32. See Pinder, C.C. 1984. *Work motivation,* Glenview, IL: Scott & Foresman.

33. In Vroom's original theory, extrinsic rewards were the focus. In some later work, intrinsic rewards were also a point of emphasis.

34. Durocher, S., Fortin, A., & Cote, L. 2007. Users' participation in the accounting standard-setting process: A theory-building study. *Accounting, Organizations, and Society,* 32: 29–59; House, R.J., Shapiro, H.J., & Wahba, M.A. 1974. Expectancy theory as a predictor of work behavior and attitudes: A reevaluation of empirical evidence. *Decision Sciences,* 5: 481–506; Kanfer, R. 1990. Motivation theory and industrial and organizational psychology. In Dunnette & Hough (Eds.), *Handbook of industrial and organizational psychology (Vol. 1);* Landy, F.J., & Trumbo, D.A. 1980. *Psychology of work behavior* (2nd ed.). Homewood, IL: Dorsey Press, pp. 343–351; Wahba, M.A., & House, R.J., 1972. Expectancy theory in work and motivation: Some logical and methodological issues. *Human Relations,* 27: 121–147; Watson, S. 2006. "A multi-theoretical model of knowledge transfer in organizations: Determinants of knowledge contribution and knowledge reuse." *Journal of Management Studies,* 43: 141–173.

35. Landy & Trumbo, *Psychology of work behavior.*

36. Korsgaard, M.A., Meglino, B.M., & Lester, S.W. 1997. Beyond helping: Do other-oriented values have broader implications in organizations? *Journal of Applied Psychology,* 82: 160–177.

37. For one revised model, see: Porter, L.W., & Lawler, E.E. 1968. *Managerial attitudes and performance.* Homewood, IL: Irwin-Dorsey.

38. See, for example, Camerman, J. 2007. The benefits of justice for temporary workers. *Group & Organization Management,* 32: 176–207; Cropanzano, R., Rupp, D.E., Mohler, C.J., & Schmincke, M. 2001. Three roads to organizational justice. In G. Ferris (Ed.), *Research in personnel and human resources management.* Oxford, UK: Elsevier Science, pp. 1–113; Greenberg, J., Ashton-James, C.E., & Ashkanasy, N.M. 2007. Social comparison processes in organizations. *Organizational Behavior and Human Decision Processes,* 102: 22–41; Wong, Y-T., Ngo, H-Y., & Wong, C-S. 2006. Perceived organizational justice, trust, and OCB: A study of Chinese workers in joint ventures and state-owned enterprises. *Journal of World Business,* 41: 344–355.

39. Pasturis, P. 2002. The corporate scandal sheet. At http://www.Forbes.com.

40. See Cox, T. 2001. *Creating the multicultural organization: A strategy for capturing the power of diversity.* San Francisco: Jossey-Bass.

41. Adams, J.S. 1965. Inequity in social exchange. In L. Berkowitz (Ed.), *Advances in experimental social psychology (Vol. 2).* New York: Academic Press, pp. 267–299.

42. Colquitt, J.A., Conlon, D.E., Wesson, M.J., Porter, C.O.L.H., & Ng, K.Y. 2001. Justice at the millennium: A meta-analytic review of 25 years of organizational justice research. *Journal of Applied Psychology,* 86: 425–445; Greenberg, Ashton-James, & Ashkanasy, Social comparison processes in organizations.

43. Greenberg, J., & Leventhal, G. 1976. Equity and the use of overreward to motivate performance. *Journal of Personality and Social Psychology,* 34: 179–190.

44. See, for example, Bing, M.N., & Burroughs, S.M. 2001. The predictive and interactive effects of equity sensitivity in teamwork-oriented organizations. *Journal of Organizational Behavior,* 22: 271–290; Huseman, R.C., Hatfield, J.D., & Miles, E.W. 1987. A new perspective on equity theory: The equity sensitivity construct. *Academy of Management Review,* 12: 222–234.

45. For details of this story, see: Boswell, T. 2000. A Texas-sized mistake involving no lone star. *The Washington Post,* December 12, p. D.01; Simmons, M. 2003. A-Rod hits the jackpot, super Mario returns. At www.askmen.com.

46. White, P. 2007. How A-Rod learned to relax and enjoy N.Y.: In a turnabout he's on a roll but Yankees aren't. *USA Today,* May 4, p. 1A.

47. Colquitt, Conlon, Wesson, Porter, & Ng, Justice at the millennium.

48. Greenberg, J. 1993. Stealing in the name of justice: Informational and interpersonal moderators of theft reactions to underpayment inequity. *Organizational Behavior and Human Decisions Processes,* 54: 81–103.

49. Distributive and procedural justice are the two most studied types of justice. A third type, however, has been distilled and has received some attention. This third type, interactional justice, relates to quality of interpersonal treatment, typically from the supervisor. In our chapter, we focus on the main two anchors of justice phenomena. For additional discussion, see, for example, Olkkonen, M-E., & Lipponen, J. 2006. Relationships between organizational justice, identification with the organization and work unit, and group related outcomes. *Organizational Behavior and Human Decision Processes,* 100: 202–215; Roch, S.G., & Shanock, L.R. 2006. Organizational justice in an exchange framework: Clarifying organizational justice distinctions. *Journal of Management,* 32: 299–322.

50. Brockner, J., & Wiesenfeld, B.M. 1996. An integrative framework for explaining reactions to decisions: Interactive effects of outcomes and procedures. *Psychological Bulletin,* 120: 189–208; Thibaut, J., & Walker, L. 1975. *Procedural justice: A psychological analysis.* Hillsdale, NJ: Lawrence Erlbaum.

51. Bies, R.J., & Moag, J.F. 1986. Interactional justice: Communication criteria of fairness. In R.J. Lewicki, B.H. Sheppard, & M.H. Bazerman (Eds.), *Research on negotiations in organizations (Vol. 1).* Greenwich, CT: JAI Press, pp. 43–55; Leventhal, G.S. 1980. What should be done with equity theory: New approaches to the study of fairness in social relationships. In K. Gergen, M. Greenberg, & R. Willis (Eds.), *Social exchange: Advances in theory and research.* New York: Plenum, pp. 27–55; Thibaut & Walker, *Procedural justice.*

52. Brockner, J., DeWitt, R.L., Grover, S., & Reed, T. 1990. When it is especially important to explain why: Factors affecting the relationship between managers' explanations of a layoff and survivors' reactions to the layoff. *Journal of Experimental Social Psychology,* 26: 389–407.

53. Locke, E.A., & Latham, G.P. 1990. *A theory of goal setting and task performance.* Englewood Cliffs, NJ: Prentice Hall.

54. Locke, E.A. 1968. Toward a theory of task motivation and incentives. *Organizational Behavior and Human Performance,* 3: 157–189.

55. Heath, C., Larrick, R.P., & Wu, G. 1999. Goals as reference points. *Cognitive Psychology,* 38: 79–109.

56. Locke & Latham, *A theory of goal setting and task performance.*

57. Locke, E.A., & Latham, G.P. 1979. Goal setting: A motivational technique that works. *Organizational Dynamics,* 8 (2): 68–80.

58. See, for example: Motowidlo, S.J., Loehr, U., & Dunnette, M.D. 1978. A laboratory study of the effects of goal specificity on the relationship between probability of success and performance. *Journal of Applied Psychology,* 63: 172–179.

59. Locke & Latham, *A theory of goal setting and task performance.*

60. Locke, Toward a theory of task motivation and incentives; Renn, R.W. 1998. Participation's effects on task performance: Mediating roles of goal acceptance and procedural justice. *Journal of Business Research,* 41: 115–125.

61. Latham, G.P., & Marshall, H.A. 1982. The effects of self-set, participatively set and assigned goals on the performance of government employees. *Personnel Psychology,* 35: 399–404; Latham, G.P., Steele, T.P., & Saari, L.M. 1982. The effects of participation and goal difficulty on performance. *Personnel Psychology,* 35: 677–686.

62. Renn, Participation's effect on task performance.

63. Becker, L.J. 1978. Joint effect of feedback and goal setting on performance: A field study of residential energy conservation. *Journal of Applied Psychology,* 63: 428–433.

64. Morse, G. 2003. Why we misread motives. *Harvard Business Review,* 81 (1): 18.

65. Ibid.

66. Deci, E.L. 1972. Effects of noncontingent rewards and controls on intrinsic motivation. *Organizational Behavior and Human Performance,* 8: 217–229.

67. See, for example: Pate, L.E. 1978. Cognitive versus reinforcement views of intrinsic motivation. *Academy of Management Review,* 3: 505–514.

68. Chuanzhi, L. Set different incentive levels. *Harvard Business Review,* 81 (1): 47.

69. Locke & Latham, *A theory of goal setting and task performance.*

70. Kerr, S. 1975. On the folly of rewarding A, while hoping for B. *Academy of Management Journal,* 18: 769–783.

71. This story is based on the following materials: Bates, S. 2003. Top pay for best performers. *HR Magazine,* 48 (1): 31–38; Leventhal, G.S. 1976. The distribution of rewards and resources in groups and organizations. In L. Berkowitz & E. Walster (Eds.), *Advances in Experimental Social Psychology* (Vol. 9). New York: Academic Press, pp. 91–131; Mizra, P., & Fox, A. 2003. Reward the best, prod the rest. *HR Magazine,* 48 (1): 34–35.

72. Bates, Top pay for best performers.

73. Ibid.

74. Aldag, R.J., & Brief, A.P. 1979. *Task design and employee motivation.* Glenview, IL: Scott, Foresman, pp. 42–43.

75. See, for example, Ford, R. 1969. *Motivation through the work itself.* New York: American Management Association; Fried, Y., & Ferris, G.R. 1987. The validity of the job characteristics model: A review and meta-analysis. *Personnel Psychology,* 40: 287–322; Walton, R.E. 1972. How to counter alienation in the plant. *Harvard Business Review,* 50 (6): 70–81; Whittington, J.L., Goodwin, V.L., & Murray, B. 2004. Transformational leadership, goal difficulty, and job design: Independent and interactive effects on employee outcomes. *The Leadership Quarterly,* 15: 593–606.

76. Hulin, C.L. 1971. Individual differences and job enrichment: The case against general treatments. In J. Maher (Ed.), *New perspectives in job enrichment.* Berkeley, CA: Van Nostrand Reinhold; Aldag & Brief, *Task design and employee motivation.*

77. Deloitte Consulting. 2005. *Who are the millennials (aka Generation Y)?* New York: Deloitte & Touche USA.

78. Hackman, J.R., & Oldham, G.R. 1974. *The job diagnostic survey: An instrument for the diagnosis of jobs and the evaluation of job design projects,* Technical Report No. 4. New Haven, CT: Yale University, Department of Administrative Sciences.

79. Hackman, J.R., & Oldham, G.R. 1976. Motivation through the design of work: Test of a theory. *Organizational Behavior and Human Decision Performance,* 16: 250–279.

80. See, for example, Abbott, J.B., Boyd, N.G., & Miles, G. 2006. Does type of team matter? An investigation of the relationships between job characteristics and outcomes within a team-based environment. *The Journal of Social Psychology,* 146: 485–507; Fried & Ferris, The validity of the job characteristics model.

81. Kanfer, Motivation; Fried & Ferris, The validity of the job characteristics model.

82. Fried & Ferris, The validity of the job characteristics model.

83. Schaubroeck, J., Ganster, D.C., & Kemmerer, B.E. 1994. Job complexity, "type A" behavior, and cardiovascular disorder: A prospective study. *Academy of Management Journal,* 37: 426–439; Dwyer, D.H., & Fox, M.L. 2000. The moderating role of hostility in the relationship between enriched jobs and health. *Academy of Management Journal,* 43: 1086–1096.

84. Kluger, A.N., & DeNisi, A.S. 1996. The effects of feedback interventions on performance: A historical review, a meta-analysis, and a preliminary feedback intervention theory. *Psychological Bulletin,* 119: 254–284.

85. Eckert, R.A. 2003. Be a broken record. *Harvard Business Review,* 81 (1): 44.

86. Miller, P. 2003. Signed, delivered: Malone cannot hide his excitement about playing for a title in L.A. *Salt Lake Tribune,* July 18, at www.sltrib.com.

7

STRESS AND WELL-BEING

The pay is good, and sales bonuses can be generous. So why did Verizon call-center service representatives go on strike for 18 days several years ago? The answer in part is *excessive stress*.

Verizon, a *Fortune* 100 telecommunications company with revenues of more than $93 billion, depends on call-center representatives to provide positive customer service. These representatives provide the service link between the company and its customers. They answer many calls each day,

©AP/Wide World Photos

EXPLORING BEHAVIOR IN ACTION
Striking for Stress at Verizon

covering a wide range of service issues. In addition, they sell products to the customers who call (such as caller ID services and DSL high-speed Internet access). The representatives are monitored electronically and in person on such factors as courtesy, length of calls, and sales of products. They are also closely monitored for tardiness, break times, and attendance. Failure to meet strict performance standards can lead to severe penalties, such as probation, suspension, or "separation from the payroll." Finally, service representatives are required to work overtime.

Call-center representatives are well paid and can earn commissions on sales. Over the years, they have voiced few complaints about the pay associated with the job. They have, however, voiced complaints about other issues. Associates said the following a few years ago:

You are constantly monitored on everything that you do. Every call is timed, how long it takes you to handle a customer. If you go off-line too long they say something about it. If you go to the bathroom too long

they say something about it. Forced overtime is another problem.

We were promised training after they closed down the other NOC centers, and we have never gotten any. The working conditions are terrible. It is very stressful because we don't have enough people. . . . People aren't treated as people anymore. The company only sees us as numbers and dollar signs. . . .

You're worried that before you let the customer go, you have to offer [sell] him something, no matter how upset he is, because the person sitting next to you or in that observation room is going to mark you off.

The call center is a gold-plated sweatshop.

In addition to the above issues, one associate complained of being forced to sell a product to a person who was calling to have phone service shut off for a dead relative.

Several associates complained that managers monitored employees for personal reasons rather than to evaluate performance.

The Communication Workers of America (CWA), representing the call-center associates, and Verizon settled the strike that partially resulted from these workplace conditions. The settlement attempted to alleviate some of the more stressful conditions. Some of the changes included:

- Advance notification of monitoring and limits on the number of calls that can be monitored based on associates' performance.
- Monitoring only during regular working hours—not during overtime hours.

- Face-to-face feedback on monitoring within 24 hours of observation.
- Permission to be away from phones for 30 minutes per day to do paperwork.
- The formation of a CWA–Verizon committee to examine stressful conditions.
- Funding for work and family support programs.
- At some locations, recording of performance at the team level rather than the individual level.
- Split shifts, job sharing, and limited flextime at various locations.
- Limits on overtime at some locations—for example, 24-hour advance notice of overtime, 7.5 hours per week limit on mandatory overtime, and 15-minute breaks for every three hours of overtime worked.

Although the new contract addressed many of the call-center associates' complaints, some still argue that not enough has been done. To that end, some call-center associates have threatened to strike again.

Overall, though, Verizon seems to have addressed the issues. It has received awards and recognition recently from *Working Mother, LATINAStyle, CEO, Training,* and several other periodicals.

Sources: Anonymous, "Union Rejects Contract Offer—Verizon Communication Workers Speak on Issues in Strike," Aug. 2000, at http://www.wsws.org/articles/2000/aug2000/cwa-a15.shtml; Communication Workers of America, "Protections against Abusive Monitoring, Adherence, and Sales Quotas in CWA Contracts," 2003, at http://www.cwa-union.org/workers/customers/protections.asp; Communication Workers of America, "Contract Improvements for CWA Customer Service Professionals: 1999–Spring 2001," 2003, at http://www.cwa-union.org/workers/customers/improv_99-01.asp; K. Maher, "Stressed Out: Can Worker Stress Get Worse?" *Wall Street Journal,* Jan. 16, 2001: B1; L. Caliri, "'The Call Center Is a Gold-Plated Sweatshop': A Retired Employee of Roanoke Center Says Verizon Strike Likely as Workers Complain about Work Stress," *roanoke.com,* August 2003, at www.roanoke.com/roatimes/news/story 152897.html; Verizon Communications, "Executive Center: Awards and Honors," 2007, at http://www22.verizon.com/about/executivecenter/besttoflists/bestoflists_index.html; Verizon Communications, "Verizon Careers," 2007, at http://www22.verizon.com/jobs/.

The Strategic Importance of *Workplace Stress*

By most standards, call-center service representatives have stressful jobs. Of course, individuals in other jobs also can experience stress, and such stress can lead to poor performance, workplace violence, sabotage, substance abuse, and other types of maladaptive behaviors, as well as increased health-care costs.[1]

It has been estimated that 75 percent of all medical problems are directly attributable to stress.[2] Time away from work is also an issue. According to the U.S. Bureau of Labor Statistics, individuals with substantial occupational stress missed 23 days of work per person (the median number), with 44 percent of absences lasting more than 31 days—much longer than absences resulting from injuries and illnesses.[3]

As suggested by the Verizon call-center case, many jobs and organizational policies can cause stress. Rapid technological changes, long work hours, repetitive computer work, work–family issues, and a growing service economy can also lead to stress. Given the many sources of stress, it is not surprising that a National Institute for Occupational Safety and Health (NIOSH) report on stress at work indicates that 26 to 40 percent of Americans find their work to be very or extremely stressful.[4] A survey by Northwestern Mutual Life found that 25 percent of people believe their jobs to be the most stressful aspect of their lives.[5] A 2006 Gallup survey indicated that 35 percent of respondents were somewhat or completely dissatisfied with the stress produced in their jobs.[6] Finally, a Marlin Company survey of attitudes in the American workplace found that 43 percent of respondents believed managers at their companies did not help associates deal with stress.[7]

Although not all stress is bad (some of it can have positive outcomes, as explained later in this chapter), much of it is dysfunctional and, as we have seen, costly to organizations in terms of lost human capital and lower productivity. As a result, managers at all levels are increasingly aware of the effects of their decisions and actions on the stress of others. Indeed, it is imperative that managers effectively deal with the stress of those around them if they are to develop/maintain a high-involvement, high-performance workforce.

Given the prevalence of stress in the workplace and the high direct and indirect costs of stress at work, it should be a priority item on the agenda of top executives. In fact, many top executives also experience significant stress. The CEO makes decisions that affect many people. The strategy adopted by the organization affects the jobs performed by managers and associates. Poor decisions concerning strategy may mean that some people lose their jobs because of decreased demand for the organization's products or services, for example.

Top executives also make decisions to acquire or merge with other firms and they must decide how many people will be laid off as a result of an acquisition or merger. Sometimes, too, they make decisions to lay off employees simply to cut costs. Layoffs create stress for the associates and managers who lose their jobs and for the survivors as well. Survivors experience stress because of job insecurity. In addition, research shows that they often feel guilty because their friends and co-workers were chosen to lose their jobs and they were not.[8] For stress to be as low as possible, those chosen to be laid off as well as survivors must view senior leader actions as fair and humane. Research has shown that communicating effectively about the layoffs, implementing layoffs by careful selection of the units (those less valuable to the organization), and helping those laid off (e.g., providing severance pay, providing services to help them find new jobs) produces better outcomes.[9] For example, these actions result in investors seeing managers as more effective and more likely to produce higher performance, and thus stock price is positively affected.[10]

In the first section of this chapter, we define stress and related concepts. In the two sections that follow, we (1) present two important models of workplace stress that explain why and when people experience stress, and (2) discuss common workplace stressors. Next, we discuss individual characteristics that can cause people to experience more stress or help them cope with stressors. We then describe individual and organizational outcomes resulting from stress reactions. Finally, we present methods that associates, managers, and organizations can use to combat the effects of stress.

KNOWLEDGE OBJECTIVES

After reading this chapter, you should be able to:

1. Define stress and distinguish among different types of stress.

2. Understand how the human body reacts to stress and be able to identify the signs of suffering from too much stress.

3. Describe two important models of workplace stress and discuss the most common work-related stressors.

4. Recognize how different people experience stress.

5. Explain the individual and organizational consequences of stress.

6. Discuss methods that associates, managers, and organizations can use to manage stress and promote well-being.

Workplace Stress Defined

Unfortunately, we all know what it feels like to be stressed. For some people, stress manifests itself as an upset stomach. For others, heart palpitations and sweaty palms signal stress. The list of stress reactions is almost endless and differs from individual to individual. Even though we know what stress feels like, we may not know just how to define it. In fact, stress is a difficult concept to define, and researchers have argued over its definition and measurement for many years.[11]

For our purposes, **stress** can be defined as a feeling of tension that occurs when a person perceives that a given situation is about to exceed her ability to cope and consequently could endanger her well-being.[12] In such situations, people first ask themselves: "Am I in trouble or danger?" and then ask, "Can I successfully cope with this situation?" If people respond with "yes" to the first question and "no" to the second, they are likely to experience stress. Extending this definition, we can define **job stress** as the feeling that one's capabilities, resources, or needs do not match the demands or requirements of the job.[13]

Consider a call-center representative who has a child in day care who must be picked up at 5:30 P.M. The representative has sole responsibility for picking up his child because his wife is out of town. At 4:58 P.M., as the representative is beginning to close down his station, his supervisor walks over and tells him that he must stay and work for another two hours. If the representative refuses to stay, he can be put on probation or even be fired, but he cannot think of anyone to call to pick up his child for him. Clearly, the demands of this situation are taxing his ability to cope, and therefore stress results. It is easy to see why being notified about overtime at least 24 hours in advance was such an important issue for Verizon's call-center representatives.

There are several important issues regarding the definition of stress. First, the level of stress experienced depends on *individual* reactions to a situation. Therefore, an event experienced by one person as stressful may not be as stressful to another person. For example, some people find stopping at a traffic light while driving to be stressful, whereas others do not. A second issue is that the source of stress, or *stressor*, can be either real or imagined. People do not actually need to be in danger to experience stress—they have only to *perceive* danger.

Stress can be defined as acute or chronic.[14] **Acute stress** is a short-term reaction to an immediate threat. For example, an associate might experience acute stress when being reprimanded by a supervisor or when not able to meet a deadline. **Chronic stress** results from ongoing situations. For example, it can result from living in fear of future layoffs or from having continuing problems with a supervisor. The constant monitoring in the call centers also is an example of a stressor likely to result in chronic stress.

Reactions involving chronic stress are potentially more severe than those involving acute stress because of the way the body responds. Stress makes demands that create an imbalance in the body's energy supply that is difficult to restore. The body reacts with a special physiological response commonly referred

stress
A feeling of tension that occurs when a person perceives that a situation is about to exceed her ability to cope and consequently could endanger her well-being.

job stress
The feeling that one's capabilities, resources, or needs do not match the demands or requirements of the job.

acute stress
A short-term stress reaction to an immediate threat.

chronic stress
A long-term stress reaction resulting from ongoing situations.

PhotoDisc, Inc./Getty Images

Exhibit 7-1	Some Stress-Related Conditions

Conditions That Can Result from Acute Stress

Alertness and excitement

Increase in energy

Feelings of uneasiness and worry

Feelings of sadness

Loss of appetite

Short-term suppression of the immune system

Increased metabolism and burning of body fat

Conditions That Can Result from Chronic Stress

Anxiety and panic attacks

Depression

Long-term disturbances in eating (anorexia or overeating)

Irritability

Lowered resistance to infection and disease

Diabetes

High blood pressure

Loss of sex drive

Source: Adapted from: Mayo Clinic, "Managing Work Place Stress: Plan Your Approach." 2003, at http://www.mayoclinic.com/invoke.cfm?id=HQ01442.

stress response
An unconscious mobilization of energy resources that occurs when the body encounters a stressor.

to as the **stress response.** A stress response is an unconscious mobilization of the body's energy resources that occurs when the body encounters a stressor.[15] The body gears up to deal with impending danger by releasing hormones and increasing the heartbeat, pulse rate, blood pressure, breathing rate, and output of blood sugar from the liver.[16] If stress is short-lived, or acute, then stress responses tend to be short term. If, on the other hand, stress lasts over a period of time, with little relief, stress responses begin to wear down the body and result in more serious problems. Exhibit 7-1 displays some of the conditions that can be caused by acute and by chronic stress.

Not all demands that associates and managers encounter on the job lead to negative stress responses. Sometimes people become energized when faced with difficulties. Hans Seyle, one of the most influential stress researchers, distinguished between eustress and dystress.[17] **Eustress** is positive stress that results from facing challenges and difficulties with the expectation of achievement. Eustress is energizing and motivating. Indeed, some research suggests that a certain level of stress is necessary for maximum performance.[18] Too little stress can produce boredom and even apathy, whereas reasonable levels of stress increase alertness and concentration. However, as stress increases, it reaches a point at which the effects become negative. If a high level of stress continues for prolonged periods, **dystress,** or bad stress, results. Note that we use the general term *stress* to refer to dystress throughout the book. This type of stress overload can lead to the physiological and psychological problems discussed here.

eustress
Positive stress that results from facing challenges and difficulties with the expectation of achievement.

dystress
Negative stress; often referred to simply as stress.

How can you tell when stress is reaching a negative level? Dr. Edward Creagan, an oncologist at the Mayo Clinic, identifies five basic signs in everyday life that indicate you are under too much stress:[19]

1. You feel irritable.

2. You have sleeping difficulties. Either you are sleepy all the time, or you have problems falling asleep and/or staying asleep.

3. You do not get any joy out of life.

4. Your appetite is disturbed. Either you lose your appetite, or you cannot stop eating.

5. You have relationship problems and difficulties getting along with people who are close to you.

 ## Two Models of Workplace Stress

We have seen that workplace stress, or job stress, can occur when individuals perceive the demands of the workplace to outweigh their resources for coping with those demands. We turn now to two popular and important models of workplace stress—the **demand–control model**[20] and the **effort–reward imbalance model.**[21]

> **demand–control model**
> A model that suggests experienced stress is a function of both job demands and job control. Stress is highest when demands are high but individuals have little control over the situation.

Demand–Control Model

The demand–control model is focused on two factors that can create situations of job strain and ultimately the experience of stress. Job strain is a function of the following two factors:

1. The workplace demands faced by an associate or manager

2. The control that an individual has in meeting those demands

> **effort–reward imbalance model**
> A model that suggests experienced stress is a function of both required effort and rewards obtained. Stress is highest when required effort is high but rewards are low.

Workplace demands are aspects of the work environment that job holders must handle. Examples of workplace demands abound in the call-center example at the beginning of this chapter and include long hours, pressure to handle calls quickly, and being subjected to monitoring. *Control* refers to the extent to which individuals are able to (or perceive themselves as able to) affect the state of job demands and to the amount of control they have in making decisions about their work. In the call-center example, one issue of the greatest concern to associates was their lack of control over how many hours they worked.

The demand–control model suggests that job strain is highest when job demands are high and control is low. In this condition, individuals face stressors but have little control over their situation. Call-center associates who must try to sell a product to every caller—with no authority to decide whether a particular caller needs or can afford the product—operate in a state of high strain and consequently experience stress. Compare this with a situation in which a call-center

**Exhibit 7-2
The Demand–Control
Model of Workplace
Stress**

Source: R. Karasek, 1989.
Control in Workplace and
its Health-Related Aspects.
In S.L. Sauter, J.J. Hurrell,
Jr., & C.L. Cooper (Eds.),
*Job Control and Worker
Health.* New York: John
Wiley & Sons, pp. 129–159.

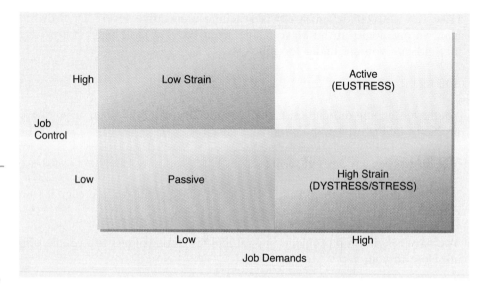

associate has a sales quota but also has the power to decide what products to try to sell and to whom to sell them. In this situation, the associate could exercise a great deal of creativity in determining how to classify customers so that their needs are met and still meet her sales goals. This situation exemplifies the "Active" condition in which both demands and control are high. The result is similar to the notion of eustress discussed earlier. Individuals are most likely to be energized, motivated, and creative in this condition.[22] Less research has been done on the other two conditions, labeled "Low Strain" and "Passive," which are characterized by low demands. In any event, people facing these conditions are unlikely to experience stress. The demand–control model is depicted in Exhibit 7-2.

Research on the demand–control model has yielded somewhat mixed results. Some research has found that people in the high-strain condition are more likely to experience stress-related health problems, such as coronary heart disease and high blood pressure.[23] Other research has found less support for the model.[24] On balance, most researchers agree that both demands and control are important factors in explaining stress. However, how they work together, what constitutes job control, and the role of other variables (such as social support) must be considered in refining the demand–control model of workplace stress.[25]

Effort–Reward Imbalance Model

The effort–reward imbalance model is focused on two factors, as depicted in Exhibit 7-3:

1. The effort required by an associate or manager

2. The rewards an individual receives as a result of the effort

Effort required relates to the performance demands and obligations of the job. It is very similar to the demand dimension in the demand–control model, but it is somewhat more narrowly focused on the job itself rather than on broader aspects of the overall work environment. Rewards include extrinsic (e.g., pay) and intrinsic (e.g., esteem) outcomes of the work.

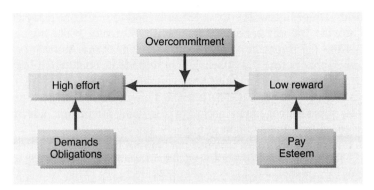

Exhibit 7-3:
The Effort–Reward Imbalance Model of Stress

Source: Adapted from: J. Siegrist, Occupational Health and Public Health in Germany, In P.M. Le Blanc, M.C.W. Peeters, A. Bussing, & W.B. Schaufeli (Eds.), Organizational Psychology and Healthcare: European Contributions. Munchen: Rainer Hampp Verlag.

The effort–reward imbalance model highlights the fact that a combination of strong required efforts and low rewards violates the principle of reciprocity. Ongoing violation of this principle results in strong negative emotions and harmful changes in the autonomic nervous system. Although an individual facing such a situation could simply exit, many stay because of (1) limited opportunities in the labor market, (2) hope for changes in the situation, and (3) excessive work-related overcommitment.[26] Overcommitment, the factor that most researchers have focused upon, is driven by achievement motivation and approval motivation.

Research has yielded generally supportive results for the effort-reward imbalance model. For example, in a recent study of hospital workers, effort–reward imbalance predicted musculoskeletal injury.[27] In a recent synthesis of 45 studies, effort–reward imbalance predicted a variety of negative outcomes.[28] The relevance of overcommitment has been questioned (it may not play an important role), but other aspects of the model appear to be valid.

Organizational and Work-Related Stressors

A great deal of research has focused on identifying the specific aspects of the work environment likely to cause associates and managers to experience stress—that is, the factors that act as **stressors.** Organizational and work-related causes of stress include role conflict, role ambiguity, work overload, occupation, resource inadequacy, working conditions, management style, monitoring, and job insecurity.[29] We examine these factors next.

stressors
Environmental conditions that cause individuals to experience stress.

Role Conflict

All of us have many roles (student, fraternity/sorority member, athlete, spouse, associate). Many times, these roles are reasonably compatible. Sometimes, however, they are not compatible and create conflicting demands and requirements. This situation, known as **role conflict,** has been demonstrated to be a significant work stressor and is often associated with dissatisfaction, tardiness, absenteeism, and turnover.[30] It has been labeled a hindrance stressor in recent stress research.[31]

A specific example of role conflict and its connection to stress is provided by the case of flight attendants after the September 11 terrorist attacks.[32] Prior to the attacks, the flight attendants' role focused on providing service to passengers—"service with a smile." However, since September 11, flight attendants, under federal rulings, have

role conflict
A situation in which different roles lead to conflicting expectations.

been required to perform extraordinary security procedures and to scrutinize passengers. It is difficult to provide friendly service (customer service role) while taking extreme security precautions (security role). Pat Friend, president of the Association of Flight Attendants, noted that before the attacks, flight attendants could ignore or "grin and bear" unruly passenger behavior. Now, however, they are required to treat the mildest infraction as a "level-one" threat. This approach has produced an increase in passenger complaints, stress-management programs for flight attendants, and a study of job stress sponsored by a major flight attendants' union.

Apart from conflict among work roles, it is not uncommon for a person's work and non-work roles to conflict. For example, a person's job demands may conflict with a role as a spouse and mother or father. Such conflict was seen in the Verizon case, and it can be quite serious. A recent study, for example, connected work–family conflict to mental issues. Individuals with high levels of such conflict exhibited mood problems, anxiety, and substance use. This was true for women and men, with single mothers and married fathers having the highest levels of work–family tension.[33] Overall, men and women seem to exhibit similar levels of work–family issues.[34]

The discussion in the *Managerial Advice* feature highlights a number of useful ideas for managing work–life conflict. Ensuring an appropriate balance between work and personal lives is crucial to the well-being and productivity of

MANAGERIAL ADVICE

Restoring and Maintaining Work–Life Balance

Jupiter Images/Banana Stock/Alamy

Work–life conflict is a serious source of stress in many parts of the world. Work demands have increased for many people because of longer working hours, heightened speed and complexity of the work world, and advances in communication technology that tie together workplaces and workers 24 hours per day. At the same time, personal lives have become more complex, particularly for those with families. Families have become complicated by increases in dual-career couples, increases in the number of long-distance relationships, and more time-consuming non-school activities for children.

To help individuals cope in today's world, organizations such as the Mayo Clinic, the National Mental Health Association, and WebMD have developed useful ideas. Their advice is particularly important for managers, professionals, and other white-collar workers who have high-demand jobs. Here is our adaptation of their advice:

- *Focus on what is truly important.* Track and record all activities for one week, those that are work-related and those that are not. Prioritize the items on the list. At work, delegate tasks that are less important or personally less enjoyable. At home, outsource less enjoyable tasks. If mowing the lawn is not an enjoyable task, outsource it if possible. At both work and home, delete nonessential tasks. Less important, non-enjoyed, and nonessential tasks clutter the days of a surprising number of people.

- *Take advantage of work-related options.* If commuting is time-consuming and stressful, consider telecommuting some days, or request longer working hours on some days to avoid going to the office on other days. If onsite daycare is offered, consider using it to simplify dropoff and pickup routines. If financial services are offered onsite or nearby through a credit union, consider using those services to avoid traveling to a financial institution for face-to-face transactions.

- *Protect non-work time.* Do not allow work-related matters to creep into non-work time. Rejuvenation is crucial. Attempt to complete less desirable personal tasks (e.g., laundry, changing the bed linen) on work days so that days off can be spent on more enjoyable activities.

- *Manage your personal time.* Rather than going out multiple times to handle different errands, use multipurpose outings. Cook multiple meals for the week during a single evening. Complete multiple chores simultaneously whenever possible and comfortable (such as washing clothes and preparing dinner).

- *Set aside specific time each week for recreation.* Stay away from cell phones and work-related computing while enjoying activities with family and friends.

If stress becomes unmanageable, employee-assistance programs might be helpful. Given the complexity of today's world, some companies now offer programs designed specifically to help managers and associates strengthen relationships with spouses and significant others. For a suite of helpful tools, techniques, and resources, see the Mayo Clinic Stress Center at http://www.mayoclinic.com/health/stress/SR99999.

Sources: Mayo Clinic, 2006, "Work-life balance: Ways to Restore Harmony and Reduce Stress," at http://www.mayoclinic.com/health/work-life-balance/WL00056; National Mental Health Association, 2007, "Finding Your Balance: At Work and at Home," at http://www.nmha.org/go/finding-your-balance-at-work-and-home; R. Silverman, "Working on Your Marriage—At Work," *Wall Street Journal*, May 31, 2007, p. D.1; E. White, "How to Balance Home-Life Issues with Work Duties," *Wall Street Journal*, Aug. 22, 2006, p. B.8; WebMD, 2006, "5 Tips for Better Work-Life Balance," at http://www.webmd.com/balance/guide/5-strategies-for-life-balance?page=1.

associates and managers. Because high-involvement organizations expect a great deal from associates, these organizations must pay particular attention to work–life balance among those individuals.

Role Ambiguity

Role ambiguity refers to the situation in which jobholders are unclear about the goals, expectations, or requirements in their jobs. Under ambiguous job demands, people are unsure of what is expected of them and how they will be evaluated. A number of management jobs have high role ambiguity; thus, ambiguity is another contributor to the high stress often experienced in managerial jobs.

> **role ambiguity**
> A situation in which goals, expectations, and/or basic job requirements are unclear.

Ambiguity on the job creates tension and anxiety.[35] Reactions to this stress are likely to be emotional. Moreover, role ambiguity has been shown to have strong negative effects on job motivation and performance, even stronger than role conflict in many instances. Further, it often has stronger effects on tardiness, absenteeism, and turnover than does role conflict.[36] Finally, role ambiguity seems to be most problematic when the job demands are perceived as quite challenging.[37]

Work Overload

Another common cause of stress in organizations is work overload. Overload can be quantitative (too much work) or qualitative (work is too complex). Research suggests that qualitative overload creates more stress than quantitative overload. For example, qualitative work overload has been found to create greater depression, less enjoyment of work, and greater hostility.[38] In a study of nurses, those with an overload of complex cases were sick more frequently.[39] Therefore, managers should be very sensitive to overloading associates with work that is too complex for them.

Occupation

In accordance with the models of stress discussed above, occupations characterized by high demands and strong required efforts can generate stress. Statistics from the U.S. Department of Labor indicate that white-collar occupations are associated with a higher proportion of stress cases than the blue-collar and service occupations combined.[40] Technical, sales, and administrative support personnel contribute most of these cases, but managerial and professional occupations also contribute a substantial number of them. Although the white-collar occupations may allow greater control and offer substantial rewards, demands and requirements for people holding these jobs are typically much greater than in other occupations. On the other hand, the effects of control and rewards are demonstrated in research findings that suggest senior managers (upper-level executives, such as CEOs) experience less stress than middle managers. Even though demands on the senior managers may be greater, these managers are also likely to have more control,[41] and they frequently have generous reward packages.

Resource Inadequacy

People may also experience job stress when they lack needed resources.[42] Having inadequate resources makes it difficult to accomplish tasks effectively and efficiently and can therefore increase job demands or lessen control. There may be too few people, too little support, or inadequate material to accomplish a task, placing pressure on the person who has responsibility for the task. Severe resource shortages caused by situations such as loss of sales may lead to other stressful events, such as layoffs. As mentioned earlier, layoff decisions are stressful for the managers who make them, for those who lose their jobs, and even for those who stay. Those who remain on the job experienced stress before the layoff decision (because of uncertainty about who would be laid off), experienced the loss of friends and co-workers who were laid off, and then must endure added pressures to accomplish tasks with fewer workers.

Working Conditions

The job environment can have major effects on job attitudes and reactions. The job environment includes both physical surroundings (lighting, temperature, noise, office arrangements, and so on) and psychological aspects (such as peer relationships, warmth, and perceived rewards). If the working conditions are unpleasant, they can be stressful. For example, working with inadequate lighting, loud noise, or uncomfortable temperatures or working in isolation from others creates pressure and stress.[43]

Management Style

Management style significantly affects the psychological climate of the workplace, and certain styles of dealing with subordinates create more stress than others. For example, one study found that high scores on Machiavellianism (managing through fear) were negatively related to job satisfaction and positively related to job tension.[44] Certain types of jobs and associate personalities may interact with managerial style to produce stress. For example, directive managerial styles may produce less stress on routine jobs and with associates who prefer a more structured environment. However, for people in professional jobs and for those who prefer more personal involvement and self-determination in their jobs, a less directive managerial style produces less stress.

Monitoring

Relatively recent developments in technology have led to an explosion of stricter monitoring of associates' behavior—both work-related and non-work-related. Organizations are able to read associates' e-mail, detect web sites they visit, listen to phone conversations, and keep track of any work they do electronically. As illustrated in our opening feature, Verizon's call-center associates frequently mentioned phone monitoring as a source of stress. Monitoring can cause associates to experience increased demands and loss of control at the same time, making monitoring extremely stressful.[45] Demands are increased because associates feel that they must always be "on" and that any mistake will be noticed. Control is lessened because associates who are being monitored may feel that they have little discretion in how they do their jobs. Call-center associates, for example, complained about having to follow strict scripts when they felt that it was inappropriate and would even hinder performance.

Job Insecurity

In the early part of the twenty-first century, the U.S. unemployment rate increased somewhat, and more organizations became involved in mergers and acquisitions, downsizing, and moving work offshore. As a result, U.S. associates today are more likely to experience insecurity about keeping their jobs. Job insecurity can be an enormous stressor.[46]

Individual Influences on Experiencing Stress

Earlier, in defining stress, we noted that individuals vary in how they respond to external stressors. For example, some individuals may be energized by quite demanding workloads, whereas others respond with negative stress reactions. A great deal of research has examined characteristics that are likely to influence how an individual reacts to stress. These characteristics include Type A versus Type B personality, self-esteem, hardiness, and gender.

Type A versus Type B Personality

Many researchers have studied people with Type A and Type B personalities and how they respond to stress. People with **Type A personalities** are competitive, aggressive, and impatient. Type A's may push themselves to achieve higher and higher goals until they become frustrated, irritated, anxious, and hostile. Type A behavior is exemplified by the driver who blasts the car horn when the car in front of him is a second too slow in moving through an intersection after the light has

type A personality
A personality type characterized by competitiveness, aggressiveness, and impatience.

turned green. In the words of the two physicians who focused attention on this phenomenon:

> Type A pattern is an action-emotion complex that can be observed in any person who is aggressively involved in a chronic, incessant struggle to achieve more and more in less and less time, and if required to do so, against the opposing efforts of other things or other persons. It is not psychosis or a complex of worries or fears or phobias or obsessions, but a socially acceptable—indeed often praised—form of conflict.[47]

People with Type B personalities are quite different. They tend to be less competitive, less aggressive, and more patient.

People with Type A personalities are more susceptible to stress-induced illness.[48] Type A individuals may experience more stress for two reasons. First, given their competitive and aggressive tendencies, they may actually create more stressors in their environments. For example, Type A people have been known to increase work overload on their own, whereas Type B people are more reasonable.[49] Second, Type A people are more likely to appraise any given event as a stressor than are Type B people.[50]

Self-Esteem

Research has found that people with high self-esteem suffer fewer negative effects from stress than people with low self-esteem.[51] People with high self-esteem, in general, experience greater well-being and may be more resistant to the effects of stressors. Furthermore, people with high self-esteem are more likely to engage in active coping behaviors when they experience stressful demands relative to those with low self-esteem. For example, when faced with a heavy workload, people with high self-esteem may break tasks down into manageable units and prioritize their work so that they can begin to tackle excessive work demands. In contrast, someone with low self-esteem may withdraw from the work or procrastinate, making the work overload even worse. Consequently, people with high self-esteem are more likely to gain control over stressful situations and decrease the amount of stress they experience.

Hardiness

hardiness
A personality dimension corresponding to a strong internal commitment to activities, an internal locus of control, and challenge seeking.

Individuals who are high in **hardiness** tend to have a strong internal commitment to their activities, have an internal locus of control, and seek challenge in everyday life. Research has shown that people who are high in hardiness experience less severe negative stress reactions than those who are low in hardiness.[52] For example, one study showed that managers in a public utility who had scored high on hardiness had fewer illnesses following exposure to significant stress.[53]

Perhaps the most important aspect of hardiness is locus of control. Recall from Chapter 5 that people with an internal locus of control are likely to view themselves as responsible for the outcomes they experience. Those with an external locus of control are more likely to view themselves as victims of fate or luck. It is not surprising that people with an internal locus of control are more likely to develop active coping strategies and to perceive that they have control when experiencing stressful work demands. However, research has shown that the relationship between stress and locus of control may be more complex because people who have an extreme internal locus of control are likely to blame themselves for negative events and thus experience more responsibility, a stressor.[54]

Gender

Although the evidence is not entirely conclusive, women and men do not seem to differ in how stressful they perceive a given stressor to be.[55] They do, however, seem to cope differently. More specifically, women seek more emotional social support (comfort and a shoulder to lean on), seek more instrumental social support (specific support to solve a problem), engage in more positive self-talk, and exhibit rumination (thinking over the situation).[56] Social support tends to be an effective coping strategy.[57]

Beyond the above issues, women might be exposed to more stressors in the workplace. In some cases, women are lower-paid than men for similar work. They are more likely than men to experience discrimination and stereotyping, and to work in service industries that are stressful (such as nursing). Research suggests that women experience a greater variety of stressors in the workplace than men.[58] Some studies directly comparing the stress experienced by men and women at work also suggest that women experience more stress overall.[59] The U.S. Bureau of Labor Statistics reported that for every case of stress leading to work absence for men, there were 1.6 cases for women.[60]

Individuals holding extreme jobs have become a key part of the business landscape. They tend to be highly valued by their companies and enjoy their work. In the *Experiencing Strategic Organizational Behavior* feature, these individuals are profiled. As one might expect, they tend to have Type A personalities, but they also exhibit hardiness and high self-esteem. Thus, extreme workers frequently handle stressors surprisingly well. While men and women can both handle extreme jobs, more men than women are in such jobs.

EXPERIENCING STRATEGIC ORGANIZATIONAL BEHAVIOR

Extreme Jobs

Many managers and associates work long hours and have challenging responsibilities. Some of these individuals, however, have extreme jobs, a concept currently receiving a great deal of attention at The Center for Work-Life Policy in New York. Individuals in extreme jobs work at least 60 hours per week and meet at least 5 of the following 10 criteria: unpredictable work flow, tight deadlines, large job scope, work-related events outside of normal business hours, constant availability to clients/customers, profit and loss responsibility, mentoring and recruiting responsibility, a great deal of travel, many direct reports, and at least 10 hours per day at the office or work site. Holders of extreme jobs can be found in many industries, but many are found in consulting and investment banking.

While it might seem that managers and associates in these types of jobs would be rushing for the exits, many are not. In fact, many holders of these jobs thrive in them. Cynthia McKay, CEO of LeGourmet Gift Basket, works more than 70 hours per week and is on call 24 hours a day for clients. She has said, "I love being at work. It becomes a lifestyle as opposed to a job. . . . It is absolutely my choice." Irene Tse, a guru in the trading area at Goldman Sachs, often works 80 hours per week while generating and sometimes losing millions of dollars in a day. In her words, "I've done this for ten years, and can count on the fingers on one hand the number of days in my career when I didn't want to come to work. Every day I wake up and I can't wait to get here." John Bishop, an investment banker at

Ghislain & Marie David de Lossy/The Image Bank/Getty Images

Citigroup, routinely works between 90 to 100 hours per week. He characterizes himself as only "a little skewed to the workaholic." In a recent survey conducted by Harris Interactive, 66 percent of extreme jobholders in the United States and 76 percent globally reported being very happy with their jobs.

With the U.S. Bureau of Labor Statistics reporting that thousands and thousands of people work more than 60 hours per week, the number of people in extreme jobs seems to be substantial. What drives them? One answer is Type A personalities. The adrenaline rush from stimulating work is another answer. In the survey mentioned above, 90 percent of men and 82 percent of women report stimulating work as a key motivator for extreme work lives. The opportunity to work with and support high-quality colleagues is the next-most-cited factor, with 52 percent of men and 43 percent of women citing it as a key motivator. Compensation was mentioned by less than half of men and women as a motivator (all of the individuals surveyed had high incomes).

What protects these individuals from high levels of stress? Intrinsic interest in the work and attraction to challenge are clearly important. When the work is enjoyable, long hours and other heavy demands are more easily handled. Alternative employment options also play a role. Extreme jobholders tend to be talented and have a sense of their own self-worth. With options always available, there is a reduced chance of feeling trapped. Control and rewards follow.

There are issues, however. At the top of the list is work–life balance. Basically, there is no balance. Personal lives suffer: 66 percent of men and 77 percent of women in extreme jobs report difficulties maintaining a home. About 50 percent of both men and women report difficulties maintaining strong relationships with spouses/partners. Also, about 50 percent of both genders report difficulties maintaining a satisfying sex life.

There is also a gender gap. Holders of extreme jobs are disproportionately men. Because companies often place high value on individuals who embrace extreme jobs, women could be left behind. Why are women less represented in extreme jobs? Sylvia Ann Hewlett, president of the Center for Work-Life Policy, is concerned with this question. Her research suggests that women are not afraid of extreme work but are not as willing as men to accept the work–life balance problem. Many companies, such as Booz Allen Hamilton and American Express, are responding by recognizing the value that women bring to their organizations even when not wanting to work extreme hours. The companies are recognizing the importance of work quality and impact per unit of time rather than total hours available.

Sources: L. Belkin, "Putting in the Hours and Paying the Price," *New York Times,* Dec. 3, 2006, p. 10.1; M. Gardner, "'Extreme' Jobs on the Rise," *The Christian Science Monitor,* Dec. 4, 2006, 14; S.A. Hewlett, & C.B. Luce, "Extreme Jobs: The Dangerous Allure of the 70-Hour Workweek," *Harvard Business Review,* 84 no. 12 (2006): 49–59; L. Tischler, "Extreme Jobs (and the People Who Love Them)," *Fast Company,* Apr. 2005, 55–60.

Individual and Organizational Consequences of Stress

It should be clear by now that stress can be detrimental to developing a high-involvement, high-performance work organization. High-involvement organizations require that associates be engaged and motivated to perform at high levels and that their individual capabilities be employed in the most productive and efficient manner. However, the consequences of work stress can sabotage managerial attempts to develop such an environment. The following discussion focuses on the individual and organizational consequences of stress.

Individual Consequences

Individual consequences of stress can be classified as psychological, behavioral, or physiological.

PSYCHOLOGICAL CONSEQUENCES

Psychological responses to stress include anxiety, depression, low self-esteem, sleeplessness, frustration, family problems, and burnout.[61] Some of these psychological reactions are more severe than others. Their importance and overall effect on individual behavior and physical condition depend on their degree or level. Extreme frustration or anxiety can lead to other, more severe behavioral and physiological problems.

One important psychological problem is **burnout.** Associates and managers experiencing burnout show little or no enthusiasm for their jobs and generally experience constant fatigue. These individuals often complain bitterly about their work, blame others for mistakes, are absent from work more and more often, are uncooperative with co-workers, and become increasingly isolated.[62] Burnout often occurs in jobs that require individuals to work closely and intensely with others under emotionally charged conditions (nursing is an example). Burnout is a major concern in American industry and governmental organizations.

> **burnout**
> A condition of physical or emotional exhaustion generally brought about by stress; associates and managers experiencing burnout show various symptoms, such as constant fatigue, or lack of enthusiasm for work, and increasing isolation from others.

BEHAVIORAL CONSEQUENCES

Behavioral consequences of stress include excessive smoking, substance abuse (alcohol, drugs), accident proneness, appetite disorders, and even violence.[63] Probably the most severe behavioral consequences are substance abuse and violence.

Substance abuse, unfortunately, has become much more common in the United States in recent years. The Department of Health and Human Services has reported that alcohol, tobacco, and other drug-related problems cost U.S. business over $100 billion every year.[64] Studies have shown that alcoholics and other drug users in the workforce exhibit the following characteristics:[65]

- They are much less productive than other associates.
- They use three times as many sick days as other associates.
- They are more likely to expose themselves and co-workers to serious safety hazards because of poor judgment and coordination. Up to 40 percent of industrial fatalities are linked to alcohol and drug consumption.
- They are five times more likely to file worker's compensation claims. In general, they are subject to higher rates of absenteeism, accidents, and sickness.
- They report missing work frequently because of hangovers.

Although there are many reasons for alcoholism and drug abuse, many people use alcohol and drugs as a means of handling stress. Alcohol and some drugs are depressants that can substantially reduce emotional reactions. Studies have shown that in small doses, alcohol has little effect. However, with moderate-to-heavy consumption, alcohol can substantially reduce tension, anxiety, fear, and other emotional reactions to disturbing situations.[66] Drugs can have the same effects. Alcohol and drugs, then, give people a means of blocking stress reactions when they cannot control the situation. Of course, emotions are suppressed only as long as the individual continues to consume large quantities of alcohol or drugs. Because the disturbing situation still exists, emotional reactions return when the effects of drugs or alcohol wear off, leading to continued usage of these substances.

MTPAStock/Masterfile

Another serious behavioral consequence of stress is workplace violence. The Occupational Safety and Health Administration (OSHA) reports that approximately two million workers are victims of workplace violence every year. Homicide is the third leading cause of workplace fatalities. Workplace violence can be either physical or mental, as in the case of excessive taunting or harassment. Many cases of tragic outbursts at work are related to stressful working conditions. The case of Mark O. Barton offers an example.

On July 31, 1999, Barton shot and killed 9 people and injured 13 more at two Atlanta day-trading organizations. In the previous days, he had killed his wife and two children by hammering them to death. After being spotted by the police at a gas station a few hours after the shootings, Barton shot and killed himself. What caused Barton to commit these unspeakable acts of violence? While the causes of such behavior are highly complex, one contributing factor was the extreme stress involved in day trading.[67]

Day trading involves the buying and selling of stocks on a very-short-term basis. Traders often use their own money, and they can experience heavy gains and losses daily. In the month before the killings, Mark Barton had lost $105,000. Day traders have no security and no regular paycheck. Some have said that day traders must have a casino mentality.[68] Christopher Farrell, author of *Day Trading Online*, states: "A day trader makes a living at the game; you live or die by your profit and loss. You never get away from it. It's on your mind twenty-four hours a day. You don't have a steady paycheck."[69] Although day trading is not as popular as it once was, it continues to be a widespread phenomenon.[70]

Stress probably was not the only factor that led to Barton's deadly outburst; he most likely suffered from personality disorders. However, the stress of trading may have been one factor that set him off. And while Barton's behavior may have been extreme, workplace violence is so prevalent that we have nicknames for it, such as "going postal," "desk rage," and "air rage" to describe it.

PHYSIOLOGICAL CONSEQUENCES

Physiological reactions to stress include high blood pressure, muscle tension, headaches, ulcers, skin diseases, impaired immune systems, musculoskeletal disorders (such as back problems), and even more serious ailments, such as heart disease and cancer.[71] Stress has also been linked to obesity, a rising health epidemic worldwide.[72] Stress can be directly related to physiological problems, or it can make existing conditions worse. As we mentioned earlier, it has been estimated that 75 percent of all medical problems are directly attributable to stress.[73] The physical ailments noted above may lower productivity while on the job and increase absences from work (thereby reducing overall productivity even more).

Rick Speckmann exemplifies the debilitating physiological effects that can result from stress.[74] Speckmann was a hard-driving entrepreneur, burned out from the stress of running his executive search company in Minneapolis. One day, at age 40, Speckmann experienced an intense tightness in his chest after exercising. He was promptly sent to the hospital in an ambulance, where he received a battery of tests. The final diagnosis: acute overstress. Luckily, Speckmann paid attention to this lesson and changed his lifestyle to a less stressful one. It is important to note that physiological stress begins with normal biological mechanisms. Recall from our earlier discussion that the stress response prepares the body to deal with impending danger by releasing hormones and increasing the heartbeat, pulse rate, blood pressure, breathing rate, and output of blood sugar from the liver. These physiological changes helped primitive human beings respond to danger.[75] Such a physiological response to stress is often referred to as the *fight-or-flight response*. However, the stress response is best adapted for dealing with acute stress. As noted earlier, it is chronic stress, and the physiological responses to it, that can lead to physical ailments. The human body has not yet adapted well to an environment of continuous stress. Therefore, individual responses to stress can be severe and costly.

Organizational Consequences

Stress has consequences for organizations as well as for individuals. These consequences follow from the effects on individuals that include lower motivation, dissatisfaction, lower job performance, increased absenteeism, increased turnover, and lower quality of relationships at work. Research has shown strong connections between stress, job dissatisfaction, turnover, and health-care costs.[76] Stress-related illnesses cost companies millions of dollars in insurance and worker's compensation claims. Employees who report high levels of stress have health-care expenditures that are 50 percent higher than those reporting lower levels of stress.[77] Exhibit 7-4 gives some perspective to these costs.

Exhibit 7-4	Managerial Costs of Job Stress

The cost of job stress to American industry can be estimated at $200 billion per year due to:	To put this figure into perspective, consider the following:
Absenteeism	Total U.S. corporate profits were $897.6 billion in 2006 (after taxes, with inventory valuation and capital accounted for).
Diminished productivity	
Compensation claims	The entire U.S. gross domestic product (the market value of the nation's goods and services) was approximately $13,246 billion in 2006.
Health insurance	
Direct medical expenses	

Sources: 2007, at http://www.bca.gov/national/txt/dpga.txt; Bureau of Economic Analysis, 2007, at http://www.bea.gov/national/xls/gdplev.xls; J. Cahill, P.A. Landsbergis, and P.L. Schnall, "Reducing Occupational Stress," 1995, at http://workhealth.org/prevention/prred.html.

Furthermore, individual consequences of stress may interact to cause organizational problems. For example, behavioral problems, such as violence, and psychological consequences, such as anxiety, can lower the quality of the relationships between co-workers, resulting in distrust, animosity, and a breakdown in communications. When individuals frequently miss work due to stress-related illness, their colleagues may become resentful at having to take over their work while they are absent.[78] We have already discussed the increased safety risks for everyone that result from one person's alcohol or drug use. Thus, the organizational consequences of stress can be dangerous as well as costly. Fortunately, many organizations and professionals, including companies, government agencies (NIOSH, OSHA), medical doctors, and psychologists, have recognized the importance of addressing stress in the workplace, and a variety of techniques have been developed to combat stress-induced problems. We now turn to a discussion of actions that can be taken to alleviate the debilitating effects of stress on individuals and organizations.

Managing Workplace Stress

Individual associates and managers can implement a number of tactics to more effectively deal with stress. Similarly, organizations can be helpful in alleviating stress. They also can be mindful of stressful working conditions that cause stress in the first place.

Individual Stress Management

Based on the models of stress discussed earlier in this chapter, associates and managers can avoid workplace stress by finding jobs that provide a personally acceptable balance between demands and control, and between effort required and rewards. They can also propose that a dysfunctional job be redesigned. Further, they can avoid or reduce some stress by following the tactics for work–life balance presented in the earlier *Managerial Advice* feature. Beyond these tactics, individuals can adopt several positive tactics for coping with existing stress. The goal is to develop healthy ways of coping. Because individuals experience multiple sources of stress, using multiple tactics for coping is beneficial.

One of the most important tactics is regular exercise. Three areas are important: endurance, strength, and flexibility.[79] Endurance activities maintain or increase aerobic capacity. Key activities include regular walking, treadmill walking, jogging, running, cycling, and swimming. Extreme amounts of endurance exercise are not required. Moderate amounts improve fitness and reduce mortality.[80] Moderate exercise has been defined as 30 minutes of sustained activity three to four times per week, at a heart rate that is above the normal rate but below the maximum rate. An individual's target heart rate can be calculated by subtracting his age from 220, and then taking 65 to 80 percent of that number.[81]

Strength activities maintain or improve muscle mass and can prevent loss of bone mass as well. Key activities include weight training and aqua-aerobics.

Twenty minutes of these types of exercises three times per week can provide important benefits.[82] Flexibility activities maintain or improve range of motion and energy. Stretching is the key activity. Stretching various muscle groups three times per week provides important and sustainable benefits.[83]

A second tactic for coping with stress is proper diet. Diet affects energy, alertness, and overall well-being. According to research conducting at the Cooper Institute, four key areas should be considered.[84] First, it is important to monitor fat intake. Adults over 30 should obtain no more than 20 to 25 percent of calories from fat per day. Younger adults also should be careful with fat consumption. Fifty to 70 percent of calories should come from complex carbohydrates (drawn from fruits, vegetables, and whole grain foods, not from candies and cakes). Ten to 15 percent of calories should come from protein (drawn from fish, poultry, and meats). Second, it is important to consume a reasonable amount of fiber, both insoluble and soluble. Third, consumption of calcium is important. Fourth, consumption of foods rich in antioxidants can be helpful. Antioxidants seem to be helpful in preventing damage caused by normal bodily operations involving oxygen.

In today's world, implementing a proper diet can be difficult. Time for grocery shopping and cooking is often limited. Many companies (not to mention school cafeterias) make the situation worse by providing or facilitating junk food. In a recent poll conducted by Harris Interactive for the Marlin Company (a workplace communications company), 63 percent of respondents reported that vending machines on the job mostly contain junk food, such as potato chips, candy bars, and cookies. In a second poll, 74 percent of respondents reported that it is common for special occasions to be celebrated with candy, cookies, or cake. Even on routine workdays, accessible candy bowls are in many cubicles and offices.

A third tactic for coping with stress involves the development and use of social-support networks. Social support is very important. Research has shown that such support is positively related to cardiovascular functioning and negatively related to perceived stress, anxiety, and depression.[85] Having friends and family to talk with about problems can be quite useful (emotional social support). Having friends and family who can offer specific suggestions, provide resources, and break down barriers can also be quite useful (instrumental social support).

A fourth tactic involves the use of relaxation techniques. For some, meditation, yoga, and visualization of serene settings work very well. For others, a simple walk in the park is more useful.

Other tactics include developing and using planning skills, being realistic about what can be accomplished, and avoiding unnecessary competition.

Organizational Stress Management

Organizations can help to reduce stress or help managers and associates deal more effectively with stress. To reduce stress, the following actions can be taken. These actions are consistent with high-involvement management:

- Increase individuals' autonomy and control. According to the demand–control model, increased control should help to keep experienced stress to manageable levels.

- Ensure that individuals are compensated properly. According to the effort–rewards imbalance model, proper compensation should help to keep experienced stress to manageable levels.
- Maintain job demands/requirements at healthy levels.
- Ensure that associates have adequate skills to keep up-to-date with technical changes in the workplace.
- Increase associate involvement in important decision making.
- Improve physical working conditions. For example, use ergonomically sound equipment and tools.
- Provide for job security and career development. Provide educational opportunities so that associates can continue to improve their skill sets. Use job redesign and job rotation to expand associates' skill sets.
- Provide healthy work schedules. Avoid constant shifting of schedules. Allow for flextime or other alternative work schedules.
- Improve communication to help avoid uncertainty and ambiguity.

In addition to actions taken to reduce stress, organizations can help associates and managers cope with stress and its effects. Specifically, they can encourage some managers to be "toxin handlers" and they can implement wellness programs. These are discussed next.

Toxin handlers, a term coined by renowned educator and consultant Peter Frost, are people who take it upon themselves to handle the pain and stressors that are part of everyday life in organizations.[86] Frost argues that toxin handlers are necessary for organizations to be successful, even though their contributions are often overlooked. Without the efforts of these organizational heroes, both individual and organizational well-being and productivity would suffer.

Managers can become more efficient, compassionate toxin handlers. Frost lists the following behaviors as necessary for handling the pain, strain, and stress of others:

- Read your own and others' emotional cues and understand the impact that emotional cues have on others. For example, be aware that when you show signs of anger, the most common response will be defensiveness or hostility. This can begin a cycle of negative emotions and nonproductive behavior that could have been avoided. The ability to avoid negative behaviors is one of the major components of emotional intelligence.
- Keep people connected. Devise ways in which people at work can react to each other as human beings. This can be accomplished by encouraging intimacy and fun.
- Empathize with those who are in pain. Actively listen with compassion.
- Act to alleviate the suffering of others. Providing a shoulder to cry on might be appropriate. Arranging for discreet financial aid to an associate in need might be useful.
- Mobilize people to deal with their pain and get their lives back on track. Actively acknowledge problems, encourage helping behavior, and celebrate achievements.
- Create an environment where compassionate behavior toward others is encouraged and rewarded.

Wellness programs are very popular and important tools that organizations use to manage stress and its effects.[87] These programs include health screenings, health advice, risk management programs, smoking cessation, weight control, and exercise. The main goal is to develop/maintain a healthy and productive workforce. In some organizations, health coaches are used to proactively monitor participating associates and managers. These coaches, often nurses, offer advice based on health-screening information as well as ongoing medical events and drug prescriptions.[88]

The wellness program at Johnson & Johnson is one of the oldest and most recognized. Originally called "Live for Life," the program has helped thousands of people lead healthier lives. In terms of company benefits, assessments have shown positive returns to the bottom line through enhanced productivity and lower healthcare costs. A recent estimate suggested that savings just from reduced medical expenditures have been approximately $224 per person per year, which translates into a total of $22.4 million per year based on J&J's employment base of 100,000.[89] Today, the health and wellness initiative has several specific goals:

- 91% of employees will be tobacco free.
- 90% of employees will have blood pressure of 140/90 or better.
- 85% of employees will have total cholesterol below 240.
- 75% of employees will be physically active, defined as 30 minutes of activity three or more times each week.
- 60% of employees will be trained in resilience/stress management.[90]

Evidence suggests that wellness programs provide benefits to both individuals and organizations. As such, organizations want as many people as possible to participate. Participation, though, is voluntary. As discussed in the next *Experiencing Strategic Organizational Behavior* feature, incentives have been used to raise participation levels. These incentives, however, have a dark side, and legal issues have arisen.

EXPERIENCING STRATEGIC ORGANIZATIONAL BEHAVIOR

Incentives for Participating in Wellness Programs

Evidence supporting the bottom-line impact of wellness programs has begun to accumulate. Overall, research suggests a return of three dollars for every one dollar spent, with some recent estimates suggesting a return of six dollars per dollar spent on a wellness program. In one recent evaluation of programs at such organizations as LL Bean, Duke University, and General Motors, returns on investment were very positive.

With substantial benefits available, incentives designed to increase participation are now offered by many companies. Because participation by associates and managers is voluntary, these incentives are very important. At Baptist Health Florida, individuals who complete the wellness program's health assessment receive an additional $10,000 in life insurance survivor benefits. At Pitney Bowes, individuals who complete a health risk assessment at the start of the year are given $75 in a healthcare spending account. At Dell, an individual who undergoes a health-risk assessment receives a $75 reduction in annual health-care premiums, and receives another $225 for medical expense if she completes a course on managing health risks.

Don Mason/ Blend Images/ Getty Images

At some companies, however, incentives have become heavy handed, and this is a source of growing concern. Employees at Weyco who failed to have mandated medical tests and evaluations in 2006 paid an additional $65 per month for insurance premiums. After 2006, additional increases have come into play for those who continue to resist the program. Employees at Scotts Miracle Gro Company who failed to have "requested" evaluations saw $40 per month added to their insurance premiums. Moreover, all employees were subjected to investigation by an outside health management company. This company used data-mining techniques and available databases to uncover any health problems or risks. Those who had issues/risks were assigned a health coach and an action plan was developed. Individuals who failed to comply with the action plan saw $67 per month added to their insurance premiums.

Although it makes sense to have people with higher risks pay more for insurance, there are some problems to consider. First, health assessments are becoming less and less voluntary and seek very personal information (e.g., information on depression, the quality of a relationship with a spouse/partner, parents' causes of death). Is it appropriate to provide, directly or indirectly, this information to an employer? Second, the use of financial incentives tied to health plan costs and the pushing of action plans based on health status may bring legal issues. Certainly, charging people in certain categories (i.e., smokers) more for health insurance can be a complex undertaking. In the United States, The Health Insurance Portability and Accountability Act (HIPAA), the Americans with Disabilities Act (ADA), and Bona Fide Wellness Program Exceptions (BFWP) must be considered, along with applicable state laws.

Overall, the use of heavy-handed incentives (and indeed punishments) is becoming more common as companies strive for a smarter, fitter workforce. Only time will tell how accepted these practices become.

Sources: L. Chapman, "Wellness Programs Hitting Their Stride," *Benefits & Compensation Digest* 43, no. 2 (2006), pp. 15–17; M. Conlin, "Get Healthy or Else: One Company's All-out Attack on Medical Costs," *BusinessWeek*, Feb. 26, 2007, pp. 58–69; R. Dotinga, "Can Boss Insist on Healthy Habits?," *Christian Science Monitor*, Jan. 11, 2006, p 15; D. Koffman, R. Goetzel, V. Anwuri, K. Shore, D. Orenstein, & T. Lapier, "Heart Healthy and Stroke Free," *American Journal of Preventative Medicine*, 29 (2005), 113–121; L. McGinley, "Health Costs: The Big Push for Wellness," *Wall Street Journal*, July 16, 2006, p. 2A; M. McQueen, "The Road to Wellness Is Starting at the Office: Employers' Efforts to Push Preventative Care Begin to Show Both Health and Cost Benefits," *Wall Street Journal*, Dec. 5, 2006, p. D1; T.M. Simon, F. Bruno, N. Grossman, & C. Stamm, "Designing Compliant Wellness Programs: HIPAA, ADA, and State Insurance Laws," *Benefits Law Journal*, 19 no. 4 (2006), 46–59; T. Walker, "Businesses Justify Worker Incentives," *Managed Healthcare Executive*," 17 no. 5 (2007), p.18.

The Strategic Lens

Stress is an important component of organizational life. Although some stress has positive effects on people's behavior, much stress is dysfunctional. Stress affects everyone in the organization—top executives, middle and lower-level managers, and associates at all levels. All of these individuals represent human capital to an organization. We know that human capital is important because it repre-sents much of the knowledge and skill in an organization and affects task performance. Effective task performance and problem solving are necessary for an organization to gain and hold a competitive advantage, which in turn results in positive outcomes for the organization and its external stake-holders. However, dysfunctional stress prevents associates and managers from fully utilizing their knowledge and applying it in their jobs. When this occurs, their productivity suffers, and organizational performance is harmed. If many associates and managers are overstressed, the organization may suffer millions of dollars in extra costs and lower profits. In short, top executives who want the strategies they develop to be successfully implemented must manage the stress in their organizations. Overall, managers' ability to prevent stress and help associates cope with the stress they experience will have a major impact on the performance of individuals and the organization as a whole.

Critical Thinking Questions

1. How can good stress be distinguished from bad stress? How much stress is too much stress?

2. How can managing stress in an organization contribute to improved strategy implementation and organizational performance?

3. How much stress do you currently experience? How can reducing your stress increase your performance in school and enhance your life in general?

What This Chapter Adds to Your Knowledge Portfolio

In this chapter, we have discussed workplace stress, focusing on its causes and consequences and what can be done to help manage it. A high-involvement, high-performance workplace requires that associates perform at their best; however, stress can prevent them from doing so. If an organization is to compete successfully, it is important both to manage the stress experienced by associates and to eliminate some of the sources of stress. In summary, we have made the following points.

- Stress is a feeling of tension experienced by an individual who feels that the demands of a situation are about to exceed her ability to cope. It can also be acute (short-term) or chronic (long-term). Not all stress has negative effects; eustress is positive stress that results from facing challenges with an expectation of achievement.

- The demand–control model of stress suggests that experienced stress is a function of both job demands and job control. Stress is highest when demands are high but control is low. The effort–reward imbalance model suggests that stress comes about when effort required is high but rewards are low.

- Organizational and work-related stressors include role conflict, role ambiguity, work overload, occupation, resource inadequacy, working conditions, management style, monitoring, and job insecurity.

- Individual differences can influence how people experience stress, react to stress, and cope with stress. These individual differences include Type A versus Type B personalities, self-esteem, hardiness, and gender.

- The consequences of stress are serious for both individuals and organizations. For the individual, stress can lead to psychological consequences, such as burnout; behavioral consequences, such as substance abuse and violence; and physiological consequences, such as high blood pressure, impaired immune systems, and heart disease. Many medical problems are attributed to stress.

- Organizational consequences of stress include lower job performance across a number of people, higher absenteeism and turnover rates, lower quality of work relationships, increased safety risks, and increased health-care and insurance costs.

- Associates and managers can do many things to help manage their own stress. Coping tactics include exercise, healthy diets, social support, and relaxation techniques.

- Organizations can reduce the stress experienced by associates and managers by reducing stressors. They also can encourage toxin handlers and implement wellness programs.

Back to the Knowledge Objectives

1. What do we mean by *stress?* What are the distinguishing features of acute and chronic stress, and eustress and dystress? Does all stress result in negative consequences?

2. How does the human body react to stress? What are the outcomes of this reaction? How can you tell if you or someone you know may be suffering from too much stress?

3. What are the general causes of workplace stress according to the demand–control model? What are the general causes of stress according to the effort–reward imbalance model? What implications do these models have for creating a high-involvement workplace? What are the most common workplace stressors?

4. What types of people are likely to experience the most stress at work? If you are experiencing too much stress, what can you do to help manage it?

5. What specific effects does workplace stress have on individuals and organizations?

6. What can organizations do to prevent and manage workplace stress? What specific changes can they make?

Thinking about Ethics

1. What responsibility do senior managers have to understand how their decisions affect the stress experienced by other managers and by associates?

2. Do managers have any responsibility to help associates manage stress caused by life events outside of work? Explain.

3. What actions should a manager take if she has an associate experiencing burnout?

4. Do organizations have a responsibility to offer programs or benefits that can help associates manage stress, such as more vacations, flexible work arrangements, and wellness programs? Why or why not?

5. Is it appropriate for employers to seek detailed personal information in order to make recommendations for wellness action plans?

Key Terms

stress, p. 225
job stress, p. 225
acute stress, p. 225
chronic stress, p. 225
stress response, p. 226
eustress, p. 226

dystress, p. 226
demand–control
  model, p. 227
effort–reward imbalance
  model, p. 227
stressors, p. 229

role conflict, p. 229
role ambiguity, p. 231
Type A personality, p. 234
hardiness, p. 234
burnout, p. 237

Building Your Human Capital

How Well Do You Handle Stress?

One of the most famous stress studies was published in 1960 and illustrated that it was possible to predict the likelihood that a person would succumb to stress-related illnesses within two years. The study resulted in the following list of life events with assigned points that can be used to predict a person's chances of becoming ill. The list is slightly modified to reflect modern life. Even though this research is almost 40 years old, the questionnaire still predicts stress-related illness.

To find out how likely you are to experience health problems due to stress, mark each life event that you have experienced in the last 12 months.

RANK	LIFE EVENT	POINT VALUE
1	Death of a spouse or life partner	100
2	Divorce or breakup with life partner	73
3	Marital separation or separation from life partner	65
4	Jail term	63
5	Death of close family member	63
6	Personal injury or illness	53
7	Marriage	50
8	Fired from job or laid off	47
9	Relationship reconciliation	45
10	Retirement	45
11	Change in health of family member	44
12	Pregnancy	40
13	Sex difficulties	39
14	Gain of new family member	39
15	Major business readjustment	39
16	Change in financial state	38
17	Death of close friend	37
18	Change in one's line of work	36
19	Change in number of arguments with spouse or partner	35
20	Taking on large mortgage or debt	31
21	Foreclosure of mortgage or loan	30
22	Change in work responsibilities	29
23	Child leaving home	29
24	Trouble with in-laws	29
25	Outstanding personal achievement	28
26	Spouse or partner's work begins or stops	26
27	Beginning or ending schooling	26
28	Change in living conditions	25
29	Revision of personal habits (e.g., diet, quit smoking)	24
30	Trouble with boss	23
31	Change in work hours or conditions	20
32	Change in residence	20
33	Change in schools	20
34	Change in recreation	19
35	Change in church activities	19
36	Change in social activities	18
37	Taking on a small mortgage or debt	17
38	Change in sleep habits	16
39	Change in number of family get-togethers	15
40	Change in eating habits	15
41	Vacation	13
42	Christmas (or other major holiday)	12
43	Minor violations of the law	11

Scoring

Total the point values of the life events that you marked. Use the total to assess your risk of health problems, as follows:

Up to 150 points	You are unlikely to experience health problems due to stress.
151–300 points	You have a 50 percent chance of experiencing health problems due to stress.
301 or more points	You have an 80 percent chance of experiencing health problems due to stress.

Source: Adapted from T. Holmes and R. Rahe, "Holmes-Rahe Social Readjustment Rating Scale," *Journal of Psychosomatic Research,* 11 (1967): 213–218.

A Strategic Organizational Behavior Moment

Friend or Associate?

Walt strode angrily to the kitchen to see Tony. Tony had begun showing up late for work and had missed several shifts altogether. In fact, Walt had had to cover his shift last night. The problem was that Walt really liked Tony despite the drinking problem. "I even named my kid after him," Walt thought to himself.

He had first met Tony when they both worked at the old Frontier Hotel. Tony was the chef, and Walt was head-waiter. Perhaps because they were both in their late thirties and headed nowhere, they really hit it off. Even in those days, Tony had a taste for the booze. Tony's marriage was breaking up, and he seemed to be lost. Walt often traveled the bars looking for Tony when he had missed a few days of work. He would get Tony sobered up and help him straighten it out with the boss. Tony would be okay for two or three months, and then it would happen all over again. Throughout all this time, Walt remained a faithful friend, believing that some day Tony would straighten himself out.

It was during one of Tony's good periods that the idea of starting a restaurant came up. Tony encouraged Walt to start a place of his own. Walt thought the idea was crazy, but Tony insisted on having Walt meet another friend, Bill, who might be interested in backing the idea. After several meetings and a lot of planning, they opened a small place, converting an old two-story home into a quaint Italian restaurant.

Walt and Bill were full partners, and Tony was to be the chef. They had both tried to convince Tony to join them in partnership, but he had refused. It had something to do with losing his freedom, but Walt was never sure what Tony had meant by that.

The restaurant had been an almost-instant success. Within a year, they had to move to a larger location. Walt couldn't believe how much money he was making. He took care of his associates, sharing his revenues generously with them and frequently acknowledging their efforts. Tony was earning nearly twice what he had made at the Frontier and seemed to be happy.

Then, about a week ago, Tony didn't come in to work. He hadn't called in sick; he just didn't show up. Walt was a little worried about him, but he covered the shift and went over to Tony's the next morning. Tony answered the door still half asleep, and Walt demanded an explanation.

Groggily, Tony explained, "I met the nicest woman you ever saw. Things were going so well, I just couldn't leave her. You understand, don't you?"

Walt laughed. It was all right with him if his friend had met someone and was happy. After all, Tony was a friend first and an associate second. "Sure, Tony. Just meet her a little earlier next time, okay? Can't do without a chef every day, you know."

Tony came to work late the next couple of nights, showed up the third night on time, but missed the last two. Although Walt was a patient man, he found it irritating to have to work Tony's shifts. After all, he was the boss. And then it happened. While complaining about Tony's "love life" to one of the other cooks, Walt nearly dropped a pizza platter when the cook said, "What love life, Walt? Tony's drinking again. I saw him last night over at Freddie's place on my way home. He was so drunk he didn't even recognize me."

Walt was worried. It had been almost two years since Tony had "gone on the wagon." He was concerned and irritable when a waitress, Irene, came up to the front and said, "Walt, Tony's in the back—drunk. He says he wants his money. He looks awful."

Discussion Questions

1. Could Tony's problem with alcohol be stress-related? Explain why or why not.

2. What should Walt do in this circumstance to help Tony cope?

3. Is Tony savable? Do the benefits outweigh the costs of trying to save him?

Team Exercise

Dealing with Stress

1. If you have not done so already, complete the assessment presented in *Building Your Human Capital*. In addition to the periodic stressors identified in that assessment, identify and list any ongoing stressors (demanding classes, a teacher who is not treating you appropriately, etc.).

2. Write down what you currently do to cope with stress. Be specific in commenting on each element found in the section entitled "Individual Stress Management" (e.g., endurance exercise, instrumental social support, meditation).

3. Give your results from Steps 1 and 2 to two classmates, as identified by your instructor (if you have privacy concerns, consult with your instructor).

4. Receive results from the same two classmates, and evaluate the effectiveness of their coping strategies in light of their stressors.

5. Team up with the other two people and discuss your evaluations.

Steps 1–4 should take about 30 minutes to complete, and step 5 should take about 20–30 minutes.

Endnotes

1. Manning, M.R., Jackson, C.N., & Fusilier, M.R. 1996. Occupational stress, social support, and the costs of health care. *Academy of Management Journal,* 39: 738–751.

2. Hughes, G.H., Person, M.A., & Reinhart, G.R. 1984. Stress: Sources, effects, and management. *Family and Community Health,* 7: 47–58.

3. U.S. Bureau of Labor Statistics. 2006. Occupational stress and time away from work. At http://www.bls.gov/opub/ted/1999/oct/wk3/art03.htm (originally published in 1999).

4. Sauter, S, Murphy, L., Colligan, M., Swanson, N., Hurrell, J., Scharf, F., Sinclair, R., Grubb, P., Goldenhar, L., Alterman, T., Johnston, J., Hamilton, A., & Tisdale, J. 1999. *Stress . . . At Work.* Publication No. 99–101. Washington, D.C.: National Institute for Occupational Safety and Health.

5. Ibid.

6. The Gallup Poll. 2006. Work and Work Place. At http://www.galluppoll.com/content/?ci=1720&pg=1.

7. The Marlin Company. 2003. Workplace behavior: Gossip, stress, rudeness. At http://www.themarlincompany.com/Media Room/PollResults.aspx.

8. Brockner, J., Grover, S., Reed, T.F., & DeWitt, R.L. 1992. Layoffs, job insecurity and survivors' work effort: Evidence of an inverted-U relationship. *Academy of Management Journal,* 35: 413–425.

9. See, for example, Hopkins, S.M., & Weathington, B.L. 2006. The relationship between justice perceptions, trust, and employee attitudes in a downsized organization. *The Journal of Psychology,* 140: 477–498; Mishra, K.E., Spreitzer, G.M., & Mishra, A.K. 1998. Preserving employee morale during downsizing. *Sloan Management Review,* 39(2): 83–95.

10. Nixon, R.D., Hitt, M.A., Lee, H., & Jeong, E. 2004. Market reactions to announcements of corporate downsizing actions and implementation strategies. *Strategic Management Journal,* 25: 1121–1129.

11. Dewe, P. 1991. Primary appraisal, secondary appraisal and coping: Their role in stressful work encounters. *Journal of Occupational and Organizational Psychology,* 64: 331–351.

12. See, for example, Lazarus, R.S., & Folkman, S. 1984. *Stress, appraisal and coping.* New York: Springer; Medline Plus Medical Encyclopedia. 2007. Stress and Anxiety. At http://www.nlm.nih.gov/medlineplus/ency/article/003211.htm.

13. Sauter et al., *Stress . . . At Work.*

14. Mayo Clinic. 2003. Managing work place stress: Plan your approach. At http://www.mayoclinic.com/invoke.cfm?id=HQ01442; Mayo Clinic. 2006. Understand your sources of stress. At http://www.mayoclinic.com/health/stress-management/SR00031.

15. Quick, J.C., & Quick, J.D. 1984. *Organizational stress and preventive management.* New York: McGraw-Hill.

16. Mayo Clinic, Managing work place stress.

17. Seyle, H. 1982. History and present status of the stress concept. In L. Goldberger and S. Breniznitz (Eds.), *Handbook of stress.* New York: Free Press, pp. 7–17.

18. McGrath, J.E. 1976. Stress and behavior in organizations. In M.D. Dunnette (Ed.), *Handbook of industrial and organizational psychology.* Chicago: Rand McNally, pp. 1351–1395.

19. From Mayo Clinic, Managing work place stress.

20. Karasek, R. 1979. Job demands, job decision latitude, and mental strain: Implications for job redesign. *Administrative Science Quarterly,* 24: 285–306; Karasek, R. 1989. Control in

the workplace and its health related aspects. In S.L. Sauter, J.J. Hurrell, & C.L. Cooper (Eds.), *Job control and worker health.* New York: John Wiley & Sons, pp. 129–159.

21. Siegrist, J. 1996. Adverse health effects of high-effort/low-reward conditions. *Journal of Occupational Health Psychology,* 1: 27–41; Siegrist, J. 1999. Occupational health and public health in Germany. In P.M. Le Blanc, M.C.W. Peeters, A. Büssing, & W.B. Schaufeli (Eds.), *Organizational psychology and healthcare: European contributions.* München: Rainer Hampp Verlag, pp. 35–44; Siegrist, J., Siegrist, K., & Weber, I. 1986. Sociological concepts in the etiology of chronic disease: The case of ischemic heart disease. *Social Science & Medicine,* 22: 247–253.

22. Ibid.

23. See, for example, Karasek, Control in the workplace and health related aspects; Stansfeld, S., & Candy, B. 2006. Psychosocial work environment and mental-health: A meta-analytic review. *Scandinavian Journal of Work Environment & Health,* 32: 443–462.

24. Daniels, K., & Guppy, A. 1994. Occupational stress, social support, job control, and psychological well-being. *Human Relations,* 47: 1523–1544; Ganster, D.C., & Schaubroeck, J. 1991. Work stress and employee health. *Journal of Management,* 17: 235–271; Perrewe, P.L., & Ganster, D.C. 1989. The impact of job demands and behavioral control on experienced job stress. *Journal of Organizational Behavior,* 10: 213–229.

25. Daniels & Guppy, Occupational stress, social support, job control, and psychological well-being.

26. Siegrist, Adverse health effects of high-effort/low-reward conditions; van Vegchel, N., de Jonge, J., Bosma, H., & Schaufeli, W. 2005. Reviewing the effort-reward imbalance model: Drawing up the balance of 45 empirical studies. *Social Science & Medicine,* 60: 1117–1131.

27. Gillen, M., Yen, I.H., Trupin, L., Swig, L., Rugulies, R., Mullen, K., Font, A., Burian, D., Ryan, G., Janowitz, I., Quinlan, P.A., Frank, J., & Blanc, P. 2007. The association of status and psychosocial and physical workplace factors with musculoskeletal injury in hospital workers. *American Journal of Industrial Medicine,* 50: 245–260.

28. van Vegchel, de Jonge, Bosma, & Schaufeli, Reviewing the effort-reward imbalance model.

29. Kahn, R.L., & Byosiere, P. 1992. Stress in Organizations. In M.D. Dunnette & L.M. Hough (Eds.), *Handbook of industrial and organizational psychology* (Vol. 3). Palo Alto, CA: Consulting Psychologists Press, pp. 571–650.

30. Jackson, S.E., & Schuler, R. 1985. A meta-analysis and occupational critique of research on role ambiguity and role conflict in work settings. *Organizational Behavior and Human Decision Processes,* 36: 16–78; Jamal, M. 1984. Job stress and job performance controversy: An empirical assessment. *Organizational Behavior and Human Performance,* 33: 1–21; Kalliath, T., & Morris, R. 2002. Job satisfaction among nurses: A predictor of burnout levels. *Journal of Nursing Administration,* 32: 648–654; O'Driscoll, M.P., & Beehr, T.A. 1994. Supervisor behaviors, role stressors and uncertainty as predictors of personal outcomes for subordinates. *Journal of Organizational Behavior,* 15: 141–155; Piko, B.F. 2006. Burnout, role conflict, job satisfaction and psychosocial health among Hungarian health care staff. *International Journal of Nursing Studies,* 43: 311–318.

31. Podsakoff, N.P., LePine, J.A., & LePine, M.A. 2007. Differential challenge stressor-hindrance stressor relationships with job attitudes, turnover intentions, turnover, and withdrawal behavior: A meta-analysis. *Journal of Applied Psychology,* 92: 438–454.

32. Barnes, B. 2003. The new face of air rage. *Wall Street Journal* (Eastern Edition), January 10: W1.

33. Wang, J.L., Afifi, T.O., Cox, B., & Sareen, J. 2007. Work-family conflict and mental disorders in the United States: Cross-sectional findings from the National Comorbidity Survey. *American Journal of Industrial Medicine,* 50: 143–149.

34. Byron, K. 2005. A meta-analytic review of work-family conflict and its antecedents. *Journal of Vocational Behavior,* 67: 169–198.

35. Glazer, S., & Beehr, T.A. 2005. Consistency of implications of three role stressors across four countries. *Journal of Organizational Behavior,* 26: 467–487; Jackson & Schuler, A meta-analysis and occupational critique of research on role ambiguity and role conflict in work settings.

36. Jamal, Job stress and job performance controversy.

37. Lang, J., Thomas, J.L., Bliese, P.D., & Adler, A.B. 2007. Job demands and job performance: The mediating effect of psychological and physical strain and the moderating effect of role clarity. *Journal of Occupational Health Psychology,* 12: 116–124.

38. Shaw, J.B., & Weekley, J.A. 1985. The effects of objective work-load variations of psychological strain and post-workload performance. *Journal of Management,* 11: 87–98; Ganter & Schaubroeck, Work stress and employee health.

39. Rauhala, A., Kivimäki, M., Fagerström, L., Elovainio, M., Virtanen, M., Vahtera, J., Rainio, A., Ojaniemi, K., & Kinnunen, J. 2007. What degree of work overload is likely to cause increased sickness absenteeism among nurses? Evidence from the RAFAELA patient classification system. *Journal of Advanced Nursing,* 57: 286–295.

40. U.S. Bureau of Labor Statistics. 1999. Issues in labor statistics: Summary 99-10. At http://www.bls.gov/opub/ils/pdf/opbils35.pdf.

41. Ivancevich, J.M., Matteson, M.T., & Preston, C. 1982. Occupational stress, Type A behavior, and physical well-being. *Academy of Management Journal,* 25: 373–391.

42. Jamal, Job stress and job performance controversy.

43. Kahn & Byosiere, Stress in organizations.

44. Holton, C.J., 1983. Machiavellianism and managerial work attitudes and perceptions. *Psychological Reports,* 52: 432–434.

45. Aiello, J.R., & Kolb, K.J. 1995. Electronic performance monitoring and social context: Impact on productivity and stress. *Journal of Applied Psychology,* 80: 339–353.

46. Reisel, W., & Banai, M. 2002. Job insecurity revisited: Reformulating with affect. *Journal of Behavioral and Applied Management,* 4: 87–96.

47. Friedman, M., & Rosenman, R.H. 1974. *Type A behavior and your heart.* New York: Knopf, p. 47.

48. Kahn & Byosiere, Stress in organizations; Ganster & Schaubroeck, Work stress and employee health; Sanz, J., Garcia-Vera, M.P., Magan, I., Espinosa, R., & Fortun, M. 2007. Differences in personality between sustained hypertension, isolated clinic hypertension and normotension. *European Journal of Personality,* 21: 209–224.

49. Froggatt, K.L., & Cotton, J.L. 1987. The impact of Type A behavior pattern on role overload-induced stress and performance attributions. *Journal of Management,* 13: 87–90.

50. Ganster & Schaubroeck, Work stress and employee health.

51. Ibid.

52. Jimenez, B.M., Natera, N.I.M., Munoz, A.R., & Benadero, M.E.M. 2006. Hardy personality as moderator variable of burnout syndrome in firefighters. *Psicothema,* 18: 413–418; Kobasa, S.C.O., & Puccetti, M.C. 1983. Personality and social resources in stress resistance. *Journal of Personality and Social Psychology,* 45: 839–850; McCalister, K.T., Dolbier, C.L., Webster, J.A., Mallon, M.W., & Steinhardt, M.A. 2006. Hardiness and support at work as predictors of work stress and job satisfaction. *American Journal of Health Promotion,* 20: 183–191.

53. Kobasa, S.C., Maddi, S.R., & Kahn, S. 1982. Hardiness and health: A prospective study. *Journal of Personality and Social Psychology,* 42: 168–177.

54. Ganster & Schaubroeck, Work stress and employee health.

55. See, for example, Martocchio, J.J., & O'Leary, A.M. 1989. Sex differences in occupational stress: A meta-analytic review. *Journal of Applied Psychology,* 74: 495–501; Tamres, L.K., Janicki, D., & Helgeson, V.S. 2002. Sex differences in coping behavior: A meta-analytic review and an examination of relative coping. *Personality and Social Psychology Review,* 6: 2–30; Vagg, P.R., Speilberger, C.D., & Wasala, C.F. 2002. Effects of organizational level and gender on stress in the workplace. *International Journal of Stress Management,* 9: 243–261.

56. Tamres, Janicki, & Helgeson, Sex differences in coping behavior: A meta-analytic review and an examination of relative coping.; Torkelson, E., & Muhonen, T. 2004. The role of gender and job level in coping with occupational stress. *Work and Stress,* 18: 267–274.

57. Daniels & Guppy, Occupational stress, social support, job control, and psychological well-being.

58. McDonald, K.M., & Korabik, K. 1991. Sources of stress and ways of coping among male and female managers. In R.L. Perrewe (Ed.), *Handbook on job stress.* New York: Select Press, pp. 185–199; Lim, V.K.G., & Thompson, S.H.T. 1996. Gender differences in occupational stress and coping strategies among IT personnel. *Women in Management Review,* 11: 20–29.

59. Nelson, D.L., & Quick, J.C. 1985. Professional women: Are distress and disease inevitable? *Academy of Management Review,* 10: 206–213.

60. Webster, Y., & Bergman, B. 1999. Occupational stress: Counts and rates. *Compensation and Working Conditions,* Fall: 38–41.

61. Nelson & Quick, Professional women.

62. For a more extensive list, see: Mayo Clinic. 2006. Job burnout: Know the signs and symptoms. At http://www.mayoclinic.com/health/burnout/WL00062.

63. Quick, J.C., & Quick, J.D. 1985. *Organizational stress and preventive management.* New York: McGraw-Hill.

64. U.S. Department of Health and Human Services. 1995. Alcohol, tobacco and other drugs in the workforce. At http://www.health.org/govpubs/m1006.

65. Ibid.; National Council on Alcoholism and Drug Dependence. 1992. NCADD fact sheet: Alcohol and other drugs in the workplace. New York: NCADD; National Institute on Drug Abuse.

1991. National household survey of drug abuse. Bethesda, MD: U.S. Department of Health and Human Services.

66. Bandura, A. 1969. *Principles of behavior modification.* New York: Holt, Rinehart & Winston; Cook, R., Walizer, D., & Mace, D. 1976. Illicit drug use in the Army: A social-organizational analysis. *Journal of Applied Psychology,* 61: 262–272.

67. Colarusso, D. 1999. Over the edge: Amateur traders stressed beyond capacity to cope. *ABC News.com,* at http://abcnews.go.com/sections/business?TheStreet/daytraders_990729.html; Immelman, A. 1999. The possible motives of Atlanta day-trading mass murderer Mark O. Barton. *Unit for the Study of Personality in Politics,* at http://www.csbsju.edu/uspp/Research/Barton.html.

68. Harmon, A. 1999. "Casino mentality" linked to day trading stresses. *New York Times,* August 1, p. 1.16.

69. Colarusso, Over the edge: Amateur traders stressed beyond capacity to cope.

70. For additional information on day trading, go to http://www.daytraders.com/.

71. Quick & Quick, Organizational stress and preventive management; Sauter, Murphy, Colligan, Swanson, Hurrell, Scharf, Sinclair, Grubb, Goldenhar, Alterman, Johnston, Hamilton, & Tisdale, *Stress . . . At Work.*

72. Chrousos, G.P., & Gold, P.W. 1992. The concepts of stress and stress system disorders. Overview of physical and behavioral homeostasis. *Journal of the American Medical Association,* 267: 1244–1252. Peeke, P. 2000. *Fight fat after forty.* New York: Penguin.

73. Hughes, G.H., Pearson, M.A., & Reinhart, G.R. 1984. Stress: Sources, effects, and management. *Family and Community Health,* 6: 47–58.

74. Margoshes, P. 2001. Take the edge off. *Fortune Small Business,* June 23, at http://www.fortune.com/smallbusiness/articles/0,15114,358931,00.html.

75. Quick & Quick, *Organizational stress and preventive management.*

76. Kemery, E.R., Bedeian, A.G., Mossholder, K.W., & Touliatos, J. 1985. Outcomes of role stress: A multisample constructive replication. *Academy of Management Journal,* 28: 363–375; Manning & Jackson, Occupational stress, social support, and the costs of health care; Parasuraman, S., & Alluto, J.A. 1984. Sources and outcomes of stress in organizational settings: Toward the development of a structural model. *Academy of Management Journal,* 27: 330–350.

77. Sauter, *Stress at work.*

78. Colella, A. 2001. Coworker distributive fairness judgments of the workplace accommodation of employees with disabilities. *Academy of Management Review,* 26: 100–116.

79. Neck, C.P., & Cooper, K.H. 2000. The fit executive: Exercise and diet guidelines for enhancing performance. *Academy of Management Executive,* 14 (2): 72–83.

80. Blair, S.N., Kohl, H.W., Paffenbarger, R.S., Clark, D.G., Cooper, K.H., & Gibbons, L.W. 1989. Physical fitness and all-cause mortality: A prospective study of healthy men and women. *Journal of the American Medical Association,* 262: 2395–2401.

81. Neck & Cooper, The fit executive: Exercise and diet guidelines for enhancing performance.

82. For additional details, see Cooper, K.H. 1995. *It's better to believe.* Nashville: Thomas Nelson, Inc.

83. For additional details, see Neck & Cooper, The fit executive: Exercise and diet guidelines for enhancing performance. For important safety tips, see Blake, R. 1998. Don't take muscle flexibility for granted. *Executive Health's Good Health Report,* 34 (12): 7–8. In general, individuals with any health concerns should consult a physician prior to beginning a new exercise program.

84. For details, see: Cooper, K.H. 1996. *Advanced nutritional therapies.* Nashville: Thomas Nelson, Inc.; Neck & Cooper, The fit executive: Exercise and diet guidelines for enhancing performance.

85. Clay, R.A. 2001. Research to the heart of the matter. *Monitor on Psychology,* 32: 42–45; Schirmer, L.L., & Lopez, F.G. 2001. Probing the social support and work strain relationship among adult workers: Contributions of adult attachment orientations. *Journal of Vocational Behavior,* 59: 17–33.

86. Frost, P.J. 2003. *Toxic emotions at work.* Boston: Harvard Business School Press.

87. For general information, see: Wellness Councils of America, 2007, WELCOA Overview. At http://www.welcoa.org/presskit/index.php. Note that we are using the term "wellness" broadly to include a number of health and general well-being initiatives.

88. See, for example: Schoeff, M. 2006. UPS employees get advice from health coaches. *Workforce Management,* 85 (16): 14.

89. Ozminkowski, R.J., Ling, D., Goetzel, R.Z., Bruno, J.A., Rutter, K.R, Isaac, F., & Wang, S. 2002. Long-term impact of Johnson & Johnson's Health and Wellness Program on health care utilization and expenditures. *Journal of Occupational and Environmental Medicine,* 44: 21–29. Note that some controversy exists over the exact benefits received by J&J, but most analysts agree that the impact as been substantially positive.

90. Johnson & Johnson. 2005. Healthy people. At http://www.jnj.com/community/health_safety/programs/Healthy_People.htm.

PART III GROUPS, TEAMS, AND SOCIAL PROCESSES

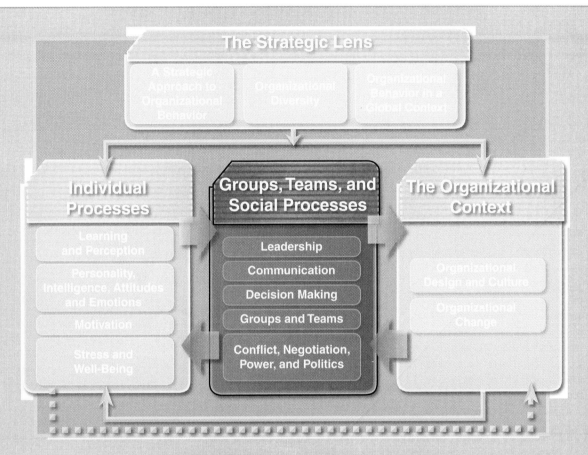

In Part II, we examined individual-level processes that affect organizational behavior. In Part III, we explore group, team, and social processes, which can directly or indirectly affect behavior in organizations. Knowledge of each of these types of processes helps managers achieve and maintain a competitive advantage. Therefore, each has important strategic implications for the organization.

Chapter 8, the first chapter in Part III, discusses various concepts related to leadership and explains what makes a leader effective. In the chapter, we pay special attention to the effects of leadership on motivation and productivity. **Chapter 9** explores communication in organizations. Communication is critical for achieving objectives because it provides the information on which people in organizations act. In addition, leaders communicate in order to motivate individuals and teams and to obtain the behavior desired.

Chapter 10 describes individual and group decision making. Decision making is a critical dimension of leadership and has substantial effects on organizational behavior. In **Chapter 11**, we turn to an examination of teams and group dynamics. Because organizations make frequent use of teams (groups of associates integrated to accomplish specified goals), understanding and managing teams can be essential to organizational success. Finally, in **Chapter 12**, we explore power, conflict, politics, and negotiations within organizations. Both the exercise of power and occurrences of conflict can have either functional or dysfunctional consequences. Chapter 12 provides an understanding of how managers can achieve functional outcomes.

LEADERSHIP

8

As the twentieth century gave way to the twenty-first, senior management in Deloitte & Touche's consulting practice faced a significant problem: the organization was ill-prepared for the e-Business revolution. It lacked the expertise and infrastructure needed to effectively consult with businesses that increasingly relied upon web and other information technologies across the value chain. Moreover, its efforts were lagging behind those of other major consulting firms.

Creatas/PictureQuest

EXPLORING BEHAVIOR IN ACTION
Cathy Benko at Deloitte Consulting

Senior managers turned to Cathy Benko for help. Benko, who had just been promoted to partner, seized the opportunity and quickly realized that information technologies would continue to fundamentally change how businesses functioned. She developed a vision and specific goals for Deloitte's future consulting efforts and set out to create major changes inside the organization.

Benko identified a number of innovative tactics to speed the strategic transformation of Deloitte Consulting. These included e-Learning technologies for training and online knowledge management for client applications. Despite her efforts and the support of senior leaders, she faced opposition from some of the firm's partners. Some inside the firm simply did not see the need for major change, and certainly not rapid change. Benko, however, knew how to deal with people. She summed up her philosophy this way:

No matter where you sit in the hierarchy of an organization, you should never try to control people or force them to do things; instead lead. Using influence always gets better results. People are far more effective when they feel they have a say and are part of a team.

In the end, Benko was very successful. Deloitte Consulting caught and surpassed its consulting rivals in e-Business capabilities, and it received a number of awards for its e-Business consulting. Benko herself attracted significant attention, being named one of the industry's 25 Most Influential Consultants by *Consulting* magazine.

She was also recognized by *Women in Technology Management*.

Cathy Benko has had a very successful career at Deloitte & Touche, leading Deloitte Consulting's work in the high-technology sector, participating as a member of the small group that advises Deloitte & Touche's CEO, and functioning as the managing director of Deloitte & Touche's Women's Initiative. Benko, however, did not follow a traditional path in obtaining such lofty positions and success in an elite firm. She came from humble beginnings and had to overcome a number of obstacles.

When she was a child, her working-class father became disabled, leaving her young mother with the responsibility of providing for five children. Despite her mother's best efforts, the family struggled and periodically had to survive on public assistance (i.e., welfare). Determined to be somebody despite the tough beginning, Benko secured a scholarship to attend Katherine Gibbs Secretarial School. After the one-year program and several months

as an executive secretary, she was able to move into her company's new and evolving information technology group. Benko also attended Ramapo College during this period as a part-time student, graduating in five years with a Bachelor's degree. She then leveraged her IT experience and college degree to obtain positions of increasing challenge and responsibility, including leadership roles. Ultimately, she defied the odds by gaining acceptance to the full-time MBA program at the Harvard Business School.

Reflecting on the Harvard experience, she said this: "I was intimidated beyond belief. . . . You introduce yourself to everyone in the section— one guy is a rocket scientist, really, another is out of West Point, another, Annapolis [U.S. Military Academy and U.S. Naval Academy, respectively]. To be honest I was embarrassed. I didn't even mention Katherine Gibbs." Although quiet at first, Benko worked hard and began to see that she had a great deal to offer, even in an elite group.

Through her life experiences, Cathy Benko developed and demonstrated the drive, confidence, and abilities needed for leadership. She also developed a philosophy that helps her to this day:

> Life is not fair. Not everybody starts at the same place or has the same opportunities and support someone else might have. Don't spend time wondering why you're in the position you're in. Just get out there and do as well as you can. . . .

Sources: Deloitte & Touche, "Meet Cathleen Benko," 2007, at http://www.deloitte.com/dtt/executive_profile/0,1010,cid%3D64697%26pv%3DY,00.html; K.L. McGinn, D.M. Kolb, & C.B. Hammer, *Cathy Benko: WINning at Deloitte (A)* (Boston: Harvard Business School Publishing, 2006); WITI, "Cathy Benko," 2000, at http://www.witi.com/center/witimuseum/womeninsciencet/2000/060400.shtml; womenworking.com, "Play the Hand You're Dealt," 2002, http://www.womenworking2000.com/success/index.php?id=14.

The Strategic Importance of Leadership

Cathy Benko displayed strong leadership in dealing with a significant strategic issue. Having developed a vision as well as specific goals, she arranged for proper resources and dealt effectively with resistance. Based at least in part on her life experiences, she had the drive and abilities for success.

Although there has been some controversy about the link between leadership and organizational performance,[1] researchers often find a positive relationship. One recent study focused on the behavior of senior leaders and showed that such behavior has positive effects on a firm's performance. These effects were especially strong for firms operating in uncertain environments. The leaders who exhibited transformational behaviors had the strongest positive effect on performance in this case.[2] We discuss transformational leadership in this chapter.

In a recent survey of CEOs conducted by the Center for Creative Leadership, almost 80 percent of respondents said that leadership development is the most important factor or one of the top five factors in achieving a competitive advantage.[3] This same survey reported that leadership quality was linked to a firm's financial performance. CEOs who reported that their companies were outperforming their peers were more likely to indicate that their companies support the development of leadership skills through HR systems, that there is a shared understanding of the nature of effective leadership, and that their leadership development practices are tailored to meet individual needs.

As originally defined, *strategic leadership* corresponds to actions taken by senior leaders.[4] Certainly, the chief executive officer (CEO) and those working with him are very important given the substantial influence they have in designing the organization's strategy and overseeing its implementation. Effective implementation, however, involves all leaders in the organization. Thus, the concept of strategic leadership has been extended in recent years to leaders from all levels.

In this context, strategic leadership covers a spectrum of behaviors. For example, some have argued that strategic leadership entails developing a vision for the unit or group led.[5] Furthermore, recent work has focused on the importance of strategic leaders' managing the resources under their direction, to include financial capital but especially human capital and valuable interpersonal relationships (social capital). Particular emphasis has been placed on the importance of providing effective leadership that enhances associates' productivity (that is, managing human capital well) and building and maintaining important relationships both within the organization (with associates and other leaders) and externally (for example, with alliance partners). Those who manage this human and social capital well are the most effective leaders.[6] Based on this work, we assert that leadership is necessary in building and maintaining a high-involvement, high-performance workforce.

In this chapter, we examine the concept of leadership. We begin by describing its fundamental nature. Next, we address three types of theories that have historically been used to explain leadership effectiveness: trait theories, behavioral theories, and contingency approaches. We then focus on the most recent developments in leadership theory: the transformational and charismatic approaches. We close with a discussion of several additional topics of current relevance.

After reading this chapter, you should be able to:

1. Define *leadership* and distinguish between formal and informal leaders.

2. Explain the trait concept of leadership.

3. Describe major behavioral theories of leadership and compare and contrast them.

4. Explain contingency theories of leadership and how they relate leadership effectiveness to situational factors.

5. Describe transformational leaders.

6. Discuss topics of current relevance, including leader–member exchange, servant leadership, gender effects on leadership, and global differences in leadership.

The Nature of Leadership

We usually attribute the success or failure of an organization to its leaders. When a company or an athletic team is successful, for example, it is the president or coach who receives much of the credit. These individuals are also subject to criticism if the company does not meet its goals or the team has a losing season.

Leadership has been defined in many ways, but most definitions emphasize the concept of influence. Here, we define **leadership** as the process of providing general direction and influencing individuals or groups to achieve goals.[7] A leader can be formally designated by the organization (formal leader) or can provide leadership without such formal designation (informal leader).

Leaders can do many things to provide direction and to influence people. These activities include providing information, resolving conflicts, motivating followers, anticipating problems, developing mutual respect among group members, and coordinating group activities and efforts.[8] Warren Bennis, who has studied leadership for a number of years, suggests that effective leaders are concerned with "doing the right things" rather than "doing things right."[9] The right things, according to Bennis, include the following:

- Creating and communicating a vision of what the organization should be
- Communicating with and gaining the support of multiple constituencies
- Persisting in the desired direction even under bad conditions
- Creating the appropriate culture and obtaining the desired results[12]

From this definition of leadership, company presidents and many managers can be identified as leaders. Coaches, basketball captains, and football quarterbacks are leaders. Army drill sergeants are leaders. The person who organizes a social gathering is also a leader. In other words, many people serve as either formal or informal leaders, and almost anyone can act as a leader. However, some positions provide more opportunities to display leadership behavior than others. On the other hand, not all people in positions that call for leader behavior (e.g., managerial positions) act as leaders. For example, a manager who merely follows rules and fails to provide direction to and support for his associates is not acting as a leader.

> **leadership**
> The process of providing general direction and influencing individuals or groups to achieve goals.

Trait Theory of Leadership

At one time, it was thought that some people were born with certain traits that made them effective leaders, whereas others were born without leadership traits.[10] The list of traits generated by this early research was substantial (in the thousands) and included physical characteristics (such as height and appearance), personality characteristics (such as self-esteem and dominance), and abilities (such as intelligence and verbal fluency). Additional traits that were thought to characterize leaders are presented in Exhibit 8-1.

Exhibit 8-1	Traits Associated with Leadership		
Energy	Achievement drive	Initiative	Sense of humor
Appearance	Adaptability	Insightfulness	Tolerance for stress
Intelligence	Aggressiveness	Integrity	Interpersonal skill
Judgment	Enthusiasm	Persistence	Prestige
Verbal fluency	Extroversion	Self-confidence	Tact

Source: Based on A.C. Jago, "Leadership: Perspectives in Theory and Research," *Management Science* 28, 1982:315–336.

Early trait research has been criticized for several reasons. For example, the methodology used to identify the traits was poor. Investigators simply generated lists of traits by loosely comparing people who were labeled as leaders with those who were not—without actually measuring traits or testing for meaningful differences. A second criticism is that the list of traits associated with leadership grew so large it became meaningless. A third criticism is that the results of this research were inconsistent—different leaders possessed different traits. Finally, no leadership trait was found to relate consistently to unit or organizational performance, and different situations seemed to require different traits.[11] Although famous leaders (for example, Abraham Lincoln, Gandhi, Martin Luther King) had "special" traits, a close examination reveals differences among them. Numerous studies conducted to determine the traits that relate to effective leadership found that not all leaders possess the same traits.

Nevertheless, the notion of leadership traits has been revived in recent years.[12] Research has demonstrated that leaders usually *are* different from other people. It is now believed, however, that many of the traits (or characteristics) that are possessed by leaders can be learned or developed (i.e., leaders are not born but are made). Moreover, possessing leadership traits is not enough to make a person a successful leader; he must also take actions necessary for strong leadership.[13] The measurement and understanding of personal characteristics have improved since the early twentieth century, and modern researchers have proposed that important leadership traits can be categorized as follows:[14]

- *Drive.* Drive refers to the amount of ambition, persistence, tenacity, and initiative that people possess. Leaders must have the energy and will to continue to act during turbulent and stressful times. Drive and ambition are also important to a leader's ability to create a vision and engage in behavior to achieve the vision.

- *Leadership motivation.* Leadership motivation refers to a person's desire to lead, influence others, assume responsibility, and gain power. We must distinguish here between two types of motives. Leaders can have a *socialized power motive* whereby they use power to achieve goals that are in the organization's best interests or in the best interests of followers. In contrast, a leader with a *personalized power motive* desires power solely for the sake of having power over others.

- *Integrity.* Leaders with honesty are truthful and maintain consistency between what they say and what they do. Followers and others in the organization are not likely to trust a leader who does not have these characteristics.

- *Self-confidence.* Leaders must be confident in their actions and show that confidence to others. People who are high in self-confidence are also able to learn from their mistakes, react positively to stress, and remain even-tempered and display appropriate emotions.

- *Cognitive ability.* Leaders who possess a high degree of intelligence are better able to process complex information and deal with changing environments.

- *Knowledge of the domain.* Knowledge of the domain in which they are engaged allows leaders to make better decisions, anticipate future problems, and understand the implications of their actions.

William Bratton, former chief of police for New York City and currently head of the Los Angeles Police Department, exhibits these traits. As discussed in the *Experiencing Strategic Organizational Behavior* feature, he has leveraged them to create positive outcomes in the areas of enhanced public safety and reduced crime. He also has exhibited the characteristics of strategic leaders that were explained earlier. For example, he engaged in strategic planning with the NYPD and effectively implemented the strategy developed from this process. To implement the strategy, he decentralized authority to use the leaders throughout the police department and used effective communication processes in the organization. He used his knowledge of policing to have a strong positive effect on the police department's performance.

EXPERIENCING STRATEGIC ORGANIZATIONAL BEHAVIOR

Reforming a "Rotten Apple"

William Bratton was appointed police commissioner of New York City in 1994 at perhaps one of the worst times in the history of the huge New York City Police Department (NYPD). New York City had experienced three decades of increasing crime rates, and some critics claimed that there was nothing the police department could do about it. Bratton, who had previously worked his way up through the Boston Police Department, faced a challenge that had been unresolved by his predecessors, and he had to handle the problem without an increase in resources.

AFP/Getty Images

To say that William Bratton exhibited successful leadership would be an understatement. Within two years, his leadership of the NYPD made New York City one of the safest large cities in the world. Felony crimes fell 39 percent, theft decreased 35 percent, and murders dropped 50 percent. Public confidence in the police department, reported in Gallup polls, soared from 37 percent to 73 percent. Not only was the NYPD effective in fighting crime, but police officers were also happier with their jobs, reporting record levels of job satisfaction. In October 2002, Bratton was appointed police commissioner of the beleaguered Los Angeles Police Department. Statistics suggest that Bratton is currently achieving results there similar to those he achieved in New York City.

Does William Bratton exhibit the leadership traits suggested by modern research? Yes, he does:

Drive. Bratton's nickname was "cannonball," which provides an idea of his drive and ambition. Bratton shows passion for his vision that police should be held accountable for reducing crime and that success should be measured by how much crime, disorder, and fear are reduced.

Leadership motivation. From his early years in the Boston Police Department, Bratton expressed the desire to lead it some day. When he was leaving the New York City commissioner's job, he entertained the idea of running for mayor.

Integrity. Bratton's actions support his words. Even in the face of opposition from political contingencies and civil liberties groups, he sticks to his commitment to police accountability and zero-tolerance policies. Bratton does not tailor his messages to his audiences. For example, he states,

"One of the things people like about me is that when I'm talking to a black audience I'm not talking any different than when I'm talking to a white audience." Furthermore, he is tough on corruption, firing officers who are dishonest.

Self-confidence. Bratton always displays self-confidence, particularly in the face of adversity. His self-confidence has sometimes been interpreted as arrogance; however, over his career he has learned the difference between the two.

Cognitive ability. One of the most telling indications of Bratton's strong cognitive ability is the strategic manner in which he approaches managing the country's largest police departments.

Knowledge of the domain. Bratton worked his way through the ranks of the Boston Police Department, gaining knowledge about how policing works from the bottom up. Even as the NYPD police commissioner, he would ride the subway to work so that he had a better understanding of what was going on in the street.

Beyond the traits listed above, Bratton undertook a number of specific actions in New York that led to success and to his being named "Police Executive of the 20th Century" (and having his photo on the cover of *Time*). His success has been attributed to four major changes:

1. He decentralized the police department, giving greater authority and autonomy to precinct commanders. Instead of having to deal with bureaucratic policies that prevented them from combating crime, they were able to deal more aggressively and decisively with it and do so with more understanding, involvement, and commitment from the communities in which they served.

2. He engaged in systematic strategic planning to analyze crime patterns and use of resources. The end result was more efficient use of resources. More police officers were assigned to higher-crime areas, and more focus was placed on common and serious crimes. Bratton reduced levels of management, improved internal and external communication, developed trust and rapport within communities, improved data collection and analysis of crime statistics, heightened accountability on the part of police officers, and rewarded positive results. He has referred to this strategy as "reengineering" the NYPD. He also worked to create an environment where officers were encouraged to provide suggestions and recommendations—many of which were followed.

3. During his leadership, the *Compstat process* was developed. This process uses computerized crime statistics, electronic maps, and management meetings where precinct heads are held accountable (and rewarded or reprimanded) for the crime activity in their precincts.

4. He instigated a controversial policy known as *zero-tolerance* crime fighting. Police officers were required to arrest people for seemingly petty crimes such as graffiti writing, panhandling, and minor vandalism. The philosophy behind this policy is that if a neighborhood is plagued by petty crime, it appears to be out of control—reducing the felt presence of the police and making criminals feel freer to commit more serious crimes.

Although there are critics of Bratton's zero-tolerance style of policing and questions about the real effect his strategy had on the rapid decline of crime in New York City, the fact remains that crime was reduced, police officer satisfaction improved, and police relations with the communities they served were strengthened. In Los Angeles, success has also followed the hiring of Bratton. Few doubt that he is an effective leader.

Sources: W.J. Bratton, & W. Andrews, "What We've Learned about Policing," *City Journal* 9, no. 2 (1999): 14–20; W.J. Bratton, & P. Knobler, *The Turnaround: How America's Top Cop Reversed the Crime Epidemic* (New York: Random House, 1998); W.C. Kim, & R. Mauborgne, "Tipping Point Leadership," *Harvard Business Review* 81, no. 4 (2003): 60–69; P. McGreevey, "Bratton Earns A's Thus Far," *Los Angeles Times*, Sept. 18, 2006, p. B.1; P. McGreevey, "Lots of Ham at Chief's Charity Roast," *Los Angeles Times*, Mar. 16, 2007, p. B.3; J. Newfield & M. Jacobson, "An Interview with William Bratton," 2000, at http://www.tikkun.org/magazine/index.cfm/action/tikkun/issues/tik0007/article/000727.html; "William J. Bratton—Police Executive of the 20th Century," at http://www.policetalk.com/bratton.html.

Most studies of leaders have concluded that the traits focused on here are important. Other traits that have been identified as important include flexibility and creativity, especially because of the importance of innovation in today's world. As noted, however, although specific traits may be necessary for a person to be an effective leader, ultimately she must take action to be successful.

Before ending this discussion of trait theory, it is important to mention charisma. Think of famous (or infamous) leaders such as John F. Kennedy, Adolf Hitler, Winston Churchill, Eleanor Roosevelt, Martin Luther King, Ronald Reagan, and Barbara Jordan. Many people believe that all of these individuals possessed charisma. Charisma is usually defined by the effect it has on followers. Charismatic leaders inspire their followers to change their needs and values, follow visionary quests, and sacrifice their own personal interests for the good of the cause. Traditionally, charisma was thought of as a personality trait. However, conceptualizing charisma as a simple personality trait has been subject to criticism. In addition, charisma has been difficult to define precisely, and different leaders have displayed charisma in different ways.

The notion of charisma has become popular again in modern theories. Charismatic leadership, though possibly based in personality to some degree, can be learned over time (at least partially) and is ultimately reflected in a leader's behavior. Thus, it is best described by the leader's behavior and her relationship to followers.[15] We discuss charisma in more detail later in this chapter in the section on transformational leadership.

Behavioral Theories of Leadership

In response to the heavy reliance in the earlier part of the twentieth century on trait theory and the notion that leaders are born and not developed, large research projects were conducted at the University of Michigan and the Ohio State University to examine what leaders actually did to be effective. This research concentrated largely on leadership style. Although both managerial thought and scholarly investigation have progressed beyond these two lines of research, this work provided the foundation for more contemporary theories of leadership, such as the transformational leadership approach discussed later in the chapter.

University of Michigan Studies

job-centered leadership style
A behavioral leadership style that emphasizes employee tasks and the methods used to accomplish them.

employee-centered leadership style
A behavioral leadership style that emphasizes employees' personal needs and the development of interpersonal relationships.

The leadership studies at the Institute for Social Research of the University of Michigan were conducted by such scholars as Rensis Likert, Daniel Katz, and Robert Kahn. The studies involved both private and public organizations, including businesses from numerous industry groups. These studies examined two distinct styles of leader behavior: the **job-centered** and **employee-centered styles.**[16]

The job-centered leader emphasizes employee tasks and the methods used to accomplish them. A job-centered leader supervises individuals closely (provides instructions, checks frequently on performance) and sometimes behaves in a punitive manner toward them. Alternatively, an employee-centered leader emphasizes employees' personal needs and the development of interpersonal relationships. An employee-centered leader frequently delegates decision-making authority and responsibility to others and provides a supportive environment, encouraging interpersonal communication.

To measure these styles, leaders completed a questionnaire consisting of a number of items. Based on their responses, they were classified as either job-centered or employee-centered. The effectiveness of these leaders was then examined by measuring factors such as the productivity, job satisfaction, absenteeism, and turnover rates of those being led.

The results of these studies were inconsistent. In some cases, units whose leaders used a job-centered style were more productive, whereas in other cases units with employee-centered leaders were more productive. The job-centered style, however, resulted in less productive units more often than did the employee-centered style. In addition, even when productivity was high, employees with job-centered leaders had lower levels of job satisfaction than those who worked with employee-centered leaders. Therefore, many of the researchers involved in the studies concluded that the employee-centered style was more effective.

The situations in which job-centered leaders were effective could not be well explained. In addition to style, then, other factors seemed to affect a leader's effectiveness. In addition, the leadership style examined in these studies was unidimensional. A leader was classified as either job-centered or employee-centered but could not possess characteristics of both styles. This oversimplification no doubt affected the results of the research.

If we consider the case of Police Commissioner William Bratton, discussed in the earlier *Experiencing Strategic Organizational Behavior* feature, it is clear why the unidimensional view of leadership behavior is problematic. Although Bratton displayed a job-centered style by carefully monitoring police officers' performance and providing rewards or punishment based on that performance, he also demonstrated an employee-centered style by decentralizing authority and opening communication channels within the department.

Ohio State University Studies

consideration
A behavioral leadership style demonstrated by leaders who express friendship, develop mutual trust and respect, and have strong interpersonal relationships with those being led.

At around the same time that the University of Michigan studies were being conducted, leadership studies were underway at Ohio State University led by such scholars as Ralph Stogdill and Edwin Fleishman. These studies emphasized a two-dimensional view of leaders' behavior. The two independent dimensions of leadership behavior were consideration and initiating structure.

Consideration refers to behavior that expresses friendship, develops mutual trust and respect, and builds strong interpersonal relationships with those being

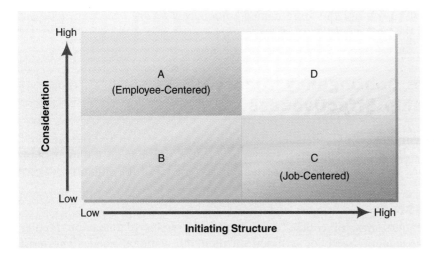

Exhibit 8-2
Comparison of
Consideration and
Initiating Structure with
Employee-Centered
and Job-Centered
Concepts

led. Leaders who exhibit consideration offer support to their employees, use employees' ideas, and frequently allow them to participate in decisions.

Initiating structure indicates behavior that establishes well-defined patterns of organization and communication, defines procedures, and delineates the leader's relationships with those being led. Leaders who initiate structure emphasize goals and deadlines and ensure that employees are assigned tasks and know what performance is expected from them.[17]

These two concepts are similar to the ones used in the Michigan studies—consideration is similar to employee-centered leadership, while initiating structure is similar to job-centered leadership. The important difference is that leaders can exhibit characteristics of both. Thus, an individual could be classified in any of the four cells shown in Exhibit 8-2, whereas the Michigan approach artificially forced a person to be classified in either Cell A or Cell C.

Various studies have examined the linkage between these two dimensions of leader behavior and effectiveness. Results of early research suggested that leaders high in both consideration and initiating structure were more effective than other leaders. However, further studies showed that the relationship between leaders' behavior and their effectiveness, as measured by such factors as employee productivity, satisfaction, and turnover, was more complicated. In addition, each of the leader-behavior dimensions might affect various outcomes in different ways (consideration seems to have stronger effects on satisfaction, for example, whereas structuring might have stronger effects on productivity). Recently, a review of studies on consideration and initiating structure showed that the basic ideas of the Ohio State studies still apply.[18] Newer theories of leadership, however, present a more complex and complete view.

> **initiating structure**
> A behavioral leadership style demonstrated by leaders who establish well-defined patterns of organization and communication, define procedures, and delineate their relationships with those being led.

Contingency Theories of Leadership

Studies of trait and behavioral leadership concepts hinted at the role of situational factors in the relationship between leaders' behavior and effectiveness. Those studies led other researchers to conclude that effective leadership practices are "contingent" on the situation. Contingency leadership concepts were then developed.

The two best known are the aptly named *contingency theory of leadership effectiveness* and the *path–goal theory of leadership*.

Fiedler's Contingency Theory of Leadership Effectiveness

The **contingency theory of leadership effectiveness** was developed by Fred Fiedler.[19] According to this theory, the effectiveness of a leader depends on the interaction of the leader's behavioral style with certain characteristics of the situation.

> **contingency theory of leadership effectiveness**
> A theory of leadership that suggests the effectiveness of a leader depends on the interaction of his style of behavior with certain characteristics of the situation.

LEADER STYLE

Different leaders may, of course, exhibit different styles of behavior. Fiedler explains that leaders' behavior is based on their motivational needs. The most important needs of leaders, according to Fiedler, are interpersonal-relationship needs and task-achievement needs. As you can see, these are similar to the concepts used in the Michigan and Ohio State studies.

The relative importance of these needs to a leader determines the leader's style. In determining which need is strongest, the esteem for the least-preferred co-worker (LPC) must be assessed.[20] If leaders describe their least-preferred co-worker mainly in negative terms (uncooperative, unfriendly), they obtain a low LPC score, which indicates a task-oriented leader whose task-achievement needs have first priority. Leaders who describe their least-preferred co-worker in positive terms (cooperative, friendly) receive a high LPC score. A high score indicates that the leader has a relationship-oriented style where interpersonal relationship needs have first priority.

Perhaps you have had a supervisor who focused mainly on the work to be done and did not engage in much personal interaction with those being led. This supervisor would probably have a low LPC score and be considered task oriented. Contrast this person with another leader you have known who really cared about others and put a great deal of effort into maintaining positive relationships with everyone. This leader would have a high LPC score and be considered relationship oriented. Which of these styles is most effective? That depends on situational characteristics.

SITUATIONAL CHARACTERISTICS

In some situations, leaders have more control over the work environment. In the context of Fiedler's contingency theory, this means that leaders can influence events in a straightforward way and work systematically toward desired outcomes. Important situational characteristics that determine a leader's level of control include leader–member relations, task structure, and position power.

> **leader–member relations**
> The degree to which a leader is respected, is accepted as a leader, and has friendly interpersonal relations.

> **task structure**
> The degree to which tasks can be broken down into easily understood steps or parts.

- **Leader–member relations** correspond to the degree to which a leader is respected, is accepted as a leader, and has friendly interpersonal relations. When a leader has the respect and admiration of those who are led, he tends to have more control over the situation. He can more easily influence events and outcomes. This is the most important of the three situational variables.

- **Task structure** is the degree to which tasks can be broken down into easily understood steps or parts. When a leader deals with structured tasks, she has more control over the situation. She can more easily influence events and drive for goal achievement.

- **Position power** is the degree to which a leader can reward, punish, promote, or demote individuals in the unit or organization. When a leader can reward and punish, he has greater control and influence over the situation.[21]

> **position power**
> The degree to which a leader can reward, punish, promote, or demote individuals in the unit or organization.

SITUATIONAL FAVORABLENESS

The amount of control a leader has determines the favorableness of the situation. In the most favorable situations, leader–member relations are good, the tasks are highly structured, and the leader has strong position power. In the least favorable situations, leader–member relations are poor, tasks are unstructured, and leader position power is weak. Situations may, of course, vary between these two extremes.

Consider leading a project team for this course. Suppose that you have the respect of team members, you are engaged in a set of tasks that can be easily managed, and you are able to assign participation grades. This represents a favorable situation in which you, as leader, could easily influence events and outcomes. Now suppose instead that you do not get along with members of the team, you are engaged in a set of tasks that are difficult to manage, and you have no power to reward or punish team members. This would be a very unfavorable situation in which you would have much less influence over events and probably would have more difficulty working toward goal achievement.

LEADERSHIP EFFECTIVENESS

The leader's effectiveness is determined by the interaction of the leader's style of behavior and the favorableness of the situational characteristics. The leader's effectiveness is judged by the performance of the group being led. The relationship between the leader's effectiveness, her style of behavior, and situational favorableness is shown in Exhibit 8-3.

Fiedler's research on the contingency model has shown that task-oriented leaders are more effective in highly favorable (I, II, III) and highly unfavorable situations (VII, VIII), whereas relationship-oriented leaders are more effective in situations

Effective Leader	Task Oriented (Low LPC)			Relationship Oriented (High LPC)			Task Oriented (Low LPC)	
Situational Favorableness	Favorable			Intermediate Favorableness			Unfavorable	
Leader–Member Relations	Good	Good	Good	Good	Poor	Poor	Poor	Poor
Task Structure	Structured	Structured	Un-structured	Un-structured	Structured	Structured	Un-structured	Un-structured
Leader Position Power	Strong	Weak	Strong	Weak	Strong	Weak	Strong	Weak
Situation	I	II	III	IV	V	VI	VII	VIII

Exhibit 8-3   Fiedler's Contingency Model of Leadership Effectiveness

of intermediate favorableness (IV, V, VI). More specifically, the correlations between LPC scores and group performance in favorable and unfavorable situations is negative (performance was higher when LPC was lower). The correlation between LPC and group performance in situations of intermediate favorableness is positive (performance was higher when LPC was higher).[22]

Fiedler has also found that leaders may act differently in different situations. Relationship-oriented (high-LPC) leaders often display task-oriented behaviors under highly favorable conditions and display relationship-oriented behaviors in situations that are unfavorable or intermediate in favorableness. Conversely, task-oriented (low-LPC) leaders often display task-oriented behaviors in situations that are unfavorable or intermediate in favorableness but display relationship-oriented behaviors in favorable situations.[23] These findings help to explain why various leadership styles are effective in different situations.

Favorable situations do not require leaders to provide strong oversight or frequent task-focused inputs. Tasks can be accomplished with less direction from the leader. The task-oriented (low-LPC) leader's interpersonal needs are activated in favorable situations; however, the relationship-oriented (high-LPC) leader's needs for task achievement are activated in favorable situations. The low-LPC leader is thus more effective in favorable situations because they require leaders to provide encouragement, support, and interpersonal trust (relationship-oriented behavior).

Unfavorable situations require stronger oversight and more task-focused inputs. In such situations, the high-LPC leader's natural needs for interpersonal relations are activated, which creates difficulties. On the other hand, the low-LPC leader's natural needs for task achievement are activated. This matches the requirements of the situation.

Situations of intermediate favorableness provide neither of these extremes. Where the task is unstructured, a naturally relationship-oriented leader may be necessary to get the group to use its creativity to solve problems. Where leader–member relations are poor, a naturally relationship-oriented leader may be better able to overcome the negative relations with the group and build trust.

According to the contingency model, then, a leader cannot be effective in all situations by exhibiting only one leadership style. Fiedler believes that individuals should be matched with situations in which their leadership styles are likely to be most effective. Lacking the ability to reassign leaders, the characteristics of the situation should be changed to provide an effective match between the leader's style and the favorableness of the situation.

Fiedler conducted extensive research on the contingency model, and most of his research provided support for it.[24] Others, however, have provided mixed support.[25] One issue is the simplicity of the model. It incorporates only two narrow behavioral styles (task and relationship). Moreover, it does not explain outcomes for the middle-LPC leader. Interestingly, some research suggests that the middle-LPC leader may be more effective than either the high- or low-LPC leader. Because the middle-LPC leader is more flexible and is not constrained by one orientation, she may better adapt to multiple situations.[26] Another concern has been the validity of the LPC measure. Critics believe that other measures of leader behavior are more reliable and valid.[27] A final concern has been the model's failure to explicitly address followers' satisfaction with leaders. Some research, however, has found the model to predict follower satisfaction.[28]

These criticisms do not reduce the importance of Fiedler's model. It represents one of the first comprehensive attempts to explain a complex subject. In addition, a significant amount of research supports the model, and researchers continue to investigate and attempt to extend it.

The Path–Goal Leadership Theory

The **path–goal leadership theory** was originally developed by Martin Evans[29] and Robert House.[30] The theory, which is based on expectancy concepts from the study of motivation, emphasizes a leader's effects on subordinates' goals and the paths used to achieve those goals. It provides a bridge to the modern study of leadership.

> **path–goal leadership theory** A theory of leadership based on expectancy concepts from the study of motivation, which suggests that leader effectiveness depends on the degree to which a leader enhances the performance expectancies and valences of her subordinates.

Recall from Chapter 6 that *expectancies* relate to the perceived probability of goal attainment and *valences* correspond to the value or attractiveness of goal attainment. Leadership can affect employees' expectancies and valences in several ways:

- Assigning individuals to tasks for which goal attainment is personally valuable (valence). In other words, leaders can assign individuals to tasks that they will find rewarding.

- Supporting employees' efforts to achieve task goals (effort → performance expectancy). Effective leaders provide individuals with opportunities (through encouragement, training, and technical support, for example) that allow them to gain confidence that their efforts on a task will lead to goal attainment.

- Tying extrinsic rewards (pay raise, recognition, promotion) to accomplishment of task goals (performance → reward instrumentality).

These actions on the part of leaders increase effectiveness; employees achieve higher performance because of their increased motivation on the job. It follows that effectiveness is enhanced in situations that allow leaders to exercise these behaviors.

LEADER BEHAVIOR AND SITUATIONAL FACTORS

The path–goal leadership theory focuses on several types of leader behavior and situational factors. The main types of leader behavior are as follows:[31]

- **Directive leadership** behavior is characterized by implementing guidelines, providing information on what is expected, setting definite performance standards, and ensuring individuals follow the rules.

- **Supportive leadership** behavior is characterized by being friendly and showing concern for well-being, welfare, and needs.

- **Achievement-oriented leadership** behavior is characterized by setting challenging goals and seeking to improve performance.

- **Participative leadership** behavior is characterized by sharing information, consulting with those who are led, and emphasizing group decision making.

> **directive leadership** Leadership behavior characterized by implementing guidelines, providing information on what is expected, setting definite performance standards, and ensuring individuals follow rules.

> **supportive leadership** Leadership behavior characterized by friendliness and concern for individuals' well-being, welfare, and needs.

> **achievement-oriented leadership** Leadership behavior characterized by setting challenging goals and seeking to improve performance.

> **participative leadership** Leadership behavior characterized by sharing information, consulting with those who are led, and emphasizing group decision making.

Directive leadership and achievement-oriented leadership are related to the earlier concepts of job-centered style (Michigan studies), initiating structure (Ohio State studies), and task orientation (Fiedler's Contingency Theory of Leadership Effectiveness). Supportive leadership and participative leadership are related to the concepts of employee-centered style (Michigan studies), consideration (Ohio State studies), and interpersonal orientation (Fiedler's Contingency Theory of Leadership Effectiveness).

There are two sets of situational factors: subordinates' characteristics (such as needs, locus of control, experience, and ability) and characteristics of the work environment (such as task structure, interpersonal relations in the group, role conflict, and role clarity). The effectiveness of various leader behaviors depends on these situational factors.

INTERACTION OF LEADER BEHAVIOR AND SITUATIONAL FACTORS

Path–goal theory specifies a number of interactions between leader behavior and situational factors, with these interactions influencing outcomes. Researchers, however, have provided only mixed support for the theory,[32] with some studies supporting it and others failing to support it.[33] Relationships that appear to be valid are listed below:

- Associates with an internal locus of control (who believe outcomes are a function of their own behavior) are likely to be more satisfied with a participative leader. Individuals with an external locus of control (who believe outcomes are a function of chance or luck) are more likely to be effective with directive leaders.

- Associates who have a high need for affiliation are likely to be more satisfied with a supportive leader. Supportive leaders fulfill their needs for close personal relationships.

- Associates with a high need for security probably will be more satisfied with a directive leader who reduces uncertainty by providing clear rules and procedures.

- Supportive and participative leaders are more likely to increase satisfaction on highly structured tasks. Because the tasks are routine, little direction is necessary. Directive leaders are more likely to increase satisfaction on unstructured tasks, where individuals (particularly those with less experience and ability) often need help in clarifying an ambiguous task situation.

- Directive leadership is often more effective on unstructured tasks because it can increase an employee's expectation that effort will lead to task goal accomplishment (particularly when employees have less experience and/or ability). Supportive leadership is often more effective on structured tasks because it can increase a person's expectation that accomplishing goals will lead to extrinsic rewards.[34]

- Associates with a high need for growth who are working on a complex task probably perform better with a participative or achievement-oriented leader. Because they are intrinsically motivated, they appreciate information and difficult goals that help in achievement. Individuals with a low growth need strength working on a complex task perform better with directive leaders.[35]

A summary of these interactions involving leader behavior and situational factors is presented in Exhibit 8-4. Although any number of situational factors could play roles in leader effectiveness,[36] those discussed here have been shown to be important.

Conclusions Regarding Contingency Theories

Contingency leadership concepts are more difficult to apply than the trait or behavioral concepts, because they are more complex. But when appropriately used, they are more practical and should therefore lead to higher levels of effectiveness. In essence, they require that leaders correctly diagnose a situation and identify the behaviors that are most appropriate (those that best fit the characteristics of the situation). Also, contingency theories imply that a leader might need to change her approach over time. Among those being led, abilities and experience levels change, as do other features of the situation, suggesting that leaders must change their approaches.[37] Finally, path–goal theory implies that leaders

| Situational Factors | | |
Subordinate Characteristics	Characteristics of the Work Environment	Effective Leader Behaviors
Internal Locus of Control		Participative
External Locus of Control		Directive
High Need for Affiliation		Supportive
High Need for Security		Directive
	Structured Task	Supportive
	Unstructured Task	Directive
High Growth Need Strength	Complex Task	Participative Achievement Oriented
Low Growth Need Strength	Complex Task	Directive
High Growth Need Strength	Simple Task	Supportive
Low Growth Need Strength	Simple Task	Supportive
	High Role Clarity and Low Role Conflict	Upward Influencing and Contingent

Exhibit 8-4
Interaction of Leader Behavior and Situational Factors

might need to treat individuals differently within the same unit or organization.[38] If individuals in a unit are different, then leaders can benefit from approaching them in different ways, at least to some degree.

In order to be successful, leaders must act in ways that fit the situation in which they find themselves. Phil Jackson, one of basketball's great coaches, leads in a way that fits his situation. His story is presented in the *Managerial Advice* feature.

MANAGERIAL ADVICE

Phil Jackson and Leadership Success

Phil Jackson's success as a coach in the National Basketball Association (NBA) is legendary. He has won nine championships, six with the Chicago Bulls and three with the Los Angeles Lakers. He has more playoff victories than anyone else in the history of the league, and has the best winning percentage in playoff games. He also sports the best winning percentage in regular season games.

Some have suggested that Jackson's success is due only to having great players, such as Michael Jordan, Kobe Bryant, and Shaquille O'Neal. But the facts do not support this. In both Chicago and Los Angeles, the great players did not win championships until Jackson arrived.

So what makes him special? One answer to this question is his philosophy of leadership. His philosophy, which has been influenced by Zen Buddhism, embraces humility, respect for others, and a belief in the interconnected nature of humankind. Jackson said this:

> In terms of leadership, this means treating everyone with the same care and respect you give yourself—and trying to understand their reality without judgment. When we can do that, we begin to see that we all share human struggles, desires, and dreams.

In essence, Jackson applies a philosophy that suggests less directive leadership, which fits the situation he faces in the NBA. His players typically have strong ability,

©AP/Wide World Photos

a great deal of experience, and strong growth needs in terms of wanting to achieve on the basketball court. Additionally, the relevant tasks are relatively structured. Under these conditions, directive leadership behaviors would be less desirable, and Jackson is known to be one of the least directive coaches during basketball games.

In Los Angeles, Jackson has helped his star player, Kobe Bryant, rebuild respect with his fellow players. Although tensions continue to arise from time to time, Jackson has helped to make the situation better. He did so by advising Bryant to exhibit fewer directive behaviors in his own leadership. In Bryant's words:

> Sometimes it's best if you just step back and kind of guide them a little bit and allow them to learn on their own. Very subtle. That's . . . one of the things he taught me this summer, is how to do that.

Within his overall approach, Jackson tailors his leadership to circumstances. If players are less experienced or have growth needs that are dormant, he is more directive. His goal is to be "invisible," but he would not advise such invisibility in all situations.

Sources: J.A. Adande, "Kobe, Phil Are on the Same Page," *Los Angeles Times,* Nov. 19, 2006, p. D.5; M. Bresnahan, "Leader Counsel," *Los Angeles Times,* Feb. 20, 2007, p. D.1; D. Dupree, "Phil Jackson: Zen and Now," USA Today.com, June 6, 2002, at http://www.usatoday.com/sports/nba/02playoffs/2002-06-05-cover-jackson.htm; D. Ferrell, "Address Him as Dr. Phil," SpokesmanRevew.com, May 15, 2004, at http://www.spokesmanreview.com/tools/story_pf.asp?ID=6669; P. Jackson, & H. Delehanty, "Sacred Hoops" (New York: Hyperion, 1995); NBA Encyclopedia, "All-Time Playoffs," 2006, at http://www.nba.com/history/records/playoff_victories_coaches.html; NBA Encyclopedia, "All-Time Regular Season Victories-Coaches," 2006, at http://www.nba.com/history/records/victories_coaches.html; J.P. Pfeffer, & R.I. Sutton, *"Hard Facts, Dangerous Half-truths, & Total Nonsense"* (Boston: Harvard Business School Press, 2006).

Although important and useful, contingency theories of leadership have received less attention in recent years. The dynamic business environment and rapid technological advancements of the past two decades have combined to create the need for a new approach to leadership.[39] We next turn to one of the most significant contemporary paradigms for leadership.

Transformational Leadership

The need for organizations to change and adapt rapidly while creating a high-performance workforce has become increasingly apparent in recent years. To stay competitive, business leaders must be able to inspire organizational members to go beyond their ordinary task requirements and exert extraordinary levels of effort and adaptability. As a result, new approaches to leadership have emerged.

transactional leadership
A leadership approach that is based on the exchange relationship between followers and leaders. Transactional leadership is characterized by contingent reward behavior and active management-by-exception behavior.

Transactional leadership[40] provides a useful starting point in this discussion. This type of leadership focuses primarily on leaders' exchange relationships with followers—that is, the degree to which leaders provide what followers want in response to good performance. Followers comply with leaders' wishes to gain desired rewards. Transactional leaders have the following four specific characteristics:[41]

1. They understand what followers want from their work, and they attempt to deliver these rewards if deserved.

2. They clarify the links between performance and rewards.

3. They exchange rewards and promises of rewards for specified performance.

4. They only respond to interests of followers if performance is satisfactory.

Transactional leaders are characterized by contingent reward behavior and active management-by-exception behavior.[42] *Contingent reward behavior* involves clarifying performance expectations and rewarding followers when those expectations are met. *Active management-by-exception* behavior is demonstrated when a leader clarifies minimal performance standards and punishes those who do not perform up to the standards. Transactional leaders consistently monitor the performance of their followers.

In contrast to this exchange-based approach, **transformational leadership** involves motivating followers to do more than expected, to continuously develop and grow, to increase their level of self-confidence, and to place the interests of the unit or organization before their own.[43] Transformational leaders do the following three things:

> **transformational leadership** A leadership approach that involves motivating followers to do more than expected, to continuously develop and grow, to increase self-confidence, and to place the interests of the unit or organization before their own. Transformational leadership involves charisma, intellectual stimulation, and individual consideration.

1. They increase followers' awareness of the importance of pursing a vision or mission, and the strategy required.

2. They encourage followers to place the interests of the unit, organization, or larger collective before their own personal interests.

3. They raise followers' aspirations so that they continuously try to develop and improve themselves while striving for higher levels of accomplishment.

Transformational leadership results from both personal characteristics and specific actions. Three characteristics have been identified with transformational leaders: charisma, intellectual stimulation, and individual consideration.[44] **Charisma** refers specifically to the leader's ability to inspire emotion and passion in his followers and to cause them to identify with the leader.[45] A charismatic leader displays confidence, goes beyond self-interest, communicates and lives up to organizational values, draws attention to the purpose of the organization or mission, and speaks optimistically and enthusiastically. The second characteristic, *intellectual stimulation,* is the leader's ability to increase the followers' focus on problems and to develop new ways of addressing them. Leaders who provide intellectual stimulation reexamine assumptions, seek out different views, and try to be innovative. Finally, *individual consideration* involves supporting and developing followers so that they become self-confident and desire to improve their performance. Leaders showing individual consideration provide individualized attention to followers, focus on followers' strengths, and act as teachers and coaches.

> **charisma** A leader ability to inspire emotion and passion in his followers and to cause them to identify with the leader.

A great deal of research has focused on how transformational leaders behave—that is, what they do to become transformational leaders. The list of common behaviors includes the following:[46]

- Transformational leaders articulate a clear and appealing vision, which is beneficial to the followers.
- They communicate the vision through personal action, emotional appeals, and symbolic forms of communication (such as metaphors and dramatic staged events).

- They delegate significant authority and responsibility.
- They eliminate unnecessary bureaucratic constraints.
- They provide coaching, training, and other developmental experiences to followers.
- They encourage open sharing of ideas and concerns.
- They encourage participative decision making.
- They promote cooperation and teamwork.
- They modify organization structure (such as resource allocation systems) and policies (such as selection and promotion criteria) to promote key values and objectives.

The proactive and energetic nature of transformational leadership hints at an opposite approach, called *laissez-faire or passive-avoidant* leadership.[47] Leaders displaying a laissez-faire style are not proactive, react only to failures or chronic problems, avoid making decisions, and are often absent or uninvolved in followers' activities. Such leaders typically do not have positive outcomes.[48] Leaders who strongly display transformational leadership do not display laissez-faire behaviors.

Commander D. Michael Abrashoff exemplified transformational leadership during his days on the USS *Benfold*.[49] First, Abrashoff's charisma was evident in several different ways. He demonstrated confidence with his informal but passionate manner. Consistent with this, he said the following: "I divide the world into believers and infidels. What the infidels don't understand . . . is that innovative practices combined with true empowerment produce phenomenal results." He focused on the vision of extreme readiness in order to protect the United States, and he communicated that vision clearly to all crew members, often meeting with them individually. He tried to link each crew member's tasks to the vision. He also went beyond self-interest, saying, "Anyone on my ship will tell you that I'm a low maintenance CO. It's not about me; it's about my crew."

Abrashoff demonstrated his ability to create intellectual stimulation by continuously reexamining the way things were done on the ship and changing procedures when a better way was found. He stated, "There is always a better way to do things." During his first few months on the *Benfold*, he thoroughly analyzed all operations. He questioned everyone involved in each operation to find out whether they had suggestions for how to do things better. They almost always did.

Finally, Abrashoff displayed individual consideration by meeting individually with all new recruits on the ship and asking three questions: "Why did he/she join the Navy? What's his/her family situation like? What are his/her goals while in the Navy—and beyond?" He said that getting to know the sailors as individuals and linking that knowledge to the vision for the ship was critical. He always treated the sailors with respect and dignity. For example, he had the ship's cooks train at culinary schools so that the food would be the best of any ship in the Navy. Furthermore, he

Getty Images

created learning opportunities for the crew. He wanted the crew to take the time to thoroughly learn their jobs and develop the skills necessary for job success and promotion.

The *Benfold* achieved notable performance, both in terms of reduced maintenance and repair budgets and in terms of combat-readiness indicators such as gunnery scores. At one point, the ship was considered the best in the U.S. Navy's Pacific Fleet, and it was awarded the prestigious Spokane Trophy. Furthermore, the commitment and satisfaction of the crew was quite high. One hundred percent of the crew signed up for a second tour of duty (the average for the Navy was 54 percent at the time).

Systematic research on transformational leadership is still in its early stages. However, several conclusions have become apparent. First, leaders can be trained to exhibit transformational leadership behaviors.[50] Second, leaders can display both transformational and transactional leadership styles.[51] William Bratton provides a clear example of this. While exhibiting many charismatic qualities and decentralizing authority (transformational leadership), he also closely monitored officers' performance and rewarded or punished that performance accordingly (transactional leadership).

Third, both transformational and transactional leadership can be positive.[52] Transactional leadership has been associated with follower satisfaction, commitment, performance, and (in some cases) organizational citizenship behaviors.[53] Transformational leadership has also been linked to follower satisfaction and commitment, unit performance, organizational performance, and individual performance.[54] There are some differences. For example, the effects of transformational leadership seem to be stronger at the unit level than at the individual level (collective unit outcomes versus the outcomes of individuals). Furthermore, transformational leaders are viewed as better leaders by their followers and are more likely to enhance the self-concepts of followers.[55] This can pay important dividends in terms of confidence and sustained efforts. Finally, transformational leaders seem to be more effective in bringing about significant change in a unit or organization,[56] which explains why this form of leadership receives so much attention in today's fast-paced world. By focusing on shared visions of the future and collective interests, transformational leaders promote change.[57]

A unique study used historical data to assess U.S. presidents' charismatic leadership (part of transformational leadership). The study found that presidential charisma was positively related to presidential performance (measured by the impact of the president's decisions and various ratings by historians).[58] Another study found that the market value (stock price) of companies led by charismatic leaders was higher than the market value of other companies. This study also found that external stakeholders were more likely to make larger investments in a firm led by a charismatic leader than in firms whose leaders did not display charismatic qualities.[59] In a recent study, transformational leaders positively affected the outcomes of a strategic acquisition.[60] Because diversification and growth strategies often involve acquisitions of other firms, this is an important finding. As mentioned, however, it appears that both types of leadership can be effective; the organizational context may determine which one should be emphasized.[61] Transactional leadership perhaps should be a greater part of the leadership mix in stable situations, where significant change is not required. Transformational leadership perhaps should be a greater part of the mix in more dynamic situations where associates must perform outside of explicit expectations, in terms of either providing extraordinary effort or being innovative. Overall,

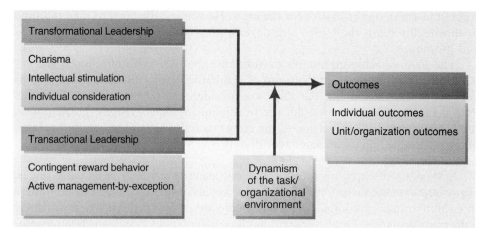

Exhibit 8-5
The Effects of
Transformational
and Transactional
Leadership

though, an integration of transformational and transactional leadership approaches seems to provide the most effective leadership strategy.[62] The basic relationships are shown in Exhibit 8-5.

Very recently, transformational leadership theory has been put to use in the pursuit of more ethical behavior in organizations. We describe this work in the *Experiencing Strategic Organizational Behavior* feature.

EXPERIENCING STRATEGIC ORGANIZATIONAL BEHAVIOR

Ethical Leadership? Authentic Leadership!

AP/Wide
World Photos

The twenty-first century seems to have brought an all-time low in ethical behavior by corporate leaders. A record number of top executives have been caught in outrageous scandals, leading to a large drop in public confidence in business leadership. Here are some examples:

- Perhaps the most colorful scandal involved Dennis Kozlowski, the ex-CEO of Tyco International, Ltd. Kozlowski is alleged to have taken $62 million in unauthorized loans from the company. He, along with Mark Swartz (former finance chief) and Mark Belnick (former general counsel), were indicted in September 2003 for illicitly using $600 million of their company's money. Stories of Kozlowski's outrageous spending of corporate funds flooded the media: a $15,000 umbrella stand; a $2,200 wastebasket; a $30 million home in Boca Raton, Florida; a severance package of over $1.2 million for an ex-mistress who had been a secretary at Tyco! Perhaps the pinnacle of the scandal was depicted in photographs of Kozlowski cavorting with toga-clad participants in an extravagant party paid for by Tyco.

- In what was probably the most widely reported scandal, numerous Enron executives—including former CEO Kenneth Lay; former COO, president, and CEO Jeffrey Skilling; and former CFO Andrew Fastow—were indicted on various charges, including conspiracy, fraud, and money laundering. Fastow alone was indicted on 788 charges and was sentenced to a 10-year prison sentence in return for pleading guilty to conspiracy and agreeing to help prosecutors with the rest of the cases. Enron declared bankruptcy in December 2001—the scandal involved, among other things, outrageous attempts to cover up the company's poor performance. Arthur Andersen LLP, the accounting firm that served as Enron's auditor, was convicted in June 2002 of justice obstruction for destroying Enron documents. The Enron fiasco had a terrible financial impact on thousands of employees, who had most of their retirement in Enron stock, as well as on shareholders and on the company's creditors, who can expect to receive little of what they are owed.

- Samuel D. Waksal, founder of ImClone Systems, pleaded guilty in October 2002 to charges of securities fraud, perjury, and obstruction of justice. He played a major role in the flurry of stock sales that occurred after he learned that the Food and Drug Administration was not going to approve one of ImClone's new cancer drugs.

- The Waksal case led to the even-more-publicized trial of Martha Stewart, the popular lifestyle guru, who stood trial on charges related to her sale of ImClone stock. As part of the trial, many personally embarrassing details about Stewart's behavior were revealed (for example, her tendency to treat employees badly). She was convicted and sent to prison.

- In 2007, Ryan Brant, CEO of Take-Two Interactive Software, pleaded guilty to falsifying financial records in a case of backdating stock options. Myron Olesnyckyj pleaded guilty to securities fraud and conspiracy for options backdating. According to many informed onlookers, these two cases represent the tip of a rather large iceberg.

The large number of scandals (and there were many more than reported here) has led to a public outcry demanding that the management community, including business schools, place more emphasis on the ethical behavior of leaders. In response to this demand, new conceptualizations of leadership have been advanced. One such conceptualization is *authentic leadership*, proposed by Fred Luthans and Bruce Avolio.

Building on the research regarding transformational leadership, which partially addresses the quality of moral behavior, Luthans and Avolio posit the need to focus attention on developing leaders who are not only transformational but authentic. An authentic leader is someone who is genuine, trustworthy, and truthful. Authentic leaders "own" their thoughts, emotions, and beliefs and act according to their true selves. These leaders have the following qualities:

- They are guided by values that focus on doing what's right for their constituencies.

- They try to act in accordance with their values.

- They remain transparent. That is, they are aware of their own shortcomings and discuss these shortcomings with others. Others are free to question them.

- They "walk the talk." That is, they model confidence, hope, optimism, and resiliency.

- They place equal weight on getting the task accomplished and developing associates.

- They continuously develop themselves.

- They have developed the values and personal strength they need to deal with ambiguous ethical issues.

The concept of authentic leadership is important in today's troubled business environment. Future leadership development and training should encompass these qualities so that leaders will be less likely to succumb to greed and dishonesty. Perhaps with this new stage in leadership development, images of CEOs from major corporations being led away in handcuffs and innocent people being emotionally and financially devastated by corporate corruption will be a less common sight!

Sources: Associated Press, "Timeline of Events in Enron Scandal," press release, Feb. 19, 2004; P. Burrows, "A Smaller Options Scandal," *BusinessWeek,* Mar. 5, 2007, pp. 28–29; K. Friefeld, "Second Tyco Mistress Testifies," *New York Newsday,* Nov. 14, 2003, at http://www.nynewsday.com/busines/nyc-tyco1114,0,34699766.story; B. George, P. Sims, A. McLean, & D. Mayer, "Discovering Your Authentic Leadership," *Harvard Business Review* 85, Feb. 2007, 129–138; F. Luthans, & B.J. Avolio, "Authentic Leadership," in K.S. Cameron, J.E. Dutton, & R.E. Quinn (Eds.), *Positive Organizational Scholarship* (San Francisco: Berrett-Koehler, 2003); "The Perp Walk," *BusinessWeek Online,* Jan. 13, 2003, at http://www.businessweek.com/print/magazine/content/03_02/bb3815660.htm; "Tyco Wants Its Money Back," *CNNMONEY,* Sept. 17, 2002, at http://money.cnn.com/2002/09/177/news/companies/tyco/.

The scandals described in the *Experiencing Strategic Organizational Behavior* feature dramatically illustrate the effects of leaders on the performance of an organization. Unfortunately, they show the negative effects of leadership. The leaders at Enron, for example, destroyed all value in a multibillion-dollar corporation, and many people lost their jobs and all retirement savings because of the unethical leadership.

Additional Topics of Current Relevance

In closing our discussion of leadership, we cover several additional topics relevant to leading in today's workplaces. We cover leader–member exchange, servant leadership, gender effects on leadership, and global differences in leadership.

Leader–member Exchange

leader-member exchange A model of leadership focused on leaders developing more positive relationships with some individuals, and having more positive exchanges with these individuals.

The **leader–member exchange** (LMX) model builds on a simple idea: leaders develop different relationships with different followers.[63] A leader develops positive relationships with some followers but develops less positive relationships with others. An individual's ability to contribute at a high level is one factor that determines the relationship with the leader. An individual's similarity to the leader, in terms of personality and interests, is another factor.[64]

Individuals who have positive relationships with the leader are members of an in-group. They experience leader–member exchange characterized by mutual trust, mutual support, and the provision of substantial resources. Individuals who have less positive relationships with the leader are members of an out-group. They experience out-group leader–member exchange characterized by more formality, less respect, lack of mutual support, and fewer opportunities for growth. Research on the LMX model indicates the obvious: members of an out-group tend to have lower levels of satisfaction, commitment, and performance.[65]

The existence of an out-group is inconsistent with high-involvement management. The high-involvement approach requires selection and retention of qualified individuals, proper training and coaching for each of them, and meaningful work for each of them. This is not simply a moral imperative. As explained in Chapter 1, organizational performance is at stake. Leaders should provide opportunities for all employees, or at least as many as possible.

Servant Leadership

Similar to authentic leadership, **servant leadership** overlaps with the transformational tradition.[66] It includes such elements as valuing individuals, developing people, building community, conceptualizing, exhibiting foresight, and displaying wisdom.[67] Its distinctive focus, however, lies with an emphasis on serving others, both inside and outside the organization. Servant leaders want to serve others. They want to serve those who follow them. Their self-concepts are those of servants rather than leaders. And they often do not seek out leadership roles. Rather, such roles are thrust upon them.

> **servant leadership**
> An approach to leadership focused on serving others.

Max De Pree, former CEO of Herman Miller, often told a story that illustrates the key idea. In his words:

> I arrived at the local tennis club just after high school students had vacated the locker room. Like chickens, they had not bothered to pick up after themselves. Without thinking too much about it, I gathered up all their towels and put them in a hamper. A friend of mine quietly watched me do this and then asked me a question that I've pondered many times over the years. "Do you pick up towels because you're the president of the company? Or are you the president because you pick up towels?"[68]

The premise of the first question is more consistent with servant leadership. It suggests a mentality of "I am the leader, therefore I serve," rather than "I am the leader, therefore I lead."[69]

Systematic research into the effects of servant leadership is very limited. A number of individuals, however, have used the approach with great success. James Blanchard, former CEO of Synovus Financial Corporation, put it this way:

> The heart of the servant-leader brings order, brings meaning to employees. When employees feel order and meaning and that they are part of a team that stands for something good, that there is a higher calling than just working to get a paycheck, that they are improving mankind, there is an energy level that explodes and great things happen.[70]

Gender Effects on Leadership

Do women lead differently relative to men? Given the increase in the number of women in the U.S. workforce since the 1970s and the concern over the glass ceiling facing women who wish to advance in U.S. corporations,[71] it is not surprising that a great deal of attention has been focused on this question. For over three decades, researchers have investigated the issue of gender and leadership, and this research has been characterized by a great deal of debate.[72] There are reasons to believe that women often lead differently (for better or worse) than men, and there are also reasons to expect no differences in how men and women lead, particularly in U.S. work organizations.

One argument suggesting that women and men behave differently as leaders is referred to as the **structural–cultural model** of leader behavior.[73] This model suggests that because women often experience lack of power, lack of respect, and certain stereotypical expectations that result from cultural norms and stereotypes, they must behave differently from men to be more effective leaders.[74] For example, followers are likely to expect different behaviors from women than from men. Thus, a female leader who acts aggressively might be viewed as mean spirited or overly emotional, whereas a man behaving in the same way might be thought of as strong, confident, or passionate. Women may also be pressured to conform to certain gender-role stereotypes, such as being more interpersonally oriented and nurturing.[75] In essence, they are required to find a way to lead while making associates comfortable by exhibiting behavior consistent with gender-role stereotypes. Women who do this will not necessarily be less effective leaders because, as we discussed above, the effectiveness of specific leader behaviors depends on situational factors. Therefore, when the situation calls for a leader who emphasizes concern and caring for followers, women exhibiting nurturing behavior and strong interpersonal skills are likely to be effective and perhaps will be better at leading than men.[76]

In contrast, the **socialization model** suggests that there should be no differences in the way male and female leaders behave.[77] According to this argument, when all newcomers enter the organization, they are socialized into the organization's norms and accepted ways of behaving. Regardless of gender, all who advance to leadership positions have experienced the same organizational socialization and therefore are likely to display similar leader behaviors.[78] Therefore, women and men who have advanced into leadership positions will behave in the same way.

Research evidence exists for both points of view. On the one hand, some studies have found that women display more interpersonal and social behaviors in small groups assembled as part of formal experiments, whereas men display more task-oriented behaviors.[79] Other studies have found women to be more democratic and participative than men.[80] On the other hand, research examining female leaders in organizational work settings found no differences in the way male and female leaders behave.[81] In a recent study of almost 700 middle-level and executive managers, female managers and executives engaged more frequently in both stereotypical female behaviors (interpersonal behaviors) and stereotypical male behaviors (task-oriented behaviors).[82] In this case, the organization highly valued both types of behaviors—and it appeared that female leaders had to demonstrate more positive leadership behaviors than men, even though those behaviors were the same. In conclusion, answering the question of whether women and men lead differently is not simple.[83] Overall, the evidence supporting stereotypical differences among actual managers is not clear.

The arguments concerning the differences or lack thereof between male and female leaders could be extended to differences between racial/ethnic minority leaders and white majority leaders. However, less research has been done on this issue than on gender differences. Results tend to show weak differences or no differences.[84] However, to address this issue more fully we need to better understand glass ceiling issues that also face racial/ethnic minority group members.

Global Differences in Leadership

As discussed in greater detail in Chapters 2 and 3, the U.S. workforce has become more diverse. In particular, globalization has produced situations in

structural–cultural model A model holding that because women often experience lack of power, lack of respect, and certain stereotypical expectations, they develop leadership styles different from those of the men.

socialization model A model proposing that all leaders in a particular organization will display similar leadership styles, because all have been selected and socialized by the same organization.

which U.S. managers lead associates socialized in different cultures, international managers lead U.S. associates, and work groups are made up of people from different cultures who must work together. Most of the theories and findings discussed so far in this chapter have focused primarily on the North American workforce, which values participation in decision making, narrow power distance (power should be equally shared), a high-performance orientation (people should be rewarded for good performance), significant individualism, and reasonably strong orientation toward the future (planning, investing, delaying gratification).[85] We can easily understand why leaders who are charismatic, engender participation, and provide relevant rewards for high performance are effective with this workforce.

Getty Images

But what happens in a culture that values collectivism (that is, the group is viewed as more important than individuals) or has a high power distance (believes that power should be hierarchically distributed)? Such views are common in Arabic cultures such as Egypt and Morocco.[86] Would effective leadership take a different form? Or are there universal truths about what makes a good leader? As Michael Marks, CEO of Flextronics, a multinational manufacturing company, points out, "I have learned that in every place we operate, in every country, the people want to do a good job [and] there is no place where people can't do a world class job. . . . This isn't to say we approach every region with cookie-cutter uniformity."[87]

The U.S. National Science Foundation funded a worldwide project, headed by Robert House, to examine whether leadership differs across different cultures and whether the effectiveness of different types of leadership varies by culture. This study is referred to as the *GLOBE* project (Global Leadership and Organizational Behavior Effectiveness).[88] It was first introduced in Chapter 3. Preliminary findings of the GLOBE project, based on surveys of thousands of people, cluster countries into groups with shared histories and values. Below is a description of the ideal leader for four cultural clusters:

1. *Anglo cluster*[89] (Australia, Canada, England, Ireland, New Zealand, South Africa [white sample], and United States): The ideal leader demonstrates charismatic influence and inspiration while encouraging participation. Ideal leaders are viewed as being diplomatic, delegating authority, and allowing everyone to have their say.

2. *Arabic Cluster*[90] (Egypt, Morocco, Kuwait, and Qatar, with Turkey also being included with these Arabic countries): Ideal leaders need to balance a paradoxical set of expectations. On one hand, they are expected to be charismatic and powerful, but on the other they are expected not to differentiate themselves from others and to have modest styles. Leaders are also expected to have a great deal of power and to direct most decisions and actions.

3. *Germanic cluster*[91] (Austria, Germany, the Netherlands, and Switzerland): The ideal leader is one who is charismatic and participative, and who conceptualizes her relationships in a team-like fashion.

4. *Southern Asia cluster*[92] (India, Indonesia, Iran, Malaysia, Philippines, and Thailand): The ideal leader is humane, participative, and charismatic. Leaders are expected to be benevolent while maintaining a strong position of authority.

The findings from the GLOBE project suggest that charismatic leadership is viewed as effective and desirable across all cultures. Other dimensions of leadership, such as participation, humaneness, and team orientation, vary in importance across cultures. As numerous CEOs of multinational firms have indicated,[93] today's managers need to develop the cultural sensitivity required to understand differences in leadership requirements across national boundaries and cultures in order to develop highly productive multinational workforces.[94]

The Strategic Lens

Leadership is a critically important concept in organizational behavior and equally important for the performance of organizations. As demonstrated in this chapter, leaders have direct and strong effects on the performance of the individuals and teams they lead. At all levels in the organization, leaders often have major goals for performance, and they provide the context and take actions that affect and support efforts to achieve those goals. Leaders at the top of organizations, with input from lower-level leaders and associates, establish the strategies designed to achieve the organization's overall goals. Furthermore, the actual achievement of those goals is based strongly on the quality of the leadership they and other leaders throughout the organization provide in the implementation of strategies. In such implementations, leaders may need to be directive while simultaneously exhibiting compassion for their associates.

For strategies to be effective, they need to be formulated and implemented within a context of appropriate organizational values and with a working knowledge of the global environment. In addition, organizational strategies can be more effectively implemented when the value of diversity is understood and used to advantage. Research has shown that while entering international markets with current products helps the firm achieve economies of scale (reduces the cost for each product sold), selling goods in international markets has additional benefits that are even greater. For example, organizations operating in international markets often gain access to new knowledge. People from different cultures develop different ways of thinking and operating. As a result, leaders can obtain new ideas from employees, customers, and suppliers in international markets and incorporate them into their domestic operations and other foreign operations as well.[95]

International operations provide an excellent opportunity to gain benefits from diversity, as discussed in Chapters 2 and 3. For example, some firms develop teams composed of people from multiple ethnic and cultural backgrounds. With effective leadership, these heterogeneous teams often produce more creative ideas and solutions to problems. Also, they can better understand diverse customers and satisfy their needs.[96] Although the global context is complex, effective leadership adjusts to it and uses the multicultural environments to benefit the organization. Thus, leaders who espouse and exhibit ethical values, understand and use a diverse workforce to benefit the organization, and adapt to and extract knowledge from different environments in international markets contribute to an organization's capability to achieve and sustain a competitive advantage. These leadership characteristics contribute to the formulation of better strategies and to more effective implementation of those strategies.[97]

Critical Thinking Questions

1. How should leaders approach individuals, units, and organizations suffering from poor performance?

2. Why is ethical leadership often of utmost importance to various stakeholders?

3. Should women and men lead in different ways?

What This Chapter Adds to Your Knowledge Portfolio

In this chapter, we have discussed ideas about what makes a leader effective. We have covered trait theories, behavioral theories, contingency theories, and transformational leadership theory. All of these theories are related and build on one another. In specific terms, we made the following points:

- Leadership is the process of providing general direction and influencing individuals or groups to achieve goals.

- Trait theories of leadership propose that a person must possess certain characteristics to become a leader. Older trait theories held that leaders were born, not made. More modern trait theories state that certain characteristics are necessary but not sufficient for a person to be an effective leader and that many leadership characteristics can be developed or learned. Six core traits of leaders are drive, leadership motivation, integrity, self-confidence, cognitive ability, and knowledge of the relevant domain. Charisma may also be important.

- The Michigan studies focused on two distinct behavioral leadership styles—job centered and employee centered. The job-centered leader emphasizes tasks and the methods used to accomplish them. The employee-centered leader emphasizes employees and their needs and the development of interpersonal relationships. Research on which style is more effective has been inconclusive.

- The Ohio State studies focused on two dimensions of leader behavior: consideration and initiating structure. A leader showing consideration expresses friendship and develops mutual trust and strong interpersonal relationships with subordinates. Leaders exhibiting initiating structure establish well-defined patterns of structure and communication, defining both the work activities and the relationship between leaders and subordinates. Leaders may possess any combination of these two dimensions. Early research indicated that leaders exhibiting high levels of both consideration and initiating structure were most effective. However, later research showed that leadership effectiveness is more complex than this simple idea suggests.

- Fiedler's contingency model of leadership suggests that effectiveness depends on the match between a leader's style and the degree of favorableness of the situation. The important situational characteristics in this model are leader–member relations, task structure, and the leader's position power. Situational favorableness is determined by the amount of control a leader has. Fiedler's research indicates that task-oriented leaders are more effective in highly favorable or highly unfavorable situations, whereas relationship-oriented leaders are more effective in situations of intermediate favorableness. Fiedler's model has been criticized, but it is one of the first contingency concepts proposed and is supported by some research.

- The path–goal leadership model proposed by Robert House is based on the expectancy concept of motivation. Leaders affect individuals' expectancies (paths) and goal valences by assigning people to tasks in which they are interested, providing support for the achievement of task goals and giving consistent rewards for task-goal achievement. Research has provided support for many of the specific predictions of the theory.

- Transformational leadership has been the subject of recent attention. Transactional leaders, who provide a useful contrast to transformational leaders, provide clear expectations and reward or punish followers based on their performance. Followers comply with leaders' wishes to gain desired rewards. Transformational leaders motivate followers to do more than expected, to continuously develop and grow, to build up their own confidence, and to put the interests of the team or organization before their own. They display charisma, intellectual stimulation, and individual consideration of followers. Research shows that both types of leadership can be positive and even necessary, with the appropriate degree of emphasis on each varying with the context (stable versus dynamic situations).

- Leader–member exchange is focused on the nature of the relationship between a leader and an individual in his unit/organization. When a positive relationship exists, the individual is a member of an in-group and experiences positive exchanges. When a less positive relationship exists, the individual is a member of an out-group and experiences less positive exchanges. Research shows that out-group members have lower satisfaction, commitment, and performance.

- Servant leadership means serving others. Research has been scant, but a number of individuals report success with the approach.

- Whereas the structural–cultural model suggests that there are significant differences in the leadership styles used by men and women, the socialization model holds that men and women experience the same organizational socialization and therefore exhibit the same leadership behaviors in U.S. work organizations. Research provides more support for the socialization model.

- The globalization of business has helped us understand that leaders must exhibit different styles to be effective in different regions of the world. For example, in the Anglo region, the ideal leader demonstrates charismatic influence and inspiration while encouraging participation, whereas in the Arabic region leaders are expected to have a great deal of power and to direct most decisions and actions.

Back to the Knowledge Objectives

1. What is leadership, and why is it important for organizations?

2. Are leaders born or made? Explain your answer. What are the core traits possessed by effective leaders?

3. Considering the findings from the Michigan and Ohio State studies, what do you think is the most effective leadership style? Give reasons to support your choice.

4. What key situational variables are related to leadership effectiveness in Fiedler's model of leadership effectiveness and in the path–goal model of leadership? In what ways do contingency models fall short in specifying a complete picture of effective leadership?

5. How do transformational and transactional leaders differ? What kind of results can be expected from each type of leader?

6. How do the leader–member exchange and servant-leadership models differ?

7. Explain why male and female leaders might engage in different leadership behaviors. What does the evidence show with respect to differences in leadership?

8. Describe the characteristics of an effective leader in each of the following clusters of countries: Anglo, Arabic, Germanic, and Southern Asia.

Thinking about Ethics

1. What ethical responsibilities do leaders have in the organizations in which they work? What are the primary ethical issues involved in the leader's relationship to the organization?

2. What is more important, associates' productivity or leaders' exhibiting ethical behaviors? Is ethical behavior more important even if the result is poor performance? Why or why not?

3. Are ethical leaders more effective than leaders who exhibit unethical behaviors? Explain why or why not.

4. Assume that you are the leader of a marketing group and have been trying for some time to acquire a large new customer in a foreign country. One of your sales representatives reports that a competitor has offered a bribe to a key official of the company to obtain the contract. If you do not respond, your organization will likely lose this major new contract and your group will probably not meet its sales goal for the year. What should you do? Explain the reasons for your recommendation.

Key Terms

leadership, p. 257
job-centered leadership style, p. 262
employee-centered leadership style, p. 262
consideration, p. 262
initiating structure, p. 263
contingency theory of leadership effectiveness, p. 264
leader–member relations, p. 264

task structure, p. 264
position power, p. 265
path–goal leadership theory, p. 267
directive leadership, p. 267
supportive leadership, p. 267
achievement-oriented leadership, p. 267
participative leadership, p. 267

transactional leadership, p. 270
transformational leadership, p. 271
charisma, p. 271
leader–member exchange, p. 276
servant leadership, p. 277
structural–cultural model, p. 278
socialization model, p. 278

Building Your Human Capital

Are You a Transformational Leader?

Individuals lead in different ways. Understanding your own leadership behavior is very useful in assessing its appropriateness. In this chapter's *Building Your Human Capital,* we provide an assessment tool for transformational, transactional, and laissez-faire leadership.

Instructions

If you currently hold or have recently held a leadership position, ask several individuals who have experienced your leadership to respond to the questions that appear below. Your leadership position could involve managing a formal work unit in a company, leading a temporary team in an organization, being captain of an intramural basketball team, being pledge chairwoman for a sorority, and so on. If you do not have recent leadership experience, then complete a self-assessment, being very honest with yourself about the behaviors that you probably would exhibit in a future leadership role. Alternatively, you could complete the assessment with another leader in mind (i.e., rate someone who has been a leader for a unit or organization in which you have been a member).

For each item, tell your respondents to rate the frequency with which you engage in the behavior described. Also tell them that few people have extreme scores (low or high) on all or even most items (a "1" or a "4" is an extreme score). Have each respondent circle the appropriate number beside the item, using the following scale (note that "L" stands for Leader):

1	2	3	4
Never	Infrequently	Frequently	Always

1. L goes beyond self-interest.	1	2	3	4
2. L has my respect.	1	2	3	4
3. L displays power and confidence.	1	2	3	4

4. L talks of values.	1	2	3	4
5. L models integrity.	1	2	3	4
6. L considers the integrity dimension of situations.	1	2	3	4
7. L emphasizes the collective mission.	1	2	3	4
8. L talks optimistically.	1	2	3	4
9. L expresses confidence.	1	2	3	4
10. L talks enthusiastically.	1	2	3	4
11. L arouses awareness about important issues.	1	2	3	4
12. L reexamines assumptions.	1	2	3	4
13. L seeks different views.	1	2	3	4
14. L suggests new ways.	1	2	3	4
15. L suggests different angles.	1	2	3	4
16. L individualizes attention.	1	2	3	4
17. L focuses on your strengths.	1	2	3	4
18. L teaches and coaches.	1	2	3	4
19. L differentiates among us.	1	2	3	4
20. L clarifies rewards.	1	2	3	4
21. L assists based on effort.	1	2	3	4
22. L rewards your achievements.	1	2	3	4
23. L recognizes your achievements.	1	2	3	4
24. L focuses on your mistakes.	1	2	3	4
25. L puts out fires.	1	2	3	4
26. L tracks your mistakes.	1	2	3	4
27. L concentrates on failures.	1	2	3	4
28. L reacts to problems but only when very serious.	1	2	3	4
29. L reacts to only the biggest failures.	1	2	3	4
30. L displays a philosophy of "If it's not broke, don't fix it."	1	2	3	4
31. L reacts to problems, if chronic.	1	2	3	4
32. L avoids involvement.	1	2	3	4
33. L is absent when he or she is needed.	1	2	3	4
34. L avoids deciding.	1	2	3	4
35. L delays responding.	1	2	3	4

Scoring

Items 1–11: These items measure **charisma.** To calculate your score, sum the points given to you by each respondent and then divide by the number of respondents (i.e., calculate the average total score given by the respondents). If your score is above 29, then you display significant charisma. If the score is greater than 41, then you score very high on charisma.

Items 12–15: These items measure **intellectual stimulation.** If the total score for these items (averaged across respondents) is greater than 10, then you display significant intellectual stimulation. If the score is greater than 14, you score very high on intellectual stimulation.

Items 16–19: These items measure **individualized consideration.** If you scored higher than 11 (averaged across respondents), you display individual consideration to a significant degree. If the score is greater than 15, then you scored very high on individual consideration.

Items 20–23: These items measure **contingent reward behavior.** If you scored higher than 10 (averaged across respondents), you display contingent reward behavior to a significant degree. If the score is greater than 14, then you score very high on contingent reward behavior.

Items 24–27: These items measure **management-by-exception behavior.** If you scored higher than 7 (averaged across respondents), you demonstrate management-by-exception behavior to a significant degree. If the score is greater than 11, then you score very high on management-by-exception behaviors.

Items 28–35: These items measure tendencies toward **laissez-faire** leadership. If you scored more than an 8 on these items (averaged across respondents), you display passive behavior to some degree. If the score is greater than 16, then you score very high on passive leadership.

Transformational leaders are characterized by charisma, intellectual stimulation, and individualized consideration. If you scored high on these three scales, then you are a good example of a transformational leader.

Transactional leaders provide contingent rewards and exhibit management-by-exception behaviors. If you scored high on these two scales, then you engage in transactional leadership. It is possible for a leader to be high on both transformational and transactional leadership.

Laissez-faire managers score high on avoidant/passive behaviors. If you scored high on the last set of items, then you are most likely a passive leader.

Source: Based on B.J. Avolio, B.M. Bass, and D.I. Jung, "Re-examining the Component of the Transformational and Transactional Leadership Using the Multifactor Leadership Questionnaire," *Journal of Occupational and Organizational Psychology,* 72 (1999): 441–462.

A Strategic Organizational Behavior Moment

The Two Presidents

Frances Workman had been president of Willard University for less than two years, but during that time she had become very popular throughout the state. Frances was an excellent speaker and used every opportunity to speak to citizen groups statewide. She also worked hard to build good relationships with the major politicians and business leaders in the state. This was not easy, but she managed to maintain favorable relationships with most.

She also had worked on the internal structure of the organization, streamlining the administrative component. She started a new alumni club to help finance academic needs, such as new library facilities and higher salaries for faculty and staff. In addition, she lobbied the state legislature and the state university coordinating board for a larger share of the state's higher education budget dollars. Her favorable image in the state and her lobbying efforts resulted in large increases in state funding for Willard. Interestingly, Frances was so busy with external matters that she had little time to bother with the daily operations of the university. However, she did make the major operational decisions. She delegated the responsibility for daily operations to her three major vice presidents.

Before Frances's arrival, Willard University had several presidents, none of whom had been popular with the state's citizens or particularly effective in managing the university's internal affairs. The lack of leadership resulted in low faculty morale, which affected student enrollment. Willard had a poor public image. Frances worked hard to build a positive image, and she seemed to be succeeding.

Another state university, Eastern State, had Alvin Thomas as president. Al had been president about three years. He was not as popular externally as Frances. He was not a particularly effective speaker and did not spend much time dealing with the external affairs of the university. Al delegated much of that responsibility to a vice president. He did work with external groups but in a quieter and less conspicuous way than Frances did.

Al spent much of his time working on the internal operation of the university. When he arrived, he was not pleased to find that Eastern was under censure by the American Association of University Professors (AAUP) and that the university had a large number of students without adequate faculty. In addition, Eastern was not involved in externally funded research. Al was committed to developing a quality university. Although he did not change the administrative structure of Eastern, he did extend considerable responsibilities to each of his vice presidents. He had high performance expectations for those on his staff, set ambitious goals, and reviewed every significant decision made in the university, relying heavily on his vice presidents and deans to implement them effectively. He developed a thorough planning system, the first of its kind at Eastern. He maintained good relations with the board of regents, but faculty viewed him as somewhat "stilted" and indifferent.

Frances projected a positive image to people in the state and along with that had built a positive image of Willard. The results of her efforts included an increase in enrollment of more than a thousand students in the last year. This occurred when enrollments were declining in most other colleges and universities in the state. Willard received the largest budget increase ever from the state university coordinating board and the state legislature. Finally, the outside funds from her special alumni club totaled almost $2 million in its first year. Faculty morale was higher, but faculty members viewed Frances warily because of her external focus.

In contrast, Eastern received an average budget increase similar to those it had received in the past. Although Eastern still had more students than Willard, its student enrollment declined slightly (by almost 300 students). However, the university was removed from AAUP censure. Externally funded research had increased by approximately $2 million during the previous year. Faculty morale was declining, and most faculty members did not believe they had an important voice in the administration of the university.

Discussion Questions

1. Based on the information provided, describe Frances's and Al's leadership styles.

2. What are the important factors that the leaders of Willard and Eastern must consider in order to be effective?

3. Compare and contrast Frances's and Al's effectiveness as leaders of their respective universities. What did each do well? What could each have done to be more effective?

Team Exercise

Coping with People Problems

The purpose of this exercise is to develop a better understanding of leadership through participation in a role play in which a leader must cope with an employee problem.

Procedure

1. Assemble into three-person teams.
2. Within each team, one person should be selected as Don Martinez, the manager; one person selected as John Williams, the subordinate; and one person as the observer.
3. Each person should read his or her role and prepare to role play the situation (allow 10 minutes for reading and preparing for roles). Each person, except the observer, should read *only* the role assigned. The observer should read all role materials.
4. After preparation, each team will engage in the role play for approximately 20 minutes.
5. Following the role play, each observer will answer the relevant questions and prepare to discuss how the leader (Don Martinez) handled the subordinate's (John Williams') problem.
6. Reassemble as a class. Each observer will describe the leadership situation in his or her team.
7. The instructor will present additional points for consideration.

Role for Don Martinez

You are manager of material control for Xenex Corp. You have had the job for five years and have almost 15 years of managerial experience. Four supervisors report to you, and John Williams is one of them. John is supervisor of inventory control. He has 22 people under his direction and has held the position for nine years. He is a good supervisor, and his unit performance has never been a problem.

However, in recent weeks you've noticed that John seems to be in a bad mood. He doesn't smile and has snapped back at you a couple of times when you've made comments to him. Also, one of his lead persons in the warehouse quit last week and claimed John had been "riding" him for no apparent reason. You think there must be some problem (maybe at home) for John to act this way. It is uncharacteristic.

John made an appointment to see you today and you hope that you can discuss this problem with him. You certainly want to deal with the problem because John has been one of your best supervisors.

Role for John Williams

You have been supervisor for inventory control for Xenex Corp. for almost nine years. You've had this job since about six months after graduating from college. When you took the job, Xenex was much smaller, but the job was a real challenge for a young, inexperienced person. The job has grown in complexity and number of people supervised (now 22).

Don Martinez, your boss, is manager of material control. He has held the job for about five years. When he was selected for the position, you were a little disappointed that you were not promoted to it, because you had done a good job. However, you were young and needed more experience, as the director of manufacturing told you.

Overall, Don has been a fairly good manager, but he seems to have neglected you during the past couple of years. You have received good pay increases, but your job is boring now. It doesn't present any new challenges. You just turned 31 and have decided that it's time to move up or go elsewhere. In past performance appraisal sessions, you tried to talk about personal development and your desire for a promotion, but Don seemed unresponsive.

You've decided that you must be aggressive. You have done a good job and don't want to stay in your present job forever. You believe that you have been overlooked and ignored and don't intend to allow that to continue.

The purpose of your meeting today is to inform Don that you want a promotion. If the company is unable or unwilling to meet your needs, you are prepared to leave. You intend to be aggressive.

Role for Observer

You are to observe the role play with Don Martinez and John Williams without participating. Please answer the following questions based on this role play.

1. Briefly describe how the situation evolved between Don and John.

2. What leadership style did Don use in trying to deal with John?

3. How was the problem resolved?

4. How could Don have handled the situation more effectively?

Endnotes

1. Pfeffer, J., & Sutton, R.I. 2006. *Hard facts, dangerous half-truths, & total nonsense: Profiting from evidence based management*. Boston: Harvard Business School Press, pp. 187–214.

2. Waldman, D.A., Ramirez, G.C., House, R.J., & Puranam, P. 2001. Does leadership matter? CEO leadership attributes and probability under conditions of perceived environmental uncertainty. *Academy of Management Journal*, 44: 134–143.

3. Haapniemi, P. 2003. Leading indicators: The development of executive leadership. http//www.ccl.org.

4. Finkelstein, S., & Hambrick, D. 1996. *Strategic leadership*. St Paul, MN: West Publishing Co.

5. Ireland, R.D., & Hitt, M.A. 1999. Achieving and maintaining strategic competitiveness in the 21st century: The role of strategic leadership. *Academy of Management Executive*, 13(1): 43–57.

6. Hitt, M.A., & Ireland, R.D. 2002. The essence of strategic leadership: Managing human and social capital. *Journal of Leadership and Organizational Studies*, 9(1): 3–14.

7. Wesley, K.N., & Yukl, G.A. 1975. *Organizational behavior and industrial psychology*. New York: Oxford University Press, pp. 109–110.

8. Kouzes, J.M., & Posner, B.Z. 2002. *The leadership challenge*. San Francisco: Jossey-Bass.

9. Bennis, W. 1982. The artform of leadership. *Training and Development Journal*, 36(4): 44–46.

10. Kirkpatrick, S.A., & Locke, E.A. 1991. Leadership: Do traits matter? *Academy of Management Executive*, 5: 48–60.

11. Stogdill, R.M. 1974. *Handbook of leadership: A survey of theory and research*. New York: Free Press.

12. Zaccaro, S.J. 2007. Trait-based perspectives of leadership. *American Psychologist*, 62: 6–16.

13. Kirkpatrick & Locke, Leadership: Do traits matter?

14. Ibid.

15. Bass, B.M., & Avolio, B.J. 1990. The implications of transactional and transformational leadership for individual, team, and organizational development. In W.A. Pasmore, & R.W. Woodman (Eds.), *Research in organizational change and development*, Vol. 4. Greenwich, CT: JAI Press, pp. 231–272; House, R.J., Spangler, W.D., & Woycke, J. 1991. Personality and charisma in the U.S. presidency: A psychological theory of leader effectiveness. *Administrative Science Quarterly*, 36: 364–396.

16. Likert, R. 1961. *New patterns of management*. New York: McGraw-Hill.

17. Stogdill, *Handbook of leadership*.

18. Judge, T.A., Piccolo, R.F., & Illies, R. 2004. The forgotten ones? The validity of consideration and initiating structure in leadership research. *Journal of Applied Psychology*, 89: 36–51.

19. Fiedler, F.E. 1967. *A theory of leadership effectiveness*. New York, NY: McGraw-Hill.

20. Ibid.

21. For additional information on situational factors, see Fiedler, F.E. 1993. The leadership situation and the black box in contingency theories. In M.M. Chemers, & R.Y. Ayman (Eds.), *Leadership theory and research: Perspectives and directions*. New York, NY: Academic Press, pp. 2–28.

22. Fiedler, F.E. 1971. Validation and extension of the contingency model of leadership effectiveness: A review of empirical findings. *Psychological Bulletin*, 76: 128–148.

23. Fiedler, F.E. 1972. Personality, motivational systems, and behavior of high and low LPC persons. *Human Relations*, 25: 391–412.

24. Chemers, M.M., & Skrzypek, C.J. 1972. Experimental test of the contingency model of leadership effectiveness. *Journal of Personality and Social Psychology*, 24: 173–177; Fiedler, F.E., & Chemers, M.M. 1972. *Leadership and effective management*. Glenview, IL: Scott, Foresman

25. For meta-analyses of LPC research, see Peters, L.H., Hartke, D.D., & Pohlmann, J.T. 1985. Fiedler's contingency theory of leadership: An application of the meta-analysis procedures of Schmidt and Hunter. *Psychological Bulletin*, 97: 274–285; Schriesheim, C.A., Tepper, B.J., & Tetrault, L.A. 1994. Least-preferred co-worker score, situational control, and leadership effectiveness: A meta-analysis of contingency model performance predictions. *Journal of Applied Psychology*, 79: 561–573.

26. Kennedy, J.K. 1982. Middle LPC leaders and the contingency model of leadership effectiveness. *Organizational Behavior and Human Performance*, 30: 1–14.

27. Green, S.C., & Nebeker, D.M. 1977. The effects of situational factors and leadership style on leader behavior. *Organizational Behavior and Human Performance*, 20: 368–377; Hare, A.P., Hare, S.E., & Blumberg, H.H. 1998. Wishful thinking: Who has the least preferred co-worker? *Small Group Research*, 29: 419–435; Shiflett, S. 1981. Is there a problem with the LPC score in leader match? *Personnel Psychology*, 34: 765–769; Singh, B. 1983. Leadership style and reward allocation: Does Least Preferred Co-Worker scale measure task and relation orientation? *Organizational Behavior and Human Performance*, 32: 178–197.

28. Rice, R.W. 1981. Leader LPC and follower satisfaction: A review. *Organizational Behavior and Human Performance*, 28: 1–25.

29. Evans, M.C. 1970. The effects of supervisory behavior on the path-goal relationship. *Organizational Behavior and Human Performance*, 7: 277–298.

30. House, R.J. 1971. A path-goal theory of leadership effectiveness. *Administrative Science Quarterly*, 16: 321–338.

31. For work that followed the original specification of the theory, see: Fulk, J., & Wendler, E.R. 1982. Dimensionality of leader-subordinate interactions: A path-goal investigation. *Organizational Behavior and Human Performance*, 30: 241–264; House, R.J., & Mitchell, T.R. 1974. Path-goal theory of leadership. *Journal of Contemporary Business*, 3: 81–99; Podsakoff, P.M., Todor, W.D., Grover, R.A., & Huber, V.L. 1984. Situational moderators of leader reward and punishment behaviors: Fact or fiction? *Organizational Behavior and Human Performance*, 34: 21–63.

32. For a quantitative synthesis of research, see: Woffard, J.C., & Liska, L.Z. 1993. Path-goal theories of leadership: A meta-analysis. *Journal of Management*, 19: 857–876. For a supportive study in Taiwan, see: Silverthorne, C. 2001. A test of path-goal leadership theory in Taiwan. *Leadership and Organizational Development Journal*, 22: 151–158.

33. For additional insight on the mixed results, see: House, R.J. 1996. Path-goal theory of leadership effectiveness: Lessons, legacy, and a reformulated theory. *Leadership Quarterly*, 7: 305–309.

34. For additional insight, see: House, R.J., & Dessler, G.A. 1974. Path-goal theory of leadership: Some post hoc and a priori tests. In J.G. Hunt & L.L. Larsen (Eds.), *Contingency approaches to leadership*. Carbondale: Southern Illinois University Press, pp. 29–59.

35. For additional insight, see: Griffin, R.W. 1979. Task design determinants of effective leader behavior. *Academy of Management Review,* 4: 215–224; and Johnsen, A.L., Luthans, F., & Hennessey, H.W. 1984. The role of locus of control in leader influence behavior. *Personnel Psychology,* 37: 61–75.

36. Podsakoff, P.M., MacKenzie, S.B., Ahearne, M., & Bommer, W.H. 1995. Searching for a needle in a haystack: Trying to identify illusive moderators of leadership behaviors. *Journal of Management,* 21: 422–470.

37. For details of one framework emphasizing this point, see: Hersey, P., & Blanchard, K.H. 1988. *Management of organizational behavior: Utilizing human resources* (5th Ed.). Englewood Cliffs, NJ: Prentice Hall.

38. See, for example: Schriesheim, C.A., Castro, S.L., Zhou, X., & DeChurch, L.A. 2006. An investigation of path-goal and transformational leadership theory at the individual level of analysis. *Leadership Quarterly,* 17: 21–38.

39. For related commentary from the key figure in path-goal theory, see: House, R.J. 1999. Weber and the neocharismatic paradigm. *Leadership Quarterly,* 10: 563–574.

40. Bass & Avolio, The implications of transactional and transformational leadership for individual, team, and organizational development.

41. Bass, B.M. 1985. *Leadership and performance beyond expectations.* New York: Free Press.

42. Bass & Avolio, The implications of transactional and transformational leadership for individual, team, and organizational development.

43. Bass, *Leadership and performance beyond expectations;* Bass & Avolio, The implications of transactional and transformational leadership for individual, team, and organizational development.

44. Others have specified four or more characteristics, but our three are grounded in the original work and have proven useful. For additional details, see: Judge, T.A., & Piccolo, R.F. 2004. Transformational and Transactional Leadership: A meta-analytic test of their relative validity. *Journal of Applied Psychology,* 89: 755–768; Rafferty, A.E., & Griffin, M.A. 2004. Dimensions of transformational leadership: Conceptual and empirical extensions. *Leadership Quarterly,* 15: 329–354.

45. Charisma has been studied as a standalone concept by a number of researchers, and has spawned its own research tradition. It is, however, an integral part of the broader concept of transformational leadership. For details of the origins of charismatic leadership research, see House, R.J. 1977. A 1976 theory of charismatic leadership. In J.G. Hunt, & L.L. Larsen (Eds.), *Leadership: The cutting edge.* Carbondale, IL: South Illinois University Press, pp. 189–207. For example research studies, see: Howell, J.M., & Hall-Merenda, K.E. 1989. A laboratory study of charismatic leadership. *Organizational Behavior and Human Decision Process,* 43: 243–269; Shamir, B., Zakay, E., Breinin, E., & Popper, M. 1998. Correlates of charismatic leader behavior in military units: Subordinates' attitudes, unit characteristics, and superiors' appraisals of leader performance. *Academy of Management Journal,* 41: 387–409.

46. Yukl, G., & Van Fleet, D.D. 1992. Theory and research on leadership in organizations. In M.D. Dunnette & L.M. Hough (Eds.), *Handbook of industrial and organizational psychology* (2nd Ed.), Vol. 3. Palo Alto, CA: Consulting Psychologists Press, pp. 147–197.

47. Avolio, B.J., Bass, B.M., & Jung, D.I. 1999. Re-examining the components of transformational and transactional leadership using the Multifactor Leadership Questionnaire. *Journal of Occupational and Organizational Psychology,* 72: 441–462.

48. Judge & Piccolo, Transformational and transactional research; Skogstad, A., Einarsen, S., Torsheim, T., Assland, M.S., & Hetland, H. 2007. The destructiveness of laissez-faire leadership behavior. *Journal of Occupational Health Psychology,* 12: 80–92.

49. LaBarre, P. 1999. The agenda–Grass roots leadership. *Fast Company,* 23 (April): 114–120.

50. Bass & Avolio, The implications of transactional and transformational leadership for individual, team, and organizational development.

51. Bass, B.M., Avolio, B.J., Jung, D.I., & Berson, Y. 2003. Predicting unit performance by assessing transformational and transactional leadership. *Journal of Applied Psychology,* 88: 207–218.

52. Bass, Avolio, Jung, & Berson, Predicting unit performance by assessing transformational and transactional leadership; DeGroot, T., Kiker, D.S., & Cross, T.C. 2000. A meta-analysis to review organizational outcomes related to charismatic leadership. *Canadian Journal of Administrative Sciences,* 17: 356–371; Judge & Piccolo, Transformational and transactional research; Lowe, K.B., Kroeck, K.G., & Sivasubramaniam, N. 1996. Effectiveness correlates of transformational and transactional leadership: A meta-analytic review. *Leadership Quarterly,* 7: 385–425.

53. Lowe, Kroeck, & Sivasubramaniam, Effectiveness correlates of transformational and transactional leadership.

54. Bass & Avolio, The implications of transactional and transformational leadership for individual, team, and organizational development; Lowe, Kroeck, & Sivasubramaniam, Effectiveness correlates of transformational and transactional leadership; Shamir, B., House, R.J., & Arthur, M.B. 1993. The motivational effects of charismatic leadership: A self-concept based theory. *Organizational Science,* 4: 577–594;

55. Shamir, House, & Arthur, The motivational effects of charismatic leadership.

56. See, for example: Nemanich, L.A., & Keller, R.T. 2007. Transformational leadership in an acquisition: A field study of employees. *Leadership Quarterly,* 18: 49–68.

57. Bass & Avolio, The implications of transactional and transformational leadership for individual, team, and organizational development.

58. House, R.J., Spangler, W.D., & Woycke, J. 1991. Personality and charisma in the U.S. presidency: A psychological theory of leader effectiveness. *Administrative Science Quarterly,* 36: 364–396.

59. Flynn, F.J., & Staw, B.M. 2004. Lend me your wallets: The effect of charismatic leadership on external support for an organization. *Strategic Management Journal,* 25: 309–330.

60. Nemanich, & Keller, Transformational leadership in an acquisition.

61. Ibid.

62. Bass, Avolio, Jung, & Berson, Predicting unit performance by assessing transformational and transactional leadership.

63. Graen, G.B. 1976. Role-making processes within complex organizations. In M.D. Dunnette (Ed.), *Handbook of industrial and organizational psychology.* Chicago: Rand McNally, pp. 1201–1245; Graen, G., Novak, M., & Sommerkamp, P. 1982. The effects of leader-member exchange and job design on productivity and satisfaction: Testing a dual attachment model. *Organizational Behavior and Human Performance,* 30:109–131.

64. For research related to factors that influence leader-member relationships, see Sparrowe, R.T., & Liden, R.C. 1997. Process

and structure in leader-member exchange. *Academy of Management Review,* 22: 522–552.

65. Chen, Z., Lam, W., & Zhong, J.A. 2007. Leader-member exchange and member performance: A new look at individual-level negative feedback-seeking behavior and team-level empowerment climate. *Journal of Applied Psychology,* 92: 202–212; Gerstner, C.R., & Day, D.V. 1997. Meta-analytic review of leader-member exchange theory: Correlates and construct issues. *Journal of Applied Psychology,* 82: 827–844; Ilies, R., Nahrgang, J.D., & Morgeson, F.P. 2007. Leader-member exchange and citizenship behaviors: A meta-analysis. *Journal of Applied Psychology,* 269–277.

66. Barbuto, J.E., & Wheeler, D.W. 2006, Scale development and construct clarification of servant leadership. *Group & Organization Management,* 31: 300–326.

67. Ibid; Smith, B.N., Montagno, R.V., & Kuzmenko, T.N. 2004. Transformational and servant leadership: Content and contextual comparisons. *Journal of Leadership & Organizational Studies,* 10 (4): 8091; Spears, L. 1995. Servant leadership and the Greenleaf legacy. In L.C. Spears (Ed.), *Reflections on leadership.* New York: John Wiley & Sons.

68. Max De Pree, quoted in: Sendjaya, S., & Sarros, J.C. 2002. Servant leadership: Its origin, development, and application in organizations. *Journal of Leadership & Organizational Studies,* 9 (2): 57–64.

69. Ibid.

70. James Blanchard, quoted in: Sendjaya & Sarros, Servant leadership.

71. Cleveland, J.N., Stockdale, M., & Murphy, K.R. 2000. *Men and women in organizations: Sex and gender issues at work.* Mahwah, NJ: Lawrence Erlbaum.

72. Ibid.

73. Dobbins, G.H., & Platz, S.J. 1986. Sex differences in leadership: How real are they? *Academy of Management Review,* 11: 118–127; Powell, G.N. 1990. *One more time: Do female and male managers differ? Academy of Management Executive,* 4: 68–75.

74. Kanter, R.M. 1977. *Men and women of the corporation.* New York: Basic Books.

75. Heilman, M.E. 1995. Sex stereotypes and their effects in the workplace: What we know and what we don't know. *Journal of Social Behavior and Personality.* 10: 3–26; Eagly, A.H., & Karau, S.J. 2002. Role congruity theory of prejudice toward female leaders. *Psychological Review,* 109: 573–598.

76. Bass, B.M., & Avolio, B.J. 1997. Shatter the glass ceiling: Women may make better managers. In K. Grint (Ed.), *Leadership: Classical, contemporary, and critical approaches.* Oxford: Oxford University Press, pp. 199–210.

77. Bartol, K.M., Martin, D.C., & Kromkowski, J.A. 2003. Leadership and the glass ceiling: Gender and ethnic group influences on leader behaviors at middle and executive managerial levels. *Journal of Leadership and Organizational Studies,* 9: 8–16.

78. Eagly, A.H., & Johnson, B.T. 1990. Gender and leadership style: A meta-analysis. *Psychological Bulletin,* 108: 233–256; Ragins, B.R., & Sundstrom, E. 1989. Gender and power in organizations: A longitudinal perspective. *Psychological Bulletin,* 105: 51–88.

79. Wheelan, S.A., & Verdi, A.F. 1992. Differences in male and female patterns of communication in groups: A methodological artifact? *Sex Roles,* 27: 1–15.

80. Eagly & Johnson, Gender and leadership style.

81. Dobbins & Platz, Sex differences in leadership; Powell, One more time.

82. Bartol, Martin, & Kromkowski, Leadership and the glass ceiling.

83. For an additional point of view see: Eagly, A.H. 2007. Female leadership advantage and disadvantage: Resolving the contradictions. *Psychology of Women Quarterly,* 31: 1–12.

84. Bartol, Martin, & Kromkowski, Leadership and the glass ceiling.

85. Hofstede, G. 1980. *Culture's consequences: International differences in work related values.* London: Sage; Ashkanasy, N.M., Trevor-Roberts, E., & Earnshaw, L. 2002. The Anglo cluster: Legacy of the British Empire. *Journal of World Business,* 37: 28–39.

86. Kabasakal, H., & Bodur, M. 2002. Arabic cluster: A bridge between East and West. *Journal of World Business,* 37: 40–54.

87. Marks, M. In search of global leaders. *Harvard Business Review,* 81 (8): 43–44.

88. House, R.J., Hanges, P.J., Javidan, M., Dorfman, P.W., Gupta, V., & GLOBE Associates. 2004. *Cultures, leadership, and organizations: GLOBE—a 62 nation study* (Vol. 1). Thousand Oaks, CA: Sage Publishing; House, R.J., Javidan, M., Dorfman, P.W., & de Luque, M.S. 2006. A failure of scholarship: Response to George Graen's critique of GLOBE. *Academy of Management Perspectives,* 20 (4): 102–114; Javidan, M., House, R.J., Dorfman, P.W., Hanges, P.J., & de Luque, M.S. 2006. Conceptualizing and measuring cultures and their consequences: A comparative review of Globe's and Hofstede's approaches. *Journal of International Business Studies,* 37: 897–914.

89. Ashkanasy, N.M., Trevor-Roberts, E., & Earnshaw, L. 2002. The Anglo cluster: Legacy of the British Empire. *Journal of World Business,* 37: 28–39.

90. Kabasakal, H., & Bodur, M. 2002. Arabic cluster: A bridge between East and West. *Journal of World Business,* 37: 40–54.

91. Szabo, E., Brodbeck, Den Hartog, D.N., Reber, G., Weibler, J., & Wunderer, R. 2002. The Germanic Europe cluster: Where employees have a voice. *Journal of World Business,* 37: 55–68.

92. Gupta, V., Surie, G., Javidan, M., & Chhokar, J. 2002. Southern Asia Cluster: Where the old meets the new? *Journal of World Business,* 37: 16–27.

93. Marks, In search of global leaders.

94. For additional information related to the GLOBE project, go to http://www.thunderbird.edu/wwwfiles/ms/globe/. Also see: Chhokar, J.S., Brodbeck, F.C., & House, R.J. 2007. *Culture and leadership across the world.* Mahwah, NJ: Lawrence Erlbaum Associates.

95. Hitt, M.A., Hoskisson, R.E., & Kim, H. 1997. International diversification: Effects on innovation and firm performance in product diversified firms. *Academy of Management Journal,* 40: 767–798.

96. Hitt, M.A., Keats, B.W., & DeMarie, S. 1998. Navigating in the new competitive landscape: Building strategic flexibility and competitive advantage in the 21st century. *Academy of Management Executive,* 12(4): 22–42.

97. Hitt, M.A., Ireland, R.D., & Hoskisson, R.E. 2007. *Strategic management: Competitiveness and globalization* (7th ed.). Cincinnati, OH: South-Western.

COMMUNICATION

9

On August 29, 2005, Hurricane Katrina ripped through the Gulf Coast, devastating hundreds of thousands of homes, leveling entire towns, and resulting in over 1,500 deaths. After the storm, several levees surrounding Lake Ponchartrain failed, causing 80 percent of the city of New Orleans to be covered in water. For blocks and blocks, all that was visible from aerial views were rooftops, often with desperate people on top trying to flag down rescue helicopters. Cars and refrigerators floated down main streets.

Paul Figura/Getty Images

EXPLORING BEHAVIOR IN ACTION
Communication Casualties

In many areas, the only way to get around was by boat. Swimming in the toxic, sludgy floodwater was extremely dangerous, even though it was the only way many people were able to save their lives. Some weren't so lucky, as dead bodies were often found floating down the streets of once-active and charming neighborhoods.

As if the disaster wasn't enough, the attempt of authorities to respond to the disaster was shockingly inept, with a few exceptions such as the efforts of the U.S. Coast Guard. Thousands of people waited on rooftops or overpasses for days to be rescued from the flood, without adequate food or water in insufferable heat. Looting was rampant in the city, with reports that even some New Orleans police officers were taking part in the festivities. About 30,000 people were trapped in the Superdome without basic necessities, under a leaking roof, and in filthy conditions. It took five days to rescue these people. Another 15,000 to 20,000 people were stranded at the Ernest N. Morial Convention Center, right outside the famed French Quarter, suffering the heat, filth, and lack of food and water like those in the Superdome. People who needed medicine for diseases such as diabetes, hypertension, or asthma became critically ill due to the lack of medical care. Rumors of rape and murder terrified the crowds. Approximately 15 percent of the police force deserted. The rest of the nation looked on in horror while watching TV reports of scenes that one would never imagine taking place in a major U.S. city.

Since that late-summer week in 2005, a great deal of examination has taken place over what went wrong. Why weren't agencies, such as the Federal Emergency Management Association (FEMA), the Red Cross, or the New Orleans Police Department able to come to the aid of New Orleanians sooner and more effectively? Blame can be placed on many, and has been. However, one factor that everyone agrees on that thwarted rescue attempts and fostered the chaos following Katrina is that there was a major communications failure.

In order to deal effectively with such a crisis, rescue agencies and first responders, such as FEMA, the New Orleans Police Department, the Red Cross, the U.S. military, and local rescue organizations, have to be able to work together, which means they also have to be able to communicate among themselves and with each other. Furthermore, there is a dire need for communication about the extent and the form of damage, what type of problems are emerging (e.g., looting, fires, stranded people), where the damage has occurred, and what type of aid is needed and where. Furthermore, in order to prevent panic and to help people survive the crisis, they must be provided with communications about what has happened, safety procedures, potential dangers, and instructions for further action. People stranded in rising floodwaters, in need of emergency medical assistance or food, were unable to call for help. The communication system needed to accomplish this was broken in the days following hurricane Katrina.

- More than three million telephone lines were knocked down in Louisiana, Mississippi, and Alabama.

- Thirty-eight 911 call centers went down.
- Local wireless networks had considerable damage, making most cell phones in the area useless. The only way to get messages through was by text messaging.
- Thirty-seven out of 41 radio stations in New Orleans were unable to broadcast.
- The NOPD's communications system was inoperable for three days. Six out of eight police headquarters were flooded, making it impossible to establish command centers. There was a severe shortage of satellite phones that allowed for communication.
- Hundreds of first responders were able to communicate through only two radio channels, jamming the system and causing great delays in the communication of vital information.
- Many areas of the city were inaccessible on land. One needed a boat or helicopter to reach them.
- Verizon wireless did have generators for its cell towers; however, a number of these were stolen and a fuel truck bringing fuel to the generators was stopped at gunpoint and its fuel taken.
- FEMA did not provide New Orleans with a mobile multimedia communications unit (used in emergencies) until four days after the storm.

The outcomes of this total communication breakdown were tragic as described above in terms of human suffering and loss of life. Specific outcomes include the inability of the federal government and Homeland Security (who oversee FEMA) to get timely and reliable information. Michael Chertoff, secretary of Homeland Security, did not know about what was going on at the convention center three days after the storm. His reports from his staff indicated that there were about 1,500 people there. However, after being questioned on the radio by a National Public Radio interviewer, he yelled at his staff, "What the hell is going on with the convention center?" It seems the public media knew that there were over 10,000 people there, but the head of Homeland Security did not. Chertoff complained consistently that every time he'd ask a question of his staff (e.g., when did the levees break?), he was given many conflicting answers.

Another direct outcome of the communications failure was the inability for rescuers to communicate and coordinate with each other. Some police officers reported not hearing from a commander for three days after the storm. Rescue crews in helicopters could not talk to those patrolling in boats. The National Guard had to use old-fashioned runners to communicate orders.

The lack of communication also caused terrifying rumors to run rampant. Citizens in the Superdome and Convention Center became terrified over accounts of rape and murder. False reports about snipers attacking rescue planes led to the aborting of several rescue missions. Then–police chief, Eddie Compass, told Oprah Winfrey that babies were being raped inside the Superdome. These rumors led to less effective rescue attempts and more terror on the part of people who were already suffering dreadful conditions. In the end, there were a few substantiated claims of rape (although rape is usually underreported), six people dead in the Superdome and four dead in the Convention Center, mostly from natural causes, and little substantiation to the claims that snipers were firing at emergency workers.

Hopefully a lesson has been learned about how to prepare for a total communication breakdown during a national crisis. In any event, the aftermath of Katrina illustrates why communication is important, not only to organizational effectiveness, but in this case, to the life and well-being of the hundreds of thousands of people affected in this catastrophe.

Sources: Select Bipartisan Committee to Investigate the Preparation for and Response to Hurricane Katrina, "A Failure of Initiative," U.S. Government Printing Office, Feb. 15, 2006, at http://www.gpoaccess.gov/congress/index.html; D. Brinkley, *The Great Deluge* (New York: Harper Collins, 2006); W. Haygood, & A.S. Tyson, "It Was as If All of Us Were Already Pronounced Dead," *Washington Post,* Sept. 15, 2005, p. A01; E. Thomas, "Michael Chertoff: 'What the Hell Is Going On?'" *Newsweek,* Dec. 26–Jan. 2, 2006, at http://www.msnbc.msn.com/id/10511927/site/newsweek; M. Hunter, "Deaths of Evacuees Push Death Toll to 1,577," *Times Picayune,* May 19, 2006, at http://www.nola. com; B. Thevenot, & G. Russell, "Rumors of Deaths Greatly Exaggerated, Widely Reported Attacks False or Unsubstantiated," *Times Picayune*, Sept. 26, 2005, at http:// www.nola.com.

The Strategic Importance of Communication

The need for communication pervades organizations. Jobs cannot be adequately accomplished, goals cannot be met, and problems cannot be solved without adequate communication. The communication breakdown after hurricane Katrina among first responders illustrates what can happen when communication fails.

In the aftermath of Katrina, communication failures prevented individuals, such as police officers and citizens, from communicating with each other, curtailed organizations from accurately reading the environment and situation they were facing, and prevented leaders from passing down any organizational strategies for dealing with the disaster so that the strategies could be implemented by the first responders at the scene of the disaster.[1] However, some private companies, such as BP PLC, an oil company, were able to avoid such communications disasters during the aftermath of the hurricane by developing a carefully arranged crisis communication plan. This plan involved providing BP associates with various channels of communication, such as providing laptops with wireless capabilities and conducting business and forwarding news via the Internet.[2]

Good communication, then, is vital to better organizational performance. Effective communication is important because few things are accomplished in organizations without it.[3] Managers must communicate with their subordinates in order for jobs to be performed effectively. Top management must communicate organizational goals to the associates who are expected to achieve them. Many jobs require coordination with others in the organization, and coordination requires communication. In fact, communication is such an important part of a manager's job that managers spend between 50 and 90 percent of their time at work communicating.[4] Top managers must digest information, shape ideas, coordinate tasks, listen to others, and give instructions. Decisions and policies are of little value unless they are fully understood by those who must implement them.[5] Good communication is also the basis for effective leadership, the motivation of subordinates, and the exercise of power and influence. It is also necessary for establishing effective relations with important external entities, such as suppliers, consumers, and government agencies.

Communication systems in organizations affect numerous outcomes that are central to an organization's functioning and competitive advantage, These include productivity,[6] quality services and products,[7] reduced costs, creativity, job satisfaction, absenteeism, and turnover.[8] In other words, organizational communication is interrelated with organizational effectiveness.[9] Indeed, surveys asking managers to give the reasons for project failures cite communication problems as an important explanation, if not the most important explanation.[10]

293

Given the importance of organizational communication, it is troubling that a number of managers find communication a challenging task. One study found that many managers underestimate the complexity and importance of superior–subordinate communications.[11] In addition, although research confirms that communication is an integral part of corporate strategy,[12] a recent survey showed that only 22 percent of line associates and 41 percent of supervisors understand their organization's strategy and that 54 percent of organizations do a poor job of communicating their strategy.[13] Thus, it appears that organizations and managers have much to learn about effective communication. Also, it is not surprising that a recent survey of corporate trainers found that 44 percent of their organizations planned to greatly increase their budgets for communication training for managers and senior leaders in the upcoming year.[14]

Communication can take many forms, such as face-to-face discussions, letters, memos, phone calls, notes posted on bulletin boards, presentations to groups of people, e-mail, and computer-based information systems. The purposes of communication are to provide information and instructions, to influence others, and to integrate activities.[15]

In this chapter, we examine communication in organizations, discuss barriers to it, and learn how to achieve it effectively. In the first section, we discuss the communication process. Next, we describe organizational communication, focusing on communication networks and the direction of communication. We then discuss interpersonal communication—that is, communication between individual associates. Finally, after describing various barriers to effective communication, we present ways in which these barriers can be overcome to build a successful communication process.

KNOWLEDGE OBJECTIVES

After reading this chapter, you should be able to:

1. Explain why communication is strategically important to organizations.

2. Describe the communication process.

3. Discuss important aspects of communication within organizations, including networks and the direction of communication flow.

4. Define interpersonal communication and discuss the roles of formal versus informal communication, communication media, communication technology, and nonverbal communication in the interpersonal communication process.

5. Describe organizational and individual barriers to effective communication.

6. Understand how organizations and individuals can overcome communication barriers.

The Communication Process

communication
The sharing of information between two or more people to achieve a common understanding about an object or situation.

Communication involves the sharing of information between two or more people to achieve a common understanding about an object or situation. Successful communication occurs when the person receiving the message understands it in the way that the sender intended. Thus, communication does not end with the message sent. We also need to consider the message that is received. Think of a time when you meant to compliment someone, but the person understood your remark as an insult. This was not successful communication—the message received was not the same as the one sent.

Communication can be viewed as a process, as shown in Exhibit 9-1. The starting point in the communication process is the sender—the person who wishes to communicate a message. To send a message, the sender must first encode it.

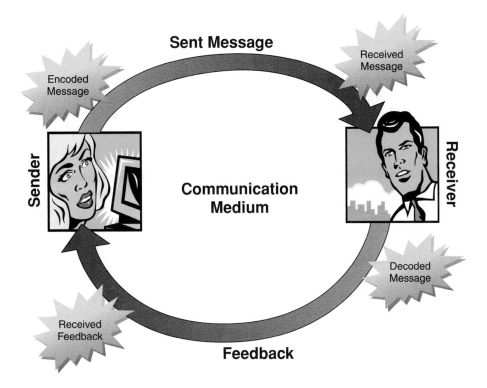

Exhibit 9-1
Sent Message

Encoding involves translating information into a message or a signal.[16] The encoded message is then sent through a **communication medium,** or **communication channel,** to the intended receiver. Communication media are numerous and include writing, face-to-face verbal exchanges, verbal exchanges without face-to-face contact (for example, phone conversations), e-mail, television, body language, facial expressions, touch (such as a pat on the shoulder), and visual symbols (such as an "okay" sign).

Once the message has been received, the receiver must decode it. In **decoding,** the receiver perceives the message and interprets its meaning.[17] To ensure that the meaning the receiver attaches to the message is the same as the one intended by the sender, feedback is necessary. **Feedback** is the process through which the receiver encodes the message received and sends it back to the original sender. Communication that includes feedback is referred to as *two-way* communication. If feedback is not present (resulting in *one-way* communication), the receiver may walk away with an entirely different interpretation than that intended by the sender.

All parts of the communication process are important. A communication breakdown can occur in any part of the process. For example, information must be encoded into a message that can be understood as the sender intended. In addition, some forms of media may not be as effective as others in communicating the meaning of a particular message. Some communication media are richer than others—that is, they provide more information.[18] Consider e-mail as an example. People often use symbols such as ":)" to indicate intent (in this case, humor) in e-mails because the medium is not very rich. If the message had been spoken, the humorous intent could have been indicated by the sender's tone of voice or facial expression. We describe more barriers to effective communication, as well as more details about media richness, later in the chapter.

encoding
The process whereby a sender translates the information he or she wishes to send in a message.

communication medium or communication channel
The manner in which a message is conveyed.

decoding
The process whereby a receiver perceives a sent message and interprets its meaning.

feedback
The process whereby a receiver encodes the message received and sends it back to the original sender.

Communication within Organizations

Communication occurs at several different levels. On one level is the communication that occurs among individuals or groups of individuals. This is referred to as interpersonal communication, and we discuss it in the next section. Here, we focus on *organizational communication*—that is, the patterns of communication that occur at the organizational level. As discussed later in this chapter, organizational communication can be either formal or informal. The purpose of organizational communication is to facilitate the achievement of the organization's goals. As we have already seen, communication is a necessary part of almost any action taken in an organization, ranging from transmitting the organization's strategy from top executives to line associates to integrating operations among different functional areas or units. Organizational communication involves the use of communication networks, policies, and structures.[19]

Centralized communication network
A communication network in which each network member only communicates with a few other members.

Decentralized communication network
A communication network in which many people can communicate with many other people.

Communication Networks

Communication networks represent patterns of communication. They describe the structure of communication flows in the organization, indicating who communicates with whom. There are a variety of possible patterns, and a few of the more common ones are presented in Exhibit 9-2. These networks are illustrated as two-way systems, although they may be one-way as well.

Networks serve various purposes in organizations; among other things they can be used to regulate behavior, promote innovation, integrate activities, and inform and instruct group members.[20] Networks also differ in the extent to which they are **centralized** or **decentralized.** In centralized networks, all communications

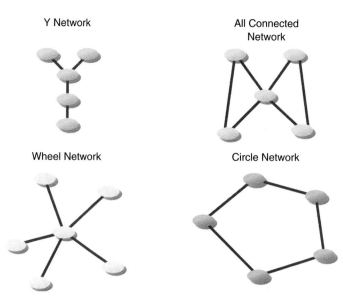

Exhibit 9-2
Communication
Networks

pass through a central point or points, so that each member of the network communicates with only a small number of others. The wheel and the Y networks depicted in Exhibit 9-2 are examples of centralized networks. Traditional organizational hierarchies, where subordinates communicate to their boss, who then communicate to his or her boss, are centralized networks. So are companies in which all units must communicate with a central headquarters, which then simultaneously coordinates all the units. In decentralized networks, many people or units can communicate with many others. The circle and all-channel communication networks depicted in Exhibit 9-2 are examples.

The results of several studies on communication networks show that the effectiveness of networks depends on situational factors.[21] For example, the wheel and the Y networks are more effective in accomplishing simple tasks. These structures promote efficiency, speed, and accuracy by channeling communication through a central person. However, the circle and the all-channel patterns are more effective for complex tasks. Communication among all parties facilitates the use of group resources to solve complex problems.

In addition, research has shown that a person's position in the network can affect personal satisfaction. Individuals in more central positions in the network tend to be more satisfied. The most central position is the one that can communicate with all members with the fewest number of links. For example, the person in the middle of the wheel network is the most central. Because individuals in the all-channel and circle networks are equally central, these two networks tend to produce higher levels of total member satisfaction.

The networks depicted in Exhibit 9-2 involve four or five individuals; however, networks are often considerably larger. In recent years, social scientists and mathematicians have been developing sophisticated theories of social networks that can be used to explain and predict such diverse phenomena as stock market crashes, the relationships between CEOs, the spread of disease, and the spread of computer viruses.[22]

For example, in the late 1990s, Toyota had a brief brush with disaster that has been attributed to its network structure. However, the situation was resolved quickly by the very network structure that caused the problem.[23] Here is what happened. Toyota actually is not a single company; rather, it is composed of about 200 separate companies that provide Toyota with the parts it needs to manufacture vehicles. The production units are independent, and each focuses on making a unique part (such as electrical components or seat covers). At the same time, the units are integrated because all follow Toyota's strict production system guidelines and protocols.

One of the businesses in the Toyota network is Aisin Seiki, which produces P-valves—brake devices that help prevent cars from skidding. The production of P-valves requires high precision, and the P-valves are a necessary component of every vehicle. If production of P-values stops, Toyota cannot complete the manufacture of any vehicles. Aisin Seiki was the sole provider of P-valves for Toyota, and all the valves were made in one plant. In 1997, this plant burned down, and it was predicted that production would stop for at least a month—which would ruin Toyota. However, because of the close coordination and effective communication among units, other plants were able to pick up the production of the precision P-valves with only about three days' preparation! Within a week, Toyota was once more manufacturing cars. Toyota's amazingly quick recovery can be attributed to the integration of all the units in its communication network.

Direction of Organizational Communication

Communication within organizations can occur in any of three directions: downward, upward, or horizontally.

downward communication
Communication that flows from supervisor to subordinate.

DOWNWARD COMMUNICATION

Downward communication, which refers to communication from supervisor to subordinate, is necessary to provide job instructions, information on organization policies, and performance feedback. Downward communication can also be used to inform associates about the organization's goals and about changes faced by the organization. (Downward communication is frequently deficient in this regard. Associates often complain about the lack of information on goals and changes being made in the organization.)

An example of the importance of downward communication can be seen in the recent merger of a large consumer-goods manufacturing company. The company was acquired by a large conglomerate, but no downward communication had taken place informing associates of what effects the merger would have on them. A rumor began to circulate among its highly professional finance department staff that the department was to be reduced to a record-keeping function. All major financial responsibilities were supposed to be transferred to the financial staff at the conglomerate's headquarters. Because of this rumor, many of the finance department's professional staff members sought and obtained jobs with other organizations. When top management realized the problem, it immediately announced that the rumor was false and assured associates that the financial responsibilities would remain in their organization. However, the company had lost almost 50 percent of its financial staff before this downward communication occurred.

upward communication
Communication that flows from subordinate to supervisor.

UPWARD COMMUNICATION

Upward communication, which flows from subordinate to supervisor, is necessary to provide feedback on downward communication. It is difficult to achieve, however; thus it is one of the least frequently used forms of communication in organizations. Common channels for obtaining upward communication include grievance procedures, departmental meetings, "open-door" policies, suggestion boxes, attitude surveys, participation in decisions, and exit interviews. Upward communication may be necessary to monitor the effectiveness of decisions, provide information, maintain associate morale, and ensure that jobs are being done properly. However, it will not occur in organizations where managers give the impression that they do not want to hear negative feedback or where subordinates do not trust superiors and fear reprisals. Upward communication can also be costly to organizations because they have to develop and implement policies and procedures to carry it out and also because it requires managers' time.[24]

Upward communication seems particularly difficult in larger organizations, probably because relationships in large organizations are more formalized.[25] Certainly larger size may inhibit the quantity of interactions between supervisor and associate; however, the quality of the interaction is the most critical element.[26] Meg Whitman, CEO of eBay, fosters upward communication through her practice of enabling associates to feel free to be totally honest with her. So successful is this approach that a newly minted MBA associate at eBay once felt free to proclaim that almost anyone could manage the company—implying that Whitman's job as CEO was easy. And because she enables associates to communicate upward, this brash young MBA is still an associate with the company.[27] Another organization, Connecticut Bank, encourages upward communication through employee attitude surveys. When survey results revealed that associates were dissatisfied with written communications in the organization, the bank focused on reducing the quantity and improving the quality of memos. Communication quality improved, and so did employee satisfaction and productivity. Finally, as illustrated in the *Experiencing Strategic Organizational Behavior* feature, J. Crew CEO Mickey Drexler makes it quite easy for his subordinates to communicate directly to him by frequently dropping in to J. Crew stores.

HORIZONTAL COMMUNICATION

Horizontal communication, which takes place between associates at the same level, is also important but is frequently overlooked in the design of organizations. Coordination among organizational units is facilitated by horizontal communication. For example, the manufacturing and marketing departments must coordinate and integrate their activities so that goods will be in inventory in anticipation of sales orders. This frequently is achieved through meetings, written memos, and informal interpersonal communication. Integrating positions may also be used to facilitate horizontal communications between units. These positions are often referred to as "boundary-spanning positions" because the position holders cross the boundaries that separate different units.[28] For example, some human resource departments have representatives or liaison members in each functional unit of the organization to coordinate and communicate staffing, compensation, and performance management activities.[29] Mickey Drexler often performs a boundary-spanning role by talking directly to customers.

> **horizontal communication** Communication that takes place between associates at the same level.

Recently, organizations have begun to use communication from all three directions in the area of performance appraisal. Almost all *Fortune* 500 companies use 360-degree multi-rater feedback to evaluate senior managers.[30] Such feedback often includes performance appraisals from peers (horizontal communication), subordinates (upward communication), and supervisors (downward communication).[31] Sometimes evaluations from customers, clients, and suppliers are also sought.

Some problems with 360-degree feedback have been observed. One problem with subordinates evaluating superiors is that they may retaliate for negative performance evaluations. Another problem is that peers may be politically motivated to either overrate or underrate their co-workers. Thus, it is usually recommended that upward appraisals be used only for training and development purposes and that the supervisor's evaluation be given more weight when appraisals are used to make personnel decisions (such as those involving promotions and pay raises).[32] However, if supervisors do take their own 360-degree feedback seriously, and change their behavior as a result of feedback from subordinates and peers, the loyalty of subordinate associates will also increase.[33]

EXPERIENCING STRATEGIC ORGANIZATIONAL BEHAVIOR

Communication at J. Crew: Mickey Drexler

Zena Olijnyk became extremely frustrated when responding to a promotional e-mail from J. Crew advertising the "retro-dot" mini skirt. She immediately tried to order the skirt online, but her size was not available. In a pique, she fired off an e-mail to J. Crew's customer service department complaining about sending promotional e-mail ads for items that were sold out. She was responded to immediately by a customer service representative who told her that the demand was much larger than expected and then apologized. She was still annoyed, so she asked that her complaint be forwarded to someone higher up—maybe even the CEO. The next day, Zena received the following e-mail from someone named Millard Drexler:

> Thx much for taking time to send email-have copied our team-it has been somewhat difficult for us to forecast demand on our fashion merchandise as have not expected the reaction we have been getting-your points about how we handle are right on-have been trying to communicate more effectively than doing right now, and obviously not doing a great job. If one of out (sic) team members not already searching your size, please let know if still interested.

Millard "Mickey" Drexler is the chairman and CEO of J. Crew. He took over the company after he was let go from the GAP in 2002, where he had been for 19 years. Drexler left the GAP because of a 29-month decline in profits. However, Drexler is the person who is credited with putting the GAP on the map, turning the company into a $14.5 billion business, and revolutionizing the way the world dresses (some say he invented "casual chic"). Mickey Drexler has done the same for J. Crew, taking the company from a failing business that lost $40 million in 2002 to one of the most profitable retail clothing companies around. He did this by cutting operating costs, bringing in his own team, raising prices while raising quality, applying his uncanny talent for spotting clothing trends, and engaging in a communication style that is somewhat unique among CEOs.

Not only does Drexler e-mail and call unhappy customers, he habitually drops in on J. Crew stores around the country to get a feel for what's selling, what's not, what is happening in individual stores, and to get input from sales associates in those stores. He walks into stores and quizzes customers about what they think and what they want. He also keeps in close contact with individual store managers. Once a week Drexler holds a conference call with store managers across the country. He asks them specific questions about what's going on in their stores, such as how customers reacted to a window display featuring suits (they liked it; sales rose dramatically). While Drexler is in his office at J. Crew headquarters, he spends most of his time running around, sticking his head into cubicles to personally talk with all associates. A recent survey found that most associates complain about a lack of face-to-face contact with the "higher-ups" and about not being asked their opinion. It seems unlikely that J. Crew team members would ever feel this way.

Drexler's communication style is also unique. He's loud, boisterous, infectiously passionate about the business, and incredibly honest when he voices his frequent opinions. A colleague from his GAP days described him as letting it all hang out—he does victory dances when pleased and yells when frustrated. In response to a pair of shorts shown to him by the design team, Drexler responded, "This is a monster! No one is doing these!" Another colleague stated "Mickey's fun, but he was making so much noise we had to close the doors. He yells and screams. . . ."

In the end, it is not surprising that Mickey Drexler has taken what was known as a failing, staid, preppy clothing company and turned it into an exciting, profitable, and much-talked-about success story. Through his direct and passionate communication with all stakeholders in the business, he seems to have channeled his energy and excitement.

Sources: Z. Olijnyk, "Now That's Service," *Canadian Business Online*, Feb. 20, 2007, at http://candianbusiness.com/shared/print.jsp?content= 20070220_130900_5412; L. Lee, "J. Crew's Smart-Looking IPO," *BusinessWeek*, June 28, 2006, at http://www.businessweek.com/print/investor/content/jun2006/pi20060628_109690.htm; T. Rozhon, "A Leaner J. Crew Is Showing Signs of a Turnaround," *New York Times*, June 24, 2004, at http://query.nytimes.com/gst/fullpage.html?res=9D02EFD6123F937A35755C0A9629C8; M. Gordon, "Mickey Drexler's Redemption," *New York* (nymag.com), at http://www.nymag.com/nymetro/news/bizfinance/biz/features/10489/index.html, accessed May 11, 2007; A. Maitland, "Employees Want to Hear It Straight from The Boss's Mouth," *Financial Times*, Dec. 1, 2006, p. 12.

Interpersonal Communication

We now move from the organizational level to the interpersonal level of communication. **Interpersonal communication** involves a direct verbal or nonverbal interaction between two or more active participants.[34] Interpersonal communication can take many forms, both formal and informal, and be channeled through numerous media. Furthermore, people can communicate without even intending to through nonverbal communication. In this section, we discuss each of these issues: formal versus informal communication, communication media, and nonverbal communication.

> **interpersonal communication**
> Direct verbal or nonverbal interaction between two or more active participants.

Formal versus Informal Communication

Much of the interaction that occurs within organizations involves interpersonal communication. Interpersonal communication can be formal or informal. **Formal communication** follows the formal structure of the organization (for example, supervisor to subordinate) and communicates organizationally sanctioned information. A major drawback of formal communication is that it can be slow. In contrast, **informal communication,** otherwise known as "the grapevine," involves spontaneous interaction between two or more people outside the formal organization structure. For example, communication between peers on their coffee break may be considered informal communication.

> **formal communication**
> Communication that follows the formal structure of the organization (for example, supervisor to subordinate) and communicates organizationally sanctioned information.

The informal system frequently emerges as an important source of communication for organization members.[35] Managers must recognize it and be sensitive to communication that travels through informal channels (such as the grapevine). In addition, managers may find that the informal system enables them to reach more members than the formal one. Another benefit of informal communication is that it can help build solidarity and friendship among associates.[36]

> **informal communication**
> Communication that involves spontaneous interaction between two or more people outside the formal organization structure.

Effective communication is crucial in implementing the organization's strategy. However, there is a downside to informal interpersonal communication—rumors

rumors
Unsubstantiated information of universal interest.

and gossip. **Rumors** are unsubstantiated information of universal interest. People often create and communicate rumors to deal with uncertainty.[37] This is why rumors are so prevalent during times of organizational upheaval, particularly during mergers and acquisitions. For example, in 2000, the Coca-Cola Company undertook a major restructuring to overcome its lagging financial performance.[38] During this period, persistent (and untrue) rumors flourished—such as "Coke is leaving Atlanta," "They're removing the flagpoles so that the American flag doesn't fly over the company," and "The CEO is leaving." These rumors resulted in dissatisfaction, loss of morale, and turnover, and top management had to spend a great deal of time overcoming and eliminating them. The impact of rumors can go beyond intraorganizational issues such as poor morale and turnover to affect the stock value and public worth of companies. For example, in 1998, a rumor that Lehman Brothers Holdings, Inc., was struggling to remain solvent led to a big reduction in the price of the investment bank's stock. In order to quell these rumors, Lehman Brothers had to release details of its financial status.[39] As discussed in the *Exploring Behavior in Action* feature on responses to hurricane Katrina, rumors of snipers, rape, and murder severely hindered rescue attempts.

gossip
Information that is presumed to be factual and communicated in private or intimate settings.

Gossip is information that is presumed to be factual and communicated in private or intimate settings.[40] Often, gossip is not specifically work related and focuses on things such as others' personal lives. Furthermore, gossip usually reflects information that is third-hand, fourth-hand, and even farther removed from the person passing it along. Gossip can cause problems for organizations because it reduces associates' focus on work, ruins reputations, creates stress, and can lead to legal problems. People are thought to engage in gossip in order to gain power or friendship or to enhance their own egos. For example, groups of low-status office workers may try to keep their supervisor in check by continuously gossiping about him and thus threatening his reputation. (Note, however, that people who gossip too much or are thought to communicate unreliable information are often evaluated poorly by others.)

To avoid rumors and gossip in the workplace, managers are advised to provide honest, open, and clear information in times of uncertainty. Rumors should be addressed by those in the position to know the truth. Gossip would be eradicated if people stopped communicating irrelevant, unsubstantiated information; however, the drive to do it can be compelling. Many offices have dealt with this by placing restrictions on idle chatter.

Communication Media

Interpersonal communication, as already mentioned, can use many different media, and different media vary in degree of richness. Recall that richness describes the amount of information a medium can convey. Richness depends on (1) the availability of feedback, (2) the use of multiple cues, (3) the use of effective language, and (4) the extent to which the communication has a personal focus.[41] Face-to-face verbal communication is the richest medium.[42] Think about all that happens during face-to-face interaction. Suppose that you (the sender) are talking to a friend. If your friend does not understand the message or interprets it inaccurately, she can let you know either verbally or nonverbally (for example, with a puzzled expression). In the interaction, you use multiple cues, including tone of voice, semantics (the words that are used), facial expressions, and body language. You use natural language and thus communicate more precise meaning. Finally, because you and your friend are face-to-face, it is easy to create a personal focus in the message.

Research has ordered common communication media in terms of richness.[43] In order of richest to least rich, they are:

1. Face-to-face communication

2. Telephone communication

3. Electronic messaging (such as e-mail and instant messaging)

4. Personal written text (such as letters, notes, and memos)

5. Formal written text (such as reports, documents, bulletins, and notices)

6. Formal numerical text (such as statistical reports, graphs, and computer printouts)

Choosing the type of media to use usually involves a trade-off between the richness of the medium and the cost (especially in time) of using it. For example, it is much easier and quicker to send someone a quick e-mail than to find his phone number, call him, and have a phone conversation, yet the phone conversation would likely yield richer information. Research on media richness suggests that effective managers will use richer media as the message becomes more equivocal.[44] *Equivocal* messages are those that can be interpreted in multiple ways. "We're having a meeting in the boardroom at 2 P.M. on Thursday" is an unequivocal message. "Your performance is not what I expected" is an equivocal message. Research has also shown that managers will use richer media when the message is important and when they feel the need to present a positive self-image (for example, when giving negative performance feedback).[45]

Another factor that influences the type of media that people choose to use is the organizational norms for what types of communication media are desireable.[46] Some organizations have strong norms that employees communicate in a face-to-face manner, resulting in many meetings and chatting in the office. Other organizations have strong norms for using electronic communications and the Internet. As mentioned at the beginning of the chapter, BP had strong norms for Internet-based communication and thus their Gulf Coast employees were better able to communicate after hurricane Katrina than were other people in the area. A recent study found that associates' use of e-mail and instant messaging was highly dependent on their organization's norms for the use of this technology.[47]

Communication Technology

Communication technology will continue to rapidly advance. E-mail, cell phones, the World Wide Web, audio, video and web conferencing, virtual private networks (VPNs), instant messaging, mobile communications (e.g., BlackBerrys), online chat rooms, social networking technology (e.g., MySpace, FaceBook) and web logs (blogs) either did not exist or were uncommon 15 years ago.[48] It is difficult to derive estimates on how common and frequently used new technology has become. However, here are some estimates that demonstrate the prevalence of technology in business organizations:

- Approximately 62 billion e-mails are sent each day.[49]
- As of May 2007, 9.2 percent of Fortune 500 companies made blogs available to the public. Many more have blogs that are available only internally for use by the company's associates. These numbers had doubled since the spring of 2006.[50]
- Hundreds of CEOs and top executives worldwide have blogs to communicate with associates, clients and customers, and the general public.[51] These include:
  - John Mackey, CEO, Whole Foods Market
  - Tom Glocer, CEO Reuters
  - Bob Lutz, vice chairman, General Motors

Exhibit 9-3	Communicating with Cutomers

22-February-2007
Dear JetBlue Customers,

We are sorry and embarrassed. But most of all, we are deeply sorry.

Last week was the worst operational week in JetBlue's seven year history. Following the severe winter ice storm in the Northeast, we subjected our customers to unacceptable delays, flight cancellations, lost baggage, and other major inconveniences. The storm disrupted the movement of aircraft, and, more importantly, disrupted the movement of JetBlue's pilot and inflight crewmembers who were depending on those planes to get them to the airports where they were scheduled to serve you. With the busy President's Day weekend upon us, rebooking opportunities were scarce and hold times at 1-800-JETBLUE were unacceptably long or not even available, further hindering our recovery efforts.

Words cannot express how truly sorry we are for the anxiety, frustration and inconvenience that we caused. This is especially saddening because JetBlue was founded on the promise of bringing humanity back to air travel and making the experience of flying happier and easier for everyone who chooses to fly with us. We know we failed to deliver on this promise last week.

We are committed to you, our valued customers, and are taking immediate corrective steps to regain your confidence in us. We have begun putting a comprehensive plan in place to provide better and more timely information to you, more tools and resources for our crewmembers and improved procedures for handling operational difficulties in the future. We are confident, as a result of these actions, that JetBlue will emerge as a more reliable and even more customer responsive airline than ever before.

Most importantly, we have published the **JetBlue Airways Customer Bill of Rights**—our official commitment to you of how we will handle operational interruptions going forward—including details of compensation. I have a <u>video message</u> to share with you about this industry leading action.

You deserved better—a lot better—from us last week. Nothing is more important than regaining your trust and all of us here hope you will give us the opportunity to welcome you onboard again soon and provide you the positive JetBlue Experience you have come to expect from us.

Sincerely,

David

Source: http://www.jetblue.com/aboutourcompany/flightlog/archive_February2007/.html.

- David Neeleman, founder and chairman of JetBlue Airways
- Jonathan Schwartz, CEO and president, Sun Microsystems
- Instant messaging is used in 85 percent of companies worldwide.[52]

This new technology allows organizations and their members to communicate more quickly, across any distance, and to collaborate more effectively than ever before.[53] Indeed, in order for organizations to remain competitive, they need to constantly keep up to date on modern communication technologies.[54] For example, after the great blackout of 2003 struck the eastern United States and Canada, IBM employees were able to fall back on instant messaging technology to continue working, while many other organizations, which did not use wireless technology, were crippled.

Technology also allows organizations and their members to communicate to new and varied audiences. Blogs (informal electronic communication sites that reach a wide audience) provide one mechanism for doing so. Twenty-seven percent of Internet users read blogs. Organizations have been creating blogs to communicate a variety of messages related to advertising, explaining corporate decisions, or learning consumer thinking in the general marketplace.[55] For example, Stonyfield Farms, the largest organic yogurt company in the world, uses blogs to interact with its customers on health-related topics relevant to the yogurt business.[56] When JetBlue Airways canceled half of its flights and kept passengers waiting in planes on the runway for up to 11 hours, they had a lot of apologizing to do—especially for a company known for its customer service.[57] One way in which the company regained its service reputation was through Chairman David Neeleman's blog message to the passengers and the general public. This message is presented in Exhibit 9-3. Another way in which organizations are using new technology is in the area of hiring and recruitment, as discussed in the following *Managerial Advice* feature.

Although the adoption of communication technologies can be beneficial to organizations and their members, they continuously evolve, and new communication technologies can also cause problems. One common problem is *information overload*, which is discussed later in this chapter. Another problem is that the new technology makes it easier to leak private or secret information to an unintended audience and often with unintended consequences. For example, Mark Jen, a programmer at Google, blogged about the company's unfavorable health plan.[58] This blog caused Jen to be fired and served as a warning to other bloggers at Google. Finally, as illustrated in the *Managerial Advice* feature, personal privacy concerns that did not exist 10 years ago are now very apparent.

MANAGERIAL ADVICE

Surfing for Applicants

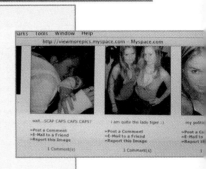

Eva Montibello, a marketing manager in a Boston consulting firm, was sorting through job applications, when a member of her staff came up and told her to check out a particular applicant's MySpace page. Eva did, and was quite shocked to find many compromising photos of the applicant, including one involving Jell-O wrestling. When this applicant was asked about the photos in her interview, she laughed it off and was quite silly about them. In the end, the unprofessional photos and unprofessional response to the photos were a factor in why this applicant was not hired by Eva's firm.

In recent years, the way in which companies recruit associates has gone through a revolution due to the availability of technology that allows employers to connect with and get information about potential job applicants. It used to be that when an individual applied for a job, the hiring organization had access only to information provided by past employers, schools, or the applicant. Now, for many people, there exists an abundance of information out there in Cyberspace and organizations are using this information to evaluate job candidates. Employers have access to information about candidates that they would never dream of asking about in an interview, such as social activities, religious activities, friends, and what people really think about their old boss.

In a 2006 survey by executive search firm ExecuNet, 77 percent of recruiters said they use search engines to check out job candidates. In a recent Career-Builder.com survey of 1,150 hiring managers, 25 percent reported using search engines to gather information on applicants and over 10 percent also check social networking sites such as FaceBook and MySpace. According to the CareerBuilder survey, recruiters found these searches quite informative. In terms of negative information about applicants, they found that:

- 31 percent lied about qualifications.
- 25 percent had poor communication skills.
- 24 percent were linked to criminal behavior.
- 19 percent badmouthed their previous employers.
- 19 percent posted information about drinking or drug use.
- 15 percent shared confidential information from prior employers.
- 12 percent lied about an absence.
- 11 percent posted provocative photographs.

There was also good news to report. In terms of positive information:

- 64 percent of hiring managers searching online found information supporting a candidate's qualifications.
- 34 percent found evidence of great communication skills.
- 31 percent could see a match between the candidate and the corporate culture.
- 23 percent saw good professional references.
- 23 percent perceived the candidate as being creative.

The message is quite clear: People need to be aware of the electronic image that they project. Services such as Jobster.com can provide help in doing this. Not only do companies screen people out based on negative information, they also look for positive information as cited in the above survey results. Some companies, such as Wal-Mart, have even hired people who did not initially apply. Wal-Mart contacted them because they liked what they had read on the individual's blog.

Sources: D. Aucoin, "MySpace vs. Workplace," *Boston Globe,* May 29, 2007, at http://www. boston.com/news/globe/living/articles/2007/05/29/myspace_vs_workplace; W.M. Bulkeley, "Technology (A Special Report)—The Inside View: Employee Blogs Can Put a Human Face on Companies, But That's Not Always a Good Thing," *Wall Street Journal* (Eastern Edition), New York: Apr. 3, 2006, p. R.7; M. Brandel, "How to 'Get Found' On the Web," *Computerworld,* Framingham: Mar. 26, 2007, vol. 41, no. 13, p. 30; Anonymous, "Using Social Networking Sites for Recruitment: Pros & Cons," *HR Focus,* New York: April 2007, vol. 84, no. 4, pp. 8–9; S.E. Needleman, "How Blogging Can Help You Get a New Job," *Wall Street Journal* (Eastern Edition), Apr. 10, 2007, p. B.1.

Nonverbal Communication

We can easily understand the concept of verbal communication, which involves written or oral language; however, **nonverbal communication** is frequently as important. Forms of nonverbal communication include facial expressions, tone of voice, personal appearance (such as dress), contact or touch, and various mannerisms. In general, nonverbal communications fall into three categories: body language, paralanguage, and gestures. *Body language* (sometimes referred to as *kinesics*) includes facial expressions; the use of hands, arms, and legs; and posture. *Paralanguage* refers to how something is said, such as how tone of voice, pitch of voice, and silence are used. *Gestures* are signs used to convey specific meanings (such as making a circle with your fingers to indicate "okay" or shrugging your shoulders to indicate "I don't know").

> **nonverbal communication** Communication that takes place without using language, such as facial expressions or body language.

All of us have had a great deal of experience with nonverbal communication. In fact, between 60 and 90 percent of all interpersonal communication is nonverbal.[59] You have probably heard the adage "actions speak louder than words" or heard someone say they received "good vibes" from someone else. These phrases refer to nonverbal communication. One of the reasons that we place so much weight on nonverbal behavior is that it is "leaky behavior." Leaky behaviors are those that we cannot control. Therefore, people may be more likely to express their true feelings through nonverbal means rather than verbal means that are easy to control.

Nonverbal communication is important because, along with the sender's verbal expressions, it provides information about the person's attitudes and emotional or mental state. For example, a person's tone of voice, facial expression, and body movements can give us information about the person's feelings (timidity, enthusiasm, anger), which may either support or conflict with the words used. Nonverbal communication can also provide a useful form of feedback. Facial expressions can show whether the receiver understands the sender's message and how he or she feels about it. For this reason, face-to-face communication is frequently more effective than written communication, as we have already seen. In general, therefore, a supervisor should try to provide job directions and discuss performance through face-to-face communication with associates.

Because nonverbal behavior is more difficult to control than verbal behavior, it can reveal whether a person is lying. This issue has been given a great deal of attention, especially in light of its practical implications. For example, U.S. Customs officials were able to increase their hit rate in spotting drug carriers from 4.2 percent to 22.5 percent after they had been trained to read body language.[60] The detection of lying is also very important in the area of negotiations. The negotiating abilities of an organization's members are critical to an organization's overall performance. It is important that people engaging in negotiations be able to read body language to identify when others are being deceptive. It is also important for negotiators to be aware of their own nonverbal cues.[61] For example, experienced negotiators often are able to determine whether their opponent is lying through nonverbal cues such as the following:

- Subtle shifts in the pitch or tone of a person's voice[62]
- Long pauses before answering a question[63]
- Certain mannerisms, such as shifting limbs, licking one's lips repeatedly, scratching, or grooming[64]
- Fleeting smiles[65]

Another issue involves cultural differences in nonverbal communication. Given the increase in diversity within U.S. organizations and the globalization of the business world, it has become highly important for people to understand these differences. Cultures vary a great deal in how they present themselves and in their norms for nonverbal communication. Some of these differences are discussed later in the chapter. However, one aspect of nonverbal communication appears to be the same for all human beings. People of all cultures seem to discern and label facial expressions showing certain basic emotions in the same way.[66] These basic emotions include fear, disgust, surprise, happiness, and anger. Therefore, people in the United States, Spain, Argentina, New Guinea, and Japan are all likely to recognize a smile as a sign of happiness and a scowl as a sign of disgust.

Barriers to Effective Communication

At the beginning of this chapter, we emphasized how important timely, accurate, and informative communication is to an organization's overall performance and to the individuals who work within the firm. We also pointed out that organizations experience many communication problems. Here, we address the barriers to effective communication. These barriers range from those in the organization's external environment to those that affect the individual.[67]

Organizational Barriers

Organizational barriers to effective communication include information overload, noise, time pressures, breakdown in the communication network, information distortion, and cross-cultural barriers.

INFORMATION OVERLOAD

In our present-day organizations, managers and associates are frequently burdened with more information than they can process. This overload occurs for several reasons. First, organizations face higher levels of uncertainty because of escalating change and turbulence in the external environment, so they obtain more information to reduce the uncertainty. Second, the increasing complexity of tasks and organization structures creates a need for more information. Again, organizations employ more specialists to provide the needed information, placing greater information-processing burdens on organizational members. Third, ongoing developments in technology—small mobile computers, the Internet, intranets, the growing number of large organizational databases—increase the amount of information available to associates and managers.

As mentioned, when associates or managers are overloaded with information, they cannot process all of it. Instead, they may try to escape the situation, or they may prioritize information so that some is attended to and the rest is ignored. Consider what happens when you are at a party and there are several conversations going on around you, music is playing, and someone is watching the game on TV. It is impossible to focus on everything. In order to focus on a specific conversation, you need to tune out everything else. Selecting only parts of the available information for use, however, can result in inaccurate or incomplete communication in the organizational context.[68]

In recent years, the development and widespread use of cell phones, e-mail, and instant messaging has further increased the information overload problem—anyone can contact anyone anywhere. People in most organizations send and receive e-mail messages at work on a regular basis. Therefore, even associates at lower levels can quickly and easily send messages to higher-level managers. Similarly, top executives can communicate messages almost instantaneously to all associates regardless of their location. Obviously, this technology contributes to information overload, particularly for managers at higher levels. With these advances in technology, we are facing two overload problems that were not so common only a few years ago: spamming and forwarding frenzies.

As you are no doubt aware, spam is unsolicited electronic junk mail. Despite anti-spam legislation in many states and increasingly sophisticated filtering systems that guard against offensive spam, the amount of spam with which people must cope at work is increasing at an alarming rate. Indeed, *InformationWeek* reported that almost 80 percent of all e-mail sent in February 2007 was spam mail.[69] A study conducted by researchers at the University of Maryland estimated that spam mail cost U.S. businesses almost $22 billion due to lost associate time spent reading and deleting the junk mail.[70]

Forwarding frenzies occur because electronic communication makes it very easy to pass on information to anyone, thereby potentially increasing information overload. One common behavior is to forward messages to anyone who might have even the remotest interest in them. Thus, we receive many messages that we need to process but in which we do not have any interest.

One way in which organizations are trying to deal with the overload caused by electronic messaging and e-mail is by adopting newer, web-based interactive technologies for internal communications. These include blogs, wiki sites, and social networking sites. With this technology, messages are all posted in one place, avoiding redundancy. Also, new anti-spam software has helped businesses cut down on the cost of unwanted e-mail.

NOISE

Information overload can lead to noise because the excess information may distract listeners from focusing on and correctly understanding any one message. **Noise** is anything that disrupts communication or distorts the message. In the case of overload, associates may receive so much information that they are unable to discern what is important or accurate and what is not. Noise can be either an organizational-level barrier or an individual-level barrier. It may occur at any step in the communication process or within any element, and it may occur in many forms. Often, it is unintentional, as when two parties have different perceptions of a message. But at times noise may be intentional. For example, research has shown that subordinates frequently withhold or distort information that is potentially threatening to them when communicating with their superiors.[71] Other examples of noise include language barriers (especially in international firms), interruptions, emotions, and attitudes.

noise
Anything that disrupts communication or distorts the message.

TIME PRESSURES

In most organizations work needs to be done under deadlines, which create time pressures and constrain an individual's ability to communicate. When people are under time pressure, they sometimes do not carefully develop a message before sending it.[72] In addition, the pressure of a deadline often does not allow for time to receive feedback, so the sender may not know whether the receiver accurately perceived the message.

NETWORK BREAKDOWNS

Breakdowns in the communication network frequently occur in large organizations because so much information flows through those networks. Many things can interfere with the flow—mail can be misplaced, messages may not be received by those targeted, and people can forget to relay pieces of information. Larger organizations have more problems because messages must flow through more people, increasing the probability that the message will be transmitted inaccurately at some point. A vivid example of a communication network breakdown confronted first responders to the Hurricane Katrina disaster, as discussed in the *Exploring Behavior in Action* case at the beginning of this chapter; they found that almost all of their traditional communication media did not work.

One other factor that can cause communication network breakdowns is the architecture of the work environment. In one study, people who were physically central and close to many others received and were able to communicate a great deal of information. However, those who were physically separated from their associates (e.g., their offices were on a different floor than the rest of their work group) did not receive as much information. Thus, the portion of the communication network linking those who were physically distant often broke down.[73]

SPECIALTY AREA JARGON

One problem in large, complex organizations concerns the proliferation of specialists. Specialists are highly knowledgeable within their own fields but frequently have limited understanding of other fields. In addition, they often have their own "language," or jargon. It may be difficult for two specialists in different fields to communicate effectively with one another because they use different terminology. For example, a financial specialist may use terms such as *NEBT, accelerated depreciation,* and *P and L statement.* A computer specialist may use terms such as *firmware, hexadecimal, bytes,* and *PLII.* Each must understand the other's terminology if the two are to communicate.

INFORMATION DISTORTION

It is common for information to be distorted, either intentionally or unintentionally. Unintentional distortion can occur because of problems cited previously, such as time pressures, or because of perceptual differences (discussed later in the chapter). However, intentional distortion often occurs because of competition between work units in an organization. Departments frequently have to compete for scarce resources in their operating budgets. Research has suggested that some units may believe that they can compete more effectively by distorting or suppressing information, thus placing their competitors at a disadvantage by keeping accurate information from them.[74] This is not a healthy situation, but it can occur if managers are not careful.

Suppression or distortion of information can (and does) also occur when an associate has more information than his or her supervisor. One study found that some associates suppress or misrepresent information about budgets when they have private information unknown to the supervisor.[75] For example, associates may suppress information about the amount of travel expenses, leaving the supervisor to discover the problem at audit time.

CROSS-CULTURAL BARRIERS

As discussed in Chapter 3, the business world is becoming more global, increasing the amount of regular cross-cultural communication. Effective cross-cultural communication is necessary to the financial success of international ventures.[76] Communication problems cause many expatriate managers to fail in their international assignments, leading to the removal of the manager or the failure of the international venture. These failures cost multinational corporations billions of dollars.[77] Many U.S. firms compete in foreign markets, and increasing numbers of foreign firms have moved into the U.S. market in recent years. Department of Labor statistics indicate that in 2004, more than 21 million workers were foreign born (one in seven U.S. workers), half of these workers were new immigrants arriving after 1990, and almost 40 percent came from Mexico and Central America and another 25 percent came from Asia (Philippines, India, China, Vietnam, and Korea).[78] This figure is expected to grow. Thus, North American workers must deal with cross-cultural communication issues even in domestic locations. Exhibit 9-4 lists common differences in communication patterns in the United States and other cultures.

Cross-cultural barriers occur for two general reasons: lack of language fluency and lack of cultural fluency.[79] Even though English is becoming an international language for business,[80] the potential for language barriers continues to exist in cross-cultural communications. One study found that U.S. firms doing business in foreign countries received 41 percent of their correspondence from foreign firms in English. Only 42 percent of these firms had associates who could interpret the

Exhibit 9-4	Examples of Cultural Differences between the United States and Other Cultures	
Communication	In the United States	Elsewhere
Eye contact	Direct	In many Asian countries, extended eye contact is unacceptable.
Time orientation	Punctual— "Time is money"	Asian and Latin American cultures have longer time horizons; resolving issues is more important than being on time.
Answering questions	Direct and factual	Many Asian cultures view being direct as rude and aggressive.
Self-presentation	Self-promotion rewarded	Many other cultures (e.g., Asian, Russian) find this rude.
Posture	Open body posture preferred (e.g., arms relaxed)	In Japan, a closed body posture is preferred (e.g., crossed arms and legs).
Indicating "no"	Shaking one's head from side to side	In Bulgaria, the "no" signal means "I'm listening," rather than "I disagree."

remaining correspondence, which was written in languages other than English. Not surprisingly, the study concluded that knowledge of the domestic language in countries where the firm has local operations is valuable.[81] In addition, those who learn the local language often earn more respect within the local culture.

Because many products are sold internationally, language is also an increasingly important consideration in product names and slogans. Major companies have experienced poor results by trying to use North American English names for products sold in foreign countries, especially when they have ignored how the name translated into other languages. For example, Enco (the former name of Exxon petroleum company) means "stalled car" in Japanese. Direct translation of advertising slogans presents similar problems. The slogan "Come alive with Pepsi," for instance, translated into "Come out of the grave" in German.

Language fluency is one dimension of what is known as **cultural fluency**—the ability to identify, understand, and apply cultural differences that influence communication.[82] Language fluency is necessary for cultural fluency but is not itself enough. Take, for example, the situation faced by Sue, an expatriate manager. When she was in Singapore, she asked a hotel clerk, who spoke English fluently, for the location of the health spa. She had seen several signs indicating that the hotel had opened a new gym, but none of the signs gave the location. The clerk responded that the hotel had no spa, although Sue kept arguing, "But I saw the signs!" After asking others and finally finding the gym, Sue concluded that the first clerk either had lied to her or was totally incompetent. Had she understood that many Asian cultures uphold the value of "face," or unwillingness to experience the embarrassment of saying "I don't know," she might have interpreted the situation differently.

Cultural fluency can affect many dimensions of organizational behavior, including negotiating styles, nonverbal behavior, personal space, and the use of symbols. The following *Experiencing Strategic Organizational Behavior* feature demonstrates cultural communication problems associates from various cultures have encountered and the issues on over which these problems commonly occur.

cultural fluency
The ability to identify, understand, and apply cultural differences that influence communication.

EXPERIENCING STRATEGIC ORGANIZATIONAL BEHAVIOR

Cultural Communication Snafus

Kevin Widlic, an internal communications manager for the Norwegian company Hydro, talks about the early days of integrating with a German company Hydro had acquired. The Norwegian associates wrote informal e-mails and memos and did not use proper titles, calling everyone by their first names. This caused a great deal of confusion on the part of the German associates because they could not figure out who was in charge and who had responsibility for what. Norway is a low power distance country and Germany has a high power distance culture.

When an international software developer assembled a team of associates from the United States and from India to work on producing a new product, trouble began immediately. The Indians estimated it would take two to three months to complete the project, whereas the Americans thought it would take only two weeks. Throughout the project, the Indian associates avoided reporting setbacks in production to the Americans, who would find out about problems only when they were working on the project. This team never learned to work together successfully by overcoming their cultural differences.

A Latin American member of a multicultural consulting team reported becoming frustrated because he felt that he was always ignored in meetings because he spoke English with an accent and was not always able to come up with the English words to fully explain what he was thinking. His partner's response was to become the dominant team member and take over, even though the two men were at the same organizational level.

Expatriate managers working in a foreign company in Thailand consistently complained that their Thai associates took on work assignments that they did not complete and did not inform their manager of the problems. This behavior is a manifestation of the Thai cultural value of *kreng jai*, where the norm is to agree to whatever your boss asks, even if you are not sure you can do it. This cultural value was foreign to the Hungarian and U.S. expatriate managers.

The above are just a few examples of the multitude of cross-cultural miscommunications that take place every day in the global business environment. Common sources of cross-cultural communication snafus are:

- *Opening and closing conversations.* Different cultures have different ways of greeting each other, showing respect, and starting off the conversation. For example, Americans shake hands; the Japanese bow. Norwegians call everyone by their first name; Germans use formal titles (*Herr Doktor*).
- *Taking turns during conversations.* Some cultures prefer to have more interactive conversations, whereas others prefer to have everyone speak their piece without comment or interruption from others.
- *The signaling of agreement.* Different cultures have different manners of signaling agreement. Traditionally, Chinese do not like to say "no," because it can mean a loss of face. Anglo cultures have no problem with saying "no" loud and clear.
- *Appropriate topics of conversation.* Cultures vary in how appropriate they consider topics such as religion, politics, family, personal lives, and money.
- *Use of humor.* In the United States, it is common to use humor in the workplace to ease tension and to make work more enjoyable. However, other cultures may consider the use of humor offensive and disrespectful.
- *Direct versus indirect communication.* Most Western cultures prefer direct communication, where the words spoken reflect what is actually meant. Other cultures, such as many Asian cultures, prefer indirect communication, where one must consider who is speaking and the context of the conversation.
- *Acknowledgment of authority and status.* Power distance was discussed as an important cultural value in Chapter 3. The extent to which a culture accepts power and status differences greatly influences communication styles. For example, in cultures with a high power distance, directive and nonparticipative managers are preferred—people expect to be told what to do. On the other hand, low power distance cultures would find this management style overbearing, preferring a much more informal and participative style.

Sources: Anonymous, 2007, "Describe a Cultural Miscommunication That You Experienced and How You Would Handle It Differently Now," *Communication World,* Jan.–Feb. 2007, p. 14; J. Brett, K. Behfar, & M.C. Kern, 2006, "Managing Multicultural Teams," *Harvard Business Review,* No. 2006, pp. 84–91; R. Sriussadaporn, 2006, "Managing International Business Communication Problems at Work," Pilot Study in Foreign Companies in Thailand, *Cross-Cultural Management: An International Journal* 13(4); pp. 330–344; D. Hannon, May 18, 2006, "Dos and Don'ts of Doing Business in China," *Purchasing,* 135(8), pp. 52–54; R.J. House, P.J. Hanges, M. Javidan, P.W. Dorfman, & V. Gupta, 2004, *Culture, Leadership, and Organizations* (Thousand Oaks, CA: Sage Publications); A.J. Schuler cited in "Cross Cultural Communication," at http://corp.americanexpress.com/gcs/travel/us/tips/CrossCultureCom.aspx.

The above *Experiencing Strategic Organizational Behavior* feature illustrates the strategic importance of managing cultural communication barriers that go beyond simply not speaking the same language. Examples of these barriers occur between peers, subordinates, and supervisors, and at every level of the organization. If organizations are to survive in a global environment, it is essential that they develop the cultural fluency of their associates.[83]

Individual Barriers

We have examined several organizational factors that can make effective communication difficult. Individual factors, however, are the most commonly cited barriers to effective communication. These factors include differing perceptual bases, semantic differences, status differences, consideration of self-interest, personal space, and poor listening skills.

DIFFERING PERCEPTIONS

One of the most common communication failures occurs when the sender has one perception of a message and the receiver has another. Differing perceptions are caused by differing frames of reference. Our expectations or frames of reference can influence how we recall and interpret information.[84]

This communication problem is vividly displayed in an exchange that recently occurred between a coach and a quarterback in a hotly contested football game. There were 16 seconds left in the game. The team was behind by one point and had the ball on its opponent's 20-yard line with no timeouts remaining. A field goal would win the game. The safest thing to do would be to call a running play and then kick a field goal. The coach decided, however, that it was necessary to risk a pass play because no timeouts were left. (If the pass was dropped, the clock would stop. If it was caught in the end zone, the game was won.)

The coach told the quarterback to call the play that they had discussed in practice for just such a situation. But they had discussed two plays (one a pass into the end zone and the other a running play). The quarterback assumed the coach wanted to take the safest course and called the running play. He handed off to the fullback, who carried the ball into the middle of the line. A big pileup ensued, and the clock continued to run. Before the quarterback could get off another play, time had run out, and the team had lost the game. The coach and the quarterback had two different perceptions of the meaning of one message.

SEMANTIC DIFFERENCES

Semantics refers to the meaning people attach to symbols, such as words and gestures. Because the same words may have different meanings to different people, semantic differences can create communication problems. For example, the word *profit* has a positive connotation to most professionals in business, but other people sometimes have a negative connotation of *profit,* interpreting it to mean "rip-off" or "exploitation." (This difference is evident in the problems oil companies have had in explaining their profits to the general public.)

One reason for semantic differences relates to the proliferation of specialists in organizations, as we mentioned earlier. Specialists tend to develop their own jargon; such terminology may have little meaning to a person outside the specialist's field.

STATUS DIFFERENCES

Status differences can result from both organizational and individual factors. Organizations create status differences through titles, offices, and support resources, but individuals attribute meaning to these differences. Status differences can lead to problems of source credibility and can create problems that block upward communication (and thus feedback).[85] Sometimes, for example, subordinates are reluctant to express an opinion that is different from their manager's, and managers—because of either time pressures or arrogance—may strengthen status barriers by not being open to feedback or other forms of upward communication. To be effective communicators, managers must overcome the status difference that exists between them and the associates reporting to them.

CONSIDERATION OF SELF-INTEREST

Often, information provided by a person is used to assess his or her performance. For example, it is not uncommon for firms to request information from managers about their units' performance. Data such as forecasts of future activity, performance standards, and recommendations on capital budgets are often used in determining the managers' compensation. Research shows that where data accuracy cannot be independently verified, managers sometimes provide information that is in their own self-interest.[86] Although this does not necessarily mean they intentionally distort information, they may provide incomplete data, selecting only information that is in their own best interests.

PERSONAL SPACE

All of us have a *personal space* surrounding our bodies. When someone enters that space, we feel uncomfortable. The size of the personal space differs somewhat among individuals; it also differs by gender and across cultures.[87] Women seem to have smaller personal spaces than men. Similarly, the typical personal space in some cultures (such as some European and South American cultures) is smaller than that in other cultures (such as the United States). Personal space affects, for example, how close together people stand when conversing. Suppose someone from a culture where the norm is to stand close together is talking with someone from a culture where the norm is to stand farther apart. The first person will tend to move forward as the second backs away, with each trying to adjust the space according to a different cultural norm. Each may consider the other discourteous, and it will be difficult for either to pay attention to what the other is saying. In this case, the difference in personal space can be a barrier to communication.

POOR LISTENING SKILLS

A frequent problem in communication rests not with the sender but with the receiver. The receiver must listen in order to hear and understand the sender's message, just as the sender must listen to feedback from the receiver. Managers spend more than 50 percent of their time in verbal communication, and some researchers estimate that they spend as much as 85 percent of this time talking. This does not leave much time for listening and receiving feedback. Perhaps more importantly, it has been estimated that managers listen with only about 25 percent efficiency.[88] Therefore, they hear and understand only 25 percent of what is communicated to them verbally. This can lead the speaker to become annoyed and discouraged, thus leaving a bad impression of the listener.[89] Poor listening is not conducive to high-involvement management, because it breaks down the communication process and will limit information sharing. Later we discuss ways in which listening can be improved.

Communication Audits

Analyzing the organization's communication needs and practices through periodic communication audits[90] is an important step in establishing effective communication. A **communication audit** examines an organization's internal and external communication to assess communication practices and capabilities and to determine needs. Communication audits can be conducted in-house (for example, by the human resource management department) or by external consulting firms. Communication audits often are used to ascertain the quality of communication and to pinpoint any communication deficiencies in the organization. Audits can be conducted for the entire organization or a single unit within the organization.

Communication audits usually examine the organization's communication philosophy and objectives, existing communication programs, communication media used, quantity and quality of personal communications, and employee attitudes toward existing communications. The following is a recommended methodology for conducting a communication audit:

* Hold a planning meeting with all major parties to determine a specific approach and gain commitment to it.
* Conduct interviews with top management.
* Collect, inventory, and analyze communication material.
* Conduct associate interviews.
* Prepare and administer a questionnaire to measure attitudes toward communication.
* Communicate survey results.[91]

Communication Climates

An organization's **communication climate** is the perception that associates have regarding the quality of communications within the organization.[92] The communication climate is important because it influences the extent to which associates identify with their organization.[93] Organizations can overcome communication barriers by establishing a communication climate where mutual trust exists between senders and receivers, communication credibility is present, and feedback is encouraged. Managers also should encourage a free flow of downward, upward, and horizontal communication.[94] People must be comfortable in communicating their ideas openly and in asking questions when they do not understand or they want to know more. Information should be available and understandable. People in organizational units should be allowed to develop their own communication systems independently for an effective communication culture.[95]

Individual Actions

Managers and associates can also act as individuals to help overcome communication barriers. Experts recommend the following ways to improve interpersonal communication.

KNOW YOUR AUDIENCE

People often engage in what communication expert Virgil Scudder refers to as "me to me to me" communication.[96] With this phrase, Scudder is describing communicating with others as if you were communicating with yourself. Such communication assumes that others share your frame of reference and, in the absence of feedback, that people interpret the message as you intend it. Take, for example, an information technology expert trying to explain to his technologically unsophisticated colleagues how to use new computer software. He may use jargon that they do not understand, not fully explain the steps, and mistake their dumbfounded silence for understanding. In the end, the IT professional believes he has done his job and taught others how to use the new program. However, because of poor communication, his colleagues learned little and are frustrated. To communicate effectively, people must know their audience, including the audience's experience, frames of references, and motivations.

SELECT AN APPROPRIATE COMMUNICATION MEDIUM

Earlier, we discussed how various communication media differ in richness. When messages are important or complex, use of rich media, such as face-to-face communication, is necessary.[97] Also, when dealing with important and/or complex information, it is best to use several communications—for example, by following a face-to-face communication with an e-mail message summarizing the discussion.

LISTEN ACTIVELY

As mentioned earlier, poor listening skills are a common barrier to effective communication. People tend to hear and understand only around 25 percent of what is communicated to them verbally.[99] Listening is not a passive, naturally occurring activity. People must actively and consciously listen to others in order to be effective communicators. Exhibit 9-5 outlines the steps in being an active listener.

Exhibit 9-5	Steps to Effective Listening

1. *Stop talking.* Often, we talk more than we should without giving the other person a chance to respond. If we are thinking about what we will say when we talk, we cannot focus attention on the person we wish to listen to. Do not interrupt.

2. *Pay attention.* Do not allow yourself to be distracted by thinking about something else. Often, we need to make an active effort to pay attention when others are speaking.

3. *Listen empathetically.* Try to take the speaker's perspective. Mirror the speaker's body language and give him or her nonjudgmental encouragement to speak.

4. *Hear before evaluating.* Do not draw premature conclusions or look for points of disagreement. Listen to what the person has to say before jumping to conclusions or judgment.

5. *Listen to the whole message.* Look for consistency between the verbal and the nonverbal messages. Try to assess the person's feelings or intentions, as well as just facts.

6. *Send feedback.* In order to make sure that you have heard correctly, paraphrase what was heard and repeat it to the person you were listening to.

ENCOURAGE FEEDBACK

Communication is a two-way process. To ensure that the received message is interpreted as intended, feedback from the recipient is necessary. Some guidelines that individuals can use to obtain feedback are as follows:

- Ask recipients to repeat what they have heard.
- Promote and cultivate feedback, but don't try to force it.
- Reward those who provide feedback and use the feedback received. For example, thank people for providing feedback.
- Respond to feedback, indicating whether it is correct.[98] In other words, obtain feedback, use it, and then feed it back to recipients.

REGULATE INFORMATION FLOW AND TIMING

Regulating the flow of information can help to alleviate communication problems. Regulating flow involves discarding information of marginal importance and conveying only significant information. That is, do not pass on irrelevant information, or else important messages may be buried by information overload or noise.

The proper timing of messages is also important. Sometimes people are more likely to be receptive to a message and to perceive it accurately than at other times. Thus, if you have an important message to send, you should not send it when recipients are about to leave work, are fully engaged in some other task, or are receiving other communication.

The Strategic Lens

Organizations cannot accomplish their goals without using effective communication practices. Managers and leaders must communicate with associates to ensure that they understand the tasks to be done. In doing so, they need to use a two-way communication process to make certain that communication is understood as intended. Without effective communication, human capital in the organization will be underutilized and will not be leveraged successfully. Organizations that do not use their human capital well usually implement their strategies ineffectively, and so their performance suffers. When firms perform poorly, they often change their strategy because they do not realize that the strategy implementation—not the actual strategy—was the problem. Of course, with continued poor performance, CEOs are likely to lose their jobs.[100]

Information serves as a base for developing organizational strategies. Usually, the organization gathers significant amounts of information on its markets, customers, and competitors to use in the selection of the best strategy. Interestingly, some organizations use blogging to gather intelligence on their competitors. In addition, before selecting a strategy, managers frequently obtain information on the organization's strengths and weaknesses. To get all of this information requires substantial communications with internal and external parties. If managers do not communicate well, they are unlikely to obtain the information needed to develop the correct strategy. Therefore, top executives must ensure that they communicate effectively and that all managers (and hopefully associates) do so as well. Good communication is the base on which most of what happens in the organization depends.

Critical Thinking Questions

1. For what tasks in a manager's job is effective communication critical? Explain.

2. Which contributes more to an organization's performance—verbal communications or written communications? Justify your answer.

3. What are the strengths and weaknesses in your communication abilities? How can you best take advantage of your strengths and overcome your weaknesses to have a successful career?

4. What impact is rapidly developing communication technology likely to have on communication in organizations?

What This Chapter Adds to Your Knowledge Portfolio

In this chapter, we have discussed the communication process and have examined both organizational and interpersonal communication issues. We have also described organizational and individual barriers to communication, along with ways of overcoming these barriers. To summarize, we have covered the following points:

- The communication process is a two-way process in which a sender encodes a message, the message travels through a communication medium to the receiver, and the receiver decodes the message and returns feedback to the sender. Effective communication occurs when the received message has the same meaning as the sent message.

- Two important aspects of organizational communication are communication networks and the direction of communication flow. Networks can have many or few members and can be centralized or decentralized. Communication can occur in a downward, upward, or horizontal direction. In the case of 360-degree feedback, it occurs in all three directions.

- Important aspects of interpersonal communication include whether it is formal or informal, what media are used, communication technology, and how nonverbal communication plays a role.

- Common barriers to effective communication that occur at the organizational level are information overload, noise, time pressures, network breakdowns, information distortion, and cross-cultural barriers.

- Common individual barriers to effective communication include differing perceptions, semantic differences, status differences, self-interest, personal space, and poor listening skills.

- Organizations can improve communication effectiveness by conducting communication audits and creating positive communication cultures.

- Individuals can improve their interpersonal communication by knowing their audience, selecting appropriate communication media, engaging in active listening, encouraging feedback, and regulating information flow and timing, and engaging in active listening.

Back to the Knowledge Objectives

1. Why is communication strategically important to organizations?

2. How would you describe an effective communication process?

3. What are the advantages and disadvantages of the various types of communication networks? How are upward, downward, and horizontal communication accomplished?

4. Define *interpersonal communication.* How do formal and informal communication processes differ?

5. What is media richness, and how do different communication media vary in richness?

6. How can technology affect the communication process?

7. How does nonverbal communication contribute to the communication process?

8. What are six organizational barriers to effective communication?

9. What are six individual barriers to effective communication?

10. What are communication audits, and how are they conducted?

11. What specific actions can individuals take to overcome communication barriers?

Thinking about Ethics

1. Do managers have a compelling reason to tell the truth to everyone (associates, customers, suppliers, and so forth)? Are there any circumstances in which it is ethically acceptable not to tell the truth? Explain.

2. Do people who are central to communication networks within organizations have a responsibility to pass on important information they receive? Explain.

3. What ethical issues are related to the use of "the grapevine" (the informal communication network in organizations)?

4. Do managers have a responsibility to use the richest media possible in their communications with associates and other stakeholders? Explain.

5. What are managers' responsibilities in overcoming organizational barriers to communication with associates?

6. In the Managerial Advice feature, we discussed how organizations are using the Internet to check up on job applicants. Are there potential legal and ethical concerns with this practice?

Key Terms

communication, p. 294
encoding, p. 295
communication medium
   or communication
   channel, p. 295
decoding, p. 295
feedback, p. 295
downward communication,
   p. 298
upward communication,
   p. 298

horizontal communication,
   p. 299
interpersonal
   communication, p. 301
formal communication,
   p. 301
informal communication,
   p. 301
rumors, p. 302
gossip, p. 302

nonverbal communication,
   p. 307
noise, p. 309
cultural fluency, p. 311
communication audit,
   p. 316
communication climate,
   p. 316

Building Your Human Capital

Presentation Dos and Don'ts

Making presentations can be one of the most challenging communication exercises faced by anyone, especially people who are not used to doing so. Below is a quiz to help you determine how you fare in giving public presentations. The first 16 questions are presentation "dos," and the second 16 items are presentation "don'ts."

Answer the questions based on your own recollections of presentations you have given. Perhaps an even better indicator of your presentation effectiveness would be to have a friend in the audience fill out this questionnaire for you when you are giving a presentation. In answering the questions, use the following scale:

1	**2**	**3**	**4**	**5**
Rarely	**Seldom**	**Sometimes**	**Frequently**	**Almost Always**

Presentation "Dos"

When you are making a presentation to a group of people, how often do you:

1. Think about their point of view?
2. Acknowledge that the audience may be different from you?
3. Do research on who comprises your audience?
4. Tailor your message to suit the audience?
5. Provide a clear outline of what you are going to discuss?
6. Provide illustrative visual information?
7. Summarize your main points?
8. Make between three and six major points?
9. Look at the audience to determine their reaction?
10. Ask the audience for feedback?
11. Stop and provide clarification when the audience seems confused?
12. Solicit questions?
13. Use body language to get your points across?
14. Maintain eye contact with the audience?
15. Modulate your tone of voice to keep people interested?
16. Show enthusiasm for your topic?

Presentation "dos" scoring:

Add together your scores on the items for each section below. If you scored less than 16 on any of the sections, you need to work on this aspect of your presentation style.

Questions 1–4: Knowing your audience. Total score on questions 1–4: _____

Questions 5–8: Structure. Total score on questions 5–8: _____

Questions 9–12: Feedback. Total score on questions 9–12: _____

Questions 13–16: Animation. Total score on questions 13–16: _____

Presentation "Don'ts"

When you are making a presentation to a group of people, how often do you:

1. Present information at the most difficult level possible, because it will make you appear knowledgeable?

2. Assume everyone in the audience agrees with you?

3. Make the presentation as simple as possible so even the least-educated person will understand?

4. Figure that if a presentation works with one crowd, it will work with another?

5. Present very detailed visual information to make sure the audience picks up on all the details?

6. Avoid a summary because it should be obvious what you have already said?

7. Get distracted by random questions?

8. Be extremely thorough in getting all your points across, even if it means you don't have time to explain all of them?

9. Look out over the heads of the people in the audience?

10. Refuse questions because it is very important that you get your message across?

11. Ignore signs of confusion or lack of interest in the audience because it will just get you off your point?

12. Focus all your attention on a friendly face in the audience?

13. Read from your notes?

14. Make nervous gestures (fidget with your hair, tap your foot, rattle your change, or the like)?

15. Speak in a monotone because it is more authoritative?

16. Speak as quickly as possible?

Presentation "don'ts" scoring:

Add together your scores on the items for each section below. If you scored more than 8 on any of the sections, you need to work on this aspect of your presentation style.

Questions 1–4: Knowing your audience. Total score on questions 1–4: _____

Questions 5–8: Structure. Total score on questions 5–8: _____

Questions 9–12: Feedback. Total score on questions 9–12: _____

Questions 13–16: Animation. Total score on questions 13–16: _____

Explanation of Section Topics

Knowing your audience: In order to reach audience members and engage their interest, you must understand their point of view, their motivation for hearing your presentation, their attitudes about what you are saying, and their level of knowledge about your topic.

Structure: To get your message across, it is usually best to keep it organized and simple—stick to a few major, important points. If some members of the audience want more details, offer to speak to them later, provide handouts, or give them a source of further information. If your visual presentation is too complicated, the audience will be reading your slides rather than listening to you.

Feedback: Remember that feedback is an essential part of the communication process. You need to be aware of how your audience is responding so that you can further tailor your presentation to ensure that audience members understand or are engaged with what you are telling them. Do not ignore their reactions.

Animation: Everyone has experienced both "good speakers" and "boring speakers." Don't be one of the latter. Be lively, animated, and show enthusiasm for your subject. If you don't, your audience won't either.

A Strategic Organizational Behavior Moment

Going North

"Roll 'em!"

"Take number 64. Lights. Camera. Action!"

"Jane, I've missed you so much these past few weeks."

"I know, my darling. I've missed you, too."

"We must make up for lost time."

"Cut, cut, cut! Tom, you're playing this scene like a frozen polar bear. This is a tender love scene!" Helen screamed in her loudest, shrillest voice. "You're supposed to play it with feeling and tenderness. You want to make people think you love Jane."

"Helen, I could play the part better if you'd just get off my back. I knew more about romance when I was a teenager than you do now. Who are you to tell me how to play a love scene?" Tom shot back.

Helen called out, "That's all for today, everybody. We can let our mechanical lover calm down and maybe get in a better mood for this scene tomorrow."

With that Tom stomped off the set, and everyone began to disperse.

Helen Reardon is the producer and director of the film *Going North,* based on a novel that had stayed on the best-seller list for 16 months. Helen is considered to be one of the best directors in Hollywood. She already has two Academy Awards to her credit and many hit motion pictures.

Tom Nesson is a promising young actor. His most recent film, *The Western Express,* was well received at the box office and thrust him into the limelight. In fact, one of the reasons he was chosen to play the leading male part in *Going North* was his current popularity. He is considered by industry insiders as a potential superstar.

All went well on the set for the first few weeks. But then problems began to arise. First came arguments between the set-design staff and wardrobe. There were feelings that the sets and the costumes didn't match. Some thought that the colors even clashed at times. The question was, "Whose fault is it?" Of course, each group blamed the other.

Later, the makeup staff walked off the job, claiming that they were being asked to work unreasonable hours. Helen did have a penchant for shooting movies at odd hours, particularly if the scene called for it. The makeup staff claimed that they had an informal agreement with studio management about the hours they would work and that this agreement had been violated. Although studio executives convinced them to return to work, the "peace" was an uneasy one. Now there was this blowup between Helen and Tom. Everyone hoped that the problems between the two were temporary.

The next day, everybody was back on the set on time except Tom. He came in about 10 minutes late. He explained that the makeup people were slow in getting his makeup on. No one questioned this, and they began where they had left off yesterday.

"Take number one. Lights. Camera. Action! . . . Take number 9. . . . Take number 19. . . . Take number 31. . . ." Finally, Helen yelled "Cut! Tom, we've got to find a way to get this right. We can't go on like this forever. What do you suggest?"

"I suggest you shoot it like it is. The scene was good. I've done it well several times, but you seem to keep finding small things wrong."

"Tom, do you really know what love is? Your acting doesn't show it."

With that Tom exploded. "Yes, I know what love is, but you obviously don't." He then left the set, shouting, "I'm not coming back on the set until you're gone!"

Helen left the set immediately, going straight to the studio executive offices. She barged into the president's office and stated, "Either you get rid of Tom Nesson on this movie, or I go!"

The studio executives were in a quandary. They did not want to lose either Helen or Tom. Neither had a history of being difficult to work with. They were not sure what was causing the problem. This movie seemed to be causing all kinds of problems, with the wildcat strike and the disagreements between wardrobe and set design. They obviously needed to examine all of the circumstances involved in the making of this film.

Discussion Questions

1. What do you suppose is really causing the problem between Helen and Tom? Explain.

2. Discuss the problems between set design and wardrobe and those with the makeup department.

3. Could any of the problems in this case have been prevented? If so, how? How can the problems now be solved?

Team Exercise

Communication Barriers

This exercise demonstrates the importance of communication in organizations and shows how barriers affect communications.

Procedure

1. With the aid of the instructor, the class will be divided into teams of three to five persons.
2. The teams will perform the following tasks:
   - Identify all of the major ways in which your institution communicates with students (catalog, registration, advising, etc.). Be as specific as possible. Write each of these down.
   - Determine instances in which communication problems arise between the institution and students (for example, where students need more or better information). Write these down.
   - Identify specific barriers that make effective communications between students and the institution difficult. Write these down.
   - Development recommendations to overcome the barriers and solve the communications problems previously noted.

The instructor will allow 30 minutes for the teams to complete their analyses.

3. The teams will present their lists of means of communication, communication problems, and recommendations, in that order. First, each team will present one item from the means of communication list, then the next team will present one, and so on, until all communication means have been presented. This same procedure will be followed for communication problems and recommendations, respectively. The instructor will compile a list of all the teams' responses.
4. The instructor will guide a discussion of this exercise, noting the similarity of communication problems or barriers in all types of organizations.

The presentation and discussion should require about 30 minutes.

Endnotes

1. Hitt, M.A., Black, J.S., & Porter, L.W. 2005. *Management.* Upper Saddle River, NJ: Pearson Prentice Hall.
2. Cambie, S. 2007. Power to succeed. *Communication World,* 24 (2): 30–33.
3. Monge, P.R., Farace, R.V., Eisenberg, E.M., Miller, K.I., & White, L.L. 1984. The process of studying process in organizational communication. *Journal of Communication,* 34: 234–243.
4. Whitely, W. 1984. An exploratory study of managers' reactions to properties of verbal communication. *Personnel Psychology,* 37: 41–59.
5. Shapiro, I.S. 1984. Managerial communication: The view from inside. *California Management Review,* 27: 157–172.
6. Clampitt, P.G., & Downs, C.W. 1993. Employee perceptions of the relationship between communication and productivity: A field study. *Journal of Business Communications,* 30: 5–28.
7. Pinto, M.B., & Pinto, J.K. 1991. Determinants of cross-functional cooperation in the project implementation process. *Project Management Journal,* 22: 13–20.
8. Ammeter, A.P., & Dukerich, J.M. 2002. Leadership, team building, and team member characteristics in high performance project teams. *Engineering Management Journal,* 14: 3–10; Henderson, L.S. 2004. Encoding and decoding communication competencies in project management—an exploratory study. *International Journal of Project Management,* 22: 469–476.

9. Snyder, R.A., & Morris, J.H. 1984. Organizational communication and performance. *Journal of Applied Psychology,* 69: 461–465.

10. Thomas, D. 2005. Poor communication makes UK workers less productive. April 6, 2005 at www.PersonnelToday.com; Computing Technology Industry Association Press Release. March 6, 2007. "Poor communications is the most frequent cause of project failure, CompTIA web poll reveals." At http://www.comptia.org/pressroom/get_pr.aspx?prid=1227.

11. Whitely, W. 1984. An exploratory study of managers' reactions to properties of verbal communication. *Personnel Psychology,* 37: 41–59.

12. Hinske, G. 1985. The uneven record of the corporate communicators. *International Management,* 40: 2.

13. Collison, J., & Frangos, C. 2002. Aligning HR with organization strategy survey. Society for Human Resource Management Research Report. Alexandria, VA: Society for Human Resource Management.

14. Dewhurst, S. 2007. Key findings from the pulse survey. *Strategic Communication Management,* 11(1): 6–7.

15. Humphreys, M.A. 1983. Uncertainty and communication strategy formation. *Journal of Business Research,* 11: 187–199.

16. Clevenger, T., Jr., & Matthews, J. 1971. *The speech communication process.* Glenview, IL: Scott Foresman.

17. Ibid.

18. Daft, R.L., & Lengel, R.H. 1986. Organizational information requirements: Media richness and structural design. *Management Science,* 32: 554–571.

19. Greenbaum, H.H. 1974. The audit of organizational communication. *Academy of Management Journal,* 17: 739–754.

20. Shaw, M.E. 1964. Communication networks. In L. Berkowitz (Ed.), *Advances in experimental social psychology.* New York: Academic Press, pp. 111–147.

21. Leavitt, H.J. 1951. Some effects of certain communication patterns on group performance. *Journal of Abnormal and Social Psychology,* 46: 38–50.

22. Watts, D. 2003. *Six degrees: The science of a connected age.* New York: W.W. Norton.

23. Ibid.

24. Bolton, P., & Dewatripont, M. 1994. The firm as a communication network. *Quarterly Journal of Economics,* 109: 809–839.

25. Freibel, G., & Raith, M. 2004. Abuse of authority and hierarchical communications. *Rand Journal of Economics,* 35: 224–244.

26. Jablin, F.M. 1982. Formal structural characteristics of organizations and superior–subordinate communication. *Human Communication Research,* 8: 338–347.

27. Sellers, P. 2004. Most powerful women in business. *Fortune,* October 4, at www.fortune.com.

28. Katz, D., & Kahn, R.L. 1978. *The social psychology of organizations* (2nd ed.). New York: John Wiley & Sons.

29. Collison, J., & Frangos, C. 2002. Aligning HR with organization strategy survey. Society for Human Resource Management Research Report. Alexandria, VA: Society for Human Resource Management.

30. Ghorpade, J. 2000. Managing five paradoxes of 360-degree feedback. *Academy of Management Executive,* 14: 140–150.

31. Lussier, R.N., & Achua, C.F. 2004. *Leadership: Theory, application, skill development* (2nd ed.). Eagan, MN: Thomson Southwestern.

32. Bettenhausen, K.L., & Fedor, D.B. 1997. Peer and upward appraisals: A comparison of their benefits and problems. *Group and Organization Management,* 22: 236–263; Freibel, G., & Raith, M. 2004. Abuse of authority and hierarchical communications. *Rand Journal of Economics,* 35: 224–244.

33. Atwater, L.E., & Brett, J.F. 2006. 360-degree feedback: Does it relate to changes in employee attitudes? *Group and Organization Management,* 31: 578–600.

34. Huseman, R.C., Lahiff, J.M., & Hatfield, J.D. 1976. *Interpersonal communication in organizations.* Boston, MA: Holbrook Press, p. 5.

35. Kurland, N.B., & Pelled, L.H. 2000. Passing the word: Toward a model of gossip and power in the workplace. *Academy of Management Review,* 25: 428–439.

36. Michelson, G., & Mouly, V.S. 2004. Do loose lips sink ships? The meaning, antecedents, and consequences of rumor and gossip in organizations. *Corporate Communications: An International Journal,* 9: 189–201.

37. Ibid.

38. McKay, B. 2000. At Coke layoffs inspire all manner of peculiar rumors, *Wall Street Journal* (Eastern Edition), October 17: p. A1.

39. Anonymous. 1998. Lehman gives regulators data gathered on rumors. *Wall Street Journal* (Eastern Edition), October 5: p. 1.

40. Kurland, N.B., & Pelled, L.H. 2000. Passing the word: Toward a model of gossip and power in the workplace. *Academy of Management Review,* 25: 428–439.

41. Sheer, V.C., & Chen, L. 2004. Improving media richness theory: A study of interaction goals, message valence, and task complexity in manager–subordinate communication. *Management Communication Quarterly,* 18: 76–93.

42. Daft, R.L., & Lengel, R.H. 1986. Organizational information requirements: Media richness and structural design. *Management Science,* 32: 554–571.

43. Trevino, L.K., Lengel, R.H., Bodensteiner, W., Gerloff, E., & Muir, N. 1990. The richness imperative and cognitive style: The role of individual differences in media choice behavior. *Management Communication Quarterly,* 4: 176–197.

44. Daft, R.L., & Lengel, R.H. 1986. Organizational information requirements: Media richness and structural design. *Management Science,* 32: 554–571.

45. Sheer, V.C., & Chen, L. 2004. Improving media richness theory: A study of interaction goals, message valence, and task complexity in manager–subordinate communication. *Management Communication Quarterly,* 18: 76–93.

46. Fulk, J. 1993. Social construction of communication technology. *Academy of Management Journal,* 36: 921–950.

47. Turner, J.W., Grube, J.A., Tinsley, C.H., Lee, C., & O'Pell, C. 2006. Exploring the dominant media: How does media use reflect organizational norms and affect performance? *Journal of Business Communication,* 43: 220–250.

48. Fontaine, M.A., Parise, S., & Miller, D. 2004. Collaborative environments: An effective tool for transforming business processes. *Ivey Business Journal Online,* May–June: 1–7.

49. Ask Yahoo! March 24, 2006. At http//ask.yahoo.com/20060324.html.

50. Anonymous, May 1, 2007. Business crawls onto Web.20. At http://www.emarketer.com/Article.aspx?id=1004868; Anonymous. May 10, 2007. Fortune 500 blog project wiki. At http://blogbusinesssummit.com/fortune500/index.php?title=Project.

51. For a full list, see: http://www.ceoblogwatch.com.

52. Turner, J.W., Grube, J.A., Tinsley, C.H., Lee, C., & O'Pell, C. 2006. Exploring the dominant media: How does media use reflect organizational norms and affect performance? *Journal of Business Communication*, 43: 220–250.

53. Fontaine, M.A., Parise, S., & Miller, D. 2004. Collaborative environments: An effective tool for transforming business processes. *Ivey Business Journal Online*, May–June: 1–7.

54. Desanctis, G., & Fulk, J. (Eds.) 1999. *Shaping organizational form: Communication, connection, and community*. Thousand Oaks, CA: Sage Publications.

55. Baker, S., & Green, H. 2005. Blogs will change your business. *BusinessWeek online*. May 2. At www.businessweek.com/print/magazine/content/05_18/b3931001_mz001.htm.

56. Gard, L. 2005. Online extra: Stonyfield's Farm's blog culture. May 2. At www.businessweek.com/print/magazine/content/05_18/b3931005_mz001.htm.

57. CBS/AP. 2007. JetBlue Attempts to calm passenger furor. CBS News. February 15. At http://www.cbsnews.com.stories/2007/02/15/national/printable2480665.shtml.

58. Baker, S., & Green, H. 2005. Blogs will change your business. *BusinessWeek online*. May 2. At www.businessweek.com/print/magazine/content/05_18/b3931001_mz001.htm.

59. Mehrabian, A. 1968. Communication without words. *Psychology Today*, 2: 53–55.

60. Davis, A., Pereira, J., & Buckley, W.M. 2002. Silent signals: Security concerns bring new focus on body language. *Wall Street Journal*, August 15: p. A.1.

61. Schweitzer, M.E., Brodt, S.E., & Croson, R.T.A. 2002. Seeing and believing: Visual access and strategic use of deception. *International Journal of Conflict Management*, 13: 258–275.

62. Streeter, L.A., Krauss, R.M.N., & Geller, V. 1977. Pitch changes during attempted deception. *Journal of Personality and Social Psychology*, 35: 345–350.

63. Kraut, R.E. 1978. Verbal and nonverbal cues in the perception of lying. *Journal of Personality and Social Psychology*, 36: 380–391.

64. Ibid.

65. Davis, A., Pereira, J., & Buckley, W.M. 2002. Silent signals: Security concerns bring new focus on body language. *Wall Street Journal*, August 15: p. A.1.

66. Ekman, P., & Oster, H. 1979. Facial expressions of emotion. In M. Rosenzweig, & L.W. Porter (Eds.), *Annual Review of Psychology*, 30: 527–554.

67. Brown, D.S. 1975. Barriers to successful communication: Part 1. *Management Review*, 64: 24–29; Brown, D.S. 1976. Barriers to successful communication: Part 2. *Management Review* 65: 15–21.

68. Marcus, H., & Zajonc, R.B. 1985. The cognitive perspective in social psychology. In G. Lindzey & E. Aronson (Eds.), *The handbook of social psychology* (3rd ed). New York: Random House, pp. 137–230.

69. Gaudin, S. 2007. Report: Spam levels rise for fifth month in a row. *InformationWeek*. March 1. At http://www.informationweek.com/story/showArticle.jhtml?articleID=197700567.

70. Claburn, T. 2005. Spam costs billions. *InformationWeek*. February 3. At http://www.informationweek.com/story/showArticle.jhtml?articleID=59300834.

71. Sussman, L. 1974. Perceived message distortion, or you can fool some of the supervisors some of the time. *Personnel Journal*, 53: 679–682.

72. Graham, J.R. 2002. Who do we thank (and curse) for e-mail? *Agency Sales* (November) 32: 23–26.

73. Allen, T.J. 2007. Architecture and communication among product development engineers. *California Management Review*, 49 (2):23–41.

74. Morgan, C.P., & Hitt, M.A. 1977. Validity and factor structure of House and Rizzo's effectiveness scales. *Academy of Management Journal*, 20: 165–169.

75. Bairman, S., & Evans, J.H., III. 1983. Pre-decision information and participative management control systems. *Journal of Accounting Research*, 21: 371–395.

76. Harvey, M.G., & Griffith, D.A. 2002. Developing effective intercultural relationships: The importance of communication strategies. *Thunderbird International Business Review*, 44: 455–476.

77. Fisher, G.B., & Hartel, C.E.J. 2003. Cross-cultural effectiveness of Western expatriate–Thai client interactions: Lessons learned from IHRM research and theory. *Cross Cultural Management*, 10: 4–29.

78. U.S. Department of Labor. 2005. Immigration Facts and Figures. November. At http://www.doleta.gov/reports/dpld_immigration.

79. Beamer, L. 1992. Learning intercultural communication competence. *Journal of Business Communication*, 29: 285–303.

80. Kranhold, K. 2004. Lost in translation?: Managers at multinationals may miss the job's nuances if they speak only English. *Wall Street Journal* (Eastern Edition), May 18: p. B.1.

81. Kilpatrick, R.H. 1984. International business communication practices. *Journal of Business Communication*, 21: 33–44.

82. Scott, J.C. 1999. Developing cultural fluency: The goal of international business communication instruction in the 21st century. *Journal of Education for Business*, 74: 140–144.

83. Briscoe, D. R., & Schuler, R.S. 2004. *International human resource management*. New York: Routledge.

84. Marcus, H., & Zajonc, R. 1985. The cognitive perspective in social psychology. In G. Lindzey & E. Aronson (Eds.), *The handbook of social psychology* (3rd ed.), Vol. 1. New York: Random House, pp. 127–230.

85. Athanassiades, J.C. 1973. The distortion of upward communication in hierarchical organization. *Academy of Management Journal*, 16: 207–226.

86. Dye, R.A. 1983. Communication and post-decision information. *Journal of Accounting Research*, 21: 514–533.

87. Cohen, L.R. 1982. Minimizing communication breakdowns between male and female managers. *Personnel Administrator*, 27: 57–58.

88. Inman, T.H., & Hook, B.V. 1981. Barriers to organizational communication. *Management World*, 10: 34–35.

89. McKechnie, D.S., Grant, J., & Bagaria, V. 2007. Observation of listening behaviors in retail service encounters. *Managing Service Quality*, 17 (2): 116-113.

90. Kopec, J.A. 1982. The communication audit. *Public Relations Journal*, 38: 24–27; Quinn, D., & Hargie, O. 2004. Internal communication audits: A case study. *Corporate Communications: An International Journal*, 9: 146–158.

91. Ibid.

92. Goldhaber, G.M. 1993. *Organizational communication.* Dubuque, IA: Brown and Benchmark.

93. Bartels, J., Pruyn, A., De Jong, M., & Joustra, I. 2007. Multiple organizational identification levels and the impact of perceived external prestige and communication climate. *Journal of Organizational Behavior,* 28: 173–190.

94. Monge, P.R., Farace, R.V., Eisenberg, E.M., Miller, K.I., & White, L.L. 1984. The process of studying process in organizational communication. *Journal of Communication,* 34: 234–243.

95. Poole, M.S. 1978. An information-task approach to organizational communication. *Academy of Management Review,* 3: 493–504.

96. Scudder, V. 2004. The importance of communication in a global world. *Vital Speeches of the Day,* 70: 559–562.

97. Trevino, L.K., Lengel, R.H., Bodensteiner, W., Gerloff, E., & Muir, N. 1990. The richness imperative and cognitive style: The role of individual differences in media choice behavior. *Management Communication Quarterly,* 4: 176–197.

98. Gelb, B.D., & Gelb, G.M. 1974. Strategies to overcome phony feedback. *MSU Business Topics,* 22: 5–7.

99. Inman, T.H., & Hook, B.V. 1981. Barriers to organizational communication. *Management World,* 10: 34–35.

100. Colvin, G. 2005. CEO knockdown. *Fortune,* April 4: 19–20.

DECISION MAKING BY INDIVIDUALS AND GROUPS

A s president of the new CW Television Network, Dawn Ostroff faced many challenges in the spring of 2006. Chief among these was programming the lineup of shows. One issue making this a difficult task was the newness of the network. Recently created through a combination of the WB network and UPN, the combined entity had no viewer base. What mix of existing shows versus exciting new shows would draw former WB and UPN viewers? What mix of shows would motivate

Frazer Harrison/Getty Images

EXPLORING BEHAVIOR IN ACTION

Dawn Ostroff's Decision Making at the CW Television Network

former WB and UPN viewers to find and watch the new network? In some markets, WB viewers would need to find the old UPN station. In other markets, UPN viewers would need to find the old WB station. In still other markets, both WB and UPN viewers would need to find a completely new station carrying CW. A second issue was the reduction in primetime hours available. The combination of WB and UPN had resulted in a shift from 23 centrally scheduled primetime hours to 13 centrally scheduled hours. Which existing shows should

be cut? With a lineup of shows such as *America's Next Top Model* (UPN), *WWE Smackdown* (UPN), *One on One* (UPN), *Veronica Mars* (UPN), *Gilmore Girls* (WB), *Reba* (WB), and *One Tree Hill* (WB), this issue was noteworthy.

Ostroff attacked the programming task with her usual zeal. As an individual, she considered a number of factors, such as the importance of retaining current WB and UPN viewers, the passion that WB and UPN viewers displayed in lobbying for particular shows, the overall popularity of

existing shows as assessed by Nielsen ratings, and the current and future preferences of the new network's demographic target group (18-to-34-year-olds). As a leader, she considered the views of others as well. Two-dozen individuals were involved in the decision making, with a group of six providing strong inputs for the final lineup of shows. Given the non-routine and complex nature of the situation, incorporating information and opinions from other people was crucial.

Although Ostroff had a great deal of information at her disposal, she did not become mired in evaluating detailed information. Instead, she tended to keep the big picture in mind and use her judgment in evaluating alternatives. In her words,

Ultimately the people who are successful in this business have a tacit ability to make right decisions based on a wide variety of inputs; they are able to integrate those inputs into what seems to be a gut decision. Deciding on programming is not formulaic. It is not purely a business decision, but also a creative decision. If this was a science I wouldn't lose sleep at night.

In the end, Ostroff and her group decided to use mostly existing shows, emphasizing the more popular ones. Although some of these shows had begun to fade and none were top performers in the overall Nielsen ratings, they believed their strategy to be the best one for developing an audience quickly. Exciting new shows would wait for the next season.

The new CW network performed as well as could be expected. Although the network had no established track record, no direct ownership of stations in large markets, and limited resources, it attracted a small but meaningful audience. Some were disappointed with the performance, believing that the network had used too many fading shows and had not established a consistent identity, but most saw a foundation for the future. CW executives and affiliate stations remained optimistic.

To aggressively pursue success in future seasons, Ostroff again has focused on the big picture and drawn from her group of advisors, particularly John Maata, the chief operating officer of the network. A number of creative and somewhat risky tactics have been adopted, including: (1) 10-second ads called "cwickies," (2) sponsors' products being embedded in one show in lieu of breaks for commercials, (3) the use of a cultural attaché who spends her time interacting with viewers via blogs and checking the latest developments on the Web, and (4) an online community for dancing, shopping, and interacting with other viewers while

watching a show called *Gossip Girls*. For new shows, Ostroff and her team "aggressively looked outside of the usual development pipeline in an attempt to find new voices."

Has success been ensured for the future? This is a difficult question. The situation is challenging, but Ostroff has made and continues to make decisions that have the potential to pay off. Given her history of accomplishments and awards, she may have a dynamic and successful network in a few years.

Sources: J. Benson, "Is This the CW's New Reality?" *Broadcasting and Cable*, Mar. 26, 2007, p. 12; A. Elberse and S.M. Young, *The CW: Launching a Television Network* (Boston: Harvard Business School Press, 2007); M. Fernandez, "Youth Must Be Served: The Revitalized CW Seeks to Regain the 18 to 34 Crowd," *Los Angeles Times*, July 11, 2007, p. E.1; C. Littleton, "Dialogue with Dawn Ostroff and John Maata," *Hollywood Reporter*, Feb. 28, 2006, pp. 1–2; M. Miller, "CW Forms a Plan of Action: 'Online Nation' and 'Gossip Girls,' with Web Components, Are Meant to Woo the 18–34 Group," *Los Angeles Times*, July 21, 2007, p. E.17; M. Schneider, "Young CW Makes Brand Stand," *Variety*, Jan. 8, 2007, p. 22; B. Steinberg, "CW Shatters the TV-Ad-as-Usual Mold," *Advertising Age*, July 30, 2007, pp. 1–2.

The Strategic Importance of Decision Making

Individuals in charge of businesses make very important decisions. When we think about these decisions, we tend to think of decisions that are strategic in nature, such as adding or deleting products and services. However, these individuals also make other important decisions that have strategic implications. For example, deciding to outsource a function can have implications for effectively implementing a strategy. As another example, deciding to hire a particular person as a senior manager can affect strategy implementation.

The decisions made by individuals at the top of an organization are important because they often have the greatest effects on the organization's performance. However, the decisions of other managers also affect performance; frequently, even decisions by lower-level managers have significant effects on the success of the organization.[1]

In particular, managers throughout the organization make decisions about the actions needed to implement strategic decisions. The quality and speed of those decisions affect the success of strategy implementation efforts.

The example of Dawn Ostroff at the CW Network provides important insights into decision making and not only for those at the top. Ostroff made many important decisions related to programming, web-based products/services, advertising formats, organizational structure, personnel, logos, and trademarks. Other managers in the firm made decisions to support her. Managers in charge of web-based offerings made some of the decisions related to the specific content and timing of online links to television shows. Managers courting and working with advertisers made decisions related to commercials. Beyond the many managerial decisions, associates made choices in areas ranging from broadcast standards to development of new comedy shows. And in many instances, joint decisions were made by groups of people.

Faced with numerous challenges in her job, Ostroff gathered information, discussed issues with managers and associates, and made choices based on the big picture and even intuition. This approach can be effective. As you will learn in this chapter, however, not all decision makers follow this approach. Indeed, personal styles vary, and different situations call for different approaches. Furthermore, cognitive biases affect decision makers, causing them to collect less information or poor information in some cases. The cognitive models used by managers to make decisions are affected by the amount and type of their education and experience. For example, a manager with an engineering degree and several years of experience in an engineering unit and a manager with a degree in marketing and several years of experience in a marketing unit are likely to approach the same problem in very different ways.[2]

In this chapter, we open with a discussion of the fundamentals of decision making, including the basic steps and the need for balance between ideal and satisfactory decisions. Following this, we cover individual decision making, focusing on individual decision styles, risk taking, and cognitive biases. Next, we examine the important area of group decision making. Key topics include techniques for improving group decisions and tools for evaluating how well groups have done. Finally, we address a crucial question: To what extent should a manager involve associates in a particular decision? While high-involvement management, an important concept presented in this book, requires managers to delegate many decisions to associates and to involve them in many others, under some circumstances a manager should make a decision alone or with limited input from associates. A framework is offered to guide managers in addressing this issue.

KNOWLEDGE OBJECTIVES

After reading this chapter, you should be able to:

1. Describe the fundamentals of decision making, including the basic steps and the need to balance ideal and satisfactory decisions.

2. Discuss four important decision-making styles, emphasizing the effectiveness of each one.

3. Explain the role of risk-taking propensity and reference points.

4. Define cognitive bias and explain the effects of common types of cognitive bias on decision making.

5. Discuss common pitfalls of group decision making.

6. Describe key group decision-making techniques.

7. Explain the factors managers should consider in determining the level of associate involvement in managerial decisions.

Fundamentals of Decision Making

Decisions are choices. We make decisions every day. We decide when we want to get up in the morning, what clothes we will wear, what we will eat for breakfast, and what our schedule of activities will be. We also make more important decisions. We decide what college or university to attend, what our major will be, what job to accept, what career path to follow, and how to manage our finances. Each time we make a purchase, a decision is involved. Clearly, decision-making activities are important to each of us.

They are also important to organizations. Making decisions is one of the primary activities for senior managers. Senior managers make decisions related to such things as entering new businesses, divesting existing business, and coordinating the units of the firm. Other managers in the firm make decisions regarding how a unit should be organized, who should lead various workgroups, and how job performance should be evaluated. In a high-involvement organization, associates also make many important decisions. They may decide on scheduling of work, job rotation schedules, vacation time, approaches to various tasks, and ways to discipline an individual for problem behavior. Overall, decision-making skills are critical to organizational effectiveness.

decisions
Choices of actions from among multiple feasible alternatives.

Basic Steps in Decision Making

As a process, decision making involves multiple steps, as shown in Exhibit 10-1. First, effective decision making begins with a determination of the problem to be solved. Problems are typically gaps between where we are today and where we

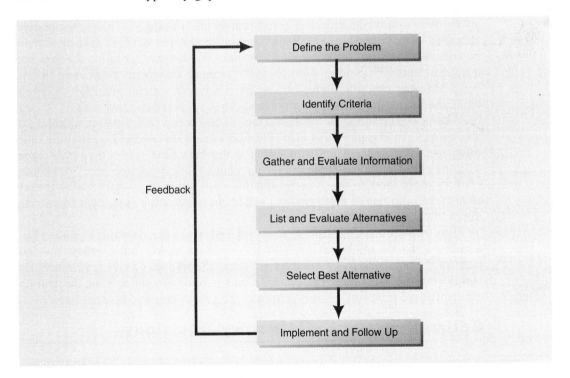

Exhibit 10-1   The Decision-Making Process

would like to be tomorrow. We need a new associate in the workgroup but do not have one. We have excess cash in the firm but do not know where to invest it. We are experiencing quality problems and must correct them.

Two individuals examining the same situation may see the problem differently. Consider the following example. A manufacturing unit has a broken machine. One person might define the problem in terms of the need to repair the machine or perhaps buy a new one. When developing possible solutions later in the process, he would focus either on a set of possible companies to do the repair work or a set of possible new machines. Another person might define the problem very broadly in terms of a need to return the manufacturing unit to an operational status. By broadening the problem, this person would gain access to a larger range of alternative solutions. Alternatives might include buying a new machine, repairing the existing machine, outsourcing the work, using a different type of machine already on hand to do the work, redesigning the workflow so that the machine is no longer needed, and so on. Overly narrow problem definitions are a chief concern in decision making, as they restrict options.[3]

The next step in decision making, identification of decision criteria, requires the decision maker to determine exactly what is important in solving the problem. In the case of purchasing a new machine to replace a broken one, she might consider price, maintenance costs, tolerance levels that can be achieved, size, delivery speed, and so on. Decision criteria determine what information the decision maker needs to collect in order to evaluate alternatives, and they help her explain the choice that she ultimately makes.[4] Failure to thoroughly identify important criteria results in faulty decision making.

After the decision criteria have been identified, the decision maker must gather and process information to better understand the decision context and to discover specific alternatives that might solve the problem. In developing the list of possible alternatives, she should be careful not to constrain or evaluate the alternatives to any significant degree because in so doing she may prematurely eliminate more creative or novel approaches. In this context, two truisms should be understood.[5] First, a decision maker cannot choose an alternative that has not been considered. Second, a decision maker cannot choose an alternative that is better than the best alternative on the list. Therefore, careful attention to developing the list of alternatives is important.

The next step in the decision-making process involves evaluating all relevant alternatives. To complete this step, the decision maker assesses each alternative using each criterion. When purchasing a new machine, she would rate each machine on the criteria of price, projected maintenance costs, tolerance levels, size, delivery speed, and so on. After evaluating each alternative, the decision maker chooses the alternative that seems to satisfy the criteria the best, thereby solving the problem in the best manner possible.

The decision-making process does not end when the decision is made. The decision must be implemented, and the decision maker must follow up and monitor the results to ensure that the adopted alternative solved the problem. By monitoring the outcomes, the decision maker may determine that the chosen alternative did not work. A new problem then must be solved.

Optimal versus Satisfactory Decisions

A decision maker typically wants to make an effective decision. For the purposes of this book, we define an effective decision as one that is timely, that is acceptable to those affected by it, and that satisfies the key decision criteria.[6] Although the systematic, logical process outlined in Exhibit 10-1 may not be ideal in all situations, such as when a decision must be made very quickly, it does serve as a useful framework for producing effective decisions.

The process of making decisions is not as simple, however, as it may seem from reviewing standard decision-making steps like those shown in the exhibit. Each step is more complex than it appears on the surface. Furthermore, individuals and groups cannot always make decisions that maximize their objectives, because to make such decisions, we must have complete knowledge about all possible alternatives and their potential results. Complete knowledge would allow us to choose the best possible alternative, but it is unlikely that we would have complete knowledge. Thus, we tend to make **satisficing decisions,** or what many psychologists and economists refer to as boundedly rational decisions.[7]

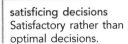

satisficing decisions
Satisfactory rather than optimal decisions.

There are two important reasons that people often make satisfactory decisions rather than optimal, maximizing ones. First, as already suggested, we do not have the capability to collect and process all of the information relevant for a particular decision. In theory, the number of alternatives that could be considered for most decisions is very large, as are the number of people who could be consulted and the number of analyses that could be completed. However, most of us, and certainly managers, lack the time and other resources required to complete these activities for most decisions. Consider the simple situation of hiring a manager to head a new public relations unit. Literally millions of people could possibly fill that role. Would the company consider millions of people so that the absolute best person could be found? No! Most likely, a convenient group of perhaps two-dozen people would be considered.

Second, we often display a tendency to choose the first satisfactory alternative discovered. Because we are busy and typically want to conserve the resources used in making any one decision, we often stop searching when we find the first workable alternative. Research has indicated, however, that some individuals are more likely than others to choose the first satisfactory option.[8] Some continue to search for additional alternatives after encountering the first satisfactory one, thereby increasing their odds of finding a better solution. This is an important individual difference that is of interest to managers and those interested in organizational behavior.

Individual Decision Making

Decision making is a cognitive activity that relies on both perception and judgment. If two people use different approaches to the processes of perception and judgment, they are likely to make quite different decisions, even if the facts and objectives are identical. Although many individual characteristics can affect an individual's decision process, the four psychological predispositions isolated by noted psychologist Carl Jung are of special importance in managerial decision making. We consider these next and then turn to other factors that influence an individual's decision making, including degree of acceptable risk and cognitive biases.

Decision-Making Styles

According to Jung's theory, an individual's predispositions can affect the decision process at two critical stages: (1) the perceiving of information and (2) the judging of alternatives. Decisions, then, reflect the person's preference for one of two

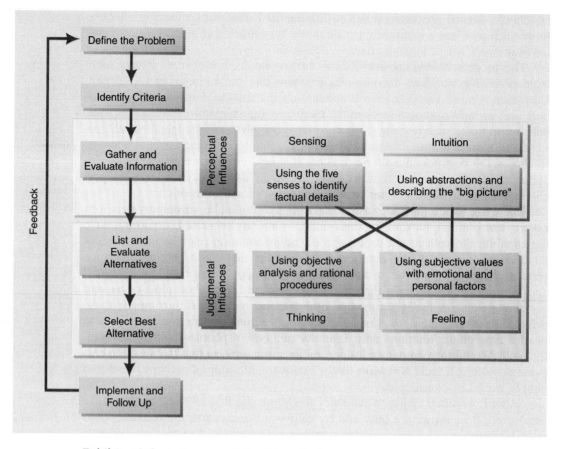

Exhibit 10-2   Influence of Decision Styles

perceptual styles and one of two judgment styles. How these styles relate to the decision process is illustrated in Exhibit 10-2. Although some have questioned the usefulness of Jung's ideas, research has offered reasonable support for those ideas,[9] and assessment tools based on his work are very popular in the corporate world.

GATHERING INFORMATION

Individuals may differ in how they gather information to use in making decisions. As described in Chapter 4, gathering information involves perceptual processes. Some individuals prefer information that is concretely grounded and readily accessible through the five basic senses, whereas others prefer abstractions and figurative examples as sources.

An associate or manager who relies on facts gathered directly by the five senses is said to use a **sensing** style.[10] Such a person believes in experience and typically wants to focus on rules and regulations, step-by-step explanations, and fact checking. Decision makers who use a sensing style are concerned primarily with developing a factual database that will support any resulting decision.

People who prefer this style of gathering information see themselves as practical and realistic. They work steadily in the early stages of the decision process and enjoy the information-gathering stage. Such persons observe the actual situation very carefully: specific details, concrete examples, real experiences, practicalities, and literal statements. They are down-to-earth people who believe that

sensing
A decision style focused on gathering concrete information directly through the senses, with an emphasis on practical and realistic ideas.

creativity involves much effort. Steve Ballmer, CEO of Microsoft, seems to fit this profile. He is attracted to facts and hard data and sees things as "black or white, on or off."[11]

Decision makers who use the **intuition** style dislike details and the time required to sort and interpret them.[12] These people become impatient with routine details and often perceive information in large chunks—for example, as holistic, integrated abstractions. A decision made using this style is often based on imagination. Such people believe that creativity comes from inspiration rather than concentrated effort.

> intuition
> A decision style focused on developing abstractions and figurative examples for use in decision making, with an emphasis on imagination and possibilities.

Although this second style may appear to be illogical and risky, many consultants and senior managers believe that it can be an effective approach. Managers with good intuition may be better able to cope with rapid change and crisis situations. They frequently have a vision for the future and can react quickly to urgent needs. Former U.S. president Bill Clinton has been classified as having the intuition style,[13] as has former British prime minister Margaret Thatcher.[14] Dawn Ostroff of the CW network also seems to fit the profile.

Overall, both the sensing and intuition styles of perception can be effective, but their effectiveness may vary depending on the context. The sensing style may be most appropriate for jobs where routine decisions are typical.[15] In one relevant study, researchers examined how loan officers handled a number of lending decisions.[16] Individuals with a sensing style used more information and made better choices. The intuition style may be most appropriate for jobs where novel decisions and a need for creativity are common. Research on innovation illustrates this point. In one recent study, individuals responsible for new business ideas in a *Fortune* 500 company were divided into two groups of equal size, with one group representing the sensing style and the other representing the intuition style.[17] In the sensing group, individuals displayed less creativity and identified ideas that resulted in only $15.2 million of profit during the time period of the study. Individuals in the intuition group displayed more creativity and delivered $197.5 million in profit.

Specific situations in which the intuition style may prove valuable include the following:

- When a high level of ambiguity exists
- When few or no precedents exist
- When facts are limited
- When facts don't clearly indicate which way to go
- When time is limited and there is pressure to make the right decision
- When several plausible alternative solutions exist with good arguments for each

EVALUATING ALTERNATIVES

Jung proposed that once information has been gathered, decision makers again diverge, tending to adopt either a thinking style or a feeling style to make their judgments. As seen in Exhibit 10-2, there is no fixed relationship between a person's information-gathering style and his judgment style. A person using a sensing style of gathering information may use either a thinking or a feeling style in evaluating and judging the alternatives. Similarly, an intuitive information gatherer may use either of the judgment styles.

Managers and associates who use an impersonal, rational approach to arrive at their judgments are said to prefer a **thinking** style.[18] Decision makers who use

> thinking
> A decision style focused on objective evaluation and systematic analysis.

the thinking style to derive conclusions from their perceptions are objective, analytical, logical, and firm.

People using a thinking style are concerned with principles, laws, and objective criteria. They find it easy to critique the work and behavior of others but are often uncomfortable dealing with people's feelings. Thinkers prefer objective analysis and fair decisions based on standards and policies. They are able to discipline and reprimand people, even fire them, if necessary. They are firm and may seem detached and impersonal to subordinates. Their apparently detached nature is likely due to the organized and structured approach they prefer. They would seldom leap to a conclusion without fully evaluating all possible alternatives. They are often conservative in their decisions.

feeling
A decision style focused on subjective evaluation and the emotional reactions of others.

At the other extreme, people who prefer to rely on their emotions and personal, subjective judgments are said to use a **feeling style**.[19] People concerned with feelings emphasize the maintenance of harmony in the workplace. Their judgments are influenced by their own or others' personal likes and dislikes. Such persons are subjective, sympathetic, and appreciative in their decisions. They also dislike decision problems that would require them to say unpleasant things to people. Managers who use a feeling approach frequently give more weight to maintaining a friendly climate in the workgroup than to effective task achievement. These managers often interpret problems as having been caused by interpersonal factors rather than by other issues.

Both the thinking and feeling styles are important in organizations. The thinking style is consistent with careful decision making, and a number of studies have shown this style to be effective. In one study, for example, real estate agents were asked to provide information on decision style as well as performance in selling properties.[20] Those who used the thinking style tailored their approach to selling based on circumstances and reported stronger performance. The feeling style, however, also can have positive effects. Concern for the feelings and morale of those around us is important.

To take advantage of the positive outcomes of each style and to balance the factors considered in a decision, a decision maker who emphasizes the feeling style should consult with one or more others who emphasize the thinking style. Similarly, decision makers who emphasize the thinking style should consult with those who use the feeling style. Because most managers at all levels in an organization tend to emphasize the thinking style,[21] they are likely to benefit from seeking out a feeling type. In addition, when a manager creates a team to address a problem and make a decision, she is likely to benefit from including both styles on the team.

USING DECISION STYLES

Although it may seem that decision-making styles are fixed, there is some flexibility in the styles used by managers and associates. As stated by Jung and later researchers, a decision style is simply a preference.[22] Many experienced decision makers are able to adjust their styles as need dictates, at least to some degree. Microsoft's Steve Ballmer, for example, clearly emphasizes the thinking style but at times seems capable of adopting the feeling style. As a thinker, he tends to be objective, logical, and analytical, and perhaps a bit impersonal as well, but he can also take into account the feelings of others. He has been known to scream, yell, and even be sarcastic and then feel badly about the behavior and attempt to make amends.[23] Dawn Ostroff appears to emphasize the thinking style, but not as strongly as Ballmer. She, therefore, probably moves more easily between thinking and feeling.

Nurturing Alternative Decision Styles

Many accounting students and practicing accountants combine the sensing and thinking styles. In fact, many accountants are attracted to the accounting field because it allows them to emphasize rules, procedures, facts, and analysis. The structure in professional accounting activities appeals to them. They must, for example, follow generally accepted accounting principles (GAAP) in creating and analyzing financial data for their companies or clients. In contrast, many marketing students and practicing marketers combine the intuition and feeling styles. Marketers are often drawn to the marketing field because it allows them to engage in creative problem solving and requires an understanding of the feelings of others.

Digital Vision

Although accountants and marketers may need to emphasize the decision styles that fit the type of work they generally do, they must be careful not to overemphasize those styles. Accountants, for example, can be too narrowly focused on standard data and analysis, thereby failing to take a strategic view of financial information in the firm. The following story, as told by the chief financial officer (CFO) of a pharmaceutical firm, illustrates the problem:

> The CEO started the meeting by attempting to get a handle on the overall financial condition of the company. He turned to our controller and asked her to give a summary of the financial situation. As I recall, she started with an explanation of how "There was a debit to this account on this date, a credit to that account on this date. . . . " As she continued, you could literally see the CEO's eyes cross. He turned in frustration and said, "No, what I mean is, where are we . . . ? What do we need to work on?"

In reflecting on this experience, the CFO concluded that (1) many accountants are biased toward a belief that having more data is better and (2) many accountants hide behind "a mass of data." He recommended that accountants focus on the strategic objectives of the firm and provide written or oral communications that interpret analyses in light of those objectives.

Some marketers also have "blind spots." For those marketers who work in the more strategic, creative areas of marketing, detailed study of a statistical market analysis is often not appealing, but such work may provide key insights. Even in areas of marketing that are more quantitative, such as marketing research, individuals may not be evaluating the data carefully enough. In the words of a successful consultant:

> That basically defines what marketing research is supposed to do—apply the scientific method to gain knowledge about consumers, buyers, competitors, markets and marketing. But many, both within and outside the profession, don't think marketing research has fulfilled its mandate. . . . Researchers have become too long on observation, description and problem identification, and too short on rigorous hypothesis testing, analysis-based conclusions and accurate predictions.

In reflecting on the state of marketing research, this consultant suggested additional training in rigorous methods, among other tactics.

To maximize effectiveness, accountants and marketers must be comfortable with alternative decision styles. They must use their "whole brains," in the words of a recent *Harvard Business Review* article. To support such efforts, several companies offer training programs and materials. The de Bono Group, for example, offers training called Six Thinking Hats. The purpose is to promote the use of different ways of thinking (go to http://debonogroup.com/). Numerous companies have used de Bono resources, including 3-M, Federal Express, Intel, Microsoft, PPG, The New York Times, and Wachovia. Herrmann International offers a brain dominance assessment and creative ideas for working with decision styles (go to http://www.hbdi.com/). Many companies have also utilized Herrmann resources, including American Express, Citibank, Coca-Cola, DuPont, General Electric, IBM, MTV, Starbucks, and Weyerhaeuser.

Sources: K.A. Brown, & N.L. Hyer, "Whole-Brain Thinking for Project Management," *Business Horizons* 45, no. 3 (2002): 47–57; de Bono Group, "What We Do," 2007, at http://debonogroup. com/what_we_do.htm; B. Hamilton, "How to Be a Top Strategic Advisor," *Strategic Finance* 84, no. 12 (2003): 41–43; Herrmann International, "Why Herrmann International," 2007, at http:www.hbdi.com/WhyUs/index.cfm; D. Leonard, & S. Straus, "Putting Your Company's Whole Brain to Work," *Harvard Business Review* 75, no. 4 (1997): 112–121; W.D. Neal, "Shortcomings Plague the Industry," *Marketing News* 36, no. 19 (2002): 37–39; P.D. Tieger, & B. Barron-Tieger, *Do What You Are: Discover the Perfect Career for You Through the Secrets of Personality Type*, 3rd ed. (New York: Little, Brown, 2001); P. Wheeler, "The Myers-Briggs Type Indicator and Applications to Accounting Education and Research," *Issues in Accounting Education* 16 (2001): 125–150.

The accounting and marketing examples discussed in the *Managerial Advice* feature represent a larger problem involving many functional areas. Associates and managers in many areas can have personal styles that work well most of the time but interfere with effectiveness on occasion. Although not all individuals working in a given functional area think in the same way, they often share some general tendencies. The mind-stretching techniques briefly discussed in the advice segment can be quite helpful in addressing the problem by extending ways of thinking about situations and broadening the decision styles used. Using the Six Thinking Hats technique, for example, enabled MDS SCIEX to save $1 million on a single project. Similarly, the brain dominance technique has been credited with helping DuPont-Mexico gain three new clients with total additional revenue of $100 million. Overall, the use of these techniques can enhance organizational performance.

Degree of Acceptable Risk

Risk exists when the outcome of a chosen course of action is not certain.[24] Most decisions in business carry some degree of risk. For example, a manager may be considering two candidates for a new position. One of them has a great deal of experience with the type of work to be performed and has been very steady, though not outstanding, in her prior jobs, whereas the other has limited experience but seems to have great potential. If the manager chooses the first candidate, the likelihood of poor work performance is relatively low but not zero. If he chooses the second candidate, the likelihood of poor work performance is higher, but there is also a chance of excellent performance, performance that would be out of reach for the first candidate. Who should be chosen?

In choosing between less and more risky options, an individual's **risk-taking propensity,** or willingness to take chances, often plays a role.[25] Two persons with

risk-taking propensity
Willingness to take chances.

different propensities to take risks may make vastly different decisions when confronted with identical decision situations and information. One who is willing to face the possibility of loss, for example, may select a riskier alternative, whereas another person will choose a more conservative alternative. U.S. businessman Donald Trump is known for taking risks. Over the years, he has made and lost and made again significant amounts of money in buying and selling real estate.[26]

In making decisions, individuals with lower risk-taking propensities may collect and evaluate more information. They may even collect more information than they need to make the decision. In one study, managers made hiring decisions in a practice exercise.[27] Managers with low risk-taking propensity used more information and made decisions more slowly. Although information is important, managers and associates with low risk-taking propensities must avoid becoming paralyzed by trying to obtain and consider too much detailed information. Conversely, those with high risk-taking propensities must avoid making decisions with too little information.

Beyond general risk-taking propensity, reference points play an important role in many decisions.[28] A **reference point** can be a goal, a minimum acceptable level of performance, or perhaps the average performance level of others, and it is used to judge one's current standing. If a particular individual's current position in an ongoing activity is below his reference point, he is more likely to take a risk in an attempt to move above the reference point. If his current position is above the reference point, he is less likely to take risks. For example, a manager of a division in a consumer products firm who is below the goal she has set for profitability may undertake a risky project in order to meet her goal. A manager who is above a reference point she has adopted is less likely to take on such a project. In an extreme case, a student in a finance course who is performing below the level he considers minimally acceptable may decide to take drugs to help him stay awake all night studying for the next exam, or he may even decide to cheat. A student who is above his reference point is less likely to engage in these types of risky behavior.

> **reference point**
> A possible level of performance used to evaluate one's current standing.

Each individual chooses, consciously or unconsciously, his own reference point in a given situation. Two different students are likely to have different minimally acceptable performance levels for a class, and these different levels can serve as their respective reference points. In a recent study, senior managers from small firms subjectively rated disappointment with their firms' business performance.[29] In some cases, managers were disappointed with a level of performance that other leaders endorsed as very positive. Clearly, reference points differed. Moreover, managers expressing dissatisfaction were more likely to undertake particularly risky projects. In another study, different reference points were examined in the context of negotiation situations.[30]

Cognitive Biases

> **cognitive biases**
> Mental shortcuts involving simplified ways of thinking.

Individuals often make mistakes in decision making. Although carelessness, sloppiness, fatigue, and task overload can be contributing factors, some mistakes are caused by simple **cognitive biases.** Such biases represent mental shortcuts.[31] Although these shortcuts can be harmless and save time, they often cause problems. Being aware of their existence is an important step in avoiding them.

The **confirmation bias** is particularly important, because it often has strong effects on the type of information gathered. This bias leads decision makers to seek information that confirms beliefs and ideas formed early in the decision

> **confirmation bias**
> A cognitive bias in which information confirming early beliefs and ideas is sought while potentially disconfirming information is not sought.

process.[32] Rather than also search for information that might disconfirm early beliefs, as a thorough decision process requires, individuals subconsciously seek only information that supports their early thinking. Failing to look for disconfirming information is particularly likely if a decision maker is revisiting a decision that has already been made and partially or fully implemented.

The following story illustrates the problem. An equities broker is concerned about a company in which many of his clients have invested. Because of some recent R&D failures, the company's long-term growth prospects are not as strong as originally expected. The broker's initial position, however, is to recommend that his clients retain the stock; he believes in the company's management and does not want to recommend divesting based only on one sign of possible trouble. Before making a decision, he calls two other brokers who are acquaintances and who also remain supporters of the company. He wants to understand why they continue to be positive about the firm. In the end, he decides to stay the course without seeking the opinions of other brokers who have recommended divesting the company's stock. In other words, he makes his decision having contacted only those who were likely to agree with his initial thinking. Research suggests that this is a common occurrence.[33]

ease-of-recall bias
A cognitive bias in which information that is easy to recall from memory is relied upon too much in making a decision.

The **ease-of-recall bias** is also important because it affects the amount and type of information that is gathered and evaluated. In the context of this bias, a decision maker gathers information from his own memory and relies on information that he can easily recall.[34] Unfortunately, easily recalled information may be misleading or incomplete. Vivid and recent information tends to be easily recalled but may not be indicative of the overall situation. In performance appraisals, for example, a supervisor may recall a vivid incident such as an angry disagreement between two associates while forgetting many common instances of good performance. When selecting a new supplier for a key raw material, a manager may find one or two informal stories of poor performance easier to remember than the comprehensive numbers in an evaluative report on the various alternative suppliers. As the brutal despot Joseph Stalin once said, "A single death is a tragedy, a million deaths is a statistic."[35]

anchoring bias
A cognitive bias in which the first piece of information that is encountered about a situation is emphasized too much in making a decision.

Another bias is the **anchoring bias.** Here, decision makers place too much emphasis on the first piece of information they encounter about a situation.[36] This initial information then has undue influence on ideas, evaluations, and conclusions. Even when decision makers acquire a wide range of additional information (thereby avoiding the confirmation bias), initial information can still have too much influence.

In one study of this phenomenon, auditors from the largest accounting firms in the United States were asked about management fraud.[37] Some of the auditors were asked if executive-level fraud occurred in more than 10 out of every 1,000 client organizations. Then they were asked to estimate the actual incidence rate. Others in the study were asked if executive-level fraud occurred in more than 200 out of every 1,000 client organizations. Auditors in this latter group also were asked to estimate the actual incidence rate. Interestingly, auditors in the first group estimated the actual fraud rate to be 16.52 per 1,000 client organizations whereas auditors in the second group estimated the fraud rate to be 43.11. Despite answering the same question about actual fraud, trained auditors in the most prestigious accounting firms appear to have anchored on arbitrary and irrelevant numbers (10 in the first group and 200 in the second).

sunk-cost bias
A cognitive bias in which past investments of time, effort, and/or money are not treated as sunk costs in deciding on continued investment.

Finally, the **sunk-cost bias** causes decision makers to emphasize past investments of time and money when deciding whether to continue with a chosen course of action.[38] Decision makers are reluctant to walk away from past investments, preferring to build on them and make them successful. Decision makers should, however, treat a past investment as a *sunk cost*—a cost that is unrecoverable and irrelevant—and focus on the future costs and benefits of continued investment. For example, when the CEO of a small business returns to a loan officer at the local bank saying that he needs another $250,000 to succeed, the loan officer should not consider the first $250,000 that was loaned. She should consider the likelihood that a new $250,000 will truly help the small firm succeed. What is the probability of success going forward? What has occurred in the past is not directly relevant to the new decision.

EXPERIENCING STRATEGIC
ORGANIZATIONAL
BEHAVIOR

Mount Everest Expeditions and the Perils of Sunk-Cost Bias

Mount Everest rises an estimated 29,028 feet above sea level, or about 5.5 miles. As the tallest mountain in the world, and as an exceedingly remote and inhospitable place, Everest is shrouded in mystery and mystique. To the Nepali people, who see the mountain from its south side, Everest is deeply respected, carrying the ancestral name of *Sagarmatha*, meaning goddess of the sky. To Tibetans, who live to the north, respect and reverence also run deep, as seen in their ancestral name, *Chomolungma*, meaning goddess of the universe. To others in the world, Everest is simply an enigma.

Famous British mountaineer George Mallory led the first known attempt to reach the summit of Mount Everest. As a British citizen, Mallory felt strongly about reaching the summit in the early 1920s. The British had lost to the Americans in the race to reach the North Pole (1909) and to a Norwegian party in the race to reach the South Pole (1911). He was forced to end his initial attempts, however, due to bad weather. His third expedition has become one of the most talked about of all Everest climbs.

On June 6, 1924, Mallory stepped out of his tent at an intermediate camp partway up the mountain. More than two months had passed since he left Darjeeling, India, for Tibet, and a month had passed since he arrived at the base camp on Everest. Weather-related problems had impeded previous pushes to the summit during the expedition. On this morning, Mallory faced a particularly troublesome set of circumstances. He and his team were short on supplies, many of their local helpers, known as *Sherpas*, were too tired or sick to climb, and the annual monsoon season with its blinding snows was expected to begin soon.

Having trained hard, invested much time and money, and traveled a long way, Mallory pressed on. He and his climbing partner, Andrew Irvine, were seen from a distance two days after leaving the intermediate camp by a teammate who had followed behind them. Mallory was near the final stretch of the journey to the summit when spotted, but he was several hours behind schedule. At that point, he was risking a dangerous nighttime descent from the uninhabitable summit.

Mallory was never seen again alive. His body was discovered in 1999 on the North Face of Mount Everest, where the frigid conditions had largely preserved the fallen mountaineer. What had gone wrong? While the exact circumstances of Mallory's death remain unknown, many friends and mountaineers have commented on how Mallory continued toward the peak after he should have turned back. With so much invested, and being so close, this is not surprising. The situation was tailor-made for the sunk-cost bias to play a role. As a later climber

Alison Wright/Photo Researchers, Inc.

said when close to the summit, "Descent was totally unappetizing. . . . Too much labor, too many sleepless nights, and too many dreams had been invested to bring us this far."

Since the loss of Mallory, several hundred people have successfully reached the summit, beginning in 1953 with New Zealander Edmund Hillary and a Nepali Sherpa named Tenzing Norgay. In 1985, a Texas businessman with limited climbing experience paid a guide to take him to the top. This marked the start of commercial expeditions whose purpose was to help less experienced climbers reach the summit. Clients are charged tens of thousands of dollars for the experience.

Rob Hall and a partner founded Adventure Consultants as a company specializing in guiding individuals to the highest peaks in the world. By the mid-1990s, Hall had guided 39 clients to the summit of Everest. To avoid a repeat of Mallory's experience, he used a prespecified turnaround time for the final leg of the journey. If the summit could not be reached by 1:00 or 2:00 in the afternoon, the party turned around. Although the technology of climbing—clothing, supplemental oxygen, tents, and so on—has improved dramatically since Mallory's day, it is still crucial to avoid nighttime descents on Everest.

Even with the prespecified turnaround time, Rob Hall lost his life and the lives of several in his party in May 1996. In part, these deaths happened because Hall ignored his own turnaround rule. In this fateful ascent, he and his party encountered delays and slow progress on the final leg. Despite the delays and the slipping schedule, Hall pressed on and failed to send back clients who were obviously struggling. These clients had invested a great deal in the effort to climb Mount Everest and did not want to be sent down after coming so far. The sunk-cost bias seemed again to play a role. Several members of the party did, however, decide to turn around without being forced down by Hall, prompting the following observation:

> In order to succeed you must be exceedingly driven, but if you're too driven you're likely to die. Above 26,000 feet, moreover, the line between appropriate zeal and reckless summit fever becomes grievously thin. Thus, the slopes of Everest are littered with corpses. Taske, Huthchison, Kasischke, and Fischbeck [party members who turned back] had each spent as much as $70,000 and endured weeks of agony to be granted this one shot at the summit. . . and yet, faced with a tough decision, they were among the few who made the right choice that day.

Sources: M. Coffey, "The Ones Left Behind," *Outside* 31, no. 9 (2006): 80–82; J. Hemmleb, *Ghosts of Everest: The Search for Mallory and Irvine* (Seattle: The Mountaineers Books, 1999); T.F. Hornbein, *Everest: The West Ridge* (San Francisco: The Sierra Club, 1966); J. Krakauer, *Into Thin Air: A Personal Account of the Mount Everest Disaster* (New York: Villard Books, 1997); M.A. Roberto, "Lessons from Everest: The Interaction of Cognitive Bias, Psychological Safety, and System Complexity," *California Management Review* 45, no. 1 (2002): 136–158; M.A. Roberto, & G.M. Carioggia, *Mount Everest—1996* (Boston: Harvard Business School Publishing, 2003); P.S. Turner, "Going Up: Life in the Death Zone," *Odyssey* 12, no. 8 (2003): 19.

The tragedies described in the *Experiencing Strategic Organizational Behavior* feature provide an extreme example of the potential effects of the sunk-cost bias. Fortunately, the effects of this bias are normally much less severe. Yet, the sunk-cost bias can have significant effects on organizational performance. For example, recent research has shown that CEOs are unlikely to sell off poorly performing businesses that they acquired. In fact, a major event, such as a change in CEO or a new outside member added to the board of directors, is frequently needed to force a change in the earlier decision. When these events occur, the firm is more likely to divest the poorly performing business.[39] Decision-making biases clearly play a role in such scenarios.

Group Decision Making

We often view decision making as an individual activity, with thoughtful individuals making good or bad organizational decisions. For example, it is easy to credit the success of Intel in the 1990s microchip industry to the effective decision making of Andy Grove, the CEO for many years. But it is common for a number of people to participate in important organizational decisions, working together as a group to solve organizational problems. This is particularly true in high-involvement organizations, where associates participate in many decisions with lower-level and middle-level managers and where lower-level and middle-level managers participate in decisions with senior-level managers. In high-involvement organizations, teams of associates also make some decisions without managerial input. In this way, human capital throughout the organization is utilized effectively.

Group decision making is similar in some ways to the individual decision making we described earlier. Because the purpose of group decision making is to arrive at a preferred solution to a problem, the group must use the same basic decision-making approach—define the problem, identify criteria, gather and evaluate information, list and evaluate alternatives, choose the best alternative, and implement it.

Groups are made up of multiple individuals, however, resulting in dynamics and interpersonal processes that make group decision making different from decision making by an individual.[40] For instance, some members of the decision group will arrive with their own expectations, problem definitions, and predetermined solutions. These characteristics are likely to cause some interpersonal problems among group members. Also, some members will have given more thought to the decision situation than others, members' expectations about what is to be accomplished may differ, and so on. Thus, a group leader may be more concerned with turning a collection of individuals into a collaborative decision-making team than with the development of individual decision-making skills. In this section, we consider these and other issues in group decision making.

Stockbyte/PictureQuest

Group Decision-Making Pitfalls

Although group decision making can produce positive outcomes, the social nature of group decisions sometimes leads to undesired results. In fact, group processes that occur during decision making often prevent full discussion of facts and alternatives. Group norms, member roles, dysfunctional communication patterns, and too much cohesiveness may deter the group, thereby producing ineffective decisions. Researchers have identified several critical pitfalls in decision-making groups. These include groupthink, common information bias, diversity-based infighting, and the risky shift (see upper half of Exhibit 10-3).

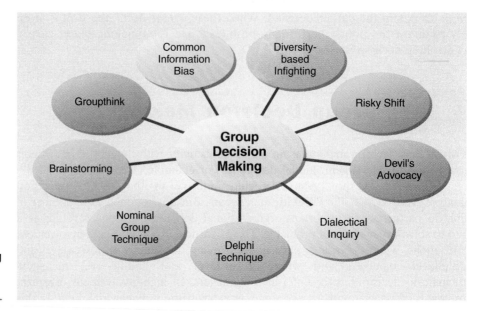

Exhibit 10-3
Group Decision-Making
Phenomena—Pitfalls
and Techniques

GROUPTHINK

When group members maintain or seek consensus at the expense of identifying and earnestly debating honest disagreements, **groupthink** is said to occur.[41] Focusing too much attention on consensus, especially early in a decision process, can result in a faulty decision. Many important ideas and alternative courses of action may not be seriously considered.

This type of group phenomenon can occur under a number of different conditions, including the following:

- Group members like one another and therefore do not want to criticize each other's ideas.[42]
- Group members have high regard for the group's collective wisdom and therefore yield to early ideas or the ideas of a leader.[43]
- Group members derive satisfaction from membership in a group that has a positive self-image and therefore try to prevent the group from having any serious divisions.[44]

In essence, then, a variety of factors can cause group members to avoid creating problems within the group.

Groupthink may be most likely when a group that has a positive image is under threat, such as when a management team faces a tough competitor or when a presidential administration faces possible military engagement.[45] At Enron, the failed energy company, managers valued being part of the leadership of a company perceived as progressive, innovative, and sophisticated. Being employed by Enron, and especially being a part of the favored group in the company, was powerfully reinforcing. This seems to have contributed to managers' tendency to agree with increasingly risky investments and accounting tricks.[46]

At least eight specific symptoms are associated with groupthink:

1. *Self-censorship*. Group members who recognize flaws or errors in the group position tend to remain quiet during group discussions and avoid issues that might upset the group.

2. *Pressure*. Group members apply pressure to any member who expresses opinions that threaten group consensus and harmony.

3. *Unanimity*. Censorship and pressure lead to the illusion of unanimous support for the final group decision. Members who have been quiet are assumed to be in complete agreement, which further discourages consideration of other decision alternatives.

4. *Rationalization*. Many group members build complex rationales that effectively discount warnings or information that conflict with their thinking. Thus, sources of negative information are discredited in group discussions. Such actions often narrow the decision alternatives considered.

5. *Invulnerability*. Group members may develop an illusion of invulnerability, which causes them to ignore any dangers. As a result, they become overly optimistic and take unwarranted risks; the group seriously overestimates its collective wisdom.

6. *Mindguards*. Certain group members take on the social role of "mindguard." They attempt to shield the group from any facts, criticisms, or evaluations that may alter the illusion of unanimity and invulnerability.

7. *Morality*. Most group members believe in the morality of the group's position. The members may even speak about the inherent morality of what they are doing and the immorality of opposing views. This can result in decisions that ignore ethical and legal issues as viewed by the broader society and lead to negative consequences for others.

8. *Stereotypes*. Group members may develop negative stereotypes of other people and groups. These stereotypes can protect their own position and block the possibility of reasonable negotiations with outsiders.

As the most discussed group decision-making phenomenon, groupthink has been linked to a number of actual decisions.[47] Many of these have been U.S. government or military decisions, in part because a great deal of groupthink research has been conducted in the United States and access to important materials for assessing U.S. decision making is reasonably good. Examples include the decision of Admiral Kimmel and his advisors to focus on training instead of defense of Pearl Harbor prior to its being attacked in 1941, the decision of President John F. Kennedy and his cabinet to authorize an invasion of Cuba at the Bay of Pigs in 1960, and the decision of President Lyndon Johnson and his inner circle to escalate the war in Vietnam in the mid-1960s.[48] At NASA, examples in which groupthink may have played a role include the decision to launch the *Challenger* Shuttle in 1986[49] and the handling of the Hubble telescope.[50] For business firms, examples abound, with many of them involving boards of directors.[51] Groupthink has also been found in self-managing work teams.[52] This has implications for high-involvement organizations.

Groupthink does not guarantee a poor decision but simply increases the likelihood of such a result. When good judgment and discussion are suppressed, the group can still be lucky. However, because the purpose of group decision making is to increase the likelihood of a good decision, managers must take steps to reduce groupthink. Such steps are discussed later in this chapter.

COMMON INFORMATION BIAS

common information bias
A bias in which group members overemphasize information held by a majority or the entire group while failing to be mindful of information held by one or a few group members.

Some information a group might consider in making a decision may be held by one or a few group members. Other pieces of information are held by most or all group members. The **common information bias** leads groups to unconsciously neglect information held by one or a few group members while focusing on more commonly held information in the group, thereby neglecting potentially important issues and ideas.[53] The common information bias defeats one of the presumed advantages of group decision making—the availability of unique information, ideas, and perspectives brought to the process by individual group members.

A recent study illustrates this phenomenon.[54] First, managers were asked to evaluate PeopleSoft as an alternative to the firm's existing accounting and enterprise management software. Next, these managers assembled to discuss whether adopting PeopleSoft would be positive for the firm. Concerns and ideas held by one or a few members received less attention than concerns and ideas held by most or all group members, resulting in a very limited group discussion.

DIVERSITY-BASED INFIGHTING

diversity-based infighting
A situation in which group members engage in unproductive, negative conflict over differing views.

When groupthink is an issue, one or more members of the group typically act to suppress diverse ideas, and many members censor themselves. With the common information bias, individuals subconsciously focus on common information and ideas. Thus, in many groups, diverse ideas are not discussed. In other groups, however, diverse ideas are emphasized. Although this is generally positive for group decision making, it can become extreme.

Instead of creating rich discussions and insight, diverse ideas can create ill will and fractured groups.[55] Such **diversity-based infighting** is likely to occur when individuals feel very strongly about their ideas and no mechanisms to channel disagreement in productive ways have been instituted. As discussed in the next section, mechanisms that can help channel diversity include formal brainstorming procedures and the formal use of devil's advocacy.

RISKY SHIFT

risky shift
A process by which group members collectively make a more risky choice than most or all of the individuals would have made working alone.

As discussed earlier, most decisions involve some degree of risk. Because decision-making groups are composed of individuals, it would seem that risk taken by a group should be the same as the average risk that would have been taken by the individual group members acting alone. But the social forces involved in group decisions make this assumption incorrect.

Research on the risk taken by groups in making decisions began in the 1960s, when investigators compared individual and group decisions on the same problems.[56] Possible solutions to the problems ranged from relatively safe alternatives with moderate payoffs to relatively risky options with higher potential payoffs. Contrary to expectations, groups made consistently riskier decisions than individuals. This finding has since been called the **risky shift** phenomenon.

Subsequent analysis of these findings and additional research have determined that decisions made by groups are not always riskier. In fact, they are sometimes more cautious. However, group decisions seem to shift toward increased risk more often than toward increased cautiousness.[57] Several explanations for such shifts have been offered, but the most common and most powerful explanation involves diffusion of responsibility. Because individual group members believe that no single person can be blamed if the decision turns out poorly, they can shift the blame entirely to others (the group). This diffusion of individual responsibility may lead members to accept higher levels of risk in making a group decision.[58]

Group Decision-Making Techniques

As the preceding discussion makes clear, groups may flounder when given a problem to solve. It is important, therefore, to understand the techniques that can be used to encourage full and effective input and discussion before the group reaches a decision. Several techniques have been developed, including brainstorming, the nominal group technique, the Delphi technique, dialectical inquiry, and devil's advocacy (see Exhibit 10-3).

BRAINSTORMING

For major decisions, it is usually important to generate a wide variety of new ideas during the data-gathering and alternative-generation phases of decision making. Increasing the number of ideas during these phases helps ensure that important facts or considerations are not overlooked. Unfortunately, if the group evaluates or critiques each new idea as it is introduced in a group meeting, individual members may withhold other creative ideas because they fear critical comments. In contrast, if ideas are not evaluated immediately, members may be encouraged to offer inputs, even if they are uncertain of the value of their ideas. This is the essence of **brainstorming.**[59]

Brainstorming within groups has the following basic features:

PhotoDisc, Inc./Getty Images

brainstorming
A process in which a large number of ideas are generated while evaluation of the ideas is suspended.

- Imagination is encouraged. No idea is too unique or different, and the more ideas offered the better.
- Using or building on the ideas of others is encouraged.
- There is no criticism of any idea, no matter how bad it may seem at the time.
- Evaluation is postponed until the group can no longer think of any new ideas.

Many companies—such as IDEO, a Silicon Valley product design firm—use this basic approach.[60] Research supports the approach, as it suggests that groups using brainstorming often generate more ideas than groups that do not use brainstorming.[61] However, research also suggests that groups following this approach do not do as well as individuals brainstorming alone.[62] In one study, for example, a brainstorming group developed 28 ideas, and 8.9 percent of them were later judged as good ideas by independent experts.[63] The same number of people engaging in solitary brainstorming developed a total of 74.5 ideas, with 12.7 percent judged as good ideas.

Why is group brainstorming often less effective than individual brainstorming? One problem may be that group members believe criticism will not be entirely eliminated but will simply remain unspoken.[64] In other words, if a member contributes a unique idea, she may believe that others are silently ridiculing it. Another problem may be that some group members are simply distracted by the significant amount of discussion in a group brainstorming session.[65]

Two techniques may be helpful in overcoming the problems of standard group brainstorming. First, *brain-writing* can be used. In brain-writing, group members stop at various points in a group meeting and write down all of their ideas.[66] Then the written ideas are placed on a flipchart or whiteboard by an individual assigned the task of pooling the written remarks. By moving from an oral to a written approach, and by introducing anonymity, this method makes many individuals feel less inhibited. Furthermore, less talking takes place in the room, so distractions are reduced. Second, *electronic brainstorming (EBS)* can be used. In a common version of EBS, group members sit around a table with computer stations in front of them.[67] Each individual attempts to develop as many ideas as possible and enter them into a database. As an idea is entered, it is projected onto a large screen that everyone can see. Because there is anonymity, individuals feel less inhibited, and because there is less talking in the room, they are not distracted. Individuals can, however, build on the ideas of others as they appear on the screen.

NOMINAL GROUP TECHNIQUE

Another technique used to overcome some of the inhibiting forces in group decision making is called the **nominal group technique.** This technique shares some features of brain-writing and electronic brainstorming. In its basic form, it calls for a decision meeting that follows four procedural rules:

nominal group technique
A process for group decision making in which discussion is structured and the final solution is decided by silent vote.

1. At the outset, individuals seated around a table write down their ideas silently and without discussion.

2. Each member presents one idea to the group. Then, each member presents a second idea. The process is repeated until all ideas have been presented. No group discussion is permitted during this period.

3. After the ideas have been recorded on a blackboard or a large flipchart or in a computer database for projection, the members discuss them. The major purpose here is to clarify and evaluate.

4. The meeting concludes with a silent and independent vote or ranking of the alternative choices. The group decision is determined by summing or pooling these independent votes.[68]

The nominal group technique eliminates a great deal of interaction among group members. Discussion and interaction occur only once during the entire process. Even the final choice of an alternative occurs in silence and depends on an impersonal summing process. Proponents of this technique believe that inhibitions are overcome at crucial stages, whereas group discussion occurs at the time it is needed for evaluation. Research has suggested that the technique yields better results than a standard group brainstorming session.[69]

DELPHI TECHNIQUE

Brainstorming and the nominal group technique generally require group members to be in close physical proximity (seated around a table, for example). However, groups using the **Delphi technique** do not meet face-to-face. Instead, members are solicited for their judgments at their various homes or places of business.[70] In the most common approach, group members respond to a questionnaire about the issue of interest. Their responses are summarized and the results are fed back to the group. After receiving the feedback, individuals are given a second opportunity to respond and may or may not change their judgments.

Delphi technique
A highly structured decision-making process in which participants are surveyed regarding their opinions or best judgments.

Some Delphi approaches use only two sets of responses, whereas others repeat the question–summary–feedback process several times before a decision or conclusion is reached. The final decision is derived by averaging or otherwise combining the members' responses to the last questionnaire; often, the members' responses become more similar over time. Although some research has been supportive of this technique,[71] it is a highly structured approach that can inhibit some types of input, especially if some individuals feel constrained by the particular set of questions posed. Even so, the Delphi technique is an option to consider, especially when members of the group are geographically dispersed.

DIALECTICAL INQUIRY AND DEVIL'S ADVOCACY

The techniques for group decision making explained above are more concerned with increasing the number of ideas generated than with improving the quality of the final solution. Although having a greater number of ideas enhances the possibility that a superior alternative will be identified, other techniques can help the group find the best choice.

Two key approaches are dialectical inquiry and devil's advocacy. These approaches counter the tendency of groups to avoid conflict when evaluating alternative courses of action and to prematurely smooth over differences within the group when they occur.[72] In its basic form, **dialectical inquiry** calls for two different subgroups to develop very different assumptions and recommendations in order to encourage full discussion of ideas. The two subgroups debate their respective positions. **Devil's advocacy** calls for an individual or subgroup to argue against the assumptions and recommended action put forth by other members of the group. Thus, both dialectical inquiry and devil's advocacy use "constructive" conflict. Proponents assert that both are learning-oriented approaches because the active debates can help the group to discover new alternatives and to develop a more complete understanding of the issues involved in the decision problems.[73] In spite of these similarities, however, there are important differences between the two approaches.

The dialectical inquiry technique requires group members to develop two distinct points of view. More specifically, one subgroup develops a recommendation based on a set of assumptions, and a second subgroup develops a significantly different recommendation based on different assumptions. Debate of the two opposing sets of recommendations and assumptions maximizes constructive conflict, and the resulting evaluation of the two points of view helps ensure a thorough review and also helps to promote the development of new recommendations as differences are bridged. Devil's advocacy, however, requires the group to generate only one set of assumptions and a single recommendation, which are then critiqued by the devil's advocate (or advocates).

Research on these techniques suggests that both are effective in developing high-quality solutions to problems.[74] At the same time, however, they can result in somewhat lower levels of group satisfaction than approaches such as brainstorming.[75] This outcome is probably due to the intragroup conflict that can arise when these methods are used. Still, both approaches are apt to be effective in controlling undesirable group phenomena that suppress the full exploration of issues. Because both approaches aim to create constructive conflict through assigned roles, they are not likely to cause major dissatisfaction among group members.

dialectical inquiry
A group decision-making technique that relies on a critique of assumptions and recommended action in order to encourage debate.

devil's advocacy
A group decision-making technique that relies on a critique of assumptions and recommended action in order to encourage debate.

Who Should Decide? Individual versus Group Decision Making

In this closing section, we first provide guidance on how a manager should approach a decision that he must make. Should he make the decision alone, should he invite limited participation by associates, or should he use a group decision-making approach with associates? From the perspective of high-involvement management, managers should try to involve associates in most of their decisions. The knowledge and skills embodied in associates (their human capital) have great value. Following the discussion of associate involvement in managerial decisions, we summarize the advantages and disadvantages of having an individual versus a group make a decision.

Associate Involvement in Managerial Decisions

Although associates in high-involvement firms make many important decisions, other decisions remain for managers to address, perhaps with the assistance of associates. For these latter decisions, managers must determine the correct level of associate involvement in the decision-making process. Two researchers, Victor Vroom and Philip Yetton, point out that the correct level of involvement depends on the nature of the decision problem itself.[76] If the manager can diagnose the nature of the problem, she can determine the degree to which a group of associates should participate.

The Vroom–Yetton method requires the manager first to diagnose the problem situation and then to determine the extent to which associates will be involved in the decision-making process. The optimal extent of involvement depends on the probable effect participation will have on: (1) the quality of the decision, (2) the acceptance or commitment subordinates exhibit when implementing the decision, and (3) the amount of time needed to make the decision.[77]

As you can see in Exhibit 10-4, there are several levels of involvement, ranging from the manager's making the decision alone to a fully participative group

Exhibit 10-4	Managerial Approaches to Associate Involvement in Decision Making

Approach

Low — A-I—Manager solves the problem or makes the decision alone, using the information to which she has current access.

A-II—Manager requests information but may not explain the problem to associates. The associates' role in the process is to provide specific information; associates do not generate or evaluate alternatives.

C-I—Manager explains the problem to the relevant associates one by one, requesting their input without discussing the problem as a group. After discussing it with each of the relevant associates, the manager makes the decision alone. It is unclear whether the decision reflects the associates' input.

C-II—Manager explains the problem to associates as a group. The manager obtains group members' ideas and suggestions. Afterwards, the manager makes the decision alone. The associates' input may or may not be reflected in the manager's decision.

G-II—Manager explains the problem to the associates in a group setting. They work together to generate and evaluate alternatives and agree on a solution. The manager acts as a facilitator, guiding the discussion, focusing on the problem, and ensuring that the important issues are examined. The manager does not force the group to accept her solution and will accept **High** and implement a solution supported by the group.

Axis label (vertical): Level of Associate Involvement in Decision

Source: Adapted from V.H. Vroom, & A.G. Jago, 1978. "On the validity of the Vroom–Yetton Model," *Journal of Applied Psychology*, 69: 151–162; V.H. Vroom, & P.W. Yetton, 1973. *Leadership and Decision Making.* Pittsburgh, PA: University of Pittsburgh Press.

A: Is there a quality requirement such that one solution is likely to be more rational than another (is it worth working hard to find the best possible solution, or will any number of solutions work reasonably well)?

B: Do I have sufficient information to make a high-quality decision?

C: Is the problem structured (do I know the questions to ask and where to look for relevant information)?

D: Is acceptance of the decision by associates critical to effective implementation (if implementation would be relatively easy, then full acceptance is less important; if implementation would be pursued out of loyalty, then full acceptance is less important)?

E: If I were to make the decision by myself, is it reasonably certain that it would be accepted by my associates?

F: Do the associates share the organization's goals to be attained in solving this problem?

G: Is conflict among associates likely in preferred solutions?

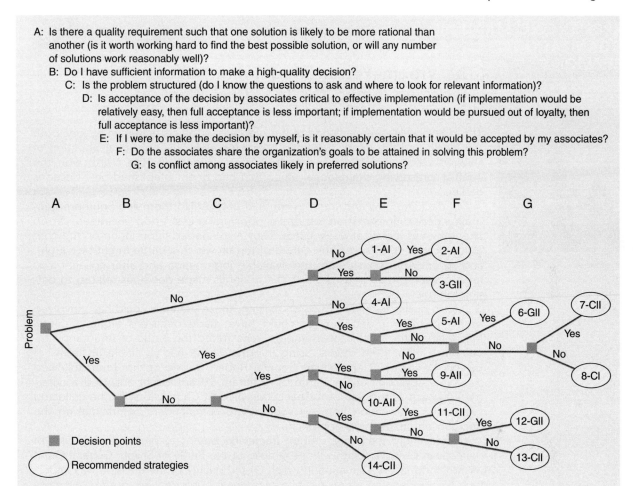

Exhibit 10-5   Decision Tree Method for Diagnosing the Appropriate Level of Subordinate Involvement in Decisions

Source: V.H. Vroom & P.W. Yetton, 1973. *Leadership and Decision Making.* Pittsburgh, PA: University of Pittsburgh Press.

approach. Vroom and Yetton suggest that managers can determine the best strategy for associate participation by asking seven diagnostic questions. This procedure yields a decision tree that indicates the most effective level of participation, as shown in Exhibit 10-5. It is not always necessary, however, to ask all seven questions to determine the level of involvement because some branches of the decision tree end after a few questions are asked.

Research has supported the Vroom–Yetton method. The method predicts the technical quality, subordinate acceptance, and overall effectiveness of final solutions.[78]

As shown in the *Experiencing Strategic Organizational Behavior* feature, the success of many Civil War generals was at least partially determined by a proper level of subordinate involvement in decisions. Like a top general during the Civil War, a CEO must decide on the level of involvement for the top management team. When, for example, the CEO needs to address a complex strategic decision (such as whether to enter a new market), she is likely to fully involve top management team members in the decision, given the need for a variety of inputs.

The Vroom–Yetton Model and Military Decisions during the U.S. Civil War

Getty Images

The U.S. Civil War remains one of the bloodiest conflicts in human history. Both the North and the South sustained heavy losses in this fight over abolition of slavery, economic issues, and states' rights. Eventually, the North won the conflict, preserving the national union that had been established only decades earlier.

In deciding how and when to conduct battles, Northern and Southern generals needed information on the opposing side's troop locations, troop strength, and logistical weaknesses. They also needed information on the condition of their own forces, the nature of terrain where a battle might be fought, and so on. After considering the available information and after collecting as much new information as desired, the generals made decisions related to battle strategy.

As in business-related decision making, these generals could have involved others in making decisions or could have made decisions alone. General McClellan of the North, for example, orchestrated the Battle of Antietam without much input from others, using information he had available (in terms of Exhibit 10-4, the AI approach). General Robert E. Lee of the South followed this same approach at the Battle of Antietam (AI approach) but used a different approach at the Battle of Chancellorsville. At Chancellorsville, he collected substantial information from his subordinate commanders before making the decision on his own (AII approach).

Interestingly, the Vroom–Yetton framework seems to predict the success of generals in Civil War battles. For example, at the Battle of Shiloh, General Grant of the North faced a situation in which (1) the quality of the decision was important, (2) the decision maker did not have enough information to make a quality decision, (3) the problem was not well structured, and (4) acceptance by subordinate officers was not crucial to effective implementation (Situation 14 in Exhibit 10-5). Grant sought information but not ideas from his officers and made the battle-strategy decision alone (AII approach). Group discussion and idea generation would have been beneficial, however, because the problem was unstructured. Grant did not meet his objectives at Shiloh.

At the Battle of Gettysburg, General Meade of the North faced a situation in which (1) the quality of the decision was important, (2) the decision maker had the crucial information, and (3) acceptance by subordinate officers was not crucial to affect implementation (Situation 4 in Exhibit 10-5). Meade alone made the key decision related to strategy, without collecting substantial new information from others (AI approach, perhaps close to an AII approach). As predicted by the Vroom–Yetton model, he met his objectives.

In the following table, a number of battles are profiled. As shown, the model correctly predicts outcomes in 10 of 12 cases.

The input from other top-level managers can be especially valuable when the team members are heterogeneous in their backgrounds and knowledge.[79] As you can see, the Vroom–Yetton model is useful not only for lower-level managers deciding on the appropriate level of involvement for associates but also for generals deciding on the level of involvement for subordinate officers and for senior managers deciding on the level of involvement for those who report directly to them.

Battle/ Commanders	Problem Type	Recommended Decision Approach	Style Used	Outcome (Relative to Original Objective)
Battle of Shiloh				
General Grant	14	CII	All	Not Achieved
General Johnston	12	GII	All	Not Achieved
Battle of Antietam				
General McClellan	5	AI	AI	Achieved
General Lee	9	AII	AI	Not Achieved
Battle of Chancellorsville				
General Hooker	14	CII	AI	Not Achieved
General Lee	5	AI	AII	Achieved
Battle of Gettysburg				
General Meade	4	AI	AI	Achieved
General Lee	11	CII	AI	Not Achieved
Battle of Chickamauga				
General Rosecrans	11	CII	AII	Not Achieved
General Bragg	11	CII	AI	Not Achieved
Battle of Nashville				
General Thomas	11	CII	AII	Achieved
General Hood	13	CII	AI	Not Achieved

Sources: Adapted from W.J. Duncan, K.G. LaFrance, & P.M. Ginter, "Leadership and Decision Making: A Retrospective Application and Assessment," *Journal of Leadership and Organizational Studies* 9 (2003): 1–20 (principal source); B.J. Murphy, "Grant versus Lee," *Civil War Times Illustrated* 43, no. 1 (2004): 42–52; United States War Department, *The War of the Rebellion: A Compilation of the Official Records of the Union and Confederate Armies*, multiple series and volumes within series (Washington, DC: Government Printing Office, 1880–1891).

One final point is important. When a group decision approach is to be used (Type GII), the manager must determine how much agreement should exist within the group. Must all the members agree on the decision, or will the manager accept the decision even though some members disagree? Typically, managers seek either a majority or a unanimous decision from the decision-making group.[80] Seeking agreement from a majority has several advantages over seeking unanimous agreement, including increased speed and reduced risk of impasse.[81] Trying to obtain unanimity, however, generally creates more discussion and often causes group members to explore the assumptions that underlie the positions and preferences held within the group.[82] Managers must balance these factors when deciding which approach to use for group decision making.

Value of Individual versus Group Decision Making

Under the proper conditions, group decision making should increase the number of ideas generated and improve the evaluation of alternatives. Such outcomes are desirable because they generally produce better decisions. However, our earlier discussion of group decision making suggested that these results are not guaranteed. Furthermore, the generation of ideas and their evaluation are not the only

ADVANTAGES	DISADVANTAGES
Groups can accumulate more knowledge and facts and thus generate more and better alternatives.	Groups take more time to reach decisions than do individuals.
Groups often display superior judgement when evaluating alternatives, especially for complex problems.	Group social interactions may lead to premature compromise and failure to consider all alternatives fully.
Group involvement in decisions leads to a higher level of acceptance of the decisions and greater satisfaction.	Groups are sometimes dominated by one or two "decision leaders," which may reduce acceptance, satisfaction, and quality.
Group decision making can result in growth for members of the group.	Managers may rely too much on group decisions, leading to loss of their own decision and implementation skills.

Exhibit 10-6
Advantages and Disadvantages of Group Decision Making

outcomes from group decision making. Commitment and satisfaction of participants must also be considered.

Important considerations for judging the overall value of group decision making as opposed to individual decision making include the time needed to reach the decision, the costs of making it, the nature of the problem, the satisfaction and commitment of employees affected by the decision, and opportunities for personal growth (see Exhibit 10-6).

TIME

Not surprisingly, groups typically take more time to reach decisions than do individuals. There are several reasons for this difference:

- Many social needs are met by the group (exchanging greetings, talking about the weekend, and so forth). The time required to meet these needs increases the time needed to reach a decision.
- More ideas and opinions are held by the group, and discussing these increases the time required. The use of techniques such as brainstorming and dialectical inquiry also adds to the time required.
- Arrangements for the group meeting place, format, and assembly must be made, taking more time.

Managers must consider the importance of time in their decisions, as well as the potential quality of the decisions. Some decisions must be made immediately. In other situations, time may be available for decision making. When time is an important consideration, the manager may elect to do one of the following:

- Make the decision alone.
- Use the group for advice only.
- Use an already-existing group to minimize the arrangement time.
- Use a majority decision rule rather than requiring unanimity.
- Use the nominal group technique to reduce lengthy discussion time.

COST

It is also inevitable that group decision making costs more than individual decision making. Time costs money, especially when expensive managers and associates are involved. The additional time must be multiplied by the number of members in the group and their respective financial compensation levels to arrive at the total cost. The additional cost of group decision making can be substantial. Therefore, managers must determine whether the decision is important enough to warrant the extra cost.

NATURE OF THE PROBLEM

Members of a group typically have more information and ideas than does a single individual.[83] If the information and ideas are discussed and integrated, group decisions will often be better informed than individual decisions. Many groups, however, have difficulty managing their collective knowledge. Groupthink and common information bias can prevent information from coming to the surface. Diversity-based infighting and the risky shift can prevent sound integration of information. However, the decision-making techniques discussed in this chapter, such as devil's advocacy, can help the group to overcome these negative social forces and create high-quality decisions.

The nature of the problem being examined should be considered in choosing the approach to use. Complex problems that require many different types of input tend to be solved more effectively by groups than by individuals. Deciding whether to develop a new product, for example, may require specialized knowledge of production facilities, engineering and design capabilities, market forces, government legislation, labor markets, and financial considerations. Thus, a group should be better at making this decision. In a recent study focused on new product decision making, groups were in fact more effective than individuals.[84]

SATISFACTION AND COMMITMENT

Even though quality is not consistently improved by group decision making, individual satisfaction and commitment to the final solution are often enhanced.[85] These outcomes may result from several factors. First, group members may change their attitudes toward the various alternatives as a result of the group's discussions. In addition, "team spirit" may develop as group members discover similarities among themselves.

Finally, it simply may be that people who share in an important activity such as decision making feel more "ownership" of the decision than when they are excluded from it. Commitment as a result of sharing in decision making has been consistently demonstrated by research, as seen in the classic work of Kurt Lewin. During World War II in the United States, there was a scarcity of good cuts of meat but an abundance of organ meats (liver, kidneys, and so forth). Lewin thought that households could be persuaded to buy organ meats if they participated in the decision to do so. He arranged to meet with two groups to test his belief.[86] One group was given an informative lecture on the value of using organ meats. The other group was given the same information, but members then were asked to discuss it among themselves and arrive at a group decision on whether to use such meat. It was found that the group decision resulted in a much higher rate of consumption (32 percent versus 3 percent). The implementation of the decision was more effective because the group had arrived at the decision. Members of the group were satisfied and committed to it because it was their decision, not someone else's.

PERSONAL GROWTH

The opportunity for personal growth provided by participation in group decision making is a benefit that is often overlooked. Advancement in a career depends on the ability to learn new skills. One of the most important skills to be learned is how to make decisions, and participation in group decision making may be an ideal opportunity for individuals to acquire this skill.

The Strategic Lens

Decision making is the essence of management. The primary task of managers is to make decisions. Top-level managers decide what products and services to provide and what markets to enter. Middle managers decide where to locate facilities and how many products to manufacture. Lower-level managers decide what tasks should be assigned to particular associates and when certain associates should be laid off. Therefore, the quality of managers' decisions at all levels has a major effect on the success of an organization. If managers decide to enter the wrong markets or to hire less than the best applicants, the organization's performance is likely to suffer. If, however, they decide on excellent products for the market and hire outstanding associates and motivate them to achieve, the organization is likely to flourish. Thus, understanding how to make effective decisions is necessary to be a successful manager; and organizations must have managers who are effective decision makers if they are to achieve their goals.[87] All strategic decisions—down to decisions regarding

what holidays to allow for associates—affect the organization's performance.

Critical Thinking Questions

1. You are a manager of a unit with 25 associates. You have just been informed that you must lay off 20 percent of the associates in your unit. What process will you follow to make the decision and to implement it?

2. If you made a decision that your manager told you was important for the organization and later you learned that you made an error in that decision, what actions would you take? Assume that others will not notice the error for some time.

3. You make decisions on a daily basis. Do you find it difficult to make decisions, especially those of importance? What can you do to improve your decision-making abilities?

What This Chapter Adds to Your Knowledge Portfolio

In this chapter, we have discussed individual and group decision making. We have covered the major steps in decision making, taking note of decision makers' tendencies to make satisficing rather than optimal decisions. In discussing individuals, we have emphasized decision styles, approaches to risk, and cognitive biases. To be successful, an organization's associates and managers must understand these elements of individual decision making. In discussing groups, we have focused on a set of problems that can affect group decision making and have described techniques for avoiding or overcoming these problems. Finally, we have discussed a model for assessing the extent to which associates should be involved in managerial decisions. In summary, we have made the following points:

- Decisions are choices. Decision making is a process involving several steps: defining the problem, identifying criteria for a solution, gathering information, evaluating alternatives, selecting the best alternative, and implementing the decision.

- Satisfactory rather than optimal decisions are common. Satisficing occurs because (1) individuals cannot gather and process all information that might be relevant for a particular decision and (2) individuals have a tendency to stop searching after the first acceptable solution has been found.

- Decision styles represent preferred ways of gathering information and evaluating alternatives. For gathering information, associates and managers can have either a sensing style or an intuition style. With the sensing style, individuals focus on concrete information that is directly available through the five senses. They also tend to focus on rules and facts and are usually practical and realistic. They often are effective in jobs requiring routine decision making. With the intuition style, individuals dislike details and tend to focus on abstractions and figurative examples. They are often effective in jobs that require nonroutine decisions and creativity. For evaluating alternatives, associates and managers can have either a thinking or a feeling style. With the thinking style, individuals focus on objective criteria and systematic analysis. With the feeling style, individuals use subjective approaches and are concerned with the emotional reactions of others. Although the thinking style is consistent with careful decision making, organizations need both thinkers and feelers to achieve a balance.

- Risk-taking propensity and reference points affect an individual's overall approach to risk. Risk-taking propensity relates to a person's willingness to take chances, whereas a reference point refers to a possible level of performance that a person uses to evaluate current standing. When a person has a strong propensity for risk and is failing to move toward his reference point, risk taking is likely.

- Cognitive biases represent mental shortcuts that often cause problems. Four important biases are: confirmation bias (information confirming early beliefs and ideas is sought, but potentially disconfirming information is not sought), ease-of-recall bias (information that is easy to recall from memory is relied on too much), anchoring bias (the first piece of information encountered about a situation is emphasized too much), and the sunk-cost bias (past investments are not treated as sunk costs).

- Several pitfalls are associated with group decision making. First, groupthink occurs when group members are too focused on consensus, particularly early in a decision process. This problem may occur because (1) group members like one another and do not want to criticize each other's ideas, (2) group members have high regard for the group's collective wisdom and therefore yield to early ideas or the ideas of a leader, and (3) group members derive satisfaction from membership in a group possessing a positive self-image and therefore they try to prevent the group from having any serious divisions. Second, the common information bias leads group members to unconsciously focus on information that is held by many members of the group while ignoring information held by only one or a few group members. Third, diversity-based infighting relates to disagreements being channeled in unproductive ways. Finally, the risky shift occurs when a group makes a more risky choice than individuals would have made (on average) when working separately.

- Several techniques exist to address the problems that may arise in group decision making. Brainstorming is a heavily used technique, but in its traditional form it fails in comparisons with individual brainstorming. Brain-writing and electronic brainstorming are useful alternatives. Nominal group technique, Delphi technique, dialectical inquiry, and devil's advocacy also can be very useful.

- Associates make many decisions in high-involvement firms. Managers address many other decisions but may involve associates in those decisions. The Vroom–Yetton model offers advice for assessing the proper level of involvement. To diagnose the situation, seven key questions are asked, and then a suggested approach is found through a decision tree.

- Groups have both advantages and disadvantages in decision making. One advantage is better quality, or at least a significant chance of better quality, particularly when complex decisions are being made. This advantage is based on the fact that groups bring more knowledge and facts to the decision and engage in a richer assessment of alternatives. Other advantages include better acceptance of decisions, greater satisfaction in the organization, and personal growth for group members. Time is one of several disadvantages associated with using a group to make a decision.

Back to the Knowledge Objectives

1. What are the basic steps in decision making? How should a decision maker approach the problem definition step? Why do decision makers usually fail to achieve optimal decisions?

2. What are the four Jungian decision styles, and how do they influence decisions and effectiveness in the workplace? Give an example of a person you know who had a decision style that did not seem to fit his or her role in an organization. This could be a person in an organization in which you have worked, or it could be a person from a school club or civic organization. What were the outcomes for this person in terms of satisfaction and performance? If you had been the individual's manager, how would you have managed the situation?

3. Describe a personal situation involving a reference point. Were you above or below your reference point? What was the effect on your behavior?

4. Which cognitive bias worries you the most, and why?

5. Compare the four primary pitfalls of group decision making. If you had to choose one, which would you prefer to deal with as a manager, and why?

6. What are the major group decision-making techniques? If you were dealing with diversity-based infighting, which of these techniques would you try first, and why?

7. What factors should a manager consider when deciding on the level of associate involvement in a decision? What shortcomings do you see in the Vroom–Yetton model?

Thinking about Ethics

1. You are a senior vice president with responsibility for a major business division in a large company. The CEO has decided that the firm has to cut costs and that a large layoff of associates is necessary. He has asked you to decide how many associates should be laid off in your division. You know that the CEO wants a significant reduction in costs, which points to the large layoff. Of course, a layoff has a substantial effect on associates' lives. Should you recommend a large layoff to please the CEO or a smaller one, justifying a smaller layoff with plans to save money in other areas and increase sales? Explain your reasoning.

2. Suppose your manager continues to invest more money in a failing project in which he has already made a significant investment. Does this decision present ethical concerns? If so, describe these concerns. If not, explain. Would you report any concerns to his boss?

3. You are charged with the responsibility of deciding the location for the new manufacturing plant in your division. The current facility is old. In addition, the new facility will use advanced technology, but the workforce in the community does not have the skill levels needed to staff it. Thus, you will likely decide on a location in another state. You also have to make decisions on when and how to close the current plant. This will mean laying off 300 associates currently working at the plant. How will you tell them that they will lose their jobs soon? Should you provide severance pay or other help? How will you make these decisions?

4. If an individual observes a group decision in which groupthink has occurred, does she have an obligation to report it to her superiors in order to prevent a serious error in the decision for the organization? Does she take any risks in taking such an action?

5. The risky shift occurs when a group makes a choice riskier than the choice group members would have made individually. Is it unethical for an individual group member to assume more risk when he is part of a group? What issues should be considered with regard to the level of risk involved in a group decision?

Key Terms

Building Your Human Capital

Decision Style Assessment

Different people use different decision styles. Understanding how you approach the gathering of information and the evaluation of alternatives can help make you a better decision maker. Such an understanding clarifies your strengths and weaknesses, which better positions you to deal effectively with them. Below, we present an assessment tool for decision styles.

Instructions

In this assessment, you will read 24 phrases that describe people. Please use the rating scale below to indicate how accurately each phrase describes *you*. Rate yourself as you generally are now, not as you wish to be in the future. Rate yourself as you honestly see yourself. Please read each item carefully, and then circle the number that corresponds to your choice from the rating scale.

1	2	3	4	5
Not at all like me	Somewhat unlike me	Neither like nor unlike me	Somewhat like me	Very much like me

	1	2	3	4	5
1. Do things in a logical order	1	2	3	4	5
2. Do things that others find strange.	1	2	3	4	5
3. Come straight to the point.	1	2	3	4	5
4. Like to get lost in thought.	1	2	3	4	5
5. Sympathize with the homeless.	1	2	3	4	5
6. Do things by the book.	1	2	3	4	5
7. Believe in a logical answer for everything.	1	2	3	4	5
8. Enjoy wild flights of fantasy.	1	2	3	4	5
9. Am not as strict as I could be.	1	2	3	4	5
10. Seldom daydream.	1	2	3	4	5
11. Get a head start on others.	1	2	3	4	5
12. Love to daydream.	1	2	3	4	5
13. Let people pull my leg.	1	2	3	4	5
14. Seldom get lost in thought.	1	2	3	4	5
15. Dislike imperfect work.	1	2	3	4	5

16. Swim against the current.	1	2	3	4	5
17. Do things in a half-way manner.	1	2	3	4	5
18. Take deviant positions.	1	2	3	4	5
19. Let my attention wander off.	1	2	3	4	5
20. Do unexpected things.	1	2	3	4	5
21. Believe in an eye for an eye.	1	2	3	4	5
22. Have no sympathy for criminals.	1	2	3	4	5
23. Reason logically.	1	2	3	4	5
24. Believe that criminals should receive help rather than punishment.	1	2	3	4	5

Scoring Key for Decision Style Assessment

To create scores, combine your responses to the items as follows:

Sensing vs. intuition =   (Item 2 + Item 4 + Item 8 + Item 12 + Item 16 + Item 18 + Item 20) + (18 − (Item 6 + Item 10 + Item 14))

Thinking vs. feeling =   (Item 1 + Item 3 + Item 7 + Item 11 + Item 15 + Item 21 + Item 22 + Item 23) + (36 − (Item 5 + Item 9 + Item 13 + Item 17 + Item 19 + Item 24))

Scores for sensing vs. intuition can range from 10 to 50. Scores below 30 suggest a sensing style, while scores of 30 and above suggest an intuition style. More extreme scores (very low or very high) indicate a stronger preference for one style over another. Scores from 26 to 34 suggest weaker preferences for a particular style.

Scores for thinking vs. feeling can range from 14 to 70. Scores of 42 and above suggest a thinking style, while scores below 42 suggest a feeling style. More extreme scores (very low or very high) indicate a stronger preference for one style over another. Scores from 37 to 47 suggest weaker preferences for a particular style.

Source: International Personality Item Pool (2001). A Scientific Collaboration for the Development of Advanced Measures of Personality Traits and Other Individual Differences (http://ipip.ori.org/).

A Strategic Organizational Behavior Moment

Decision Making at a Nuclear Power Facility

Part A. Harry, the Reluctant Maintenance Man

Harry opened his lunch bucket and was disappointed to find two tuna fish sandwiches again. "Damn," he muttered to himself, "four days in a row." He would have to get on his daughter, Susan, again. She graciously prepared his lunch most days but did not always provide the variety he liked. Of course, Susan would explain that she had other things to do besides providing him with a full lunch menu.

Across the cafeteria, Dan Thompson was eating with one of the design engineers, Marty Harris. Dan didn't like to talk shop while eating, but today had decided to continue a previous discussion over lunch. Dan was the supervisor of technical maintenance and had noticed that several of his people were reluctant to follow maintenance procedures. He had been told that the specifications were too complex to understand, that the procedures were often unnecessary, and that the plant engineers did not really appreciate maintenance problems. On the one hand, Dan realized that most of their complaints were just excuses for "doing things their own way." On the other hand, he didn't really know which procedures were important and which were not. That's why he had asked Marty to meet with him.

"Look, Dan," Marty was saying, "I know these procedures are complex. But damn it, nuclear power plants are complex—and potentially risky. Every specification, every procedure has a reason for being there. If your maintenance people ignore one procedure, they might get by with it and nothing happens. But one of them just might do it at the wrong time, and something could go haywire. You might explain that we have safety and cost to consider. If we lost expensive equipment, how'd they like to pay for it? Not much, I bet. If they lose a finger or get exposed to too much radiation, they wouldn't like that either. Now, just tell your people that the specifications and procedures, if followed, are the guarantee that things won't go wrong. They can count on it. If they take shortcuts, I won't guarantee a thing."

Dan nodded. This really wasn't what his maintenance staff wanted. They had hoped for a little flexibility, but he was going to have to tell them to follow the procedures. They wouldn't like it, but they would have to do it.

Later that afternoon, Dan met with his unit and relayed the instructions. He reminded them of the rules and disciplinary actions for not following procedures. At the end of the meeting, he couldn't decide whether it had done any good.

On Thursday, Harry noticed that he had been assigned the routinely scheduled maintenance on the three auxiliary feedwater (AFW) pumps. These pumps were normally used only for startup and shutdown and as emergency backup. When the main feedwater system malfunctioned, these pumps would activate to keep the steam generator from "drying out." The procedure also specified that the pumps should be serviced and tested one at a time and that, at most, one pump should be out of service at a time.

"That's horse manure," Harry thought. "Takes three hours to service the pumps that way. I can do it in two if I shut 'em down together. Two's better than three. Those stupid design people have probably never tried to service one of these things."

Harry didn't bother to open the manual for pump servicing. He had serviced these pumps several times in the past and felt no need to do it from the book any longer. He reached over and shut off three discharge valves, set out his equipment, and got to work. Two hours later he was done. He packed up his tools and hurried to get home.

Part B. System Breakdown

Marv Bradbury was working the graveyard shift. Most technicians didn't like this shift, but Marv didn't mind it at all. In fact, he thrived on it. Over the past few months, he had discovered that he enjoyed the solitude. He also liked to sleep in the mornings. Many of his co-workers thought he was nuts, but he didn't mind. He especially liked the extra responsibility that the graveyard shift put on the technician position.

Marv's job in the nuclear generating plant was particularly important. His primary job was to monitor a series of dials and readouts in the control room. Most of the time, the job was a little monotonous because the system was so automatic. However, if the readings indicated some variance in the system, Marv's responsibilities were great. He would have to interpret the readings, diagnose the problem, and—if the automatic correcting system failed—initiate corrective actions. For two reasons, Marv never worried about the enormous responsibilities of his job. First, the system was fault-free and self-correcting. It was a good system with no weaknesses. Second, Marv was exceptionally qualified and had a great deal of understanding about the system. He always knew what he had to do in the event of a problem and was capable of doing it. Several years of training had not been wasted on him.

It was about 4 A.M. when he noticed the feedwater dial reading begin to move rapidly. Temperature in the system was increasing quickly. The readings alerted Marv that the main system was malfunctioning, and he knew just what to do. He glanced over to the AFW indicator lights to be sure they were activated. The lights switched on, and he knew everything was in order. Obviously, he would have to find the malfunction in the main system, but for the time being everything was okay. The temperature in the cooling system should drop back down to normal as the AFW pumps took over.

Suddenly, the indicator light for the pressurizer electromatic relief valve showed that it had opened. In rapid succession the high reactor tripped, and the hot leg temperature in the primary loop increased to about 607 degrees Fahrenheit.

Marv knew the system was in severe trouble and got on the phone to get help. Before he could get back, the high-pressure injection pump had started, and he could feel an unusual and threatening vibration that shouldn't be there. Indicators showed that the steam generators were drying out, but that didn't make sense—the auxiliaries were running. He knew that if they dried out, the temperature was really going to go up and that the core was going to be damaged. "Why the hell isn't that secondary loop running?" he yelled to himself.

It took eight minutes to get someone down to the auxiliary pump room and discover that the three valves were still closed. They opened the valves, but it was too late. Now no one seemed to know what to do.

Discussion Questions

1. Analyze the critical problem in Part A of the case. Did Dan handle it in the best way? What decision styles did he use?

2. In what important ways is Harry's behavior different from Marv's?

3. How might group decision making be applied at the end of Part B?

4. What alternatives do you see for reducing the possibility of a similar problem in the future?

Team Exercise

Group Decision Making in Practice

In this chapter, we discussed several techniques for group decision making. The purpose of this exercise is to demonstrate two of the techniques and to show how they facilitate group decision activities. The exercise should take about 40 minutes to complete.

Procedure

1. The instructor will assign you to either a group that will use brain-writing and dialectical inquiry (BD group) or a group that will engage in general discussion (GD group).

2. All groups will list as many ideas as possible concerning the general problem, "How can the college of business enhance its reputation among the business leaders in the regional business community?" This should take no more than 20 minutes. Each BD group will follow the rules of brain-writing to generate the list of ideas. Each GD group will discuss the issue in a group setting.

3. All groups will develop a final recommendation. Each BD group will follow the dialectical inquiry method. Each GD group will again engage in general discussion.

4. The instructor will lead a discussion about your experiences.

Endnotes

1. Hitt, M.A., Ireland, R.D., & Hoskisson, R.E. 2007. *Strategic management: Competitiveness and globalization* (7th ed.). Cincinnati, OH: South-Western.

2. Hitt, M.A., & Tyler, B.B. 1991. Strategic decision models: Integrating different perspectives. *Strategic Management Journal,* 12: 327–351.

3. Bazerman, M.H. 2006. *Judgment in managerial decision making* (6th ed.). New York: John Wiley & Sons.

4. Hammond, J.S., Keeney, R.L., & Raiffa, H. 1999. *Smart choices: A practical guide to making better decisions.* Boston: Harvard Business School Press.

5. Ibid.

6. Based on Huber, G.P. 1980. *Managerial decision making.* Glenview, IL: Scott, Foresman.

7. Simon, H. 1957. *Administrative behavior.* New York: Macmillan.

8. Cecil, E.A., & Lundgren, E.F. 1975. An analysis of individual decision making behavior using a laboratory setting. *Academy of Management Journal,* 18: 600–604; Schwartz, B., Ward, A., Monterosso, J., Lyubomirsky, S., White, K., & Lehman, D.R. 2002. Maximizing versus satisficing: Happiness is a matter of choice. *Journal of Personality and Social Psychology,* 83: 1178–1197.

9. Most research based on Jung's ideas has used the Myers–Briggs Type Indicator. For a review of relevant research in organizational behavior, see Gardner, W.L., & Martinko, M.J. 1996. Using the Myers-Briggs Type Indicator to study managers: A literature review and research agenda. *Journal of Management,* 22: 45–83. For supportive research on the internal consistency and test-retest reliability associated with the MBTI, see Capraro, R.M., & Capraro, M.M. 2002.

Myers-Briggs Type Indicator score reliability across studies: A meta-analytic reliability generalization study. *Educational and Psychological Measurement,* 62: 590–602; and see Myers, I.B., & McCaulley, M.H. 1989. *Manual: A guide to the development and use of the Myers-Briggs Type Indicator.* Palo Alto, CA: Consulting Psychologists Press. For research on the construct validity associated with the MBTI, see Carlyn, M. 1977. An assessment of the Myers-Briggs Type Indicator. *Journal of Personality Assessment,* 41: 461–473; and see Thompson, B., & Borrello, G.M. 1986. Construct validity of the Myers-Briggs Type Indicator. *Educational and Psychological Measurement,* 60: 745–752. For research on temporal stability, see Salter, D.W., Evans, N.J., & Forney, D.S. 2006. A longitudinal study of learning style preferences on the Myers-Briggs type indicator and learning style inventory. *Journal of College Student Development,* 47: 173–184; For criticism of the MBTI, see, for example, Pittenger, D.J. 1993. The utility of the Myers-Briggs Type Indicator. *Review of Educational Research,* 63: 467–488.

10. Gardner & Martinko, Using the Myers-Briggs Type Indicator to study managers; Jaffe, J. Of different minds. *Association Management,* 37 (October 1985): 120–124.

11. Leibovich, M. 2000. Alter egos: Two sides of high-tech brain trust make up a powerful partnership. *The Washington Post,* December 31: A.01.

12. Gardner & Martinko, Using the Myers-Briggs Type Indicator to study managers; Jaffe, Of different minds.

13. Lyons, M. 1997. Presidential character revisited. *Political psychology,* 18: 791–811.

14. Kiersey.com. 2007. The rationals. http://keirsey.com/personality/nt.html.

15. Gardner & Martinko, Using the Myers-Briggs Type Indicator to study managers.

16. Rodgers, W. 1991. How do loan officers make their decisions about credit risks? A study of parallel distributed processing. *Journal of Economic Psychology,* 12: 243–365.

17. Stevens, G.A., & Burley, J. 2003. Piloting the rocket of radical innovation. *Research Technology Management,* 46: 16–25.

18. Gardner & Martinko, Using the Myers-Briggs Type Indicator to study managers; Jaffe, Of different minds.

19. Ibid.

20. McIntyre, R.P. 2000. Cognitive style as an antecedent to adaptiveness, customer orientation, and self-perceived selling performance. *Journal of Business and Psychology,* 15: 179–196.

21. Gardner & Martinko, Using the Myers-Briggs Type Indicator to study managers; Jaffe, Of different minds.

22. Jaffe, Of different minds.

23. See the following: Leibovich, Alter egos; Lohr, S. 2007. Preaching from the Ballmer pulpit. *The New York Times,* January 28: 3.1; Schlender, B. 2004. Ballmer unbound. *Fortune,* 149 (2): 117–124; Schlender, B. 2007. The wrath of Ballzilla. *Fortune,* 155 (8): 70.

24. Bazerman, *Judgment in managerial decision making;* Hammond, Keeney, & Raiffa, *Smart choices.*

25. Dahlback, O. 1990. Personality and risk taking. *Personality and Individual Differences,* 11: 1235–1242; Dahlback, O. 2003. A conflict theory of group risk taking. *Small Group Research,* 34: 251–289; March, J.G. 1994. *A primer on decision making.* New York: The Free Press.

26. Lashinsky, A. 2004. For Trump, fame is easier than fortune. *Fortune,* 149(4): 38; Shawn, T. 1996. Donald Trump: An exloser is back in the money. *Fortune,* 134(2): 86–88.

27. Taylor, R.N., & Dunnette, M.D. 1974. Influence of dogmatism, risk-taking propensity, and intelligence on decision-making strategies for a sample of industrial managers. *Journal of Applied Psychology,* 59: 420–423.

28. Jegers, M. 1991. Prospect theory and the risk-return relation. *Academy of Management Journal,* 34: 215–225; Kahneman, D., & Tversky, A. 1979. Prospect theory: An analysis of decision under risk. *Econometrica,* 47: 263–291; Tversky, A., & Kahneman, D. 1986. Rational choice and the framing of decisions. *Journal of Business,* 59: 251–278; Wakker, P.P. 2003. The data of Levy and Levy. 2002. Prospect theory: Much ado about nothing? actually support prospect theory. *Management Science,* 49: 979–981.

29. Simon, M., Houghton, S.M., & Savelli, S. 2003. Out of the frying pan…? Why small business managers introduce high-risk products. *Journal of Business Venturing,* 18: 419–440.

30. Gimpel, H. 2007. Loss aversion and reference-dependent preferences in multi-attribute negotiations. *Group Decision and Negotiation,* 16: 303–319.

31. Tversky, A., & Kahneman, D. 1974. Judgment under uncertainty: Heuristics and biases. *Science,* 185: 1124–1131.

32. Bazerman, *Judgment in managerial decision making;* Hammond, Keeney, & Raiffa, *Smart choices;* Hogarth, R. 1980. *Judgment and choice.* New York: John Wiley & Sons.

33. Einhorn, H.J., & Hogarth, R.M. 1978. Confidence in judgment: Persistence in the illusion of validity. *Psychological Review,* 85: 395–416; Jones, M., & Sugden, R. 2001. Positive confirmation bias in the acquisition of information. *Theory and Decision,*

50: 59–99; Wason, P.C. 1960. On the failure to eliminate hypotheses in a conceptual task. *Quarterly Journal of Experimental Psychology,* 12: 129–140.

34. Bazerman, *Judgment in managerial decision making.*

35. Time.com. 2004. Person of the year: Notorious leaders—Joseph Stalin. http://www.time.com/time/personoftheyear/archive/photo history/stalin.html.

36. Bazerman, *Judgment in managerial decision making.*

37. Joyce, E.J., & Biddle, G.C. 1981. Anchoring and adjustment in probabilistic inference in auditing. *Journal of Accounting Research,* 19: 120–145.

38. Hammond, Keeney, & Raiffa, *Smart choices;* Roberto, M.A. 2002. Lessons from Everest: The interaction of cognitive bias, psychological safety, and system complexity. *California Management Review,* 45(1), 136–158.

39. Shimizu, K., & Hitt, M.A. 2005. What constraints or facilitates the divestitures of formerly acquired firms? The effects of organizational inertia. *Journal of Management,* 31: 50–72.

40. For an excellent example of social interactions in decision making, see Anderson, P.A. 1983. Decision making by objection and the Cuban missile crisis. *Administrative Science Quarterly,* 28: 201–222.

41. For the original formulation of groupthink, see the following: Janis, I.L. 1972. *Victims of groupthink: A psychological study of foreign-policy decisions and fiascos.* Boston: Houghton Mifflin; Janis, I.L. 1982. *Groupthink: Psychological studies of policy decisions and fiascos* (revised version of *Victims of groupthink).* Boston: Houghton Mifflin. For later variants of the groupthink model, see the following examples: Hart, P.T. 1990. *Groupthink in government: A study of small groups and policy failure.* Amsterdam: Swets & Zeitlinger; Turner, P.E., & Pratkanis, A.R. 1998. A social identity maintenance model of groupthink. *Organizational Behavior and Human Decision Processes,* 73: 210–235; Whyte, G. 1998. Recasting Janis's groupthink model: The key role of collective efficacy in decision fiascos. *Organizational Behavior and Human Decision Processes,* 73: 163–184. For an interesting critique of some past groupthink research, see Henningsen, D.D., Henningsen, M.L.M., Eden, J., & Cruz, M.G. 2006. Examining the symptoms of groupthink and retrospective sensemaking. *Small Group Research,* 37: 36–64. Also see: Haslam, S.A., Ryan, M.K., Postmes, T., Spears, R., Jetten, J., & Webley, P. Sticking to our guns: Social identity as a basis for the maintenance of commitment to faltering organizational projects. *Journal of Organizational Behavior,* 27: 607–628.

42. See, for example: Callaway, M.R., & Esser, J.K. 1984. Groupthink: Effects of cohesiveness and problem-solving procedures on group decision making. *Social Behavior and Personality,* 12: 157–164; Courtright, J.A. 1978. A laboratory investigation of groupthink. *Communication Monographs,* 45: 229–246; Janis, *Victims of groupthink.*

43. Whyte, Recasting Janis's groupthink model.

44. See, for example, Turner & Pratkanis, A social identity maintenance model of groupthink; Turner, M.E., & Pratkanis, A.R. 1997. Mitigating groupthink by stimulating constructive conflict. In C. De Dreu, & E. Van de Vliert (Eds.), *Using Conflict in Organizations.* London: Sage.

45. Turner & Pratkanis, A social identity maintenance model of groupthink; Turner & Pratkanis, Mitigating groupthink by stimulating constructive conflict.

46. Stephens, J., & Behr, P. 2002. Enron's culture fed its demise: Groupthink promoted foolhardy risks. *The Washington Post*, January 27: A.01.

47. For summaries of published case research, see: Esser, J.K. 1998. Alive and well after 25 years: A review of groupthink research. *Organizational Behavior and Human Decision Processes*, 73: 116–141; Park, W. 2000. A comprehensive empirical investigation of the relationships among variables of the groupthink model. *Journal of Organizational Behavior*, 21: 873–887.

48. Janis, *Victims of groupthink;* Tetlock, P.E., Peterson, R.S., McGuire, C., Chang, S., & Field, P. 1992. Assessing political group dynamics: A test of the groupthink model. *Journal of Personality and Social Psychology*, 63: 403–425.

49. Moorehead, G., Ference, R., & Neck, C.P. 1991. Group decision fiascos continue: Space Shuttle *Challenger* and revised groupthink framework. *Human Relations*, 44: 539–550.

50. Chisson, E.J. 1994. *The Hubble wars*. New York: Harper-Perennial.

51. Horton, T.R. 2002. Groupthink in the boardroom. *Directors and Boards*, 26(2): 9; Hymowitz, C. 2003. Corporate governance: What's your solution? *Wall Street Journal*, February 24: R8.

52. Manz, C.C., & Sims, H.P. 1982. The potential for "groupthink" in autonomous work groups. *Human Relations*, 35: 773–784.

53. Kim, P.H. 1997. When what you know can hurt you: A study of experiential effects on group discussion and performance. *Organizational Behavior and Human Decision Processes*, 69: 165–177; Stasser, G., & Titus, W. 1985. Pooling of unshared information in group decision making: Biased information sampling during discussion. *Journal of Personality and Social Psychology*, 48: 1467–1478.

54. Hunton, J.E. 2001. Mitigating the common information sampling bias inherent in small-group discussion. *Behavioral Research in Accounting*, 13: 171–194.

55. De Dreu, C.K.W., & Weingart, L.R. 2003. Task versus relationship conflict, team performance, and team member satisfaction: A meta-analysis. *Journal of Applied Psychology*, 88: 741–749; Miller, C.C., Burke, L.M., & Glick, W.H. 1998. Cognitive diversity among upper-echelon executives: Implications for strategic decision processes. *Strategic Management Journal*, 19: 39–58.

56. Stoner, J. 1968. Risky and cautious shifts in group decisions: The influence of widely held values. *Journal of Experimental Social Psychology*, 4: 442–459.

57. See, for example: Dahlback, A conflict theory of group risk taking.

58. Dahlback, A conflict theory of group risk taking; Mynatt, C., & Sherman, S.J. 1975. Responsibility attribution in groups and individuals: A direct test of the diffusion of responsibility hypothesis. *Journal of Personality and Social Psychology*, 32: 1111–1118; Wallach, M.A., Kogan, N., & Bem, D.J. 1964. Diffusion of responsibility and level of risk taking in groups. *Journal of Abnormal and Social Psychology*, 68: 263–274.

59. Osborn, A.F. 1957. *Applied imagination* (revised edition). New York: Scribner.

60. Thompson, L. 2003. Improving the creativity of organizational work groups. *Academy of Management Executive*, 17(1): 96–109.

61. Bouchard, T. 1971. Whatever happened to brainstorming? *Journal of Creative Behavior*, 5: 182–189.

62. Mullen, B., Johnson, C., & Salas, E. 1991. Productivity loss in brainstorming groups: A meta-analytic integration. *Basic and Applied Social Psychology*, 12: 3–23; Stroebe, W., & Nijstad, B.A. 2004. Why brainstorming in groups impairs creativity: A cognitive theory of productivity losses in brainstorming groups. *Psychologische Rundschau*, 55: 2–10; Taylor, D.W., Berry, P.C., & Block, C.H. 1958. Does group participation when using brainstorming facilitate or inhibit creative thinking? *Administrative Science Quarterly*, 3: 23–47.

63. Diehl, M., & Stroebe, W. 1987. Productivity loss in brainstorming groups: Toward a solution of a riddle. *Journal of Personality and Social Psychology*, 53: 497–509.

64. Camacho, L.M., & Paulus, P.B. 1995. The role of social anxiousness in group brainstorming. *Journal of Personality and Social Psychology*, 68: 1071–1080; Thompson, Improving the creativity of organizational workgroups.

65. Thompson, Improving the creativity of organizational workgroups.

66. Ibid.

67. Ibid. Also see: DeRosa, D.M., Smith, C.L., & Hantula, D.A. 2007. The medium matters: Mining the long-promised merit of group interaction in creative idea generation tasks in a meta-analysis of the electronic group brainstorming literature. *Computers in Human Behavior*, 23: 1549–1581.

68. Van de Ven, A., & Delbecq, A. 1974. The effectiveness of nominal, Delphi, and interacting group decision processes. *Academy of Management Journal*, 17: 605–621.

69. For supporting evidence, see: Gustafson, D.H., Shukla, R., Delbecq, A., & Walster, W. 1973. A comparative study in subjective likelihood estimates made by individuals, interacting groups, Delphi groups, and nominal groups. *Organizational Behavior and Human Performance*, 9: 280–291.

70. Van de Ven & Delbecq, The effectiveness of nominal, Delphi, and interacting group decision processes.

71. See, for example: Landeta, J. 2006. Current validity of the Delphi method in social sciences. *Technology Forecasting & Social Change*, 73: 467–482; Van de Ven & Delbecq, The effectiveness of nominal, Delphi, and interacting group decision processes.

72. For early research on these two techniques, see the following: Mason, R. 1969. A dialectical approach to strategic planning. *Management Science*, 15: B403–B411; Mason, R.O., & Mitroff, I.I. 1981. *Challenging strategic planning assumptions*, New York: Wiley; Schweiger, D.M., Sandberg, W.R., & Ragan, J.W. 1986. Group approaches for improving strategic decision making: A comparative analysis of dialectical inquiry, devil's advocacy, and consensus. *Academy of Management Journal*, 29: 51–71.

73. Cosier, R.A. 1983. Methods for improving the strategic decision: Dialectic versus the devil's advocate. *Strategic Management Journal*, 4: 79–84; Mitroff, I.I. 1982. Dialectic squared: A fundamental difference in perception of the meanings of some key concepts in social science. *Decision Sciences*, 13: 222–224.

74. Schwenk, C. 1989. A meta-analysis on the comparative effectiveness of devil's advocacy and dialectical inquiry. *Strategic Management Journal*, 10: 303–306; Valacich, J.S., & Schwenk, C. 1995. Structuring conflict in individual, face-to-face, and computer-mediated group decision making: Carping versus objective devil's advocacy. *Decision Sciences*, 26: 369–393.

75. Schweiger, Sandberg, & Ragan, Group approaches for improving strategic decision making.

76. Vroom, V.H., & Yetton, P.W. 1973. *Leadership and decision making*. Pittsburgh, PA: University of Pittsburgh Press.

77. Vroom & Yetton, *Leadership and decision making*.

78. Field, R.H.G. 1982. A test of the Vroom-Yetton normative model of leadership. *Journal of Applied Psychology*, 67: 523–532; Field, R.H.G., & House, R.J. 1990. A test of the Vroom-Yetton model using manager and subordinate reports. *Journal of Applied Psychology*, 75: 362–366; Tjosvold, D., Wedley, W.C., & Field, R.H.G. 1986. Constructive controversy, the Vroom–Yetton model, and managerial decision-making. *Journal of Occupational Behaviour*, 7: 125–138; Vroom, V.H., & Jago, A.G. 1978. On the validity of the Vroom-Yetton Model. *Journal of Applied Psychology*, 69: 151–162.

79. Hitt, Ireland, & Hoskisson, *Strategic management*.

80. For discussions of consensus vs. majority rule, see: Hare, A.P. 1976. *Handbook of small group research* (2nd edition). New York: Free Press; Miller, C.E. 1989. The social psychological effects of group decision rules. In P.B. Paulus (Ed.), *Psychology of Group Influence*. Hillsdale, NJ: Erlbaum; Mohammed, S., & Ringseis, E. 2001. Cognitive diversity and consensus in group decision making: The role of inputs, processes, and outcomes. *Organizational Behavior and Human Decision Processes*, 85: 310–335.

81. Mohammed & Ringseis, Cognitive diversity and consensus in group decision making.

82. Ibid.

83. Maier, N.R.F. 1967. Assets and liabilities in group problem solving: The need for an integrative function. *Psychological Review*, 74: 239–249.

84. Schmidt, J.B., Montoya-Weiss, M.M., & Massey, A.P. 2001. New product development decision-making effectiveness: Comparing individuals, face-to-face teams, and virtual teams. *Decision Sciences*, 32: 575–600.

85. Maier, Assets and liabilities in group problem solving.

86. Weiner, B. 1977. *Discovering psychology*. Chicago: Science Research Associates.

87. For an interesting history of the study of decision making, see: Buchanan, L., & O'Connell, A. 2006. A brief history of decision making. *Harvard Business Review*, 84 (1): 32-41.

11 GROUPS AND TEAMS

Stephen Schauer/The Image Bank/Getty Images

By any measure, Starbucks is one of the most successful business stories in recent history. The company's growth and financial success have been nothing short of phenomenal. As of early 2007, Starbucks has more than 12,440 retail outlets in 37 countries. In 2006, their net revenues were $7.8 billion. For the past 15 years, Starbucks has reported at least a 5 percent store sales growth. In addition to its retail coffee shops and kiosks, with which you are probably familiar, the company has entered several successful joint ventures and partnerships. For example, a partnership with PepsiCo produces the bottled coffee drink Frappuccino, and a joint venture with Dreyer's Ice Cream produces Starbucks coffee-flavored ice cream, which is sold in grocery stores. A partnership with Capitol Records resulted in a series of Starbucks jazz CDs. Furthermore,

EXPLORING BEHAVIOR IN ACTION
Teamwork at Starbucks

Starbucks has partnered with other companies, including United Airlines, Barnes & Noble Bookstores, and Nordstrom department stores—all of which exclusively serve or sell Starbucks coffee. The list of industry awards is also impressive, including national and international awards for best management, humanitarian efforts, brand quality, and providing a great place to work.

Much has been written about the success of Starbucks. Several factors have been singled out for attention—effective branding, superior product quality, product innovation, superior customer service, innovative human resource practices, effective real estate strategies, and exceptional corporate social responsibility, for example. However, to anyone who has ever visited a Starbucks, another factor for its success is apparent—the teamwork of Starbucks "baristas" (the associates who take orders and who make and serve coffee and food).

Watching the baristas at work in a busy Starbucks can be like watching a well-choreographed ballet. Baristas are making elaborate coffee drinks, serving up dessert, taking orders at record speed, answering customer questions, helping each other out when needed, and seemingly enjoying their work. Starbucks is legendary for its customer service, and teamwork is an important part of how this service is delivered. The extent to which baristas work together as a team, then, is an important aspect of Starbucks' success. And baristas are not only part of their shop's team—they are also part of the corporate Starbucks team. Indeed, all of Starbuck's associates are referred to as *partners*.

Starbucks fosters a teamwork-based culture in many ways. It begins by hiring baristas who have the desires and skills to be successful team players. Starbucks states to potential job applicants:

We look for people who are adaptable, self-motivated, passionate, creative team players. If that sounds like you, why not bring your talents

and skills to Starbucks? We are growing in dynamic new ways and we recognize that the right people, offering their ideas and expertise, will enable us to continue our success.

Training is an important element in this culture as well. Within their first month, all baristas receive 24 hours of training (most other coffee shops barely train their counter staffs). New baristas are trained in the exact methods for making Starbucks drinks, care and maintenance of machinery, and customer service practices. In addition, they receive training in how to interact with each other. One of the guiding principles in Starbucks' mission statement is to "provide a great work environment and treat each other with respect and dignity." Accordingly, all baristas are trained in the "Star Skills": (1) maintain and enhance (others') self-esteem; (2) listen and acknowledge; and (3) ask questions.

Another factor leading to increased teamwork and commitment to the company is Starbucks' generous benefits package. Baristas receive higher pay, better health benefits, and more vacation time than the industry norm. Even part-time employees receive benefits. Furthermore, Starbucks has a

stock option plan (the Bean Stock plan) in which baristas can participate if they wish to. Starbucks is the only company that offers such a plan unilaterally to all employees.

Yet another way in which Starbucks fosters teamwork is by providing numerous communication channels so that every barista can communicate directly with headquarters. These communication channels include e-mail, suggestion cards, and regular forums with executives.

These are some of the most telling signs of Starbucks' desire to create a teamwork culture.

Sources: Information at http://www.starbucks.com; M. Schilling and S. Kotha, "Starbucks Corporation," in M.A. Hitt, R.D. Ireland, & R.E. Hoskisson, *Strategic Management: Competitiveness and Globalization* (Cincinnati: South-Western College Publishing, 1999); "Starbucks in 2004: Driving for Global Dominance," in A.A. Thompson, J.E. Gamble, & A.J. Strickland, *Strategy: Winning in the Marketplace* (Chicago: McGraw-Hill, 2006); M. Gunther, "How UPS, Starbucks, Disney Do Good," *Fortune*, February 25, 2006, at http://cnnmoney.printhis.clikckability.com/pt/cpt?action=cpt&title=Companies+that+make; G. Weber, "Preserving Starbucks Counter Culture," *Workforce Management*, February 2005, pp. 28–34; Starbucks Corporation Fiscal 2006 Annual Report, at http://www.starbucks.com.

The Strategic Importance of Groups and Teams

U.S. organizations, following popular practice in other countries such as Japan, have adopted teamwork as a common way of doing work. The focus on teams in U.S. organizations developed during the 1980s. By 1993, 91 percent of *Fortune* 1000 companies used work teams, and 68 percent used self-managed work teams.[1] The presence of teamwork in business has only become greater since then. Indeed, after complaints from recruiters and advice from executives concerning the lack of interpersonal skills and teamwork skills of new graduates, many elite MBA programs have added teamwork training to the MBA curricula.[2]

Effective work teams have a synergistic effect on performance. **Synergy** means that the total output of a team is greater than the output that would result from adding together the outputs of the individual members working alone. Working in a team can produce synergy for several reasons. Team members are given more responsibility and autonomy; thus, they are empowered to do their jobs. Greater empowerment can produce higher motivation and identification with the organization.[3] Work teams also allow employees to develop new skills that can increase their motivation and satisfaction.[4] In addition, work teams can provide a means for employees to be integrated with higher levels in the organization, thereby aligning individual goals with the organization's strategy.[5] Finally, work teams can promote creativity, flexibility, and quick responses to customer needs.[6] These outcomes can be seen in the teams of baristas that work in Starbucks' stores.

Organizations have reported a great deal of success with work teams. Studies have documented tenfold reductions in error rates and quality problems, product-to-market cycles cut in half, and 90 percent reductions in response times to problems.[7] Extremely effective teams, often known as *high-performance work teams,* are able to achieve extraordinary results. A team of this kind seems to act as a whole rather than as a collection of individuals.[8]

In many companies, the organization's strategy is developed by a top management team. Research has shown that heterogeneous teams that work together effectively develop strategies that lead to higher organizational performance.[9] Heterogeneity of backgrounds and experiences among team members has been shown to produce more and diverse ideas, helping to resolve complex problems more effectively. The quality of strategic decisions made by the top management team affects the organization's ability to innovate and to create strategic change. Teams of top executives are used to make strategic decisions because of the complexity and importance of such decisions.[10] The top management team at Starbucks, for example, made the strategic decisions to develop new products (such as Cinnamon Dolce Latte) and to enter new international markets (such as Russia and India). To make such important decisions, the team must work together effectively.

For the reasons noted above, the development and management of teams is highly critical to organizational performance. However, simply having people work together as a team does not guarantee positive outcomes. Teams must be effectively composed, structured, developed, managed, and supported in order to become high-performance work teams. In this chapter, we begin by exploring the nature of teams and their effectiveness. We then examine the factors that affect team performance. Next, we describe how teams develop and change over time. Finally, we explain how to develop an effective team and how to manage teams.

KNOWLEDGE OBJECTIVES

After reading this chapter, you should be able to:

1. Describe the nature of groups and teams and distinguish among different types of teams.

2. Explain the criteria used to evaluate team effectiveness.

3. Discuss how various aspects of team composition influence team effectiveness.

4. Understand how structural components of teams can influence performance.

5. Explain how various team processes influence team performance.

6. Describe how teams develop over time.

7. Know what organizations can do to encourage and support effective teamwork.

8. Understand the roles of a team leader.

The Nature of Groups and Teams

For over 100 years, social science research has focused on studying collections of people interacting together. It is often said that human beings are social animals and that we seek out interactions with others. Organizations provide many opportunities for such interactions. Business transactions such as planning and coordinating require that individuals interact. Also, because associates are assigned to work units on the basis of their work skills and backgrounds, they are likely to find others with whom they share common interests. Furthermore, organizations frequently structure work so that jobs are done by associates working together. Two terms are used to define these clusters of associates: *groups* and *teams*.

synergy
An effect wherein the total output of a team is greater than the combined outputs of individual members working alone.

Groups and Teams Defined

There are many definitions for both *group* and *team*, with most researchers using the terms interchangeably.[11] For our purposes, the term **group** can be defined in very general terms as "two or more interdependent individuals who influence one another through social interaction."[12] In this chapter, however, our focus is more specific: we are mainly interested in teams—groups of individuals working toward specific goals or outcomes.[13] The common elements in the definition of a **team** are as follows:[14]

1. Two or more people,

2. with work roles that require them to be interdependent,

3. who operate within a larger social system (the organization),

4. performing tasks relevant to the organization's mission,

5. with consequences that affect others inside and outside the organization,

6. and who have membership that is identifiable to those who are in the team and to those who are not in the team.

group
Two or more interdependent individuals who influence one another through social interaction.

team
Two or more people, with work roles that require them to be interdependent, who operate within a larger social system (the organization), performing tasks relevant to the organization's mission, with consequences that affect others inside and outside the organization, and who have membership that is identifiable to those on the team and those not on the team.

This definition helps us understand what a team is and is not. For example, mere assemblies of people are not teams. A crowd watching a parade is not a team because the people have little, if any, interaction, nor are they recognized as a team. A collection of people who interact with and influence each other, such as a sorority or a book club, can be thought of as a general group. When the goals of a group become more specific, such as winning a game, we refer to the groups as a team (baseball team, project team, top management team, and so forth). The baristas at Starbucks work as a team because they work interdependently toward the goal of serving customers, are recognized by others as a team, and most likely perceive themselves as a team.

Several types of groups and teams exist within organizations that differ in important ways. These differences may affect how the group or team is formed, what values and attitudes are developed, and what behaviors result. In the discussion that follows, we describe various types of groups and teams.

Formal and Informal Groups

formal groups
Groups to which members are formally assigned.

Both formal and informal groups exist within organizations. People become members of **formal groups** because they are assigned to them. Thus, in our terminology, teams are formal groups. To complete their tasks, members of these teams must interact. They often share similar task activities, skills, and assigned goals. They recognize that they are part of the team, and the team exists as long as the task goals remain.[15] Examples of such teams are a faculty department, a highway crew, a small unit of production workers in an aircraft plant, and an assigned class project team.

informal groups
Groups formed spontaneously by people who share interests, values, or identities.

Many groups that are not formally created by management arise spontaneously as individuals find others in the organization with whom they wish to interact. These are **informal groups** that form because their members share interests, values, or identities. Membership in an informal group depends on voluntary commitment. Members are not assigned, and they may or may not share common tasks or task goals. They do, however, share other social values and attitudes, and their group goals are often related to individual social needs. For example, groups of employees may develop to go to Happy Hour on Friday afternoons or to play in a fantasy football league. The informal group may exist regardless of any formal purpose, and it endures as long as social satisfaction is achieved. Because of their various characteristics, informal groups are not considered teams.

Identity Groups

identity groups
Groups based on the social identities of members.

In Chapter 2, we discussed the importance of social identity. Associates often form groups based on their social identities, such as gender identity, racial identity, or religious identity. These groups are referred to as **identity groups.**[16] Individuals belong to many identity groups that are not based on membership in the organization (for example, Hispanic, female, Catholic). Thus, any member of a team is also a member of several identity groups. Effective team performance can be more difficult to achieve when team members belong to different identity groups or when their identification with these groups conflicts with the goals and objectives of the team.[17] For example, suppose most of the members of a team are white North Americans who prefer a decision-making process in which all arguments are open and group members are encouraged to debate and question each other publicly. Some of the team members, however, identify with the Japanese culture, in which publicly contradicting someone is viewed as impolite. These team members will likely find the team's decision-making process to be uncomfortable and disrespectful, and they may not participate. Thus, team functioning will be impaired.

Virtual Teams

virtual teams
Teams in which members work together but are separated by time, distance, or organizational structure.

A **virtual team** is made up of associates who work together as a team but are separated by time, distance, or organizational structure.[18] Exhibit 11-1 displays common technology through which virtual teams operate. The benefits of virtual teams are obvious—they allow people who are physically separated to work together. Virtual teams have been shown to be less effective than actual

Exhibit 11-1	Technology Commonly Used by Virtual Teams

Audio teleconferencing

Video communication systems, which may connect people either room to room or via desktop computers

Real-time electronic communication (e.g., chat groups)

Different-time electronic communication (e.g., e-mail, bulletin boards)

Keypad voting systems

Group project management software

Wireless communication devices (e.g., BlackBerries)

Instant messaging

Messaging boards

Web conferencing

Blogs and wiki sites

Sources: D. Mittleman, & R.O. Briggs, 1999. "Communicating Technologies for Traditional and Virtual Teams." In E. Sundstrom, & Associates (Eds.), *Supporting Work Team Effectiveness*, pp. 246–270; W. Combs, & S. Peacocke. February 2007, T&D, 61: pp. 27–28.

teams on many important indicators of effectiveness, however.[19] There are several reasons for this outcome. First, because fewer opportunities exist for informal discussions, trust is slower to develop among virtual team members. Second, virtual team members rely on communication channels that are less rich than face-to-face interactions. (Chapter 9 discussed communication richness.) Consequently, misunderstandings are likely to occur among team members. Third, it is more difficult for virtual teams to develop behavioral norms. Finally, it is easier for some members to be free riders (those who do not contribute effectively to the team's work), thereby causing frustration among other team members. Thus, it is very important that virtual teams be managed well, because they have a tendency to fall apart if care is not taken to maintain the team.

Research has shown that the effectiveness of virtual teams increases as a function of the number of face-to-face meetings members actually have.[20] Also, virtual teams in which members have a great deal of empowerment (authority to make their own decisions and act without supervision) are more effective than virtual teams with little empowerment. The impact of empowerment becomes even more important when virtual teams have little face-to-face interaction.[21]

When implemented properly, virtual teams can increase productivity and save companies millions of dollars.[22] For example, virtual technology has saved the Marriott Corporation over $1 million per year in person-hours. IBM has shortened its project completion time by 92 percent and decreased person-hours by 55 percent with virtual teams. By using same-time, different-place technology, Hewlett-Packard has connected research and development teams in California, Colorado, Japan, Germany, and France so that all teams can participate in the same presentation. The following *Managerial Advice* feature suggests steps to take to ensure that a virtual team functions well.

Managing Virtual Teams

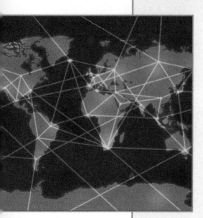

*Gregor
Schuster/
Stone/Getty
Images*

What happens when you desperately need information from a team member who lives half a world away and is probably in bed sound-asleep? How about if you can't tell by your team partner's e-mail whether she is serious or just kidding when she says that your idea is the most brilliant idea she has heard in a long time. What would you do if you know you have to work on your virtual team project, but your co-worker in the next office needs your help on another project and keeps coming into your office and asking your opinion? How difficult is it to not look at your e-mail messages while someone is giving a presentation at a video-conference and you are the only person in your physical location? How often do you feel guilty when you have forgotten to respond to a team member's instant message query and now a week has gone by?

These are just some of the problems faced by members of virtual teams. Here are some suggestions on how to make virtual teams most effective:

1. Develop a virtual team charter that describes everyone's roles, the decision-making process, and the goals of the team project. This makes it clear as to who is supposed to be doing what and to what end.

2. Provide reports on how the whole project is progressing. When people are working apart, they may lose track of how the entire project is progressing and what contributions others are making.

3. Set up communication rules such as blackout times when, due to time-zone differences, everyone is not available. These rules should also include acceptable time periods for responding to other inquiries and requests.

4. Early on, humanize everyone on the team by sharing pictures and personal information. Create a social networking site so that people can chat off the job.

5. All serious conflicts should be handled face-to-face.

6. Call for as much face-to-face communication as possible.

7. Reward positive team behavior and celebrate team successes. When most interaction takes place electronically, it is easy to forget about congratulating others for a job well done. Take time to celebrate the team's successes.

Sources: D. Mittleman, & R.O. Briggs, 1999, "Communicating Technologies for Traditional and Virtual Teams," in E. Sundstrom, & Associates (Eds.), *Supporting Work Team Effectiveness,* pp. 246–270; W. Combs, & S. Peacocke, February 2007, *T&D,* 61, pp. 27–28; B. Snyder, May 2003, "Teams That Span Time Zones Face New Work Rules," Stanford Business, at http://www.gsb. stanford.edu/news/bmag/sbsm0305/feature_virtual_teams.shtml; T. Brake, March 3, 2004, "Leading Virtual Teams: Ten Principles," TMA, at http://tmaworld.com/viewpoint/default.cfm?intviewpointid=2.

Functional Teams

Teams can be distinguished by the type of work they do and the purpose they serve. Types of functional teams include the following:[23]

- *Production teams*—groups of associates who produce tangible products (for example, automotive assemblers or a team of restaurant chefs)

- *Service teams*—groups of associates who engage in repeated transactions with customers (for example, sales teams or Starbucks baristas)

- *Management teams*—groups of senior-level managers who coordinate the activities of their respective units (for example, top management teams)

- *Project teams*—groups of associates (often from different functional areas or organizational units) who temporarily serve as teams to complete a specific project (for example, new product development teams)

- *Advisory teams*—groups of associates formed to advise the organization on certain issues (for example, disability groups who advise on the technical aspects of various products)

Self-Managing Teams

Self-managing teams have a great deal of autonomy and control over the work they do.[24] Usually self-managing teams are responsible for completing a whole piece of work or an entire project. For example, rather than working on only one part of an automobile, a self-managing auto-assembly team builds the whole automobile. Although self-managing teams often do have a formal leader, the leader's role is to facilitate team performance and member involvement rather than to direct the team. The members of the team make important decisions that in other types of teams are made by the leader, such as assigning members to specific tasks, setting team performance goals, and even deciding the team's pay structure. Team members are also held more accountable for team performance.

Self-managed work teams can lead to many benefits, including more satisfaction on the part of workers, lower turnover and absenteeism, increased productivity, and higher-quality work.[25] These benefits result because members of self-managed work teams are more engaged in their work and more committed to the team. However, the effectiveness of self-managed teams can be thwarted by several factors, including leaders who are too autocratic.[26]

A well-known example of a self-managed work team is the Orpheus Chamber Orchestra, the orchestra without a conductor. Orpheus musicians collaborate to take on leadership roles usually reserved for the conductor. The orchestra is incredibly flexible, with members moving into and out of roles as the need arises. As a result of this collaboration and flexibility, orchestra members always give their best performance, rather than acting passively as they might when working under the direction of a conductor. The Orpheus Chamber Orchestra is more successful (sells many tickets, takes in more money, and receives highly positive reviews) and has lower turnover and greater member loyalty than many other orchestras.[27]

 Team Effectiveness

How do we know when a team is effective? When a team reaches its performance goals, does this alone mean it was effective? Consider a class project in which a team turns in one report and everyone on the team receives the same grade. If the project earns an A, can we say the team was effective? What if only one person on the team did all the work and everyone else loafed? The person who did all the work is likely to be angry and dissatisfied, while the others have learned nothing and walk away with the idea that it pays to loaf, especially when they have a conscientious teammate. In this case, it would have been better to have individuals work separately, even though the final product was successful. Because outcome by itself is not enough, team effectiveness is measured on several dimensions: knowledge criteria, affective criteria, and outcome criteria. A final consideration in team effectiveness is whether a team is needed to perform the work at all, or whether the work is best performed by individuals.

Knowledge Criteria

Knowledge criteria reflect the degree to which the team continually increases its performance capabilities.[28] Teams are more effective when team members share knowledge and understanding of the team's task, tools and equipment, and processes, as well as members' characteristics.[29] This shared knowledge is referred to as the team's *mental model*.[30] Shared mental models allow team members to have common expectations and agreed-upon courses of action, improve information processing and decision making, and facilitate problem solving.[31] Another knowledge-based criterion for team effectiveness is team learning—the ability of the team as a whole to learn over time.[32] Clearly, in the class project example discussed above, this criterion was not met.

Affective Criteria

Affective criteria address the question of whether team members have a fulfilling and satisfying team experience.[33] One important affective criterion is the team's affective tone, or the general emotional state of the team.[34] It is important that the team, as a whole, have a positive, happy outlook on their work. Unfortunately, it is easy for even one member to contaminate the mood of a team.[35] The team's affect influences the way they communicate and their cohesion, as discussed later.

Outcome Criteria

Outcome criteria refer to the quantity and quality of the team's output [36] or to the extent to which the team's output is acceptable to clients.[37] The outcome should reflect synergy, as described earlier in the chapter. Another important outcome criterion is team viability—that is, the ability of the team to remain functioning as long as needed.[38] Research has shown that teams have a tendency to "burn out" over time. One study, for example, found that the performance of research-and-development teams peaks at around years 2 to 3 and shows significant declines after year 5.[39] This decline in performance can be due to teams' becoming overly cohesive (which can lead to groupthink, as discussed in Chapter 10) or to breakdowns in communication between team members. Often teams are created to deal with changing environments and uncertainty. Consider, for example, a military special operations team that must operate secretly in a foreign and hostile environment. In this case, a team's ability to adapt to the environment becomes an extremely important outcome.[40]

Is the Team Needed?

As stated earlier, teamwork has become very popular in business, as well as other types of organizations. However, is teamwork always the best way to accomplish a job? According to Jon Katzenbach, a popular team consultant to companies such as Citicorp, General Electric, and Mobil Oil, some situations do not call for teamwork and are better handled by individuals working alone.[41] He argues that because teams are popular, managers often "jump on the team bandwagon" without giving thought to whether a team is needed in the first place. He offers the following diagnostic checklist to determine whether a team should be created:

- Does the project really require collective work? If the work can be done by individuals without any need for integration, teamwork is not necessary and merely adds to the burden by creating additional coordination tasks.
- Do team members lead various aspects of the project? If so, then it might be more efficient to assign specific duties to individuals, rather than make the team responsible for all duties.
- Do people on the team hold one another accountable? Mutual accountability signals greater commitment to the team.

If there is a situation where these criteria are not met, then perhaps it is better to not use a team to accomplish the job.

Factors Affecting Team Effectiveness

As discussed in the opening section on the strategic importance of teams, when used properly, teams can yield great performance benefits to organizations. Teams create synergy for several reasons, including greater goal commitment, a greater variety of skills and abilities applied to task achievement, and a greater sharing of knowledge. However, teamwork can also lead to poorer performance than individuals working alone, as suggested above. In addition to performing their regular work-related tasks and achieving organizational goals, team members must also manage, coordinate, and develop effective communication within the team. This extra "teamwork" entails a **process loss**[42] because of the time and energy members spend maintaining the team. Thus, if teams are not able to achieve synergy, the extra work necessary to keep the team going will result in process loss.

process loss
Time and energy that team members spend on maintaining the team as opposed to working on the task.

To ensure that the benefits of teamwork outweigh the process loss that occurs from it, teams must be structured and managed properly. Literally thousands of studies in almost every type of organizational context have examined factors that influence team effectiveness. We focus on three factors: team composition, team structure, and team processes.

Team Composition

Team composition is important because it addresses who are members of the team and what human resources (skills, abilities, and knowledge) they bring to the team.

When managers assign associates to teams, they often make three common assumptions, which can lead to mistakes:[43]

1. They assume that people who are similar to each other will work better together, and so they compose homogeneous teams.

2. They assume that everyone knows how or is suited to work in a team.

3. They assume that a larger team size is always better.

In this section, we address these issues.

DIVERSITY

In Chapter 2, we explored in depth the impact of demographic diversity on group performance. Some studies have found negative effects for demographic diversity,[44] others have found positive effects,[45] and still others have found no effect.[46] Another type of diversity that can impact team performance is differences in important values among team members. Much of the research on values diversity has taken place on top management teams, exploring how differences in values regarding such things as profit maximization, innovation, customer service, and organizational growth impact top management team performance, and consequently firm performance. As with research on demographic diversity, the impact of values diversity on performance has been mixed.[47] The effects of demographic and value diversity on team performance seem to depend on several factors:[48]

- *Type of task.* Diversity has the best effects when the team's tasks require innovation and creativity.[49]
- *Outcome.* Diversity may have a positive effect on performance but a negative effect on members' reactions to the team and subsequent behaviors, such as turnover.[50]
- *Time.* Diversity can have negative effects in the short run but positive effects in the long run.[51]
- *Type of diversity.* If team members are diverse on factors that lead them to have different performance goals or levels of commitment to the team, or to form subgroups, the relationship between diversity and performance will be negative.[52]

PERSONALITY

The relationship between members' personalities and team performance can be quite strong, but the exact relationship depends on the type of task that the team is trying to accomplish. Researchers have several ways of determining the personality of the team; however, all methods are based on aggregating individuals' scores. The personality traits that have important effects on team performance include agreeableness (the ability to get along with others and cooperate) and emotional stability (the tendency to experience positive rather than negative emotions).[53] Also, the greater the degree of conscientiousness among team members, the higher the team's performance tends to be.[54] This is particularly true when the team's task involves planning and performance rather than creativity. It appears that agreeable team members contribute to team performance by fulfilling team maintenance roles, whereas conscientious team members perform critical task roles.[55] Team-level extraversion and openness to experience are positively related only to performance on decision-making and creative tasks.[56] (All these personality traits are discussed in Chapter 5.)

TEAM ORIENTATION

Some individuals are better at working on teams than others because they like working on teams and have the requisite skills. **Team orientation** refers to the extent that an individual works well with others, wants to contribute to team performance, and enjoys being on a team.[57] When a team is comprised of many members who have a positive team orientation, that team will adapt and perform better than a team whose members do not have such an orientation.[58] Notice that the three companies that rely on teamwork mentioned in this chapter's cases— Starbucks (chapter opening case), Herman Miller, Inc., and Cirque du Soleil (see the two *Experiencing Strategic Organizational Behavior* features on pp. 378 and 385)—all hire associates based on their teamwork orientation, among other things.

> **team orientation**
> The extent to which an individual works well with others, wants to contribute to team performance, and enjoys being on a team.

SIZE

There is no one ideal number of team members for all situations. Many studies have examined the relationship of team size and team performance, and two lines of thought have emerged. These two ideas are depicted in Exhibit 11-2.

The first suggests that the relationship between team size and team performance is shaped like an inverted U.[59] Thus, as teams become larger, the diversity of skills, talents, ideas, and individual associate inputs into the task is greater, leading to improved performance. However, as the number of team members increases, the need for cooperation and coordination also increases. At some point, the effort that goes into managing the team will outweigh the benefits of having more members, and team performance will begin to decline.

Other researchers, however, have found that performance increases linearly with team size without ever showing a downturn.[60] This linear relationship most likely results when a team avoids the problems associated with too many members, such as social loafing (to be discussed later in the chapter), poor coordination, and

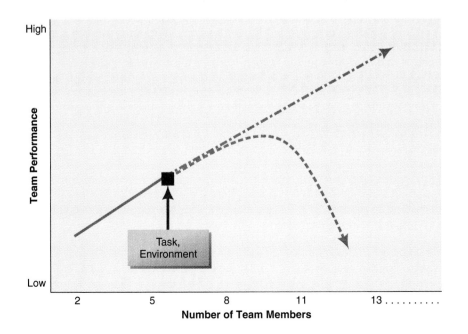

Exhibit 11-2
The Relationship
between Team Size
and Team Performance

worsening communication. Thus, the relationship between team size and team performance depends on other factors, such as the task or the environment.[61]

Team Structure

Team structure refers to the usual means of coordinating formal team efforts. Leaders are appointed, work rules and procedures are detailed, and job descriptions specify individual task responsibilities. The contribution of structure to team achievement is evident. For example, consider a bank with a loan department and a collection department. One department is assigned tasks related to making loans, such as credit analysis, interest computation, loan closing, and filing. These are sequential but somewhat dissimilar tasks. Loans cannot be closed until credit analysis has been performed and interest computed. The other department may be assigned phone collections, field collections, and repossessing tasks. These tasks are less sequential but more similar to one another. In both cases, it is necessary to coordinate the efforts of individuals assigned to the different tasks. Otherwise, tasks may not be performed in the correct sequence, and employees may duplicate their efforts or work against each other. Important aspects of team structure include roles, norms, task structure, and communication structure. In the *Experiencing Strategic Organizational Behavior* feature that follows, the importance of the physical layout of the work space is also discussed. In order to have a team that functions well, there must also be a physical environment that allows members to work as a team.

EXPERIENCING STRATEGIC ORGANIZATIONAL BEHAVIOR

Herman Miller, Designing for Teamwork

Masterfile

Herman Miller, Inc. was elected to *Fortune* magazine's most admired companies in 2007, for the nineteenth time in the past 21 years. The company, which designs furniture, primarily for the workplace, and provides consulting and research services for office design, consistently wins awards for being a great place to work, corporate citizenship, and, of course, design. Herman Miller was founded in 1923 by D.J. DePree, is the second-largest office furniture company in the world, and had net sales of $1.74 billion in 2006. Thus, the company itself serves as its own best advertisement for the products and services it sells. Its mission statement is:

We study work and living environments and design and deliver products and services that make these environments work better.

Part of its foundation of providing great work environments is to foster teamwork through the physical design of the company's offices, the knowledge of and products for which they are known. The company makes the following suggestions for arranging an office that is conducive to teamwork:

First it is important to delineate boundaries, so that everyone has their own private space over which they feel ownership. At the same time, associates should always be able to see each other, which makes for easier collaboration. Next, a collaborative workspace should be created in a quiet secluded space. Holding team meetings in more public, central spaces, allows "outsiders" to intrude on the team's meeting. It is also important that team members be provided with furniture they can arrange themselves. This allows the team to reconfigure itself to suit the task. For example, when one person on the team is presenting information to the others, that would require a different furniture arrangement than if everyone were working collectively on the same document. Finally, it is important for team members to create ways to signal each other that they are unavailable and should not be disturbed.

Herman Miller follows these suggestions in the design of its own workspaces, particularly those in which creative teams are working. However, the design team is quick to point out that simply arranging the physical outlay of the office space is not enough to support teamwork, although it greatly facilitates it. Rather, the company must also have a culture, management system, and reward system that fosters teamwork. Herman Miller accomplishes this in many ways—one of which is by having an employee-participation and profit-sharing plan whereby all employees are taught during orientation about how to link their team's performance to the profits of the company.

Sources: http://www.hermanmiller.com, accessed June 10, 2007; Herman Miller, 2007, "Making Teamwork Work," research report at http://www.hermanmiller.com; J.C. Sarros, B.K. Cooper, & J.C. Santora, May–June 2007, "The Character of Leadership," *Ivey Business Journal,* at http://www.iveybusinessjournal.com/article.asp?intArticle_ID=689.

TEAM MEMBER ROLES

Team **roles** are expectations shared by team members about who will perform what types of tasks and under what conditions.[62] Roles can be formally assigned, or they can be informally adopted by team members. Some members primarily serve in leadership roles, and others take the roles of followers. The leadership role does not need to be formally assigned or to be a function of formal authority. Leaders can emerge in groups.

> **roles**
> Expectations shared by group members about who is to perform what types of tasks and under what conditions.

Apart from leadership roles, all teams need to have members fulfilling both task roles and socioemotional, or expressive, roles.[63] **Task roles** involve behaviors aimed at achieving the team's performance goals and tasks. **Socioemotional roles** require behaviors that support the social aspects of the team. A team member may also fill an *individual role,* which consists of behaviors that place that individual's needs and goals above those of the team.[64] As we would expect, these roles impede team performance rather than facilitate it. Exhibit 11-3 depicts examples of specific task, socioemotional, and individual roles.

> **task roles**
> Roles that require behaviors aimed at achieving the team's performance goals and tasks.

> **socioemotional roles**
> Roles that require behaviors that support the social aspects of the organization.

As a team becomes more stable and structured, the roles of individual members often become resistant to change.[65] Group social pressures tend to keep members "in their place," and the team resists outside forces that would change members' roles, even if these roles were not the ones assigned by the formal organization.

NORMS

Norms are rules or standards that regulate the team's behavior. Norms tend to emerge naturally in a team and are part of the team's mental model, although occasionally they are formally recorded. Norms serve the purpose of regulating team members' behavior and providing direction. When individual team members violate team norms, some type of punishment or sanction is usually applied. For

> **norms**
> Rules or standards that regulate the team's behavior.

Exhibit 11-3	Team Member Roles
Role	**Function**
Task Roles	
Initiator/Contributor	Suggests new ideas, solutions, or ways to approach the problem
Information Seeker	Focuses on getting facts
Information Giver	Provides data for decision making
Elaborator	Gives additional information, such as rephrasing, examples
Opinion Giver	Provides opinions, values, and feelings
Coordinator	Shows the relevance of various specific ideas to the overall problem to be solved
Orienter	Refocuses discussion when the team gets off topic
Evaluator/Critic	Appraises the quality of the team's work
Energizer	Motivates the team when energy falters
Procedural Technician	Takes care of operational details, such as technology
Recorder	Takes notes and keeps records
Socioemotional Roles	
Encourager	Provides others with praise, agreement, warmth
Harmonizer	Settles conflicts among other members
Compromiser	Changes his or her position to maintain team harmony
Gatekeeper	Controls communication process so that everyone gets a chance to participate
Standard Setter	Discusses the quality of the team process
Observer	Comments on the positive or negative aspects of the team process and calls for changes
Follower	Accepts others' ideas and acts as a listener
Individual Roles	
Aggressor	Attacks others
Blocker	Unnecessarily opposes the team
Dominator	Manipulatively asserts authority
Evader	Focuses on expressing own feelings and thoughts that are unrelated to the team goals
Help Seeker	Unnecessarily expresses insecurities
Recognition Seeker	Calls unnecessary attention to himself or herself

Sources: K.D. Benne and P. Sheets, "Functional Roles of Group Members," *Journal of Social Issues* 4 (1948): 41–49. D.R. Forsyth, *Group Dynamics* (Belmont, CA: Wadsworth Publishing Company, 1999).

example, Hudson Houck, the offensive line coach for the 1996 Dallas Cowboys, stated that anyone on the team who didn't work hard all the time (a team norm) was shunned.[66]

Team norms can become very powerful and resistant to change. Witness a situation such as a regular team meeting, or even a college class, where everyone sits in the same seat at every meeting. Any change in seating can cause unease on the part of group or team members. In these situations, seating norms develop to curb the social unease that could result from choosing a seat every day. No one has to wonder why someone is or is not sitting next to her. Nor does anyone have to worry about how others will interpret his motives for his seating choice.

Although norms allow teams to function smoothly, they can sometimes be harmful to team members. Research on the causes of eating disorders in young women illustrates this fact.[67] Certain groups, such as cheerleading squads, sororities, and dance troupes, have particularly high rates of bulimia among their members. Examination of these groups has indicated that they often develop group norms of binging and purging. Instead of considering this behavior to be abnormal and unhealthy, team members come to view it as a normal way of controlling weight. Because norms are not always positive, it is important that teams develop norms that both foster team productivity and performance and promote the welfare of individual members.

TASK STRUCTURE

Task structure has been shown to be an important determinant of how teams function and perform.[68] Several typologies have been proposed on how to categorize tasks. One of the most popular typologies classifies tasks according to (1) whether they can be separated into subcomponents, (2) whether the task has a quantity or quality goal, and (3) how individual inputs are combined to achieve the team's product.[69]

First, then, we consider whether a task can be broken down into parts. Tasks such as playing baseball, preparing a class project, and cooking a meal in a restaurant are **divisible tasks** because they can be separated into subcomponents. Thus, different individual associates can perform different parts of the task. **Unitary tasks** cannot be divided and must be performed by a single individual. Examples of unitary tasks are reading a book, completing an account sheet, and talking to a customer on the phone. If a particular goal or mission requires the completion of unitary tasks, it may not be advantageous for a team to complete the mission.

> **divisible tasks**
> Tasks that can be separated into subcomponents.

> **unitary tasks**
> Tasks that cannot be divided and must be performed by an individual.

The second classification element concerns the goals of the task. Tasks with a quantity goal are called **maximization tasks.** Examples of maximization tasks include producing the most cars possible, running the fastest, and selling the most insurance policies. Tasks with a quality goal are referred to as **optimization tasks.** Optimization tasks often require innovation and creativity. Examples of optimization tasks include developing a new product and developing a new marketing strategy. As mentioned earlier, diverse teams tend to perform better on optimization tasks.

> **maximization tasks**
> Tasks with a quantity goal.

> **optimization tasks**
> Tasks with a quality goal.

Finally, we consider how individual inputs are combined to achieve the team's product. The manner in which this is done places a limit on how well the team can perform. We can classify how inputs are combined by determining whether the task is additive or compensatory and whether it is disjunctive or conjunctive.

Additive tasks are those in which individual inputs are simply added together—for example, pulling a rope or inputting data. When members' inputs are additively combined, the team performance will often be better than the best individual's performance because of social facilitation processes (discussed later in the chapter).[70] *Compensatory tasks* are those in which members' individual performances are averaged together to arrive at the team's overall performance. For example, members of a human resource management team may individually estimate future labor demands in the organization, and the total projection may then be based on the average of the managers' estimates. The potential team productivity on this type of task is likely to be better than the productivity of most of the individual members.

Disjunctive tasks are those in which teams must work together to develop a single, agreed-upon product or solution. A jury decision is an example of a disjunctive task. Usually, disjunctive tasks result in team performance that is better than that of most of the individual members but not as good as the best member's performance.[71] *Conjunctive tasks* are those in which all members must perform their individual tasks to arrive at the team's overall performance. Examples of conjunctive tasks are assembly lines and trucks moving in a convoy. Teams working on conjunctive tasks cannot perform any better than their worst individual performers. For example, an assembly line cannot produce goods at a rate faster than the rate at which its slowest member performs.

Team Processes

Team processes are the behaviors and activities that influence the effectiveness of teams. Team processes are why teams are effective or ineffective. Team processes include cohesion, conflict, social facilitation, social loafing, and communication.

COHESION

interpersonal cohesion
Team members' liking or attraction to other team members.

task cohesion
Team members' attraction and commitment to the tasks and goals of the team.

Team cohesion refers to members' attraction to the team.[72] **Interpersonal cohesion** is the team members' liking or attraction to other team members. **Task cohesion** is team members' attraction and commitment to the tasks and goals of the team.[73] Team cohesion is an important criterion because research indicates that cohesion is positively related to team performance outcomes and viability.[74] Furthermore, as stated earlier, team members' satisfaction with membership in the team is one criterion for judging effective team performance. Members of cohesive teams are more likely to be satisfied with their teams than are members of noncohesive teams.[75] We should note, however, that too much cohesion can lead to dysfunctional team performance,[76] such as groupthink (discussed in Chapter 10).

Cohesive teams are likely to have the highest performance when there is task cohesion.[77] When there is only interpersonal cohesion, and performance goals are low, cohesiveness will lead to poor performance. In other words, if the team members really like each other and enjoy spending time together, but are not committed to their organizational tasks and goals, they will perform worse than if they were not interpersonally cohesive. A classic study of factory workers found that the more cohesive the team, the less variability there was in performance among individual members.[78] Cohesive teams with high performance goals performed the best, whereas cohesive teams with low performance goals performed the worst—even worse than noncohesive teams with low performance goals. Cohesion also has a stronger effect on performance when there is a great deal of interdependence among team members.[79]

CONFLICT

When the behaviors or beliefs of a team member are unacceptable to other team members, conflict occurs. Conflict is discussed in more detail in Chapter 12. Several types of intragroup (within-team) conflict exist; they include personal conflict, substantive conflict, and procedural conflict.

Personal conflict results when team members simply do not like each other. As we might expect, people assigned to a team are more likely to experience this sort of conflict than people who choose to belong to the same informal group.

Personal conflict may be based on personality clashes, differences in values, and differences in likes and dislikes. No disagreement over a specific issue is necessary for personal conflict to occur. A recent study of business executives found that 40 percent of their conflicts resulted from personal dislike rather than disagreement over a specific issue.[80]

Substantive conflicts occur when a team member disagrees with another's task-related ideas or analysis of the team's problem or plans. For example, a design team whose task is developing a better product may disagree about whether they should focus on making the product more attractive or making it easier to use. Substantive conflicts can often lead to greater creativity and innovation, if they do not become personal conflicts.[81]

Finally, *procedural conflicts* occur when team members disagree about policies and procedures. That is, they disagree on how to work together. For example, a member of a virtual team may believe that the correct way to work as a team is to check in by e-mail with other members at least twice a day. Furthermore, he may believe that team members should respond immediately to such e-mails. Other team members, however, may believe that checking in so frequently is a waste of time and may only contact each other when necessary. Group norms develop as a way to avoid procedural conflicts. Teams may also develop specific policies or rules to avoid conflicts of this kind. Robert's Rules of Order are one such device because they specifically define how group meetings should be conducted.

Conflict can have positive consequences for team effectiveness, especially if the conflict is resolved by cooperation among team members. Apart from leading to creativity and innovation, conflict can also help teams develop cohesion by identifying differences to be resolved. Conflict can also be beneficial when teams work through it to develop norms and a consistent team mental model.[82]

SOCIAL FACILITATION

In the late 1890s, Norman Triplett, a bicyclist and early social scientist, noticed that cyclists performed better racing against others than when they were timed cycling alone.[83] This effect—that is, when the presence of others improves individual performance—has been termed the **social facilitation effect.** Social facilitation suggests that teamwork can lead to increased performance because others are present.

> **social facilitation effect**
> Improvement in individual performance when others are present.

Several reasons for the social facilitation effect have been suggested. One is that the presence of human beings creates general arousal in other human beings.[84] This general arousal then leads to better performance. Another explanation is that the presence of others arouses evaluation apprehension, so that people perform better because they think they are being evaluated.[85] Whatever the reason, social facilitation seems to occur only when people are performing well-learned, simple, or familiar tasks.[86] The presence of others can actually decrease performance on tasks that are complex or unfamiliar. For example, someone who is not accustomed to giving speeches is likely to perform more poorly when speaking in front of others than she would if she were practicing alone.

SOCIAL LOAFING

Research suggests that the simple act of grouping individuals together does not increase their total output; in fact, people working together on a common task may actually perform at a lower level than they would if they were working alone. This phenomenon is called **social loafing**[87] or shirking,[88] and it can obviously result in serious losses. There are three primary explanations for the social loafing effect.

> **social loafing**
> A phenomenon wherein people put forth less effort when they work in teams than when they work alone.

First, associates can get away with poor performance because their individual outputs are not identifiable. Second, associates, when working in teams, expect their team members to loaf and therefore reduce their own efforts to establish an equitable division of labor.[89] In this case, individual team members do not have a team identity and place their own good (working less) over the good of the team. Finally, when many individuals are working on a task, some individuals may feel dispensable and that their own contributions will not matter.[90] This is likely to happen when individuals think that they have low ability and cannot perform as well as other team members.[91]

Research on this phenomenon illustrates these explanations. In one study, individuals were asked to pull alone as hard as possible on a rope attached to a strain gauge. They averaged 138.6 pounds of pressure while tugging on the rope. When the same individuals pulled on the rope in groups of three, however, they exerted only 352 pounds of pressure, an average of 117.3 pounds each. In groups of eight, the individual average dropped even lower, to an astonishing 68.2 pounds of pressure. This supports the first explanation of social loafing—that the less identifiable the individual's output is, the more the individual loafs.[92] Also, if the people with the least physical strength decrease their pressure the most, then there would also be support for the dispensability explanation.

In a second study, subjects expected to work on a group task. Some of the subjects were told by a co-worker (a confederate of the researchers) that the co-worker expected to work as hard on the group task as she had on an individual task. Other subjects were told that the co-worker expected to work less hard on the group task than on the individual task. In a third condition, nothing was said about the co-worker's intention. In the group task, the subjects who had been told to expect lower performance from their co-worker reduced their efforts. However, the subjects who had been told to expect no slacking of effort from the co-worker maintained their effort during the group task.[93] This supports the second explanation of social loafing—that individuals reduce their efforts to establish an equitable division of labor when they expect their co-workers to slack off in their efforts.

Students often experience social loafing. It occurs frequently when students are assigned to team projects in one of their courses. Inevitably, when student teams work on a class project, one or two members coast along, not "pulling their own weight." These "loafers" frequently miss the project team's meetings, fail to perform their assigned tasks, and so on. They rely on the fact that the more motivated members will complete the project without their help. The loafers still expect to share the credit and obtain the same grade, since the professor may not be concerned about determining who worked and who did not. A recent study examining social loafing in student groups found that the most common reasons for loafing were perceptions of unfairness (i.e., others were loafing) and perceived dispensability because one was not as talented as others.[94]

Social loafing is always a possibility in work teams, especially in teams that are not cohesive. For example, in a study of almost 500 work team members, 25 percent expressed concern that members of their teams engaged in social loafing. This can be extremely costly to organizations, because creating and supporting work teams requires investments in such things as new technology to aid teamwork, coordination efforts, more complicated pay systems, and restructuring of work. Thus, when teams perform worse than individuals, not only are performance and productivity lower, but costs are also higher.

Social loafing can occur in any team at any level in an organization. And because social loafing clearly results in lower productivity, it is a serious problem. At the least, when social loafing occurs, the organization's human capital is underutilized. Fortunately, managers can use several methods to address this problem.[95] First they can make individual contributions visible. This can be accomplished by using smaller rather than larger teams, using an evaluation system where everyone's contributions are noted, and/or appointing someone to monitor and oversee everyone's contributions. The second thing that can be done is to foster team cohesiveness by providing team-level rewards, training members in teamwork, and selecting "team players" to be on the team. In the following *Experiencing Strategic Organizational Behavior* feature, we discuss behavior that is the opposite of social loafing—*backing-up behavior*. As in many jobs, performers in the Cirque du Soleil not only refrain from engaging in social loafing, they must also be ready to take over for their team members at a moment's notice and do more than their fair share.

EXPERIENCING STRATEGIC ORGANIZATIONAL BEHAVIOR

Backup at Cirque Du Soleil

Chances are that you have seen a performance by Cirque du Soleil (eight million people saw their performances in 2007 alone). What started out as a band of street performers in 1984 in Quebec, Canada, has grown into a business with over 3,000 employees (900 are performing artists), six touring companies that perform all over the world, and seven resident shows in Las Vegas, Orlando, and New York, with another to open soon in Tokyo, Japan. Cirque du Soleil has come to redefine what we mean by the term *circus*. There are no animals, the shows are aimed to attract adult audiences, and performances provide visuals not seen before, such as the shows conducted under water ("O"), amazing costumes, and unique music. The company builds its brand on creativity and teamwork.

Cirque du Soleil hires people from all over the world, searching for people with various talents, ranging from being an acrobat *and* scuba certified, to doing gymnastics on rollerblades. It does not just look for run-of-the mill acrobats, jugglers, and trapeze artists. Everyone must meet certain artistic qualifications and be predisposed to teamwork. Indeed, since about 20 percent of the artists turn over (due to injury or retirement) every year, Cirque has resorted to creating its own training camps, such as a camp for contortionists in Mongolia, to make sure it has a constant supply of talent.

Once artists are cast, they go through an eight-week boot-camp where they learn how to operate as a team. One important aspect of this teamwork is to be able to be flexible, creative, and work off other performers. Their coach, Boris Verkhovsky, states that this is not always easy, because many are trained athletes who are used to performing on their own and follow strict protocols rather than engaging in artistic performances. An important part of a Cirque performer's job is to be able to back up other performers. As with many jobs, such as police officers or retail sales clerks, it is important that these performers be able to monitor the performance of all of their team members and be able to step in when there is trouble, a team member is overtaxed, or the artistic role requires it. Thus, providing backup to other performers is an essential component of all Cirque du Soleil artists' jobs. Consider the job of an aerialist who relies on her team members for safety support should she make a mistake during her routine.

Recent research has addressed the issue of who is likely to provide backup, who is likely to receive it, and under what conditions backing-up behaviors are

Sarah Krulwich/The New York Times/Redux Pictures

likely to occur. When team members are highly conscientious and emotionally stable, they are more likely to provide backup to team members in need. Team members must also be knowledgeable about others' job responsibilities, as well as their own, in order to provide backup. When the team member who needs help is highly conscientious and extraverted, he or she will more likely receive backup from other team members. Finally, when team members perceive that the person who needs backing up has a larger workload or fewer resources to accomplish his or her work, they are more likely to provide the support needed. Cirque du Soleil achieves these conditions through both training and selection.

Sources: L. Tischler, "Join the Circus," *Fast Company,* July 5, 2005, at http://www.fastcompany. com/magazine/96/cirque-du-soleil; http://www.cirquedusoleil.com/CirqueDuDSoleil/en/Pressroom/ cirquedusoleil/factsheets/cds; R.M. McIntyre, & E. Salas, "Measuring and Managing for Team Performance: Emerging Principles from Complex Environments," in R.A. Guzzo et al. (Eds.), *Team Effectiveness and Decision Making in Organizations* (San Francisco: Jossey-Bass, 1995, pp. 9–45; C.O.L.H. Porter et al., "Backing Up Behaviors in Teams: The Role of Personality and Legitimacy of Need," *Journal of Applied Psychology* 88 (2003): 391–403.

The support that team members provide to each other can be quite important in the performance of the team and the unit in which it operates. The *Experiencing Strategic Organizational Behavior* feature describes the necessity of backing-up behavior by Cirque du Soleil performers. However, this behavior is necessary in almost all teams. Think of the need for backup among police officers. Backing-up behavior may be one of the strongest indicators of team effectiveness, because not only is everyone on the team doing his or her share, but he or she is willing to take on others' work when colleagues need assistance and to fill in gaps. Teams who engage in backing-up behavior are displaying high-involvement management behavior by going beyond what is merely necessary to get the job done.

COMMUNICATION

Team members must communicate to effectively coordinate their productive efforts. Task instructions must be delivered, results must be reported, and problem-solving discussions must take place. Because communication is crucial, teams create many formal communication processes, which may include formal reports (such as profit-and-loss statements), work schedules, interoffice memoranda, and formal meetings.

But informal communication also is necessary. Associates need and want to discuss personal and job-related problems with each other. Informal communication is a natural consequence of group processes. The effectiveness and frequency of communication are affected by many of the same factors that lead to group formation and group structure. For example, frequency of communication is partially the result of the opportunity to *interact.* People who share the same office, whose jobs are interconnected, and who have the same working hours are likely to communicate more frequently. Thus, the opportunity to interact leads to both group formation and frequent communication. This is why virtual teams are more likely to be effective when they have more face-to-face interaction.[96]

In addition to affecting task performance, communication frequency and effectiveness are related to team member satisfaction, particularly in cohesive teams.

Communication becomes more rewarding as team membership increases in importance and satisfaction to associates.[97] At the same time, increased communication enhances team members' satisfaction with their membership on the team.

Team Development

The nature of interactions among team members changes over time. Teams behave differently when they meet for the first time than when they have been together long enough to be accustomed to working together. At the beginning of a team's life cycle, members may spend more time getting to know each other than they do on the task. As time progresses, however, the team often becomes more focused on performance. According to Bruce Tuckman's group development model, teams typically go through four stages over their life cycle: forming, storming, norming, and performing.[98]

During the *forming* stage, associates come to teams without established relationships but with some expectations about what they want in and from the team. The new team members focus on learning about each other, defining what they want to accomplish, and determining how they are going to accomplish it. Sometimes personality conflicts or disagreements arise about what needs to be done or how the team should go about doing it. At this point, the team has entered the *storming* stage, marked by conflict among team members. If the team is to be successful, team members need to resolve these conflicts and to reach agreement on performance outcomes and processes. In resolving conflicts, the team will establish rules, procedures, and norms for team behavior and roles. This is the *norming* stage, in which team members cooperate with each other and become more cohesive. Once the team has established norms and is working as a cohesive whole, it enters the *performing* stage. In this stage, team members are more committed to the team, focus on task performance, and are generally more satisfied with the team experience.[99]

Most teams experience some sort of end. Individual members may leave, or the team may be formally disbanded when its mission has been accomplished. Thus, teams ultimately go through a fifth stage, *adjourning,* when individuals begin to leave the team and terminate their regular contact with other team members. Adjourning can result from voluntary actions on the part of team members, as when a team member takes a job with another organization or retires. It can also result from actions over which team members have little control, such as reassignment by the parent organization or the end of a project. When individual members of a cohesive team leave, the remaining members often experience feelings of loss, and the team becomes less cohesive and less structured, until it no longer exists, unless new members replace the members who have left. In this instance, the group is similar to a new group, and the process of group development is likely to begin again.

Teams may not go through all of the stages described above in all situations. For example, the members of a newly formed team belong to the same organization and may already know each other. They are also likely to be familiar with performance expectations and may even share similar work-related values. Thus, the forming and storming stages are not needed. Furthermore, the nature of the project on which the team is working can influence the formation of the team. Most research on Tuckman's stage theory has focused on simple teams that worked on a single project and whose members were relative strangers.[100] Thus, the theory may not apply to teams that work on complex projects or that have members who have had a long history together.

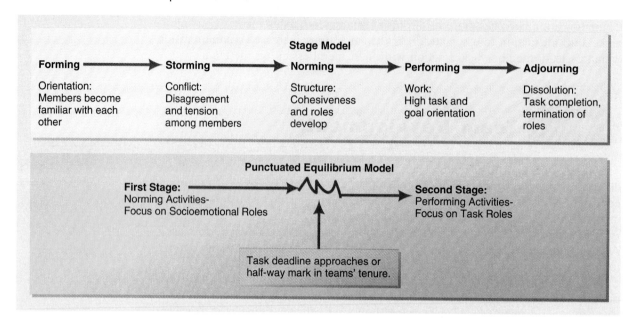

Exhibit 11-4   Models of Team Development

Sources: B.W. Tuckman, "Developmental Sequences in Small Groups," *Psychological Bulletin,* 6 (1965): 384–399; B.W. Tuckman, & M.A.C. Jensen, "Stages of Small Group Development," *Group and Organizational Studies,* 2 (1977): 419–427; C.J.G. Gersick, "Time and Transition in Work Teams: Toward a New Model of Group Development," *Academy of Management Journal,* 31(1988): 9–41; C.J.G. Gersick, 1989. Marking Time: Predictable Transitions in Task Groups. *Academy of Management Journal,* 32: 274–309; D.R. Forsyth, *Group Dynamics* (Belmont, CA: Wadsworth Publishing Company, 1999).

punctuated equilibrium model (PEM)
A model of group development that suggests that groups do not go through linear stages but that group formation depends on the task at hand and the deadlines for that task.

The **punctuated equilibrium model (PEM)** of group development takes these factors into account.[101] This model suggests that groups do not go through linear stages but that group formation depends on the task at hand and the deadlines for that task. The PEM is essentially a two-stage model representing two periods of equilibrium "punctuated" by a shift in focus. In the first stage, team members get to know one another and engage in norming activities. The focus at this stage is the development of socioemotional roles. When the deadline for the team's work approaches, the team undergoes a dramatic change in functioning. This is the point at which the "punctuation" occurs. After this point is reached, the team refocuses its activities on performing the task at hand. Thus, the focus shifts to task roles. This model contrasts with Tuckman's stage model because it suggests that team life-cycle stages are determined by the task, not by social dynamics within the team. Exhibit 11-4 compares the two models.

Research suggests that the PEM model best describes the development of teams working on a specific, limited task.[102] To fully describe the development of teams in complex work environments, some researchers have proposed that Tuckman's stage model and the PEM should be integrated.[103] More recent models of team development that integrate the stage approach with the PEM propose a two-part process punctuated by a change in focus, as in the PEM. In the first stage, the team goes through the forming, storming, norming, and performing stages while focusing on teamwork skills.[104] Teamwork skills allow team members to work interdependently, as in coordinating activities, developing communication norms, and assigning roles to members. After the shift in focus has occurred, the team goes through similar stages while focusing on performance skills—the knowledge and skills needed to perform the team's task.

Managing for Effective Teams

To experience the potential gains of teamwork, organizations must provide support for teams to work effectively. An organization cannot simply declare that it will increase the level of teamwork—as pointed out in the earlier *Experiencing Strategic Organizational Behavior* feature about Herman Miller—without planning, training, selecting, and rewarding people for teamwork. Following are several "best practices" for managing effective teams.

Top Management Support

Effective teamwork requires support from the top of the organization.[105] All organizations that are known for their teamwork, such as Xerox, Harley-Davidson, FedEx, and Boeing, have top management teams that actively promote teamwork. Several management practices can help top management to support team effectiveness:[106]

- Have an explicit vision and strategic plan that serves as the basis for determining desirable team outcomes.
- Use results-oriented measurement of outcomes and expect all leaders in the organization to do the same.
- Actively include associates at all levels in the decision-making process.
- Make an explicit decision about using teams and tie the decision to business objectives.
- Actively manage and review support systems for teams.

Top management at Starbucks, described in the chapter opening case, clearly follows these recommended practices. For example, two of the company's stated missions are to make profits and to be environmentally sensitive. These missions are incorporated into the baristas' performance assessments. The company also provides mechanisms that enable baristas to regularly communicate and share their ideas with top management.

Support Systems

Support systems are aspects of organizational life that allow a team to function well. Support systems include technology, information systems, selection of team members, training, rewards, and leadership.

TECHNOLOGY

It is important that teams have access to the technology they need to do their work. This includes the technology necessary to carry out tasks (such as tools and computer software) and also technology to help team members coordinate their work. Many technologies are designed to help teams communicate and interact more fully and efficiently. Examples can be found in the U.S. Air Force's Innovation Center.[107] The center is similar to a regular meeting room but also contains several advanced technologies that enhance teamwork. For example, networked personal computers at participating associates' workstations allow team members to engage in immediate, structured, and anonymous interactions. This anonymity helps to avoid groupthink pressures. Having appropriate technology is also essential for the success of virtual teams. In any case, team members should have input into the adoption or development of communication technologies.[108]

INFORMATION SYSTEMS

Teams must have the necessary information to act, but they frequently need more information than they possess. An example is provided by the now-defunct People Express Airlines, which used customer service teams to conduct much of the airline's business.[109] The customer service teams needed important information, such as future bookings, to do their work; however, executives were reluctant to allow them access to this information because they were afraid that it might leak out to their competitors.

Teams can also suffer from receiving too much information.[110] Often, information technology can provide people with a flood of information; but as discussed in Chapter 9, too much information creates overload. In such situations, associates may not know to what information they should attend, they may become overwhelmed and not attend to any information, or they may even shut the system down entirely. A related problem is information unavailable in the form most useful to the team. To address this problem, it is important that teams have "user-friendly" information systems.

SELECTION OF TEAM MEMBERS

Traditionally, it is recommended that organizations select team members with the knowledge, skills, and abilities to perform their jobs and with values that fit well with the organizational culture.[111] However, team members also have other roles to fulfill. For example, they may perform teamwork roles, such as energizing the team or soliciting and elaborating on the ideas of others. Furthermore, because teamwork often involves a variety of tasks, a broader set of skills may be necessary for team-based jobs. Thus, teamwork selection needs to consider more factors than selection for a traditional job. Following are some suggestions for selecting team members:[112]

- Tailor the staffing process to the type of team. For example, paper-and-pencil personality tests may be appropriate for service teams but not for top management teams.
- Conduct a teamwork analysis to identify the knowledge, skills, and abilities needed to perform both task work and teamwork.
- Consider political issues. It may be important to have members representing different constituencies on a team. For example, a university's internal review board that evaluates whether faculty research is ethical in its treatment of human subjects includes a community member who does not have ties to the university community and does not do research.
- Carefully consider who is to do the assessment of potential team members' knowledge, skills, and abilities and who will decide whom to select. It is often useful to have other team members involved in the selection process.

TRAINING

The thousands of team training programs and methods that exist speak to the criticality of adequate team training. Recall from an earlier section that one of the false assumptions held by managers is that people know how and are suited to work on teams. Team-building training generally focuses on four different types of skills:[113] (1) goal-setting skills; (2) interpersonal skills, especially communication, supportiveness, and trust; (3) problem-solving skills, which allow team members to identify problems, generate solutions, and evaluate solutions; and (4) role-clarification skills, which allow members to articulate role requirements and responsibilities.

A great deal of research has been done on the effectiveness of team training in improving team performance. This research shows that training has weak effects on actual performance outcomes, although training tends to have positive effects on team members' evaluations of their team.[114] We should note that most of this research was conducted on intact teams that had considerable experience working together. As a result, these teams had existing structures, roles, and norms, which probably made them more difficult to change. Training is likely to have a greater impact on the performance of newly formed teams.

REWARDS

If people are to work together effectively as a team, they must be rewarded as a team. Team members have little motivation to engage with and support each other if they are rewarded only for their individual performance. Thus, it is important that the reward system for teams have multiple components, some of which reflect team performance. One such reward system is a profit-sharing plan in which associates receive bonuses based on the profits generated by their team. Furthermore, if the teamwork requires cross-functional work and knowledge, team members should receive skill-based or knowledge-based pay. Such pay is determined by what skills and knowledge an associate acquires rather than by how he or she performs on specific tasks. Finally, team-based pay should be provided for only those aspects of performance under the team's control.[115]

LEADERSHIP

A team's leadership is crucial to the effectiveness of the team.[116] Team leaders can naturally emerge, or they can be assigned based on special skills or authority. Even self-managing teams have leaders, although these leaders delegate a great deal of decision-making authority to the team members. Successful team leaders must fulfill three roles.[117]

The first role, team liaison, requires the leader to network with information sources both inside and outside the team. Outside sources include suppliers, clients, customers, other teams, and higher levels of management. In the liaison role, a team leader also acts as a representative of the team and watches out for the team's interests. In essence, the team leader connects the team to the outside world.

Another leader role involves direction setting. Based on external information and personal vision, the leader needs to develop a direction for team action. This means that the leader must develop short-term action strategies based on the long-term organizational strategies developed by the top management team. Thereafter, the leader must translate the long-term strategies into directions, goals, and action plans for team members.

Finally, the team leader must serve as the team's operational coordinator. This role represents the management of the team's work and processes. The major responsibilities of this role are to recognize each member's contributions and decide how to best integrate the various team members' contributions; to monitor team performance and functioning and make necessary changes if feedback indicates problems; and to ensure that the team is operating in a psychological climate that will enable it to function effectively.

The Strategic Lens

Organization structure is typically characterized by formal groups, such as divisions and departments. In recent times, however, much of the organization's work has been accomplished by teams. The work begins with the top management team, which develops the organization's vision and the strategies intended to help realize the vision. These strategies are implemented by teams composed of members within and across departments and units throughout the organization. For example, when the organization's goal is innovation, cross-functional teams are often assigned to develop new products. Members of these teams commonly represent research and development, marketing, and manufacturing units. Sometimes additional team members are drawn from external suppliers, who will provide materials for the new products.

Because of the pervasive use and importance of teams, an organization's performance ultimately depends on its teams' effectiveness. The effectiveness of the baristas in Starbucks stores, for example,

has been largely responsible for the success of the overall organization. The design of teams, the selection of team members, and team leadership and management are all critical for organizational success. As a result, strategic leaders should invest significant effort in developing and managing teams.

Critical Thinking Questions

1. Think of some teams of which you have been a member. How successful were they? To what do you attribute your teams' success or lack thereof?

2. Why do organizations use teams to accomplish the work that needs to be done? What value do teams provide?

3. Someday you will be a leader of a team. What processes will you use to select team members? What specific actions will you take to manage the team to ensure high team productivity?

What This Chapter Adds to Your Knowledge Portfolio

This chapter discussed the importance of teams and teamwork in organizations. We began by discussing the nature of groups and teams and their different forms. Then, we addressed the criteria that should be used to determine whether a team is effective and the factors that influence team effectiveness. Next, we examined how teams develop over time. Finally, we described ways in which organizations and leaders can promote team effectiveness. To summarize, we focused on the following points:

• A group can be defined in very general terms as "two or more interdependent individuals who influence one another through social interaction." A team is a group that consists of two or more people, working interdependently within an organization, with tasks that are relevant to the organization's mission, and who are considered as a team by people within and outside the team.

• Groups and teams can be classified in a number of ways. Both formal and informal groups arise in organizations. People in organizations also often belong to identity groups based on their social identities, such as gender identity, racial identity, or religious identity. Types of teams include virtual teams, functional teams, and self-managing teams. The type and purpose of the team can affect how the team develops and functions.

• Team effectiveness is measured in terms of the team's productivity and also in terms of team learning and cognition, team members' feelings about the team, and team viability.

• The composition of the team influences the team's effectiveness. The diversity of members, their personality, and the size of the team all influence team effectiveness.

- The structure of a team, including the roles held by members, the norms, and the task structure, can all influence a team's effectiveness.

- The processes employed and experienced by the team also influence team performance. Team processes include team cohesion, conflict among team members, social facilitation, social loafing, and communication.

- Teams change and develop over time. The stage model of development proposes that teams experience four developmental stages: forming, storming, norming, and performing. A fifth stage, in which the team disbands, is adjourning. The punctuated equilibrium model of team development holds that teams undergo a shift from interpersonally focused to task focused when the deadline for the team project is nearing. Most teams follow a combination of these two models of development.

- Organizations can promote effective teamwork by providing top management support, ensuring technical and informational support, selecting people for teamwork, training people in teamwork skills, and rewarding team performance.

- Effective team leaders act as liaisons, provide direction, and operationally coordinate team activities.

Back to the Knowledge Objectives

1. What makes a collection of people a team? How does a team differ from a group? What are some different types of teams?

2. To determine whether a team is effective, what should be measured?

3. What composition factors should a manager consider in designing an effective team? Would these factors differ depending on the type of team being formed?

4. What are the important aspects of team structure? How does each affect team performance?

5. What types of team processes can have a positive influence on team performance? What processes can have negative effects?

6. How do the stage model and the punctuated equilibrium model of team development differ?

7. What can organizations do to encourage and support effective teamwork?

8. What are some important team leader roles? Describe an example from your own experience of a team leader who filled one or more of these roles.

Thinking about Ethics

1. Should associates be required to work in teams if they prefer not to do so—that is, if they prefer to be evaluated based only on their individual efforts? What are the implications of allowing people such choices (positive or otherwise)?

2. Is it appropriate to exclude some members from teams when status and long-term rewards (such as promotions) in an organization are based largely on team performance?

3. What types of sanctions (if any) should be imposed on team members identified as engaging in social loafing? Who should apply those sanctions (if any)?

4. What roles should leaders play in the development of team values and norms in self-managed teams?

5. What are team leaders' responsibilities with regard to political processes within the organization? That is, when other individuals outside of the team promote their own self-interests at the expense of the organization, especially when these actions have negative effects on the team's productivity, what should team leaders do? How can they best fulfill these responsibilities to the team and to the organization?

Key Terms

Synergy, p. 369
Group, p. 369
Team, p. 369
Formal groups, p. 370
Informal groups, p. 370
Identity groups, p. 370
Virtual teams, p. 370
Process loss, p. 375
Team orientation, p. 377

Roles, p. 379
Task roles, p. 379
Socioemotional roles, p. 379
Norms, p. 379
Divisible tasks, p. 381
Unitary tasks, p. 381
Maximization tasks, p. 381

Optimization tasks, p. 381
Interpersonal cohesion, p. 382
Task cohesion, p. 382
Social facilitation effect, p. 383
Social loafing, p. 383
Punctuated equilibrium model (PEM), p. 388

Building Your Human Capital

Do You Have a Team?

The benefits of teamwork are clearly outlined in this chapter. Not only can teams increase organization-related performance and contribute to the competitive advantage of the organization, but they can also increase individual well-being. This has led the business world to adopt teamwork whenever possible. However, sometimes what we call a team is not functioning as a team. Think of a team that you belong to, whether it is a sports team, a class project team, or a work team. Answer the following questions below to determine whether what you think of as your team is really operating as a team:

1. To what extent is your team interdependent?
   • Do team members work well together?
   • Are there problems in coordinating the team's activities?
   • Do people work together, or do they mostly do their work independently of one another?
   • What happens when a team member does not perform up to standards?

2. Is your team structured as a team?
   • Is the team organized?
   • Is it clear who is supposed to be doing what?
   • Are there conflicts over who is in charge?

3. Is your team cohesive?
   • Is your team close or tight-knit?
   • Do team members like each other?
   • Do team members frequently quit the team?

4. Does your team have an identity?
   • Does your team have a name (either formal or informal)?
   • Are team members proud to tell others that they are a part of this team?
   • Do the team members have a sense of shared identity with each other?

5. Does your team have goals?
- Do team members put the team goals above their own personal goals?
- Do team members work hard to reach the team's goals?
- Does the team have a specific mission that everyone is clear about?

Source: Information adapted from and based on D.R. Forsyth, *Group Dynamics* (Belmont, CA: Wadsworth, 1999).

A Strategic Organizational Behavior Moment

The New Quota

"One club." Jack closed his hand and, almost imperceptibly, leaned forward a little. To most people, such a movement would have gone unnoticed. But all three of the others knew that Jack's opening bid was a little weak.

"Pass."

"Three no trump." Bill was gleeful. He had 16 points, and this would be the first hand he had played this lunch hour. He watched as Jack spread his hand and noted that the play would be uneventful.

"Bid three, making four," Dennis said as he penciled down the score. "Got time for another?"

"Not really. Gotta get back to the grind," Steve grimaced as he spoke. "Listen, what do you guys think about the new quota?"

"It's ridiculous!" Bill was anxious to find out how his co-workers felt, and he also wanted to express his own opinion. "When I came here five years ago, we were supposed to wire three assemblies an hour. Now we're supposed to do eight. They aren't paying me that much more. I think it stinks."

"I do, too." Dennis was usually pretty low key. But as he spoke, his eye began to twitch, revealing his anxiety. "I'm not sure that I could meet it even if I tried, and I'm sure as hell not going to try. They can have my stinking job if they want. Only reason I stick around here, anyway, is because you guys are such lousy bridge players."

They all laughed. Then Jack, seeing that Steve was waiting, said, "Eight's possible, but I think some of us are going to be laid off if we all do it. I was talking to this guy over in engineering the other day, and he explained how to make a jig that lets you just lay those wires in real easy. I tried it and it really works. It saved me about six minutes on the first assembly. Of course, I went back and told him it didn't work. I just don't want to do eight—won't help any of us if we do."

Steve looked curiously at Jack. "So that's what you were up to! I saw you really humping a couple of days ago and thought you'd lost your screws. Anyway, I'm glad you guys

feel the same as me. It makes me feel a lot better. Don't figure the boss will do much to us if he thinks an old pro like Jack can't do eight."

It was several days later when Dave, the shop supervisor, was called to the manager's office. Dave knew that it was going to be about the quota, and he didn't know exactly what he was going to say. Mr. Martin was on the phone but motioned for him to sit down.

When he hung up, he faced Dave and said, "That was Pacific Electronics. They want to know if we can meet the shipping schedule or not. What do I tell them when I call back?"

"I don't know, honestly. The guys have picked their speed up some, but I don't think we're going to do better than six-and-a-half, maybe seven."

"That won't cut it, Dave. This new business is important. If we can't handle it, we'll have to cut back some workers. We have too many budget problems without it. Are you sure they're really trying?"

"Yes!" Dave responded. "Jack even tried a new jig that engineering thought up, but it didn't seem to help. Maybe if we added some more incentive bonus it would help. I don't know."

"We can't do that. Costs are already too high. We're being hurt on scrappage, too. You just go back there and really push them. I'm going to tell Pacific that we can meet the schedule. Now you get that crew of yours to do it!"

Discussion Questions

1. What factors seem to be influencing team performance here?

2. Identify the team norms and goals. Are they compatible with organizational objectives?

3. How does the team function to meet individual needs? If you were Dave, what team concepts would you apply? Why?

Team Exercise

Virtual versus Real Teams

As discussed in this chapter, the use of virtual teams is becoming increasingly common in the business world. Although the use of virtual teams can save an organization time and money, they can also have their disadvantages. The purpose of this exercise is to explore the different dynamics that occur between teams meeting face-to-face and virtual teams.

Procedure

Day 1

1. The instructor will randomly divide the class into teams of five to seven people. The instructor will designate one-half of the teams to be "real" teams and the other half to be "virtual" teams.
2. Each team is responsible for developing a new school logo and branding slogan. They will have approximately one week to do this.

Interim Period (approximately one week)

1. Each team is responsible for completing its task outside of class. Real teams can meet face-to-face any time they desire and can also use electronic means of communication. Virtual teams may not meet face-to-face but can use any form of electronic communication to complete their task. Virtual teams also should not discuss the task in class. In addition, it is not necessary for all team meetings to include everyone on the team but several members should be present and all members should participate in some of the meetings.
2. The task is to develop a new school logo and branding slogan. Each team must also develop a three- to five-minute presentation of its product to present in class on Day 2 of the exercise.
3. Before class, each team should prepare answers to the following questions:
   a. How many meetings between team members took place? To what extent were these meetings productive?
   b. What were the most frustrating aspects about working on this project?
   c. To what extent did everyone contribute to the project?
   d. What type of communication problems arose in your team?
   e. To what extent was your team congenial? Were there misunderstandings? How well do team members now understand each other?
   f. How difficult was it to coordinate your work?

Day 2 (approximately one week after day 1)

1. Each team presents its logo and slogan to the class.
2. The class votes on which logo slogans are the best.
3. The instructor leads the class in a discussion of their answers to the above questions and the different dynamics between teams that meet face-to-face and virtual teams.

Endnotes

1. Lawler, E.E., III, Mohrman, S.A., & Ledford, G.E. 1995. *Creating high performance organizations: Practices and results in Fortune 1000 companies*. San Francisco: Jossey-Bass.

2. Fisher, A. 2007. The trouble with MBAs. *Fortune*, April 23, at http://cnnmoney.printhis.clickability.com/pt/cpt?action=cpt&title=The trouble+with+MBAs.

3. Kirkman, B.L., Rosen, B., Tesluk, P.E., & Gibson, C.B. 2004. The impact of team empowerment on virtual team performance: The moderating role of face-to-face interaction. *Academy of Management Journal,* 47: 175–192.

4. Hackman, J.R., & Oldham, G.R. 1980. *Work redesign.* Reading, MA: Addison-Wesley.

5. Cohen, S.G., Ledford, G.E., & Spreitzer, G.M. 1996. A predictive model of self-managed work team effectiveness. *Human Relations,* 49: 643–679.

6. Sundstrom, E. 1999. The challenges of supporting work team effectiveness. In E. Sundstrom, & Associates (Eds.), *Supporting work team effectiveness: Best management practices for fostering high performance.* San Francisco: Jossey-Bass, pp. 3–23.

7. Ibid.

8. Labich, K. 1996. Elite teams get the job done. *Fortune,* February 19: 90–99.

9. Finkelstein, S., & Hambrick, D.C. 1996. *Strategic leadership: Top executives and their effects on organizations.* St. Paul, MN: West Publishing Company.

10. Ireland, R.D. Hoskisson, R.E., & Hitt, M.A. 2005. *Understanding business strategy.* Mason, OH: South-Western Thomson Publishing.

11. Koslowski, S.W.J., & Bell, B.S. Work groups and teams in organizations. In W.C. Borman, D.R. Ilgen, & R.J. Klimoski, (Eds.), *Handbook of psychology, Vol. 12: Industrial and organizational psychology.* Hoboken, NJ: Wiley, pp. 333–374; West, M.A. 1996. Preface: Introducing work group psychology. In M.A. West (Ed.), *Handbook of work group psychology.* Chichester, UK: John Wiley & Sons, pp. xxvi–xxxiii; Guzzo, R.A. 1995. Introduction: At the intersection of team effectiveness and decision making. In R.A. Guzzo, E. Salas, & Associates (Eds.), *Team effectiveness and decision making in organizations.* San Francisco: Jossey-Bass, pp. 1–8.

12. Forsyth, D.R. 1999. *Group dynamics.* Belmont, CA: Wadsworth, p. 5.

13. Guzzo, R.A. 1995. Introduction: At the intersection of team effectiveness and decision making. In R.A. Guzzo, E. Salas, & Associates (Eds.), *Team effectiveness and decision making in organizations.* San Francisco: Jossey-Bass, pp. 1–8.

14. Ibid.

15. Mitchell, T. 1978. *People in organizations: Understanding their behavior.* New York: McGraw-Hill, p. 176.

16. Alderfer, C.P. 1987. An intergroup perspective on group dynamics. In J. Lorsch (Ed.), *Handbook of organizational behavior.* Upper Saddle River, NJ: Prentice-Hall, pp. 190–210.

17. Chao, G.T. 2000. Levels issues in cultural psychology research. In K.J. Klein & S.W.J. Koslowski (Eds.), *Multilevel theory, research, and methods in organizations.* San Francisco: Jossey-Bass, pp. 308–346.

18. Mittleman, D., & Briggs, R.O. 1999. Communicating technologies for traditional and virtual teams. In E. Sundstrom, & Associates (Eds.), *Supporting work team effectiveness.* San Francisco: Jossey-Bass, pp. 246–270.

19. Furst, S.A., Reeves, M., Rosen, B., & Blackburn, R.S. 2004. Managing the life cycle of virtual teams. *Academy of Management Executive,* 18: 6–20.

20. Kirkman, B.L., Rosen, B., Tesluk, P.E., & Gibson, C.B. 2004. The impact of team empowerment on virtual team performance: The moderating role of face-to-face interaction. *Academy of Management Journal,* 47: 175–192.

21. Ibid.

22. Mittleman, D., & Briggs, R.O. 1999. Communicating technologies for traditional and virtual teams. In E. Sundstrom, & Associates (Eds.), *Supporting work team effectiveness.* San Francisco: Jossey-Bass, pp. 246–270.

23. Sundstrom, E., McIntyre, M., Halfhill, T., & Richards, H. 2000. Work groups: From the Hawthorne studies to work teams of the 1990s and beyond. *Group Dynamics: Theory, Research, and Practice,* 4: 44–67.

24. Hackman, J.R. 1986. The psychology of self-management in organizations. In M.S. Pollack, & R.O. Perlogg (Eds.), *Psychology and work: Productivity change and employment.* Washington, DC: American Psychological Association, pp. 85–136; Manz, C.C. 1992. Self-leading work teams: Moving beyond self-management myths. *Human Relations,* 45: 1119–1140.

25. Cohen, S.G., & Ledford, G.E., Jr., 1994. The effectiveness of self-managing teams: A quasi-experiment. *Human Relations,* 47: 13–43; Manz, C.C., & Sims, H.P., Jr. 1987. Leading workers to lead themselves: The external leadership of self-managing work teams. *Administrative Science Quarterly,* 32: 106–128.

26. Stewart, G.L., & Manz, C.C. 1995. Leadership for self-managing work teams: A typology and integrative model. *Human Relations,* 48: 347–370.

27. Seifert, H. 2001. The conductor-less orchestra. *Leader to leader,* No. 21, http://www.pfdf.org/leaderbooks/121/summer2002/seifter.html; Hackman, J.R. 2002. *Leading teams: Setting the stage for great performances.* Boston; Harvard Business School Press.

28. Hackman, J.R. 2002. *Leading teams: Setting the stage for great performances.* Boston; Harvard Business School Press.

29. Canon-Bowers, J.A., Salas, E., & Converse, S.A. 1993. Shared mental models in expert team decision making. In N.J. Castellan (Ed.), *Individual and group decision making.* Hillsdale, NJ: Erlbaum, pp. 221–246.

30. Klimoski, R.J., & Mohammed, S. 1994. Team mental model: Construct or metaphor? *Journal of Management,* 20: 403–437.

31. Edwards, B.D., Day, E.A., Arthur, W., Jr., & Bell S.T. 2006. Relationships among team ability composition, team mental models, and team performance. *Journal of Applied Psychology,* 91: 727–736.

32. Koslowski, S.W.J., & Bell, B.S. Work groups and teams in organizations. In W.C. Borman, D.R. Ilgen, & R.J. Klimoski, (Eds.), *Handbook of psychology, Vol. 12: Industrial and organizational psychology.* Hoboken, NJ: Wiley, pp. 333–374.

33. Hackman, J.R. 2002. *Leading teams: Setting the stage for great performances.* Boston: Harvard Business School Press.

34. George, J.M. 1990. Personality, affect, and behavior in groups. *Journal of Applied Psychology,* 75: 107–116.

35. Barsade, S.G., Ward, A., Turner, J., & Sonnenfeld, J. 2000. To your heart's content: A model of affective diversity in top management teams. *Administrative Science Quarterly,* 45: 802–836.

36. Shea, G.P., & Guzzo, R.A. 1987. Groups as human resources. In K.M. Rowland, & G.R. Ferris (Eds.), *Research in personnel and human resource management (Vol. 5).* Greenwich, CT: JAI Press, pp. 323–356.

37. Hackman, J.R. 2002. *Leading teams: Setting the stage for great performances.* Boston: Harvard Business School Press.

38. Hackman, J.R. 1987. The design of work teams. In J. Lorsch (Ed.), *Handbook of organizational behavior.* New York: Prentice Hall, pp. 315–342.

39. Katz, R., & Allen, T.J. 1988. Investigating the not invented here (NIH) syndrome: A look at performance, tenure, and communication patterns of 50 R&D project groups. In M.L. Tushman, & W.L. Moore (Eds.), *Readings in the management of innovation.* New York: Ballinger, pp. 293–309.

40. Burke, C.S., Stagl, K.C., Salas, E., Pierce, L., & Kendall, D. 2006. Understanding team adaptation: A conceptual analysis and model. *Journal of Applied Psychology,* 91: 1189–1207.

41. Katzenbach, J., 1997. *Teams at the top.* Boston, MA: Harvard Business Press.

42. Steiner, I.D. 1972. *Group processes and productivity.* New York: Academic Press.

43. Hackman, J.R. 2002. *Leading teams: Setting the stage for great performances.* Boston: Harvard Business School Press.

44. Kochan, T., et al. 2003. The effects of diversity on business performance: Report of the diversity research network. *Human Resource Management,* 42: 3–21.

45. Ely, R.J., & Thomas, D.A. 2001. Cultural diversity at work: The effects of diversity perspectives on work group processes and outcomes. *Administrative Science Quarterly,* 46: 229–274; Bantel, K.A., & Jackson, S.E. 1989. Top management and innovations in banking: Does the composition of the top team make a difference? *Strategic Management Journal,* 10: 107–124; Jackson, S.E., Brett, J.F., Sessa, V.I., Cooper, D.M., Julin, J.A., & Peyroonnin, K. 1991. Some differences make a difference: Individual dissimilarity and group heterogeneity as correlates of recruitment, promotions, and turnover. *Journal of Applied Psychology,* 76: 675–689; Pelled, L.H., Eisenhardt, K.M., & Xin, K.R. 1999. Exploring the black box: An analysis of work group diversity, conflict, and performance. *Administrative Science Quarterly,* 44: 1–28.

46. Campion, M.A., Medsker, G.J., & Higgs, A.C. 1993. Relations between work group characteristics and effectiveness: Implications for designing effective work groups. *Personnel Psychology,* 46: 823–850.

47. Ward, A.J., Lankau, M.J., Amason, A.C., Sonnenfeld, J.A., & Agle, B.R. 2007. Improving the performance of top management teams. *MIT Sloan Management Review,* Spring: 84–90; Simons, T., Pelled, L.H., & Smith, K.A. 1999. Making use of difference: Diversity, debate, and decision comprehensiveness in top management teams. *Academy of Management Journal,* 42: 662–673; Barkema, H.G., & Shvyrkov, O. 2007. Does top management team diversity promote or hamper foreign expansion? *Strategic Management Journal,* 28: 663–680; Perretti, F., & Giacomo, N. 2007. Mixing genres and matching people: A study in innovation and team composition in Hollywood. *Journal of Organizational Behavior,* 28: 563–586.

48. Argote, L., & McGrath, J.E. 1993. Group processes in organizations: Continuity and change. In C.L. Cooper, & I.T. Robertson (Eds.), *International review of industrial and organizational psychology (Vol. 8).* New York: John Wiley & Sons, pp. 333–389.

49. Jackson, S.E., May, K.E., & Whitney, K. 1995. Understanding the dynamics of diversity in decision making teams. In R.A. Guzzo, E. Salas, & Associates (Eds.), *Team effectiveness and decision making in organizations.* San Francisco: Jossey-Bass, pp. 204–261.

50. Koslowski, S.W.J., & Bell, B.S. Work groups and teams in organizations. In W.C. Borman, D.R. Ilgen, & R.J. Klimoski, (Eds.), *Handbook of psychology, Vol. 12: Industrial and organizational psychology.* Hoboken, NJ: Wiley, pp. 333–374.

51. Watson, W.E., Kumar, K., & Michaelson, L.K. 1993. Cultural diversity's impact on interaction process and performance: Comparing homogeneous and diverse task groups. *Academy of Management Journal,* 36: 590–602.

52. Barkema, H.G., & Shvyrkov, O. 2007. Does top management team diversity promote or hamper foreign expansion? *Strategic Management Journal,* 28: 663-680.

53. Mount, M.K., Barrick, M.R., & Stewart, G.L. 1998. Five-Factor model of personality and performance in jobs involving interpersonal interactions. *Human Performance,* 11: 145–165.

54. Barrick, M.R., Stewart, G.L., Neubert, M.J., & Mount, M.K. 1998. Relating member ability and personality to work-team processes and team effectiveness. *Journal of Applied Psychology,* 83: 377–391; Bell, S.T. 2007. Deep-level composition variables as predictors of team performance: A meta-analysis. *Journal of Applied Psychology,* 92: 595.

55. Stewart, G.L. 2003. Toward an understanding of the multilevel role of personality in teams. In M.R. Barrick, & A.M. Ryan (Eds.), *Personality and work: Reconsidering the role of personality in organizations.* San Francisco: Jossey-Bass, pp. 183–204.

56. Neuman, G.A., & Wright, J. 1999. Team effectiveness: Beyond skills and cognitive ability. *Journal of Applied Psychology,* 84: 376–389.

57. Burke, C.S., Stagl, K.C., Salas, E., Pierce, L., & Kendall, D. 2006. Understanding team adaptation: A conceptual analysis and model. *Journal of Applied Psychology,* 91: 1189–1207.

58. Ibid.

59. Nieva, V.F., Fleishman, E.A., & Reick, A. 1985. *Team dimensions: Their identity, their measurement, and their relationships. (Research Note #12).* Washington, DC: U.S. Army Research Institute for the Behavioral and Social Sciences.

60. Campion, M.A., Medsker, G.J., & Higgs, A.C. 1993. Relations between work group characteristics and effectiveness: Implications for designing effective work groups. *Personnel Psychology,* 46: 823–850.

61. Koslowski, S.W.J., & Bell, B.S. Work groups and teams in organizations. In W.C. Borman, D.R. Ilgen, & R.J. Klimoski, (Eds.), *Handbook of psychology, Vol. 12: Industrial and organizational psychology.* Hoboken, NJ: Wiley, pp. 333–374.

62. Porter, L., Lawler, E., III, and Hackman, J. 1975. *Behavior in organizations.* New York: McGraw-Hill, p. 373.

63. Forsyth, D.R. 1999. *Group dynamics.* Belmont, CA: Wadsworth, p. 5.

64. Benne, K.D., & Sheets, P. 1948. Functional roles of group members. *Journal of Social Issues,* 4: 41–49.

65. Hackman, J.R. 2002. *Leading teams: Setting the stage for great performances.* Boston: Harvard Business School Press.

66. Labich, K. 1996. Elite teams get the job done. *Fortune,* February 19: 90–99.

67. Crandall, C.S. 1988. Social contagion of binge eating. *Journal of Personality and Social Psychology,* 55: 588–598.

68. Hackman, J.R. 1987. *The design of work teams.* In J. Lorsch (Ed.), *Handbook of organizational behavior.* New York: Prentice Hall, pp. 315–342.

69. Steiner, I.D. 1972. *Group processes and productivity.* New York: Academic Press.

70. Forsyth, D.R. 1999. *Group dynamics.* Belmont, CA: Wadsworth.

71. Ibid.

72. Evans, C.R., & Jarvis, P.A. 1980. Group cohesion: A review and re-evaluation. *Small Group Behavior,* 11: 359–370.

73. Ibid.

74. Barrick, M.R., Stewart, G.L., Neubert, M.J., & Mount, M.K. 1998. Relating member ability and personality to work-team processes and team effectiveness. *Journal of Applied Psychology,* 83: 377–391; Hambrick, D.C. 1995. Fragmentation and other problems CEOs have with their top management teams. *California Management Review,* 37: 110–127; Mullen, B., & Copper, C. 1994. The relationship between group cohesiveness and performance: An integration. *Psychological Bulletin,* 115: 210–227.

75. Hackman, J.R. 1992. Group influences on individuals in organizations. In M.D. Dunnette & L.M. Hough (Eds.), *Handbook of industrial and organizational psychology (Vol. 3).* Palo Alto, CA: Consulting Psychologists Press, pp. 199–267.

76. Ibid.

77. Mullen, B., & Copper, C. 1994. The relationship between group cohesiveness and performance: An integration. *Psychological Bulletin,* 115: 210–227.

78. Seashore, S.E. 1954. *Group cohesiveness in the industrial work group.* Ann Arbor: University of Michigan, Institute for Social Research.

79. Gully, S.M., Devine, D.J., & Whitney, D.J. 1995. A meta-analysis of cohesion and performance: Effects of levels of analysis and task interdependence. *Small Group Research,* 26: 497–520.

80. Morrill, C. 1995. *The executive way.* Chicago: University of Chicago Press.

81. Forsyth, D.R. 1999. *Group dynamics.* Belmont, CA: Wadsworth.

82. Ibid.

83. Ibid.

84. Zajonc, R.B. 1980. Compresence. In P.B. Paulus (Ed.), *Psychology of group influence.* Hillsdale, NJ: Erlbaum, pp. 35–60.

85. Cottrell, N.B. 1972. Social facilitation. In C.G. McClintock (Ed.), *Experimental social psychology.* New York: Holt, Rinehart, & Winston, pp. 185–236.

86. Bond, M.H., & Titus, L.J. 1983. Social facilitation: A meta-analysis of 241 studies. *Psychological Bulletin,* 94: 265–292.

87. Latane, B., Williams, K., & Harkins, S. 1979. Many hands make light the work: The causes and consequences of social loafing. *Journal of Personality and Social Psychology,* 47: 822–832.

88. Alcian, A.A., & Demsetz, H. 1972. Production information costs, and economic organization. *American Economic Review,* 62: 777–795.

89. Price, K.H., Harrison, D.A., & Gavin, J.A. 2006. Withholding inputs in team contexts: Member composition, interaction processes, evaluation structure, and social loafing. *Journal of Applied Psychology,* 91: 1375–1384; Jackson, J.M., & Harkins, S.G. 1985. Equity in effort: An explanation of the social loafing effect. *Journal of Personality and Social Psychology,* 49: 1199–1206.

90. Karau, S.J., & Williams, K.D. 1993. Social loafing: A meta-analytic review and theoretical integration. *Journal of Personality and Social Psychology,* 65: 681–706.

91. Kerr, N., & Bruun, S. 1983. Dispensability of effort and group motivational losses: Free rider effects. *Journal of Personality and Social Psychology,* 44: 78–94.

92. Latane, B., Williams, K., & Harkins, S. 1979. Many hands make light the work: The causes and consequences of social loafing. *Journal of Personality and Social Psychology,* 47: 822–832.

93. Jackson, J.M., & Harkins, S.G. 1985. Equity in effort: An explanation of the social loafing effect. *Journal of Personality and Social Psychology,* 49: 1199–1206.

94. Price, K.H., Harrison, D.A., & Gavin, J.A. 2006. Withholding inputs in team contexts: Member composition, interaction processes, evaluation structure, and social loafing. *Journal of Applied Psychology,* 91: 1375– 1384.

95. Vermeulen, P., and Benders, J. 2003. A reverse side of the team medal. *Team Performance Management: An International Journal,* 9: 107–114.

96. Kirkman, B.L., Rosen, B., Tesluk, P.E., & Gibson, C.B. 2004. The impact of team empowerment on virtual team performance: The moderating role of face-to-face interaction. *Academy of Management Journal,* 47: 175–193.

97. Reitz, J. 1977. *Behavior in organizations.* Homewood, IL: Richard D. Irwin, p. 301.

98. Tuckman, B.W. 1965. Developmental sequences in small groups. *Psychological Bulletin,* 63: 384–399; Tuckman, B.W., & Jensen, M.A.C. 1977. Stages of small group development. *Group and Organizational Studies,* 2: 419–427.

99. Koslowski, S.W.J., & Bell, B.S. Work groups and teams in organizations. In W.C. Borman, D.R. Ilgen, & R.J. Klimoski, (Eds.), *Handbook of psychology, Vol. 12: Industrial and organizational psychology.* Hoboken, NJ: Wiley, pp. 333–374.

100. Ibid.

101. Gersick, C.J.G. 1988. Time and transition in work teams: Toward a new model of group development. *Academy of Management Journal,* 31: 9–41; Gersick, C.J.G. 1989. Marking time: Predictable transitions in task groups. *Academy of Management Journal,* 32: 274–309.

102. Chang, A., Bordia P., & Duck, J. 2003. Punctuated equilibrium and linear progression: Toward a new understanding of group development. *Academy of Management Journal,* 46: 106–117.

103. Morgan, B.B., Salas, E., & Glickman, A.S. 1993. An analysis of team evolution and maturation. *Journal of General Psychology,* 120: 277–291.

104. Ibid.; Wheelan, S.A. 1994. *Group processes: A developmental perspective.* Sydney, Australia: Allyn and Bacon.

105. Hitt, M.A., Nixon, R.D., Hoskisson, R.E., & Kochhar, R. 1999. Corporate entrepreneurship and cross-functional fertilization: Activation, process and disintegration of a new product design team. *Entrepreneurship, Theory & Practice,* 23: 145–167.

106. Sundstrom, E. 1999. Supporting work team effectiveness: Best practices. In E. Sundstrom, & Associates (Eds.), *Supporting*

work team effectiveness: Best management practices for fostering high performance. San Francisco: Jossey-Bass, pp. 301–342.

107. Mittleman, D., & Briggs, R.O. 1999. Communicating technologies for traditional and virtual teams. In E. Sundstrom, & Associates (Eds.), Supporting work team effectiveness: Best management practices for fostering high performance. San Francisco: Jossey-Bass, pp. 246–270.

108. Sundstrom, E. 1999. Supporting work team effectiveness: Best practices. In E. Sundstrom, & Associates (Eds.), Supporting work team effectiveness: Best management practices for fostering high performance. San Francisco: Jossey-Bass, pp. 301–342.

109. Hackman, J.R. 1992. Group influences on individuals in organizations. In M.D. Dunnette, & L.M. Hough (Eds.), Handbook of industrial and organizational psychology (Vol. 3). Palo Alto, CA: Consulting Psychologists Press, pp. 199–267.

110. Ibid.

111. Heneman, H.G. III, & Judge, T.A. 2003. Staffing organizations. Middleton, WI: Mendota House.

112. Klimoski, R.J., & Zukin, L.B. 1999. Selection and staffing for team effectiveness. In E. Sundstrom, & Associates (Eds.), Supporting work team effectiveness: Best management practices for fostering high performance. San Francisco: Jossey-Bass, pp. 63–91.

113. Salas, E., Rozell, D., Driskell, J.D., & Mullen, B. 1999. The effect of team building on performance: An integration. Small Group Research, 30: 309–329.

114. Ibid.

115. Sundstrom, E. 1999. Supporting work team effectiveness: Best practices. In E. Sundstrom, & Associates (Eds.), Supporting work team effectiveness: Best management practices for fostering high performance. San Francisco: Jossey-Bass, pp. 301–342.

116. McIntyre, R.M., & Salas, E. 1995. Measuring and managing for team performance: Emerging principles from complex environments. In R.A. Guzzo, E. Salas, & Associates (Eds.), Team effectiveness and decision making in organizations. San Francisco: Jossey-Bass, pp. 9–45.

117. Chen, G., Kirkman, B.L., Kanfer, R., Allen, D., & Rosen, B. 2007. A multilevel study of leadership, empowerment, and performance in teams. Journal of Applied Psychology, 92: 331–346; Zaccaro, S.J., & Marks, M.A. 1999. The roles of leaders in high-performance teams. In E. Sundstrom, & Associates (Eds.), Supporting work team effectiveness: Best management practices for fostering high performance. San Francisco: Jossey-Bass, pp. 95–125.

CONFLICT, NEGOTIATION, POWER, AND POLITICS

12

After speaking at the Consumer Electronics show in Las Vegas in 2003, Michael Dell was confronted by a group of angry environmental activists (the Silicon Valley Toxics Coalition) dressed up as prisoners and shackled to PCs. The protest was against Dell's then-practice of using prison labor and unsafe practices to recycle old computers while competitors such as Hewlett-Packard were using much safer and more effective means. In 2007, the Center for Health, Environment, and Justice

Jakub Mosur/Zuma Press

EXPLORING BEHAVIOR IN ACTION
Green Conflict

staged a huge protest against Target stores for using PVC vinyl. The protest included newspaper ads against Target, a petition to the CEO, letters to store managers, and picketing at individual stores. In 2003, Greenpeace activists claimed that they had sabotaged 100 Esso gas stations in the United Kingdom, forcing many of the stations to close. Protestors then chained themselves to gasoline pumps at several stations. The protests were

against "environmental crimes" committed by Esso and its parent company, ExxonMobil. In 2005, Greenpeace activists dumped hundreds of used PCs outside of Wipro headquarters in Bangalore, India, to protest the computer assembler's lack of a "take-back" recycling practice. Greenpeace mounted a different type of campaign to get Apple computers to become more environmentally responsive by creating the "Green My Apple" web

site in 2006 to get Apple computer users to put pressure on the company to become more environmentally responsible.

These are just six out of thousands of examples where the conflict between the goals of environmental and conservation groups and the goals of business corporations has surfaced. Traditionally, the goals of the environmentalist and conservationist groups have included reducing carbon emissions, protecting wildlife and natural habitats, avoiding the use of poisonous substances and introducing them into the environment, recycling, and the use and development of sustainable products and energy sources. Corporate goals usually center on providing value to shareholders—meaning that they benefit from using the least expensive products, processes, energy sources, and labor practices to produce their goods and services. Typically, environmentally sound business practices are not the most cost (or profit) effective. Thus, it is no surprise that there is a long history of conflict between environmentalist and conservationist groups and business firms.

However, things are beginning to change, with environmentalist organizations working together with business corporations to obtain mutual benefit. In fact, in order for many organizations to survive now, they must work with environmentalist groups. For example, when William K. Reilly was contemplating a private equity takeover of TXU corporation, a Texas utilities firm, a major drawback was that TXU did not have support from environmentalist organizations. In order for the deal to go through, TXU had to win support from environmentalist organizations. TXU had been doing battle with Environmental Defense, a major environmentalist organization, over the opening of 11 coal-fired power plants. As part of the deal negotiation, Environmental Defense was brought in. After harrowing negotiations, the new owners

of TXU agreed to Environmental Defense's terms and dropped 8 of the original 11 proposed plants. When asked why environmentalists' support was so important for the TXU deal, Reilly responded, "We all swim in the same culture—and the culture is going green." So, what did TXU gain by making these concessions? It garnered public praise from Environmental Defense and other environmentalist organizations—an outcome that is becoming more important to business corporations.

TXU is not the only company forming partnerships with environmentalist organizations. Shortly after the 2003 protest against their recycling policies, Dell joined together with Silicon Valley Toxics Coalition to develop a state-of-the-art recycling plan. DuPont, which is known as a green leader in its industry, employs Paul Gilding, the former head of Greenpeace, to work on its environmental policies and practices. In a much-publicized campaign, Wal-Mart is working with Conservation International and the consulting firm BlueSkye to become a leader in environmentally sound retail practices. Wal-Mart's CEO, Lee Scott, stated that what started out as a defensive strategy in response to public protests over Wal-Mart's environmental practices has turned out to be exactly the opposite. Wal-Mart has found that its new environmental policies and practices have led Wal-Mart associates and the public to feel better about the company and saved their customers money, which is

Wal-Mart's prime business strategy. Given the enormous influence Wal-Mart has on food suppliers, energy usage (the company is the biggest private user of electricity in the United States), and the products people buy, the company can have a huge impact on environmentalists' goals. Thus, what has traditionally been a conflict-ridden relationship between environmentalists and big business has turned into a win-win collaboration. As Al Gore stated after meeting with Wal-Mart executives, "There need not be any conflict between the environment and the economy."

Sources: J. Carey, & M. Arndt, "Hugging the Tree-Huggers: Why So Many Companies Are Suddenly Linking Up with Eco Groups—Hint: Smart Business," BusinessWeek, Mar. 12, 2007, no. 4025, pp. 66–67; M. Gunther, "The Green Machine," Fortune, July 31, 2006, at http://money.com/magazines/fortune/fortune_archive/2006/08/07/8382593/index.htm; Associated Press, "Environmentalists at Vegas Trade Show Protest Dell's Recycling," press release, Jan. 9, 2003; Greenpeace, "Green My Apple Bears Fruit," June 1, 2007, at http://www.greenpeace.org/use/news/green-my-apple-bears-fruit; J. Ribeiro, "Greenpeace Protests Recycling Policies," PCWorld, Sept. 6, 2005, at http://www.pcworld.com/printable/article/id.122419/printable.html; Staff, "Greenpeace Protest Closes Esso Pumps Across UK," Guardian Unlimited, Feb. 24, 2003, at http://www.guardian.co.uk/antiwar/story/0,12809,901865,00.html; Center for Health, Environment, and Justice, "Target Faces Mounting Pressure to Phase Out Toxic Products & Packaging on Day of Annual Shareholder Meeting," news release, May 24, 2007, at http://www.besafenet.com/pvs/newsreleases/target_may_24_doa_release.htm.

The Strategic Importance of Conflict, Negotiation, Power, and Politics

The relationship between environmentalists and business described in the above *Exploring Behavior in Action* feature illustrates a conflict between environmentalists and business that was once believed to be a zero-sum game where one side had to win and the other had to lose. It was thought that either corporations acted responsibly toward the environment and thus decrease profits (environmentalists win) or that businesses operate to increase profits at the expense of the environment (business wins). However, many environmentalist groups and businesses are handling this conflict in a different manner, through cooperation, so that win-win outcomes are achieved. Environmentalists have learned to work with businesses to develop more environmentally friendly practices rather than to protest and embarrass them. Many businesses, on the other hand, have come to view being environmentally responsible as a profitable business strategy.[1]

For those businesses that have been able to solve this conflict, the payoff has been immense. First, many practices that are environmentally sound have also served to save businesses money. For example, DuPont has saved over $2 billion from reductions in energy use since 1990.[2] Another way in which companies benefit is by improving sustainability of the environment. This is a long-term perspective whereby companies operate so as not to deplete their resources so that they can operate in the future. For example, Wal-Mart, one of the largest purveyors of seafood, has developed a program of sustainable fishing practices to maintain commercial stocks of fish, which usually become depleted.[3] Finally, companies' reputations are bolstered by acting in an environmentally responsible manner.[4] There are many very public "report cards" (e.g., the Dow Jones Sustainability Index and the FTSE4Good Index) that evaluate how well companies perform in terms of environmental responsibility as well as other types of social responsibility.[5] Company reputation has been linked to profits,[6] associates' morale,[7] and the ability to recruit top talent.[8] In this case, effectively dealing with and resolving conflict has been shown to have a very important strategic impact on firm performance.

In this chapter, we examine the nature of conflict, the process of negotiation, the exercise of power, and the political behavior that is common in organizations. We begin by defining conflict and differentiating among different types of conflict. We then turn to the causes of conflict, its outcomes, and various responses to it. After discussing conflict-resolution techniques in organizations, we conclude with a discussion of power and politics.

KNOWLEDGE OBJECTIVES

After reading this chapter, you should be able to:

1. Explain how conflict can be either functional or dysfunctional, and distinguish among various types of conflict.

2. Discuss common causes of conflict.

3. Describe conflict escalation and the various outcomes of conflict.

4. Explain how people respond to conflict and under what circumstances each type of response is best.

5. Understand how organizations can manage conflict.

6. Describe the basic negotiation process, strategies, and tactics.

7. Explain why organizations must have power to function, and discuss how people gain power in organizations.

8. Define organizational politics and the tactics used to carry out political behavior.

The Nature of Conflict

conflict
The process in which one party perceives that its interests are being opposed or negatively affected by another party.

Conflict is a process in which one party perceives that its interests are being opposed or negatively affected by another party.[9] An individual can experience internal conflict—for example, role conflict, wherein various demands in a person's life compete for the person's time and attention.[10] In this chapter, we focus on interpersonal conflict, which occurs between individuals or groups. As we noted in the opening discussion, some conflicts are dysfunctional and some are not. In this section, we look more closely at the difference between functional and dysfunctional conflict and then describe three major types of conflict.

Dysfunctional and Functional Conflict

dysfunctional conflict
Conflict that is detrimental to organizational goals and objectives.

Dysfunctional conflict is conflict that interferes with performance. Conflict can be dysfunctional for several reasons. First, conflict among important constituencies can create doubt about the organization's future performance in the minds of shareholders, causing stock prices to drop.[11] For example, this happened when Greenpeace protested Shell Oil's sinking of the oil rig, Brent Spar, in the North Sea.[12] Second, conflict can cause people to exercise their own individual power and engage in political behavior directed toward achieving their own goals at the expense of attaining organizational goals. Third, conflict can have negative effects on interpersonal relationships, as shown in Exhibit 12-1. Finally, it takes time, resources, and emotional energy to deal with conflict, both on an interpersonal and an organizational level. Thus, resources that could be invested in achieving the organization's mission are used in the effort to resolve the conflict. One survey showed that managers spend approximately 25 percent of their time dealing with conflict. In some fields (such as hospital administration and management of municipal organizations), managers can spend as much as 50 percent of their time managing conflict. Managers rate conflict management as equal to or higher in importance than planning, communication, motivation, and decision making.[13]

Exhibit 12-1	Effects of Conflict	
Effects on Individuals	**Effects on Behavior**	**Effects on Interpersonal Relationships**
• Anger	• Reduces motivation and productivity	• Distrust
• Hostility	• Avoidance of other party	• Misunderstandings
• Frustration	• Emotional venting	• Inability to see other's perspective
• Stress	• Threats	• Questioning of other's intentions
• Guilt	• Aggression (psychological or physical)	• Changes attitudes toward others
• Low job satisfaction	• Quitting	• Changes in the amount of power
• Embarrassment	• Absenteeism	• Changes in the quality of communication
	• Biases perceptions	• Changes in the amount of communication
	• Stereotyped thinking	
	• Increases commitment to one's position	
	• Demonizing others	

As mentioned, however, conflict need not be dysfunctional. Conflict that has beneficial results for both the organization and the individual is considered **functional conflict.**[14] An organization without functional conflict frequently lacks the energy and ideas to create effective innovation. Indeed, to encourage functional conflict in groups, some managers have implemented a formal devil's advocate approach (described in Chapter 10). The person serving as devil's advocate has the responsibility of questioning decisions to ensure that as many alternatives as possible are considered.[15]

Conflict can have a number of functional consequences for organizations, including the following:

- Facilitation of change
- Improved problem solving or decision making
- Enhanced morale and cohesion within a group (based on conflict with other groups)
- More spontaneity in communication
- Stimulation of creativity and, therefore, productivity[16]

Types of Conflict

Three types of conflict occur in the workplace: personal conflict, substantive conflict, and procedural conflict.[17] As shown in Exhibit 12-2, although personal conflict and procedural conflict tend to be dysfunctional, substantive conflict can prove constructive.

Personal conflict refers to conflict that arises out of personal and relationship differences between people—differing goals, values, personalities, or the like. Individuals involved in personal conflict often report disliking one another, making fun of one another, being angry with or jealous of one another, having problems with

functional conflict
Conflict that is beneficial to organizational goals and objectives.

personal conflict
Conflict that arises out of personal differences between people, such as differing goals, values, or personalities.

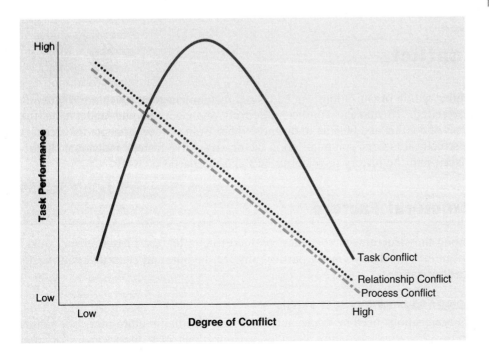

Exhibit 12-2
The Effects of Different Types of Conflict on Task Performance

each other's personalities, or perceiving each other as enemies.[18] Personal conflict is likely to result in poor performance.[19] This form of conflict creates distrust, misunderstanding, and suspicion and reduces goodwill.[20] As a result, associates who have trouble focusing their attention fully on their job responsibilities find it difficult to work together toward organizationally relevant goals.

substantive conflict
Conflict that involves work content and goals.

The second type of conflict, **substantive conflict,** occurs over work content, tasks, and goals.[21] One example of task conflict was an event described as the "Great Petunia War."[22] Two types of military retailers sell goods to military personnel: commissaries and post exchanges. In 1997, these retailers entered into a turf war over who had the right to sell garden plants and flowers. The battle soon escalated to include cooking oil, fruits and vegetables, and other types of food. These retailers were in conflict over their work goals. The conflict became so heated that two generals had to get involved because the conflict was threatening a proposal to reduce costs by integrating the operations of both retailers in the same facility on some bases. Substantive conflicts do not have to result in poor performance, if managed correctly.[23] Moderate levels of substantive conflict have actually been shown to increase performance.[24] We discuss this issue later in this chapter.

Bruce Coleman Inc./Alamy

procedural conflict
Conflict that arises over responsibilities and how work should be completed.

The third type of conflict, **procedural conflict,** concerns responsibilities and how work should be completed.[25] Procedural conflict occurs, for example, when students working together on a project disagree about who will work on which parts of the project or whether they should meet face to face or communicate by e-mail. Procedural conflict has been found to negatively affect performance. If individuals cannot decide who should be responsible for completing a task or how it should be done, there is little chance that they will accomplish their goals or even complete the project.[26]

Causes of Conflict

Conflict within organizations can be caused by many factors, which are frequently interrelated. To manage conflict effectively, managers should understand the causes of conflict and be able to diagnose them. Some of the more common causes are structural factors, communication factors, cognitive factors, individual characteristics, and the history of relations between the parties.

Structural Factors

Among the structural factors that can lead to conflict are increased specialization, interdependency among parties, physical layout, and centralization versus decentralization.

INCREASED SPECIALIZATION

As organizations become larger and more diverse, they require more specialization for effective operation. Smaller organizations may have general human resource managers who perform most or all of the human resource management functions, for example, but larger organizations frequently have specialists for employment, labor relations, training and development, compensation, and affirmative action. This situation represents specialization within one function. Organizations also add new functional areas as they serve a more diverse public. Dividing up the work in this manner is referred to as *differentiation*. Effective organizations become more differentiated as they grow larger or as their external environment becomes more uncertain.[27]

Increasing specialization has many positive benefits, but it also creates a greater potential for conflict. Specialized units frequently view issues from different perspectives. The specialists also often differ with regard to time perspectives and goals. For example, a research and development department often operates within a long-term time frame because developing a product and preparing it for manufacture often require several years. However, a production department operates within a much shorter time frame, perhaps a few weeks (the time required to produce the products for a given order). Conflict can result when the research and development department is late in developing and testing product prototypes, thereby creating scheduling delays for the production department.

INTERDEPENDENCY

In most organizations, work must be coordinated between groups (such as departments) or individuals. The more interdependent two groups or individuals are, the more the potential for conflict exists. A good example of interdependence can be found within state governments. Many state employees work under what is referred to as a *merit system*. This system is designed to alleviate political patronage; employment is based on a person's merit. A human resource management agency based on the merit system is used to screen applicants for state employment and to maintain lists of those who are eligible for certain jobs within state government. When a state agency has a job opening, it must request a list of eligible applicants from the merit system. The state agency, then, depends on the merit system, and the merit system exists to serve state agencies. If the merit system is slow in responding to a request, conflict can occur.

Interdependency can result from limited resources or from required coordination in the timing and sequencing of activities. All organizations have limited resources and attempt to find the most efficient way to divide the resources and accomplish tasks. For example, an organization orders new computers for many of its associates. However, before the associates can use the computers, the company computer technician must hook them up. If there is only one technician and each job takes an hour, competition will arise among associates for the technician's time. One study found that competition for limited resources often leads to dysfunctional conflict. In this case, such competition caused units to distort and suppress information needed by other units.[28]

PHYSICAL LAYOUT

The physical layout of work environments can produce conflict through several mechanisms. In the previous chapter, we discussed how virtual work teams, whose members are physically separated from one another, are more likely to suffer from poor communication that can lead to conflict. Conflict can also arise when associates must work too closely together.[29] Associates commonly work in small, crowded cubicles that do not allow for privacy or personal space—a phenomenon sometimes termed the "Dilbertization effect" (after the comic-strip character).[30] Associates in such environments experience a stressful type of interdependency.

Image100/Alamy

Because everyone is continuously in view and can be easily overheard when talking, even in private conversations, conflict can arise. Conflict is especially likely if associates are unaware of the effect their behavior is having on others around them. For example, someone with a loud phone voice can be particularly irritating to co-workers. Furthermore, such environments do not allow associates to handle sensitive matters in private, a situation that can further increase conflict.[31]

CENTRALIZATION VERSUS DECENTRALIZATION

Both centralization and decentralization of authority can cause conflict, but each causes a different form of conflict. Centralized authority means that one individual makes decisions for all units or that one higher unit makes decisions for all other units. Centralization can lessen conflict between units because all units are more likely to share the same goals and perspectives in a centralized system. However, conflict between individual associates and their supervisors or individual units and the decision-making unit can arise because individuals and units have less control over their own work situations.

For example, many organizations have centralized recruiting; that is, the human resource department recruits associates for jobs in all departments. Centralized recruiting has many advantages for the organization. For example, it ensures that Equal Employment Opportunity Commission rules are followed, and it can save the organization money by avoiding duplication of effort.[32] However, many units may resent the human resource department's control over whom they hire (after all, the people in the unit have to work with the new hires). The hiring goals of the human resource department may be different from those of the individual department. Thus, conflict can arise between individual units and the human resource department.

Decentralization is more common in large, diverse organizations that have many highly specialized units (differentiation, as described earlier). Decentralized authority means that each division manager can make important decisions. Although decentralized authority can reduce conflict between superiors and subordinates within a unit, because subordinates have more control over their work situations, it also creates the potential for more conflict between units because decisions made by one unit may conflict with decisions made by another. Furthermore, these decisions may reflect biased perceptions associated with the specialties of the separate units.

Communication

As discussed in Chapter 9, a common cause of conflict is poor communication, which can lead to misunderstandings and allow barriers to be erected.[33] Probably the easiest way to prevent conflict is to ensure good communication. One of the authors observed conflict caused by poor communication a few years ago in a consulting case. The situation involved two company vice presidents who did not communicate well with one another. They would *talk* to each other, but neither of them would *listen* to the other. As a result, misunderstandings occurred and were never resolved. There were frequent heated arguments in meetings. This hostility extended to their respective departments, and problems of coordination became evident. The conflict became so bad the chief executive officer asked one of the vice presidents to resign.

Both too little and too much communication can lead to conflict.[34] On the one hand, when there is too little communication, associates do not know enough about each other's intentions, goals, or plans. Coordination becomes difficult, and misunderstandings are more likely to occur, which can result in conflict. On the other hand, too much communication can also result in misunderstandings that cause conflict. Other factors leading to poor communication are discussed in Chapter 9.

Cognitive Factors

Certain beliefs and attitudes can lead to conflict. Two such cognitive factors involve differing expectations and one party's perceptions of the other party.

DIFFERING EXPECTATIONS

People sometimes differ in their expectations about jobs, careers, and managerial actions. A common example of such differences involves professional associates (such as research scientists, accountants, or attorneys) and managers. Professional associates often perceive themselves as being loyal to their profession and define their careers as extending beyond a particular organization. In so doing, they focus on those activities valued by the profession, which the management of the organization does not necessarily value. This can lead to lower organizational loyalty and potentially to conflict between these associates and management. If the differences in expectations are great and conflict ensues, the associates may even leave the organization.[35] Thus, managers must be aware of this potential problem and work to reduce differences in expectations between groups.

PERCEPTIONS OF THE OTHER PARTY

The perceptions that one party holds about another can set the stage for conflict. One person may perceive that another has extremely high goals and that these goals will interfere with his own goal attainment.[36] For example, if Smith perceives that a co-worker, Johnson, desires to be promoted at any cost, Smith might fear that Johnson will try to steal his work or sabotage his performance to "beat the competition." Other perceptions that result in conflict include the perception that the other party's intentions are harmful, violate justice norms, are dishonest, or are counter to one's own intentions.[37]

Individual Characteristics

Individual characteristics that may lead to conflict include personality factors, differences in values, and differences in goals.

PERSONALITY

The Type A personality trait has been linked to increased conflict. Recall from Chapter 5 that people with Type A personalities are competitive, aggressive, and impatient.[38] One study found that managers with Type A personalities reported more conflict with subordinates.[39] Because people with Type A personalities are more competitive, they are more likely to perceive others as having competing goals, even when this is not the case.

Another type of personality characteristic likely to influence how people experience and react to conflict is *dispositional trust*. Some people are more likely than others to become vulnerable because they have positive expectations about the motives of others.[40] People who are low in trust are less likely to cooperate with others[41] and less likely to try to find mutually beneficial solutions when conflict arises.[42] When people are high in trust, they are more likely to concede to another party during conflicts, especially when it appears that the other party is upset or disappointed.[43]

Differences in personality can also facilitate conflict. People high in conscientiousness plan ahead, are organized, and desire feedback. While working on a project, a person high in conscientiousness wants to plan the project out, start early, set clear goals, and consistently seek feedback. Someone who is low in conscientiousness may see these actions as unnecessary, creating the potential for procedural conflict. Note that it is not the degree of conscientiousness per se that leads to conflict here; it is the difference on this trait between two people who must work together.

VALUE DIFFERENCES

People vary in the degree to which they value conflict. Some people think conflict is necessary and helpful, whereas others avoid it at all costs. There are important cultural differences as well in the way people view conflict.[44] People in Western cultures tend to view conflict as an inevitable and sometimes beneficial aspect of life. Those in some Asian cultures (such as Chinese) believe that conflict is bad and should be avoided.[45] These value differences make it more difficult to resolve conflicts when the parties are from different cultures. Value differences are most likely to get in the way of conflict resolution when the parties have a high need for closure.[46] That is, when associates desire for there to be closure to a situation or conflict, they will resort to their strongest cultural norms to guide their decision making. So an American with a high need for closure might seek out solutions that put him at the best advantage, whereas a Chinese associate with a high need for closure would focus on avoiding the conflict and maintaining harmony.

GOALS

By definition, when individuals have competing or contrary goals, they often engage in conflict. In addition, certain aspects of individual goals make conflict more likely.[47] Associates with high goals, rigid goals, or competitive goals are more likely to experience conflict, especially when they are strongly committed to the goals.

Differences in goals can result from structural characteristics of the organization, such as increased specialization and interdependency. Recall our earlier example of the merit system for state government employees. The merit system has the goal of ensuring that only qualified candidates are on the eligible-for-hire list and that all applicants are given a fair chance. A state agency wants qualified applicants for a job opening, but it also needs the position filled quickly so that the required work is done. It takes time to be fair to all and to be cautious about who is on the eligible list, which can delay getting the list to the state agency. Meanwhile, the agency may have a vacant job and a work backlog during the delay. In this case, differences in goals generate conflict. As the difference between the goals of two units becomes greater, the likelihood that conflict will occur increases. Organizations with structures that align individual and subgroup goals with those of the organization experience less conflict.[48]

In the following *Experiencing Strategic Organizational Behavior* feature, the battles between labor and management at United Airlines illustrate the impact of competing goals in generating conflict. From management's perspective, the only way the company's financial woes could be solved was by obtaining salary and pension concessions from the unions. In contrast, the unions and their members sought to protect current salaries and pension plans. In their view, the company's financial woes could be solved only by better executive decision making and more sacrifices on the part of management.

EXPERIENCING STRATEGIC ORGANIZATIONAL BEHAVIOR

Un-United

On September 11, 2001, United Airlines lost 2 airplanes and 18 employees in the terrorist attacks. Following this tragedy, United experienced a $2.2 billion loss, the largest in aviation history. But the setback caused by the terrorist attacks was not the only problem facing United; the firm had been experiencing financial difficulties before the attacks.

In 2000, United tried to buy US Airways, much to the displeasure of United employees. In response, the pilots participated in a work slowdown and refused to work overtime. Flights were frequently canceled or late, and customers became irate. In spite of the fact that United was losing business and falling to the bottom of the industry's performance rankings, the pilots were granted a 28 percent pay raise, making them the highest-paid pilots in the industry. Meanwhile, the deal with US Airways fell through.

The pilots' union, mechanics' union, and flight attendants' union were at odds with the company and with each other. Problems dated back at least to 1994, when members of some of the unions had agreed to pay cuts in exchange for stock ownership. Twenty-five percent of the company's stock went to pilots, 20 percent to mechanics, and 10 percent to nonunion employees. The flight attendants' union would not agree to a salary decrease in exchange for stock, however, which caused problems with the other unions.

After the September 11 tragedy, the conflict among unions and between unions and management subsided for a bit. However, United's CEO, Jim Goodwin, soon made matters worse. Goodwin was an operations expert who disliked appearing in public. He did little to address weary employees, attending only one memorial service. However, he did write a letter to employees that caught everyone's attention, including the media. The letter said that the company was "hemorrhaging" money and that major cost cuts and sacrifices would have to be made to keep United in the skies. Wall Street also got wind of the letter, and stock prices immediately fell 20 percent. Goodwin was soon fired.

John W. Creighton replaced Goodwin. He was previously the CEO of Weyerhaeuser, where he was known for changing the fragmented, infighting culture to a united company working toward a single mission. Creighton had the same challenge facing him at United. By 2002, however, United was losing $7 million a day. Creighton retired in September, after 11 months on the job, and was succeeded by Glenn Tilton, the fourth CEO in six years. Tilton described his new company as follows: "Years of decisions based on expediency and the interests of disparate constituencies had a corrosive effect on the culture of United Airlines. . . . Cynicism and dysfunction permeated the workforce."

Late in 2002, UAL Corporation, United's parent company, applied for an Air Transportation Stabilization Board (ATSB) loan of almost $2 billion to cover its debt. A condition of the loan was that United would have to make major cutbacks, largely from reductions in wages. For this to occur, all unions would have to agree

United's dive
Monthly stock price of UAL Corp., parent of United Airlines:

Nov. 1, 2001
$16.87

Friday
$2.45

NewsCom

to pay cuts. The message from management was that everyone had to sacrifice to save the company. Because employees owned 55 percent of the airline, they had reasons other than saving their current jobs to keep United in the skies. The pilots' and flight attendants' unions agreed to pay cuts. The mechanics' union, however, refused. United did not get the ATSB loan and filed for bankruptcy. Many blamed the mechanics' "no" vote, increasing tension again among the unions.

Once under bankruptcy, the pilots' union agreed to a 29 percent pay cut, flight attendants to a 9 percent decrease, and dispatchers and meteorologists to a 13 percent decrease. The mechanics' union still refused to negotiate a pay cut and was ordered to take a 14 percent reduction by the federal bankruptcy court. At this point, Tilton announced that employee sacrifices would help get United back on track and out of bankruptcy. During this period, United laid off thousands of employees (a 40-percent decrease between 2001 and 2003) and outsourced many of its jobs.

Despite these cutbacks, United still was not out of bankruptcy by late 2003. The company was denied another federal loan and was performing poorly. The SARS epidemic, the war in Iraq, and increasing gasoline prices did not help. Employees were asked to make additional sacrifices. In the fall of 2004, United proposed to end its pension plan and further reduce pay, causing the mechanics' union to sue top executives and the flight attendants' union to request that a judge allow outsiders to take over the airline's plan to exit from bankruptcy.

Management–labor relations were at an all-time low. Management believed that the unions were impairing United's ability to survive by fighting further pay cuts, pension cuts, layoffs, and outsourcing. The unions felt that high-level managers were making incompetent decisions, ignoring their input, and not assuming their fair share of sacrifices (because they were still receiving bonuses and generous executive pay). At this point, United was heading into two years of bankruptcy without an agreed-on plan on how to get out.

United Airlines finally emerged from bankruptcy on February 1, 2006 after 3 years and 51 days. However, internal conflicts still remained, leading to falling stock prices and increasingly dissatisfied customers. United had the highest number of passenger complaints in 2006 and scored the lowest in the airline industry on the University of Michigan's 2007 American Customer Satisfaction Index.

Sources: M. Allison, "Messages of Unity Sounded at United, CEO: Work Won't 'Be Undermined,'" *Chicago Tribune,* Aug. 4, 2004, at http://www.chicagotribune.com/classified/jobs/promo/chi-0408040232aug04,0,2386882.story; M. Allison, "Flight Attendants Target United's Leaders, Liens Filed against 3 UAL Subsidiaries," *Chicago Tribune,* Sept. 1, 2004, at http://www.chicagotribune.com/classified/jobs/promo/chi-0409010201sep01,0,2714564.story; M. Allison, "United Needs $500 Million More in Cuts," 0409170123sep17,0,1071580.story; API, "Pay Cuts Ordered for United Mechanics," CBSNEWS.com, Jan.10, 2003, at http://www.cbsnews.com/stories/2002/12/27/national/main534447.shtml; J. Helyar, "United We Fall," *Fortune,* Feb. 18, 2002, pp. 90–96; M. Skertic, "United Asks Cuts in Pay of Up to 18%," *Chicago Tribune,* Nov. 6, 2004, at http://www.chicagotribune.com/classified/jobs/promo/chi-0411060211nov06,0,973948,print.stor.; Reuters, "UAL Asks for Delay on Bankruptcy Plan," *New York Times,* Apr. 10, 2005, at http://www.nytimes.com/2005/04/10/business/10ual.html; M. Adams, "United Passengers Air Their Bitter Grievances," *USAToday,* June 18, 2007, at http://usatoday.com/travel/flights/2007-06-18-ual-service-usat_N.htm; Associated Press, "Timeline of United Airline's Bankruptcy," *USAToday,* Feb. 1, 2006, at http://usatoday.com/travel/flights/2007-02-01-united-timeline_x.htm.

The case of United Airlines illustrates how differing goals can lead to conflict. It also shows how unresolved conflict such as that which occurred between the unions and management can have devastating effects on firm performance. The long history of this conflict did not help much either; thus we next discuss the effect of history on conflict.

History

Previous relationships between two parties can influence the likelihood of conflict in the future. Past performance and previous interactions are two such relationship factors.

PAST PERFORMANCE

When individuals or groups receive negative feedback because of poor past performance, they often perceive it as a threat.[49] When a threat is perceived, individuals frequently attempt to deal with it by becoming more rigid, exerting more control over deviant group members and ideas, and restricting the flow of communication.[50] When people become more rigid and communicate less, both task conflict and relationship conflict can result. Thus, when past performance is poor, the chances for both these types of conflict are greater.[51]

PREVIOUS INTERACTIONS

Individuals who have experienced conflict in the past are more likely to experience it in the future.[52] This was illustrated in the United Airlines case, where there were continuous conflicts between labor and management for over 12 years. Previous conflict can influence the probability of future conflict in several ways. First, the parties often engage in the same conflict-inducing behaviors. Second, the parties likely distrust one another. Third, they may expect conflict, and this expectation may become a self-fulfilling prophecy. Think of the old story of the warring Hatfield and McCoy families. These two families had been fighting so long that younger members of each family did not know what had caused the initial conflict. All they had learned was to engage in conflict with the other family.

Later in the chapter we discuss the negotiation process, which is an illustration of how associates attempt to resolve conflict. Negotiation situations are influenced by the negotiators' previous interactions. Research has shown that negotiators' past negotiation history in terms of the quality of deals they arranged influences how they negotiate in other situations—even if they are negotiating with a different person.[53] Negotiators who had a history of not being able to reach a satisfactory conclusion during previous negotiations were much more likely to reach unfavorable solutions in future negotiations than those who had had a successful negotiation history.

 # Conflict Escalation and Outcomes

As we have just seen, conflict has many causes, and they are often interdependent. For example, structural factors such as specialization are related to differences in goals and perceptions. The physical environment can cause conflict because it can interfere with communication. However a conflict begins, though, there are only a certain number of ways in which it can end.

Fortunately, most cases of conflict are resolved, although not necessarily in a manner satisfactory to both parties or to the organization (as in the earlier example, where two vice presidents were in conflict and one was fired by the CEO). The conflict between Rosie O'Donnell and Donald Trump, which was not resolved, illustrates how two individuals' reputations were besmirched with possibly negative impact on their business (the TV shows *The View* and *The Apprentice*). The "Rosie vs. Donald" case described in the *Experiencing Strategic Organizational Behavior* feature is a good example of how a conflict can grow over time. We begin this section with a discussion of conflict escalation and then focus on conflict outcomes.

Rosie vs. Donald

Stephen
Lovekin/Getty
Images

Retna

If you were watching television during December 2006 and January 2007, you probably could not avoid hearing about the escalating feud between *The View* talk-show host, Rosie O'Donnell, and businessman and TV personality, Donald Trump. This was an incredible example of escalation of conflict that eventually led to the bewilderment or boredom of just about everyone.

The fight started on December 20, 2006. Trump, who co-owns the Miss USA contest, had just given Miss USA, Tara Conner, a second chance after she was found to be partying too much in defiance of her Miss USA contract. During *The View*, O'Donnell questioned Trump's morality and right to be a "moral compass." She also made disparaging remarks about his business and called him a "snake-oil sales-man." She followed this with an entry on her blog implying Trump was bankrupt.

The next morning Trump called into the morning show *Good Day L.A.* and made remarks about Rosie's sexual orientation and called her "an unattractive woman," a "loser," and a "bully." He also said he would sue her.

Rosie O'Donnell and Donald Trump continued throughout the spring of 2007 to appear on very public forums (talk shows, *David Letterman*, *Larry King Live*, etc.), each time leveling more and more personal insults at each other and making unsubstantiated claims about each other. For example, Trump implied that Barbara Walters (the creator of *The View*) was embarrassed by Rosie. Rosie claimed that Trump's businesses were failing. Both were accused by the media of engaging in this behavior to increase the ratings of their TV shows (*The View* and *The Apprentice*).

In the end, the feuding did not bode well for either of their roles on their TV shows. O'Donnell left *The View* in June 2007, amid rumors (many from Trump) that she was fired. However, the official statement was that she could not reach a settlement with the network in her contract negotiations. This was unfortunate for the TV show, because she had greatly increased the ratings in the 10 months that she was on the show. When NBC failed to put *The Apprentice* on its Fall 2007 schedule, Trump replied that they could not fire him—he quit.

The conflict between Rosie and Donald escalated extremely quickly. In fact, they skipped the initial stage of conflict where both parties act in a rational and controlled manner. Cooperation should have been attempted, and overt conflict avoided.

The conflict essentially began in the second phase, where the parties cannot solve the conflict and distrust and tension develop. Hostility and lack of respect characterized the exchanges. Also attempts were made to enter into coalitions with other parties. Both O'Donnell and Trump claimed in various ways that Barbara Walters was on their side. She ended up publicly supporting Rosie, but rumors abound about how this event caused conflict between the two women and may have led to Rosie's leaving *The View*.

Finally, the confrontations between parties became extremely aggressive and hostile. Each saw the other as an evil person. One could argue that both Rosie and Donald were willing to risk their own welfare to harm the other party, since the feud was bringing negative press to both of them. In the end, there was no chance for a satisfactory resolution. When asked by Larry King whether there was any chance of a reconciliation, Trump replied, "Zero chance. Is there such a thing as less than zero?" Ultimately, each of the parties harmed the other but did equal harm to themselves.

Source: F. Glasl, "The Process of Conflict Escalation and Roles of Third Parties," in G.B.J. Bomers, & R. Peterson (Eds.), *Conflict Management and Industrial Relations* (Boston:

Kluwer-Nijhoff, 1982), pp. 119–140; transcripts from CNN's *Larry King Live,* aired Jan. 16, 2007; D. Bauder, "Rosie O'Donnell Leaving ABC's 'The View,'" *USAToday,* Apr. 25, 2007, at http://usatoday.com/life/television/2007-04-25-4088890135_x.htm; anonymous, "Clash of TV Hosts: Rosie vs. Donald," *USAToday,* Jan. 11, 2007, at http://usatoday.com/life/people/2007-01-10-trump-rosie-feud-timeline_x.htm; *USAToday* at http://usatoday.com/life/television/2007-04-25-4088890135_x.htm; Associated Press, "Trump and Rosie Argue Over Miss USA," *USAToday,* Dec. 21, 2006, at http://usatoday.com/life/people/2006-12-21-rosie-donald_x.htm; J. Steinberg, "Back to 'Talking Smack' with Rosie, Donald and Barbara," *New York Times,* Jan. 11, 2007, at http://www.nytimes.com/2007/01/11/arts/television/11feud.html.

Conflict Escalation

Conflict escalation, as indicated by the feud between Rosie O'Donnell and Donald Trump, is the process whereby a conflict intensifies over time. Escalation is characterized by several features. Tactics become increasingly severe, and the number of issues grows. In addition, the parties become more and more deeply involved in the conflict. Eventually, as their goals shift from caring about their own welfare and outcomes to trying to harm the other party, they lose sight of their own self-interests.[54]

Many reasons have been proposed for conflict escalation. Some experts feel that escalation is inevitable unless direct measures are taken to resolve the conflict.[55] Others believe that conflicts do not have to escalate. Rather, there are certain conditions that make escalation more likely. These include the following:

- Cultural differences exist between the parties.[56]
- The parties have a history of antagonism.[57]
- The parties have insecure self-images.[58]
- Status differences between the parties are uncertain.[59]
- The parties have strong ties to each other.[60]
- The parties do not identify with one another.[61]
- One or both parties have the goal of escalating the conflict in order to beat the other party.[62]

conflict escalation
The process whereby a conflict grows increasingly worse over time.

Conflict Outcomes

There are five ways in which conflict can end in terms of how the outcome satisfies each party's concerns, goals, or wishes: lose-lose, win-lose, lose-win, compromise, and win-win.

LOSE-LOSE

In this conflict outcome, neither party gets what was initially desired. In the first *Experiencing Strategic Organizational Behavior* feature, United Airlines was headed for a lose-lose outcome. In order to come out of bankruptcy and save the company, both management and unions needed to make concessions. If the company remained in bankruptcy and ultimately went out of business, management would fail and lose their interests in the company. Union members would lose their jobs as well as the money they had invested in United Airlines stock. If neither side gave in, then all would lose. United Airlines has come out of bankruptcy, but still continues to face many problems, such as dropping stock prices and poor customer satisfaction.

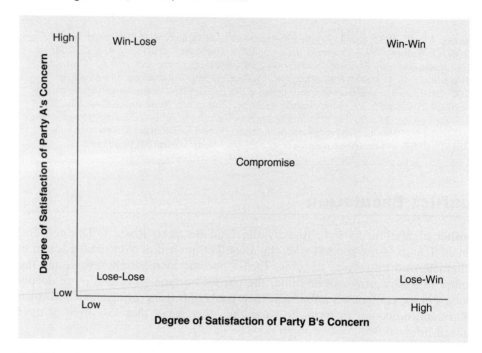

Exhibit 12-3   Possible Conflict Outcomes

Source: Adapted from K.W. Thomas, 1992. "Conflict and Negotiation Processes." In M.D. Dunette, & L.M. Hough (Eds.), *Handbook of Industrial and Organizational Psychology, Vol. 3* (Palo Alto, CA: Consulting Psychologists Press), pp. 651–717.

WIN-LOSE OR LOSE-WIN

In either of these outcome scenarios, one party's concerns are satisfied, whereas the other party's concerns are not. This type of outcome is obviously not advantageous for the losing party, and it often is not particularly advantageous for the organization. Such outcomes are not always avoidable, however. Some conflicts involve "zero-sum," or distributive, issues, in which one party can gain only at the expense of the other. For example, consider a situation in which two opposing parties are competing for a limited number of resources. The more of the resources one party obtains, the less of the resources the other party can receive. In the view of United Airlines' unions, distributive issues were at the heart of their conflict with management. That is, the unions believed that by making concessions in terms of salaries and pensions, they were giving more resources to management.

COMPROMISE

Compromise occurs when both parties give up something in order to receive something else. Had management at United Airlines been willing to give the unions something valuable in return for their salary and pension concessions, a compromise might have been achieved. Indeed, a compromise was actually achieved several times during the travails at United. For example, a compromise resulted in employees' accepting pay cuts and receiving stock ownership in return. Compromise is a desirable solution to conflict.

WIN-WIN

A win-win situation occurs when both parties get what they want. Consider a situation in which a union bargains for increased pay, but management does not have the resources to increase pay. A win-win situation would occur if the union decided to adopt specific productivity incentives. Increases in productivity would be accompanied by cash bonuses, thus increasing union members' pay. Management would win because productivity (and consequently profit) would be expected to increase, in turn justifying the higher pay. In the opening case, we described how environmentalist organizations and some businesses (Dell, Wal-Mart, DuPont) had moved from win-lose outcomes to win-win outcomes. Exhibit 12–3 depicts the five conflict outcomes.

Responses to Conflict

People respond to conflict in different ways. One person may try to win at all costs, whereas another person may try to ensure that both her own concerns and those of the other party are met. There are five potential responses to conflict, as well as situations in which each response is appropriate.[63] Each response is described in terms of assertiveness and cooperativeness.[64] Here, *assertiveness* refers to the extent to which a party tries to satisfy his or her own concerns. *Cooperativeness* refers to the extent to which a party attempts to satisfy the other party's concerns.

1. *Competing.* A party with a competing response attempts to win at the expense of the other party. Other names for this response include *forcing* and *dominating*. This style is useful when quick, decisive action is required, when an unpopular course of action must be taken, or when the other party will take advantage of noncompetitive behavior. For example, some countries have more lenient copyright laws than the United States, leading to a proliferation of imitative (knockoff) goods (such as fake Gucci purses, Adidas sneakers, and Rolex watches). The Calvin Klein Company used a competitive conflict response in dealing with counterfeiters by establishing a worldwide network to investigate and take legal action against any organization counterfeiting its goods.[65]

2. *Accommodating.* An accommodating response is the opposite of a competitive style. A person using an accommodating response will forgo his own concerns so that the concerns of the other party can be met. For example, when someone has to work on a holiday, an associate agrees to work on the holiday so that a co-worker can have the holiday off, in order to avoid conflict. An accommodating style may be used by a party who believes that he cannot win. It may also be useful when the issue is less important to one party than to the other. This party can adopt an accommodating style in return for a favor at a future time.

3. *Avoiding.* A party who exhibits an avoiding response neglects both her own concerns and those of the other party. An avoiding style may be necessary to allow emotions to cool down or as a means of delaying decisions until effective solutions can be found. IBM has avoided conflict by refusing to do business in countries that allow bribery of public officials.[66]

4. *Compromising.* Compromising responses are those in which a party tries to partially meet both his own concerns and those of the other party. Each party gives up something but gets something in return. A compromising response is best used when the parties are of relatively equal power, when temporary settlements to complex problems are required, when there is time pressure, and as a backup when collaboration (described next) is unsuccessful.

5. *Collaborating.* Collaborating responses are attempts to fully meet the concerns of both parties. To use a collaborating response, the parties must work together to identify solutions in which both parties can win.[67] This type of response is most likely to result in the win-win outcome described earlier. A collaborating response is best used when both parties' concerns are too important to ignore and when the objective is to learn and to gain commitment.

Negotiation

negotiation
A process by which parties with different preferences and interests attempt to agree on a solution.

The resolution of conflict usually requires negotiations between the conflicting parties. **Negotiation** is a process by which parties (individuals, groups, or representatives of groups) with different preferences and interests attempt to agree on a solution. Furthermore, the parties are committed to achieving a peaceful means of dispute resolution.[68]

In the resolution of conflict, the parties often engage in bargaining that requires them to engage in several reactions to conflict such as compromise, collaboration, accommodating, or competing. Although each party usually approaches negotiations with the intent to gain the most benefits for their side, for negotiations to be successful, all parties must bargain in good faith. Managers should build their skills in negotiation because they will be called on to negotiate in many situations. The political skill explained later can be useful to managers in negotiations if they use them for the benefit of the organization to achieve a negotiated agreement whereby both parties gain benefit and agree to abide by the decision. Depending on the circumstances, a manager can serve as a mediator or an arbitrator in the negotiations. A mediator acts as a neutral third party who facilitates a positive solution to the negotiations, whereas an arbitrator acts as a third party with the authority to require an agreement. In reality, managers often serve in both roles simultaneously, and require tact and strong interpersonal skills to achieve negotiated agreement in a conflict situation. The skills and means of negotiation depend on the negotiator's bargaining strategy.

Negotiation Strategies

distributive bargaining
A negotiation where one party's goals are in direct conflict with the goals of another party.

integrative bargaining
A negotiation strategy where the nature of the problem permits a solution that is attractive to both parties—in other words, a win-win outcome.

Negotiators enter negotiations with one of two different strategies.[69] A **distributive bargaining** strategy occurs when one party's goals are in direct conflict with the goals of another party. This type of negotiation strategy usually calls for a competing response and results in a win-lose outcome. For example, if a buyer and a supplier are negotiating over the price of a product, the higher the agreed-upon price, the bigger the win for the supplier and the bigger the loss for the buyer. On the other hand, an **integrative bargaining** strategy occurs when the nature of the problem permits a solution that is attractive to both parties—in other words, a win-win outcome. Sometimes what appears to be a distributive situation at the beginning can be turned into an integrative strategy by broadening the issues under consideration. For example, if the above buyer were to also offer the supplier bigger orders and offer to buy additional products in return for a lower price on the product under negotiation, then an integrative solution could be reached. The buyer would get a lower price; the supplier would get more business. Depending on what type of strategy a negotiator is using, different types of tactics are appropriate and likely to be effective. These tactics are listed in Exhibit 12-4.

Exhibit 12-4	Negotiation Tactics

Distributive Tactics

- Convince the other that breaking off negotiations would be costly for the other or for yourself.
- Convince the other that you feel very committed to reaching your target outcome.
- Prevent the other from making a firm commitment to an outcome close to the other's target.
- Allow the other to abandon his position without loss of face or other cost.
- Convince the other that your own target outcome is fair.
- Convince the other that their target outcome is unfair.
- Convince the other that important third parties favor your own target outcome.
- Use nonhostile humor to build positive affect.
- Distract the other to impair the other's ability to concentrate.

Integrative Tactics

- Show the other that their concerns are important to you.
- Show the other that your target outcome is too important to compromise.
- Show the other that a win-win outcome is a possibility.
- Demonstrate that you are flexible with respect to various solutions.
- Insist on fair criteria for deciding among possible solutions.
- Make collaborative norms salient.
- Minimize use of behaviors or tactics that would cause negative emotions.
- Provide an emotionally supportive climate.
- Shield the other from emotional distractions.

Attitudinal Structuring Tactics

- Use similar language.
- Disassociate oneself from others not liked by the opponent.
- Reward opponent's behavior.
- Express appreciation.
- Remind opponent of role obligations.
- Assist opponent in working through negative attitudes.
- Return favors.
- Fight the antagonism, not the antagonist.
- Associate oneself with others the opponent likes.

Sources: K.W. Thomas, "Conflict and Negotiation Processes," in M.D. Dunette & L.M. Hough (Eds.), *Handbook of industrial and organizational psychology, Vol. 3* (Palo Alto, CA: Consulting Psychologists Press, 1992), pp. 651–717; R.E. Walton, & R.B. McKersie, *A Behavioral Theory of Labor Negotiations* (New York: McGraw-Hill, 1965).

Apart from the issues directly under negotiation, there is often the long-term relationship between parties to consider. Another outcome of negotiations is the relationship between the two parties. Most often during negotiations, the parties desire to remain friendly, trustful, and respectful of each other. For example, if a company were negotiating with an environmentalist group and the negotiations turned hostile, future relationships between the two groups would remain antagonistic. The company might do only what is absolutely required to meet the terms of negotiations and fail to develop new ways in which to protect the environment. The environmentalist group might then give only a weak endorsement to the company or refuse to work with it on environmental practices. The activities aimed at influencing the attitudes and relationships of the negotiating parties are referred to as **attitudinal structuring.**[70] Examples of tactics to use for attitudinal structuring are presented in Exhibit 12-4.

attitudinal structuring
Activities aimed at influencing the attitudes and relationships of the negotiating parties.

The Negotiation Process

There are generally four stages that a negotiation process should follow:[71]

1. *Preparation.* Prior to any negotiation, each party outlines the specific goals he or she hopes to achieve. At this point, negotiators must determine their *best alternative to a negotiated agreement* (BATNA). This is the least that the negotiator is willing to accept. Also, during the preparation stage, negotiators should engage in self- and opponent analysis. It is important for negotiators to understand their own behavior during negotiations as well as that of the opponent. At this stage the following questions should be asked about one's opponent:
   a. What is the opponent's position and power? Does the opponent have to confer with others to make concessions?
   b. What does the opponent consider a "win"?
   c. What is the history of the opponent's negotiating style? Does he or she tend to focus on distributive strategies or rely on integrative strategies?

2. *Determining the negotiation process.* Determine the timeline, place, and structure of the negotiations. Also agreements should be made about confidentiality, the sharing of information, and how agreements will be approved. At this point it should also be clarified who will be present during the negotiation process.

3. *Negotiating the agreement.* During this stage the actual negotiation takes place and negotiation strategies and tactics are chosen and employed.

4. *Closing the deal.* At this stage both parties should be quite clear about the conclusion of the negotiations and the particulars of the final agreement. Final agreements should be formalized and it should be made clear what each party's responsibility is in implementing the agreement.

The process outlined above appears to be quite formal. However, it should be followed in any form of negotiation, ranging from negotiating one's pay increase to negotiating major merger and acquisition deals. In the following *Managerial Advice* feature, we explore a common type of negotiation scenario—that of negotiating one's salary when taking a new job.

A Costly Conflict Resolution: The Importance of Negotiation

Jane and Rob are very happy today. Both were offered jobs at ABSCO in the management trainee program. Because Jane and Rob had the same qualifications, ABSCO offered them the same salary of $40,000 per year. This was Rob's dream job, so he accepted right away. This was also Jane's dream job; however, she realized that she would be working in an area where the cost of living was high, and when this was taken into consideration, she would be making less than many of her colleagues in similar positions. So Jane negotiated her salary up to $42,500.

At ABSCO, pay increases are calculated as a percentage of salary. As can be seen in the chart, given the pay-raise schedule, Jane's initial increase over Rob of $2,500 will grow to nearly $3,500 at the end of a five-year period. Over that time, Jane will make almost $14,700 more than Rob. Should they both stay at ABSCO, Jane's salary will continue to grow faster than Rob's, even if they receive the same percentage increases. Thus, Rob's failure to negotiate a higher salary will mean that he is likely to receive less compensation than Jane for the rest of his career at ABSCO.

Royalty-Free/Corbis

	Raise	Rob's Salary	Jane's Salary
Year 1	—	$ 40,000.00	$ 42,500.00
Year 2	5%	42,000.00	44,625.00
Year 3	10%	46,200.00	49,087.50
Year 4	10%	50,820.00	53,996.25
Year 5	10%	55,902.00	59,395.88

Salary negotiations are a classic case of conflict. The hiring organization wants to minimize its costs (lower compensation), whereas the applicant wants to earn as much as possible. This involves a distributive issue, as described earlier, in which two parties are contesting a limited resource. The conflict must be resolved. When you negotiate your salary, how can you participate effectively in this resolution? Advice abounds for how to negotiate your salary, and most writers agree. Below are some common steps you can take:

1. Do your homework. Know what you are worth on the job market and what the industry standards are for the position you are being offered. Numerous sources of information exist to help you with this task, including:
   - Salary survey information at your university's career services center.
   - Job listings that indicate salaries for similar positions.
   - Web sites that allow you to calculate the cost of living for various parts of the country; $40,000 goes a lot further in Houston than it does in New York City.
   - Talking to friends, other students, and networking contacts.
   - On-line salary surveys such as JobSmart.

2. Determine your best alternative to a negotiated agreement (BATNA). This is the lowest offer you will consider; you will reject any offer lower than your BATNA. Your BATNA is a dynamic cutoff. You should always strive to increase it. One way to do this during salary negotiations is to have alternative job offers. The best current offer becomes your BATNA.

3. Know what salary you want—your target salary. Your BATNA is your least acceptable outcome. Your target salary is your most preferred outcome.

4. Never make vague counteroffers, such as "I need more money." Be prepared to offer a specific salary range and a justification for the salary range. This is where your homework will come in handy. Ensure that the range you specify does not limit your possibilities for negotiation. For example, if you specify your BATNA (say, $30,000) as the low end of your range, you may not be able to get more than your minimal acceptable amount. This does not mean you should communicate an unrealistically high figure, however. Suggesting unrealistically high figures leaves a bad impression with the organization.

5. Although you should not be vague, neither should you say, "I need X amount of dollars." This indicates that you are unwilling to negotiate. On the one hand, the organization can say no and withdraw the offer. On the other hand, if the organization accepts immediately, you may experience "winner's remorse," whereby you feel that your offer was too low.

6. Be realistic. Often, when organizations offer salaries for entry-level positions, they leave little room for negotiation. The higher you go in the organization, the more room there usually is for negotiation.

7. Be polite and direct during negotiations.

8. Never inflate your past salary or experience. Be honest in all aspects of the negotiation.

9. Remember to calculate benefits as part of the offer package. One offer may have a lower salary figure but a much more generous retirement plan. Again, do your homework.

10. Do not play "hard to get" when you have little bargaining power.

Sources: D. Gordon, "Suggested Salary Negotiation Guidelines for Recent College Graduates," 2004, at http://www.adguide.com/pages/articles/article257.htm; C. Krannich, & R.L. Krannich, "30 Salary Negotiation Mistakes to Avoid," 2004, at http://www.washingtonpost.com/wl/jobs/Content?Content=/Career_Advic.../impactadvice8.html; L.L. Thompson, *The Mind and Heart of the Negotiator*, 3rd ed. (Upper Saddle River, NJ: Prentice Hall, 2005).

As suggested in the *Managerial Advice* feature, the natural conflict over salaries and its resolution are important to both the organization and the individual involved. Jane negotiated a higher salary before accepting the job offer, but Rob did not do so. Therefore, even though Rob and Jane had equal qualifications, they were compensated differently. Furthermore, assuming that they perform at equal levels over time and thus receive the same percentage pay increase, the gap between Jane's salary and Rob's will grow. Furthermore, although the organization may save almost $14,700 over a five-year period, it may also lose a productive associate. Rob is likely to be unhappy about the difference in pay if he discovers it (which is likely). As we explained in Chapter 6, in the discussion of equity theory, Rob will feel that he is not being treated equitably. Consequently, he might search for a job with another organization. Unfortunately, if it leads to conflict between Rob and the organization, he is likely to depart for a job elsewhere. In this case, the organization loses valuable human capital.

Before closing this section on negotiation, it is important to point out that associates negotiate all the time in everyday work life. When we think of negotiations, we tend to think of formalized negotiations such as labor–management bargaining or merger-and-acquisition talks. However, negotiations take place whenever there are two parties who need to come to an agreement about a proposed course of action. Negotiation is just a means of trying to influence others to obtain outcomes that one desires. Thus, a major issue that underlies all negotiations as well as conflict situations is power.[72] When two parties try to influence each other to attempt to maximize their own outcomes or attain a target outcome, the issue of power can be critical to resolving the conflict.

Power

The concept of power is one of the most pervasive in the study of organizational behavior.[73] **Power** is generally defined as the ability of those who hold it to achieve the outcomes they desire.[74] Power can also be thought of as the ability of one person to get another person to do something that he or she would not normally do.[75] Thus, any time someone persuades another person to do something, he or she is exercising power. For example, a coach who requires players to do pushups is exercising power. A secretary who has the boss change her schedule to accommodate an associate is also exercising power.

Often, power is thought to be negative. However, little would be accomplished if power were not exercised on a regular basis.[76] Whether or not the exercise of power is harmful depends on the intent of the person holding the power. A manager who exercises power to meet organizational goals is using power in a positive, productive way. In contrast, a manager who exercises power to promote his or her personal interests, at the expense of others, is misusing power.

Power exists on different levels. Individuals and organizational units can have power. For example, a student body president can have power to influence university policy. Powerful subunits such as academic departments that bring in a great deal of external money can also influence university policy, as can the alumni association. It is generally easy to identify people in an organization or social unit who have power.[77] Think of an organization to which you belong, for example, and identify who has the power in that organization.

> **power**
> The ability to achieve the desired outcomes.

Bases of Individual Power

Power in organizations can come from many sources. John French and Bertram Raven developed one of the most commonly used typologies for describing the bases of power.[78] It includes five categories: legitimate power (formal authority), reward power, coercive power, expert power, and referent power.

LEGITIMATE POWER

People derive **legitimate power** (or formal authority) from the positions they hold in the organization. Legitimate power is narrow in scope because it can be applied only to acts that are defined as legitimate by everyone involved. For example, after being elected to a second term in 2004, President George W. Bush replaced many of the cabinet members from his first term. This was an exercise in legitimate power because the president has the formal authority to choose his cabinet members. However, when Attorney General Alberto Gonzales fired many U.S. attorneys, he came under fire because he was viewed as not having the legitimate authority to do so and his motives were questioned.[79]

> **legitimate power**
> Power derived from position; also known as formal authority.

REWARD POWER

reward power
Power resulting from the ability to provide others with desired outcomes.

Reward power results when one person believes that another has the ability to provide him or her with desired outcomes (that is, the person controls desired resources). Reward power is limited by the person's actual ability to supply desired outcomes. For example, a supervisor may have power because she can assign pay raises to associates. However, if the company has a bad year, and the supervisor is not permitted to give pay raises, then she loses this source of power. Reward power is not limited to formal sources, such as the supervisor's power to give raises; it can also come from informal sources. For example, a secretary who often controls his boss's schedule may then reward associates with access to the boss.

COERCIVE POWER

coercive power
Power resulting from the ability to punish others.

Coercive power exists when one person believes that another person has the ability to punish him or her. Coercive power is usually considered a negative form of power; thus, its use should be limited. Overuse or inappropriate application of this type of power can produce unintended results. For example, associates might respond with negative or undesired behaviors. Like reward power, coercive power can be derived from informal as well as formal sources. For example, an associate who spreads negative gossip about others may have coercive power because others fear that he will spread negative gossip about them.[80] Coercive power is limited by the fact that those being influenced must be highly dependent on the person wielding the power.[81]

EXPERT POWER

expert power
Power resulting from special expertise or technical knowledge

Expert power arises from special expertise or technical knowledge that is valuable to others or the organization. Expert power is limited by the degree to which this expertise is irreplaceable. For example, an associate can gain power by becoming the only person in the unit who knows how to use certain software. However, if others learn to use the software, this person's power will be diminished.

REFERENT POWER

referent power
Power resulting from others' desire to identify with the referent.

People are said to have **referent power** when others are attracted to them or desire to be associated with them. For example, it has been found that executives who have prestigious reputations among their colleagues and shareholders have greater influence in the strategic decision-making process in their firms, thus, giving them greater power because others want to associate with them.[82] Referent power is the most resilient type of power because it is difficult to lose once it has been achieved. In addition, referent power can be used to influence a wide range of behaviors.[83]

An Example of Power

The use of different power bases is not mutually exclusive. Associates can use multiple bases at one time. The past CEO of Disney, Michael Eisner, is an example of someone who drew power from a variety of sources.[84] During the years of Eisner's reign (1984–2006) at Disney, the entertainment giant went through a number of ups and downs. Owing to his efforts, in Eisner's early years, the company's performance improved dramatically. In recent years, Disney had experienced hostile takeover threats; the acquisition of Miramax Studios and Capital Cities/ABC; conflict with Bob and Harvey Weinstein of Miramax; a successful alliance with Pixar Animation studios; the dissolution of the alliance with Pixar; the very public and contentious resignation of Jeffrey Katzenberg as president of Disney;

constant battles with Disney family member Roy Disney; and the expensive hiring and resignation of Eisner's friend, Michael Ovitz.

Until recently, Eisner had been incredibly successful in maintaining power over Disney, despite opposition from shareholders, other Disney companies, the Disney family, and even his own executives. How did he do it? Numerous reports exist about Eisner's strategies to increase and hold his power.

First, Eisner had a great deal of legitimate power. He was both the chairman of the board of directors and the CEO. These positions allowed him to make managerial decisions while at the same time having the authority to evaluate those decisions. He also had the power to hire and fire executives and board members, almost guaranteeing that he was surrounded by people who supported him. This led to complaints by Eisner's detractors that he dominated the board by filling it with his own people, who often did not work in the best interest of other shareholders.

A second way in which Eisner obtained power was by lavishing attention on board members, important investors (like Warren Buffett and Sid Bass), members of the Disney family, and even the widows of former executives. In this way, he was able to curry favor with important Disney stakeholders. Thus, he was able to gain referent power with at least some important players.

Eisner was also a genius at limiting access to and controlling information. He wooed board members to support him by constantly supplying them with information. He stated "If I filled them in, made them my partner, if things didn't go so well, the likelihood of, 'I told you so' and those kind of reactions would not exist." At the same time, he controlled communication between executives and board members so that any disagreements, important discussions, or decisions had to go through him. When Eisner wanted to fire Michael Ovitz only months after hiring him, he went through elaborate procedures, talking to board members without Ovitz's knowledge and spreading the word that Ovitz wasn't working out.

Another way that Eisner maintained power was to divide those who might oppose him and to make himself indispensable. He encouraged and allowed rivalries between executives and board members to develop so that other important decision makers were unable to form a cohesive unit. He also refused to train or plan for who would succeed him in the chairman and CEO roles, thus making his departure a problem for Disney.

Finally, Eisner maintained power by restricting the power of others. One of the reasons that the Weinstein brothers wanted to separate Miramax from Disney was that Eisner tried to stop them from releasing the movie *Fahrenheit 911*, which was critical of the Bush administration. According to Michael Ovitz, when Eisner made the deal to hire Ovitz in 1995, he implied that the chief financial officer and the corporate operations chief would report to Ovitz. However, Ovitz soon learned at a dinner party that both of these men would report to Eisner.

By March 2004, Disney shareholders had become highly dissatisfied. Led by Roy Disney, among others, they participated in a 43 percent no-confidence vote to oust Eisner as the chairman of the Disney board. One of the major factors leading to this vote was the $140 million severance pay package that Eisner gave to Ovitz after Ovitz had been at Disney for only 15 months. Shareholders argued that they had not been given enough information about this deal and that the cost was detrimental to the company. They believed that Disney board members had buckled under Eisner's pressure at shareholders' expense. By December 2005, Eisner had stepped down as chairman; however, he stated that he planned to remain as CEO of Disney until his retirement in 2006.

It appears that Michael Eisner's use of power was sometimes inappropriate. This was a special concern because Eisner was both chairman and CEO of Disney.

Thus, he already had significant legitimate power. Furthermore, his position also gave him reward power throughout the entire company. Because of his efforts in turning around Disney after he became CEO, many perceived him to have expert power. In addition, his prominent position afforded him referent power. His actions regarding Michael Ovitz suggest that he used coercive power as well. He fired Ovitz but only after conducting a negative campaign with members of the board of directors. He then gave Ovitz an exceptionally large severance pay package. It seems that Eisner may often have acted in his own best interests and not in the best interests of the company or its shareholders. This story perhaps suggests why Disney's performance suffered during the last years of Eisner's reign.

Strategic Contingencies Model of Power

strategic contingencies model of power
Model holding that people and organizational units gain power by being able to address the major problems and issues faced by the organization.

Individuals and organizational units can also obtain power by being able to address the strategic problems that an organization faces. This is referred to as the **strategic contingencies model of power.**[85] For example, when an organization is in a highly innovative industry, where success depends on being able to develop new products, the research and development (R&D) department has a great deal of power. The R&D unit has the knowledge (human capital) critical for the success of the firm's strategy to produce innovations and compete effectively in its industry. Consider the pharmaceutical industry. Pharmaceutical firms must introduce valuable new drugs regularly, especially as their patents on their current drugs expire. Without new drugs, their revenues will decrease, and the firms will eventually die. The knowledge and expertise needed to develop new drugs is highly important to the companies' strategy. Thus, the R&D units in pharmaceutical firms often have significant power. Essentially, these units control resources that are valuable to the organization.[86]

Individuals or units may obtain power, then, by identifying the strategic contingencies faced by an organization and gaining control over them. For example, in the United Airlines case discussed earlier in this chapter, management (which controls the financial resources) gained more power by arguing that financial difficulties could be solved only by the unions' agreement to salary and pension concessions. However, the unions (which control the human capital) gained power by causing work slowdowns, so that the most immediate problem for the organization was to get its flights running on schedule again. The strategy of operating flights on time and satisfying customers was negatively affected by the union's exercise of its power. Thus, the unions controlled the most important of the resources for the strategy and had more power at that point.

If people or units are able to identify the resources or other contingencies important to the organization's strategy and performance and control them, they should be able to maintain their bases of power. They can then use that power to require the organization to act in ways that benefit them. Take, for example, an athletic department that brings a great deal of alumni money to its university. Because of its ability to provide the university with financial resources, the athletic department has power. The department then uses that power to demand that the university provide more resources to the athletic department. In so doing, the athletic department gains even more power.

Strategic contingency power also comes from dependency.[87] Dependency occurs when someone has something that another person wants or needs and is in control of the desired resource. For example, in the popular TV show *The Sopranos,* all the gangsters are dependent on Tony Soprano, the mob boss. Because Tony controls all of the mob's "businesses" (such as phone-card fraud rings and truck-hijacking operations), the gangsters are able to make a living only if Tony allows them to operate one of these businesses.

Another source of controlling critical contingencies is the ability to cope with uncertainty.[88] Uncertainty creates threats for the organization. Anyone who can help reduce this uncertainty will gain power. In the opening case, it was implied that environmental organizations have achieved greater power and influence with businesses. There are several reasons for this, including the uncertainties of tougher environmental regulations and the growing public concern with environmental issues. Environmental organizations gain power because they can help businesses deal with these uncertainties.

Yet another way in which people or units can control critical contingencies is by being irreplaceable.[89] One of the power moves made by Michael Eisner at Disney was to avoid developing a succession plan. After all, if no one was prepared to replace him, the board would be unlikely to ask him to resign.[90] In contrast, Jack Welch, the former CEO of General Electric, announced 10 years before stepping down that finding a successor was the most important job he had to do.[91]

Finally, strategic contingency power can result from controlling the decision process, either by setting parameters on the types of solutions that are acceptable or by controlling the range of alternatives to be considered.[92] For example, consider a class project in which student project teams must choose a company to analyze. If a team member states that he knows what types of projects the professor prefers and what types of projects have received good grades in the past, he can gain a great deal of control over the group's decision regarding the type of project on which they will work.

Organizational Politics

When conflict is present in organizations, associates are likely to engage in political behavior. Indeed, politics are a fact of life in most organizations.[93] **Organizational politics** involve behavior that is directed toward furthering one's own self-interests without concern for the interests or well-being of others.[94] The goal of political behavior is to exert influence on others. A recent survey of top-level executives and human resource managers indicates that organizational politics are on the rise.[95] Seventy percent of respondents to this survey said that they had been harmed by the political behavior of others and 45 percent said they had gained power and influence by acting politically. In the following, we discuss the conditions under which political behavior is more likely to occur.[96]

Political behavior can occur at several levels. At the individual level, it involves an associate who uses politics to suit his best interests, such as an individual who attempts to take sole credit for a project that was jointly completed. Political behavior at the group level often takes place in the form of coalitions. **Coalitions** are groups whose members act in an integrated manner to actively pursue a common interest. For example, when a new CEO must be chosen for an organization, groups of shareholders may act together to influence the board of directors' choice of a particular successor. Politics can also occur at the organizational level, such as when particular organizations hire lobbyists who try to influence congresspersons' votes on issues important to that organization.

organizational politics
Behavior that is directed toward furthering one's own self-interests without concern for the interests or well-being of others.

coalition
A group whose members act together to actively pursue a common interest.

Political tactics can also be aimed at any target. Upward political influence refers to individual or group influence on those in a superior position, such as their manager. Lateral politics refers to attempts to influence targets at the same hierarchical level. Finally, downward influence refers to attempts to influence those lower down in the hierarchy.

What do politics look like in organizations? In other words, what do people do to engage in political behavior? A great deal of research has examined the political tactics used within or by organizations.[97] These tactics include the following:

- *Rational persuasion.* A rational persuasion tactic involves using logical arguments or factual information to persuade targets that the persuader's request will result in beneficial outcomes. For example, a sales associate who is the number-one seller may tell her boss all the benefits of switching to a purely commission-based compensation system while ignoring the potential disadvantages.

- *Consultation.* A consultation tactic requires getting the target to participate in the planning or execution of whatever the politician wants accomplished. For example, a CEO who wants to implement a specific strategy would consult associates at every relevant organizational level to gain their support of her plan.

- *Personal appeal.* A personal appeal tactic often focuses on the target's loyalty or affection immediately prior to asking for her help in doing something. For example, an associate may remind targets about how he has always supported their ideas and causes before asking them to support his idea.

- *Ingratiation.* An ingratiation tactic makes the target feel good by flattering or helping him. For example, a person may tell a colleague how valuable he is before asking for his help to do something.

- *Inspirational appeal.* An inspirational appeal tactic is used to generate the enthusiasm and support of targets by appealing to their important values and ideals. For example, to obtain a target's support for her new web-based advertising plan, a person may appeal to an ecology-conscious target by explaining how electronic advertising saves trees as opposed to advertising in newspapers and magazines.

- *Exchange.* Using an exchange tactic, a person volunteers a favor in order to gain a favor in return. This is exemplified by the old axiom, "I'll scratch your back if you'll scratch mine."

- *Coalition.* As discussed above, a coalition tactic is used when people with common interests join together to pursue their common interests. For example, a coalition is represented by ethnic and minority group members who band together to promote organizational diversity.

- *Legitimizing.* A legitimizing tactic involves making a request seem legitimate or official. For example, an associate who wants to complete a project in a certain manner will try to convince targets that this is "how management wants it done."

- *Pressure.* A pressure tactic involves threats, nagging, or demands as a means of influencing targets. For example, an associate who threatens to expose a target's secret if the target does not comply with her wishes is using pressure tactics.

Recent events at Morgan Stanley, the large financial services firm, illustrate the use of some of these political tactics.[98] Over the five-year period ending in April 2005, Morgan Stanley stock lost one-third of its value, and the company was performing worse than its major competitors. In March 2005, a group of eight disgruntled Morgan Stanley ex-executives initiated a process intended to oust the CEO, Philip Purcell. Because they collectively owned only 1.1 percent of Morgan Stanley shares, they needed to convince other shareholders that Purcell should go.[99] One action they took involved sending a letter to other shareholders blaming the company's poor performance solely on Purcell's leadership. Because there are likely to be many causes for an organization's poor performance, this statement can be seen as a legitimizing tactic because they state the cause of the problem with assumed expertise (substantial experience in Morgan Stanley and the industry). The dissenters also personally courted shareholders, displaying ingratiation. Another tactic used by the dissenters was to speak passionately about the future of Morgan Stanley. This was done by Robert Scott, who was the ex-president and would-be-CEO of the company. Unfortunately for Scott, many investors were concerned only with short-term profit, so his inspirational appeal held little sway over investors. As one independent analyst noted, "People who hold those shares are going to want something concrete before they give up their votes"[100]; he suggested that the dissenters use an exchange tactic instead. As of late April 2005, Purcell continued as CEO, but the walls were beginning to crumble. Many important Morgan Stanley executives and senior analysts were deserting for competitors, and a large shareholder publicly expressed support for the dissenters. Thus, it was unclear whether the Morgan Stanley dissenters would be successful in their political actions to oust the CEO.

Research has examined the issue of who is better or more successful in behaving politically. One line of research has found that personality is related to the types of political tactics people are likely to use.[101] For example, extraverts are likely to use inspirational appeals and ingratiation, whereas people high on conscientiousness are most likely to use rational appeals. Also, people have varying abilities to engage in political behavior. Some people are quite good at it, but others are more transparent in their actions, thus alerting the target to their intentions. Recent research has identified an individual difference known as political skill that affects the successful use of political tactics. **Political skill** is the ability to effectively understand others at work and to use this knowledge to enhance one's own objectives.[102] People with strong political skills have the following qualities:[103]

political skill
The ability to effectively understand others at work and to use this knowledge to enhance one's own objectives.

- They find it easy to imagine themselves in others' positions or take another's point of view.
- They can understand situations and determine the best response. They can adjust their behavior to fit the situation.
- They develop large networks and are known by a great many people.
- They can easily gain the cooperation of others.
- They make others feel at ease.

Individuals with strong political skills can use them to the advantage of the organization (e.g., gaining the cooperation of diverse groups). Using political skills for one's own political gain, however, can harm the organization. Therefore, political skills can be positive, but only if used to achieve the appropriate goals.

The Strategic Lens

Managing conflict and the exercise of power are important to the success organizations enjoy. As we learned in the chapter opener, companies such as Dell, DuPont, and Wal-Mart have learned to develop win-win solutions with environmentalist organizations, which not only has had a positive impact on the companies' performance but will also benefit society. In an *Experiencing Strategic Organizational Behavior* feature, it was shown how United Airlines' inability to manage conflict led to difficulties that may eventually prove insurmountable. Most strategic leaders must deal with conflict while making decisions. Some of this conflict is functional; it produces better decisions because it forces consideration of a broader range of alternatives. Much of the conflict that occurs in organizations is dysfunctional, however. If the organization's strategy is to be effectively implemented, this conflict must be resolved, or at least managed. Negotiation is one way to resolve conflict.

Some conflict can be resolved through the exercise of power. In addition, people and units that have power because they control critical contingencies or resources can add a great deal of value to the organization. Most strategic leaders have considerable power, especially legitimate power, and their use of power is necessary for the achievement of their organizations' goals. Yet they must exercise their power appropriately, or it could produce undesired consequences. Michael Eisner exercised his power primarily for his own benefit rather than in the best interests of the organization. By exercising power in this way, he created considerable internal politics (e.g., others vying for influence and working in their own best interests) throughout the organization. As a result, Disney's performance suffered. Similarly, the exercise of political behavior at Morgan Stanley cost the organization the loss of valuable human capital from which it may not be able to recover. The use of political tactics often has negative consequences for the organization. However, the attributes of people with political skills are not negative. These skills, such as easily gaining cooperation from others, can be especially helpful to managers. The skills are negative only if they are used for personal gain at the expense of others and the organization. They are especially bad when exercised by the CEO or other top managers (e.g., at Morgan Stanley) because they tend to have significant effects on the organization and others.

Critical Thinking Questions

1. Can you describe a situation in which conflict was functional (i.e., it had positive outcomes)? If so, in what ways was the conflict functional?

2. A strategic leader must use power in many actions that she takes. In what ways can she exercise this power to achieve positive outcomes?

3. How can knowledge of conflict, negotiations, power, and politics in organizations help you be more successful in your career? Please be specific.

What This Chapter Adds to Your Knowledge Portfolio

This chapter has explored conflict, negotiation, power, and politics in organizations. It has covered the nature and types of conflict, causes of conflict, outcomes of conflict, responses to conflict, and how organizations can manage conflict. The chapter has also discussed various sources of power. In summary, we have made the following points:

- Conflict can be either functional or dysfunctional for organizational effectiveness. Functional conflict leads to creativity and positive change. Dysfunctional conflict detracts from the achievement of organizational goals.

- Conflict is the process in which one party perceives that its interests are being opposed or negatively affected by another party. Conflict can be classified as personal, substantive, or procedural conflict. Personal conflict occurs when there are personal differences between parties; substantive conflict concerns the work that is to be done; and procedural conflict concerns how work is to be accomplished.

- Causes of conflict include structural causes (for example, increased specialization), communication problems, cognitive factors (for example, differing expectations), individual differences (for example, personality), and the history of the parties (for example, their previous interactions).

- Conflict escalation occurs when the conflict is not resolved and becomes worse. Resolution outcomes of conflict include lose-lose, win-lose/lose-win, compromise, and win-win.

- Parties to a conflict can adopt one of several responses to the conflict: competing, accommodating, avoiding, compromising, or collaborating. These responses vary to the degree in which they reflect assertiveness and cooperativeness on the part of conflicting parties.

- Often negotiations are required to resolve the conflict. Managers may act as a third party, using both mediator and, if necessary, arbitrator roles to achieve a negotiated settlement.

- Distributive and integrative negotiation strategies focus on either winning or reaching a mutually beneficial outcome. Attitudinal restructuring focuses on developing positive feelings and relationships between negotiating parties.

- Power is the ability of those who hold it to achieve the outcomes they desire. Nothing would be accomplished in organizations if individuals did not exercise power.

- Individuals can obtain power through several means. The bases of power include legitimate power, reward power, coercive power, expert power, and referent power. Referent power can influence a wider range of behaviors than the other four types of power.

- The strategic contingencies model of power suggests that individuals or units can obtain power by being able to address the important problems or issues facing the organization. Power can be obtained by defining the critical contingencies facing an organization, creating dependency, being able to cope with uncertainty, being irreplaceable, and controlling the decision-making process.

- Organizational politics is a fact of life in most organizations. Political behavior can be carried out through a wide range of tactics. The extent to which a politician is successful in achieving his or her own goals depends on political skill.

Back to the Knowledge Objectives

1. Under what circumstances can conflict be functional? When is conflict dysfunctional? Which of the basic types of conflict are likely to be dysfunctional, and why?

2. Why does conflict often develop?

3. What is conflict escalation, and what conditions make it likely? What are other possible outcomes of conflict?

4. How do people respond to conflict, and under what circumstances is each type of response most effective?

5. What can organizations do to manage conflict?

6. Describe basic negotiating strategies and the tactics most likely to accomplish those strategies.

7. Why is the exercise of power necessary for organizations to operate effectively? What are some of the ways in which people gain power in organizations?

8. Why is political behavior common in organizations? How do people go about carrying out political behavior, and what makes them successful at it?

Thinking about Ethics

1. Under what circumstances is it ethically appropriate to use coercive power? When should managers not use coercive power to deal with problems in organizations?

2. How can a manager know when conflict is functional? How can conflict be managed to ensure that it remains functional? Do managers have a responsibility to ensure that conflict is functional or to eliminate dysfunctional conflict?

3. You are chairman of the board and CEO of a major corporation. Is it appropriate for you to select the other board members? Why or why not?

4. If you control resources that are critical to an organization, you have power. Are there circumstances in which it would be acceptable to use that power to garner more resources for your unit (and thus more power)?

5. You have recently hired five new associates in your unit, all of whom have excellent knowledge and skills. Each was offered a beginning annual salary of $100,000. Four of them accepted the salary offered, but one negotiated for $5,000 more. Should you give each of the other associates $5,000 more as well? Over time, such an action would cost your unit and the organization considerable money. If you take no action, what do you expect the long-term consequences to be?

Key Terms

Conflict, p. 404
Dysfunctional conflict, p. 404
Functional conflict, p. 405
Personal conflict, p. 405
Substantive conflict, p. 406
Procedural conflict, p. 406
Conflict escalation, p. 415

Negotiation, p. 418
Distributive bargaining, p. 418
Integrative bargaining, p. 418
Attitudinal structuring, p. 420
Power, p. 423
Legitimate power, p. 423
Reward power, p. 424

Coercive power, p. 424
Expert power, p. 424
Referent power, p. 424
Strategic contingencies model of power, p. 426
Organizational politics, p. 427
coalition, p. 427
political skill, p. 429

Building Your Human Capital

Are You Ready to Manage with Power?

Any type of managerial task requires the exercise of power. After all, power is the ability to get others to do something you want them to do. Thus, any time you find yourself in a situation in which you need to get others to do something, you need to exercise power. However, many people are uncomfortable thinking about using power. The next time you find yourself in a situation in which you need to influence others, consider the following questions before acting:

1. What are your goals? What are you trying to accomplish?
2. Diagnose patterns of dependency. Who will be influential in allowing you to achieve your goal? Who is dependent on you for certain outcomes?

3. What do you think others will feel about what you are trying to do? Do you think there will be resistance?

4. What are the power bases of those you wish to influence? For example, do they have reward power? referent power?

5. What are your bases of power and influence? What rewards or valued outcomes can you control? What type of power can you exert to gain more control over the situation?

A Strategic Organizational Behavior Moment

The Making of the Brooklyn Bluebirds

The Brooklyn Bluebirds is a professional baseball team. Years ago, it was the best team in professional baseball. Then it hit a period of almost 10 years without a pennant. Recently, though, things have been looking up. A new owner, Trudy Mills, acquired the Bluebirds and proclaimed that she intended to make them world champions again.

Trudy quickly began to use her wealth to rebuild the team by acquiring big-name players in the free-agent draft. She also signed a manager well known for his winning ways, Marty Bellman. Marty was also known for his "fighting ways" on and off the field. However, Trudy was more concerned with his winning record.

The first year of Trudy's and Marty's tenure, the Bluebirds came in second in the division, showing it was a team to be reckoned with. Trudy acquired even more big-name players in the free-agent draft. Everyone was predicting a pennant for the Bluebirds in the coming year.

The year began with great expectations. During the first month, the Bluebirds looked unstoppable. At the end of the month, the team was in first place with a record of 20 wins and 7 losses. But then problems began. Rumors of conflict between players were reported in the sports columns. Russ Thompson, a five-year veteran and starting first baseman, publicly stated that he wanted to renegotiate his contract. (He was unhappy that Trudy had brought in so many players at much higher salaries than his.) He and his lawyer met with Trudy and the Bluebirds' general manager, but the meeting ended in disagreement. Both Russ and Trudy were angry.

The team's record began to deteriorate, and by the All-Star Game at midseason, the Bluebirds had lost as many games as they had won and were back in fourth place. Right after the All-Star break, Marty decided he had to make a move. He benched both Russ Thompson and Mickey Ponds, a well-known player with a multimillion-dollar contract. Marty called them to his office and said, "You guys are not playing baseball up to your abilities. I think you've been loafing. When you decide to start playing baseball and quit counting your money or worrying how pretty you look on television, I'll put you back in the starting lineup. Until then, you can sit on the bench and cheer for your teammates."

Russ responded hotly, "The owner won't pay me what I'm worth, and now you won't play me. I don't want to play for the Bluebirds anymore. I'm going to ask to be traded."

Mickey was no happier than Russ. "I'm going to Trudy. You can't bench me. You're the biggest jerk I've ever played for!"

At that, both players left his office, got dressed, and left the ballpark. Later, a few minutes before game time, Marty received a phone call in his office. It was Trudy, and she was upset. "Why did you bench Russ and Mickey? I hired you to manage the team, not create more problems. They're two of our best players, and the customers pay to see them play. I want you to apologize to them and put them back in the starting lineup."

Marty was not known for his diplomacy. "You hired me to manage, and that's just what I'm doing. Keep your nose out of my business. You may own the team, but I manage it. Russ and Mickey will stay benched until I say otherwise!" With that, Marty slammed the receiver down and headed for the field to get the game under way.

Discussion Questions

1. Describe the types of conflict that seem to exist within the Bluebirds organization. What are the causes?

2. Is the conflict functional, dysfunctional, or both? Explain.

3. Assume that Trudy has hired you as a consultant to help her resolve the conflict. Describe the steps that you would take.

Team Exercise

Managing Conflict

The purpose of this exercise is to develop a better understanding of the conflict-management process by examining three different conflict situations.

Procedure

1. With the aid of the instructor, the class should be divided into four- or five-person teams.
2. The teams should read each case and determine:
   a. What conflict response should be used to manage the conflict (this may require starting with one style and moving to others as the situation changes).
   b. What resolution tactics should be used to resolve the conflict.
3. Each team should appoint a leader to explain its results to the class.
4. The instructor should call on the teams to explain the conflict response and resolution tactics recommended. The recommendations should be recorded on a board or flipchart for comparisons. The situations should be discussed one at a time.
5. The instructor will lead a general discussion regarding the application of conflict responses and resolution tactics.

This exercise usually requires about 25 minutes for case analyses and another 20 to 30 minutes (depending on the number of teams) for class discussion.

Case Incident 1

You are James Whittington, manager of internal auditing. The nature of your position and of your unit's work often put you in conflict with managers of other units. Most of your audits of unit operations support the actions taken, although a few do not. However, the managers seem to resent what they consider an intrusion on their authority when the audits are conducted. You have come to accept this resentment as a part of your job, although you would prefer that it didn't occur. One case has been a particular problem. Bill Wilson, manager of compensation in the personnel department, has created problems every time your auditors have worked in his department. He has continually tried to hold back information necessary for the audit. Unfortunately, during the last year and a half, you have had to audit activities in his department several times.

Your department now has been assigned to audit the incentive bonus calculations for executives made by Bill's department. Bill was irate when he discovered that you were again going to audit his employees' work. When he found out about it, he called your office and left a message for you not to send your employees down, because he was not going to allow them access to the information. You are now trying to decide how to respond.

Case Incident 2

Irene Wilson is manager of corporate engineering and has a staff of 17 professional engineers. The group is project oriented and thus must be flexible in structure and operation. Irene likes to hire only experienced engineers, preferably with division experience in the firm. However, during the last several years, the market for engineers has been highly competitive. Owing to shortages of experienced personnel, Irene has had to hire a few young engineers right after college graduation.

Robert Miller was one of those young engineers. Robert was considered a good recruit, but his lack of experience and arrogance have created some problems.

Irene has tried to work with him to help him gain the needed experience but has not yet discussed his arrogant attitude with him.

Last week, Robert got into an argument with several engineers from the International Division with whom he was working on a project. One of them called Irene, and she met with Robert and discussed it with him. Irene thought Robert would do better after their discussion. However, a few minutes ago, Irene received a call from the project manager, who was very angry. He and Robert had just had a shouting match, and he demanded that Robert be taken off the project. Irene did not commit to anything but said she would call him back. When Irene confronted Robert about the phone call that she had just received, he turned his anger on her. They also had an argument. Irene believes Robert has potential and does not want to lose him, but he has to overcome his problems.

Case Incident 3

Steve Bassett, a supervisor in the marketing research department, is scheduled to attend a meeting of the budget committee this afternoon at 1:30. Sarah McDonald, supervisor of budget analysis, is also a member of the committee. It has been a bad day for Steve; he and his wife argued about money as he left the house, one of his key employees called in sick, and the company's computer system went down at 9:00 this morning. Steve is not fond of being a member of this committee and really does not care to waste his valuable time listening to Sarah today. (He thinks that Sarah talks too much.)

Steve arrives at Sarah's office at 1:38 P.M. After glancing at her watch and offering a few harmless pleasantries, Sarah begins her assessment of the budget committee's agenda. Although not exciting, everything seems to be all right until she mentions how poorly Steve's unit has been responding to the budgeting department's requests for information. Steve becomes visibly irritated and tells Sarah that nothing good has ever come out of these committee meetings and that she places entirely too much emphasis on them. Sarah responds by noting that Steve has not followed company policy about preparing budget information. These failures, she reasons, are the causes of his inability to achieve positive results. Having heard this comment, Steve states, in a loud voice, that whoever designed the company's policy did not know a thing about the budgeting process.

Sarah realizes that she and Steve are in disagreement and that she should try to deal with it. How, she wonders, should she deal with Steve?

Endnotes

1. Dechant, K., & Altman, B. 1994. Environmental leadership: From compliance to competitive advantage. *Academy of Management Executive*, 8: 7–27; Porter, M.E., & Kramer, M.R., 2006. The link between competitive advantage and corporate social responsibility. *Harvard Business Review*, 84(12): 78–92.

2. Porter, M.E., & Kramer, M.R., 2006. The link between competitive advantage and corporate social responsibility. *Harvard Business Review*, 84(12): 78–92.

3. Shatwell, J. 2007. The net loss of overfishing. At http:www.conservation.org/xp/frontlines/partners/06060601.xml.

4. Grayson, D., & Hodges, A. 2004. *Corporate social opportunity*. Greenleaf.

5. Chatterji, A., & Levine, D. 2006. Breaking down the wall of codes: Evaluating non-financial performance measurement. *California Management Review*, 48(2): 29–51.

6. Orlitzky, F., Schmidt, F., & Rynes, S. 2003. Corporate social and financial performance: A meta-analysis. *Organizational Studies*, 24: 403–411.

7. Collier, J., & Esteban, R. 2007. Corporate social responsibility and employee commitment. *Business Ethics*, 16(1): 12–31.

8. Turban, D.B., & Greening, D.W. 1997. Corporate social performance and organizational attractiveness to perspective employees. *Academy of Management Journal*, 40: 848–868.

9. Wall, J.A. Jr., & Callister, R.R. 1995. Conflict and its management. *Journal of Management*, 21: 515–558.

10. Jackson, S.E., & Schuler, R. 1985. A meta-analysis and occupational critique of research on role ambiguity and role conflict in work settings. *Organizational Behavior and Human Decision Processes*, 36: 16–78.

11. Orlitzky, F., Schmidt, F., & Rynes, S. 2003. Corporate social and financial performance: A meta-analysis. *Organizational Studies*, 24: 403–411; Bromiley, P. 1990. On the use of finance theory in strategic management. In P. Shrivastava and R. Lamb (Eds.), *Advances in strategic management (Vol. 6)*. Greenwich, CT: JAI Press, pp. 71–98; Nixon, R.D., Hitt, M.A., Lee, H., & Jeong, E. 2004. Market reactions to announcements of corporate downsizing actions and implementation strategies. *Strategic Management Journal*, 25: 1121–1129.

12. Porter, M.E., & Kramer, M.R., 2006. The link between competitive advantage and corporate social responsibility. *Harvard Business Review*, 84 (12): 78–92.

13. Lippitt, G.L. 1982. Managing conflict in today's organizations. *Training and Development Journal*, 36: 66–72, 74.

14. Pelled, L.H. 1996. Demographic diversity, conflict, and work group outcomes: An intervening process theory. *Organizational Science*, 6: 615–631; Tjosvold, D. 1991. Rights and responsibilities of dissent: Cooperative conflict. *Employee Responsibilities and Rights Journal*, 4: 13–23.

15. Herbert, T.T. 1977. Improving executive decisions by formalizing dissent: The corporate devil's advocate. *Academy of Management Review*, 2: 662–667.

16. Eisenhardt, K., & Schoonhoven, C. 1990. Organizational growth: Linking founding team, strategy, environment, and growth among U.S. semiconductor ventures: 1978–1988. *Administrative Science Quarterly*, 35: 504–529.

17. Jehn, K.A. 1997. A qualitative analysis of conflict types and dimensions in organizational groups. *Administrative Science Quarterly*, 42: 530–557.

18. Ibid.

19. Jehn, K.A., & Mannix, E.A. 2001. The dynamic nature of conflict: A longitudinal study of intragroup conflict and group performance. *Academy of Management Journal*, 44: 238–251.

20. Deutsch, M. 1969. Conflicts: Productive and destructive. *Journal of Social Issues*, 25: 7–41.

21. Jehn, K.A. 1997. A qualitative analysis of conflict types and dimensions in organizational groups. *Administrative Science Quarterly*, 42: 530–557.

22. Smolowitz, I. 1998. Organizational fratricide: The roadblock to maximum performance. *Business Forum*, 23: 45–46.

23. Jehn, K.A. 1995. A multimethod examination of the benefits and detriments of intragroup conflict. *Administrative Science Quarterly*, 40: 256–282; Schweiger, D., Sandberg, W., & Rechner, P. 1989. Experiential effects of dialectical inquiry, devil's advocacy, and consensus approaches to strategic decision making. *Academy of Management Journal*, 29: 745–772; Tjosvold, D. 1991. Rights and responsibilities of dissent: Cooperative conflict. *Employee Responsibilities and Rights Journal*, 4: 13–23.

24. Eisenhardt, K., & Schoonhoven, C. 1990. Organizational growth: Linking founding team, strategy, environment, and growth among U.S. semiconductor ventures: 1978–1988. *Administrative Science Quarterly*, 35: 504–529.

25. Jehn, K.A. 1997. A qualitative analysis of conflict types and dimensions in organizational groups. *Administrative Science Quarterly*, 42: 530–557.

26. Jehn, K.A., Northcraft, G., & Neale, M. 1999. Why differences make a difference: A field study of diversity, conflict, and performance in workgroups. *Administrative Science Quarterly*, 44: 741–763.

27. Lawrence, P.R., & Lorsch, J.W. 1967. *Organization and environment: Managing differentiation and integration*. Boston: Harvard University Press.

28. Morgan, C.P., & Hitt, M.A. 1977. Validity and factor structure of House—Rizzo's effectiveness scales. *Academy of Management*, 20: 165–169; Hitt, M.A., & Morgan, C.P. 1977. Organizational climate as a predictor of organizational practices. *Psychological Reports*, 40: 1191–1199.

29. Wall, J.A. Jr., & Callister, R.R. 1995. Conflict and its management. *Journal of Management*, 21: 515–558.

30. Moline, A. 2001. Conflict in the work place. *Plants, Sites, and Parks*, 28: 50–52.

31. Ibid.

32. Heneman, H.G. III, & Judge, T.A. 2003. *Staffing organizations*. Boston: McGraw-Hill/Irwin.

33. Filley, A.C. 1975. *Interpersonal conflict resolution*. Glenview, IL: Scott Foresman, p. 10.

34. Putnam, L.L., & Poole, M.S. 1987. Conflict and negotiation. In F.M. Jablin, L.L. Putnam, K.H. Roberts, & L.W. Porter (Eds.), *Handbook of organizational communication: An interdisciplinary perspective*. Newbury Park, CA: Sage, pp. 549–599.

35. Shafer, W.E., Park, L.J., & Liao, W.M. 2002. Professionalism, organizational-professional conflict, and work outcomes: A study of certified accountants. *Accounting, Auditing, and Accountability Journal*, 15: 46–68.

36. Kaplowitz, N. 1990. National self-images, perception of enemies, and conflict strategies: Psychopolitical dimensions of international relations. *Political Psychology*, 11: 39–81.

37. Wall, J.A. Jr., & Callister, R.R. 1995. Conflict and its management. *Journal of Management*, 21: 515–558.

38. Kahn, R.L., & Byosiere, P. 1992. Stress in organizations. In M.D. Dunnette, & L.M. Hough (Eds.), *Handbook of industrial and organizational psychology (Vol. 3)*. Palo Alto, CA: Consulting Psychologists Press, pp. 571–650.

39. Baron, R.A. 1990. Countering the effects of destructive criticism: The relative efficacy of four interventions. *Journal of Applied Psychology*, 75: 235–245.

40. Rousseau, D.M., Ditkin, S.B., Burt, R.S., & Camerer, C. 1998. Not so different after all: A cross-discipline view of trust. *Academy of Management Review*, 23: 393–404.

41. Yamagishi, T. 1986. The provision of a sanctioning system as a public good. *Journal of Personality and Social Psychology*, 50: 110–116.

42. De Dreu, C.K.W., Geibels, E., & Van de Vliert, E. 1998. Social motives and trust in integrative negotiation: The disruptive effects of punitive capability. *Journal of Applied Psychology*, 83: 408–422.

43. Van Kleef, G.A., & De Dreu, C.K.W. 2006. Supplication and appeasement in conflict and negotiation: The interpersonal effects of disappointment, worry, guilt, and regret. *Journal of Personality and Social Psychology*, 91: 124–142.

44. Augsberger, D.W. 1992. *Conflict mediation across cultures: Pathways and patterns*. Louisville, KY: Westminster/John Knox.

45. Leung, K. 1995. Negotiation and reward allocations across cultures. In P.C. Earley, & M. Erez (Eds.), *New perspectives on industrial/organizational psychology*. San Francisco: Jossey-Bass, pp. 640–675.

46. Fu, J.H., Morris, M.W., Lee, S., Chao, M., Chiu, C., & Hong, Y. 2007. Epistemic motives and cultural conformity: Need for closure, culture, and context as determinants of conflict judgments. *Journal of Personality and Social Psychology*, 92: 191–207.

47. Wall, J.A. Jr., & Callister, R.R. 1995. Conflict and its management. *Journal of Management*, 21: 515–558.

48. Ibid.

49. Staw, B., Sandelands, L., & Dutton, J. 1981. Threat-rigidity effects in organizational behavior: A multi-level analysis. *Administrative Science Quarterly*, 26: 501–524.

50. Ibid.

51. Peterson, R.S., & Behfar, K.J. 2003. The dynamic relationship between performance feedback, trust and conflict in groups: A longitudinal study. *Organizational Behavior and Human Decision Processes,* 92: 102–112.

52. Wall, J.A. Jr., & Callister, R.R. 1995. Conflict and its management. *Journal of Management,* 21: 515–558.

53. O'Connor, K.M., Arnold, J.A., & Burris, E.R. 2005. Negotiators' bargaining histories and their effects on future negotiation performance. *Journal of Applied Psychology,* 90: 350–362.

54. Pruitt, D.G., & Rubin, J.Z. 1986. *Social conflict: Escalation, stalemate, and settlement.* New York: McGraw-Hill.

55. Deutsch, M. 1990. Sixty years of conflict. *International Journal of Conflict Management,* 1: 237–263.

56. Fisher, R.J. 1990. *The social psychology of intergroup and international conflict resolution.* New York: Springer-Verlag.

57. Ember, C.R., & Ember, M. 1994. War, socialization, and interpersonal violence: A cross-cultural study. *Journal of Conflict Resolution,* 38: 620–646.

58. Pruitt, D.G., & Carnevale, P.J. 1993. *Negotiation in social conflict.* Pacific Grove, CA: Brooks/Cole.

59. Ibid.

60. Morrill, C., & Thomas, C.K. 1992. Organizational conflict management as disputing process. *Human Communication Research,* 18: 400–428.

61. Retzinger, S.M. 1991. Shame, anger, and conflict: Case study of emotional violence. *Journal of Family Violence,* 6: 37–59.

62. Brockner, J., Nathanson, S., Friend, A., Harbeck, J., Samuelson, C., Houser, R., Bazerman, M.H., & Rubin, J.Z. 1984. The role of modeling processes in the "knee deep in the big muddy" phenomenon. *Organizational Behavior and Human Performance,* 33: 77–99.

63. Thomas, K.W. 1976. Conflict and conflict management. In M. Dunnette (Ed.), *Handbook of industrial and organizational psychology.* Chicago: Rand McNally, pp. 889–935.

64. Thomas, K.W. 1992. Conflict and negotiation processes. In M.D. Dunnette, & L.M. Hough (Eds.), *Handbook of industrial and organizational psychology (Vol. 3).* Palo Alto, CA: Consulting Psychologists Press, pp. 651–717.

65. Buller, P.F., Kohls, J.J., & Anderson, K.S. 2000. When ethics collide: Managing conflict across cultures. *Organizational Dynamics,* 28: 52–66.

66. Ibid.

67. Lippitt, G.L. 1982. Managing conflict in today's organizations. *Training and Development Journal,* 36: 66–72, 74.

68. Lewicki, R.J., Barry, B., & Saunders, D.M. 2006. *Negotiation* (5th ed.). Boston: McGraw-Hill/Irwin.

69. Walton, R.E., & McKersie, R.B. 1965. *A behavioral theory of labor negotiations.* New York, NY: McGraw-Hill.

70. Ibid.

71. Thompson, L.L. 2005. *The mind and heart of the negotiator* (3rd ed.). Upper Saddle River, NJ: Prentice-Hall; Cormack, G.W. 2005. *Negotiation skills for board professionals.* Mill Creek, WA: CSE Group; Dietmeyer, B. *Negotiation: A breakthrough four-step process for effective business negotiation.* Chicago: Dearborn Trade; Sperber, P. 1983. *Fail-safe business negotiating.* Englewood Cliffs, NJ: Prentice-Hall.

72. Somech, A., & Drach-Zahavy, A. 2002. Relative power and influence strategy: The effects of agent-target organizational power on superiors' choices of influence strategies. *Journal of Organizational Behavior,* 23: 167–181.

73. Dahl, R.A. 1957. The concept of power. *Behavioral Science,* 2: 201–215.

74. Salancik, G.R., & Pfeffer, J. 1977. Who gets power and how they hold on to it: A strategic contingency model of power. *Organizational Dynamics,* 5: 3–21.

75. Dahl, R.A. 1957. The concept of power. *Behavioral Science,* 2: 201–215.

76. Pfeffer, J. 1992. Understanding power in organizations. *California Management Review,* 34: 29–50.

77. Salancik, G.R., & Pfeffer, J. 1977. Who gets power and how they hold on to it: A strategic contingency model of power. *Organizational Dynamics,* 5: 3–21.

78. French, J.R.P., & Raven, B. 1959. The bases of social power. In D. Cartwright (Ed.), *Studies in social power.* Ann Arbor: University of Michigan Institute for Social Research, pp. 160–167.

79. Eggen, D. 2007. Deputy attorney general defends prosecutor firings. *Washington Post,* February 7, at http:// washintonpost.com/wp-dyn/content/article/2007/02/06/AR2007020600732.htm.

80. Kurland, N.B., & Pelled, L.H. 2000. Passing the word: Toward a model of gossip and power in the workplace. *Academy of Management Review,* 25: 428–438.

81. Bacharach, S.B., & Lawler, E.J. 1980. *Power and politics in organizations.* San Francisco: Jossey-Bass.

82. Finkelstein, S. 1992. Power in top management teams: Dimensions, measurement, and validation. *Academy of Management Journal,* 35: 505–539.

83. French & Raven, The bases of social power. In Cartwright (Ed.), *Studies in social power.*

84. Crawford, K. 2004. "Eisner vs. Ovitz: This time in court," *CNN Money,* October 15, at http://money.cnn.com/2004/10/15/news/fortune500/ovitz; Levine, G. 2004. "Eisner: Disney, Miramax talks staggered," *Forbes,* May 12, at http://www.forbes.com/2004/05/12/0512autofacescan03.html; McCarthy, M. 2004. "Eisner foes keep up the pressure," *USA Today,* March 16, at usatoday.com/money/media/2004-03-16-eisner_x.htm; McCarthy, M. 2004. "Disney strips chairmanship from Eisner," *USA Today,* March 3, at http://www.usatoday.com/money/media/2004-03-03disney-shareholder-meeting_x.htm; Orwall, B. 2004. "Behind the scenes at Eisner's Disney: Beleaguered CEO, Ovitz, we're headed in opposite directions from the start," *Los Angeles Daily News,* November 23, at http://www.dailynews.com/cda/article/print/0,1674,200%257E20950%257E2554402,00.html; Surowiecki, J. 2004. "Good grooming," *The New Yorker,* October 4, at http://www.newyorker.com/talk/content/?011004ta_talk_surowiecki.

85. Salancik, G.R., & Pfeffer, J. 1977. Who gets power and how they hold on to it: A strategic contingency model of power. *Organizational Dynamics,* 5: 3–21.

86. Hillman, A.J., & Dalziel, T. 2003. Boards of directors and firm performance: Integrating agency and resource dependence perspectives. *Academy of Management Review,* 28: 383–396.

87. Pfeffer, J. 1981. *Power in organizations.* Marshfield, MA: Pitman Publishing.

88. Ibid.

89. Ibid.

90. Surowiecki, J. 2004. Good grooming. *The New Yorker,* October 4, at http://www.newyorker.com/talk/content/?011004ta_talk_surowiecki.

91. Ibid.

92. Pfeffer, J. 1981. *Power in organizations.* Marshfield, MA: Pitman Publishing.

93. Mintzberg, H. 1985. The organization as political arena. *Journal of Management Studies,* 22: 133–154.

94. Kacmar, K.M., & Baron, R.A. 1999. Organizational politics: The state of the field, links to related processes, and an agenda for future research. In G.R. Ferris (Ed.), *Research in personnel and human resource management (Vol. 17).* Stamford, CT: JAI Press, pp. 1–39; Zivnuska, S., Kacmar, K.M., Witt, L.A., Carlson, D.S., & Bratton, V.K. 2004. Interactive effects of impression management and organizational politics on job performance. *Journal of Organizational Behavior,* 25: 627–640.

95. Anonymous. 2002. Politics at work: Backstabbing, stolen ideas, scapegoats. *Director,* 56: 74–80.

96. Poon, J.M.L. 2003. Situational antecedents and outcomes of organizational politics perceptions. *Journal of Managerial Psychology,* 18: 138–155.

97. Yukl, G., Kim, H., & Falbe, C.M. 1996. Antecedents of influence outcomes. *Journal of Applied Psychology,* 81: 309–317.

98. Popper, M. 2004. Morgan Stanley's board must end inaction, investor Matrix says. *Bloomberg.com,* April 21, at www.bloomberg.com/apps/news?pid=10000103&sid=aluJZFE02LOA&refer=us.

99. Martinez, M.J. 2005. Uphill fight for Morgan Stanley dissidents. *Associated Press,* April 8, at www.biz.yahoo.com/ap/0504080morgan_stanley.html.

100. Ibid.

101. Cable, D.M., & Judge, T.A. 2003. Managers' upward influence tactic strategies: The role of manager personality and supervisor leadership style. *Journal of Organizational Behavior,* 24: 197–214.

102. Ahearn, K.K., Ferris, G.R., Hochwater, W.A., Douglas, C., & Ammeter, A.P. 2004. Leader political skill and team performance. *Journal of Management,* 30: 309–327.

103. Ferris, G.R., Treadway, D.C., Kolodinsky, R.W., Hochwater, W.A., Kacmar, C.J., Douglas, C., & Frink, D.D. 2005. Development and validation of the political skill inventory. *Journal of Management,* 31: 126–152.

PART IV THE ORGANIZATIONAL CONTEXT

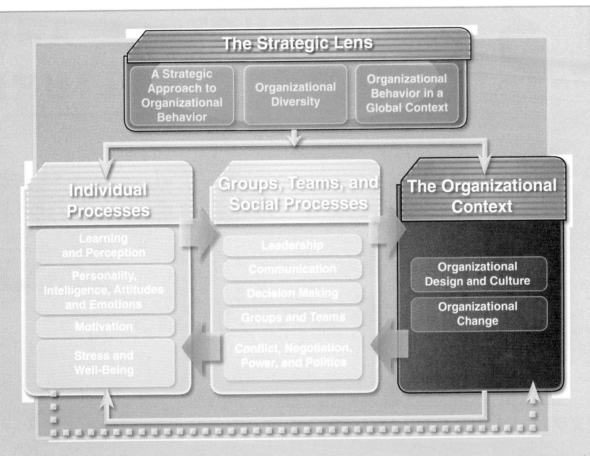

In the final part of the book, we examine the organizational context for the individual and group processes discussed in Parts II and III. Thus, we began the book with a chapter that presented the strategic lens for managing behavior in organizations, and we end with two chapters that explain the organizational processes and context for that behavior.

In **Chapter 13**, we discuss structure and organizational culture. The organization's structure can have a significant effect on behavior. Organizational culture is based on shared values in the organization. Therefore, the fit between individual values and organizational values is important. Organizational culture can significantly influence associates' and managers' behavior. It can affect individuals' motivation and attitudes as well as team processes such as leadership and conflict.

Chapter 14, the last chapter in the book, focuses on organizational change and development. Most organizations exist in dynamic environments requiring them to change regularly in order to adapt to environmental changes. Shifting environments also require that organizations develop flexibility in their strategies. Being flexible, however, necessitates taking an approach to change that associates and managers in the organization will accept. Most people dislike and resist change because of the uncertainty involved. This chapter explains how managers can develop a change process that unfreezes associates' attitudes and allows them to accept change. The chapter also discusses organization development, a form of internal consulting aimed at improving communication, problem solving, and learning in the organization. The problem-solving process involves diagnosing the problem, prescribing interventions, and monitoring progress. The change processes and problem-resolution processes discussed in this chapter draw on many of the concepts explored in the previous chapters of this book.

ORGANIZATIONAL STRUCTURE AND CULTURE

Most companies have goals designed to achieve growth and diversification of the markets they serve, both product and geographical. Growth can be achieved by developing new products and services internally or by acquiring other organizations. Growth by external acquisition has been popular because it is often a faster and less risky means of achieving the desired growth. FedEx's corporate strategy involved both of these approaches.

In 1971, Federal Express Corporation was founded in Little Rock, Arkansas.

Robert Sullivan/AFP/Getty Images

EXPLORING BEHAVIOR IN ACTION

Growth and Structure to Provide an Integrated Portfolio of Services at FedEx

Early in its history, FedEx used internal development to achieve rapid growth. In 1983, Federal Express became the first U.S. company to obtain $1 billion in revenue without making an acquisition. However, in 1984 the company made its first acquisition in buying Gelco Express International which launched operations in the Asia Pacific region. Five years later, Federal Express purchased Flying Tigers to expand its international presence. That same year, Roberts Express (now FedEx Custom Critical) began providing services to Europe. In 1993, RPS (now FedEx Ground)

exceeded $1 billion in annual revenue, recording the fastest growth of any ground transportation company. In 1995, FedEx acquired air routes from Evergreen International with authority to serve China and opened an Asia Pacific Hub in Subic Bay, Philippines, launching the FedEx AsiaOne Network. By 1996, FedEx Ground achieved 100 percent coverage in North America. In 1998, FedEx acquired Caliber Systems, Inc. and created FDX Corporation. This series of acquisitions made FedEx a $16 billion transportation powerhouse. But the acquisitions and growth continued.

In 1999, Federal Express Corporation acquired Caribbean Transportation Services. In January 2000, FDX Corporation was renamed FedEx Corporation. Federal Express became FedEx Express, RPS became FedEx Ground, Roberts Express became FedEx Custom Critical, and Caliber Logistics and Caliber Technology were combined to make up FedEx Global Logistics. Also in 2000, FedEx Trade Networks was created with the acquisitions of Tower Group International and WorldTariff. FedEx Custom Critical also acquired Passport Transport and introduced customer technology solutions including a redesigned fedex.com, FedEx e-Commerce Builder, FedEx Global Trade Manager, and FedEx Ship Manager. In 2001, FedEx acquired American Freightways, which is a less-than-truckload carrier servicing the 40 eastern states in the United States. In addition, by 2004, FedEx Corporation had acquired Kinko's for $2.4 billion and also Parcel Direct, which was a leading parcel consolidator. FedEx Corp completed its acquisitions in 2007 with its purchase of Chinese shipping partner DTW Group in order to obtain more control over and access to services in secondary Chinese cities.

As suggested by the large list of acquisitions and other changes, FedEx's strategy to achieve growth was realized. It also diversified the company's portfolio of services. An example was the acquisition of Kinko's. The goal of this acquisition was to expand the company's retail services through the 1,200-plus Kinko's stores. In addition, by acquiring Parcel Direct, FedEx was able to expand services for customers in the

e-tail and catalog segments. This acquisition complemented the FedEx alliance with the U.S. Postal Service and provides a proven, cost-effective solution for low-weight, less time-sensitive residential shipments. All of the companies acquired by FedEx Corp were carefully selected to ensure a corporate culture with a positive service-oriented spirit, thereby providing a good fit with FedEx.

Because of the growth and additional services, FedEx had to change its structure. It adopted a multidivisional structure. FedEx Corporation provides strategic direction and consolidated financial reporting for the operating companies that are collectively under the FedEx name worldwide (FedEx Express, FedEx Ground, FedEx Freight, FedEx Kinko's Office and Print Services, FedEx Custom Critical, FedEx Trade Networks, and FedEx Services). Because of the growth in the size and scope of the company, FedEx delegated significant authority to the divisions. Together, the various divisions are FedEx, but independently, each division offers flexible,

specialized services that represent an array of supply chain, transportation, and business and related information services. Operating independently, each FedEx company manages its own specialized network of services. The FedEx Corporation acts as the hub, allowing its decentralized divisions to work together worldwide. FedEx coordinates the activities of operating divisions in ways that integrate them to provide customers a unique and powerful portfolio of services globally that FedEx believes differentiates the company from competitors.

Sources: David Goulden, 2006, "Managing IT for a Flat World," *BusinessWeek*, Oct. 2, www.businessweek.com; Christopher Shevlin, 2004, "Move Out of Range to Think Out of the Box," *Financial Times*, Aug. 19, www.ft.com; Associated Press, 2007, "FedEx Completes Acquisition of DTW Group," *BusinessWeek*, Feb. 28, www.businessweek.com; Sarah Murray, 2006, "Putting the House in Order," *Financial Times*, Nov. 8, www.ft.com; Dean Foust, 2006, "Taking Off Like 'a Rocket Ship,'" *BusinessWeek*, Apr. 3, www.businessweek.com; 2007, "About FedEx," *FedEx Homepage*, www.fedex.com.

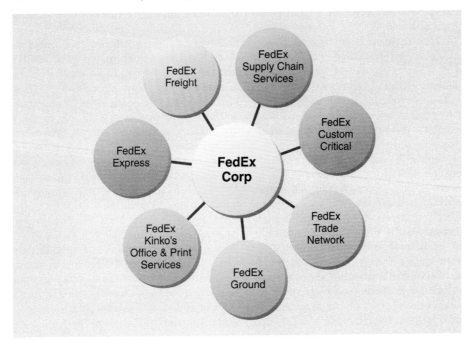

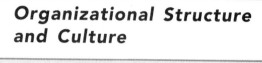

Organizational Structure and Culture

When considering the implementation of organizational strategies, we often focus on the roles of strong leaders, talented managers and associates, and effective processes such as communication and conflict management. Although all these factors are important, as emphasized in prior chapters, they provide only part of the support for implementing an organization's strategy. The organization's structure and culture have crucial effects on strategy implementation.

Organizational structure refers to the formal system of work roles and authority relationships that govern how associates and managers interact with one another.[1] To properly implement a strategy, an organization must have or build a useful structure to ensure that formal and even informal activities and initiatives support strategic goals. Structure influences communication patterns among individuals and groups and the degree to which individuals are free to be innovative. If, for example, a strategy calls for rapid responses in several dynamic and different markets, it is important to create divisions around those markets, and delegate authority to those divisions so that managers can act as they deem necessary, similar to the decentralized divisions created by FedEx as described in the *Exploring Behavior in Action* feature. Firms that fail to design and maintain effective structures experience problems. FedEx also coordinates activities across its divisions in order to achieve synergies across its various services and geographical markets. Doing this enhances FedEx's performance.

An appropriate culture is also required for effective strategy implementation and strong overall performance. **Organizational culture** involves shared values and norms that influence behavior.[2] It is a powerful force in organizations. When AT&T was forced to divest its Bell system operating companies in order to create more competition and innovation in the telecommunications industry, its strategy and culture had to change. Before the court-ordered divestiture, AT&T had a strategy focused on universally available and reliable phone service (at any cost) and incremental innovation.[3] Its culture matched the strategic and industry context by emphasizing steady but slow progress, abiding by rules, and maintaining traditions. After the breakup, with deregulation and increased competition looming, AT&T had to adopt a more innovative strategic posture and needed a culture that emphasized flexibility and adaptability, as well as a willingness to take risks.[4] Although AT&T experienced problems along the way, the company was able to adjust over time. Yet, recently AT&T experienced difficult times and was acquired by one of its former Bell companies, SBC. The newly merged firm took on the name of AT&T because it is so well known and respected.

FedEx grew rapidly early in its existence by internally expanding its services and especially by reaching new geographical markets. It then began to expand into international markets, partly by acquisition (e.g., its acquisition of Flying Tigers). It also used acquisitions to diversify the services that it offered. An example of this expansion was the acquisition of Kinko's with its 1,200 retail outlets across the United States to support the diversification strategy and divisional structure. Over time, FedEx had to adopt a new structure in order to manage its diversified portfolio of services and geographical markets. The new divisional structure granted significant autonomy to each operating business (division) with corporate coordination across the divisions to achieve synergy in offering customers integrated services. FedEx was careful in its acquisitions to ensure that the acquired firms fit well with its positive customer-oriented culture. Both organizational structure and culture influence the behavior of managers and associates and therefore play a critical role in the success of an organization's strategy and its overall organizational performance.

In this chapter, we explore issues related to structure and culture. We open with a discussion of the fundamental elements of structure, emphasizing how they influence the behavior and attitudes of individual managers and associates. Next, we discuss the link between strategy and structure as well as the structural implications of environmental characteristics, internal technology, and organizational size. In the second part of the chapter, we focus on culture. Cultural topics include the competing values model of culture, socialization, cultural audits, and subcultures. We close with a discussion of person–organization fit.

After reading this chapter, you should be able to:

1. Define key elements of organizational structure, including both structural and structuring dimensions.

2. Explain how corporate and business strategies relate to structure.

3. Explain how environment, technology, and size relate to structure.

4. Define organizational culture, and discuss the competing-values cultural framework.

5. Discuss socialization.

6. Describe cultural audits and subcultures.

7. Explain the importance of a fit between individual values and organizational culture.

Fundamental Elements of Organizational Structure

The structure of an organization can be described in two different but related ways. First, **structural characteristics** refer to the tangible, physical properties that determine the basic shape and appearance of an organization's hierarchy,[5] where **hierarchy** is defined in terms of the reporting relationships depicted in an organization chart. Essentially an organization's structure is a blueprint of the reporting relationships, distribution of authority, and decision making in the organization.[6] These characteristics influence behavior, but their effects are sometimes subtle. Second, **structuring characteristics** refer to policies and approaches used to directly prescribe the behavior of managers and associates.[7]

Structural Characteristics

Structural characteristics, as mentioned, relate to the basic shape and appearance of an organization's hierarchy. The shape of a hierarchy is determined by its height, spans of control, and type of departmentation.

Height refers to the number of levels in the organization, from the CEO to the lower-level associates. Tall hierarchies often create communication problems, as information moving up and down the hierarchy can be slowed and distorted as it passes through many different levels.[8] Managers and associates can become demotivated as decisions are delayed and faulty information is disseminated, causing lower satisfaction and commitment. Tall hierarchies also are more expensive, as they have more levels of managers.[9]

A manager's **span of control** corresponds to the number of individuals who report directly to her. A broad span of control is possible when a manager can effectively handle many individuals, as is the case when associates have the skills

organizational structure
Work roles and authority relationships that influence behavior in an organization.

organizational culture
The values shared by associates and managers in an organization.

structural characteristics
The tangible, physical properties that determine the basic shape and appearance of an organization's hierarchy.

hierarchy
The reporting relationships depicted in an organization chart.

structuring characteristics
The policies and approaches used to directly prescribe the behavior of managers and associates.

David McNew/
Reportage/Getty Images

and motivation they need to complete their tasks autonomously. Broad spans have advantages for an organization. First, they result in shorter hierarchies (see Exhibit 13-1), thereby avoiding communication and expense problems.[10] Second, they promote high-involvement management because managers have difficulty micromanaging people when there are larger numbers of them. Broad spans allow for more initiative by associates.[11] In making employment decisions, many individuals take these realities into consideration.

Spans of control can be too broad, however. When a manager has too many direct reports, she cannot engage in important coaching and development activities. As tasks become more complex and the direct reports more interdependent, a manager can be more effective with a relatively narrow span of control. It has been argued that a CEO's span of control should not exceed six people, due to the complexity and interdependency of work done by direct reports at this level.[12]

Many older companies have removed layers of management and increased spans of control in recent years, whereas younger companies, such as AES, avoided unnecessary layers and overly narrow spans from the beginning.[13] Because of their profound effects on behavior and attitudes among associates and managers, spans of control draw the attention of many organizations such as PriceWaterhouseCoopers (PWC).[14] Through their Saratoga Institute, managers and consultants at PWC track spans of control in various industries and use the

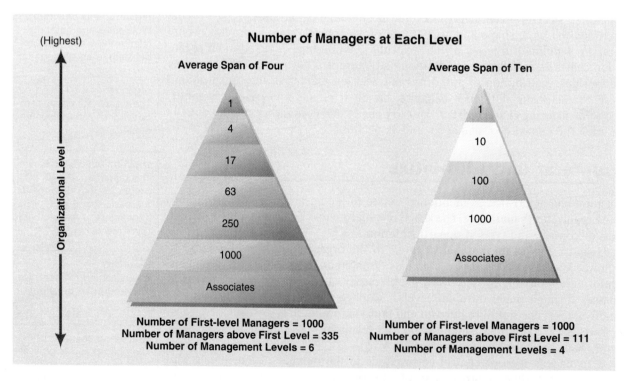

Exhibit 13-1   Average Span of Control: Effects of Height of the Hierarchy

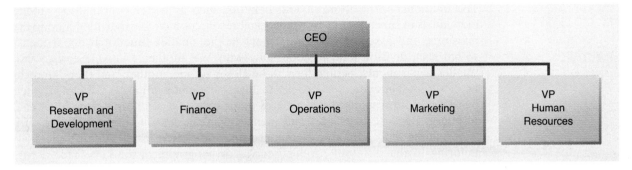

Exhibit 13-2   Simplified Functional Organization

resulting insights in various reports and consulting engagements. They reported a few years ago that the median span for all managers in all industries was seven. An earlier *Wall Street Journal* report indicated an average span of nine.

Departmentation describes the approach used in grouping resources within an organization. As highlighted in the opening case, one of the two basic options is the functional form of departmentation, in which resources related to a particular functional area are grouped together (see Exhibit 13-2). The functional form provides several potential advantages, including deep specialized knowledge in each functional area (because functions are the focus of the firm) and economies of scale within functional areas (resources can be shared by all individuals working within each functional area).[15] This form, however, also has a potential major weakness: managers and associates in each functional department can become isolated from those who work in other departments, which harms coordinated action and causes slow responses to major industry changes that require two or more functional areas to work together.[16] Lateral relation tools, discussed in a later section, can help to overcome this weakness.

If an organization has multiple products or services or operates in multiple geographical areas, it can group its resources into divisions (see Exhibit 13-3).

height
The number of hierarchical levels in an organization, from the CEO to the lower-level associates.

span of control
The number of individuals a manager directly oversees.

departmentation
The grouping of human and other resources into units, typically based on functional areas or markets.

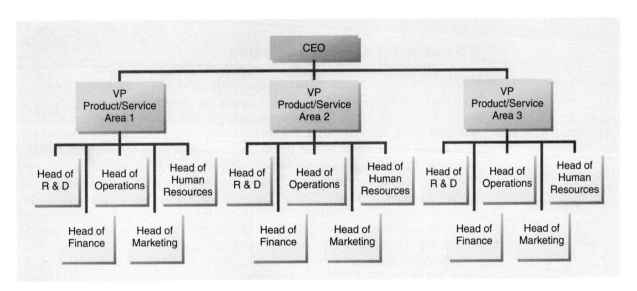

Exhibit 13-3   Simplified Divisional Organization

The divisional form offers several benefits, such as better coordination among individuals in functional areas. Functional resources have been divided among the divisions, and associates and managers in the smaller functional departments within each division tend to coordinate with one another relatively easily. With smaller departments, people tend to be closer to one another, and there tends to be fewer bureaucratic roadblocks to direct communication. A second, related benefit is rapid response to changes in the industry that call for a cross-functional response. Because associates and managers in the various functional areas are coordinating more effectively, response times are often faster. A third benefit is tailoring to the different product/service or geographical markets. This occurs because the people in each division are dedicated to their own markets.[17] The divisional form is not without its drawbacks, however. Two of the most important are (1) lack of collaboration across the product/service or geographic markets (individuals in one division can become isolated from those in other divisions) and (2) diseconomies of scale within functional areas (individuals in a given functional area but working on different markets cannot share resources as they can in the functional structure).[18] As described in the *Exploring Behavior in Action* feature, FedEx developed a diverse set of businesses offering a portfolio of services. To manage these businesses efficiently and to offer customers the most effective services, FedEx implemented a divisional structure.

Hybrid forms also exist, with some functional areas divided across divisions, while others remain intact at the corporate level, often for cost reasons. *Network* organizations are another option, where many or most functional areas are outsourced to other organizations.[19] Home builders are usually network organizations, as they often do not complete their own architectural work and typically outsource to subcontractors much of the actual construction work. Nike is generally considered to be a network organization because it outsources manufacturing and other types of work.

The network approach has been emphasized by a number of firms in recent years, at least to some degree. Its chief benefit lies in allowing a firm to focus on what it does best while outsourcing the rest.[20] Quality control, however, is sometimes an issue, and coordination of internal and external efforts is often a substantial problem. Effective information technology that facilitates coordination across organizational boundaries is crucial.

Structuring Characteristics

Whereas structural characteristics indirectly affect behavior, *structuring* characteristics relate to policies and approaches used to directly prescribe the behavior of managers and associates. This second category of structure includes centralization, standardization, formalization, and specialization.

Centralization refers to the amount of decision-making authority that is held at the top of the organization.[21] In centralized organizations, top-level managers retain most authority, leaving less for mid- and lower-level managers and very little for associates. This is not consistent with high-involvement management, and research suggests that centralized organizations generally perform less well.[22] There are several conditions, however, that call for a significant degree of centralization. We discuss this issue in a later section.

Standardization refers to the existence of rules and standard operating procedures. When standardization is high, managers and associates are expected to follow prearranged approaches to their work. Under these circumstances, their behavior is very predictable. Although standardization is sometimes necessary for

---

centralization
The degree to which authority for meaningful decisions is retained at the top of an organization

standardization
The degree to which rules and standard operating procedures govern behavior in an organization.

efficiency and safety, it reduces opportunities for individual initiative, creativity, and self-directed collaboration with others inside and outside the organization. This negatively affects motivation and satisfaction for many. **Formalization** is a closely related phenomenon; it is the degree to which rules and procedures are documented. **Specialization** is the degree to which managers and associates have narrow jobs that use focused skills; usually these jobs offer little variety. As discussed in Chapter 6, narrow jobs can negatively affect motivation, satisfaction, and performance for individuals who want to be challenged and to grow in the workplace.

formalization
The degree to which rules and operating procedures are documented on paper or in company intranets.

specialization
The degree to which associates and managers have jobs with narrow scopes and limited variety.

The Modern Organization

Structural and structuring characteristics combine to create very different types of organizations. Some in the field of organizational behavior label the two fundamental types *organic* versus *mechanistic*.[23] Others label these types *learning* versus *nonlearning*.[24] Still others use the labels *boundaryless* versus *traditional* to make the same basic distinction.[25] In all cases, the more flexible empowering type of structure (i.e., organic, learning, or boundaryless) is associated with fewer management levels; broader spans of control; and lesser amounts of centralization, standardization, formalization, and specialization. Departmentation at the top of the firm can be either functional or divisional. The flexible approach provides freedom for lower-level managers and associates to think for themselves, to communicate with anyone who could be helpful, and to try new ideas.

Although substantial freedom may exist, it is not unlimited, nor should it exist without alternative mechanisms designed to ensure that managers and associates are working for the common good of the organization. First, freedom is not unlimited. Even in relatively organic firms there is some standardization, and some decisions are made by middle and senior-level managers. At Lincoln Electric, the Cleveland maker of welding equipment, factory workers are free to experiment with process innovations, but there are limits to how far they can go.[26] They must work with other factory workers if process innovations would affect them, and if the innovation would radically change production flows, managers must be consulted. At Southwest Airlines, pilots and flight attendants have more freedom than at other airlines, but they still must follow applicable laws and safety rules.[27] Interestingly, research shows that new-venture firms need structure and thus often are more successful if their organization structure is less organic.[28]

Second, alternative mechanisms are used to ensure that individuals are working for the good of the organization. These mechanisms include selection systems, socialization schemes, and leadership processes. Selection systems should be designed to identify individuals who share the values of the organization. Socialization schemes, discussed later in this chapter, should be designed to further shape values and to promote a shared vision of the organization's future. Similarly, strong leadership at the top of the firm instills shared purpose among managers and associates. Shared values and vision act as guides to behavior, and reduce the chances of lower-level managers and associates acting in ways that are counterproductive. Reward systems also are used to promote appropriate behavior. Although lower-level managers and associates may not realize it, powerful forces guide their behavior in organizations characterized by relative freedom of thought and action.

Through the 1960s and into the 1970s, freedom in most organizations was severely limited. Over time, however, the value of unleashing human capital throughout an organization became widely recognized. Today, senior leaders in modern organizations tend to favor organic structure. Although this is positive, given that organic structures are closely aligned with high-involvement management, there are situations in which some aspects of this approach are not appropriate.

Factors Affecting Organizational Structure

Senior managers must choose structural arrangements for their firms. Middle and lower-level managers often are involved in these choices and are always involved in implementing the choices. Factors that should be considered in designing the structure of the firm include strategy, external environment, internal technology, and organizational size.

The Role of Strategy

An organization's task environment is composed of customers, suppliers, competitors, government regulatory agencies, and perhaps unions. These are external elements with which the organization frequently interacts and that have an effect on the organization.[29] Organizations adapt to their environments through formal strategies. In turn, these strategies affect the organization's structure.

CORPORATE STRATEGY

corporate strategy
The overall approach an organization uses in interacting with its environment. The emphasis is placed on growth and diversification.

growth
Relates to increases in sales as well as associates and managers.

Corporate strategy is the overall, predominant strategy of the organization. It determines the direction for the total organization. Senior managers formulating corporate strategies focus on the organization's stockholders and other critical external constituents. Their strategies can be oriented toward growth, diversification, or both.[30]

Almost all types of organizations use **growth** as a measure of success. Awards are given for growth, such as the Growth Strategy Leadership Award given by the consulting firm Frost and Sullivan.[31] Under some circumstances, senior leaders are even willing to trade profits for increasing sales. Growth can be achieved through internal development or by external acquisition. Although the internal growth strategy is an attractive option, growth by external acquisition is popular with many companies.[32] Frontier Insurance Group, for example, has acquired many firms in order to grow.[33] Cisco Systems, a maker of telecommunication equipment, is known for its frequent acquisitions.[34] Acquisition is often a faster method of achieving growth, but it does carry some risk in part because cultural differences between firms often cause difficulties in post-acquisition integration of operations.[35] Some firms that have diversified through multiple acquisitions later retrenched and sold off prior acquisitions because of poor performance.[36]

Each of these two growth strategies has implications for structure. For example, firms using an internal-growth strategy are likely to have larger marketing and R&D departments. It is also probable that authority for decisions is decentralized to the heads of these departments. In contrast, firms following an external acquisition strategy are likely to have the more well-developed financial and legal functions required to analyze and negotiate acquisitions. These firms may even have a separate specialized planning and acquisitions department. For example, given the number of acquisitions completed by FedEx over time, the company likely enhanced these functions in order to do them effectively.

Diversification has also been a common and popular corporate strategy. Diversification involves adding products or services different from those currently in the firm. Firms may diversify for several reasons, but the primary one is to reduce overall risk by decreasing dependency on one or a few product markets.[37] Thus, if demand for one of the firm's products falls, the other products may continue to sell. Most companies start out as *single-product firms,* which are firms where more than 95 percent of annual sales come from one product. *Dominant-product firms* obtain 70 to 94 percent of their sales from one product. Most companies following a diversification strategy move on to become *related-product firms,* where less than 70 percent of annual sales come from one product and the various products are related to one another. The most diversified firms are classified as *unrelated-product firms.* In these firms, less than 70 percent of annual sales come from any one product, and the firm's various products are unrelated to the primary core business.[38]

As firms become more diversified, research suggests that they should adopt the divisional form.[39] In other words, they should develop divisions for each of their end-product businesses. Also, as firms become more diversified and divisionalized, authority should be delegated to the divisions.[40]

Matches between diversification and structure are shown in Exhibit 13-4. Single-product and most dominant-product firms should use a functional structure, where the major units of the organization are based on the functions performed (marketing, production, finance) rather than on products. Related-product and most unrelated-product firms should use a divisionalized structure. Large, highly diversified unrelated-product firms may use a *holding company* structure, in which the operating divisions are extremely autonomous.[41] Firms with functional structures are sometimes referred to as *U-form* (unitary) *organizations* and firms with divisionalized structures as *M-form* (multidivisional) *organizations.* Over time, FedEx changed from a single-product firm to a related-product firm. As such, it implemented the divisional structure and decentralized primary authority to make decisions to the heads of each division. Because the businesses are all related, the corporate office coordinated activities across the divisions to offer customers the full portfolio of FedEx's services (as described in the *Exploring Behavior in Action* feature).

> **diversification**
> Related to the number of different product lines or service areas in the organization.

Exhibit 13-4	Matches between Diversification Strategy and Structure
Diversification	**Structure**
Single product	Functional
Dominant product (few products)	Functional
Dominant product (several products)	Divisional
Related product	Divisional
Unrelated product	Divisional
Unrelated product	Holding Company

BUSINESS STRATEGY

business strategy
How a firm competes for
success against other
organizations in a particular
market.

Firms must formulate business strategies in addition to corporate strategies. A **business strategy** is formulated for a particular product/service market and is a plan of action describing how the firm will operate in a particular market.[42]

Business strategies are necessary to ensure effective competitive actions in the different markets in which a firm intends to operate. One popular competitive strategy involves maintaining low internal costs as a basis for low prices offered to customers. Consumers interested in buying the least expensive goods in a particular market are targeted. To effectively implement this strategy, efficiency and control are important inside the firm or division utilizing this approach, and a somewhat more mechanistic structure is useful if not taken to an extreme.[43] The structure used to implement a low-cost strategy often emphasizes functions and the decisions are also centralized to maintain economies of scale in operations.[44] A second popular competitive strategy involves product/service differentiation. Consumers are targeted who are willing to pay more for a product/service that is different in some meaningful way (higher quality, superior technology, faster availability). To effectively implement this strategy, flexibility and initiative are useful for staying ahead of the competition, and a more organic structure can be helpful in supporting these needs.[45]

In the *Experiencing Strategic Organizational Behavior* segment, IDEO illustrates three key points. First, this firm shows how a differentiation strategy can be used in the business of designing products and services. IDEO has distinguished itself in this industry through its unique approach to working with clients, and it promotes the innovation and initiative required to maintain its edge by using an organic structure. Second, the firm highlights the fact that companies occasionally supplement their internal human capital as they work to create a competitive advantage in the marketplace. All or most of IDEO's clients have talented associates and managers. Yet on occasion they still need outside assistance. Finally, the IDEO case again illustrates the value of teams with diverse members, as explained in Chapters 2 and 11. Teams provided invaluable help for IDEO and its client firms to implement a strategy of innovation designed to create or maintain a competitive advantage.

EXPERIENCING STRATEGIC ORGANIZATIONAL BEHAVIOR

IDEO and the Differentiation Strategy

Courtesy of IDEO

The computer mouse, stand-up toothpaste containers, Palm V, i-Zone cameras, patient-friendly waiting rooms, and shopper-friendly intimate apparel displays. Differentiation is not easy, but these products and services helped to differentiate Apple Computer, Procter & Gamble, Palm Inc., Kaiser Permanente, and Warnaco. In cooperation with IDEO, Shimano, a global company headquartered in Japan, developed an innovative new bicycle introduced in 2007. What is the secret of their success? It may have something to do with the associates and managers at IDEO, a design firm based in Palo Alto, California.

The people of IDEO have a long history of helping firms design award-winning products and services. More recently, they have begun offering consulting and training in innovation and culture change. To make a difference, IDEO's associates and managers rely upon a simple concept—empathy. Although this concept may sound attractive to some students, IDEO's record of success is difficult to question.

Empathy for the customer is created in clients through a set of time-tested, systematic research methods. First, IDEO forms a diverse team composed of client and IDEO members. Team members from IDEO may represent the disciplines of cognitive psychology, environmental psychology, anthropology, industrial design, interaction design, mechanical engineering, and business strategy. Team members from the client firm are key decision makers. With the team in place, observations in the real world are orchestrated. Team members observe how people use relevant products and services. For a project focused on intimate apparel, team members followed women as they shopped for lingerie, encouraging the shoppers to verbalize everything they were thinking. Team members may even act as customers themselves. For a health-care project, team members received care at various hospitals and documented their experiences by video and other media.

Second, team members engage in brainstorming. After some preliminary work, the designers, engineers, social scientists, and individuals from the client company engage in intense interactions to develop a rich understanding of an existing product/service design or of the needs in a novel product category. Unlike some group sessions, IDEO's brainstorming sessions have been compared to managed chaos.

Third, team members engage in rapid prototyping. This is one of the characteristics that have made IDEO famous. IDEO associates and managers believe in the power of trying many different ideas rather than just talking about them. Rudimentary versions of products and services are quickly constructed and examined. In the words of IDEO's managers:

> Prototyping is the language of innovation and a way of life at IDEO. Prototyping is problem solving in three dimensions. You can prototype just about anything—a new product or service, a website or a new space. Ranging from simple proof-of-concept models to looks-like/works-like prototypes that are practically finished products, prototyping allows you to fail early in order to succeed sooner.

Finally, team members implement the fruits of their labor. Detailed design and engineering work is completed, and the team works closely with clients to ensure a successful launch. In many other design firms, team members simply turn over their work with little follow-up.

IDEO has become so popular that many firms send their managers to the firm to observe the organic structure and to be trained in innovative thinking and action. These managers use what they have learned to enhance the operations and structures of their own firms. The founder of IDEO, Bill Moggridge, has written a book describing how designers now interact with technology to create innovative products and services.

Sources: "Coasting Bicycle Design Strategy for Shimano," 2007, http://www.ideo.com/ideo.asp, Apr. 16; B. Moggridge, 2006, *Designing Interactions*, Boston: MIT Press; IDEO, "About Us: Methods," 2004, at http://www.ideo.com/about/index.asp?x=3&y=3; B. Nussbaum, 2004, "The Power of Design: IDEO Redefined Good Design by Creating Experiences, Not Just Products," *BusinessWeek*, May 17, p. 86; D.H. Pink, 2003, "Out of the Box," *Fast Company* 75: 104; H. Reeves, 2003, "Building a Better Bra Shop," *New York Times Magazine*, Nov. 30, pp. 44–45; T. Sickinger, 2003, "True Innovation Goes Beyond Invention, Silicon Valley Entrepreneur Says," *Knight Ridder Tribune Business News*, May 21, p. 1.

A more advanced form of the divisional structure, strategic business units (SBUs) are sometimes used for more complex firms. Large firms with multiple diversified businesses sometimes group their businesses into SBUs. At General Electric, for example, businesses are grouped into SBUs that include GE Advanced Materials, GE Commercial Finance, GE Consumer Finance, GE Consumer and Industrial Products, GE Energy, GE Healthcare, GE Infrastructure,

GE Insurance Solutions, GE Transportation, and NBC Universal.[46] A business strategy is then formulated for each separate SBU, thus allowing the complex organization to be more effectively managed. The key to developing effective strategies for each SBU is the appropriate grouping of businesses. Each group must have commonalities among its businesses for a coherent strategy to be developed. These commonalities may correspond to market relatedness, shared technology, or common distinctive competencies.[47]

The Role of the Environment

Environmental forces account for many differences between organizations, and they have a marked effect on the way organizations conduct business. Because organizations must obtain their inputs from the external environment, their relationships with suppliers and customers are critical. They also must satisfy governmental regulations, adapt to changes in the national and world economies, and react to competitors' actions.

ENVIRONMENT AND BASIC STRUCTURE

Managers must closely monitor their organization's external environment. However, some environments are more difficult to monitor than others because they are more uncertain (complex and changing). A number of researchers have found that the degree of **environmental uncertainty** experienced by managers is related to the type of structure an organization utilizes. The classic studies of two researchers, Paul Lawrence and Jay Lorsch, indicated that effective organizations exhibit a match between environmental characteristics and organizational structures.[48] Although the evidence is not entirely consistent, a number of other researchers have found similar results, using mostly small organizations or units of larger ones.[49]

In their study of the plastics, food-processing, and can-manufacturing industries, Lawrence and Lorsch reported the following important findings:

- Effective organizations experiencing high environmental uncertainty tend to be more organic because lower-level managers and associates must be able to think for themselves. They must be able to respond to events quickly.

- Effective organizations experiencing low environmental uncertainty tend to be less organic. Mid- and senior-level managers in conjunction with operations specialists can create efficient and effective rules and operating procedures. They can gain sufficient insight to understand and anticipate most situations that will arise and carefully create procedures to handle those situations.

Lawrence and Lorsch also examined differences in functional departments within an organization. Because separate departments focus on different areas of the external environment, they often exhibit different patterns of structure. Research and development, for example, is focused on technological advances and the changing pool of knowledge in the world. The relatively high level of uncertainty involved can result in a more organic structure with longer time horizons for decision making and planning and a greater emphasis on interpersonal relationships to promote important discussions and information sharing. In contrast, accounting is focused on more slowly evolving developments in accounting standards. The relatively low level of uncertainty can result in a less organic structure, with shorter time horizons and less emphasis on interpersonal relationships. In

environmental uncertainty The degree to which an environment is complex and changing; uncertain environments are difficult to monitor and understand.

effective organizations, then, differences in the level of uncertainty in subenvironments create differences in functional departments.

Recent work suggests that environmental uncertainty also affects the way resources should be managed in organizations. For example, organizations operating in uncertain environments need to constantly enrich their current capabilities and even create new ones. Thus, they continuously train their managers and associates to upgrade their skills and are on the lookout for new associates with "cutting-edge" knowledge that can add to the organization's stock of knowledge. They also need to search for opportunities in the environment and to engage in entrepreneurial behavior to maximize the use of their capabilities to provide products and services that create value for their customers.[50] IDEO, as explained in the *Experiencing Strategic Organizational Behavior* feature, is helping firms to be more entrepreneurial and create products that are valued by the customers. All of the research then suggests that managers must continuously scan their firm's external environment to identify factors that may affect how the firm should act. Their scanning behavior is even more important in dynamic environments.[51]

ENVIRONMENT AND INTEGRATION

Functional departments within a single-product firm or a division of a larger firm must be integrated. They must share information and understand one another in order to coordinate their work. Thus, organizations must be structured to provide the necessary information, or perhaps to reduce the need for it. Structural arrangements that address information needs are particularly important when the environment is uncertain. Useful arrangements include (1) creation of slack resources, (2) creation of self-contained tasks, (3) investment in information technology, and (4) creation of traditional lateral relations.[52] Exhibit 13-5 shows the relationship of these elements of organizational structure and information processing needs.

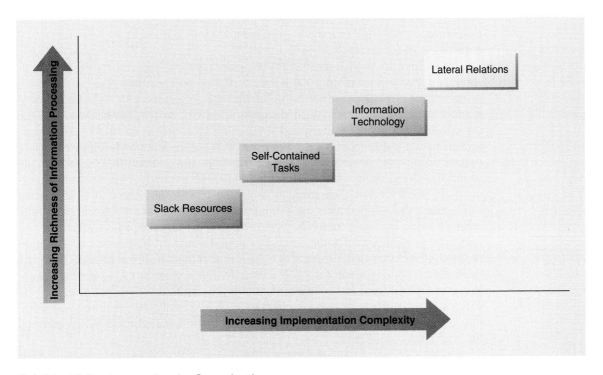

Exhibit 13-5   Integration in Organizations

slack resources
An integration technique whereby a department keeps more resources on hand than absolutely required in order to reduce the need for tight communication and coordination with other departments.

self-contained tasks
An integration technique whereby a department is given resources from other functional areas in order to reduce the need to coordinate with those areas.

information technology
An overall set of tools, based on microelectronic technology, designed to provide data, documents, and commentary as well as analysis support to individuals in an organization.

The creation of **slack resources** reduces the need for interdepartmental information processing. Departments can operate more independently. Examples of slack resources include having extra time to complete tasks that other departments need as inputs and maintaining large inventories of raw materials provided by others. Although these extra resources reduce information exchange needs, they are costly.

The creation of **self-contained tasks** reduces the need for interdepartmental processing of information. This approach provides departments with more of the resources they need to do the job. For example, a department's tasks may require the help of a design engineer and a process engineer on a part-time basis. Instead of having a group of design engineers to which various departments would come when they need help, a design engineer is specifically assigned to each department, with nonengineering work used to fill any unused time. This method reduces the need for coordination between groups (for example, the engineering group and other groups needing engineering services) and thereby reduces information-processing requirements.

Unlike the two elements of structure discussed above, **information technology** facilitates the processing of information rather than reducing the need to process it. This technology can help to transfer information up and down the hierarchy as well as horizontally from department to department. E-mail, web-based discussion boards, and chat rooms are examples of simple tools that facilitate communication and coordination. An information repository is a more complex tool for integration. Such a repository requires individuals in various departments to deposit documents, data, and commentary in an open-access central database. An enterprise resource planning (ERP) system is an even more complex tool. ERP systems provide a common set of planning and analysis capabilities across departments, as well as a platform for electronically sharing evolving plans and analyses. This type of system has provided important benefits in the integration of departments,[53] particularly when the system has been explicitly designed to support the organization's strategy. An ERP system has even been used to coordinate the cross-functional curriculum of a business school.[54]

In addition to facilitating integration across existing departments in an organization, information technology has helped to flatten organizations and has promoted project-based structures.[55] Shorter hierarchies are consistent with high-involvement management because they push decision authority to the lowest levels of the organization and increase the speed and quality of decisions as a result. Such hierarchies would not be possible, however, without information technology to ensure that associates and lower-level managers have the information they need to make sound decisions. Project-based structures utilize individuals from various departments to work on complex projects requiring intense and integrated efforts. In some cases, these individuals are temporarily assigned to a project on a full-time basis. In other instances, individuals participate part-time as project members and part-time as members of their functional departments. In both cases, information technology ensures that project participants working on different aspects of the overall project understand the goals and activities of those working in other areas. Without sophisticated information technology, individuals could not integrate the various aspects of the project as effectively or as rapidly, resulting in some complex projects not being undertaken and others being handled more slowly through the traditional hierarchy.

lateral relations
Elements of structure designed to draw individuals together for interchanges related to work issues and problems.

Relations among departments are based on the need for coordinating their various tasks. Because **lateral relations** increase information flow at lower levels, decisions requiring interdepartmental coordination need not be referred up the hierarchy. Lateral relations are traditional elements of structure used to help organizations process more information. These relations may be facilitated by information technology but often are based on face-to-face communication. A number of alternative lateral processes can be used. Listed in order of least complex to most complex, they are as follows:

- *Direct contact* involves two individuals who share a problem and work directly with one another to solve it.
- *Liaison roles* are temporary coordination positions established to link two departments that need to have a large amount of contact.
- *Task forces* are temporary groups composed of members from several departments who solve problems affecting those departments.
- *Teams* are permanent problem-solving groups for continuous interdepartmental problems.
- *Integrating roles* are permanent positions designed to help with the coordination of various tasks.
- *Managerial linking roles* are integrative positions with more influence and decision-making authority.
- *Matrix designs* establish dual authority between functional managers (marketing manager, engineering manager) and project or product managers (leisure furniture manager, office furniture manager).

The Role of Technology

Within an organization, technology refers to the knowledge and processes required to accomplish tasks. It corresponds to the techniques used in transforming inputs into outputs. The relationship of technology and structure has been described in several ways.

TECHNOLOGY AND STRUCTURE: A MANUFACTURING FRAMEWORK

The relationship between technology and organization structure was first identified by Joan Woodward. She examined small British manufacturing organizations and defined technology in terms of three types of production processes: small-batch production, mass production, and continuous-process production.[56]

Small-batch technology is associated with custom, made-to-order products. Automation and overall technological complexity tend to be low, as associates handcraft products using simple tools and equipment, as seen in an organization that builds furniture by hand for individual customers. Associates typically are highly skilled craftsmen and craftswomen with a great deal of autonomy. Stewart-Glapat, the Zanesville, Ohio, maker of telescoping conveyors, has historically relied on this type of technology.[57]

Mass-production technology results in large quantities of relatively standardized products. In traditional mass-production organizations, products are highly standardized, as in the manufacturing of razor blades, cans, and even automobiles. Associates in these organizations often have relatively narrow jobs and rely heavily on sophisticated equipment in their work. Automation is higher than in small-batch organizations, resulting in higher technological complexity. General Motors and other auto manufacturers use this technology.[58]

small-batch technology
A manufacturing technology used to produce unique or small batches of custom products. Automation trends to be low; skilled craftsmen and craftswomen are essential.

mass-production technology
A manufacturing technology used to produce large quantities of standardized products. Automation is moderately high.

Process-production technology is the most complex, involving almost complete automation of the process that converts inputs to outputs. Associates do not physically touch units of throughput in process facilities; instead, machines do the work. Examples include organizations focused on oil refining, chemical production, and power production. DuPont relies on this type of technology.[59]

Woodward found that technological complexity influenced structure in her small manufacturing organizations and that effective organizations exhibited matches between technology and structure. Other researchers have found supporting results.[60] Woodward's findings can be summarized as follows:

- Firms using small-batch technology have few management levels and few managers. Skilled craftsmen and craftswomen perform their work in an organic environment. The work is varied and requires the judgment of associates.

- Firms using mass-production technology have more management levels and more managers per associate. Associates handle relatively routine jobs in a less organic environment. Staff specialists and managers design procedures in advance.

- Firms using process technology have still more management levels and more managers per associate. Tall hierarchies are designed for monitoring various aspects of the organization because safety and a unified response to unforeseen events are paramount. Despite the tall hierarchy and the emphasis on monitoring, lower-level associates enjoy some level of discretion, as they must be free to act in emergencies. Lower-level associates in process organizations are plant operators and maintenance specialists with strong training.

Woodward's findings are useful, but they apply only to smaller manufacturing firms—those with fewer than 500 associates and managers. Yet today we see changes in technology that affect small and larger manufacturing operations alike. Technology can equalize the competition between smaller and larger organizations. The use of advanced manufacturing technology (AMT), computer-aided design (CAD), and computer-aided manufacturing (CAM) helps firms of all sizes to customize their strategies by manufacturing products of high variety at lower costs and to commercialize new products in a shorter amount of time.[61] These technologies have been integrated to create forms of "mass customization." **Mass customization** is a process that integrates sophisticated information technology and management methods in a flexible manufacturing system with the ability to customize products in a short time cycle.[62] Organizations using mass customization need a more flexible and organic structure.[63]

TECHNOLOGY AND STRUCTURE: A BROADER FRAMEWORK

Charles Perrow proposed a link between technology and structure using a broader description of technology than Woodward used, and Perrow's approach is useful in both manufacturing and service organizations. He defined technology as the number of different problem types that are encountered over time *(task variability)* and the degree to which problems can be solved using known steps and procedures *(task analyzability)*.[64] Based on these two dimensions, he delineated four types of technology:

1. *Routine:* There is little variation in the fundamental nature of problems encountered over time, but any new problems can be solved using readily available methods.

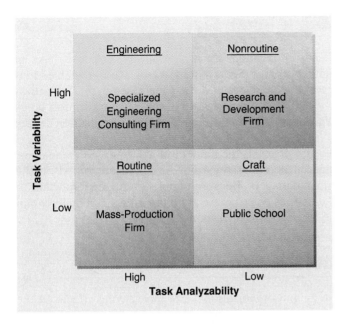

Exhibit 13-6   Organizations and Technology

2. *Craft:* There is little variation in the fundamental nature of problems encountered over time, but any new problems often require a novel search for unique solutions.

3. *Engineering:* There is significant variation in the fundamental nature of problems encountered over time, and new problems can be solved using readily available methods.

4. *Nonroutine:* There is significant variation in the fundamental nature of problems encountered over time, and new problems often require new methods to find unique solutions.

Exhibit 13-6 provides examples of organizations with these types of technologies. Perrow explains that for firms to be most effective, they should match their structure to the technology employed. Nonroutine organizations should adopt an organic structure; craft and engineering organizations should adopt a moderately organic structure; and routine organizations should adopt the least organic structure.[65] Essentially, as routineness increases, organic structures become somewhat less useful.

Perrow's technology concepts can be applied to an organization as a whole or to units within the organization. For example, the technology of W. L. Gore, the maker of Gore-Tex fabric, can be described as a mixture of routine and craft technology at the level of the overall firm, but its R&D area can be described as nonroutine. Any unit can be assessed with respect to task variability and task analyzability and placed into one of the four technology categories. A number of studies have shown that technology influences structure at the unit level and that effective units exhibit a significant match between technology and structure.[66] Indeed, many organizational researchers believe that technology has a larger role at the unit level than at the overall organization level, because a single dominant technology is more likely to exist in specific units.[67] Strong technology effects also occur in small organizations, because a single dominant technology is likely to exist there as well.

The Role of Organizational Size

It is not surprising that size has implications for organizational structure.[68] As an organization grows, it generally becomes taller; otherwise, the average span of control for managers becomes too large. As organizations increase in size, formalization also tends to increase to help maintain order. However, centralization tends to decrease, as senior managers cannot comprehend all of the organization's work and make all decisions.

The most important measure of size is the number of associates and managers. Research shows that managerial decisions regarding structure are based on the factors that are most salient to managers. Because people are highly important to most managers, managerial decisions on structure are often influenced by the number of people for whom the managers have responsibility.[69]

Summary of Effects on Structure

In summary, corporate strategy and organizational size have strong effects on the structural characteristics of organizations—those that determine the shape and appearance of the hierarchy. Corporate strategy is a particularly strong determinant of departmentation, and size is an especially strong determinant of height and spans of control. Business strategy, environmental uncertainty, and technological nonroutineness have strong effects on unit structuring within organizations, as well as overall organizational structuring in small organizations.

An important study has shown how business strategy, environmental uncertainty, technological nonroutineness, and structure work together to influence performance in organizational units as well as in small organizations.[70] In this study, strong performance was associated with consistency among these factors:

- Uncertain environments led to strategies based on differentiation and innovation, which in turn led to nonroutine work, all of which were matched by organic structure.

- More certain environments led to strategies based on low costs and efficiency, which in turn led to routine work, all of which were matched by a less organic structure.

Other studies have provided similar results,[71] suggesting that managers in effective firms create consistency across strategy, environment, technology, and structure.

Organizational Culture

Culture is closely related to most other concepts in organizational behavior, including structure, leadership, communication, groups, motivation, and decision making.[72] Culture is affected by and can also affect these other areas of organizational functioning and it is related to social, historic, and economic issues as well.[73] Thus, it is an important and encompassing concept.

Google's organizational culture is described in the *Experiencing Strategic Organizational Behavior* feature. Google's culture is highly informal, with a decentralized structure designed to enhance associates' creativity. Google must be doing something right because it is a highly successful company. Its culture and structure,

Google Culture Attracts High-Quality Associates

Larry Page and Sergy Brin graduated from Stanford University in 1995 with computer science degrees. They wanted to build a search engine that would retrieve selective information from the vast amount of data available on the Internet. In 1997, they named their search engine "Backrub," and in 1998 they renamed it to "Google" (*Google* is a play on *googol*, the mathematical term for a 1 followed by 100 zeros—a reference to organizing the seemingly infinite Web). By 2003, it was the most preferred search engine in the world, due to its precision and speed in delivering the desired data in searches. But their success was also attributed to Google's organizational culture.

*Kate Lacey/The
New York Times/
Redux Pictures*

Google's work environment was successful because Page and Brin avoided all unnecessary managerial hierarchies, creating a decentralized structure, and gave their engineers complete autonomy to encourage creative thinking. Google has no management structure and most engineers work in teams of three, with project leadership rotating among them. These teams had complete autonomy and freedom to create, reporting directly to the vice president. Open communication is encouraged and employees are free to approach top management as desired. They are allowed to communicate with anyone in any department. Employees were also asked to eat in the cafeteria so they could meet others in the company and create opportunities for them to share and discuss technical ideas or issues. In addition, every Friday afternoon all employees are provided information about new products and how the company is financially performing. Google's emphasis on innovation and commitment to cost containment means each employee is a hands-on contributor. The decentralized model of management and open lines of communication are essential parts of Google's organizational culture. And the organizational structure and culture have helped the firm attract and retain the most talented individuals in the field. Google's work culture has become legendary in Silicon Valley.

Larry and Sergy also felt it was important to create a fun place to work and incorporate incentives that could attract top talent. Google headquarters, known as the *Googleplex*, was decorated with lava lamps, giant plastic balls, and bright colors. Employees are also allowed to bring their pets to work and are provided free snacks, lunch, and dinner, prepared by an award-winning former chef to the Grateful Dead. The founders said that the free, healthy meals came about after calculating the time saved from driving off-site and reduced health-care costs. They have even provided a Webcam that monitors the cafeteria lunch line, so employees can avoid a long wait. Employees are also provided recreational activities, which include workout gyms, assorted video games, pool tables, Ping Pong tables, and roller-skater hockey. Additional benefits include flexible work hours, company-paid, midweek ski trips to Squaw Valley, and maternity/paternity leave with 75 percent pay.

A few people have criticized Google's organizational culture and management model. Some believe that Google has outgrown the informal culture and that it will not be able to sustain the growth and still maintain the informal lines of communication. Critics argue that even though engineers are free to pursue individual projects, the informality makes it difficult to coordinate and plan activities.

But Google continues to defend the consensus-management structure suggesting that partnerships make better decisions. In addition, Google's focus on maintaining a flat organization, where any employee can address company co-founders on a weekly basis, and its impressive perks still makes it one of the most desirable companies. As a result, it continues to attract some of the top talent in the industry.

Google's culture and its talented associates has allowed it to continue to enhance its Internet search capabilities maintaining its competitive advantage over formidable rivals such as Microsoft and Yahoo!. The culture and structure encourages and facilitates the development of innovative new services by associates helping Google to become one of the most successful companies in the world.

Sources: Carmine Gallo, 2006, "How to Run a Meeting Like Google," *BusinessWeek,* Sept. 27, www.businessweek.com; B-School News, 2006, "They Love it Here, and Here, and Here," *BusinessWeek,* June 4, www.businessweek.com; Matt Marshall, 2003, "See Google," *Mercury News,* May 4, www.keepmedia.com; Jade Chang, 2006, "Behind the Glass Curtain," *BusinessWeek,* July 18, *www.businessweek.com;* corporate info, 2007, Google website, www.google.com/intl/en/about; Ben Elgin, 2004, "Google: Why the World's Hottest Tech Company Will Struggle to Keep Its Edge," *BusinessWeek,* May 3, www.businessweek.com.

along with its interrelated management model, have attracted significant human capital and that is probably one of the reasons for its success. Google's approach is highly similar to a high-involvement organization.

Organizational cultures are based on shared values as described earlier.[74] As noted, culture begins with shared values, which then produce norms that govern behavior. Behavior produces outcomes that are reinforced or punished, thereby bolstering the culture. Thus, any culture, positive or negative, becomes self-reinforcing and difficult to change. The process of culture development and reinforcement is shown in Exhibit 13-7.

The strength of an organization's culture is based to some degree on the homogeneity of associates and managers and the length and intensity of shared experiences in the organization.[75] The longer a culture is perpetuated, the stronger it becomes because of its self-reinforcing nature. The self-reinforcing nature of culture is evident in a story told at IBM. A young woman of slight build (98 pounds) had the job of ensuring that all people entering security areas had appropriate clearance identification. On one occasion, she was approached by

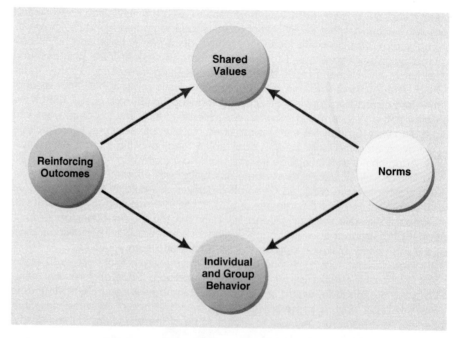

Exhibit 13-7   Process of Developing Organizational Culture

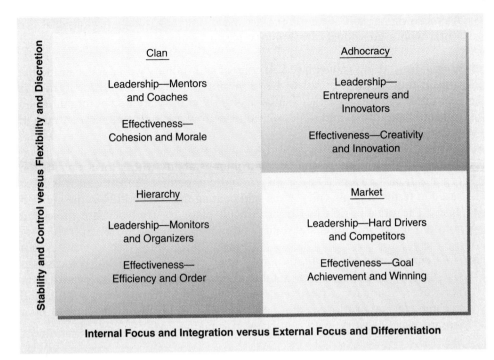

Exhibit 13-8 Competing Values Model of Organizational Culture

Thomas Watson, Jr.—who was chairman of the board at the time—and several other executives. Watson did not have the proper clearance identification to enter the area, and the young woman stopped him. One of the accompanying executives asked her if she knew who Watson was. Of course, she did know and was quite afraid, but she stood her ground. Watson urged his colleagues to be silent and to obtain the necessary clearance identification for him to enter. The young woman was doing her job and was praised for it. All associates and managers were expected to obey the rules, even the chairman of the board. And all employees, regardless of their rank, were expected to uphold and enforce the rules.[76]

Competing Values Model of Culture

Several models of culture have been proposed; one of the most popular in business firms is the competing values model, in which two value dimensions are central.[77] The first dimension relates to the value placed on *flexibility and discretion* versus *stability and control*. In some organizations, managers and associates believe in the power and usefulness of flexibility and discretion, while in other organizations individuals believe in the power of a stable work situation where control is strongly maintained. The second dimension relates to the value placed on an *internal focus* coupled with *integration* versus an *external focus* coupled with *differentiation* in the marketplace. In some organizations, associates and managers prefer to focus internally; in other organizations, individuals have an external orientation.

From these two dimensions, four types of culture emerge (see Exhibit 13-8):

1. *Clan*—strong value placed on flexibility and discretion with a focus inside the organization. Leaders tend to be mentors and coaches. Effectiveness is evaluated in terms of the cohesion and morale of individuals inside the firm and

tacit knowledge held. Overall, the organization tends to be a friendly place to work, with a great deal of commitment and loyalty.

2. *Hierarchy*—strong value placed on control and stability with a focus inside the organization. Leaders tend to be monitors and organizers. Effectiveness is measured in terms of efficiency and orderly coordination. The organization tends to be a formal and standardized place to work with emphasis on explicit knowledge.[78]

3. *Market*—strong value placed on control and stability with a focus outside the organization. Leaders tend be driven and competitive. Effectiveness is measured in terms of goal achievement and beating the competition in the marketplace. The organization can be a difficult place to work because there is a constant focus on results and doing better than colleagues.

4. *Adhocracy*—strong value placed on flexibility and discretion with a focus outside the organization. Leaders tend to be entrepreneurial and innovative, perhaps even visionary. Effectiveness is evaluated in terms of creativity and leading-edge innovation in the marketplace. The organization tends to be a vibrant place to work, with significant risk taking.

Organizations usually possess elements of all four cultural types. In fact, organizations need all four because morale, innovation, success relative to competitors in the marketplace, and efficiency are all important for long-term performance and survival.[79] In most cases, however, an organization emphasizes one cultural type over another. Each culture can be useful as a point of emphasis, depending on circumstances. Hierarchy, for example, might be emphasized in an organization pursuing a low-cost business strategy in all of its product lines. In such an organization, however, managers must be careful not to allow the emphasis on hierarchy to become too great. If hierarchy is overemphasized, it will be difficult to incorporate the decision- and team-related aspects of high-involvement management.[80] Furthermore, research suggests that the hierarchy culture can reduce commitment and satisfaction. Market culture could be useful in industries that are highly competitive. Clan culture is often more useful for organizations operating in regulated industries or in small new-venture firms where working with good colleagues and positive working relationships are emphasized more than financial compensation. Google has used such a culture since its startup. However, even as a large, more established organization, Google continues to use this culture successfully. Adhocracy might be emphasized in an organization pursuing the differentiation strategy in its product lines.

Clearly, organizational cultures affect managers' and associates' behaviors and thus organizational performance. The core values of an organization serve to attract new associates that share similar values or at least are comfortable with them.[81] For example, research has shown that organizational culture affects the extent to which associates are willing to accept changes in an organization. Specifically, associates who perceived an organizational culture that positively valued human relations are more willing to participate in and accept changes made by the organization.[82] Additionally, other studies have shown that when the organizational culture promotes respect for people, associates are more likely to view relationships with leaders more positively and to perceive that the organization treats associates fairly. Therefore, such cultures are likely to support an organization's competitive advantage because of a motivated workforce and low turnover among associates.[83]

Cultural Socialization

Newcomers are taught an organization's culture through **socialization**—the imparting of the organization's values. Socialization can take several forms. Based on groundbreaking work by noted culture researchers John Van Maanen and Ed Schein, researchers have focused on three sets of issues: context, content, and social dynamics.[84]

Context refers to whether newcomers are exposed to key values through a collective or individual process, and whether they experience a formal or informal approach. In a collective process, all newcomers experience the same socialization events (videos, senior leadership greetings, exercises, receptions, stories, and so on). In an individual process, the experiences are unique. With a formal approach, newcomers learn about the organization away from the jobs they will be taking (off-the-job learning and training), whereas an informal approach puts them in their jobs immediately (on-the-job learning and training). To maximize absorption of an organization's values, a collective, formal approach may be best. This approach ensures that newcomers are exposed to a standard set of tactics in a focused manner away from the pressures of the new job. Bain and Company, a management consulting firm, illustrates this approach. It uses a formal standard induction program to provide specific training and to build cohesiveness and a sense of identity with the firm. This is supported by excellent materials on the Bain website that explain the company's culture and provide consultants' journals with valuable information on the jobs the new recruits will likely hold. In the program and on the website, information is provided to reinforce the idea that senior colleagues serve as mentors and coaches.[85]

Content refers to whether newcomers are provided information on the probable sequence of development activities and job rotations for the first year or two in the organization, and whether they are given specific information on the likely duration of each activity. With detailed information on upcoming development activities, newcomers experience less uncertainty. They have a better sense of where they are going in the organization. When information provided to newcomers conveys a variable and random situation (no set sequence of development activities and no estimates of duration times), newcomers are less able to discern a clear path to success and advancement. This latter situation can create satisfaction and commitment issues.

Social dynamics refer to whether newcomers experience serial or disjunctive processes and whether they are exposed to an investiture or divestiture approach. Newcomers experiencing a serial approach have experienced organizational members as role models. The disjunctive process does not formally establish contact with experienced associates and managers, forcing newcomers to make sense of the situation on their own. With the investiture approach, positive social support is provided from the beginning rather than negative information through a hazing process. The combination of serial and investiture techniques yields better socialization experiences.

In a high-involvement organization, socialization is usually an easier task, as the process begins before employment, during the selection process. Most applicants are rigorously screened with the purpose of discouraging those who may not fit the culture. For example, at Southwest Airlines, the socialization process begins well

socialization
A process through which an organization imparts its values to newcomers.

Michael Newman/Photo Edit

before the applicant is hired. Applicants are exhaustively screened by a number of interviewers. The interview team does not oversell Southwest but describes both the advantages and disadvantages of working for the firm. The purpose is to make sure that the applicant's values and objectives mesh with those of the airline.[86] The process has been highly effective, as Southwest's culture is often given credit for the company's success. In 2006, Southwest Airlines was ranked for the tenth straight year as one of the best corporations in the United States by *Fortune* magazine.[87]

Integrating new associates into the organization's culture is important, especially for maintaining the culture. Research has shown that organizations with highly integrative cultures, whether they are focused on associate development and harmony or customer orientation and innovation often perform better than organizations that pay less attention to their cultures.[88]

Cultural Audits

cultural audit
A tool for assessing and understanding the culture of an organization.

Managers must understand and monitor their organization's current culture to develop and effectively manage it.[89] Thus, a **cultural audit** should be conducted periodically. This type of audit is an analysis designed to uncover shared values and beliefs in an organization. It should identify the strengths and weaknesses of the current culture with respect to the support it provides for the achievement of the organization's goals.[90]

The following five steps may be used in conducting a cultural audit:[91]

1. Analyze the process and content of the socialization of new associates and managers (interview those directly involved in socialization).

2. Analyze responses to critical incidents in the organization's history (construct an organizational biography from documents and interviews of past and present associates and managers).

3. Analyze the values and beliefs of culture creators (founders) and carriers (current leaders) (observe and/or interview the founders and current leaders).

4. Explore anomalies or puzzling features discovered in other analyses (initiate joint problem-solving sessions with current leaders in the organization).

5. Examine the linkage of the current organizational culture to its goals.

A cultural audit is a complex and sometimes lengthy process that should be conducted only after careful planning and preparation. The results of an audit might indicate a culture that is not well developed or might disclose the presence of subcultures. An underdeveloped culture poses less of a problem than one that is dysfunctional, fully developed, and self-reinforcing, because the less-developed culture can be more easily influenced and its path altered if necessary.

Subcultures

subcultures
In the organizational context, groups that share values that differ from the main values of the organization.

It is possible for **subcultures** to develop in an organization, particularly when no dominant organizational culture exists or when the organization is diverse and geographically dispersed.[92] Subcultures are based on values shared by a group rather than by an organization as a whole. Some of the values of the subculture are similar to and others are dissimilar from the organization's values and the values of other groups. The existence of subcultures complicates the development and management of an organizational culture.

In large, diverse organizations, some researchers advocate viewing organizational culture as a system of integrated subcultures rather than a unified set of values.[93] In such cases, senior managers need to understand each subculture, ensure that it is appropriate for its market segment, and decide whether it fits with critical organizational values. Thus, a manager's purpose is to encourage the integration of critical organizational values in each subculture.

When subcultures exist, at least one could include values that are substantially counter to those of the overall organization. Such a counterculture may be difficult to manage. Although a counterculture often creates problems, it can also produce positive outcomes. For example, a counterculture can induce a revolution, forcing change in a staid, outmoded culture. It also may encourage the development of new and creative ideas not allowed by existing norms of the organizational culture.[94]

MANAGERIAL ADVICE

Finding a Fit at Home Depot

Research indicates that similarity in values and goals draws individuals to specific organizations. When an individual's management style and values are not congruent with the organization's culture, problems can develop. This is the reason why problems developed after Home Depot hired Bob Nardelli as CEO in 2000. Home Depot wanted to remain adaptive and make some necessary changes to increase stock prices by bringing in a key individual that the board of directors felt could accomplish this. In addition, the board believed that Bob Nardelli's ideas might prompt reflection and help Home Depot make needed changes to impress investors and "pump up" its stock price.

In the early years, Home Depot founders Bernie Marcus and Arthur Blank took it personally if a customer left without buying something. Home Depot's culture was similar to a clan, as the founders placed strong value on flexibility, leaders tended to be mentors and coaches, and they worked to achieve group cohesion and high morale among the associates. The organization was known to be a friendly place to work and they established a decentralized, entrepreneurial business model. Home Depot was famous for its freewheeling, entrepreneurial spirit, with individual stores operated in a highly autonomous manner. Every aspect of the store operations was the responsibility of local management. Using that model, it became the fastest-growing retailer in U.S. history, expanding from a three-store startup in 1979 to a $45 billion chain in 2000. But with the growth, the company found that it struggled with its internal systems and controls and change was necessary in order to accommodate and manage more growth.

Nardelli's changes were too strong and conflicted with the Home Depot culture. After five years with Nardelli as CEO, the company began looking and feeling like a military organization. He embarked on an aggressive plan to centralize control, and to support this change Home Depot invested more than $1 billion in new technology. To help generate the desired data, the company purchased self-checkout aisles and inventory management systems. He felt it was important to measure everything that occurred in the company and hold executives accountable for meeting "their numbers." Nardelli implemented a military management model that imported

Scott Olson/
Gettty Images

ideas, people, and platitudes from the military, which was a key part of the move to reshape Home Depot into a more centralized organization. The culture he was trying to create would value hierarchy, control, and stability with leaders emphasizing monitoring and organizing in an efficient manner. In making these changes, Nardelli failed to keep the entrepreneurial spirit alive in the company.

Some former executives said that Nardelli had created a "culture of fear" and a demoralized staff, which in turn caused customer service to wane. While some praise Nardelli for bringing greater discipline and structure, others blame him for eroding the entrepreneurial culture at Home Depot. Many on Wall Street felt that Nardelli never understood the value of the previous organizational culture. Associates did not embrace his military-style leadership and some feel this was the reason Home Depot struggled with customer satisfaction and performance in the stock market. As much as Nardelli attempted to change the company culture from a decentralized model to a centralized model, employees and even stockholders were unwilling to accept his leadership style. Thus, the fit between an individual and the organization was unsuccessful and had debilitating effects on the company's performance. In early 2007, it was announced that Nardelli departed the company in a disagreement with the board of directors. Many were pleased to see him go.

Sources: Theresa Forsman, 2000, "The Maverick's Manual for Entrepreneurial Success," *BusinessWeek,* Dec. 5, www.businessweek.com; Brian Grow, 2006, "Renovating Home Depot," *BusinessWeek,* Mar. 6, www.businessweek.com; Andrew Ward, 2007, "Two More Executives Quit Home Depot," *Financial Times,* Mar. 2, www.ft.com; 2007, investor relations, Home Depot website, www.ir.homedepot.com; Julie Creswell & Michael Barbaro, 2007, "Home Depot Ousts Chief," *International Herald Tribune,* Jan. 4, www.iht.com.

The *Managerial Advice* segment provides an example of a misfit between a key manager and the company's culture. Bob Nardelli was hired as CEO of Home Depot to make some changes. He did so, but went further than desired by the board. His changes strongly revised the culture of the firm, making it control oriented, whereby the entrepreneurial spirit among store managers and associates was lost. While Home Depot likely needed better control systems, Nardelli's changes went too far. This example shows the importance of a person–organization fit, discussed next.

Person–Organization Fit

As suggested throughout this discussion of structure and culture, the fit between an individual and the organization has important implications for satisfaction, commitment, intent to turnover, and job performance.[95] **Values** are abstract ideals related to proper life goals and methods for reaching those goals. As such, individual values often underlie groups of attitudes. Although people may have thousands of attitudes, most likely they have only a few-dozen values.[96] Thus, values are more general than attitudes and form the basis for how we should behave. For example, we could have the underlying value that family time is highly important and a corresponding negative attitude toward a colleague who works most nights and many weekends.

Values emerge as individuals mature and as they develop the ability to form general concepts from their accumulated experiences. Also, during value formation, the value judgments of people we respect influence the nature of our values. Finally, as discussed in Chapter 2, national and ethnic culture affects the development of values.

Once formed, values serve as frames of reference that help guide people's behavior in many different contexts. Values may be modified or refined as a result of new

values
Abstract ideals that relate to proper life goals and methods for reaching those goals.

experiences but are much more resistant to change than are attitudes. Thus, individuals will not change their values to join a particular organization. Rather, they make choices based on the agreement between their personal values and those of the organization. Many organizations try to select new associates who share the values consistent with their organization culture. For example, the individuals who work at Southwest Airlines are likely to share values concerning equality, hard work and having fun at work, partly because of the recruitment practices of Southwest and partly due to the choices made by individuals on where they prefer to work.

Values develop along two dimensions: (1) the types of personal goals that one ought to have and (2) the types of behaviors that one ought to use in reaching those goals.[97] These two dimensions are sometimes referred to as the end–means dimensions of values. Thus, individuals may develop an end value that they should seek a life of prosperity and a means value that they should be ambitious and hardworking to achieve that goal. These values complement each other by specifying a general goal in life and identifying acceptable behaviors for reaching it. A list of "end" values and "means" values is shown in Exhibit 13-9.

Research has shown that basic personal values affect individual reactions to job situations.[98] Our satisfaction with the type of work we do, the rules imposed by the organization, career advancement opportunities, and other organizational factors are evaluated in terms of our values. Workers' reactions to jobs in different cultures may vary because of differing basic value systems. For example, the basic value systems in the United States emphasize self-reliance and initiative, whereas in Japan basic value systems emphasize self-sacrifice, obedience, and cooperation. As

Exhibit 13-9	Types of Personal Values
End (Goal) Values	**Means (Behavior) Values**
Prosperity	Ambition and hard work
Stimulating, active life	Open-mindedness
Achievement	Competence
World peace	Cheerfulness
Harmony in nature and art	Cleanliness
Equality	Courageousness
Personal and family security	Forgiving nature
Freedom	Helpfulness
Happiness	Honesty
Inner peace	Imagination
Mature love	Independence and self-reliance
National security	Intelligence
Pleasure and enjoyment	Rationality
Religion and salvation	Affection and love
Self-respect	Obedience and respect
Social respect	Courtesy
Friendship	Responsibility
Wisdom	Self-discipline

Source: Adapted from M. Rokeach, *The Nature of Human Values* (New York: The Free Press, 1973).

explained in Chapter 3, this difference has implications for how high-involvement management systems should be developed in different cultures.

When an individual's values and preferences do not fit prevailing structural arrangements, she may be a less satisfied, less positive contributor to the organization. Similarly, and perhaps more importantly, when an individual's values are not congruent with the organization's culture, problems are likely to develop. In fact, when the lack of fit is between the CEO and the organization's culture, the problems are likely to be more severe as in the case of Home Depot and Bob Nardelli. The outcomes are consistent with a great deal of research suggesting that similarity in values and goals draws individuals to one another and to organizations.[99] Job applicants as well as associates and managers in an organization should assess applicant fit with structure and culture prior to making final employment decisions. Selection for fit is a key aspect of high-involvement management, as discussed in Chapter 1.

Interestingly, socialization can bridge some differences between newcomer preferences and organizational structure, and between newcomer values and organizational culture. Socialization achieves this function by highlighting how a person's preferences and values may fit in unseen or partial ways. To some small degree, socialization also may alter a newcomer's preferences. In a recent study based on the socialization framework presented earlier, individuals exposed to strong socialization efforts exhibited more congruence between their personal attributes and the organization's structure and culture. (This was true even after taking into account the initial level of congruence.)[100]

Although fit with structure and culture is important, two issues must be addressed. First, an organization that hires only those who fit existing organizational characteristics may find it difficult to transform itself if this becomes necessary.[101] With individuals throughout the organization sharing preferences and values, the organization may be resistant to change. To remain adaptive, an organization may want to hire a few key individuals who do not fit. Their ideas may prompt reflection and may help an organization change if necessary. These issues are addressed more fully in the next chapter. Second, an organization that hires only those who fit may inadvertently discriminate against minorities or foreign nationals.[102] Such an organization would fail to experience the benefits of being multicultural, as discussed in Chapter 2. Perhaps the best advice is to hire for fit, but with a relatively broad definition of fit allowing exceptions and a specific plan for nurturing the exceptions, no matter what their differences.[103]

The Strategic Lens

We have emphasized that an organization's structure and culture play important roles in the implementation of its strategy. For example, if an organization's business strategy is to be a "first mover" in the market, it must be innovative in order to develop and introduce new products before competitors do so. To be entrepreneurial and innovative, the organization needs a flexible decentralized structure, one that is organic. A centralized mechanistic structure would not allow managers and associates the freedom to be creative and take the risks necessary to identify market opportunities and develop innovative products. Similarly, the culture of the organization must allow for the use of intuition and risk-taking behaviors because associates and managers should not be afraid of making errors or failing.

In the chapter, we mentioned that Southwest Airlines has been highly successful because of its culture and its ability to hire new associates and managers who fit well with the culture. Southwest has followed an integrated low-cost/differentiation business strategy since its founding. Many airlines have tried to imitate this strategy but have been unable to reproduce Southwest's success. These competitors have failed to realize that Southwest employs a differentiation strategy of delivering high-quality service through its associates in addition to the low cost. Southwest's associates have fun at work and work together as a team. These attributes come through in the service provided and also help the airline to hold down its costs. Thus, Southwest Airlines' unique strategy, which integrates low cost and differentiation, is implemented effectively because of its culture and human resource management system.[104] Other airlines could not reproduce this integrated strategy because they could not imitate Southwest's culture.

A strategy will be only as effective as its implementation. If the strategy is well formulated, and the structure and the culture fit the strategy well, the organization will achieve higher performance. Congruence among strategy, structure, and culture is necessary for the highest possible organization performance.

Culture's effects on strategy are also often evident in mergers and acquisitions. Many mergers between companies fail. Often these failures occur not because of financial or technical problems but because the companies involved have vastly different organizational cultures.[105] One company may be entrepreneurial and flexible, for example, whereas the other may be traditional and rigid. Merging these two cultures is problematic at the least.

Therefore, senior managers who expect their firm to acquire another firm should understand the target firm's culture and what must be done to integrate it. They must also act immediately after the completion of the acquisition to merge the cultures. Doing so will require developing shared values between the two firms. Cisco Systems is well known for its ability to integrate acquisitions.[106] This firm assigns key people to preacquisition integration teams and carefully includes individuals from the firm being acquired.

Critical Thinking Questions

1. Consider an organization of which you are a member or an associate. What is the structure in this organization? Is it centralized or decentralized? Is it organic and flexible? How would you change the structure in this organization to make it more effective?

2. How would you describe the culture in the organization discussed in question #1? How does the culture affect members' behavior in the organization?

3. When you become a manager, what type of culture will you establish in your unit? What values do you want to emphasize? Why?

What This Chapter Adds to Your Knowledge Portfolio

In this chapter, we have described several aspects of structure and explained how strategy, environment, technology, and firm size influence structure. We have also discussed the competing values culture framework, as well as socialization, subcultures, and cultural audits. Person–organization fit has also been addressed. In summary, we have made the following points:

- Organizational structure is the formal system of work roles and authority relationships that govern how associates and managers interact with one another. Structure can be described using structural characteristics, which determine the shape and appearance of an organization's hierarchy. These characteristics include height, spans of control, and departmentation (functional versus divisional grouping of resources). Structure can also be described using structuring characteristics, which directly prescribe behavior. These include centralization (the amount of decision authority held at the top of the organization), standardization (the existence of rules and standard operating procedures), formalization (the degree to which rules and procedures exist in written form), and specialization (the degree to which associates and managers have narrow jobs). Modern organizations tend to emphasize configurations of structural and structuring characteristics that yield a substantial amount of freedom for lower-level managers and associates.

- Strategy plays an important role in organizational structure. Corporate strategy corresponds to the emphasis placed on growth and diversification in a firm. An emphasis on growth through internal development suggests the need for substantial research and development and marketing departments. An emphasis on growth though acquisition suggests the need for well-developed financial and legal functions. Diversification must be matched by type of departmentation, with a single business strategy and a dominant-product strategy calling for a functional structure and higher levels of diversification calling for a divisional structure. Business-level strategies represent the method of competing in a particular product or service market. Low-cost and differentiation are two popular strategies, with low-cost calling for a less organic structure and differentiation requiring a more organic structure.

- The external environment also plays a role in structure. Uncertain environments (those that are complex and changing) create a need for organic structure. They also increase the need for integration among functional departments focused on the same market. Elements of structure that address integration include slack resources, self-contained tasks, information technology, and lateral relations. Furthermore, different levels of uncertainty may be experienced by different functional departments, resulting in a need to differentiate the departments, with some being more organic than others.

- Technology, too, plays a role in structure. An early framework suggests that technological complexity determines the structure required in small manufacturing firms. More recent work demonstrates that mass customization can be used in manufacturing firms of all sizes and that organic structure facilitates this approach. Recent work has also focused on technological nonroutineness in manufacturing and service organizations, suggesting that high levels of nonroutineness in small organizations and units of larger ones should be matched with more organic structures.

- Finally, organizational size plays a role in structure. Large organizations must be taller and more formalized in order to ensure smooth functioning. Centralization tends to decrease, however, because senior managers cannot make all decisions.

- Organizational culture represents shared values that influence behavior. The competing values culture model is an important and popular framework for analyzing cultural phenomena in organizations. The model is based on two value dimensions: (1) flexibility and discretion versus stability and control and (2) internal focus coupled with integration versus an external focus coupled with differentiation in the marketplace. Based on these two dimensions, four culture types emerge: clan, hierarchy, market, and adhocracy.

- Socialization involves imparting an organization's values to newcomers. Socialization is accomplished by exposing individuals to experiences that highlight the organization's values. In designing socialization activities, managers and associates should consider context (collective and formal versus individual and informal), content (sequential and fixed versus variable and random), and social dynamics (serial and investiture versus disjunctive and divestiture).

- Culture audits are formal analyses designed to uncover shared values in an organization. They involve (1) analyzing the process and content of socialization, (2) analyzing how the organization has responded to critical incidents in its history, (3) analyzing the values and beliefs of founders and current leaders, and (4) exploring any puzzling findings from the earlier analyses.

- Subcultures can develop in an organization. In large, diverse organizations, the organizational culture can be seen as a system of integrated subcultures rather than a unified set of values. Although subcultures can sometimes cause problems when they are substantially inconsistent with the overall culture of the organization, they can also help to produce fresh insights and ideas.

- Individuals bring values to the organization. The fit between individual values and organization values can be important. If there is a misfit, individuals are likely to be unproductive or become dissatisfied and leave.

Back to the Knowledge Objectives

1. Compare and contrast the structural and structuring aspects of organizational structure.

2. Assume you manage a firm with three substantially different product lines. A differentiation strategy is used for each product line. What structure choices would you make, and why?

3. Assume you manage a small R&D department. When making choices concerning structure, would you be more concerned about the external environment, more concerned about technology, or equally concerned about the external environment and technology? Explain your answer.

4. What are the four types of culture in the competing values model? In which would you prefer to work, and why?

5. What is socialization? Describe a situation in which you were socialized into an organization (a club, a business firm, a church, or a volunteer organization).

6. What is a cultural audit? Why should organizations conduct cultural audits?

7. How does an organization ensure a fit between its associates' values and its organizational culture?

Thinking about Ethics

1. Organizations can have some units with organic structures and others with mechanistic structures. Is it equitable to allow some associates a great deal of freedom and flexibility and to tightly control the behaviors of the others? Why or why not?

2. Intuit's CEO, Steve Bennett, is fond of saying, "If you don't involve me in the takeoff, don't involve me in the crash." When a firm performs poorly, do managers who design and implement a mechanistic structure have responsibilities to protect the jobs of associates who have relatively little involvement and opportunity to affect the firm's results?

3. An organization, such as Southwest Airlines, might not hire a person who is fully qualified for the job but who is thought not to fit the organizational culture. What are the ethical implications, if any? Explain your answer.

4. In a market organizational culture, associates may be encouraged to compete against one another, with the emphasis on winning. What are the ethical implications, if any? Explain your answer.

5. An organization with an adhocracy culture encourages risk taking and allows associates to make errors. How do managers operating in such a culture decide when an associate is doing a poor job and should be laid off? Should the organization specify a maximum acceptable number of errors? Explain your answer.

Key Terms

organizational structure,
    p. 442
organizational culture, p. 442
structural characteristics,
    p. 443
hierarchy, p. 443
structuring characteristics,
    p. 443

height, p. 443
span of control, p. 443
departmentation, p. 445
centralization, p. 446
standardization, p. 446
formalization, p. 447
specialization, p. 447
corporate strategy, p. 448

growth, p. 448
diversification, p. 449
business strategy, p. 450
environmental uncertainty,
    p. 452
slack resources, p. 454
self-contained tasks.
    p. 454

Building Your Human Capital

An Assessment of Creativity

Many organizations use a differentiation strategy that calls for initiative and creativity. Many of these same organizations have an adhocracy culture, where innovation and risk taking are valued. Not all individuals, however, are equally suited for these organizations. This assessment focuses on creativity. Although an individual's propensity to be creative can vary from situation to situation, his or her general tendencies provide useful insight.

Instructions

In this assessment, you will read 50 statements that describe people. Use the rating scale below to indicate how accurately each statement describes you. Rate yourself as you generally are now, not as you wish to be in the future; and rate yourself as you honestly see yourself. Read each item carefully, and then circle the number that corresponds to your choice from the rating scale.

1	2	3	4	5
Strongly Disagree	Disagree	In-Between or Don't Know	Agree	Strongly Agree

1. I always work with a great deal of certainty that I am following the correct procedures for solving a particular problem.   1   2   3   4   5
2. It would be a waste of time for me to ask questions if I had no hope of obtaining answers.   1   2   3   4   5
3. I feel that a logical step-by-step method is best for solving problems.   1   2   3   4   5
4. I occasionally voice opinions in groups that seem to turn some people off.   1   2   3   4   5
5. I spend a great deal of time thinking about what others think of me.   1   2   3   4   5
6. I feel that I may have a special contribution to give to the world.   1   2   3   4   5
7. It is more important for me to do what I believe to be right than to try to win the approval of others.   1   2   3   4   5
8. People who seem unsure and uncertain about things lose my respect.   1   2   3   4   5
9. I am able to stick with difficult problems over extended periods of time.   1   2   3   4   5
10. On occasion I get overly enthusiastic about things.   1   2   3   4   5
11. I often get my best ideas when doing nothing in particular.   1   2   3   4   5
12. I rely on intuitive hunches and the feeling of "rightness" or "wrongness" when moving toward the solution of a problem.   1   2   3   4   5
13. When problem solving, I work faster analyzing the problem and slower when synthesizing the information I've gathered.   1   2   3   4   5
14. I like hobbies that involve collecting things.   1   2   3   4   5
15. Daydreaming has provided the impetus for many of my more important projects.   1   2   3   4   5

16. If I had to choose from two occupations other than the one I now have or am now training for, I would rather be a physician than an explorer.   1   2   3   4   5

17. I can get along more easily with people if they belong to about the same social and business class as myself.   1   2   3   4   5

18. I have a high degree of aesthetic sensitivity.   1   2   3   4   5

19. Intuitive hunches are unreliable guides in problem solving.   1   2   3   4   5

20. I am much more interested in coming up with new ideas than in trying to sell them to others.   1   2   3   4   5

21. I tend to avoid situations in which I might feel inferior.   1   2   3   4   5

22. In evaluating information, the source of it is more important to me than the content.   1   2   3   4   5

23. I like people who follow the rule "business before pleasure."   1   2   3   4   5

24. One's own self-respect is much more important than the respect of others.   1   2   3   4   5

25. I feel that people who strive for perfection are unwise.   1   2   3   4   5

26. I like work in which I must influence others.   1   2   3   4   5

27. It is important for me to have a place for everything and everything in its place.   1   2   3   4   5

28. People who are willing to entertain "crackpot" ideas are impractical.   1   2   3   4   5

29. I rather enjoy fooling around with new ideas, even if there is no practical payoff.   1   2   3   4   5

30. When a certain approach to a problem doesn't work, I can quickly reorient my thinking.   1   2   3   4   5

31. I don't like to ask questions that show my ignorance.   1   2   3   4   5

32. I can more easily change my interests to pursue a job or career than I can change a job to pursue my interests.   1   2   3   4   5

33. Inability to solve a problem is frequently due to asking the wrong questions.   1   2   3   4   5

34. I can frequently anticipate the solution to my problems.   1   2   3   4   5

35. It is a waste of time to analyze one's failures.   1   2   3   4   5

36. Only fuzzy thinkers resort to metaphors and analogies.   1   2   3   4   5

37. At times I have so enjoyed the ingenuity of a crook that I hoped he or she would go scot-free.   1   2   3   4   5

38. I frequently begin work on a problem that I can only dimly sense and cannot yet express.   1   2   3   4   5

39. I frequently tend to forget things, such as names of people, streets, highways, and small towns.   1   2   3   4   5

40. I feel that hard work is the basic factor in success.   1   2   3   4   5

41. To be regarded as a good team member is important to me.   1   2   3   4   5

42. I know how to keep my inner impulses in check.   1   2   3   4   5

43. I am a thoroughly dependable and responsible person.   1   2   3   4   5

44. I resent things being uncertain and unpredictable.   1   2   3   4   5

45. I prefer to work with others in a team effort rather than solo.   1   2   3   4   5

46. The trouble with many people is that they take things too seriously.   1   2   3   4   5

47. I am frequently haunted by my problems and cannot let go of them.   1   2   3   4   5

48. I can easily give up immediate gain or comfort to reach the goals I have set.   1   2   3   4   5

49. If I were a college professor, I would rather teach factual courses than those involving theory.   1   2   3   4   5

50. I'm attracted to the mystery of life.   1   2   3   4   5

Scoring Key

Combine the numbers you have circled, as follows:

Item 4 + Item 6 + Item 7 + Item 9 + Item 10 + Item 11 + Item 12 + Item 15 + Item 18 + Item 20 + Item 24 + Item 29 + Item 30 + Item 33 + Item 34 + Item 37 + Item 38 + Item 39 + Item 40 + Item 46 + Item 47 + Item 48 + Item 50 + [162 − (Item 1 + Item 2 + Item 3 + Item 5 + Item 8 + Item 13 + Item 14 + Item 16 + Item 17 + Item 19 + Item 21 + Item 22 + Item 23 + Item 25 + Item 26 + Item 27 + Item 28 + Item 31 + Item 32 + Item 35 + Item 36 + Item 41 + Item 42 + Item 43 + Item 44 + Item 45 + Item 49)]

Total scores can be interpreted as follows:

210–250	Very creative
170–209	Somewhat creative
130–169	Neither creative nor noncreative
90–129	Not very creative
50–89	Noncreative

Source: Adapted from D.D. Bowen, R.J. Lewicki, D.T. Hall, & F.S. Hall, *Experiences in Management and Organizational Behavior* (New York: John Wiley & Sons, 1997).

A Strategic Organizational Behavior Moment

How Effective Is Hillwood Medical Center?

Sharon Lawson is the administrator of Hillwood Medical Center, a large hospital located in Boston, Massachusetts. She has been its administrator for almost five years. Although it has been a rewarding position, it has not been without its frustrations. One of Sharon's primary frustrations has been her inability to determine how she should measure the effectiveness of the hospital.

The chief medical officer, Dr. Ben Peters, thinks that the only way to measure the effectiveness of a hospital is the number of human lives saved, compared with the number saved in other, similar hospitals. But the board to which Sharon reports is highly concerned about the costs of running the hospital. Hillwood is nonprofit but has no outside sponsors, and so it must remain financially solvent without contributions from another major institution.

In order to be reimbursed for Medicare and Medicaid patients, the hospital must meet the licensing requirements of the state health department, as well as the requirements of the U.S. Department of Health and Human Services. Sharon finds that some of these requirements reflect minimum standards, whereas others are more rigid. She also finds that the demands of the administrative board and those of doctors on the staff frequently conflict. She must mediate these demands and make decisions to maximize the effectiveness of the hospital.

Sharon's day begins when she arises at 6:00 A.M., exercises, showers, has a quick breakfast, and heads for the office. She usually arrives at the office around 7:15 A.M. She likes to get there before others so that she can review and plan her day's activities without interruption. Today she sees that she has an appointment at 8:30 A.M. with a member of the state health department concerning its recent inspection. At 10:00 A.M., she has an administrative staff meeting. At 2:00 P.M., she has scheduled a meeting with the medical staff, and at 4:00 P.M. she has an appointment with the hospital's attorney. (She also has a luncheon appointment with an old college friend who is in town for a few days.) It looks as if her day is well planned.

At 8:15, Sharon receives a call from Dr. Ramon Garcia, chief of surgery.

"Sharon, I must see you. Do you have time now so that we could talk about an important matter?"

"Ramon, I have an appointment in fifteen minutes and probably won't be free until about eleven this morning. Would that be okay?"

"I guess so. I don't have much choice, do I?" With that, he hangs up.

At 8:30, Sharon ushers in Holly Wedman from the state health department. She learns that Hillwood has passed the general inspection but that some areas need to be improved. The kitchen meets only minimum standards for cleanliness, and some other areas are questionable. The inspectors also questioned hospital procedures that allow many people access to the drug supplies. (Sharon recalls that she tried to tighten up those procedures only two months ago, but the medical staff complained so strongly that she relented and made no change.) The state health department representative requests that appropriate changes be made and notes that these areas will be given especially rigorous scrutiny at the next inspection in six months. As the meeting ends, Sharon looks at her watch. It is 9:55—just enough time to make it to the conference room for her next meeting.

The administrative staff meeting begins normally, but after about 30 minutes, Helen Mathis, controller, asks to speak.

"Sharon, when are we going to get the new computer hardware we requested six months ago?"

"I don't know, Helen. I've discussed it with the board, but they've been noncommittal. We'll have to try to build it into next year's budget."

"But we need it now. We can't process our billing efficiently. Our accounts receivable are too large. We're going to run into a cash-flow problem soon if we don't find other ways to increase our billing efficiency."

Sharon thought, "Cash-flow problems. I wonder how those fit into Dr. Peters's definition of effectiveness."

It is finally decided that Sharon will make a new and stronger request to the board for the computer hardware.

At 11:00 sharp, Dr. Garcia comes stomping into Sharon's office, exhibiting his usual crusty demeanor. "Sharon, we have a serious problem on our hands. I've heard through the grapevine that a malpractice suit will be filed against one of our surgeons, Dr. Chambers."

"That's nothing new; we get several of those a year."

"Yes, but I think this one may have some merit, and the hospital is jointly named in the suit."

"What do you mean?"

"Well, I've suspected for several months that Dr. Chambers has been drinking a lot. He may have performed an operation while under the influence. I've talked to several people who were in the operating room at the time, and they believe that he was drunk."

"Oh, no! If you suspected this why didn't you do something?"

"What was I supposed to do? Accuse one of the oldest and most respected members of our surgical staff? You just don't accuse a person like that without proof. We've got to meet with Chambers now and confront him."

"Well, set up a meeting."

"I already have. His only free time was at lunch, so I took the liberty of scheduling a meeting with him for you and me at that time."

"I already have an engagement. I can't do it today. Try to set one up tomorrow."

Dr. Garcia, obviously feeling a great deal of stress, explodes, "You administrators are never available when we need you. Your only concern is holding down costs. We're talking about human lives here. Chambers may do it again before tomorrow."

Sharon seethes at his insinuation. "If that mattered to you, why did you wait until you heard of the malpractice suit to do something about it?"

Garcia leaves, slamming the door.

Sharon goes to lunch with her friend, but she can't enjoy it. Her mind is on problems at the hospital. She can hardly wait for the 2:00 P.M. medical staff meeting.

The meeting begins with only about half of the doctors in attendance, which is not unusual. Most of them will show up before the meeting is over. Much of the time is taken up discussing why the hospital has not purchased an upgraded piece of standard diagnostic equipment used in body scanning. Of course, it "only" costs $700,000. The meeting ends without resolving the problem. Sharon agrees to buy the equipment next year but does not have the money for it in this year's budget. The doctors do not fully understand why it cannot be purchased now if it can be purchased next year.

As soon as Sharon gets back to her office, her secretary gives her a message to call Terry Wilson, one of the third-floor pediatric nurses. Terry had said it was urgent.

"Terry, this is Sharon Lawson. What can I do for you?"

"Ms. Lawson, I thought you should know. The nurses in pediatrics are planning a walkout tomorrow."

"What? A walkout? Why?" Sharon is beginning to get a headache.

"Yes, a walkout. The nurses feel that Supervisor Tyson is a tyrant, and they want her replaced."

"Terry, can you get a group of those nurses together and meet me in my office in fifteen minutes? Be sure to leave several to cover the floor while you're gone."

"Okay. See you in a few minutes."

Sharon and the nurses meet and discuss the situation. The nurses are quite adamant but finally agree to give Sharon a week to investigate the situation and attempt to resolve it. A meeting is scheduled for next week to review the situation.

The hospital's attorney has to wait for almost 20 minutes because Sharon's meeting with the nurses runs past 4:00 P.M. Finally they meet, and as Sharon feared, he brings news of the malpractice suit filed against Dr. Chambers and Hillwood. They discuss the steps that should be taken and how the situation with Dr. Chambers should be handled from a legal viewpoint. Obviously, some hard decisions will have to be made.

The attorney leaves at 5:30, and Sharon sits in her office pondering the day's problems. She also thinks of her original problem: how to measure Hillwood's effectiveness.

Discussion Questions

1. Describe the culture or cultures at Hillwood. Are there subcultures?

2. How would you recommend that Sharon measure effectiveness at Hillwood? What do you think some of the effectiveness criteria might be?

Team Exercise

Words-in-Sentences Company

In this exercise, you will form a "mini-organization" with several other people. You will also compete with other companies in your industry. The success of your company will depend on your planning and organizational structure. It is important, therefore, that you spend some time thinking about the best design for your organization.

Step 1: 5 Minutes

Form companies and assign workplaces. The total class should be divided into small groups of four or five individuals. Each group should consider itself a company.

Step 2: 10 Minutes

Read the directions below and ask the instructor about any points that need clarification. Everyone should be familiar with the task before beginning Step 3.

You are members of a small company that manufactures words and then packages them in meaningful (English-language) sentences. Market research has established that sentences of at least three words but not more than six words are in demand.

The "words-in-sentences" (WIS) industry is highly competitive in terms of price, and several new firms have recently entered the market. Your ability to compete depends on efficiency and quality control.

Group Task

Your group must design and participate in running a WIS company. You should design your organization to be as efficient as possible during each 10-minute production run. After the first production run, you will have an opportunity to reorganize your company if you want to.

Raw Materials

For each production run, you will be given a "raw material word or phrase." The letters found in the word or phrase serve as the raw materials available to produce new words in sentences. For example, if the raw material word is *organization,* you can produce the following words and sentence: "Nat ran to a zoo."

Production Rules

Several rules must be followed in producing "words-in-sentences." If these rules are not followed, your output will not meet production specifications and will not pass quality-control inspection.

1. A letter may appear only as often in a manufactured word as it appears in the raw-material word or phrase; for example, *organization* has two *o*'s. Thus, *zoo* is legitimate, but *zoology* is not—it has too many *o*'s.
2. Raw-material letters can be used over again in new, different manufactured words.
3. A manufactured word may be used only once in a sentence and in only one sentence during a production run; if a word—for example, *zoo*—is used once in a sentence, it is out of stock.
4. A new word may not be made by adding *s* to form the plural of an already used manufactured word.
5. A word is defined by its spelling, not its meaning.
6. Nonsense words or nonsense sentences are unacceptable.

7. All words must be in the English language.
8. Names and places are acceptable.
9. Slang is not acceptable.

Measuring Performance
The output of your WIS company is measured by the total number of acceptable words that are packaged in sentences in the available time. The sentences must be legible, listed on no more than two sheets of paper, and handed to the quality-control review board at the completion of each production run.

Delivery
Delivery must be made to the quality-control review board 30 seconds after the end of each production run.

Quality Control
If any word in a sentence does not meet the standards set forth above, all the words in the sentence will be rejected. The quality-control review board (composed of one member from each company) is the final arbiter of acceptability. In the event of a tie vote on the review board, a coin toss will determine the outcome.

Step 3: 15 Minutes
Design your organization's structure using as many group members as you see fit to produce your words-in-sentences. There are many potential ways of organizing. Since some are more efficient than others, you may want to consider the following:

1. What is your company's objective?
2. How will you achieve your objective? How should you plan your work, given the time allowed?
3. What degree of specialization and centralization is appropriate?
4. Which group members are more qualified to perform certain tasks?

Assign one member of your group to serve on the quality-control review board. This person may also participate in production runs.

Step 4: 10 Minutes—Production Run 1

1. The instructor will hand each WIS company a sheet with a raw material word or phrase.
2. When the instructor announces "Begin production," you are to manufacture as many words as possible and package them in sentences for delivery to the quality control review board. You will have 10 minutes.
3. When the instructor announces "Stop production," you will have 30 seconds to deliver your output to the quality-control review board. Output received after 30 seconds does not meet the delivery schedule and will not be counted.

Step 5: 10 Minutes

1. The designated members of the quality-control review board will review output from each company. The total output should be recorded (after quality-control approval) on the board.
2. While the review board is completing its task, each WIS company should discuss what happened during Production Run 1.

Step 6: 5 Minutes
Each company should evaluate its performance and organization. Companies may reorganize for Run 2.

Step 7: 10 Minutes—Production Run 2

1. The instructor will hand each WIS company a sheet with a raw-material word or phrase.

2. Proceed as in Step 4 (Production Run 1). You will have 10 minutes for production.

Step 8: 10 Minutes

1. The quality-control review board will review each company's output and record it on the board. The total Runs 1 and 2 should be tallied.

2. While the board is completing its task, each WIS company should prepare an organization chart depicting its structural characteristics for both production runs and should prepare a description of its structuring characteristics.

Step 9: 10 Minutes

Discuss this exercise as a class. The instructor will provide discussion questions. Each company should share the structure information it prepared in Step 8.

Source: Adapted from D.D. Bowen, R.J. Lewicki, D.T. Hall, & F.S. Hall, *Experiences in Management and Organizational Behavior* (New York: John Wiley & Sons, 1997).

Endnotes

1. Etzioni, A. 1964. *Modern organization.* Englewood Cliffs, NJ: Prentice Hall; Jones, G.R. 2007. *Organizational theory, design and change (5th edition)* Englewood Cliffs, NJ: Pearson Prentice Hall.

2. Bookbinder, S.M. 1984. Measuring and managing corporate culture. *Human Resource Planning,* 7 (1): 47–53; Ravashi, D. & Schultz, M. 2006. Responding to organizational identity threats: Exploring the role of organizational culture. *Academy of Management Journal,* 49: 433–458.

3. Evans, D.S. 2000. Sorry, wrong model: Splitting AT&T worked—Microsoft is a different story. *The Washington Post,* May 7, B01.

4. Brooke, T.W. 1986. The breakup of the Bell system: A case study in cultural transformation. *California Management Review,* 28: 110–124.

5. Campbell, J.P., Bownas, D.A., Peterson, N.G., & Dunnette, M.D. 1974. The measurement of organizational effectiveness: A review of the relevant research and opinion. Report Tr-71-1, San Diego, Navy Personnel Research and Development Center; Dalton, D.R., Todor, W.D., Spendolini, M.J., Fielding, G.J., & Porter, L.W. 1980. Organization structure and performance: A critical review. *Academy of Management Review,* 5: 49–64.

6. Keats, B. W. & O'Neill, H. 2001. Organizational structure: Looking through a strategy lens, in M.A. Hitt, R.E. Freeman, and J.S. Harrison (eds.), *Handbook of strategic management,* Oxford, UK: Blackwell Publishers, 520–542.

7. Campbell, Bownas, Peterson, & Dunnette, The measurement of organizational effectiveness; Dalton, Todor, Spendolini, Fielding & Porter, Organization structure and performance.

8. Child, J. 1984. *Organization: A guide to problems and practices (2nd ed.).* London: Harper & Row; Larson, E.W., & King, J.B. 1996. The systematic distortion of information: An ongoing challenge to management. *Organizational Dynamics,* 24 (3): 49–61; Nahm, A.Y., Vonderembse, M.A., & Koufteros, X.A. 2003. The impact of organizational structure on time-based manufacturing and plant performance. *Journal of Operations Management,* 21: 281–306.

9. Child, *Organization: A guide to problems and practices.*

10. Ibid.

11. Bohte, J., & Meier, K.J. 2001. Structure and the performance of public organizations: Task difficulty and span of control. *Public Organization Review,* 1: 341–354; Worthy, J.C. 1950. Organizational structure and employee morale. *American Sociological Review,* 15: 169–179.

12. Jones, *Organizational theory, design and change.*

13. Paine, L.S., & Mavrinac, S.C. 1995. *AES Honeycomb.* Boston: Harvard Business School Publishing; AES Corporation 2005 Annual Report, www.aes.com, March 3, 2007.

14. Davison, B. 2003. Management span of control: How wide is too wide? *The Journal of Business Strategy,* 24 (4): 22–29.

15. Duncan, R. 1979. What is the right organization structure? Decision tree analysis provides the answer. *Organizational Dynamics,* 7 (3): 59–80.

16. Ibid.

17. Ibid.

18. Ibid.

19. Daboub, A.J. 2002. Strategic alliances, network organizations, and ethical responsibility. *S.A.M. Advanced Management Journal,* 67 (4): 40–63; Maria, J., & Marti, V. 2004. Social

capital benchmarking system: Profiting from social capital when building network organizations. *Journal of Intellectual Capital*, 5: 426–442; Miles, R.E., Snow, C.C., Mathews, J.A., Miles, G., & Coleman, H.J. 1997. Organizing in the knowledge age: Anticipating the cellular form. *Academy of Management Executive*, 11 (4): 7–20.

20. Daboub, Strategic alliances, network organizations, and ethical responsibility. Maria, & Marti. Social capital benchmarking system: Profiting from social capital when building network organizations. Hitt, M.A., Ireland, R.D., & Hoskisson, R.E., 2007. *Strategic management: Competitiveness and globalization* (Cincinnati, OH: Thomson South-Western Publishing Co.).

21. Mintzberg, H. 1993. *Structuring in fives: Designing effective organizations*. Englewood Cliffs, NJ: Prentice-Hall, Inc.; Zabojnik, J. 2002. Centralized and decentralized decision making in organizations. *Journal of Labor Economics*, 20: 1–21.

22. Huber, G.P., Miller, C.C., & Glick, W.H. 1990. Developing more encompassing theories about organizations: The centralization-effectiveness relationship as an example. *Organization Science*, 1: 11–40; Tata, J., & Prasad, S. 2004. *Journal of Managerial Issues*, XVI: 248–265.

23. Burns, T., & Stalker, G.M. 1966. *The management of innovation*. London: Tavistock Institute; Jones, *Organization theory, design and change*.

24. The term "learning organization" has been defined in many different ways. As it stands, there is considerable confusion and disagreement concerning its proper definition. Many *users* of the term, however, focus on aspects of structure just as we do here. See, for example, Dodgson, M. 1993. Organizational learning: A review of some literatures. *Organization Studies*, 1: 375–394. Also see Goh, S.C. Toward a learning organization: The strategic building blocks. *S.A.M. Advanced Management Journal*, 63 (2): 15–22; For general insights, see Garvin, D.A. 1993. Building a learning organization. *Harvard Business Review*, 71 (4): 78–91.

25. The term "boundaryless organization" has been defined in various ways. Users of the term, however, generally refer to individuals having freedom and incentives to work across internal and external organizational boundaries. For a broad discussion, see Ashkenas, R., Ulrich, D., Jick, T., & Kerr, S. 1995. *The boundaryless organization*. San Francisco, CA: Jossey-Bass.

26. Berg, N.A., & Fast, N.O. 1975. *Lincoln Electric Company*. Boston: Harvard Business School Publishing.

27. Freiberg, K., & Freiberg, J. 1996. *Nuts!: Southwest Airlines' crazy recipe for business and personal success*. Austin, TX: Bard Press.

28. Sine, W.D., Mitsuhashi, H., & Kirsch, D.A., 2006. Revisiting Burns and Stalker: Formal structure and new venture performance in emerging economic sectors, *Academy of Management Journal*, 49: 121–132.

29. Thompson, J.P. 1967, *Organizations in action*. New York: McGraw-Hill.

30. Hitt, M.A., Ireland, R.D., & Palia, K.A. 1982. Industrial firm's grand strategy and functional importance: Moderating effects of technology and uncertainty. *Academy of Management Journal*, 3: 265–298.

31. Anonymous. 2004, December 19. Growth Strategy Leadership Award Given to Technology Company. *Medical Devices & Surgical Technology Week*, Atlanta, p. 25.

32. Hitt, M.A., Harrison, J.S., & Ireland, R.D. 2001. *Mergers and acquisitions: A guide to creating value for stakeholders*. New York: Oxford University Press.

33. Niedzielski, J. 1997. Frontier targets growth by acquisition. *National Underwriter*, 101 (47): 18–19.

34. Holloway, C.A., Wheelwright, S.C., & Tempest, N. 1999. *Cisco Systems, Inc.: Acquisition integration for manufacturing*. Palo Alto: Stanford Graduate School of Business.

35. Weber, Y., & Menipaz, E. 2003. Measuring cultural fit in mergers and acquisitions. *International Journal of Business Performance Management*, 5: 54–72.

36. Shimizu, K., & Hitt, M.A. 2005. What constrains or facilitates the divestiture of formerly acquired firms? The effects of organizational inertia. *Journal of Management*, 31: 50–72.

37. Palich, L.E., Cardinal, L.B., & Miller, C.C. 2000. Curvilinearity in the diversification-performance linkage: An examination of over three decades of research. *Strategic Management Journal*, 21: 155–174.

38. Hitt, M.A., & Ireland, R.D. 1986. Relationships among corporate level distinctive competence, diversification strategy, corporate structure and performance. *Journal of Management Studies*, 23: 401–416.

39. Grinyer, P.H., Bazzaz, S.A., & Yasai-Ardekani, M. 1980. Strategy, structure, environment, and financial performance in 48 United Kingdom companies. *Academy of Management Journal*, 23: 193–220; Rumelt, R.P. 1974. *Strategy, structure, and economic performance*. Cambridge, MA: Harvard University.

40. Hitt, Ireland, & Hoskisson, 2007. *Strategic management: Competitiveness and globalization*.

41. Grinyer, Bazzaz, & Yasai-Ardekani. Strategy, structure, environment, and financial performance in 48 United Kingdom companies; Hitt, & Ireland. Relationships among corporate level distinctive competence, diversification strategy, corporate structure and performance.

42. Porter, M.E. 1980. *Competitive strategy: Techniques for analyzing industries and competitors*. New York: The Free Press.

43. See, for example: Govindarajan, V. 1988. A contingency approach to strategy implementation at the business unit level: Integrating administrative mechanisms with strategy. *Academy of Management Journal*, 31: 828–853; Jones. *Organizational theory, design and change*.

44. Hoskisson, R.E., Hitt, M.A., Ireland, R.D., & Harrison, J.S. 2008. *Competing for advantage*, Cincinnati, OH: Thomson South-Western.

45. See, for example: Govindarajan, A contingency approach to strategy implementation at the business unit level: Integrating administrative mechanisms with strategy; Jones. *Organizational theory, design and change*; Vorhies, D.W., & Morgan, N.A. 2003. A configuration theory assessment of marketing organization fit with business strategy and its relationship with marketing performance. *Journal of Marketing*, 67: 100–115.

46. General Electric. 2004. Our company: Business directory. http://www.ge.com/en/company/ businesses/index.htm.

47. Bourgeois, L.J. 1980. Strategy and environment: A conceptual integration. *Academy of Management Review*, 5: 25–29.

48. Lawrence, P.R., & Lorsch, J.W. 1967. *Organization and environment*. Boston: Harvard Business School Press.

49. Burns & Stalker, *The management of innovation;* Child, J. 1975. Managerial and organizational factors associated with company performance—Part II. *Journal of Management Studies,* 12: 12–27; Naman, J.L., & Slevin, D.P. 1993. Entrepreneurship and the concept of fit: A model and empirical tests. *Strategic Management Journal,* 14: 137–153; Negandhi, A., & Reimann, C. 1973. Task environment, decentralization and organizational effectiveness. *Human Relations,* 26: 203–214; Priem, R.L. 1994. Executive judgement, organizational congruence, and firm performance. *Organization Science,* 421–437.

50. Sirmon, D.G., Hitt, M.A., & Ireland, R.D. 2007. Managing firm resources in dynamic environments to create value: Looking inside the black box. *Academy of Management Review,* 32: 273–292.

51. Garg, V.K., Walters, B.A., & Priem, R.L. 2003. Chief executive scanning emphases, environmental dynamism, and manufacturing firm performance. *Strategic Management Journal,* 24: 725–744.

52. Galbraith, J. 1973. *Designing complex organizations.* Reading, MA: Addison-Wesley.

53. Al-Mudimigh, Zairi, M., & Al-Mashari, M. 2001. ERP software implementation: An integrative framework. *European Journal of Information Systems,* 10: 216–226; Davenport, T. 2000. *Mission critical: Realizing the promise of enterprise systems.* Boston: Harvard Business School Press.

54. Johnson, T., Lorents, A.C., Morgan, J., & Ozmun, J. 2004. A customized ERP/SAP model for business curriculum integration. *Journal of Information Systems Education,* 15: 245–253.

55. Huber, G.P. 2004. *The necessary nature of future firms: Attributes of survivors in a changing world.* Thousand Oaks, CA: Sage Publications.

56. Woodward, J. 1965. *Industrial organization: Theory and practice.* London: Oxford University Press.

57. Clawson, J. 1991. *Stewart-Glapat Corporation (A).* Charlottesville, VA: Darden Business Publishing.

58. See http://www.gm.com/. Note that many companies such as General Motors and Dell now use advanced manufacturing techniques that allow more customization to specific orders. Mass customization allows these organizations to handle custom orders to some degree (see, for example, Selladurai, R.S. 2004. Mass customization in operations management: Oxymoron or reality? *Omega.* 32: 295-300.

59. See http://www.dupont.com.

60. See, for example: Harvey, E., 1968. Technology and the structure of organizations. *American Sociological Review,* 33: 241–259; Zwerman, W.L. 1970. *New perspectives on organizational effectiveness.* Westwood, CT: Greenwood.

61. Hitt, M.A., Keats, B.W., & Demarie, S.M. 1998. Navigating in the new competitive landscape: Building strategic flexibility and competitive advantage in the 21st century. *Academy of Management Executive,* 12(4):22–42.

62. Kotha, S. 1995. Mass customization: Implementing the emerging paradigm for competitive advantage. *Strategic Management Journal,* 16: 21–42; Pine, B. 1993. *Mass customization.* Boston, MA: Harvard Business School Press.

63. Hitt, M.A. 2000. The new frontier: Transformation of management for the new millennium. *Organizational Dynamics,* 28 (3): 7–17.

64. Perrow, C. 1970. *Organizational analysis: A sociological view.* Belmont, CA: Wadsworth.

65. Ibid.

66. See, for example: Argote, L. 1982. Input uncertainty and organizational coordination in hospital emergency units. *Administrative Science Quarterly,* 27: 420–434; Drazin, R., & Van de Ven, A.H. 1985. Alternative forms of fit in contingency theory. *Administrative Science Quarterly,* 30: 514–539; Schoonhoven, C.B. 1981. Problems with contingency theory: Testing assumptions hidden within the language of contingency theory. *Administrative Science Quarterly,* 26: 349–377.

67. Comstock, D.E., & Scott, W.R. 1977. Technology and the structure of subunits: Distinguishing individual and workgroup effects. *Administrative Science Quarterly, 22: 177–202;* Randolph, W.A., & Dess, G.G. 1984. The congruence perspective of organization design: A conceptual model and multivariate research approach. *Academy of Management Review,* 9: 114–127.

68. Child, *Organization: A guide to problems and practices.*

69. Ford, J.D., & Hegarty, W.H. 1984. Decision makers' beliefs about the causes and effects of structure: An exploratory study. *Academy of Management Journal,* 27: 271–291.

70. Doty, D.H., Glick, W.H., & Huber, G.P. 1993. Fit, equifinality, and organizational performance: A test of two configurational theories. *Academy of Management Journal,* 36: 1196–1250.

71. See, for example: Burton, R.M., Lauridsen, J., & Obel, B. 2002. Return on assets loss from situational and contingency misfits. *Management Science,* 48: 1461–1485.

72. Smircich, L. 1983. Concepts of culture and organizational analysis. *Administrative Science Quarterly,* 28: 339–358.

73. Deetz, S. 1985. Critical-cultural research: New sensibilities and old realities. *Journal of Management,* 11: 121–136.

74. Chatman, J.A., & Cha, S.E. 2003. Leading by leveraging culture. *California Management Review,* 45 (4): 20–34; Keeley, M. 1983. Values in organizational theory and management education. *Academy of Management Review,* 8: 376–386.

75. Tetrick, L.E., & Da Silva, N. 2003. Assessing culture and climate for organizational learning. In S.E. Jackson, M.A. Hitt, & A. DeNisi (Eds.), *Managing knowledge for sustained competitive advantage.* San Francisco, CA: Jossey-Bass, 333–359; Schein, E.H. 1984. Coming to a new awareness of organizational culture. *Sloan Management Review,* 25 (2): 3–16.

76. Martin, J., Feldman, M.S., Hatch, M.J., & Sitkin, S.B. 1983. The uniqueness paradox in organization stories. *Administrative Science Quarterly,* 28: 438–453.

77. Cameron, K.S., & Quinn, R.E. 1999. *Diagnosing and changing organizational culture: Based on the competing values framework.* Reading, MA: Addison-Wesley.

78. Turner, K.L., & Makhija, M.V. 2006. The role of organizational controls in managing knowledge. *Academy of Management Review,* 31: 197–217.

79. Quinn, R.E. 1988. *Beyond rationale management.* San Francisco, CA: Jossey-Bass.

80. Goodman, E.A., Zammuto, R.F., & Gifford, B.D. 2001. The competing values framework: Understanding the impact of organizational culture on the quality of work life. *Organization Development Journal,* 19 (3): 59–68.

81. van Rekom, J., van Riel, C.B.M., & Wierenga, B. 2006. A methodology for assessing organizational core values. *Journal of Management Studies,* 43: 175–201.

82. Jones, R.A., Jimmieson, N.L., & Griffiths, A. 2005. The impact of organizational culture and reshaping capabilities on change implementation success: The mediating role of readiness for change. *Journal of Management Studies,* 42: 361–386.

83. Erdogan, B., Liden, R.C., & Kraimer, M.L. 2006. Justice and leader-member exchange: The moderating role of organizational culture. *Academy of Management Journal,* 49: 395–406.

84. Cable, D.M., & Parsons, C.K. 2001. Socialization tactics and person-organization fit. *Personnel Psychology,* 54: 1–23; Jones, G.R, 1986. Socialization tactics, self-efficacy, and newcomers' adjustments to organizations. *Academy of Management Journal,* 29: 262–279. Also see Van Maanen, J., & Schein, E.H. 1979. Toward a theory of organizational socialization. *Research in Organizational Behavior,* 1: 209–264.

85. Bain & Company. 2007. http://www.bain.com/, April 17.

86. Freiberg, K., & Freiberg, J. 1996. *Nuts! Southwest Airline's crazy recipe for business and personal success.* Austin, TX: Bard Press.

87. Southwest Airlines' recognitions. 2007. http://www.southwest.com/about_swa/press/factsheet.html#Distinctions, *April 19.*

88. Tsui, A.S., Wang, H., & Xin, K.R. 2006. Organizational culture in China: An analysis of culture dimensions and culture types. *Management and Organization Review,* 2: 345–376.

89. Wilkins, A.L. 1983. The culture audit: A tool for understanding organizations. *Organizational Dynamics,* 12: 24–38.

90. Culture Audit. 2007. Smith Weaver Smith Accelerated Cultural Transformation, http://www.smithweaversmith.com.

91. Schein, Coming to a new awareness.

92. Wilkins, A.L. 1983. Efficient cultures: Exploring the relationship between culture and organizational performance. *Administrative Science Quarterly,* 28: 468–481.

93. Riley, P. 1983. A structurationist account of political culture. *Administrative Science Quarterly,* 28: 414–437.

94. Martin, J., & Siehl, C. 1983. Organizational culture and counterculture: An uneasy symbiosis. *Organizational Dynamics,* 12: 52–64.

95. Chatman & Cha, Leading by leveraging culture; Kristof, A.L. 1996. Person-organization fit: An integrative review of its conceptualizations, measurement, and implications. *Personnel Psychology,* 49: 1–48; O'Reilly, C.A., Chatman, J.A., & Caldwell, D.F. 1991. People and organizational culture: A profile comparison approach to assessing person-organization fit. *Academy of Management Journal,* 14: 487–516; Tziner, A. 1987. Congruency issue retested using Fineman's achievement climate notion. *Journal of Social Behavior and Personality,* 2: 63–78; Vandenberghe, C. 1999. Organizational culture, person-culture fit, and turnover: A replication in the health care industry. *Journal of Organizational Behavior,* 20: 175–184.

96. Ronen, S. 1978. Personal values: A basis for work motivation set and work attitude. *Organizational Behavior and Human Performance,* 21: 80–107.

97. Rokeach, M. 1973. *The nature of human values.* New York: The Free Press.

98. Ronen, Personal values: A basis for work motivation set and work attitude.

99. Schneider, B. 1987. The people make the place. *Personnel Psychology,* 40: 437–453.

100. Cable & Parsons, Socialization tactics and person-organization fit.

101. See, for example, Bowen, D.E., Ledford, G.E., & Nathan, B.R. 1991. Hiring for the organization, not the job. *Academy of Management Executive,* 5 (4): 35–51.

102. See, for example, Lovelace, K., & Rosen, B. 1996. Differences in achieving person-organization fit among diverse groups of managers. *Journal of Management,* 22: 703–722.

103. For additional insights, see Powell, G. 1998. Reinforcing and extending today's organizations: The simultaneous pursuit of person-organization fit and diversity. *Organizational Dynamics,* 26 (3): 50–61.

104. Hitt, M.A., Ireland, R.D., & Hoskisson, R.E. 2007. *Strategic management: Competitiveness and globalization.* Mason, OH: Thomson South-Western.

105. Hitt, M.A., Harrison, J.S., & Ireland, R.D. 2001. *Mergers and acquisitions: Creating value for stakeholders.* New York: Oxford University Press; Cartwright, S., & Cooper, C.L. 1993. The role of culture compatibility in successful organizational marriage. *Academy of Management Executive,* 7 (2): 57–70.

106. Holloway, Wheelwright, & Tempest, Cisco Systems, Inc.: Acquisition integration for manufacturing.

14

ORGANIZATIONAL CHANGE AND DEVELOPMENT

Il Giornale Coffee Company of Seattle began as most firms do, as a small collection of individuals with many ideas and a pressing need for financial capital. Howard Schultz, the entrepreneurial force behind the organization, provided the guiding vision and a golden touch in raising funds. Dave Olsen, the founding partner, provided expertise in upscale specialty coffees and European-style coffee bars and coffee houses. Dawn Pinaud, the first manager, provided ideas for day-to-day operations. All three invested their personal sweat and tears.

When the doors to the company's first coffee bar opened, the three did not know what to expect. They had done little advertising, relying instead on Seattle's established coffee culture to provide initial interest among potential customers. As opening day unfolded, the three adventurers were pleased to see nearly 300 individuals become customers. Within six months, 1,000 customers per day entered the Il Giornale coffee bar.

To handle the increasing customer traffic, Shultz and his friends hired additional people and planned for expansion. "Everyone did everything," said Olsen of this time period. Olsen himself sliced sandwich meat at his desk in the business office, while Schultz waited on customers, cleaned tables, and obtained additional financial capital. Everyone worked long hours, but motivation was high. Owners, managers, and baristas (who made and served the various coffee drinks) were in this venture together and were inspired by the possibility of fundamentally elevating the coffee experience in Seattle and beyond.

Frances Roberts/Alamy

EXPLORING BEHAVIOR IN ACTION
The Evolution of Starbucks

The partners had opened a few more coffee bars under the Il Giornale name when they learned that the owners of Starbucks, Schultz's previous employer, were considering selling their small firm. Schultz quickly raised additional funds to acquire Starbucks' principal assets. The acquisition made sense strategically because Il Giornale emphasized selling premium coffee drinks while Starbucks emphasized roasting and selling premium coffee beans. Starbucks was a supplier to Il Giornale, and its purchase came at the same time that Schultz recognized the need for an in-house roasting plant.

After adopting the name Starbucks and reconfiguring the six existing

Starbucks retail outlets so that each could sell coffee drinks in addition to coffee beans, Schultz and Olsen planned further growth. With a customer base that had embraced their products and with word-of-mouth advertising creating new demand, the two entrepreneurs succeeded in growing the firm rapidly. Within 11 years of its founding, the company had 1,000 locations, a reputation for being chic, and a loyal following.

As the firm grew, informal communication, coordination, and management techniques were no longer adequate and had to be supplanted by formal systems, a strict division of labor, and professional management. These changes proved difficult. In Schultz's words:

> If you're a creative person, an entrepreneur at heart, introducing systems and bureaucracies can be painful, for they seem like the antithesis of what attracted you to business in the first place. But if you don't institute the right processes, if you don't coordinate and plan, if you don't hire people with MBA skills, the whole edifice could crumble. So many companies do [crumble at that point].

Schultz had to reinvent himself to accommodate the changes. Many entrepreneurs are unable to do so, and they move on or are forced out when a firm reaches a certain size. In the end, Schultz made the transition by understanding the needs of the business, by understanding his limitations, and by having faith in the people around him.

Schultz was not alone in his struggle with change. He said, "Within the company, people who had helped me grow Starbucks in the early years became fearful and threatened." Some left the company, while others stayed but were never quite as happy as before. Still others adapted and thrived. To help individuals feel connected to the organization as it grew and changed, the leadership of Starbucks emphasized employee stock ownership programs, superior fringe benefits, and well-defined communication channels where associates and lower-level managers had easy access to middle and senior-level managers. Recently, Starbucks has emphasized health and wellness among its employees (and customers, for example, by eliminating trans fats from its products). Starbucks' efforts paid off, as illustrated by the company's frequent inclusion in *Fortune*'s list of "The 100 Best Companies to Work For."

Despite the successful transition from small to large company, Starbucks today faces a number of new challenges. As a mature company with more than 13,000 locations in numerous countries and growing at about 2,000 stores annually, Starbucks is no longer considered so exotic or chic. Because of its market dominance and its presence on "every street corner," some perceive Starbucks as just another large multinational company concerned only with the bottom line. Howard Schultz recently expressed concerns that in the drive to increase its size and gain the economies of scale, the company may have compromised the "soul" of its original stores.

Sources: J. Useem, ". . . Get Bigger," *Fortune,* Apr. 30, 2007, pp. 82–84; H. Jung, "Peet's Offers Change from Usual Grind on Starbucks' Home Turf," *Los Angeles Times,* Feb. 18, 2003, p. C.3; N.F. Koehn, *Howard Schultz and Starbucks Coffee Company* (Boston: Harvard Business School Publishing, 2001); K. MacQueen, "Café Society: The Sweet Side of a Bitter Dispute," *Macleans,* Nov. 10, 2003, p. 66; A. McLaughlin, "Brewing a Tempest in a Coffee Cup," *Christian Science Monitor,* Feb. 25, 1998, p. 3; Y. Moon, & J. Quelch, *Starbucks: Delivering Customer Service* (Boston: Harvard Business School Publishing, 2004); B. Richards, "Café Au Revoir? Some Say Coffee Has Become Too Cool," *Wall Street Journal,* Jan. 13, 1995, p. A.1; J. Rose, & S. Beaven, "Vandalism Strikes Controversial Starbucks in Portland, Ore., Neighborhood," *Knight Ridder Tribune Business News,* May 6, 2004, p. 1; H. Schultz, & D.J. Yang, *Pour Your Heart into It* (New York: Hyperion, 1997); J. Simons, "A Case of the Shakes," *BusinessWeek,* July 14, 1997, pp. 42–44; Starbucks Coffee Company, "Starbucks Timeline and History," 2004, at http://www.starbucks.com/aboutus/timeline.asp; "Starbucks Corporate Social Responsibility Annual Report," 2006, at http://www.starbucks.com/aboutus/csrannualreport.asp.

The Strategic Importance of Organizational Change and Development

Few, if any, organizations can remain the same for very long and survive. For example, Polaroid Corporation has become a classic case, showing the outcome of being too slow to change. Polaroid introduced instant photography to the market and at one time was among the top 50 corporations in the United States. However, in 2001, it declared bankruptcy, and in 2002, what was left of the company was sold to Bank One's OEP Imaging Unit and then sold again in 2005 to the Petters Group. Polaroid's problem was its failure to adapt in a timely way to technological change. The company lost its market because it was too slow in recognizing the importance of digital imaging technology and then too slow in changing after competitors developed digital cameras.[1]

The development of a new technology created the need for change at Polaroid. Although top managers are responsible for instituting such changes, managers and associates lower in the organization must help because of their knowledge of the environment (markets, customers, competitors, technology, government regulations, and so forth). All managers should actively scan the environment for changes and help to identify external opportunities and threats. Unfortunately, Polaroid's managers did not perceive the threat to their existing business quickly enough to transform the firm. After learning of the need for a change, these managers began the difficult process of designing and implementing a new approach, but they were unable to do so in time to avoid failure. Competitors developed and introduced new cameras using digital technology before Polaroid could do so and it lost a substantial share of its market.

In contrast, Starbucks has had many admirers over the years. Numerous awards have been given to Starbucks' founders and managers as well as to the company as a whole. The company has been recognized for its high-involvement management practices (the manner in which it has valued and managed its human capital), environmentally conscious policies, accessibility to those with disabilities, and high-quality coffees. Starbucks' positive work environment is exemplified by its rating as among the best 100 companies to work for by *Fortune* magazine. (It was ranked 29th in 2006 and 16th in 2007.[2]) Starbucks has also enjoyed significant financial success.

None of these accomplishments would have been possible if Starbucks' founders and early managers had not recognized the need for change and acted to make necessary changes. Starbucks encountered a predictable set of problems as it grew, but its people responded to these problems in effective ways. As Starbucks continued to develop past its infancy and adolescence, its leaders maintained high-involvement management practices while implementing more formal systems and processes. Continued commitment to high-involvement practices, which effectively use the talents of associates and enhance their motivation, helped to reduce resistance to change by lower-level managers and associates. Some experts believe that effective management of human capital and developing effective ways of dealing with change have contributed significantly to Starbucks' ability to build and maintain a competitive advantage. And, Starbucks' leaders show their concern by maintaining the soul of the company that has made it successful and yet continuing to change.

Change often involves an entire firm, as in the Starbucks case. In other instances, a single division or work group must change. To be prepared for either situation, managers must understand and appreciate change and possess the skills and tools necessary for implementing it. In high-involvement organizations, associates also play key roles in planning and implementing change, and they, too, must possess appropriate skills and tools.

In this chapter, we discuss organizational change and renewal. First, we examine internal and external pressures for change. Such pressures must be properly understood for effective change to occur. Next, we describe the basic process of planned change and consider important tactical decisions involved in a change effort. Building on this foundation, we then address the important topic of resistance to change. Individuals and groups often resist change, and the ability to diagnose causes of resistance and deal with them effectively is crucial. Finally, we discuss a set of assessment techniques and change tactics, collectively known as *organizational development*.

After reading this chapter, you should be able to:

1. Describe two major internal pressures for change.

2. Identify and explain six major external pressures for change.

3. Describe the three–phase model of planned change.

4. Discuss important tactical choices involving the speed and style of a change effort.

5. Explain the four general causes of resistance to change and the tactics that can be used to address each cause.

6. Discuss the role of the DADA syndrome in organizational change.

7. Describe the basic organization development (OD) model and discuss OD interventions, including relationship techniques and structural techniques.

 ## Pressures for Organizational Change

Organizations constantly face pressure for change, and to cope, they must be agile and react quickly.[3] Organizations that understand and manage change well tend to be the most effective.[4] As suggested by Exhibit 14-1, pressures for change can be categorized as internal or external.

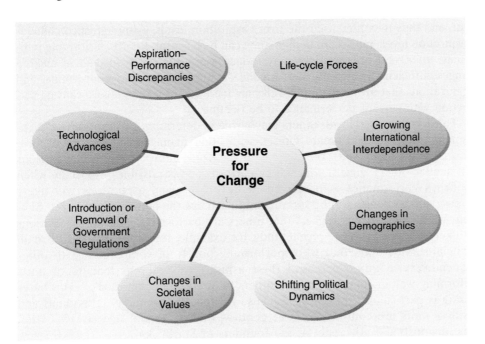

Exhibit 14-1
Internal and External Pressures for Organizational Change

Internal Pressures for Change

Although many pressures for change exist in the external environments of organizations, some pressures are more closely identified with internal dynamics. Aspiration–performance discrepancies and natural life-cycle forces are two of the most important pressures.

ASPIRATION–PERFORMANCE DISCREPANCIES

aspiration–performance
discrepancies
Gaps between what an
individual, unit, or organization wants to achieve and
what it is actually achieving.

Perhaps the most fundamental pressure for change involves **aspiration–performance discrepancies,** or differences between aspirations and current performance.[5] When an individual, work group, division, or organization is not meeting its own expectations, changes in tactics, strategies, and processes often follow. Failing to live up to one's own expectations is an uncomfortable state that often motivates change. One study, for example, found that radio stations were more likely to make major format changes (say, from rock to jazz) when aspirations were not being met.[6] Another study found that firms increased risk taking when aspirations were not being met.[7]

To fully appreciate the role of aspirations, it is important to understand how they develop. Research has identified three factors.[8] First, past aspirations play a role in current aspirations. Thus, if an associate had high expectations of herself yesterday, she is likely to have high expectations today as well. This point underscores an important phenomenon: stickiness in aspirations. *Stickiness* exists when individuals, units, and organizations are slow to revise their aspirations even when those aspirations appear to be too high or too low. One study, for example, found that units of a company adjusted performance aspirations less than might be expected in the face of information suggesting that greater change, either up or down, was warranted.[9]

Second, past performance plays an important role. If performance in the recent past was below target levels, aspirations are likely to be reduced, although stickiness places limits on the degree of adjustment in the short run. Conversely, if performance has been above target levels, it is common for aspiration levels to be increased to some degree. For example, in the early days, Starbucks' executives learned that it was relatively easy to perform well in a high-growth environment, and thus they increased the firm's aspiration levels. Although such changes in aspiration levels may seem benign, they can be harmful. Poorly performing individuals, units, and organizations may reduce aspiration levels instead of making changes sufficient to increase performance. Alternatively, individuals, units, and organizations that are performing well may increase aspiration levels, causing satisfaction with current performance to be fleeting.

Third, comparisons with others play a role in determining aspirations. A management trainee may compare himself with other management trainees. A firm often compares itself with other firms in the same industry. When comparisons with similar others suggest that better performance is possible (especially when the firm's performance is perceived to be below par), aspirations will likely increase and strategies will be formulated to achieve the higher aspirations.[10] Similarly, when comparisons suggest that others are performing less well, aspirations are likely to decrease. One recent study, for example, found that leaders of retail financial-service units that were performing poorly in comparison with other financial-service units increased their aspirations, whereas leaders of units performing well in comparison with others lowered their aspirations.[11] This latter finding is particularly intriguing, because it suggests that many individuals and business units are content to be as good as others but not necessarily better. This obviously did not apply to the founders of Starbucks.

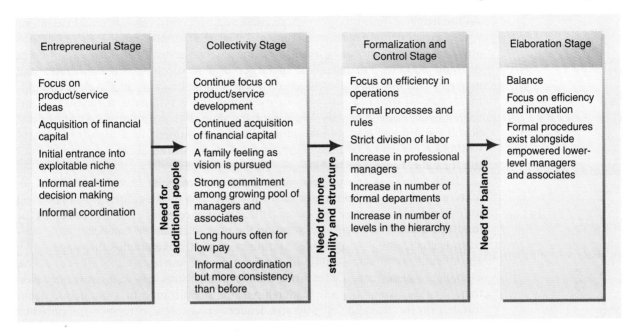

Exhibit 14-2 Integrative Life-cycle Model

Source: Based on R. E. Quinn, & K. Cameron, 1983. "Organizational Life Cycles and Shifting Criteria of Effectiveness," *Management Science,* 24:33–51.

LIFE-CYCLE FORCES

Organizations tend to encounter predictable **life-cycle forces** as they grow.[12] Not every organization experiences the same forces in the same way as others, but most organizations face similar pressures. Although several models of the organizational life cycle have been proposed, an integrative model best highlights the key pressures that organizations experience. This model has four stages: entrepreneurial, collectivity, formalization and control, and elaboration (see Exhibit 14-2).

In the *entrepreneurial stage,* founders and perhaps a few initial managers and associates develop ideas for products or services, acquire financial capital, and take actions to enter a niche in the marketplace. This is an exciting time, but after the market is entered and success is achieved, growth requires founders to add managers and associates. Processes must be introduced for selecting, training, and coordinating these individuals. Dave Olsen handled these tasks in the early days at Il Giornale.

In the *collectivity stage,* founders, managers, and associates continue to emphasize product or service development and fund raising. Individuals in the young firm tend to feel like a family as they pursue the vision that attracted them to the firm. Individuals often work long hours for relatively low pay, and they tend to be highly committed. Informal communication and coordination are important, but founders often begin to handle more managerial responsibilities and fewer entrepreneurial responsibilities than they would like. As the firm continues to grow, professional managers and formal processes must be incorporated to resolve or prevent coordination and control problems.

In the *formalization and control stage,* managers and associates are guided by formal processes and rules, a strict division of labor, and a stable organizational structure. And they emphasize efficiency more than innovation. Functional disciplines such as accounting and operations management are elevated in status.

life-cycle forces
Natural and predictable pressures that build as an organization grows and that must be addressed if the organization is to continue growing.

As the firm continues to grow, more rules and procedures are often added, along with a greater number of management levels. Eventually, managers and associates can become alienated from the firm, partly because they lose discretion in decision making. Furthermore, in larger organizations, newer associates and managers do not have a connection to the original vision, and overall commitment may be lower. To prevent or overcome these problems, a renewed effort to empower both managers and associates should be considered. At Starbucks, Schultz and other leaders maintained their commitment to a high-involvement workplace, which helped the company avoid some of the negative side effects of the formalization stage.

In the *elaboration stage,* managers and associates experience a more balanced, mature organization. Formal rules and processes exist alongside empowered lower-level managers and associates. Efficiency concerns coexist with concerns for innovation and renewal. As discussed in the previous chapter, balancing these concerns is challenging but possible. Starbucks currently exemplifies this stage.

Overall, some firms handle life-cycle forces reasonably well; Starbucks is one example of such firms. Other firms handle these issues less well. In these cases, there is often a change in the leadership of the organization that can trickle down through the organization. If effective leaders are chosen to replace the previous ones and the transition is handled in an orderly manner, the organization can experience positive outcomes from the change.[13]

External Pressures for Change

Along with internal pressures, organizations face external pressures for change. Organizations must be sensitive to these external pressures, or they may not survive. For example, if an organization does not react to changes in the market for its product, the demand for its product probably will decrease. Such was the case for Polaroid, as discussed earlier. The new digital cameras introduced to the market by Polaroid's competitors greatly reduced the demand for Polaroid's products. When Polaroid was unable to respond quickly, it filed for bankruptcy and ceased to exist as an independent business.

External pressure for change comes from several sources, including technological advances, the introduction or removal of government regulations, changes in societal values, shifting political dynamics, changing demographics, and growing international interdependency (see Exhibit 14-1).

TECHNOLOGICAL ADVANCES

Scientific knowledge, produced by both companies and universities, has been developing rapidly over the past 50 years.[14] As an indication of this growth, consider that the number of pages published in scientific journals per U.S. scientist increased by 70 percent between 1975 and 1995.[15] With advances in research methods and a continuing need for answers to many important research questions, the rapid development of knowledge is expected to continue.

Technological advances are based on advances in scientific knowledge. Such advances can lead to incremental or radical changes in how services and products are designed, produced, and delivered. Two facts illustrate the point that scientific knowledge drives technology. First, scientific knowledge is routinely cited in patent applications, with the number of scientific articles cited per patent on the increase in the United States, Germany, France, Britain, and other countries.[16] Second, the number of patents granted by the U.S. Patent Office is increasing at a growing rate, which matches the growth in science. In the first half of the twentieth century, patents increased by 50 percent.[17] In the second half of the twentieth century, they quadrupled.[18] These rapid changes can be seen in technologies of recent origin, such as cellular phones, videoconferencing, and Gore-Tex fabric. New technologies are being developed faster than they can be implemented. A prime example is provided by new developments in microelectronic technology, which occur before previous developments can be fully implemented.

Photodisc/Getty Images

Firms must adapt to technological advances or risk becoming outdated and ineffective.[19] Manufacturing firms, for example, must adopt new manufacturing technologies or suffer disadvantages in cost, quality, or speed. Firms that failed, or were slow, to take advantage of computer-aided manufacturing, computer-aided design, and modern manufacturing resource planning experienced competitive disadvantages. Even BMW, a maker of high-end automobiles, had to adopt computer-aided design of its products to compete effectively with other German and Japanese luxury-auto producers. This technology was inconsistent with the existing BMW culture, causing resistance to change among managers and associates.[20]

INTRODUCTION AND REMOVAL OF GOVERNMENT REGULATIONS

The U.S. government has the responsibility to regulate commerce for the common good. Much of the regulation is initiated because of societal pressures. Major regulation has been implemented over the years in such areas as civil rights and equal opportunity, environmental protection, and worker safety and health.

In recent times, regulations have been implemented that establish fuel efficiency standards for automobile manufacturers, requirements for regional telephone companies to provide competitors access to their hardwired networks, and rules limiting telemarketers' ability to call people's homes.[21] The Drug-Free Workplace Act was passed to encourage employers to test associates for drugs and to implement employee assistance programs for substance abuse. Additional rules and regulations have been enacted since the original legislation to enhance effects. However, these regulations have been only partially effective in achieving the goals. For one thing, it covers only employers with federal contracts. In addition, the programs implemented by employers vary in their effectiveness.[22] Without question, however, organizations must adapt to regulatory changes.

The U.S. government also occasionally removes regulations created in earlier times. The airline, trucking, and communication industries, for example, have been largely deregulated. Such deregulation also requires changes. For example, firms in deregulated industries typically must adapt to a more competitive environment, which many firms in these industries have found difficult to do. Many airlines that prospered in the regulated era, such as Pan Am and Braniff, failed under deregulation.

CHANGES IN SOCIETAL VALUES

Changes in societal values are normally seen in four ways. First, changing values influence consumer purchases, affecting the market for an organization's products or services. Second, society's values are evidenced in employee attitudes, behaviors, and expectations. Third, they affect potential investors in the company. Finally, society's values are represented in government regulations.

Companies' Responses to Pressures for "Green" Policies and Practices

Michael Stravato/The New York Times/Redux Pictures

While in times past, financing or regulatory approval were the most critical issues of concern for many major investments, in current times a growing number of investors are focused on environmentalists' support for the company. Companies have begun to realize that changing their environmental policies—making them more green—will in turn help their bottom line, improve their public image, and make them more attractive to many investors. *Sustainability* in simple terms means meeting our current human needs without harming future generations. It is a major cause among environmentalists, human rights activists, and economic development experts. In the past, sustainability often meant higher costs for companies, but they are now realizing that better environmental and social practices can yield strategic advantages. Customers are beginning to shift their loyalties to those companies that embrace the concept of sustainability.

Environmental activists have started using the power of publicity as people have become more sensitive to the need for environmentally friendly practices, especially in the twenty-first century. For example, in 2000, Coke sponsored the Olympics, and during this event, Greenpeace launched an e-mail campaign that criticized the company for using a potent greenhouse gas in its coolers and vending machines. In response to this negative publicity, Coca-Cola announced significant investments to develop a more environmentally friendly system. Coca-Cola recognized the need to change how it conducted business in order to avoid the negative impact on its reputation. In addition, Coke is now supporting a new organization named RecycleBank, which is an innovative incentive-based recycling program, and has co-founded a food-and-beverage organization called Refrigerants Naturally to promote HFC-free refrigeration technology in order to reduce emission of greenhouse gases. The management of each of Coca Cola's organizational units is required by the company to issue an environmental policy or mission statement that specifically addresses the commitment to preserve and protect the environment.

Because of changes in the marketplace (customers) and in the equity markets (investors), incorporating environmental values in policies and practices is contributing to a competitive advantage for companies. Companies are changing their missions, goals, and values in order to address "green" issues and partnering with environmental organizations such as Greenpeace. Some companies, exemplified by Wal-Mart, have used Conservation International to help shape their environmental goals targeting the reduction of energy use. Dow Chemical identified a market for low-cost housing and is developing technologies such as eco-friendly Styrofoam to be used in their construction. Philips Electronics is also promoting "green" strategies by developing low-cost water-purification technology and a smokeless wood-burning stove. By doing this, the company hopes to reduce the 1.6 million deaths annually worldwide from pulmonary diseases linked to cooking smoke. Philips Electronics considers sustainability as a business imperative. In addition, there is an increasing demand from investors to provide information on companies' sustainability practices. The number and size of mutual funds that primarily invest in those companies that have effective sustainability practices have grown dramatically in the past 10 years. California and other states have pledged to place emphasis on sustainability practices in their investment decisions. Shareholders are experiencing more environmental resolutions in proxy statements.

IBM and some other companies have created new business units that specifically focus on environmental matters. Even car rental companies are responding to climate change regulations by making green cars available in their fleets. Although U.S. regulators do not require companies to quantify the effects of their environmental practices, these practices have become a powerful indicator of future market performance. Thus, responding positively to environmental pressures may help companies achieve long-term survival.

Sources: J. Carey, "Hugging the Tree-Huggers," *BusinessWeek*, Mar. 12, 2007, at www.businessweek.com; speeches, 2007, at www.thecoca-colacompany.com/presscenter; P. Engardio, "Beyond the Green Corporation," *BusinessWeek*, Jan. 29, 2007, www.businessweek.com; E. Beck, "Do You Need to Be Green?," *BusinessWeek*, Summer, 2006, at www.businessweek.com; R. Golding, "Regulation: Greener Rules Bear Fruit," *Financial Times*, May 9, 2007, at www.ft.com; S. Hamm, "Big Blue's Big Green Plans," *BusinessWeek*, Apr. 24, 2007, at www.businessweek.com; J. Eaglesham, "Green and Business Lobbies Gear Up for Final Battle Over Bill," *Financial Times*, Sept. 25, 2006, at www.ft.com; M. Herbst, "The Greening of the Proxy Season," *BusinessWeek*, Mar. 12, 2007, at www.businessweek.com.

Because of the increasing concerns about global warming, many people throughout the world have become sensitive to environmental issues. The importance of "green" issues is reflected by consumers' buying behaviors, investors' purchases of stock in companies, and in other ways as well. The interest in green issues has encouraged Coca-Cola, Wal-Mart, Philips Electronics, and IBM to develop environmentally sensitive policies and practices as explained in the Managerial Advice segment. For example, Coca-Cola is supporting an innovative incentive-based recycling program, and has co-founded a food-and-beverage organization that promotes HFC-free refrigeration technology in order to reduce emission of greenhouse gases.

The influence of societal values on consumer purchases can have a major effect on organizations. For example, Americans have become increasingly hostile to products manufactured by companies using questionable practices in foreign countries. Such practices include child labor, periods of intense overwork, and very low wages. In past decades, individuals thought less about these issues, and firms could neglect them as well. Today, firms must be very careful. Nike, for example, has been under pressure for its lack of clear commitment to avoiding questionable labor practices in underdeveloped countries.[23]

Other influences of societal values are more indirect. They affect politicians who enact laws such as the Drug-Free-Workplace Act. With over $200 billion in costs to organizations because of associates' substance abuse, the employee-assistance programs promoted by the Act are important to save lives and reduce costs to organizations from substance abuse.[24] Thus, societal values also influence government regulation, which in turn places external pressures on the organization.

SHIFTING POLITICAL DYNAMICS

Political pressures, both national and international, can influence organizational operations. The political philosophy of those elected to office affects legislation and the interpretation of existing legislation and government policies. For example, President Ronald Reagan's views on U.S. defense spending created massive shifts in government expenditures that affected firms in several industries. These firms had to gear up to meet the government demand. International politics also influence organizational change. Disagreements over proper tariffs between the European Union and the United States, for example, can cause uncertainty and perhaps higher costs for a firm if tariffs increase. Faced with increased tariffs in an important export market, a firm may need to enhance its efficiency to avoid being forced to raise prices to noncompetitive levels. Alternatively, it may need to shift exports to other markets.

CHANGES IN DEMOGRAPHICS

As discussed in Chapter 2, the average age of U.S. citizens has been increasing, along with the proportion of U.S. residents who belong to groups other than non-Hispanic whites. To deal with these changes, many organizations have altered internal practices to ensure fair treatment for people of all races and ages. Diversity programs designed to increase understanding across different groups have become common. Further changes in the demographic profile of the nation may require additional organizational changes.

Firms also have introduced products and marketing tactics designed to appeal to a broader mix of individuals or to a particular targeted niche that has grown in importance. In North Carolina, where the Hispanic population is growing fast compared to most other states, auto dealers and service businesses have added Spanish-speaking associates; and Time-Warner Cable has created a special TV package targeting Hispanic viewers in the state.[25]

GROWING INTERNATIONAL INTERDEPENDENCE

You have probably heard someone say that "the world is getting smaller." Clichés such as this are frequently used to describe the growing interdependency among countries in the world today. The United States is no longer as self-sufficient as it once was. Growing interdependencies are created by many factors. At the national level, countries may share mutual national defense goals, which are implemented through organizations such as the North Atlantic Treaty Organization (NATO). At the organizational level, a company may need natural resources that it cannot obtain in its own country, or a firm from one country may establish operations in another.[26] One result of interdependency is that organizations must be concerned about what happens throughout the world, even if they have no operations outside the United States. For example, events in the Middle East have an effect on most major organizations in the United States in some way. International interdependencies provide both opportunities and constraints.[27] Many firms have found that international markets present more opportunities for sales growth than U.S. markets, as discussed in Chapter 3.

Planned Change

planned change
A process involving deliberate efforts to move an organization or a unit from its current undesirable state to a new, more desirable state.

How does an organization respond to pressures for change? One possibility is **planned change,** which involves deliberate efforts to move an organization or a subunit from its current state to a new state. Planned change may be evolutionary over time, or can be more revolutionary, involving major changes in a shorter period of time.[28] To effectively move the organization from one state to another, those managing the change must consider a number of issues in three distinct parts of the change process. Resistance to change may develop along the way, however.

Process of Planned Change

Change is typically thought of as a three-phase process that moves an organization from an undesirable state through a difficult transition period to a desirable new state. Although researchers tend to agree on the nature of these three phases,[29] different names for the phases have been used by different people. One pair of noted researchers called them *awakening, mobilizing,* and *reinforcing.*[30]

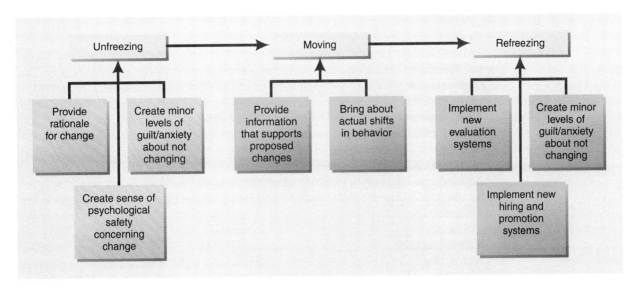

Exhibit 14-3 Process of Planned Change

Another set called them *energizing, envisioning,* and *enabling.*[31] Kurt Lewin, a noted social psychologist, provided the most commonly used labels: *unfreezing, moving,* and *refreezing.*[32] That is, the change process involves unfreezing an organization from its current state, moving (changing) it to a new state, and refreezing it in the new state (see Exhibit 14-3).

UNFREEZING

Unfreezing involves three activities.[33] First, change leaders provide a rationale—a reason why individuals in the organization should de-commit from the status quo. The leaders may accomplish this by providing information on poor financial performance, an impending regulatory change, or a new technological development. Second, leaders create at least minor levels of guilt or anxiety about not changing. Although causing undue negative emotion is not the intent, creation of psychological discomfort can be motivating. Leaders may create such a feeling by discussing the negative outcomes that the organization and its managers and associates will suffer if changes are not made. Third, leaders create a sense of psychological safety concerning the change. Managers and associates must believe they can successfully change.[34] Tactics that change leaders might use include the following:

- Reminding individuals that they have successfully changed in the past
- Communicating to individuals that managers and associates in other organizations in similar circumstances have successfully changed
- Letting individuals know that support and training will be available for the specific changes to be made

MOVING

Moving involves three key activities.[35] First, change leaders must provide information and evidence that supports the proposed changes. Without supporting information, managers and associates may not have faith in what they are being asked to do, and they will not be committed. Pilot tests, outside experts, and data on how others have benefited from similar changes can be effective tactics. Furthermore,

unfreezing
A phase in the change process in which leaders help managers and associates move beyond the past by providing a rationale for change, by creating guilt and/or anxiety about not changing, and by creating a sense of psychological safety concerning the change.

moving
A phase in the change process in which leaders help to implement new approaches by providing information that supports proposed changes and by providing resources and training to bring about actual shifts in behavior.

as noted in our discussion of transformational leaders in Chapter 8, a compelling vision of the future also can be useful in building commitment to proposed changes. Indeed, such a vision is likely to be crucial for creating change. Second, any potential constraints to making the change must be removed by the change leaders. This might require investing more money to reduce financial constraints or providing more training to remove constraints due to associates' capability limitations.[36] Third, change leaders must be able to shift behavior and implement the change.[37] They must arrange for the resources required for change, such as new equipment or budgets, and they must ensure that education and training are available. With resources and training in place, actual change can begin. Feedback on progress can be used to make any necessary adjustments along the way. Small wins, or quick and highly visible successes, can be helpful in supporting this stage of the change process.

REFREEZING

refreezing
A phase in the change process in which leaders lock in new approaches by implementing evaluation systems that track expected behaviors, by creating reward systems that reinforce expected behaviors, and by ensuring that hiring and promotion systems support the new demands.

Refreezing involves three interrelated activities.[38] First, change leaders implement evaluation systems that track expected behaviors after the change, and they implement permanent training systems to continuously upgrade relevant knowledge and skills. If, for example, working in teams is part of a new approach to production work in a particular organization, an individual's willingness to contribute to a team must be measured and must also be enhanced when necessary. Second, change leaders arrange for permanent reward structures, involving both monetary and nonmonetary rewards, to positively reinforce the new behaviors. As many managers have said, "You get what you reward."[39] Third, change leaders ensure that new hiring and promotion systems and other forms of support are designed to satisfy the altered demands.[40]

EXPERIENCING STRATEGIC ORGANIZATIONAL BEHAVIOR

Coca-Cola Is Finding a New Fizz

In April 2006, the CEO of Coca-Cola, Neville Isdell, explained to investors that potential failure exists with the development and introduction of new products to the market. This possibility is greater when the company is simultaneously making other changes such as in its structure. Isdell believes that Coke must take bigger risks than it has done in the past. This approach required an alteration of the firm's traditional risk-adverse culture. This change will be accomplished by ensuring that employees and shareholders feel secure in initiating change and feel confident that failure will be tolerated. In general, people not only fear the failure of their ideas, but more so the consequences of those failures. Coca-Cola is changing its culture, and also adapting its product lines to better satisfy its consumers' desire for a healthier lifestyle. Coke has organized its North American operations and created a unit that is specifically dedicated to developing new products outside of the company's traditional soft-drink product lines. Coca-Cola is shifting from the traditionally sugar-laden carbonated drinks to healthier alternatives, partly to address society's concern for obesity.

Isdell's goal is to transform Coca-Cola into a more innovative, risk-taking company. An example of the company's changed approach to diversification was Coke Black. This product is a coffee-flavored cola hybrid that was launched in the United States and France in 2006. Coca-Cola Black is designed to appeal to the

20- to 30-year-old market with fashionable, figure-conscious consumers desiring a more sophisticated, low-calorie, caffeinated-flavored experience. Isdell believes more risks are required to regenerate the company. In order for Coca-Cola to compete in the global marketplace, they must explore, experiment, and at times fail in order to maintain the pace of other companies' creativity and speed in introducing new products to the market.

Sandy Douglas, President of Coca-Cola North America, stated that the objective is to become the U.S. growth and profit leader in emerging ideas, brands, and categories. Though Coke has been slower than its rival PepsiCo to respond to changes in the beverage market for more healthy alternatives, it is beginning to make up lost ground by expanding noncarbonated brands such as PowerAde sports drinks, Minute Maid juices, and Dasani bottled water. In 2006, Coca-Cola's noncarbonated beverage sales increased. In February, the company agreed to buy Fuze Beverages, a fast-growing U.S. maker of teas and juices, to help the company expand its product portfolio to compete more effectively with PepsiCo. The company has also decided to create a new structure for its domestic portfolio, splitting it among three new business units (sparkling beverages, still beverages, and emerging brands). The executives hope that by separating these units, each one will incubate new products and increase response time to the rapid changes in the U.S. beverage market. In other words, the changes in the structure are designed to make the firm more nimble and competitive.

Many analysts believe that Coca-Cola is beginning to become more innovative in its product lines. The company has changed its organizational culture and product portfolio to compete more effectively with rivals and meet the changing needs of our society. Isdell is committed to revive the company through innovations that reduce the firm's dependency on sugary soft drinks and to do so with research and experimentation. Coca-Cola's overall performance has steadily improved since Neville Isdell was appointed chief executive, so these changes appear to be on the right track.

Sources: V. Manning-Schaffel, "Coca-Cola: Is the Legend Enough?," *BusinessWeek*, June 7, 2006, at www.businessweek.com; A. Ward, "Coca-Cola Looks Beyond the Fizz," *Financial Times*, Mar. 10, 2007 at www.ft.com; Coca Cola news release, 2007, www.thecoca-colacompany.com/presscenter; J. Wheatley, "Coke Pops the Top Off an Emerging Market," *BusinessWeek*, May 2, 2005, at www.businessweek.com; J. McGregor, "How Failure Breeds Success," *BusinessWeek*, July 3, 2006, at www.businessweek.com; A. Ward, "Coca-Cola Revamps U.S. Business," *Financial Times*, Jan. 5, 2005, at www.ft.com.

The *Experiencing Strategic Organizational Behavior* feature illustrates the process of change that we have been discussing. In particular, Coca-Cola is working through the unfreezing-moving-refreezing process of change. For example, CEO Isdell explained the need to change in order to remain competitive. Without change, Coca-Cola was losing market share to PepsiCo and others in different product markets. This was designed to unfreeze managers, associates, and other stakeholders and motivate them to support the changes. The moving phase involved changing the firm's culture, making it more risk oriented, changing its structure, and developing new and significantly different products (e.g., Coke Black). The company remains in the refreezing stage. However, the successful performance plays an important role in reinforcing the value of the changes made. Organizational change thus can be critical for firm performance. Coca-Cola's attempts to take more risk parallel the actions of Apple Computers. In a recent book written about Apple's efforts, the development and introduction of the iPod was described as risk shaping for competitors, and not as taking risk. In other words, Apple created risk for its competitors with the introduction of this new product because they would have to adapt and respond or lose significant market share.[41]

The time and attention change leaders spend on the unfreezing phase can be significant in order to be successful. When change leaders fail to treat unfreezing as a distinct and crucial phase, they often encounter problems. Without explicit attention to unfreezing, resistance to change is likely to be strong. Failure to focus attention on this phase, however, is common and is a source of failure in many change efforts. Two additional points are important. First, managers and associates should not expect all change activities to occur sequentially. Thus, activities important in one phase of the process may overlap activities necessary in the next phase.[42] For example, change leaders may engage in various activities in the moving phase while continuing to convince people of the need to change, an activity associated with the unfreezing phase. Although it is very useful to think in terms of three distinct phases, a measure of flexibility is required in actually creating change.

Second, a team of change leaders rather than a single individual should guide an organization through a major change effort. Relying on a single leader is risky because there is too much work required for one person.[43] Deciding how best to unfreeze people, developing a vision, communicating a vision, generating small wins, and overseeing numerous change projects require more than one key change leader.[44]

In constructing the team, several factors should be considered. According to a well-known researcher and business consultant, John Kotter, four factors are crucial:[45]

1. *Position power* plays a role. Individuals with power based on their formal positions can block change or at least slow it down. Including some of these individuals on the team will leave fewer potential resisters who have the power to slow or resist the change.

2. *Informal credibility* is important. Individuals who have credibility are admired and respected and can be effective in selling change. Associates often are selected as change leaders based on this criterion.

3. *Expertise* is a relevant factor. Individuals on the team should possess knowledge related to the problems requiring the change effort and should have diverse points of view on potential solutions.

4. *Proven leadership* is crucial. The team needs individuals who can lead other managers and associates through the transition.

The size of the team is also a concern. There is little agreement on how large or small the team of change leaders should be, but the size of the organization that will be changed plays a role.[46] Six may be sufficient in a smaller organization or in a division of a larger organization. Fifteen or more may be required in a larger organization. However, as the team grows, it will be more difficult to coordinate and manage.

Important Tactical Choices

Change leaders must make many decisions. Among these are two important tactical decisions, the first involving speed and the second involving style.[47] Whereas these issues have no right or wrong answers, certain criteria must be considered when making informed choices.

SPEED OF CHANGE

A fundamental decision in any change effort involves speed. A fast process, where unfreezing, moving, and refreezing occur quickly, can be useful if an ongoing problem will cause substantial damage in the near term.[48] Senior managers, for example, often initiate rapid change when they realize that organizational strategies or structure no longer provide value to customers. When Charlotte Beers became CEO of Ogilvy and Mather, a global advertising firm, the firm was out of step with the needs of the advertising industry, was losing important customers, and was suffering from declining overall performance. To save the firm, she and her circle of senior advisors created a vision, designed transformational change, and orchestrated its implementation in a matter of months.[49]

Overall, criteria that can be usefully considered when deciding on speed include:[50]

- *Urgency:* if the change is urgent, a faster pace is warranted.
- *Degree of support:* if the change is supported by a wide variety of people at the outset, a faster pace can be used.
- *Amount and complexity of change:* if the change is small and simple, a faster pace often can be used; but if the change is large, more time may be required.[51]
- *Competitive environment:* if competitors are poised to take advantage of existing weaknesses, a faster pace should be considered.
- *Knowledge and skills available:* if the knowledge and skills required by the new approach exist in the firm or can be easily acquired, a faster pace can be used.
- *Financial and other resources:* if the resources required by the change are on hand or easily acquired, a faster pace can be considered.

STYLE OF CHANGE

A second fundamental decision involves style. When using a top-down style, change leaders design the change and plan its implementation with little participation from those below them in the hierarchy. In contrast, when using a participatory style, change leaders seek the ideas and advice of those below them and then use many of those ideas. Leaders at Glaxo Wellcome in the mid-to-late 1990s followed a participatory style in fundamentally changing their company's strategy and structure.[52]

In a high-involvement organization, leaders use a participatory style whenever possible. Participation can be useful in generating ideas and developing commitment among those who will be affected by a change.[53] Participation, however, can be time consuming and expensive, as meetings, debates, and synthesis of multiple sets of ideas take significant time. Overall, the following criteria are useful in evaluating the degree to which a participatory approach should be used:[54]

- *Urgency:* if the change is urgent, a participatory approach should not be used, as it tends to be time consuming.
- *Degree of support:* if the idea of changing is supported initially by a wide variety of people, a participatory approach is less necessary.
- *Referent and expert power of change leaders:* when change leaders are admired and are known to be knowledgeable about pertinent issues, a participatory approach is less necessary.

Resistance to Change

resistance to change
Efforts to block the introduction of new approaches. Some of these efforts are passive in nature, involving such tactics as verbally supporting the change while continuing to work in the old ways; and other efforts are active in nature, involving tactics such as organized protests and sabotage.

Although organizations experience both internal and external pressures to change, they frequently encounter strong resistance to needed changes. **Resistance to change** involves efforts to block the introduction of new ways of doing things. Dealing with resistance is one of the most important aspects of a manager's job. In a high-involvement organization, associates also must take responsibility for helping to motivate change among their peers.

Resistance may be active or passive.[55] Individuals may actively argue and use political connections in the firm to stop a change. In extreme cases of active resistance, resisters may sabotage change efforts through illegal means. In other cases, individuals passively resist change, which is more difficult to detect. Resisters may act as if they were trying to make the change a success, but in reality they are not. This often occurs in organizations that have attempted to change too frequently in the recent past, because individuals in these organizations have become tired of change.[56]

Resistance to change can usually be traced to one or more of the following four causal factors: lack of understanding, different assessments, self-interest, and low tolerance for change.[57]

LACK OF UNDERSTANDING

The first possible cause is lack of understanding. In some cases, individuals are unsure of what a change would entail. They resist because they do not understand the change.[58] For example, change leaders may decide to redesign jobs in a factory using job enrichment. Such a redesign can result in substantial benefits to associates in the affected jobs, as discussed in Chapter 6. If, however, change leaders fail to explain the expected changes, some associates may begin to make false assumptions. They may, for example, believe that if job enrichment is implemented, their pay status will change from hourly wages to established salaries (with no overtime or incentive pay provided). Thus, they resist the change.

The key to avoiding or handling resistance to change based on lack of understanding is to communicate clearly what the change entails.[59] Many organizational researchers have emphasized the importance of rich communication for successful change. Meetings, articles in newsletters, and articles on company intranets are examples of possible communication tools.

DIFFERENT ASSESSMENTS

A second possible cause of resistance involves differing assessments of the change. Associates and managers who resist on this basis believe the change would have more costs and fewer benefits than those desiring the change claim.[60] In this case, resisters often do not have inaccurate or insufficient information. Rather, they understand the change but disagree with change leaders about the likely outcome. For example, a mid-level manager may resist an increase in product diversification because she sees more costs in terms of loss of focus than do those who are pushing for the change. Furthermore, she may see less potential for synergy across product lines than others do. Increased diversification may or may not be beneficial to a firm. Many factors are involved, and the situation is usually quite complex. Thus, honest disagreements are common when a firm is considering product line expansion. Obviously, this is true for many other changes as well.

To prevent or deal with resistance based on different assessments, change leaders should consider including potential or actual resisters in the decision-making process.[61] This focus on participation serves two purposes. First, change leaders can ensure that they have all of the information they need to make good decisions.[62] Individuals resisting on the basis of different assessments may have more and better information than change leaders, making their resistance to change positive for the organization. Change leaders must explore why resisters feel the way they do.

Second, by emphasizing participation, change leaders can help to ensure procedural justice for actual or potential resisters.[63] In the context of organizational change, **procedural justice** is defined as perceived fairness in the decision process. Individuals are more likely to believe the process is fair and are more likely to trust the organization and change leaders if they are included in the decision process. A recent study showed the potential power of procedural justice. Associates in two U.S. power plants who believed they had input into change-related decisions felt more obligated to treat the organization well, trusted management to a greater degree, and expressed an intention to remain with the organization.[64]

procedural justice
In the context of organization change, the perceived fairness of the change process.

SELF-INTEREST

Individuals who resist change because of self-interest believe that they will lose something of value if the change is implemented. Power, control over certain resources, and a valued job assignment are examples of things that could be lost. For example, the head of marketing in a small, rapidly growing firm might resist the establishment of a unit devoted to new product development. If such a unit were established, he would lose his control over product development. Another example of self-interest is when individuals oppose an appointment to a higher-level position on the basis of gender or ethnicity.[65]

To combat this type of resistance, change leaders can try to reason with resisters, explaining that the health of the organization is at stake. Leaders can also transfer resisters or, in extreme cases, ask them to leave the organization. Another option is to adopt a more coercive style and insist on compliance. In rare cases, when the resisters are extremely valuable to the organization and other tactics have failed or are unavailable, change leaders can negotiate in an effort to overcome the resistance.[66] Valuable resisters who are managers can be offered larger budgets or a valued new assignment for favored subordinates, for example. In the case of associates, additional vacation time might be offered. These actions, however, should be undertaken only under exceptional circumstances because they may create expectations on the part of other managers or associates.

LOW TOLERANCE FOR CHANGE

Associates and managers who resist on the basis of low tolerance for change fear the unknown. They have difficulty dealing with the uncertainty inherent in significant change. Such resistance leads to organizational inertia (very slow or no change). A manager, for example, may resist a change that seems good for the organization but that will disrupt established patterns. He may not be able to cope emotionally with the uncertainty and be concerned about having the capability to perform in the new situation.[67] Change leaders should offer support to these resisters.[68] Kind words, emotional support, and attention to training and education that properly prepare the individuals for the planned changes are appropriate tactics.

Research has shown that certain individual characteristics are associated with low tolerance for change. Lack of self-efficacy is perhaps the most important of these characteristics.[69] An associate or manager low in self-efficacy does not believe he or she possesses or can mobilize the effort and ability needed to control events in his or her life. In the workplace, this translates into uncertainty about the capacity to perform at reasonable levels. Another factor is low risk tolerance.[70] Individuals who do not tolerate risk very well often dislike major change. In a recent study of 514 managers from companies headquartered in Asia, Australia, Europe, and North America, poor views of self and low risk tolerance were found to harm the ability to deal with change.[71] In particular, openness to change is critical for organizations to be innovative.[72]

British Airways: The Yin and Yang of Organizational Change

Daniel
Berehulak/
Getty Images

Thanks to the drastic changes implemented by the previous chief executive, new British Airways CEO Willie Walsh is reaping the benefits. In 2006, Walsh announced that for the first time in 10 years, British Airways enjoyed a strong increase in profits, even with the higher fuel costs. Still, change is needed to achieve the company goal for operating margin of 10 percent in 2008; it was 8.3 percent in 2006. To reach this achievement, British Airways (BA) has gone through considerable change over time.

For example, one of the first major changes was the privatization of BA. As the new prime minister in 1979, Margaret Thatcher was not supportive of government-owned companies. She announced her intentions to privatize the company. In addition, international air traffic was being deregulated in a number of countries, including the United States, which in turn created more competition among the airlines. Prior to these changes, British Airways was notorious for poor customer service and treated customers more like cargo than passengers. Leaders in the organization knew it was time to change, so the company began implementing new approaches and started to properly realign resources and provided training to help bring shifts in employee behavior. Top executives completed major downsizing at this time (approximately 22,000 associates and managers). They also implemented programs to help associates learn good customer service skills. In addition, they implemented employee incentive programs to reward employees for good customer service. They also worked hard to change involvement levels by top management in redefining business strategies and rethinking their perspectives about being a service-oriented airline. These changes produced a structure and approach to decision making similar to a high-involvement organization. Overall, these changes were very positive and helped BA to become a competitive and well-performing organization.

Organizations must continue to respond to environmental pressures that may require adaptation. One such pressure for the global airline industry emanated from the tragic events that occurred on September 11, 2001. Many airlines suffered significantly reduced demand, causing massive losses, especially U.S. and western European airlines. British Airways clearly suffered and had to make large reductions in its flights and staff in response to the lower demand and thus to manage its costs. BA announced layoffs of 7,000 associates, but other airlines announced even larger layoffs (e.g., 20,000 at both United and American Airlines). BA also decommissioned 20 aircraft, cut flights by 10 percent, and reduced the pay of 36,000 associates. Despite these reductions, it continued to struggle in the fall of 2001; Standard & Poors downgraded its debt rating to junk-bond status, thereby greatly increasing the airline's debt costs. Even though there was a strong and obvious rationale for these changes, BA encountered resistance to the changes made. The Transport and General Workers' Union expressed disappointment at the rapid and deep cuts made by BA. The pilots were disappointed because they felt that their pay was almost 20 percent below the market prior to the changes made in response to the events of 9/11. Therefore, while the changes may have been justified, they encountered resistance and harmed morale among the associates.

British Airways shareholders did not receive dividends for five years following 9/11. Furthermore, the new CEO, Willie Walsh, knew that additional changes were needed to show a full recovery for investors and to earn greater returns for the shareholders. The changes made by Walsh included increasing the space devoted to premium passengers by converting some economy seats into larger business-class cabins on some aircraft. British Airways installed seats that would flatten for sleeping and modernized in-flight entertainment that included audio and video in the business-class cabin. The premium passenger generates a good portion of the profits enjoyed by the airline. The company is taking steps to reform its pension plan. British Airways is cutting pension benefits and increasing the employee's contribution. The company was contributing five times more than the employee to the pension funds compared with the recommended ratio of two to one. Finally, the firm invested significant time, money, and effort in top management training. For example, Willie Walsh spent six months shadowing the outgoing CEO Rod Eddington.

Organizations need to change regularly. On average, companies make big structural changes every two or three years. British Airways is one of the largest international airlines, carrying almost 36 million passengers worldwide each year. To survive and remain profitable requires that it change regularly to be competitive and respond to other important environmental demands. Despite its progress, BA continues to face challenges. For example, it is struggling to meet its targeted goal to cut $300 million in employee costs in 2007. Its seats that flattened for sleeping were uncomfortable and led to many customer complaints. So, it continues to change in response to demands by its stakeholders.

Sources: K. Done, "British Airways Adds More Business Class," *Financial Times*, at www.ft.com, Nov. 16, 2005; British Airways History, British Airways website, www.britishairways/bapress/-public.com, Jan. 1, 2006; J. Fitzgerald, "British Airways' Lesson on How Not to Out," 2005; A. Campbell, "To Split Up or Stay Together?," *Financial Times*, at www.ft.com, Aug. 9, 2005; "How Failure Breeds Success," *BusinessWeek*, at www.businessweek.com, July 10, 2006; "British Airways Cuts 7,000 Jobs," British Broadcasting Company, bbc.com, Sept. 20, 2001; "Fresh Blow for British Airways," British Broadcasting Company, bbc.com, Nov. 30, 2001.

Anticipating resistance to change can give leaders a major advantage in managing change. The discussion in the *Experiencing Strategic Organizational Behavior* feature suggests that British Airways has had different experiences over time. For example, the top managers seemed to overcome resistance to the changes made when the airline was privatized. They did so by providing information and training, and involving associates in the decision processes. As such, they provided understanding of the changes and their value. Additionally, they were able to overcome the inertia that exists in a government-owned and thus highly regulated organization. They seemed to develop into a high-involvement workplace. However, it seems that this type of approach dissipated over time. It is evident by the dissatisfaction voiced by the pilots and the union representatives of other BA associates. Their concerns seem to be based on self-interest but also might be related to different assessments (by associates and by management) that could also suggest a lack of trust between associates and managers. The training and preparation of the current CEO to take over the role will hopefully help the organization to make changes more effectively in the future.

The DADA Syndrome

DADA syndrome
A sequence of stages—denial, anger, depression, and acceptance—through which individuals can move or in which they can become trapped when faced with unwanted change.

Beyond the resistance to change discussed above, change leaders must realize that associates and managers can become trapped in the so-called **DADA syndrome**—the syndrome of *d*enial, *a*nger, *d*epression, and *a*cceptance.[73] This syndrome highlights what can occur when individuals face unwanted change. In the denial stage, individuals ignore possible or current change; in the anger stage, individuals facing unwanted change become angry about the change; and in the depression stage, they experience emotional lows. Finally, in the acceptance stage, they embrace the reality of the situation and try to make the best of it. Not all individuals who experience this syndrome move through all of the stages sequentially, but many do. Some, however, remain in the anger or depression stage, resulting in negative consequences for them and the organization.

In a well-known incident, Donna Dubinsky at Apple Computer experienced the DADA syndrome.[74] Dubinsky headed the distribution function at Apple in the mid-1980s. She had performed well in her time at Apple and was considered to be a valuable part of the organization. Even so, Steve Jobs, chairman of the board at the time, began to criticize distribution and called for wholesale changes in the way this unit functioned. Dubinsky, incredulous that her unit was being questioned, decided the issue would go away on its own (denial stage). But the issue did not go away. Instead, Jobs asked the head of manufacturing in one of the operating divisions to develop a proposal for a new approach to distribution. Dubinsky still could not believe her unit would be changed, particularly without her input. Over time, however, she became defensive and challenged the criticisms (anger stage).

Concerned with the process through which Jobs was attempting to change distribution, senior management in the company protested, which led to the creation of a taskforce to examine distribution issues. Dubinsky continued to be defensive as a member of this taskforce. As it became clear that the taskforce would endorse Jobs' proposed changes, however, Dubinsky reached an emotional low (depression stage). She was eventually revived by conversations at a retreat for executives. There, Dubinsky realized she had not invested her considerable talents in effectively handling the criticisms and plans for change in the distribution function. She went on the offensive and asked that she be allowed to develop her own proposal for change (acceptance). She was allowed to do so, and after examining the concerns and alternatives, she recommended major changes—changes that were different from Jobs' original ideas. Dubinsky's ideas were incorporated in the final plan.

Change leaders should be sensitive to the potential for the DADA syndrome. To prevent associates and managers from entering the DADA stages or to ensure they do not become mired in the anger or depression stage, leaders must monitor their organizations for actual or potential resistance to change. If resistance is discovered, the cause of the resistance must be diagnosed and addressed.

Organization Development

Leaders must recognize internal and external pressures for change and introduce initiatives designed to cope with them. In addition, leaders can proactively position their organizations to better recognize the need for change and to more easily implement change when necessary. In other words, leaders can develop their organizations so that communication, problem solving, and learning are more effective.

To achieve these goals, **organization development (OD)** is useful. Although researchers have not always agreed on the specific features of organization development, they agree that its purpose is to improve processes and outcomes in organizations.[75] OD has had its share of critics in recent years but has produced some worthwhile results as well.[76]

OD can be defined as a planned, organizationwide, continuous process designed to improve communication, problem solving, and learning through the application of behavioral science knowledge.[77] With its roots in humanistic psychology, OD is grounded in values of individual empowerment and interpersonal cooperation. Thus, it is fully consistent with the high-involvement management approach.

> **organization development (OD)**
> A planned organization-wide continuous process designed to improve communication, problem solving, and learning through the application of behavioral science knowledge.

The Basic OD Model

The basic OD model uses a medical approach in which organizations are treated when they suffer ill health. OD researchers and practitioners diagnose the illness, prescribe interventions, and monitor progress.[78] Exhibit 14-4 provides an overview.

DIAGNOSIS

Diagnosis is an important step in organization development. Without effective diagnosis, managers will not understand what their organization really needs, and the chosen course of action will likely be ineffective.

Although the diagnostic approaches used by physicians and managers are similar, the tools they use vary. Over the years, physicians' diagnostic tools have become quite sophisticated (laboratory tests, CT scans, MRIs, electrocardiograms, and so on). Those of the manager, though useful, are less precise. Even so, our knowledge of diagnostic tools has increased rapidly in recent years.

Diagnostic devices for managers include interviews, surveys, group sociometric devices, process-oriented diagnosis, and accurate records (for example, performance records). Of these tools, the most frequently used are surveys and individual and group interviews.[79] Managers can conduct many different surveys, including job satisfaction surveys (such as the Job Description Index), organization climate surveys (such as the Organizational Practices Questionnaire), job design measures (such as the Job Diagnostic Survey), and assessments of leaders (such as the Leadership Practices Inventory). In many cases, standard survey forms may be used; in other cases, surveys may need to be designed specifically for the situation. These diagnostic tools can be useful in determining needed interventions. Some organizations administer surveys to employees on a regular basis, such as annually, to identify problems.

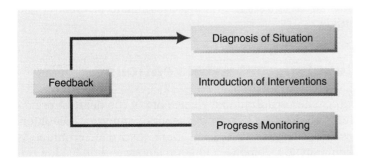

Exhibit 14-4
Basic Organization
Development Model

INTERVENTIONS

After the situation has been diagnosed, interventions can be prescribed. Organization development interventions include different forms of group training, team building, and job redesign.[80] Which technique is most appropriate will vary with the situational factors involved. Unfortunately, there are no ready-made answers that can be used for all situations. Several of the more important techniques are described later in this chapter.

Proper implementation is crucial in organization development. For example, job enrichment may be useful when individuals desire more challenging jobs and more responsibility. Providing such jobs can enhance intrinsic motivation and satisfaction, yielding empowered individuals who are better positioned for effective problem solving and learning. OD leaders must properly prepare the individuals for job enrichment, however, even though they may have requested it. Overall, the interventions must be well planned. Increased job responsibilities often raise the question, "Don't I deserve more pay if I'm performing a more responsible job?" OD leaders must be prepared to answer such questions.

A well-trained organization development specialist should play an important role in any intervention.[81] Often, managers who understand only one or two specific OD techniques attempt to use these approaches to solve whatever problem exists. But the techniques must match the situation, or the likelihood of failure is high. Furthermore, people who are not fully knowledgeable about organization development frequently have problems implementing a successful program. For example, only experts in sensitivity training, team building, or conflict resolution should implement those particular OD change techniques.

PROGRESS MONITORING

The effects of the interventions must be evaluated after an appropriate time interval.[82] The evaluation is important to ensure that the objectives have been met. A common evaluation technique is the survey, which may be used to diagnose a problem and then reused after an OD technique has been implemented to determine what progress has been made toward resolving the problem. Other evaluation tools may be used as well. In any case, the main criterion for evaluation is whether the original objectives have been accomplished.

If the evaluation shows that objectives have not been accomplished, further efforts may be necessary. A new or modified approach may be designed and implemented. The type and degree of these actions depend on why the objectives were not reached and by how far they were missed. Questions such as "Was the original process correct?" and "Was it correctly implemented?" must be answered.

Frequently, some modifications are needed to increase the positive benefits of OD work, but if care has been taken in the OD process, wholesale changes at this stage are unnecessary. Because a comprehensive organization development program is continuous, the process of sensing the organization's need for development is continuous. In this way, an organization is in a constant state of renewal and regularly checks its health.

Organization Development Interventions

The interventions used to create organizational change are at the heart of organization development. Here, we describe several of the more important OD intervention techniques. Research suggests that using more than one technique is generally superior to using a single technique.[83] For convenience of discussion, we

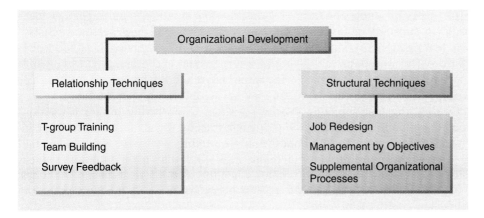

Exhibit 14-5
Organization Development Interventions

have placed the interventions into two groups: techniques directly focused on how individuals relate to one another[84] and techniques focused on structure and systems[85] (see Exhibit 14-5).

RELATIONSHIP TECHNIQUES

Relationship techniques focus on how individuals perceive and respond to one another. T-group training, team building, and survey feedback are among the most important techniques in this category.

In **t-group training,** individuals participate in various interpersonal and group situations to better understand how they act, how others perceive their actions, and how others react to them.[86] For example, individuals may be asked to sit in a circle and discuss values. To promote honest behavior, rather than behavior designed to yield positive impressions, the group meets in a safe setting away from regular work duties. In many cases, individuals involved in this type of training do not know one another before the group experience. Participating with strangers rather than work colleagues helps to promote honest behavior. T-group training is aimed at helping individual associates and managers learn about themselves in a group setting and then transfer that learning to the workplace. An individual often is able to learn about unintended negative effects created by certain types of behavior, for example, and then change that behavior, resulting in a positive effect on the workplace environment.

T-group training must be used carefully and only with a trained, qualified facilitator. The facilitator plays an important role in increasing the chances of success. In addition, not everyone should participate in t-group training sessions. Some individuals, such as those who are highly insecure or not open to deep introspection, may experience negative effects. Thus, group participants must be chosen with great care. Neglecting to take such care is one reason that organization development efforts fail.

Team building, a cornerstone of organization development, is a technique that requires members of a team to work together to understand their problems and implement solutions.[87] A team is any group of associates and/or managers who come together to accomplish a task (see Chapter 11 for additional details). The problems faced by teams usually involve substantive team tasks (for example, technical design problems for a new product development team), the processes of the team (for example, weaknesses in problem solving), and interpersonal relationships among team members (for example, difficulties based on differences in personality).

t-group training
Group exercises in which individuals focus on their actions, how others perceive their actions, and how others generally react to them; participants often learn about unintended negative consequences of certain types of behavior.

team building
A process in which members of a team work together and with a facilitator to diagnose task, process, and interpersonal problems within the team and create solutions.

In successful applications of OD-based team building, team members focus mostly on substantive tasks rather than on process and interpersonal issues.[88] While team members concentrate on substantive problem solving, a skilled leader or third-party consultant can introduce interpersonal and other process guidance as needed. Allowing the group to focus on task-related issues can help to reduce the skepticism some group members may have concerning team building.

Overall, the team-building process can help to positively reinforce relations among team members and may be particularly useful for teams experiencing conflict, lack of leadership, lack of cohesiveness, or ambiguous goals. New leaders taking over the responsibility for a team often find that team building reduces suspicion, increases trust, and promotes a healthy working relationship. At times, the use of a third-party consultant may be necessary to guide the process, particularly when conflict is present.

In summarizing their experiences, two OD researchers have offered a useful list of team-building tips:[89]

1. Get the *right people* together for

2. a *large block of uninterrupted time*

3. to work on *high-priority problems or opportunities* that

4. *they have identified* and have them work

5. in *structured ways* to enhance the likelihood of

6. *realistic solutions and action plans,* which are then

7. *implemented* enthusiastically and

8. *followed up* to assess actual versus expected results.

survey feedback
Data obtained from questionnaires; managers receive the data for their units and are expected to hold unit meetings to discuss problems.

The **survey feedback** technique emphasizes the collection and use of data from questionnaires.[90] Although all OD efforts involve collecting data through surveys and interviews as part of diagnosing the organization's situation, surveys can also be used as an intervention following diagnosis. If, for example, the diagnosis suggests that poor motivation among associates is driven partly by a feeling of lack of input, using surveys more frequently may be helpful in changing this feeling.

The first step in the survey feedback technique involves collecting data on how individuals feel about various aspects of leadership and interpersonal relations within the unit, as well as broader organizational issues. Each manager in the organization receives a summary of the survey results for her unit. An internal or external OD consultant meets with the manager to discuss the results. A second meeting is then arranged for the manager to present the findings to associates and lower-level managers. The OD consultant often attends this unit meeting to explain any technical aspects of the data. The unit members then work together to interpret the findings, understand problems, and find solutions.

It is important that all information from a survey be discussed. Positive information is crucial in helping to build and maintain a positive climate. Negative information is critical for understanding problems.

STRUCTURAL TECHNIQUES

Structural OD techniques, as the name implies, involve adjustments in the organization's structure. In the field of organization development, some structural interventions are focused on changing tasks; others are focused on changing the method of setting task objectives; and still others are broadly focused on communication, problem solving, and learning. Commonly used techniques include job redesign, management by objectives (MBO), and supplemental organizational elements.

The **job redesign** technique may include job enlargement, job enrichment, or both.[91] As discussed in Chapter 6, job enlargement involves adding tasks that offer more variety and that may require the use of different skills. The additional tasks, however, are not of greater complexity. Some refer to this as *horizontal loading*. Job enrichment involves adding more complex tasks, generally by incorporating tasks formerly handled by managers (for example, scheduling of maintenance on a production machine) and staff specialists (for example, making quality-control decisions). Thus, associates whose jobs are enriched have greater responsibility because they begin to manage their own jobs individually or as members of self-managing teams.

> **job redesign**
> Enlargement or enrichment of jobs; enrichment is the better method to enhance motivation for effective problem solving, communication, and learning.

Much of the emphasis on the redesign of jobs in organization development grew out of controversy surrounding boring, repetitive tasks often seen in mass-production systems. Many observers, believing that repetitive tasks led to an alienated workforce, proposed to enrich jobs by providing more challenging tasks. Through enrichment, associates become more engaged problem solvers. Because managers no longer need to closely supervise the routine activities of associates, they can focus more of their attention on helping to solve key organizational problems and helping to establish a learning orientation in their units.

When an organization uses **management by objectives (MBO),** individuals negotiate task objectives with their managers, and this occurs at each level of the organization. (See Chapter 6 for a more detailed discussion of participation in setting goals and the motivational properties of goals.) This technique changes the objective-setting structure from one determined by the supervisor to one in which both supervisor and subordinates participate. Once set, objectives are used in performance assessments.

> **management by objectives (MBO)**
> A management process in which individuals negotiate task objectives with their managers and then are held accountable for attainment of the objectives.

As an organization development technique, MBO involves several specific steps.[92] First, information collected from organization members, senior managers, and perhaps others is used to diagnose organizational problems. This diagnosis provides a focus for MBO efforts. After diagnosis, senior managers and others can define major organizational objectives. Next, workshops about the MBO process are conducted for all managers to help them understand and use the technique correctly.

Objectives for middle managers are then defined by teams of middle and senior managers. Objectives for lower-level managers are set by teams of lower-level and middle managers, with senior managers also possibly involved. Finally, objectives for associates are established by teams of associates and managers. The participatory approach embedded in MBO often yields associates and managers who are more satisfied with and committed to the organization and therefore more likely to be enthusiastic problem solvers open to learning.

Management by objectives can be a useful technique, but it does carry risks.[93] First, objectives can be rather static and inflexible, while the environment is constantly changing. People may have to change their focus and what they do in order to meet changing environmental demands. Second, an associate's accomplishments are often influenced by factors outside of his control. Thus, performance assessments tied to meeting objectives can be unfair. Third, a strong focus on objective attainment may mean that intangible aspects of the job for which objectives have not been set are ignored.

Finally, senior managers can create **supplemental organizational processes** to enhance communication, problem solving, and learning. Examples of such processes include quality circles, safety councils, regular union-management meetings, and periodically scheduled management retreats. At the core, these supplemental processes involve ongoing meetings of associates and/or managers for the purpose of understanding and addressing important problems. Team building, with its attention to process and interpersonal issues, sometimes is involved.

Senior managers at General Electric used a number of organization development interventions to improve honest communication, problem solving, and learning. Their efforts had remarkable results.[94] The management–union meetings implemented in the transportation division constituted a supplemental organizational process. Work-out was also a supplemental process, and it involved aspects of team building as well. The boundaryless organization involved job redesign, as individuals were expected to search across unit lines for ideas—an activity formerly outside of their domain. Many analysts believe that the work-out and boundaryless organization concepts contributed to GE's phenomenal performance during the 20 years of Jack Welch's tenure as CEO. During this time, GE created more value for shareholders than any other company in the world.[95]

Beginning with the efforts of Thomas Edison, over the years General Electric has provided significant advances in many useful products, including the incandescent light bulb, X-ray equipment, the electric fan, radios, TVs, and turbines. But despite GE's history of innovation in product development and its overall success, the company had become stale and out of step with its environment by the time Welch took over as CEO in 1981. Many associates and managers were unhappy and unproductive, and financial performance was beginning to decline. Internal processes and structures were hindering rather than helping. But, organization development interventions helped to create a healthier company. Through these interventions, associates and lower-level managers became more motivated to help identify needed changes; middle and senior managers had better forums for information exchange; and everyone had greater incentives to develop, borrow, and share ideas. The outcome was highly positive for GE's shareholders, managers, and associates.

Organizational Learning

Most organizational development and change require learning. The changes may be based on learning new capabilities, new processes, or adding new knowledge that helps the organization more effectively use its current capabilities and processes. Thus, managing organizational change entails managing knowledge transfers and development.[96] Learning how to more effectively use current knowledge is referred to as **exploitative learning.** Alternatively, **exploratory learning** involves creating new knowledge and being innovative.[97]

As explained earlier, some of the OD techniques also involve learning about relationships and building relationship skills.[98] Some of this learning can eventually be integrated into and enrich current organizational routines (e.g., regular processes and approaches for problem solving) or create new ones.[99] But, it is critical to emphasize that organizational change is successful in the long term only if learning occurs. For example, the changes that enhanced GE's phenomenal performance during Jack Welch's tenure as CEO were based in managers learning how to make effective decisions that created value for the organization.

---

supplemental organizational processes Processes in which associates and/or managers have ongoing meetings for the purpose of understanding and addressing important problems.

exploitative learning Learning how to more effectively use current knowledge.

exploratory learning Creating new knowledge and being innovative.

Organization Development across Cultures

The growth of multinational corporations and the global marketplace suggests that the cultural implications of OD programs must be considered. Behavioral science techniques may not work the same way in different cultures, and methods of managing successful organizations may vary across cultures. Managers hoping to implement an OD program in a culture different from their own must avoid an ethnocentric attitude (assuming that everyone is similar to those back home) as well as stereotyping.[100]

To implement OD successfully in different cultures, those involved should demonstrate the following qualities:

* *Flexibility*—openness to new approaches, ideas, and beliefs and willingness to change one's own behavior
* *Knowledge of specific cultures*—understanding of the beliefs and behavior patterns of different cultures (see Chapter 3 for a discussion of cultural differences)
* *Interpersonal sensitivity*—the ability to listen to and resolve problems with people from different cultures[101]

The Strategic Lens

Organizations must adapt to their external environments in order to survive, grow, and achieve financial success. Organizations design their strategies to help them act in ways that give them an advantage over their competitors. Because most organizations exist in dynamic environments, they have to adjust their strategies regularly. Implementing strategies and adjustments to them requires the involvement and support of all managers and associates in the organization. Therefore, identifying the need for major changes and implementing those changes are critical determinants of organizational success. Managers must overcome resistance to change and effectively use the human capital in the organization to achieve and sustain a competitive advantage. Yet, according to John Kotter, the largest challenge in creating organizational change is in changing the behavior of people. This conclusion is supported by Edward Miller, dean of the medical school at Johns Hopkins University. Dr. Miller stated that 90 percent of people who have very serious heart disease find it highly difficult to change their lifestyle even though they understand the importance of doing so for their personal health.[102] One can easily surmise that if they cannot change their lifestyle when it affects their health, changing their behavior for the good of the organization is likely to be even more difficult. Research shows that events causing substantial change (often referred to as discontinuous change) rarely trigger a response until they are perceived as a threat to survival.[103]

The examples of major changes implemented at GE show the importance of managing organizational change, as well as the potential importance of organization development interventions. The major organizational changes implemented at GE are reportedly the primary reason that Jack Welch enjoyed so much success as CEO during his 20-plus years in that role. Developing and implementing effective organizational strategies and managing organizational change are interdependent.

Critical Thinking Questions

1. Why do organizations need to make changes on a regular basis? What are the major causes of these changes?

2. Why is it so difficult for people to change their behavior, even when they know it is important to do so?

3. If you were in a managerial position and believed that a major change in your unit's structure was needed, what actions would you take to ensure that the change was made effectively?

What This Chapter Adds to Your Knowledge Portfolio

In our final chapter, we have discussed change in organizations. More specifically, we have discussed pressures for change, a three-phase change model, two critical tactical decisions, and resistance to change. We have also examined organization development, offering a definition and basic model, along with a set of techniques. In summary, we have made the following points:

- Organizations experience pressures for change, some of which are internal. Aspiration–performance discrepancies constitute one internal source of pressure. These discrepancies are simply differences between desired and actual performance. Past aspirations, past performance, and comparisons with others affect today's aspirations. Life-cycle forces constitute a second internal source of pressure. When organizations grow, pressure tends to build at certain predictable points, forcing organizations to respond. If an organization responds effectively, it tends to move through several stages: entrepreneurial, collectivity, formalization, and elaboration.

- Organizations experience a host of external pressures for change. Such pressures originate with technological advances, the introduction or removal of government regulations, changes in societal values, shifting political dynamics, changes in demographics, and growing international interdependencies.

- Planned change entails deliberate efforts to move an organization or a subunit from its current state to a new state. Such change is typically thought of as a three-phase process comprising unfreezing, moving, and refreezing. Unfreezing involves providing a rationale for change, producing minor levels of guilt or anxiety about not changing, and creating a psychological sense of safety concerning the change. Moving involves providing information that supports the proposed change and creating actual change. Refreezing focuses on implementing evaluation systems to track expected new behaviors and training systems to ensure continuous upgrading of relevant knowledge and skills. It also involves creating permanent reward structures to reinforce the new behaviors, as well as hiring and promotion systems that support the new approaches.

- Decisions related to speed and style must be made in all planned change projects. Whether movement toward change should be fast or slow depends on the urgency of the change, the degree of support for changing, the amount or complexity of the change, the competitive environment, the knowledge and skills available to support the change, and the availability of financial and other resources necessary to implement the change. Style involves using a top-down or participatory approach. Key criteria for this decision are the urgency of the change, the degree of support for changing, the referent and expert power of change leaders, and organizational norms.

- Resistance to change can be traced to a general set of causes: lack of understanding, different assessments, self-interest, and/or low tolerance for change. To address lack of understanding, change leaders should ensure proper communication about proposed changes. To address different assessments, leaders should include actual or potential change resisters in the decision-making process in order to learn as much as possible about their thinking and to create a sense that all voices are being heard. To address self-interest, leaders must consider a host of tactics, including transferring resisters or even terminating them, using a coercive style to ensure compliance, and in rare situations, negotiating compliance. Finally, to address low tolerance for change, change leaders should offer emotional support and ensure proper education and training to break the inertia.

- Individuals facing unwanted change may move through a series of stages known as denial, anger, depression, and acceptance. Change leaders must understand this so-called DADA syndrome. To prevent associates and others from experiencing it, they must monitor their organizations for potential and actual resistance to change and deal effectively with resistance when it is identified.

- Organization development is an applied field of study focused on improving processes and outcomes in organizations. It can be formally defined as a planned, organization-wide, continuous process designed to improve communication, problem solving, and learning. Because it has roots in humanistic psychology, it is grounded in values of individual empowerment and interpersonal cooperation. The basic OD model has three steps: diagnosis, intervention, and progress monitoring.

- The various interventions used in organization development can be classified as either relationship techniques or structural techniques. Relationship techniques, which focus on how individuals perceive and respond to one another, include t-group training, team building, and survey feedback. Structural techniques, which involve adjustments to the structural aspects of an organization, include job redesign, management by objectives, and supplemental structural elements. OD techniques involve organizational learning in order to create the desired change.

- Cultural differences must be considered when organization development techniques are being used. Techniques must be chosen in light of the prevailing culture. To implement OD successfully in different cultures, those involved should be flexible, understand the various cultures, and possess interpersonal sensitivity.

Back to the Knowledge Objectives

1. What are the two major sources of internal pressure for organizational change? In your opinion, which of these two is most difficult to handle? Why?

2. What are the six major sources of external pressure for organizational change? In your opinion, which of these is most difficult to handle? Why?

3. What is involved in each phase of the unfreezing–moving–refreezing model of planned change?

4. What are the factors to consider in deciding whether a fast or slow approach to change is best? What are the factors to consider in deciding whether a top-down or participatory approach to change is best? Describe a situation where you were either a change recipient or a change leader and a poor choice was made for at least one of these two decisions (use an example from an organization in which you currently work or formerly worked, or use a voluntary organization, a church, a sports team, or a fraternity/sorority).

5. Compare the four basic causes of resistance to change. If you had to choose one, which would you prefer to deal with as a manager, and why?

6. What is the DADA syndrome?

7. What is organization development? Provide a definition as well as a basic model. A number of interventions can be used in organization development. As a manager, which of these interventions would you prefer to use, and why?

Thinking about Ethics

1. The entrepreneurial stage of an organization's life cycle is an exciting time. But while the founders are deciding how they will enter new markets and what products they will offer, do they have any obligation to consider the general public's interests in these decisions?

2. In this chapter, we suggested that managers can adopt a coercive style to overcome resistance to change when it is based on self-interest. Do managers have any responsibility to people whose resistance is based on self-interest? Explain.

3. When implementing OD interventions, how should managers deal with people who have low self-efficacy?

4. What ethical issues are involved in implementing major organizational changes in which a large number of associates are laid off? How should these issues be handled?

5. Suppose you identify a person going through the DADA process in response to an organizational change. Should you intervene or leave the person alone to move through the stages on his or her own? Explain your answer. If the person is in the anger stage, how can you intervene successfully?

Key Terms

Aspiration–performance discrepancies, p. 486
Life-cycle forces, p. 487
Planned change, p. 492
Unfreezing, p. 493
Moving, p. 493
Refreezing, p. 494
Resistance to change, p. 498

Procedural justice, p. 499
DADA syndrome, p. 502
Organization development (OD), p. 503
T-group training, p. 505
Team building, p. 505
Survey feedback, p. 506
Job redesign, p. 507

Management by objectives (MBO), p. 507
Supplemental organizational processes, p. 508
Exploitative learning, p. 508
Exploratory learning, p. 508

Building your Human Capital

An Assessment of Low Tolerance for Change

People differ in their tolerance for change. Low self-efficacy and low risk tolerance are two important factors that affect tolerance for change. Although an individual's self-efficacy and risk tolerance may vary from situation to situation, overall scores on these factors provide insight into general tendencies. Understanding these tendencies can help you to understand how and why you behave as you do. In this installment of *Building Your Human Capital*, we present an assessment tool for efficacy and risk.

Instructions

In this assessment, you will read 19 phrases that describe people. Use the rating scale below to indicate how accurately each phrase describes you. Rate yourself as you generally are now, not as you wish to be in the future; and rate yourself as you honestly see yourself. Keep in mind that very few people have extreme scores on all or even most of the items (a "1" or a "5" is an extreme score); most people have midrange scores for many of the items. Read each item carefully, and then circle the number that corresponds to your choice from the rating scale that follows.

1	2	3	4	5
Not at all like me	Somewhat unlike me	Neither like nor unlike me	Somewhat like me	Very much like me

1. Enjoy being reckless.	1	2	3	4	5
2. Become overwhelmed by events.	1	2	3	4	5

3. Would never go hang-gliding or bungee-jumping.	1	2	3	4	5
4. Readily overcome setbacks.	1	2	3	4	5
5. Take risks.	1	2	3	4	5
6. Am often down in the dumps.	1	2	3	4	5
7. Would never make a high-risk investment	1	2	3	4	5
8. Can manage many things at the same time.	1	2	3	4	5
9. Seek danger.	1	2	3	4	5
10. Feel that I am unable to deal with things.	1	2	3	4	5
11. Stick to the rules.	1	2	3	4	5
12. Can tackle anything.	1	2	3	4	5
13. Know how to get around rules.	1	2	3	4	5
14. Am afraid of many things.	1	2	3	4	5
15. Avoid dangerous situations.	1	2	3	4	5
16. Think quickly.	1	2	3	4	5
17. Am willing to try anything once.	1	2	3	4	5
18. Need reassurance.	1	2	3	4	5
19. Seek adventure.	1	2	3	4	5

Scoring Key

To determine your score, combine your responses to the items above as follows:

Self-efficacy = (Item 4 + Item 8 + Item 12 + Item 16) + (30 − (Item 2 + Item 6 + Item 10 + Item 14 + Item 18))

Tolerance for risk = (Item 1 + Item 5 + Item 9 + Item 13 + Item 17 + Item 19) + (24 − (Item 3 + Item 7 + Item 11 + Item 15))

Scores for self-efficacy can range from 9 to 45. Scores of 36 and above may be considered high, while scores of 18 and below may be considered low. Scores for risk tolerance can range from 10 to 50. Scores of 40 and above may be considered high, while scores of 20 and below may be considered low.

Source: International Personality Item Pool. (2001). A Scientific Collaboration for the Development of Advanced Measures of Personality Traits and Other Individual Differences (http://ipip.ori.org/).

A Strategic Organizational Behavior Moment

Organization Development at KBTZ

KBTZ is a large television station located in a major metropolitan area in the United States. The station is one of the largest revenue producers in its market and employs more than 180 people, considerably more than its closest competitors. It is a subsidiary of a large conglomerate corporation that has diversified interests in other businesses as well as the communications field. KBTZ represents a significant portion of the conglomerate's profit base.

Over the past few years, substantial investments have been made in the television station by the parent corporation. These investments not only have resulted in significant tax advantages but also have established KBTZ as the local television leader in the use of sophisticated electronic equipment. The station's physical plant was remodeled at considerable expense to accommodate the new equipment and to boost its image as the leader in the market. KBTZ is a successful business and a respected member of the metropolitan community. However, in part because of the recent changes in the station and in part because of its desire to maintain its established success, the station has requested that a consultant examine important problems. You are the consultant.

In your initial meeting with Valerie Diaz, the president and general manager of KBTZ, she explained her perceptions of key problems facing the station.

One of our biggest problems is the high stress to which our managers and associates are exposed. This is especially true with respect to time deadlines. There is no such thing as slack time in television. For example, when it is precisely six o'clock, we must be on the air with the news. All of the news material, local reporting, news interviews, and so on must be processed, edited, and ready to go at six. We can't have any half-prepared material or extended deadlines, or we lose the audience and, most likely, our sponsors. I believe this situation causes a great deal of conflict and turnover among our employees. We have a number of well-qualified and motivated employees, some of whom work here because of the glamour and excitement. But we also have a lot of problems.

Valerie concluded by saying, "I've asked you here because I believe the station needs an outside viewpoint. Our employee turnover is about 35 percent, which is too high. We are having trouble hiring qualified people who fit our culture and who can help us deal with the challenges. We must eliminate the conflicts and develop a cohesive organization to retain our profit and market-leading positions. I would like to hire you as a consultant for this job. I would like you to monitor our operations and diagnose our problems."

You have now collected data within each department (there are seven departments based on function, as discussed below). All department heads have been interviewed, while other employees have responded to questionnaires concerning organizational climate and job satisfaction. The information collected during this diagnosis phase has been summarized as follows.

Interviews with Department Heads

Business Manager: "I'm very new in this job and haven't really learned the ropes yet. I previously worked in sales and in the general manager's office. This is my first managerial position, and I need help in managing my department, since I don't have any management training."

News Director: "Let me be frank with you. I've worked for the big network, and the only reason I'm here is because I wanted to come back home to live. I don't think we need you here. We don't need any new 'management programs.' My department functions smoothly, my people are creative, and I don't want you messing us up with some newfangled program."

Operations Manager: "We truly have the best department in the station. I believe in Valerie's management of the station. I also believe in working my people hard. Nobody lags in this department, or out they go. Our only problems are with the news director's people, who are confused all of the time, and the engineering group, which is lazy and uncooperative. Our effectiveness depends on these groups. I think the chief engineer is incompetent. Get rid of him, shape up the news group and the engineers, and you'll have done a great job."

Chief Engineer: "Things go pretty well most of the time, except for the unreasonableness of certain people in other departments. Some people expect us to drop whatever we're doing and immediately repair some malfunctioning equipment in their area. Hell, this is sophisticated equipment, and it can take several hours just to determine the cause of the failure. The news people just have to treat their equipment better, and the operations manager—he's up here nearly every day screaming about something. One of these days I'm going to punch his lights out!"

Program Director: "My department is okay, but the station is missing a lot of opportunities in other areas. We have a lot of people problems in some departments, especially news and sales. The chief engineer is incompetent, and the operations manager pushes his lower-level managers and associates too hard—never lets them make any decisions or take any responsibilities. The general manager, Valerie Diaz, doesn't want to face up to these problems."

Promotion Manager: "We're a small, friendly group. We have few problems—except with the news group people, who think they know more than we do. But that's just a small problem. I would like a little training in how to deal with people—motivation, communication, and that sort of stuff."

Sales Manager: "Things are just great in our department. To be sure, the sales reps complain sometimes, but I just remind them that they're the highest-paid people in the station. I think Mom [Valerie Diaz] is doing a great job as general manager of the station."

Survey of Departments

Business Office and Programming Departments. The survey showed individuals in these departments to have generally positive attitudes. Job satisfaction was somewhat mixed but still positive. These individuals did, however, have two important negative perceptions of their task environment. First, they thought that their department heads and the general manager could handle downward communication better. Second, there were several unsolicited comments about being underpaid relative to other station employees.

News Department. Managers and associates in the news department reported very high satisfaction with their jobs but extreme dissatisfaction with the department head (the news director) and very negative attitudes toward their overall work environment. Communication between managers and associates was perceived to be almost nonexistent. Associates complained of very low rewards, including pay, promotion opportunities, and managerial praise. They also complained of constant criticism, which was the only form of managerial feedback on performance. In addition, in spite of their high job satisfaction, they believed that the negative factors led them to be poorly motivated.

The severity of the problems in this department was highlighted when some associates reported that they weren't sure who their immediate manager was, since both the assignments editor and the assistant news director gave them assignments. They also reported that creativity (thought to be important in their jobs) was discouraged by the director's highly authoritarian and structured style. Many employees resented the news director, referring to him as erratic, caustic, and alcoholic.

Operations Department. Most of the operations associates were satisfied with their jobs and reported pride in their department. However, satisfaction with immediate managers was mixed. Furthermore, some associates had very positive feelings about the department head, but most held him in low regard. The associates tended to feel overworked (reporting a 74-hour workweek) and thought the department head expected too much. They also thought they were underpaid relative to their task demands and criticized managerial feedback on their performance. They noted that the department head never praised positive performance—he only reprimanded them for poor performance. They also reported concern over the conflict with engineering, which they believed should and could be resolved.

Engineering Department. The survey revealed that members of this department were very dissatisfied with their jobs and immediate managers. Responses also showed that department members perceived a high level of conflict between themselves and the operations and news departments, especially the operations department. They also believed the department head did not support them and that managers and associates in other departments held them in low regard. They noted that they never had department meetings and that they rarely received feedback on their performance from the chief engineer.

Promotions Department. The survey showed this department to have very positive attitudes. Job satisfaction was high, and everyone viewed their task environment positively. The few negative attitudes were primarily directed toward the "ineffectiveness" of the news department.

Sales Department. Very few individuals from the sales department responded to the survey. To find out why they hadn't received responses, the consultants approached several salespersons for private discussions. Nearly all of them indicated that they couldn't complete the survey honestly. As one stated, "My attitudes about this place are somewhat negative, and my department head is the station manager's son. I'd lose my job today if he knew what I really thought about him."

Discussion Questions

1. Identify the basic problems at KBTZ.

2. Which OD techniques would you consider using, and why?

Team Exercise

Identifying Change Pressures and Their Effects

Procedure

1. With the aid of the instructor, the class will be divided into four- or five-person groups.

2. The groups will be assigned several tasks:
   - Each group should identify several specific change pressures that are acting on their institution (e.g., college, university). The group should record these pressures as external or internal.
   - Once the change pressures have been identified, the group should determine and record the effects of each change pressure on the institution.

- Each group should prepare a list of recommendations concerning what the institution should do to deal with these change pressures.
- Finally, each group should conduct an analysis of possible resistance to change. Who or what groups might resist each recommendation and why? How should the possible resistance be handled?

3. The instructor will call on each group in class, asking it to present its lists of (1) change pressures, (2) effects of change pressures, (3) recommendations, and (4) people/groups that might resist change.

4. The instructor will guide a discussion of this exercise.

Endnotes

1. Hitt, M.A., Ireland, R.D., & Hoskisson, R.E. 2009. *Strategic management: Competitiveness and globalization* (8th ed). Mason, OH: South-Western.

2. "100 Best Companies to Work For 2007," *Fortune,* http://money.cnn.com/magazines/fortune/bestcompanies/2007.

3. Walsh, J.P., Meyer, A.D., & Schoonhoven, C.B. 2006. A future for organization theory: Living in and living with changing organizations. *Organization Science,* 17: 657–671; Fiss, P.C., & Zajac, E.J. 2006. The symbolic management of strategic change: Sensegiving via framing and decoupling. *Academy of Management Journal,* 49: 1173–1193.

4. Huber, G.P. 2004. *The necessary nature of future firms: Attributes of survivors in a changing world.* Thousand Oaks, CA: Sage Publications.

5. Chen, W.-R., & Miller, K.D. 2007. Situational and institutional determinants of firms' R&D search intensity. *Strategic Management Journal,* 28: 368–381; Cyert, R.M., & March, J.G. 1963. *A behavioral theory of the firm.* Englewood Cliffs, NJ: Prentice-Hall.

6. Greve, H.R. 1998. Performance, aspirations, and risky change. *Administrative Science Quarterly,* 43: 58–86.

7. Bromiley, P. 1991. Testing a causal model of corporate risk taking and performance. *Academy of Management Journal,* 34: 37–59.

8. Cyert & March, *A behavioral theory of the firm;* Mezias, S.F., Chen Y-R., & Murphy, P.R. 2002. Aspiration level adaptation in an American financial services organization: A field study. *Management Science,* 48: 1285–1300.

9. Mezias, S.J., Chen, Y.-R., & Murphy, P.R. 2002. Aspiration level adaptation in an American financial services organization: A field study. *Academy of Management Best Paper Proceedings,* CE-ROM—MOC:D1.

10. Morrow, J.L., Jr., Sirmon, D.G., Hitt, M.A., & Holcomb, T.R. 2007. Creating value in the face of declining performance: Firm strategies and organizational recovery. *Strategic Management Journal,* 28: 271–283.

11. Mezias, Chen, & Murphy, Aspiration level adaptation in an American financial services organization.

12. de Figueiredo, J.M., & Kyle, M.K. 2006. Surviving the gales of creative destruction: The determinants of product turnover. *Strategic Management Journal,* 27: 241–264; Greiner, L.E. 1998. Evolution and revolution as organizations grow. *Harvard Business Review,* 76(3): 55–68; Flamholtz, E., & Hua, W. 2002. Strategic organizational development, growing pains and corporate financial performance: An empirical test. *European Management Journal,* 20: 527–536; Lynall, M.D., Goleen, B.R., & Hillman, A.J. 2003. Board composition from adolescence to maturity: A multitheoretic view. *Academy of Management Review,* 28: 416–431.

13. Arthaud-Day, M.L., Certo, S.T., Dalton C.M., & Dalton, D.R. 2006. A changing of the guard: Executive and director turnover following corporate financial restatements. *Academy of Management Journal,* 49: 1119–1136.

14. Huber, *The necessary nature of future firms.*

15. Tenopir, C., & King, D. 1998. Designing electronic journals with 30 years of lessons from print. *Journal of Electronic Publishing,* 4(2): http://www.press.umich.edu/jep/04-02/king.html.

16. Narin, F., & Olivastro, D. 1998. Linkage between patents and papers: An interim EPO/U.S. Comparison. *Scientometrics,* 41: 51–59.

17. U.S. Patent and Trademark Office. 1977. Technology assessment and forecast report. Washington, DC: U.S. Government Printing Office; U.S. Patent and Trademark Office. 2000. U.S. patent studies report. Washington, DC: Government Printing Office.

18. U.S. Patent and Trademark Office, U.S. patent statistics report.

19. Lin, Z., Zhao, X., Ismail, K.M., & Carley, K.M. 2006. Organizational restructuring in response to crises: Lessons from computational modeling and real-world cases. *Organization Science,* 17: 598–618; Huber, G.P. 1984. The nature and design of post-industrial organizations. *Management Science,* 30: 928–951.

20. Thomke, S., & Nimgade, A. 1998. *BMW AG: The digital car project (A).* Boston: Harvard Business School Publishing.

21. Bell, J., & Power, S. 2004. Nissan is seeking U.S. exemption on fuel efficiency. *Wall Street Journal,* March 10: D.12; Draper, H. 2004. "Do not call" list forces marketers to seek new ways to get attention. *Wall Street Journal,* July 7: 1; Latour, A., & Squeo, A.M. 2004. FCC to urge telecoms to settle on local network-access issue. *Wall Street Journal,* March 31: D.4.

22. Spell, C.S., & Blum, T.C. 2006. Adoption of workplace substance abuse prevention programs: Strategic choice and institutional perspectives. *Academy of Management Journal,* 49: 1125–1142.

23. Back, B.J. 2002. Nike watchdogs attacking each other. *The Business Journal,* 19(2): 1.

24. Spell & Blum, Adoption of workplace substance abuse prevention programs.

25. Spanish Resources: Overview—Hispanics in North Carolina, 2007. CarolinasAGC, http://www.cagc.org/spanish_res/hisp_nc.cfm, May 21; Hummel, M. 2004. Speaking the language: Booming Spanish-speaking population alters business strategies. *Greensboro News Record,* May 16: E.1.

26. Hitt, M.A., Tihanyi, L., Miller T., & Connelly, B. 2006. International diversification: Antecedents, outcomes and moderators. *Journal of Management, 32:* 831–867; Meyer, K.E. 2006. Globalfocusing: From domestic conglomerates to global specialists. *Journal of Management Studies, 43:* 1109–1144.

27. Mathews, J.A., & Zander, I. 2007. The international entrepreneurial dynamics of accelerated internationalisation, *Journal of International Business Studies, 38:* 387–403; Szulanski, G., & Jensen, R.J. 2006. Presumptive adaptation and the effectiveness of knowledge transfer. *Strategic Management Journal, 27:* 937–957.

28. Koka, B.R., Madhavan, R., & Prescott, J.E. 2006. The evolution of interfirm networks: Environmental effects on patterns of network change. *Academy of Management Review, 31:* 721–737.

29. See, for example, Kanter, R.M., Stein, B.A., & Jick, T.D. 1992. *The challenge of change: How companies experience it and leaders guide it.* New York: The Free Press.

30. Tichy, N., & Devanna, M. 1986. *The transformational leader.* New York: John Wiley & Sons.

31. Nadler, D., & Tushman, M. 1989. Organizational framebending: Principles for managing reorientation. *Academy of Management Executive, 3(3):* 194–204.

32. Ford, M.W. 2006. Profiling change. *Journal of Applied Behavioral Science, 42:* 420–446; Hayes, J. 2002. *The theory and practice of change management.* New York: Palgrave; Lewin, K. 1951. *Field theory in social science.* New York: Harper & Row; Lewin, K. 1958. Group decisions and social change. In E.E. Maccobby, T.M. Newcomb, & E.L. Hartley (Eds.), *Readings in social psychology* (3rd ed.). Austin, TX: Holt, Rinehart & Winston.

33. Based on Goodstein, L.D., & Burke, W.W. 1993. Creating successful organizational change. *Organizational Dynamics, 19(4):* 5–18; Kanter, Stein, & Jick, *The challenge of change;* Lewin, *Field theory in social science;* Lewin, Group decisions and social change; Schein, E.H. 1987. *Process consultation* (Vol. II). Boston: Addison-Wesley; Sitkin, S. 2003. *Notes on organizational change.* Durham, NC: Fuqua School of Business.

34. Reay, T., Golden-Biddle, K., & Germann, K. 2006. Legitimizing a new role: Small wins and microprocesses of change. *Academy of Management Journal, 49:* 977–998.

35. Based on Goodstein, & Burke, Creating successful organizational change; Kanter, Stein, & Jick, *The challenge of change;* Lewin, *Field theory in social science;* Lewin, Group decisions and social change; Schein, *Process consultation* (Vol. II); Sitkin, *Notes on organizational change.*

36. Filatotchev, I., & Toms, S. 2006. Corporate governance and financial constraints on strategic turnarounds. *Journal of Management Studies, 43:* 407–433.

37. Lavie, D. 2006. Capability reconfiguration: An analysis of incumbent responses to technological change. *Academy of Management Review, 31:* 153–174.

38. Based on Goodstein, & Burke, Creating successful organizational change; Kanter, Stein, & Jick, *The challenge of change;* Lewin, *Field theory in social science;* Lewin, Group decisions and social change; Schein, *Process consultation* (Vol. II). Sitkin, *Notes on organizational change.*

39. See, for example, Schuster, J.R. 2004. Total rewards. *Executive Excellence,* 21(1): 5.

40. Anand, N., Gardner, H.K., & Morris, T. 2007. Knowledge-based innovation: Emergence and embedding of new practice areas in management consulting firms. *Academy of Management Journal,* 50: 406–428.

41. Slywotzky, A.J. 2007. *The upside: The 7 strategies for turning big threats into growth breakthroughs.* New York: Crown Business.

42. See, for example, Kotter, J.P. 1996. *Leading change.* Boston: Harvard Business School Publishing.

43. See, for example, Kotter, *Leading change.*

44. Ibid.

45. Ibid.

46. Ibid.

47. See Hailey, V.H., & Balogun, J. 2002. Devising context sensitive approaches to change: The example of Glaxo Wellcome. *Long Range Planning,* 35: 153–178; Kanter, Stein, & Jick, *The challenge of change;* Nohria, N., & Khurana, R. 1993. *Executing change: Seven key considerations.* Boston: Harvard Business School Publishing.

48. See Hailey, & Balogun, Devising context sensitive approaches to change; Kanter, Stein, & Jick, *The challenge of change.*

49. Ibarra, H., & Sackley, N. 1995. *Charlotte Beers at Ogilvy and Mather (A).* Boston: Harvard Business School Publishing.

50. Kanter, Stein, & Jick, *The challenge of change.*

51. Durand, R., Rao, H., & Monin, P. 2007. Code and conduct in French cuisine: Impact of code changes on external evaluations. *Strategic Management Journal,* 28: 455–472.

52. Hailey, & Balogun, Devising context sensitive approaches to change.

53. Marrow, A.J., Bowers, D.F., & Seashore, S.E. 1967. *Management by participation.* New York: Harper and Row.

54. Kanter, Stein, & Jick, *The challenge of change.*

55. Judson, A.S. 1991. *Changing behavior in organizations: Minimizing resistance to change.* Cambridge, MA: Basil Blackwell.

56. Abrahamson, E. 2004. Avoiding repetitive change syndrome. *Sloan Management Review,* 45(2): 93–95.

57. Kotter, J.P., & Schlesinger, L.A. 1979. Choosing strategies for change. *Harvard Business Review,* 57(2): 106–114.

58. Elliott, D., & Smith, D. 2006. Cultural readjustment after crisis: Regulation and learning from crisis within the UK soccer industry. *Journal of Management Studies,* 43: 290–317.

59. Kotter & Schlesinger, Choosing strategies for change.

60. David, P., Bloom, M., & Hillman, A.J. 2007. Investor activism, managerial responsiveness, and corporate social performance, *Strategic Management Journal,* 28: 91–100.

61. Kotter & Schlesinger, Choosing strategies for change.

62. See Vroom, V.H., & Yetton, P.W. 1973. *Leadership and decision making.* Pittsburgh: University of Pittsburgh Press.

63. Korsgaard, M.A., Sapienza, H.J., & Schweiger, D.M. 2002. Beaten before begun: The role of procedural justice in planning change. *Journal of Management,* 28: 497–516; Saunders,

M.N.K., & Thornhill, A. 2003. Organizational justice, trust, and the management of change: An exploration. *Personnel Review,* 32: 360–375.

64. Korsgaard, Sapienza, & Schweiger, Beaten before begun.

65. Ryan, M.K., & Haslam, S.A. 2007. The glass cliff: Exploring the dynamics surrounding the appointment of women to precarious leadership positions. *Academy of Management Review,* 32: 549–572.

66. See Kotter & Schlesinger, Choosing strategies for change.

67. Henderson, A.D., Miller, D., & Hambrick, D.C. 2006. How quickly do CEOs become obsolete? Industry dynamism, CEO tenure and company performance. *Strategic Management Journal,* 27: 447–460.

68. Kotter & Schlesinger, Choosing strategies for change.

69. Judge, T.A., Thoresen, V.P., & Welbourne, T.M. 1999. Managerial coping with organizational change: A dispositional perspective. *Journal of Applied Psychology,* 84: 107–122; Malone, J.W. 2001. Shining a new light on organizational change: Improving self-efficacy through coaching. *Organizational Dynamics,* 19(2): 27–36; Morrison, E.W., & Phelps, C.C. 1999. Taking charge at work: Extrarole efforts to initiate workplace change. *Academy of Management Journal,* 42: 403–419; Bandura, A. 1977. Self-efficacy: Toward a unifying theory of behavioral change. *Psychological Review,* 84: 191–215; Judge, T.A., Thoresen, V.P., & Welbourne, T.M. 1999. Managerial coping with organizational change: A dispositional perspective. *Journal of Applied Psychology,* 84: 107–122; Malone, J.W. 2001. Shining a new light on organizational change: Improving self-efficacy through coaching. *Organizational Dynamics,* 19(2): 27–36.

70. Judge, Thorenson, & Welbourne, Managerial coping with organizational change: A dispositional perspective.

71. Ibid.

72. Laursen, K., & Salter, A. 2006. Open for innovation: The role of openness in explaining innovation performance among U.K. manufacturing firms. *Strategic Management Journal,* 27: 131–150.

73. Jick, T.D. 1991. *Donna Dubinsky and Apple Computer (A) (B) (C): Note.* Boston: Harvard Business School Publishing. For the original basis of these ideas, see Kubler-Ross, E. 1969. *On death and dying.* New York: Macmillan.

74. Ibid.

75. French, W.L., & Bell, C.H. 1999. *Organization development: Behavioral science interventions for organization improvement* (6th ed.). Upper Saddle River, NJ: Prentice-Hall.

76. Worley, C.G., & Feyerherm, A.E. 2003. Reflections on the future of organization development. *Journal of Applied Behavioral Science,* 39: 97–115; Robertson, P.J., Roberts, D.R., & Porras, J.I. 1993. An evaluation of a model of planned organizational change: Evidence from a meta-analysis. In R.W. Woodman & W.A. Passmore (Eds.), *Research in organizational change and development (Vol. 7).* Greenwich, CT: JAI Press.

77. See Egan, T.M. 2002. Organization development: An examination of definitions and dependent variables. *Organization Development Journal,* 20(2): 59–70; French & Bell, *Organization development: Behavioral science interventions for organization improvement* (6th ed.); Schifo, R. 2004. OD in ten words or less: Adding lightness to the definitions of organizational development. *Organization Development Journal,* 22(3): 74–85; Worley & Feyerherm, Reflections on the future of organization development.

78. See Beckhard, R. 1969. *Organization development: Strategies and models.* Reading, MA: Addison-Wesley.

79. See French & Bell, *Organization development.*

80. Ibid.

81. Worley & Feyerherm, Reflections on the future of organization development.

82. French & Bell, Organization development.

83. Guzzo, R.A., Jette, R.D., & Katzell, R.A. 1985. The effects of psychologically based intervention programs on worker productivity. *Personnel Psychology,* 38: 461–489; Neuman, G.A., Edwards, J.E., & Raju, N.S. 1989. Organization development interventions: A meta-analysis of their effects on satisfaction and other attitudes. *Personnel Psychology,* 42: 461–489.

84. See the "human processual" approaches in Friedlander, F., & Brown, D. 1974. Organization development. *Annual Review of Psychology,* 25: 313–341; Also see Porras, J.I., & Berg, P.O. 1978. The impact of organization development. *Academy of Management Review,* 3: 249–266.

85. See structural interventions in French & Bell, *Organization development.*

86. Argyris, C. 1964. T-groups for organizational effectiveness. *Harvard Business Review,* 42(2): 60–74; French & Bell, *Organization development.*

87. Porras & Berg, The impact of organization development.

88. See team-building interventions in French & Bell, *Organization development*; also see Hackman, J.R. 2002. *Leading teams: Setting the stage for great performances.* Boston: Harvard Business School Press.

89. Bell, C., & Rosenzweig, J. 1978. Highlights of an organization improvement program in a city government. In W.L. French, C.H. Bell, Jr., & R.A. Zawacki (Eds.), *Organization development theory, practice, and research.* Dallas: Business Publications.

90. Bowers, D.G., & Franklin, J.L. 1972. Survey-guided development: Using human resources management in organizational change. *Journal of Contemporary Business,* 1: 43–55.

91. Hackman, J.R., Oldham, G., Janson, R., & Purdy, K. 1975. A new strategy for job enrichment. *California Management Review,* 17(4): 57–71.

92. Steps based on French, W., & Hollman, R. 1975. Management by objectives: The team approach. *California Management Review,* 17(3): 13–22.

93. Levinson, H. 2003. Management by whose objectives? *Harvard Business Review,* 81(1): 107–116.

94. Bartlett, C.A., & Wozny, M. 2004. *GE's two-decade transformation: Jack Welch's leadership.* Boston: Harvard Business School Publishing.

95. Hitt, M.A., Ireland, R.D., & Hoskisson, R.E. 2003. *Strategic management: Competitiveness and globalization* (5th ed.). Mason, OH: South-Western.

96. Meyer, K. 2007. Contextualizing organizational learning: Lyles and Salk in the context of their research. *Journal of International Business Studies,* 38: 27–37.

97. Gupta, A., Smith, K.G., & Shalley, C.E. 2006. The interplay between exploration and exploitation. *Academy of Management Journal,* 49: 693–706.

98. Kang, S.-C., Morris, S.S., & Snell, S.A. 2007. Relational archetypes, organizational learning and value creation: Extending the human resource architecture. *Academy of Management Review,* 32: 236–256.

99. Espedal, B. 2006. Do organizational routines change as experience changes? *Journal of Applied Behavioral Science,* 42: 468–490.

100. Bourgeois, L.J., & Boltvinik, M. 1981. OD in cross-cultural settings: Latin America. *California Management Review,* 23(3): 75–81.

101. See Lippitt, G., Lippitt, R., & Lafferty, C. 1984. Cutting edge trends in organization development. *Training and Development Journal,* 38(7): 59–62.

102. Deutschman, A. 2005. Change or die. *Fast Company,* May: 52–62.

103. Gilbert, C.G. 2006. Change in the presence of residual fit: Can competing frames coexist? *Organization Science,* 17: 150–167.

Glossary

achievement motivation The degree to which an individual desires to perform in terms of a standard of excellence or to succeed in competitive situations.

achievement-oriented leadership Leadership behavior characterized by setting challenging goals and seeking to improve performance.

acute stress A short-term stress reaction to an immediate threat.

affective commitment Organizational commitment due to one's strong positive attitudes toward the organization.

agreeableness The degree to which an individual is easy-going and tolerant.

anchoring bias A cognitive bias in which the first piece of information that is encountered about a situation is emphasized too much in making a decision.

approval motivation The degree to which an individual is concerned about presenting him- or herself in a socially desirable way in evaluative situations.

ascribed status Status and power that is assigned by cultural norms and depends on group membership.

aspiration–performance discrepancies Gaps between what an individual, unit, or organization wants to achieve and what it is actually achieving.

associates The workers who carry out the basic tasks.

attitude A persistent tendency to feel and behave in a favorable or unfavorable way toward a specific person, object, or idea.

attitudinal structuring Activities aimed at influencing the attitudes and relationships of the negotiating parties.

authoritarianism The degree to which an individual believes in conventional values, obedience to authority, and legitimacy of power differences in society.

brainstorming A process in which a large number of ideas are generated while evaluation of the ideas is suspended.

burnout A condition of physical or emotional exhaustion generally brought about by stress; associates and managers experiencing burnout show various symptoms, such as constant fatigue, or lack of enthusiasm for work, and increasing isolation from others.

business strategy How a firm competes for success against other organizations in a particular market.

centralization The degree to which authority for meaningful decisions is retained at the top of an organization.

charisma A leader's ability to inspire emotion and passion in his followers and to cause them to identify with the leader.

chronic stress A long-term stress reaction resulting from ongoing situations.

coalition A group whose members act together to actively pursue a common interest.

coercive power Power resulting from the ability to punish others.

cognitive biases Mental shortcuts involving simplified ways of thinking.

cognitive dissonance An uneasy feeling produced when a person behaves in a manner inconsistent with an existing attitude.

common information bias A bias in which group members overemphasize information held by a majority or the entire group while failing to be mindful of information held by one or a few group member(s).

communication audit An analysis of an organization's internal and external communication to assess communication practices and capabilities and determine needs.

communication climate Associates' perceptions regarding the quality of communications within the organization.

communication medium or communication channel The manner in which a message is conveyed.

communication The sharing of information between two or more people to achieve a common understanding about an object or situation.

competitive advantage An advantage enjoyed by an organization that can perform some aspect of its work better than competitors or in a way that competitors cannot duplicate, such that it offers products/services that are more valuable to customers.

confirmation bias A cognitive bias in which information confirming early beliefs and ideas is sought while potentially disconfirming information is not sought.

conflict escalation The process whereby a conflict grows increasingly worse over time.

conflict The process in which one party perceives that its interests are being opposed or negatively affected by another party.

conscientiousness The degree to which an individual focuses on goals and works toward them in a disciplined way.

consideration A behavioral leadership style demonstrated by leaders who express friendship, develop mutual trust and respect, and have strong interpersonal relationships with those being led.

contingency theory of leadership effectiveness A theory of leadership that suggests the effectiveness of a leader depends on the interaction of his style of behavior with certain characteristics of the situation.

continuance commitment Organizational commitment due to lack of better opportunities.

continuous reinforcement A reinforcement schedule in which a reward occurs after each instance of a behavior or set of behaviors.

corporate strategy The overall approach an organization uses in interacting with its environment. The emphasis is placed on growth and diversification.

cultural audit A tool for assessing and understanding the culture of an organization.

cultural fluency The ability to identify, understand, and apply cultural differences that influence communication.

cultural intelligence The ability to separate the aspects of behavior that are based in culture as opposed to those unique to the individual or all humans in general.

culture Shared values and taken-for-granted assumptions that govern acceptable behavior and thought patterns in a country and that give a country much of its uniqueness.

culture shock A stress reaction involving difficulties coping with the requirements of life in a new country.

DADA syndrome A sequence of stages—denial, anger, depression, and acceptance—through which individuals can move or in which they can become trapped when faced with unwanted change.

decisions Choices of actions from among multiple feasible alternatives.

decoding The process whereby a receiver perceives a sent message and interprets its meaning.

Delphi technique A highly structured decision-making process in which participants are surveyed regarding their opinions or best judgments.

demand–control model A model that suggests experienced stress is a function of both job demands and job control. Stress is highest when demands are high but individuals have little control over the situation.

departmentation The grouping of human and other resources into units, typically based on functional areas or markets.

devil's advocacy A group decision-making technique that relies on critiques of single sets of assumptions and recommendations in order to encourage debate.

dialectical inquiry A group decision-making technique that uses debate between very different sets of assumptions and recommendations in order to encourage full discussion.

directive leadership Leadership behavior characterized by implementing guidelines, providing information on what is expected, setting definite performance standards, and ensuring individuals follow rules.

discrimination Behavior that results in unequal treatment of individuals based on group membership.

distributive bargaining A negotiation where one party's goals are in direct conflict with the goals of another party.

distributive justice The degree to which people think outcomes are fair.

diversification Related to the number of different product lines or service areas in the organization.

diversity A characteristic of a group of people where differences exist on one or more relevant dimensions such as gender.

diversity-based infighting A situation in which group members engage in unproductive, negative conflict over differing views.

divisible tasks Tasks that can be separated into subcomponents.

downward communication Communication that flows from supervisor to subordinate.

dysfunctional conflict Conflict that is detrimental to organizational goals and objectives.

dystress Negative stress; often referred to simply as stress.

ease-of-recall bias A cognitive bias in which information that is easy to recall from memory is relied upon too much in making a decision.

effort–reward imbalance model A model that suggests experienced stress is a function of both required effort and rewards obtained. Stress is highest when required effort is high but rewards are low.

emotional contagion Phenomenon where emotions experienced by one or a few members of a work group spread to other members.

emotional intelligence The ability to accurately appraise one's own and others' emotions, effectively regulate one's own and other's emotions, and use emotion to motivate, plan, and achieve.

emotional labor The process whereby associates must display emotions that are contrary to what they are feeling.

emotional stability The degree to which an individual easily handles stressful situations and heavy demands.

emotions Complex subjective reactions that have both a physical and mental component.

employee-centered leadership style A behavioral leadership style that emphasizes employees' personal needs and the development of interpersonal relationships.

encoding The process whereby a sender translates the information he or she wishes to send into a message.

environmental uncertainty The degree to which an environment is complex and changing; uncertain environments are difficult to monitor and understand.

equity theory A theory that suggests motivation is based on a person's assessment of the ratio of outcomes she receives (e.g., pay, status) for inputs on the job (e.g., effort, ability) compared to the same ratio for a comparison other.

ERG theory Alderfer's theory that suggests people are motivated by three hierarchically ordered types of needs: existence needs (E), relatedness needs (R), and growth needs (G). A person may work on all three needs at the same time, although satisfying lower order needs often takes place before a person is strongly motivated by higher level needs.

ethnocentrism The belief that one's culture is better than others.

eustress Positive stress that results from meeting challenges and difficulties with the expectation of achievement.

expatriate An individual who leaves his or her home country to live and work in a foreign land.

expectancy The subjective probability that a given amount of effort will lead to a particular level of performance.

expectancy theory Vroom's theory that suggests motivation is a function of an individual's expectancy that a given amount of effort will lead to a particular level of performance, instrumentality judgments that indicate performance will lead to certain outcomes, and the valences of outcomes.

expert power Power resulting from special expertise or technical knowledge.

exploitative learning Learning how to more effectively use current knowledge.

exploratory learning Creating new knowledge and being innovative.

extinction A reinforcement contingency in which a behavior is followed by the absence of a previously encountered positive consequence, thereby reducing the likelihood that the behavior will be repeated in the same or similar situations.

extraversion The degree to which an individual is outgoing and derives energy from being around other people.

feedback The process whereby a receiver encodes the message received and sends it back to the original sender.

feeling A decision style focused on subjective evaluation and the emotional reactions of others.

formal communication Communication that follows the formal structure of the organization (for example, supervisor to subordinate) and communicates organizationally sanctioned information.

formal groups Groups to which members are formally assigned.

formalization The degree to which rules and operating procedures are documented on paper or in company intranets.

functional conflict Conflict that is beneficial to organizational goals and objectives.

fundamental attribution error A perception problem in which an individual is too likely to attribute the behavior of others to internal rather than external causes.

glass border The unseen but strong discriminatory barrier that blocks many women from opportunities for international assignments.

globalization The trend toward a unified global economy where national borders mean relatively little.

global strategy A strategy by which a firm provides standard products and services to all parts of the world while maintaining a strong degree of central control in the home country.

goal-setting theory A theory that suggests challenging and specific goals increase human performance because they affect attention, effort, and persistence.

gossip Information that is presumed to be factual and communicated in private or intimate settings.

group Two or more interdependent individuals who influence one another through social interaction.

groupthink A situation in which group members maintain or seek consensus at the expense of identifying and debating honest disagreements.

growth Relates to increases in sales as well as associates and managers.

halo effect A perception problem in which an individual assesses a person positively or negatively in all situations based on an existing general assessment of the person.

hardiness A personality dimension corresponding to a strong internal commitment to activities, an internal locus of control, and challenge seeking.

height The number of hierarchical levels in an organization, from the CEO to the lower-level associates.

hierarchy The reporting relationships depicted in an organization chart.

hierarchy of needs theory Maslow's theory that suggests people are motivated by their desire to satisfy specific needs, and that needs are arranged in a hierarchy with physiological needs at the bottom and self-actualization needs at the top. People must satisfy needs at lower levels before being motivated by needs at higher levels.

high-context cultures A type of culture where individuals use contextual clues to understand people and their communications and where individuals value trust and personal relationships.

high-involvement management Involves carefully selecting and training associates and giving them significant decision-making power, information, and incentive compensation.

horizontal communication Communication that takes place between associates at the same level.

human capital imitability The extent to which the skills and talents of an organization's people can be copied by other organizations.

human capital rareness The extent to which the skills and talents of an organization's people are unique in the industry.

human capital The sum of the skills, knowledge, and general attributes of the people in an organization.

human capital value The extent to which individuals are capable of producing work that supports an organization's strategy for competing in the marketplace.

hygienes Job factors that can influence job dissatisfaction but not satisfaction.

identity groups Groups based on the social identities of members.

implicit person theories Personal theories about what personality traits and abilities occur together and how these attributes are manifested in behavior.

informal communication Communication that involves spontaneous interaction between two or more people outside the formal organization structure.

informal groups Groups formed spontaneously by people who share interests, values, or identities.

information technology An overall set of tools, based on microelectronic technology, designed to provide data, documents, and commentary as well as analysis support to individuals in an organization.

initiating structure A behavioral leadership style demonstrated by leaders who establish well-defined patterns of organization and communication, define procedures, and delineate their relationships with those being led.

instrumentality Perceived connections between performance and outcomes.

integrative bargaining A negotiation strategy where the nature of the problem permits a solution that is attractive to both parties—in other words, a win-win outcome.

intelligence General mental ability used in complex information processing.

intermittent reinforcement A reinforcement schedule in which a reward does not occur after each instance of a behavior or set of behaviors.

international ethics Principles of proper conduct focused on issues such as corruption, exploitation of labor, and environmental impact.

interpersonal cohesion Team members' liking or attraction to other team members.

interpersonal communication Direct verbal or nonverbal interaction between two or more active participants.

intuition A decision style focused on developing abstractions and figurative examples for use in decision making, with an emphasis on imagination and possibilities.

job enlargement The process of making a job more motivating by adding tasks that are similar in complexity relative to the current tasks.

job enrichment The process of making a job more motivating by increasing responsibility.

job redesign Enlargement or enrichment of jobs; enrichment is the better method to enhance motivation for effective problem solving, communication, and learning.

job stress The feeling that one's capabilities, resources, or needs do not match the demands or requirements of the job.

job-centered leadership style A behavioral leadership style that emphasizes employee tasks and the methods used to accomplish them.

lateral relations Elements of structure designed to draw individuals together for interchanges related to work issues and problems.

leadership The process of providing general direction and influencing individuals or groups to achieve goals.

leader–member exchange A model of leadership focused on leaders developing more positive relationships with some individuals, and having more positive exchanges with these individuals.

leader–member relations The degree to which a leader is respected, is accepted as a leader, and has friendly interpersonal relations.

learning A process through which individuals change their behavior based on positive or negative experiences in a situation.

legitimate power Power derived from position; also known as formal authority.

life-cycle forces Natural and predictable pressures that build as an organization grows and that must be addressed if the organization is to continue growing.

locus of control The degree to which an individual attributes control of events to self or external factors.

low-context cultures A type of culture where individuals rely on direct questioning to understand people and their communications and where individuals value efficiency and performance.

management by objectives (MBO) A management process in which individuals negotiate task objectives with their managers and then are held accountable for attainment of the objectives.

managing organizational behavior Actions focused on acquiring, developing, and applying the knowledge and skills of people.

mass customization A manufacturing technology that involves integrating sophisticated information technology and management methods to produce a flexible manufacturing system with the ability to customize products for many customers in a short time cycle.

mass-production technology A manufacturing technology used to produce large quantities of standardized products. Automation is moderately high.

maximization tasks Tasks with a quantity goal.

modern racism Subtle forms of discrimination that occur despite people knowing it is wrong to be prejudiced against other racial groups and despite believing they are not racist.

monochronic time orientation A preference for focusing on one task per unit of time and completing that task in a timely fashion.

monolithic organization An organization that is homogeneous.

motivation Forces coming from within a person that account for the willful direction, intensity, and persistence of the person's efforts toward achieving specific goals, where achievement is not due solely to ability or to environmental factors.

motivators Job factors that can influence job satisfaction but not dissatisfaction.

moving A phase in the change process in which leaders help to implement new approaches by providing information that supports proposed changes and by providing resources and training to bring about actual shifts in behavior.

multicultural organization An organization in which the organizational culture values differences.

multidomestic strategy A strategy by which a firm tailors its products and services to the needs of each country or region in which it operates and gives a great deal of power to the managers and associates in those countries or regions.

need for achievement The need to perform well against a standard of excellence.

need for affiliation The need to be liked and to stay on good terms with most other people.

need for power The desire to influence people and events.

negative reinforcement A reinforcement contingency in which a behavior is followed by the withdrawal of a previously encountered negative consequence, thereby increasing the likelihood that the behavior will be repeated in the same or similar situations.

negotiation A process by which parties with different preferences and interests attempt to agree on a solution.

noise Anything that disrupts communication or distorts the message.

nominal group technique A process for group decision making in which discussion is structured and the final solution is decided by silent vote.

nonverbal communication Communication that takes place without using language, such as facial expressions or body language.

normative commitment Organizational commitment due to feelings of obligation.

norms Rules or standards that regulate the team's behavior.

OB Mod A formal procedure focused on improving task performance through positive reinforcement of desired behaviors and extinction of undesired behaviors.

openness to experience The degree to which an individual seeks new experiences and thinks creatively about the future.

operant conditioning theory An explanation for consequence-based learning that assumes learning results from simple conditioning and that higher mental functioning is irrelevant.

optimization tasks Tasks with a quality goal.

organization A collection of individuals forming a coordinated system of specialized activities for the purpose of achieving certain goals over some extended period of time.

organization development (OD) A planned organization-wide continuous process designed to improve communication, problem solving, and learning through the application of behavioral science knowledge.

organizational behavior The actions of individuals and groups in an organizational context.

organizational culture The values shared by associated and managers in an organization.

organizational politics Behavior that is directed toward furthering one's own self-interests without concern for the interests or well-being of others.

organizational structure Work roles and authority relationships that influence behavior in an organization.

participative leadership Leadership behavior characterized by sharing information, consulting with those who are led, and emphasizing group decision making.

path–goal leadership theory A theory of leadership based on expectancy concepts from the study of motivation, which suggests that leader effectiveness depends on the degree to which a leader enhances the performance expectancies and valences of her subordinates.

perception A process that involves sensing various aspects of a person, task, or event and forming impressions based on selected inputs.

personal conflict Conflict that arises out of personal differences between people, such as differing goals, values, or personalities.

personality A stable set of characteristics representing internal properties of an individual, which are reflected in behavioral tendencies across a variety of situations.

planned change A process involving deliberate efforts to move an organization or a unit from its current undesirable state to a new, more desirable state.

plural organization An organization that has a diverse workforce and takes steps to be inclusive and respectful of differences, but where diversity is tolerated rather than truly valued.

positive organizational behavior Nurtures individual's greatest strengths and helps people use them to their and the organization's advantage.

political skill The ability to effectively understand others at work and to use this knowledge to enhance one's own objectives.

polychronic time orientation A willingness to juggle multiple tasks per unit of time and to have interruptions and an unwillingness to be driven by time.

position power The degree to which a leader can reward, punish, promote, or demote individuals in the unit or organization.

positive reinforcement A reinforcement contingency in which a behavior is followed by a positive consequence, thereby increasing the likelihood that the behavior will be repeated in the same or similar situations.

power The ability to achieve the desired outcomes.

prejudice Unfair negative attitudes we hold about people who belong to social or cultural groups other than our own.

procedural conflict Conflict that arises over responsibilities and how work should be completed.

procedural justice In the context of organization change, the perceived fairness of the change process.

procedural justice The degree to which people think the procedures used to determine outcomes are fair.

process loss Time and energy that team members spend on maintaining the team as opposed to working on the task.

process-production technology A manufacturing technology used to produce large amounts of products such as electricity and gasoline in a highly automated system where associates and managers do not directly touch raw materials and in-process work.

projecting A perception problem in which an individual assumes that others share his or her values and beliefs.

punctuated equilibrium model (PEM) A model of group development that suggests that groups do not go through linear stages but that group formation depends on the task at hand and the deadlines for that task.

punishment A reinforcement contingency in which a behavior is followed by a negative consequence, thereby reducing the likelihood that the behavior will be repeated in the same or similar situations.

reference point A possible level of performance used to evaluate one's current standing.

referent power Power resulting from others' desire to identify with the referent.

refreezing A phase in the change process in which leaders lock in new approaches by implementing evaluation systems that track expected behaviors, by creating reward systems that reinforce expected behaviors, and by ensuring that hiring and promotion systems support the new demands.

resistance to change Efforts to block the introduction of new approaches. Some of these efforts are passive in nature, involving such tactics as verbally supporting the change while continuing to work in the old ways; and other efforts are active in nature, involving tactics such as organized protests and sabotage.

reward power Power resulting from the ability to provide others with desired outcomes.

risk-taking propensity Willingness to take chances.

risky shift A process by which group members collectively make a more risky choice than most or all of the individuals would have made working alone.

role ambiguity A situation in which goals, expectations, and/or basic job requirements are unclear.

role conflict A situation in which different roles lead to conflicting expectations.

roles Expectations shared by group members about who is to perform what types of tasks and under what conditions.

rumors Unsubstantiated information of universal interest.

satisficing decisions Satisfactory rather than optimal decisions.

self-contained tasks An integration technique whereby a department is given resources from other functional areas in order to reduce the need to coordinate with those areas.

self-efficacy An individual's belief that he or she will be able to perform a specific task in a given situation.

self-monitoring The degree to which an individual attempts to present the image he or she thinks others want to see in a given situation.

self-serving bias A perception problem in which an individual is too likely to attribute the failure of others to internal causes and the successes of others to external causes. Whereas, the same individual will be too likely to attribute his own failure to external causes and his own successes to internal causes.

sensing A decision style focused on gathering concrete information directly through the senses, with an emphasis on practical and realistic ideas.

servant leadership An approach to leadership focused on serving others.

simulation A representation of a real system that allows associates and managers to try various actions and receive feedback on the consequences of those actions.

slack resources An integration technique whereby a department keeps more resources on hand than absolutely required in order to reduce the need for tight communication and coordination with other departments.

small-batch technology A manufacturing technology used to produce unique or small batches of custom products. Automation trends to be low; skilled craftsmen and craftswomen are essential.

social facilitation effect Improvement in individual performance when others are present.

social identity A person's knowledge that he belongs to certain social groups, where belonging to those groups has emotional significance.

social learning theory An explanation for consequence-based learning that acknowledges the higher mental functioning of human beings and the role such functioning can play in learning.

social loafing A phenomenon wherein people put forth less effort when they work in teams than when they work alone.

socialization A process through which an organization imparts its values to newcomers.

socialization model A model proposing that all leaders in a particular organization will display similar leadership styles, because all have been selected and socialized by the same organization.

socioemotional roles Roles that require behaviors that support the social aspects of the organization.

span of control The number of individuals a manager directly oversees.

specialization The degree to which associates and managers have jobs with narrow scopes and limited variety.

standardization The degree to which rules and standard operating procedures govern behavior in an organization.

stereotype A generalized set of beliefs about the characteristics of a group of individuals.

stereotyping A perception problem in which an individual has preconceived ideas about a group and assumes that all members of that group share the same characteristics.

strategic contingencies model of power Model holding that people and organizational units gain power by being able to address the major problems and issues faced by the organization.

strategic OB approach An approach that involves organizing and managing people's knowledge and skills effectively to implement the organization's strategy and gain a competitive advantage.

stress A feeling of tension that occurs when a person perceives that a situation is about to exceed her ability to cope and consequently could endanger her well-being.

stress response An unconscious mobilization of energy resources that occurs when the body encounters a stressor.

stressors Environmental conditions that cause individuals to experience stress.

structural characteristics The tangible, physical properties that determine the basic shape and appearance of an organization's hierarchy.

structural–cultural model A model holding that because women often experience lack of power, lack of respect, and certain stereotypical expectations, they develop leadership styles different from those of men.

structuring characteristics The policies and approaches used to directly prescribe the behavior of managers and associates.

subcultures In the organizational context, groups that share values that differ from the main values of the organization.

substantive conflict Conflict that involves work content and goals.

sunk-cost bias A cognitive bias in which past investments of time, effort, and/or money are not treated as sunk costs in deciding on continued investment.

supplemental organizational processes Processes in which associates and/or managers have ongoing meetings for the purpose of understanding and addressing important problems.

supportive leadership Leadership behavior characterized by friendliness and concern for individuals' well-being, welfare, and needs.

survey feedback Data obtained from questionnaires; managers receive the data for their units and are expected to hold unit meetings to discuss problems.

swift trust A phenomenon where trust develops rapidly based on positive, reciprocated task-related communications.

synergy An effect wherein the total output of a team is greater than the combined outputs of individual members working alone.

t-group training Group exercises in which individuals focus on their actions, how others perceive their actions, and how others generally react to them; participants often learn about unintended negative consequences of certain types of behavior.

task cohesion Team members' attraction and commitment to the tasks and goals of the team.

task roles Roles that require behaviors aimed at achieving the team's performance goals and tasks.

task structure The degree to which tasks can be broken down into easily understood steps or parts.

team building A process in which members of a team work together and with a facilitator to diagnose task, process, and interpersonal problems within the team and create solutions.

team orientation The extent to which an individual works well with others, wants to contribute to team performance, and enjoys being on a team.

team Two or more people, with work roles that require them to be interdependent, who operate within a larger social system (the organization), performing tasks relevant to the organization's mission, with consequences that affect others inside and outside the organization, and who have membership that is identifiable to those on the team and those not on the team.

thinking A decision style focused on objective evaluation and systematic analysis.

transactional leadership A leadership approach that is based on the exchange relationship between followers and leaders. Transactional leadership is characterized by contingent reward behavior and active management-by-exception behavior.

transformational leadership A leadership approach that involves motivating followers to do more than expected, to continuously develop and grow, to increase self-confidence, and to place the interests of the unit or organization before their own. Transformational leadership involves charisma, intellectual stimulation, and individual consideration.

transnational strategy A strategy by which a firm tailors its products and services to some degree to meet the needs of different countries or regions of the world but also seeks some degree of standardization in order to keep costs reasonably low.

two-factor theory Herzberg's motivation theory that suggests job satisfaction and dissatisfaction are not opposite ends of the same continuum but are independent states, and that different factors affect satisfaction and dissatisfaction.

type A personality A personality type characterized by competitiveness, aggressiveness, and impatience.

unfreezing A phase in the change process in which leaders help managers and associates move beyond the past by providing a rationale for change, by creating guilt and/or anxiety about not changing, and by creating a sense of psychological safety concerning the change.

unitary tasks Tasks that cannot be divided and must be performed by an individual.

upward communication Communication that flows from subordinate to supervisor.

valence Value associated with an outcome.

values Abstract ideals that relate to proper life goals and methods for reaching those goals.

virtual teams Teams in which members work together but are separated by time, distance, or organizational structure.

virtual electronic teams Teams that rely heavily on electronically mediated communication rather than face-to-face meetings as the means to coordinate work.

Organization Index

Name Index

Subject Index